Knight's Master Book

of

New Illustrations

Knight's
MASTER BOOK
of
NEW ILLUSTRATIONS

by

WALTER B. KNIGHT

Author and Compiler of:
3,000 *Illustrations for Christian Service*

WM. B. EERDMANS PUBLISHING COMPANY
Grand Rapids, Michigan

KNIGHT'S MASTER BOOK
OF NEW ILLUSTRATIONS

Compiled by Walter B. Knight

ISBN 0-8028-1699-1

Set up and printed, March 1956

Reprinted, October 1982

PHOTOLITHOPRINTED BY EERDMANS PRINTING COMPANY
GRAND RAPIDS, MICHIGAN, UNITED STATES OF AMERICA

Dedication

To my three devoted daughters, Alice,
Mary Nell, and Ruth, who early in life
invited Christ into their hearts, and
who, through the years, have lived for
Him; and to my loyal sister, Sara, this
book is affectionately and
gratefully dedicated.

"But the path of the just is as the shining light, that shineth more and more unto the perfect day." (PROVERBS 4:18)

Preface

Since its publication, my first book, 3,000 *Illustrations for Christian Service,* has found its place in the hearts and hands of tens of thousands of ministers, teachers, and Christian workers.

Now the time has come for its successor, *Knight's Master Book of New Illustrations,* to make its appearance. It is complementary to its predecessor, and much effort has been expended to avoid duplication.

For years, my wife, Alice Marie Knight, author of 1,001 *Stories for Children and Children's Workers,* and I have spared no effort to make this new book the greatest aid of its kind yet to appear.

Having been a pastor and writer for more than thirty years, I experimentally know the need of busy pastors, evangelists, teachers, and writers, for heart-stirring illustrations.

Knight's Master Book of New Illustrations is a well-balanced book, not topheavy in some sections, and skimpy in other sections. The replete index, with its cross references, puts at the user's finger tips just the illustrations needed to clinch his thought and help others to see, in clarity, eternal truths.

Painstaking care has been exerted to delete from the illustrative material superfluous sentences and paragraphs. This has made it possible to increase the number of illustrations more than a thousand over my previous book of illustrations, with only a slight increase in cost.

Having been a news correspondent in my earlier years, I have been ever alert for new stories and illustrations wherever they have occurred. This fact has made for freshness and relative up-to-dateness in the illustrative material of this book.

May the greatest of story tellers, the gracious Saviour, bless this book and use it to bring inspiration and illumination to God's children, and to awaken in the hearts of the unsaved the desire to know Him, whom to know is life everlasting.

WALTER BROWN KNIGHT

Chicago, Illinois.
January, 1956

Contents

Knight's Master Book

of

New Illustrations

ASSURANCE

"His Word Tells Me, and My Heart Tells Me!"

A dear little girl came to me in one of my meetings and said, "I want to be a Christian." Taking her aside, I read from God's Word this verse, among others, "But as many as received Him, to them gave He power to become the sons of God" (John 1:12a). Having read this verse, I asked the little girl, "Do you believe this verse?" She said, "I believe it!" Then I asked her, "Will you receive Jesus as your Saviour?" Said she, "I will receive Jesus as my Saviour!" Then I asked her, "Are you saved?" "Yes, I am one of God's children! I know it because of two things: This (pointing to her Bible) tells me I am, and this (pointing to her heart) tells me I am, too!"

—Rev. Roy Gustafsen

* * *

"I Am of Paul's Persuasion!"

A pastor asked a dying man, "Brother, of what persuasion are you?"

The man replied, "I am of Paul's persuasion."

"You don't understand me. Of what persuasion are you?"

"I understood you. I am of Paul's persuasion."

The preacher shaking his head said, "Brother, I'm afraid I do not understand you. You said you are of Paul's persuasion. What do you mean? There is a Methodist persuasion, and a Baptist persuasion, and an Episcopalian persuasion, and a Lutheran persuasion, and a Christian persuasion, and a Nazarene persuasion, but what is Paul's persuasion? What is the persuasion of Paul?"

The man, smiling, quoted, "I know whom I have believed, and am persuaded that he is able to keep that which I have committed unto him against that day" (II Tim. 1:12).

—Dr. Hyman Appelman

Rest Secure

"On Christ salvation rests secure,
The Rock of Ages must endure;
Nor can that faith be overthrown
Which rests upon the 'Living Stone.'

"No other hope shall intervene,
To Him we look, on Him we lean;
Other foundation we disown,
And build on Christ, the 'Living Stone.'

"In Him it is ordained to raise
A temple to Jehovah's praise,
Composed of all the saints who own
No Saviour but the 'Living Stone.' "

—*Selected*

* * *

"Have You Any Certainties?"

Said Goethe, "If you have any certainties, let us have them. We have doubts enough of our own!"

—*Selected*

* * *

Grandmother's Translation

A young man was home from the theological school to visit his grandmother. To have a bit of fun at her expense, he said, "Grandmother, you know the Bible that you say you believe was written in Hebrew and Greek. It had to be translated by great scholars into our language. How do you know those who translated it got it right?" "Ah," she answered, "never mind the great men. I have translated a few of the promises myself!"

—*Overcomer*

* * *

Statement of Shakespeare's Belief
(From his last will and testament)

"I, William Shakespeare, of Stratford-upon-Avon, in the county of Warrick, gentleman in perfect health and memory, God be praised, do make and ordain this my last will and testament in manner and form following, that is to say, first, I commend my soul into the hands of God, my Creator, hoping and assuredly believing, through the only merits of Jesus Christ, my Saviour, to be made partaker of life everlasting, and my body to the earth whereof it is made."

—Selected

* * *

Why She Was Unconcerned

An aged lady left Buffalo by boat for Cleveland, Ohio, to visit a daughter. A terrible storm arose, and the passengers, fearing death, gathered for prayer. But the aged lady seemed quite unconcerned. She sat praising the Lord. Some of the passengers, after the storm subsided, became curious to know the reason for the old lady's calmness. They gathered around her and asked her the secret. "Well, children," she replied, "It is like this. I had two daughters. One died and went home to Heaven; the other moved to Cleveland. When the storm arose, I wondered which daughter I might visit first, the one in Cleveland or the one in Heaven, and I was quite unconcerned as to which."

—Wesleyan Methodist

* * *

The One Important Word.

Dr. S. D. Gordon tells of an old Christian woman whose age began to tell on her memory. She had once known much of the Bible by heart. Eventually only one precious bit stayed with her. "I know whom I have believed, and am persuaded that he is able to keep that which I have committed unto him against that day." By and by part of that slipped its hold, and she would quietly repeat, "That which I have committed unto him." At last, as she hovered on the borderline between this and the spirit world, her loved ones noticed her lips moving. They bent down to see if she needed anything. She was repeating over and over again to herself the one word of the text, "Him, Him, Him." She had lost the whole Bible, but one word. But she had the whole Bible in that one word.

—American Holiness Journal

Secure and Assured

Some years ago the world's longest bridge was completed at San Francisco at a cost of seventy-seven million dollars. During the construction of the first part of the bridge no safety devices were used and twenty-three men fell to their death in the waters far below. In the construction of the second part it was decided to install the greatest safety net in the world, even though the cost amounted to $100,000. It saved the lives of at least ten men who fell to it without injury. In addition to that the work went on from 15 to 25 percent faster with the men relieved from the fear of falling. The knowledge that they were safe left the men free to devote their energies to the particular tasks in hand.

To be assured that neither things present nor things to come can separate me from Christ's love sets me gloriously free to serve with glad alacrity.

—Moody Monthly

* * *

Luther's Assurance.

Some one told Martin Luther, when he was going out on one of his hard tasks, that the Pope was after him. He replied: "If it is a matter between Martin Luther and the Pope, it is all up with Martin Luther; but if it is a matter between the Pope and God, it's all up with the Pope."

—Watchman-Examiner

* * *

One Thing He Knew

William James Taylor, alias Bill Hennessy, alias Ed Lynch, alias Tom O' Brien, learned that he couldn't hide from God. At the age of three, behind his father's saloon he acquired a taste for liquor by dipping his baby fingers into the dregs of glasses and bottles. Small wonder that by twelve he was a drunken street urchin. After two years in a reform school he lived aimlessly until a second arrest placed him in an industrial institution. Gambling, drugs, and drink provided a livelihood and made him a constant fugitive from the law that kept him constantly on the move, whenever he wasn't serving sentence. The night he arrived in Chicago, he hurried into the Pacific Garden Mission to avoid what he thought were suspicious glances of a policeman. He returned a second night. Again he heard the testimonies of what God had done for such as he. He knelt at the altar and repeated, "God be merciful to me, a sinner, and save me now for Jesus' sake." "I cannot tell all Jesus Christ has done for me. But one thing I can do, and that is tell others about Him. And there's a lot of things I don't know. But there's one thing I do know. That is that God ain't any picker of persons."

—Carl F. H. Henry
The Pacific Garden Mission

* * *

Minister's Sermon Topic Too Short

The Rev. R. I. Williams telephoned his sermon topic to the *Norfolk Ledger Dispatch.*
"The Lord is my Shepherd," he said.
"Is that all?" he was asked.
He replied, "That's enough."
And the church page carried Mr. William's sermon topic as: "The Lord is my Shepherd—that's enough."
The minister rather liked the idea. He used the expanded version as his sermon title that Sunday at Fairmount Park Methodist Church.

—*Gospel Herald*

* * *

Feeling or Believing?

Someone asked Luther, "Do you feel that you have been forgiven?"
He answered, "No! but I'm as sure as there's a God in heaven.
"For feelings come and feelings go, and feelings are deceiving;
My warrant is the Word of God, nought else is worth believing.
Though all my heart should feel condemned for want of some sweet token,
There is One greater than my heart whose word cannot be broken.
I'll trust in God's unchanging Word till soul and body sever;
For though all things shall pass away His Word shall stand forever."

—*Moody Monthly*

Fact, Not Feeling.

In a Gospel meeting a penitent woman was seeking salvation. The evangelist quoted to her anxious soul the assurance of Isaiah 53:6, and led her to simply take God at His Word, and to depend upon Christ for the remission of sin. She went home rejoicing, but the next morning came downstairs with tears in her eyes. Her little boy, who had been with her in the meeting the night before, asked, "Mamma, what is troubling you?" "Oh," was the answer, "last night I *felt* that I was saved. But now it seems like a dream. I fear I am deceived." "Mamma," said the little lad, "get your Bible and turn to Isaiah 53:6." She did so, and read, "The Lord hath laid on him the iniquity of us all." "Mamma, *is the verse still there?*" "Yes, my son." "Then your sins *were laid on Jesus*," said the wise lad. The mother saw the truth. She took God's Word without regard to her feelings, and then God's peace came to stay.

—*"Faith,"* James H. McConkey

* * *

Never Say "Good-by"

In ancient Rome a guard felt sorry for a Christian prisoner, who was soon to die because of his faith in Christ. He secretly allowed his daughter to visit him. After she was gone the guard stared at his prisoner. "Why do you gaze at me?" he asked. "Because you do not seem worried," was the answer. "You are to die tomorrow. Tonight you saw your daughter for the last time." "Oh, but you are wrong," exclaimed the prisoner. "I shall see her again. My daughter is a Christian, too. She will soon follow me. Christians never see one another for the last time. They meet in heaven, there to live forever. Now do you understand why I am happy and why I am ready to die for my Christian faith?"

—*Choice Gleanings*

* * *

We Know the Way

A traveler in Switzerland, uncertain of his way, asked a small lad by the wayside where Kandersteg was, and received, so he remarks, the most significant answer ever given him. "I do not know, sir," said the boy, "where Kandersteg is, but there is the road to it." There are a great many things I cannot tell about the life to come, but I know where lies the road. As I know Christ, the hope of glory, I have the certain assurance of immortality.

—*Herald and Presbyter*

* * *

My Anchor Holds

"A sailor in Gloucester, Mass., had been wounded in a wreck and was brought ashore. The fever was great, and he was dying. His comrades gathered around him in a little fishing house, and the physician said: 'He won't live long.' The sailor was out of his mind until near the close. But within a few minutes of his death he looked around, and calling one comrade after another, bade them goodby, and then sank off to sleep. Finally as it was time for the medicine again, one of the sailors rousing him, said, 'Mate, how are you now?' He looked up to the face of his friend and said, 'My anchor holds!' These were his last words. And when they called upon a friend of mine to take charge of the funeral service, how powerful was the impression made upon his hearers when he quoted the dying words: 'My anchor holds!' "

—*Gospel Herald*

* * *

Inside Information

In a British army discussion period on the religions of the world, men began to voice their opinions concerning Jesus. To one He was "a good enough man"; to another, "an impossible idealist"; to another, "a revolutionary"; and to another, "a **fanatic.**"

At last a lad got to his feet and, with flushed face and stammering tongue, said: "Excuse me, but you're all wrong. He is more than that." Then he paused, and a wit who knew the lad interposed with: "He's got inside information!"

"So I have!" flashed back the young Christian. "You see, I know Him!"

The men did not laugh. They recognized the fact that the lad had got hold of something beyond their surface appraisals.

—*War Cry*, Essex

* * *

Safer Than in His Arms

Some years ago at the great Keswick Convention in England, a brother said to the Rev. George Silwood, "Is it not blessed to be safe in the arms of Jesus?" "Yes," said Brother Silwood, "but I am safer than that." "Why," said his friend in astonishment, "how could you be safer than in the arms of Jesus?" "Why, I am as safe as an arm of Jesus," said the preacher; nor did he overemphasize this great and glorious fact, "for we are members of his body, of his flesh, and of his bones."

—Rev. P. W. Philpott

* * *

Better Examine the Bridge!

An extract from a letter written by a minister to a brother minister whose faith was failing through illness: "Are you not making the mistake of examining your faith rather than the promises upon which that faith should rest? If you were traveling a new public highway and should approach a bridge of whose strength you were not satisfied, would you stop to examine your faith in that bridge, or dismount and examine the structure itself? Common sense would tell you to examine the bridge, and then, when satisfied of its strength, you would cross over with confidence. So now I beg you, dear brother, look away to the promises that were made by God whom you have served so long, and trust Him though He slay you. Remember the bridge."

—*King's Business*

* * *

"It Is Well With My Soul!"

"Saved, Alone!" This was the cablegram which Horatio Gates Spafford, author of the hymn, "It Is Well With My Soul," received. It meant that his four children had gone down to a watery grave in mid-Atlantic, and that his wife only had been rescued. In his deep sorrow he was wondrously sustained by the God of all grace. Out of his sorrowing heart, he gave to the world the great hymn of assurance:

"When peace, like a river, attendeth my way,
When sorrows, like sea-billows, roll;
Whatever my lot, Thou hast taught me to say,
It is well, it is well with my soul!"

—W. B. K.

* * *

His Shepherd Forever

A Scottish minister was instructing a small boy in the home of one of his parishioners, and he was having him read the Twenty-third Psalm. "The Lord is my shepherd," began the little boy; but he was interrupted by the old minister. "Nae, nae," he said, "ye dinna read it richt." Again the little boy began, slowly and earnestly, "The—Lord—is—my—shepherd." But again he was stopped. "Nae, ye dinna read it richt yet," the old minister said, shaking his head. "Now watch me"—and holding up his left hand he placed the forefinger of his right hand on the thumb of the left and said, "The"—then to the next finger, "Lord"—and to the next, "is"—and then grasping firmly the fourth finger, he said, "You TAKE HOLD on the fourth one and say, 'My.'" "Oh," exclaimed the little boy, "it's 'The Lord is MY shepherd!'" Not long afterward the little boy followed the sheep out to pasture one morning, and later the broken little body was found at the foot of a steep cliff, over which he had evidently fallen by accident. The life was gone, but the grief-stricken parents saw one thing that cheered their hearts, for the little right hand, though cold in death, was clasped firmly upon the fourth finger of his left, and they knew that their little laddie was safe in the arms of HIS Shepherd.

From a radio program broadcast
—Rev. Hilmore Cedarholm

The Doctor's Dog

There was once an English doctor whose dog always accompanied him when he made the round of visits to his patients. One night when he was called to see a dying man, the dog followed him into the house. The doctor went into the sick room, closing the door behind him, leaving the dog in the hall outside. The sick man, realizing that death was very near and being unprepared to die, said to the doctor, "Doctor, how can we know what lies beyond death?"

The doctor, taken off guard by the unexpected question, yet being a Christian man and desiring to help the patient paused for a moment to think how best to answer. Just then there was a noise at the door. The little dog was sniffing at the crack and scratching on the closed panels. This gave the doctor an idea.

He said, "My little dog is outside. He followed me into the house, and I left him behind when I came into this room. He doesn't know what's here; he has never been into the house and certainly never into this room; but he wants to come in because he knows I am here and he loves and trusts me. We may not know a great deal about what lies beyond the door of death; but if we *love God* and trust Him, knowing He is there, we need have no fear of going where He is."

—Dr. Bob Jones, Jr.

* * *

When the Props Go

"See, Father," said a small boy who was walking with his father by the river, "they are knocking the props away from under the bridge. What are they doing that for? Won't the bridge fall?" "They are knocking them away," said the father, "that the timbers may rest more firmly upon the stone piers which are now finished." God often takes away our earthly things that we may rest more firmly on Him.

—*Choice Gleanings Calendar*

The Eternal Goodness

I know not what the future hath
Of marvel or surprise,
Assured alone that life and death
His mercy underlies.

And if my heart and flesh are weak
To bear an untried pain,
The bruised reed He will not break,
But strengthen and sustain.

And so, beside the Silent Sea,
I wait the muffled oar;
No harm from Him can come to me
On ocean or on shore.

I know not where His islands lift
Their fronded palms in air;
I only know I cannot drift
Beyond His love and care.

—John G. Whittier

* * *

The Basis of His Faith

A friend questioned one of God's servants of the other years: "Mr. Mackenzie, you are a man to be envied: you know nothing of doubts and fears; you always enjoy the full assurance of hope." The old man replied at once: "Yes, yes, I understand you. Many a man speaks of my strong faith that does not know all it has to struggle with. But I shall tell you what my faith is. I am the emptiest, vilest, poorest sinner I know on the face of this earth. I feel myself to be so. But I read in His own Word that He heareth the cry of the poor, and I believe Him, and I cry unto Him, and He always hears me, and that is all the faith or assurance I have got."

—*Sunday School Times*

* * *

He Said He Would

At a certain church a boy of ten years of age was examined for membership. After he had spoken of his sense of guilt, came the question, "What did you do when you felt yourself so great a sinner?" and the eyes of the boy brightened as he answered, "I just went to Jesus and told Him how sinful I was, and how sorry I was, and asked Him to forgive me." "And do you hope at times that Jesus heard you and forgave your sins?" "I don't only hope so, sir, I know He did." The oldest of them raised his glasses and peered into the face of the little candidate, and said, "You say you 'know' that Jesus forgave your sin?" "Yes, sir," was the prompt answer. "You mean, my son, that you hope Jesus has pardoned your sins." "I hope he has, and I know it, too," said the boy, with a bright smile on his manly face. "How do you know it, my son?" Every eye was intent on the little respondent. "He said he would," said the boy, with a look of astonishment, as if amazed that anyone should doubt it.

—*Earnest Worker*

* * *

"Thou Remainest!"

When winter reigns, and flowers are
    dead,
And song birds with their songs have
    fled;
When trees are etched on leaden skies,
And poverty in anguish cries,
And funeral trains go o'er the snow,
O God, how good it is to know—
    That Thou remainest!

When man his courage would reveal,
When he would build his towers of steel
And granite blocks to pierce the sky,
And would the hand of time defy;
While here is strength, yet he doth know
That these as well some day must go;
For ruins fill the ancient world,
And to the depth man's pride is hurled
    But Thou remainest!

Why should I grieve and be afraid
When in the grave my hopes are laid?
Well do I know that death must be
Unless my Lord shall come for me;
Therefore, build I my life on Thee,
Foundation of eternity—
    For Thou remainest!

—Rev. J. G. W. Kirschner

I Know I Have

They had been talking with Dr. W. H. Griffith-Thomas night after night, endeavoring to win him, then a young doctor, for Christ. Nothing they said seemed to cut through the mental fog that blocked the way to a clear understanding of salvation. Finally realizing that the young man's difficulty was his own inability to "feel" saved, Mr. Poole took a coin, and handing it to Dr. Griffith-Thomas asked him to put it in his vest-pocket.

"Do you *feel* you've got it?" Mr. Poole asked.

"No," replied the young doctor, "I *know* I have."

"So," Mr. Poole rejoined, "we know we have Christ when we accept Him and believe His Word, without feeling it."

Dr. Griffith-Thomas testified later, "When I awoke the next morning my soul was overflowing with joy, and since then I have never doubted that it was on that Saturday night I was 'born again'—converted to God."

—Power

* * *

Sure of His Salvation

It is a long time since Herodotus described the little folk of distant Central Africa, but the Gospel has at last reached them. Miss Bell of the Africa Inland Mission describes one to whom she had often preached, asking him if he had at last received the words of God. "Yes, we have," he answered. "Every night we meet for prayer. We sing, 'Jesus Loves Me' and 'What Can Wash Away My Sins?' and then call on God to protect us in the night." Miss Bell then inquired if he were sure that, on death, he would go to Heaven. The Pygmy stood at attention, hand at salute, and said, "When I die I will go to God's village. I will salute, and say, 'Greetings, God. I am come to my house in Your village.' And when He asks me what permission I have to enter, I will tell Him that His Son Jesus Christ died for me and washed my heart clean in His blood. Then He will tell me, 'Enter; your house is waiting for you.'" Miss Bell's comment: "He was perfectly sure about his salvation—and so am I!"

—Sunday School Times

* * *

Dropping the Burden

A Negro, carrying a bag of potatoes on his back, was asked by a skeptic:

"How do you know you are saved?"

The Negro took a few steps and then dropped the bag. Then he said:

"How do I know I have dropped the bag? I have not looked around."

"No," replied the man. You can tell by the lessening of the weight."

"Yes," went on the Negro, "that is how I know I am saved. I have lost the guilty feeling of sin and sorrow, and have found peace and satisfaction in my Lord and Saviour."

—The Elim Evangel

* * *

George Whitefield:

"I go to my everlasting rest. My sun has risen, shone, and is setting — nay, it is about to rise and shine forever. I have not lived in vain. And though I could live to preach Christ a thousand years, I die to be with Him, which is far better."

—Sunday School Times

* * *

Safe Hiding

When Martin Luther was in the throes of the Reformation and the Pope was trying to bring him back to the Catholic church, he sent a cardinal to deal with Luther and buy him with gold.

The cardinal wrote to the Pope, "The fool does not love gold." The cardinal, when he could not convince Luther, said to him, "What do you think the Pope cares for the opinions of a German boer? The Pope's little finger is stronger than all Germany. Do you expect your princes to take up arms to defend you—you, a wretched worm like you? I tell you no. And where will you be then?"

Luther's reply was simple. "Where I am now. In the hands of Almighty God."

—Pentecostal Herald

He Cannot Deny Himself

Spurgeon used to tell the story of an illiterate old woman who was a humble follower of the Lamb. A skeptical neighbor loved to poke fun at her, especially at the assurance she displayed regarding her own salvation. "How do you know that?" he asked. "God tells me so a hundred times," she answered, and then she quoted one promise after another, especially from John's first Letter, the Epistle of Christian assurance, where the phrase, "We know," is used fourteen times in five short chapters. The question was then shot at her, "Suppose God doesn't keep His word?" Quickly she answered: "His loss would be greater than mine. I would lose my soul. He would lose His honor." She was right. Oh, we have a great God, a wonderful God! He cannot deny Himself.

—*United Presbyterian*

* * *

Absolutely Certain

Some years ago I had a boys' club mostly made up of newsboys; they were mostly tough little fellows, but so loyal to each other. One ten-year-old accepted Christ as his Saviour, and turned out to be a splendid Christian; he witnessed everywhere. One of his customers said to him, "Peter, maybe you only think you are saved." "Oh, no, sir," replied Peter; "I don't 'only think'; I'm absolutely certain. Jesus said He wouldn't cast anybody out who came to Him, and I came to Him, and I'm saved for keeps. Jesus couldn't make a mistake."

—*Personal*

An Arab Proverb

1. He that *knows not* and *knows not* that he *knows not;*
   He is a fool—shun him!
2. He that *knows not* and *knows* that he *knows not;*
   He is simple—teach him!
3. He that *knows* and *knows not* that he *knows;*
   He is asleep—wake him!
4. He that *knows* and *knows* that he *knows;*
   He is a wise man—follow him!

—*Gospel Herald*

* * *

The Voice That Stilled the Crowd

On the morning of Lincoln's death, a crowd of fifty thousand people gathered before the Exchange Building in New York. Feeling ran high, natural enough in the circumstances, and there was danger of its finding expression in violence. Then a well-built man in officer's uniform stepped to the front of the balcony, and in a voice that rang like a trumpet call, cried: "Fellow citizens! Clouds and darkness are round about Him. His pavilion is dark waters, and thick clouds of the skies. Justice and judgment are the establishment of His throne. Mercy and truth go before His face. Fellow citizens! God reigns! And the Government at Washington still lives!" Instantly the tumult was stilled, as the people grasped the import of those sublime words. The speaker was General James A. Garfield, himself to become a martyr-president sixteen years later.

—*Moody Monthly*

ATHEISM

Did You?

Never did I hear anyone state, "I was undone and outcast but I read Tom Paine's 'Age of Reason' and I was saved from the power of sin." Did you?

Never did I hear of one who declared, "I was in darkness and despair and knew not where to turn until I read 'Robert Ingersoll's Lectures' and found liberty and peace." Did you?

Never did I hear an atheist telling that his atheism had been the means by which he had been freed from the bondage of drink and set in holiness and happiness. Did you?

But I have heard many testify that when as hopeless and helpless sinners they had turned in their need to the Son of God and cast themselves upon Him for forgiveness and for victory over sin, that He set them in freedom as worshippers at His pierced feet. Have you?

—*Evangelical Tract*

* * *

Losing Faith in God!

A small boy, new to the Sunday school, was greatly pleased with his picture card and its text, "Have faith in God." On the homeward way, however, the precious possession slipped from his fingers and fluttered from the open streetcar window. Immediately a cry of distress arose: "I have lost my 'Faith in God!' Stop the car!'" The good-natured conductor signaled, and the card was recovered amid the smiles of the passengers. One of them said something about the "blessed innocence of childhood," but a more thoughtful voice answered: *"There would be many happier and truer lives if only we older ones were wise enough to call a halt when we find ourselves rushing ahead on some road where we are in danger of leaving our faith in God behind us."*

—*Presbyterian of the South*

* * *

Fooling Those Who Were Robbed

An Illinois thief stole five hundred dollars worth of shoes, the entire stock of a store, and in addition played a trick on the dealer by leaving all the empty boxes, putting them back just where they belonged. One after another the customers arrived the next day, and the dealer pulled out box after box, only to find that each was empty. That was a unique theft, but something much like it takes place all the time in the spiritual world. *For there are many thieves of faith, writers and speakers who make it their business to destroy belief in God, in Christ, in the Church, in religion. But they always leave the boxes. They always leave the shell of what they have taken, in order to fool people into thinking that they have taken nothing at all.* But pull out the boxes, try to get any

comfort and strength out of what they have left, and you will see that the theft has been complete.

—*Christian Endeavor World*

* * *

"Any Brains?"

It is not at all uncommon in our day to meet people who insist that no intelligent person can accept what is not in complete agreement with human reason or what lies outside the realm of human experience.

Which reminds us of how an aged Quaker once confounded a young "rationalist." This young man declared: "I will not believe in the existence of what has never been seen; we are creatures of reason, you know." "Didst thee ever see France?" queried the old Quaker. "No, sir, but others have, and so my reason allows me to believe in its existence upon their testimony." "Ah, thou wilt believe only in what thee or another hast seen." "That's it, you have my idea exactly." "Didst thee ever see thy brains?" "No, sir." "Didst thee ever see anyone who has seen them?" "No, sir." "Dost thee believe thee has any?"

—*The Christian Home*

* * *

"Taste and See!"

An infidel was lecturing to a great audience and, having finished his address, he invited any who had questions to ask to come on the platform. After a short interval, a man who had been well known in the town as a notorious drunkard, but who had lately been converted, stepped forward, and taking an orange from his pocket, coolly began to peel it. The lecturer asked him to propound his question, but without replying to him the man finished peeling his orange, and then ate it. When he had finished his orange he turned to the lecturer and asked him if it was a sweet one. Very angry, the man said, "Idiot, how can I know whether it was sweet or sour, when I never tasted it?" To this the converted drunkard retorted, "And how can you know anything about Christ, if you have not tried Him?"

—*Christian Herald*

Startling Judgment!

An unbeliever got up on one of the heights of the Catskill Mountains, and in the presence of some atheistic companions defied the God of Heaven to show Himself in battle. He swung his sword to and fro, and challenged the Almighty to meet him in single combat. The Almighty paid no attention to him, of course, but He just commissioned a little gnat, so small that it could scarcely be seen by a microscope, to lodge in his windpipe and choke him to death."

—Dr. Arthur T. Pierson

* * *

Hen or Egg?

A young skeptic said to an elderly lady: "I once believed there was a God, but now since studying philosophy and mathematics I am convinced that God is but an empty word."

"Well," said the lady, "I have not studied such things, but since you have, can you tell me from whence comes this egg?" "Why, of course, from a hen," was the reply. "And where does the hen come from?" "Why, from an egg." Then the lady inquired: "Which existed first, the hen or the egg?" "The hen, of course," rejoined the young man. "Oh, then a hen must have existed without having come from an egg?" "Oh, no, I should have said the egg was first."

"Then I suppose you mean that one egg existed without having come from a hen?" The young man hesitated: "Well, you see—that is—of course, well the hen was first!"

"Very well," said she, "Who made that first hen which all succeeding eggs and hens have come?"

"What do you mean by all this?" he asked.

"Simply this, I say that He who created the first hen or egg is He who created the world. You can't explain the existence even of a hen or egg without God, and yet you wish me to believe that you can explain the existence of the whole world without Him!"

—*Now*

The Perfect Squelch!

An Atheist sent a young man a parcel of infidel literature, advising him to read it in preference to the Bible. The young man's reply could not be excelled: "If you have anything better than the Sermon on the Mount, the Parable of the Prodigal Son, and that of the Good Samaritan, or if you have any code of morals better than the Ten Commandments, or anything more consoling and beautiful than the twenty-third Psalm, or on the whole, anything that will throw more light on the future and reveal to me a Father more merciful and kind than the New Testament, send it along."   —*Power*

* * *

Trusting God to Know Some Things

Dr. Talmage once told a story of how, when a young man, he was inclined to be rather skeptical. One day, after he had asked an old minister "why" this, and "how" that, the aged man replied, "Talmage, you must let almighty God know some things you don't know." He acted on the advice, trusted, and preached to thousands afterward.

—*Sunday Companion*

* * *

A Contrast

Out of the night that covers me,
Black as the pit from pole to pole,
I thank whatever gods may be
For my unconquerable soul.

In the fell clutch of circumstance
I have not winced, nor cried aloud,
Under the bludgeoning of chance
My head is bloody, but unbowed.

Beyond this place of wrath and tears
Looms but the horror of the shade;
And yet the menace of the years
Finds, and shall find, me unafraid.

It matters not how strait the gate,
How charged with punishment the scroll,
I am the master of my fate;
I am the captain of my soul.

—*Invictus* by Wm. E. Henley

Out of the light that dazzles me,
Bright as the sun from pole to pole,
I thank the God I know to be
For Christ, the conqueror of my soul.

Since His the sway of circumstance
I would not wince nor cry aloud.
Under that rule which men call chance
My head, with joy, is humbly bowed.

Beyond this place of sin and tears,
That life with Him! and His the aid,
That, spite the menace of the years,
Keeps, and shall keep, me unafraid.

I have no fear though strait the gate;
He cleared from punishment the scroll.
Christ is the Master of my fate;
Christ is the Captain of my soul.

—*My Captain* by Dorothea Day
(*Note*: Wm. Henley died a suicide!)

* * *

The Failure of Atheism

Dr. Jacks tells the story of two friends who had rather blatantly proclaimed themselves to be atheists. When mortal sickness visited one of them, the other came to see him and, perhaps a little afraid lest at the last he should abandon his atheism, said to him, "Stick to it, Bill!" "But," replied the stricken man, "*there is nothing to stick to!*"
—J. D. Jones, in *Morning and Evening*

* * *

"Nobody Made It! It Just Happened!"

Sir Isaac Newton had a replica of our solar system made in miniature. In the center was the sun with its retinue of planets revolving around it. A scientist entered Newton's study one day, and exclaimed, "My! what an exquisite thing this is! Who made it?" "Nobody!" replied Newton to the questioner who was an unbeliever. "You must think I am a fool. Of course somebody made it, and he is a genius." Laying his book aside, Newton arose and laid a hand on his friend's shoulder and said: "This thing is but a puny imitation of a much grander system whose laws you and I know, and I am not able to convince you that this mere toy is without a designer and maker; yet you profess to believe

that the great original from which the design is taken has come into being without either designer or maker. Now tell me, by what sort of reasoning do you reach such incongruous conclusions?"
—W. G. Polack in *"Lutheran Witness"*

* * *

The Perfect Answer

When D. L. Moody was conducting evangelistic meetings across the country, he frequently faced hecklers who were in rather violent disagreement with his tenets.

In the final service of one campaign, an usher handed the famed evangelist a note as he entered the auditorium. Supposing it to be an announcement, Moody quieted the large audience and prepared to read the notice. He opened it to find a single word: "Fool!"

But the colorful preacher was equal to the occasion. Said he, "This is most unusual. I have just been handed a message which consists of but one word—the word 'fool.' I repeat, this is most unusual. I have often heard of those who have written letters and forgotten to sign their names—but this is the first time I have ever heard of anyone who signed his name and *forgot to write the letter!*"

And, taking advantage of the situation, Moody promptly changed his sermon to the text: "The fool hath said in his heart, 'There is no God.' "
—*Moody Monthly*

* * *

The Lesson of the Meat Chopper

The *American Magazine* once published an article giving a businessman's statement of why he knows there is a God. He had been frankly facing the wonders of the stars and planets, their system and order; then he said, "It takes a girl in our factory about two days to learn to put the seventeen parts of a meat chopper together. It may be that these millions of worlds, each with its separate orbit, all balance so wonderfully in space—it may be that they just happened; it may be that by a billion years of tumbling about they finally arranged themselves. I don't know. I am merely a plain manufacturer of cutlery. But this I do know, that you can shake the seventeen parts of a meat chopper around in a washtub for the next seventeen billion years and you'll never have a meat chopper."

—*Christian Herald*

* * *

One of Ingersol's Stunts:

It was usually the custom of Robert Ingersol, at the close of his lectures, to "prove" the non-existence of God by taking his watch from his pocket, and arrogantly say, "If there is a God, I defy Him to strike me dead within the next five minutes!" Standing before the audience, with watch in hand, he could count off the minutes: "One minute; two minutes; three minutes; four minutes; five minutes!" And, then with a smirk of satisfaction wreathing his face, he would triumphantly say, "There, I told you there was no God!" Hearing of Ingersol's blatant blasphemy, Joseph Parker said, "Does the gentleman from America think that he can exhaust God's patience in five minutes?"

—W. B. K.

* * *

No Further Discussion Needed

Charles Bradlaugh, the agnostic, was speaking in a great hall, and after his attack on the Christian faith, he said, "If there is any Christian who would like to come to the platform and say a word in defense of the Christian religion, he has the opportunity." All the men were motionless, but one old woman walked feebly to the platform and said, "I am the woman to speak, for I *know.* Fifty years ago I was left a widow with

three children. I had not a penny in the world, but I believed in God as my Father, and in Jesus Christ as my Saviour. I committed my life to His care. I have, by His blessed help, reared all my children, and all are today in positions of trust. Soon I shall leave this world, and I know my Lord is waiting to meet me on the shores of Eternity. I *know* what my religion has done for me. What has your agnosticism done for you?" With the instinct of one who is beaten, Bradlaugh replied, "Well, Grandma, we will not discuss that tonight."

—*Grace and Truth*

* * *

Case of the Braggart

A notorious infidel had a considerable following in a certain town. He was one of the braggart stamp, and seemed to revel in his outpourings of a blasphemy against God. One day, in the height of his folly, he challenged God, if such a Being existed, to fight him in a certain wood.

The day came, and he went defiantly to the wood, stayed for some time, and returned home again apparently all right, and jubilant of his seeming success.

But when in the wood there had alighted on his eyelid a tiny midge, which he brushed away, paying no attention to it. At night his eye swelled. Soon blood poisoning set in and he died. "The fool hath said in his heart, There is no God." God sent one of His tiniest insects, and the boasting braggart fell before it. It is worthy of being pondered, especially in the fact that a long-suffering God did not strike the blasphemer dead upon the spot, but gave him four days' warning, and space for repentance.

—*Faithful Words*

BIBLE

Science Catching Up With Bible!

Observe some of the belated discoveries of science:

1. The "north" above our earth is "empty." The Bible flashed out this fact 3460 years ago: Job 26:7;

2. "Air has weight." The Bible flashed this into radio land 3460 years ago: Job 28:25;

3. "Earth must balance." The Bible gave this information 2650 years ago: Isa. 40:12;

4. "Earth hangs on nothing." The Bible told this 3460 years ago: Job 26:7;

5. "Stars do not deviate in their courses." The Bible flashed this fact 3236 years ago in this phrase: "The stars in their course": Judg. 5:20;

6. Science: "Sand keeps the ocean in." Bible: "The sea is bound in by sand and cannot pass it": Jer. 5:22.

—*Selected*

* * *

The Power of the Word of God

When Jacob de Shazer went as one of Jimmy Doolittle's raiders on Japan on April 18, 1942, he was an atheist. He was captured and imprisoned by the Japanese. He saw two of his companions shot by a firing squad. He saw another die of slow starvation.

During the long months he pondered the question of why the Japanese hated him and why he hated them. He began to recall some of the things he had heard about Christianity.

Boldly, he asked his jailers if they could get him a Bible. At first they laughed boisterously, as at a good joke, grew ugly, and warned him to stop making a nuisance of himself. But he kept on asking.

A year and a half later — May 1944 — a guard brought him a Bible, flung it at him, and said, "Three weeks you have. Three weeks, then I take away."

True to his word, in three weeks the guard took the Bible away and de Shazer never saw it again.

In 1948, de Shazer, his wife, and infant son were on their way back to Japan as missionaries, all because he asked for a Bible and a Japanese guard gave him one for three weeks.

—*The Teacher*

* * *

The One and Only Remedy!

"A contagious enthusiasm among Christians for the Word of God and a return in faith and obedience to its precepts would do more to point the way out of present world distress and despair than all the plans and strivings of men!"

—Dr. Merrill F. Unger, in *Eternity*.

Without Comparison

"Nothing can stop the Bible. It is useless to call it the world's best seller, though it is, because that term implies comparison — and there is nothing else that even remotely compares with the Bible in popular circulation."

The Bible, or parts of it, has now been translated into 1,027 languages. It is the most wonderful book the world has ever seen. It is estimated that there are over 200,000,000 Bibles. Placed end to end they would make a line 17,000 miles long.

—*San Francisco Chronicle*

* * *

How Readest Thou?

A young lady, asked by her friend to explain what is meant by devotional reading of the Bible, made answer as follows:

"Yesterday morning I received a letter from one to whom I had given my heart and devoted my life. I freely confess to you that I have read that letter five times, not because I did not understand it at the first reading, nor because I expected to commend myself to the author by frequent reading of his epistle. It was not with me a question of duty, but simply one of pleasure. I read it because I am devoted to the one who wrote it.

"To read the Bible with the same motive is to read it devotionally, and to one who reads it in that spirit it is indeed a love Letter."

—*United Presbyterian*

* * *

He Learned on His Knees

The *Pilgrim* reports Dr. Harry A. Ironside as a young preacher visiting the aged Alexander Fraser and listening enthralled as one truth after another was opened up from God's Word by Mr. Fraser, until he could constrain himself no longer and cried out, "Where did you learn these things?" "On my knees on the mud floor of a little sod cottage in the north of Ireland," replied Mr. Fraser. "There, with my Bible open before me, I used to kneel for hours at a time, and ask the Spirit of God to reveal Christ to my soul and to open the *Word* to my heart. He taught me more on my knees on that mud floor than I could have learned in all the colleges and seminaries in the world."

—*Evangel*

* * *

"There It Stands!"

(A Tribute to the Indestructibleness of God's Word)

Century follows century — There it stands.

Empires rise and fall and are forgotten — There it stands.

Dynasty succeeds dynasty — There it stands.

Kings are crowned and uncrowned — There it stands.

Emperors decree its extermination — There it stands.

Atheists rail against it — There it stands.

Agnostics smile cynically — There it stands.

Profane prayerless punsters caricature it — There it stands.

Unbelief abandons it — There it stands.

Higher critics deny its claim to inspiration — There it stands.

The flames are kindled about it — There it stands.

The tooth of time gnaws but makes no dent in it — There it stands.

Infidels predict its abandonment — There it stands.

Modernism tries to explain it away — There it stands.

—Rev. A. Z. Conrad,
Park Street Church, Boston

* * *

"This Precious Book!"

This precious book I'd rather own
Than all the golden gems
That e'er in monarchs' coffers shone,
Or on their diadems.
And were the seas one chrysolite,
This earth a golden ball,
And gems were all the stars of night,
This book were worth them all.

Ah, no, the soul ne'er found relief
In glittering hoards of wealth;
Gems dazzle not the eye of grief;
Gold can not purchase health.
But here a blessed balm appears
For every human woe,
And they that seek that book in tears—
Their tears shall cease to flow.

—Sam Jones, in *Quit Your Meanness.*

* * *

Bible Kicks Me

A heathen Chinese gave a gift Bible back to the missionary. "Every time I read it," he said, "it kicks me."

—*Biblical Research Monthly*

* * *

Bible Reading and Hoeing Potatoes

"Some people read their Bibles like I used to hoe potatoes when I was a boy: When the dinner bell rang, I had to put down a stick at the place in the row where I left off hoeing so when I returned an hour later, I could know where I left off hoeing. We read our Bibles with so little concentration that we do not know where we left off when the reading is resumed."

—W. B. K.

* * *

Bible Knowledge Better Than College Course

William Lyon Phelps of Yale University — called the most beloved professor in America — has on more than one occasion stated: "I thoroughly believe in a university education for both men and women, but I believe a knowledge of the Bible without a college course is more valuable than a college course without the Bible."

* * *

"Be Ye Doers of the Word"
James 1:22

There is a story of a missionary in Korea who had a visit from a native convert who lived a hundred miles away, and who walked four days to reach the mission station. The pilgrim recited proudly, without a single mistake, the whole of the Sermon on the Mount. The missionary was delighted, but he felt that he ought to warn the man that memorizing was not enough — that it was necessary to practice the words as well as to memorize them.

The Korean's face lit up with happy smiles. "That is the way I learned it," he said. "I tried to memorize it, but it wouldn't stick. So I hit upon this plan — I would memorize a verse and then find a heathen neighbor of mine and practice it on him. Then I found it would stick."

—*Earnest Worker*

* * *

A Haifa Policeman

A Haifa policeman, well versed in the Bible, managed to track down a band of smugglers by applying a passage from the Prophets. The gang used an ass-drawn caravan to cross the border into Israel and the policeman was able to capture some of the asses but the smugglers got away. The cop let the beasts of burden go without food for several days and then turned them free. And just as predicted in Isaiah: "The ox knoweth his owner, and the ass his master's crib," the starving animals led police directly to the smuggler's hideout.

—*The American Zionist*

* * *

The Safe Compass

A country lad, who was about to leave his Sunday School and friends to go up to the Metropolis to take a situation there, was accompanied to his starting place by a Christian friend, who kindly said to him: "Now, my boy, recollect you are going to launch your craft on a dangerous ocean."

"Yes, I know it," said the boy; and taking a Bible out of his pocket, and holding it up, he added, "but you see I have got a safe compass to steer by." The guide of young Timothy is still the best guide of youth (II Tim 1:5; 2:1).

—*Sunlight for the Young*

Saved by a Fragment

A colporteur traveling in Bohemia through a Roman Catholic district was surprised to come upon a locksmith who knew the Bible well. He learned that seventeen years before, a priest had gathered all the copies of the Bible together and made a bonfire of them. A gust of wind carried away two burning pieces out of the bonfire, which the locksmith had picked up and read. The first words that caught his eyes were, "Heaven and earth shall pass away, but my words shall not pass away." So impressed was he that he and his father saved a whole Bible out of the burning, and became Bible readers and Bible students.

—Rev. F. B. Meyer

* * *

"Our God Whom We Serve Is Able to Deliver Us"
Daniel 3:17

A man was compelled one night to cross a wide, frozen river. Notwithstanding the assurances of those who were thoroughly familiar with the region and repeatedly crossed on the solid ice, the traveler feared to undertake the trip, but finally began to crawl his way over. When near the middle of the frozen stream he was startled by a sound in the distance, and caught sight of a Negro driving a heavy team of horses pulling a great load of pig iron; yet there was not the least sign of a crack in the ice. Will the Word of God hold? Some fear to trust it. Why, man, it can't fail!

—*Sunday School Times*

* * *

Words About the "Word"

In a recent issue of the *Bible Society Record*, the following quotations from prominent and well-known Americans appear concerning "God's Word."

George Washington:

It is impossible to rightly govern the world without God and the Bible.

Abraham Lincoln:

I am profitably engaged in reading the Bible. Take all of this Book upon reason that you can, and the balance by faith, and you will live and die a better man.

Woodrow Wilson:

I have a very simple thing to ask of you. I ask every man and woman in this audience that from this day on they will realize that part of the destiny of America lies in their daily perusal of this great Book.

Dr. Helen Keller:

Unless we form the habit of going to the Bible in bright moments as well as in trouble, we cannot fully respond to its consolations, because we lack equilibrium between light and darkness.

Captain Eddie Rickenbacker:

The Bible is "one Book" for "one world". . . . Today I realize that I probably would not be here, had it not been for the spiritual light and the moral power learned from this Book, which has carried me through the many crises of my life.

John Foster Dulles:

The Bible means to me that there is a God, that He has purposes for men and that each of us has the task to find and immerse himself in the stream of the Divine purpose.

Douglas MacArthur:

Believe me, sir, never a night goes by, be I ever so tired, but I read the Word of God before I go to bed.

Herbert Hoover:

The whole of the inspirations of our civilization springs from the teachings of Christ and the lessons of the Prophets. To read the Bible for these fundamentals is a necessity of American life.

J. Edgar Hoover:

The Bible is the unfailing guide which points the way for men to the perfect life. The lessons of charity, justice and equality which enrich its pages should be learned well by all men in order that greed, avarice, and iniquity can be blotted out.

Dwight D. Eisenhower:

To read the Bible is to take a trip to a fair land where the spirit is strengthened and faith renewed.

Senator Styles Bridges:

All citizens of our Republic must constantly be reminded that the American heritage is a Biblical heritage; that the American present is a Biblical present and the American destiny is a Biblical destiny.

—*Gospel Herald*

* * *

Reading the Bible

The great effective instrument of the Holy Spirit by which the truth is authoritatively taught is the inspired Word of God. Satan is gaining victories by holding men back from a loving, searching study of the Bible.

My own daily life is as full as that of any man I know, but I found long since that as I allowed the pressure of professional and other engagements to fill in every moment between rising and going to bed, the spirit would surely starve; so I made a rule, which I have since stuck to in spite of many temptations, not to read or study anything but my Bible after the evening meal, and never to read any other book but the Bible on Sunday.

—Dr. Howard M. Kelly

* * *

John's Bible

When he had become one of the country's greatest merchants, John Wanamaker once said, "In my lifetime, I have made many purchases. I have bought things which have cost me thousands of dollars. But the greatest purchase I ever made was when I was a boy twelve years old. Then I bought a Bible for two dollars and fifty cents. That was my greatest purchase, for that Bible made me what I am today."

John Wanamaker became a great man because he, as a poor boy, loved God and His Word. He loved the Bible, read it, and followed its teachings.

—*Gospel Herald*

* * *

The Word Lives

Ingersoll held up a copy of the Bible and said, "In fifteen years I'll have this book in the morgue." Fifteen years rolled by, Ingersoll was in the morgue, and the Bible lives on. Voltaire said that in one hundred years the Bible would be an outmoded and forgotten book, to be found only in museums. When the one hundred years were up, Voltaire's house was owned and used by the Geneva Bible Society. And recently ninety-two volumes of Voltaire's works —a part of the Earl of Derby's library —were sold for two dollars!

—Rev. Eugene M. Harrison, in *Moody Monthly*

* * *

Turtle Christians

Prof. J. A. Carlson, in "Your Body," speaks of hunger. A bird can go nine days without food. A man twelve days. A dog twenty days. A turtle five hundred days. A snake eight hundred days. A fish one thousand days. Insects twelve hundred days. But food is necessary for all of God's creatures. There are some "turtle" Christians, who go five hundred days without much real Bible meat. And many "bird" Christians, who go more than nine days without food. And not a few "fish" Christians, who go one thousand days without eating much of the honey and meat and bread of the Bible. Classify yourself!

—"*Pickings*," by Robert G. Lee, D.D.

* * *

No Masterpiece

An elderly gentleman, who was very nearsighted, prided himself on his ability as an art critic. While accompanying some friends through a large gallery, he sought to display his real or fancied knowledge of pictures to these friends. He had left his glasses at home and was not able to see things very clearly. Standing before a large frame, he began to point out the inartistic features of the picture there revealed. "The frame," he said, "is altogether out of keeping with the subject, and as for the subject itself (it was that of a man), it is altogether too homely, in fact, too ugly, ever to make a good picture. It is a great mistake for any artist to choose so homely a subject for a picture if he expects it to be a masterpiece." The old gentleman was going on like this when his wife managed to get near enough to interrupt. She exclaimed, "My dear, you are looking into a mirror." He was quite taken back to realize that he had been criticizing his own face. Now the word of God is such a mirror. It does not hide our deformities.

—Dr. Harry A. Ironside

* * *

Said Henry Ford:

"All the sense of integrity, honor, and service I have in my heart I got from hearing the Bible read by a school teacher in the three years I was privileged to go to a little, old-fashioned grammar school. The teacher read the Bible every morning to start the day right. I got a great deal out of that influence. I was brought up in the church. I belong to the church. I attend church. I never go to hear a sermon, whether it is by a preacher in a small church or a large one, that I do not get help."

—*Gospel Herald*

* * *

Falling In Love With the Author

A young lady once laid down a book which she had just finished, with the remark that it was the dullest story she had ever read. In the course of time, she became engaged to a young man, and one night she said to him: "I have a book in my library whose author's name, and even initials, are precisely the same as yours. Isn't that a singular

29

coincidence?" "I do not think so," he replied. "Why not, pray?" "For the simple reason that I wrote the book." That night, the young lady sat up until two o'clock reading the book again. And this time it seemed the most interesting story she had ever read. The once dull book was now fairly fascinating because she knew and loved the author. So, a child of God finds the Bible interesting because he knows and loves the Author! It is His Father's message, addressed to him.

—*Record of Christian Work*

* * *

"Don't Let Me Go Back Empty-Handed!"

Said Robert Moffat, missionary to Africa, "A woman came to me after having walked fifteen miles, and said that she wished for a New Testament. I said to her:

" 'My good woman, there is not a copy to be had.'

" 'What! Must I return empty-handed?'

" 'I fear you must.'

" 'Oh,' she said, 'I borrowed a copy once, but the owner came and took it away, and now I sit with my family, sorrowful, because we have no Book to talk to us. Now we are far from any-one else. We are living at a cattle out-post, and no one to teach us but the Book. Oh, go and try to find a Book! Oh, my elder brother, do go and try to find a Book for me! Surely there is one to be found. Do not let me go back empty.'

"I felt deeply for her, for she spoke so earnestly, and I said: 'Wait a little and I will see what I can do.'

"I searched here and there and at last found a copy and brought it to the good woman. Oh, if you could have seen how her eyes brightened, how she clasped my hands and kissed them over and over again. Anyway she went with the Book, rejoicing, with a heart overflowing with gratitude."

—*Pilgrim Holiness Advocate*

Two Hundred Lives

A few years before the war, a humble villager in eastern Poland received a Bible from a colporteur who visited his small hamlet. He read it, was con-verted, and passed the book on to others. Through that one Bible two hundred more became believers. When the col-porteur, Michael Billester, revisited the town in the summer of 1940, the group gathered to worship and listen to his preaching. Billester suggested that in-stead of giving the customary testimonies they all recite verses of Scripture.

Thereupon a man arose and asked, "Perhaps we have misunderstood. Did you mean verses or chapters?"

"Do you mean to say there are people here who can recite chapters of the Bible?" asked Mr. Billester in astonish-ment.

That was precisely the case. Those vil-lagers had memorized, not only chapters, but whole books of the Bible. Thirteen knew Matthew and Luke and half of Genesis. One had committed all the Psalms to memory. Together, the two hundred knew virtually the entire Bible. Passed around from family to family and brought to the gathering on Sun-days, the old Book had become so worn with use that its pages were hardly legible.

—*Sunday School Times*

* * *

Hearing It Through

A certain wayward young man ran away from home and was not heard of for years. In some way, hearing that his father had just died, he returned home and was kindly received by his mother. The day came for the reading of the will; the family were all gathered to-gether, and the lawyer began to read the document. To the surprise of all present, the will told in detail of the wayward career of the runaway son. The boy in anger arose, stamped out of the room, left the house, and was not heard from for three years. When eventually he was found he was in-formed that the will, after telling of his waywardness, had gone on to bequeath him $15,000. How much sorrow he would have saved himself and others, if he had only heard the reading through! Thus many people only half read the Bible, and turn from it dissatisfied. The Bible says, "The wages of sin is death," yes, but it says more, it says, "but the gift of God is eternal life."

—*Herald and Presbyter*

* * *

The Bible Is the Book

A noted orator asked Dickens for the most pathetic story in literature, and he said it was that of the prodigal son. Mr. Coleridge was asked for the richest passage in literature, and he said it was the first sixteen verses in the fifth chapter of Matthew. Another asked Daniel Webster for the greatest legal digest, and he replied that it was the Sermon on the Mount. No one has equaled Moses for law, nor David for poetry, nor Isaiah for visions, nor Jesus for ethics, nor Peter for holy zeal, nor Apollos for fiery oratory, nor Paul for logic, nor John's statements of sanctified love. What a ridiculous statement that to study the Bible "marks a step backward in education!" God's Word is the very greatest of all books, and its Author is the very greatest of all teachers. We do well to stay close to its pages. It is *the* Book.

—*Christian Action*

* * *

All in the Bible

"The religious knowledge of too many adults resembles, I am afraid, the religious knowledge of little Eve," said Bishop Hoss at a Nashville picnic.

"So you attend Sunday School regularly?" the minister said to little Eve.

"Oh, yes sir."

"And you know your Bible?"

"Oh, yes sir."

"Could you perhaps tell me something that is in it?"

"I could tell you everything that's in it."

"Indeed," and the minister smiled. "Do tell me, then."

"Sister's beau's photo is in it," said little Eve, promptly, "and ma's recipe for vanishin' cream is in it, and a lock of my hair cut off when I was a baby is in it, and the ticket for pa's watch is in it."

—*Los Angeles Times*

* * *

The Power of God's Word

Away in a little town in the far south of Argentina one day a soldier, attracted by the sound of singing, entered a little mission hall and heard the Gospel preached. He stayed behind and spoke to the missionary who asked him if he was a Christian.

"Yes, I am," he replied.

"Where did you hear the Gospel?"

"From my mother."

"Where does she live?"

"She is a long way off, but will you come and see her? She has never heard a preacher, and she will be glad to see you."

The missionary went, and found on a distant farm, where no missionary had ever been, an old Christian woman. She told him that years before a colporteur, passing that way, had left a copy of the Word of God. She had read it, her eyes had been opened, and she had come to know Jesus Christ as her Saviour. She had had no teacher but the Spirit of God. That old woman was the mother of fourteen children. At the time the missionary visited her, the youngest was twelve years old, and she had led every one of those children to Christ through the reading of the Scriptures left by an unknown colporteur.

—*Selected in God's Revivalist*

* * *

The Hammer

God's Word has been a hammer for nineteen centuries and when other hammers today try to break God's eternal anvil of truth we remember the inscription on the monument to the Huguenots at Paris: "Hammer away, ye hostile hands; Your hammers break; God's anvil stands."

—*Samuel M. Zwemer*

Going By The Book

Two men, the one a foreman, the other, one of the carpenters under him, were standing on the deck of a steamship then on the stocks, in one of the shipbuilding yards on the Clyde. "Well, S—," said the foreman, "I have been anxious to have a conversation with you. I'm told you are one of those people who say they know for certain that they are saved. Is that true?" "Yes," said S—, "quite true; thank God, I know I'm saved; in fact, there is nothing I'm more sure of, than that I'm saved." "Well, now," said the foreman, "that is something I cannot see through, how any man can say that he is saved as long as he is in this world. I think it is rather presumptuous for anyone to say so . . ." "Well," said S—, "I'm not at all surprised at you, but there *is a reality in being saved*, in being a child of God, and in knowing it. What is the breadth of this waterway?" The foreman, astonished at the apparent sudden change in the conversation, said "Why, fourteen inches all around, to be sure; what makes you ask that, when you know?" "But are you quite sure that it is to be fourteen inches?" "Certainly." "But what makes you so sure?" *"Why, I'm going by the book,"* and, as he said so, he pulled a book out of his pocket, in which were marked the sizes and position of the various things on the deck. "I'm sure it is fourteen inches, for it is here in the book, and I got the book from headquarters." "Oh! I see," said S—; "now look here; that is exactly how I know I'm saved. *I'm just going by the Book.* It came from headquarters—it is God's Word."

—*Traveler's Guide*

* * *

The Shipwrecked Bible

Alexander Duff, the great missionary sailed for India on the *Lady Holland*. His clothes, his prized possessions, his library of eight hundred volumes were all on board. And then within a few miles of India, a shipwreck occurred.

The passengers were all saved. But the possessions of all the passengers were lost at the bottom of the sea. On the seashore, Alexander Duff looked out to sea, hoping against hope that some part of his possession might be cast up on the shore.

Then they saw something—something small, floating on top of the water. Nearer and nearer it came, while anxious eyes watched it. What would it be? The missionary waded into the water, got hold of the floating object and returned. What was it?

The Bible! Of all his books, of all his possessions, that single Book was worth saving! Alexander Duff took the rescued Book to be a token from his Lord—took it to mean that this one Book was worth all his books, and all his possessions.

So, heartened, Alexander Duff began his career as a missionary in India. The very next day, reading from the Bible, he began his first class—a group of five boys meeting under a banyan tree. A week later the class had swelled to three hundred listeners!

And several years later a beautiful church stood on the spot where the banyan tree had been—and one thousand students of the Gospel raised their voices in prayer and hymns to Jesus Christ.

—*Youth's Comrade*

* * *

"Life in Blood"

In 1615, William Harvey discovered the circulation of the blood and that the life principle resided therein. Scientists regarded this as an amazing discovery, revealed over three hundred years ago. Says the Bible, "The life of the flesh is in the blood" (Lev. 17:11). "This is the most comprehensive and up-to-date physiological generalization that has ever been made. The life and wellbeing of every organ, gland, and tissue depends upon the condition and rate of the blood stream," writes a modern scientist.

—*Selected*

* * *

Man and Soil of Earth:

Modern Science says, "The identical sixteen elements found in the human body are also found in ordinary soil of the earth." The Bible says, with scientific accuracy, "Man is formed of the dust of the ground!" (Gen. 2:7). "Dust thou art and unto dust shalt thou return" (Gen. 3:19). Said a scientific lecturer, "If it were possible for the human body to instantly lose all of its electrical values, that body would instantly fly into dust!"

* * *

—Selected

Meditating upon the Word

Andrew Bonar tells of a simple Christian in a farm house who had "meditated the Bible through three times." This is precisely what the psalmist had done; he "had shaken every tree in God's garden and gathered fruit therefrom." The idea of meditation is to "get into the middle of a thing." *Meditation is to the mind what digestion is to the body. Unless the food be digested, the body receives no benefit from what we read or hear; there must be that mental digestion known as meditation.* If we would "buy the truth," we must pay the price which Paul intimated when he wrote to Timothy: "Meditate upon these things, give thyself wholly to them." David meditated in God's Word because he loved it, and he loved it because he meditated in it.

—*Moody Monthly*

* * *

Power of the Word

It was in a meeting where they were giving personal testimony. One man arose, holding a New Testament in his hand. "My story," said he, "is unlike other men. I was a pickpocket, and one day I saw a man with a definite bulge in his hip pocket. 'A fat purse,' thought I, and soon it was in my pocket. But when I arrived home, behold, it was a Book. In disgust I threw it aside, but afterward, out of curiosity, I opened it and began to read. Before many days had passed I discovered Christ as my Saviour and Lord."

Listening to this testimony, one of the volunteer colporteurs of the Bible Society became interested. After the service he asked to see the New Testament. It was the one he had carried with him for years, the one he had considered lost. Is not this evidence of the power of the Word to change and to transform man's life? What has the Word done for you?

—W. H. McCutcheon
in *Gospel Herald*

* * *

The History of Judson's Bible

Twenty years after Adoniram Judson reached Burma the New Testament was translated into the Burmese tongue. In 1824, when war was waged between England and Burma, Mr. Judson was thrown into prison, and Mrs. Judson buried the precious manuscript, just ready for the printer, in the earth beneath their house. But as mold was gathering upon it, on account of the dampness caused by heavy rains, with a woman's ready wit, she sewed the treasure inside a roll of cotton, put on a cover and took it to the jail to be used by Mr. Judson as a pillow.

In nine months he was transferred to the inner prison, where five pairs of fetters were upon his ankles, and it was announced that he, with a hundred others, fastened to a bamboo pole, were to be killed before morning. During this terrible night, much prayer ascended for the precious pillow. It had fallen to the share of the keeper of the prison, but Mrs. Judson, producing a better one, induced him to exchange.

Mr. Judson was not killed, but was hurried away to another place, and again the pillow was his companion. But one of the jailers untied the mat that served as its cover and threw the roll of cotton into the yard as worthless. Here a native Christian, ignorant of its value, found and preserved it as a relic of his beloved master, and with him months afterward its contents were discovered intact. After the close of the war this New Testament was printed, and in 1834 the whole Bible was translated into the Burmese language—a language peculiarly difficult on account of its construction and curious combinations.

—*Stories of Bible Translation*

33

Bible

When an Infidel Corroborated the Scriptures

"David, a man after God's own heart!" said an infidel, "a pretty specimen; a liar, an adulterer, a murderer." "You are a proof of the truth of God's Word," quietly answered the one to whom the words were addressed, "for the Bible says that Nathan said to David, 'By this deed thou hast given great occasion to the enemies of the Lord to blaspheme.'"

—*Christian Reader's Digest*

* * *

T. N. T.

A minister recently sent a number of books, among them a copy of the New Testament, to be rebound. He was surprised on the return of the books to find on the backbone of the New Testament a label in gilt letters, "T.N.T." There was no room to spell out "The New Testament," so the bookbinder inscribed merely "T.N.T.," the first letters of the three words.

Not a bad name for the New Testament! It is T. N. T.—it is spiritual dynamite.

—*Moody Monthly*

* * *

Patrick Henry's Regret

Patrick Henry, near death, said: "Here is a Book, the Bible, worth more than all others that were ever printed; yet it is my misfortune never to have found time to read it."

—*Prairie Overcomer*

* * *

Stabbed Through

Dr. Malon of Geneva, on a journey got into conversation with an unbeliever. At last the man said, "Don't you see that I don't believe in your Bible?" The doctor said, "If ye believe not that I am he, ye shall die in your sins." Years after the doctor received a letter. "You took the Sword of the Spirit and stabbed me through and through."

—*Christian Herald*

A Complete Entity

Let us beware that we do not forget that the Old Testament and the New Testament alike tell of Jesus. It can be truly said of the Bible: "The glory of God did lighten it, and the Lamb is the light thereof. The name of Jesus, the supreme personality, the center of the world's hope, is on every page."

—Matthew Henry

* * *

When the Truth Hurts

Years ago, before "civilization" had penetrated the remote regions of Africa, a white man presented a mirror to the chief of a tribe. He did not know what it was. He looked into it and saw a frightfully ugly face; then sensing that he was seeing the image of himself, he dashed it to the ground and broke it into fragments. Someone might say of him, "He was only a savage; an educated person wouldn't be so foolish." Wait a moment! In the city of Boston, at a society of artists, was mentioned one who painted beyond the skin-deep beauty and expression of his subjects, and where the character warranted it had brought out the latent traits and portrayed almost the very soul of the person. Among his patrons was a Boston lady. When she received her portrait from him, she studied it awhile. Then she recognized the fact that the artist had laid bare her true character on the canvas. Furiously she seized a knife and cut the face from the painting and destroyed it. Why should an African slave and a cultured Bostonian both act in this extraordinary manner? Is it not that men and women of all sorts cannot bear to be told the truth about themselves?

—*From a tract of the Good News Publishers.*

* * *

Dr. Howard A. Kelly's Remedy for Taut Nerves:

A woman of nervous temperament visited the world-renowned physician, Dr. Howard A. Kelly. The cares of life threatened her physical strength and even her reason. Having given her symptoms to the physician, she was greatly astonished at his prescription: "Madam, what you need is to read the Bible more!" "But, Doctor—" began the bewildered woman. "Go home and read your Bible an hour a day," the great man reiterated with kindly authority, "then come back to me a month from today."

At first, the woman was inclined to be angry. But she reflected with a pang of conscience that she had neglected the daily reading of God's Word, and "the secret place of the most High," where formerly she communed with her Lord. In coming back to her God, and His Word, the joys of her salvation returned. When she presented herself to the doctor a month later, he said, "Well, I see you have been an obedient patient. Do you feel as if you needed any other medicine now?" "No, Doctor, I feel like a *different* person. But how did you know what I needed?" Taking up his own worn and well-marked Bible, he said, "If I would omit my daily reading of God's Word, I would not only lose my joy, but I would lose my greatest source of strength and skill . . . Your case called not for medicine, but for a source of peace and strength *outside* your own mind. My prescription, when tried, *works wonders!*"

—W. B. K.

* * *

The Bible

Within this awful volume lies
The mystery of mysteries.
Happiest they of the human race
To whom God has granted grace
To read, to fear, to hope, to pray,
To lift the latch and force the way.
And better had they ne'er been born
Who read to doubt, or read to scorn.

—Sir Walter Scott

* * *

Literature's Source

So closely is the Bible allied with the literature of the world that DeWitt Talmage said, "Every great book that has been published since the first printing press was lifted has directly or in-directly derived much of its power from the Sacred Oracles. Milton's 'Paradise Lost' is borrowed from the Bible; Spenser's writings are imitations of the parables; John Bunyan saw in a dream what Saint John had previously seen in a vision; Macauley crowns his most gigantic sentences with Scripture quotations; Walter Scott's characters are Bible men and women under different names; Hobbs stole from this 'Castle of Truth' the weapons with which he afterward attacked it; and the writings of Pope are saturated with Isaiah. The Bible is the fountain of truth from which other good books dip their life."

—*Herald of Holiness*

* * *

An Accurate Portrait

A prominent photographer of Milwaukee, Wis., says that there are actually few beautiful women or handsome men in the world. It takes a good photographer, by careful lighting and posing, to make almost any human face attractive, he contends. "It is interesting to see the number of persons who do not know that they have a crooked nose, one eye smaller, or a lopsided face, or some other fault," this authority said, and he added: "When people look into a mirror they usually are combing their hair, shaving, or otherwise in motion. Motion is the great deceiver, and when in motion the faults are minimized. It is when the face is stationary, as in a photograph, that the faults become apparent." The Lord has taken a life-sized photograph, so to speak, of man in his natural condition. He shows it in Romans 3:9-18. We have not yet heard of a person who called it beautiful, but we have heard of some who said it was not a true picture of them. We must not blame God's camera. It is perfect. How true, as this man says, that "motion is a great deceiver." Sinners are so busy doing this and that, going hither and yon, seeking to establish their own righteousness. They do not care to stop and look intently at the photograph taken of them.

—Tom. M. Olsen, in *Now*

"Snakebite Remedy"

A black snake slithered out of a cave, and the old timer in the Tennessee hills watched it pause a short distance from the mouth of the cave. The reptile took a few bites of a certain plant and wended its way back into the cave. Mr. Old Timer watched the snake repeat this performance two or three times, each time biting on the plant and returning to the cave.

"I'll venture the black snake is fighting with a deadly rattler in there," he thought to himself. "He comes out here and bites this plant to offset the poison of those fangs, I believe. Just to make sure, I'll make a test." Waiting until the black snake returned to the cave again, he slipped from behind his bush of observation, uprooted the plant and removed it, and returned to watch the results. He regretted his deed, but his suspicions were confirmed when he saw the heroic snake search in vain for the plant, and then curl up and die.

A specific remedy has been provided for the bite of "that old serpent . . . the Devil"—the Eternal Word of God. Let him come with his poisonous "Go ahead and do it—thou shalt not surely die," and the Christian may run to the Word of Life and find the antidote.

—Marie Manire Chapman, in
Gospel Herald

* * *

The Bible — There It Stands!

Where childhood needs a standard
  Or youth a beacon light,
Where sorrow sighs for comfort
  Or weakness longs for might,
Bring forth the Holy Bible,
  The Bible! There is stands!
Resolving all life's problems
  And meeting its demands.

Though sophistry conceal it,
  The Bible! There it stands!
Though Pharisees profane it,
  Its influence expands;
It fills the world with fragrance
  Whose sweetness never cloys,
It lifts our eyes to heaven,
  It heightens human joys.

Despised and torn in pieces,
  By infidels decried—
The thunderbolts of hatred
  The haughty cynics' pride—
All these have railed against it
  In this and other lands,
Yet dynasties have fallen,
  And still the Bible stands!

To paradise a highway,
  The Bible! There it stands!
Its promises unfailing,
  Nor grievous its commands;
It points man to the Saviour,
  The lover of his soul;
Salvation is its watchword,
  Eternity its goal!

—James M. Gray

* * *

"It Will Light You Home"

A minister went far into a backwoods settlement to hold a meeting and it was necessary that he return late in the very dark night. A woodsman provided him with a torch of pitch-pine wood. The minister, never having seen anything of the kind, said, "It will soon burn out." "It will light you home," answered the other. "The wind may blow it out," said the preacher. "It will light you home," was again the answer. "But what if it should rain?" "It will light you home," was the answer a third time. And, contrary to the minister's fears, the torch did last him all the way home. The Word of God is a torch given into the hands of each of us. What if it rains? What if the wind blows? What if the fires of persecution come? If you will hold the torch high it will light you home.

—*Christian Union Herald*

* * *

An Inheritance Incorruptible

Many years ago a Brazilian gave hospitality to a traveler who, before leaving, gave his host a Bible. Being a "Protestant" version, this Bible was placed in the drawer of the kitchen table and left there many years. When this man died, his son-in-law, Guilhermino, inherited the Bible along with other effects. He was a staunch Roman Catholic, but he commenced reading the Bible and through it was led to the Lord. During the next ten years he did not meet another Christian. One day he set out to find someone who would baptize him. After two days' travel on horseback, he came across an evangelical woman, the first Protestant he had ever met, and was overjoyed to find that she believed the same as he did. Several months later a missionary went to his home to baptize him and his wife and two of his children. No one could be persuaded to come to his baptism, and his father would not enter his house for eight months as a result of this open confession.

Years have passed since Guilhermino was baptized. Now, his father also has confessed Christ and has been baptized, all as a result of the testimony of one man!

—*Scripture Gift Mission News Bulletin*

* * *

Wealth Untold!

Precious things of wealth untold,
Stores of silver and of gold,
God hides oft within the ground,
Till by seeking they are found.
In His Word He's hidden, too,
Riches that He means for you.

Search the Scripture's precious store
As the miner digs for ore,
Finding wisdom not of earth,
Far above a ruby's worth.
Search, and you will surely find
Treasures to enrich the mind.

Search the Scriptures every day,
Search, and find there hidden away,
Like a pearl within its shell,
Promises that fears dispel.
Search, and find God's words impart
Treasures to enrich the heart.

Search the Scriptures, finding there
Christ, its chiefest Treasure rare,
Through whom God makes wealth abound
In each life where He is found.
Search, and find what Christ will do
To enrich all life for you.   —*Selected*

For Limited Packing Space

A certain Christian traveler was packing his suitcase when about to proceed on a journey, when he remarked to a friend: "There is still a little corner left open in which I desire to pack a guidebook, a lamp, a mirror, a telescope, a book of poems, a number of biographies, a bundle of old letters, a hymn book, a sharp sword, a small library, containing thirty volumes,—all these articles must occupy a space of about three by two inches." "How are you going to manage that?" queried his friend, and the reply was, "Very easily; for the Bible contains all these things."

—*Gospel Herald*

* * *

"Does the Bible Tell About Peanuts?"

Dr. Carver, the great Negro scientist of Tuskegee Institute, has gone to be with Christ after spending his life for others. For years he urged his people in the South to plant crops besides cotton, for if that crop failed all was lost. He finally persuaded them to plant peanuts. However, they raised more peanuts than they knew what to do with. Carver then prayed for wisdom whereby the peanut might be put to new uses. His prayer was answered, and he discovered how to make oils, varnishes, colorings, medicines, and a hundred other things from peanuts. He was invited to testify before a Senate Committee, and there he was asked, "Dr. Carver, how did you learn all these things?" He replied, "From an old Book." The chairman asked, "What book?" He said, "The Bible." He was asked, "Does the Bible tell about peanuts?" He answered, "No, Mr. Senator, but it tells about the God who made the peanut. I asked Him to show me what to do with the peanut, and He did."

—*Christian Life*

* * *

What Glory Gilds!

What glory gilds the sacred page!
Majestic, like the sun;
It gives a light to ev'ry age;
It gives, but borrows none.

The pow'r that gave it still supplies
　The gracious light and heat.
Its truths upon the nations rise;
　They rise, but never set.

Lord, everlasting thanks be Thine
　For such a bright display
As makes a world of darkness shine
　With beams of heavenly day.

Our souls rejoicingly pursue
　The steps of Him we love,
Till glory breaks upon our view
　In brighter worlds above.
　　　　　　　　—William Cowper

* * *

The Book Conquered

Some years ago a Spaniard found a torn book by the side of a railway. On reading it he soon found it was no ordinary book, but he did not know that it was part of the Bible. The words so interested him he decided to follow its teachings, and so pleased was he with his new found treasure, that he called in his neighbors, and read to them out of the Book. One day the orchard next to his was sold, and the new owner turned aside a water course that had also watered his land, and it was not long before his trees began to suffer. His friends told him what he ought to do to punish his neighbor, but no, he would not think of doing any harm. He would stand by his Book. One morning, going into the orchard, he noticed in a far corner one tree quite fresh and green. At once he got his spade and dug around, and to his joy found a spring of water, and soon ditches were carrying the life-giving water to all corners of his orchard. The Book had conquered.

　　　　　　　　—*Faithful Words*

* * *

Bible Penetration

No one has a better chance to learn how the Bible finds men out than the missionaries. And what testimonies do they give!

Once when Dr. Chamberlain had read to the natives of an East Indian city the first chapter of the Epistle to the Ro-

mans, an intelligent Brahmin said to him, "Sir, that chapter was written by one of you missionaries about us Hindus; *it describes us exactly.*" But nobody disputes that that chapter was written by the apostle Paul eighteen hundred years before our missionaries went to India.

At another time a learned Chinese was employed by some missionaries to translate the New Testament into Chinese. At first the work of translating had no effect upon the scholarly Chinese. But after some time he became quite agitated and said, "What a wonderful book this is!" "Why so?" said the missionary. "Because," said the man, "*it tells so exactly about myself. It knows all that is in me. The One who made this book must have made me!*"

　　　　　　　—Frank M. Goodchild, in
　　　　　　　　　Can We Believe?

* * *

How the Word Was Cut into His Heart

When the Christians in Lahore, India, wanted to stamp Matthew 11:28 on the back of Gospels they had printed, they found they could not obtain a rubber stamp with which to do it. The only way to obtain this stamp with the words of the Lord Jesus on it, "Come unto me, all ye that labor and are heavy laden, and I will give you rest," was to get a clever Mohammedan to cut the words in rubber for them. This follower of the false prophet did a good job for the saints. He also cut according to instructions the address of the church in the rubber. But while the Indian was doing his work on the soft rubber, God by His Spirit was doing a work in the heart of this Oriental. What was the surprise and joy of the missionary when the rubber stamp was finished to hear the Mohammedan say: "While I was cutting those words in the rubber, God was cutting them in my heart."

　　　　　　　　　　—*Good News*

* * *

Not Only for the Dying

Mr. Tompkins was obliged to stop overnight at a small country hotel. He was shown to his room by the one boy the place afforded, a colored lad. "I'm glad there's a rope in case of fire," commented Mr. Tompkins, as he surveyed the room; "but what's the idea of putting a Bible in the room in such a prominent place?" "Dat am intended foh use, suh," replied the boy, "in case de fire am too far advanced foh yo' to make yo' escape, suh." The Bible is not only for the dying, it is for the living. It shows the way of life to all; it shows how to walk in that way of life. It should be read daily, and studied as a treasure map.

—*Christian Victory*

* * *

The Why of the Reformation

In the dawn of the English Reformation, when the great Bible, just translated, stood on its desk chained to a pillar in the cathedral, the people gathered in throngs, and standing on the stone floor, listened attentively, hour after hour, and if the reader paused would cry out, "Read on! Read on!"

—*Bible Readings*

* * *

The Unchanging Word

"The empire of Caesar is gone; the legions of Rome are moldering in the dust; the avalanches that Napoleon hurled upon Europe have melted away; the pride of the Pharaohs has fallen; the pyramids they raised to be their tombs are sinking every day in the desert sands; Tyre is the rock for bleaching fishermen's nets; Sidon has scarcely left a wreck behind; but the Word of God still survives. All things that threatened to extinguish it have only aided it; and it only proves every day how transient the noblest monument that man can build, how enduring is the least Word God has spoken. Tradition has dug for it a grave; intolerance has lighted for it many a faggot; many a Judas has betrayed it with a kiss; many a Demas has forsaken it, but the Word of God still endures."

—Dr. John Cumming

Not the Paintings, but the Visitors

There is no city in the world, perhaps, where the treasures of art are more appreciated than Florence, Italy. It is told that an American visitor to the Pitti Palace in Florence, after viewing some of the paintings there, said to his guide: "Are these the great masterpieces that everyone tells me about? I don't see much in them to arouse such enthusiasm."

"It is not these paintings that are on trial, sir," the guide answered, "but it is you, who view them."

So it is with the Word of God. Sometimes we run across scoffers, men who sneer at divine revelation, who say that they cannot get up much enthusiasm about the Bible. *But the Bible is not on trial.* Whether men believe it or not, it is the Word of God, "which liveth and abideth for ever." (1 Pet. 1:23).

—*The Pilgrim*

* * *

Unpleasant Application

When our Lord returned to Nazareth and read the Scriptures in the synagogue of His boyhood, there passed through the congregation a thrill of pleasure, but how their pleasure gave way to anger, their welcome to a violent expulsion from Nazareth. They loved to hear the Scriptures read; they disliked their application to themselves. So long as Jesus sounded the swelling notes of Isaiah they were thrilled but when He brought Isaiah's message up-to-date and illustrated it from present conditions they were offended. They reveled in the ancient Scriptures—but let them be left ancient. When God's Word became a two-edged sword, piercing heart and conscience, they rebelled. Is this our trouble today?

—*"The Book for Today."*
by John A. Patton,
in *Christian Digest*

* * *

From Library Shelf to Heart

Charles G. Finney was reported "a hardened case" by ministers who labored in the communities of New York State in which he lived. At 29 years of age he was a rising young lawyer who had never owned a Bible but added one to the reference books in his law library. Gradually the Bible replaced his interest in Blackstone and the Statutes of New York, his heart was changed and he bade farewell to his clients with the announcement that he "had a retainer from the Lord Jesus Christ to plead his cause." And plead it he did in America and the British Isles to the lasting benefit of multitudes. This lawyer turned evangelist, who was permanently retained by Jesus Christ, founded the Broadway Tabernacle, New York City, became the second president of Oberlin College and urged the claims of the Gospel upon more hearers than any other man of his generation. It happened because a "reference book" somehow got from a library shelf into Charles G. Finney's heart.

—*The Chaplain*

* * *

In Which Stage Are You?

There are three stages of Bible study: first, the cod-liver oil stage, when you take it like medicine, because it is good for you; second, the shredded wheat biscuit stage, dry, but nourishing; third, the peaches and cream stage. Have you reached the third stage?

—*Moody Monthly*

* * *

A Statesman's Tribute

"If asked *what* is the remedy for the deeper sorrows of the human heart, *what* a man should chiefly look to in his progress as the power that is to sustain him under trials and enable him to confront his inevitable afflictions, I must point him to something which in a well-known hymn is called 'The old, old story,' told in an old, old Book, which is the greatest and best gift ever given to mankind."

—Wm. E. Gladstone,
three times Premier of Great Britain

* * *

It Works

A mechanic was called in to repair the mechanism of a giant telescope. During the noon hour the chief astronomer came upon the man reading the Bible.

"What good do you expect from that?" he asked. "The Bible is out of date. Why, you don't even know who wrote it?"

The mechanic puzzled a moment. Then he looked up. "Don't you make considerable use of the multiplication table in your calculations?"

"Yes, of course," returned the other.

"Do you know who wrote it?"

"Why no, I guess I don't."

"Then," said the mechanic, "how can you trust the multiplication table when you don't know who wrote it?"

"We trust it because—well, because it works," the astronomer finished testily.

"Well, I trust the Bible for the same reason—it just works."   —*Selected*

* * *

Hearing God's Word

A caller found a young mother with her babe in her lap and her Bible in her hand. "Are you reading to your baby?" was the humorous query. "Yes," the young mother replied. "But, do you think he understands?" "I am sure he does not understand now, but I want his earliest memories to be that of hearing God's Word." God's Word is the "sword of the Spirit." Only by His Word are we purified and strengthened to do His will. It is impossible to overestimate the importance of reading the Word all through life.   —*King's Business*

* * *

Where He Got It

Roger W. Babson, the statistician, sent to his customers a leaflet entitled, "Essentials of Business Success." They consisted entirely of the Ten Commandments plus the "new commandment" given by Christ. Among the letters of acknowledgement that poured in from all parts of the country was one from a Western businessman whose enthusiasm could hardly be restrained. "I have never seen," he wrote, "such a fine statement of the essentials for success. Where did you get it?"

—*Congregationalist*

The Depths of the Bible

"I am glad there is a depth in the Bible I know nothing about," says Mr. Moody; "that there is a height there I cannot climb to if I should live to be as old as Methuselah; I venture to say that if I should live for ages on earth I would only have touched its surface. I pity the man who knows all the Bible, for it is a pretty good sign he doesn't know himself. A man came to me with what he thought was a very difficult passage, and he said:

" 'Mr. Moody, how do you explain it?'
"I said: 'I don't explain it.'
" 'But how do you interpret it?'
" 'I don't interpret it.'
" 'Well, how do you understand it?'
" 'I don't understand it.'
" 'But what do you do with it?'
" 'I don't do anything with it.'
" 'You don't believe it?'
" 'Yes, I believe it. There are lots of things that I believe that I do not understand. In John three, Christ says to Nicodemus: "If you do not understand earthly things, how can you understand Heavenly things"? About my own body I do not understand. I don't understand nature; it is filled with wonderful things I don't comprehend. Then why should I expect to know everything spiritually?'

"But men ask, 'How can you prove the Book is inspired?' I answered, 'Because it inspires me.' "

That is one of the best proofs. It does inspire us.

—Way of Faith

* * *

A Radiogram Answered

A Presbyterian youth from New Orleans was a naval "wireless" operator during the war. Early one morning, after a night on duty, he snatched a few minutes for his "Quiet Hour" when no message was going over, and he was reading the Twenty-third Psalm. Suddenly the thought came to him to send the Psalm out over the water and see if any ship would take it up. He did, and as he sent the last word sixteen ships answered a wireless "Amen."

—Christian Life

A Fellow Needs Reminders

"Sometimes I think I am not a Christian," said a boy one day. "I don't seem to have the same interest that I had when I joined the church. It isn't easy for me to remember God." "What about the time your father was away from home so long? Was it hard for you to remember him?" asked the minister slowly. "Not a bit," said the boy. "We had letters from him and kept thinking about him and talking about him and looking forward to the time when he'd come home. No, there wasn't much chance to forget him." "Suppose there had been no letters. Suppose your father's name had been dropped from the conversation," said the minister thoughtfully. "That would have made a difference," answered the boy slowly. "Well, don't you see it's the same with God? We can't see Him. It isn't to be wondered at if we forget him when we allow so many other things to crowd in upon us. But God has given us his Holy Word—something like your father's letters—and his house where the members of the family can meet and talk about Him." "I see what you mean, and you're right. A fellow needs all the reminders of God he can have in a world like this."

—Youth's Companion

* * *

Wherein the Bible Is Different

In Exeter Hall, London, Sir Monier-Williams addressed a large gathering of missionaries about to leave for India and the East. He spoke on "The Sacred Books of the East," on which subject he was the greatest living authority: "Those non-Christian bibles are all developments in the wrong direction. They all begin with some flashes of light, but end in utter darkness. Pile them, if you will, on the left side of your study table, but place your own Holy Bible on the right hand side —all by itself, all alone, and with a wide gap between. I would illustrate the absolutely unique character of the Bible by reminding you, first: Where else do we read of a sinless Man who was 'made sin'? Secondly, Where else do we read of a dead and buried Man who is 'Life'? It requires some courage to appear intolerant in these days of flabby compromise and milk-and-water concessions, but I contend that the two unparalleled declarations quoted by me from our Holy Bible make a gulf between it and the so-called sacred books of the East which severs the one from the other utterly, hopelessly, and forever." —*Sunday School Times*

* * *

The Best Commentary

Matthew Henry, the great commentator, loaned one of his works to Mose, a Negro helper. Several days later he came to return the book; he laid it upon Dr. Henry's desk and started backing out of the room. "Well, Mose, how did you like my commentary?" asked Dr. Henry. "Strange how much light the Bible do throw on your commentary," replied Mose. The Bible is indeed the best commentary on the Bible.

—H. M. Miller, in *Christian Digest*

* * *

"The Gospel Truth About Great Books"

Wrote a lady to Dr. George W. Crane: "Some years ago, Chancellor Hutchins of the University of Chicago stated that people are woefully ignorant of the great books of the past. He urged us to study them if we wished to become cultured people. So I've thought about organizing a 'Culture Club' for this purpose. Don't you think it would be a good idea?" "Yes, it is always desirable to improve your mind by good reading," replied Dr. Crane. "Before you tackle Aristotle or Plato or other writers whom Dr. Hutchins glorifies, you better read the four books that have had 10,000 times more influence on mankind than all those other volumes he advocates. I refer to the four Gospels: Matthew, Mark, Luke and John, which are a small part of the Bible.

"Most people, even with college diplomas, haven't read the four Gospels! Yet, those four books are responsible for most of the colleges in North America."

—Dr. George W. Crane,
a Columnist, in *Chicago Daily News*

Fireproof

A friend of an infidel left a Bible in the infidel's home, in the hope that he might begin to read it and get converted. His wife placed it on his study desk.

The sight of the book made the infidel furious. He tore off the covers, ripped out the pages and flung it into the fireplace.

A leaf from the burning Bible blew out of the flames and landed at his feet. He picked it up as though it was poisonous, intending to throw it back into the fire. But a few words on the page went like a dagger through his heart: "Heaven and earth shall pass away, but my word shall not pass away."

He read all the words on the page and was unable to escape from its message. It wasn't long before he bowed before the Author of the Bible and became a born-again believer.

—*The Standard*

* * *

How Do You Read Your Bible

A little boy who was in the habit of attending the Gospel preaching every Lord's Day evening, was unable to go one evening, so he stayed at home and read his Bible.

His mother was upstairs attending to the little ones and did not know what her boy was doing, but noticing how quiet he was, and thinking perhaps he was up to some mischief—as little boys often are when they are quiet — she called downstairs, "What are you doing, Henry?" The dear lad replied, "I am *watching* Jesus raise Lazarus from the dead." What a beautiful answer. He was of course reading the 11th chapter of John, and it was all very real to him. Do you *read your Bible like this?*

—J. G. Mathieson

* * *

My Bible and I

We've traveled together, my Bible and I,
Through all kinds of weather, with smile
        or with sigh,
In sorrow or sunshine, in tempest or calm,
Thy friendship unchanging, my lamp
        and my psalm.

We've traveled together, my Bible and I,
When life had grown weary, and death
  even was nigh,
But all through the darkness, of mist
  or of wrong
I found there a solace, a prayer and a
  song.

So now who shall part us, my Bible
  and I,
Shall "isms" or "schisms" or "new
  lights" who try?
Shall shadow for substance, or stone
  for good bread,
Supplant thy sound wisdom, give folly
  instead?

Ah! no, my dear Bible, exponent of
  light!
Thou sword of the Spirit, put error to
  flight!
And still through life's journey, until
  my last sigh,
We'll travel together, my Bible and I.

—*Selected*

* * *

Bible for Writers

William Lyon Phelps, distinguished
emeritus professor of English literature
at Yale University, says, "The English
Bible has been a greater influence on
the course of English literature than all
other forces put together. It is impossible to read standard authors intel-
ligently without knowing something
about the Bible, for they all assume
familiarity with it on the part of their
readers. Not only standard but contemporary authors exhibit, consciously
or unconsciously, intimacy with the
Scriptures. So universally true is this
that to any young man or woman eaten
with ambition to become a writer I
should advise, first of all, 'Know the
Bible.' I read an enormous number of
contemporary books. I do not think I
have read a single author who does not
show familiarity with the greatest of
books."

—*Selected*

The More He Read

It is said of old Edwin Rushworth,
who, having been a skeptic all his life,
resolved to read for an hour a day the
book that he had so long derided. "Wife,"
he said, as he looked up from his first
perusal, "if this book is right, we are all
wrong!" He continued his readings for
another week. "Wife," he exclaimed at
the end of that time, "if this book is
right, we are lost!" He went on reading
with more avidity than ever. "Wife!"
he said earnestly a few nights later, "if
this book is right, we may be saved!"
And they were! And in entering the
Kingdom of Heaven, they left all their
"ifs" behind them.

—*"The Fiery Crags," by
Dr. F. W. Boreham*

* * *

"This Deathless Book!"

The deathless Book has survived three
great dangers: the negligence of its
friends; the false systems built upon it;
the warfare of those who have hated it.

—Isaac Taylor

* * *

When the Enemy Attacks

We are told that the gray heron has
a very singular mode of defense. When
attacked by the eagle or falcon it simply
stands quiet and firm, using its bill as
a sword, allowing the enemy to pierce
himself through by his own force. The
Christian's method of defense is very
similar. We have the sword of the
Spirit. When attacked by the enemy,
stand firm and display the Word; hold
it forth. The more fiercely the foe
attacks, the more surely will he pierce
himself with it. —*Sunday School Times*

* * *

Worth of Bible

"This Holy Book I'd rather own,
  Than all the gold and gems
That e'er on monarch's coiffure shone,
  And all their diadems.

"Nay! were the sea one chrysolite,
  The earth one golden ball,
And diamonds all the stars of night,
  This Book is worth them all!"

—Tom M. Olsen, in *Now*

What Am I?

"I speak every language and enter every corner of the earth.

"I bring information, inspiration and recreation to all who heed my words.

"I treat all persons alike, regardless of race, color, creed, or condition.

"I have power to stretch man's vision, to deepen his feeling, and to enrich his life.

"I am a true friend, a wise counselor, and faithful guide.

"I am as silent as gravitation, pliant and powerful as the electric currents, and enduring as the everlasting hills.

"I am the Bread of Life with the message of salvation for every lost soul. "I am the Bible."

—*The War Cry*

* * *

The Best From the Word

Study it through. Never begin a day without mastering a verse from its pages.

Pray in it. Never lay aside your Bible until the verse or passage you have studied has become a part of your being.

Put it down. The thoughts that God gives you put down in the margin of your Bible or in your notebook.

Work it out. Live the truth you get in the morning through each hour of the day.

Pass it on. Seek to tell somebody else what you have learned.

—J. Wilbur Chapman

A Boy's Tribute to the Power of the Word

Dr. Moffat, the celebrated missionary to South Africa, tells the amusing story of a lad who had been converted by reading the New Testament. One day he came to Dr. Moffat in great distress to tell him that their big watchdog had got hold of the book and torn a page out of it. Dr. Moffat tried to comfort him by saying he could get another New Testament. But the boy was not comforted at all. "Think of the dog," he said. Dr. Moffat supposing the boy thought the paper would do the dog harm, said, "If your dog can crunch an ox bone he's not going to be hurt by a piece of paper." "Oh, Papa Moffat," he cried, "I once was a bad boy. If I had an enemy I hated him, and everything in me wanted to kill him. Then I got the New Testament in my heart, and began to love everybody, and forgive all my enemies; and now the dog, the great big hunting dog, has got the blessed Book in him, and will begin to love the lions and tigers, and let them help themselves to the sheep and oxen." What a beautiful tribute that boy, out of the simplicity of his heart, paid to the power of the Bible.

—*King's Business*

CARE, GOD'S

"I Should Really Like to Know!"

Said the Robin to the Sparrow:
"I should really like to know,
Why these anxious human beings,
Rush about and worry so."

Said the Sparrow to the Robin:
"Friend, I think that it must be
That they have no heavenly Father,
Such as cares for you and me!"

—Elizabeth Cheney

"There Ought to Be Such A God!"

A Japanese woman whose heart was yearning for someone on whom to lean said, "I went to the temple and drew lots to see if I could not get some comfort. I opened the little package which fell to me and inside it said, 'There is no help for you. Lean on your own shadow and go on.'

"I was more desperate than ever. I looked at the great sun by day and the moon by night and felt there should be someone somewhere who would care for one so needy as I."

As the missionary told her of our Heavenly Father she burst out with a joyful shout, while tears of relief rolled down her face. "I thought there ought to be such a God," she cried. "Oh, I have found Him at last!"

—R. Mabel Francis

* * *

Somebody Forgets

A little fellow in the slum section of a large city was induced to attend a mission Sunday School, and by-and-by became a faithful little Christian. He seemed quite settled in his Christian faith, but some one, surely in a thoughtless mood, tried to test or shake his simple faith in God, asking him, "If God loves you, why does He not take better care of you? Why doesn't He tell someone to bring you shoes and a warm coat and better food?" This little fellow thought a moment, then with tears starting in his eyes, said, "I guess He does tell somebody, but somebody forgets."

—Gospel Herald

* * *

A Good Sermon!

During the blitz an old London lady refused to move from the top front room, where she had lived for twenty years, to a safer place. Her explanation was: "I says my prayers to God every night and I goes to sleep. There's no need for us both to keep awake."

—World Christian Digest

* * *

"They Comfort Me"

Dr. H. W. McLaughlin, of Richmond, Va., tells a lovely story of an experience while in Palestine. In talking to an old shepherd he inquired in what sense it could be said that his staff was for the comfort of the sheep. The old shepherd proceeded to explain that in daylight he always carried the staff across his shoulder, and when the sheep saw it, it spoke of the presence of the shepherd, and thus was a means of comfort. On the other hand, if night overtook him with the sheep on the mountainside, or if they were caught in a heavy mountain mist so that the sheep could no longer see the staff, then he would lower it, and as he walked he would tap with it on the ground, so that by hearing if not by sight the staff comforted the sheep by speaking of the presence of the shepherd.

David remembered these things and said in effect to himself, "*It would be unreasonable to suppose that God has less care for me than I had for the sheep!*" "Yea, though I walk through the valley of the shadow of death, I will fear no evil; for thou art with me; thy rod and thy staff they comfort me."

—F. Crossley Morgan, in
A Psalm of An Old Shepherd

* * *

Falling Sparrow!

It was a beautiful winter day. I was sitting on the veranda of a southern hotel enjoying the sunshine and sky. Suddenly I became conscious of the swift flight of some small object before my eyes. Then came a dull thud as of something falling. There before my eyes, not ten feet away, lay the crumpled body of a sparrow. He turned upon his back. His little claws stretched appealing toward the sky. There was a convulsive shiver as though in pain. Then the tiny eyelids closed over the death-dimmed eyes. A quick, short gasp and all was over. A tell-tale spot of crimson on the little breast gave the story of the tragedy. His swift flight through the air had evidently brought him into a death collision with a pole or buttress and his sparrow life had been the price. It was only a passing incident, this death of a tiny sparrow. Seemingly no one but myself, sitting there alone, had noticed it. But like a flash came to mind a wondrous text, with its marvelous truth—
"*Not a sparrow falleth without your Father.*"

—James McConkey

* * *

He Has Not Forgotten Israel

A Jewish man told this story of his son who came home recently to spend the week end with his parents: He sat down to eat, and to their great surprise, he bowed his head to pray. When he had finished, his father said, "Son, what does this mean? You never did that before." The son replied: "No, Father, I have never believed in God before. But now, after what I have experienced in the war, I can never again doubt God's existence. In the midst of the fighting in the Negev, three divisions of Egyptian troops came to attack a point that was held by only about twenty of us. We knew that it was an absolutely impossible situation, but we decided to fight to the last man. We had hardly begun to fire at the enemy when two divisions of them turned and fled, and the third held up their hands and surrendered. Afterward, they were greatly surprised to find there were so few of us. They said to us, 'Where are the others?' We replied, 'What others do you mean?' The Egyptians said, 'We saw others with you. Where are they?' We answered, 'There were no others with us.'" The son ended his story by saying, "Then we knew that God had worked a miracle for us."

—George T. B. Davis, in
The Sunday School Times

* * *

Passing Through

"When thou passeth through the waters"
Deep the waves may be and cold,
But Jehovah is our refuge
And His promise is our hold;
For the Lord Himself hath said it,
He, the Faithful God and true—
"When thou comest to the waters
Thou shalt not go down, but through."

Seas of sorrows, seas of trial,
Bitterest anguish, fiercest pain,
Rolling surges of temptation
Sweeping over heart and brain—
They shall never overflow us
For we know His Word is true;
All His waves and all His billows
He will lead us safely through.

Threatening breakers of destruction,
Doubt's insidious undertow,
Shall not sink us, shall not drag us
Out to ocean depths of woe;

For His promise shall sustain us,
Praise the Lord, whose Word is true!
We shall not go down, or under,
For He saith, "Thou passeth *through*."

—Annie Johnson Flint, in
Gospel Herald

* * *

More Than All Our Struggling

Bound by natural desires and carnal appetites, and sick at heart for my oft failings, I forfeited my lunch one noon while a student at the Missionary Training Institute, and climbed the mountain behind the main dormitory. There at a natural rock altar I knelt, lifted my heart and hands toward Heaven, and cried out in desperation of soul: "O God! What can I do?" Bending my head downward again, and opening my eyes a little, I observed through the blur of tears the web of a spider directly in front of my gaze on the grass. At that moment a tiny fly, buzzing past, entangled one foot in the web. Violent struggles ensued and captivated my interest. The more he struggled, the more entangled he became! At last the weary little thing attracted the attention of the spider, who rushed out and proceeded to wrap strand after strand of sticky thread about him, preserving him alive but helpless. That little insect, for all his struggles, could not free himself, but I put down my little finger, and with the slightest effort I freed the captivated struggler. Then God spoke, and I saw that God's little finger was worth more than all my vain struggles. Oh, the joy that flooded my soul!

—Charles Weston Shepson

* * *

Acquainted With All My Ways

Many, many years ago the King of England visited Norwich to lay the foundation stone of a new hospital. Thousands of school children greeted the king and sang for him. Soon after King Edward had passed the multitude of children a teacher saw a little girl crying. She asked, "Why are you crying, did you not see the king?" The little girl sobbed out, "Yes, but please, teacher, the king *did not see me.*"

True enough. An earthly king cannot see nor watch over each individual. But blessed be God our Lord in Glory, while we do not see Him with our natural eyes, He constantly seeth us.

—*Our Hope*

* * *

Too Muddy for the Dance

One evening after a rain I was walking to the home of a Christian friend, where a few of us gathered weekly to have fellowship with our Lord.

I noticed my neighbor's son ahead of me and quickened my pace to catch up with him. He was going to a dance and was really dressed for the occasion. To save his shoes he had on a pair of high-topped rubbers. I tried to persuade him to come with me, but he would have none of it.

When we neared the gate he accidentally slipped and fell into the mud. Since he could not very well go to the dance, he grudgingly went with me.

He was fidgety during the service and grumbled all the way home. His attitude changed, however, when several days later he learned that three of the toughest bullies were waiting for him at the dance. Rumor had it that they were armed with pipe wrenches, and were ready to get even with him for something he was supposed to have done.

This boy became firmly convinced that it was the hand of Jesus that kept him from attending that dance. He began to attend our meetings regularly, and soon was saved.

—Wm. Grasiuk, in *Power*

* * *

He Will Not Fail

The late Dr. J. H. Jowitt said that he was once in a most pitiful perplexity, and consulted Dr. Berry of Wolverhampton.

"What would you do if you were in my place?" he entreated.

"I don't know, Jowitt, I am not there, and you are not there yet. When do you have to act?"

"On Friday," Dr. Jowitt replied.

"Then," answered Dr. Berry, "you will find your way perfectly clear on Friday. The Lord will not fail you."

And sure enough, on Friday all was plain. Give God time, and even when the knife flashes in the air the ram will be seen caught in the thicket. Give God time, and even when pharaoh's host is on Israel's heels, a path through the waters will be suddenly open. Give God time, and when the bed of the brook is dry, Elijah shall hear the guiding voice.

—F. W. Boreham

* * *

The Difference: Jesus Cares!

"When you've met some disappointment,
 And you're tempted to feel blue,
When your plans have all been side-tracked,
 Or some friend has proved untrue;
When you're toiling and you're struggling
 At the bottom of the stairs,
It will seem a bit like Heaven,
 Just to know that *Jesus* cares!

Oh, this life is not all sunshine,
 Some days darkest clouds disclose
There's a cross for every joy-bell,
 And a thorn for every rose.
But the cross is not so grievous,
 Nor the thorn the rose-bud wears,
And the clouds have silver linings
 When we know that *Jesus cares!*"

—*Selected*

* * *

Is God Too Busy?

"Do you suppose," querried Johnny, as his little cousin laid away her rosiest apple for a sick girl, "that God cares as much about such things as we do? Isn't He too busy taking care of the big folks to notice us?"

Winnie shook her head and pointed to mother, who had just lifted the baby from his cot.

"Mother is not so busy with the big folks that she forgets the baby," she answered. "She thinks of him first 'cause he's the smallest. Surely God thinks as much of little folks."

—*Exchange*

Care, God's

"With The Saviour for A Friend!"

In a very humble cot,
In a rather quiet spot,
In the suds and in the soap,
Worked a woman full of hope;
Working, singing, all alone,
In a sort of undertone:
"With the Saviour for a friend,
He will keep me to the end."

Sometimes happening along,
I had heard the semi-song,
And I often used to smile,
More in sympathy than guile;
But I never said a word
In regard to what I heard,
As she sang about her friend
Who would keep her to the end.

Not in sorrow nor in glee
Working all day long was she,
As her children, three or four,
Played around her on the floor;
But in monotones the song
She was humming all day long:
"With the Saviour for a friend,
He will keep me to the end."

Just a trifle lonesome she,
Just as poor as poor could be;
But her spirits always rose,
Like the bubbles in the clothes,
And though widowed and alone,
Cheered her with a monotone,
Of a Saviour and a friend
Who would keep her to the end.

I have seen her rub and scrub,
On the washboard in the tub,
While the baby, sopped in suds,
Rolled and tumbled in the duds;
Or was paddling in the pools,
With old scissors stuck in spools;
She still humming of her friend
Who would keep her to the end.

Human hopes and human creeds
Have their root in human needs;
And I would not wish to strip
From that washerwoman's lip
Any song that she can sing,
Any hope that song can bring;
For the woman has a friend
Who will keep her to the end.

—Eugene F. Ware (*"Ironquill"*)

God's Blank Check

Who ever conceived a more beautiful illustration for the sublime words, I AM, than the following by Bishop Beveridge? "He does not say, *I am* their light, their guide, their strength, or tower, but only 'I AM.' He sets, as it were, His hands to a blank, that his people may write under it what they please that is good for them. And as if He should say, Are they weak? *I am* strength. Are they poor? *I am* riches. Are they in trouble? *I am* comfort. Are they sick? *I am* health. Are they dying? *I am* life. Have they nothing? *I am* all things. *I am* wisdom and power. *I am* justice and mercy. *I am* grace and goodness. *I am* glory, beauty, holiness, eminency, super-eminency, perfection, all-sufficiency, eternity. Jehovah, *I am.* Whatsoever is amiable in itself, or desirable unto them, that *I am.* Whatsoever is pure and holy, whatsoever is great or pleasant, whatsoever is good or needful to make men happy, that *I am.*"

—*Ladies' Repository*

* * *

Weakness Appealing to Strength

Speaking of how the weakness of God's children appeals to God's strength, the late Dr. A. C. Dixon gave the following illustration: "A friend of mine in America was very fond of the chase, and lived in a country where the woods abounded with wild deer. One morning, as he was walking across his field, he heard the sound of hounds in the distance, and as they approached, looking through the cracks of a high fence, he saw a little fawn, very wearied, its tongue hanging out, and its sides lathered with foam. The little thing had just strength enough to leap over the fence, and stood there for a moment, with its great liquid eyes gazing about in a frightened manner. When it saw a hound leap over the fence not far away, its first impulse seemed to cause it to run again, but, instead of running away, it came and fell down in a heap at the feet of my friend. He said, 'I stood there and fought dogs for nearly half an hour. I just felt that all the dogs in that country could not capture the little fawn after its weakness had appealed to my strength.' "

—In *"Through Night to Morning"*

* * *

Who Told the Hen?

John Brentz, a friend of Luther, and one of the stalwarts of the Reformation, incurred the hatred of Charles V who made many attempts to kill the minister. Hearing that a troop of Spanish cavalry was on the way to arrest him, he cast himself upon God in prayer. At once the guidance came: "Take a loaf of bread and go into the upper town and where thou findest a door open, enter and hide thyself under the roof." He acted accordingly, found the only open door, and hid himself in the loft. For fourteen days he lay there while the search continued. The one loaf of bread would have been insufficient, but day by day, a hen came up to the garret, and laid an egg without cackling. The fifteenth day it did not come, but John Brentz heard the people in the street say, "They are gone at last," and he came out.

—*Sunday School Times*

* * *

Bread from a Stone

One morning Mary said to her grandmother, whose only companion she was, "Granny, what shall we do this morning? We have nothing for breakfast." "We will light the fire and put on the kettle and set the table, and tell our Heavenly Father. Even if He turns stones into bread we will have our breakfast," answered her grandmother. Soon came a knock at the door. It was a little old man. "Have you got such a thing as an old grindstone you could sell me?" he said. Granny had, and he bought it for ten shillings. "Let us kneel down again," said Granny, "and give thanks, then you can run to the shop and buy some food for breakfast, Mary." So the Lord did turn a stone into bread.

—*Christian's Guide*

"More Good Than Sermons!"

A widow and her six children were stricken with a contagious illness. One morning at breakfast the minister's wife announced that she was going to take care of the stricken family. Her own family protested, but she only quoted a part of the 91st Psalm: "Nor for the pestilence that walketh in darkness; nor for the destruction that wasteth at noon-day." And, "There shall no evil befall thee, neither shall any plague come nigh thy dwelling."

"I believe that Psalm means just what it says," she told the others. "It is a clear call for me to go. God will take care of you."

She went, and was in that home for five weeks. When they were practically well again she went back home. Neither she nor her family contracted the disease. Her kindly act did more to raise the spiritual level of that community than all the sermons her husband preached.

—*Free Methodist*

* * *

"Yes, God Will Take Care of You."

Years ago when we appointed the first two single girls to pioneer work where it was a "man's job," and an experienced missionary objected, saying that no missionary had ever gone to that dangerous area before, I turned to the girls in deep concern, and said, "Perhaps you had better not go." I shall never forget the surprised expression on their faces as they replied with a question that put me on the spot, "Won't God take care of us?" For me to have answered "No" would have knocked the props out from under our whole movement. We had nothing to stand on for the solution of all the impossible problems that lay ahead of us except God's miraculous power. An affirmative answer meant that the girls could go in spite of the dangers. I looked at the expression of wounded faith upon the face of those young girls and, replied, "Yes, God will take care of you." They went, and God protected them. Today the

Mazateca Indians have the Word because Eunice Pike and Florence Hansen (now Mrs. George Cowan) dared to trust God.

—*Sunday School Times*

* * *

God Is Mindful of His Own

When distress and cares oppress you,
And you seem to walk alone;
Look up, friend, for God will bless you,
"He is mindful of His own."

You may walk with Him forever,
He's a never-failing Guide;
He will not forsake you, never,
He will keep right at your side.

What a word of consolation;
Sweetest theme you've ever known;
In the time of fierce temptation,
"God is mindful of His own."

—*Good Tidings*

* * *

Praying Ice From Heaven

A native African Christian moaned and tossed with a raging high fever. The missionary used what simple remedies he had. He longed, however, for an ice pack. No ice was possible, he thought, and dismissed the longing. The mother of the fevered boy, asked, "Cannot the Great-God send ice for my dear son?" Then she reminded him of one of his sermons when he said that God delights to do miracles. "But," he protested, "Ice! Ice!" She gave no heed to his doubts, and said, in a tone of implicit faith, "Shall we not pray?" Down on their knees they went, he praying first, telling the Lord things He already knew, and making very general requests. But the mother plainly said, "Lord, if ice is necessary to his healing, Thou canst send it. I do believe." When the prayer ended, a hailstone the size of a walnut rolled into the hut, and when they looked out, they saw drifts of hailstones beyond the door. Sekunzi seized and shook her pastor, and exclaimed, "Did not the Great-God answer in His own wonderful way?" The hailstorm was local—the crops of the neighbors were not harmed—the son recovered completely — the miracle increased the faith of all who heard it—the pastor learned never to limit the power of God.

—Alan Livingstone Wilson, in
Moody Monthly

* * *

The Weaker Ones

In every family, there are the weaker ones. They are the objects of our special care and watchfulness. Likewise, in God's great family, there are the weaker ones. How their helplessness touches the heart of God!

In the great state of Texas is located the far-famed Buckner Orphanage, an institution that has mothered and fathered thousands of orphaned children. In the beginning years of the Orphanage, Dr. Buckner would be away from the home for weeks, raising funds for the institution. When it was announced to the children that "Father" Buckner was to return at some definite time, the home became all abuzz with excitement, and all hearts were aflutter with anticipation. The children would put on their best clothes, and all would gather beautiful bouquets for the returning superintendent. In that home in those days was a little half-witted girl. She didn't know the difference between sticks and weeds, and flowers. When Dr. Buckner would return, hundreds of little children would press about him, trying to be the first to place kisses of affection and esteem upon his cheek, and to show their love in the presentation of their bouquets. As the kind-hearted man stood in their midst, he seemed to be looking for some one, some special one. Yes, there she stood on the fringe of the crowd of children, holding in her little hands her "bouquet" of sticks and weeds. Dr. Buckner, pushing aside all the other children, would go to the small half-witted girl, enfold her in his strong arms, receive first her bouquet of sticks and weeds, and speak comforting, tender words to her little heart. I tell you, my friends, that Dr. Buckner was never more like Christ than when he thus acted!

—W. B. K., in
God's Presence With His People

Because of the Fifth Sparrow

The direct appeal of the Gospel to a young, fresh heart is the subject of a delightful story. A little Spanish boy in Vigo who became a devout Christian was asked by an Englishman what had been the influence under which he acted. "It was all because of the odd sparrow," the boy replied. "I do not understand," said the Englishman in surprise. "What odd sparrow?" "Well, Senor, it is this way," the boy said, "A gentleman gave me a Testament, and I read in one Gospel that two sparrows were sold for a farthing. And again in Luke, I saw, 'Are not five sparrows sold for two farthings . . .?' And I said to myself that Nuestro Senor ('our Lord') Jesus Christ knew well our custom of selling birds. As you know, Sir, we trap birds, and get one chico for two but for two chicos we throw in an extra sparrow. That extra sparrow is only a makeweight, and of no account at all. Now, I think to myself that I am so insignificant, so poor, and so small that no one would think of counting me. I'm like the fifth sparrow. And yet, oh, marvelous, Nuestro Senor says, 'Not one of them is forgotten before God.' I have never heard anything like it, Sir. No one but He could ever have thought of not forgetting me."

—King's Business

* * *

"God Knows His Business!"

There were three children in the home, one of whom was much younger than the others. A terrific storm came up and the two older ones were greatly frightened and cried very hard. The little fellow paid no attention to the storm and finally said to them: "Oh, stop your bawlin'! Don't you s'pose God knows His business?"

The small boy realized that God can take care of you just as well in a storm as when the sun shines.

—Gospel Herald

* * *

Moody and Twenty-five Dollars

An interesting incident is told of an earnest Christian who was yearning for a more vivid proof that God heard prayer. He was also eager for a greater conviction of the reality of the Holy Spirit.

One morning he asked the Lord: "What can Thy servant do for Thee this day? Teach him that he may gladly minister to anyone in Thy Name."

In the course of the day there came to him the thought of Mr. Moody and his revival services in Brooklyn. He thereupon sat down and wrote a letter to Mr. Moody, saying: "I know not how you are supported, or anything of your needs; but I feel like helping you in your work. Enclosed please find check for twenty-five dollars; take it and use it if you need it for yourself; if not, then do some good with it."

The day afterward there came this wonderful reply from Mr. Moody: "Your letter came to hand in the same mail, at the same instant of time, with a letter from a brother in distress wanting the same amount. And now you have made him happy, and my heart glad, and the Lord will bless you for it."

Note the words: "In the same mail, at the same instant of time . . . the same amount."

—Elim Evangel

* * *

"It Matters To Him!"

My child, I know thy sorrows,
　Thine every grief I share:
I know how thou art tested,
　And, what is more—*I care.*

Think not I am indifferent
　To what affecteth thee;
Thy weal and woe are matters
　Of deep concern to Me.

But, child, I have a *purpose*
　In all that I allow;
I ask thee then to trust Me,
　Though all seems dark just now.

How often thou hast asked Me
　To purge away thy dross!
But this refining process
　Involves for thee—*a cross.*

Care, God's

There is no other pathway
If thou would'st really be
Conformed unto the image
Of Him Who died for thee.

Thou canst not be like Jesus
Till *self* is crucified;
And as a *daily process*
The cross must be applied.
—*Selected*

* * *

"Lord Pulled Fast One!"

The plane had caught fire like a torch.

"I was still conscious," said the pilot, "and I tried to get through the little window next to my seat. Flames licked at my back and legs. I got halfway through, but the chute on my back wedged me in. I had to go back into the fire and try to get it off. But I couldn't. My fingers were numb. The last thing I remembered was shouting, 'Please help me, God.' And the next thing I knew I was lying on the ground, with the doctor bending over me. Nobody knows yet how I got out of that window."

He hesitated for a moment, and then added, "My theory, of course, is that the Lord pulled a fast one."
—*Reader's Digest*

* * *

He Lets God Care

Once, when Martin Luther felt very despondent, he heard a bird singing its evening song. Then he saw it tuck its head under its wing and go to sleep. He remarked: "This little bird has had its supper and now is getting ready to go to sleep, quite content, never troubling itself as to what its food will be or where it will lodge on the morrow. Like David, it abides under the shadow of the Almighty. It sits on its little twig content and lets God care."
—W. B. K.

* * *

What Do You Cast Away?

It is His will that I should cast
My care on Him each day,
He also bids me *not* to cast
My confidence away.

But oh! how foolishly I act,
When taken unaware,
I cast away my confidence
And carry all my care.
—*Selected*

* * *

In God's Care

Bishop Gobat, while laboring among the wild tribes of the Druses, was one day invited by the chief to visit him. Now, he long had desired to gain some influence over this man, and was eager to accept the invitation. But he was ill when the invitation came and was obliged to decline. When the invitation was repeated, he was again unable to accept. A third came, and he set out with a guide to go to the home of the chief. But the guide first lost his way and, soon after he had found it, a hyena crossed his path and the superstitious man would go no farther. Thus hindered, the bishop was obliged to forego the visit, for the next day he sailed for Malta. Some time later he learned that by these means he had been hindered from falling into the hands of the enemies who purposed murdering him. The treacherous chief himself acknowledged, "That man must be the servant of God; for though I sent messenger after messenger to bring him, he was always hindered."
—*Pilgrim Holiness Advocate*

* * *

A Prayer for Food Answered

In February, 1931, our district was reduced to a state of famine, and there was yet another month to wheat harvest. We had helped many, but one day when the Christians came for help we had to tell them we had nothing left. I told them that God was a prayer-hearing and prayer-answering God. They proposed to come and join in prayer each afternoon. On the fourth day of intercession I was called out of the meeting to see what was happening. Away in the north was a dark cloud appearing, and as we watched, it crossed our district and rained heavily. It was not an ordinary rain, but a deluge of little black seeds in such abundance they could be shoveled up. They asked, "What is it?" reminding us of the children of Israel in the wilderness who asked a similar question. The seeds proved edible, and the supply so great it sustained the people until harvest. We learned later that the storm had arisen in Mongolia and wrecked the places where this grain was stored. The seed was carried fifteen hundred miles to drop on the district where prayer was being answered.

—*Evangelical Christian*

* * *

Our Five Per Cent

A farmer one fall brought in a beautiful ear of corn, and showing it to his wife said, "A man deserves some credit for raising corn like that." Thought the corn: "God gave him the soil to start with, and gave health to him and life to the seed, and while the farmer tended us intermittently, God never ceased His care. He taught my rootlets to push down and get life out of the soil. He guided my sprouts upward and to breathe in the air. He gave the sunshine and dew and rain and sent the wind to help me pollinize every growing kernel. In due time every kernel filled with milk and he changed my color to gold to show how he loved and cared for me." A famous teacher of agriculture has figured out that man does only about five per cent of the work on an ear of corn like that, and that God does ninety-five per cent. So it is with wheat, or oats, or clover, or potatoes, or any other product of the soil. —*United Presbyterian*

* * *

His Hand on the Water

"The long dark lines of men on the beaches waited for them, neck-deep in water. They dragged them aboard. One ship was shelled. She shivered and then she pulled herself together, and the men turned her around and started back to England. There were holes just above the water line, and they were bad ones. But so long as the sea got no rougher she might make it. She did make it, and the tired, wet soldiers dragged themselves off at Ramsgate, singing in croaking brave voices. 'You'll have to dock her now,' somebody said. 'She's badly hit.' Her amateur crew, tired and dirty and aching, scrambled out on the dock to have a look at the holes. 'A little swell awash her, and she would go down,' they admitted. Then they looked at each other, and at that strangely calmed Channel whose nasty disposition was such a byword to them. 'She'll make it,' they said. 'God's got His hand on that water.' And without hesitation they turned her around and went back to Dunkirk for another load."

—*"The Great Answer,"* by Margaret Lee Runbeck

* * *

"God Cares!"

A Frenchman incurred the displeasure of Napoleon and was put into a dungeon. He seemer to be forsaken by his friends and forgotten by everyone in the outside world. In loneliness and despair he took a stone and scratched on the wall of his cell, "Nobody cares."

One day a green shoot came through the cracks in the stones on the floor of the dungeon and began to reach up toward the light in the tiny window at the top of the cell. The prisoner kept part of the water brought to him each day by the jailer and poured it on the blade of green. It grew until at last it became a plant with a beautiful blue flower. As the petals opened in full blossom, the solitary captive crossed out the words previously written on the wall and above them scratched, "*God* cares."

—*The Chaplain*

* * *

"They Shall Never Overflow!"

Has a sorrow come upon you
That no other soul can share?
Does the burden seem too heavy
For your aching heart to bear?
There is One whose love and comfort,
If you'll trust Him with your load,
There's a Burden-Bearer ready,
If you'll give Him an abode;
Lo! the precious promise reaches
To the depth of human woe
That however deep the waters
They shall never overflow!

Care, God's; Children

Does your flesh seem worn and weary
And your spirits grow depressed?
Does life's tempest sweep upon you,
Like a storm on ocean's breast?
Let me whisper there's a haven
Open for the weary bird,
And a refuge for the tempted
In the promise of God's Word;
Let the standard of His Spirit
E'er be raised against the foe—
Then however deep the waters,
They shall never overflow.

Do you ever grow discouraged
As you journey on your way?
Does there seem to be more darkness
Than there is of sunny day?
Ah, 'tis hard to learn the lesson
As you pass beneath the rod,
That the shadow and the sunshine
Are alike the will of God.
Let me speak a word of promise
Like the promise in the bow—
That however deep the waters
They shall never overflow.

When the sands of life are ebbing,
And you near the Jordan's shore,
When you see the billows rising
And you hear the waters roar,

Just reach out your hand to Jesus
In His tender bosom hide,
Then 'twill only be a moment
Till you reach the other side;
Then indeed the fullest meaning
Of His promise you shall know—
When thou passeth through the waters
They shall never overflow!
—*Selected*

* * *

Why the Clothes Would Fit

What a simple yet wonderful faith was that of Billy Bray, the eccentric Cornish preacher. On one occasion he was met by a member of the Society of Friends. "Mr. Bray," said the kind-hearted Quaker, "I have often observed thy unselfish life, and feel much interested in thee, and I believe the Lord would have me help thee; so if thou wilt call at my house, I have a suit of clothes to which thou art very welcome—that is, if they'll fit thee." "Thank'ee!" said Billy. "I will call. But I have no doubt that the clothes will fit me. If the Lord told thee they were for me, they're sure to fit, for He knows my size exactly."
—*Christian Herald*

CHILDREN

How Moody Won Them

"What will you have?" asked a saloon keeper of Moody. "These children for my Sunday school," Moody replied. Said the saloon keeper, "If you come down here next Thursday night, and meet the boys in the infidel club, which meets here, you may have the children." Said Moody, "Agreed! I'll be here!" Moody was there. He opened the meeting by saying, "Gentlemen, it is our custom to open our meeting with prayer. Tommy, jump on that barrel and pray," whereupon Tommy perched himself on the barrel, turned his little face up toward Heaven, and how he did pray! As the tears stole down his cheeks the more tenderhearted beat a retreat, and finally

those more rock-like, subdued by the pathos and spiritual power of the occasion, slowly retired, until there was none left except the barkeeper, Moody and the praying boy.

"That will do, Tommy," exclaimed the evangelist. "I claim the children," said he, turning to the father. "They are yours according to contract," replied the father, "but it is a queer way to fight."

"It is the way I win my battle," said Moody. He had instructed the boy not to cease praying until he had prayed them all out. It was a piece of strategy full of tactfulness. The reality, the venturesomeness, the tact of such a man is worth emulating.
—*Gospel Herald*

The Chap at Home

"To feel his little hand in mine,
So clinging and so warm,
To know he thinks me strong enough
To keep him safe from harm;
To see his simple faith in all
That I can say or do,
It sort o' shames a fellow,
But it makes him better, too;
And I'm trying hard to be the man
He fancies me to be,
Because I have this chap at home
Who thinks the world o' me.

I would not disappoint his trust
For anything on earth,
Nor let him know how little I
Just naturally am worth.
But after all, it's easier
That brighter road to climb,
With the little hands behind me
To push me all the time.
And I reckon I'm a better man
Than what I used to be
Because I have this chap at home
Who thinks the world of me."

—*Selected*

* * *

The Wolf Prefers Lambs

Dr. W. B. Riley told of spending a brief vacation years ago on the premises of a Scottish sheep herder. His host had met him courteously at the station, but in the long drive to the ranch had seemed strangely disinclined to talk. There had seemed to be a heavy burden on his heart. Pressed for the reason for his silence, the old shepherd had wept as though his own children had been snatched from him. "I lost sixty-five of my best lambs last night," he said. "Wolves got in." The sympathetic pastor expressed his own grief over this great loss of his friend's. "And how many sheep did they kill besides?" he asked. The shepherd looked surprised. "Don't you know," he answered, "that a wolf will never take an old sheep so long as he can get a lamb?" The "lambs" are being cruelly ruined by the enemy of souls today. Who is there with the shep-

herd heart to weep over this loss, to se about to bring to the lambs and th sheep the protection that is to be foun only in Christ?

—*King's Busines*

* * *

A Piece of Plastic Clay

"I took a piece of plastic clay
And idly fashioned it one day,
And as my fingers pressed it still,
It moved and yielded to my will.
I came again when days were passed;
The bit of clay was hard at last,
The form I gave it still it bore,
But I could change that form no more.

"I took a piece of living clay
And touched it gently day by day,
And molded with my power and art
A young child's soft and yielding heart.
I came again when years were gone;
It was a mind I looked upon;
That early impress still he wore,
And I could change that form no more."

—*Selected*

* * *

A Twelve-year Old Missionary

Years ago when Robert Moffat was in Africa, he traveled far into the interior. One day he came to a tree upon which a board was fixed, saying that a Christian school was to be found in a village not far away.

He was amazed, for he believed himself to be the first white man in that part. Making his way toward the village, he met a little native girl about twelve years of age, to whom he said, "I saw a board fastened to a tree saying that there was a Christian school held in the village. Would you be so good as to lead me to the teacher?"

The little girl hung her head shyly and made no reply.

"Do you know the teacher?" he asked. She replied this time with a nod.

"Well, who is the teacher?" he persisted. Looking up into his face now, but still shyly, she answered, "I am the teacher."

Mr. Moffat discovered that the little girl had once been taken to a distant tribe, where she heard a missionary tell the people of the love of Jesus; and she had now become the first missionary to her own people.

—*Gospel Herald*

* * *

Wonder Stories of Mary Slessor and William Quarrier

Little five-year-old William stood barefoot, cold and hungry, in a street in Glasgow, and wondered why no one gave him food, when he had had nothing to eat for a day and a half. At the ripe age of six and a half years, he went to work in a factory, putting the heads on pins for twelve hours a day, and earning a shilling a week. What chance in life had such a poor, starved little creature? When he was seventeen he heard the Gospel for the first time, believed it, and received the Saviour. He has been in Glory for many years now, but his monument on earth still stands. It is the Orphan Homes of Scotland, at Bridge of Weir. For that little boy was William Quarrier.

Little Mary went to work in a factory when she was eleven, to help to supply the needs of her younger brothers and sisters, because her father was a drunkard. She was not tall or strong, and of course not well educated. How could such a sorrowful and thwarted childhood lead to a useful and blessed womanhood? But a poor old woman warned her to escape the fire that never shall be quenched and she gave heed, and came to the children's Saviour. That little girl was Mary Slessor who brought so great blessings to Calabar in West Africa.

—*Sunday School Times*

* * *

Am I Too Little?

In a meeting, the minister invited the little children to come to Jesus. "But I am too little," said one of the children afterwards.

"Too little for what, my dear?" he kindly asked. Timidly the little girl answered, "Am I too little to come to Jesus?"

Moved by the child's question, the servant of Christ took her up in his arms, saying, "No, my dear, not too little; it was to very little ones that Jesus said, 'Suffer little children to come unto Me, and forbid them not, for of such is the Kingdom of Heaven.'"

The dear child wiped her tears and went to her mother, telling her she had come to Jesus, and that she was saved. How glad was the mother to hear her child confess her simple faith in the Lord.

The next day she brought another little girl to the meeting, saying, "She wants to be saved, too." You, too, dear children, are welcome to the Saviour. He longs to have you come. He will make you happy in His love. Then you can tell others of Him, too, as this little girl did.

—*The Sunday School Visitor*

* * *

Little Fingers

"If we knew the little fingers
Pressed against the window pane,
Would be cold and stiff tomorrow,
Never trouble us again,—
Would the bright eyes of our darling
Catch the frown upon our brow?
Would the prints of rosy fingers
Vex us then, as they do now?

"Ah, those little ice cold fingers—
How they point our memories back
To the hasty words and actions
Strewn along our backward track!
How those little hands remind us,
As in snowy grace they lie,
Not to scatter thorns, but roses,
For our reaping by and by."

—*R. T. Cross*

* * *

Why He Was Sure

Someone said, "Children are so ignorant when you think they understand." Later, he went with Mr. Spurgeon to see some children, who said to one of them, "Well, my boy, have you a good heart?" "Yes, sir," replied the boy. "There you are," said the gentleman, turning to Mr. Spurgeon, "you see he does not know the first thing about the Gospel! He doesn't know he is a sinner." Whereupon Mr. Spurgeon addressed the boy, "How do you know you have a good heart?" "Well," said the boy, "when I took the Lord Christ as my Saviour, He gave me a NEW HEART, and I am sure it was a good one!"

—*The Christian*

* * *

She Knew What It Meant

A little girl had learned the verse, "Suffer the little children to come unto me," to repeat at a meeting. She stood on a platform and began. "Suffer"—it was her first attempt at speaking in public. She was frightened, and stopped for a moment. Then she began again. "Suffer little"—again her fear overcame her. But being a determined little one, she made a third attempt, and said, "Suffer little children." With a last grand effort, she said, not exactly the verse, but these words: "Jesus wants us all to come to him; and don't anybody try to stop us."

—*King's Business*

* * *

"It's Different With the Bairns"

An old sexton in a cemetery took special pains with the little graves. When asked why, he said, "Sir, about those larger graves, I don't know who are the Lord's and who are not, but, you know, it's different with the bairns."

—*Sunday Circle*

* * *

A Child's Prayers

Morning

I thank thee, Lord, for sleep and rest,
For all the things that I love best;
Now guide me through another day,
And bless my work and bless my play,
Lord, make me strong for noble ends,
Protect and bless my loving friends;
Of all mankind good Christians make;
All this I ask for Jesus' sake. Amen.

Evening

Lord, send me sleep that I may live;
The wrong I've done this day forgive;

Bless every deed and thought and word,
I've rightly done, or said, or heard;
Bless relatives and friends alway;
Teach all the world to watch and pray;
My thanks for all my blessings take,
And hear my prayer for Jesus' sake.
Amen.

—*The Churchman*

* * *

"A Man in the Making!"

There comes a boy a-down the pike,
Sauntering along, so careless-like;
Scuffing the dust with a brownied foot;
His pockets bulge with woodland loot.
Thinking, dreaming, he moves along
Scarcely aware of the linnet's song.
All unaware of the powers awaking,
A boy today; but a man a-making.

Who can but love that jaunty air,
The roguish smile, the mop of hair,
The graceful tilt of that torn brim.
A style that's only just for him.
Don't be fooled by outward show,
There's something fine you ought to know.
Etiquette laws he may be breaking;
Never-the-less, here's a man a-making.

O, laddy-man, could you but see
The character that you may be,
And deeply purpose in your heart
In noble life to play a part.
If all of us who smile at you
Would lend a hand to help you through
And all together use the plan,
That changes a Boy to a noble Man.
—*S. S. Hotchkiss, Fairmont, Ind.*

* * *

The Fifth Commandment

An old schoolmaster said one day to a clergyman, who came to examine his school, "I believe the children know the catechism word for word."

"But do they understand it? That is the question," said the clergyman.

The schoolmaster bowed respectfully, and the examination began. A little boy had repeated the fifth commandment, "Honor thy father and thy mother," and he was asked to explain it. Instead of trying to do so, the little boy, with his face covered with blushes, said, almost in a whisper, "Yesterday I showed some strange man over the mountain, and the sharp stones cut my feet. The man saw they were bleeding, and gave me some money to buy shoes. I gave it to my mother, for she had no shoes either, and I thought I could go barefooted better than she could."

—Selected

* * *

To the New Baby

A sweet little miniature weaver
Came into our home one day,
Like a wee little queen of the cradle,
God grant her a long, long stay.

Such is the spell she has woven,
We scarce know how it came to be,
Into the meshes of every heart,
Knitting herself tenderly.

Dear little helpless struggler
What strength for such tiny fist,
A fountain of love, and a teacher
Whose lessons so few can resist.

Like wee midge glamorous conjurer
You reign from your magic bed,
A queen from the tip of your tiny toes
To the top of your fuzzy head.

A delegated prophet, whose office
Is to brighten, and deepen home love,
We welcome you, little sojourner
As a loan from the Father above.

A harbinger and herald of good tidings;
You make, with your smiles and your tears,
Young again hearts well nigh wearied
By the cares and the toil of the years.

—Velma B. Hofman

* * *

A Child's Conversion

A little girl in America, when she was asked by the church committee as to her knowledge of Jesus Christ, and asked to recite her experience, said, "I do not know if I have any 'experience.' All I know is that Jesus said, 'Come unto Me,' and I came, and He said, 'I will give you rest,' and He gave me rest." One of the older men said: "But you don't seem to know much about the Slough of Despond, my dear." She dropped a curtsey and said: "Please, sir, I did not come that way."

—A. T. Pierson

* * *

Diamonds!

"They shall be Mine when I make up My jewels." (Mal. 3:16)
"A diamond in the rough,
Is a diamond sure enough;
For before it ever sparkles,
It is made of diamond stuff!
Of course some one must find it,
Or it never will be found;
And then some one must grind it,
Or it never will be ground;
But when it's found, and when it's ground,
And when it's burnished bright,
It sparkles everlastingly,
Just shooting forth its light!
Ah, teacher in the Sunday school,
Don't say, 'I've done enough,'
That worst boy in your Bible class,
May be a diamond in the rough!
Perhaps you think he's grinding you,
And maybe you're right,
But possibly you need the grinding,
To finish you out bright!"

—Selected

* * *

"The Hole in the Fence"

A story is told of a father who took his boy on his knee and told him the story of the lost sheep; how it found a hole in the fence and crawled through; how glad it was to get away; how it skipped and played in the sunshine until it wandered so far that it could not find its way back home. And then he told him of the wolf that chased the sheep, and how, finally, the good shepherd came and rescued it and carried it back to the fold.

The little boy was greatly interested and when the story was over, he surprised his father by asking, *"Did they nail up the hole in the fence?"*

How often we overlook the "hole in the fence!"

—*The Circuit Rider*

That Most Discouraging Boy

Some years ago a manufacturer of Scotland told the Sunday school teacher of a class of poor boys that he would get them each a new suit of clothes. The worst and most unpromising boy in the class was a lad named Bob. After a few Sundays he was missing. His teacher hunted him up, but found his new clothes torn and dirty. The manufacturer gave him a second suit, but after attending once or twice, Bob again absented himself. Utterly discouraged, his teacher reported to the manufacturer that they must give him up. But he wanted to try him once more, and gave him a third suit if he'd promise to attend regularly. Bob did promise, and attended faithfully, and later found Jesus as his Saviour. The end of the account is that that discouraged boy — that forlorn, ragged Bob — became the Rev. Robert Morrison, the great missionary to China, who translated the Bible into the Chinese language, and by so doing opened the Kingdom of Heaven to the teeming millions of that country.

—*"Church of Scotland's Children's Review"*

* * *

A Prayer List

There was once a little cripple who lay upon her deathbed. She had given herself to God and was distressed because she could not labor for Him actively among the lost. Her pastor visited her, and hearing her complaint, told her that from her sick bed she could pray earnestly. He went away and thought of the subject no more. Soon a feeling of religious interest sprung up in the village and the churches were crowded nightly. The little cripple heard of the progress of the revival and inquired anxiously for the names of the saved. A few weeks later she died and among a roll of papers that was found under her pillow was one bearing the names of fifty-six persons, every one of whom had been converted in the revival. By each name was a little cross, by which the poor crippled saint had checked off the names of the converts as they had been reported to her.

—*Gospel Herald*

* * *

"Suffer Little Children To Come"

Dr. Horatius Bonar said concerning the spiritual history of 253 converts with whom he was familiar, "Saved under 20 years of age, 138; between 20 and 30 years, 85; between 30 and 40 years, 22; between 40 and 50 years, 4; between 50 and 60. 3: between 60 and 70 years 1; over seventy, NOT ONE!"

* * *

Children Evangelists!

It happened in Orleans, Indiana. Two children, a girl of twelve, and a boy of ten years, were among those who early confessed Christ in the meeting. They made their way to the outer door, and brought their father, a railroad engineer, just off his engine. They knelt beside him and pointed him to Christ. He was brightly converted! The world has no more beautiful scene!

—T. J. Bassett

* * *

Edith in the Bible

One day in London, a group of children were feeling the cold and slipped inside a church to get warm. To their surprise, a service soon began, and the vicar arose to read the lesson. "This man (Christ Jesus) receiveth sinners and eateth with them."

After the service, a little girl about 8 years old went up to the vicar.

"Please, sir," she said, "I didn't know my name was in the Bible."

"And what is your name, little girl?" he asked.

"Edith, sir."

"No," he said, "Edith doesn't come in the Bible."

"Oh, yes sir," she replied, "you read this afternoon that this man Christ Jesus receiveth sinners and EDITH with them."

—*Prairie Pastor*

Gentle Jesus

Gentle Jesus, meek and mild,
Look upon a little child;
Pity my simplicity,
Suffer me to come to Thee.

Lamb of God, I look to Thee:
Thou shalt my example be;
Thou are gentle, meek and mild;
Thou wast once a little child.

Fain I would be as Thou art;
Give me Thy obedient heart.
Thou art pitiful and kind,
Let me have Thy loving mind.

Loving Jesus, gentle Lamb,
In thy gracious hands I am;
Make me, Saviour, what Thou art;
Live Thyself within my heart.

Let me above all fulfil
God my heavenly Father's will;
Never His good Spirit grieve,
Only to His glory live.

I shall then show forth Thy praise;
Serve Thee all my happy days;
Then the world shall always see
Christ, the Holy Child, in me.
—Charles Wesley

* * *

Thirty-Six Million Spiritual Orphans!

In our land alone, there are thirty-six million children and adolescents attending no church or Sunday School, and receiving no definite Christian teaching. What makes the tragedy worse, is that statistics show that eighty percent of the children drop out of the Sunday School before they are won to Christ.
—*Selected*

* * *

His Hands Over Ours

A teacher of children had told them that their daddies sometimes allowed them to take the wheel of the car, but that they always placed their hands over their little ones to be sure there would be no mistake. Sometime afterward, a little fellow, eight years old, was asked if he would like to lead in prayer. This is what he said, "Dear Lord, will you please put your hands over the hands of our President so he will know how to turn the wheel for our country."
—*Sunday School Times*

* * *

A Teacher's Prayer

Give me a little child to point the way,
Over the strange sweet path that leads
to Thee;
Give me the little voice to teach to pray;
Give me two shining eyes Thy face to see.

The only crown I ask, dear Lord, to wear,
Is this: that I may teach a little child.
I do not ask that I may ever stand
Among the wise, the worthy, or the
great—
I only ask that softly, hand in hand,
A child and I may enter at the gate.
—C. A. Fields

* * *

Paul Rader Went In
On Moody's Coat-Tail!

Paul was then a lad of ten. Moody was holding meetings in Denver, Col. Little Paul wanted so badly to hear Mr. Moody preach. At the door the usher pushed him gently back, saying: "No room for boys any more." The boy started crying, and lingered around the building. Finally, arriving at a door again, anew he was pushed aside, with: "No boys in here!" Overwhelmed with grief, the boy started weeping bitterly. Then very suddenly a neatly dressed gentleman approached him. A man wearing a coat with a long tail. In a very sympathetic tone, this man said: "My boy, why are you weeping so bitterly? If there is any way I can help you, say so, and I'll gladly do it!"

The boy stuttered in sobs: "I was going to hear Mr. Moody preach, and I was so anxious for it, for he is the best preacher in America. And now the usher pushed me back, saying, 'No room for the boys!' "

Mr. Moody smiled, and grasping the boy's hand, said, "Here, my boy, you grasp with this hand my coat-tail, and thus I can pull you in. You sure ought to hear Mr. Moody preach."

A large audience was looking on in a bewildered amazement. Mr. Moody explained something like this: "Here, my friends, is a boy who cried bitterly outdoors because the usher had pushed him back, saying, 'No room for boys!' Well, I said, 'Boy, you hang on to my coattail and I'll pull you way up to the platform!' So, here we are, and I sure will give this boy tonight on this platform the highest place of honor, and call him the best boy in America!" A loud amen came from the crowd as a pleasant response.

Paul Rader grew up to become a very prominent evangelist. Thousands of sinners learned through his preaching to seek and love the Lord.

—*Gospel Herald*

* * *

Lacked Good Health, Yet Gave Gospel to Millions!

Hudson Taylor, founder of the China Inland Mission, had a good Christian father, a happy and prosperous home, plenty of books and food, suitable clothing, a careful training, and above all, much love. But he was without one earthly blessing—good health. He was often too ailing to go to school until he was eleven, and then was absent because of illness much of the time, until the attempt was abandoned. He obtained a post as a bank clerk when he was fifteen. But in two years he had to relinquish it because of persistent inflammation in his eyes. Then he was converted, in answer to the prayers of his mother and sister, through reading a tract concerning the finished work of Christ. But how could such a frail little fellow be of much use in extending the Kingdom of God?

When he was twenty-one he sailed for China, the only passenger on a cargo boat, to carry God's message of salvation to the millions of that vast land. Before he died of old age his God had used him to found the China Inland Mission, and lead out a thousand other missionaries to open inland China to the Gospel.

—*Sunday School Times*

* * *

A Little Girl's Answer

The King of Prussia, while visiting a village in his land, was welcomed by the school children of the place. After their speaker had made a speech for them, he thanked them. Then taking an orange from a plate, he asked: "To what kingdom does this belong?"

"The vegetable kingdom, sir," replied a little girl.

The king took a gold coin from his pocket and asked, "To what kingdom does this belong?"

"To the mineral kingdom," said the little girl.

"And to what kingdom do I belong, then?" asked the king.

The little girl colored up deeply, for she did not like to say "the animal kingdom," as he thought she would, lest his Majesty should be offended. Just then it flashed into her mind that "God made man in His own image," and looking up with a brightening eye she said: "To God's Kingdom, sir."

The king was deeply moved. A tear stood in his eye. He placed his hand on the child's head, and said, most devoutly: "God grant that I may be accounted worthy of that Kingdom."

—*Gospel Herald*

* * *

A Real Cause for Amazement

A few years ago there appeared a newspaper account of a Southern girl of sixteen, the daughter of a poor farmer, who made her way to Memphis, where for the first time in her life she saw such things as electric lights, trolley cars, moving pictures, and heard a radio. She was described as intelligent, but had never heard of leading world characters. She said, "I knew it couldn't be a dream, because I never dreamed anything as wonderful as this." This led *America* to moralize a bit: "The country is astonished on discovering a girl ignorant about radios and electric lights and trolley cars, but it is not astonished at seeing millions of boys and girls ignorant about God and their own souls. One American girl does not know who Hitler is; that's simply amazing. Millions of American girls do not know who Christ is; that's not amazing at all in this so-called Christian country."

—*The Presbyterian*

* * *

I Would Gather Children

"Some would gather money
Along the path of life,
Some would gather roses,
And rest from worldly strife;
But I would gather children
From among the thorns of sin,
I would seek a golden curl,
And a freckled, toothless grin.
For money cannot enter
In that land of endless day,
And roses that are gathered
Soon will wilt along the way.
But oh, the laughing children,
As I cross the sunset sea,
And the gates swing wide to heaven
I can take them in with me!"

—*Selected*

* * *

My Boy

He's not my boy, but when his hand
Is held in mine I understand
The problems that he has to face;
I glimpse his goal in life's long race,
And then a thrill akin to joy
Sweeps over me—
He IS my boy.

He's not my boy, he has no dad;
He's just a lonely, little lad
Who'll have to battle all the way.
And so, in trust, if he will lay
His hand in mine, I'll count it joy
To help that lad—
I call my boy.

—*Selected*

* * *

"Reformation Fires Slumbering in Tow-Headed Boy!"

Said a dejected, discouraged Sunday School teacher to Mr. Moody: "I went to the school and found only a little boy, and so I came away!" "Only a little

lad?" exclaimed Mr. Moody. Then he added, "Think of the value of one such soul! The fires of a Reformation may be slumbering in that tow-headed boy! There may be a young Knox, or a Wesley, or a Whitfield in your class!"

—W. B. K.

* * *

Ideals in Construction

A builder builded a temple,
He wrought it with grace and skill,
Pillars and groins and arches,
All fashioned to work his will.
Men said as they saw its beauty,
"It shall never know decay.
Great is thy skill, O Builder,
Thy fame shall endure for aye."

A teacher builded a temple
With loving and infinite care,
Planning each arch with patience,
Laying each stone with prayer.
None praised his unceasing efforts,
None knew of His wondrous plan,
For the temple the teacher builded
Was unseen by the eyes of man.

Gone is the builder's temple,
Crumbled into the dust;
Low lies each stately pillar,
Food for consuming rust.
But the temple the teacher builded
Will last while the ages roll,
For that beautiful unseen temple
Is a child's immortal soul.

—*Selected*

* * *

Too Young?

A new missionary on a foreign field was examining some candidates for baptism. He had examined all except one and found their answers to his questions satisfactory. He looked at the last candidate doubtfully and suggested that as he was so young he wait awhile before coming into the church. Immediately the others protested, "Why, he was the one who led us to the Lord!"

—*Sunday School Times*

Where Are The Souls?

I read of a certain evangelical pastor in a fashionable city church who started a work among slum boys. He succeeded in getting a lot of them into the church parlors for meetings, and taught them the way of salvation. Unfortunately the boys soiled the parlor carpets and upholstery. The pastor was called before the church officers to give an account of the damage done. His defense was something like this: "Brethren, when called to give an account to my Master, what shall I say?—'Here, Lord, is the church which thou didst entrust to me. It is in good shape. The church parlor carpets are as good as new, all nice and clean.' May He not say to me, 'Where are the *souls* which I sent you to win for Me? Where are the boys?'"

—*Sunday School Times*

* * *

Begin With the Boy

If you are ever going to do anything permanent for the average man, you must begin before he is a man. The chance of success lies in working with the boy—not with the man. That applies peculiarly to those boys who tend to drift off into courses which mean that unless they are checked they will be formidable additions to the criminal population when they grow older.

—Theodore Roosevelt

CHOOSING

"Wanting To Get Away From It All"

"While backstage in my dressing room in a theater off Broadway, I happened to have turned on the radio and recognized your opening hymn—'Wonderful Words of Life.' It was a great inspiration to me. A year and a half ago, I thought I was the happiest person in the universe, when I was offered a position on the stage. My mother, being saved, objected to this, but having a stubborn streak in me, I signed a contract with the agent and on the stage I went. As I said before, I thought I was the happiest person since I had everything my heart desired—money, clothes, the so-called good times, etc. Everything went fine for a half year, but within the past year I've been living in misery. I thought I'd escape this by going to Hollywood, but my greatest misery took place there, so I returned to New York. If you were to ask me what I remembered in your broadcast, I would have to say nothing, except the following words, 'choose you this day whom you will serve.' Just before curtain time these words were ringing in my ears. When I was told to be ready to go on in three minutes, a fear came over me. Out of all the lines I had memorized, I could think of none but 'Choose you this day, whom you will serve.' That night instead of going out with the rest of the actors and actresses, I went home, wanting to get away from it all."

—Jack Wyrtzen

* * *

God's Second Best

G. Christian Weiss tells how one day, while he was a student in Christian training, one of his teachers startled them in class by saying, "I have lived most of my life on God's second best." Following this remark, instead of devoting the class period to the lesson, he told them his story. God had manifestly called him to be a missionary in his younger days, but he turned aside from this course through marriage. In fact, he practically gave up Christian work and began a selfish business life as a cashier in a bank, with the primary purpose of setting up a nice home and making money. The Spirit of God kept dealing with him, but there was no yielding. Then after a number of years one day there came a message to him at the bank. His little child had toppled over in her high chair, and was dead. It took that bitter experience to bring

63

Choosing

this Christian to the place of surrender. After he spent a night alone with God on his knees, in tears and agony, the surrender came. But it was too late now to go to the mission field. With a broken and contrite heart, he pleaded with the Lord to take up the tangled threads of his disobedient life and make of the wreckage whatever He could.

—*Sunday School Times*

* * *

Watch Your Can't's and Can's.

If you would have some worthwhile plans
You've got to watch your can't's and can's;
You can't aim low and then rise high;
You can't succeed if you don't try;
You can't go wrong and come out right;
You can't love sin and walk in light;
You can't throw time and means away
And live sublime from day to day.

You can be great if you'll be good
And do God's will as all men should;
You can ascend life's upward road,
Although you bear a heavy load;
You can be honest, truthful, clean,
By turning from the low and mean;
You can uplift the souls of men
By words and deeds, or by your pen.

So watch your can't's and watch your can's,
And watch your walks and watch your stands,
And watch the way you talk and act,
And do not take the false for fact;
And watch indeed the way you take,
And watch the things that mar or make;
For life is great to every man
Who lives to do the best he can.

—Walter E. Isenhour, in
The Wesleyan Youth

* * *

Decision

The late Admiral Foote, the hero of the West African Coast in breaking up the slave trade, and of the Mississippi in cleaning out the Confederate batteries and gunboats, when a midshipman on the old warship *Natchez*, fought the grandest battle of his life. Pacing the deck one midnight he was tempted by all the fiends that lodge in the hot blood of youth. With compressed lips, and emphasizing each syllable with his footfall, he made this splendid resolve: "*Henceforth, Andrew Foote serves God.*" It was a repetition of the ancient scene when Jacob by a sublime act of consecration became Israel: "*For as a prince thou hast favor with God and with men, and hast prevailed.*"

—James M. Ludlow

* * *

Have You Been Chosen?

Christ was at the everlasting council: He can tell you whether you were chosen or not, but you cannot find it out in any other way. Go and put your trust in Him, and His answer will be, "I have loved thee with an everlasting love: therefore with lovingkindness have I drawn thee." There will be no doubt about His having chosen *you*, when you have chosen *Him*.

—C. H. Spurgeon

* * *

When a Young Jew Found Him

Jacob Gartenhaus began preparation for the rabbinate at the tender age of three in a strict Jewish home. This was followed by further training in the strictest Jewish institutions under private tutors. But the very strictness of the discipline defeated its purpose, for all work and no play flouted the arrangement and launched the lad upon the sea with the helmsman bearing his ship straight for America, for was it not the land of gold? A brother followed him all the way to America to win him for Christ, and later several members of his family traveled the same five thousand miles to try to take him away from Christ. At the Moody Bible Institute he prepared for missionary work. While in the Southern Baptist Theological Seminary, an uncle and aunt offered him $10,000 in cash to start him off in business if he would renounce Christianity. "No," he said, "not for $100,000!" "But," said his uncle, "although you will not hear me, you will listen to your mother." So he had her come on. Then, in the midst of his relatives he was subjected to unbelievable pressure to apostatize . . . But for the love of Christ he spurned the lure of wealth and broke the tender ties that bound him to his family, for he had found Him of whom Moses and the prophets did write. In season and out of season he has preached Christ . . . by voice and pen, until many converts have been won from Jewry to Christ.

—*Moody Monthly*

* * *

No Intention of Obeying

A young man at college in England, a true believer, had been discussing Biblical Christianity with another student, a young man of exceptionally keen intellect. Finally, he said to him: "Look here! I am no match for you in argument. But suppose that I could prove to you beyond the shadow of a doubt that Christ is what He claims to be; would you then be willing to acknowledge Him as your Lord?" The immediate response was, "No! Certainly not!" And this is the end toward which human intellect moves. It is not that the knowledge of God cannot be maintained against all the attacks of a false science, but that there is no desire to retain such knowledge.

—*Moody Monthly*

* * *

Reversed Sentence

A few years ago a Jewish merchant died. He had a Christian friend who had been in the same business, and they had often, without any prejudice, talked of the claims of Jesus Christ. The Jewish merchant had never accepted Christ as Saviour, and when he was dying his family did not want to allow any Gentile to get near him; but the Christian associate was eager to see him, and they felt that they could not refuse him because he had been a close friend. But they said, "You must not talk religion to him; you must not excite him." He went in and sat for a moment by the bedside, touched the hand of his friend, and then knelt by the bed and silently lifted his heart to God. Soon there was a movement on the bed. The old man opened his eyes, tried to sit up, lifted up his hand, and struggling to speak, said, "Not Barabbas, but this Man," and he fell back dead. Do you see what he had done? He had reversed the sentence of his nation. His nation had said, "Not this man, but Barabbas," but he had said, "Not Barabbas, but this Man."

—From *The Unchanging Christ*, by Dr. Harry A. Ironside.

* * *

Saved for 24 Hours

A minister once said to a German Jew in Bulgaria: "I want you to consent to be a Christian for 24 hours; then you will see how it seems and how you like it. Will you do so?"

"Oh, yes; I will for 24 hours."

"Well, then, first, I want you to believe that Jesus was born of the Virgin Mary."

The Jew threw up his hands and exclaimed, "Oh, no, I could not do that!"

"But it's only for 24 hours—"

"Very well, then, I will."

"Second, I want you to believe that Jesus died on the cross for the sins of the world."

"Impossible, impossible! I could not believe that."

"But it's only for 24 hours—"

"Well, all right; I will until tomorrow."

"Third, I want you to believe that Jesus rose from the dead."

"Oh, that I could not do!"

"But just for the time being?" So he consented.

"Fourth, I want you to believe that Jesus ascended into Heaven."

"Oh, impossible! No man could do that."

"But just believe it till tomorrow. Fifth, I want you to kneel down with me and pray to Christ the Saviour."

The old Jew prayed, "O God, Jehovah! If Christ be the true Son of God let Him save me!"

When he arose, the Jew, putting his hand upon his heart, said to the pastor, "I feel so strange right here." He had received a touch of the divine Spirit in his soul. The next day he came to the minister and said with a smile upon his face and peace in his heart, "I will take Him for another 24 hours!"

—*Power*

* * *

Letting Him Make Choice

Years ago I lived in a town where I could never buy anything to fit me. I used to send away occasionally to a certain large store for what I needed, and they would send me printed order forms. At the bottom of the forms were some such words as these: "If we have not the article you order in stock, may we substitute?" Once I said, "Yes," and they wrote, "We are sorry we have not in stock the article you ordered, but we are substituting—," and they sent me something that was worth double the price I paid. They made it a rule, if they could not supply the article ordered, to substitute with one of a much better quality. Ever after that I printed it out boldly so they would understand it—"Y-E-S." When we pray to God, we had better put on the order form that we are quite willing to let Him substitute, for every time He does He sends us something far better, "Exceeding abundantly above all that we ask or think."

—*Gospel Witness*

* * *

A Choice That Affected Generations

"*As for me and my house, we will serve the Lord*" (Josh. 24:15).

It was these words that the Holy Spirit brought to the mind of young James Taylor on the morning of his wedding day, February 1, 1776. Though he had lived a gay, worldly life, and was a leader in all that was opposed to the neighborhood Methodist revival, God dealt with him as he worked alone that momentous day. He yielded, was born again, and said, "Yes, we will serve the Lord." His bride was dismayed, but

he soon won her to Christ, and a Christian home was established. This was the great-grandfather of James Hudson Taylor, founder of the China Inland Mission. Holy influences from this right choice flowed down through the generations to come, and resulted in untold good. What if the decision had been different?

—"*Hudson Taylor in Early Years,*" by Dr. and Mrs. Howard Taylor

* * *

Heirs of God

"*Seek ye first the kingdom of God*"— Matthew 6:33

A king once said to a particular favorite, "Ask what thou wilt, and I will give it to thee."

The courtier thought: "If I ask to be made a general, I shall readily obtain it. If, for half the kingdom, he will give it to me. I will ask for something to which all these things shall be added." So he said to the king, "Give me thy daughter to wife." This made him heir to all the wealth and honors of the kingdom.

So, choosing Christ makes us heirs to all the wealth and glory of the Father's kingdom.

—*The King's Business*

* * *

Right or Wrong?

A thing is right, or a thing is wrong,
   And there is no in-between.
We sometimes wish that it wasn't so,
   But it's plain what both words mean.

If it's "not quite right," then it must
   be wrong,
If "it wouldn't be wrong," then it's
   right,
Though sometimes it's very hard to
   choose
When the difference seems very slight.

But no matter how old you live to be,
   And no matter where you go,
There are no half measures with right
   or wrong,
   And it always will be so.

—Alfred I. Tooke, in
Olive Plants

Jenny Lind's Choice

The Swedish Nightingale, Jenny Lind, won great success as an operatic singer, and money poured into her purse. Yet she left the stage while she was singing her best, and never returned to it. She must have missed the money, the fame, and the applause of thousands, but she was content to live in privacy. Once an English friend found her sitting on the sea sands with a Bible on her knee, looking out into the glory of the sunset. They talked, and the conversation drew near to the inevitable question: "Oh, Madame Goldschmidt, how is it that you came to abandon the stage at the very height of your success?" "When, every day," was the quiet answer, "it made me think less of this (laying a finger on the Bible) and nothing at all of that (pointing to the sunset), what else could I do?"

—From *Springs in the Valley*, by Mrs. Charles E. Cowman

Nothing To Merit His Choice

An old woman, hearing of some preachers who dwelt on the doctrine of predestination, said: "Ah, I have long settled that point, for if God had not chosen me before I was born, I am sure He would have seen nothing in me to have chosen me afterward."

—*United Presbyterian*

* * *

The Contrast

In the home of Mr. and Mrs. Oxley, Liverpool, Brother Oxley told us that the funeral procession of David Livingstone was one of the greatest London has ever seen. He said, "In the great throng a shabbily dressed bum fought his way through the crowd to see the funeral procession go by. He was rebuked by the crowd, but he cried out, 'I have a right to see David Livingstone, I know him better than any of you. We were in Sunday school together. He decided for Christ; I decided against Him.' "

—*Sunday School Times*

CHRISTIAN EXAMPLE — INFLUENCE

Hopelessly Handicapped?

Some years ago the late Mr. Gokhals, in conversation with Dr. Hume, after speaking of Christ with the deepest reverence, remarked: "But the Lord Jesus Christ is hopelessly handicapped by His connection with the West." To which Dr. Hume replied, "For nineteen centuries the Lord Jesus Christ has been handicapped by His connection with His followers; but *hopelessly*, never!"

—*Sunday School Times*

* * *

"According To You"

"We are living a Gospel
    A chapter each day,
By deed that we do,
    By word that we say;
Men read what we live,
    Whether faithless or true,
Say! What is the Gospel
    According to you?"

—*Selected*

The World's Need

A young Buddhist who had made a very careful study of Christianity, and particularly of Christ, said to a Christian regarding his study: "*Your Christ is wonderful, oh, so wonderful; but you Christians, you are not like Him.*" Without knowing it, the Buddhist pointed out the greatest need of present-day Christianity—more of Christlikeness in those who bear His name.

—*Earnest Worker*

* * *

"My Rule for Christian Living"

Dr. J. Wilbur Chapman had this which he called "My rule for Christian living": "The rule that governs my life is this: anything that dims my vision of Christ, or takes away my taste for Bible study, or cramps my prayer life, or makes Christian work difficult, is wrong for me, and I must, as a Christian, turn away from it." This simple rule may help you find a safe road for your feet along life's road.

—*Watchman-Examiner*

* * *

The Best Way

Not long ago a Hindu woman was converted, chiefly by hearing the Word of God read. She suffered very much persecution from her husband. One day a missionary asked her, "When your husband is angry and persecutes you, what do you do?" She replied: "Well, sir, I cook his food better; when he complains, I sweep the floor cleaner; and when he speaks unkindly, I answer him mildly. I try, sir, to show him that when I became a Christian I became a better wife and a better mother."

The consequence of this was that, while the husband could withstand all the preaching of the missionary, he could not stand the practical preaching of his wife, and gave his heart to God with her.

—*Evangelical Visitor*

* * *

True Epistles

An African prince, after interpreting the missionary's message, said, "I can't read this Book myself but I believe the words of it because I have watched the missionaries for two years and they have told me no lies about anything else, so when they tell me this Book is God's Word I believe it and I believe that Jesus died for me and I am going to follow this Jesus."

—*Inland Africa*

* * *

Why She Did Her Best

A young woman from my Bible class, only converted a short time, was called in to the president's office, where she is employed. He told her the firm was so pleased with the skillfulness of her work that they wished to let her know of their appreciation; he said that he was interested in knowing why anyone would put so much of themselves into the work as she did. She saw the opportunity to witness for her Lord, so she quickly said: "Sir, a few months ago I accepted the Lord Jesus Christ as my Saviour and Lord. I want everything about me to tell for Him."

—*Sunday School Times*

* * *

A Big Difference

Two sisters had been living in different cities. They came home on a visit. While away from home, one of the girls had become a Christian. After a few days the other girl said, "I don't know what causes it, but you are a great deal easier to live with than you used to be."

When Jesus comes in, it should make a difference!   —*Counsellor*

* * *

It's Always the Other Fellow

Dr. and Mrs. Paul James of Atlanta have a little lad, Edward, some five or six years of age. Next door to their home in Atlanta there lives another Christian family with a boy of Edward's age. One day play developed into a misunderstanding. The quarrel between the boys waxed warm and long. Suddenly little Edward drew himself up and said, "It's time one of us acted like a Christian. How about you?"

—*Moody Monthly*

* * *

Living What You Teach

I was present on one occasion when a group of teen-age girls were discussing a new leader for their Bible class. Their frank comments on the lady in question amused me. Said one girl, "If you kids pick Mrs. L— to be our teacher, I'm quitting." "Why, what's wrong with her?" asked several of the group. "Plenty," was the reply. "Remember how I used to go to help her with her housework on Saturdays? Well, she still owes me money, and she won't pay me. Also, she talks a lot about being a good Christian, and, boy, you should hear her say nasty things about some of her neighbors. Honest, kids, I know I shouldn't talk about her, but, please, let's wait until we find a teacher who lives what she teaches us on Sunday."

—*Sunday School Times*

The Worst Hurt

We who have believed can hurt Christ more than can the unbeliever. Enemies within the fort are more dangerous than enemies without. God's worst enemies when He sought the world through His Son were not the unbelieving Romans, but the Jews who believed in God and had worshipped Him for centuries.

What a responsibility this truth puts upon those who bear Christ's name. For the damage is just as severe from unintentional disloyalty as from open enmity. Every lowering of our standard is a worse stab at our best Friend and Saviour than can be dealt by scoffers or unbelievers.

—*Selected*

* * *

Knowing and Walking

You must not only know the way yourself, you must walk in it. Example is greater than precept. A gentleman was seeking the directions in a strange city, and the person of whom he inquired was vague and unsatisfactory. Another, coming up and seeing the stranger's perplexity, asked him where he wished to go. On being told, he replied, "Just come along with me, I am going that way myself." When parent and teacher can say to the child, "Come along with me, I am going that way myself," they talk in a language any child can understand.

—*Moody Monthly*

* * *

Life's Mirror

"There are loyal hearts, there are spirits brave,
There are souls that are pure and true;
Then give to the world the best you have,
And the best will come back to you.

"Give love, and love to your life will flow,
A strength in your utmost need;
Have faith, and a score of hearts will show
Their faith in your word and deed.

"Give truth, and your gift will be paid in kind,
And honor will honor meet;
And a smile that is sweet will surely find
A smile that is just as sweet.

"Give sorrow and pity to those who mourn,
You will gather in flowers again,
The scattered seeds of your thought outborne,
Though the sowing seemed but vain.

"For life is the mirror of king and slave;
'Tis just what you ARE and DO;
Then give to the world THE BEST YOU HAVE,
And the BEST will come back to you!"

—Madeline S. Bridges, in *St. Paul Dispatch*

* * *

Seen Through the Doctor

A Navajo woman was taken to a hospital in a dying condition. She was tenderly cared for for some time. Finally, when she seemed on the road to life again, the missionary, in simple words presented the claims of Christ for some time, but there was no answer. The woman lay there perfectly quiet, but it was evident that she was thinking things over. After some little time the door at the end of the ward opened and the doctor looked in just to make sure that everything was all right with his patient. She looked up and her bright eyes expressed the gratitude she felt as she softly replied in the liquid tongue of the Navajos, "If Jesus is anything like the doctor, I can trust Him forever." She had seen Christ magnified in a man, and her heart was won.

—*Sunday School Times*

* * *

Law Breaking When Convenient

One day as I was waiting to cross a street with the traffic signal, two girls were waiting also. They each carried a Bible. The light was red, and one girl said, "Let's go; there's not much traffic coming." The other girl said: "We had better stay until the light is green. It certainly wouldn't look good for us, carrying our Bibles, to cross against the light, when we know perfectly well we are breaking the law."

—*From a personal experience*

* * *

Next Door to God

An English traveler in Jerusalem was trying to find someone who could speak both English and Arabic. He heard of an American missionary who lived near by. Accosting an Arab boy who knew a little English, he asked him if he could direct him to the missionary's home. The face of the boy lit up, and he said, "You mean the lady who lives next door to God." If an uncouth Arab boy could detect one who walked with God, why cannot we so live here that the world can see Jesus in us?

—*Gospel Herald*

* * *

"Mother, You Haven't Lived the Life!"

Dr. Philpot was called to the bedside of a dying girl. In life, she had lived for the sinful things of the Christ-rejecting world. The faithful minister did his best to cause her to see her need of the Saviour, pleading, praying and quoting God's Word to her. Seemingly he could make no impression on the dying girl. As a final effort, he called in her mother. The mother, with heart-breaking sorrow, also pled with the girl to accept Christ as her Saviour. The girl listened stonily, and then she said these indicting words to her mother, "Mother, you can't talk to me now. YOU HAVEN'T LIVED THE LIFE BEFORE ME!" Ah, how great will be OUR accountability before God if we, by low, lustful living cause others to stumble into hell over us!

—W. B. K.

* * *

"I Won't Marry A Corpse!"

A fellow, trying to tell his sweetheart how much he loved her, exclaimed, "Why, I would DIE for you!" Promptly replied the sensible girl, "It's off! I don't want to marry a corpse!"

The Lord Jesus does not often ask us to DIE for Him. He asks that we LIVE for Him, "And He died for all, that they which live should not . . . live unto themselves, but unto Him which died for them" (II Cor. 5:15). There isn't a greater lack among God's children than simple faithfulness; unwearied continuance in well doing; a day-by-day living for Him and others!

—W. B. K.

* * *

Courage to Stand for Convictions

A distinguished Christian lady was recently spending a few weeks at a hotel at Long Branch, and an attempt was made to induce her to attend a dance, in order that the affair might have prestige bestowed by her presence, as she stood high in society. She declined all the importunities of her friends, and finally an honorable senator tried to persuade her to attend, saying, "Miss B., this is quite a harmless affair, and we want to have the exceptional honor of your presence." "Senator," said the lady, "I cannot do it. I am a Christian. I never do anything during my summer vacation, or wherever I go, that will injure the influence I have over the girls of my Sunday School class." The senator 'bowed, and said, "I honor you; if there were more Christians like you, more men like myself would become Christians."

—Dr. George Pentecost

* * *

"Like Christ"

I find that the greatest hindrance to the Gospel and the greatest hindrance to many precious truths taking effect in the hearts and consciences of un-believers is the un-Christlike lives of those who profess the truth. Oh, give me a hundred people that are making it the business of their lives to be "like Christ"—reading His Word and crying to God to show them the right way—and I will show you a place where there will be permanent blessing.

—J. R. Caldwell

Someone Else Is Watching

A friend of mine, who had been a hold-up man and a kidnaper for twelve years, met Jesus Christ in prison. Christ said, "I will come and live in you and we will serve this sentence together," and they did. Several years later he was discharged, and just before he went out he was handed a two-page letter written by another prisoner. After the salutation, it said in effect, "You know perfectly well that when I came into this jail I despised preachers, the Bible, and everything. I went to the Bible class and the preaching service because there wasn't anything else interesting to do. Then they told me you were saved, and I said, 'There's another fellow taking the Gospel road to get a parole'; but, Roy, I've been watching you for two and a half years. You did not know it, but I watched you when you were in the yard exercising, when you were working in the shop, when you played, while we were all together at meals, on the way to our cells, and all over, and now I'm a Christian, too, because I watched you. The Saviour who saved you has saved me. You never made a slip." Roy said to me, "When I got that letter and read it through I came out in a cold sweat. Think of what it would have meant if I had slipped, even once."

—*Sunday School Times*

* * *

The Mystery of Truth

In the Christian life we must lose to gain; we must give to obtain; we must be last to be first; we must be humble to be exalted; we must be least to be greatest; we must die to live.

—E. H. Blake, in
The Missionary Worker

* * *

How He Knew

A boy and girl, who played a good deal together, both learned to love the Saviour.

One day the boy said to his mother, "Mother, I know that Emma is a Christian!"

"What makes you think so?"

"Because, Mother, she plays like a Christian."

"Plays like a Christian!" said the mother, to whom this sounded odd. "Why what do you mean?"

"You see," said the child, "she used to be selfish and get angry at any little thing; now she is not selfish any more and doesn't get angry if you take everything she has got."

—*Y. P. Leader*

* * *

Not After the Pattern

A short time ago a Salvation Army captain was preaching in Hyde Park (London) when a man in the crowd interrupted him. "We haven't anything agin' Jesus of Nazareth," said the interrupter, "but we have something agin' you Christians *because you ain't up to sample.*"

—*Sunday School Chronicle*

* * *

"Whatsoever Ye Do, Do All"

Whatever you read, though the page may allure,
Read nothing of which you are not perfectly sure
Consternation at once would be seen in your look
If the Lord should say solemnly, "Show Me that book."

Whatever you write, in haste or with heed,
Write nothing you would not like Jesus to read.
Whatever you sing in the midst of your glee,
Sing nothing that God's listening ear could displease.

Wherever you go, never go where you'd fear
God's asking the question, "What doest thou here?"
Whatever the pastime in which you engage,
For the cheering of youth or the solace of age,

Turn away from each pleasure you'd
  shrink from pursuing
Were the Lord to look down and say,
  "What are you doing?"
            —Selected

* * *

Proof of Pudding

Gustav Dore, the famous artist, lost
his passport while traveling in Europe.
He was at a certain boundary post between two countries and the officer in
charge asked him for his passport. Dore
fumbled about and finally announced,
"I have lost my passport, but it is all
right. I'm Dore, the artist. Please let
me go in."

The officer replied, "Oh, no. We have
plenty of people representing themselves
as this or that great person! Here is
a pencil and paper. Now, if you are
Dore, the artist, prove it by drawing me
a picture!"

Dore took the pencil and drew some
pictures of scenes in the immediate area.

"Now, I am perfectly sure that you are
Dore. No one else could draw like that!"
said the officer as he allowed the great
artist to enter the country.

So it is with professing followers of
Christ. You say you are a Christian.
But can you really produce evidence?
            —Power

* * *

The Right Way

More than a century and a half ago,
the Highland Brigade of the British
Army was obliged to march across the
Egyptian desert by night to Tel-el-
Kebir. It would have been quite easy
to lose the route, but a young naval
officer volunteered to lead by stellar
observation. So the soldiers looked to
the sailor, and the sailor looked to the
stars.

The journey was completed by dawn
and the Brigade charged the enemy's
trenches and took them. The naval officer fell in the battle, however. As he
lay dying, he turned his face to the
general, who was visiting the wounded,
and asked: "Sir, I led them straight,
didn't I?"

Are we as Christians, leading men and
women straight?   *—The Pilgrim*

Revealing Christ

"Not merely in the words you say,
  Not only in your deeds confessed,
But in the most unconscious way
  Is Christ expressed.

"For me 'twas not the truth you taught,
  To you so clear, to me so dim,
But when you came to me you brought
  A sense of Him.

"And from your eyes He beckons me,
  And from your heart His love is shed,
Till I lose sight of you and see
  The Christ instead."
            —Selected

* * *

Christian Fronts

A young doctor said a terrible thing
a few years ago to somebody who was
talking to him about accepting Christ.
He remarked, "I think I might have
become a Christian if I had not met so
many people who said they were." The
tragedy is that so often our lives deny
our profession; our low standards, our
compromises, bickerings, impatience, ir-
ritability, censoriousness, ill-temper, and
selfishness belie our profession. We need
to pray, "Create in me a clean heart."
Spurgeon once said, "Some Christians
are like jerry-built houses: they are
Queen Anne in front, and Mary Ann at
the back."
            —Keswick Week

* * *

The Best Translation!

Four clergymen were discussing the
merits of various translations of the
Bible. One liked the King James Version best because of its simple beautiful
English.

Another liked the American Revised
Version best because it is more literal
and comes nearer the original Hebrew
and Greek.

Still another liked Moffat's translation best because of its up-to-date vo-
cabulary.

The fourth minister was silent. Finally he said, "I like my mother's translation best. She translated it into life,
and it was the most convincing translation I ever saw."
       —N. A. E. News Bulletin

Responsibility

"Yours must be a very responsible position," said a traveler to a switchman who had charge of the switches where five lines converge. "Yes," was the reply, "but it is as nothing compared to yours as a Christian."—

—*Christian Herald*

* * *

Who Do They See in You?

A greatly beloved medical missionary was Dr. Fred Douglas Shepard of Aintab, Asia Minor. His magnificent courage and undying zeal enabled him to accomplish an enormous and varied work for suffering humanity. "I have never seen Jesus," once said a poor Armenian, "but I have seen Dr. Shepard." That was the next thing to seeing Jesus. Let us strive to live so that men and women will talk about us in that way.

—*Immanuel Messenger*

* * *

"Ask the Skipper!"

Dr. Grenfell, of Labrador, tells about his calling to see a dying man on a fishing vessel off this coast. As he left the cabin another invalid called out, "You've forgotten me, Doctor. I'm the man who was converted at — two years ago." "Well," said Grenfell, "what difference has it made in your life?" "Ask the skipper," he replied. Ah, friends, that's the test. *Can others testify as to the difference conversion has made in your life?*

—Leonard Trap, in *The Banner*

* * *

Showcases.

It has been well said that "God has great and wonderful things to display if he finds suitable showcases." Are you a showcase for the Lord Jesus?

—*Sunday School Times*

* * *

How He Died:

So he died for his faith. That is fine—
More than most of us do.
But say, can you add to that line
That he lived for it, too?

In his death he bore witness at last
As a martyr to truth.
Did his life do the same in the past
From the days of his youth?

It is easy to die. Men have died
For a wish or a whim—
From bravado or passion or pride:
Was it harder for him?

But to live — every day to live out
All the truth that he dreamt,
While his friends met his conduct with doubt
And the world with contempt;

Was it thus that he plodded ahead,
Never turning aside?
Then we'll talk of the life that he led,
Never mind how he died.

—*Selected*

* * *

"It's the Life that Counts"

If we would show decision for the truth we must not only do so by our tone and manner, but by our daily actions. A man's life is always more forcible than his speech; when men take stock of him they reckon his deeds as pounds and his words as pence. If his life and his doctrine disagree the mass of lookers-on accept his practice and reject his preaching. We must show our decision for the truth by the sacrifices we are ready to make.

—C. H. Spurgeon

* * *

Is It Visible?

A youngster, who gave his heart to the Lord Jesus Christ in a Child Evangelism meeting, hurried home afterward and said to his little sister: "I have a new heart."

"Have you?" she asked him, and then, quite naively, added: "Let me see it."

A tree is known by its fruits. If we are Christians, if we possess the new life that we profess to have, the fact should be visible to others. Conversion to Christ issues in conduct that shows for the new life in Christ.

—*The Pilgrim*

Worthless Unless Seen

I would not give much for your religion unless it can be seen. Lamps do not talk, but they do shine. A lighthouse sounds no drums, it beats no gong; and yet far over the water its friendly spark is seen by the mariner.

—C. H. Spurgeon

* * *

How to Express Christianity

In the home — by love and unselfishness.

In business — by honesty and diligence.

In society — by purity, courtesy and humility.

Toward the unfortunate — by sympathy and mercy.

Toward the weak — by helpfulness and patience.

Toward the wicked — by overcoming evil, without compromise.

Toward the strong — by trust and cooperation with good.

Toward non-Christians — by witnessing to Christ and His Gospel.

Toward the penitent — by forgiveness and restoration.

Toward the fortunate — by rejoicing with them without envy.

Toward God — by reverence, love and obedience.

—*Sunday School Digest*

* * *

"Making Christians by Being Christians!"

Years ago Dr. Temple in an address to a group of newly-ordained ministers said: "Young men, believe me, you will make more people Christians by being Christians yourselves than you will by all the sermons you will ever preach."

—S. G. Harwood, in *Gospel Herald*

* * *

Christians Living the Christ Life

Having a room to rent, a Jew desired it, and referred me to a neighbor with whom he had boarded. She advised me not to take him, but the words of Jesus, "Inasmuch as ye have done it unto one of the least of these my brethren," kept ringing in my ears. I knew I must let him have it. John 3:16, printed in large, glowing letters I hung where he could see it each time he entered the house, and prayed much that I might lead him to know Jesus Christ. The Jew borrowed my Bible to read, and later told me he believed in my Jesus. He said, "The Jews are looking to see if they can find any *Christians living* the Christ life."

—*The Sunday School Times*

* * *

He Didn't Sleep

One night just before the late Captain Bickel was retiring to rest he met at the deckhouse door a ruffian who had been wonderfully converted on one of his voyages. Mr. Bickel was very tired, but he had a little talk with the man. He asked him if he would take a Bible to a certain man on the morrow. He shook his head. "No, no, Captain; he does not need that." "But why not?" "Because it is too soon. That is your Bible, and thank God! it is now mine; but it is not his Bible." "What do you mean by that?" "Why simply that he has another Bible; you are his Bible; he is watching you. As you fail, Christ fails. As you live Christ, so Christ is revealed to him." Writing of this incident, Captain Bickel said: "Friends, I did not sleep that night. I had been called a thief, liar, foreign spy, traitor, devil, in public and private, and had not flinched; but to face this. 'As you live, so Christ lives — in that man's soul, in that house, in that village, in four hundred villages. As you fail to live Christ, Christ is crucified again.' What wonder that I slept not!" All of us are being watched by someone. What kind of a witness do we give by our lives?

—*The Evangelist*

* * *

Livingstone's Living

Henry M. Stanley found Livingstone in Africa and lived with him for some time. Here is his testimony: "I went to Africa as prejudiced as the biggest atheist in London. But there came for me a long time for reflection. I saw this solitary old man there and asked myself, 'How on earth does he stop here — is he cracked, or what? What is it that inspires him?' For months after we met I found myself wondering at the old man carrying out all that was said in the Bible — 'Leave all things and follow Me.' But little by little his sympathy for others became contagious; my sympathy was aroused; seeing his piety, his gentleness, his zeal, his earnestness, and how he went about his business, I was converted by him, although he had not tried to do it."

—The Australian Baptist

CHRISTMAS

Christmas Eve in "No Man's Land!"

'Twas Christmas Eve in "no man's land!" The time was World War I. A most unusual and wondrous thing occurred: Battle-weary men in one trench began singing:

"Silent night, holy night,
All is calm, all is bright!"

Enemies, in the opposite trench, answered by singing:

"O little town of Bethlehem,
How still we see thee lie!"

Cannon ceased their booming. The Spirit of Christ became all-pervasive! Peace reigned 'midst scenes of carnage! For the time, foes became friends! The incident is prophetic of that wondrous day when Jesus, "the Prince of Peace," will return to our war-wrecked, sin-sodden world as "Lord of lords and King of Kings!" Then prophecy will become history: "They shall beat their swords into plowshares, and their spears into pruninghooks: nation shall not lift up sword against nation, neither shall they learn war any more!" (Micah 4:3). The heart-cry of God's children around the world is this: "Even so, come, Lord Jesus!" (Rev. 22:20b).

—W. B. K.

* * *

Christmas Bells

I heard the bells on Christmas Day
Their old familiar carols play,
And wild and sweet the words repeat
Of peace on earth, good-will to men!

I thought how, as the day had come,
The belfries of all Christendom
Had rolled along the unbroken song
Of peace on earth, good-will to men!

And in despair I bowed my head;
"There is no peace on earth," I said;
"For hate is strong, and mocks the song
Of peace on earth, good-will to men."

Then pealed the bells more loud and deep;
"God is not dead, nor doth He sleep!
The wrong shall fail, the right prevail,
With peace on earth, good-will to men!"

—Henry Wadsworth Longfellow

* * *

The Star In God's Window

One night, a man and his small son were walking slowly down the streets of a large American city. The child was delighted to see the many service stars hanging in the windows of homes — each star proudly proclaiming the fact that a son was in the service of his country. He clapped his hands excitedly as he approached each new star, and was duly impressed by those homes with more than one star in the window.

Finally they came to a wide gap between houses, through which the black velvet of the sky was clearly discernible, with the evening star shining brightly. "Oh look, Daddy," cried the little boy, "God must have given His Son, for He has a star in His window!"

—Harry Lauder

* * *

Carols Changed Christmas!

Before the advent of the Christmas carol, celebrations of Christmas had become so depraved and rowdy that the observance of the joyous season was once forbidden by the English Parliament. The meaning of Christmas had become lost in a maelstrom of revelings, drunkenness, riotings, and depravity. Decent people found it necessary to stay indoors for safety. The situation became so shameful that in 1644 Parliament passed strict laws making it illegal to commemorate the season in any way whatsoever! How empty and devoid of meaning is a Christless Christmas! KEEP CHRIST IN CHRISTMAS!

—W. B. K.

* * *

A Bed In My Heart

"Ah, dearest Jesus, holy Child,
Make Thee a bed, soft, undefiled,
Within my heart, that it may be
A quiet chamber kept for Thee.
My heart for very joy doth leap,
My lips no more can silence keep,
I too must sing, with joyful tongue,
That sweetest ancient cradle song,
Glory to God in highest Heaven,
Who unto man His Son hath given
While angels sing with pious mirth.
A glad New Year to all the earth."

—Martin Luther

* * *

Christ the Light of the World

An artist once drew a picture of a winter twilight — the trees heavily laden with snow, and a dreary, dark house, lonely and desolate in the midst of the storm. It was a sad picture. Then, with a quick stroke of yellow crayon, he put a light in one window. The effect was magical. The entire scene was transformed into a vision of comfort and cheer. The birth of Christ was just such a light in the dark world.

—*Sunday School Chronicle*

* * *

The Child of Long Ago

For the sake of one small child of long
   ago
I shall go down dark alleyways and dim
To find the children there and give the
   gifts
I cannot bring to Him.

And for His sake I shall go seeking those
Who have forgotten stars may shine
   for them,

To tell them of one everlasting star:
The Star of Bethlehem.

—Grace Noll Crowell

* * *

"Happy Birthday"

"On Christmas morning my little daughter was downstairs opening her packages before anyone else was out of bed. To my surprise, I heard her singing the Happy Birthday song. 'Happy Birthday on Christmas morning'? I thought that she, aware of festivity in the air, was confused as to the occasion. But as she sang on, I realized that it was I who had been confused. 'Happy Birthday, dear Jesus,' the little voice caroled, 'Happy Birthday to You.' "

—*Reader's Digest*

* * *

Christmas Everywhere

Everywhere, everywhere, Christmas tonight!
Christmas in lands of the fir tree and
   pine,
Christmas in lands of the palm tree and
   vine,
Christmas where snow-peaks stand
   solemn and white,
Christmas where cornfields lie sunny
   and bright,
Everywhere, everywhere, Christmas tonight!

Christmas where children are hopeful
   and gay,
Christmas where old men are patient
   and gray,
Christmas where peace, like a dove in
   its flight,
Broods o'er brave men in the thick of
   the flight;
Everywhere, everywhere, Christmas tonight!

Then let every heart keep its Christmas
   within,
Christ's pity for sorrow, Christ's hatred
   of sin,
Christ's care for the weakest, Christ's
   courage for right,
Christ's dread of the darkness, Christ's
   love of the light,
Everywhere, everywhere, Christmas tonight!

—Phillips Brooks

Startling Contrasts

This little message the editor discovered a few years ago in a tract. We want to share it with you. "Jesus Christ was born in the meanest circumstances, but the air above was filled with the hallelujahs of the heavenly host. His lodging was a cattle pen, but a star drew distinguished visitants from afar to do Him homage. His birth was contrary to the laws of life. His death was contrary to the laws of death. No miracle is so inexplicable as His life and teaching. He had no cornfields or fisheries, but He could spread a table for 5,000 and have bread and fishes to spare. . . . Three years He preached His Gospel. He wrote no book, built no church, had no money back of Him. After 1,900 years, He is the one central character of human history, the perpetual theme of all preaching, the pivot around which the events of the age revolve, the only regenerator of the human race. Was it merely the son of Joseph and Mary who crossed the world's horizon 1,900 years ago? Was it merely human blood that was spilled on Calvary's hill for the redemption of sinners, and which has worked such wonders in men and nations through the centuries? What thinking man can keep from exclaiming, 'My Lord and my God!' "

—Essex

* * *

Latch String Out!

My latch is on the string tonight
  The hearth fire is aglow
I seem to hear swift passing feet —
  The Christ Child in the snow.
My heart is open wide tonight
  For stranger, kith or kin.
I would not close a single door
  Where Christ may enter in.

—Selected

* * *

Keeping Christmas

Are you willing to forget what you have done for other people, and to remember what other people have done for you; to ignore what the world owes you, and to think what you owe the world; to put your rights in the background, and your duties in the middle distance, and your chances to do a little more than your duty in the foreground; to see that your fellow men are just as real as you are, and try to look behind their faces to their hearts, hungry for joy; to own that probably the only good reason for your existence is not what you are going to get out of life, but what you are going to give to life; to close your book of complaints against the management of the universe, and look around you for a place where you can sow a few seeds of happiness — are you willing to do these things even for a day? Then you can keep Christmas.

Are you willing to believe that love is the strongest thing in the world — stronger than hate, stronger than evil, stronger than death — and that the blessed life which began in Bethlehem nineteen hundred years ago is the image and brightness of the Eternal Love? Then you can keep Christmas.

And if you keep it for a day, why not always?

But you cannot keep it alone.

—Henry Van Dyke

* * *

Give Me These Gifts

I want no frankincense, myrrh and
  gold
Like the Wise Men brought to the Child
  of old,
But this I crave with a great desire —
These gifts I ask with my soul on fire:
Peace of mind in this heart of mine,
Comrade-love as a light to shine
Like the golden gleam of an afterglow
Of sunset over a field of snow;
A woodfire, bright in the twilight gloam,
And the holy warmth of a loving home;
Friends who will take my reaching hand
Like the star of old in a distant land,
And guide my steps to a manger shrine
And the heart of a lowly Child, Divine!

—Wm. L. Stidger

* * *

The Loveliest Thing About Christmas

"For this cause I bow my knees" (Eph. 3:14a). A group of noblemen were gathered together in London, when the King of Great Britain entered. They all knew him, personally, yet they all honored him as their king. So when he entered they stood solemnly to their feet. "Take your seats, gentlemen," said the king, "I count you my personal friends." And then jokingly he added, "I am not the Lord, you know." Then up spoke one of the noblemen, a true Christian at heart, "No, sir, if you were our Lord, we would not stand to our feet. He would fall on our knees."

The loveliest thing about the Christmas story is not the simple faith of the lowly shepherds who were keeping their flocks by night; not the singing of the angel hosts; but the fact, rather, that when the Wise Men found the baby Jesus, they fell on their knees before Him and worshipped Him.

—*Baptist Young People's Union Quarterly*

* * *

Keep Christ in Christmas

As now we celebrate His birth,
The coming of the Christ to earth,
May we, amid our joyous mirth,
   Keep Jesus first in Christmas!

As chiming bells ring out their lay,
And hearts are merry, light, and gay,
Remember it is His birthday —
   Keep Jesus first in Christmas!

Let's sing of Him in carols sweet,
Let's lay our best gifts at His feet
And make the season's joy complete —
   With Jesus first in Christmas!

Selected

* * *

What He Wants Most of All

"Mommie," asked Jane, "what makes everybody so happy at Christmas?" "Well, because it is the Lord Jesus' birthday . . . and because we love Him . . . and because we are happy about His coming to this world." Jane thought a minute and then said, "And is the Lord happy about you?" Oh, little girlie, what a question you've asked! Is the Lord Jesus happy about us on His birthday? Really happy because He sees within our hearts a deep, true love for Him? A satisfying love and not just a seasonal affection stirred up by the festivities of Christmas? . . . What He wants more than anything else on His birthday is the love of our hearts.

—From Doris Coffin Aldrich, in *Moody Monthly*

* * *

The Express Image of His Person

In the Rospigliosi Palace in Rome is Guido Reni's famous fresco, "The Aurora," a work unequaled in that period for nobility of line and poetry and color. It is painted on a lofty ceiling. As you stand on the pavement and look up at it, your neck stiffens, your head grows dizzy, and the figures become hazy and indistinct. And so the owner of the place has placed a broad mirror near the floor. In it the picture is reflected, and you can sit down before it and study the wonderful work in comfort. Jesus Christ does precisely that for us when we try to get some notion of God. He is the mirror of Deity. He is the express image of God's person. He interprets God to our dull hearts. In Him God becomes visible and intelligible to us. We cannot by any amount of searching find out God. The more we try, the more we are bewildered. Then Jesus Christ appears. He is God stooping down to our level, and He enables our feeble thoughts to get some real hold on God Himself.

Frank M. Fairchild, in *Moody Monthly*

* * *

What Each One Did

In a rude stable cold,
The friendly beasts their stories told:
"I," said the donkey, shaggy and brown,
"Carried His mother up hill and down,
Carried her safely to Bethlehem town."
"I," said the cow all white and red,
"Gave Him my manger for His bed,
Gave Him my hay to pillow His head."
"I," said the sheep, with the curly horn,
"Gave Him wool for His blanket warm;
He wore my coat on Christmas Morn."
"I," said the camel, all yellow and black,
"Over the desert, upon my back,
Brought Him a gift in the Wise Man's pack."

"I," said the dove, "from my rafter high,
Cooed Him to sleep, that He should not
   cry,
We cooed Him to sleep, my mate and I."
And every beast, by some good spell
In the stable darkness, was able to tell
Of the gift he gave to Emmanuel.

                —Robert Davis

* * *

Better Than Gold

"I shall give that to the missionaries,"
said Billy; and he put his fat hand on a
little gold dollar, as he counted the contents of his money-box.

"Why?" Susie asked.

" 'Cause it's gold. Don't you know
the Wise Men brought Jesus gifts of
gold? The missionaries work for Jesus."

Stillness for a little bit, then Susie
said, "The gold all belongs to Him anyhow. Don't you think it would be better to go right to Him and give Him
just what He asks for?"

"What's that?" Billy asked.

Susie repeated softly, " 'My son, give
Me thine heart.' "

         —*The King's Highway*

* * *

How Do You Look?

A poor little street girl was taken ill
one Christmas and carried to the hospital. While there she heard the story
of Jesus coming into the world to save
us. One day she whispered to the nurse:
"I'm having real good times here.
S'pose I'll have to go away from here
just as soon as I get well; but I'll take
the good time along — some of it anyhow. Do you know about Jesus being
born?" "Yes," replied the nurse. "I
know. Sh-sh-sh! Don't talk any more."
"You do? I thought you looked as if
you didn't, and I was going to tell you."
"Why, how did I look?" asked the nurse,
forgetting her own order in her curiosity. "Oh, just like most folks — kind
o' glum. I should think you'd never look
glum if you knew about Jesus being
born."

         —*Sunday at Home*

Why He Was Laid in a Manger

Thank God, none are too bad or too
low-down to take Jesus Christ into their
hearts. There was once a poor drunkard
who wakened one morning in a strange
kind of bed, feeling something near him
warm and soft. Finally it dawned on
him that he was in a stable close beside
a cow. He laughed grimly as he thought
of breakfast. In his mind he went over
those who might be persuaded to help
him with a meal. "No, I can't ask any
of them; they would say I have fallen
too low." Then he heard the bells ringing, and began to realize it was Christmas Day. "What was that story about
the shepherds — the angels — and a
manger?" Well, he wasn't the first one
who had slept in a stable. He thought,
"Mebbe the reason He slept in a manger was so He could help a fellow like
me — a fellow too low for anyone else
to help." There and then the poor outcast knelt and prayed the prayer of the
publican, "God, be merciful to me a sinner."

         —*Baptist Standard*

* * *

Would You Wish to Live There?

Little Hattie had a model village, and
she never tired of setting it up. "What
kind of village is that, Hattie?" asked
her father. "Oh, a Christian town,"
Hattie answered quickly. "Suppose we
make it a heathen town," her father
suggested. "What must we take out?"
"The church," said Hattie, taking it to
one side. "Is that all?" "I suppose so."
"No, indeed," her father said, "the public school must go. Take the public
library out also." "Anything else?"
Hattie asked sadly. "Isn't that a hospital over there?" "But, Father, don't
they have hospitals?" "Not in heathen
countries. It was Christ who taught us
to care for the sick and the old." "Then
I must take out the Old Ladies' Home,"
said Hattie soberly. "Yes, and that
Orphans' Home at the other end of the
town." "Why, Father," Hattie exclaimed, "then there's not one good thing
left! I would not live in such a town
for anything." Does having room for
Jesus make so much difference?

         —*Moody Monthly*

CHURCH

It's You!

'Sez I to myself, as I grumbled and
   growled,
'I'm sick of my church,' and then how I
   scowled.
'The members unfriendly, the sermons
   too long;
In fact, it seems that everything's wrong.
I don't like the singing; the church —
   a disgrace,
For signs of neglect are all over the
   place.
I'll quit going there, and won't give a
   dime:
I can make better use of my money and
   time.'
Then my conscience sez to me, sez he,
'The trouble with you is, you're blind
   to see
That your church reflects you, whatever
   it be.
Now come, pray, and serve cheerfully;
Stop all your faultfinding and boost
   it up strong;
You'll find you'll be happy and proud to
   belong.
Be friendly, be willing, and sing as you
   work,
For churches are not built by members
   who shirk."

—*Selected*

* * *

An Impure Church

Said David Livingstone: "Nothing
will induce me to form an impure
church. Fifty added to the church
sounds well at home, but if only five are
GENUINE what will it profit in the
Great Day?"

—*Western Recorder*

* * *

A Strong Congregation

"Is it a strong congregation?"

"Yes," was the reply.

"How many members are there?"

"Thirty."

"Thirty! Are they so wealthy?"

"No, many of them are poor."

"How, then, can you say it is a strong
church?"

"Because they are earnest, devoted, at
peace, loving each other, following the
Word of God in all things, instant in
prayer, and striving together to do the
Lord's work. Such a congregation is
strong, whether composed of thirty or
three hundred members."

—*Lutheran Annual*

* * *

Where Are the Dead?

I spoke one night on "Where are the
dead?" My audience, I think, expected
me to deal with the question of the
future state. They were greatly surprised. Declaring that ninety per cent
of the dead were in the churches, I gave
them quite a few facts to think over.
There are big dead churches everywhere,
and to them the Lord's injunction certainly applies. "Because thou sayest, I
am rich and increased with goods, and
have need of nothing; and knowest not
that thou art wretched, and miserable,
and poor, and blind, and naked; I counsel thee to buy of Me gold tried in the
fire." —*Edwin Orr*

* * *

Churches

Thank God for the sight of them,
The beauty, the dreams, and the right
   of them.
Churches that silently testify
With spires and crosses reared to the
   sky,
That make us think every time we look
Of God, and right, and the Holy Book.

—*Chauncey R. Piety*

* * *

Old Paths

In a section of a certain city, all the
churches but one closed their doors on

Sunday evenings for the summer months. A newspaper sent a young woman reporter to call on the minister. She found him a very plain, humble man. When she asked him why his church could still get a fair-sized crowd on Sunday evenings during the summer, and the other churches have to close, the minister said: "In our church we have stayed to the 'old paths.' We haven't tried to use worldly methods to attract crowds; we believe the Lord Jesus can draw people to Himself when He is truly lifted up. *He still has that power*, you know."

—*As told by the Reporter*

* * *

Be Careful!

Aunt Alice came downstairs frowning with a miserable headache. She was advised to go back to bed and rest.

"But I can't," she replied. "You see, I have to read a paper at my Saturday morning Club, and I just have to go. I'll take a couple of headache pills and get by somehow."

The next morning (Sunday), she said: "I simply can't go out today with this headache. Somebody else will have to take my Sunday school class. No, you needn't phone the superintendent. There will be someone he can get. Anybody can take it."

Small Dorothy was observing it all, and doing some significant learning. Later in life she may be one of those people about whom we ask wonderingly, "Why are so many Christians so indifferent?"

—*Sunday School Times*

* * *

Dead Men?

Have you ever read "The Ancient Mariner"? I dare say you thought it one of the strangest imaginations ever put together, especially that part where the old mariner represents the corpses of all the dead men rising up to man the ship, — dead men pulling the rope, dead men steering, dead men spreading sails. I thought what a strange idea that was.

But do you know, I have lived to see that time. I have gone into churches, and I have seen a dead man in the pulpit, a dead man as deacon, a dead man handling the plate, and dead men sitting to hear.

—C. H. Spurgeon

* * *

Omnipresent

One day the telephone in the office of the rector of President Roosevelt's Washington church rang, and an eager voice said, "Tell me, do you expect the President to be in church this Sunday?"

"That," the rector explained patiently, "I cannot promise. But we expect God to be there, and we fancy that will be incentive enough for a reasonably large attendance."

—*Reader's Digest*

* * *

What Kind Are YOU?

There are three kinds of church members: There are the "Old Faithfuls." Heaven bless them! Then, there are the "Once-in-a-Whilers." They are also known as "Up and Downers," or, "In and Outers." They come one Sunday, and stay away five. There are also the "Almost Nevers." They never come! Perhaps, I should not have said, "Never." They do come on Easter, or on Christmas.

—Rev. Harold F. Stoddard, in
Watchman-Examiner

* * *

A Multitude of "Jiners"

Dr. Theodore L. Cuyler used to give the following account that has a far wider application than ever imagined by the poor Negro who was interviewed. Dr. Cuyler said: "We asked an old Negro preacher how his church was getting on, and his answer was 'Mighty poor, mighty poor, brudder.' We ventured to ask the trouble, and he replied: 'De 'sieties, de 'sieties. Dey ist jist drawin' all de fatness and marrow outen de body and bone of de Lord's Body. We can't do nuffin without de 'siety. There is de Lincum 'siety, wid Sister Jones and Brudder Brown to run it. Sister Williams mus' march right in front of de Daughters of Rebekah. Den dar is de Dorcases, de Marthas, de Daughters of Ham, and Liberian Ladies.' 'Well, you have your brothers to help in the church,' we suggested. 'No, sah, dar am de Masons, de Odd Fellows, de Sons of Ham, and de Oklahoma Promised Land Pilgrims. Why, brudder, by de time de brudders and sisters pay all dues, an' tend all de meetings, der is nuffin left for Mount Pisgah Church but just de cob! De co'n has all been shelled off and frowed to de speckled chickens.' "

—*Bible Expositor and Illuminator*

* * *

All Active

A minister was once asked by an old-time friend, whom he met in a distant city: "How many members do you have in your church?"

"One thousand," the preacher replied.

"Really!" the friend exclaimed. "And how many of them are active?"

"All of them are active," was the response. "About two hundred of them are active for the Lord; the balance are active for the devil."

—*Free Methodist*

* * *

Back Seat Problem

"I wonder," said good parson Jones
With a little troubled frown,
If there is any way to get
You folks seated farther down?

You see I have to talk across
So many empty pews,
Before my voice can reach the back,
I fear my point you lose.

And then I feel so lonesome,
Way up here — you clear back there,
Its hard to feel you're with me
When I come to God in prayer.

I wonder If you folks are scared
Of what I'm going to preach
That you hurry so to park
In the fartherest seat?

Or do you fear the church some day
Will suddenly catch afire?
Or do you want to slip out quick
If of my subject you tire?

I wish you'd come up closer
So I wouldn't have to shout —
If you don't I'm going to have
Those back-seats taken out!"

—*Selected*

* * *

The Wrecking Crew

Two classes of people manifest themselves in every church. Some are constructive and others are destructive. Some are positive and others are negative. And what a difference their attitudes make in the work of Christ!

The immediate occasion of this homily is the following which has just come to my attention:

"A good thing to remember
And a better thing to do,
Is to work with the construction gang
And not the wrecking crew."

The wrecking crew is usually present in church business meetings. If a proposal is made by the board or by an individual, the members of the wrecking crew are on their feet to oppose the measure. They never analyze a proposition constructively, but simply assume that the plan is to be resisted. They are "born in the objective case and kickative mood." They are like the deaf brother who used to cup his ear in a business meeting and call out, "I didn't hear what the brother said, but I'm against it." To be sure, there are times in which we must oppose propositions and resist individuals on scriptural grounds, but there is no necessity for opposing everything and resisting everybody.

—*King's Business*

* * *

A Minister's Dream

It is said that a minister dreamed he was hitched to a covered wagon, and was laboriously, but slowly, pulling it along, until he reached a place in the road where the mud seemed to get deeper, and it was with much difficulty that he moved the wagon a few inches at a time. He thought it rather peculiar, as the last time he looked back he thought he saw the entire congregation pushing. But the longer and harder he pulled, the more difficult it became to move the wagon. Finally, almost exhausted, he went to the rear to examine the source of the trouble. All the church members had quit pushing. Not only had they quit pushing but they were sitting in the wagon and were criticizing the pastor for not pulling the church along faster.

Well, was it a dream . . . ?
—*Cumberland Presbyterian*

* * *

The Meeting

Think not, my friend, because I seek
This quiet shelter twice a week
I better deem its pine-laid floor
Than breezy hill or sea-sung shore.
But nature is not solitude:
She crowds us with her thronging wood,
Her many hands reach out to us,
Her many tongues are garrulous,
She will not leave our senses still
But drags them captive at her will.
And so I find it well to come
For deeper rest to this still room,
For here the habit of the soul
Feels less the outer world's control,
And from this silence — multiplied
By these still forms on either side —
The world which Time and Sense have
    known
Falls off, and leaves us God alone.
—J. G. Whittier

* * *

Why Sambo Went to Church

An aged Negro who was a faithful church-goer was urged by his friends one cold, rainy day to stay at home, lest his rheumatism should become worse. But the old Negro answered,

"But I must go. Who knows but de blessin' may come to-day, an' I don't want to miss it."
—*War Cry*

* * *

No Substitutes for Church

Harmon B., aged 45, is a successful business executive.

"Dr. Crane, you've put me in a tough spot," he smilingly informed me, as I was having luncheon at his Kiwanis club.

"You have urged parents to set a good example before their children even as regards going to church or Sunday school with them.

"Well, I have two youngsters, now in high school, but Sunday is about my only time to fish or play golf. Isn't it as inspiring to commune with God in the woods as in a church auditorium?"

It is possible to commune with God in the outdoors, but not very likely if you hold a golf club or fishpole in your hand. And Thoreau's fallacy about communing with Divinity on a hike through the woods is chiefly rationalization.

Moreover, no collection plate is passed when you are on the hike, nor do you give as well as receive the reciprocal stimulation of worshiping with other people.

And you aren't so likely to teach your children unselfishness and moral lessons by a Sunday stroll.

Civilized Americans try to take a bath at least once a week, and they feel much refreshed afterwards.

But just as this regular cleansing of the body becomes a worthwhile habit, and even makes us feel uncomfortable if we fail to carry it out, so we can learn the habit of spiritual refreshment by regular attendance at church.

The inspiration of music, plus the tonic of a good sermon, as well as the social stimulation of seeing our friends in similar attendance at a place of worship, serve as a refreshing bath for the soul.

Everybody would profit from at least one such soul cleansing per week. It is far more relaxing on the blood pressure than half a day on the golf links.

A person who thus sets a good positive example before his children and possibly many wavering neighbors or associates feels happy in knowing that he has helped influence others who are looking for strong leadership.

Millions of neurotics and hypochondriacs are wasting money and time, as well as shortening their lives by fear and its resulting high blood pressure, just because they don't form the habit of leaning upon God.
—Dr. George W. Crane, in
Chicago Daily News

"I Voted to Close the Church"

Last Sunday I voted to close the church; not intentionally, not maliciously, perhaps, but carelessly, thoughtlessly, lazily, indifferently, I voted. I voted to close its doors that its witness and its testimony might be stopped. I voted to close the open Bible on its pulpit — the Bible that had been given us by years of struggle and by the blood of martyrs who died that we might have it to read.

For, you see, I could have gone and I should have gone, but I didn't. I stayed away from Church last Sunday.

—*Selected*

* * *

"Closed For Summer"

Read an announcement on a church bulletin board, "This church is the gateway to heaven!" Summer came. The following words were added, "Closed for the summer!"

—W. B. K.

* * *

Food for Thought

The world's opinion of the church may not always be correct, but it is a good thing for the church to know what that opinion is. Here is what a secular paper out in Oregon has to say about the church's appeal to the physical man:

"Behold! The lodge lodgeth together — *and they eat.* The club clubbeth together — *and they eat.* The church hath a social — *and they eat.* The Young People's Society elects officers — *and they eat.* And even when the Missionary Society meeteth together — *they eat.* But this latter is in a good cause, because they eat in remembrance of the poor heathen who have not much to eat.

"Behold! Hath man's brains gone to his stomach, and doth he no longer regard intellectual dainties that thou canst no longer call an assembly or get together a quorum or even a 'baker's dozen' except that thou hold up the baker's dainties as a bait? Be it true, that the day cometh that to get a crowd

at prayer meeting, the preacher must hold up a biscuit?

"Yea, verily, thou hast heard of the child races of the world. But, behold, it is nigh thee, even at the door. For as one calleth unto the child and sayeth, 'Come hither, sweet little one, and I will give thee a stick of candy,' even so must thou say to the grown-up Papa and Mamma, 'Assemble ye together and we will serve refreshments!' And lo, they come like sheep in a pen."

—*"Christiana" Tract*

* * *

Parable of the Vacationists

Now it came to pass, as summer drew nigh, that Mr. Church Member lifted his eyes unto the hills and said: "Lo, the hot days come and even now are at hand. Come, let us go unto the heights, where cool breezes refresh and glorious scenes await."

"Thou speakest wisely," quoth Mrs. Church member. "Yet three or four things must we do before we go."

"Three things I can think of, but not four," responded Mr. Church Member. "We must arrange for the flowers to be watered, the chickens fed, and the mail to be forwarded, but the fourth eludes my mind."

"The fourth is like unto the first three, yet more important than all. Thou shalt dig down into thy purse and pay thy church pledge, that the good name of the church be preserved, and that it may be well with thee, for verily I say unto thee, thou hast more money now than thou wilt have when thou dost return."

And it came to pass that Mr. Church Member paid his pledge for the summer, and the treasurer rejoiced greatly, saying, "Of a truth, there are those who care for the Lord's work." And it was so.

—J. V. Jacobs in
Christian Messenger

* * *

The City Church

God bless the church on the avenue
   That hears the city's cry,

The church that sows the Seed of the
Word
Where the masses of men go by;
The church that makes midst the city's
roar
A place for an Altar of Prayer,
With a heart for the rich and a heart
for the poor,
And rejoices in their burdens to share.
The church that's true to the call of
Christ,
Who wept o'er the city's need,
And who sent His disciples to labor
for Him
Where the forces of evil breed.
The church that gives and the church
that lives,
As seen by the Master's eye —
God bless the church on the avenue
That answers the city's cry!

—*Selected*

* * *

It's You

"If you want to work in the kind of a
church
Like the kind of a church you like,
You needn't slip your clothes in a grip
And start on a long, long hike.

"You'll only find what you left behind,
For there's nothing that's really new;
It's a knock at yourself when you knock
your church,
It isn't your church — it's YOU.

"Real churches aren't made by men
afraid
Lest somebody else go ahead;
When everyone works and nobody shirks,
You can raise a church from the dead.

"And if while you make your personal
stake
Your neighbor can make one, too.
Your church will be what you want to
see —
It isn't your church — it's YOU!"

—*Selected*

* * *

Potency in Repetition

It is said that in the Zulu churches of
South Africa, it is the custom for the
believers, both men and women, to go
out after hearing the sermon and repeat
as much of it as possible to anyone who
will listen. *In giving the message to
others, they retain more of it themselves
and therefore receive a double blessing.*
Is not this the way to get more of the
Holy Spirit and all spiritual blessings
from God?

—*S.S. Illustrator*

* * *

Trunk Member

Someone asked an old lady about her
son-in-law, "And is he a church member?"

"Well, yes," said the old lady hesitant-
ly. "At least he's a 'trunk' member."

When asked for an explanation the
old lady replied:

"That's what I've always called those
church members who join a church and
then put their membership letter in the
bottom of the trunk. There it lays
whether they move about or stay in one
place for thirty years. They seldom go
to church. They take little or no part in
the services. They contribute irregular-
ly, if at all. They aren't active members
working for the Lord. They're just
trunk members."

—Elsie Williams, in *Gospel Herald*

* * *

No One Could Qualify

A new Sunday school was to be opened
by a certain church named All Saints.
The neighborhood was canvassed for
pupils. On the appointed Sunday the
superintendent and teachers arrived,
and put up a blackboard outside, with
the inscription, "All Saints' Sunday
School." However, no pupils came, and
when they came out, somewhat crest-
fallen, they found that someone, with a
piece of chalk, had altered the inscription. It now read, "All Saints (and no
Sinners) Sunday School." Alas, in
people's own estimation, many churches
have congregations like that. But what
is right in a man's own eyes is not
necessarily right in the sight of God.

—*Selected*

* * *

A Church on Fire

"Billy" Sunday, the eccentric evangelist so recently gone to his reward,

used to relate a graphic story of a well-known village atheist who was seen running vigorously to a burning church building intent on joining with others in subduing the flames. A neighbor observing him exclaimed facetiously, "This is something new for you! I never saw you going to church before." The atheist replied, "Well, this is the first time I have ever seen a church on fire." *Who can tell how many might be drawn to the people of God if they were only on fire for Christ and burning with zeal to win the lost?*

—Dr. Harry A. Ironside, in
Except Ye Repent

* * *

Meet the 'Tater Family

Practically every church has some interesting families in the membership. Others have some rather outstanding families in them. Still other churches number among their constituency families which are both interesting and outstanding. The latter is especially true of the TATER family. Arthur Flake is credited with saying that the family includes: Dic-Tater, Hesi-Tater, Agi-Tater, Imi-Tater, and Spec-Tater.

Uncle Dic-Tater has some very lovable characteristics, and is usually easy to get along with, especially if he is allowed to have his own way. The truth of the matter is that he is going to have his own way or else. His policy seems to be that of "rule or ruin," and he usually ruins.

Aunt Hesi-Tater is the amiable wife of Uncle Dic-Tater. She, too, has some very lovable qualities, but her greatest fault seems to be that of always waiting for someone else to go ahead. This characteristic is probably due in part to the dominant attitude of her husband. She is a rather timid soul, and quite hesitant about advancing her ideas or doing anything without waiting for the advice of someone else, especially her husband.

Cousin Imi-Tater is quite an attractive young lady, and has some qualities which are not seen in any other member of the family. Perhaps her greatest lack is that of originality. She always

wants to do what other people do, and that in spite of what God says in Exodus 23:2, "Thou shalt not follow a multitude to do evil."

Cousin Agi-Tater is the other girl in the family, and is quite different from her mother or sister. Although she seems to be possessed of unflagging zeal and unlimited energy, she is constantly stirring up trouble. She is somewhat of a loose-tongued busy-body. Apparently, she has not learned what God means when He says, "Thou shalt not go up and down as a talebearer among thy people" (Lev. 19:16).

Cousin Spec-Tater is the only son in the family, and seems to be obsessed with the idea that he is outnumbered by the feminine portion of the family. He is a quiet, humble, unassuming sort of fellow. His worst fault is that he never does anything. He simply sits or stands quietly by and looks on without much comment about what the others do.

Do you belong to the Tater family? If so, which member are you?

—R. F. Hallford, in
Baptist Standard

* * *

More Zeal Than Christians

"We will not accept into membership anyone with any reservations whatsoever," declared Lenin, the founder of Russian communism. "We will not accept into our membership anyone unless he is an active, disciplined, working member in one of our organizations."

"I wonder how far we would get if we applied that to our churches — nobody allowed in church membership unless he is an active worker, disciplined and proven in one of the organizations?"

—W. B. K.

* * *

"We're Holding Our Own!"

Dr. Len G. Broughton, founder and first pastor of the great Tabernacle Baptist Church, Atlanta, Georgia, used to chuckle as he related the following story to different gatherings of Southern Baptists:

Among the annual reports read one year at an associational meeting was one which ran as follows:

Additions to church during the year by profession of faith, none; additions by restoration, none; additions by transfer of letter, none; losses by transfer of letters, none; losses by withdrawal of fellowship, none; losses by death, none; marriages, none!

The report closed with the following notation:

"BRETHREN, WE ARE HOLDING OUR OWN! PRAY FOR US!"

—W. B. K.

* * *

Palace Beautiful

The finest name ever given outside the Bible to the church is Bunyan's "Palace Beautiful." Yet the churches with which he was acquainted were only the Baptist meetinghouses in Bedfordshire. No better than barns they seemed to common eyes, but in his eyes each of them was a "Palace Beautiful," because, when seated on one of its benches, the eye of his imagination would look up through the dingy rafters and descry the gorgeous roof and shining pinnacles of the church universal. Love to God, whose house it is, can make the humblest material structure a home of the Spirit.

—Rev. F. Stalker

* * *

Like a Mighty Army?

A minister asked a returned GI to speak in his pulpit. He said: " 'Like a mighty army moves the church of God.' The trouble is that about 10,000,000 men know exactly how an army moves. Suppose the army accepted the lame excuses that many of you think good enough for not attending the church parade. Imagine this: Reveille at 7 a. m. — squads on parade ground. Sergeant barks out, 'Count fours.' 'One, two, three,' four is missing. 'Where's Private Smith?' 'Mr. Smith was too sleepy to get up. He said to tell you he would be with you in spirit.' 'That's fine,' said the sergeant. 'Where's Brown?' 'He's playing golf. You know how important recreation is.' 'Sure, sure,' says the sergeant cheerfully. 'Hope he has a good game. Where's Robinson?' 'He is sorry,

but he is entertaining guests today. Besides, he was at drill last week.' 'Tell him he is welcome any time he finds it convenient to drop in for drill.' If any GI pulled that stuff he would get twenty days in the brig. Yet you hear stuff like that every week in church. 'Like a mighty army!' Why, if this church moved like a mighty army, a lot of you folks would be court-martialed within an hour."

—Abridged from the
Evangelical Christian

* * *

Slowing Down

A boy named Donald observed that the grandfather's clock was striking the hour very slowly, and heard his Uncle John remark, "Sounds as if the striking part of it is nearly run down." The following Sunday morning Uncle John's wife came into the room where he was reading, and asked him if he were going to church. He replied, very slowly, "Oh, I — I suppose so." Then Donald remarked: "Why, Uncle John, that sounds as if the chapel part of you is nearly run down. Is it?" Uncle John flushed as he threw the paper aside, saying, "Maybe it is, Donald; but we'll wind it up again, and get a little stronger movement."

—*Methodist Recorder*

* * *

Why She Came

We have in the church of which I am a member a woman who is very old, very deaf, and whose eyes are bad, but she is always at church, even though she does not hear a word. On Saturday she is given a church bulletin and she looks up and reads the hymns and Scripture lesson. One day she remarked that all she gets out of the service is that received from the bulletin, and I told her what a fine thing it is that she comes. She replied, "Well, you know, the Psalmist said, 'The Lord is in his holy temple,' and I come here to meet the Lord." Of how many who attend church can that be said, I wonder.

—*Sunday School Times*

An Age-Old Problem — Absenteeism

Absenteeism is not the problem of industry alone, the church knows a great deal of it as well. As far back as the resurrection of the Lord Jesus Christ, Thomas was an absentee, and he missed one of the most eventful weeks in history. His absenteeism tended to unbelief. . . . We recently heard of a brother in a place where a gathering was to be held who asked another brother, "Do you know whom we are to have with us today?" The latter began naming one prominent speaker after another until the first brother said, "Why, no — the Lord Himself!" He has vouchsafed His presence in the midst of His saints. Absenteeism means the missing of His blessed presence at the service.

—*Now*

* * *

The Dying Fire

A certain Sunday school superintendent felt very keenly the absence from the Sunday school of a once faithful member. After some time had passed, he called at the home of the absentee and found him sitting before the fire.

Somewhat startled by the intrusion, the member hastily placed a chair for the visitor, and then waited for the expected rebuke. But not a word did the superintendent say. Taking a seat before the fireplace, he silently took the tongs and, lifting a glowing coal from the midst of its fellows, laid it by itself on the hearthstone. Remaining painfully silent, he watched the blaze die out.

Then the truant murmered: "You needn't say a single word; I'll be there next Sunday morning."

—*Rod and Staff*

* * *

Keeping Balance

One of our friends is a policeman. He is a regular church-goer and gives liberally of his time when it would be very easy to beg off because of the nature of his job. Because this is a somewhat uncommon combination, we asked him why his church meant so much to him. "Well," he said, "I'll tell you exactly what I tell our young recruits when they come on the force. I tell them that in the job they have chosen, most of their contacts will be on the seamy side. That they won't meet too many folks they will want to invite in for Sunday dinner. That even some of our 'best people' are not exactly sweetness and light when caught in a minor traffic violation. So I suggest that they tie up with some church to give them balance, to give them something to hang on to when circumstances of their work make them think the whole world is drunk or crooked. A policeman without something of spiritual value to lean on soon becomes a poor policeman."

—K. V. P. *Philosopher*

* * *

Try Tears

When General Booth received a communication from one of his captains, that the work was so hard he could make no progress, the General sent a telegram back, "Try tears." We are told success came to that corps. If the church of God followed the same advice more frequently, she might reap a larger harvest of souls.

—Wm. Olney

* * *

Why He Returned

Jim was a barber in our village. He, his wife, and their three children were the prize family of our Sunday school. It was clear to all who knew him that Jim had prepared for advancement. We were not surprised when he announced that he had been offered an agency in another state. Shortly before they left for their new home, our little church gave Jim and family a farewell reception, and sent them on their way with blessings, prayers, and high hopes — with a few tears for them to remember us by. You can easily imagine the mixture of surprise and shock in our small community when, a few months later, Jim was back at his barber's chair. But he didn't seem in the least troubled. He greeted his friends with his old-time broad smile. And while he clipped hair, he explained: "No church or Sunday school in that big, new, mushroom town. Not one. People there too busy making money, gambling, and drinking to need church. Such a day Sunday was! The kids cried for Sunday school. I couldn't raise my boy and little girls there. That's how Jennie felt about it, too." But God did not forget Jim; nor did businessmen. In a short time he was offered a better position — within walking distance of Sunday school.

—Secret Place

What the Church Is For:

The church is not a gallery for the exhibition of eminent Christians but a school for the education of imperfect ones, a nursery for the care of weak ones, a hospital for the healing of those who need assiduous care.

—Henry Ward Beecher

CIGARETTES—TOBACCO

Dishonest Advertising

The Sunday School Times has verified the accuracy of this statement by correspondence with the editor of the *Plain Dealer*. Some reporters had called on Martinelli, the famous tenor, for an interview. " 'No, no, no,' exclaimed Giovanni Martinelli, the opera star. 'The pipe, the cigar, the cigarettes!' Reporters who had come to interview the famous singer hastily extinguished the three evils, when he explained that the smoke made his throat sore. 'But didn't you endorse a cigarette once?' asked a reporter. 'Si, si' (Yes, yes), admitted the smiling tenor. 'But remember what I said. I said: "These cigarettes never make my throat sore." And that is true. They never do.' 'Because,' a reporter suggested, 'you never smoke them?' 'Si, si,' laughed Martinelli. 'I never smoke them. I never smoked anything in my life.' "

—Homer Rodeheaver, in *Sunday School Times*

* * *

Tobacco Does Shorten Life

The story which the American press will never mention is the scientific truth that tobacco impairs the life span. People who smoke more than a pack of cigarettes a day not only die sooner than non-smokers, but throughout their lifetime, from age thirty, they make themselves much more liable than non-smokers to all the ills to which flesh is heir; and even mild smokers impair their lives to an extent which, according to Johns Hopkins, "is measurable and significant."

This is the story which *Time* magazine said was enough to "scare the life out of tobacco manufacturers and make the tobacco users' flesh creep," but the Associated Press and United Press correspondents either suppresed or buried it.

Worse than that, when Secretary of the Interior Ickes offhandedly mentioned the suppression of this story (facts furnished by editor of *In Fact*) the very newspapers which had suppressed it accused him of error, and when the facts were sent Associated Press, New York *Times*, Columnist Pegler, *Saturday Evening Post*, and numerous papers throughout the country, all of which had either suppressed the story or attacked Ickes on false information, they refused to publish the scientific facts as supplied by *In Fact*'s editor.

The tobacco advertisers share with peacetime automobile advertisers first place in spending money in newspapers and magazines. This is without doubt the reason the press suppressed the story.

The story proves scientifically that between the ages of thirty and sixty no less than 61 per cent more heavy smokers die than non-smokers.

—*Narcotic Review*

* * *

Dwarf Dogs

"When I was in Paris some years ago," said a noted lecturer, "I met a man who had very tiny dogs for sale. I asked him why they were so abnormally small.

"At first he refused to tell me, fearing that I would divulge his secret or become his business competitor. I convinced him that I was simply in pursuit of knowledge. Then, with many cautions, he confided to me his process for producing these very tiny dwarfs.

" 'You see, I put a little speck of *nicotine* in their food when they are quite young. Then I add a little more, and a little more, and then they never get big.' "

"But doesn't the nicotine ever kill them?"

" 'Oh, yes many of them die; but I get a big price for the little fellows that live.' "

Poor dogs, thus poisoned for the sake of gain.

—*White Ribbon*

* * *

A Study

"In a study of two thousand smokers and nonsmokers by the Life Extension examiners, some interesting observations were made.

"Smokers complained of cough 300 per cent more often than nonsmokers. Smokers complained of irritation of the nose and throat 167 per cent more often than nonsmokers. Smokers complained of palpitation 50 per cent more often than nonsmokers. Smokers complained of pain over the heart 73 per cent more often than nonsmokers. Smokers complained of shortness of breath 140 per cent more often than nonsmokers. Smokers complained of heartburn 100 per cent more often than nonsmokers. Smokers complained of excessive gas 62 per cent more often than nonsmokers. Smokers complained of nervousness 76 per cent more often than nonsmokers.

"From these figures it is evident that smoking is the cause of much suffering and that it does influence health . . .

"Many people believe that smoking facilitates relaxation and helps them overcome nervousness. Nothing could be farther from the actual truth. Smoking causes a stimulation, not a relaxation."

—*Harry J. Johnson, M.D.*

Herbert Hoover Says:

"There is no agency in the world that is so seriously affecting the health, education, efficiency, and character of boys and girls as the cigarette habit. Nearly every deligent boy is a cigarette smoker. Cigarettes are a source of crime. To neglect crime at its source is a shortsighted policy, unworthy of a nation of our intelligence."

—Former President Herbert Hoover

* * *

Doctor Cites Cigarettes As Lung Cancer Factor

The possibility of cigarette smoking as one of the factors causing a sharp rise in lung cancer was cited here Sunday by Dr. Evarts Graham of St. Louis.

Speaking to the Inter-American Congress of Surgery at the Stevens Hotel, Dr. Graham declared pipe tobacco and cigars "do not appear to bear the same important relationship."

Dr. Graham, who is commonly referred to as the "father of chest surgery," added:

"It would seem, therefore, that if smoking is an etiological (causative) factor, it is something in the composition of cigarettes which contains the carcinogenic (cancer producing) agent.

"Various possibilities suggest themselves, perhaps something used in the curing of tobacco, insecticides employed during its growth, or maybe even something in the paper."

Another surgeon, Dr. Alton Ochsner of New Orleans, raised the same speculation in a talk to the Rotary Club here. "The rise in the incidence of lung cancer," he said, "parallels the increasing sales of tobacco."

Dr. Graham said that in his own study of 400 bronchial cancers to date, it was "very rare" to find a patient who had not smoked excessively.

—*Chicago Daily News*

* * *

How He Was Cured

Several years ago a young man went to the Mayo clinic because of pain in the left foot which became worse on walking. After a thorough study, it was concluded that for at least five years he had been suffering from Buerger's disease, which was becoming progressively worse. He smoked 20 cigarettes a day and every physician consulted advised him to give up the habit. Nevertheless he disregarded all this advice. He returned to the clinic two years later and admitted that, altho his consumption of tobacco had been reduced, he had not abstained. By then, the pain in the left foot and right calf was more severe.

Another year slipped by and on his third visit to the clinic the condition had not changed. Again tobacco was interdicted and the patient dismissed. He was not seen for 12 years, at which time the clinic physicians were surprised when they learned that after his previous admittance he had given up tobacco entirely. Shortly after he stopped smoking pain subsided and circulation improved. The tests were repeated and it was found that the arteries were again pulsating, indicating a normal blood flow. He had been cured without medicines, baths, lamps, or suction pressure treatments.

—Dr. Theodore R. VanDellen, in "How To Keep Well" column in *Chicago Daily Tribune*

* * *

Chewing Tobacco and Heaven

"Can a man chew tobacco and go to Heaven?" was a question put to Mr. Moody. His reply, though not elegant and a bit jolting, about covers the situation. "Yes," answered Mr. Moody, "but he would have to go to hell to spit!"

—W. B. K.

* * *

To His Satisfaction

A tobacco company sent packs of cigarettes to high school boys accompanied with this explanation: "We are sending you a pack of our finest cigarettes. We hope you will use them to your satisfaction and want more." One of the boys wrote back, "I received the package of cigarettes and used them to my satisfaction. I steeped them in a quart of water and sprayed our bug infested rose bushes. Every bug died.

These cigarettes are sure good poison. I want more next spring if we have more bugs."

—*Youth Today*

* * *

Tobacco Pouch and Pipe Goes

I was once staying with another man, a pastor. I had said nothing about smoking, — I never do single out sins, — I had not alluded to the habit; but one day we were walking along a street that led over a river, and to my surprise as we got to the apex of the bridge he took his tobacco-pouch and pipe and threw them over, and said: "There, I have settled that."

Then, turning to me, he said: "I know, Mr. Meyer, you have said nothing about it; but for the last few months God has been asking me to set a new example to my young men, and I said: 'Why should not I do as I like, and they as they like?' God was searching me. and I was fighting Him, but it is all settled now, sir, it is all done now."

—F. B. Meyer

* * *

Smoking and Diseases of Heart and Blood Vessels

The connection between smoking and the onset of diseases of the heart and blood vessels was discussed by Dr. Grace M. Roth of the Mayo foundation at the University of Minnesota. Extensive tests indicate it is nicotine, and not other factors in smoke, which cause increases of blood pressure and pulse, and decreases of skin temperatures in susceptible persons. She said any person with a tendency toward blood or vessel disease should stop smoking.

The use of tobacco may mean the difference between life and death for persons with diseases of the circulation, the report stated.

All speakers agreed the causative factor in lung cancer is smoking, and not polluted city air or some other environmental condition.

—*Chicago Daily Tribune*, Dec. 10, 1953

Links Cigarettes to Rising Rate of Lung Cancer

The correlation between smoking and cancer was stated in unusually strong terms by leading medical specialists speaking at the 29th annual Greater New York dental meeting.

Dr. Alton Ochsner, chairman of the department of surgery at Tulane university school of medicine in New Orleans, said medical men are "extremely concerned about the possibility that the male population of the United States will be decimated by cancer of the lung in another 50 years, if cigaret smoking increases as it has in the past, unless some steps are taken to remove the cancer producing factor in tobacco."

More than 5,000 patients with cancer of the lung have been studied in England, Germany, Switzerland, Denmark, Czechoslovakia and the United States, Dr. Wynder said. There were some variations in the independent studies, he reported, but the ultimate conclusion is that "the prolonged and heavy use of cigarettes increases up to 20 times the risk of developing cancer of the lung."

—*Chicago Daily Tribune,*
Dec. 15, 1953

* * *

Spurgeon and Smoking

Since many Christians have made excuses for their smoking by stating that Charles Haddon Spurgeon smoked, it is necessary to give the following explanation:

I was a member of the entertainment committee of the World Baptist Alliance in the Baptist Temple of Philadelphia in 1911. Some months prior to these meetings, Dr. Shakespeare, General Secretary of the Alliance, came to give instruction and advice in regard to the conduct of these gatherings.

At that time there came to Philadelphia a Baptist minister who had been the chief secretary of the late Charles Haddon Spurgeon. In his discussion of Spurgeon's life and of his loyalty to Christ, he told this story to Dr. Shakespeare and me:

"One Saturday morning Mr. Spurgeon went out for a walk, and when he came back, he said to me, 'I saw in a shop window down the street a can of tobacco, and on it a printed card reading: *Spurgeon's Tobacco.*' Then he asked me, 'When the Lord calls me home, shall I be remembered by the tobacco I smoked or by the Lord I preached? I can never again smoke to the glory of God.' Immediately he picked up all of his smoking paraphernalia and threw it upon the fire. For nine months, to the day of his departure to glory, he never smoked again."

I was myself present when these statements were made. It was known that Spurgeon suffered greatly from gout and he may have thought that smoking eased the pain. However, in spite of this, he had finally come to the conclusion that his smoking dishonored the Lord, and had given it up.

—Dr. L. Sale-Harrison

* * *

Said Connie Mack:

"It is my candid opinion and I have watched very closely the last twelve years or more, that boys at the age of ten to fifteen who have continued smoking cigarettes do not as a rule amount to anything. They are unfitted in every way for any kind of work where brains are needed. No boy or man can expect to succeed in this world to a high position and continue the use of cigarettes."

—Connie Mack,
Former Manager of
Philadelphia Athletics

COMMUNION WITH GOD

"Be Still and Know!"
Dear Child, God does not say today,
"Be strong;"
He knows your strength is spent: He knows how long

The road has been, how weary you have grown,
For He who walked the earthly roads alone,

Each bogging lowland, and each rugged
   hill,
Can understand, and so He says, "Be
   still,
And know that I am God." The hour
   is late,
And you must rest awhile, and you
   must wait
Until life's empty reservoirs fill up
As slow rain fills an empty upturned
   cup.
Hold up your cup, dear child, for God
   to fill
He only asks today that you be still.
              —Selected

* * *

Listening

I once heard Dr. A. T. Pierson say
that he called upon a clergyman who
was laid on his back for six months. The
doctor said to his friend, "You are a
very busy man. It may be that God had
something to say to you, but you are
too busy to listen, so God had to lay
you on your back, that you might hear
His voice and receive His message."

As he was leaving the house it struck
Dr. Pierson that he himself was a very
busy man, and did not give much time
to listening for the voice of God. So he
determined to practice what he had
preached. "And from that time," said
he, "I have sat at the close of each day
for an hour in the quiet of my study
— not to speak to God, but to listen to
what God has to say to me, and to lay
the day's life and work open to the gaze
of God."
              —Elim Evangel

* * *

"The Morning Hour"

Alone with God, in quiet peace,
From earthly cares I find release;
New strength I borrow for each day
As there with God, I stop to pray.

Alone with God, my sins confess'd
He speaks in mercy, I am blest.
I know the kiss of pardon free,
I talk to God, He talks to me.

Alone with God, my vision clears
I see my guilt, the wasted years
I plead for grace to walk His way
And live for Him, from day to day.

Alone with God no sin between
His lovely face so plainly seen;
My guilt all gone, my heart at rest
With Christ, my Lord, my soul is blest.

Lord keep my life alone for Thee;
From sin and self, Lord, set me free.
And when no more this earth I trod
They'll say, "He walked alone with God."
            —Bruce Fogarty

* * *

Stopping To Listen

A man working in an ice plant amid
the ice, and the sawdust in which it
was stored, lost a valuable watch. His
fellow workmen searched with him for
more than two hours, but were unable
to find it. They left the plant for lunch
and returned to find a little boy with
the watch in his hand. "How ever did
you find it?" they inquired. He replied,
"I just lay down in the sawdust and
heard it ticking." We, too, cannot find
God by intensive, bustling search, but
must "be still, and know that I am
God."
          —Rev. C. E. Travis

* * *

With God Alone

He who opens the doors of the day
with the hand of mercy draws around
His people the curtains of the night,
and by His shining presence makes the
outgoings of the morning and of the
evening to rejoice. A promise at dawn
and a sure word at sunset crown the
day with light, sandal its feet with
love. To breakfast with Jesus, and to
sup with Him also, is to enjoy the days
of heaven upon the earth. It is dangerous to fall asleep till the head is leaned
on Jesus' bosom. When divine love puts
its finger on the weary eyelids, it is
brave sleeping.
         —C. H. Spurgeon

Silence! God Is Now Speaking!

Years ago, a mighty earthquake rocked the city of Charleston, South Carolina. It is said that an aged Negro preacher was just beginning the delivery of his sermon when the first tremor was felt. All was silence for a moment. Then, a second and a mightier upheaval was felt. Lifting his eyes from his sermon notes, the aged Negro minister exclaimed, "God is now speaking! It is time for us to be silent!" In the midst of earth's upheavals, blessed indeed are God's children who are sufficiently close to Him to shut out earth's confusing and contradictory voices, hearing only the soothing, sustaining voice of God. "Speak, Lord, for Thy servant heareth!"

—W. B. K.

* * *

Evening Quiet

The twilight deepens into night,
   The day has reached its close,
And passing now the rays of light
   With the western sky of rose.

O Spirit of all truth Divine,
   Now let us feel Thy power,
In spirit to commune with Thee
   In this most quiet hour.

Hush all the clamoring of our hearts,
   Make us to look to Thee,
That in this holy eventide
   We purified may be.

May our small voices be made still,
   That we may list to Thine;
And our weak spirit wilt thou fill
   With the loving strength of thine.

Thus may we feel each eventide
   Thy helpful grace and power,
That on the morrow we may serve
   Thy children every hour.

And when have passed the day and night
   Which to us mortals come,
Oh, may we see in clearer light
   Our souls with thine at Home!

—Virgie Mendenhall

Alone With God!

It is a good deal better, my friends, if you are going to work for God, to be constantly with Him. There are two lives for the Christian, one before the world, and one *alone with God*. If you dwell constantly at the feet of Jesus, it will save you many a painful hour. The sweetest thoughts of God I ever got were not found in a great assembly like this but when alone, sitting at the feet of Jesus.

—D. L. Moody

* * *

Deep Living

We love to spread our branches,
   The root-life we neglect;
We love to shine in public,
   And human praise expect;
While in the inner chamber,
   Where creature voices cease,
We may meet God in silence,
   And breathe in heaven's peace.

The secret of deep living
   Lies in the secret place —
Where, time and sense forgotten,
   We see God face to face;
Beyond mere forms and symbols,
   Beyond mere words and signs —
Where in that hidden temple
   The light eternal shines.

—Max I. Reich

* * *

The Radiance of His Presence

I remember reading years ago a simple story of an old violinist. He was poor, but possessed an instrument which never failed to charm by its soothing mellowness. Played as he could play, it never failed to awaken responsive chords in the heart! Asked to explain its charm, he would hold out his violin and, tenderly caressing its graceful curves, say: "Ah, a great deal of sunshine must have gone into this wood, and what has gone in comes out."

How much of God's sunshine has entered your life? How much time have you spent in the radiance of His presence? It is only too true of all of us that if more of God's radiance had entered into our souls we should be better able to radiate peace and hope to the crowds around us.

—E. Townley Lord

* * *

Consider Him

Hebrews 12:3

When the storm is raging high,
When the tempest rends the sky,
When my eyes with tears are dim,
Then, my soul, "consider Him."

When my plans are in the dust,
When my dearest hopes are crushed,
When is passed each foolish whim,
Then, my soul, "consider Him."

When with dearest friends I part,
When deep sorrow fills my heart,
When pain racks each weary limb,
Then, my soul, "consider Him."

When I track my weary way,
When fresh trials come each day,
When my faith and hope are dim,
Then, my soul, "consider Him."

Clouds or sunshine, dark or bright,
Evening shades, or morning light,
When my cup flows o'er the brim,
Then, my soul, "consider Him."

—*Selected*

* * *

Quietness

Around the great issues of life there is quietness. Silence characterizes the highest in art, and the deepest in nature. The surest spiritual search is made in silence. Moses learned in Midian, and Paul in Arabia, what would have eluded them in the busy haunts of men.

Silence reaches beyond words. The highest point in drama is silence. The most valid emotions do not cry aloud. The most effective reproof is not a tongue lashing. The most poignant grief is not expressed in loud shriekings. The sincerest sympathy is not noisy. The best preparation for an emergency is quietness. It is the highest duty to play "The Still," and every

man's duty to remain perfectly quiet for a moment, collecting his senses in preparation for intelligent action. The best proof of greatness is silence. The great engine is almost noiseless, but the cheap model is a "rattletrap."

The best proof of confidence is silence. The man who is confident of his position does not strive nor cry aloud, nor try to explain everything.

"In quietness and in confidence shall be your strength."

—*Gospel Herald*

* * *

Religion on the Run

In the middle of the track of a transcontinental railroad at a certain point in Ohio, there is a metal trough. It runs along for a quarter of a mile or more. It is kept filled with water. Through trains as they rush along do not stop at water tanks to take on water. When they reach the place where the water trough is, the fireman presses a lever which drops a scoop from the bottom of the tank and takes up the water as the train keeps going. No stop, no pause, they just keep going on the dead run and scoop up the water. Isn't that pretty much like a lot of folks try to do with their religion, scoop it up on the run? They haven't time for their soul's needs. They are too busy. "Take time to be holy," bids the hymn. Time must be given to receive, to hold, and to increase the content and possession of true, genuine, living religion in our hearts and lives. You cannot get religion on the run.

—*Lutheran*

* * *

"Be Still and Know"

How can God give us visions when life is hurrying at a precipitate rate? I have stood in the national gallery and seen people gallop round the chamber and glance at Turner's picture in the space of five minutes. Surely we might say to such trippers, "Be still and know Turner!" Gaze quietly at one little bit of cloud or at one branch or at one wave of the sea or at one ray of the drifting moon. "Be still, and know Turner." But God has difficulty in getting us still.

That is perhaps why he has sometimes employed the ministry of dreams. Men have had "visions in the night." In the daytime I have a Divine visitor in the shape of some worthy thought or noble impulse or hallowed suggestion, but I am in such feverish haste that I do not heed it and pass along. I do not "turn aside to see this great thing," and so I lose Heavenly vision. If I would know more of God, I must relax the strain and moderate the pace. I must be "still."

—J. H. Jowett

* * *

Highly Recommended

A young man came to London bearing a letter of introduction to Baron Rothschild with the request that he would give him employment. The great banker received him warmly, but expressed his regret that he had no position for him. As the young man was going, the baron put on his hat and walked along with him, pointing out the various objects of interest. Passing the bank, the rich man went in to transact some business. Afterward the young man applied at that very bank for work, and was asked, "Are you not the young man who was walking with the baron this morning? Well, you were in good company; and since we need a young man, we will consider this a sufficient recommendation." To walk with God is after all a good recommendation. And when men of the world have need of a Christian's services in sickness or death, they will be likely to consider such a fact as a high recommendation.

—Alfred P. Gibbs in
Choice Gleanings

* * *

Occupied WITH or FOR Him?

Weary, anxious, and burdened with toil,
Martha is serving a meal for her Lord;
Mary, with love that no doubt can despoil,
Eagerly feedeth her soul on His word.
Food for the body sustains for a day,
Food for the spirit will nourish alway.

—Melvin J. Hill

Saving Time by Praying

When Edward Payson was a student at college he found himself overtaxed with study and preparation for examinations. There was little or no time for private prayer. But aware of the lack in his spiritual life, he deliberately took time that seemed rightfully to belong to other things, and devoted it to communion with God. His dairy discloses the fact that when he did so, *he did more in his studies in a single week after he had spent time with God in prayer than he had accomplished in twelve months before.*

—From *Christian Victory*

* * *

Is Grass Growing On Your Path?

In some parts of Africa, where the natives live in small crowded mud huts, with little chance of privacy, the Christians choose each one a tree in the forest, where they may go to pray and be alone with God. If one becomes unfaithful and neglects his place of prayer, another says, "Brother, the grass grows on your path."

—*Oklahoma City Star*

* * *

Divine Companionship

Man is the greatest marvel in the universe. Not because his heart beats forty million times a year, driving the blood stream a distance of over sixty thousand miles in that time; not because of the wonderful mechanism of eye and ear; not because of his conquest over disease and the lengthening of human life; not because of the unique qualities of his mind, but because he may walk and talk with God.

—*Selected*

* * *

Be Alone Sometimes

Secure for yourself some privacy of life. As George Herbert says, "By all means use some time to be alone." God has put each into a separate body. We should follow the divine hint, and not lapse into the general flood of being.

Many people cannot endure being alone; they are lost unless there is a clatter of tongues in their ears. It is not only weak, but it fosters weakness. The gregarious instinct is animal; to be alone is spiritual. We can have no clear, personal judgment of things till we are somewhat separate from them.

Daniel Webster used to say of a difficult question, "Let me sleep on it." It was not merely for morning vigor, but to get the matter at a distance where he could measure the proportions and see its relations. So it is well at times to get away from our world — companions, actions, work — in order to measure it and ascertain our relations to it. The moral value of the night is in the isolation it brings, shutting out the world from the senses, that it may be realized in thought.

This is very simple advice but worth heeding: Get some moments each day to yourself; take now and then a solitary walk; get into the silence of thick woods, or some other isolation as deep, and suffer the mysterious sense of selfhood to steal upon you as it surely will.

—T. T. Munger, in
The Fellowship News

* * *

The Secret

Earl Granville, who was a prominent figure in British politics in the latter half of Queen Victoria's reign, once asked the Countess Cairns (wife of Earl Cairns, then Lord Chancellor), "Can you tell me how it is that no matter what business is on, no matter how he may be pressed, your husband always comes down to the House (of Lords) so quietly and so full of vigor and power?"

"Oh, yes," Lady Cairns replied, "I can tell you; he always spends a time alone with his God before he goes into the House."

—*Prairie Overcomer*

Walking With God

There are two men who are said to have walked with God, Enoch and Noah. Many people think that Enoch had a very delightful time of it, sitting on clouds and singing hymns all day! But we are told by Jude that he had a very severe time in testifying against ungodliness; and, therefore, I do not think that even Enoch had altogether a delightful experience. But whatever you may think about Enoch, remember that Noah was a practical man of affairs, and for 120 years, probably, he preached the gospel of righteousness without getting a single convert; and all the while he was walking with God. *That is the life that is intended for us, the life of perpetual fellowship.*

—W. H. Griffith Thomas

* * *

Listening to the Voice from Above

At the corner of two busy thoroughfares, where the traffic was noisiest, the writer watched a man who was working quietly at the foot of a telephone pole. He seemed to know by instinct what was wanted by his mate, who was at work away up at the top of the pole; first one tool, then another, or a bit of wire would be sent up, and the two were working together in such harmony that I looked more carefully, and saw that the man on the sidewalk had clamped on his head what looked like a small telephone apparatus; one ear could hear the sounds around him, but the other was deaf to them, and was listening all the time to the voice from above. Being in constant communication they could work together in wonderful unity; and then I realized anew the need for us as Christians to be ever listening for the voice from above.

—Homera Hodgson

CONFESSION

"I Want to Show Old Life Gone, New Life Begun!"

Yataro Yamaguchi, upon hearing the Gospel, was convicted of sin and was soundly converted to the Saviour. He poured out his heart to God, saying, "O God, I give up. I take Him now as my Saviour. Forgive all my sins. Save me now for Jesus' sake. Amen!" Immediately, he wanted to be baptized. Said he, "I read in Bible about bury with Jesus when we trust Him. Now, I like bury under water, show that old life all gone and new life begun!

I told him we would endeavor to make arrangements for his baptism by the following Lord's Day. He looked up surprised and said, "Mr. Katsamatsu tell me Jesus Christ coming back again. So?"

"Yes," I answered, "He is to return again."

"Mr. Kasamatsu tell me He coming soon. So?"

"Yes, He says, 'Surely, I come quickly.' "

"He not come before next Sunday?"

"I cannot say that."

"Maybe He be back before next Sunday?"

"Yes, He might come at any time."

"Then I no like to wait till next Sunday. I like do today what He want me to do. I fight too long already. Now I like obey at once."

"Forgive me!" I exclaimed. "We will arrange your baptism for today. Can we meet, brethren, at the Sacramento River at 2:30 this afternoon?" All agreed to this. "Then if you meet us there we will see that you are baptized at once."

—Dr. Harry A. Ironside

* * *

Someone Else To Blame

Charles Spurgeon once said, "Could excellent spines be inserted into certain brethren, it would be well; but backbone would render them unfashionable." So the cry goes on, "He made me do it." A minister once asked a young man in San Quentin Prison, "Why did you do it?" The answer was the same old story: "Bad company. They put me up to it." The minister's answer was thought-provoking. He said: "So you admit you are just a follower, and have no will power of your own; you just do what you are told? Suppose they told you to cut off your hand?" The boy replied, "O.K., parson, you win; I was to blame; I did it, and I'm sorry now, but it's too late. I did cut off my very life to go with the crowd. If I had had that will power I wouldn't be here."

—*Sunday School Times*

A Little Indian Girl's Prayer

In "Memories of Yesterdays," by Isabella M. Alden, is related a story which Mrs. Alden heard Dr. Maud Allen, a missionary to India, tell. Nonine was a girl rescued among the famine sufferers, and cared for in the mission. The little girl was very fond of jewelry, and she yielded to the temptation to take some flour from the mission's supply and trade it to a peddler for a shiny ring. Finally, she confessed with great bitterness of soul, and Mrs. Allen said: "Finally, we kneeled down to pray, and that little girl, just one year removed from the lowest depths of heathenism, prayed these words: 'Oh, dear Lord, my Jesus, do make me care much less about jewels for my body, and much more about jewels for my heart.' "

—Mrs. I. M. Alden

* * *

Blanket Confessions

An illustration used by a Chinese evangelist: A woman with a bundle of dirty washing had taken it to the riverside with the purpose of washing it. But she was ashamed to open it for fear someone would see how dirty it was; so she just plunged the whole bundle into the water, jogged it up and down several times, and then went home with it. A lot of people are like that foolish woman. They have many sins that need to be cleansed, but they are not willing to bring them out and confess them one by one. They just say, "Lord, I am a sinner, forgive me." So, they cover up all their sins, their thefts, and their lies, and their jealousies, and their hatred. But they have to be brought out and confessed, and only then can they be cleansed.

—Abridged from *China's Millions*

* * *

Only a Plain Ticket Will Do

"So, John, you've got fairly into the kingdom. You have been long seeking; how did you get in at last?" "Oh, it was the simplest thing in the world; it was just by presenting the right ticket . . . . It was as plain a ticket as you ever bought for a public meeting: it had

nothing on it but the words "Admit the Bearer — A SINNER." . . . What kept me so long from getting in was that I always *added* something to the words on the ticket, when I presented it. Whenever the Lord saw anything of my adding, it was refused. The first time I went, I wrote at the bottom, 'But not so great a sinner as many of my neighbors.' That would not do, so I rubbed it out and put down, 'But is doing the best he can to improve.' That would not do, either, so I became anxious, and prayed and wept awhile, and then, under the words, 'Admit the bearer — a sinner,' I wrote, 'Who is praying and weeping for his sins.' Even that wouldn't do. After that I began to despair, and wrote down, 'Too great a sinner to be saved.' That only made matters worse, and I had almost given up, when I looked at Christ and heard Him say, 'Him that cometh to me I will in no wise cast out.' . . . I remembered that Jesus had said, 'I came . . . to call . . . sinners to repentance,' so I pulled out the old ticket, and, without adding a word, presented it, and, was accepted, and I entered." Go thou and do likewise.
—*Traveler's Guide,*
    compiled by Mrs. Stephen Menzies

* * *

Not Until the Blight Was Removed

A young missionary wrote to the Rev. W. H. Aldis of England: "When I was before the candidates' committee, I told a lie. I was so anxious to get to the mission field; and I feared if I answered that question as I ought to have answered it, I would never have got there, so I said what was not true. Ever since I arrived in this land where I am seeking to witness for God, that lie has been like a blight upon me, a blight as I try to learn the language, as I commence learning my ministry, and every time I kneel to pray, the Lord puts His finger on that lie which I told. At last, in desperation, I am writing to you, as I owe it to you. I must get right." He added, "From the very moment I determined by God's grace to write the letter, everything has changed, and God is

beginning to use me, and I know that souls are going to be saved."
    —*Life of Faith*

* * *

All Life Changed

An influential Chinaman who held high office in the educational life of China accepted Christ. He had magnificent prospects before him: position, influence, opportunity, all were his. The study of the New Testament brought to him the conviction that Christ was the Saviour of men, and his Saviour. After a period of struggle and of counting the cost, he determined upon his confession before men. His dearest friend pleaded with him earnestly, agonizingly. He pleaded in vain. Then he urged him to secret discipleship. "Bow to the tablet of Confucius; it is only an empty form, and you can believe what you like in your heart." It was a struggle, but he replied: "A few days ago one came to dwell within my heart; He has changed all life for me forever. I dare not bow to any other, lest He depart."
    —*The Regeneration of China,*
    by Nelson Bitton

* * *

"A Tow-Headed Norwegian Boy Stood Up"

In one of our meetings a little tow-headed Norwegian boy stood up. He could hardly speak a word of English, but he got up and came to the front. He trembled and the tears trickled down his cheeks as he said, "If I tell the world about Jesus, He will tell the Father about me." That was all he said, but in those few words he said more than all the rest of them, young and old together. They went straight down into the heart of every one present. "If I tell the world" — yes, that's what it means to confess Christ.
    —D. L. Moody

* * *

In Unconscious Ways

Not merely in the words you say,
Not merely in the deed confessed,
But in the most unconscious way
Is Christ confessed.

99

For me, 'twas not the truth you taught,
   To you, so clear, to me so dim,
But when you came to me you brought
   A sense of Him.

And from your eyes He beckons me,
   And from your heart His love is shed,
Till I lose sight of you — and see
   The Christ instead.

—*Selected*

* * *

Two Different Martins

At the beginning of the Reformation, Martin of Basle came to a knowledge of the truth, but, afraid to make a public confession, he wrote on a leaf of parchment: "O most merciful Christ, I know that I can be saved only by the merit of thy blood. Holy Jesus, I acknowledge thy sufferings for me. I love thee! I love thee!" Then he removed a stone from the wall of his chamber and hid it there. It was not discovered for more than a hundred years. About the same time Martin Luther found the truth as it is in Christ. He said: "My Lord has confessed me before men; I will not shrink from confessing Him before kings." The world knows what followed, and today it reveres the memory of Luther but as for Martin of Basle, who cares for him?

—*Sunday School Times*

* * *

When He Came to the End of Self

A young lad was troubled in soul. He had attended some services where the preacher used many passages concerning the utter depravity of the human heart. The preacher quoted: "All have sinned"; "There is none righteous, no, not one"; "All we like sheep have gone astray"; "Dead in trespasses and sin." The lad refused the application of these Scriptures to himself. His philosophy was this: "I know there is some bad about me, but I am not utterly bad. I have just about as much good about me as bad." In this frame of mind, he sought salvation, but could not find it. For six months this striving in his soul continued, until finally he was so wearied with the struggle that he sat down

beside the road to see whether he was really honest in his heart. The more he considered himself, the more he condemned himself, until finally he cried out: "O God, Thou art righteous. I am just utterly bad from head to foot. If You sent me to hell, that is what I deserve!" As soon as this confession had burst from his heart and lips, the Holy Spirit revealed the Saviour to him. He trusted his soul to Christ and went on his way with peace.

—*Evangelical Christian*

* * *

Something in It After All

There is nothing that so takes the joy out of life like unconfessed sin on the conscience. I once heard the late Dr. F. E. Marsh tell that on one occasion he was preaching on this question and urging his hearers on the importance of confession of sin, and, wherever possible, of restitution for wrong done to others. Afterward a young man came up to him and said: "Pastor, you have put me in a sad fix. I have wronged another and am ashamed to confess it or to try to put it right. I am a boat-builder and the man I work for is an infidel. I have talked to him often about his need of Christ and have urged him to come and hear you preach, but he scoffs and ridicules it all. In my work copper nails are used because they do not rust in the water, but they are quite expensive, so I had been carrying home quantities of them to use on a boat I am building in my back yard." The pastor's sermon had brought him to face the fact that he was just a common thief. "But," said he, "I cannot go to my boss and tell him what I have done, or offer to pay for those I have used. If I do he will think I am just a hypocrite, and yet those copper nails are digging into my conscience, and I know I shall never have peace until I put this matter right." One night he came again to Dr. Marsh and exclaimed, "Pastor, I've settled for the copper nails, and my conscience is relieved at last." "What happened when you confessed?" asked the pastor. "Oh, he looked queerly at me, and then said, 'George, I always did think you were just a hypocrite, but now I begin to feel there's something in this Christianity after all. Any religion that makes a dishonest workman confess that he has been stealing copper nails, and offer to settle for them, must be worth having."

—Dr. Harry A. Ironside

* * *

God's Good News

A thief broke into a Buffalo, N. Y., church and got away with some valuable equipment and several dollars from a collection box. The next day the church's outside bulletin board carried the words, "If the person who burglarized this church will contact the pastor, he will receive important news." Interested, reporters called on the pastor. "What's the good news?" they wanted to know. Replied the pastor, "If we confess our sins, he is faithful and just to forgive us our sins, and to cleanse us from all unrighteousness."

—*From Heart-to-Heart Talk,* by Charles E. Fuller

* * *

As Bad As Others

His name was Whittle, Major Whittle. He was a major in the Civil War. He said, "When I left home, my mother sent me away with prayer. I was not a Christian. I was in frequent encounters and in one was wounded and had to have my arm amputated. My mother had given me a Bible. I started reading at Matthew and the more I read the more interested I became. I saw as plain as day the way of salva-

tion, but I didn't have the slightest desire to follow that way or believe it. One day as I lay there the nurse came in and said, "There is a lad of 19 here dying and he wants some one to pray with him. You are the only one I know." I told her that I was just as bad as any of them. She replied, "I hadn't heard you curse and thought you might know something about this. Won't you come and do what you can?" He was a lovely boy but the delirium was in his eyes and he was saying, "I can't die the way I am." Something within me said, "You kneel down and confess your sin and be saved and pray with that boy." I confessed my sins and believed on Christ and then poured promises into that boy's ears."

—Dr. R. A. Torrey

* * *

She Did Want Her Name Known

George Pentecost used to tell of a timid little girl who came to the leader of a meeting and said, "Will you pray for me at the meeting, please, but do not mention my name." When every head was bowed and there was perfect silence he prayed for her and said, "O Lord, there is a little girl here who does not want her name known, but Thou dost know her; save her precious soul." There was stillness for a moment and then way back in the congregation a little girl arose and a little pleading voice said, "Please, it's me, Jesus, it's me." She did not want to have a doubt. She wanted to be saved and she was not ashamed to say, "Jesus, it's me."

—*Sunday School Times*

CONSCIENCE

God Sees and Knows

Some years ago two brothers, running a general store in a country town, were perplexed by the discovery that many small items on their shelves were gone, though an inventory showed that they had not been sold. The brothers drew their conclusions, and for some time sought a solution to the problem, and

finally one of them hit upon a plan. They climbed up into the attic above the store ... bored a hole in the ceiling. And then each of them took turns watching through the hole, while the other waited on the trade. What they discovered about some of the townspeople was amazing! However, no open accusations were made; instead, they simply dropped the gentle hint around that there was a hole in the ceiling. Almost immediately the pilfering ceased! But occasionally the brothers noticed with amusement some casual shopper strolling about the store suddenly shifting his eyes toward the ceiling, and this somewhat guiltily.

—*Sunday School Times*

* * *

If the Heart Is Right

It doesn't so much matter
  What path our feet may tread,
Or whether the cheering hopes we knew
  In youth are vanished — dead.
We shall find a gleam in the darkness
  To guide in the dreary night,
And a joyful song as we journey along,
If we go with a heart that's right.

We sip from the cup of sweetness
  And then the bitter gall;
Blossoms and friends are swept away,
  Dreams are forgotten — all.
And you have known the tugging
  That comes to the heart strings tight,
Know of the balm, the peace and calm
  That comes from a heart that's right.

The thorns that beset the causeway
  May fester and wound the feet;
The cup you drink may end with gall,
  Drowning the cherished sweet;
But the nectar for which you hunger,
  The roses that suffered blight,
Will be yours to taste and smell again
If you go with a heart that's right.

—*Selected*

* * *

Conscience

An Indian's definition of conscience, given by a missionary, is not only amusing but very significant:

"It is a little three-cornered thing inside of me. When I do wrong it turns round and hurts me very much. But if I keep on doing wrong, it will turn so much that the corners become worn off and it does not hurt me any more."

—*Samuel M. Zwemer, in*
It Is Hard to Be a Christian

102

Forgetting to Look Up

A man went to steal corn from his neighbor's field. He took his little boy with him to keep a lookout, so as to give warning in case anyone should come along. Before commencing he looked all around, first one way and then the other. Not seeing any person, he was just about to fill his bag, when his son cried out, "Father, there is one way you haven't looked yet!" The father supposed that someone was coming, and asked his son which way he meant. He answered, "You forgot to look up!" The father, conscience-stricken, took his boy by the hand, and hurried home without the corn which he had designed to take.

—*Prairie Overcomer*

* * *

Better Not Get Familiar

A colored man had applied for a job as teamster. "Are you familiar with mules?" asked the employer. "No, sah!" replied the applicant, "for Ah knows mules too well to get familiar wid 'em." There is great danger of our getting used to sinful practices because of their commonness. Let us insist on keeping a concience which will not grow dull to sin because it is prevalent. We should have convictions and follow them.

—*Alliance Full Gospel Quarterly*

* * *

Conscience Free

"I desire so to conduct the affairs of this administration that if at the end, when I come to lay down the reins of power, I have lost every other friend on earth, I shall at least have one friend left, and that friend shall be down inside of me."

—Abraham Lincoln

* * *

Never Go Against Conscience

In the primitive days of our American history a wealthy man came to a poor sadler on Saturday night, leaving a bridle with orders that it should be finished Monday. "That is not possible," said the proprietor of the shop. "What nonsense! There is all day tomorrow." "We do not work on Sunday, sir." "Then I shall go to those who do." "We can get it done by Tuesday." "That will not do, put it in the carriage." Not a moment did the sadler linger. Quietly he did as he was told. Hours afterward a neighbor came and said, banteringly, "I thought the least I could do was to come and thank you, and tell you I should be glad of as many more customers as you like to send." "I shall not send you those I can keep, but God helping me, I will never go against my conscience, not for any man, nor for any money." Weeks went by, weeks of trouble to this faithful sadler, and a military man came into his shop. "So you are the impudent fellow who will not work on Sunday." "I do not work on Sunday, but I hope I am not wanting in respect to my employers." "My friend said you refused to do his work, do you not call that impertinence?" "I had no choice, sir." "Yes you had, you were free to choose between serving God and pleasing man, and you made your choice, and because of that I am here today. I am General Downing. I have been looking for a man on whom I could rely, to execute a large government order. The moment I heard of you, I made up my mind you should have it, for I felt sure the man who would serve God fearlessly would serve his neighbor faithfully." The general gave him the order, and it laid the foundation of the sadler's prosperity.   —*Selected*

* * *

A Principle Within

I want a principle within,
    Of jealous, godly fear;
A sensibility of sin, —
    A pain to feel it near:
I want the first approach to feel
    Of pride, or fond desire;
To catch the wandering of my will,
    And quench the kindling fire.

From Thee that I no more may part,
    No more Thy goodness grieve,
The filial awe, the fleshly heart,
    The tender conscience, give.
Quick as the apple of an eye,
    O God, my conscience make;
Awake my soul when sin is nigh,
    And keep it still awake.
                —**Charles Wesley**

Your Conscience

Oh child of many prayers; Oh child of baptism and covenants; Oh child of the Sabbath-school and the early Church — if you are going from glory to glory, how joyful is your lot! But if you are going on from insensibility to insensibility, if you sin more and feel less, if you are becoming harder and harder, if moral waste is more and more manifest in you, if death already begins to show itself in the supernal and superior part of your nature, if conscience ceases any more to speak and hope is gone, and faith is lost, and wreck and ruin have come upon the crystalline sphere of your being — then woe is you!

                —Henry Ward Beecher

* * *

Fit for Myself

I have to live with myself, and so
I want to be fit for myself to know.
I want to be able, as days go by,
Always to look myself in the eye.
I don't want to stand with the setting
    sun,
And hate myself for the things I've done.

I don't want to keep on a closet shelf
A lot of secrets about myself,
And fool myself as I come and go
Into thinking that nobody else will know
The kind of a person I really am;
I don't want to dress myself up in a
    sham.

I want to go out with my head erect,
I want to deserve all men's respect;
But here in the struggle for fame and
    pelf,
I want to be able to like myself.
I don't want to look at myself and know
That I'm bluster and bluff and empty
    show.

I never can hide myself from me;
I see what others may never see;
I know what others may never know;
I can never fool myself, and so,
Whatever happens, I want to be
Self-respecting and conscience-free.

                —*Selected*

The Better Way

It is better to lose with a conscience clean
  Than win with a trick unfair;
It is better to fall and to know you've
    been,
  Whatever the prize was, square.
Than to claim the joy of a far-off goal
  And the cheers of the standers-by,
And to know down deep in your inmost
    soul
  A cheat you must live and die.

Who wins by trick may take the prize,
  And at first, he may think it sweet,
But many a day in the future lies
  When he'll wish he had met defeat.
For the man who lost shall be glad at
    heart
  And walk with his head up high,
While his conqueror knows he must play
    the part
  Of a cheat and a living lie.

The prize seems fair, when the fight is
    on,
  But save it is truly won
You will hate the thing when the crowds
    are gone.
  For it stands for a false deed done.
And it's better you never should reach
    your goal
Than ever success to buy,
  At the price of knowing down in your
    soul,
  That your glory is all a lie.
        —*Detroit Free Press*

* * *

Guilty Conscience

At a missionary conference in a southern church, Rev. Leon Cramer was leading the singing. Many of the poorer folk had no money to give to missions, but they laid aside a hen, pig, calf, or sheep and brought in the money when the animal was sold. One brother had promised a calf, but meat prices went a-soaring and said he to himself, I'll not give it. Even the rich won't give that much." Many came with their offerings but he still refused. One Sunday afternoon Mr. Cramer led in singing, "The Half Has Never Yet Been Told."

This brother was coming up over the hill. He heard the singing and came running in onto the platform shouting, "Stop singing about it and I'll bring the money in for missions tomorrow." A guilty conscience needs no accuser. He thought they were singing, "The Calf Has Never Yet Been Sold." Perhaps some of us have "a calf" on hand that should be given to God.
        —W. Leon Tucker

* * *

Signal Lights

"It was well you stopped when the red
    light flashed,"
  She said as we drove along.
"For an officer stood on the corner there,
  In charge of the traffic throng."
And I smiled, and said to my daughter
    fair
  As we waited on the spot:
"I always stop when the red light shows,
  Be an officer there, or not."

Then she sat in thought as we drove
    along,
  And suddenly she said:
"There ought to be lights for us all
    through life —
  The amber, the green and the red
What a help 'twould be if a red light
    flashed
When danger and shame were near,
And we all might wait till the green
    light came
  To show that the road is clear."

"My dear," said I, "We have tried to
    light
Life's road for your feet to fare,
And we pray you'll stop when the red
    light glows,
  Though none of us may be there.
We have tried to teach you the signs of
    wrong,
  And the way to a life serene,
So STOP, when your conscience-post
    shows red,
  And GO when it flashes green."
        —Edgar A. Guest

* * *

Three $1 Bills

According to the *Chicago Tribune*, H. R. Sampson, general traffic manager of the Chicago and Eastern Illinois railroad got a letter from Los Angeles not long ago with three $1 bills enclosed. The accompanying note said: "Years ago I rode on one of your trains without paying. I am getting along in years and since I have gone west and become a Christian I want to clear my conscience."

"And herein do I exercise myself, to have always a conscience void of offense toward God, and toward men." Acts
—*Power*

* * *

Conscience Not Infallible:

An Hindu said to a British administrator in India, "Our consciences tell us to burn our widows on the funeral pyres of their husbands!" The Englishman replied, "Our consciences tell us to hang you if you do!"   —W. B. K.

CONSECRATION

Dedication

Lord, can I dare sit idly by
And watch the millions Christless die;
Doing nothing to save the lost,
Afraid of what might be the cost;
Like Peter, warming at the fire —
Sheltering under the church's spire?
Dare I sit and waste the years,
Sharing Thy joys, but not Thy tears;
Unheeding Thy low, tender plea,
"Take up thy cross and follow Me;"
While Thy footprints leave crimson stains
In city streets and country lanes,
As Thou dost carry Thy cross anew,
Seeking the lost as I should do?
O Lord, forgive. I weep in shame,
I love Thee truly; in Thy name,
I turn my back upon the past
To wholly follow Thee at last!

—William Atherton, in
Moody Monthly

* * *

All Yours

There was a dramatic moment in the world's history when General Pershing placed the American Army under the command of General Foch, who had just been made Commander of the Allied Forces in the field. One sentence that he uttered at that time, although not widely quoted, is most significant: "Infantry, artillery, aviation — all that we have are yours. Dispose of them as you will." God wants to hear his Church make such a consecration as

that. It will then be as irresistible as "an army with banners."
—*Christian Herald*

* * *

Whom Do You Acknowledge as Owner?

The Rev. J. Alexander Clark, a Scotch missionary from Africa, told in this country a very striking story of an African who had been mauled by a lioness and was well-nigh dead. Mr. Clark cared for his wounds, and when he got well he left. After three months he came back to Mr. Clark, and said, "You know the law of the African forest, that the redeemed belongs to the redeemer. I was dead, but I am now alive. I am yours. Here are my six wives and my children and my cattle; do with me as you will." Are *we* willing to surrender all to Christ like that? The secret of our lack of power and service is just this — we do not acknowledge that we, the redeemed, belong to the Redeemer.

—*Christ Life*

* * *

He Will Not Crush Those Who Trust Him

A young lady stood talking to an evangelist on the subject of consecration. "I dare not give myself wholly to the Lord," she said, "for fear He will send me out to China." The man of God said: "If some cold, snowy morning a little bird should come, half frozen, pecking at your window, and should let you take it in and feed it, thereby putting itself

105

entirely in your power, what would you do? Would you grip it in your hand and crush it? Or would you give it shelter, warmth, food, and care?" A new light came into the girl's eyes. "Ah, I see, I see!" And her face shone as she went away. Two years later she again met the clergyman and recalled to him the incident. With a countenance all aglow with holy joy, she said, "And, do you know, I am going to China!"

—*Record of Christian Work*

* * *

"What Is the Title, 'Lord'?"

There have been many who have laid aside all earthly gain for Christ's sake, to find in Him richer gain and fuller joy, and that nothing given up for Him is lost; for He gives better things. Such was the Apostle Paul, who counted all things but loss for the excellency of the knowledge of Christ Jesus his Lord (Phil. 3:8). Another such was Baron von Welz, who renounced his title and wealth to become a missionary in Dutch Guiana and there give his life in service. Said he, when he gave up his title and riches:

"What to me is the title 'well-born,' when I have been born again in Christ? What to me is the title 'lord,' when I desire only to be a servant of the Lord Christ? What is it to me to be called, 'Your Grace,' when I have need of God's grace, help, and succor? All these vanities I will away with, and all else I will lay at the feet of Jesus, my dearest Lord, that I may have no hindrance in serving Him aright."

—*The Pilgrim*

* * *

Brainerd's Surrender

The saintly Brainerd tells how that on one Sunday night he offered himself to God to be used only for His glory. "It was raining," he says, "and the roads were muddy; but the desire to surrender to God grew so strong that I stopped my horse and kneeled down by the side of the road and told God about it. I told Him that my hands should work for Him, my tongue speak for Him if He would only use me as His

instrument, when suddenly the darkness of the night lit up and I knew God had answered my prayer, and I felt that I was accepted into the inner circle of His will."

—From *Springs in the Valley* by Mrs. Charles Cowman

* * *

Utter Surrender

Let us give up our work, our thoughts, our plans, ourselves, our lives, our loved ones, our influence, our all, right into His hand, and then, when we have given all over to Him, there will be nothing left for us to be troubled about, or to make trouble about.

—J. Hudson Taylor

* * *

Consecration of the Best

An evangelist was preaching to the Indians. He had made a strong appeal that assistance be given to other Indians, and a collection was to be taken. Through an interpreter he asked them to make the very best gift they had. When the baskets had been passed down the aisle there came to the front a big Indian, his wife walking by his side and a little bit of a boy between them. Securing the attention of the evangelist, the Indian said, "You told us to give the very best we had to God. Our best in not money, but it is this little child." And without a suggestion of a smile he said, "We could not put him into the basket, so we brought him to you. You may take him away if you please, and we will never see him again. Only remember he is God's child." *There is many a life of blessing which if traced back to its source would come to parental consecration.*

—J. Wilbur Chapman, in *Awakening Sermons*

* * *

Send Me

Send me to the hearts without a home, to the lives without a love, to the crowds without a compass, to the ranks without a refuge. Send me to the children whom none have blessed, to the famished whom none have fed, to the sick whom none have visited, to the demoniac whom none have calmed, to the fallen whom none have lifted, to the leper whom none have touched, to the bereaved whom none have comforted.

Then shall I have the birthright of the first-born; then shall I have the blessing of the mighty God of Jacob!

—George Matheson

* * *

What Are You Holding On To?

The Christians of "God's Invasion Army" give a whole year of their life to house-to-house soul-winning. One thing demonstrated is that the greatest asset to the work of God is a yielded life. God has called many young people to this work and answering such a call has rarely been easy, as they have ambitions. Yet there has been a response which shows that the spirit of sacrifice has not died out in the Christian youth of our day. One girl went to see the Invasion Army group which was visiting her church, and said: "As I listened to their testimonies, I wanted an unselfish life of service. I realized that to be happy in my Christian life, I must be used of the Lord. Still," she admits, "as I went home to bed, I kept thinking of job, home, friends, and the other things I held so dear. It seemed too much to give up, but I couldn't sleep. All through the night a voice kept saying, 'They left all, and followed Jesus.' Finally I could stand it no longer. I slipped down by the side of my bed and whispered to Jesus, 'I will leave all, and follow Thee.'"

—*Moody Monthly*

* * *

"Crown Him Lord!"

Friends at the bedside of a noble and aged missionary noticed her lips move feebly. Bending low, they caught the faintly uttered word, "Bring!"

Asked they, "Bring What? Your medicine?" Then, with smiles wreathing her face, the missionary said with her latest breath, "Bring forth the royal diadem and crown Him Lord of all!"

—W. B. K.

When He Gave Himself

James H. McConkey related this experience: "The winter was ending. The ice was breaking in our native river. The freshets were piling it up in great gorges along the banks. A few miles above our home was a little town at which an immense ice gorge had imprisoned eleven men, women and children. The instant this huge ice gorge should break, it would sweep those lives out of existence. My brother learned of the situation. Putting fifty dollars in his pocket he hastened to the little town. Arriving there he found the people waiting on the banks of the river for the catastrophe which seemed inevitable. Stepping up to the crowd he offered the fifty dollars to any man who would attempt the rescue of the imperiled ones. But not a man stirred. Then he sent a little lad into a nearby store for a line. When he brought it out, my brother tied one end of it around his waist, and offered to join with any man who would rope himself to him in an effort to rescue the lives that were in instant jeopardy of death. Immediately four men leaped to his side. They roped themselves to the same line of peril with himself, and these five men, picking their way over the dangerous gorge at the imminent hazard of their own lives, brought in safety to the shore every man, woman, and child upon the ice. When my brother offered money, not a man stirred. But when they saw him give himself and saw the love for those imperiled, it drew them to his side in an instant."

—*Gospel Herald*

* * *

The Master Potter

Have you ever watched a potter
Fashion vessels out of clay?
He takes the formless substance
And in a wondrous way,
With patience, skill, and pressure,
Makes perfect works of art;
That which was clay is now a joy
To please the potter's heart.

So too the Master Potter
Takes clay so rough and rude,
And fashions perfect patterns
From forms that have been crude.
He shows such skill and patience,
Uses gentle pressure too,
In molding lives for service
His daily work to do.

—Sarah Ingham, in
Moody Monthly

* * *

Burning Bridges

A young woman who was converted several years ago wrote me a letter. She had made a profession of salvation, but had never gone on. Her experience is just what keeps many from walking in close fellowship with Christ. In her letter she said: "I had so many idols, I wasn't willing to face the ridicule of my office associates, yes, and of my own relations; also I belonged to several worldly clubs. I loved the friendship of worldly people whom I was sure would scorn me if I was a true Christian. I loved too well the good things of the world, like clothes, beyond what I could afford, but as this year draws near its close, by God's help, I am going to 'burn my bridges' and tear every idol from my heart, and from henceforth be a true Christian."

—*Sunday School Times*

* * *

A Divided Heart

Is there a thing beneath the sun
That strives with Thee my heart to share?
O tear it thence, and reign alone,
The spring of every motion there!
Then shall my joyful heart be free,
And find its deep repose in Thee!

—*Selected*

* * *

No Hands of His Own

A white man was desirous of teaching a native (Solomon Islands) lad how to gamble. "Me no got any hands," said the Christian boy. "But you have two hands. What do you mean?" said the puzzled European. "Yes, you look 'im two fella hands," was the reply, "but two fella hands you look 'im no belong me, two fella hands they belong Jesus."

—*Moody Monthly*

* * *

Her Last Surrender

In a letter from Dr. and Mrs. George R. Cousar, of Lubondai, Africa, we read the following: "Recently an old, old woman was being examined by our native pastor for baptism. Her face was radiantly happy. She finished answering all the questions satisfactorily, showing that she understood the plan of salvation. When the time came for those who were to be baptized to enter the church, this old woman said that she wanted to get something in her house. Everyone else had gone into the church shed and was waiting expectantly for the old woman to come back. When she did come, she walked right up to the front of the church, laid a small fetish on the ground and quietly took her seat among the other women present at the service. Serious looks were on every face, for each native in that village knew that the 'medicine' she had put up there was lightning medicine, the last medicine that any of them is willing to give up. This woman's father had been killed by lightning years before, and never had she been without her fetish to protect her against the same fate. But when she found Jesus as her Lord and Saviour she was not willing to give Him less than all."

—*Christian Observer*

* * *

How Real Holiness Came

One of the saintliest ministers in our Free Church once told me the story of his sanctification. They had a child, an only child, and God was pleased to let it sicken till it was near death. There was no hope, and the father's and mother's hearts rebelled, and they cried that this was hard. But only for a little. Their trust in God was in eclipse, not quenched. "Wife," said the husband, "we must not let God *take* our child, we must *give* him." So, kneeling down beside the bed together, they humbly gave to God again what he had lent them for a little space. Death came, a stranger to that home, and knocked. And in the fragrance of two consecrated lives, never a man or child in all their parish but knew they entertained an angel unawares.

—*"Flood Tide,"*
by G. H. Morrison

* * *

Christ In Full Possession

Mendelssohn, it is said, once visited the cathedral at Fridbourg, and, having heard the great organ, went into the organ loft and asked to be allowed to play it. The old organist, in jealousy for his instrument, at first refused, but was afterward prevailed on to allow the great German composer to try the colossal "thunder" of the cathedral. And after standing by in an ecstasy of delight and amazement for a few moments, he suddenly laid his hands on the shoulders of the inspired musician and exclaimed: "Who are you? What is your name?" "Mendelssohn," replied the player. "And can it be! that I had so nearly refused to let Mendelssohn touch this organ!" How little the Lord's people know what they are doing when they refuse to let Christ have full possession of their entire life and evoke the full melody and harmony of which it is capable!

—*Gospel Herald*

* * *

Wholly Consecrated

How unlike the spirit of the hour is the story of Chinese Gordon. For his services in China the government sought to reward him, but he declined all honors. Money and titles he scorned, but he accepted a medal inscribed with his name and his thirty-three engagements because it could not well be refused.

After his tragic death the medal could nowhere be traced. What a revelation of the great soldier's unselfishness unfolds when we learn that the medal was sent to the poor of Manchester during the famine, with an anonymous letter requesting the ore be melted down and used for the hungry children of the city.

Then in his diary he wrote these words: *"The last and only thing I have in this world that I value I have given over to the Lord Jesus Christ."*

—*Evangelical Christian*

* * *

"I'll Go, But —"

"I'll go where you want me to go, dear
    Lord,
Real service is what I desire.
I'll say what you want me to say, dear
    Lord —
But don't ask me to sing in the choir,
I'll say what you want me to say, dear
    Lord,
I like to see things come to pass.
But don't ask me to teach girls and boys,
    dear Lord —
I'd rather just stay in my class.
I'll do what you want me to do, dear
    Lord,
I yearn for the kingdom to thrive.
I'll give *you* my nickels and dimes, dear
    Lord —
But please don't ask me to tithe.
I'll go where you want me to go, dear Lord,
I'll say what you want me to say.
I'm busy just now with myself, dear
    Lord —
I'll help you some other day."

—*Decatur Christian*

* * *

How Dr. Carey Paid Expenses

A characteristic incident is told about Dr. Carey, the pioneer missionary in India, who, before he left this country, was a shoemaker, or, rather, as he himself put it, a cobbler.

He used to go about from village to village preaching, for his soul was filled with the love of God. One day a friend came to him and said: "Mr. Carey, I want to speak to you very seriously." "Well," said Carey, "What is it?" The friend replied, "By your going about preaching as you do you are neglecting your business. If you only attended to your business more you would be all right, and would soon get on and prosper, but as it is you are simply neglecting your business." "Neglecting my business," said Carey, looking at him steadily. "My business is to extend the

Kingdom of God. I only cobble shoes to pay expenses."

—*Gospel Herald*

* * *

Can You Say:

"The SERVICE of Christ is the business of my life,
The WILL of Christ is the law of my life,
The PRESENCE of Christ is the joy of my life,
The GLORY of Christ is the crown of my life."

—*C.B.M.C. Prayer Quarterly*

* * *

Do We?

A missionary in India was hurrying along the street one day by the Ganges River when he saw a native woman looking at the water. In her arms was a sickly infant, while at her side stood a beautiful, healthy boy. The missionary on questioning her found she was in deep distress and was trying to make up her mind to give an offering to her god. He tried to dissuade her, telling her of the love of Jesus and His sacrifice fer her. After a time he had to leave her, and hours later he saw her with the sickly babe in her arms. The beautiful boy was gone. He knew what had happened. She had thrown the boy to the crocodiles in the river. "I made an offering to my god," the woman said. "But why did you give your boy, why not this sickly little one?" asked the missionary. Rising to her feet the woman replied: "We give our gods our best."

—*Wonderful Word*

* * *

Have You Forgotten?

There is a song the children sometimes sing, "Praise Him, praise Him, all ye little children." Sitting at the piano a father and his little boy were singing it together. It is one of those children's songs that run on through endless verses, satisfying and suggestive. The father had sung it through (as he thought): "Praise Him, praise Him, all ye little children. Love Him, love Him," etc.

"Serve Him, serve Him," etc. When he stopped the boy looked up into his face surprised, still expectant, and said, "But Father, you forgot to crown Him!" And so they sang, "Crown Him, crown Him, all ye little children." When we began to think it over we are confident that the little lad is right. We have forgotten to crown Him. We have forgotten that He is King. He is Lord of all.

—*"Forward, Day by Day"*

* * *

Constitutional, or Absolute Sovereign?

"I remember," says the Rev. G. W. Moore in one of his books, "at one of our testimony meetings, a man stood and he said he had received a great blessing at Keswick. They asked him, 'What can you say about it?' 'Well,' he replied, 'I can say this: I was a Christian before I came to Keswick: Christ was my King; but I am afraid He was a constitutional sovereign, and I was a prime minister. Now He is absolute Lord, and that has made all the difference in my life, and brought a blessing.' "

—*Sunday School Times*

* * *

The Inspiration of a Great Life

I will place no value on anything I have or may possess except in relation to the Kingdom of Christ. If anything will advance the interests of that Kingdom, it shall be given away or kept, only as by the giving or keeping of it I shall most promote the glory of Him to whom I owe all my hopes in time and eternity. May grace and strength sufficient to enable me to adhere faithfully to this resolution be imparted to me, so that, not in name only, all my interest may be identified with His cause."

—David Livingstone

* * *

In The Hand of God!

When Richard Baxter lay dying, his friends, pitying his pain, liked to comfort him by speaking of the good that he had achieved by means of his writings. Baxter shook his head. "No," he said, "I was but a pen in God's hand, and what praise is due to a pen?"

When Saladin saw the sword with which Richard Coeur de Lion had fought so bravely he marveled that so common a blade should have wrought such mighty deeds. "It was not the sword," replied one of the English officers, "it was the arm of Richard."

When Paganini appeared for the first time at the Royal Opera House in Paris, the aristocracy of France was gathered to hear him. In his peculiar *ghostly* manner he *glided* on to the stage amidst the breathless silence of the expectant throng. Commencing to tune his violin, a string snapped. The *audience tittered.* Commencing again, a second string broke; and a moment later, a third gave way. The people stared in consternation. Paganini paused for a second, and then, giving one of his grim smiles, he lifted his instrument, and, from the single string, drew music that seemed almost Divine.

Only a pen — but a pen in the hand of a poet.

Only a common sword — but a sword in the hand of Richard!

Only a broken violin — but a violin in the hand of a master!

—F. W. Boreham

* * *

"It Pays to Put God First"

Robert G. LeTourneau writes: "Our young people had been going regularly to a mission to hold a Gospel service, and I had been going with them. One night I had some special work to do. I was operating a small factory at the time, and machinery had to be built the next day for which I had to make the design that night in order that a crew of men on contract could build it the next morning. How could I do my work and attend the meeting at the mission? The Lord and I had quite a struggle while I was trying to decide what to do. Although I could not understand how I was going to get the plan drawn for the next morning, I went with the young people and we had a profitable time. I returned home about ten o'clock. Up to that time I had been unable to make a single plan. I sat down

at the drafting board, and in about five minutes the outline and plan was as plain as it could be. What is more, the little piece of machinery designed that night has been the key machine in all that I have been building since. It pays to put God first."

—*King's Business*

* * *

George Muller's Secret:

To one who asked him the secret of his service, George Muller said: "There was a day when I DIED, utterly died: Died to George Muller, his opinions, preferences, tastes, and will, died to the world, its approval, or censure, died to the approval or blame even of my brethren and friends, and since then I have studied ONLY to show myself approved unto God!"

—*Selected*

* * *

Clear Gain

At a dinner given by a Grand Army Post, a veteran soldier was introduced as one of the speakers. In making the introduction, the presiding officer referred to the fact that the man who was to speak had lost a leg in the war, and the veteran was greeted with loud cheering as he arose to make the address. He began by disavowing the introduction. "No," he said, "that is a mistake. I lost nothing in the war, for, when we went into the war, we gave our country all that we had, and all we brought back was so much clear gain."

—From Hart's *Pearls for Preachers*

* * *

Which One Was Successful?

A successful writer and a foreign missionary, invalided home, met in the college town where they had been classmates. The missionary, as a youth of twenty-one, had gone to blaze a path in a new and unhealthful field. Now, twenty years later, he was back in the homeland trying to patch up the ruins of a magnificent constitution so that he might return for another sojourn, feeling that, with his knowledge of the people and language, he might be able to crowd his last days with useful work

111

even in weakness. The writer, fresh from a visit to London, where he had been acclaimed and feted as a brilliant novelist and essayist, gazed on his old friend's wasted form and features marked by suffering, and, seeming to have a moment of insight, exclaimed, "Dick, you are the only one of our class that has had a career!"

—*Sunday School Times*

* * *

Christ Speaks

Thus speaketh Christ our Lord to us:
Ye call me Master, and obey Me not;
Ye call me Light, and see Me not;
Ye call me Way, and walk Me not;
Ye call me Fair, and love Me not;
Ye call me Rich, and ask Me not;
Ye call me Eternal, and seek Me not;
Ye call me Gracious, and trust Me not;
Ye call me Just, and fear Me not —
If I condemn ye, blame Me not.

This epitaph was engraved on an ancient slab in the Cathedral of Luebeck, Germany.

—*Gospel Banner*

* * *

Just "Things"

Some one asked John Wanamaker: "How do you get time to run a Sunday school with your four thousand scholars, in addition to the business of your stores, your work as Postmaster-General, and other obligations?" Instantly Mr. Wanamaker replied: "Why, the Sunday school is my business! All other things are just *things*. Forty-five years ago I decided that God's promise was sure: 'Seek ye first the kingdom of God, and his righeousness; and all these *things* shall be added unto you.' "

—*King's Business*

* * *

Really Given to God

A sacrifice is something really given to God. We cannot take it back again. A man could not lay a lamb on God's altar and in a few minutes come and claim it. So we cannot be God's today and our own tomorrow. We are His al-

ways or His not at all. We are to give ourselves, a living sacrifice. Of old the sacrifice was killed and placed on God's altar; we are to present ourselves living. The fire consumed the ancient offerings; we are purified by divine love and filled with a new life. The sacrifice of old died; we live. It is easier to die for Christ than to live for Him. It is easier to suffer for Christ in days of enthusiasm than to endure the petty trials of daily life. We belong to God. Our first duty is to Him.

—*Christian Life*

* * *

Nothing Too Precious

A memory of his American tour that lingered in Mr. Taylor's heart with special sweetness was an incident of one of the first farewell meetings. The father of a dear girl in the party of missionary recruits had come over from Pittsfield, Mass., and was sitting near the platform. Seeing a wonderful light on his face, Mr. Taylor invited him to say a few words. "He told us with a father's feeling," Mr. Taylor loved to recall, "what his daughter had been in the home, to him and to her mother; what she had been in the mission hall in which he worked, and something of what it meant to part with her now. 'But I could only feel,' he said, 'that I have nothing too precious for my Lord Jesus. He has asked for my very best, and I give, with all my heart, my very best to Him.' That sentence was the richest thing I got in America, and has been an untold blessing to me ever since. The thought has been a real help to me on such occasions as when leaving my loved ones in England; indeed, I could never tell how many hundreds of times God has given me a blessing through those words — 'Nothing too precious for my Lord Jesus.' "

—Hudson Taylor

* * *

Anywhere for God

Being present at a missionary meeting when Bishop Handley Moule was speaking, the Rev. Thomas Walker decided that the call had come to him to volunteer for any field in which he was wanted. Dr. Moule had spoken of the servant whose ear was to be bored in token that he would not go out free; and it was noted by friends afterward that when asked what had brought him to India, Mr. Walker always replied in the same words, that Dr. Moule, "*asked us to put both our hands quite within the Master's hands.* And that meant doing anything, going anywhere: and so I am here."

"Here," as so many know, was the Tinnevelly District of South India, where he was much used of God.

—*Gospel Herald*

* * *

What God Claims

    What God claims, I yield;
    What I yield, He accepts;
    What He accepts, He fills;
    What He fills, He uses;
    What He uses, He blesses.
    —*Moody Monthly*

* * *

Belief Versus Discipleship

To believe costs nothing; to follow Christ is expensive.

I believe in Christ's work for me, but discipleship is the result of His work in me.

Believers consider themselves first; disciples consider Christ first.

Believers (only) produce no perfect fruit, but disciples are known by their fruit.

Belief saves my soul, but discipleship glorifies Christ.

Believers (only) are not necessarily known as Christians, but disciples are known as Christians.

Believers go to heaven; disciples are richly rewarded there.

—*Calvary Church News*

* * *

The Master's Hand

" 'Twas battered and scarred, and the auctioneer
Thought it scarcely worth his while
To waste much time on the old violin,
But held it up with a smile.
'What am I bidden, good folks,' he cried,
'Who'll start bidding for me?

A dollar, a dollar — now two, only two —
Two dollars and who'll make it three?

" 'Three dollars, once, three dollars, twice,
Going for three' — but no
From the room far back a gray haired man
Came forward and picked up the bow;
Then wiping the dust from the old violin,
And tightening up all the strings,
He played a melody pure and sweet,
As sweet as the angels sing.

"The music ceased, and the auctioneer,
With a voice that was quiet and low,
Said: 'What am I bid for the old violin?'
And he held it up with the bow,
'A thousand dollars — and who'll make it two?
Two thousand, and who'll make it three?
Three thousand once, and three thousand twice —
And — going, and gone,' said he.

"The people cheered, but some of them cried,
'We do not quite understand —
What changed its worth?' The man replied,
'The touch of the master's hand.'
And many a man with life out of tune,
And battered and torn with sin,
Is auctioned cheap to a thoughtless crowd,
Much like the old violin.

"A mess of pottage, a glass of wine,
A game and he travels on,
He's going once, and he's going twice,
He is going, and almost gone.
But the Master comes, and the foolish crowd,
Never can quite understand
The worth of a soul, and the change that's wrought
By the touch of the Master's hand."
    —*Myra Brooks Welch*

* * *

The Vital Connection

One day when the late Doctor Truett was preaching to the cattlemen in the Southwest, a ranchman came to him at the close of the sermon and said: "I never knew until you preached today that the ranch land and thousands of cattle, that I have called mine, are not really mine, but that they belong to Christ, and that I am simply His steward. Never until today did I know that. I have not been a Christian long, and I don't know much about what Christ expects of me. I want you to bow down here," said he, "and tell Christ for me that I will take my place, I will accept my stewardship." Doctor Truett then prayed, and the ranchman, as soon as he could control his emotions, ended his prayer thus: "Master, am I now in a position to give my son to you along with all else? I do give him to you.

Save him for your glory." That night a spiritual atmosphere was present, and before the preacher was halfway through his message, a young man on the outskirts of the great crowd rose up and said, "I cannot wait until that man is done with his sermon to tell you that I have found the Lord." He was the ranchman's son. "Do you doubt," says this discerning pastor, "that there was a vital connection between the right relation of that ranchman to Jesus Christ and the homecoming of his son?"

—Sunday School World

CONVERSION

Infinite Gain In Seeming Loss!

"That's the place, right there," he said to me pointing to a large building, as we rode by in the trolley car.

"You don't mean that whole block, do you?" I asked my travelling companion, a man of sixty-odd.

"Yes, it was all mine. I began in a small way. I worked hard. I was successful. Hundreds of men were working — two shifts. Orders were piling up. I was fast becoming a rich man. Then — well, overnight I was stripped of everything. It was like turning off the only light in a room on a dark, stormy night. Everything went black as midnight. The storm was terrible — in my heart I mean." Then he paused.

"Too bad," I exclaimed.

"Too bad?" he repeated, turning to me sharply, with eyes glistening. "Say, I shall never quit thanking God for that experience."

"I don't understand," I said.

"In the terrible darkness of that hour," he explained, "I saw a great light. In the storm I heard a sweet voice. The light took form; it was the Saviour. The Saviour was speaking to me — oh, so gently. The loss awakened my sleeping soul and brought me to God!"

—Guy Edward Mark, D.D.

"I'd Rather Have Jesus!"

It was in the thirties. Business curves were still heading downward and there was rumor of a salary cut at the New York insurance office where 22-year-old Beverly Shea was employed as a clerk. Possessor of a deep melodious voice, the young man was offered a radio contract and immediately saw opportunities for fame and possible riches in his regular appearance on a secular program.

Shea had been pondering the matter for several days when he sat down to the piano early one Sunday morning to rehearse a hymn he was to sing in church that morning. As he played and sang his eyes fell on a piece of paper, on which was written:

"I'd rather have Jesus than silver or gold,
I'd rather be His than have riches untold!"

The poem, by Mrs. Rhea Miller, had been placed where Beverly would see it by his mother, a minister's wife, who knew of the offer her son was pondering. Above all, she wanted her son, a Christian, to become wholly consecrated in His service.

As his eyes raced over the words, "I'd rather have Jesus than men's applause" and "I'd rather have Jesus than worldwide fame" were sentences which struck his very heart.

His fingers unconsciously left the tune he was rehearsing and began to find the melody which is today known to millions.

Several days after, the director who spoke to Shea in behalf of the radio network was amazed to receive a firm "no" in response to the offer. "No" was a strange word to the director's ear as thousands of singers would have leaped at such an opportunity as was proposed to the young bass-baritone.

From that time forward, the words of the poem "I'd rather Have Jesus" set to music became his testimony. Today Shea is realizing his ambition to sing the gospel on the radio. He is sponsored on a hymn program and is heard on many youth programs.

—*Power*

* * *

Franklin's Story of the Speckled Ax

Benjamin Franklin, in his autobiography, tells of the man who bought an ax from the local blacksmith. The purchaser wanted the whole of its surface as bright as its edge, and this the smith consented to do, provided the man would turn the wheel while he ground it. It was a hard, wearisome job and often the man stopped to see how the ax was getting on. "Turn on, turn on," said the smith; "we shall have it bright by and by; as yet it is only speckled." "Yes," said the man, "but I think I like a speckled ax best."

Is this not the case with many of God's children? Instead of going all the way into the fully consecrated and victorious Christian life, they become satisfied with "a speckled ax" Christian experience, God's second best for them.

—*Christian Victory*

* * *

Inside Your Heart

Two little Zulu boys in South Africa heard a missionary speak and one of them, when asked later by his mistress what he had heard, said: "Oh, there was a wonderful Man, and people were very unkind to Him, and He died and went up to Heaven; but He came down again and was like a little child in people's hearts."

The lady asked him what he did when he heard this and, with shining face, he answered: "I opened my heart and let the little Babe Christ in; He came in and my heart closed over Him and He is inside."

Later that little heathen boy went back to his own people and was cruelly ill-treated because of his love for Jesus. They tried every way to get the love of Christ out of his head and heart, but they could not do it. The little boy would keep saying, "He is inside, and you cannot get Him out, and you must be very careful not to hurt Him."

—*The Junior King's Business*

* * *

The Miracle of Opening

In the sixteenth chapter of Acts, we have the story of two conversions. It took an earthquake to convert the jailer, but the heart of Lydia opened like a flower to the kiss of the Son of Righteousness. All down through the centuries, the Spirit of God has been at the work of conversion. Back in the third century Cyprian the Bishop of Carthage wrote to his friend Donatus: "It is a bad world, Donatus, an incredibly bad world. But I have discovered, in the midst of it, a quiet and holy people who have learned a great secret. They have found a joy which is a thousand times better than any of the pleasures of our sinful life. They are despised and persecuted, but they care not. They are masters of their souls. They have overcome the world. These people, Donatus, are Christians — and I am one of them."

—*Sunday School Times*

* * *

A Very Definite Transaction

"There came to me here one day a fine looking fellow. I did not need to ask whether he did business on the water, for the sea breeze had kissed his brow so often that it had left its mark there. I said, 'Where did you find the Lord?' In a moment he answered, 'Latitude 25, longitude 54.' I confess that rather puzzled me. I had heard of people finding Jesus Christ in these galleries and down these aisles, but here was something quite different. 'Latitude 25, longitude 54! What do you mean?' He said, 'I was sitting on deck, and out of a bundle of papers before me I pulled one of Spurgeon's sermons. I began to read it. As I read it I saw the truth and I received Jesus into my heart. I jumped off the coils of rope, saved. I thought if I were on shore, I would know where I was saved, and why should I not on the sea? And so I took my latitude and longitude.' "

—From *The Pastor His Own Evangelist*, by F. M. Barton

* * *

A Sacred Spot

One day, some years ago, a policeman walking his beat in Chicago, observed a man standing before a little building, with bared head, acting — as the cop thought — "pretty queer."

"Either sick — er drunk," he concluded, eyeing the man suspiciously. Then he walked up, to where the man stood with eyes closed, and grunted: "What's the matter, Mac? Sick?"

The man opened his eyes, and smiled. "No, officer. My name's Bill Sunday, and I was converted right here in that little mission. I never come by here that I don't take off my hat and say a prayer."

The cop grinned now, reached a giant hand to Billy, and said, heartily: "Put 'er there, Bill! I've heard about it. You keep right on with your prayer, and' I'll keep the crowd away."

—Chester Shuler

* * *

Dr. Robert G. Lee's Conversion

One morning when I was a boy the preacher preached .a sermon which I think now must have been on the subject, "The Gates of Heaven." In the sermon he asked, "If the gates of heaven were opened, would you enter?"

The question startled me. I knew that if the gates of heaven were opened that day I could not enter, because I could not claim to be a Christian boy.

That night the preacher's text was, "What then shall I do with Jesus who is called the Christ?" He said very simply and earnestly that to accept Christ as Saviour meant heaven, that to reject Him as Saviour meant hell.

I went home that night with the most wretched feeling. I could not sleep. I got up in the night, slipped out of the window that opened on the back porch, and went down to the moonlit watermelon patch. It was a beautiful clear night, and I thought of the heaven beyond the stars and of the hell somewhere in some vast region below.

At the breakfast table next morning, my mother said, "Son, you look like you didn't sleep much last night."

"No, ma'am," I said, "I didn't."

"What was the matter?"

"I feel awfully sinful," I admitted.

I had to plow that day. My misery grew until finally I drove out to the end of a long row and dropped the plow down by the side of Barney, my old white mule. I got down in the fence corner, the corner of an old rail fence, and told God I felt awfully bad — awfully sinful — and that I wanted to be saved.

"If one must accept Jesus to be saved," I prayed, "then I accept Him."

There in a fence corner the Lord saved me.

That night — the text of the preacher's sermon I do not now remember — I walked right down the church aisle and let it be known that the Lord had saved me.

I do remember the hymn they sang:

"Out of my bondage, sorrow, and night;
Jesus, I come! Jesus, I come!
Into thy freedom, gladness, and light;
Jesus, I come to Thee."

The peace which came to me in the fence corner is in my heart until this day.

—*Selected*

* * *

Said Dr. C. I. Scofield of his conversion:

"I was a drunken lawyer; I was thirty-seven years old. One day one of my clients, Tom McPhetters, was in my office. When he started to go out, with his hand on the knob of the door, he turned and said:

" 'Scofield, I'm the biggest coward on earth.'

" 'Why, Tom, what do you mean? I never had you down as a coward.'

" 'Well, for a whole year I have had a question in my mind that I have wanted to ask you, and I have never had sand enough to ask it until today.'

"Then I said, 'Tom, come back here and sit down and ask me any question you like.'

" 'It is this, Why aren't you a Christian?'

" 'Well, Tom, doesn't the Bible say something about no drunkard ever going to Heaven?'

" 'Scofield, that isn't the answer to my question. Now tell me, why aren't you a Christian?'

" 'The fact is, Tom, I don't know how to go about it.'

"He took from his pocket a New Testament and began to read. He read John 3:16; 5:24; 6:47; 10:28, etc."

" 'I imply from what you have read that I must believe on the Lord Jesus Christ.'

" 'Right, and will you do it now?"

"I will think about it; you have set me thinking.'

" 'Scofield, you've thought about it long enough. Will you take the Lord Jesus Christ as your personal Saviour?'

" 'Yes, I will.' "

He later wrote to his biographer, Mr. Trumbull: *"It was a Bible conversion. Instantly the chains of sin were broken never to be forged again; the passion for drink was all gone. Divine power did it, wholly of grace."*

—*Selected*

* * *

The Mastering Christ

There was a man in New York who had been so fortunate as to get a copy of Hoffmann's "Jesus in the Temple," soon after it was painted, and he kept it on his desk in his office. A judge of one of the superior courts of Massachusetts went to this lawyer's office on a matter of business. As the two men talked, the judge's eyes rested on this picture until it seemed hard for him to attend to business; but at last the business was settled and the judge left the

office. Several hours later he returned to the office and asked "to look at that Boy again." For an hour he sat and looked at that picture. The next day he came again into the man's office and said, "I want to see that Boy again." He was given the picture, and retired into a private room adjoining the office. Having occasion later to go into the room, the man found the judge sitting with the picture on his knees, his eyes being filled with tears. When the judge came back into the office, he handed back the picture and said, *"That Boy has mastered me."*

—*Epworth Herald*

* * *

"Gentle Jesus, Meek and Mild"

Ike Miller was the terror of a North England mining district.

Gospel services were being held and many miners were listening to the old, old message. The love of Christ was the theme of the young preacher, Henry Moorhouse, one evening. Ike Miller had said that he would break up the meetings, and coming in to the service, he took his seat near the front.

The preacher and all his fellow workers were in fear lest a disturbance should be created.

Unknown to them, a disturbance was created. It was in the depths of Ike's soul. As he listened to the sweet message of a Saviour's love his proud heart was broken. The light of the Gospel shown in.

The meeting was over and Ike left it for his home.

Several of the older Christians surrounded the young evangelist, telling him that he had missed a great opportunity. They thought that a warning word of judgment, and not a winsome message of love, should have been sounded. "What does he care about the love of Christ?" they asked.

"I am real sorry I did not preach to him right," said young Moorhouse, "I did want so to help him."

Little those well-meaning men knew of the power of the *good* news of the Gospel.

Ike Miller reached his home, where he had been a terror oftentimes.

"Home so early?" his wife cried, as he entered. She had come forward to meet him and shelter their children who had fled into a corner. Then, to her astonishment, she saw that he was not drunk but perfectly sober. To her greater astonishment he put his arms round her and kissed her. "Lass," he said, "God has brought your husband back to you." Taking up his children, he said to them, "My little boy and girl, God has brought your father back to you. Now let us all pray."

"Gentle Jesus, meek and mild,
Look upon a little child;
Pity my simplicity,
Suffer me to come to Thee."
—Inglis Fleming, in
Gospel Herald

* * *

Gipsy Smith's Conversion

Cornelius Smith, father of the great evangelist Gipsy Rodney Smith, became greatly impressed with his need of salvation. On one of his journeys, he camped at Shepherd's Bush, and attending a service in a mission hall, he heard the people sing Cowper's stirring hymn:

There is a fountain filled with Blood
Drawn from Immanuel's veins;
And sinners, plunged beneath that flood,
Lose all their guilty stains.

The chorus ran:
I do believe, I will believe,
That Jesus died for me,
That on the Cross He shed His Blood
From sin to set me free.

Soon the father, who was seeking salvation, exclaimed, "I am converted!" Reaching home, he told his motherless children what had happened, placed his arms around the five of them, kissed them, and fell on his knees and began to pray. That first prayer was never forgotten; and many years afterward Gipsy Smith said: "I still feel its sacred influence on my heart and soul." The next morning the converted man was pleading with others, and thirteen

gypsies professed to find Christ that day.

When Gipsy Smith was a little older, he attended a service in a Primitive Methodist Chapel in Cambridge, and a prayer meeting followed the sermon. When an invitation was given, the gypsy lad went forward. By a coincidence, the congregation sang the chorus which was sung when his father was converted:

I do believe, I will believe,
That Jesus died for me,
That on the Cross He shed His Blood
From sin to set me free.

There and then he trusted in Christ, and from that time he rejoiced in Him as his Saviour.
—*Elim Evangel*

* * *

Various Channels

The Philippian jailer was converted through fear; Lydia through the emotions; the Ethiopian eunuch through intellectual conviction; Saul of Tarsus through his conscience. The Holy Spirit uses various channels.
—F. C. White, in
Moody Monthly

* * *

Charles Fuller, Director of the Old-Fashioned Revival Hour" Led to Christ by Paul Radar

"Back in 1917 I was a successful young business man from a Christian home, but I had had my faith in God shattered in college. One Sunday in that year (and by the way it was the third Sunday in July) I went, out of curiosity, to hear Paul Radar preach at the Church of the Open Door. I entered that place a lost sinner; I came out under deep conviction because Paul preached Christ and Him crucified in such a spirit-empowered message that I saw myself a lost, undone sinner. He preached from Ephesians 1:18, 19.

Leaning my head on the seat in front of me, I trembled there under deep conviction, though I did not then know what was the matter with me. I left the afternoon meeting and went out to a park in Hollywood, where I got down on my knees in the back of my touring car and there, in prayer, after a real struggle, I asked God to save my soul, which He did — and to use me in some capacity to reach others for Himself.

I became a new creation, then and there, and I went back to the evening meeting to hear Paul Rader preach another sermon, which seemed to me like manna from Heaven. My heart was fairly bursting with joy, and all desire to get ahead in the business world and to make money left me. I just wanted God to use me if He could win souls for Himself.

Later I had blessed fellowship with Brother Paul in conference work in McPherson, Kansas, and in Indianapolis. He wrote his name in a Bible which I use constantly, and beneath it he wrote "Days of Heaven upon earth." Truly our days of fellowship together in those conferences were heavenly days.

I wish to say that I, with other thousands of souls, will look him up in the Glory and say, "Brother Paul, I'm here because the Holy Spirit used the Word of God as you gave it forth to bring me under conviction, and to save my soul."

—Charles E. Fuller, in
The Peoples Magazine

* * *

"My Bungling Work"

"I'm one of your converts," hiccoughed a drunken man to Sam Jones, the farfamed evangelist and winner of souls of other years. "Yes," said Sam Jones, "you look like some of my bungling work!" Only God can save: "Which were born, not of blood, nor of the will of the flesh, nor of the will of man, but of God" (Jn. 1:13). Said Paul, "I have planted, Apollos watered; but God gave the increase" (I Cor. 3:6). Said an aged Negro, in explaining his conversion, "I did my part, and God did His part: I did the sinning, and God did the saving!"

—W. B. K.

The Mexican Mayor's Surprise

When the new religious law of Mexico was promulgated, the mayor of a certain city in the state of Morelos undertook to suspend the services of the Methodist church, because they were held in a private house and not in a chapel. The Mexican Methodist pastor replied that that was the habitual place of meeting and that according to law it was therefore the church, and added, "The law requires the Mayor to keep watch of the places of worship, and as we are now in our meeting, and you are the Mayor, we invite you to come and see what we do and hear what we say." "Very well," said the Mayor, and he remained, with the result that he was so pleased with what he saw and heard that the next Sunday he brought his whole family and they were converted and baptized.

—*Sunday School Times*

* * *

Saved By Testing God

Some years ago there was a man called Tambring, who lived in a little town on the border between Holland and Germany. He worked in a spinning mill and was a socialist and an atheist.

One day his little niece fell ill. His sister, who wanted to fetch a doctor, asked Tambring to stay with the child. While she was tossing feverishly, the little one said, "Uncle, pray that I may get well again." He could not *pray*, "Uncle, pray!" the child begged. Much embarrassed, he tried to calm her, but in vain. "Uncle, if you don't pray I shall have to die." Then, strong man that he was, he fell down beside the little bed and cried, "O God, if there is a God, hear me and heal the child."

The little one smiled, and laid her head on the pillows. She fell asleep, and her breathing grew more regular. A profuse perspiration broke out, and when her mother returned some hours later with the doctor he said in astonishment, "The child is saved."

Tambring went quietly into his room and locked the door. He prayed again, and the God who heard his prayer for

119

the child likewise answered his cry for salvation. He came out of the room a new man.

—*Gospel Herald*

* * *

Nothing too Hard for God

"The conversion of Newt Harrison in a Salvation Army corps in Missouri," relates the late Henry F. Milans, "fairly shouts the truth that the power of Jesus is the same today as yesterday. People who knew Newt Harrison say that it was impossible to expect that such a life could ever be changed for the better. Rather, there was general speculation as to just how far down he would sink before death took him." Yet when the Harrison of this century, like Peter of old, "lifted his great hairy face to Heaven and in a loud, firm voice cried, 'O God, take me as I am. I don't know how to pray . . . have mercy on me and *save* me,' that very same Jesus touched his life and no one ever saw Newt Harrison drunk again."

—*Gospel Herald*

* * *

Robert Moffat's Conversion

When Robert Moffat, the great missionary was about twenty, he wrote this: "Living alone in an extensive garden, my leisure was my own. While poring over the Epistle to the Romans, I could not help wondering over a number of passages which I had read many times before. They appeared altogether different. I exclaimed with a heart nearly broken, 'Can it be possible that I have never understood what I have been reading?' turning from one passage to another, each sending light into my darkened soul. The Book of God seemed to be laid open, and I saw at once what God had done for the sinner. I felt that, being justified by faith, I had peace with God through the Lord Jesus Christ."

—*Selected*

* * *

"Oh, Thou Blessed Epilepsy!"

In their futile effort to explain away the FACT of Paul's conversion, unbelievers say that he had an epileptic

seizure. Observe Paul BEFORE the alleged seizure: a blasphemer, a murderous persecutor, "breathing out threatenings and slaughter against the disciples of the Lord" (Acts 9:1). Observe Paul AFTER the alleged seizure: an utterly transformed man, imbued with a deathless love for all mankind, especially Israel, his "kinsmen according to the flesh" (Rom. 9:3b), and for Christ for whom he "suffered the loss of ALL things!" (Phil. 3:8). If Paul had epilepsy, we can but say, "Sail on, O thou blessed epilepsy! All power to thee in thy character-ennobling, heart-transforming mission!"

—W. B. K.

* * *

The Conversion of George Whitefield

George Whitefield, the great preacher, was born in the county of Gloucester, England, on the 16th December, 1714. During his early years he was the subject of serious impressions, but according to his own account they were not sufficient to restrain the evil propensities of his nature. At the age of sixteen he says: "I began to fast twice in the week for nearly thirty-six hours together, prayed many times a day, received the sacrament every Lord's Day, fasting myself almost to death all the forty days of Lent, during which I did not go less than three times a day to public worship, besides seven times to private prayers, yet I knew no more that I needed to be born again, born a new creature in Christ Jesus, than if I never was born at all. Then by God's grace Charles Wesley put a book in my hand whereby God showed me that I must be 'born again' or damned."

This is a most extraordinary testimony, showing how far a man may go and not be saved. The words of the Lord Jesus are plain: "Except a man be born again, he cannot see the Kingdom of God" (*John* 3:3).

After his conversion to God Whitefield became an eloquent and powerful preacher of the Gospel. He is said to have preached over a thousand times from the text, "Ye must be born again," and to all kinds of audiences, from the very roughest to that of the highest and noblest in the land. The effect of his preaching was so remarkable that great audiences are described as being "drenched in tears." "How can I help weeping," he said to them, "when you have not wept for yourselves," and they began to weep.

A preacher sat in his study one night after returning from preaching, and began to question himself: "I have preached to others, but have I been converted myself? If so, where was I converted? When was I converted? How was I converted?" Reader, put these questions to yourself, and if you are honest you will soon discover your true state. —F. W. B., in
The Home Evangel

* * *

The Bishop and the Bowl

During the war of 1914-18, the Chaplain General to the Forces, Bishop Taylor Smith, had been visiting a military hospital. On his way out he passed a party of convalescents who were seated around a table on which his quick eyes spied a bowl turned upside down. He said to the men, "Do you know the two things inside that bowl? No? *Darkness and uselessness.*" Then he turned it the right way up. "Now," he aid, "it is full of light, and ready to hold porridge, or soup, or anything you like to use it for. It is a converted bowl. Which are you men like? The inverted, dark, useless bowl? or the converted, lighted, useful bowl, because you have turned from darkness to light, from Satan to God?"
—As heard in a sermon

* * *

The Tears Touched Him

It is grief over the unsaved that is often one of the most powerful elements in their salvation. A home missionary in a barracks offered a soldier a tract. The man tore it up in his face, and the missionary's eyes filled with tears. The soldier saw it. On the worker's next visit to the barracks the soldier came up to him and begged his pardon and asked for conversation. Nothing touched him but the tears.
—*Sunday School Times*

God's Great Leveler

At an evangelistic service conducted in London by Dr. G. Campbell Morgan, a hardened criminal came forward to the altar seeking salvation. Dr. Morgan knelt beside him and pointed him to Jesus the Lamb of God who could cleanse him from all his sins, and he who had been a great sinner believed and was converted. Then Dr. Morgan saw the Mayor of the city, a man of high morals and greatly respected, kneeling at the same altar, and to him, as to the criminal, he pointed out the Lamb of God who alone could take away sins. In humble self-surrender, the Mayor, too, accepted Jesus as his Saviour. A short time before this, the Mayor had sentenced the criminal to imprisonment; and there at the altar the two shook hands while tears of joy ran down their cheeks. For the worst of sinners and the best of moralists there is the same Saviour. In none other is there salvation, for "there is none other name under heaven given among men, whereby we must be saved."
—Dr. Campbell Morgan

* * *

He Was There When It Happened

I heard Mel Trotter tell how one time when in the Pacific Garden Mission in Chicago where the Lord Jesus found him, he was giving his testimony, a half-drunk fellow in the back of the hall yelled, "How do you know you are converted?" "Why, bless your dear heart, old fellow, I was right there when it all happened," was the prompt reply.
—Wm. H. Ridgway, in
Sunday School Times

* * *

Billy Sunday's Conversion:

"I walked down a street in Chicago in company with some ball players who were famous in this world . . . and we went into a saloon. It was Sunday afternoon and we got tanked up (no games were played on Sunday then) and then went and sat down on a corner. I never go by the street without thanking God for saving me. It was a vacant lot at that time. Across the street a company of men and women were playing on instruments — horns, flutes, and slide trombones — and the others were singing the gospel hymns that I used to hear my mother sing back in the log cabin in Iowa and back in the old church where I used to go to Sunday School.

"And God painted on the canvas of my recollection and memory a vivid picture of the scenes of other days and other faces.

"Many have long since turned to dust. I sobbed and sobbed and a young man stepped out and said, 'We are going down to the Pacific Garden Mission. Won't you come down to the mission?'

"I arose and said to the boys, 'I'm through. I am going to Jesus Christ. We've come to a parting of the ways,' and I turned my back on them. Some of them laughed and some of them mocked me; one of them gave me encouragement; others never said a word.

"I turned and left that little group on the corner of State and Madison Streets and walked to the little mission and fell on my knees and staggered out of sin and into the arms of the Saviour.

"The next day I had to get out to the ball park and practice. Every morning at 10 o'clock we had to be out there. I never slept that night. I was afraid of the horse-laugh that gang would give me because I had taken my stand for Jesus Christ.

"I walked down to the old ball grounds. I will never forget it. I slipped my key into the wicket gate and the first man to meet me after I got inside was Mike Kelly."

Mike Kelly was a Catholic, and Billy expected almost anything. "Billy," said Mike Kelly, "I've read in the papers what you've done. Religion isn't my long suit. It's a long time since I've been to mass. But I won't knock you, and if anyone does, I'll knock him."

As for the other players, Billy said: "Up came Anson, the best ball player that ever played the game; Pfeffer, Clarkson, Flint, Jimmy McCormick, Burns, Williamson and Dalrymple. There wasn't a fellow in that gang who knocked; every fellow had a word of encouragement for me." —*Power*

Sam Hadley's Conversion:

To his companions, Hadley said, 'Boys, listen to me! *I am dying*, but I will die in the street before I will ever take another *drink*' — and I felt as though this would happen before morning. A voice said to me, 'If you want to keep that promise, go and have yourself locked up.' There was no place on earth I dreaded more than a police station, for I was living in daily dread of arrest; but I went to the police station and asked the captain to lock me up. 'Why do you want to be locked up?' asked he, as I gave him an assumed name.

" 'Because,' said I, 'I want to be placed somewhere so I can die before I can get another drink of *whisky*.' They locked me up in a narrow cell, Number 10 in the back corridor. That has become a famous cell to me since. For twenty years I have visited that same cell on the anniversary of that *awful night of darkness*, and have had sweet communion there with *Jesus*.

"It seemed that all the demons that could find room came in that place with me that night. They were not all the company I had, either. No, praise the Lord, the dear Saviour who came to me in the saloon was present, and said, 'Pray.' I said, '*God be merciful to me a sinner.* ' "

Instantly, Hadley became a new creature in Christ Jesus!

—*Gospel Herald*

* * *

The Powerful Word

Father Chiniquy of St. Anne was very devout, but his soul was filled with unrest. Like Luther in his days as a monk, he had made strenuous efforts but he had no assurance of salvation. As Father Chiniquy read his Bible one Saturday night, he was converted and transformed as he read Romans 6:23. For hours he paced the room saying, "Accept the gift and love the Giver." The next morning he told his congregation of his spiritual dissatisfaction and of his conversion, and urged them also to "accept the gift and love the Giver."

Many of them did so and joined him in establishing a Protestant church.

—Rev. Eugene M. Harrison, in
Moody Monthly

* * *

Conversion: What? How? When? Where?

A parishioner asked his pastor to preach on the text, "Except ye be converted, and become as little children, ye shall not enter into the kingdom of heaven." The pastor readily consented. He thought, "Let me see, how will I divide it? Conversion: What? Conversion: How? Conversion: When? Conversion: Where? He thought cf conversion — what? Well, conversion must be the turning of the heart to God, and he elaborated on that. And then he came to conversion — how? How is a man converted? A little perplexed, he thought, "Well, let me see, how was I converted? Why, I don't know. I think I'll pass over that just now." He came to the next point: Conversion — when? "Well, one may be converted as a child; as a youth; or, one may be converted in mature years." But then the thought came constantly to him, "WHEN WAS

I CONVERTED? Was I converted when I was a child? I can't ever remember. Well, was I converted when I was a youth? No, I am sure I was not, for I got far away from God out in the world. No, not as a youth. Was I converted when I came to more mature years? I do not recall." And so he passed on to the next point: Conversion — where? It might take place in the home, in the church, or in the Sunday School, or out in the open. God is ready to meet men wherever they may be. Then the thought came to him, "Where did it take place with ME? Was I converted at home? Was I converted in church? Have I ever been converted?" Suddenly, it came to him with tremendous power, "I am preaching to other people, and I have never been converted myself. I don't know when I was converted. I don't know how I was converted. I don't know where I was converted. I HAVE NEVER BEEN CONVERTED AT ALL!" He preached his own sermon to himself, and got on his knees and told the Lord Jesus that he would trust Him as his Saviour. That was the beginning of a new life, and a NEW MINISTRY!

—Dr. Harry A. Ironside

COOPERATION

In Asylum Because Couldn't Get Heads Together!

A visitor to an institution for the mentally sick was astounded to observe one lone man guarding some hundred inmates. He was armed only with a small stick. Asked the visitor, "Are you not afraid that these insane people will get their heads together and plan to attack you?" "Ah," replied the guard, "these people are here because of their inability to get their heads together, and work cooperatively!" We do not know whether a psychiatrist would agree with the guard. The story, however, is most suggestive.

—W. B. K.

* * *

"Who Flies the Kite?"

A preacher talked to the children about making and flying kites. He

quoted some lines about kite-flying. Here they are:

Who flies the kite?
"I," said the boy; "it is my joy;
I fly the kite."

Who flies the kite?
"I," said the wind; "it is my whim,
I fly the kite."

Who flies the kite?
"I," said the string, "I am the thing
That flies the kite."

Who flies the kite?
"I," said the tail, "I make it sail;
I fly the kite."

Who flies the kite?
All are wrong; all are right;
All fly the kite.

Now, belonging to a church or Sunday school is like that. Paul says the church is like a body, with hands and feet, and

123

eyes and ears and nose, and it takes every one of these parts, and more, to make a body. In the church there are apostles and prophets and evangelists and pastors and teachers, and there is *you*. Jesus needs every one of us to do His work, and each must play his part. Don't forget — all fly the kite.

—G. Osborn Gregory,
in the *Methodist Recorder*.

* * *

'We're Acting Like Human Fools!"

"Two tough old mules said, 'Get this dope,
We're tied together with a piece of rope'.
Said one to the other, 'You come MY way,
While I take a nibble of that new-mown hay'.

'I won't,' said the other, 'You come with ME,
I have some hay over this way, you see'.
So they got nowhere, just pawed up the dirt,
Pulling each way, how that rope did hurt!

Then faced they about, those stubborn mules,
And said, 'We're acting just like human fools,
Let's pull together, I'll go your way,
Then you come with me, and we'll both eat hay'.

So they ate their hay, and liked it, too,
And said, 'Let's be comrades, good and true'.
As the sun went down they were heard to bray,
'Ah, this is the end of a perfect day' "

—*Selected*

* * *

Persistence Won Him

I once made my way into the office of a doctor to ask him to come to Christ. The meetings were in progress in the church, and I thought he was interested.

He received me kindly, but firmly declined even to talk of Christ, and, utterly discouraged, I left him. The next night this man gave his heart to Christ, and for this reason, I believe: We had made him, in a little company of church officers, a subject of prayer; and you cannot pray earnestly for one for any length of time without speaking to him concerning his salvation. Without having had any conference, four men determined to see the doctor, and they all called upon him within two hours' time. When the first came the doctor laughed at him; when the second came, his prominence, in the business world at least commanded the doctor's respect. When the third came, having driven four miles in from the country, he began to be interested; and with the coming of the fourth there was awakened in him a deep conviction. He closed his office, went to his home, and before the evening hour of the service came he had accepted Christ.

—J. Wilbur Chapman

* * *

Toilers with God

God can grow trees, and lift mountains, and fill space with singing stars, and people the earth with bright-eyed babies, and stretch the seas from continent to continent, and weigh the nations as dust in the balance, and fill the earth with His glory; but He has so aranged things that He needs our help in the salvation of a lost world, in comforting a broken heart, in making the desert place blossom as the rose for those out of whose lives the light has gone and into whose lives the night has come. Let us help God with His work.

—*Selected*

* * *

Making A Garden

"Man plows and plants, and digs and weeds,
He works with hoe and spade;
God sends the sun and rain and air —
And thus a garden's made.

"He must rejoice who tills the soil,
And turns the heavy sod,
How wonderful a thing to be
In partnership with God!"

—*Selected*

COURAGE

Some Are Watching You, Too

In a large office where are several young Christians, there is among them one young woman whose earnest Christian life is noted and felt. The date for the annual office "at-home" was drawing near, and this young woman was asked to help arrange the banquet. She said, "I'm sorry; it isn't possible for me to do that, as there's to be drink served this year." The office manager was quite offended, but this fine girl held out, and answered, "Mr. L........, I dare not do it. Some of the young people in this office are watching me, and will follow my lead; also my Master expects I do nothing that will cause anyone to stumble."
—As told to Mrs. J. Shields, Toronto

* * *

"I Am Attacking!"

We are told that just before the first battle of the Marne in the first World War, Marshal Foch, the great French General, reported: "My centre is giving; my left wing is retreating; the situation is excellent; I am attacking!" This was not mere military bombast, for the Marshal realized that apparent defeat could be turned into victory by acting with resolution and alacrity at the very moment when the enemy seemed to be triumphant.
—Dr. Harry A. Ironside

* * *

Show Your Colors

Some years ago a follower of the Lord Jesus Christ was riding in a railway carriage, when two men entered the car and took the seat in front of him. One of them took a bottle out of his pocket, drank of its contents, and passed it over to his companion. This was repeated a number of times. By and by the men began to swear — a very torrent of profanity issued from their mouths. Meanwhile the Christian held a little conversation with himself somewhat after this fashion.

"Henry, that man belongs to the devil."
"There is no doubt of that."
"He is not ashamed of it."
"Not a bit ashamed."
"Whom do you belong to?"
"I belong to the Lord Jesus Christ."
"Are you glad or sorry?"
"I am glad — very glad."
"Who in the car knows that man belongs to the devil?"
"Why, everybody knows that, for he has not kept it a secret."
"Who in the car knows you belong to the Lord Jesus Christ?"
"Why, no one knows it, for you see I am a stranger around here."
"Are you willing they should know whom you belong to?"
"Yes, I am willing."
"Very well, will you let them know it?"
The Christian took a good breath and began to sing.

"There is a fountain filled with blood
Drawn from Immanuel's veins;
And sinners, plunged beneath that
flood,
Lose all their guilty stains."

The singer had not concluded with the verse when the blasphemer turned around and looked at him with a face resembling a thunder cloud. The following conversation ensued:
"What are you doing?"
"I am singing."
"Well, any fool can understand that."
"I am glad you understand it."
"What are you singing?"
"I am singing the religion of the Lord Jesus."
"Well, you quit."
"Quit what?"
"Quit singing your religion on the cars."
"I guess not," said the Christian, "I don't belong to the Quit family; my name is Mead. For the last half hour you have been standing by your master; now for the next half hour I am going to stand up for my Master."
"Who is my master?"
"The devil is your master — while Christ is mine. I am as proud of my Master as you are of yours. Now I am going to have my turn, if the passengers have no objection."
A chorus of voices encouraged him with: "Sing on, stranger, we like that." Song after song followed, and the Christian had won the day. —*Gospel Herald*

"Won't You Recant?"

When I was in Scotland I went a long way out of my path to visit the city of Sterling. Having only a short time to stay, I went at once to the spot I sought — the old cemetery — and I gazed upon that monument. Looking back through the mist of years, it brought to my mind the story of the Covenanters. It was the monument of Margaret Wilson. It told how that dear young saint, that girl in her teens, held so to her love of Jesus that the pleadings of father and mother and friends kept her not back from death.

"Only one little word, Margaret, one little word, and your life will be spared," they said. "I cannot speak the word that shall dishonor Jesus," she replied. "Remember your father's grief," he begged, the night before she died. She stroked his gray hairs, and said, "I cannot speak the words you bid me speak." And then the next morning they took her out, those rude men, and tied her to a stake and put it into the sea. And they tied another to the stake, a gray-haired old saint, and they put her a little farther out in the wild sea, so that Margaret could first see her die. And they said, "Margaret Wilson, if you speak that word you shall be free." And then they left her to the billows of the rising sea.

Nearer and nearer they came to the aged martyr; they reached her waist, they reached her shoulders, they swept her face, but she stood there with her countenance lifted to Heaven. And they said, "Margaret Wilson, don't you see her? Won't you still recant?" And she said, "No; I do not see her: I only see Jesus Christ in His suffering servant wrestling there"; and as she lifted her eyes the chariot of the Lord was waiting to bear the martyr home.

—A. B. Simpson

* * *

Lincoln's Business

One day a stranger called to secure Lincoln's services. "State your case," said Lincoln. A history of the case was given, when Lincoln astonished him by saying, "I cannot serve you, for you are wrong, and the other party is right." "That is none of your business, if I hire and pay you for taking the case," said the man. "Not my business!" exclaimed Lincoln. "My business is never to defend wrong. I never take a case that is manifestly wrong." "Not for any amount of pay?" said the stranger. "Not for all you are worth," replied Lincoln.

—*Christian Herald*

* * *

Tell Me Thy Secret

How we spiritually face life determines, in a marked way, what life will bring us. We must decide to make the best of harsh realities.

There are two interesting memorials in Edinburgh. One is a statue of Livingstone. Looking at it, one is reminded that when the odds were all against him, Livingstone kept noble and strong, brave and true. And then there is that remarkable memorial to Walter Scott. Facing the very difficulties that he had planned to avoid, Scott, nevertheless, did not lose heart. He was of good cheer. What a great soul he was!

There is nothing more important for us than to face life as Christ faced it. But we can do this only when we have the same divine spirit that swept Him to victory — even on Calvary! He really knew how to face life, and we are able to meet it in the same way when He possesses our very souls.

Tell me thy secret; help me bear
The strain of toil, the fret of care,
In hope that sends a shining ray
Far down the future's broadening
*   way;*
In peace that only Thou canst give,
With Thee, O Master, let me live.
        —*Christian Digest*

* * *

One Thing Christianity Did

Shortly after Ingersoll, the noted infidel, was defeated in his race for governorship of Illinois, he was one day proclaiming his infidelity on board a railroad train between Chicago and Peoria. After being for some time offensively voluble, he turned to a gentleman near him, and defiantly demanded, "Tell me one great result that Christianity has ever accomplished." The gentleman, not wishing to open an argument with the boaster, hesitated to answer. The train had stopped and all was silent in the car. Just then an old lady of eighty who sat just behind the infidel touched his arm with trembling hand, and said, "Sir, I do not know who you are, but I think I can tell you of one great and glorious thing which Christianity has done." "What is it, Madam?" asked Ingersoll. "It has kept Robert G. Ingersoll from being governor of the State of Illinois." If a stroke of lightning had flashed through the car the effect could not have been more marked. Ingersoll turned literally pale with rage, and remained silent.

—*Sunday School Times*

* * *

A Boy's Example

Our pastor, Dr. Harold Purdy, said that some years ago he heard a peacher tell over the radio of an experience he had on a Pullman. He was talking with two businessmen when a young boy got on the train. His parents were with him, but they kissed him good-by and left him, and they guessed that the boy was going away to school. One could tell that the boy was not accustomed to traveling on a Pullman, but he watched the other passengers and when he saw them push a button and get the porter, he pushed his button and asked the porter to make down his berth. After the berth was ready, the boy took down his suitcase and took out a Bible. He sat on the edge of his berth and read from the Bible. His face was a bit red as he saw so many eyes fastened upon him, but he knelt beside his berth in prayer before he retired. One of the businessmen remarked to the preacher that it had been a long time since he had seen anything like that, in fact, not since he had seen his own mother kneel in prayer. He admitted that he had drifted from her teaching, and asked the preacher to help him back into the right way. The preacher said he was able to lead both of those businessmen to the Lord, then added that he was not the one who had done this; but that boy who was not ashamed to kneel in prayer there on the train had really led them to Christ.

—As told by Dr. Harold J. Purdy

* * *

Have Courage, My Boy, to Say "No"

You're starting, my boy, on life's journey
    Along the grand highway of life;
You'll meet with a thousand temptations
    Each city with evil is rife;

This world is a stage of exitement —
    There's danger wherever you go;
But if you are tempted in weakness,
    Have courage, my boy, to say, "No."

The bright, ruby wine may be offered —
    No matter how tempting it be,
From poison it stings like an adder:
    My boy, have the courage to flee.
The billiard saloons are inviting,
    Decked out in their tinsel and show;
But if you are tempted to enter,
    Have courage, my boy, to say, "No."

In courage alone lies your safety,
    When you the long journey begin;
Your trust in the Heavenly Father
    Will keep you unspotted from sin.
Temptations will keep on increasing,
    As streams from a rivulet flow;
But if you'd be true to your manhood,
    Have courage, my boy, to say, "No."
    —*Selected*

* * *

Good Timber

The tree that never had to fight
For sun and sky and air and light,
That stood out in the open plain
And always got its share of rain,
Never became a forest king,
But lived and died a common thing.
The man who never had to toil,
Who never had to win his share
Of sun and sky and light and air,
Never became a manly man,
But lived and died as he began.

Good timber does not grow on ease
The stronger wind, the tougher trees,
The farther sky, the greater length,
By sun and cold, by rain and snows,
In tree or man good timber grows.
Where thickest stands the forest growth,
We find the patriarchs of both,
And they hold converse with the stars
Whose broken branches show the scars
Of many winds and much of strife,
This is the common law of life.
    —Douglas Malloch, in
        The Wesleyan Methodist

* * *

Courage

"Little crosses bravely carried,
    Little duties daily done,
To the heart of God are precious,
    And He counts them one by one.

Little things that fret and worry,
   Little slights that hurt and pain,
Humbly borne without a murmur
Turn at length to golden grain —
Into crowns of priceless worth,
   For the souls who loved and served
      Him
Here on earth."
                         —*Selected*

* * *

"Fight On!"

"It matters not how deep entrenched
   the wrong,
How hard the battle goes, the day, how
   long;
Faint not, fight on! Tomorrow comes
   the song."
                    —Maltbie D. Babcock

* * *

"He Kept Climbing!"

Charles P. Steinmetz, who rivaled
Thomas A. Edison in his discoveries and
inventions in the field of electrical engi-
neering, was terribly deformed. He
did most of his work half standing, half
leaning upon a stool. However, he did
not allow his handicap to embitter or
discourage him. He knew he would have
to fight his way. There was no personal
popularity, no pleasant social contacts
to speed him along. He tortured his
brain into headaches and his eyes into
burning balls of pain. Time after time
he was defeated and undone, but Steinmetz kept climbing until he became the
greatest electrical wizard of his time.
                         —*Selected*

* * *

The Real Rebel Was Caught

During what was known as the killing
times in Scotland, John Welsh was
chased unrelentingly. He hardly knew
where to flee; but relying on Scottish
hospitality he knocked one night at the
door of a landlord bitterly opposed to
the field preachers, and to himself in
particular, although he had never actually set eyes on him.

The stranger, being unrecognized, was
received with kindness. In the evening's
talk reference was made to Welsh, and
the host complained of the difficulty of
capturing him.

"I am sent," the visitor said; "to
apprehend rebels. I know where he is
to preach tomorrow. I will put his
hand into yours."

Overjoyed, the gentleman agreed to
accompany his informant next morning.
When they arrived at the appointed
spot, the congregation had assembled.
The people made way for the minister,
whom they trusted, and for his comrade.

Welsh desired his entertainer to sit
down on the solitary chair which had
been provided for himself, and, to his
companion's utter bewilderment, took
his own stand beside it, and rang out
the story of sin and salvation. The
Spirit of God was there, and the landlord was heartbroken. When at the
close, Welsh, fulfilling his promise, gave
him his hand, that he might do with
him whatever he wished, the landlord
said:

"You told me that you were sent to
apprehend rebels; and I, a rebellious
sinner, have been apprehended this day."
                    —*Men of the Covenant*

* * *

True to His Promise

The new errand boy was sent out by
the proprietor of a store to deliver a suit
of clothes. When he reached the place
of delivery he found it was a saloon.
He asked a man to tell the proprietor to
come outside to get his package. The
saloonkeeper was angry and telephoned
his indignation to the clothing store.
Upon his return the boy was threatened
with the loss of his job if he ever disobeyed orders again. "Job or no job,"
replied the lad, "I won't go into such a
place. I promised my mother that I
would never go into a saloon; and I
won't." The time came when that boy
owned that same clothing store.
                       —*Free Methodist*

* * *

They All Voted To Die

In the days of war the Japanese policeman who had absolute power said that
within three days everyone in a certain
Formosan mountain village must come
to the police station and swear that he

would not be a Christian, or he would be tied hand and foot, and stones tied to him, and he would be thrown from the high bridge into the rushing river below. The Christians met at midnight to decide what to do. Some said, "We'll have to give it up. We cannot be Christians now. He will surely kill us." Then a young boy arose. "But don't you remember that Jesus said not to be afraid of those who can only kill the body, but to be afraid of those who kill body and soul? If he kills us, it will only be our bodies — our souls will go to be with Jesus." They all said, "That's true." When the vote was taken, every hand was raised — all voted to die. Next day the policeman laughed cruelly, and said, "Tomorrow you die." Now the policeman liked to fish, and waded out into the river. A rock or tree in the current struck his leg and broke it. While the mountain people were praying, a messenger rushed in, and said, "The man who was to kill you tomorrow has been drowned in the river."

—Abridged from *Child Evangelism*

* * *

A Pastor's Courage

A minister was asked to perform a wedding ceremony in a wealthy home. The members of the family seldom attended any church. After the ceremony the minister was asked to propose a toast at the reception. "What do you use?" asked the minister. "Oh, we can get ginger ale for you," replied the bride's father, somewhat irritably. "But what will the others drink?" persisted the minister. "Oh!" came the impatient reply, "don't think you'll start anyone here on a drinking career. They all take their drinks." "I'm sorry," said the minister, "but I have just asked God's blessing on your daughter's marriage, and I cannot conscientiously propose a toast with the use of liquor since it is the greatest enemy of the home I know. If you'll get my hat and coat I'll be excused." It took courage and conviction to take that stand. But listen to the sequel. A few weeks later the bride's father sent a check for one hundred dollars to the church served by this earnest minister, and a year later he asked the same man to officiate at the marriage of a second daughter. He did so, and this time proposed a toast to the bride in ginger ale, and all the guests were provided with the same!

—Rev. J. E. Harris, in
The Sunday School Times

* * *

Prayer Before Turning In!

A Christian man went to camp and was placed in a tent with two or three other men who were not Christians. He wanted to be true to Jesus, and he asked the preacher to pray that he would not be ashamed of Jesus before the rough, ungodly men in his tent. On reaching his tent that night, the man said: "Friends, I am a Christian, and as such, I am, of course, going to pray before I turn in." Not a word was said, and our man dropped on his knees and began to pray. Instead of praying silently, he prayed aloud. Nothing happened until the next night, when, on returning to the sleeping quarters, our man was greeted with these words, from one of the un-Christian men, "Matey, we have been waiting for you to come. We want you to pray again tonight; and we want you to pray for us, before we turn in." This man was not ashamed of Jesus, and he was used of God to lead his tent-mates to the Saviour. May you, boys and girls, always confess Jesus before your little friends and playmates, and may you never be ashamed of Him.

—*Gospel Herald*

* * *

"Everything Gone?"

Dr. John Watson once called on a man of his church who had suffered great financial reverses. The man was utterly broken.

"Everything is gone," he said.

"What!" said his pastor, "I'm sorry to hear your wife is dead."

The man looked up in surprise. "My wife?" he queried.

"And I'm doubly grieved to hear you have lost your character," said Watson, and went on remorsefully naming one thing after another, till at last the man protested that all these things still remained. "But I thought you said you lost everything? Man, you have lost none of the things which are worth while."

—*Sunday School Times*

* * *

"Here I Stand!"

When Luther was called before the Diet of Worms and his enemies demanded that he recant his writings, the reformer boldly declared, "Unless I am convinced by Scripture or by right reason, for I trust neither in popes nor in councils since they have often erred and contradicted themselves — unless I am thus convinced, I am bound by the texts of my Bible, my conscience is captive to the Word of God, I neither can nor will recant anything, since it is neither right nor safe to act against conscience. Here I stand! I can do no other! God help me. Amen!"

—*Moody Monthly*

* * *

A Moro's Steadfastness

Kailing was a young Moro of the Sulu Archipelago who came to Jolo for his high school education, and, hearing the story of the cross, he was preciously saved. After he was publicly baptized he became even more devoted to Him who died on the cross. His family tried in vain to dissuade him from following the Christian life. One evening Kailing's brothers broke into his room and, with poised knives, said, "Kailing, if you don't recant we will kill you!" Looking steadfastly into his brothers' faces, Kailing replied: "Brothers, kill me if you must. I cannot deny Christ." God miraculously intervened, and the brothers departed without further word or action.

—*Alliance Weekly*

* * *

How Much Do You Suffer for Him?

He came walking up the aisle on little fat, brown legs, with serious determination in his eyes. I stopped speaking and the congregation was quiet as death. "You asked me what I would have done if I had been in the crowd when Jesus fell under the weight of His cross." He looked earnestly up at me. "Please, sir, I would have helped carry it." He was a Mexican lad eight years of age. His father was a miner and his mother was an outcast from decent society. I had been preaching on Simon of Cyrene; and when I asked the audience to determine in their own hearts their reaction to that scene, little Pedro moved toward me. . . . I lifted my arm and cried: "Yes, and if you had helped Him to carry His cross, the cruel Roman soldiers would have beaten down across your back with their whips until the blood ran down to your heels!" . . . He never flinched. Meeting my look with one of cool courage, he gritted through clenched teeth: "I don't care. I would have helped Him carry it just the same." Two weeks later, at the close of the service in the same building, I stood at the door, greeting people as they left. When Pedro came by, I patted him affectionately on the back. He shrank from me with a little cry. "Don't do that. My back is sore." I stood in astonishment. I had barely touched his shoulders. I took him into the cloak room and stripped his shirt from his body. Crisscrosed from his neck to his waist were ugly, bloody welts. "Who did that?" I cried in anger. "Mother did it. She whipped me because I came to church."

—Harold Dye, in
the Teacher, S.B.C.

* * *

They Fell Facing Enemy

After a bloody battle in World War I, won at terrific cost of life, a General walked over the field of carnage. The field was widely bestrewn with American dead. It was observed, however, that the heroic dead fell with their faces toward the enemy! What a lesson for God's children in this hour of cowardly compromise of the eternal verities of God's Word, whelming apostasy, and blatant denials of the only Lord God! May each soldier of the Cross face forward, marching triumphantly 'neath the all-conquering banner of the Captain, or "File-Leader" of our salvation! When we fall in death, should the Lord delay His coming, may our faces, with flint-like steadfastness, be toward the enemy!

—W.B.K.

* * *

What If He Had Kept Silent?

James Haldane, when a young man, commanded the man of war, the *Melville Castle*. In a fierce battle with an enemy ship, he ordered new men on deck to take the place of those who had been killed or wounded. The men, seeing the mangled bloody bodies of their comrades, fell back in horror. Captain Haldane began to swear frightfully and wished them all in hell. At the close of the fight a Christian soldier stepped up and said respectfully to the young captain, "Sir, if God had answered your prayer just now where should we have been?" This faithful word of rebuke went home to the conscience of Haldane. It led to his sound conversion. He abandoned his career in the Navy and became a preacher of the Gospel and labored for fifty-four years. But this was not all: James led his brother Robert to Christ who also became a preacher and an able commentator of the Bible. Nor was this all. Robert Haldane was the means of the conversion of Felix Neff a philanthropic Swiss preacher and leader of Protestantism. What if that Christian soldier had remained silent instead of rebuking Captain Haldane?
—*Triumphs of Faith*

* * *

God Hears You

A man working in the baggage room of a large railroad station dropped a heavy parcel on his foot and began to curse. A little girl, standing at the doorway of the room, called to him: "Please, mister, don't talk that way. Don't you know that God hears you?"

Her words gripped the man and convicted him of his sinfulness. Throughout the balance of the day, and through the night, her question plagued him. "Don't you know that God hears you?" Again and again these words rang in his ears. It was the turning point in his life.

Within a few days this man cried out to God in faith and was converted. The witness of a little child convicted him of his need and he found the way of life through the Gospel which he had often heard but had never heeded until this time.
—*The Pilgrim*

* * *

Higher Orders

In Formosa, an aboriginal woman was wonderfully saved. She studied the Bible a little while, then she went back up in the hills to preach the Gospel of the Lord Jesus. The Japanese police said: "You cannot preach. If you preach you will be thrown into prison." But she said, "I have higher orders." They said, "Never mind; if we catch you, you will be thrown into prison." She said, "You won't catch me." She traveled by night up into those native, aboriginal wild villages. Then the evening of the second night she sent her runners to gather in the people, arriving back in her village at one o'clock in the morning, and from one to three they studied the Word of God by tallow candle light. Then at three o'clock while it was yet dark they would go back so that when day dawned and the Japanese police checked, everybody would be doing his work in the field. As a result, when missionary Jim Dickson returned to Formosa, he found several thousand aboriginal people had turned to Christ, and the work has been carried through, and today over 150,000 of those people have turned to Jesus Christ — one of the mightiest harvests of this generation.
—Rev. Dick Hillis, in the *Sword of the Lord*

* * *

Greater Than Thou

Frederick the Great was a scoffer, but his great general, Von Zealand, was a Christian. One day at a gathering, the king was making coarse jokes about Jesus Christ and the whole place was ringing with guffaws.

Von Zealand arose stiffly and said, "Sire, you know I have not feared death. I have fought and won 38 battles for you. I am an old man; I shall soon have to go into the presence of One Greater than thou, the mighty God who saved me from my sin, the Lord Jesus Christ whom you are blaspheming against. I salute thee, sire, as an old man, who loves his Savior, on the edge of eternity."

With trembling voice, Frederick replied: "General Von Zealand, I beg your pardon. I beg your pardon!"

The company silently dispersed.
—*Sunday*

* * *

God Cares for His Own

"Mr. Shauffler," said the Russian Ambassador to the old-time missionary in Constantinople, "I will say to you frankly that my master, the Czar of all the Russias, will never suffer Christian missions to set their feet in the Turkish Empire." The old missionary looked at him for a moment, and then replied, "Your Excellency, my Master, the Lord Jesus Christ, will never ask the Czar of all the Russias where He may set His feet." And he went on with his mission unintimidated by any agencies working in the dark against him. He was confident that the living God whose he was and whom he served would care for His own work.
—*Choice Gleanings Calendar*

* * *

A Lad's Courage To Say "No"

A young Italian lad, who had gone far in the ways of sin, was converted. He turned rightabout-face. A Chautauqua came to town. He purchased a ticket. A magician furnished the entertainment one evening. He needed a helper, and the lad volunteered. Presently the magician produced a deck of cards and asked the lad to cut the deck. He said, "No, I will not touch them; never again." "Oh," said the magician, "they will not hurt you. I am not asking you to play cards, bet, or anything like that. Use your head. Don't be a fool. I cannot do this trick if you do not co-operate." There they stood before a large audience. The elite of the town was there. What would you have done under the circumstances? The lad said: "No, I will not touch those cards. They almost ruined my life." The magician threw

up his hands, and the audience burst out in prolonged applause. Do you have the courage to say no?
—*Christian Union Herald*

* * *

It's Best to Take A Stand!

During the Civil War, it is said that there was a man who was sympathetic to both sides. He lived, you see, in a border-line state. Finally, he decided that he would effect a compromise. He put on a mixed uniform, wearing the Confederate gray coat, and the Union blue trousers.

All went well, it seems, until he became engaged in a hard-fought battle, when the Federals shot him in the coat, and the Confederates shot him in the trousers! Now, here's the moral of this highly improbable story: It's best not to compromise. It's best to "stand up and be counted!"
—W.B.K.

* * *

A Disconcerting Question

A story that carries its own application to Christian faithfulness has been told of a question and anwer that passed between Martin Niemoeller and a chaplain who visited him in his detention: "Why are you here?" asked the chaplain. "Why are you not here?" asked Dr. Niemoeller.
—*Christian Faith and Life*

* * *

In But Not Out

I remember when I was a little boy, how my mother would draw me to her knee and speak to me so solemnly of the importance of trusting the Lord Jesus Christ as my Saviour, and I would say, "Well, Mamma, I would like to do it, but the boys will all laugh at me."

Mother used to say, "Harry, remember, they may laugh you into hell, but they can never laugh you out of it." And oh, how that used to go home to me, and it stayed with me all through the years! Yes, men may sneer and ridicule and not understand us as we come out for Christ, but after all, His is the only approval worth having.
—Dr. Harry A. Ironside

"The Unexpected!"

"I know not what may come to-day,
Some needy soul may cross my way;
Lord, give me words of cheer, I pray,
    To meet the unexpected.

"Perhaps some loss may come to me,
Some care, or some perplexity,
Then He my strength and stay shall be
    To face the unexpected.

"How oft within the trivial round
So many trying things are found;
But He can make all grace abound
    For all the unexpected.

"No matter what the call may be,
Or changes that may come to me;
His Hand of love in all I see
    From sources unexpected."
                                    —Selected

* * *

Bad Reading — but Good Theology

A speaker recalled a story of Spurgeon's concerning a class of boys who were having a Scripture lesson on Daniel. One of the boys was asked to read some verses aloud, and presently he came to verse 3 in chapter 6, which reads, " . . . because an excellent spirit was in him," but by mistake the boy rendered it, " . . . because an excellent *spine* was in him." It was undoubtedly bad reading, but it was excellent theology, for Daniel was a man of real backbone — strong, courageous.
                                    —*Moody Monthly*

* * *

A Scottish Covenanter's Reply

John Ross . . . was summoned before the king for preaching a sermon in which he said that the king was a traitor to God for taking the part of the wicked. The king asked him, "Will ye stand and bide by all that you have spoken?" and Ross replied, "The heart thought it; the mouth spake it; the hand subscribed it; and if need be, by God's grace, the blood shall seal it."
                        —Stephen E. Slocum, Ph.D., in
                            Sunday School Times

* * *

The Missing Note

C. T. Studd once wrote: "Heroism is the lost chord, the missing note of present-day Christianity. Had we the pluck and heroism of the flyers, or the men who volunteered for the North or South Polar expeditions, or for the Great War, or for any ordinary daredevil enterprise, we could have every soul on earth knowing the name and salvation of Jesus Christ in less than ten years."
                                    —*Moody Monthly*

COVETOUSNESS

"He Left Everything!"

Is covetousness a disease? We believe it is. It is a disease of the soul which stultifies every noble impulse, shrivels the soul, and whelms it, at last, 'neath the bleak, black waters of defeat and despair. One day I had the funeral of an aged man who lived in squalor and in aloofness from his brother man. His clothes were tattered and torn. He lived on public relief. His clutching, covetous spirit hardened into hatred for mankind. He died, as he had lived, without friends and without God. There was not a flower or a mourner at his funeral. Now we come to the crux of our story: Among his personal belongings, ten thousand dollars were discovered, which will go to the state, along with some twenty additional thousands of dollars which this miser had hoarded!

"That man may breathe, but never live,
Who much receives, but nothing gives;
Whom none can love, whom none can
    thank,
Creation's blot, creation's blank!"
                                    —W. B. K.

* * *

The Whole World Has the Same Trouble

A story is told of Abraham Lincoln, the great President. A Springfield

133

neighbor was drawn to his door one day by the crying of children. When he got there, he saw Lincoln passing by with his two sons, both crying lustily. "What is the matter with the boys?" asked the man. "Just what is the matter with the whole world!" answered Lincoln. "I have three walnuts and each boy wants two." Surely this spirit is abroad still today. We all need to learn more earnestly that covetousness and greed are sins that bring only trouble and pain.

—*Christian Herald* (*London*)

* * *

When Military Despots Spoke the Truth

Once when Frederick the Great was about to declare war, he instructed his secretary to write the proclamation. The secretary began: "Whereas in the providence of God," etc., etc. "Stop that lying," Frederick thundered; "simply say, 'Frederick wants more land.' "

—*Earnest Worker*

* * *

Holding It for Life's Short Day

"The wealthy owner of a large business in Sweden had been a poor boy. His task had been the tending of cattle. One day he wanted to be away and asked his sister to tend the cattle, promising to let her hold for the day a small coin, worth less than two annas, to be returned at night. She consented. The very sight of money was a rarity. She spent a long, hard day caring for his cattle, holding the bright coin, and returned it at night, quite content with the day's pay. Later the brother, who had grown very wealthy, was telling the story. He had allowed the love of money to crowd out the Christ passion, to which he was not a stranger. He told the story with great glee, laughing at his sister's simplicity. My friend said quietly, 'That is all you get; you hold your wealth to the end of the day of your life; then you give it up and have as little as before, and the whole of your life is gone!' And the man's startled face showed he quite understood."

—*King's Business*

Seeing Only Self

One day a certain old, miserly, rich man visited a rabbi, who took him by the hand and led him to a window. "Look out there," he said. And the rich man looked out into the street. "What do you see?" asked the rabbi. "I see men, and women, and little children," answered the rich man. Again the rabbi took him by the hand, and led him to a mirror. "What do you see now?" "Now I see myself," the rich man replied. Then the rabbi said, "Behold, in the window there is glass. But the glass of the mirror is covered with silver, and no sooner is the silver added than you fail to see others, but see only yourself."   —*Dawn*

* * *

The Old Nature Must Go

A stingy Christian was listening to a charity sermon. He was nearly deaf, and was accustomed to sit facing the congregation, right under the pulpit, with his ear trumpet directed upward, toward the preacher. The sermon moved him considerably. At one time he said to himself, "I'll give ten dollars;" again he said, "I'll give fifteen." At the close of the appeal, he was very much moved, and thought he would give fifty dollars. As they passed the collection plates along, his charity began to ooze out. He came down from fifty to twenty, to ten, to five, to zero. He concluded that he would not give anything. "Yet," said he, "this won't do — I am in a bad fix. This covetousness will be my ruin." The plate was getting nearer and nearer. The crisis was upon him! What should he do? The plate was now under his chin — all the congregation were looking. He had been holding his pocketbook in his hand during this soliloquy, which was half audible, though, in his deafness, he did not know that he was heard. In the agony of the final moment, he took his pocketbook and laid it in the plate, saying to himself as he did it, "Now squirm, old natur'!" This was victory beyond any that Alexander ever won — a victory over himself. Here is a key to the problem of covetousness. The old natur' must go under.   —*Moody Monthly*

**Ragged Peddler Dead
With $61,000 Hoard in House!**

How soul-shrivelling is the sin of COVETOUSNESS! How ugly is grasping greed, clutching covetousness. It is a sin which tightens its grasp upon its victims with the passing of the years. Too few, alas, heed the warning words of the Saviour: "Take heed and beware of covetousness" (Luke 12:15a). An Associated Press dispatch from Hutchinson, Kansas, gave to the world the following story:

A ragged peddler who told a friend he didn't have $5 to pay a debt, was found dead the next morning in his apartment here amongst littered filth — and $61,000 in bonds and currency. The man, Ramond Mishler, 48, died of malnutrition. Police and executors today confirmed a report that the money had been found in a cluttered old store building which had been converted into two dwelling units.

Detective Ed May, who went to investigate when Mishler's body was discovered, noticed a piece of paper sticking in a door sill. It was a $1,000 government bond. May and Patrolman Bob Adams then found $40,000 in bonds in a dresser drawer and $3,000 in currency, nearly all of it old, large size bills, in tobacco cans and a trunk. Also found were passbooks from three banks showing deposits of $8,890 and papers showing he had several thousand dollars in postal savings and in savings and loan deposits.

—W. B. K.

* * *

"He Left It All!"

A famous millionaire died of cancer. For weeks he suffered intolerable agony. Although surrounded by every luxury and receiving every possible care, he died as wretchedly as a pauper. There was the usual publicity, flowers, telegrams, an expensive bronze casket and a towering beautifully carved tombstone. After the funeral a relative turned to another and said, "How much do you suppose that Harry left?" Back came the reply, "He left everything he had." Yes, Harry could take not one thing with him. He worked harder than a slave would. He grasped, saved, cheated, lied and where legally possible, he stole as he amassed his great fortune. He lived for self. He left all he had. He faced God without hope or plea. Harry was a poor fool. "What shall it profit a man, if he shall gain the whole world, and lose his own soul?"

—C. Leslie Miller, in
Gospel Herald

* * *

It's Always the Other Fellow

I once knew a small storekeeper with a bad reputation for parsimony. His business was prospering, but there was no increase in his contributions. As his pastor, I was much concerned about him. Finally, I prepared the strongest sermon I could on the love of money. I preached it with all possible earnestness, and he listened with absorbed attention. I was sure a profound impression had been made. Downtown the next day he crossed the street to speak to me. "Brother Egbert," he said, "I greatly enjoyed that sermon of yours yesterday morning?" "Why?" I asked. Said he: "Did you notice that Mr. — was in the congregation? Well, you certainly did give it to him! You did not leave him a leg to stand on. I don't see how he could have stayed in church under that sermon." Just there lies the deadliness of the money peril — that we never think of it in connection with ourselves. Of all temptations, it is the most insidious, the most utterly unsuspected. La Salle, the most popular confessor of the Middle Ages, has left it on record that of the tens of thousands that confessed to him their sins, not one ever confessed the love of money. Yet the prevalence of this sin is taught from one end of the Bible to the other. In Isaiah's time, what sin was it that brought the chastisement upon Israel? God tells Isaiah: "For the iniquity of his covetousness was I wroth, and smote him." In Jeremiah's time, what was the prevalent sin? God tells Jeremiah: "From the least of them even unto the greatest of them every one is given to covetousness."

—Egbert Smith, in the
Western Recorder

"Why Dost Thou Want My Land?"

We've heard of an old Quaker who advertised that he would give 40 acres of rich farm land to anyone who was perfectly satisfied with that which he had. One seeker came to see the Quaker. "Are thee perfectly satisfied with what thee hast?"

"Yes," answered the hopeful guest.

"Then why dost thee want this land?" was the old Quaker's significant reply.

—*Gospel Herald*

* * *

Love of Money the Root of Evil

There is a painting which portrays the lust for gold and its consequence in an unforgettable way. Here is a description of it written by Harry Earl Montgomery:

"It depicts a narrow highway along which is rolling a golden coin, surmounted by a shadowy, beckoning, graceful figure. The road is crowded with men and women who are rushing madly after the golden coin. Their eyes are aflame with eagerness and their faces are drawn with intense desire."

On a galloping horse rides a man whose eyes are fixed upon the golden coin, whose body is bent over the neck of his steed, and whose thoughts are focused on the wealth ahead.

Clinging to him is his wife, who with love, devotion, anxiety and fear written on her face, is endeavoring to remain close to her husband. But he, in his eagerness to obtain the coveted gold, is unconsciously, unwittingly, and roughly pushing her from him as he feels that she is becoming a drag on him in his race for wealth. He appears to be oblivious of the men and women in his path, and is urging his horse onward toward the golden goal, trampling on all who are in his way, leaving behind him a line of broken, bleeding and crushed men and women."

—*Christian Observer*

A Common Sin

As it has been well said, "When a man gets rich, God gets a partner or the man loses his soul." Dictionaries give the meaning of covetousness as "avaricious," "grasping," "greedy of gain," "greed of wealth with a view of hoarding it." These expressions describe a sin which is most common among all classes. The young and the old, the poor as well as the rich, generally speaking, are all guilty of this sin.

—Oscar Lowery, in *The Sin We're Afraid to Mention*

* * *

Death in Life

He always said he would retire
When he had made a million clear,
And so he toiled into the dusk
From day to day, from year to year.

At last he put his ledgers up
And laid his stock reports aside —
But when he started out to live
He found he had *already died!*

—*Earnest Worker*

* * *

"Wife, Had We Owned These!"

In the other years, a capitalist came up to death's door. Commanded he of his wife who stood at his bedside, "Wife, bring me the strong box!" Obeying his behest, she brought to the dying man the safety box in which his stocks and bonds reposed. Fumbling at the lock, he opened the box. Clutching the stocks and bonds, with a tenacious, icy death-grip, he exclaimed, with ghoulish glee, "Wife, had we owned these on the day of our wedding, the State of Georgia would be ours today!" Then, he fell back on his pillow, a lifeless corpse! The condemning words of the rich fool's Judge need no explanation: "Thou fool, this night thy soul shall be required of thee! . . . So is he that layeth up treasure for HIMSELF, and is not rich toward God" (Lk. 12:20-21).

—Dr. T. W. Callaway

CRIME

Crime—Broken Boys and Girls

"As a jurist who judges thousands of crime-broken boys and girls each year I know that religious interests for young people are essential for their moral welfare and future as worth-while American citizens. Religion is necessary to the happiness of American youth, but it is not enough merely to send children to church. Parents must attend church, for the child inevitably follows the examples set by its father and mother."

—Judge Hill, Presiding
Justice, N. Y. Juvenile
Delinquency Court

* * *

Our Greatest Need:

Said J. Edgar Hoover, "Doubt, uncertainty, and fear are dulling men's minds and perverting their souls. The individual, the community, and the nation have great need for a reawakening to the eternal truths of life, truths found in the greatest book in history — the Bible. Religious instruction is the rod and staff which brings forth, in triumphant glory, the teachings of God and of men. America could have no greater need."   —J. Edgar Hoover

* * *

93% From Broken Homes

Public delinquency takes many forms, but — again according to Mr. Hoover — disintegration of the American home is the greatest single factor.

Statistically, some 93 percent of the country's delinquents come from broken homes. In addition, there are many from homes which have been tragically affected by the death of one parent or by the inability of parents to live and work in harmony.

—Dorothy C. Haskin, in
Moody Monthly

* * *

Where Criminals Come From

Where do our criminals come from? Plainly from bad or inferior homes, or lack of any homes. The home directs the youth into the road he is apt to

follow throughout life. J. Edgar Hoover is quoted as saying on this point: "Criminals are home-grown. So are law-abiding, honorable citizens. Character, good or bad, gets its original 'set' in the home. Criminal tendencies are mostly picked up outside the home, perhaps on the street — because of a lack of proper teaching in the home. There is no real substitute for a good home."

—*United Presbyterian*

* * *

The Answer

Why has the world been sinking so steadily into a slough of despond? Why does even a casual study of crime in our own America give us pictures that both appall and sicken? The answer of the *Brethren Evangelist* is not acceptable to a large section of the modern pulpit — but it is the true answer nevertheless. Modern religious movements for a generation have centered their efforts toward bringing world peace, tolerance between the races, and a new social order. Not only have these efforts ended in failure, but all these ideals are further from realization than when churchmen stopped the preaching of salvation and shifted to the social emphasis. Modernism can be credited with nothing but failure.

—*The Presbyterian*

* * *

The Cause of Delinquency

A pastor asked a man of the world what he considered the cause of the crime wave of the past few years, and received this reply, "The church and you preachers are responsible." With some spirit the minister said, "What do you mean by that?" "I mean that you ministers preach about everything but sin. You talk about philosophy and morality, but not of sin and its terrible consequences. The church must impress the world that she has something, and is going somewhere. To the average person the church is only one among many good institutions."

—*Christ Life and Word of the Cross*

Killed Mother! "Why Did I Do It?"

Often the delinquents themselves do not know. Not long ago a fourteen-year-old walked into a police station and calmly announced, "I've just shot and killed my mother and father. Tell me why I did it. I don't know."

The stunned police, usually hardened to cases of confessed murder, stared into the eyes of a medium-sized, fine-looking boy and shook their heads in astonishment. Yet he voiced the attitude of most of the juveniles who find themselves in trouble. They do not know why they have committed the crimes they did.

—Dorothy C. Haskin, in
Moody Monthly

* * *

Movies

J. Edgar Hoover shows his wisdom also when he turns upon this money-mad industry:

Today's movies, many of them dealing with crime, exert a tremendous influence upon pliable young minds. Law enforcement files are replete with the stories of juvenile offenders who confess to have derived the ideas for their crimes from motion pictures. After having seen a particularly atrocious crime picture which had been skillfully exploited as the enactment of a 'public enemy's life,' four teen-age boys emulated the examples. Their car ran out of gas; they needed money, so one of the group snatched a purse. In another instance two boys, nine and ten, were caught throwing lighted matches into the gas tank of a car. They said they got the idea from the movies. Still another case — the arrest of four boys, ages fixteen and sixteen, solved a wave of burglaries. Each boy had a good school record and came from a home of good repute; each boy said he got the idea from the movies.

—*Christian Victory*

* * *

Crime Breeders

"Why the American people will continue to spend thousands of millions on schools and teachers," says Roger Babson, "to train the children of our cities, and then permit a bunch of irresponsible men to exhibit each night crime-breeding pictures within the shadow of the school building, just to make a few dollars, is beyond my comprehension. Such pictures in one night uproot all the good seed which the schools can plant in a month. It is exactly like appropriating money for a fire department, and then permitting every one to set the buildings on fire to collect insurance."

—*Alliance Weekly*

* * *

Why They Needed the Gospel

After making an appeal to munition workers in their factory canteen, an evangelist invited questions. A man stood up, and said bluntly: "We don't need religion. We have everything we want. We have plenty of money. The firm provides recreation. Food is put before us, and we don't even have to clear away or wash up the crockery. What need have we of religion?" The evangelist found his reply in the poster prominently displayed in the canteen. "Twelve hundred knives and forks have been stolen from this canteen during the past month. In the future, those using the canteen must bring their own cutlery."

—*Moody Monthly*

* * *

The Family Altar

With juvenile crime steadily on the increase, Americans must "clean up democracy at home" by rebuilding their religious fiber and restoring their home values, is the view of J. Edgar Hoover, Director of the Federal Bureau of Investigation.

Mr. Hoover asserts, "This country is in deadly peril. A creeping rot of moral disintegration is eating into our nation. I am not easily alarmed or shocked, but today like thousands of others, 1 am both alarmed and shocked. The arrests of teen-age boys and girls are staggering and they are danger signals which every parent, every responsible American should heed.

"It is not too late to correct the situation. If every home were awakened to its responsibility, over night there would be a renaissance of that virile, indomitable spirit which is only found in

free and God-fearing peoples. I am
sure if more emphasis were placed on
the Gospel of salvation, and less on social justice, the latter would be a greater reality.

"What we need is a return to God,
more specifically a return to the practice of religion. That without doubt is
the greatest need in America today."
—*Sword of the Lord*

CRITICISM

It's You!

How quick we are to censure and
criticize others! How prone we are to
detect the "mote" in our brother's eye,
and overlook the "beam" in our own
eye. A lady in Switzerland bought a
small package of greatly aged cheese.
Putting it into her handbag, she continued her shopping in different stores.
She was greatly repelled at what she
thought to be the malodor of the different clerks encountered. Her thoughts
ran something like this: "How can these
ill-smelling clerks maintain their positions?" Imagine her embarrassment
when, upon opening her hand bag, she
discovered that it was she, not others,
who was responsible for the offensive
odor!

—W. B. K.

* * *

Watch Dogs

"There are in every community and
every church, watch dogs, who feel
called upon to keep their eyes on others
and growl. They are always the first to
hear of anything wrong. Vultures are
always the first to smell carrion. They
are self-appointed detectives. I lay this
down as a rule without an exception,
that those people who have the most
faults themselves are the most merciless
in their watching of others. From
scalp of head to soles of foot, they are
full of jealousies, of hypercriticism.
They spend their life hunting for musk-
rats and mud turtles, instead of hunting for rocky mountains and eagles, always for something mean instead of
something grand. They look at their
neighbors' imperfections through a telescope upside down."

—T. DeWitt Talmadge

How To Escape Criticism:

"Say Nothing;
Do Nothing;
Be Nothing!"
—W. B. K.

* * *

A Talent To Be Buried

One of the best stories told at a missionary conference in Shanghai was of
a man who said he was afraid he was
going to be of no use in the world because he had only one talent. "Oh,
that need not discourage you," said his
pastor. "What is your talent?" "The
talent of criticism." "Well, I advise
you," said his pastor, "to do with it what
the man of one talent did with his. Criticism may be useful when mixed with
other talents, but those whose only activity is to criticize the workers might
as well be buried, talent and all."

—*Expositor*

* * *

Will You Sign Your Name to It?

A preacher had on his desk a special
book labeled "Complaints of members
against one another." When one of his
people called to tell him the faults of
another he would say, "Well, here's my
complaint book. I'll write down what
you say, and you can sign it. Then
when I have to take up the matter officially I shall know what I may expect
you to testify to." The sight of the
open book and the ready pen had its
effect, "Oh, no, I couldn't sign anything
like that!" and no entry was made.
The preacher said he kept the book for
forty years, opened it probably a thousand times, and never wrote a line in
it.

—*Moody Monthly*

Judging Ourselves

A man was complaining of his neighbors. "I never saw such a wretched set of people," he said, "as are in this village. They are mean, greedy of gain, selfish, and careless of the needs of others. Worst of all, they are forever speaking evil of one another."

"Is it really so?" asked an angel who happened to be walking with him.

"It is indeed," said the man. "Why, only look at this fellow coming toward us! I know his face, though I cannot just remember his name. See his little shark-like, cruel eyes, darting here and there like a ferret's, and the lines of covetousness about his mouth! The very droop of his shoulders is mean and cringing, and he slinks along instead of walking."

"It is very clever of you to see all this," said the angel, "but there is one thing which you did not perceive; that is a looking glass we are approaching."
—Laura E. Richards, in
Gospel Herald

* * *

Misdirected Skill

During the Peninsular War, an officer of artillery had just served a gun with admirable precision against a body of men posted in a wood to his left. When the Duke rode up, after turning his glass for a moment in the direction of the shot, he said, in his cool way: "Well aimed, Captain. But no more. They are our own 39th!" This blunder has been repeated sadly too often in the Lord's army. With what fatal frequency have great guns of the church, which might have battered down the citadel of Satan been misdirected against the Christian brethren!
—*Choice Gleanings Calendar*

* * *

The Critic Choses

A little seed lay in the ground,
    And soon began to sprout;
• "Now which of all the flowers around,"
    It mused, "Shall I come out?
The lily's face is fair, and proud,
    But just a trifle cold;
The rose, I think is rather loud,
    And then, its fashion's old.

The violet is all very well,
    But not a flower I'd choose,
Nor yet the Canterbury bell,
    I never cared for blues."
And so it criticized each flower,
    This supercilious seed,
Until it woke one summer hour,
    AND FOUND ITSELF A WEED!
—*Messiah's Advocate*

* * *

The World's Color Blindness

A minister was asked by a Quaker lady, "Does not thee think that we can walk so carefully, live so correctly, and avoid every fanaticism so perfectly, that every sensible person will say, 'That is the kind of religion I believe in?' " He replied, "Sister if thee had a coat of feathers as white as snow, and a pair of wings as shining as Gabriel's, somebody would be found somewhere on the footstool with so bad a case of color blindness as to shoot thee for a black-bird."
—*Biblical Illustrator*

* * *

The Critic

The man who had a good opinion of his own abilities, so much so that he thought he could do a thing better than anyone else, was once taught a good lesson. He was standing in front of a taxidermist's, in the window of which there was an owl which had attracted quite a lot of sight-seers.

Anxious to display his knowledge he said, with a pompous air, "Well, if I couldn't stuff an owl better than that, I would quit the business. The head isn't right, the poise of the body isn't right, the feathers are not on right, the feet are not placed right." Before he could finish, the owl turned his head and winked at him. The crowd laughed, and the critic moved on.
—*The Home*

* * *

Rowland Hill's Answer

Rowland Hill was once shamefully attacked in the public press. He was urged by a friend to start a libel action and to seek justification in a court of law, but he replied: "I shall rather answer the libel, not prosecute the writer: 1. Because in doing the one I might be led into unbecoming violence. 2. Because I have learned from long experience that no man's character can be eventually injured but by himself." It requires particular but supremely attractive grace to return good for evil, to meet a censorious person with unruffled patience, to face criticism uncritically. But the Spirit of God instructs us to render to no man "evil for evil." The victory we feel we need over others is often to be found in conquering ourselves.

—*Watchman-Examiner*

* * *

Do You Agree?

"There is so much good in the worst of us,
And so much bad in the best of us,
That it hardly becomes any of us
To talk about the rest of us."

—*Selected*

* * *

The Unimportance of Faultfinding

You should refuse to attach too much importance to criticism. Lincoln declared that if he read all the criticisms directed at him, he would have had time for nothing else. James Whitcomb Riley, when criticized by Ambrose Bierce, noted for his fierce temper, said, "I hit him with a chunk of silence." I once had an experience with an old man who did not hesitate at the vilest slander, and the poison of his temper is described in these lines:

A viper bit a slanderer in the side,
The slanderer lived, but the viper died.

An indignant Bostonian rushed into the office of Edward Everett Hale, excited and angered over some criticism that had appeared in a newspaper. Mr. Hale said to him, "Now calm yourself, not half the people in this city take that paper, not half of those who take it read it, not half of those who read it saw that particular item, not half of those who read the statement believed it, and not half of those who believed it are of any consequence."

—*Southern Methodist Layman*

A Better Method

There have been many who have criticized the method of Moody in asking men and women after his service to signify publicly their intention to take their stand for Christ.

A minister on one occasion took the evangelist to task for it. Moody listened to his objection, and said: "I agree with you, brother. I don't altogether like the method myself, and I am always looking for a better. What is yours?"

Considerably taken aback, the clergyman confessed he had no method, and did not invite men and women to make a public profession of their faith in the Saviour.

—*The Reaper*
Auckland, N. Z.

* * *

Wesley's Mistake

John Wesley tells of a man whom year after year he thought of contemptuously as covetous. One day when he contributed to one of Wesley's charities a gift that seemed very small, Wesley's indignation knew no bounds, and he raked him fore and aft with blistering condemnation. Wesley tells us in his diary that the man quietly said: "I know a man who at each week's beginning goes to market and buys a penny's worth of parsnips and takes them home to boil in water, and all that week he has parsnips for his food and water for his drink; and food and drink alike cost him a penny a week." The man had been skimping in order to pay off debts contracted before his conversion.

—*Christ's Ambassadors Herald*

* * *

After the Criticisms

A preacher announced a men's meeting in his church, proposing to give the men a chance to air their objections to Christianity. Over twelve hundred were present. The first objector said, "Church members are no better than others." "The ministers are no good," said another. And so the objections were mentioned one after another, and the pastor wrote them down on paper: "Hypocrites in the church," "The church is a rich man's club," "Christians don't believe the Bible any more" — twenty-seven in all. When they were through the pastor read off the whole list, then tossed it aside, saying, "Boys, you have objected to us *pastors, to church members, to the Bible, and other things, but you have not said a word against my Master!*" And in a few simple words he preached Christ to them as the faultless One, and invited them to come to Him, and believe on Him. Forty-nine men responded.

—*Record of Christian Work*

* * *

The Fortunate Passengers

A train was crowded, and numbers were standing in the aisles and on the platform. They took the opportunity to express themselves in no very patient tones in regard to the railway company. Some declared they had been standing for three hours. At a station others came aboard, and one was an invalid who was being carried in. As the passengers made way for him one repeated his complaint. "Yes, we've been standing here three hours." The invalid looked at him, and quietly said, "You are fortunate." They were tired, it's true, but the rebuke so honestly and gently given did its work, and there was a great change in the looks and tones of the passengers.

—*Sunday School Times*

* * *

How to Take Criticism

There are several things to do when we are criticized. Human nature resents it, but the Christian cannot be governed by the impulses of his old nature. Both Dr. Henry Clay Trumbull and Dr. Charles G. Trumbull, the illustrious Editors of *The Sunday School Times* from 1875 to 1941, used to say that when criticism comes we ought to see whether there is any truth in it, and learn from that truth, and not let our thoughts be distracted by the fact that the criticism may not have been given in the right spirit. In the face of criticism, by word or by letter, it is well to (1) Commit the matter instantly to God,

asking Him to remove all resentment or counter-criticism on our part, and teach us needed lessons; (2) "Consider him that endured such contradiction of sinners against himself, lest ye be wearied and faint in your minds," remembering that we ourselves are very great sinners, and that the one who has criticized us does not really know the worst; (3) Take account of the personal bias of the speaker or writer; (4) Remember that "a soft answer turneth away wrath: but grievous words stir up anger" (Prov. 15:1); (5) If the criticism is true, and we have made a mistake or committed a sin, let us humbly and frankly confess our sin to Him, and to anyone whom we may have injured; (6) Learn afresh that we are fallible, and that we need His grace and wisdom moment by moment to keep up in the straight path; (7) Then, — and not until then — "forgetting those things which are behind, and reaching forth unto those things which are before . . . press toward the mark for the prize of the high calling of God in Christ Jesus."

—*Sunday School Times*

* * *

Heedless of Passing Opinion

Travelers in the northern lane of ocean traffic have frequently observed the icebergs traveling in one direction in spite of the fact that the strong winds are blowing in the opposite way. The icebergs were moving *against* the winds. The explanation is that the great bergs, with eight-ninths of their hulk under the waters, were caught in the grip of mighty currents that carried them forward, no matter which way the winds raged.

So the ideal Christian leader has the greater part of his being thrust down into the deep places of God. The currents move him toward righteousness no matter how the winds of passing opinion blow.

—*Westminster Teacher*

* * *

"Judge Not"

Judge not: the work of his brain
And of his heart thou canst not see;

What looks to thy dim eyes a stain,
  In God's pure light may only be
A scar, brought from some well-fought
  field
Where thou wouldst only faint and yield.

The look, the air, that frets thy sight,
  May be a token that below
The soul has closed in deadly fight
  With some internal fiery foe,
Whose glance would scorch thy smiling
  grace,
And cast thee shuddering on thy face.
                                —Selected

* * *

Impossibility of Pleasing Everyone

Oliver Goldsmith tells the story of a painter of eminence who was resolved to finish a piece which should please the whole world. When therefore he had drawn a picture, in which his utmost skill was exhausted, it was exposed in the public market place, with directions at the bottom for every spectator to mark with a brush, which lay by, every limb and feature which seemed erroneous. The spectators came, and in general applauded; but each, willing to show his talent at criticism, marked wherever he thought proper.

At evening, when the painter came, he was mortified to find the whole pic-ture one universal blot; not a single stroke that was not stigmatized with marks of disapprobation. Not satisfied with this trial, the next day he was resolved to try them in a different manner, and exposing his picture as before, desired that every spectator would mark those beauties he approved or admired. The people complied, and the artist returning, found his picture replete with the marks of beauty; every stroke that had been yesterday condemned, now received the character of approbation.

"Well," cries the painter, "I now find that the best way to please one-half of the world is not to mind what the other half says; since what are faults in the eyes of these, there shall be by those regarded as beauties."
                        —New S. S. Illustrator

* * *

What They Paid For It

When the family returned from Sunday morning service, father criticized the sermon, daughter thought the choir's singing atrocious, and mother found fault with the organist's playing. But the subject had to be dropped when the small boy of the family piped up: "But it was a good show for a nickel, don't you think, Dad?"
                          —The Illinois Farmer

CROSS, THE BLOOD

The Stick That Reached Leland's Heart

One of the most comforting of Scriptural doctrines is that our salvation rests not alone upon God's mercy, but upon His justice. In His mercy and love, "he gave his only begotten Son, that whosoever believeth in him should not perish, but have everlasting life." But when the Son took our place, He bore the punishment that should have fallen on every sinner. . . . Therefore God is righteous in setting free from guilt and penalty every sinner who believes in the Lord Jesus Christ as his own personal Saviour. . . . Leland Wang, the Chinese evangelist, told recently of an incident of his childhood which vividly illustrates the substitutionary work of Christ. On one occasion he had been very naughty and his mother, with a stick in her hand, called him to her to be punished. But he ran off, taunting his mother because she could not catch him. She had little chance of catching her small, lively son. So she stood still and said, "I feel ashamed of myself that I have brought up a boy who is not willing to be disciplined by his mother when he does wrong, so I must punish myself," and she began to whip her bare arm. This so touched Leland's heart that he ran back to his mother, threw

143

himself into her arms, and pleaded with her not to hurt herself but to punish him. But no further punishment was necessary. . . . Mr. Wang says that, as he grew older, the memory of this incident helped him to understand the great love of the Lord Jesus Christ who willingly took our place on the cross.

—*Sunday School Times*

* * *

The Evidence of His Claim

There is a story told of a cottage in a little country village, in which lived a family of four: father, mother, and two small children. One evening something happened, what, no one knows — and the little cottage caught on fire. In a few seconds the thatched roof, and wooden timbers were ablaze. There was no fire engine in this remote spot, and the villagers stood round helpless. But suddenly a young man, who had only recently come to the place, came striding up. "What, can nothing be done to rescue the inmates?" he cried, and as no one responded, he dashed through the flames. A moment later, he emerged bearing under each arm a little child. They were unhurt, for Andy had hidden them under his coat — but he was terribly burned. Scarcely had he got out before the roof of the cottage fell in with a sickening crash, and the parents of the children were never seen alive again. A kind old woman took Andy into her home and nursed him carefully. Meanwhile, there was much discussion in the village as to what was to become of the two rescued children. It was decided that a council should meet to decide what was to become of them. When the day of the decision arrived, there were two who claimed the little ones. The first was the squire of the village. He had money, position, and a home to offer the children. The second claimant was — Andy! When asked what right he had to the little ones, he said never a word, but held up his hands — burned and scarred for them. Friends, the Lord Jesus comes and just holds up His pierced hands as His reason for claiming you and yours.

—*Christian Life*

Consumed for Us

A great artist once sought to paint the scene of the Crucifixion. With marvelous skill he sketched the skull-shaped hill crowned by three crosses, and with true delineation pictured the two thieves hanging in agony upon their emblems of shame; but when he came to depict the figure upon the central cross, he found his hand had lost its cunning, and that he was impotent to portray the figure of the world's great Redeemer. Finally, in despair, he simply enveloped the central cross in a sunburst of glory, and left it thus. But what conception could have been more appropriate, for as the sun burns itself up in giving light, heat, and life to the planets of the solar system which it shepherds, so the Sun of Righteousnes was consumed that man might have eternal life, and through His sacrificial death might learn that "without shedding of blood is no" — anything. The supreme fact of the age remains — "Christ died for our sins."

—*Royal Road to Royalty*
by Lewis R. Akers

* * *

Not The Crucifix, But the One Who Died!

Dr. H. A. Ironside, in his booklet, "Full Assurance," tells of a visit which James Parker of Plainfield, N. J., made to a hospital. The nurse indicated a bed surrounded with white screens, and whispered: "The poor man is dying. The priest has been here and administered the last sacrament. He cannot live long." Mr. Parker begged to go inside the screen, and permission was granted. As he looked down upon the dying man he observed a crucifix on his bosom. He stooped over and lifted it. The sick man lifted his eyes and looked distressed. "Put it back," he whispered, "I want to die with it on my breast." The visitor pointed out the figure pictured on the cross, and said fervently, "He's a wonderful Saviour!" "Yes, yes, I love the crucifix. Put it back, please. I hope it will help me to die well." "Not the crucifix, but the One who died on the cross, the Lord Jesus; He died to save you." The man looked bewildered, then his face brightened; "Oh, I see; not the crucifix, but the One who died. He died for me. I see, sir, I see. I never understood it before." Mr. Parker replaced the crucifix, offered a brief prayer, and left. In a few minutes he saw the body being wheeled out of the ward.

—*Sunday School Times*

* * *

God's Plus Sign

A crowd of university students were coming home from an evening of so-called pleasure. Their drunken leader noticed on the steeple of a church a cross, illuminated by the moonlight. Suddenly he shouted, "Ye mathematicians, look at God's plus sign!" One of those students could not sleep that night. Toward morning he stepped into the leader's room, and said that the vision of the cross as God's plus sign — the symbol of His abundant love for mankind — had made him decide to uphold that Cross. Seven others of those university men followed in his steps.

—*Watchman-Examiner*

* * *

It Includes All

Beelzebub berates us for the blunders we make; the gentle Holy Spirit speaks of the precious blood that washes whiter than snow. The accuser once reminded Martin Luther of his many transgressions, and tabulated them. "Is that all?" asked Luther. "No, there are many more," sneered Satan, who added more. "Is that all?" "Yes, and now what?" "Now," said the rugged reformer, "write beneath them all, 'The blood of Jesus Christ cleanseth from all sin.'"

—*Christian Digest*

* * *

He Took My Whipping for Me

Rev. A. C. Dixon, the Baptist preacher, who was born in the mountains of Virginia, relates the following:

Years ago there was a certain school in his section which no teacher could

handle. The boys were so rough that the teachers resigned.

A young, grey-eyed teacher applied, and the old director scanned him, then said, "Young feller, do you know what you are asking? An awful beatin'! Every teacher you have had for years has had to take it."

He replied, "I'll risk it."

Finally, he appeared for duty. One big fellow, Tom, whispered, "I won't need any help, I can lick him myself."

The teacher said, "Good morning boys, we have come to conduct school!" They yelled at the top of their voices. "Now, I want a good school, but confess I do not know how unless you help me. Suppose we have a few rules. You tell me and I will write them on the blackboard."

One fellow yelled, "No stealin'!" Another yelled, "On time." Finally ten rules appeared.

"Now," said the teacher, "a law is no good unless there is a penalty attached. What shall we do with the one who breaks them?"

"Beat him across the back ten times without his coat on."

"That is pretty severe, boys. Are you ready to stand by it?"

Another yell, and the teacher said, "School comes to order!"

In a day or so "Big Tom" found his dinner was stolen. Upon inquiry the thief was located — a little hungry fellow about ten. The next morning the teacher announced, "We have found the thief and he must be punished according to your rule — ten stripes across the back! Jim, come up here!"

The little fellow, trembling, came up slowly with a big coat fastened up to the neck and pleaded, "Teacher, you can lick me as hard as you like, but please don't make me take my coat off!"

"Take that coat off; you helped make the rules!"

"Oh, teacher, don't make me!" He began to unbutton, and what did the teacher behold! Lo, the lad had no shirt on, but strings for braces over his little bony body.

"How can I whip this child?" thought he. "But I must do something if I keep this school." Everything was quiet

145

as death. "How come you to be without a shirt, Jim?"

He replied: "My father died and mother is very poor. I have only one shirt to my name, and she is washing that today, and I wore my brother's big coat to keep warm."

The teacher, with rod in hand, hesitated. Just then "Big Tom" jumped to his feet and said, "Teacher, if you don't object, I will take Jim's licking for him."

"Very well, there is a certain law that one can become a substitute for another. Are you all agreed?"

Off came Tom's coat, and after five hard strokes the rod broke! The teacher bowed his head in his hands, and thought "How can I finish this awful task?"

Then he heard the entire school sobbing, and what did he see? Little Jim had reached up and caught Tom with both arms around the neck. "Tom, I am awful hungry. Tom, I'll love you till I die for taking my licking for me! Yes, I'll love you forever!"

Sinner, friend, you have broken every rule and deserve eternal punishment! But Jesus Christ took your scourging for you, died in your stead, and now offers to clothe you with His garments of salvation. Will you not fall at His feet and tell Him you will love and follow Him forever? "The wages of sin is death, but the gift of God is eternal life through Jesus Christ our Lord."

—Dr. L. G. Broughton

* * *

God's Safety Zone

An old preacher, who was preaching on a village green in England, had lived on the American prairies. He had a fascination for my boyish ears as he told of a prairie fire. He described the way the Indians saved their wigwams from the blaze by setting fire to the dry grass adjoining the settlement. "The fire cannot come," he cried, "where the fire has already been."

"That is why I call you to the Cross of Christ," he continued. "Judgment has already fallen and can never come again. He who takes his stand at the Cross is safe evermore. He can never come into condemnation. He is in God's safety zone." —*Religious Digest*

Millionaire's Will

When Mr. J. Pierpont Morgan, the American financier, the multi-millionaire, died some years ago, it was found that the year before his death, he had made his will. It consisted of about 10,000 words and contained thirty-seven articles.

But we are left in no doubt as to what Mr. Morgan considered to be the most important clause in his will, nay, the most important affair in his whole life.

He made many transactions — some affecting such large sums of money as to disturb the financial equilibrium of the world — yet there was one transaction that evidently stood out in Mr. Morgan's mind as of supreme importance:

"I commit my soul in the hands of my Saviour, full of confidence that, having redeemed me and washed me with His most precious Bood, He will present me faultless before the throne of my Heavenly Father.

"I entreat my children to maintain and defend, at all hazard and at any cost of personal sacrifice, the blessed doctrine of complete Atonement of sins through the Blood of Jesus Christ once offered, and through that alone."

In the matter of his soul's eternal blessing his vast wealth was as powerless as the beggar's poverty. In this he was as dependent upon mercy as the dying robber at Calvary.

—*The B. C. Shantyman*

* * *

Who Was the Pierced One?

Dr. A. J. Gordon relates the comments of the Hebrew Christian scholar, Rabinowitz, on the first and last letters of the Hebrew alphabet: Do you know what questioning and controversies the Jews have kept over Zechariah 12:10 — "They shall look upon me whom they have pierced?" They will not admit that it is Jehovah whom they have pierced. Hence the dispute about the "whom." But this word "whom" is in the original, simply the first and last letters of the Hebrew alphabet, aleph and tav. Do you wonder then that I was filled with awe and astonishment when I opened to Revelation 1:7, 8, and there read, "Behold, he cometh with clouds; and every eye shall see him, and they also which pierced him," and then read on and heard the glorified Lord saying, "I am Alpha and Omega?" The Lord Jesus seemed to say to me, "Do you doubt who it is 'whom' you pierced? I am the Aleph and the Tav of Zechariah 12:10, the Alpha and Omega, Jehovah the Almighty." The one who was "pierced" is in both passages Alpha and Omega or Aleph and Tav.

* * *

Second-Hand Clothes

Fred Jordan once went into Oviatt's, one of Los Angeles exclusive men's stores. He says, "A clerk came up to me: 'Can I help you?' he asked. 'Yes, if you sell secondhand clothing,' I answered. He looked around the well-appointed shop and murmured, 'I'm afraid we don't.' Then he studied my clothes, and said, 'If you wear secondhand clothes, they are pretty good.' 'They are secondhand all right.' I glanced at my shoes. 'They used to belong to a cow, and my coat once belonged to a sheep.' The man laughed, but I had made my point, and was able to explain that as an animal died that we might have clothes, so the Son of God had to die that we might be clothed in His righteousness." —*Moody Monthly*

* * *

Just Like God

A little girl was reading with her mother in the New Testament, and this was one of the verses of the chapter: "For God so loved the world, that he gave his only begotten Son, that whosoever believeth in him should not perish, but have everlasting life." Stopping for a moment in the reading, her mother asked, "Don't you think it is wonderful?"

The girl, looking surprised, said, "No." The mother, somewhat astonished, repeated the question, so the little girl said, "Why no. It would be wonderful if it were anybody else, Mother. But it is really just like God."

—*War Cry*

A Child's Understanding

A mother said to her little boy, after the chapter describing the Passover had been read in church, "You might have gone out before that, for you could not understand it." "Oh, yes, I did," said the little lad. "It was a beautiful story — I loved hearing it. It was about the blood of the Lamb, and they were all safe."

—*The Quiver*

* * *

The Only Face She Could See

You remember the story that is told of one of the generals of Cyrus the Great, king of Persia. . . . One of his generals came home from a campaign and was shocked to find that in his absence his own wife had been arrested and was languishing in prison, charged with treachery against her country, and the trial was to be held that very day. The general hastened to the court of Cyrus, and the guards brought in his own beloved wife. She, poor woman, pale and anxious, tried to answer the charges brought against her, but all to no avail. Her husband, standing near, heard the stern voice of the Persian ruler pronounce the death sentence. In a moment, as they were about to drag her away to behead her, he ran forward and threw himself down at the feet of the Emperor. "Oh, sire," he cried, "not she, but me. Let me give my life for hers. Put me to death, but spare my wife." And as Cyrus looked upon him, he was so touched by his deep devotion and his love for his wife that his heart was softened. He remembered, too, how faithful this servant had been, and he gave the command that the wife should go free. She was fully pardoned. As her husband led her out of the room, he said to her, "Did you notice the kind look in the eyes of the Emperor as he pronounced the word of pardon?" She said, "I did not see the face of the Emperor. The only face that I could see was that of the man who was willing to die for me." Oh, when we get Home, when we see the face of the Man who did die for us, how our hearts will praise him! How we will rejoice in His pres-

ence as we say, "The Son of God . . . .
loved me, and gave himself for me."
—*Great Words of the Gospel*,
by Dr. Harry Ironside

* * *

"I Know Now How"

"I know not how that Bethlehem's Babe,
Could in the Godhead be,
I only know the manger child
Has brought God's life to me.

"I know not how Calvary's Cross
A world from sin could free.
I only know its matchless love,
Has brought God's love to me."
—*Selected*

* * *

God's Son Upon the Tree

Before the cross in awe I stood,
Beholding brow and pierced hand;
For me it was He bled and died,
No other price for sin beside
Could pay the price for me.

His precious blood, there flowing red,
Was love's best gift, most freely shed;
No one but He the price could pay,
Or save from death and point the way
For sinners, you and me.

And as I gaze, I seem to hear
Him gently say, "My son, draw near;
New life I give and power withal,
Free unto all who on Me call,
Now and eternally."
—Ernest O. Sellers

* * *

Have You Thanked Him?

During the war a minister, going
along a street in London, saw a wounded
British soldier painfully hobbling along.
Stopping him, the minister astonished
the soldier by saying, "Thank you for being wounded for me." The man could
only look his surprise. People had sent
him cigarettes, and had given him entertainment, but no one before had ever
thanked him for what he had suffered
on others' behalf. Then the minister
continued, "I know Someone who was
wounded for *you*." "Wounded for me,
sir?" said the soldier, now more sur-

prised. "Who could that be?" "It was
our Lord Jesus," replied the minister.
"The Bible says, 'He was wounded for
our transgressions.' " With that the
man of God was on his way, leaving
the soldier to think about the One who
was wounded for him. I wonder if he
ever thanked the Saviour.
—J. E. Harris,
Sunday School Times

* * *

The Only Solvent

In the chemistry class we learned
how acids act on different substances.
In the course of our experiment the professor gave us a bit of gold and told us
to dissolve it. We left it all night in the
strongest acid we had, and tried combinations of acids, then finally told him
we thought gold could not be dissolved.
He smiled. "I knew you could not dissolve gold," he said; "none of the acids
you have there will attack it; but try
this," and he handed us a bottle labeled
"Nitromuriatic Acid (Aqua Regia)."
We poured some of its contents into the
tube that held the piece of gold; and
the gold that had resisted so easily all
the other acids quickly disappeared in
the "royal water." The gold at last had
found its master. The next day in the
classroom the professor asked, "Do you
know why it is called Royal Water?"
"Yes," we replied, "it is because it is
the master of gold, which can resist almost anything else that can be poured
on it." Then he said, "Boys, it will not
hurt the lesson today if I take time to
tell you that there is one other substance that is just as impervious as gold;
it cannot be touched or changed, though
a hundred attempts are made upon it.
That substance is the sinful heart.
Trial and affliction, riches and honor,
imprisonment and punishment will not
soften or master it. Education and culture will not dissolve and purify it.
There is but one element that has
power over it — the blood of Christ the
Saviour, the aqua regia of the soul."
—*Reformatory Record*

* * *

The Difference

The one thing which distinguishes the
gospel of God's grace and extinguishes

the religions of the world is that in the religions of the world the blood is flowing from the devotees to the gods to appease them, but in Christianity the blood is flowing from God to the sinners.

"See from His head, His hands, His feet,
Sorrow and love flow mingled down;
Did e'er such love and sorrow meet,
Or thorns compose so rich a crown?"

God himself meets his own requirements in the death of Christ. He is not acting apart from him, therefore his action is God's act.

—*Moody Monthly*

* * *

Imitating Christ

At the close of a Gospel service an intelligent-looking man came to the minister and said, "I do not see any necessity for the Blood of Christ in my salvation. I can be saved without believing in His shed Blood."

"Very well," said the minister, "how then do you propose to be saved?"

"By following His example," was the answer. "That is enough for any man."

"I suppose it is," said the minister. "And you propose to do just that in your life?"

"I do, and I am sure that that is enough."

"Very well. I am sure that you want to begin right. The Word of God tells us how to do that. I read here concerning Christ, 'Who did no sin, neither was guile found in His mouth.' I suppose that you can say that of yourself too?"

The man became visibly embarrassed. "Well," he said, "I cannot say that exactly. I have sometimes sinned."

"In that case you do not need an Example, but a Saviour; and the only way of salvation is by His shed Blood."

—*The Chaplain*

* * *

Has It Broken Your Heart?

A group of candidates were being examined in Korea. Among the missionaries in charge of the service was a sweet young woman from Wellesley. She feared to frighten and embarrass an elderly Korean woman by difficult questions, so placing her arms across her shoulder, she said quietly, "Tell me a story about Jesus." And the Korean woman with face aglow began her simple recital. She came to the Calvary scene. She told it all bravely till the time when the nails were driven into His feet and hands, and she broke down utterly, and with sobs and broken voice she murmured, "I can't tell that part. It breaks my heart." Oh, for a larger realization of Calvary! Oh, for a heart broken with the thought of the anguish of our blessed Lord!

—*Uplook*

* * *

It Took Calvary

An English soldier was converted in the trenches during the first World War and wrote home to his mother, "This war had to occur that I might be saved." The mother showed the letter to her minister, remarking that her boy was unduly magnifying the importance of his salvation. The minister agreed with the boy. "Madam," he said, "not only this war, but Calvary, had to occur to save your boy." God used the wrath which raged both at Calvary and through that awful war experience to bring the lad to his Saviour.

—*Presbyterian*

* * *

Rock of Ages

A young English curate set out one fine afternoon in the spring for a walk. His path led through a limestone gorge about two and a half miles long. As he was enjoying the exercise and the scenery he did not notice the storm clouds gathering overhead. But, finally, he did look up, and seeing the dark, overcast sky, he turned and made haste for home. But the storm overtook him. The rain descended in torrents and the young curate found shelter in a cleft of a great limestone rock. As he stood there in the place of shelter and heard the thunder roar and saw the lightning flash, he was deeply impressed. He drew from his pocket a pencil and a scrap of paper, and wrote:

"*Rock of Ages, cleft for me,
Let me hide myself in Thee.*"

This was the inspiration that led Augustus M. Toplady to write one of our greatest hymns — a hymn of faith and love and hope. It is a hymn that expresses simply and beautifully the gospel truth that trust in the Cross of Christ is our only refuge.

Is Christ to us all that is claimed for Him in our text — a refuge, a river and a rock? "And a man shall be as a hiding place from the wind, and a covert from the tempest; as rivers of water in a dry place, as the shadow of a great rock in a weary land."

—Rev. C. D. Honeyford

* * *

Made White by the Blood

One Christmas we had a tree which we trimmed on Christmas eve. The whole lighting effect was to be accomplished with red bulbs, and, when our work was finally done, we turned out all the other lights in the room so that the bulbs on the trees should give out the only illumination. We saw a startling thing! Near the base of the tree was a poinsettia plant, having some red flowers and some white ones. When the other lights were turned out and the red lights turned on, it was absolutely impossible to determine which of the poinsettia flowers had red petals and which had white — they were all white in the red light. What a perfect illustration that was of what happens to our sins when they are washed in the blood of Christ! They may be as scarlet, but when the red of Christ's shed blood is applied they become as white as snow.

—E. Schuyler English, in
Our Hope

* * *

"Died In Substitute"

During the Civil War the government drafted men into service. A man in Mercer County, Pennsylvania, was drawn. Because of sickness at home he felt he could not leave. The administration permitted him to secure some one to take his place. The substitute enlisted and went out in place of the man who was drafted. In a short time he was killed and buried, and the government made a record of it. But by some oversight on the part of the officials, the name of the man who was excused was placed in another draft and he was drawn a second time. He went before the authorities and said to them, "You cannot draft me. I am a dead man." "What do you mean?" came the reply. "Look up the records. You will see I enlisted, I fought, I died in the person of my substitute." In the eyes of the law that man was dead. The substitute fought and died in his place, and the government could not touch him.

The Lord Jesus Christ is the sinner's substitute. Christ took the sinner's place and paid the penalty at the cross for his sin, so that the law of death can no longer claim him.

—*Senior Teacher, S. B. C.*

* * *

What Chances Have You?

A legend is told of a dying man to whom Satan brought a parchment containing a list of the man's sins throughout all his life. His actions were pictured and the story was made vivid to him as the tempter demanded an answer to this question, "Where are your virtues among so many sins? What chances have you in judgment before God?" The dying man answered, "You have not kept the full account. That is only the debit side. There is a credit side. Opposite your dark picture, you should have painted a Cross and opposite that long list of sins you should have written these words: 'The Blood of Jesus Christ His Son cleanseth us from all sin.' " At the mention of the Name of Christ and the efficacy of His Blood, Satan vanished.

—*Gospel Herald*

* * *

"We Want You To Leave India!"

An old Hindu priest sat on the ground with the rest of the congregation. He became increasingly restless as the word picture developed. So this Christ, who came to save the world, had been seized and mocked by the very persons He had sought to help — had endured the trial, the judgment, the cross.

Finally as he heard the words spoken by the suffering, deserted Saviour:

"Father, forgive them, for they know not what they do," the old man could stand it no longer. Rushing forward, he fell prostate, exclaiming, "We want you to leave India! We want you to leave India!"

When the speaker asked why, the Hindu implored, "Because we have no story like this — no Saviour who lived a sinless life, died for His enemies and prayed for those who took His life. If you keep on telling this story to our people, they will forsake our temples and follow your Saviour."

—*Evangelical Christian*

* * *

"Not Pupular, But . . ."

Dr. George F. Pentecost is said to have gone to Boston once to deliver a series of Gospel addresses. The committee met him and asked him what his theme would 'be. He told them that he thought he would take something fundamental and speak on the blood of Christ. Said they, "Doctor, hadn't you better change your subject and make it the death of Christ, for the term blood is not very popular with many of the people in Boston." The Doctor replied, "Jesus might have died in bed without shedding His blood and 'without shedding of blood is no remission.' I expect to stick to the blood as my theme."

—*Paul's Conversion*,
by Chas. Reitzel

* * *

It Is Finished

Between two thieves, one either side,
The Lord of Life was crucified;
Men marvelled at a sight so rare,
And, sitting down, they watched Him there.

And none that saw could understand
Why darkness covered all the land;
And none who heard that cry, "I thirst,"
Knew why the Sinless One was cursed.

Nor understand these words so true:
"Father, they know not what they do";
For God alone, and none beside,
Knew what was done when Jesus died.

But ever since that blood-stained day
The eyes of men have turned that way,
And owned that life itself were loss
Without the glory of that Cross.

—F. W. Pitt

* * *

A Sea as Well as a Fountain

The Rev. Dr. Alexander Whyte, of Free St. George's Church, Edinburgh, once made a running comment on Cowper's famous hymn — a hymn which some ministers wished excluded from the New Hymnary, as offensive to good taste and fine feeling. This great divine and devout minister, when he read, "There is a fountain filled with blood," paused and said, "My sins for their cleansing call for a sea, not a fountain." Said a minister who heard Dr. Whyte's comment, "Is not that the sea in which God cast our sins?"

—*British Weekly*

* * *

Where the Worst and Best Meet

Some of the people in Central Africa speak of the death of Christ as "the victory of Golgotha." When Dan Crawford asked one of them why they did so, he improvised a cross with two sticks and said, 'Just here at the cross when Satan did his very worst, just here, just then, God did his very, very best. At the cross the very worst and the very best meet."

—*Florida Baptist Witness*

* * *

What's News?

In one of his letters the poet Tennyson furnishes a delightful autobiographical item. Upon arriving to spend a few days on the Lincolnshire coast with two "perfectly honest Methodists," the poet said to his hostess, "Well, what is the news?"

"Why, Mr. Tennyson!" said she, "haven't you heard? There is but one bit of news — that Christ died for our sins."

"That," said the poet, "is old news, and *new* news, and good news."

—*New Century Leader*

One to Die By

Lady Powerscourt lay dying in her castle. A friend who was on intimate terms with her came into her room, and said, "How are you today, Lady Powerscourt?"

"Very well; I will tell you what I have been thinking of. I have been thinking that one needs a great many scriptures to live by, but only one to die by."

"And what is that, your ladyship?"

"The only scripture that a person needs to die by is this: 'The blood of Jesus Christ, His Son, cleanseth from all sin,' and that verse was never sweeter to my soul than at this moment."

—*High School Christian*

* * *

"He Died For Me!"

Testified Ned Wright, a converted drunkard and thief:

"Previous to the Boer War I was sitting in a saloon in London drinking and gambling when a recruiting serjeant of the Army came in and asked me to join the army. I was so drunk I did not know what I was saying or doing. I told him I would, so he took me to the Barracks, where I was rigged out in a full soldier's uniform. It was not until the next morning that I realized what I had done.

"Soon after this the Boer war broke out and I was to be drafted out to South Africa. I did not want to go, but a friend was wanting to go badly, who had been refused by the doctors. So we agreed that he should take my name and uniform as we were about the same in height and build, and I should take his name and clothes.

"It was not long after, that it was reported Ned Wright had been killed."

At this juncture of his address I well remember he paused for a moment, looked all over the church, and then said, " 'He died for me.' Had I not exchanged with him I would have stood in the same place that he stood. I would have received the same bullet that he received, He died for me."

152

"Jesus the Son of God came down upon earth, took upon Himself our human flesh that we might be clothed with His righteousness, was tempted in all points like as we are, yet without sin, conquered death and hell, and has risen victorious for our justification, "He died for me."

—W. Barker

* * *

The Only Way To Remove the Spot

During the first World's Fair, held in Chicago over fifty years ago, there was an exhibit, or exposition, called, "The Parliament of Religions." Dr. Joseph Cook represented the Christian Religion. One by one, the representatives of the various world religions spoke in behalf of their beliefs. Dr. Cook was the last to speak. He turned to English literature for his example, and told the story of Lady Macbeth. In conclusion, he asked, "Gentlemen, does your religion have anything that will remove the spot of blood from Lady Macbeth's hand?" One by one, the various men shook their heads. Theirs was a *negative* religion, not positive like Christianity. "Gentlemen," said Dr. Cook, "the religion of Christ has: 'The Blood of Jesus Christ ...cleanseth us from all sin' (I John 1:7)." When he had finished the Bible verse, the great trained choir from Moody's Church rose from the balcony and sang the "Hallelujah Chorus" from Handel's oratoria, *The Messiah*.

"And He shall reign forever — King of kings, Lord of lords, Hallelujah! Hallelujah!"

And when the last hallelujah had been finished, Dr. Cook raised his head. All the representatives of the various other religions had filed out in the face of a religion like that!

—*Intermediate Leader,* S. B. C.

* * *

The Forgotten Scar!

Down South where his memory is still revered they tell you this story of the late General John B. Gordon. Years after the Civil War, Gordon was a candidate for the United States senatorship. The day came when his name was to be put in nomination in his state legislature. In that body was a man who had been a comrade of Gordon during the war. But for some reason the latter had incurred his resentment and the man had decided to vote against the general. When the time came, the roll was being called for the voting. Presently this old soldier's name was reached, and he arose to cast his vote against the man with whom he had fought all through the great struggle of four years. General Gordon was seated at the time upon the Speaker's platform in full view of all the legislators. As the man arose his eyes fell upon a scar upon Gordon's face, the mark of his valor and suffering for the cause to which he had literally given his life-blood in battle. Immediately the old soldier was stricken with remorse. As he saw this token of the sacrifice and suffering of the man by whose side he had himself fought he cried out with great emotion: "I cannot vote against him; I had forgotten the scar — I had forgotten the scar!"

—Dr. Robert G. Lee

* * *

Where Was God?

When a father received word that his son, a brilliant lad, had been killed in a railway accident, he turned to his pastor and cried in desperation, "Tell me, sir, where was God when my son was killed?" And in that tense and terrible moment guidance was given to the counseling pastor. "My friend," said he, "God was just where He was when His own Son was killed!"

—*Christian Digest*

* * *

I Know That It Does

A preacher was speaking from the text, "The blood of Jesus Christ his Son cleanseth us from all sin." Suddenly he was interrupted by an atheist who asked, "How can blood cleanse sin?"

For a moment the preacher was silent; then he countered, "How can water quench thirst?"

"I do not know," replied the infidel, "but I know that it does."

"Neither do I know how the blood of Jesus cleanses sin," answered the preacher, "but I know that it does."

—*Sunday School Times*

* * *

Hopelessness of a Perect Example

Dr. Joseph Parker, on one occasion, referred to the Unitarian conception of Jesus Christ as a great example only, and then went on to say: "We have been to hear Paderewski play. It was wonderful, superb, magnificent. Then we went home and looked at the piano. We would have sold it to the first man who would have been fool enough to buy it. That is the effect of your great examples upon us. I want not only a great example, but a great Saviour, one who can deliver me from my weakness and my sins." To follow a good example in the future will not blot out the black record of the past; we need the blood of Christ's atoning sacrifice to accomplish that. To hear a Paderewski play will not make us like a Paderewski. Could a Paderewski incarnate himself within one, he could play like himself. So the Christian life is not Christ and I, but Christ in me. We need the Christ within to live the Christ without.

—*Moody Monthly*

* * *

"Satisfied Completely!"

A converted Jewess, daughter of a New York rabbi, tells this story. "My father taught me to read the Bible in Hebrew as a young child. We began at Genesis. When we came to Isaiah, he skipped the fifty-third chapter. I asked him why. He said it was not necessary for Jews to read that chapter. I became more curious. I asked him who it was for, and he said Christians. I asked him what the Christian Bible was doing in our Bible. He became angry and told me to keep quiet. I wondered why God would put unnecessary things in the Bible. I copied that fifty-third chapter on paper, and carried it in my stocking for two years, until I came to America — the free country. I looked at it at night, and every chance I could without being seen. I took better care of that paper than people do of money. Through reading this wonderful chapter I was led to accept Christ as my Saviour. I was walking in New York one day and heard a lady reading this chapter. She explained that it referred to Jesus Christ. It satisfied me completely."

—*The Illustrator*

* * *

Glorying in the Cross

All who have heard the sacred hymn, "In the Cross of Christ I Glory," love it; and it adds to its beauty to learn about how it was written. Sir John Bowring, the noted naturalist, linguist, statesman, financier, was the author. This gifted man was at one time the governor of Hong Kong. It was he who invented the florin, a two-shilling piece greatly used in England. He could write in thirteen different languages and dialects. His education was of the right sort, for it led him to a deeper worship of the Crucified One.

One time when he was in the Orient, he was gazing at a tract of land which had been devastated by an earthquake. He noticed the tower of a church standing among the ruins, and on the top of the tower a cross. The sight of this prompted him to write the great hymn.

—*Our Youth*

* * *

Beside the Cross

Oppress'd with noonday's scorching heat,
  To yonder Cross I flee;
Beneath its shelter take my seat;
  No shade like this for me!

Beneath that Cross clear waters burst,
  A fountain sparkling, free;
And there I quench my desert thirst;
  No spring like this for me!

A stranger here, I pitch my tent
  Beneath this spreading tree;
Here shall my pilgrim life be spent;
  No home like this for me!

For burdened ones a resting-place
  Beside that Cross I see;
Here I cast off my weariness;
  No rest like this for me!

—Horatius Bonar

* * *

Much More Needed!

I have a friend in the City of Glasgow, who, many years ago, found himself in Barlinnie prison because of his sin. He was given to drunkenness, became a sot, and grieved the heart of his godly mother. After serving his term of imprisonment, he found his way back again to the old home, and the mother who loved him pleaded with him to sign the pledge. But, like the honest man he was, he said, "No, Mother, I have signed enough pledges to paper the wall; I need something more than a pledge." But she said to him, "Sinclair, perhaps if you sign it this time it may help you," and having a pledge near at hand, she urged her wayward boy to sign the paper. But again he said, "No, Mother, I am not going to sign another pledge. I need a power that can make me a sober man, and change my life." Growing desperate, his mother took a knife and opened one of her veins, and dipping a pen into her flowing blood, she said, "Sinclair, sign it with your mother's blood, and that may help you." I heard him say one night before a crowded audience, "What the blood of my mother could not do, the blood of Jesus Christ accomplished," and that man tonight is preaching the Gospel of the Redeemer.

—Herbert Lockyer, in
London Christian Herald

* * *

"That's What I Want!"

Dr. Chamberlain, one of the oldest missionaries in India, says that one day while he was preaching in Benares, among the devotees who came to bathe in the sacred stream, was a man who had journeyed wearily on his knees and elbows from a great distance with the pain of conviction at his heart. He hoped by washing in the Ganges to be relieved of his "looking for judgment." Poor soul! He dragged himself to the river's edge, made his prayer to Gunga, and crept in. A moment later he emerged with the old pain still tugging at his heart. He lay prostrate on the bank in his despair, and heard the voice of the missionary. He raised himself and crawled a little nearer. He listened to the simple story of the Cross. He was hungry and thirsty for it. He rose upon his knees, then upon his feet, then clapped his hands and cried, "That's what I want! That's what I want!" The story of the Cross is what our dying world needs!

—*Watchman-Examiner*

* * *

How Paul and the Infidel Agreed

An earnest Christian man and faithful reader of the Bible was assailed by an infidel. "I do not understand nor do I believe," said he, "that the blood of Jesus Christ can wash away my sin." "You and St. Paul quite agree on that subject," answered the Bible student. "How?" "Turn to the first chapter of First Corinthians and read the eighteenth verse: 'For the preaching of the cross is to them that perish foolishness; but unto us which are saved it is the power of God.' " The infidel hung his head and began to study the Bible. He soon found it to be God's power unto salvation.

—*The Lutheran*

* * *

Why We May Have Peace

A young lady was dying, and one Scripture which she had heard in health came to her at this time: "He was wounded for our transgressions, he was bruised for our iniquities: the chastise-

ment of our peace was upon him; and with his stripes we are healed," and she was led by the Holy Spirit to rest in him of whom it spoke, for salvation. A friend said to her one day, "You suffer much, I fear." "Yes," she said, "but," pointing to her hand, "there is no nail there. He had the nails; I have the peace." Laying her hand on her brow, she said, "There are no thorns here. He had the thorns; I have the peace." Touching her side she said, "There is no spear here. He had the spear; I have the peace."

—*Young People's Delight*

* * *

The Cure Is in the Blood

The International News Service has published a count of Mrs. Rose L. McMullin, who has traveled from coast to coast, donating her blood for more than 400 transfusions in forty states. She just arrived in New York to aid in a transfusion for a twenty-five-year-old mother, having hurried east from Salt Lake City on an urgent wire from doctors in New York. The donor is a phenomenon in the medical world. She is one of the very few persons whose blood can resist staphylococcus aureus, a disease of the blood stream. She is said also to be the only person who has been able to offer blood simultaneously for two transfusions; this was done in Portland, Oreg. While over 400 persons thank generous Mrs. McMullin for her blood, unnumbered hosts sing the praises of the Lord Jesus Christ for the shedding of his precious blood which cleanses from all sin. Sin is the real disease in the blood stream of humanity.

—*Now*

* * *

Cheapening Lord's Sacrifice

When John McNeill, the Scottish evangelist, landed in France for Y. M. C. A. duty during the World War, he was introduced to the general in command, who said that he would like to give him suggestions about his preaching to the men. Mr. McNeill's biographer, Alexander Gammie, describes the incident: "What the general wanted him to do was to instruct the men that, when they went over the top, if they fell, it would be all right for them in the next world — they had died for their country. Mr. McNeill . . . replied: 'General, if one of the men under your command were to win the Victoria Cross for valor, and I were to belittle the deed by which the decoration was won, you would not like it. And I want to tell you, General, that you are cheapening my Lord's sacrifice.' The incident ended at that point."

—*Selected*

* * *

"One Has Died for Me!"

There was once a Roman patrician girl of high birth and finished culture. "No one," she said, "shall ever win my hand, unless he gives me proof that he would die for me." Years passed, and one day, in one of the Roman streets, she heard an outcast Christian speaking of his Lord. When she heard, with amazement breaking on her soul, she exclaimed: "Here is One Who *has* died for me; to Him alone shall my heart's love be devoted forever."

—**D. M. Panton**

* * *

The Message of the Cross Conquered

It is said that when the Moravians began their mission in Greenland, they found the natives so ignorant that they decided to begin by educating them. The results were so utterly disappointing that they decided to leave. While waiting for a vessel, one of the missionaries began translating a portion of the Gospels, and thought he would test his translation by reading it. After he had read of the sufferings and death of Jesus, there was a period of silence. Then the chief rose and asked the missionary to read it again. When he had finished, the chief said: "What you read — is it true? You say, 'It is true?' Then why did you not tell us that at first? You must not leave us now. We will

listen to the words of the Man who suffered for us." So the Cross conquered where education failed. The missionaries remained to see much fruit from their labors.

—*Evangelical Christian*

* * *

"Calvary Covers It All"

The Scotch patriot, Robert Bruce, was once hiding in the mountains from the forces of King Edward of England, when he heard the baying of bloodhounds. Bruce suddenly recognized the baying as that of his own dogs. His English enemies had put them on his track, sure that they would lead straight to their owner. Although worn out from hardships and lack of food, the Scotch patriot rose up at once and fled as rapidly as possible. But in vain; only one end seemed possible. The baying dogs came closer and closer. The fugitive was at the point of despair when suddenly he came upon a brook. Quickly he entered the water and walked downstream. Shortly afterward the dogs were at the bank. The tone of the barking changed as they worked upstream and down without finding the continuation of the trail. Bruce was able thus to elude his enemies because the dogs were unable to find the trail under the water.

Surely this is a picture of the sinner. Robert Bruce's own hounds were his pursuers. The sinner is pursued by his sins. Every man's own sins are sure to track him down and destroy him. What to do?

There is only one way; but thank God, there is one in which the guilty sinner can be saved from the judgment of God. He must hide himself in the current that flows from Calvary. There Jesus Christ paid with His own blood in order to freely offer pardon to every sinner. The bloodhounds of sin are at your heels — but here is hope for you. God loves you still. "The blood of Jesus Christ his Son cleanseth us from all sin" (I John 1:7).

—*Missionary Norman Lewis, in The Sword of the Lord.*

Man's Work in Heaven

A minister, going through a mental institution, was stopped by a woman, who asked: "Mr. Minister, what work of man will there be in Heaven?" "None, my dear lady," he said, thinking to answer as quickly as possible and get away. "Oh, yes, there will! Can't you tell me?" "No, I cannot; but will you tell me?" said the minister. "Oh, sir," she replied, "it will be the prints of the nails of the hands and feet of the Master, the Lord Jesus Christ. That is the only work of man that there will be in Heaven."

—*Christian Herald*

DEATH
(See also: Resurrection)

What They Said At Death's Door:

Charles Dickens. — 1870 — whose works are world-famed, wrote in his will: "I commit my soul to the mercy of God, through our Lord and Saviour Jesus Christ."

Brownlow North. — 1875. — Profligate nobleman who became a preacher, said: " 'The Blood of Jesus Christ His Son cleanseth us from all sin.' That is the verse on which I am now dying. One wants no more."

Henry Moorhouse. — 1880. — "If it were God's will to raise me up I should like to preach from the text John 3:16. Praise be to the Lord."

John Nelson Darby. — 1882. — "Well it will be strange to find myself in Heaven; but it won't be a strange Christ — One I have known these many years. I am glad He knows me. I am a demonstrative man, but I have a deep, deep peace, which you know."

Earl Cairns. — 1885. — Lord High Chancellor of England. — "God loves me and cares for me. He has pardoned all my sins for Christ's sakes, and I look forward to the future with no dread."

Lord Congleton. — 1893. — Irish Christian worker. — "Lord Jesus, receive my spirit."

Sidney Cooper. — 1902. — Royal Academician, wrote when 98: "I have full faith in Thy atonement, and I am confident of Thy help. The precious Blood I fully rely on. Thou art the source of my comfort. *I have no other. I want no other.*"

John Pierpont Morgan. — 1913. — American millionaire. — First paragraph of his will. "I commit my soul into the hands of my Saviour, in full confidence that having redeemed it and washed it in His most precious Blood, He will present it faultless before the throne of my Heavenly Father, and I entreat my children to maintain and defend at all hazards and at any cost of personal sacrifice the blessed doctrine of the complete atonement for sin through the Blood of Jesus Christ, once offered, and through that alone."

Lord Roberts, V. C. — 1914. — Who died among his loved Indians in France, commending the Bible to his troops said: "I ask you to put your trust in God. You will find in this Book guidance when you are in health, comfort when you are in sickness, and strength when you are in adversity."

William Pitt. — 1778. — Earl of Chatham, statesman, and orator. — "I throw myself on the mercy of God through the merits of Christ."

Augustus Toplady. — 1778. — Author of "Rock of Ages." — "The consolations of God to such an unworthy wretch are so abundant that He leaves me nothing to pray for but a continuance of them. *I enjoy Heaven already in my soul.*"

Countess af Huntingdon. — 1791. — "I have no hope but that which inspired the dying malefactor. And now my work is done, I have nothing to do but go to my Father."

John Wesley. — 1791. — Almost his last words were, "The best of all, God is with us."

John Bacon. — 1799. — Eminent English sculptor, whose monument of Lord Chatham stands in Westminster Abbey. — "What I was as an *artist* seemed to be of some importance while I lived; but what I really was as a *believer* in the Lord Jesus Christ is the only thing of importance to me now."

George Washington. — 1799. — First President of the United States of America. — "Doctor, I am dying, but I am not afraid to die."

Lady Powerscourt. — 1800. — "One needs a great many Scriptures to live by, but the only Scripture that a person needs to die by is, I John 1:7, and that verse never was sweeter to me than at this moment."

Sir Walter Scott. — 1832. — The famous author on his death-bed begged his son-in-law to read to him. "What shall I read?" said Lockhart. "Can you ask?" replied the dying man; "there is only one Book."

William Wilberforce, M. P., — 1833. The champion of the slave. — "My affections are so much in Heaven that I can leave you all without a regret; yet I do not love you less, but God more."

Captain Hedley Vicars. — 1855. — The Crimean hero. — "The Lord has kept me in perfection peace and made me glad with the light of His countenance. In the Lord Jesus I find all I want of happiness or enjoyment."

Sir Henry Havelock. — 1857. — Who relieved Lucknow. — When felled by an attack of malignant cholera, and told that he could not survive, he calmly replied, "I have prepared for this for forty years." *"Prepare to meet thy God."*

Paul the Apostle. — A.D. 66: — "I have fought a good fight, I have finished my course, I have kept the faith: henceforth there is laid up for me a crown of rigteousness" (*II Tim.* 4:7,8).

Polycarp. — A. D. 155. — Christian martyr and disciple of John. — "Eighty and six years have I served Him, and He has done me nothing but good. How could I curse Him, my Lord and Saviour?"

Philip Melanchthon. — 1560. — When several portions of Scripture had been read to him, he was asked by his son-in-law if he would have anything else, and his reply was in these emphatic words, "Nothing else but Heaven!"

Michael Angelo. — 1564. — Eminent sculptor wrote in his will, "I die in the faith of Jesus Christ, and in the firm hope of a better life."

Samuel Rutherford, — 1615. — "Mine eye shall see my Redeemer. He has pardoned, loved, and washed me, and given me joy unspeakable and full of glory. I feed on manna. Glory, glory, glory to my Creator and Redeemer for ever! Glory, glory shines in Immanuel's land!"

John Bunyan. — 1688. — Author of *The Pilgrim's Progress.* — "Weep not for me, but for yourselves. I go to the Father of our Lord Jesus Christ, who will, through the mediation of His blessed Son, receive me, though a sinner, where I hope we shall meet to sing the new song, and remain everlastingly happy, world without end."

David Brainerd. — 1747. — Well known missionary. — "I am going into eternity; and it is sweet to me to think of eternity; the endlessness of it makes it sweet. But O! what shall I say of the eternity of the wicked? The thought of it is too dreadful!"

Michael Faraday. — 1867. — Chemist, electrician and philosopher. — A distinguished scientist, calling on him, put this question, "Have you conceived to yourself what will be your occupation in the next world?" Hesitating a while, Faraday answered, "Eye hath not seen, nor ear heard, neither have entered into the heart of man, the things that God hath prepared for them that love Him." And then he added, in his own words, "I shall be with Christ, and that is enough."   *—Gospel Herald*

*   *   *

What They Said at Death's Door:

Voltaire, the famous infidel who spent most of his life fighting Christianity, cried out with his dying breath, "I am abandoned by God and man: I shall go to hell!"

Mirabeau, noted French statesman: "Give me more laudanum, that I may not think of eternity! O Christ, O Jesus Christ!"

Charles IX, King of France: "What blood, what murders, what evil councils I have followed. I am lost! I see it well!"

Mazarin, French Cardinal and statesman: "O my poor soul! what will become of thee? whither wilt thou go?"

Hobbes, the atheist: "I am taking a fearful leap in the dark!"

Sir Thomas Scott, Chancellor of England: "Until this moment, I thought there was neither God nor hell; now I know and feel that there are both, and I am doomed to perdition by the just judgment of the Almighty!"

Edward Gibbon, author of "History of the Decline and Fall of the Roman Empire:" "All is dark and doubtful!"

Sir Francis Newport: "Oh, that I was to lie a thousand years upon the fire that never is quenched, to purchase the favor of God, and be united to Him again! But it is a fruitless wish. Milions of millions of years would bring me no nearer to the end of my torments than one poor hour. Oh, eternity, eternity! forever and forever! Oh, the insufferable pangs of hell!"

Abbott: "Glory to God! I see Heaven sweetly opened before me!"

Dwight L. Moody: "This is glorious! Earth receding, Heaven opening. God calling me!"

John Antler: "The chariot has come, and I am ready to step in."

John Wesley: "Best of all, God is with us!"

John Knox: "Live in Christ and the flesh need not fear death."

John A. Lyth: "Can this be death? Why, it is better than living! Tell them I die happy in Jesus!"

Martin Luther: "Our God is the God from whom cometh salvation. God is the Lord by whom we escape death! Into Thy hands I commit my spirit: God of truth, Thou hast redeemed me!"

Margaret Prior: "Eternity rolls before me like a sea of glory!"

Martha McCrackin: "How bright the room! How full of angels!"

Mary Frances: "Oh, that I could tell you what joy I possess! The Lord doth shine with such power upon my soul. He is come! He is come!"

Philip Heck: "How beautiful! The opening Heavens around me shine!"

Sir David Brewster, inventor of the kaleidoscope: "I will see Jesus: I shall see Him as He is. I have had the light for many years. Oh, how bright it is! I feel so safe and satisfied!"

—*Sunday School Times*

* * *

"The Last of the Ninth for Me!"

"The doctor knows what his trained eyes see,
And he says it is the last of the ninth for me;
One more swing while the clouds loom dark,
And then I must leave this noisy park.

"'Twas a glorious game from the opening bell,
Good plays, bad plays and thrills pell-mell;
The speed of it burned my years away,
But I thank my God that He let me play!"

—Wm. F. Kirk, columnist, written just before his death, and couched in terms of the baseball diamond.

* * *

Moody and Death

Are we witnessing such glorious death-bed scenes in our age as the records of the past reveal? We fear not. People who would die triumphantly must live victoriously. Mr. Moody lived a wonderful life of consecration, service and victory; his death was glorious. The story of his death-bed has been given as follows:

"A few hours before entering the 'Homeland' Dwight L. Moody caught a glimpse of the glory awaiting him. Awakening from a sleep, he said, 'Earth recedes, Heaven opens before me. If this is death, it is sweet! There is no valley here. God is calling me, and I must go!' His son who was standing by his bedside said, 'No, no, father, you are dreaming.'

" 'No!' said Mr. Moody, 'I am not dreaming: I have been within the gates: I have seen the children's faces.' A short time elapsed and then, following what seemed to the family to be the death struggle he spoke again: 'This is my triumph; this my coronation day! It is glorious!' "   —G. W. Ridout

* * *

When the Clock Stops

Miss Tweedle, a missionary in India, writes: "At a village, a dear old woman noticed my wrist watch, so I put it to her ear. You should have seen her face! She called to the other women, and said, 'Come, come! Here's a machine that keeps on saying, Quick, quick, quick.' (The Tamil word for 'quick' sounds similar.) I was then able to tell them that we kept a watch to remind us how quickly time is going. One day that watch would stop, so would her heart; and then she would have to meet God. What would she do? It was such a solemn time, and she said with tears in her eyes, 'I will worship Jesus, so that when the clock stops I need not fear.' "
—*Sunday School Chronicle*

* * *

Trapped in a Closet

Awakened when his bed caught fire, Edward Sweeney of New York City ran to the door, opened it, went through and slammed it behind him, only to discover that he was in a clothes closet and could not get out. Meanwhile other tenants smelled smoke, sounded the alarm, and the firemen not only extinguished the blaze but released Mr. Sweeney from the closet when they heard him pounding on the door.

How like human beings! Caught in the sleep of death, they race to any door and rush through only to be trapped in their false hope. Is it any wonder that the Lord cries through the prophet, "Turn you to the stronghold, ye prisoners of hope" (Zech. 9.12)? Christ is the Stronghold and the only Door. Any man who attempts to find safety by any other door will find himself trapped forever.   —*Revelation*

Two Kinds of Death

Dr. Walter Wilson, a great personal worker, tells of how he was called to conduct a funeral service for a poor family. The day of the funeral was rainy and the roads were muddy, so he asked the undertaker if he could ride with him. As the two were riding along the preacher asked the undertaker whether he ever read in the Bible the verse that says, "Let the dead bury their dead." "There is no such passage in the Bible," he promptly replied. "If there is it must be a wrong translation, because it does not make any sense. How can a dead person bury another dead person?" "No, it is not a wrong translation," the doctor said. "These words were spoken by the Lord Jesus himself who always spoke words of truth." "What does the passage mean?" asked the undertaker. "You say that you are not a Christian, so you are a dead undertaker in front of this hearse, driving out to the cemetery to bury this dead friend in the back of the hearse. That friend is dead to his family and you are dead to God. He does not respond to their caresses, their calls, and their commands; neither do you respond to the love and call of God." After this it was an easy matter for the doctor to lead this undertaker to Christ.
—*Gospel Herald*

* * *

No Regrets!

No man ever repented of being a Christian on his death-bed.
—Hannah More

* * *

What Makes A Death Bed Terrible!

When Garrick showed Dr. Johnson his fine mansion, gardens, statues and pictures at Hampton Court, what ideas did they awaken in the mind of that great man? "Ah! David, David!" said the Doctor. "these are the THINGS which make a deathbed terrible!"
—W. B. K.

* * *

"Call The Missionary!"

An Oriental girl of 17 years was dying of tuberculosis in an American hospital. As death's cold fingers touched her she screamed with fear. Her Buddha seemed indifferent to her fear. The nurses had no medicine that would quiet her troubled heart. A missionary talked with her about Jesus. Over and over she read, "He that believeth on the SON hath life." She closed her tired eyes and prayed. Then as she counted the words out on her thin fingers she whispered, "The Lord is *my* Saviour." The missionary was about to leave, but her plea arrested him — "Oh, don't go, tell me more about Jesus." He told her more and she drank in every word.

"She spent her waking hours reading John's Gospel. The next day he saw her again and told her of the place Jesus had prepared for her. "Are you afraid to die?" "No, the fear is all gone, I am ready to die." Early the next day her weary eyes closed, her tired heart stopped and she slipped away into His everlasting arms. Before she went she whispered, "Call the missionary."

—*Gospel Herald*

* * *

Moved Out!

Joseph S. Flacks, a devoted Hebrew Christian, prepared a triumphant testimony to be mailed to his friends at the time of his death, and caused it to be written on postal cards, in readiness for the time it would be needed. On August 14, 1940, the day the Lord took Mr. Flacks to be with Himself, the cards required only the addition of the date line before they were posted. The message read:

August 14, 1940

Triumphant through Grace. This is to announce: I moved out of the old mud house (2 Cor. 5:1). Arrived in Glory-land instantly, in charge of the angelic escort (Luke 16:22). Absent from the body, at home with the Lord (2 Cor. 5:6). I find as foretold (Psa. 16:11), in His presence fullness of joy . . pleasures for evermore! Will look for you on the way up at the redemption of the body (Rom. 8:23). Till then, look up!

—J. S. Flacks

"To Die Is Gain!"

Many phrases have been coined by literary genius, tending to soften the harshness of the word death. Whitman called it: "Cool-enfolding death;" Ingersol, "The fine serenity of death;" Shakespeare, "A necessary end." How different are the words of Scripture! Paul says: "To die is gain." "O death, where is thy sting?"

Death, to the children of God, means something vastly different from the meaning given it by unbelievers, no matter how cultured, admired, and respected they may be. Different, too, are the ceremonials connected with the burials. The ancient Christians gathered round their departed loved ones in the Catacombs and sang:

"Good night, beloved, sleep and take your rest.
Lay down your head upon the Savior's breast."

On her death bed, Queen Victoria called for the hymn:

"Rock of Ages, cleft for me.
Let me hide myself in Thee."

A great life is a wonderful thing; but infinitely greater is a great death — in the Lord.

—*Gospel Herald*

* * *

Into The Sunset

Let me die, working,
Still tackling plans, unfinished, tasks undone!
Clean to its end, swift may my race be run,
No laggard steps, no faltering, no shirking;
Let me die, working!

Let me die, thinking.
Let me fare forth still with an open mind,
Fresh secrets to unfold, new truths to find,
My soul undimmed, alert, no question blinking;
Let me die, thinking!

Let me die, laughing.
No sighing o'er past sins; they are
forgiven.
Spilled on this earth are all the joys of
Heaven;
Let me die, laughing!

—S. Hall Young, in
Watchman-Examiner

* * *

We Are Immortal

Death is not the end; it is only a beginning. Death is not the master of the house; he is only the porter at the King's lodge, appointed to open the gate and let the King's guests into the realm of eternal day. And so shall we ever be with the Lord.

The range of our threescore years and ten is not the limit of our life. Our life is not a landlocked lake enclosed within the shorelines of seventy years. It is an arm of the sea. And so we must build for those larger waters. We are immortal! How, then, shall we live today in prospect of eternal tomorrow?

—J. W. Jowett

* * *

Death Insurance

When I asked the man what he was selling, he said, "Life insurance."

"That's not *life*, but *death* insurance."

"What do you mean?"

"You have to die to win."

"Not always. You get your money back with big interest in 10 or 20 years if you live, but if you die your family is protected for a number of years."

"Fine. The Bible says, 'But if any provide not for his own, specially for those of his own house, he has denied the faith and is worse than an infidel,' but it's more important to carry *life* insurance."

"Say, what are you selling?"

"Life insurance. Eternal life. Nothing to pay, and you begin to get big dividends immediately, of peace, joy, contentment, and an understanding of God's plan for your life."

—Selected

A Welcome on Both Sides

He was a Scotch soldier, terribly wounded, and the great surgeon, who was also a great Christian, said to him: "Jock, lad, I have to operate; and I think I ought to tell you — you have one chance in a hundred of living through the operation. Have you anything you want to say to me?"

And the brave lad looked up and said, "No, doctor, just get on with it." He came through. He is alive today.

To a friend who asked him afterwards how he felt when he submitted himself to the surgeon, Jock said: "I knew it was all right. *I knew whichever side I came out there would be a welcome for me. If I came back, mother was there; and if I went on, Jesus was there.*" —*Christian Union Herald*

* * *

No Provision for Winter of Death

Among the many thrilling stories told in connection with the search of gold in the Klondyke is one which impressed me more than all the others. A prospecting party, penetrating far into the country, came upon a miner's hut. All without was as quiet as the grave. Entering the cabin, they found the skeletons of two men, and a large quantity of gold. On a rough table was a letter telling of their successful search for the precious ore. In their eagerness to get it, they forgot the early coming of winter in that northern land. Each day, the gold was found in more abundance. One morning, they awoke to find a great snowstorm upon them. For days the tempest raged, cutting off all hope of escape. Their little store of food was soon exhausted, and they lay down and died amidst abounding gold! Their folly was not in finding and gathering the gold, but in neglecting to provide against the inevitable winter. Neither are men to be classed as fools today who are diligent in business and successful in the accumulation of property. The folly is in permitting these to so occupy the attention that provision for the greater winter of death, so soon to fall, is entirely neglected. —W. W. Weeks, in *The Heart of God*

An Inch of Time

"Millions of money for an inch of time!" cried Elizabeth, the gifted but ambitious Queen of England, upon her dying bed. Unhappy woman, reclining upon a couch, with ten thousand dresses in her wardrobe, a kingdom on which the sun never sets, at her feet — all now are valueless; and she shrieks in anguish and she shrieks in vain, for a single "inch of time." She had enjoyed threescore and ten years. Like too many among us, she had devoted them to wealth, to pleasure, to pride, and ambition, so that her whole preparation for eternity was crowded into a few moments; and hence she, who had wasted more than half a century, would barter millions for an inch of time.

—*The Biblical Museum*

* * *

Safe Either in Life or Death

"But," I said, "some of your sons were drowned, for all that you say about safety." "Well, sir," she answered with a sigh, "I trust they are none the less safe for that. It would be a strange thing for an old woman like me to suppose that safety lay in not being drowned. What is the bottom of the sea, sir?" "The hollow of His hand," I replied, and she said no more.

—*King's Business*

* * *

"Yours Forever!"

Remember that what you possess in this world will be found at the day of your death and belong to someone else; what you are will be yours forever.

—Henry Van Dyke

* * *

Possible, but Improbable

One of our greatest preachers was speaking on deathbed repentances recently when he said something like this: "I think the reason that God set the stage for Jesus to be crucified between two thieves was not just to fulfill a prophecy, but to teach a great lesson, namely, that it is *possible* for a man to be saved on his deathbed as the thief

who appealed to Jesus received the assurance, "To day shalt thou be with me in paradise.' " On the other hand, it teaches us that it's *highly improbable*, for you will remember there are thousands of conversions recorded in the Bible and this is the sole record of a deathbed conversion. God expects us to give Him our lives and not just our souls.

—*Teacher, S.B.C.*

* * *

"Eternal Spring In My Heart!"

In the face of death a genuine Christian manifests a calm and victorious spirit. Shortly before his passing, a friend asked John Quincy Adams how he was. The old man, feeble but not despondent, answered: "Mr. Adams was never better, but the house in which he lives is weather-beaten and showing signs of age and decay. So, Mr. Adams is getting his effects together, preparatory to moving out."

As Victor Hugo's life drew near its close, he said: "Winter is on my head, but eternal spring is in my heart. When I go down to the grave I cannot say: 'I have finished my life.' My day's work will begin again the next morning. The tomb is not a blind alley; it is a thoroughfare. It closes on the twilight to open with the dawn."

Paul in his last letter wrote: "I am now ready . . . the time of my departure is at hand." The word translated "departure" literally means "unloosing," as when sailors unloose their boats and put out to sea.

—*Gospel Herald*

* * *

"Like Muffled Drums"

"Art is long, and time is fleeting,
    And our hearts, though stout and
        brave,
Still, like muffled drums, are beating
Funeral marches to the grave!"
        —Henry Wadsworth Longfellow

* * *

Franklin's Epitaph

Benjamin Franklin wrote the following epitaph for his own tomb: "The Body of Benjamin Franklin, Printer,

Like the Cover of an Old Book, Its Contents Torn Out and Stripped of Its Lettering and Gilding, Lies Here, Food for Worms. Yet the Work Itself shall not be Lost; for it will, as He Believed, Appear once More in a New and More Beautiful Edition, Corrected and Amended by The Author."
—*Wesleyan Methodist*

* * *

"Well Done!"

Servant of God, well done;
Rest from thy loved employ;
The battle fought, the vict'ry won,
Enter thy Master's joy.

The voice at midnight came;
He started up to hear;
A mortal arrow pierced his frame;
He fell, but felt no fear.

The pains of death are past;
Labor and sorrow cease;
And life's long warfare closed at last,
His soul is found in peace.

Soldier of C' rist, well done;
Praise be ·j new employ;
And, while eternal ages run,
Rest in thy Saviour's joy.
—James Montgomery

* * *

The Land of the Living

When the Puritan Owen lay on his deathbed his secretary wrote (in his name) to a friend, " 'I am still in the land of the living.' Stop, alter that," said Owen. " *'I am yet in the land of the dying, but I hope soon to be in the land of the living.'* "
—J. L. Hurlbut

* * *

"Living or Dying"

An aged Scotchman, while dying, was asked what he thought of death, and he replied, "It matters little to me whether I live or die. *If I die I will be with Jesus, and if I live Jesus will be with me.*"
—A. C. Dixon, in
The Bright Side of Death

The Only Faith

An old woman who lay dying was visited by her minister. "You know that I am not long for this world," she whispered, "but I am not afraid to die. The Master knows *I have taken him at his word.*" Was not this a beautiful faith?
—*Sunday Circle*

* * *

Death Ends All

I was talking to an atheist one day, and he said, "I do not believe, Dr. Wilson, what you are preaching." I said, "You have told me what you do not believe; perhaps you will tell me what you do believe." He replied, "I believe that death ends all." "So do I," I said. "What! You believe death ends all?" "I certainly do," I answered. "Death ends all your chance for doing evil; death ends all your joy; death ends all your projects, all your ambitions, all your friendships; death ends all the gospel you will ever hear; death ends it all for you, and you go out into the outer darkness. As for myself, death ends all my wanderings, all my tears, all my perplexities, all my disappointments, all my aches and pains; death ends it all, and I go to be with my Lord in glory." "I never thought of it that way," he said. The outcome was that I led that man to Christ by just agreeing with him that "death ends all."
—Dr. Walter L. Wilson, in
The Sunday School Times

* * *

True, Indeed!

A newspaper cutting referred to a striking story in an anonymous book of memoirs published not long ago. The writer met the woman who nursed the great agnostic, Professor J. H. Huxley, through his last illness. She said that as he lay dying the great skeptic suddenly looked up at some sight invisible to mortal eyes, and, staring a while, whispered at last, "So it *is* true."
—From *Fingertips on Glory,*
by Reginald Kirby

* * *

Going to Bed in the Dark

Dr. Guthrie tells of a dying woman who missed all sense of the presence of

Him whom she had served with exceptional faithfulness and enjoyment, and who, when questioned as to her state, replied, "If God please to put his child to bed in the dark, his will be done." Nothing could be better than that saying. In it we see the victory of faith over feeling, of reason over mood.

—Dr. Kelman

* * *

The Meaning of Death

The story is told by William H. Ridgeway that when a boy, he with other boys would go berrying, and, having filled their baskets, would wait beside the railroad track, as the sun was dipping toward the west, and have the train "run over them." But the train didn't run over them at all. It was only the shadow that enveloped them. There they sat, knowing they were in no danger but keyed up to the highest pitch in anticipation of the oncoming of the thundering locomotive and the long passenger cars. As it swept by them, *they were in the shadow for just a few split seconds, and then the shadow was gone. I know of no better illustration of the meaning of death to the Christian.*

—*Western Recorder*

* * *

Legally Dead

A prisoner, who had been sentenced to death for murder, was sitting in his cell one day when the doctor passed. The prisoner requested him to secure some paper and pen and ink for him, as he had forgotten to make his will, and wished to do it before he was executed. "But," said the doctor, "that will be of no use. *It is too late now for you to make a will. Ever since the judge passed sentence of death upon you, you have been a dead man in the eyes of the law. The fact that the sentence has not been actually executed makes no difference. No court of law in the land can regard as valid any document that you may now produce."* The poor fellow buried his head in his hands as he realized his condition. He was dead, even though he lived. Trace this important principle through the Bible, and you will discover

that here are two things which God hath joined together, and no one can part them asunder: SIN and DEATH.

—Capt. Reginald Wallis, in
The London Christian Herald

* * *

A Convincing Test

Whatever may be thought of the truth of the doctrine of Christianity, no candid man will question its power in the house of mourning and in the hour of death. "The world," wrote Wesley, "may not like our Methodists and evangelical people, but the world cannot deny that they die well."

—*King's Business*

* * *

"Should You Go First"

"Should you go first and I remain
To walk the road alone,
I'll live in memory's garden, dear,
With happy days we've known.
In spring I'll wait for roses red,
When fades the lilac blue;
In early fall when brown leaves call
I'll catch a glimpse of you.

"Should you go first and I remain
For battles to be fought,
Each thing you've touched along the way
Will be a hallowed spot!
I'll hear your voice, I'll see your smile,
Though blindly I may grope,
The memory of your helping hand
Will buoy me on with HOPE.

"Should you go first and I remain
To finish with the scroll,
No length'ning shadows shall creep in
To make this life seem droll.
We've known so much of happiness,
We've had our cup of joy,
And memory is one gift of God
That death cannot destroy.

"Should you go first and I remain,
One thing I'd have you do:
Walk slowly down the path of death,
For soon I'll follow you.
I'll want to know each step you take
That I may walk the same,
For some day down that lonely road,
You'll hear me call your name!"

—*Congressional Record*, June 9, 1941

The Last Hour

A minister named Winstanley was the means of comforting and edifying the great Dr. Samuel Johnson on his deathbed. In a letter to a friend, Hannah Moore, alluding to this, says: "I cannot conclude without remarking what honor God has hereby put upon the doctrine of faith in a crucified Saviour. The man whose intellectual powers had awed all around him, was in his turn made to tremble when the period arrived at which all knowledge appears useless and vanishes away, except the knowledge of the true God, and of Jesus Christ whom He has sent. Effectually to attain this knowledge, this giant in literature must become a fool that he might be wise."

What a comment is this upon that word: *"The loftiness of man shall be bowed down, and the haughtiness of men shall be made low, and the Lord alone shall be exalted in that day!"*

—*Fellowship News*

DEVIL

Shepherd or Butcher, Which?

This interesting little story we pass on to our readers: A party of tourists was on its way to Palestine and its guide was describing some of the quaint customs of the East.

"Now," said he, "you are accustomed to seeing the shepherd following his sheep through the English lanes and byways. Out in the East, however, things are different, for the shepherd always leads the way, going on before the flock. And the sheep follow him, for they know his voice."

The party reached Palestine, and, to the amusement of the tourists, almost the first sight to meet their eyes was that of a flock of sheep being driven along by a man. The guide was astonished and immediately made it his business to accost the shepherd.

"How is it that you are driving these sheep?" he asked. "I have always been told that the Eastern shepherd leads his sheep."

"You are quite right, sir," replied the man. "The shepherd does lead his sheep. But you see, I'm not the shepherd, I'm the butcher."

—*Church of God Evangel*

* * *

The Barrier Between

When I was in England, during one of the conferences, a woman told me she was once awakened by a very strange noise of pecking, or something of the kind. When she got up, she saw a butterfly flying back and forth inside the window pane in a great fright, and outside a sparrow pecking and trying to get in. The butterfly did not see the glass, and expected every minute to be caught, and the sparrow did not see the glass, and expected every minute to get the butterfly. Yet all the while that butterfly was as safe as if it had been millions of miles away, because of the glass between it and the sparrow. So it is with Christians. Satan cannot touch the soul that has the Lord Jesus Christ between itself and him.

—*Josiah Strong in Earnest Worker*

* * *

What to Preach Against

A Christian captain once invited a Calvinist clergyman to preach on his vessel. The preacher replied, "Oh, I could not do that; for you see I am a Calvinist and you are an Arminian, and I might say something to hurt your feelings." "Sir," was the reply, "what we wish you to do is to come and preach against the Devil."

—*Sunday School Times*

* * *

Is the Devil Afraid of You?

A distinguished clergyman said, in vindication of his course as a Christian preacher and reformer, "I am not afraid of the devil."

Another said in reply, "That is not the point, but this: Is the devil afraid of you, doctor?"

If the father of lies is afraid of us, we may be sure that we are right and ought to go ahead.

—*Moody Monthly*

* * *

Change Your Hitching Post

A young Western farmer, who had frequented the village barroom, was converted to Christ, but on his visits to the village continued to tie his team to the hotelman's hitching post. The trained and watchful eye of a good old deacon noticed this, and after congratulating the youth upon his conversion, he said: "George, I am a good deal older than you, and will be pardoned, I know, if I make a suggestion out of my wider experience. No matter how strong you think you are, take my advice and at once change your hitching post." Do not stop to parley with the Tempter, as many a one has been ruined in this way. Christ made no mistake when He said, "Watch!"

—*Expositor*

* * *

When Christ is in Control

Martin Luther was often very graphic in his description of the activities of the Devil. Asked one time how he overcame the Devil, he replied, "Well, when he comes knocking upon the door of my heart, and asks 'Who lives here?' the dear Lord Jesus goes to the door and says, 'Martin Luther used to live here but he has moved out. Now I live here.' The Devil seeing the nail-prints in the hands, and the pierced side, takes flight immediately." It is surely good for every life and for every home to have Jesus as a permanent resident. This assured, heavenly blessings are sure to fall upon such bodies.

—*Sword of the Lord*

* * *

When Satan Growls

"The best evidence of God's presence is the Devil's growl." So said Mr. C. H. Spurgeon, and that little sentence has helped many a tried and tired child of God to stand fast and even to rejoice under the fiercest attacks of the foe. We read in the Book of Samuel that the moment David was crowned at Hebron, "all the Philistines came up to seek David." And the moment we get anything from the Lord worth contending for, then the Devil comes to seek us.

—A. B. Simpson, in *Alliance Weekly*

* * *

Demons

A missionary in the South Sea Evangelical Mission, working in the Solomon Islands, thinks that *those who scoff at the reality of Satan and demons would revise their theology if they could be in a heathen village for a few days.* He tells of a notorious old witch doctor whose mind was incapable of grasping spiritual ideas. When he was convicted of sin and he accepted Christ his mind cleared, and his joy was unbounded. But Satan did not easily release him. Next day a man hurried to the mission, crying: "Come quick! Old Mae-hue shake-shake too much; old fella devil come back." The old man was found grasping the rafters of his low dwelling, shaking the building with great power, and crying out in an unearthly way. Prayer was offered and soon Mae-hue called out, "Lord Jesus, save me from this devil's power." Immediately he fell exhausted to the floor and slept heavily for a few hours. He soon recovered and has gone on since a happy Christian.

—*Missionary Review of the World*

* * *

Why He Wasn't Afraid

In the old slave days, says the *Home Herald*, there was a colored man who was a faithful Christian, and his master often tried to bother him. "Sam, aren't you afraid the Devil will get you?" "No, massa, not a bit afraid he will get me." "But," said the master, "isn't the Devil much stronger than you?" "Oh, yes, massa, Devil much stronger than me." "But aren't you afraid he will get you?" "No, massa." "Why not, if he's so much stronger than you?" "Because, massa, just as soon as I see the Devil getting

167

after me, I simply look up there and say, 'Lord, look after your property.' An' I believe the Lord am able to look after his property."

—*Sunday School Times*

* * *

Recipe for Devil's Food

Take one fine boy of tender years,
Remove the ties of love,
Mix with parental neglect and bad company in equal parts,
Sift in a few foul stories,
Add a dash of deviltry, and a measure of mischief,
Allow to soak in, then beat into a fury;
Add a pinch of hate, then crush with brute force, putting in a pound of parental cussing;
Shake well, then turn into the street to harden;
Garnish with ungodliness.
Serve with six months in the workhouse.

—*Used by permission of* Dr. C. H. Williamson

* * *

Ensnaring Funnels

Boys often entrap and catch sparrows by a simple device. They roll a piece of paper into the form of a funnel and stick it in the ground, putting seed at the bottom. The bird thrusts its head down into the funnel to get at the seed, and when it would lift its head the funnel sticks on, and it cannot see to direct its flight. *Satan is continually getting men ensnared in his funnels to get at his seed, and so he blinds them and they cannot fly.*

—*Arthur T. Pierson, in* Bible and Spiritual Life

* * *

"Talking Against God"

We are told that Billy Bray, the Cornish miner, was noted far and near for his piety. One year his potato crop was almost a failure. As he was digging the potatoes, Satan said, "There, Billy, isn't that poor pay for serving your Father the way you have all this year? Just see those small potatoes!"

"Ah, Satan," said Billy, "at it again talking against my Father? Bless His Name! Why, when I served you I did not have any potatoes at all. I thank my dear Father for small potatoes."

Those who thank God for the little things soon find their blessings multiplying.

—*Gospel Herald*

* * *

The Riddle

A lady in the west of England, on reading out the riddle from her cracker at a tea party, surprised her friends as well as herself at the great truth so jestingly written. "Question: Why is the Devil like a pawnbroker? Answer: Because he claims all the unredeemed." Surely this would startle and arouse some poor careless souls. How often God uses the foolish things of this world for his wise purposes!

—*Christian Herald* (*London*)

* * *

Do You Believe in the Devil?

A friend of mine once asked me if I believed in a personal Devil, to which I replied with some emphasis, "No!" His only answer was a lifting of eyebrows as though wondering at my heterodoxy; whereupon I proceeded to clear myself: "I most certainly believe there *is* a personal Devil, but far be it from me to believe *in* him. He is a liar and the father of lies, and how he has lied about the Word of God! It has been the method of Satan from the beginning to tamper with, distort, and otherwise cast doubts upon the Word. 'Yea, hath God said . . . ?' was the crafty, doubt-sowing utterance by which he deceived Eve."

—*Dr. E. J. Pace*

* * *

Why the Devil Hates Genesis

Dr. Graham Scroggie, of Edinburgh, spoke at one of the sessions on the text, "In the volume of the book it is written of me." Among other things, he said that modern criticism tells us that Genesis is a myth and Revelation a mystery." He then asked, "I wonder who it was that inspired that theory." A voice in the tent shouted out, "The Devil!" "Quite, right," exclaimed Dr. Scroggie; "and I will tell you why the Devil is so anxious to get rid of Genesis and Revelation; because in Genesis his sentence is declared and in Revelation it is executed."

—*Moody Monthly*

* * *

Destroying Satan's Power — but Not with a Machete

Two young Chorti Indians of Guatemala, descendants of the ancient Mayas, heard that in the meeting of the "*evangelicos,*" while preaching was going on, the Devil came and showed himself to those present. Consequently they came across the river to the little meeting of believers and sat on the front bench, each armed with his long machete, with the determination to put an end to the Devil when he should appear. They waited expectantly but did not see the Devil. However, as the Gospel message was given they saw Jesus Christ, and soon came to know His power to deliver from the works of the Devil, and their feet have been "beautiful upon the mountains" of Honduras as they have pastored the flocks of God and preached the message of life to the unevangelized.

—*Sunday School Times*

* * *

The Devil Breaks Forth!

M. Barbezat, working in the Lake Tchad region of French Central Africa, tells of fevers and tropical infections, the hostility of Moslems, the tracks of lions, jealous Catholic competition, and demonic possession. Of the last he says: "I was profoundly moved and uncomfortable. This contact with the powers of darkness was repugnant, like a breath from hell. When I retired I put myself under the protection of the blood.

"Each time we go into these villages, which are under the power of demon worship and Islam, the Devil breaks forth. The first night, in an Arab village, we had a meeting around the fire and the principal men of the village were there. They heard me well until the first mention of Jesus' name. 'We like to hear you talk of God. Of Jesus we will not hear.' Some rose and spit on the ground, going away. Others mocked and laughed, even when I spoke of God's judgments.

"But at another village, Paul and Mareina gave their personal witness to the change which God had effected in their life by the power of His Spirit through the new birth. We talked long. Finally one of the men said: 'What strange words! It would be well if God changed our hearts also.' Others said the same, and we stayed on until the moon was high in heaven, and in spite of mosquitoes, speaking to these blacks who had never heard the name."

—*Sunday School Times*

* * *

How To Deal With Satan

A number of simple people were talking of temptation, and the part which Satan takes in the believer's temptations came into discussion. Many good things were uttered. A quaint old pilgrim was appealed to. The old man rose and said: "Well, my friends, you ask me what I think to be the best way to deal with Satan. I'll tell you. Now, if you'll take an old pilgrim's advice, you'll never parley with him. He ain't wise; for if he had been, he'd have stopped in Heaven. But he's artful, and he's had a pretty long spell these six thousand years in studying the weak points of human nature. And so sure as you begin to parley with him, he'll outwit you and throw you. I'll tell you what I have done with him these many years; I never speak to him at all, but just as soon as he comes to me, I always introduce him to my betters."

—A. B. Simpson, in
The Alliance Weekly

* * *

Mrs. Chiang's Deliverance

Mr. Chiang had heard the Gospel when in the army, but had never taken it to heart. After returning home he married, only to find that his wife was demon-possessed. They burned incense in vain efforts to appease the demons which were determined to kill her. Several times she tried to hang herself. Her husband realizing there was nothing else he could do, brought her into the Gospel hall. While she was here, a very fine doctor from another mission visited us. I asked him if he ever had dealings with demon-possessed people. He replied that he had not, so I asked him to see this woman. While he was with me, I questioned the demon, who answered in a high-pitched voice — very different from the woman's ordinary soft voice. He told us his name was "the Hanger," that he had already killed several people, and wanted to kill this woman, too, but he dared not stay at the Gospel hall. He was the leader, and there were four other demons with him. After listening to this for a while, I asked the doctor, 'Is this insanity or demon-possession?" He replied, "Demon-possession." The next day the demons told us that Jesus had bound their leader, and they were looking for a place to go. They said they feared our Heavenly Father, and that He was punishing them. They even wept aloud because Jesus was "hurting" them. In less than a week dear Mrs. Chiang was completely delivered, and she is now a bright little Christian. Praise God for the power of Jesus' matchless name!

—*Moody Monthly*

* * *

"Good News Too Much!"

As Banfield of Nigeria sat with his native teacher translating the twentieth chapter of Revelation, he reached the verse that speaks of Satan being bound for a thousand years. The native had been listening spellbound, and suddenly made a rush for the door and ran up and down the yard in a state of ecstatic joy. When the translator followed to find the cause of his joy the pundit

said, "Good news too much, Master; no Devil for a thousand years!"

—*Evangelical Christian*

* * *

Not Much To Worry About

One effect of faithful preaching is the attention of the Devil; he never overlooks a thrust at him or at his interests. Two things should discourage the preacher: no response from the unsaved and no opposition from the Devil. In Ephesus the Devil used Demetrius and the craftsmen to perpetrate a riot in the city. A disturbed Devil is positive evidence of good preaching. We sometimes wonder whether the Devil is doing much worrying about the present attack of the churches.

—Dr. John L. Hill, in
the Teacher, S. B. C.

* * *

He Silenced the Devil

If you find yourself getting miserly, begin to scatter, like a wealthy farmer in New York State that I heard of. He was a noted miser but he was converted. Soon after, a poor man who had been burned out and had no provisions, came to him for help. The farmer thought he would be liberal and give him a ham from his smokerhouse. On his way to get it, the tempter whispered to him: "Give him the smallest one you have." He had a struggle whether he would give a large ham or a small ham, but finally he took down the largest he could find.

"You are a fool," the devil said.

"If you don't keep still," the farmer replied, "I'll give him every ham I have in the smokehouse."

—*Gospel Herald*

* * *

So Is The Devil

On one occasion, when he visited Boston, a prominent clergyman remarked, "I am very sorry to have you come here, Mr. Whitefield." To which the evangelist replied, "So is the Devil, sir!"

—*Sunday School Times*

DELIVERANCE, GOD'S

Rickenbacker's Rescue

Captain Edward V. Rickenbacker, foremost American airman in World War I, has recently returned from his harrowing experiences in the South Pacific. His story of 21 days afloat in the sea is most remarkable.

He, with seven others left Hawaii by airplane for a certain island, but when the time had elapsed for them to arrive, there was no land in sight. Their compass had failed them and their radio was not working properly. They were lost! And their gas was about exhausted.

They finally exhausted their gas and had to land on the water. They were so eager to get away from the airplane before it sank that they failed to take water and rations. They only had four scrawny oranges between them.

They had three rubber boats. Three men were put in the first one, three in the second (including Captain Rickenbacker), and two in the third. They tied the boats together.

Private Bartek in Captain Rickenbacker's boat had a Bible in the pocket of his jumper and the second day out prayer meetings were organized in the evening and morning and the men took turns reading passages from the Bible. Captain Rickenbacker said: "I know things about these men's lives that probably no other living soul knows; any sins of commission or omission were confessed."

Again he said: "Frankly and humbly we prayed for deliverance. After the oranges were gone, there showed up a terrific lot of pangs of hunger and we prayed for food."

He continued: "If it weren't for the fact that I had seven witnesses, I wouldn't dare tell this story because it seems so fantastic. Within an hour after prayer meeting, a sea gull came and landed on my head and you can imagine my nervousness in trying to turn around and get him; which I did. We wrung his head and feathered him and carved up his carcass and distributed it, and used his innards for bait."

With this bait they succeeded in catching two fish. They ran into rain storms and caught the water with their shirts, socks, and handkerchiefs; and then wrung it out. For several days this meant two sips of water per man each day! During the last days their supply of water increased.

On the 13th day one man died and had to be buried at sea.

On the 17th day they saw an airplane — more on the 18th and 19th days. But the planes did not discover them.

On the 20th day they cut the boats apart and Captain Cherry was found in his boat alone, three of the men landed on an uninhabited island and were there a day and a half before being rescued.

On the 21st day American planes found and rescued Captain Rickenbacker and the men in his boat.

—Selected

* * *

Hymn and a Pill Save Doomed Sub

The British Press Association reported this strange incident:

A British submarine lay disabled on the ocean floor. After two days, hope of raising her was abandoned. The crew on orders of the commanding officer began singing:

"Abide with me! fast falls the eventide,
The darkness deepens — Lord, with me abide!
When other helpers fail and comforts flee,
Help of the helpless, oh, abide with me!"

The officer explained to the men that they did not have long to live. There was no hope of outside aid, he said, because the surface searchers did not know the vessel's position.

Sedative pills were distributed to the men to quiet their nerves. One sailor was affected more quickly than the others, and he swooned. He fell against a piece of equipment and set in motion

171

the submarine's jammed surfacing mechanism.

The submarine went to the surface and made port safely.

—*Gospel Herald*

* * *

When the Missionaries Prayed

The missionaries at a certain Chinese mission were ordered by the British legation to leave Sanyuan because of the dangers from conflicting soldiery. "Carts were ordered, and all was ready to start the next day. Then it came over the missionaries that it would be dishonoring God to go to a place of safety, leaving their flock exposed. So a prayer meeting was held, with the result that the carts were sent away and they stayed. They were kept in peace of mind, although a robber band, a thousand strong, was marching on the city and was within twelve miles. Then came a terrific downpour of rain, such as had not been known for years, scattering the robbers and making the roads impassable." It was a small scale representation of the story of Sennacherib's host.

—*Glad Tidings*

* * *

Prayer Averts A Massacre

Prayer saved the congregation of the first church ever built in Madison county from an Indian massacre.

This information was found by W. T. Cash, state librarian, in an old letter which is a part of the historical manuscripts he has collected at the state library.

Cash said the date of the incident is not given in the letter, but that it occured between 1830, when the church was built, and 1848 when the Florida Indian war ended. The church stood in Hickstown, about five miles west of the present town of Madison. The town was named after a Seminole Indian chief, Billy Hicks, Cash said.

The Indians determined to surround the Hickstown church one Sunday when a large congregation had assembled and massacre the entire assemblage, the letter said. When the Indians had gath-

ered close to the church they noticed the congregation was kneeling in prayer.

The Red Men then said to each other, "They are talking to the Great Spirit and He will be very angry with us if we kill them."

The letter said the Indians then slipped away quietly, but one of them captured later related to the whites how narrowly they had escaped being massacred in the Hickstown church.

—*Tampa (Fla.) Tribune*

* * *

Prayer and Lions

A faithful pastor, in the dead of the night, was whelmed with a burden of prayer for a missionary in Africa. He arose and gave himself for hours to earnest intercession for the safety of his friend. At that very time this was happening in the heart of Africa: The missionary, accompanied by a native, had started out to hunt. As they journeyed they ran upon two lions and a lioness. The missionary fired, killing one of the lions, and wounding the other. The lioness seemingly fled. In fact she had only hidden in the jungle. The missionary now advanced and fired again upon the wounded lion. The rifle had scarcely cracked when the great brute lioness leaped upon him from her ambush. With one blow she struck him to the ground. In an instant her teeth were sunk in his arm, and her claws tore fiercely at his shoulder. He cried out to the native to shoot, but the latter could not, as the missionary was between him and the lioness. In his panic, however, the native fired his rifle in the air. At once the lioness looked up. She dropped the missionary from her jaws. He rolled over into the bottom of a shallow ditch. And then instead of leaping upon him and finishing her work, the lioness turned and trotted into the jungle. The bleeding missionary was helped into camp. There, after six weeks, he recovered completely from an experience which it is given to but few men to pass through. God had indeed "stopped the mouths of lions" for him. The tidings of his wonderful escape went back home to his faithful pastor. And he who had *prayed* now *saw.*

He saw the peril which had menaced his friend. He *saw* why God had aroused him at midnight to pray. He *saw* the miraculous deliverance which had come to pass. Because he prayed, and prayed in faith, he saw the glory of God in wondrous answer. And so may you — if you pray likewise.

—James McConkey

* * *

A Chinese Christian's Faith

A Chinese village was on fire. A Christian old woman went onto the roof of her little dwelling and cried out so that all around could hear: "Jesus, save this house!" Next day, amid the charred ruins and desolation, her cottage alone was standing, a monument to the power of prayer. The heathen around were much impressed by such an object lesson on the foreign doctrine.

—*Wonderful Word*

* * *

God Controls Droughts

Joao Mbaxi, a native convert, was placed in charge of work among a cannibal African tribe, among whom work had been begun only a few months before. It was in the dry season when he took charge. Soon the rainy season came, but month after month went by without rain. Then came the dry season again. Every one was suffering from hunger, and starvation was near. The native chief told Joao that in all the years they had worshiped their fathers' gods, rain had never failed them to this extent. The mission workers must leave the country and take the white man's God with them. Joao refused to go. The chief said, "If your God is good, and rules the sky, why doesn't it rain? If it does not rain by sunrise tomorrow, we will drink your blood and eat your flesh." Joao thought of Elijah, and he went to his hut and prayed to Elijah's God, while the heathen were waiting for sunrise and their cannibal feast. Toward daylight came thunder, lightning, and torrential rain.

"Miracles in Black"
by John C. Wengatz, D.D.

How They Learned That God Answers

A lad who had not been reared in a Christian home, knew nothing about prayer, and cared less, had been on a torpedoed ship, when all on board were thrust out into the water to swim for their lives. Twelve of the boys kept together. Suddenly, horrified, they saw a lake of burning oil coming toward them. It was impossible to escape. What could they do? Just then a Lutheran, the only Christian in the group, began to pray aloud. It was the heart cry of one in dire need to the God of mercy whom he knew: "O God, save us! O God, save us! O God, save us!" And with that, every one of the eleven, who had never known or thought about our God of love, followed aloud with, "Please, God! Please, God!" Immediately the flaming oil parted, leaving a clear, wide path directly in front of them. And what do you think our gracious Lord had placed in this path? A raft! The lad who told the story ended with, "And no one can persuade these boys that God does not hear prayer."

—*Sunday School Times*

* * *

God's Care for His Own

One afternoon we were walking on Jaffa Read — the main street of modern Jerusalem — just returning from visiting the homes of some of our Arab believers. We were passing through the busiest section of the city and the street was packed with people — all Jews — when suddenly I remembered that we intended to do a bit of shopping but had already passed the particular locality. Mrs. Fried suggested that we turn back and attend to it, but I thought that the matter was of very little importance and could be taken care of next day, and so I suggested that we continue homeward, since it was close to suppertime. We walked only a few steps when I was strangely pressed to return, after all, and attend to the shopping. We turned back and had walked in the opposite direction only about a hundred feet when back of us we heard the most terrific explosion that seemed to be right beside us, but actually was about

173

two hundred feet away. A bomb had been thrown, probably from a passing car, into the midst of the crowd. Next day we went to the scene, and, as far as we were able to calculate, had we failed to turn back at the time we did, we would have been at the very spot where the explosion took place!

—*Sunday School Times*

* * *

Petition Denied, But Need Supplied:

Mr. James H. McConkey, in his book on prayer, says that one summer when he was ill he spent the summer on the shores of the Great Lakes. Sailing was the only recreation possible. One day, when sailing in the midst of the bay, the wind suddenly died out. His boat was utterly becalmed, with not a breath of air astir. The hot rays of the August sun beat down mercilessly upon his weak body. He had come out with a stiff breeze, and naturally he began to pray for a breeze to take him back. For an hour he prayed, but no breeze came. Then he espied a boat coming toward him. An old fisherman, realizing that Mr. McConkey would be helpless out in the bay with no wind, came out to row the sailboat to harbor. Then Mr. McConkey says that he learned his lesson. His real need had been for deliverance, and while God had denied the words of his petition, He provided for his need.

—*Sunday School Times*

ENCOURAGEMENT

"What Would You Have Done?"

A member of the young minister's official board had fallen into disgrace. He had sinned grievously. The young minister called together his board. With Jesus' compassion in his heart, he sorrowed for the erring, sinning one. He wanted to bring him back to the One against whom he had sinned so terribly. Standing before his board, he questioned them one by one. Beginning with the first member of his board, he asked, "If you had been tempted as was our brother, what would you have done?" "O, pastor," he exclaimed, "I would have never fallen into sin as did our fellow member!" Others, in answering the pastor's question, made the selfsame declaration, being firmly convinced of their powers to resist temptation, and seemingly oblivious of the Scriptural warnings, "Wherefore let him that thinketh he standeth take heed lest he fall" (I Cor. 10:12); "Pride goeth before destruction, and an haughty spirit before a fall" (Prov. 16:18); "Watch and pray, that ye enter not into temptation: the spirit indeed is willing, but the flesh is weak" (Matt. 26:41).

Finally, the minister addressed the question to the last member of the board.

This was his answer to the pastor's question, "Pastor, I feel in my heart that if I had been tempted and tested as was our brother, I would have fallen even lower than he has fallen!" Said the pastor to this one, "You are the only member of this board fit to go with me to our sinning brother, and restore him to fellowship and acceptance with the Lord, whose loving heart grieves with ours over the fallen one!"

"Brethren, if a man be overtaken in a fault, ye which are SPIRITUAL, restore such an one in the spirit of meekness; considering thyself, lest thou also be tempted" (Gal. 6:1).

—W. B. K.

* * *

I Know Something Good About You

Wouldn't this world be better,
　If folks whom we meet would say
"I know something good about you,"
　And treat you just that way?

Wouldn't it be splendid,
　If each handshake, good and true,
Carried with it this assurance:
　"I know something good about you?"

Wouldn't life be happier,
If the good that's in us all,
Were the only thing about us
That people would recall?

Wouldn't our days be sweeter,
If we praised the good we see;
For there is a lot of goodness,
In the worst of you and me?

Wouldn't it be fine to practice,
This way of thinking too;
You know something good about me,
I know something good about you?
—*Church of Christ Advocate*

* * *

One Talent

I have no voice for singing
I cannot make a speech,
I have no gift for music,
I know I cannot teach.

I am no good at leading,
I cannot "organize,"
And anything I write
Would never win a prize.

But at roll call in meetings
I always answer, "Here."
When others are performing
I lend a listening ear.

After the program's over,
I praise its every part.
My words are not to flatter,
I mean them from my heart.

It seems my only talent
Is neither big nor rare,
Just to listen and encourage
And to fill a vacant chair.

But all the gifted people
Could not so brightly shine,
Were it not for those who use
A talent such as mine!
—Alice Barbour Bennett
in *Christian Observer*

* * *

To Have This Mind

One of the greatest musicians that the world has ever known was Ludwig von Beethoven. Born into a musical family in Germany, Beethoven was compelled to spend a lonely childhood while he practised his music for hours upon hours every day. His genius soon showed itself. At the age of eleven he was composing his own music and conducting an orchestra, and in his late teens he went to Vienna for further study. There he reached fame if not fortune. There he composed what was perhaps his most bewitching composition.

Beethoven was passing a cobbler's cottage early one evening and heard someone practicing one of his compositions. As he paused to listen, he overheard the girl express the desire to hear a real musician render it properly. He entered the house and discovered that the young lady was blind. Offering to play for her, he sat at the piano and did so for an hour or more. Dusk had settled into evening. The lone candle in the room went out. But the moonlight glistened in the room and, under its inspiration and that received from the blind girl who so loved his music, Beethoven composed the "Moonlight Sonata."
—*The Pilgrim*

* * *

"Cheer Him, Boys!"

There was a fire in the big city, and the firemen flung their ladders together, and went up in their brave fashion to the very topmost story to rescue the people in peril. One after another was rescued by the brave fire laddies. All had been rescued, it seemed. No! Yonder is a white face at that upper window. They wrapped something about one of their firemen, and, breasting the fierce flames, he went again to that window, and put a robe around the little woman and started down. Then they saw him tremble as the fire raged around him, and it seemed that he would fall with his precious burden, but the fire chief cried to his men: "Cheer him, boys! Cheer him, boys!" And they cheered him, cheer after cheer, and heart came back, and he came down, with the precious life saved! Oh, you and I are to give our lives cheering a needy world! Ponder this beautiful sentence from

Isaiah: "They helped every one his neighbour; and every one said to his brother, Be of good cheer"!

-—George W. Truett

* * *

"That Was Fine!"

I once met a mother walking with a little crippled boy, whose frail limbs were covered with steel braces up to his thighs. He was hobbling along in a pitiable way, but his mother was encouraging him at every step. "That's good! that's fine! Why, you're doing splendidly!" she would say, and then the poor little one would try so hard to do still better than he had done, not to show off, but just to please his mother. Presently he said, "Mamma, watch me; I'm going to run."

"Very well, darling, let me see you run," said the mother in a most encouraging tone. Some mothers would have said, "You'd better not try it or you'll break you neck!"

I watched almost as eagerly as his mother to see how he would do. He took two or three steps that did pretty well, and then he caught one foot against the brace on his other leg, and would have fallen headlong over the curb, but his mother caught him, and put him back on his feet.

Then she stroked his hair, kissed his pale cheek and said, "That was fine! That was splendid! You can do better next time!"

Just so our Heavenly Father often does with us when we stumble in our hobbling efforts to please Him. The little boy's performance was perfect in the eyes of his mother, for she knew only too well the weakness of his frame. In a similar way can the weakest of us fully please God.

—Free Methodist

ENEMIES, TREATMENT OF

"My Opinion of Him"

Hearing General Lee speak in highest terms to President David about a certain officer, another officer, greatly astonished, said to him, "General, do you know that the man of whom you spoke so highly to the president is one of your bitterest enemies, and misses no opportunity to malign you?" "Yes,", replied General Lee, "But the President didn't ask his opinion of me, but my opinion of him!"

—Arthur T. Pierson

* * *

"So Low as to Hate!"

Said Booker T. Washington, one of America's greatest citizens, "No man is able to force me so low as to make me hate him!" Love and hate cannot dwell in the same heart at the same time. O, the havoc worked among God's children in allowing the "root of bitterness" to rankle in their hearts! "This is My commandment, That ye love one another, AS I HAVE LOVED YOU" (Jn. 15:12).

—W. B. K.

* * *

Zamperini's Search for His Tormentors

Louis Zamperini of Compton, California, a former Olympic runner, who ditched his plane off Oahu Hawaii, during World War II and drifted 2,000 miles in 47 days on a life raft, was picked up by a Japanese vessel. He was a prisoner for the two remaining years of the war. He was starved and tortured by his captors . . . At home he was given up for dead. He is in possession of his own death certificate signed by President Roosevelt. Zamperini said he left Japan in 1945 with hatred in his heart against his captors. But in 1949 he was saved at one of Billy Graham's meetings in Los Angeles. "There is such a change in my life that I feel I have a duty to perform," Zamperini told his friends. "That duty is to return to Japan and tell them of the saving power of the Lord Jesus Christ. For now I believe it is Christ or Communism for the nations, Christ or atomic annihilation for the world. Our only remedy for these threats is Christ for the individual." Zamperini is now in Japan with a list of his Japanese guards and captors — and a Bible. He says he returned to seek out the persons who mistreated him and win them to the Saviour. This case is an example of the transforming power of the Gospel of Christ; for the Saviour not only grants the believer the forgiveness of sins, deliverance from judgment, the gift of eternal life, and the Holy Spirit, but also implants the desire in his heart to see others — even his enemies — in possession of the same spiritual blessings.

—Tom M. Olson, in *Now*

* * *

General Lee's Forgiveness

A Union soldier, bitter in his hatred of the Confederacy, lay wounded at Gettysburg. At the close of the battle General Lee rode by, and the soldier, though faint from exposure and loss of blood, raised his hands, looked Lee in the face, and shouted as loudly as he could, "Hurrah for the Union!" The General heard him, dismounted, and went toward him, and the soldier confesses: "I thought he meant to kill me. But as he came up, he looked at me with such a sad expression upon his face that all fear left me, and looking right into my eyes, he said, 'My son, I hope you will soon be well.' If I live a thousand years, I shall never forget the expression on General Lee's face. There he was, defeated, retiring from a field that had cost him and his cause almost their last hope, and yet he stopped to say words like those to a wounded soldier of the opposition who had taunted him as he passed by. As soon as the General left me I cried myself to sleep there upon the bloody battleground."

—W. S. B., in
New Century Leader

Hidden Sin

I heard of a lady who suddenly came out in a rash all over her face and neck and body. She could not go out, for she felt too ashamed. She sent for the doctor, and he prescribed this and that, but she did not get better. The doctor came week after week, and she grew only worse. Her nerves became strained; she lacked fresh air, exercise, and fellowship with her friends. The doctor could not make out the reason for the hideous rash. A specialist was called in and he could not understand the reason. One day when the doctor came this lady said, "You know that woman next door. I wish I could kill her," and she shook with passion as she spoke. The doctor said, "I have discovered the reason for this corruption which has broken out in your body and caused this discoloration of the skin. Now you get things right with your neighbour, and I will come to see you again." When the doctor came again, the trouble had started to clear up, and a few weeks later she was healed.
—Rev. Francis W. Dixon
in *Keswick Week*

* * *

Spurgeon's Deafness

C. H. Spurgeon, while still a young man and a village pastor, was passing the house of a woman known as the village termagant, who greeted him with a volley of words the reverse of polite. Smiling, the young man said, "Yes, thank you; I am quite well." She burst into another string of expletives. "Yes, it does look as if it's going to rain," he replied. Surprised as well as exasperated, the woman exclaimed, "Bless the man, he's as deaf as a post! What's the use of talking to him?"
—*Christian Herald*

* * *

Lincoln and the Harsh Letter

Few people have the tact that President Lincoln had, when dealing with a situation that tempts one to use harsh measures.

When the darkest clouds of the Civil War were hovering over the capital, many things done by the generals were not approved by either Lincoln or Secretary Stanton. Lincoln would take a long time to ponder over situations, but Stanton would, at times, lose his temper and explode. One day Stanton came to see Lincoln about the doings of a certain general. Listening quietly, Lincoln let Stanton show his anger, and when the latter exclaimed, "I would like to write him a letter and tell him what I think of him!" Lincoln remarked quietly, "Well, why not do so? Sit down and write him a letter, saying all you have said to me."

Stanton was surprised for he thought that President Lincoln would object to this. He declared that he would take the President at his word.

Two days later he brought Lincoln the letter he had written, and read it to him. When Stanton had finished, Lincoln smiled and remarked, "That is all right. You have said all you told me you would. Now, what are you going to do with this letter?"

"Why, I am going to give it to him, of course."

"I wouldn't," replied the President quietly. "Throw it in the waste basket."

"What, after spending two days on it," exclaimed Stanton.

"Yes. It took you two days to write it, and it did you a lot of good. You feel a great deal better now, and that is all that is necessary."

The letter went to the waste basket, and Stanton learned an important lesson.

—Young People

* * *

Kills Himself by Ill-Will!

There was a man whose health was good; he was sturdy and strong, his heart action and blood pressure were fine. Then his father died, and he got into a prolonged legal dispute with his sister about their father's will. The case went to court, and the sister won.

From that day on the man could think about nothing but the lawsuit and his sister. He talked about it, thought about it, filled himself with it; it became his obsession. And, each day, he grew to hate his sister more.

Then he began to have difficulty with his heart and his blood pressure. Next his kidneys bothered him. Before many months, various complications killed him.

In commenting on this case, the doctor said, "It seems obvious that he died from bodily injuries wrought by powerful emotion." The man killed himself with ill will — literally committed suicide.

—Gospel Herald

* * *

"Killed" By Love

There is a story of a deacon, who, goaded beyond endurance by the persistent malice of an enemy, vowed he would kill him. It came to the ears of the enemy, who waited to see what the harmless old man would do. Actually the deacon sought every opportunity to do his enemy good. It was first an amusement to the enemy, but when at last the deacon gave costly and sacrificial service to save the man's wife from drowning, the death lock was broken. Said the enemy, "You've done what you said you would, you've killed me — or at least you've killed the man that I was. Now what can I do for you?"

—Young People's Weekly

* * *

Livingstone's Forbearance

Misjudged by a fellow missionary, Livingstone gave up his house and garden at Mabotsa, with all the toil and money they had cost him, rather than have any scandal before the heathen, and began in a new place the labor of house and school building, and gathering the people around him. His colleague was so struck with his generosity that he said had he known his intention, he never would have spoken a word against him. Parting with his garden cost him a great pang. "I like a garden," he wrote, "but Paradise will make amends for all our privations here."

—Choice Gleanings Calendar

The Generalissimo's Forgiveness

A Red Cross official in China, who recently returned to the United States, tells of a visit he made to Chungking to pay his respects to the Generalissimo and Madame Chiang Kai-shek before sailing. Seven times that day Japanese planes had raided the city and dropped bombs. The Generalissimo explained they were trying to find out where he was staying. After a simple dinner the visitor was asked to remain for evening devotions. They knelt together, and first Madame Chiang offered a prayer, then the guest prayed, and finally the Generalissimo. He prayed for the American people to whom his guest was going, then for his own Chinese people, and finally for the Japanese who that day seven times had tried to kill him. Here is a man in whose heart is no bitterness and no spirit of unforgiveness.

—*The Upper Room*

* * *

"He Served Me Cruelly!"

A man came to me and said: "I cannot understand it, sir, but it seems as if God is blotted out of my life. I used to be so happy."

I said: "How is it?"

Said he: "I think it has to do with my treatment of my brother. He served me cruelly over my father's will, and I said I would never forgive him. I am sorry I said it, but he has been going from bad to worse, has lost his wife and child, and is now on a bed of death, and I cannot go to him because I said I never would."

I said: "My friend, it is better to break a bad vow than keep it. Go."

He went, and the smile of God met him just there.

—F. B. Meyer

* * *

Christian "Enemies"

During the fighting in New Guinea, a Digger was left for dead by the side of a trail. Later he recovered consciousness and lay there expecting every moment that Japanese soldiers would arrive and finish him off. Finally four Japanese soldiers did arrive. To his surprise, instead of killing him they lifted him gently and carried him to the side of a track in another part of the forest. Before leaving him one of them said, "You will be quite safe here. Some of your countrymen will arrive soon and pick you up. We are Christians, and hate war."

—*Herald of Hope*

* * *

Something His Neighbor Didn't Have

Two men lived near each other. The river divided their farms. One day when the corn in the beautiful river bottoms was in roasting-ear stage, the cows of one neighbor got out of the pasture and crossed the river into the waving field of corn. They slashed and ruined perhaps a half acre. The man who owned the damaged corn rounded up the cattle and put them in his barn. He made the neighbor pay for every ear of corn that they had destroyed and then made him pay a good price for the cattle before he would return them to him. In the fall of that year the hogs of the man whose corn had been eaten got out and crossed the river into the potato patch of the neighbor. They played havoc with it. This neighbor saw the hogs damage his potato patch, and got the hogs back across the river to the barn where they belonged. The owner saw them coming, got his gun, and hid himself with the avowal that if his neighbor harmed the hogs, he would shoot him. When he saw that he had no intentions of harming the hogs, he was surprised. He came out from his hiding, and said: "You have something I do not have. What is it?" The neighbor replied, "I am a Christian." That night the unregenerate man and his wife went across the river and visited the neighbor. They were both converted before they left the home. On the next Lord's Day they both joined the local church.

—R. C. Campbell,
in *The Teacher*

Bury the Past!

John Wesley, who had continually to settle quarrels, gives some sound advice. In his Journal for Monday, May 28, 1787, he tells of fourteen people who had been "read out" of one of the Societies at once. He said: "I could not find, upon the strictest inquiry, that they had been guilty of any fault of meeting together that evening. So I willingly received them all again; requiring only one condition of the contenders on both sides, to say not one word of anything that was past. The spirit of peace and love gloriously descended on them all at the evening preaching, while I was explaining the 'fruit of the Spirit.' They were again filled with consolation at the Lord's Supper; and again in the morning, while Mr. Broadbent, applied 'Comfort ye, comfort ye my people, saith the Lord.' " When all has been done that can be done to heal a breach, that is a simple but very wise principle, "to say not one word of anything that was past." We need more of that healing medicine today. It is compounded of the ingredients in Paul's prescription: "Forbearing one another, and forgiving one another, if any man have a quarrel against any: even as Christ forgave you, so also do ye" (Col. 3:13).

—Sunday School Times

* * *

A Noble Revenge

An officer in the army one day struck a common soldier. He was young and hot-tempered. The soldier whom he struck was a young man, too, and noted for his courage. He felt the insult deeply, but military discipline forbade that he should return the blow; he could only use words. "I will make you repent it," he said.

One day in the heat of a furious engagement the young soldier saw an officer, who was wounded and separated from his company, gallantly striving to force his way through the enemies who surrounded him. He recognized his insulter and rushed to his assistance. Supporting the wounded man with his arm, together they fought their way through to their own lines.

Trembling with emotion the officer grasped the hand of the soldier and stammered out his gratitude.

"Noble man! What a return for an insult so carelessly given!"

The young man pressed his hand in turn and with a smile said gently, "I told you I would make you repent it." And from that time on they were as brothers. How beautifully that young soldier followed Romans 12:20-21.

—High School Christian

* * *

"If He Thirst, Give Him Drink!"

In one of the mighty battles in old Virginia, a Union officer fell severely wounded in front of the Confederate breastworks. He lay crying piteously for water. A noblehearted Confederate soldier heard his cry, and resolved to relieve him. He filled his own canteen with water, and though the bullets were flying across the field, and he could only go at the risk of his life, yet he went. He gave the suffering officer the much needed drink, and it so touched his heart that the officer instantly took out his gold watch and offered it to his generous foe, but the noble Confederate soldier refused to take it. "Then give me your name and address," said the officer. "My name is James Moore, of Burke County, North Carolina," said the soldier. Then they parted, and the soldier was subsequently wounded by losing a limb. In due time the war was over, and the wounded Union officer returned to his business in New York. And not long after, the Confederate soldier received a letter from the officer to whom he had given the "cup of cold water" telling him that he had settled on him $10,000, to be paid in four annual payments of $2,500 each. Ten thousand dollars for a drink of cold water! That was noble on the part of the Union officer, but to give that drink of water at the risk of his life was still more noble on the part of the brave Confederate soldier!

—Baptist Standard

Praying First

Two Christian men "fell out." One heard that the other was talking against him and he went to him and said: "Will you be kind enough to tell me my faults to my face, that I may profit by your Christian candor and try to get rid of them?"

"Yes, sir," replied the other; "I will do it." They went aside, and the former said: "Before you commence telling what you think wrong in me, will you please bow down with me and let us pray over it, that my eyes may be opened to see my faults as you will tell them? You lead in the prayer."

It was done, and when the prayer was over the man who had sought the interview said: "Now proceed with what you have to complain of in me." But the other replied, "After praying over it, it looks so little that it is not worth talking about. The truth is, I feel now that in going around talking against you, I have been serving the devil myself and have need that you pray for me and forgive me the wrong I have done you." Here and there in almost every community is a man or woman who might profit by this incident.

—*Christian Index*

* * *

The Blight of Unforgiveness

Many years ago I visited an old man on his deathbed. He was a man whom nobody liked — hard, sullen, taciturn, and sour. If you met him on the street and wished him good-day, he would keep his eyes straight in front of him, grunt sulkily and pass on. He lived in a tumbled-down old hut away back in the bush. He spoke to nobody, and he made it perfectly plain that he wished nobody to speak to him. Even the children shunned him.

Some said he was a hermit; some that he was a miser; some that he was a woman-hater; some that he was a fugitive from justice, a man with a guilty secret. But they were all wrong. The simple truth was that in his youth a companion had done him a grievous injury. "I'll remember it to my dying day," he hissed, in a gust of passionate resentment.

And he did. But when his dying day actually came, he realized that the rankling memory of that youthful wrong had soured and darkened his whole life. "I've gone over it by myself every morning," he moaned, as he lay gasping in his comfortless shanty, "and I've thought of it every night. I've cursed him a hundred times each day. I see now," he added brokenly, a suspicion of moisture glistening in his eye, "that my curses have eaten out my soul; they've been like gall on my tongue and gravel in my teeth. My hate has hurt nobody but myself. But, God knows, it's turned my life into hell!" It was true.

The man at whom he had spat out his venomous maledictions, having done all a man could do to atone for the suffering that he had thoughtlessly caused, had dismissed the matter from his mind a generation back. Upon *him* my gnarled old friend's bitterness had produced little or no effect. *It was the man who cherished the sinister memory who suffered most. It shadowed his life; it lent a new terror to death; it expelled every trace of brightness and excluded every ray of hope; and at last, a grim and ghostly companion, it lay down with him in his cold and cheerless grave.*

—F. W. Boreham

* * *

"Jesus Held His Peace"

(Mark 15:3).

The day when Jesus stood alone
And felt the hearts of men like stone,
And knew He came but to atone —
　　That day "He held His peace"

They witnessed falsely to His Word,
They bound Him with a cruel cord,
And mockingly proclaimed Him Lord;
　　"But Jesus held His peace."

Dear friend, have you for far much less,
With rage, which you called "righteousness,"
Resented slights with great distress?
　　Remember — "Jesus held His peace."

—A. B. Simpson

* * *

The Time for Revenge

The haughty favorite of an Oriental monarch threw a stone at a poor priest.

181

The dervish did not dare to throw it back, for the favorite was very powerful. So he picked up the stone and put it carefully in his pocket, saying to himself: "The time for revenge will come by and by, and then I will repay him." Not long afterward, walking in one of the streets, he saw a great crowd, and found to his astonishment that his enemy, the favorite, who had fallen into disgrace with the king, was being paraded through the principal streets on a camel, exposed to the jests and insults of the populace. The dervish seeing all this, hastily grasped at the stone which he carried in his pocket, saying to himself: "The time for my revenge has come, and I will repay him for his insulting conduct." But after considering a moment, he threw the stone away saying: *"The time for revenge never comes:* for if our enemy is powerful, revenge is dangerous, and if he is weak and wretched, then revenge is worse than foolish. It is mean and cruel and in all cases it is forbidden."

—Arthur T. Pierson

* * *

What We "Deserve" — and Get

The only thing we ever did to "deserve" salvation was to be rebels against God. One day a little girl, dressed in white, carrying a bunch of flowers, passed a small boy who was playing in a dusty street. The boy threw a handful of dirt at the girl. It struck the edge of her dress and fell on her shoes. She stood still. Her face flushed as though she would cry, but instead she smiled and threw a flower at the boy who waited to see what she would do. He was surprised and ashamed because in return for dirt he had received a flower. Man is a rebel against God, but all that he has ever received from God was the gift of the Lord Jesus Christ.

—*Revelation*

* * *

Nature Solves a Problem

"If two goats meet each other in a narrow path above a piece of water, what do they do?" asks Luther. "They cannot turn back, and they cannot pass each other; and there is not an inch of spare room. If they were to butt each other both would fall into the water below and be drowned. What will they do, do you suppose? What would you do?"

Well, nature has taught the one goat to lie down and let the other pass over it, and then they both get to the end of the way safe and sound.

Now, Paul was meeting goats on narrow ledges of rock with the sea below, and so are you, and so am I. If I am willing to lie down and let you pass over my prostrate body, then we shall both be saved. *What a lesson of love and concern for our fellow men!*

—Alexander Whyte

* * *

No Place for Hate

Eileen B. Beath in the *Presbyterian Survey* shared this episode with her readers. During the first year of the Chinese-Japanese War, a boy of nine years, Chin Chen, was starting for bed when he said to his mother, "Shall I pray for the Chinese soldiers tonight?" "No, Chin, pray for the little Japanese children whose fathers are fighting and dying in China tonight." Many, many times I have heard Chinese Christians praying for the Japanese. Hate has never had a place in their hearts. If Christianity can do this for individuals, can it not do it for nations?

—*Mennonite*

* * *

It Was He Who Taught Me

John Selwyn, who became the Bishop of the South Pacific, was renowned for his boxing skill in his university days. On a certain occasion he had to utter grave words of rebuke and warning to a professed convert. The man, removed from savagery only by a generation or two, struck the Bishop a violent blow on the face with his clenched fist. All Selwyn did in return was to fold his arms and look into his face. With his powerful arm and massive fist he could have easily knocked him down, but instead he waited calmly for another blow. It was too much for his assailant; he was ashamed and fled into the jungle.

Years afterward the Bishop came home seriously ill. One day the man who had struck him came to his successor to confess Christ in baptism. Convinced of the genuineness of his conversion, he was asked what new name he desired to take as a Christian. "Call me John Selwyn," he replied, "for it was he who taught me what Jesus Christ is like."

　　　　　—Southport Methodist

* * *

Kicking Back

One frosty morning a little girl stood looking out of the window into the farmyard. In the farmyard there stood many cows, oxen and horses, waiting to drink. The cows stood very still until one of them attempted to turn around. She happened to hit the cow nearest her whereupon that cow kicked and hit another. In five minutes all of the cows were kicking one another in fury! The mother of the little girl laughed and said, "My dear, do you see what comes from 'kicking' when you are hit? Just so, I have seen one cross word set a whole family saying angry words!" Later, when the little girl and her brothers were irritable, Mother said, "Take care, my children; remember how the fight in the barnyard began. Never give back a kick for a hit, and you will avoid lots of trouble."

　　　　　—Gospel Herald

* * *

When Struck by a Potato

A Salvation Army officer tells of an old Maori woman who had won the name of "Warrior Brown" by her fighting qualities when in drink or enraged. She was converted, and gave her testimony at an open air meeting, whereupon some foolish person hit her a nasty blow with a potato. A week before, the cowardly insulter would have needed to make himself scarce for his trouble; but what a change! "Warrior" picked up the potato without a word and put it in her pocket. No more was heard of the incident until the harvest festival came around, and then "Warrior"

brought a little sack of potatoes and explained that she had cut up and planted the insulting potato, and was now presenting to the Lord its increase.

　　　　　—Sunday Companion

* * *

Better Than Having Revenge

"A little boy, being asked what forgiveness is, gave the beautiful answer: 'It is the odor that flowers breathe when they are trampled upon.' Philip the Good, when some of his courtiers would have persuaded him to punish a prelate who had used .him ill, declined, saying, 'It is a fine thing to have revenge in one's power; but it is a finer thing not to use it."

　　　　　—Baptist Leader

* * *

Pardon for An Enemy

Two boys were at the same school: George Washington and Peter Miller. Washington became the first president of the United States and Peter Miller became a preacher of the Gospel. Washington lived at Philadelphia, and Miller at Ephrata, a village seventy miles from the capital. For many years the preacher endured much persecution from a man named Michael Wittman, who did all in his power to distress the servant of God. He even inflicted personal violence, injured the building, and publicly denounced the preacher's testimony.

At length Wittman was involved in treason, was arrested, and sentenced to death. Upon this the old preacher walked the seventy miles to Philadelphia to plead for the life of his persecutor. "Well, Peter, what can I do for you?" "For our old acquaintance' sake, George, I have come to beg the life of the traitor Wittman." "No, Peter; this case is too black: I cannot give you the life of your friend." "My *friend!* he is the bitterest enemy any man ever had." And then he told the president what he had suffered from this man for over twenty years. "Ah, then, Peter; this puts another aspect upon the matter. I could

183

not give you the life of your *friend;* but I will freely pardon your *enemy.*"

On the third day the preacher and the persecutor walked back the seventy miles to Ephrata. The man was melted by the pardon; he was soundly converted; Peter baptized him; and the criminal was brought into the joy of God's salvation.　　　　　*—Western Recorder*

Destroying Enemies — The Friendly Way

President Lincoln was once taken to task for his attitude toward his enemies. "Why do you try to make friends of them?" asked an associate. "You should try to destroy them."

"Am I not destroying my enemies," Lincoln gently replied, "when I make them my friends?"　　　　　*—Power*

FAITH

Wesley's Cow Sermon

One day John Wesley was walking with a troubled man who expressed his doubt as to the goodness of God. He said, "I do not know what I shall do with all this worry and trouble." At the same moment Wesley saw a cow looking over a stone wall. "Do you know," asked Wesley, "why that cow is looking over the wall?" "No," said the man who was worried. Wesley said, "The cow is looking over the wall because she cannot see through it. That is what you must do with your wall of trouble — look over it and avoid it." Faith enables us to get above circumstances and look to Christ who is over all, blessed forever.

　　　　　—Wonderful Word

* * *

Our First Good Work

He flipped a page in an old musty volume called "Marshall's Gospel Mystery of Sanctification," and suddenly his eyes were fixed on a passage that stood out like fire from the rest: "The first good work you will ever perform is to believe on the Lord Jesus Christ. Until you do this, all your works, your prayers, tears, and good resolutions are vain. To believe on the Lord Jesus Christ is to believe that He saves you here and now, for He has said, 'Him that cometh to me I will in no wise cast out.'" That was enough. A heart as hungry as his and a mind as keen needed no more. With rapture he slid to his knees and closed with the promise,

and there came to his soul such a sweet restful knowledge of sins forgiven as swept away his fears like a flood. (He was A. B. Simpson).

　　　　　—From Wingspread,
　　　　　by A. W. Tozer

* * *

Seeing — and Believing

Two children were playing on a hillside, when they noticed that the hour was nearing sunset, and one said, wonderingly: "See how far the sun has gone! A little while ago it was right over that tree, and now it is low down in the sky." "Only it isn't the sun that moves; it's the earth. You know, Father told us," answered the other. The first one shook his head. The sun did move, for he had seen it, and the earth did not move, for he had been standing on it all the time. "I know what I see," he said triumphantly. "And I believe Father," said his brother. So mankind divides still — some accepting only what their senses reveal to them, the others believing the Word of God.

　　　　　—Christian Herald

* * *

Who Works the Cure?

A great professor said at the dedication of a new operating amphitheater: "Every patient entering here should bring us the faith and hope that the God of grace and compassion *can* and *will* heal him of his sufferings. Every operator who takes knife in hand should feel a full sense of responsibility; and if he has the joy of receiving thanks of a recovered patient, he can use the words of the famous Huguenot physician addressed to a king: 'I have treated thee: *God has cured thee.*' "

—*King's Business*

* * *

Regulated By God!

"I have no hesitation in saying," says Prof. C. A. Chant, professor of Astro-Physics at Toronto University, "that at least ninety per cent of astronomers have reached the conclusion that the universe is not the result of any blind law, but is regulated by a great Intelligence."

—*Power*

* * *

"Saved By Being Good"?

I asked a little girl of ten if she were a Christian. She replied that she did not know. I next asked her if she were saved. Again she said that she did not know.

I then asked her, "How do we get saved?"

"By being good."

"How good do you have to be?" I questioned.

"You have to be awful good."

"How awful good?"

"Awful, awful good," she answered.

"Are you that good?"

She said she was not.

"Well, I guess then, that you are not saved."

I added, "I am not that good, either." She had known me as the minister in her community. I shall never forget how big her eyes became while she looked at me, as much as to say, "Well, if you are not that good, then you are not saved, and if you are the preacher and you are not saved, pray, then, who is saved?"

Aloud she asked with great earnestness, "How may I get saved?"

What a joy it was to tell her of God's way of salvation.

Only the Lord Jesus saves us. "Believe on the Lord Jesus Christ and thou shalt be saved."

—J. Irvin Overholtzer, in *Handbook on Child Evangelism*

* * *

Faith the Victory

Dr. A. C. Dixon, once a well-known pastor in Boston, found his church needed $2,000 to square accounts. He and his deacons prayed about it. One deacon arose and said, "Brethren, God has answered our prayers. God will send the money in next Sunday's collections." That Sunday it rained very much, and some deacon suggested not to take the collection. The other replied, "I did not trust the weather; I trusted God!" The collection amounted to $2,600. Faith is the victory!

—Joseph T. Larson, in *Christ, The Healer of Broken Hearts.*

* * *

Sheep, Calves, and Such

A young gentleman of very profound intellect and high culture announced to a group of friends in Missouri one day that he would believe nothing that he could not understand. An old farmer chanced to overhear the remark and, turning to the young man, said: "As I was riding into town today, I passed a common on which some sheep were feeding. Do you believe it?"

"Yes," replied the young man.

"Not far from the sheep," said the farmer, "some calves were feeding. Do you believe it?"

"Yes."

"Not far from the calves, some pigs were feeding. Do you believe it?" the farmer continued.

"Yes," was the reply.

"Not far from the pigs some geese were feeding. Do you believe it?"

"Yes."

"Well," said the farmer, "the grass that the sheep ate will turn into wool; the grass that the calves ate will turn into hair; the grass that the pigs ate will turn into bristles; and the grass that the geese ate will turn into feathers. Do you believe that?"

"Yes," the young man answered promptly.

"Do you understand it, though?"

"No," the young man replied.

"Young man," said the farmer, "if you live long, you will find that there are a great many things you will believe without understanding."

—Our Hope

* * *

Will You?

An evangelist tells how when he was conducting a gospel service, a woman who was anxious about her soul's salvation, came to him. She had long said that she could not understand the plan of salvation. The evangelist asked: "Mrs. Franklin, how long have you been Mrs. Franklin?" "Why, ever since I was married," she replied. "And how did you become Mrs. Franklin?" he asked. "When the minister said, 'Wilt thou have this man to be thy wedded husband?' I just said, 'Yes.'" "Didn't you say, 'I hope so,' or 'I'll try to'?" asked the evangelist. "No," she replied, "I said, 'I will.'" Then pointing her to God's Word, he said, "God is asking you if you will receive His Son as your personal Saviour. What will you say to that?" Her face lighted up, and she said, "Why, how simple that is! Isn't it queer that I didn't say, 'Yes' long ago?" That is the simple faith the Bible calls for. God's part is to make us "sons."

—King's Business

* * *

Expectant Prayers

A beautiful little book, "Expectation Corners," tells us of a King who prepared a city for some of his poor subjects. Not far from them were large storehouses, where everything they could need was supplied if they but sent in their requests. But on one condition — they should be on the outlook for the answer, so that when the king's messengers came with the answers to their petitions, they should always be found waiting and ready to receive them. The

sad story is told of one desponding one who never expected to get what he asked, because he was too unworthy. One day he was taken to the King's storehouses, and there, to his amazement, he saw, with his address on them, all the packages that had been made up for him, and sent. There was the garment of praise, and the oil of joy, and so much more. They had been to his door, but found it closed. He was not on the outlook. From that time on, he learned the lesson Micah would teach us: "I will look to the Lord; I will wait for the God of my salvation; my God will hear me!"

—Andrew Murray

* * *

Why She Was Waiting for Him

What simple faith! Joseph did not question the angel's message or doubt God's purpose. Many of us need to be more like the little girl whom the farmer found lost in his meadow. The farmer said to her, "Do not cry; I'll take you home." The little child snuggled up to him, and with a smile, said, "I knew you would; I was waiting for you." "Waiting for me?" said the man. "What made you think I was coming?" "I was praying you would," she said. "Praying? When I first heard you, you were saying A B C D E F G. What was that for?" She looked up again, and said, "I'm just a little girl. I was praying all the letters of the alphabet and letting God put them together the way He wanted to. He knows I was lost, and He knows how to put them together better than I do." What a difference, if we would only let God put the letters of our lives together, and, like Joseph, trust Him regardless of man's opinion.

—Bible Friend

* * *

From Hand to Mouth

Mr. Müller, the founder of the Bristol Orphanage, was relating to a friend some of the difficulties he had to contend with, in providing the orphans with food, day by day, and when he had finished, his friend said to him, "You seem to live from hand to mouth!" "Yes," said Mr. Müller, "it is my mouth, but God's hand."

—*London Church Herald*

* * *

The Supreme Mystery

Dr. Len G. Broughton said that when he was a medical student he could not accept the supernatural generation of Christ. He went to a doctor of divinity, who reasoned with him and left him in greater perplexity than ever. His medical education finished, he went to the backwoods to begin his practice, and one Sunday morning a backwoods preacher at an old country meeting-house, knocked out more skepticism in one-half hour than he had gotten in three years, and this is the way he did it. He said: "If there is anybody here troubled about the mystery of God's becoming man, I want to take you back to the first chapter of Genesis and the first verse, 'In the beginning God'!" He looked down into the audience very searchingly, and, said the doctor, "I felt that he was looking directly at me." He continued: "My brother, let me ask you this: Do you believe God was in the beginning? That is to say, that before the beginning began, God was?" I said to myself, "Yes, I believe that." "Now," he said, "if you believe that God was ahead of the beginning, you believe the only mysterious thing of this universe." If I believed that, God knows I could believe anything else in the world. I had gone to college and traveled through the mysteries of the theory of reproduction and the cell formation, and had come to realize that I was just a common fool; that if God was in the beginning, that was the one supreme mystery of all mysteries of this mysterious universe of God.

—*Moody Monthly*

* * *

As Long As He Is Awake

A mother and her little four-year-old daughter were preparing to retire for the night. The child was afraid of the dark, and the mother, on this occasion alone with the child, felt fearful also. When the light was out, the child caught a glimpse of the moon outside the window. "Mother," she asked, "is the moon God's light?" "Yes," said the mother. The next question was, "Will God put out His light and go to sleep?" The mother replied, "No, my child, God never goes to sleep." Then out of a simplicity of a child's faith, she said that which gave reassurance to the fearful mother, "Well, as long as God is awake, I am not afraid."

—Tom. M. Olson,
in *Sunday School Times*

* * *

"Sign My Name to Dat Verse"

The late Dr. J. R. Howerton used to tell his congregation in Charlotte, N. C., how old "Uncle Charlie" illustrated his faith in the Gospel of the cross for sinners. On his death-bed this former slave, who could not read, sent for Dr. Howerton, asking him to read John 3:16, and then said, "Marse Jim, sign my name to dat verse and lemme tech de pen." "Uncle Charlie" had had a cabin and lot deeded to him and understood the making of a contract. In delirium, when he was dying, the old Negro cried out, "I ain't got nothin' to do to be saved but to believe on de Lord Jesus Christ, and I done signed de Bible to show dat I do."

—*Sunday School Times*

* * *

Love That Prayed Through

Several years ago Dr. J. W. Beagle, field secretary of the Home Mission Board, while in attendance at the Mexican Baptist Convention of Texas, received a message that his wife had been stricken. Hastily he left the meeting to catch the train to Atlanta. Next morning the conductor came with a telegram for him. "It must be important," the conductor remarked, "for it was hooked on as we ran through the last station." "Yes, it's a death message," Dr. Beagle replied, as he took the yellow envelope and held it a moment unopened. The conductor sat down to offer his sympathy. Slowly trembling hands opened and unfolded the missive. Then eyes filled with tears — not with sorrow, but with love and deep joy — as these words were read: "Mexican convention in session all night praying for your wife. She will get well." When Dr. Beagle arrived in Atlanta he found that his wife had shown sudden and decided improvement from the hour he left the meeting in Texas. Dr. Beagle knew the abiding joy of Christian love and fellowship, which, through a long night of prayer, had saved his wife's life.

—The Teacher, S. B. C.

* * *

Faith Outrides Storm and Stress!

The great thing is that faith will carry you through every day. This is all. God's people need that to-day. The past two years have brought them to see it. "Unless I had believed" — what would you have done? I talked with a man who for years was a big business man in New York City, and he said, "I went to bed one night two years ago worth a million and a half. I felt that I was ready to retire, for I was over sixty years of age, and had plenty to carry me through. Then I had quite a little sum coming from stocks, which I could use in the Lord's work." He was a generous man and liked to give to the Lord. That man went to bed worth a million and a half, and woke up the next morning worth nothing. He found everything swept away, everything he had been piling up. As he told me of this, he said, "If I had not known the Lord, I would have gone up to the top floor of the office building, on the 26th floor, and I would have jumped out the window. Four other brokers did that very thing the day things collapsed here." So there it is. "If I had not believed, I would have committed suicide." He trusted the Lord when he had plenty of money, and now he is going to trust Him still.

I was talking to a woman some time ago. She said good-by to her husband and child one morning, and they went away in an automobile. A few hours later came the message of the terrible crash in which both were killed. She said to me, "Oh, my brother, if it had not been for the Lord I would have gone mad, I would have lost my senses!" Here it is again, "I would have gone insane, if I had not believed." You see, this verse will fit everybody, every circumstance, every condition. How truly we sing, "Faith is the victory that overcomes the world."

—Gospel Herald

* * *

"Set the Sails!"

When Hudson Taylor, the famous missionary, first went to China, it was in a sailing vessel. Very close to the shore of cannibal islands the ship was becalmed, and it was slowly drifting shoreward unable to go about and the savages were eagerly anticipating a feast.

The captain came to Mr. Taylor and besought him to pray for the help of God. "I will," said Taylor, "provided you set your sails to catch the breeze." The captain declined to make himself a laughing stock by unfurling in a dead calm. Taylor said, "I will not undertake to pray for the vessel unless you will prepare the sails." And it was done.

While engaged in prayer, there was a knock at the door of his stateroom. "Who is there?" The captain's voice responded, "Are you still praying for wind?" "Yes," "Well," said the captain, "you'd better stop praying, for we have more wind than we can manage."

And sure enough, when but a hundred yards away the cannibals were cheated out of their human prey.

*—Oriental and Inter-
American Missionary Standard*

* * *

God Revealed — Not Discovered

A Christian worker was trying to lead a young man to accept the grace of God in Christ by faith alone. The young man suddenly turned upon him and said, "I will never believe until I have an experience." The Christian worker flashed back, "You will never have an experience until you believe." And he was right. The manifestation of Jesus Christ in salvation comes to the man who obeys His command to believe. Here, as elsewhere, it is "If ye keep my commandments . . . I will manifest myself unto you."

—James H. McConkey

* * *

The Omniscient Captain

A story is told that once the passengers of a vessel steaming along the St. Lawrence River were very angry because, in spite of the fact that heavy fog was encircling the boat, full speed ahead was maintained. At last they went to the first mate, and complained. "Oh, don't be afraid!" the mate replied, with a smile. "The fog lies low, and the captain is high above it, and can see where we are going."

Are you tempted to complain of the way your Great Captain is leading you? Believe that He can see the end of the way. Then, declare, "Thou, Lord . . . makest me dwell in safety."

—*Sunday Circle*

* * *

"Can You Feel the Tug?"

A boy was busy flying his kite. The wind was strong and it soared upward in a way to delight any lad's heart. Finally it had vanished entirely from sight.

A gentleman came along and noticed the boy hanging onto the strong cord which anchored the kite to the earth.

"What are you doing, son?" he asked, smiling.

"Flying my kite," answered the boy proudly.

"Your kite? But I cannot see any kite."

"It's up there, sir — 'way up out of sight!" declared the boy.

"How do you know it's up there?"

"I can feel it tug, mister! That's how I know it," was the apt answer.

Shortly afterward, this Christian man met an infidel. A discussion of religion ensued, because the infidel never lost an opportunity to try to undermine some Christian's faith, if possible.

"You believe in a God?" he said, laughing lightly. "Well, I don't see how you know there's a God up there in Heaven."

"I know it by the Spirit, my friend," the Christian replied. Then, remembering the kite incident, he quickly added: "I can feel the tug of Heaven and God. I know they are up there!"

—Chester E. Shuler

* * *

What More Do You Want?

A coachman, whom I met in the Channel Islands on one occasion, told me how he got peace with God. For years his wife, who is a Christian, took him here and there to hear the Gospel preached. He knew the plan of salvation well, and became increasingly anxious to have peace with God, yet never seemed to get any further than desire.

"About three months ago," he said, "I stopped behind at the close of a Gospel meeting, and told the preacher what I wanted."

The preacher said to him, "Did the Lord Jesus die for you?"

"Yes, I believe that," he answered.

"And was He raised for you?"

"Yes," he replied.

"What more do you want?" was the preacher's earnest question.

At once the scales fell from his eyes, he appropriated to himself the blessing by faith, and he went away rejoicing in salvation. The Lord Jesus had died for him, and was raised for him; what more did he want? Surely nothing! And what more do you want, anxious reader? And what more can you have? Surely nothing.

—*Elim Evangel*

* * *

"IN" and "ON"

A correspondent, who did not furnish his address, asks us what is the difference between believing in and believing on Jesus Christ. We reply that as we look upon it, to believe in Jesus Christ means to commit ourselves unto Him in order to be saved, and to believe on Jesus Christ is to rest on Him with perfect confidence as the foundation of that salvation.

—*Sunday School Times*

* * *

A Dog's Appeal

F. B. Meyer told of once having a dog which he used to feed at the table, until his wife objected. The dog seemed to sense the cause of being refused food while the family were at their meal, so he used to crawl under the table when the wife was not looking and sit with his nose resting upon his master's knee. The silent, expectant faith of that dog's appeal was too much for Dr. Meyer and when the wife was not looking, he used to slip choice morsels of food under the table and into the waiting, expectant mouth of the dumb animal. Reach the hand of faith up to God in expectancy and He will not fail. "According to your faith be it unto you."

—*Western Recorder*

* * *

When Faith Is Fallacious

An Irish bishop had taken a country walk with a friend. On their return journey the friend urged the bishop to hurry, fearing that they might miss the train which would take them home in good time. The bishop consulted his watch. "Oh, we have plenty of time," he said. "But is your watch reliable?" asked his friend. "I have complete faith in it," replied the bishop. They arrived at the station to find they had missed the train by a few minutes. "Ah," commented the bishop's friend, "faith and good works are both necessary in this world. You had 'faith,' but it seems to me that in this case" — tapping the bishop's watch, — "the good works were the more important."

—*Christian Herald*

* * *

But God Never Removes His Sign

Next to an iced exhibit of prize winning fish in a sporting goods store in Seattle, was a box containing vacation

pamphlets and a big sign — "Take One." So many persons took one that the pamphlets soon disappeared. Along came a woman. She unfolded a newspaper, took one of the big fish, and went home with her dinner problem solved. The proprietor took down the sign! That's how simple a matter faith is! The woman saw the splendid specimens of fish — and the invitation to "Take One." She believed the sign meant what it said — and said what it meant — for there was no literature in the box when she appeared on the scene . . . To use somewhat the same figure, alongside the fountain of the water of life can be seen a sign saying: "Whosoever will, let him take the water of life freely" (Rev. 22:17). All who believe God take the water of life and have their thirst slaked.

—*Now*

* * *

Have You "Believed" and "Committed"?

Years ago there lived a famous tightrope walker, named Blondin, who performed most astonishing feats.

On one occasion he walked from one end of the center transept of the Crystal Palace, in London, to the further side, along a rope stretched across at a tremendous height, and not only so, but he stopped in the middle and cooked an omelet.

On another occasion a rope was stretched across a ship-building yard, also very high, and Blondin carried a man across, at this dizzy height, on his back, thousands of spectators gazing with awe and wonder at the remarkable performance. When he had completed his perilous journey, and descended to terra firma, he noticed a boy gazing at him in speechless amazement and admiration. So, approaching the lad, he said, "You saw me carry a man across safely, do you think I could carry you?" "Certainly you could, for I'm only a little fellow, and he's a big man." "Well, then," returned Blondin, "jump up, and I will take you," whereupon he suited the action to the word, and bending down, said, "Well, jump up!" But the boy instead of doing so, speedily disappeared in the crowd. He did not care to trust himself to him; he was afraid to do so.

—*Sunday School Times*

* * *

"Jesus Said He Would"

An evangelist was holding special meetings for boys and girls. One day after the children's meeting, little Helen came home, rushed into her father's study, threw her arms around his neck, and said, "Daddy, I am a Christian!"

"Well, Helen," said her father, "I am so glad to hear that. When did you become a Christian?"

"This afternoon," she said.

He asked her to tell him what had occurred.

"Oh," she said, "Mr. —, the evangelist, said that Jesus Christ was there in the room, and that if we would receive Him, He would come in and live in our lives and make us His own; that He would receive us."

"Well," he said, "go on; tell me what else happened."

"Why," she said, "I received Him as my Saviour and Jesus took me in."

"Well, Helen," he said, "that is all very interesting, but how do you know that when you received Jesus as your Saviour, He took you in?"

And he said he would never forget the look on the face of his little girl as she drew herself up, and said, "Why, Daddy, because He said He would!"

—Will H. Houghton,
in *The Living Christ*

* * *

A Walk of Faith

The Rev. George Grubb tells in his book, "What God Hath Wrought," the following incident. During one of his campaigns he entered the tent a little earlier than usual one evening, and found the colored tent attendant walking up and down the rows of seats. "What are you doing?" Mr. Grubb asked. "Well," he said, "I am claiming all the people who sit in these seats tonight for Jesus, for God says that

'every place that the sole of your foot shall tread upon, that have I given unto you,' so I am walking up and down these seats and claiming them for God."

—*King's Business*

* * *

Youthful Confidence

The following incident is related by Miss Mary L. Lord, a teacher among the Sioux Indians: An Indian baby was dying. It lay in its father's arms, while near by stood another little daughter a few years older, who was a Christian. "Father," said the little girl, "little Sister is going to heaven tonight. Let me pray." As she said this she kneeled at her father's knee, and this sweet little prayer fell from her childish lips: "Father God, little sister is coming to see You tonight. Please open the door softly and let her in. Amen!"

— *Baptist Teacher*, S. B. C.

* * *

Living Up to Our Faith

In a very large manufacturing town a low infidel propaganda was being very actively carried on. One of the ministers decided to deliver a Sunday evening sermon on the "Evidences of Christianity." Among the congregation the preacher was surprised to see the local infidel champion. A few days later the minister saw the man standing at his shop door and spoke with him, asking him to accept the proofs that he had given of the truths of Christianity. But the man replied:

"What! Believe? Certainly not, nor you either. Why, if I believed what you and your party profess to believe, I should scarcely be fit for business; my whole soul would be absorbed in the tremendous consequences at stake. But you and your folk are not different from other people. No, I tell you, you don't believe."

—*Christian Advocate*

* * *

He Never Disappoints

"You seem in unusual pain today," I said one afternoon to a lady who suffered terribly and was also blind. Her response amazed me. "I once heard Pastor Hood preach, sir. It was in the days when I could see. He told us in his sermon of a visit to a friend who was dying, and when he asked him how he was, the answer came: 'My head is resting very sweetly on three pillows — infinite power, infinite love, and infinite wisdom! And my poor head is on those same pillows now, so that my heart is at rest. I go to God for comfort, and He never disappoints me."

—Linton Romaine, in *The Sunday at Home*

* * *

Our Two Feet

Evan Hopkins said to a friend who was earnestly seeking victory over sin: "You know our hymns are called, 'Hymns of Consecration and Faith,' and those are the two feet we have got to walk on. You are trying to walk on one foot only — consecration. Do not worry so much . . . go and have a good believing time."

—*Sunday School Times*

* * *

Learning

"You will never learn faith in comfortable surroundings. God gives us the promises in a quiet hour; God seals our covenants with great and gracious words, then He steps back and waits to see how much we believe; then He lets the tempter come, and the test seems to contradict all that He has spoken. It is then that faith wins its crown. That is the time to look up through the storm, and among the trembling, frightened seamen cry, "I believe God, that it shall be even as it was told me." —From *Streams in the Desert* by Mrs. Charles E. Cowman

* * *

When a Dog's Trust Won

C. H. Spurgeon once said: "A dog used to come through a broken fence in my garden, doing gardening I did not like. One day I flung a stick at him. The creature seized the stick and laid it at my feet. He beat me by trusting. I

patted him on the head, and said, 'Good dog; come as often as you like.' Faith will bring even God's thunderbolts and lay them at His feet."

—C. H. Spurgeon

* * *

What We Reveal to Others

I was aboard a large air liner some time ago which ran into an extremely severe wind and rainstorm. Despite the size of the plane and the tremendous power of its four wasp motors, the ship was being tossed violently. A little nine-year-old fellow was my seat companion. It was his first experience in the air, and he was desperately afraid. Suddenly he looked up at me and said, "Are you afraid?" I smiled and replied, "No, this is real fun." An immediate change came over the little chap — fear and tension left him. He, too, had fun. This taught me a real lesson in living. What he detected in my voice, what he discerned in my face, helped him over that rough spot in life. How many people during times of trial watch my face for what it may reveal, I do not know. This I do know — my face and my life must reveal to those who observe me or need me, my faith in God.

—*Christian Advocate*

* * *

It's the Plank That Counts

A successor of George Müller said a striking thing about "little faith" and "great faith." In a recent letter from George Allen, founder and director of the Bolivian Indian Mission, he told of a visit that he and his late wife made to the Muller Orphan Homes in Bristol. When Mrs. Allan, looking at the five large buildings, said, "Dr. Burton, it must take a lot of faith to keep all this going," Dr. Burton said, "Mrs. Allan, little faith in a strong plank will carry me over the stream; great faith in a rotten plank will land me in it."

—*Prayer Letter of Columbia Bible College*

* * *

The Antidote for Fear

Faith in the Word of promise is the antidote for fear. Many a saint has stayed afloat amid the floods of mortal ills on an "I am with thee." Hudson Taylor, sleeping on the temple steps outside inland cities in China with bandits feeling for his throat which they intended to cut, was kept in perfect peace by promises of God's presence. Faith bolstered up with the prop of promises cannot fail.

—*Sunday School Times*

* * *

How to Keep Faith Bright

A woman who was showing a massive piece of family silver apologized as she took it from the cupboard, "Dreadfully tarnished!" she said, "I can't keep it bright unless I use it." That is just as true of faith as it is of silver. Tucked away in the Sunday closet of the soul, and only brought out for show, it needs apology. You can't keep faith bright unless you use it.

—*Christian Herald*

* * *

Do Faith and Science Mix?

Some smart assistant professor said to his students, "If you have science and faith in your mind, you had better keep them in watertight compartments, for if by any chance they should intermingle, faith would disappear in the precipitation that would take place."

Pasteur, the greatest of French scientists, however, has said: "It is not a question of faith and science, but it is a question of the size of the mind. If you have only a little bucket of a mind and get a lot of science into it, the little faith that you may have may come up floating out at the top and be lost; but if you have a good sized bucket of a mind there will be plenty of room for both science and faith."

—*Good News*

* * *

How Faith Came

Moody once said: "If all the time that I have spent praying for faith was put together it would be months. I thought that some day faith was going to come down and strike me like lightning. But

faith did not come. One day I read in the tenth of Romans, 'So then faith cometh by hearing and hearing by the word of God.' I had closed my Bible, and prayed for 'faith.' I now opened my Bible and began to read God's Word, and faith has been growing ever since."

—*Triumphs of Faith*

* * *

"If Blind Put Their Hand in God's" — Helen Keller

Helen Keller, shortly before her sixtieth birthday, expressed pity for the real unseeing, for those who have eyes yet do not see. Her long years of physical blindness have given her a spiritual insight which enables her to enjoy life in all its fulness. She says: "If the blind put their hand in God's they find their way more surely than those who see but have not faith or purpose."

—*Western Recorder*

* * *

He Bears

Gypsy Smith in one of his sermons tells of being in South Wales and lodging in a house on a side of a lovely mountain in the Rhondda Valley. One morning he received a letter from a man who said he had heard Gypsy preach three months before. He had never had a day of peace since, for it had revealed to him his sinful double life, and, though he had abandoned it, he could not find peace. "Do you think there is hope, that God will have mercy on me?" Gypsy laid down the letter and watched the snowflakes dancing before his window until he imagined one paused midway in air and said to the mighty mountain opposite: "O mountain, I want a place to rest. If I fall, can you bear me?" and the mountain answered: "Little snowflake, I have my roots in God. Fall on me, and see." Then Gypsy penned this parable to the man, and later a letter came saying. "I am on the mountain, and the mountain bears." Can a mountain bear a snowflake? Venture on God. He made the snowflake

193

and the mountain. and will make a new creature of you if you will trust Him.

—Sunday School Times

* * *

Faith Took the Remedy

A skeptical physician said to his Christian patient: "I could never understand saving faith. I believe in God and I suppose I believe in Jesus Christ — I am not conscious of any doubts. I believe that Jesus Christ was the Son of God, and I believe in the Bible, yet I am not saved. What is the matter with me?" "Well," said the patient, "a week ago I believed in you as a very skillful physician. I believed that if I should get sick and put myself in your hands I would be healed. In other words I trusted you. For two days now I have been taking some mysterious stuff out of a bottle. I don't know what it is, I don't understand it, but I am trusting in you." Now, whenever you turn to the Lord Jesus Christ and say, "Lord Jesus, Christianity seems to me to be full of mysteries. I do not understand them, but I believe Thou art trustworthy and I trust Thee; I commit myself to Thee," that is faith. A very simple thing, is it not? The faith of the patient did not heal him; it was the remedy that healed him; but the faith took the remedy!

—C. I. Scofield,
in Moody Monthly

* * *

Faith's Victory

George Frederick Handel, the great musician, lost his health; his right side was paralyzed; his money was gone; and his creditors seized and threatened to imprison him. Handel was so disheartened by his tragic experiences that he almost despaired for a brief time. But his faith prevailed, and he composed his greatest work, "The Hallelujah Chorus," which is part of his great "Messiah." The Apostle John wrote, "This is the victory that overcometh the world, even our faith."

—Sunday School Times

Faith Only A Link:

Your salvation comes, not because your faith saves you, but because it links you to the Savior who saves, and your believing is really nothing but the link.

—W. B. K.

* * *

A Wise Child

When someone told Dr. Emmons' little daughter that the moon was made of green cheese, she went to her father about it. But the wise old man told her to go and read, and find out. She went to her Bible, and soon came back in triumph, and said the moon was not made of green cheese, for the Bible said that the moon was made the *fourth* day, and the cows were not made till the *sixth* day, and so the moon could not have been made of green cheese!

But it may be doubted whether some older persons today would know where to look to settle such a momentous question.

—H. L. Hastings

* * *

When Our Faith in Prayer is Gone

Dr. McCormick, in "The Heart of Prayer," tells of a good woman whose daughter had died after a painful illness. She came to her minister and said, "I fear I have lost my faith in prayer. I used to believe that anything I asked for in the name of Christ I would receive. When my child was sick I besought God with an agony of desire for her recovery. I believed that God would grant my prayer. When she died I was stunned, not merely because of my grief, but because it seemed to me that God had failed me. I pray still, but the old faith in prayer is gone." This good woman was the victim of wrong teaching. She had in a word been led to substitute faith in prayer for faith in God. If our faith in prayer is uppermost, then any disappointment will shake that faith. But if faith in God is the great fact of life, then no matter what may be the outcome of our petitions we will still trust.

—The Presbyterian

Pull on Both Oars

An old Scotsman operated a little rowboat for transporting passengers. One day a passenger noticed that the good old man had carved on one oar the word "Faith," and on the other oar the word "Works." Curiosity led him to ask the meaning of this. The old man, being a well-balanced Christian and glad of the opportunity for testimony, said, "I will show you." So saying, he dropped one oar and plied the other called Works, and they just went around in circles. Then he dropped that oar and began to ply the oar called Faith, and the little boat just went around in circles again — this time the other way round, but still in a circle. After this demonstration the old man picked up Faith and Works, and plying both oars together, sped swiftly over the water, explaining to his inquiring passenger, "You see, that is the way it is in the Christian life. Dead works without faith are useless, and 'faith without works is dead' also, getting you nowhere. But faith and works pulling together make for safety, progress, and blessing."

—*Bible Friend*

* * *

How Much Have You?

A friend tells of overhearing two little girls, playmates, who were counting over their pennies. One said, "I have five pennies." The other said, "I have ten." "No," said the first little girl, "you have just five cents, the same as I." "But," the second child quickly replied, "my father said that when he came home tonight, he would give me five cents, and so I have ten cents." The child's faith gave her proof of that which she did not as yet see, and she counted it as being already hers, because it had been already promised by her father.

—*Otterbein Teacher*

FAITHFULNESS, OUR

Collie Keeps Eight-Year Vigil At Boy's Grave!

The papers over the Nation carried this touching story: King was the Collie's name. How KINGLY he acted in daily visiting, for more than eight years, the grave of his master! His master, Angelo Del Plato, was killed in a motor vehicle accident. King had delighted in romping with his master. At the graveside, King stood at the outskirts of the scene, and, as the casket was lowed into the ground, the bewildered dog watched with wonderment, seemingly a chief mourner at the solemnities. Admiring friends said of King, "I can't remember a single day, in the last eight years, that he hasn't gone to the cemetery. He usually lies on Angelo's grave a little while, and then comes home. When tied, he broke ropes and pulled down posts to get away to go to the master's grave!" The faithful dog has found a way to be as close as possible to the boy he loved. Love always finds a way!

—W. B. K.

* * *

The Blackest Mark

We might think less harshly of Judas if he had not used the cloak of professed love to betray his Lord. Right well has the scholarly James Stalker observed, "That night and the next day His face was marred in many ways: it was furrowed by the bloody sweat; it was bruised with blows; they spat upon it; it was rent with thorns; but nothing went so close to His heart as the profanation of this kiss." The token of warmest affection froze on the cheek of Jesus, and His words of rebuke must have burned into the very soul of the betrayer. . . . Judas' betrayal is commonly called the blackest crime in history, and so it is. But we would remind ourselves that Judas has no monopoly

195

on betrayals. We never had the chance
to betray the person of Christ; but opportunities for betrayal are all about
us, and too many of us take advantage
of them. The conformist in the social
circle, the money-grabber in business,
the stickler for regularity in politics —
these and many other classes are often
found in the ranks of modern betray-
ers. Wouldn't it be a wonderful thing
if every Christian would put loyalty to
Christ above every other loyalty of
life?   —John L. Hill, in
                                the Teacher

* * *

A Teacher's Reconsecration

Canon Hague tells of a chaplain who
was ministering to a dying boy in the
last war. He asked him if he had any
message for his mother. "Yes," he said,
"tell her I am dying happy." "Anything
else?" "Yes. Write to my Sunday
school teacher." "What shall I say?"
"Tell her I died a Christian, and I have
never forgotten her teaching." A few
weeks later the chaplain received a letter from this Sunday school teacher. It
went something like this: "God have
mercy upon me. Only last month I resigned from my Sunday school class,
for I felt that my teaching was doing
no good; and scarcely had I, through my
cowardly, faithless heart, given up my
appointed work than I got your letter
telling me that my teaching had been
the means of winning a soul to Christ.
I am going back to my rector at once
to tell him that I will try again in
Christ's name, and I will be faithful to
the end."   —*Moody Monthly*

* * *

God Reigns! I Will Be True

What matter if the clouds hang low?
What matter if the bleak winds blow?
What matter if I may not know
The reason why these things are so?
    God reigns! I will be true.

What matter if my friends are few?
What matter where they are, or who?
What matter what men say or do?
What matter what God leads me
    through?
He reigns! I will be true.

What matter if this life is brief?
What matter if I've toil or grief?
I, in my Saviour, find relief.
Of all my joy, He is the chief.
    God reigns! I will be true.

No matter what I must resign;
No matter how the fire refine,
If I but with His image shine.
By faith I clasp His hand Divine.
    God reigns! I will be true.

No matter if my bark is frail,
In Jesus' Name I breast the gale.
No matter if all else shall fail,
My anchor holds within the vail.
    God reigns! I will be true.
                                —*Selected*

* * *

Faithulness Required

I recall a message from a devoted
young missionary in Central America.
It came in a letter in which he gave a
peep into the deeps of his own heart as
well as into the trials of the work. "The
work is hard," said he. "I go about on
fishing boats through the day. At night
I sleep on piles of hides on the decks.
The people do not seem much interested
in the Gospel message I bring. Sometimes the adversary tempts me to discouragement in the face of seeming lack
of success. But I take courage and press
on anew as I remember that *God does
not hold me responsible for success but
for faithfulness.*"
                        —James H. McConkey

* * *

**A Baby—David Lloyd George, and Over-
Worked Physician**

One stormy night, a clamorous knock
was heard at the door of the town's
over-worked physician. He was needed
urgently in the home of a poor miner.
The doctor's first impulse was to offer
some excuse for not going. He reasoned
thus, "A new life is coming into the
world only to live in poverty and filth.
The world will be none the poorer if I
fail to go." However, the call of duty
and humanity prevailed, and presently
the doctor was breasting the terrors of
the stormy night. As day dawned, a

baby boy was ushered into the world! That baby boy grew into manhood, and became one of the world's greatest Christians and statesmen — David Lloyd George, England's World War I Premier.

—W. B. K.

* * *

Better than Going Fast

That was a bright suggestion of a little boy who made the following answer to the question of a passer-by. Seeing the little fellow patting his father's horse that was standing in front of his house, the man asked, "Can your horse go fast, my boy?" "No, not very." he replied; "but he can stand fast." That is a virtue not to be despised in either a horse or a man.

—*Selected*

* * *

The Prime Minister's Promise

Lord Palmerston, Queen Victoria's Prime Minister, was crossing Westminster Bridge when a little girl ahead dropped a jug of milk. The jug broke into fragments, and she dissolved into tears. Palmerston having no money with him dried her eyes by telling her that if she came to the same spot next day at that hour he would pay for both jug and milk. The following morning, in the midst of a cabinet meeting, he suddenly remembered his promise to the little girl, left the bewildered ministers, dashed across the bridge, popped half a crown into the waiting child's hand and hurried back.

—*All Nations Missionary Review*

* * *

Some Carry the Potatoes

A poor man plodded along toward home in an Irish town carrying a huge bag of potatoes. A horse and wagon carrying a stranger came along, and the stranger stopped the wagon and invited the man on foot to climb inside. This the poor man did, but when he sat down in the wagon he held the bag of potatoes in his arms. And when it was suggested that he should set it down, he said very warmly: "Sure, I don't like to trouble you too much. You're giving me a ride. I'll carry the potatoes!"

Sometimes we think we are doing the Lord a favor when we carry the burden. But the work is His, and the burden is His, and He asks us only to be faithful.

—Isaac Page

* * *

Are We Sentinels?

When Pompeii was destroyed by the eruption of Mt. Vesuvius there were many persons buried in the ruins who were afterward found in very different positions.

There were some found in deep vaults, as if they had gone there for security. There were some found in lofty chambers. But where did they find the Roman sentinel?

They found him standing at the city gate where he had been placed by the captain, with his hands still grasping the weapon. There, while the earth shook beneath him; there, while the floods of ashes and cinders overwhelmed him, he had stood at his post; and there, after a thousand years, he was found.

So let Christians stand by their duty in the post at which their Captain places them.

—*Gospel Trumpet*

* * *

Livingstone's Faithfulness:

When Henry M. Stanley found Livingstone, the great missionary who spent thirty years in darkest Africa, and who had been lost to the world for over two years, he wanted him to come back home to England with him, but Livingstone refused to go. Two days later he wrote in his diary, "March 19, my birthday; my Jesus; King; my Life; my All. I again dedicate my whole self to Thee. Accept me, and grant, O gracious Father, that ere the year is gone I may finish my work. In Jesus' Name I ask it. Amen." A year later his servants found him on his knees dead. It was said of him:

"He needs no epitaph to guard a name
Which men shall prize while worthy
　　work is known;
He lived and died for good — be that
　　his fame;
Let marble crumble: this is Living-
　　Stone."

　　　　　　　　　　—*Glad Tidings*

* * *

I'll Stay Where You Have Put Me

I'll stay where You've put me; I will,
　　dear Lord,
Though I want so badly to go,
I was eager to march with the "rank and
　　file,"
Yes, I wanted to lead them, You know.
I planned to keep step to the music loud,
　To cheer when the banner unfurled,
To stand in the midst of the fight,
　　straight and proud,
Victorious before the whole world.

I'll stay where You've put me; I'll work,
　　dear Lord,
Though the field be narrow and small,
And the ground be fallow, and the
　　stones lie thick,
And there seems to be no life at all.
The field is Thine own; only give me the
　　seed;
I'll sow it with never a fear;
I'll till the dry soil while I wait for the
　　rain,
And rejoice when the green blades
　　appear.

I'll stay where You've put me; I will,
　　dear Lord;
I'll bear the day's burden and heat,
Always trusting Thee fully! when even
　　has come
I'll lay heavy sheaves at Thy feet.
And then when my earth work is ended
　　and done,
In the light of eternity's glow,
Life's record all closed, I surely shall
　　find
It was better to stay than to go!
　　　　　　　　　　　　—*Selected*

* * *

A Commonplace Life

"A commonplace life," we say, and we
　　sigh;

Yet why should we sigh as we say?
The commonplace sun in the common-
　　place sky
Makes lovely the commonplace day.

The moon and the stars, they are com-
　　monplace things,
The flower that blooms, and the robin
　　that sings;
Yet sad were the world and unhappy
　　our lot
If flowers all failed and the sunshine
　　came not!
And God, who considers each separate
　　soul,
From commonplace lives makes a beau-
　　tiful whole.
　　　　　　　　　　　　—*Selected*

* * *

Beaten Severely, Yet Faithful!

A little boy, in the prayer sessions of
one of Dr. Hyman Appelman's meetings
would stand daily and make this prayer
request, "Pray for my daddy. He keeps
the saloon!" What the boy did was reported to his sinful father. He threatened to beat the boy if he did not "pipe
down," and stay away from the meetings. The threats were of no avail. The
inhumane father beat the boy severely.
But his punishment did not silence him.
He still made requests for prayer for His
unsaved daddy. In time, God's Spirit
convicted the father. He received Christ
as his personal Saviour and went out
of the saloon business, thus giving evidence to a change of heart.
　　　　　　　　　　　　W. B. K.

* * *

Message Delivered

During the war this advertisement
appeared in a newspaper in England,
calling for help: "Boys, 16 and over, to
run messages — Apply A.R.P. Warden."
Derrick Belfall was only fourteen, but
he felt that he could help. He was
turned down because of his age. This
did not stop him; he went back again
and again until the official passed him
and gave him the necessary badge. He
was given the job of delivering messages to A.R.P. workers, who could not
be reached while on duty except by boys

on bicycles. After each trip he had to report whether or not he had succeeded in getting the message through. His usual report was, "Derrick Belfall reporting — I've delivered the message." One day he was delivering a message during a "blitz," and succeeded in getting it through. On the way back to report he passed a building that had crumbled under the explosion of a bomb. The workers were clearing away the debris. Derrick thought that he could help. He heard the cry of a child, and worked frantically to clear away the bricks and beams across the cellar door. He climbed down and lifted the child to safety, but he was not so fortunate. Before he could get out, the wall collapsed and completely buried him. He was past all help. When asked if he wanted to send word to anyone, he replied, "Yes, just say, 'Derrick Belfall reporting — I've delivered the message.' " We have our orders to deliver a message. The order comes from our own Saviour. We are to deliver this great message to all people.

—*World Comrades*

* * *

Sweet Hour of Prayer

A crowded gathering of distinguished scientists had been listening spellbound to the masterly expositions of Michael Faraday. For an hour he had held his brilliant audience enthralled as he demonstrated the nature and properties of the magnet. He had brought his lecture to a close with an experiment so novel, so bewildering, and so triumphant, that for some time after he resumed his seat, the house rocked with enthusiastic applause. And then the Prince of Wales — afterwards King Edward VII — rose to propose a motion of congratulation. The resolution, having been duly seconded, was carried with renewed thunders of applause.

Suddenly the uproar ceased and a strange silence settled over the audience. The assembly waited for Faraday's reply.

But he did not appear.

Only his most intimate friends knew what had become of him. He was an elder in a little Sandemanian church — a church that never boasted more than twenty members.

The hour at which Faraday concluded his lecture was the hour of the weeknight prayer meeting.

—*Christus Medicus Magnus*

* * *

Failed to Hold Rope

Off the coast of Nova Scotia, a ship, caught in the jaws of a violent storm, went to pieces. There was a frightful loss of life! Seemingly, only one man survived. 'Midst the whelming waves, he clung to debris from the wrecked vessel. Anxious ones, gathered on shore, seemed powerless to do anything, until a brave young man requested that a rope be tied about his body, the people on shore holding onto it while he would swim out to where the lone survivor floundered. With great effort, he finally reached the imperiled man. Grasping him, he signalled to be pulled in. 'Midst their wild cheers and excitement, those on shore had failed to hold onto the rope! Both the would-be rescurer and the rescued were swallowed up by the merciless waves! Many have gone forth into the regions beyond with the message of life in Christ. Are we, in the homeland, failing to hold the rope?

—W. B. K.

* * *

Roly-Poly Pigs Become Lean Pigs

A farmer's herd of swine was often spoken of admiringly by neighboring farmers. They were sleek and roly-poly. In feeding his pigs, the farmer would go to the edge of the pasture, knock sharply with a stick on the trough which was filled with grain. All over the pasture, the pigs, hearing the farmer's knock, would lift their swinish snouts. Then they would run squealingly in the direction of the well-filled trough. All was well with the pigs until some woodpeckers began to make their homes in the dead trees scattered over the pasture. The pigs mistook the pecking on the dead trees for the farmer's knock on the trough. They ran from one dead tree to another. Rapidly, they became poor and scrawny.

How many of God's dear children become spiritually lean — running hither, thither and yon, "Carried about with every wind of doctrine," sampling this speaker and that one. Unanchored, and unsettled, they are never able to say, "My heart is fixed, trusting in the Lord!"   W. B. K.

* * *

Provided It Be Forward

In exploring the interior of Africa, Livingstone met with difficulties indescribable, amid frightful scenes — the havoc wrought by war, famine, wild beasts, and, worst of all, by the slave trade. Sometimes he would preach to a thousand people, sometimes to a few; and when it was seemingly to little purpose, he would console himself thus: "But for the belief that the Holy Spirit works and will work, I should give up in despair. I am a missionary, heart and soul. I am ready to go anywhere — provided it be *forward*. I would venture everything for Christ. Can the love of Christ not carry the missionary where the slave trade carries the trader? I shall open up a path into the interior or perish. I wish only that my exertions may be honored so far that the Gospel may be preached and believed in all this dark region."

—*Monthly Visitor*

* * *

Loving Christ More

To many, Christ's words as to hating one's parents or other relatives is a hard saying, which they find it difficult to accept. But what we need to realize is that our love for and loyalty to Him should be so intense that we will not permit the dearest of earth's relationships to interfere with it. I recall a young Jewish girl confessing Christ. Her mother, who loved her tenderly, was scandalized, and pleaded with tears for the daughter not to be baptized as a Christian. "If you do," she declared, "you show that you hate your mother." "No, Mother dear," was the reply, "I love you tenderly, but I love Christ more." This, I think, illustrates exactly what Jesus meant.

—H. A. Ironside

"Teacher Held On!"

A sixteen-year-old girl told me the following: "Only God knows what my Sunday school teacher has done for me. I was saved when I was fourteen, but my people made fun of me, and I guess I was a weak Christian, and was soon back to my old ways again. Most of the church people turned against me, but Miss M— held on to me, even when I was rude and mean to her. One evening she put her arms around me, and said with the tears running down her face: "Oh, my dear, I love you so much, and Jesus understands all you have had to fight. Someone held on to me, too, when I was your age, and saved me from a life of sin. I understand so well."

—*Sunday School Times*

* * *

My Teacher

A Sunday school teacher,
    I don't know his name.
A wonderful preacher
    Who never found fame.
So faithful, so earnest
    When I was a boy —
He stuck to his task
    Tho' I tried to annoy.
He never was missing,
    In cold or in heat,
A smile his face lighted
    The moment we'd meet.
He taught by example
    As well as by word,
This splendid old teacher
    Who honored his Lord.
He helped my young life
    More than ever he knew.
Later years I remembered
    And tried to be true.
I suppose he has gone now
    To join Heaven's ranks,
May it be my good fortune
    Some day to say thanks.
            —Dr. Will Houghton

* * *

Constrained by Love

A hindu convert was once asked if, for a certain salary, he was willing to go and try to commence a mission in a neighboring district where he would be sure to meet with great difficulties, and perhaps be persecuted and put to death. "I cannot do it for money," he replied, "but I can do it for *Christ*," and he went. "The love of Christ constraineth" (*II Cor.* 5:14).

—*Glad Tidings*

* * *

"Mind the Light"

Years ago John Walker was the keeper of the light on the Robin's Reef at Staten Island under the United States Government. There he lived happily in the faithful discharge of his duties for four years. He was then taken with severe pains and Catherine — his wife — sent to the shore for medical help. When this was forthcoming the physician ordered that John should be removed to a hospital at once.

As he was being carried to the boat which was to bear him to the shore he called to his wife, as a parting direction, "Mind the light." He was faithful to his trust to the end.

The poor fellow never returned to the lighthouse. Catherine stayed on to "Mind the light," and carried out the duties so well that she was appointed keeper. Then for more than thirty years she stayed in that lonely spot, caring for the warning beacon to keep mariners from damage on the cruel rocks.

"Mind the light." The words recall for us our duty and privilege as Christians. In the midst of a crooked and perverse generation we are set to "Shine a lights in the world."

—*Gospel Herald*

* * *

Answer Delayed — but Granted

In the city of Washington, many years ago, a teacher had in his class a mischievous boy who not only would not listen, or behave well, but who interfered with the other scholars' giving their attention. The teacher became discouraged regarding that boy. Later on the boy left Washington for the West, and there wasted his life in reckless dissipation. Years afterward he came to Baltimore and spent the night in debauchery, and next morning, while un-

der the weakening spell of his dissipation, he started walking along the streets of Baltimore. He soon found himself in one of the city's cemeteries and suddenly noticed on a tombstone the name of his old Sunday school teacher. A flood of memories rushed upon him. Things that the teacher said came back to him. His heart melted, he pulled himself over the little railing, went to the grave, and there he gave his life to Christ as he knelt down and kissed the very dirt on the grave of his faithful old teacher. He entered the ministry and became the pastor of one of the most prominent churches in Virginia, and one of the most greatly beloved of all the Virginia pastors. And yet his old teacher had gone to his grave years before, feeling that his work was a failure as far as that boy was concerned.

—*Sunday School Times*

* * *

No Recanting!

Jane Welsh, the wife of John Welsh and daughter of John Knox, was told by some officers in authority, "that if she used her influence to induce her husband, then in prison, to disown the Protestant faith, his life might be spared. She was wearing an apron when this proposition was brought to her, and gathering it up at the corners, she held it out as a receptacle, saying, 'No, your lordships,; *I would rather catch his head in this apron than that he or I should renounce my Savior.*' "

—*Gospel Herald*

* * *

Back to the Same Old Boat

Back to the same old boat, the self-same net,
And even to the self-same fishing ground
Where they had toiled all night in vain: and yet,
How great success this time their effort crowned.

So full the net it brake. They were amazed
To find what difference He had for them wrought.

201

With wondering eyes they at each other
gazed
And back to land the glittering spoil
they brought.

The gracious Master did not change the
scene
Nor give to them a new environment.
More gracious still — *back where they
late had been*
A so great failure were the seven sent,
That they may learn how near to fail-
ure lies,
For faithful souls, most glorious sur-
prise.

—*Selected*

* * *

He Only Needed to Hear

When Shackleton, the great explorer,
was planning what proved to be his
last expedition to the Arctic seas, an interesting incident is said to have occurred. Shackleton was seated in an
office in London, speaking to a friend
about his forthcoming expedition. The
friend said, "I am surprised at the publicity you are giving to your new venture. It is rather unlike you." And
Shackleton replied, "I have a purpose
in doing so. I want my colleague, Mr.
Wild, to hear about my plans. He has
buried himself in the heart of Africa,
and has left no address, but I thought
that if I would broadcast the news that
I was going it might filter though into
the very center of Africa, and if Wild
knows I am going, he will come." . . .
They both turned, and standing in the
doorway was Mr. Wild. It was a dramatic moment as Wild and Shackleton
shook hands — the handshake of loyalty.
"I heard you were going," said Wild;
"the news found its way into the heart
of Africa, and when I knew, I dropped
my gun, picked up a bit of baggage, and
made straight for home, and here I am.
What are your orders?" Would you
do that for Jesus Christ? Would you go
to the ends of the earth for Him?

—*Evangelical Christian*

The Boy Who Promised Mother

The school was out and down the street
A noisy crowd came thronging;
The hue of health, and gladness sweet,
To every face belonging.

Among them trode a little lad,
Who listened to another,
And mildly said, half grave, half sad,
"I can't — I promised mother."

A shout went up, a ringing shout,
Of boistrous derision,
But not one moment left in doubt
That manly, brave decision.

"Go where you please, do what you will,"
He calmly told the other;
"But I shall keep my word, boys, still;
I can't — I promised mother."

Ah! Who could doubt the future course
Of one who thus had spoken?
Through manhood's struggle, gain and
loss
Could faith like this be broken?

God's blessings on that steadfast will,
Unyielding to another,
That bars all jeers and laughter still,
Because he promised mother.

—Geo. Cooper

* * *

Not Wasted

A young woman who was a great lover
of flowers had set out a rare vine at the
base of a stone wall. It grew vigorously
but it did not blossom. Day after day
she cultivated it and watered it and
tried in every way to coax it into bloom.
One morning as she stood disappointed before it, her invalid neighbor, whose
back lot adjoined her own, called over
and said, "You cannot imagine how
much I have been enjoying the blooms
of that vine you planted." The owner
looked and on the other side of the
wall was a mass of bloom. The vine
had crept through the crevices and
flowered luxuriantly on the other side.
There is a lesson for every Christian
here. So often we think our efforts
thrown away because we do not see their
fruit. We need to learn that in God's

service our prayers, our toil, our crosses are never in vain. Somewhere they bear their fruit and some heart will receive their blessing and their joy.

—Forward

* * *

Niemoeller's Faithfulness!

Prison walls cannot bind the Gospel. Nero could not confine the influence of the Apostle Paul, and Hitler couldn't quench the testimony of the brave German pastor, Martin Niemoeller. News occasionally filtered through the screen of censorship during the recent War. Life and Liberty wrote: "For over two years the brave pastor has been in continuous solitary confinement, interrupted only by the daily three-quarters of an hour's exercise in the yard. He is carefully segregated from those inmates of the camp who do open-air work. On various occasions he has been offered his freedom — at a price. The price is his promise to preach only as — he is bidden. That he steadfastly refused to do."

—Sunday School Times

* * *

Faithful to the End

There are those who begin well in the Christian life but who do not "carry through." It is a joy to see faithfulness maintained to the end. A beautiful incident was told in a personal letter to the editor last summer from the widow of Dr. Perry Valiant Jenness, the well-known Presbyterian pastor of Denver who was taken home to be with the Lord, at seventy-four years of age, after an operation in the hospital. Mrs. Jenness wrote:

"On the night before the operation, after the floor nurse had made him comfortable for the night and I went back to his room, he said: 'What do you think has happened?' His face was radiant. 'This dear girl, who has made me comfortable for my night's rest said, as she worked over me: "Dr. Jenness, I'm a good girl, and I go to church and Sunday School when I can get away from

my work, but I'm not a Christian. Can you tell me how to be one?" And then he said: 'I had her hand me my Bible, and I read some passages to her and prayed with her, and gave her several little tracts that were in my handbag, and she has promised to read them, and I'll talk with her again when I'm better.' 'Valiant' — yes, valiant to! the end for the Lord he loved so dearly and served so faithfully. I stood by his bed and held his dear hand till he entered the gates of the city that hath foundations, whose builder and maker is God!"

—Moody Monthly

* * *

Faithfulness

On an occasion Mr. Spurgeon prefaced a sermon he preached on the Atonement somewhat as follows:

"I suppose I am something like Mr. Cecil when he was a boy. His father once told him to wait in a gateway till he came back, and the father being very busy went about the city, and amid his numerous cases and engagements, forgot the boy. Night came on, and at last, when the father reached home, there was a great inquiry as to where Richard was. The father said, 'Dear me! I left him in the morning standing under such and such a gateway, and I told him to stay there till I came for him. I could not wonder but that he is there now.' So they went, and there they found him.

—United Evangelical

* * *

How Play the Game

We can't all play a winning game,
Someone is sure to lose,
But we can all play so that our name
No one may dare accuse.

For when the Master Referee
Scores against our name,
It won't be whether we've won or lost,
But how we played the game.

—Selected

* * *

When Failure is Success

A Moravian missionary named George Smith went to Africa. He had been there only a short time and had only one convert, a poor woman, when he was driven from the country. He died shortly afterward, on his knees, praying for Africa. He was considered a failure.

But a company of men stumbled onto the place where he had prayed and found a copy of the Bible he had left. Presently they met the one poor woman who was his convert.

A hundred years later his mission counted more than 13,000 living converts who had sprung from the ministry of George Smith.

—A. J. Gordon

* * *

The Need for "Holders-On"

A British white book on labor conditions in the shipyards mentions two classes of workmen whom it calls "riveters" and "holders-on." The riveters, we know well, for the iterant blows of the pneumatic hammer ring out from every new building that thrusts its steel skeleton against the sky. His note is that of the woodpecker, magnified a million times. The holder-on, whose pincers grip the red-hot iron and hold it steady, must be his silent and unnoticed mate. These two smiths stand for two classes of people we meet everywhere — those who are active and noisy that someone might think that they were doing all the work unassisted, and the "holders-on," who make no fuss, but are always to be depended on to be in their places, who meet their full responsibility, and who are really needed to make effective the energy of the "riveters." Pastors and Sunday school superintendents are always on the lookout for teachers who can be classified as "holders-on."

—*Illustrator*

FAMILY ALTAR

Family Altar Fragrance

How far the holy fragrance of
The family altar goes!
When childhood days are far behind
The beauty of it glows.

Though some things to my memory
Are indistinct and blurred,
I still can hear my father's voice
Expound the Holy Word.

I did not heed its counsel then,
Nor realize its worth,
But now I know that shrine to be
The sweetest place on earth.

It proved a shield to keep my faith
Undimmed through joy and care;
The mem'ry of that hallowed place —
My father's voice in prayer.
—*The Family Altar*

* * *

Ten Reasons for a Family Altar

Because it will send you forth to your daily task with cheerful heart, stronger for the work and truer to duty, and determined in whatever is done therein to glorify God.

Because it will give you strength to meet the discouragements, the disappointments, the unexpected adversitites, and sometimes the blighted hopes that may fall to your lot.

Because it will make you conscious throughout the day of the attending presence of the unseen Divine One, who will bring you through more than conqueror over every unholy thought or thing that rises up against you.

Because it will sweeten home life and enrich home relationship as nothing else can do.

Because it will solve all the misunderstandings and relieve all the frictions that sometimes intrude into the sacred precincts of family life.

Because it will hold the boys and girls as nothing else, when they have gone out from underneath the parental roof, and so determine very largely the eternal salvation of your children.

Because it will exert a helpful, hallowed influence over those who may at any time be guests within your home.

Because it will enforce, as nothing else can do, the work of your pastor, and stimulate the life of your church in its every activity.

Because it will furnish an example and stimulus to other homes for the same kind of life and service and devotion to God.

Because the Word of God requires it, and in thus obeying God we honor Him who is the giver of all good and the source of all blessings.

—*The Family Altar*

* * *

Dad Was Right!

Teen-aged Rodney got up late and had just time enough to gulp down some hot chocolate and a piece of toast before rushing off to school. He arose from the table hastily.

"Where are you going, Son?" asked his father.

"To school, of course, Dad."

"No, my boy. You do not go to school without first looking to God. Sit down for our devotions."

Rodney was restless during the Bible reading, and shuffled his feet during the prayer, squirming impatiently. But when he was forcing his jalopy down the street at top speed toward school, some thoughts were crystallizing down underneath his resentment. They ran something like this:

"Dad is right. God is managing our lives, and we should always commit ourselves and our day to Him. I'm glad now that Dad made me wait."

—*Selected*

* * *

It Interfered With His Prayers

There was once an old codfish dealer, a very earnest and sincere man, who lived prayerfully every day. One of the great joys of his life was the family worship hour. One year two other merchants persuaded him to go into a deal with them by which they could control all the codfish in the market and greatly increase the price. The plan was

succeeding well, when this good man learned that many poor people in Boston were suffering because of the great advance in the price of codfish. It troubled him so that he broke down in trying to pray at the family altar, and he went straight to the men who had led him into the plot and told them that he could not go on with it. Said the old man: "I can't afford to do anything which interferes with my family prayers. And this morning when I got down on my knees and tried to pray, there was a mountain of codfish before me high enough to shut out the throne of God, and I could not pray. I tried my best to get around it or over it, but every time I started to pray that codfish loomed up between me and my God. I won't have my family prayers spoiled for all the codfish in the Atlantic Ocean. and I shall have nothing to do with this market control business, or with any money made from it."

—*Pentecostal Evangel*

* * *

Daily Family Prayers

What America needs more than railway extension and western irrigation, and a lower tariff, and a bigger wheat crop, and a merchant marine, and a new navy, is a revival of piety, the kind mother and father used to have; piety that counted it good business to stop for daily family prayers before breakfast, right in the middle of the harvest; that quit work a half hour earlier on Thursday night, so as to get the chores done and go to prayer meeting; that borrowed money to pay the preacher's salary and prayed fervently in secret for the salvation of the rich man who looked with scorn on such unbusiness-like behavior. That's what we need now to clean this country of the filth of graft and greed, petty and big; of worship of fine houses and big lands and high office and grand social functions.

What is this thing which we are worshiping but a vain repetition of what decayed nations fell down and worshiped just before their light went out? Read the history of Rome in decay and you'll find luxury there that could lay a big dollar over our little doughnut that looks so large to us. Great wealth never made a nation substantial nor honorable. There is nothing on earth that looks good that is so dangerous for a man or a nation to handle as quick, easy, big money. If you do resist its deadly influence the chances are that it will get your son. It takes greater and finer heroism to dare to be poor in America than to charge an earthworks in Manchuria.

—*Wall Street Journal*

* * *

God Knew Where The Water Was

Years ago there was a great drought in Connecticut. The water disappeared from the hills, and the farmers drove their cattle into the valleys. Streams there began to fail, and neighbors said to a certain man of God, "You must not send your flocks down here any more." The old man gathered his family around the family altar on their knees before God. They cried with tears and supplications for water that the flocks and herds might not perish. Afterward he went out into the hills, and in a place that he had walked scores of times before he saw that the ground was dark and moist; when he turned up the soil, water started. The family came with pails and watered the stock; then they made troughs reaching to the house. Water was plentiful.

—*Sunday School Times*

* * *

Five Important Minutes

When I was a child we had a "five minute rule" in our house. What it meant was that we were all to be ready for school five minutes before we actually had to leave.

We were a large family and that extra five minutes was prayer time for Mother and us children. The place was wherever Mother happened to be when we were all ready to leave. Sometimes it was the kitchen, other times the living room or bedroom, or even out on the porch. But we all kneeled while Mother asked a blessing on each of us individually and thanked the Lord for His provision for us. Often all of our names

were spoken and some special blessing asked for each.

If a neighborhood child dropped in to walk to school with us (and neighbors often did), they were included in our prayer circle, too.

When the prayer was finished, there came a kiss for each, and we were off. Those were Five Important Minutes to each of us.

—Adelaide Blanton

* * *

It Worked!

Sarah A. Cooke in her splendid book, *Wayside Sketches*, gives this experience:

While holding meetings some years ago in Valparaiso, Indiana, a mother gave this testimony: "I was left with five children. My oldest boy became wicked and I could do nothing with him; he would lie and steal, and I began to think that I would have to put him in the reformatory. One night I dreamed that a voice came to me telling me to read the Bible with my children. I had never read the Bible with my children, though I had a beautiful one for an ornament on the parlor table. I began to read it with the children, and, oh, what a difference it made in our home! The children would gather around me as gentle as kittens, and my eldest boy, two or three days after I commenced, broke down and, putting his arms around my neck, promised he would be a good boy and be saved. Truly, 'the entrance of thy words giveth light.' "

Norman V. Williams

* * *

"I Carried with Me a Picture"

Several years ago, five young men left their homes in Western Pennsylvania and went out into the great Northwest. They found things quite different from what they were in the old home town, and the temptations were many. Some time later they all had returned to their former homes. Four of the five showed that they were much the worse because of their experiences in a strange country. But the other young man came back seemingly all the stronger and better because of the experiences through which he had passed.

When asked why he, too, had not gone the way of the other four, he calmly replied, "Because *I carried with me a picture.*" "Oh, yes, the picture of some young maiden back home, I presume?" remarked a friend. "Oh, no! Not that kind of a picture," said the young man. "It was a picture of quite a different kind. It was my last morning at home. We all sat down to breakfast as usual; Father at one end of the table and my precious mother at the other. Realizing that there was to be a breaking of home ties in a few hours, conversation was not very brisk that morning. After breakfast, as was my father's custom, he took down the old Bible and started to read the morning lesson. But he didn't get very far. A lump kept coming up in his throat, and he was so blinded by tears that he could not read, and handed the Book over to my mother, motioning to her to finish the reading. "After she had finished the chapter we all knelt to pray. Father started his prayer as was his custom, but he didn't get far until that same lump came up in his throat and choked back further expression. Then Mother reached over and put her hand on my shoulder and began to pray, saying, 'O God, we thank Thee for our son. We thank Thee for our son. We thank Thee that Thou hast kept him true and faithful, and that we are able to send him out from our home chaste and clean. Keep him pure and clean and may his feet never stray from the paths of virtue, purity and the truth in which we have tried to bring him up. Bring him back to us as pure and true as he is going out from us.' It was the vision of my last morning in the atmosphere of a Godly home and the remembrance of my precious mother's prayer. I could not bear the thought of breaking the heart of my father and mother and dishonoring my Lord and Saviour Jesus Christ whom they taught me to love."

—Extract from *A Virtuous Woman*, by Oscar Lowry

* * *

The Family Circle"

"The picture of the family circle, the father, mother and children sitting together reading the Bible, is a scene of inspiring beauty. There the Word of God is at work — molding character, lighting the path of good, inspiring deeds of service. Religion has a vital meaning, touching every aspect of life. God is there in the home, working through purposeful lives to create His kingdom."

—J. Edgar Hoover, Chief: F. B. I.

FATHERS

God Waiting To Give

In one of Dr. J. Wilbur Chapman's meetings a man arose to give the following remarkable testimony: "I got off at the Pennsylvania depot as a tramp, and for a year I begged on the streets for a living. One day I touched a man on the shoulder and said, 'Mister, please give me a dime.' As soon as I saw his face, I recognized my father. 'Father, don't you know me?' I asked. Throwing his arms around me, he cried, 'I have found you; all I have is yours.' Men, think of it, that I, a tramp, stood begging my father for ten cents, when for eighteen years he had been looking for me to give me all he was worth!"

So the heavenly Father is waiting for you. Why not receive the unsearchable riches in Christ now?

—*Moody Monthly*

* * *

Does Every Father Do This?

We all know Gipsy Smith, the evangelist. Before he and Mrs. Smith left for a mission at Cambridge once, his aged father went to see him. At the moment of parting the Gipsy said, "Daddy, will you present me at the throne of grace every day?" The aged saint, with twinkling eyes, replied, "No, my son, I did that years ago, and I have never taken you away; but I will keep you there." Said Gypsy Smith, "With an old saintly father like that behind me, the Lord has to do something."

—*Christian Herald*

* * *

Father Stood, Too!

Dr. P. W. Philpott tells the story of a father he once knew. A fine Scottish Christian and successful businessman had a son: a splendid, well educated, and respected young fellow, who was arrested for embezzlement. At the trial, when he was found guilty, the youth appeared unconcerned and nonchalant until the judge told him to stand for sentence, whereupon he looked over at the lawyer's table and saw that his father, too, was standing. The once erect head and straight shoulders of an honest man were now bowed low with sorrow and shame as he stood to receive, as though it were himself, his son's condemnation. The son looked and wept bitterly.

—*Moody Monthly*

* * *

A Father's Prayer

Dear God, my little boy of three
Has said his nightly prayer to Thee;
Before his eyes were closed in sleep,
He asked that Thou his soul would keep.
And I, still kneeling at his bed,
My hand upon his tousled head,
Do ask, with deep humility,
That thou, dear Lord, remember me.
Make me, kind Lord, a worthy Dad,
That I may lead this little lad
In pathways ever fair and bright,
That I may keep his steps aright.
O God, his trust must never be
Destroyed or even marred by me.
So, for the simple things he prayed
With childish voice so unafraid,
I, trembling, ask the same from Thee.
Dear Lord, kind Lord, remember me.

—*Selected*

* * *

That Dad of Mine

His shoulders are stooped with strife
    and care,

His life's work is almost thru;
He sits alone in an easy chair
Dreaming of Home beyond the blue.
Those snowy locks are a noble crown,
Those eyes are dimmed with the years;
He calmly awaits the Harvest Lord,
He knows no cares or fears,
    That Dad of mine!

Years ago when he was young
I was his pride and joy,
He always prayed that God some day
    Would save his wandering boy;
God saw in him a life so pure —
His prayers are answered now,
He is ready for a crown of gold
To adorn his snowy brow,
    That Dad of mine!

When I was but a lad so small
    I thought my Daddy grand;
I would be just like him
    When "I grow to be a man."
Those days are fled and vanished,
    When I sat upon his knee,
But I look back on yesterday —
    He was a pal to me,
    That Dad of mine!
—Gwendolin A. Edge, in
    The Church of God Evangel

* * *

On His Father's Ground

Colonel Fred N. Dow tells the following story to illustrate how the son of a father devoted to a great principle is likely to follow in his father's steps. Colonel Dow once visited friends at Quebec, and, while seeing the sights of the city and its surroundings, he took a public carriage to visit the Falls of Montmorency. At a halfway house on the road the driver pulled up his horse and remarked, "The carriage always stops here." "For what purpose?" asked the Colonel. "For the passengers to treat," was the reply. "But none of us drink, and we don't intend to treat." The driver had dismounted, and was waiting by the roadside. Drawing himself up to his full height, he said impressively: "I have driven this carriage now for more than thirty years, and this happened but once before. Some time ago I had for a fare a crank from Portland, Maine, by the name of Neal Dow, who said he wouldn't drink; and, what was more to the point, he said he wouldn't pay for anybody else to drink." The son found himself occupying the same ground as that on which his father had stood.   —*New Century Leader*

* * *

Unrestrained

They "made themselves vile," and God's charge against Eli was, "he restrained them not." For the lack of a little timely correction on the part of parents many a lad is ruined for time and possibly for eternity. Samuel succeeded Eli in the office of priest, and he also had two sons, of whom it is said, "they walked not in the ways of their father." We do not read, however, of any blame being attached to Samuel for the conduct of his sons. In cases of family life it is difficult to offer judgment. Grace does not run in the blood. Still, in connection with the training of children, precept and promise are closely allied in God's Word:

"Train up a child in the way he should go: and when he is old he will not depart from it" (Prov. 22:6).
   —*Watchman-Examiner*

* * *

His Lesson

Joseph had been sent to bed by his mother for using profane language. When his father came home she sent him upstairs to punish the boy. "I'll teach that young fellow to swear," he roared, and started up the stairs. He tripped on the top step and even his wife held her ears for a few moments. "You'd better come down now," she called to him after the air had cleared somewhat, "he's had enough for his first lesson."
   —*Illinois Farmer*

* * *

The Father's Concern

One Sunday night D. L. Moody preached in a big circus tent near the Columbian Exposition in Chicago from the text, "The Son of man is come to seek and to save . . . lost." After he had finished, a little boy was brought to the platform by an officer who had found the child wandering in the crowd, lost. Mr. Moody took him in his arms and asked the crowd to look at the lost child. Said he: "The father is more anxious to find the boy than the boy is to be found. It is just so with our Heavenly Father, for long years He has been following you, oh, sinner. He is following you still!" At that moment a man with a blanched face elbowed his way to the platform. The boy saw him and, running, threw himself into his father's outstretched arms. The multitude, that witnessed the scene, broke into a mighty cheer. "Thus," cried Mr. Moody, "will God receive you if you will only run to Him today."   —*King's Business*

* * *

Only A Dad

"Only a dad with a tired face,
Coming home from the daily race,
Bringing little of gold or fame,
To show how well he has played the game,
But glad in his heart that his own rejoice,
To see him come home and hear his voice.

"Only a dad of a brood of four,
One of ten million men or more,
Plodding along in the daily strife,
Bearing the whips and scorns of life,
With never a whimper of pain or hate,
For the sake of those who at home do wait!

"Only a dad, neither rich nor proud,
Merely one of the surging crowd,
Toiling, striving, from day to day,
Facing whatever may come his way,
Silent whenever the harsh condemn,
And bearing it all for the love of them!

"Only a dad, but he gives his all,
To smooth the way for his children small,
Doing with courage stern and grim,
The deeds that his father did for him.
This is the line that for him I pen:
Only a dad, BUT THE BEST OF MEN!"
   —*Edgar A. Guest**

*Used by permission of the copyright owners, Reilly & Lee Co., Chicago.

"Have I Ever Seen A Christian?"

A father was one day teaching his little boy what manner of man a Christian is. When the lesson was finished, the father got the stab of his life, when the boy asked, "Father, have I ever seen a Christian?"

—W. B. K.

* * *

Learning to Pray

The following testimony was given by a convert in a meeting: "One night when I was about to retire, my little three-year-old girl, who was awake, said to me, 'Papa, don't you know how to pray?' I said thoughtlessly, 'No.' In a moment she was by my bedside, saying, 'I will teach you how to pray.' With all my excuses she would not sleep until I arose and, kneeling by her side, repeated after her, 'Now I lay me down to sleep.' Then she went to bed, and was soon in the land of dreams. I didn't sleep that night. God had spoken to me through my baby girl, and I felt that if I died before I waked my soul would be lost. All this day I have been miserable, but tonight I have found peace. I expect to pray that little prayer with my child tonight, knowing that living or dying I am the Lord's."

—*Epworth Herald*

* * *

Afraid of His Father

A splendid story is told of a seven-year-old lad who went to visit his aunt in another city. He became acquainted with some boys in the neighborhood, and spent much of his time playing with them. One day his new friends decided to do something that his father had taught him not to do. He withdrew from the group, but one boy called after him, "What's the matter, are you afraid?" "Yes," the boy answered, "I am afraid of my father." "Aw, he's miles away; he won't know," one of the other boys said. "I know that, but my father has always been good to me, and I don't want to do what I know would hurt his feelings." They said no more after that;

possibly feeling condemned for not entertaining the same fine ideal toward their fathers.

—Tom M. Olson, in
The Sunday School Times

* * *

"Daddy, I'm A-comin' in Your Steps!"

In the other years, in the city of Chicago, it was the custom of a father, enroute to his work in the morning, to go by the saloon for a drink. One morning, as he was tracking his way over the newly-fallen snow, he heard the piping voice of his little boy exclaiming, "Daddy, I'm a-comin' in your steps; daddy I'm a-comin' in your steps!" Looking around, he saw his little boy striding in his footsteps which he had just made and which led in the direction of the saloon. The father cried out, "Oh, God, if my boy is coming in my steps, by Thy help, I'll track them in another direction!"

W. B. K.

* * *

The Influence of a Father's Love

C. F. Andrews, beloved missionary to India, tells of a crisis in his boyhood home. A trusted friend made away with all the family savings. The Scripture lesson for family devotions that night was the Fifty-fifth Psalm: "For it was not an enemy . . . then I could have borne it. . . . But it was thou, . . . mine acquaintance. . . We . . . walked unto the house of God in company." Some terrible verses then follow, calling down a curse upon such a traitor. "My father never read those verses," Mr. Andrews relates. "Instead, he began to pray at once, and, as he did so, his voice broke with compassion for the friend." Whether the money was recovered or the friend restored, we do not learn, but one thing is certain — that the Christian love of such a father had its effect upon the loving character of his missionary son.

—From a personal account
by C. F. Andrews

"All I Could Ask!"

Press dispatches brought the sad news of the death of Ensign Neal Anderson Scott, son of a Presbyterian minister of Goldsboro, N.C. Ensign Scott was graduated with honors from Davidson College in 1940. He then entered the Harvard School of Business Administration. When the war came he promptly enlisted in the Navy.

During the naval battle around the Solomon Islands a Japanese bomber made a suicide dive right onto the deck of Ensign Scott's ship. Young Scott was mortally wounded. Evidently he knew he had only a few minutes to live. First he gave the order, *"Keep those guns firing, mates."* After that he dictated a farewell message to his father: *"To have had you and Mother for these twenty-four years has been all I could ask for in this world."* Then he was gone.

These last words are a wonderful tribute to his parents. Would that every son could give this testimony concerning those who nurtured him. These words will no doubt go down to coming generations. One finds it hard to imagine the feelings of his parents. But it is safe to say they will treasure those words among their most precious possessions. Considering the circumstances under which they were spoken, Ensign Scott's last words deserve to live and to be passed on to the young people of America and the world for generations to come.

—Moody Monthly

* * *

Patrick Henry's Will

Patrick Henry wrote in his will: "I have now disposed of all my property to my family; there is one thing more I wish I could give them, and that is the Christian religion. If they have that, and I had not given them one shilling, they would be rich; and if they have not this, and I had given them all this world, they would be poor."

—Christian Index

A Son's Surprised Gratitude

As is always the case, God's commands are a part of His gracious program for our temporal and our eternal welfare. We are to learn what is worth while and what is harmful through "nurture," t h r o u g h "chastening," and through "admonition." In Hebrews we are told that whom the Lord loveth He chasteneth and that if we be without chastisement then we are not sons. A young man, away at college, wrote his father a birthday letter, and said that his desire was to give expression to his love and gratitude for the parental program. "There was a time," said the son, "when I thought you were hard on me, and I resented it, and determined that when I was out from under the home roof, I would do my own way. Since I have been at college I have found that I have so many worthwhile things which others do not have. . . . I am writing to thank you and to express my gratitude, and to say that if I ever have a home of my own I want it to be like the one in which I grew up."

—The Teacher, Southern Baptist Convention

* * *

If Others Are to Be Helped

A boy said to his mother, "When I grow up I am going to be a Christian like Father. Nobody knows whether he is a Christian or not." That man was like the clock in a certain courthouse tower we used to see. It had no hands. It may have been working inside, but how were we to know it?

—Presbyterian

* * *

Dear Daddy:

When I'm a great big man like you,
I want to do just like you do;
I's goin' to go just where you go,
I want to know all that you know;
I's just a-growing awful big,
And walking in the tracks you dig;
I think it won't be very long,
I's growin' fast, and getting strong,
And soon I'll go to town with you
And be your partner all day through;
I'm just a little, great big man,
A' gettin' like you fast 's I can.

Dear Son:

I'm glad you want like me to be,
Yet, I must change some things I see;
If you will do just what I do,
And follow me the whole length through,
Then, I will pray for stength and power,
To walk the Christ life every hour,
And leave tracks all along my way,
Which lead to joy and endless day.
—Dr. R. E. Neighbour

* * *

Bound Up with His Child

Pliny tells of the raising of one of the world's historic obelisks. Twenty thousand workmen were to aid in raising the great stone, and great risks were involved. To make the engineer doubly responsible the anxious king devised an expedient. He ordered that the son of the engineer in charge should be bound to the apex of the obelisk. The safety of the obelisk meant the safety of the boy. The day for the raising was an anxious one for the engineer. The whole man was in the work. He looked to every detail of his best workmen. The obelisk was raised to safety and his son to life. Even so God has bound your child to every act you do and every thought you think.
—C. J. Boppell, in
Sunday School Times

* * *

"Still On Mountain Time!"

A contributor to the *Reader's Digest* tells this one:

"One evening in Albany, New York, I asked a sailor what time it was. He pulled out a huge watch and replied, 'It's 7:20.' I knew it was later. 'Your watch has stopped, hasn't it?' I asked.

" 'No,' he said, 'I'm still on Mountain Standard Time. I'm from southern Utah. When I joined the navy, Pa gave me this watch. He said it'd help me remember home.

" 'When my watch says 5 a. m., I know Dad is rollin' out to milk the cows. And any night when it says 7:30 I know the whole family's around a well-spread table, and Dad's thankin' God for what's on it and askin' Him to watch over me. I can almost smell the hot bis-

cuits and bacon.

" 'It's thinkin" about those things that makes me want to fight when the goin' gets tough,' he concluded. 'I can find out what time it is where I am easy enough. What I want to know is what time is it in Utah.' "
—*Reader's Digest*

* * *

Wish't You Was My Father!

In Chicago a boy was sent by a drunken father to buy something at a store. Somehow the lad lost the money, and he dared not go home, for when drunk his father got dreadfully angry about the slightest thing. A man who saw the boy shivering in a doorway learned his trouble and gave him the dollar he had lost. Thanking the kind stranger, the boy went off to the store, but suddenly he turned back, and looking wistfully at the man, said, "I wish't *you* was my father!" He had just had a glimpse of the difference it would make to have a good father instead of a drunken one.
—Joseph Edwin Harris,
in *Sunday School Times*

* * *

A Prayer Finished in Glory

Several years ago a minister in Cincinnati, Ohio, at the close of his sermon, felt led to do an unusual thing. He said, "If there is someone here that is sick of sin, and wants us to pray for you, raise your hand." A young man sprang to his feet, and said, "Pray for me, sir. I am sick and tired of sin." The minister learned later that for eight years the boy had been a wanderer on the earth. The minister advised him to write home and tell his parents what he had done. He did, and after several days of anxious waiting, a letter came from his mother, but it was bordered with black. With tear-dimmed eyes he read: "My dear son: The joy which your letter brought to our hearts was only exceeded by the sadness which was there at the same time, for as nearly as we can figure, the same hour that you found Jesus Christ as your Saviour, your father was

going out into the skies. All day long he tossed upon his bed. Every little while he would cry out in misery, 'Oh God, save my poor wandering, drunken boy today!' We would try to divert his attention from your waywardness and sin, but his mind would roam from place to place, and he would cry out in sorrow, 'Oh, God, save my poor wandering, wayward boy today!' Just as he passed away he cried: 'Oh, God, save . . .' and he finished the prayer in the presence of Jesus." Down at the bottom of the letter the mother added a note saying, "You are a Christian tonight because your father would not let God go."
—*Prairie Pastor and Overcomer*

* * *

Watch Your Step

"Father, there's a call for you; watch
       your step!
Little eyes see all you do; watch your
       step!
Little feet go Daddy's way
Follow you from day to day,
Lead, O lead them not astray; watch
       your step!

"Walk the safe and narrow way; watch
       your step!
Let the children hear you pray; watch
       your step!
Would you ways of wisdom teach;
With God's truth their young hearts
       reach?
Then be faithful, I beseech; watch
       your step!

"Father, near your journey's end; watch
       your step!
Let the Saviour be your friend; watch
       your step!
He will guide your feet aright,
To the land of pure delight;
Would you walk with Him in white?
Watch your step!"
—*Selected*

* * *

"I'm Shot Through the Heart"

A general whose troops won a battle in a fiercely contested conflict was called after the victory to be worthily recognized and rewarded. He could not be found. After a long search his staff officers finally located him in his tent where he sat with folded arms in utter dejection. The officers showered congratulations upon him, commending him for his brilliant generalship, adding, "The commanding general wants to see you at once. He is waiting to give you your newly earned medal." "Oh, no," said the desponding general, "don't congratulate me, I can't bear it. Tell the commanding general that I cannot come. Tell him that I care nothing, absolutely nothing, for reward, or promotion." The officers replied, "You should know we cannot go back with any such answer. You are all right. You haven't even a scratch, or a wound!" Then came the agonized reply, "Oh, I am wounded. I am mortally wounded. I am shot through the heart!" Then he walked over to the corner of the tent, turned back a blanket and exposed the dead body of his only son, who rode with him through the battle and who had been shot through the heart. For that father the shouts of victory seemed like hollow mockery. His heart was broken and crushed in the death of his precious son!

If our sons and daughters are unsafe and unsaved through our failures to live the right kind of lives before them as parents, how mockingly empty and hollow are the passing recognitions and rewards of this world.
—W. B. K.

* * *

His Greatest Sermon

Many years ago a farmer had an unusually fine crop of grain. Just a few days before it was ready to harvest, there came a terrible hail and wind storm. The entire crop was demolished. After the storm was over, the farmer, with his little son went out on the porch. The little boy looked at what was formerly the beautiful field of wheat, and then with tears in his eyes he looked up at his dad, expecting to hear words of despair. All at once his father started to sing softly, "Rock of ages, cleft for me, let me hide myself in Thee." Years after, the little boy, grown to manhood, said, "That was the greatest sermon I ever heard." The farmer lost a grain crop, but who knows but that that was the turning point in the boy's life? He saw the faith of a godly father in practice.

—*Sunday School Times*

* * *

"Desirable" Parents

A newspaper comments on a questionnaire recently sent to 369 high school boys and 415 girls, who were asked to check a list of ten desirable qualities in a father. The quality receiving the second largest vote was, "Respecting his children's opinions." Others were: "Never nagging his children about what they do; making plenty of money; being prominent in social life; owning a good-looking car." The Scriptures, with their unfailing accuracy, predict that we are seeing today as a fact of the end of the age, that "perilous times shall come" when "men (meaning mankind, including young and old) shall be lovers of their own selves . . . boasters, proud, . . . disobedient to parents."

—*Sunday School Times*

* * *

Influence of Godly Parents

A certain preacher was invited by a young preacher to speak at a family reunion at his old home. The young preacher met the guest speaker at the railroad station and drove him out through the country to the old country home. The children were all there. The sweet-faced old mother was radiant with joy. The preacher son assembled them all in the living room. A Bible was given the visiting preacher. He read a passage and then said, "As we are in the home of a dear preacher of the Gospel who has gone on to his reward, suppose we have an experience meeting." The eldest son arose and pointing to a picture on the wall said: "There is the best father God ever gave a family of children. I can feel his hand on my head now, and I can hear him pray. I have sought to honor his name." Each son and daughter referred to the father and mother. When they came to the youngest son, his face was buried in his hands. At first he would not speak. Finally, he

arose, and said: "They tell you that you have come to rededicate this old home to the Lord. That cannot be, for our mother has not let it get an inch from God since Father went away. They tell you that you have come that my brothers and sisters might rededicate their lives to the Lord. I know them; they serve the Lord and honor our parents. I am the only black sheep in the group. I, too, can feel that hand on my head. From this day forward I shall live for the Lord in honor of my parents."

—R. C. Campbell, in
The Teacher

* * *

Think This Over

A little girl, with shining eyes and little face aglow, said, "Daddy, it is almost time for Sunday school. Let's go! They teach us there of Jesus' love, and how He died that we might all have everlasting life by trusting in Him!" "Oh, no," said Daddy, "not today. I have worked so hard all the week. I am going to go into the woods, and to the creek. There I can relax and rest. I must have one day of rest, and fishing is fine, they say. So run along. Don't bother me. We'll go to church some other day!" Months and years have passed, but Daddy hears that plea no more: "Let's go to Sunday school!" Those childish years are over and now that Daddy is growing old, when life is almost through, he finds time to go to church. But what does daughter do? She says, "Oh, Daddy, not today. I stayed up almost all last night, and I've got to get some sleep!"

—*The Bible Friend*

* * *

"A New Daddy!"

Gipsy Smith tells of trying to push his way through a great crowd in the north of Scotland and feeling a tug at his coat sleeve. At first he thought it was only someone else trying to get into the meeting with him and paid little or no attention, but as the tugging increased and became more and more insistent, he turned as best he could in the jam to find out what was wanted. Imagine his astonishment to find close beside him a little Scotch lassie, clad in rags, holding in her uplifted hand something wrapped in tissue paper, moist and grimy from the clutch of her little fingers.

"What is it, my dear?" he asked and she answered, "I want you to have my candy."

"Why?" he asked.

"Oh, sir!" she cried, " 'cause we've got a new daddy at our house! He has never been sober till Saturday! We've never known him to be sober; but he was in your meeting last Saturday, and, oh, it's so wonderful now at home, 'cause he's sober!"

Didn't Gipsy Smith take that candy? and didn't he take the giver of it up in his arms and hold her close to his glad, thankful heart? She was so grateful for a sober daddy that she was willing to part with her dearly loved candy; and he was so thankful for a soul saved, a slave set free, a husband and father clothed in his right mind and returned to his family through his efforts, that tears not only filled his eyes but ran down his cheeks.

—*The Alliance Weekly*

* * *

My Lad

You're growing big and strong my lad
And that's so pleasing to your dad,
But I'll admit, through coming days,
I'll miss your simple childish ways.
When first you walked by daddy's side,
How small you were, how short your stride;
But now — O how the years flit by!
You're most as tall and strong as I.
And now when we go for a walk,
You step right up with me and talk
As man to man, not as a child,
And thus are many hours beguiled.
No more you'll ride on daddy's back,
Nor stride my foot and trot and rack,
And in the dark when fear alarms,
No more you'll cuddle in my arms.
But though you're growing up so fast,
I want that simple love to last,

That child-like trust in me my lad,
Will always comfort your old dad.
—C. G. Spindler, *Exchange*

* * *

Heaven Indeed

"It was a Sunday afternoon. I had taken my little boy of four summers for a walk to our village cemetery to see the grave of an infant recently buried there. We were walking homeward hand in hand, and had been silent for some minutes, when the little lad said: "Papa, when you die and go to Heaven, will you take me, too?" Somewhat in wonder at his artless question, I replied, "Why, my son?" He gripped my hand more closely as he looked up with the light of love in his eyes, and said tenderly, " 'Cause I want to go with you." What answer could I make him? To go with me! Then he would fear not. Heaven would be home for him if I were there. There flashed into my mind the Saviour's word, "Thou shalt be WITH ME in paradise."

—*Sunday School Times*

* * *

Untrustworthy Sons

God is often unable to give because man is not worthy to receive. A pastor was called to a home one evening to counsel with troubled parents. With much difficulty and deep emotion the father presented their great sorrow. With tears streaming down he said: "I have accumulated a business. Mother and I have now come to the years when we feel we should step out of active work and pass this business over to our son. Our son, however, is not trustworthy, and we cannot give him what we have for him." As the heart of this father was grieved that he could not give what his love prompted him to give, so the heart of God must be grieved because so often men are not trustworthy.

—*Pastor*

* * *

It Makes a Difference In Whom You Put Your Trust

Looking through binoculars in the Alps, a group of scientists saw a healthy specimen of a rare plant which they wanted. It was located, however, on a valley floor. Although they had ropes and climbing equipment, the cliffs appeared too steep for anyone of their weight. Just then a young lad with his dog came bounding down the path. They stopped him with this proposition: for a certain amount of money they would tie a strong rope around his waist, lower him to the valley floor, and draw him up again when he had uprooted the plant. He considered a moment, then without a word returned the way he had come. In a few minutes, however, he again appeared, leading by the hand a burly Swiss mountaineer. "All right, gentlemen," he said, "I will get your plant. But my father will hold the rope."

—Tomorrow

* * *

A Self-Righteous Prodigal

On one of Mr. Moody's western campaigns, he was followed from city to city by an aged and broken man of venerable appearance who, in each place, asked the privilege of saying a word to the great congregations. He would stand up and in a quavering voice would say: "Is my son George in this place? George, are you here? O George, if you are here, come to me. Your old father loves you, George, and can't die content without seeing you again." Then the old man would sit down. One night a young man came to Mr. Moody's hotel and asked to see him. It was George. When the great evangelist asked him how he could find it in his heart to treat a loving father with such cruel neglect, the young man said: "I never thought of him; but Mr. Moody, I have tried to do all the good I could." *That*

is a good picture of a self-righteous prodigal in the far country. He was generous with his money and with his words — yet every moment of his infamous life he was trampling on the heart of a loving father.

—C. I. Scofield

* * *

Dad

His shoulders are a little bent,
His youthful force a trifle spent,
But he's the finest man I know,
With heart of gold and hair of snow,
He's seldom cross and never mean;
He's always been so good and clean;
I only hope I'll always be
As kind to him as he is to me.
Sometimes he's tired and seems forlorn
His happy face is lined and worn;
Yet he can smile when things are bad:
That's why I like my gray-haired dad.
He doesn't ask the world for much —
Just comfort, friendliness, and such;
But from the things I've heard him say,
I know it's up to me to pay
For all the deeds he's done for me
Since I sat on his rocking knee;
Oh, not in dollars, dimes, or cents —
That's not a father's recompense;
Nor does he worship wealth and fame —
He wants his pay in my good name.

—Boy Life

* * *

Niemoeller's Sons

Once the three eldest of the five Niemoeller boys came to their mother. When she smilingly inquired the meaning of the delegation, their elected spokesman said: "Mother, the three of us have decided to go into the Christian ministry, we admire Father so much."

—Presbyterian

FEAR

Divided Vision

A vicar was preaching one Sunday, and he rather startled the congregation with the way he began, "I want to give you some good advice," he said. "Don't

squint." He described how Peter stepped out of the boat and walked on the sea toward his Lord. Then he began to sink, and Christ stretched out His hand and saved him, and brought him back again into the boat. The Lord said to him, "Wherefore didst thou doubt?" The root meaning of that word "doubt" is looking two ways at once. Why did Peter begin to sink? Because he had one eye upon Christ, and the other eye upon the billows and the storm around him.

—*Christian Herald,*
(London)

* * *

Prisoners of Fear

Needy miners and settlers in British Columbia, engaged in stripping abandoned Fort Alcan of lumber, electrical appliances, and plumbing, made an amazing discovery. While dismantling the jail they found that the mighty locks were attached to the heavy doors, and two-inch steel bars covered the windows, but the walls of the prison were only patented wallboard of clay and paper, painted to resemble iron. A good old heave against the walls by a man not as strong as a football tackle would have burst the wall out. Nobody ever tried it because nobody thought it possible. Many Christians are prisoners of fears that are nothing when pushed against. Satan cannot do anything against a child of God, but he loves to put barriers of papier-mache in the path of a believer to make him think that there is no progress in the direction of the will of the Lord. When by faith we push against it we will be free.

—*Eternity*

* * *

Fear Not!

The Scotch preacher, John McNeill, tells of an experience with his father in boyhood days. As a lad, he had been to town and was late in starting the tramp of six or seven miles through the lonely glen to his home. The night was very dark and the road had a bad name. "In the densest of the darkness," says McNeill, "there suddenly rang out a great, strong, cheery voice: 'Is that you, Johnny?' It was my father — the bravest, strongest man I ever knew." And then the minister adds: "Many a time since when things have been getting very black and gloomy about me,

I have heard a voice greater than any earthly father cry: 'Fear not; for I am with thee.' "

—*Christian Index*

* * *

Never Fear!

Though at times the clouds hang low,
    Never fear!
Though the winds may fiercely blow,
    Never fear!
God is still upon His throne,
He is mindful of His own,
Let this blessed truth be known,
    Never fear!

Though at times the way seems long,
    Never fear!
Murmur not but sing a song,
    Never fear!
If you trust in God and pray,
Help to you He will convey,
You'll find roses by the way,
    Never fear!

Though a friend may prove untrue,
    Never fear!
Seek his friendship to renew,
    Never fear!
This one thing remember well:
Christ is our Immanuel,
He will ever with you dwell,
    Never fear!

Though the river may seem dark,
    Never fear!
With the Pilot you'll embark,
    Never fear!
"Jesus Saviour, pilot me,
Over life's tempestuous sea,"
Hear Him whisper tenderly,
    "Never fear!"
—David F. Nygren, Litt.D.

* * *

Who Has the Keys?

One day in Central Africa a missionary and I visited an outstation where a short time before the witch doctor, Kalamba, had accepted the Saviour. The implements of his craft, constituting a fortune to those people, he had publicly burned. We found him in sore fear and distress. His heathen neighbors, now that he had no "medicines" for defense, were predicting his speedy death. "Our medicines will eat you," they said. And in dreams, to which pagan peoples have always attached a dread significance, he had been hearing his wife say to him, "I have dug your grave." The missionary spent an hour or more trying to talk him out of his agony of fear, but the terror was still visibly there. I then suggested to the missionary that he turn, in his Baluba Testament, to Revelation 1:17, 18, and show Kalamba, who could not read, the Saviour's assurance, "Fear not; I . . . have the keys of . . . death." "Have him put his finger on it," I said, "have him memorize it, and explain to him that those keys are held not in the hand of his enemies, or of dreams, or of hostile 'medicines,' but in the hand of his Saviour, whose personal word to him is, 'Fear not, Kalamba, I, your Friend and Saviour, have the keys of death.' " This was done, and as Kalamba placed his finger and glued his eyes on that assurance and heard it explained, most beautiful it was to see the anguish of fear lifted and his face grow radiant with peace and courage and joy.

—From *Paul's Ways in Christ,*
by Egbert W. Smith

*   *   *

"Our God Whom We Serve Is Able to Deliver Us"

A man was compelled one night to cross a wide, frozen river. Notwithstanding the assurances of those who were thoroughly familiar with the region and repeatedly crossed on the solid ice, the traveler feared to undertake the trip, but finally began to crawl his way over. When near the middle of the frozen stream he was startled by a sound in the distance, and caught sight of a negro driving a heavy team of horses pulling a great load of pig iron; yet there was not the least sign of a crack in the ice.

What a foolish thing to fear and crawl like that! Will the Word of God hold? Some fear to trust it. Why, man, it can't fail!

—*Sunday School Times*

Stopped by a Smile

Miss C. Leffinwell, a missionary in China, gave the following account of deliverance from death by the Boxers: "There was a lady missionary whom the Boxers told to kneel down and have her head cut off. She knelt as told, but as she did so, she looked up into the man's face and actually smiled. As she looked at him a moment, thus smiling, it seemed as if his face began to change and to reflect the smile. He stepped back a little, and then continued to withdraw, together with his companions, until after a little they all fled, leaving the ladies alone. As the Boxers were retreating the leader turned and said to her: 'You cannot die. You are immortal.' If her face had shown fear, they would have killed her without hesitation. I suppose the smile seemed supernatural. She afterward said, 'I did not know that I smiled.'"   —*Life of Missionary*

*   *   *

Faith is not CLINGING — It is LETTING GO

Somewhere we have read a story like this. A traveler upon a lonely road was set upon by bandits who robbed him of his all. They then led him into the depths of the forest. There, in the darkness, they tied a rope to the limb of a great tree, and bade him catch hold of the end of it. Swinging him out into the blackness of surrounding space, they told him he was hanging over the brink of a giddy precipice. The moment he let go he would be dashed to pieces on the rocks below. And then they left him. His soul was filled with horror at the awful doom impending. He clutched despairingly the end of the swaying rope. But each dreadful moment only made his fate more sure. His strength steadily failed. At last he could hold on no longer. The end had come. His clenched fingers relaxed their convulsive grip. He fell — *six inches,* to the solid earth at his feet! It was only a ruse of the robbers to gain time in escaping. And when he let go it was not to death, but to the safety which had been waiting him through all his time of terror.   —James H. McConkey, in *Faith*

FELLOWSHIP

Three Words in Common

The story has been told of three men of different nationalities who met, not understanding one another's languages. There was one thing however, that they all knew, and could say with the blind man in John 9, "One thing I know, that, whereas I was blind, now I see." At length one of them ventured to speak, and in so doing uttered a word which struck a chord in all their hearts and brought a glow to their faces. Then the second uttered a word which seemed to increase their pleasure; and finally the third added a word which resulted in their falling on one another's necks and weeping for joy. What could those three words be which could produce such an extraordinary result? They were, *"Jesus," "Hallelujah,"* and *"Amen."* Is there another name given among men that could produce those results?

— *Illustrator*

* * *

Why They Could Live Together Happily

Genuine Christian fellowship can be enjoyed even when war is raging! A ranch in California had been leased to a Japanese family for a period of years. When we became involved in World War II, the Japanese were ordered into the interior of the state. This brought dismay to both the family and owner of the ranch. The owner desperately needed help; and finally succeeded in hiring a Chinese family. The Chinese family arrived on the scene a week before the Japanese family had to vacate. With but one ranch house on the place, the owner was in a dilemma as to what to do. But it was discovered that both the Japanese and Chinese families were devout Christians, in the enjoyment of the fellowship of the Father and the Son — so they decided they could live happily together in the same house. Each day they worshipped and prayed together, using the English language, which both understood. The Japanese

helped the Chinese to get started with the work, and the Chinese helped the Japanese to get packed and ready to go. When the time came for the separation, both families promised to pray for each other.

— *Sunday School Times*

* * *

At High Tide

Dr. J. H. Jowett spoke of the uniting of sundered people in these words: "At low tide there are multitudes of separated pools along the shore. At high tide they flow together, and the little distinctions are lost in a splendid union. — *Missionary Monthly*

* * *

That Single Thread

J. Stuart Holden was being shown through a large factory where hundreds of looms were spinning very fine linen thread.

The manager of the mill said to Mr. Holden, "So delicate is this machinery that if a single thread of the entire 30,000, which at this moment are being woven, should break, all of these looms would instantly stop."

He stepped to one of the machines and broke a single thread. Suddenly every loom was still and remained so until the thread was rejoined, whereupon the machinery was again in motion.

The mechanical wonder exhibited in the factory that day clearly illustrates that which is spiritual. It is through one act of disobedience, one departure from the will and fear of God, that the blessings of our fellowship with Him are stopped. Not until that thread is rejoined will the joy of the Lord flow again in our hearts.

—*Good News Broadcaster*

* * *

Who Walks With God

Who walks with God must take His way
Across far distances and gray

To goals that others do not see,
Where others do not care to be.
Who walks with God must have no fear
When danger and defeat appear,
Nor stop when every hope seems gone,
For God, our God, moves ever on.

Who walks with God must press ahead
When sun or cloud is overhead,
When all the waiting thousands cheer,
Or when they only stop to sneer;
When all the challenge leaves the hours
And naught is left but jaded powers.
But he will some day reach the dawn,
For God, our God, moves ever on.
— *Heart and Life*

* * *

The Value of Church Attendance

A certain governor of Surinam once asked his Negroes why they always wanted to go to church in order to sing and pray together when they could do so privately at home. They were standing by a coal fire, and a Negress answered: "Dear master, separate these coals and they will at once die out, but what a pleasant fire they afford when they all burn together!" Going to church is not simply the act of going to *church;* it is more. When you go to church you testify that you love the Word of God; when you go to church you preach a sermon to the nonchurchgoer that he is not a beast of burden, but a human being, rational and spiritual. Merely going to church can save no man, but not going to church damns many a person. — *Expositor.*

* * *

With God

To talk with God no breath is lost;
    Talk on.
To walk with God no strength is lost;
    Walk on.
To toil with God no time is lost;
    Toil on.
Little is much, if God is in it;
Man's busiest day not worth God's
    minute.
Much is little everywhere
If God the business doth not share.
So work with God, then nothing's lost
Who works with Him does well and
    most.   —An Old English Verse

Christ, the "Hub"

We like to think of the Lord Jesus as being the "hub" in a great wheel, and of God's children as being the "spokes." The closer we get to Christ, the "Hub," the closer we get to one another! Born-again believers are "One in Christ!" When we feel a growing coldness in our hearts toward our brothers and sisters in Christ, let us "steal away" to the "secret place of the Most High," and there pray: "More love, O Christ, to Thee!"
— W. B. K.

* * *

Fortunate for the Sailor

When an Australian destroyer reached a port in the Solomons after many adventures the crew was given shore leave, and a young Christian sailor found himself free for the day. He decided to spend it quietly by himself in Bible study, and seeing a trail running through a forest he followed it until he came to a quiet spot where he sat down and began to read his Bible. So immersed was he that he did not notice, until he was already by his side, a huge, almost naked native, pointing to the open book, asked, "That Bible?" When the sailor replied, "Yes," the native remarked, "Me read Bible, too — me Christian," and taking the Bible from the sailor he read aloud a chapter of Isaiah. Then handing back the Bible with a smile, he went on his way.
— *The Bible in the World.*

* * *

The Companionship of Jesus

Among the Dutch the rose was sometimes cultivated by planting an inferior rose close to a rose of superior quality. The rose of inferior quality was carefully watched and its anthers removed so as to avoid self-pollenization; the object being that it should be pollenized by the superior rose. Gradually the rose thus treated took upon itself the characteristics of the superior life of its companion. This is indeed a beautiful illustration of the blessing that comes to the life that knows the companionship of Jesus. If our lives are pollenized, as it were, by his righteousness; if his life-transforming truth is received into the heart, and self be sacrificed to make room for the incoming of his superior life, it cannot be other than that gradually the life loses its own inferior characteristics and develops the characteristics of the blessed life of him who is himself the Rose of Sharon. O Lord, let my life receive the pollen of divine righteousness, that more and more I may become like my blessed Master! —A. S. Gumbart, D. D.

* * *

No Room

My gracious Master knocked one day
Upon my heart's closed door.
He longed to come up and sup with me
As He had supped before.
I bade Him enter, but He said,
"I see no room, today,"
And with a sad reproachful look,
He turned and went away.

Dismayed I looked within my heart —
Unlovely things were there.
For while I slept the enemy
Had entered unaware.
I saw a root of bitterness,
Of envy, wrath and pride,
And for my Lord no room was left,
So fast they multiplied.

I prayed, "O Father, cleanse my heart,"
And hearing this my prayer
The devil fled, nor left he ought —
He feared to tarry there.
My Lord no longer knocks without,
Sweet fellowship have we,
For naught impure, unholy, stands
Between my Lord and me.
— *Moody Monthly*

* * *

Walking in Him

An American traveler was staying once with the good Bengel of Germany.

One night he took a little advantage of occupying the next room to the saint, and he listened closely to hear the last devotional murmurings of this beloved servant of Christ. He thought surely Bengel would pray some rapturous prayer, and he wanted at least to catch some of its notes.

After the day was over, the good man gathered up his books and kneeling, he prayed, "Lord Jesus, I thank Thee that things are still the same between us." He arose, retired, and fell asleep. As he received Christ Jesus, so he was walking in Him. It was the same fellowship still, moment by moment.

Beloved, are we living this simple trust life, companionship with our best Friend? —A. B. Simpson

* * *

His Face Shone

Biographers of Fenelon tell us that he lived in such intimate fellowship with God that his very face shone. Lord Peterborough, a skeptic, was obliged to spend the night with him at an inn. In the morning he rushed away, saying, "If I stay another night with that man, I shall be a Christian in spite of myself!" Some one else said of him, "His manners were full of grace, his voice full of love, and his face full of glory." — Elisha Safford.

* * *

Tie That Binds

It was Sunday in occupied Kiangsu. The morning service proceeded smoothly until a stir in the rear of the church caused a turning of heads. Women uttered suppressed cries of fear, clutching their children to them. Men half rose from their seats.

A Japanese soldier stalked up the aisle. He reached the front of the church and in the silence which followed every ear awaited the expected edict, declaration or warrant.

221

In the stillness the enemy soldier pulled his hand out of his pocket and laid an offering upon the table. All could hear the clink of a coin on the collection plate. He picked up a hymn book, turned the pages and pointed out to the organist a number which he evidently desired to join with the Chinese congregation in singing.

It was the Chinese translation of "Blest be the tie that binds our hearts in Christian love."

—*Christian World Facts*

* * *

The Shortest Way

"Which is the shortest way to London?" was the question for the best answer to which a London newspaper offered a substantial cash prize. The answer which won the prize was, "The shortest way to London is *good company*." All travelers know how true that answer is. Good company shortens any journey, however long. In such company time flies, miles slip rapidly past, and the end is reached almost before one is aware of it. The journey to heaven is very much shortened, the road made easier, when Jesus Christ is our traveling companion.

— H. K. Downie, in *Choice Gleaning*

* * *

Flowing Together

A man, through whose land ran a mountain stream, went into the business of raising ducks. He made stout pens, and into each pen he put a distinct breed of ducks. All was well until a flood came. Then the waters rose over the pens and the ducks were seen swimming together.

Today we are fenced off in our denominational coops, but as we pray for the downpours and floods of the Spirit, we will be lifted above the barriers of creed and dogma and experience, — and Christ's prayer will be answered, — we will be one as He and the Father are One.

—*Sword of the Lord*

Why the Sentence Was Revoked

The Lord has united all believers with an eternal bond, and it is His desire that that unity should be manifest in a practical way so that the world may see and believe. A practical demonstration of that unity occurred in a certain section of China where some missionaries had been laboring. One man came often to the services and seemed convicted of the Holy Spirit. One day he openly confessed that he was a believer in the Lord Jesus Christ and could no longer worship his ancestors in the usual manner. It was just at the New Year time that this occurred, at which time he was supposed to perform the usual rites of burning paper and incense to his ancestors. When he refused, the decision was given out by the head of his clan that unless he would recant within fifteen days he would be beaten with a thousand stripes. They would have been permitted to wreak this vengeance upon one of their own clan. As the fifteen days drew near, another native Christian went to visit the head of the clan; he said in substance, "You don't understand this Christian religion. When a man believes in the Lord Jesus Christ, God is his father and every other believer is his brother or sister. We are one family, and I could not see my brother beaten and stand idly by. What all we Christians propose to do is this: If you insist on carrying out your sentence, all of us in the country round about who are brothers and sisters are going to come and share those stripes with him. The parley went on all night. The head of the clan knew there would be trouble if members of another clan were beaten by them, so he finally sent apologies, saying that they did not understand the Christian religion or such a verdict would never have been passed. The unity of the Christians proved greater than the heathen powers, and the Lord was glorified. — *Sunday School Times*.

FORGETTING GOD

Answer to World's Tension: An Educated Heart

"We have educated our heads and our hands. Now, the need seems to be for an educated heart. Never before have so many Americans possessed college degrees. Never have we had so much wealth per capita. Never have we been so physically comfortable. Yet, never have we lived under such tension, Never have so many of our people occupied hospital beds for the mentally ill. Never have we felt so insecure. Never have we felt so close to a general failure of the human spirit; never so close to moral bankruptcy! One does not need to be a theologian to know that the person who would keep sane, happy and balanced under the extreme stress of modern living MUST enjoy an active partnership with a POWER that is higher than he!"
— Dr. Kenneth McFarland, Educational Consultant to General Motors, in *Chicago Daily News.*

* * *

Needed: "A Peace Conference With the Prince of Peace!"

The late Arthur Brisbain, world-renowned columnist and journalist, wrote: "We may sweep the world clean of materialism. We may scrub the earth white of autocracy. We may carpet it with democracy, and drape it with the flags of republicanism. We may hang on the walls the thrilling pictures of freedom — here the signing of America's independence, there the thrilling portrait of Joan of Arc, yonder the Magna Charta, on this side the inspiring picture of Garibaldi. We may spend effort and energy to make the world a Paradise, itself where the lion of capitalism can lie down with the proletariat lamb. But if we turn into that splendid room, mankind with the *SAME OLD HEART*, 'deceitful and desperately wicked,' we may expect to clean house again not many days hence. What we need is a 'peace conference' with the Prince of Peace!"
— *Selected*

Defeated by Snowflakes

Napoleon proposed to invade Russia and bring its Czar under his sway. It is said that someone ventured to say of his purpose, "Man proposes, but God disposes." On hearing the remark, Napoleon is said to have replied, "I propose, and I dispose." But that was to leave God out of the reckoning, and it proved fatal. For God dealt with Napoleon through one of the tiniest, most fragile creations, the snowflake. By the snows of Russia God defeated the presumptuous Napoleon. "Russia shall be mine," his proud heart had said — whereas the Lord was there. And because of God, the Corsican's proudly conceived invasion came to disaster and defeat. Emperors, kings, dictators, generals, and statesmen who leave God out of their reckoning are fools.
— *Sunday School Times*

* * *

Reminders

"Sometimes I think I am not a Christian," said a boy one day. "I don't seem to have the same interest that I had when I joined the church. It isn't easy for me to remember God." "What about the time when your father was away from home so long? Was it hard for you to remember him?" asked the minister slowly. "Not a bit," said the boy. "We had letters from him and kept thinking about him and talking about him, and looking forward to when he'd come home. No, there wasn't much chance to forget him." "Suppose there had been no letters. Suppose your father's name had been dropped from the conversation," said the minister thoughtfully. "That would have made a difference," answered the boy slowly. "Well, don't you see it is the same with God? We can't see Him. It isn't to be wondered at if we forget Him when we allow so many other things to crowd in upon us. But God has given us His Holy Word — something like your father's letters — and His house where the members of the family can meet and talk about Him." "I see what you mean,

223

and you're right. A fellow needs all the reminders of God he can have in a world like this."

—*Bible Expositor and Illuminator*

* * *

Hopeless, Confused

Dr. Robert Maynard Hutchins, former chancellor of the University of Chicago, said, "The world we have created is too much for us. The intelligence of the race has failed before the problems the race has raised. We cannot tell who or what is responsible for anything. We have more money, more food, more things, more power, than any time in history; yet, we are poorer, hungrier, more helpless, and more confused than ever before!" —*Selected*

* * *

Have You Forgotten God?

In the glare of earthly pleasure,
In the fight for earthly treasure,
'Mid your blessing without measure,
Have you forgotten God?

You are thoughtful of the stranger
From the palace or the manger;
And the weak you shield from danger—
Have you forgotten God?

While His bounties you're accepting,
Are you His commands neglecting
And His call to you rejecting?
Have you forgotten God?

See the shades of night appalling
On your pathway now are falling.
Hear you not those voices calling?
Have you forgotten God?

— Robert J. Koffend

* * *

Only for an Emergency

Some Christians seem to look upon God as a kind of spare tire. A spare tire is forgotten for months at a time until suddenly we have a flat on the road. Then we want the spare tire to be in good condition, ready for use. Just so, many forget God during all the times when things go well, then in an emergency they want God to be on hand, immediately ready to hear and answer their cry of distress.

—*Sunday*

* * *

The Napkin Must Be Unwrapped

The story is told of two brothers who, brought up in a Christian home, were sent to the same college to prepare themselves for their life-work. One of the brothers decided to enter the ministry. The other determined to study law. They completed their university training at the same time and each went his way into the world.

The brother, who was now a minister of the Gospel, did not make any great name for himself. He was, however faithful to the Lord in the place of his calling, serving for many years in a small church in a small town.

The other brother prospered seemingly in every way. He developed a large practice, handled some famous cases, wrote several noteworthy legal books, and was, at a comparatively early age, appointed to a judgeship.

A day came when things went wrong for the lawyer. His fortune slipped away through some unwise investments, and his health failed. At length he went to visit his brother. One day while the minister-brother was reading in his study, he heard his lawyer-brother weeping, in another part of the house, as if his heart would break. The minister went to the lawyer and inquired as to the trouble. "Oh," exclaimed the lawyer, "it is near the end, and I am not ready to go!"

"You received Christ as your Saviour yeas ago," the pastor replied. "Don't tell me that you do not trust Him to keep you!"

"It isn't that," the broken man sobbed. "I know that my sins are gone, that God has forgiven me. But still I'm not ready to go. As I think back over my life I can't recall a single soul that I have led to Christ or of ever having been a good witness to Him."

—*The Pilgrim*

"Only Forgotten Son!"

A chaplain, in a poorly lighted railway station, was endeavoring to show a soldier the way of life eternal in Christ. Opening a New Testament to John 3:16, the chaplain said, "Read it." Here's how the soldier rendered the verse, "For God so loved the world that He gave His only FORGOTTEN Son." How forgotten and neglected is He!

—W. B. K.

FORGIVENESS, GOD'S

Only the King Can Pardon

Only the rightful king or ruler can issue a pardon. In Sir Walter Scott's "Ivanhoe," the story is told of Richard the Lionhearted coming in disguise, upon a sheriff and his men who were about to execute a prisoner. Reining in his horse and raising his hand, Richard exclaimed, "Hold! I spare that man's life." But his very act of mercy revealed his identity, for instantly the men recognized that this one, with authority to pardon, must be none other than Richard himself. Who is He that forgiveth sins? It is the coequal with the Father.

—*Sunday School Times*

* * *

God Both Forgives and Justifies

When God forgives through the risen, glorified Jesus, He not only forgives, but He justifies. It is impossible for an earthly judge to both forgive and to justify a man. If a man is justified, he does not need to be forgiven. Imagine a man charged with a crime going into court, and, after the evidence is all in, he is pronounced not guilty, and the judge sets him free. Someone says, as he leaves the building, "I want to congratulate you. It was very kind of the judge to forgive you." "Forgive? He did not forgive me; I was justified. There is nothing to forgive." You cannot justify a man if he does a wicked thing, but you can forgive. God not only forgives but He justifies the ungodly, because He links the believer with Christ, and we are made "accepted in the Beloved."

—Dr. H. A. Ironside

"Absolutely Worthless!"

A friend once showed John Ruskin a costly handkerchief on which a blot of ink had been made. "Nothing can be done with it now," said the owner. "It is absolutely worthless."

Ruskin made no reply but carried it away with him. After a time he sent it back, to the great surprise of his friend, who could scarcely believe his eyes. In a most skillful and artistic way Ruskin had made a design in India ink, using the ugly blot as a center for the design.

A blotted life is not necessarily a useless life. Jesus can make a life beautiful if it is yielded to Him.

—*Moody Monthly*

* * *

East From West

Dr. J. Wilbur Chapman was wont to tell of a man who had been a professor of mathematics in a German University, but who became a wreck from strong drink. He came to one of Dr. Chapman's meetings forlorn and dejected and took a seat in the rear of the room. He was converted and became a member of the church. It was Dr. Chapman's custom to meet the men of his church every Sunday morning, before going into his pulpit, for a short conference on things pertaining to the Christian life.

One morning he told his men that our sins were taken from us as far as the East is from the West, and then seeing the old professor before him he said, "Professor, that is a mathematical proposition for you. How far is the East from the West?" The professor reached for his pencil and notebook, when he suddenly stopped and burst into tears; and facing the crowd of men he said, "Men, you cannot measure, for if you put your stake here and keep the East ahead of you and West behind you, you can go around the world and come back to your stake and East will still be ahead of you and West behind you. The distance is immeasurable. And thank God, that is where my sins have gone."

—Christ for the World Messenger

* * *

Remission of Sin

D. L. Moody had a great many friends among the high officials in the United States. One day he met the governor of a certain state, who said, "Moody, I have decided to respond to a petition of a great many people to pardon a well-known criminal. You are offering pardon to all sinners, I would like you to take my pardon to this man."

When Moody went, all the men were called together in the chapel, and Moody said, "I have a pardon for one of you. I do not know you by face, but here is the name."

Oh, what a breathless interest! Those five or six hundred men scarcely breathed, wondering, "Is it for me?"

When Mr. Moody read the name of the man, something like a shriek came out of the crowd. It was almost more than the man could bear. Mr. Moody talked to him later and offered him remission of his sins *through faith in Christ.*

The governor had a legal right to pardon that man. He gave the document to Mr. Moody, who announced the pardon in the name and with the authority of the state and nation. The governor remitted, and Mr. Moody announced the governor's remission. Only in that sense can any man remit sins.

—R. L. Moyer, in Pilot

* * *

A Clean Slate

A lad was told by his mother not to play near a certain pond. One day the temptation was too much, and, venturing too close, he fell into the water. He was very conscious of his wrongdoing, and most uncomfortable. So he wrote on his school slate: "Dear mother, I am sorry

I have been bad. If you forgive me, please rub it out." Back came the slate, perfectly clean! How like the love of God who said, "I have blotted out, as a thick cloud, thy transgressions, and, as a cloud, thy sins" (Isa. 44:22).

—King's Business

* * *

Mother's Abundant Pardon

Out in a certain town in Pennsylvania there was a young man who got tired of home and the farm; so he went to the city. He ran wild and plunged to the depths of sin. His parents had never heard from him. By and by sin began to pall, and he wondered if he could find welcome if he went back. So he went to work, and obtained enough money to take him back home. When he got to the old home station, he was so ashamed of his rags that he boarded the train again and went on a few stations farther. Then he sat down and wrote a letter home. It was the first in years. He confessed how sinful he had been, and asked his parents' forgiveness. He told them he would be coming by the next day, and if they would forgive and welcome him again, they should hang a sheet on the clothesline as a token. What did that mother do? She got all the sheets in the house and hung them on the line. That was the sign of abundant pardon. And that is just how God does things — on a large scale.

—Moody Monthly

* * *

"Every Footprint Crooked!"

A writer walked across the valley of Dead Men in the South Sea Islands. Looking back over the way, he saw his tracks in the sand and marked how crooked his path was, though he had intended to walk straight. It became a parable to him. He said, "This is my life. Every footprint, CROOKED"! Then I fell asleep. When I awakened hours afterwards, I could see no marks on the sand. Every footprint was GONE. Not one to be seen. The tide had been in, and when it receded there was no sign of the crooked steps. I said to my soul,

'That is my fresh reminder of what God has done for me.' "

How hope-engendering, gloom-dispelling are His gracious words of promise: "I have botted out, as a thick cloud, thy transgressions, and, as a cloud, thy sins"!

—W. B. K.

* * *

Pardon for All Sins!

"Sister," said a dying girl, "please get the Bible and read for me that passage about the Blood which cleanseth from sin. I fear some of my sins are too great to be forgiven. Look whether it says 'all sin' or only 'sin,' for I do not remember." "Yes," replied the sister, "these are the exact words, "The Blood of Jesus Christ His Son cleanseth us from all sin.' " "Oh, how sweet!" said the girl whose fire of life was almost out. "Now there is pardon for all my sins."

—*Gospel Herald*

* * *

When a Man Cannot Be Pardoned

God is gracious, but he will not force the acceptance of His grace upon men. In 1829 George Wilson, in Pennsylvania, was sentenced to be hanged by a United States Court for robbing the mails and for murder. President Andrew Jackson pardoned him, but this was refused, and Wilson insisted that it was not a pardon unless he accepted it. That was a point of law never before raised, and the President called the Supreme Court to decide. Chief Justice John Marshall gave the following decision: "A pardon is a paper, the value of which depends upon its acceptance by the person implicated. It is hardly to be supposed that one under sentence of death would refuse to accept a pardon, but if it is refused, it is no pardon. George Wilson must be hanged!" And he was hanged. Provisionally the Gospel of Christ which is the power of God unto salvation is for every one irrespective of what he may be or what he may have done. Potentially, it is only to "every one that believeth."

—*Sunday School Times*

The Lord's Answer

A man once said to a servant of the Lord: "I am such a helpless, miserable sinner; there is no hope for me. I have prayed, and resolved and tried, and vowed until I am sick of my unavailing efforts."

"Do you believe that Christ died for our sins, and rose again?" was the reply.

"Of course I do."

"If he were here on earth in bodily and visible form, what would you do?"

"I would go to Him at once."

"What would you say to Him?"

"I would tell Him that I am a lost sinner."

"What would you ask Him?"

"I would ask Him to forgive and save me."

"What would He answer?"

The man was silent.

"What would He answer?"

At last the light came into his eyes, and a smile of peace stole over his face as he whispered, "He would answer, 'I will.' " And the man went away believing, rejoicing "with joy unspeakable and full of glory." Since then he has been working faithfully for the Christ who saved him for nothing.

—*Sunday School Times*

* * *

Present Tense, Indicative Mood

An elderly lady was converted at a mission in Dublin, and she told her family that she was saved, and her sins forgiven, and she knew it. Later she was taken ill and asked that Dean Bagot should come to see her. Her niece, Lady Castle-Stuart, thought she should warn the Dean. She said, "You know my aunt has got the idea that her sins are forgiven, and that she is saved." Dean Bagot said, "Been to school?" "Yes." "Do you know how to parse?" "Yes." "Got a Bible?" She got the Bible. "Now," said Bagot, "open it at Ephesians 1:7 and read the verse, and please parse the word 'have'." She began "Indicative mood, present tense of the verb 'to have.' " "What does 'have,' indicative mood, present tense, mean?" "It means that I possess, that I have got." "What have you got?" "In whom we have redemption through his blood, the forgiveness of sins." She left the visitor, and, going to her room, there laid hold of the indicative mood and present tense of the verb "to have." On returning, she said, "I have the forgiveness of my sins according to the riches of His grace. I thank God for it." The Dean said, "Go and tell your aunt that; it will do her more good than I can."

—Shantyman

* * *

When Forgiveness Was Sought

A young man who had sinned against his mother became convicted after she was on her death-bed. He went to her room, knelt, and sobbed for forgiveness. With her last departing strength she drew close to him, placed her lips near his ear, and said, "My dear boy, I would have forgiven you long ago if you had only accepted it." Jesus has made atonement for the sins of the whole world, and we all would have been forgiven long ago had we accepted his pardon.

—Arnold's Commentary

* * *

When God Forgives, He Forgets

How different God's pardon is from ours! So often we forgive as did the aunt of the little girl who had been good a whole week, and asked some favor. "I know," was the answer, "that you have been good all this week, but you know you were bad last week." In a passionate burst of feeling the little one exclaimed: "Oh, Auntie, you are not one bit like God. When He forgives He doesn't keep throwing it up afterward."

—Christian Endeavor World

FORGIVING OTHERS

What Christ Had Done for Her

The wife of a Zulu chief attended a Salvation Army meeting and heard and responded to the call of Jesus. When her husband heard of this he forbade her to go again on pain of death. However, eager to hear more about Jesus, she dared to go, and when her husband knew of this he met her on her return journey and beat her so savagely that he left her for dead. By and by his curiosity moved him to go back and look for her. She was not where he had left her, but he noticed broken twigs and found her lying under a bush. Covering her with his cruel eyes he leered, "And what can your Jesus Christ do for you now?" She opened her eyes, and looking at him, said gently, "He helps me to forgive you!"

—From In the Land of His Love,
by Mrs. M. L. Carpenter

* * *

The "More Excellent Way"

In the troublesome days of the Boxer Rebellion in China, the late Dr. Frank A. Keller suffered much loss in hospital equipment because of the rebels. Being young, he felt that there should be some compensation for the riot. He went to state his case to Dr. Hudson Taylor, who was too busy to see him, being on his knees in prayer for the young doctor's work and personal safety. Before an interview could take place, he himself was convinced that the China Inland Mission principle of claiming no compensation was right, even in his case. Returning to his station, waiving all claim to any indemnity, he was amazed at his reception. The Mandarin became Dr. Keller's warm friend. Through him he was taken to a place of safety. When he returned to the work a year later, he found that his forbearance was the means of opening up the whole Province of Hunan for Christian work, and his experience proved to be a turning point in his whole life.

—Prophecy

* * *

Wounded Dog Teaches Christian Love and Forgiveness!

A man hurled a stone at his dog. So terrific was the blow that the dog's leg was shattered! Whining and limping, the wounded creature came sadly to the man, fell at his feet, and LICKED the hand which had hurled the merciless stone! That's like Christian love and forgiveness. O, that more of God's children were as loving and forgiving as that dog!

—W. B. K.

* * *

A Conscience Void of Offense

One night when Mr. Moody was leading the singing and Mr. Sankey was playing the organ, Moody looked over to Sankey and said: "Excuse me; I see there a friend coming in to the meeting. I offended him today downtown, and I want him to forgive me." Mr. Moody walked down from the platform, and the other man got up from his seat and walked out into the aisle and met Mr. Moody about halfway, and said, "Mr. Moody, I forgive you heartily." Moody went back to the platform, and an eyewitness said, "I never saw such a meeting; it was wonderful." That is why God so richly used Mr. Moody. He kept a conscience that was void of offense toward God.

—*Moody Church News*

* * *

Why He Couldn't Forgive Her

Ethel and Tom are two children in a family. Ethel quarrels with Tom, and their father is grieved by their quarrel. Ethel is very unhappy. So, in tears she goes to her father and says, "Daddy, I am truly sorry. I can see I have made you unhappy." But while her father's arms go round her, the minx is putting out her tongue at Tom behind his back. The father wants to forgive her, but he cannot forgive her if she will not forgive Tom. "You've got to make it up with Tom first," the father wisely says. "If you shut Tom out, you keep me out, for I love Tom as well as you." "If ye forgive not men their trespasses," said the Master, "neither will your Father forgive your trespasses."

—Dr. Leslie D. Weatherhead,
in *In Quest of a Kingdom*

Both Needed the Grace of God

A shamefaced employee was summoned to the office of the senior partner to hear his doom. The least that he could expect was a blistering dismissal; he might be sent to prison for years. The old man called his name and asked him if he were guilty. The clerk stammered out that he had no defense. "I shall not send you to prison," said the old man. "If I take you back, can I trust you?" When the surprised and broken clerk had given assurance and was about to leave, the senior partner continued: "You are the second man who has fallen and been pardoned, in this business. I was the first. What you have done, I did. The mercy you have received, I received. It is only the grace of God that can keep us both."

—*Emergency Post*

* * *

A Cure for Bad Tempers

The manager of a large laundry business cured two if his men who could never agree with each other on account of their bad tempers. These men's duties caused them to work side by side in the laundry; and, owing to their quarrelsome natures, they were constantly in hot water in more senses than one. At last their employer hit upon the following plan to cure them:

He put the two men, one inside the building and the other outside, to clean all the windows on the premises. There they were, face to face with each other, without being able to exchange a word. At last the charm began to work, for the whole of the work people were laughing at them. Noticing this, the two men could not help but smile at each other, and at last broke out in a hearty roar of laughter. The cure was permanent, for they have been good-tempered friends since.

—*Gospel Herald*

* * *

Pardon and Forgiveness

Too often people forget to extend forgiveness to others, nor do they expect to receive forgiveness themselves.

Louis XII, king of France, had many enemies, who having opposed him before his ascending the throne now feared his resentment, especially as they heard he had made a list of his foes, placing a black cross against the name of each. They lost no time in getting away from Paris, dreading condign punishment.

Judge of their astonishment when tidings reached their retreat that the king recalled them with assurance of pardon, explaining that the black cross placed by the side of each man's name was not a menace, but token of clemency and forgiveness — the emblem being so placed to remind the king that as he expected to gain eternal life through the Blood of the Cross, so he must follow Christ's example, who though competent to summon a legion of angels, forebore, and instead prayed for His murderers, "Father, forgive them; for they know not what they do."

For us, as for the king, it is written: "Forgive if ye have aught against any, that your Father . . . may forgive you."

— F. J. Mallett, in
Southern Churchman

* * *

Which Place Will You Take?

Doing an injury puts you below your enemy; revenging one makes you but even with him; forgiving it sets you above him.

— Benjamin Franklin, in the
Immanuel Missionary

* * *

The Dividing Line Obliterated

I remember when as a young Christian worker I held an evangelistic campaign in a church at a crossroad, way out on the prairie. It was just a little church. There was a center aisle, and the seats went over against the wall from that aisle. We had very good congregations, but nothing else. After several nights of trying to preach, and giving an invitation, the pastor said to me: "Years ago a family in this church quarreled, and the community has taken sides in the matter. The members of the family do not speak to each other and that aisle down the center of the church divides the factions. The people on the one side will not speak to those on the other." One night — I don't know what happened — but when the meeting ended, the two who had a grievance against each other met in front of the pulpit, asking each other for forgiveness. Then the thing broke loose. There were just two nights left. The night we closed the campaign, the pastor stood with me on the doorstep of that little church. He said, "Look out there over the prairie" — and all who have been on the prairies of Nebraska know that you can see for miles — "I don't believe there is a single unsaved man left in any farmhouse in sight." God gathered them all during the last two or three nights, when the Christians got right with each other and with God.

— Dr. Will M. Houghton

* * *

Can We Pray the Lord's Prayer?

At the close of a conference, the Bible teacher was asked by a girl of seventeen if she could have a talk with him. "You know that girl who said in her testimony that there was a girl she had not been speaking to for six weeks? Well, I am that girl she was talking about." "Have you decided now to go and make up with her?" "I don't see why I can't have victory in my life. I have surrendered everything else except that." "Let us sit here and talk about it. But first let us pray. You pray." After a moment of silence, he said, "Pray the Lord's prayer." The young woman obediently began to pray, in a rather petulant way: "Our Father, who art in heaven. Hallowed be thy name. Thy Kingdom come. Thy will be done, on earth as it is in heaven. Give us this day our daily bread . . ." Then there was silence. "What is the matter?" No answer. "Why don't you go on?" Still no answer. "How have you been praying for the last six weeks?" "Haven't prayed." And thus did the Holy Spirit convict by this Word of the living God. She did surrender her life, and asked forgiveness for her sin.

From *Studying Our Lord's Parables* by Dr. R. C. McQuilkin

* * *

The Golden Rule

A war was raging in southeastern Europe more than two centuries ago. It was not strictly a religious war; nevertheless, many Turks who were Moslems were on one side, and many Christians on the other. At the first the Moslems were getting the better of the conflict, and it so happened that among those taken captive was at least one Christian, who was made a prisoner of a Turkish official. This Turk treated the Christian with the utmost cruelty. A little later the fortune of war changed, and the Turkish officer fell into the hands of his enemies. Just then word was sent him by his former Christian prisoner, assuring him that he could be at peace and that revenge would not be taken. So surprised was he, and so grateful, that he renounced his former faith, declaring, "I will not die a Moslem, but I will die a Christian; for there is no religion but that of Christ which teaches forgiveness of injuries."

—*Gospel Herald*

* * *

Able to Forgive Wrongs

Of all English kings, Richard seems to have been the bravest. History tells us that he was a great warrior, and because of his daring and prowess upon the battlefield he was surnamed Coeur-de-Lion, or the Lion-hearted. Like many another brave man, he was also very generous, and able to forgive wrongs. It is recorded that, when his treacherous brother John, who had tried to rob him of his crown, pleaded for mercy, he said, "I forgive him, and I hope to forget his injuries as easily as he will forget my pardon." After he had reigned about ten years, one of his French vassals, Vidomar, Viscount of Limoges, rebelled against him. Richard at once marched his army against him, and besieged him in his castle of Chaluz.

During the siege, with his usual disregard of danger, Richard approached very near the castle walls, almost wholly unattended. Seeing this, a young man, named Bertrand de Gurdun, fitted an arrow to his bow and took aim at the King. The arrow pierced Richard's left shoulder and proved to be a fatal wound. While the King lay in his tent, the castle was taken, and Bertrand made a captive; heavily ironed, he was led to the bedside of the suffering and dying monarch. Richard looked calmly into his face and said, "Youth, I forgive you my death." Then turning to his soldiers standing by he said, "Let him go free, and give him a hundred shillings."

—*Gospel Herald*

* * *

Why Revival Was Blocked

I remember one town that Mr. Sankey and myself visited. For a week it seemed as if we were beating the air; there was no power in the meetings. At last, one day, I said that perhaps there was someone cultivating the unforgiving spirit. The chairman of our committee, who was sitting next to me, got up and left the meeting right in view of the audience. The arrow had hit the mark, and gone home to the heart of the chairman of the committee. He had had trouble with someone for about six months. He at once hunted up this man and asked him to forgive him. He came to me with tears in his eyes, and said: "I thank God you ever came here." That night the inquiry-room was thronged. The chairman became one of the best workers I have ever known, and he has been active in Christian service ever since.

—D. L. Moody, in
Prevailing Prayer

* * *

"I Freely Forgive"

A young Greenlander said to a missionary: "I do love Jesus — I would do anything for him; how good of him to die for me!" Said the missionary: "Are you *sure* you would do anything

231

for our dear Lord?" Yes, I would. What *can* I do?"

The missionary showing him the Bible said, "This book says, 'Thou shalt do no murder.' " "Oh, but that man killed my father." "Our dear Lord himself says, 'If ye love me, keep my commandments,' and this is one of them." "Oh," exclaimed the Greenlander, "I do love Jesus! but I — I must —" "Wait a little, calm yourself; think it well over, and then come and let me know." He went out, but presently came back, saying, "I cannot decide; one moment I will, the next I will not. Help me to decide." The missionary answered, "When you say, 'I will kill him,' it is the evil spirit trying to gain the victory; when you say, 'I will not,' it is the Spirit of God striving within you." And so speaking, he induced him at length to give up his murderous design. Accordingly the Greenlander sent a message to the murderer of his father, telling him to come and meet him as a friend. He came, with kindness on his lips, but treachery in his heart. For, after he had stayed with him a while, he asked the young man to come and visit him on this side of the river. To this he readily assented, but, on returning to his boat, found that a hole had been pierced in the boat, and cleverly concealed by his enemy, who hoped thereby to destroy him. He stopped the hole, and put off in his boat, which to the surprise and warmth and indignation of the other, who had climbed a high rock on purpose to see him drown, did not sink, but merrily breasted the waves. Then cried the young man to his enemy, "I freely forgive you, for our dear Lord has forgiven me."

—*Biblical Illustrator*

* * *

Abraham Lincoln and the Spy

When I was preaching in the Southern States of America, the minister called my attention to one of the elders. He said: "When the Civil War broke out, that man was in one of the far Southern States, and he enlisted in the Southern Army. He was selected by the General and sent to spy the Northern Army. As you know, armies have no mercy on spies if they are caught. This man was caught, tried by court-marshal, and ordered to be shot. While he was in the guardroom awaiting the day of execution, he would call Abraham Lincoln by every vile name that he could think of.

"One day while he was in prison, a Northern officer came into his cell. The prisoner, full of rage, thought his time was come to be shot. The officer, when he opened the door, handed him a free pardon, signed by Abraham Lincoln. He told him he was at liberty; he could go to his wife and children. The man who had before been so full of bitterness and malice and rage suddenly quieted down, and said: 'What! has Abraham Lincoln pardoned me? I have never said a good word about him.' The officer replied: '*If you got what you deserved, you would be shot.* But some one interceded for you at Washington, and obtained your pardon. You are now at liberty.' "

—*Christian Endeavor World*

* * *

His Forgiveness Won Him

In the home of Dr. Goheen, a missionary in India, a native was dusting the furniture and carelessly upset a beautiful vase, which fell to the floor, breaking in many pieces. The frightened native dropped on his knees before Doctor Goheen, begging for mercy. The doctor smiled and said, "Never mind; I forgive you." The astonished servant looked for a moment upon the quiet face of the Christian man, where there was not the slightest trace of anger; then leaping to his feet he cried, "I believe! I believe!" He then told how, as a servant in the home, he had been gradually coming to know Christ through the doctor, and now his readiness to forgive had won him completely to the Master.

—*Christian Work*

* * *

Why He Was Not Killed

A white settler in South Africa found a native of the Kaffir tribe near his stable, and accused him of trying to steal a horse. The native declared that he was simply taking a short cut home, but the white man was not a Christian, he had no faith in Kaffirs, and decided he would make them afraid of him. So he tied the poor native to a tree and cut off his right hand. Months afterward the white man was overtaken by darkness and storm far from his cabin. Seeking shelter in a Kaffir hut he was given food and a place to sleep. When he awoke a tall Kaffir was standing over him. As their eyes met the native held up his arm without any hand. The white man felt his time had come. He knew the Kaffirs were cruel and revengeful. He waited expecting each moment to be his last. Slowly the right arm dropped, and the Kaffir said: "This is my cabin and you are in my power. You have maimed me for life, and revenge is sweet; but I am a Christian, and I forgive you."

—Pansy Magazine

* * *

Why He Lost His Pardon

A man named Samuel Holmes, who was in the Frankfort, Kentucky, jail undergoing punishment for murder, received a visit from an old schoolfellow of his, Lucien Young. The Kentucky legislature had recorded some years previously its appreciation of Young's bavery in rescuing several lives from a wrecked vessel; and when Young, moved by Holmes' condition, made an appeal to Governor Blackburn for his pardon, the governor, remembering his brave action, relented and signed the pardon for his sake.

With the document in his pocket, Young hastened back to the prison to tell the good news to his friend. Before intimating, however, that he had power to make him a free man, Young commenced a conversation. After talking awhile upon other subjects, he finally said:

"Sam, if you were turned loose and fully pardoned, what would be the first thing you would do?"

The convict very quickly responded. "I would go to Lancaster, and kill Judge Owsley and a man who was a witness against me."

Young uttered not a word, but turned mournfully away, went outside the prison wall, took the pardon from his pocket, and tore it into fragments.

This is the story as it was told in the Richmond Register.

Holmes lost his pardon simply because when he was forgiven he would not forgive. He had no penitence with which to meet pardon and no godly sorrow with which to respond to proffered mercy.

—Florida Baptist Witness

* * *

There Must Be No Bitterness

We admire Saul's magnanimity toward his enemies. There are those today who have shown a like magnanimity. Madame Chiang Kai-shek's Christian words admonish us: "There must be no bitterness in the reconstructed world. No matter what we have undergone and suffered, we must try to forgive those who have injured us, and to remember only the lessons we have gained thereby." Booker T. Washington once said, "I am determined to permit no man to narrow or degrade my soul by making me hate him."

—The Teacher,
S. B. C.

* * *

A Hardened Heart Softened

A gentleman saw a boy thief in his flower garden. He went forth quietly in a roundabout way to meet the boy and, coming up behind him, laid his hand on the boy's shoulder, saying: "Now, my boy, answer me one question: Which is the best flower in my garden?" The boy, finding no escape, looked around and after a few minutes' pause, said, "That rose is best," as he pointed to a beautiful moss rose. The gentleman, still keeping one hand on the boy's shoulder, reached out his other hand and, plucking the rose in all its beauty, gave it to the boy. As he released him he said, "There, take it, my boy." The boy was amazed. Looking into the face of his strange benefactor, he said, "Ain't you going to have me punished, sir?" "No," was the reply; "but as I am going to give you the best flower in my garden, you will never steal from my flower beds again, will you?" "Never, sir, as long as I live," was the emphatic reply; "but, please, sir, ain't there some little errand I can do for you?" Free forgiveness and a token of love had won the hardened boy's heart, and from that hour he was the willing servant of his friend.

—*Christian Herald (London)*.

Forgive and Forget

The woman who said, "I can forget and forgive, but I shall always remember it," has far too many imitators. True forgiveness is not based on forgetfulness; nor are we to wait till time has worn away the sense of wrong, before we pardon a penitent offender. When we do forgive that should forever end the matter. Forgetfulness should follow forgiveness.

Remembering wrongs benefits no one. If we have a sore finger we bind it up, and let it alone. Is there any use in pulling off the rag ten times a day, and showing the hurt to every man we meet? Talking over a wrong often does more hurt than suffering it, recollecting it is worse than receiving it.

—*Florida Baptist Witness*

FREEDOM

Washington on Spiritual Tyranny:

"If I could have entertained the slightest apprehension, that the constitution framed in the convention, where I had the honor to preside, might possibly endanger the religious rights of any ecclesiastical society, certainly I would never have placed my signature to it; and, if I could now conceive that the general government might ever be so administered as to render the liberty of conscience insecure, I beg you will be persuaded, that no one would be more zealous than myself to establish effectual barriers against the horrors of spiritual tyranny, and every species of religious persecution — For you doubtless remember, that I have often expressed my sentiments, that every man, conducting himself as a good citizen, and being accountable to God alone for his religious opinions, ought to be protected in worshiping the Deity according to the dictates of his own conscience."

—From a letter to United Baptist Churches of Virginia, dated May 10, 1789.

Freedom Follows the Flag

Reading the "Book of the Law" is a privilege which not all have. When the Americans first occupied Manila, the prison doors were opened for "political offenses." One of these crimes, according to the Spanish government, which then ruled the Philippines, was reading the Bible. One day a man came to Dr. Homer Stuntz, and asked to see him in strict privacy. He then asked in a whisper if it were true that he could now read his Bible without danger of imprisonment. Dr. Stuntz took him to the door and asked him to look at the American flag floating near by. Then he said, "So long as you see that flag floating over your country, you can sit on the ridgepole of your house, if you want to, and read the Bible, and no one can molest you."

—*Gospel Herald*

* * *

Chain and All

A minister was talking to a man in the inquiry room. The man said, "My heart is so hard it seems as if it was chained, and I cannot come." "Come along, chain and all," said the minister, and he just came to Christ, hard heart, chain, and all, and Christ snapped the fetters, and set him free. If you are bound by Satan it is the work of God to break the fetters. You cannot break them.

—D. L. Moody

* * *

Church Divisions Praised

Not many voices are raised in praise of the wide diversity of denominations and sects in America. Recently the Minnesota Methodist pastors' school heard a historian say that the country should be proud, not ashamed, that it has 350 different denominations.

Main reason for this large number is the complete religious liberty enjoyed here, said Dr. William Warren Sweet of Southern Methodist University.

The individualism of the frontier also stimulated the multiplication of church groups, he said. "As people moved west, they simply created a new denomination if they didn't like their old one."

—Selected

* * *

How an African Woman Was Freed

Mrs. Dan Crawford in an address in London told about an African woman who from her earliest years had been conscious of a strange presence within her. When she visited a village, disaster overcame the inhabitants and chiefs would give her large presents to keep away from their village. Under the influence of this madness she committed all sorts of crimes. One day she chanced to enter the mission house. The preacher was a young minister who had but little knowledge of the native language, and when the time came for him to deliver his sermon words completely failed him, so taking up his Bible, he carefully read through the fifth chapter of Mark, and when he had finished it, not knowing what else to do, he read it again. All this time the woman was listening with profound attention to the freeing of the Gadarene demoniac, and

at the conclusion she started up and began praying loudly to the unknown Power to release her also from her curse. In her intense praying she foamed at the mouth, and at one time the onlookers thought she would fall down in a fit. But at last she sank on the ground whispering, "I am freed! I am freed!" And freed she was, and for a long time she lived with Mrs. Crawford, a living testimony to the power of God to bring peace to the troubled soul.

—*Wonderful Word*

* * *

Freedom To Worship God!

"The breaking waves dashed high
  On a stern and rockbound coast,
And the woods against a stormy sky
  Their giant branches tossed;
And the heavy night hung dark
  The hills and waters o'er,
When a band of exiles moored their bark
  On the wild New England shore.

"Not as the conqueror comes,
  They, the truehearted came;
Not with the roll of the stirring drums,
  And the trumpet that sings of fame;
Amidst the storm they sang,
  And the stars heard, and the sea;
And the sounding aisles of the dim woods rang
  To the anthem of the free.

"What sought they thus afar?
  Bright jewels of the mine?
The wealth of seas, the spoils of war? —
  They sought a faith's pure shrine!
Ay, call it holy ground,
  The soil where first they trod;
They have left unstained what there they found, —
  Freedom to worship God."

—Selected

* * *

Bought To Be Freed

A young mulatto girl was being sold at auction one day. She was a beautiful girl, tall and slender. The bidding was keen, and quickly mounted higher and higher until at last only two men were left bidding for her ownership: the one a low, uncouth fellow who swearingly raised his bid every time to outbid the other, a quiet man of refinement. Finally the bidding stopped, and to the gentleman who had bid so very earnestly were given the papers which made him the lawful owner of the young girl. With a shove the auctioneer presented her to her new master. Proudly, defiantly, she stood before him, hating him with every part of her being. Suddenly, a change came over her face: first there was a look of pure amazement closely followed by one of utter incredulity. Her owner was ripping up the papers of ownership, and, with a smile of kindness, said to the now trembling girl, "My dear, you are free. I bought you that I might free you." Too stunned for speech, the girl merely stared till finally, with a cry of happiness too deep for words, she cast herself at the man's feet, and through her tears exclaimed, "Oh, master, I'll love you and serve you for life!" What the papers of ownership could not do, the man's kindness had won completely. The Lord Jesus has loved you and has paid such a price that He might buy you from the slavery of Sa-

tan and *free* you. Will you not tell Him, "Master, I'll love Thee and serve Thee for life?"

— *Evangelical International High School Quarterly*

* * *

Heart Freedom!

"A little bird I am,
　Shut out from fields of air,
And in my cage I sit and sing
　To Him who placed me there;
Well pleased a prisoner to be,
　Because, my God, it pleased Thee.

"My cage confines me round,
　Abroad I cannot fly;
But though my wing is closely bound,
　My heart's at liberty.
My prison walls cannot control
The flight, the freedom of my soul.

"Oh, it is good to soar
　These bolts and bars above,
To Him whose purpose I adore,
　Whose providence I love,
And joy, the freedom of the mind."

—Madam Guyon

FRIENDSHIP

Danny's Best Friend

As Mother's Day drew near Miss Smith asked her first-graders, "Who is your best friend, children?"

Danny's hand popped up with a quick jerk for he was positive he knew the answer.

"All right, Danny," said his teacher kindly, "Stand up and tell the children who your best friend is?"

"It's God," answered Danny with finality.

"Well, yes," said Miss Smith, "That's right, Danny, but who is your best friend at home? Who does everything for you and cares for you at home?"

"There was no hesitation in Danny's voice as he answered, "It's Jesus."

Happy boy, blessed mother whose child is taught to put the friendship of the Father-God and the love of Jesus Christ even above the friendship of Mother.

—Sarah Schuster, in
Gospel Herald

* * *

A Fellow's Mother

A fellow has a lot of friends
　Of boys and girls to play with,
And aunts and uncles that he spends
　An afternoon or day with.
I like the folks across the street,
　And men with smiling faces,
And pleasant people that you meet
　In church and other places.

A daddy's good, so big and tall,
 A sister, or a brother,
But one friend is best of all —
 And that's a fellow's mother!

The other friends are nice to know,
 To visit and to chatter,
But, oh, you want your mother so
 When something is the matter!
Perhaps a finger you may hit,
 Because the hammer misses;
Your mother always fixes it
 With tape and thread — and kisses.
A mother takes the hurt away,
 She can, somehow or other;
One friend you need, need every day —
 And that's a fellow's mother!
　　　　—Douglas Mallock, in
　　　　　　Woman's World

* * *

A Friend

"When troubles come your soul to try,
You love a friend who just stands by;
Perhaps there's nothing he can do,
The thing is strictly up to you;
For there are troubles all your own,
And paths the soul must tread alone,
Times when love can't smooth the road,
Nor friendship lift the heavy load.
But just to feel you have a friend,
Who will stand by until the end,
Whose sympathy through all endures,
Whose warm handclasp is always yours,
It helps somehow to pull you through,
Although there's nothing he can do.
And so with fervent heart we say:
'God bless the friend who just stands
　by.' "
　　　　　　　　—*Selected*

* * *

Friendship

The kind of friend you have been to me,
Is the type of friend I would be to thee;
Your faithful spirit, your radiant face
Has added just a touch of grace;
When trouble came and things looked
　drear,
'Twas then your helpfulness would cheer
Never a murmur, always a smile,
Friends like that are sure worth while;
So gladly a friend I would be to thee,

Yes, the kind of friend you have been
to me.
　　　　　—F. Sumner Ettinger

* * *

Who Is A Friend?

"A friend is one to whom we may
pour out the contents of our hearts,
chaff and grain together, knowing that
the gentlest of hands will sift it, keep
what is worth keeping, and with a
breath of kindness blow the rest away!"
　　　　　—An Arabian Definition

* * *

Faithful in Adversity

Adversity is the wind or the fan which
separates the chaff of flattery from the
grain of solid friendship. The Shadow
once said to the Body: "Who is a friend
like me? I follow you wherever you
go. In sunlight or in moonlight I never
forsake you." "True," answered the
Body, "you go with me in sunlight and
moonlight. But where are you when
neither sun nor moon shines upon me?"
The true friend is one who is faithful
in adversity and who abides with us
in the darkness of the night.
　　　　—Clarence E. Macartney, in
　　　　　　Moody Monthly

* * *

Grant's Faithful Friend

General Grant's faithful friend, his
chief of staff, the Galena lawyer, John
A. Rawlins . . . was closer to Grant
than any other during the war. It was
to Rawlins that Grant gave his pledge
that he would abstain from intoxicating liquors. When he broke that pledge
Rawlins went to him and with great
earnestness pleaded with him, for the
sake of himself, and for the sake of the
great and holy cause of the nation, to
refrain from strong drink. Faithful
were the wounds of that friend. In
front of the Capitol at Washington
today there stands the magnificent monument of General Grant, sitting on his
horse in characteristic pose and flanked
on either side by stirring battle scenes.
But at the other end of Pennsylvania
Avenue, a little to the south of the

avenue, is Rawlins Park, where there stands a very ordinary, commonplace statue of Rawlins. Whenever I stand before the great monument of Grant on his horse there in front of the Capitol, I think of that other monument. I think of that faithful friend who kept Grant on his horse.

—Clarence E. Macartney, in
Moody Monthly

* * *

Friends of His

A Christian lady visited a young girl who was blind. The lady taught her to read the Bible in raised letters.

"I went into her room one morning, and before I had time to reach her hand and let her know that someone was present, I found her speaking to Christ about the verse which she had just spelled out, *'Ye are My friends, if ye do whatsoever I command you'.* Lifting her sightless eyes to the Lord, she said, 'Oh, I like to hear You say that! You only told me before that You were my Friend, the sinner's Friend — I did not know that we were friends of Yours.' "

Isn't it wonderful to know that if we do those things which He has told us to do, He calls us His friends?

Seventy-One and No Friends!

A clergyman visiting in the sick wards of a workhouse in a crowded city was asked by one of the nurses to say a word to a sick man whose bed was near the door of the ward. He said, "With pleasure, Nurse, but he is asleep." "No," she said, "he is dying." The clergyman went to the bed and noticed the name-card at the bed-head. "Robert Browning, aged seventy-one; no friends." "What does this mean, Nurse?" he asked. "Just what it says," she answered. "If he dies tonight we do not know anyone who knows him. Do speak to him." The clergyman bent over the bed and quietly said, "How sweet the name of Jesus sounds in a believer's ear." In a moment the closed eyes opened, and a joyous whisper was heard. "Yes, Jesus is my Saviour, my Friend." "No friends," said the card; but the poor man claimed the friendship of the matchless Son of God. The promise of this ever-present-never-failing Friend is SURE: "And even to your old age I am He; and even to hoar hairs will I carry you: I have made, and I will bear; even I will carry, and will deliver you!" (Isa. 46:4).

—W. B. K.

GIVING

How the Fine Was Paid

Once, when Mr. LaGuardia, the famous ex-mayor of New York, was presiding at a police court, they brought a trembling old man before him, charged with stealing a loaf of bread. He said his family was starving. "Well, I've got to punish you," said Mr. LaGuardia. "The law makes no exception, and I can do nothing but sentence you to a fine of ten dollars." Then he added, after reaching into his pocket, "and here's the ten dollars to pay your fine. And now I remit the fine." Then, tossing the ten-dollar bill into his famous outsize hat, he said, "Furthermore, I'm going to fine everybody in this courtroom

fifty cents, for living in a town where a man has to steal bread in order to eat. Mr. Bailiff, collect the fines, and give them to this defendant." The hat was passed, and an incredulous old man, with a light of Heaven in his eyes, left the courtroom with forty-seven dollars and fifty cents.

—*Methodist Recorder*

* * *

Two Epitaphs

In Warwickshire, England, near an ivy-grown church, may be found a stone on which is the following inscription:

"Here lies a miser who lived for himself

And cared for nothing but gathering pelf,
Now where he is or how he fares,
Nobody knows and nobody cares."

The other epitaph is in St. Paul's Cathedral, London. It is a simple and plain monument. Beneath a figure are these words:

"Sacred to the memory of Charles George Gordon, who at all times and everywhere gave his strength to the weak, his substance to the poor, his sympathy to the suffering, his heart to God."
—*Teacher's Lesson Quarterly*

* * *

Generous

Teofilo ("Friend of God") said to Christobel ("Christbearer"), the new convert in the little mission chapel in Cuba:
"Christobel, if you had a hundred sheep, would you give fifty of them for the Lord's work?"
"Yes, I would."
"Would you do the same if you had a hundred cows?"
"Yes, Teofilo, I would."
"Would you do the same if you had a hundred horses?"
"Yes, of course."
"If you had two pigs, would you give one of them to Him?"
"No, I wouldn't; and you have no right to ask me, Teofilo, for you know I have two pigs."
"*If there be first a willing mind, it is accepted according to that a man hath, and not according to that he hath not*" (II Cor. 8:12).
—*Selected*

* * *

Her Alabaster Box

Hudson Taylor tells us that after a great missionary meeting at Cardiff he received a letter from a widow, who said: "I could not put into your hand yesterday any money or jewels, for my husband is dead and we have hard shifts to live. But I have one jewel — my daughter. She has long wanted to go,

I could not let her go from my care, but last night I gave my alabaster box of very precious ointment to Christ; and if you will see to her going out now, I will be glad to send her."
—*Southern Presbyterian Journal*

* * *

A Collection not an Offering

A certain small boy had a dog which he named Fido. The boy was very fond of Fido. One day at dinner the boy's father noticed that he took the best of the portion of roast beef which had fallen to his lot and placed it on another plate. Upon inquiry, the father learned that the meat was for the dog Fido. "My son," said father, "it would be better if you ate that meat yourself and gave Fido some of the scraps that are left." The boy protested, but his father was obdurate. At the conclusion of the meal the boy took out to Fido a plate heaped with the scraps of the roast. "Here, Fido," said the boy, "I wanted to make you an offering, but here is only a collection." Love for the Master should be great enough to prompt an offering at each attempted service.
—*Albany Journal*

* * *

Where Curtailment Usually Begins

A man said to me, "I am sorry that I shall not be able to subscribe to the budget of the church this year — depression, you know." "Well," I replied, "I am sorry, too, because it certainly will mean a curtailment of much in your life." "How so?" he questioned, "I do not understand you." "Simply this," I replied, "that means you will, of course, have to cut out your golf club, your fraternal connection, and probably drop many of your social activities." "Oh, no, I cannot do that, they mean too much to me." I have known that man for over eight years. During that time things have been quite easy for him, and for the most part he has been a man who considered himself quite a loyal son of the church. It is now dawning upon him that when he sang, "All to Jesus I surrender, all to Him I freely give," he was waving the magic wand of pretense over his soul. When it came to cutting down, Jesus as of old, was called first to suffer.

—Christian Herald

* * *

Wanted Pocketbook Baptized, Too!

Dr. R. E. Neighbour was in the baptismal pool with a railway engineer. The pastor was ready to proceed with the baptismal service. "Wait!" whispered the engineer; "I forgot something. I want to return to the robing room, and get my pocketbook and let you baptize it with me!" O, that more of our pocketbooks were "baptized." O, that more of God's children were taking, with seriousness, their financial responsibilities to God's work!

—W. B. K.

* * *

A Little Girl's Pennies

Hattie Wiatt, a little girl, came to a small Sunday school and asked to be taken in, but it was explained there was no room for her. In less than two years she fell ill, and slipped away on her own little last pilgrimage, and no one guessed her strange little secret until beneath her pillow was found a torn pocketbook with fifty-seven pennies in it, wrapped in a scrap of paper on which was written, "To help build the little Temple bigger, so that more children can go to Sunday school." For two years she had saved her pennies for the cause which was nearest her heart. The pastor told the incident to his congregation, and the people began making donations for the enlargement. The papers told it far and wide, and within five years those fifty-seven pennies had grown to be $250,000, and today in Philadelphia, can be seen a great church, the Baptist Temple, seating 3,300, a Temple College with accommodations for more than 1,400 students, a Temple Hospital, and a Temple Sunday school so large that all who wish may come and be comfortable. She was only a little girl, but who can estimate the result of her unselfishness, and her fifty-seven pennies?

—Christian Herald

* * *

"Go Easy!"

My six daughters sometimes gather around me, telling me how they need shoes, money for music lessons and for many other things. Sometimes I have been compelled to say, "Go easy! I am not made out of money. We will just have to get what we can afford and go without the rest." But I never read in God's Word where He ever told anybody, "Go easy! I don't have very much. I have already strained Myself giving to others. I cannot give as much as you ask." No, no! One of our greatest sins about praying is that we do not ask for enough. We do not take what God is willing to give. . . . . God forgive us our little, stingy, unbelieving prayers!

—John R. Rice, in
Prayer — Asking and Receiving

* * *

Poor Little Cent!

A big silver dollar and a little brown cent,
Rolling along together they went,
Rolling along the smooth sidewalk,
When the dollar remarked — for the dollar can talk;
"You poor little cent, you cheap little mite,
I'm bigger and more than two times as bright,
I'm worth more than you — a hundredfold,
And written on me, in letters so bold,
Is the motto drawn from the pious creed,
'In God we trust,' which all can read."

"Yes, I know" said the cent, "I'm a cheap little mite,
And I know I'm not big or good or bright,
And yet," said the cent, with a meek little sigh,
"You don't go to church half so often as I!"

—Selected

"Be Ye Not As the" — Cow

Giving not of necessity, if it can be called giving, reminds one of Father Applegate's cow. "How much milk does that cow give?" asked the summer boarder. "Wal," replied Father Applegate, "ef you mean by voluntary contribution, she don't give none. But ef ye kin get her cornered, so's she can't kick none to hurt, an able-bodied man kin take away about 'leven quarts a day from her."

—*Christian Herald*

* * *

Churches Doesn't Die Dat Way

A devout colored preacher, whose heart was aglow with missionary zeal gave notice to his congregation that in the evening an offering would be taken for missions, and asked for liberal gifts. A selfish, well-to-do-man in the congregation said to him before the service: "Yer gwine to kill this church ef yed goes on sayin' 'give!' No church can stan' it. Yer gwine ter kill it."

After the sermon the colored minister said to the people: "Brother Jones told me I was gwine to kill this church if I kep' a askin' yer to give; but, my brethren, churches doesn't die that way. Ef anybody knows of a church that died 'cause it's been givin' too much to de Lord, I'll be very much obliged ef my brother will tell me whar dat church is for I'se gwine to visit it, and I'll climb on the walls of dat church, under de light of de moon and cry, 'Blessed am de dead dat die in de Lord.' "

—*Florida Baptist Witness*

* * *

How Young Cyrus Hamlin Settled It

When Cyrus Hamlin was ten years old, his mother gave him seven cents to celebrate a great holiday. The money was for gingerbread, buns, etc. "Perhaps, Cyrus," said she, "you will put a cent or two into the missionary box at Mrs. Farrar's." As he trudged along he began to ask: "Shall I put in one cent or two? I wish she had not said one *or* two." He decided on two. Then conscience said: "What, five cents for your

stomach and two for the heathen! Five for gingerbread and two for souls!" So he said, "Four for gingerbread and three for souls." But presently he felt it must be three for gingerbread and four for souls. When he came to the box he dumped in the whole seven, to have no more bother about it. When he went home, hungry as a bear, he explained to his mother his unreasonable hunger. And, smiling through tears, she gave him an overflowing bowl of bread and milk. And he pathetically asks: "*What was the meaning of mother's tears?*"

—*Sunday School Times*

* * *

Her Responsibility

A poor man was once obliged to seek financial aid of a wealthy Christian woman. After hearing of the need, the lady made out a check for the amount, and, as she handed it to the man, told him that he need not return the money. Then she made a strong remark: "This is more than God ever gave me," she said. The man looked at her in surprise and said: "Mrs. D —, I am surprised to hear you say that. You have abundance, and God has given you all you have." She smiled and replied: "I speak the truth, for God has not *given* me but *lent* unto me what I have, that I may in his name, bestow it upon those who are in need."

—*King's Business*

* * *

With All Their Hearts

An old sailor emptied into the missionary's lap a stockingful of coins. "What does this mean? ' she exclaimed. "For you," he said, "for lassies that nobody loves." "But you are not able; I must not take it," the missionary said. Then he explained, "It were two years ago since they carried our lassie to the cemetery. We fixed a trim little mound many a time, but the wind is strong and the sand drifted over it, and we are all the time losin' the place where she be. So we says, we'll try to save a bit here an' there, till we get a stone for the head — a marble one, pure an' glistenin' white like yourself, with 'Lassie Nell' an' a verse from the Good Book on it . . . . . We had been to see the marble man. We just about had the thirty dollars; but when you told us about the lassies with nobody to love 'em, and that jest thirty dollars would take 'em away from lives o' shame an' sufferin', I went home an' told Wife, an' we talked it over. We knew 'twouldn't make any difference with Lassie Nell, bein' she was safe in the Good Shepherd's arms, an' you'll jest take it, seein' it's all in small bits, we'd be glad to thank Him this way." Speechless, the missionary turned to the old man's wife. Tears were rolling down her cheeks, but she smiled and said, "Aye, lady, an' it's worth all our hearts, too."

—*Junior B.Y.P.U. Quarterly*,
S. B. Convention

* * *

A List of Her Losses

A well-to-do lady who had become a Christian late in life was one time walking along the city street accompanied by her granddaughter. Presently a beggar accosted them. The old lady listened to his tale and then, putting her hand in her purse, took out a half-dollar and placed it in his palm. At the next corner a woman of the Salvation Army was waiting and the old lady dropped a dollar in her kettle. As she did so her granddaughter looked at her curiously and then said: "Grandma, I guess you have lost a good deal since you have become a Christian, haven't you?" "Yes," said the old lady, "I have. I have lost a hasty temper, a habit of criticizing others, a tendency to spend all my spare time in social frivolities and pleasures that mean nothing. I have also lost a spirit of avarice and selfishness. Yes, indeed, I have lost a good deal."

—*Christian Advocate*

* * *

Gain By Giving

Of a lake in Central Africa one writer says: "When this lake was first discovered there was no outlet, and the

water was brackish. When Cameron and Stanley visited the lake it was commencing to dribble into the Lukuga, and thence into the Congo. Shortly afterward it burst the barrier and flowed out in a full stream, which it has maintained ever since. Eighteen years ago, when I first lived on the shore, the water was still slightly mineral; today, however, it is pure and wholesome. Fish abound, and afford sustenance to many of the people, as well as to innumerable birds."

Many lives are suffering for want of an outlet. Beneficence to others reacts upon the quality and happiness of our own lives.

—*P. H. Advocate*

* * *

Give and Have no Loss

Never try to save out of God's cause; such money will canker the rest. Giving to God is no loss; it is putting your substance in the best bank. Giving is true having, as the old gravestone said of the dead man: "What I spent I had; what I saved I lost; what I gave I have."

—Charles H. Spurgeon

* * *

"The Beggar Died, and was Carried. . ."

At a large public meeting Dr. A. T. Pierson told how once when he was collecting for some object a wealthy man said to him: "If I had to preach your funeral sermon, I should take the text, 'The beggar died.' "

Dr. Pierson replied: "I should have no objection if you will go on with the text, '*and was carried by the angels into Abraham's bosom.*' "

—*Sunday School Times*

* * *

Another Unknown Widow

Charles Haddon Spurgeon tells us that a little old woman, ill clad, came into his study one day shortly after he had made a great plea for his work, and she said in a strange way as she laid a little package on the table: "Thus saith the Lord, behold, I have commanded a widow woman there to sustain thee." Before he had time to unwrap the package the woman was gone. He never knew her name, but she left her gift of fifty pounds!

—*Watchman-Examiner*

* * *

"Before They Call"

In the spring of 1875, Hudson Taylor, the beloved founder of the China Inland Mission, was returning to London from Bighton, where he had been attending some meetings. Waiting for his train at the station, he was accosted by a Russian nobleman who had also attended the meetings, and who, on learning that Mr. Taylor was going to London, suggested that they should find seats together.

"But I travel third class," said the missionary.

"My ticket admits of my doing the same," was the courteous reply.

They seem to have found a carriage alone together, for presently Count Bobrinsky took out his pocketbook, with the words, "Allow me to give you a trifle toward your work in China."

Glancing at the bank note as he received it, Mr. Taylor felt there must be some mistake — it was no less than fifty pounds.

"Did you mean to give me five pounds," he said at once. "Please let me return this note; it is for fifty pounds."

"I cannot take it' back," replied the other, no less surprised. "It was five pounds I meant to give, but God must have intended you to have fifty pounds; I cannot take it back."

Impressed with the incident, Mr. Taylor reached Pyrland Road, the London home of the Mission, to find a prayer meeting going on. A remittance was about to be sent to China, and the money in hand was short of forty-nine pounds, eleven shillings, of the sum it was felt would be required. This deficiency was not accepted as inevitable. On the contrary, it called together those who knew of it for special prayer. Forty-nine pounds, eleven shillings, was being

asked for in simple faith, and there upon the office table Mr. Taylor laid his precious bank note for fifty pounds. Could it have came more directly from the Heavenly Father's hand? "Whoso is wise, and will observe these things, even they shall understand the lovingkindness of the Lord."

—*The Elim Evangel*

* * *

He Approved the Mission's Product

Testimony from a businessman in Salisbury, Southern Rhodesia, is given in *Life and Work* of Edinburgh, with comment on the old criticism that businessmen would far rather have heathen than Christian servants and employees, as more honest and efficient. "Recently the Presbyterian missionary in Chasefu received this letter: 'Our native messenger boy is from your part of the country. He has asked me to forward to you the sum of —— as a contribution to his own home church. I do so with pleasure. I have, however, decided to make up his contribution to 5 pounds, for he is the best boy we ever had. If your mission can produce men of his stamp you deserve all the support you can get from people like me and firms like mine' "

—*Sunday School Times*

* * *

A Child's Understanding Gift

A large church needed a new building. They were all agreed about that, but whenever they began to plan to build, the members got into all sorts of disagreements about how and what to build. The minister was at his wit's end, and appointed a day of prayer, to which very few members came. But one devout woman went and took her little five-year-old girl, as she had no one with whom to leave her. As they prayed, the child began to understand that it was about building a new church. When they went home, she asked many questions about it, and then she was very quiet. The next morning her mother missed her, and in a frenzy went to find her. It was not hard to follow her little foot tracks to the minister's house, and there in the front yard was little Mary with her wheelbarrow, a toy one, and in it were two bricks. She was talking to the minister, and the tears were running down his cheeks. She had brought the two bricks to start the new church. He told the story in the morning service on the following Sunday. God touched hearts, and multiplied Mary's two bricks into a beautiful new church building.

—Sunday School Times

* * *

To Whom She Gave

A well-known preacher was making an appeal for funds before a large congregation, and invited them to bring their gifts and lay them on the altar. The aisle was filled with people who came bringing their offerings. A little lame girl came slowly toward the front. She pulled a little ring from her finger and laid it among the other gifts on the altar. Adjusting her crutch she started back up the aisle. An usher was sent to bring her into an anteroom following the service. The preacher met her there and said, "My dear, I saw the thing which you did tonight. It was beautiful, but, you know, the response of the people tonight has been large, and in figuring up we find that we have money enough to take care of all the things we want to do, and have some money left over, so we don't need your ring, and I have brought it back to you." The little girl looked up with rebuke in her eyes and said, "I didn't give that ring to you." Once again from the lips of a child came a great spiritual truth that mocks our unbiblical, unbusiness-like methods of church finance. In our efforts to get bills paid we forget that our gifts are offerings not to man but to God.

—Watchman-Crusader

* * *

Honoring God With Our Money

Mr. W. R. Spight, wholesale grocer of Decatur, Ala., passed away in 1936. Shortly after his departure the trustee-

ship of the Spight estate came into being. Representatives of the eight beneficiaries of the estate met recently, reviewed the activities of the trustees, and found that out of an original estate worth a million dollars, the beneficiaries have received $1,040,000 and there is still an approximate million's worth left in the estate. A friend who knew Mr. Spight said that he gave $500 to the Lord every Sunday of the year, while he lived. The Lord has said, "Them that honour me I will honour" (1 Sam. 2:30). To be worth a million, and give a million, and leave a million to be given away is a record. Only eternity will reveal the vast amount of good accomplished by the million given, and the million now being given! Money simply cannot be put to a higher use than that of honoring the Lord.

—Now

* * *

He Repays Many Times

The old German shoemaker had just sent his boy with a basket of garden stuff to a poor widow. He worked hard at his trade and cultivated his little garden patch, yet nothing was more common in his life than some such deed as this. "How can you afford to give so much away?" I asked him. "I give nothing away," he said. "I lend it to the Lord, and He repays me many times. I am ashamed that people think I am generous when I am paid so much. A long time ago, when I was very poor, I saw someone in want, and I wondered if I could give, but I could not see how. I did give, and the Lord helped me. I have had some work, my garden grows well, and never since have I stopped to think twice when I have heard of some needy one. No, if I gave away all, the Lord would not let me starve. It is like money in the bank, only this time the bank never breaks, and the interest comes back every day."

—Log of the Good Ship Grace

* * *

Handing on the Torch

The Mayo brothers are Christian stewards in all their work. They believe that money must go back into the service of that humanity which paid it to them. "We try," says Dr. William Mayo, "to take up the medical and surgical education of selected and promising men where the state leaves off. From 1894 onward we have never used more than half our incomes on ourselves and our families, latterly much less. The very roof of my house goes out of the possession of my family when I die. I wouldn't want my children deprived of the fun and benefit of wanting something and going out to fight for it."

—Westminster Teacher

* * *

The True Motive

It is said that when Andrew Fuller went into his native town to collect for the cause of missions, one of his old acquaintances said, "Well, Andrew, I'll give you five pounds, seeing it's you." To him replied the preacher, "No, I can't take anything for this cause, seeing it's I," and handed back the money. The man realized the reproof, but quickly said, "Andrew, you're right. Here are ten pounds, seeing it's for the Lord Jesus Christ."

—Biblical Illustrator

* * *

How Much Do You Give?

A missionary at home on furlough was invited to a dinner at a great summer resort where he met many women of prominence and position.

After dinner he went to his room and wrote a letter to his wife. He said:

"Dear Wife: I've had dinner at the hotel. The company was wonderful. I saw strange things today. Many women were present. There were some who, to my certain knowledge, wore one church, forty cottage organs, and twenty libraries."

In his great longing for money to provide the gospel for hungering millions, he could not refrain from estimating the silks, satins, and the diamonds of the guests at the dinner in terms of his people's need.

If God sends us money to send to perishing millions the good news of the Saviour from sin, and we spend it for needless luxuries, what does He think of it?

—Moody Monthly

* * *

Bankbook or Account Book?

A woman, working as a housekeeper, sent $300 to the mission in the Sudan. She had received this sum as a legacy. Later, after her death, relatives, who had regarded her as being overreligious, and had had very little to do with her, came to her funeral, and asked for her possessions. They went through her trunk looking for a book, evidently a bankbook, for she had been long employed at good wages. The little book they found was quite a different one, and told its own story. On the one side she had entered her wages, month after month, and on the opposite side, following the small amounts of her expenditures, were such entries as these: "For Bible woman in India, $50." "For native worker in China, $50." Turning over the pages to the date she had received her $300 legacy, they found opposite it, "Paid out for the Sudan, $300." She needed no executors; all had been administered right up to date. Some day we will wish we could produce such a book in the presence of Him to whom we must all account for our stewardship.

Evangelical Christian

* * *

"Nothin' for Nobody"

"The boy gave all his lunch to the Master," young Margaret concluded her review of the feeding of the five thousand, for the other members of the Primary class at Trinity Mission, Columbia, S. C., "and because He blessed it, there was enough for everybody." "And what do you think would have happened," the teacher asked, "if the boy had said, 'I can't share this; there is only enough for me'?" Margaret considered, and then said, "It would have squinched up and squinched up, and there wouldn't have been nothin' for nobody."

—Moody Monthly

Only a Boy's Marbles

You can't guess how much good the Lord may do with even your dime or nickel in these days, especially if that dime or nickel you give Him to use for others is something you really take from yourself. One time a poor little boy saw all the big people putting money into the offering plate. He didn't have anything to give but five marbles in his pocket. He put them into the plate! People around must have smiled as they saw the strange offering drop in. After the meeting, one of the deacons asked the child if he wanted his marbles back. "Oh, no, I gave them to the Lord Jesus." As the story was told from one to another, a rich man said, "I'll give a hundred dollars for that boy's marbles." That was another kind of miracle change, from 5 cents to $100. You may never know just how much your little gift is worth in God's eyes, but be sure if you really give with love to help, the Lord will use it and it will look big in Heaven.

—Ruth E. Dow, in
Sunday School Times

* * *

Placing Money in Christ's Hand

A pastor was taking a missionary collection recently when he said, "I want each of you to give today as though you were putting your money right into the pierced hand of Jesus Christ." A lady came up afterward, and said, "I was going to give a half-dollar, but I did not do so." "Why did you not do it?" the preacher asked. Do you think I would put a half-dollar into his pierced hand? I have ten dollars at home, and I am going to give that." If we were putting our money into the pierced hand of our Lord our contributions would amount to millions, and the world would be evangelized in ten years. — *Religious Herald.*

* * *

Giving and Receiving

So long as we live we must give. And that is one of the joys of living. Perhaps some of us have wished that the time might come when we need not "give" any more. Then we need to read this true little message in verse:

" 'For giving is living,' the angel said,
'Go feed to the hungry sweet charity's bread.'
'And must I keep giving again and again?'
My selfish and querulous answer ran.
'Oh, no!' said the angel, piercing me through,
'Just give 'till the Master stops giving to you.' " — *Sunday School Times.*

* * *

Losing Their Home for His Sake

Dr. Truett of Texas was invited to a church that was raising $6,500 to dedicate a church building. After $3,500 had been promised, the offerings ceased. Then a plainly dressed woman arose and spoke to her husband who was taking the names. "Charley, I wonder if you would be willing to give our little cottage, just out of debt. We were offered $3,500 for it yesterday. Would you be willing to give our little house for Christ that his house may be free?" The fine fellow responded in the same high spirit: "Jennie, dear, I was thinking of the same thing. Then looking up at me with his face covered with tears, he said, "We will give the $3,500." Then there followed a scene beggaring all description. Men and women sobbed aloud, and almost in a moment the $3,500 was provided. Then without invitation there came down the aisle men and women, saying, "Sir, where is the Saviour, and how can we find him?"

—From *Every-Member Evangelism* by J. E. Conant.

* * *

At Least Worth a Nickel

A man was once complaining of a missionary address which a poor, tired, furloughed missionary was trying to make to a comfortable, well-dressed congregation, after spending seven years in a foreign jungle district among illiterate people for whom he tried to make the story of the good news of Christ's love so plain and simple that even their childish minds might understand. The church officer, who was in a position to know how much the com-

plainer contributed to the great cause of making Christ known in all the world, listened long enough to get the gist of the remarks, then said, "Well, how much do you expect for a nickel?"
—*Sunday School Times*

* * *

Where Money Is Not Mentioned

Did you ever see a tombstone with a dollar sign on it? Neither did I. I have known hundreds of men who lived as though their only ambition was to accumulate, but I have never known one who wanted a final judgment of himself to be based on what he got. A man wants people to read in his obituary, not a balance sheet of his wealth, but a story of his service to humanity.
— *Homilope (Church envelope)*

* * *

Is This Our Spirit in Giving?

The Rev. J. M. Baker, a missionary of South India, writes this pathetic incident: An old man, thirty-five miles north of Ongole, had a great desire to give something to Jesus. The only thing he had to give was a magnificent pumpkin he had grown with great care and had protected a long time from thieves. But how was he to get it to the Lord? The hamlet had no Christian teacher to tell him, and the touring evangelist of that section was not liable to visit his village for some time. His conclusions were: "I will take it to the missionary. He will know what to do." In India this vegetable is worth about four cents. The old man walked seventy miles, and one-half of the distance carried on his head a weight of about thirty pounds and the food for his journey, that he might present to the Lord an acceptable gift of four cents.
—*Christian Endeavor World*

* * *

"Pigtail Christians."

Mr. Fred Paton reporting mission work in the New Hebrides tells how the Christians of Matmissa were getting slack in giving and needed exhortation. Mr. Weir therefore preached on the Christian's financial obligation. In his address he referred to a heathen custom of Epi, where, at their sacrifice of pigs, the sacred men cut off the pig's tail and presented it to the spirits as their share of the feast, — the rest being kept for themselves. Mr. Weir specially emphasized the fact that God does not want *"pigtail Christians."* The striking epithet caught the native imagination and has passed as current coin into their everyday speech.
—*Record of Christian Work*

* * *

Her "Lord's Treasury"

Years ago Dr. Henry Jessup, a faithful missionary in Syria, was calling on Mr. John H. Converse of Philadelphia, seeking help for the Syrian Protestant College in Beirut. After giving him a generous check, Mr. Converse handed him the name and address of a friend, asking Dr. Jessup to call on her, saying he believed that she would help him financially. Dr. Jessup was astounded to locate her residence on the top floor of a tenement house. Entering the door he found an elderly lady putting bristles in the wood backs of scrubbing brushes. Eagerly she listened to his story. Taking one of two bags from a nail on the wall, she said: "This is the Lord's treasury. I am able to lay by something for Him, after I have met my needs. Whatever is in His bag today is for you." She counted out thirty-seven cents into his hands, as the tears rolled down his face, saying she was so glad to be able to give it, and that she was certain the Lord would bless its use. They knelt in prayer together. Then Dr. Jessup took those thirty-seven cents up and down this land and told their story. They brought thousands of dollars for his Syrian college. She loved much. She drew the line between her wants and her needs with eager joy.
— *Gospel Herald.*

* * *

"I'll Hide Under the Bench!"

When the time for the offering came in one church, a little girl noticed a rather buxom lady fingering over the conglomerate treasures of her handbag in search of a small coin. Failing in this, the woman closed her purse, and folded her hands, intending to appear in an attitude of worship while the plate passed in front of her. The little girl, who had brought her envelope from home, realized the seriousness of the situation — that someone should be at church without an offering. So the little tyke pushed her envelope into the woman's hands with the word, "You put this in and I'll hide under the bench!"

— Warren Filkin.

* * *

Why He Gave So Much

An Indian chief, who had been converted from heathenism, was exceedingly fervent in his prayers and praises during worship, and extremely generous in his kindness and gifts to the missionary and his work. The missionary at length asked the Indian why he was so jubilant in his devotions, and so lavish in his gifts. The convert made this pathetic reply: "Ah! you have never been in the darkness."

—*Sunday School Chronicle*

* * *

Hilarious Giving

A pastor instructed the ushers, on passing plates, to emit a good-sized whistle when a dollar bill or any larger amount was placed thereon. Soon the church resounded with shrill sounds of rejoicing and laughter. The ushers found it difficult to pucker up their lips and grin at the same time, but the collection was about three times as large as usual. I do not suppose the pastor ever tried that plan again. Probably he merely used it as a sample of the "hilarious giving" (for that is the literal rendering of "cheerful giving") enjoined by Paul. At any rate, he woke up his congregation to the gaiety of giving.

—*Christian Herald*

* * *

A Dangerous "Apology"

A gentleman called on a well-to-do merchant for a contribution to a char-

itable object. "Yes, I must give you my mite," said the man. "Do you mean the widow's mite?" asked his friend. "Certainly," answered the merchant. "I shall be satisfied with half as much as she gave," said the solicitor. "Now how much may you be worth?" "Oh," said the merchant, "about seventy thousand dollars." "Then," said the friend, "give me your check for thirty-five thousand dollars; that will be half as much as the widow gave, for she gave, you remember, 'all that she had, even all her living.'" The man was not the first person who has tried to shelter himself behind the widow's mite. But it is a dangerous refuge.

—*Church Business*

* * *

Giving That Which Costs

After a missionary meeting in Brighton, England, a poor widow of the parish presented herself before the pastor and gave him a sovereign. He knew the poor woman's great poverty, and accordingly refused to accept the coin, remarking at the same time that it was too much for her to give. The widow now seemed greatly agitated, and with the irresistible eloquence of an overflowing heart, she begged him to accept it.

"Oh, sir," added she, "I have often given pieces of copper to the Lord. Two or three times I have had the joy to give Him pieces of silver; but it was the grand desire of my life to give Him a piece of gold before I die. For a long time I have been putting by all that I was able to make this sum. Take it, I pray you, for the missionary cause." The minister did not refuse further. He added to the collection this precious offering of a loving heart.

—*Gospel Herald*

* * *

Well Said

A clergyman wrote a wealthy and influential business man requesting a subscription to a worthy charity. He promptly received a curt refusal which ended by saying, "As far as I can see, this Christian business is just one continuous give, give, give."

After a brief interval the clergyman answered, "I wish to thank you for the best definition of the Christian life that I have yet heard."

— *New Century Leader*

* * *

"It's Money, Money, Money!"

The Bishop of Nelson (New Zealand) once told of a conversation between two men. The one was appointed to ask the other for a pledge to their church. The reply was that the church was always wanting money. Said he, "It's money, money, money." The other friend said, "When my lad was a boy, he was costly; he always wanted boots and shoes, stockings and clothes, and wore them out fast, and the older he grew the more money had to be spent on him. But he hasn't cost me a penny now for more than a year." "How's that?" inquired his friend. "He died."

"Yes," said the Bishop, "a live church will always need money." — In *Store House Tithing*, by Rev. Paul Sell.

* * *

Prayers and Alms-Deeds

The venerable Father Sewall of Maine once entered a meeting in behalf of foreign missions just after the offering had been taken. The chairman of the meeting requested him to lead in prayer. The old gentleman stood hesitatingly, as if he had not heard the request. The request was repeated and Mr. Sewall was seen fumbling in his pockets. Presently he produced a piece of money, which he deposited on the plate. The chairman, thinking he had misunderstood, said "I didn't ask you to give, Father Sewall, I asked you to pray." "Oh, yes," he replied, "I heard you, but *I can't pray until I have given something*."

A strict observance of this rule would place us in a class with the deacon who, being unable to attend the prayer meeting appointed in behalf of a brother who was sick, sent his son with a load of potatoes, meat, and flour, with the statement that he was sending his prayers.

Many professing Christians would make better headway in praying if their purse strings were less tightly drawn.

—*Arnold's Practical Commentary*

* * *

Cheaper Than the Matinee

I once attended a convention in Atlanta, Ga., and heard a speaker tell this true story in illustration of her address on stewardship. A woman in the congregation to which the speaker belonged took her two small children one Saturday afternoon to a matinee to see Maude Adams in Peter Pan. The tickets were priced at $2.50 each. The children saw their mother open her purse, take out seven one dollar bills, pile them on the shelf, put a 50 cent piece on the pile of bills, push all under the window, take the three little pieces of cardboard and lead them into the theater to their seats. The next day she took her little daughter to church with her. When the offering was taken, the child saw her mother open her purse, take out a quarter, and put it on the plate as it passed them. As the organ played the soft, religious music, the little daughter looked up into her mother's face, and said in a clear stage whisper which everyone around them could hear, "Mother! Church comes a heap cheaper than matinees, doesn't it?"

—*Sunday School Times*

* * *

"Not A Mite Would I Withhold!"

Frances Havergal wrote her famous hymn, "Take My Life" in 1874. It was not until 1878 that the lines were put into print. When she read the second stanza:

"Take my silver and my gold,
Not a mite would I withhold,"

she was suddenly convicted of her failure to do just that. She had an amazing collection of exquisite jewelry, most of which came by gift or inheritance. Immediately, she packed the jewels, and sent them to her church missionary society. Then, just to be sure, she included a check to cover the monetary value of the jewels she had chosen to keep! "I don't think I need to tell you I have never packed a box with such pleasure!" she exclaimed.

—Christian Index

* * *

Money Needed

A rummage sale and an oyster stew—
(The pastor's salary is overdue!)
A hard time's party next on the card—
(Have to fix up the old church yard!)
A display of dolls, both cute and quaint—
(The parsonage needs a coat of paint!)
A bridge party, next thing on the docket—
(*Again*, the pastor has an empty pocket!)
A basket social with bidder and buyer—
(New hymnals needed for the choir!)
A style parade with the public invited—
(The church's missionary must not be slighted!)
Some Mickey Mouse films for awhile—
(New carpets needed for each aisle!)
An opera singer last on the slate—
(The church's pipe organ is out of date!)
Christ described His House as a House of prayer,
And drove them out that made merchandise there!
I feel quite sure that Apostle Paul
Would never approve of such methods at all!
The need for all this would fade away
IF the people of God would tithe and pray!

—Roy Judson Wilkins

* * *

Parsimony Begets Poverty

We are taught that getting is in order to giving, and consequently that giving is the real road to getting. God is an economist. He entrusts larger gifts to those who use the smaller well. Perhaps one reason of our poverty is that we are so far slaves of parsimony. The future may reveal that God has been withholding from us because we have been withholding from Him.

—Arthur T. Pierson

God's Way of Raising Men

A well-known writer on Christian stewardship says: "Giving is not just a way of raising money. It is God's way of raising men."

—Christian Herald

* * *

Different Kinds of Givers

Some witty person once said: "There are three kinds of givers — the flint, the sponge, and the honey-comb."
To get anything out of the flint you must hammer it, and then you can get only chips and sparks.
To get water out of a sponge you must squeeze it, and the more you squeeze the more you will get.
But the honeycomb just overflows with its own sweetness.

—Florida Baptist Witness

* * *

Where He Got the Money

A church in Texas owed $260. The note was due, and there wasn't a dollar in the treasury to pay on it. No one in the church seemed to be disturbed about it except one deacon. He talked to the pastor about his anxiety concerning the debt, then went away and soon returned and put $260 into the pastor's hands. The pastor wondered where he got the money. Finally he learned that this deacon, a poor man with a large family, had mortgaged his growing cotton crop and borrowed the money. He had a proper sense of his stewardship. Out of this home have come three preachers and one foreign missionary.

—Teacher, S.B.C.

* * *

Would You Give More?

The story is told of a visitor in a large, wealthy New York City Church. When the time came to take the offering, he reached into his wallet and selected a five dollar bill, and waited for the usher. He observed that the man taking the offering in his aisle was none other than a certain multimillionaire of national reputation. Wishing to make a good impression, he exchanged the five-dollar bill for a one hundred dollar bill, and placed it on the plate. If, instead of the deacon in your church, the one who passed up and down the aisles receiving the offering was the Lord Jesus Christ Himself, and the hand that passed the offering basket to you was scarred with a nailprint, would it make any difference in the size of the offering you contributed?

—King's Business

* * *

Giving Is Living

The health of a human body depends upon the exhalations as well as upon its inhalations. It is reported that a boy who was to personate a shining cherub in a play, on being covered over with a coating of gold leaf, which entirely closed the pores of his skin, died in consequence, before relief could be afforded. Woe to the Christian who gets so gold-leafed over with his wealth that the pores of his benevolence are restrained. He is henceforth dead spiritually, though he may have a name to live.

"That man may breathe,
    but never live,
Who much receives,
    but nothing gives;
Whom none can love,
    whom none can thank,
Creation's blot,
    creation's blank!"

—A. J. Gordon,
in God's Tenth

* * *

Scorn for His Sake

A missionary tells of a poor girl in Ceylon who had received a little patrimony as her marriage portion, because without her dowry she could not hope to be wedded. But when the Lord saved her soul, and the little native church wanted to build a chapel, she brought her entire fortune and handed it over to purchase the site for the chapel, and so she not only gave her all, but all the prospects of her future marriage and home, and went back to her life of lonely toil and the scorn of her people because of her love for Him who had given His life and all His earthly honors and comforts for her salvation.

—Alliance Weekly

* * *

How to Save

The story is told of a man who contributed the money to build a church. Later on he lost all his property. "If you had the money you put into that church," some one said to him, "you could start again." But the good man wisely replied: *That is the only money I have saved. If I had not given it to the Lord it would have gone with the rest. Now it will always be mine."*

——Moody Monthly

* * *

Three Books to Bring

A negro preacher walked into the office of a newspaper in Rocky Mount, N. C., and said: "Mista Edito, they is forty-seven of my congregation which subscribe fo' your paper. Do that entitle me to have a chu'ch notice in yo Sadday issue?"

"Sit down and write," said the editor.

"I thank you."

And this is the notice the minister wrote:

"Mount Moriah Baptist Church, the Rev. John Obadiah, pastor. Preaching morning and evening. In the promulgation of the Gospel three books is necessary: The Bible, the hymn book, and the pocket book. Come tomorrow and bring all three."

Other pastors than Pastor Obadiah and other churches than Mount Moriah may well send out word to everybody to bring these three books to church.

—S. S. Friend

GOSPEL FOR EVERY ONE

Cleaning Up Corruption

A young pastor went to a church in a city of 25,000. Soon some of his church leaders told him they thought he should attack the city administration, for the mayor, department chiefs, and members of the council were so corrupt the city had become notorious. Asking for time, he prayed about it, decided on his course of action, and secured a ten-minute appointment with the mayor. When he kept the appointment, after some general remarks, he said to the mayor: "I want to congratulate you on the honor and responsibility that were laid on you when you were chosen mayor of this city. But I want to tell you that there is a greater honor waiting for you, something far bigger than the office of mayor of a city like this." Thinking this stranger might represent some high-up politician, the mayor listened with evident interest. "You ought to be a servant of Jesus Christ," said the young minister. In astonishment the mayor said, "No one ever spoke to me like this before." The time being up, the minister left, but the next day the agitated voice of the mayor said to him over the telephone, "Won't you come and talk with me? I have thought of what you said ever since you left. I must see you." Two weeks later, not only did the mayor come into that pastor's church, but the chief of police, the fire department chief, and five aldermen also yielded themselves to Christ. That city was cleaned up.

—From *The Growing Menace of the Social Gospel*, by J. E. Conant

* * *

Souls, or Tigers?

A story is told of two men who got into conversation on a boat when returning from India. One was an English sport and the other was a missionary. Said the sport to the missionary, "I've been in India for twenty-five years, and I never saw one of the natives converted." "That's queer," said the mis-sionary, "did you ever see a tiger?" "Hundreds of them," was the reply, "and I have shot dozens in the hunt." "Well, I have been in India for many years," said the missionary, "but I have never seen a tiger. But under the power of the Gospel of Christ, I have seen hundreds of the natives of India turn to the Saviour!" You see, one was looking for *tigers*, and the other was looking for *souls*! For what are *you* looking? The Bible says, "And they that be wise shall shine as the brightness of the firmament; and they that turn many to righteousness as the stars for ever and ever." (Dan. 12:3).

—*The Chaplain*

* * *

What Was Needed First

When the first Moravian missionaries went to Greenland to preach the Gospel of Jesus Christ, they thought it was necessary, first of all, to instruct the people in the doctrines of natural religion. The result was that they were there seventeen years before they had a single convert. But one day a man called Kajarnak, who was a very wicked man, entered the missionary's hut and by accident heard him read the story of the last week in the life of Christ. Somehow this wicked Greenlander got a glimpse of the fact that Jesus suffered and died for sinners and that through Him a sinner might be saved. "How was that?" he said. "Tell me that again, for I, too, wish to be saved." The missionary was astonished. It was not long before Kajarnak, his wife, and two children were happily converted to Christ and became the firstfruits of Greenland unto the Saviour. It also taught the missionaries that the first thing to preach to a sinning man anywhere is the atoning sacrifice of Christ.

—*The Teacher*

* * *

Not a "New Religion"

When George Whitefield was shaking England with the thunders of his revival preaching, a certain baronet said to a friend: "This man Whitefield is truly a great man. Surely he will be the founder of a new religion." "A new religion!" exclaimed the friend. "Yes," said the baronet, "if it is not a new religion, what do you call it?" "I say of it that it is nothing but the old religion revived and heated with divine energy in a man who really means what he says." The old-fashioned Gospel produces old-fashioned conversions when it is preached under the power of the divine Spirit.

—*Pentecostal Herald*

* * *

"There Is No Difference"

Remember, the man on Skid Row is not different in kind from the rest of us. He is merely *worse in degree*. On Skid Row we see fallen man at his dismal worst. In the better neighborhoods we see him at his polished best, but he is the same man for all his disguise. In the gutter we find him chained by dope and drink and dirt. On the Avenue we find him bound by pride and greed and lust. To God there is no difference. He sees beyond appearances and he knows what is in every man. His remedy for every man is the same, a new birth and the impartation of a new kind of life.

The Gospel is the power of God operating toward the moral and spiritual transformation of man. And it works! Thousands will testify that it does. No man who wants to climb up out of his past and find a new and better life should overlook the Gospel. It is God's way out, and there is no other.

—*Pacific Garden Mission News*

* * *

On the Level

"The rich and poor meet together: the Lord is the maker of them all" (Prov. 22:2). This truth was strikingly illustrated at a reception of members in Calvary Baptist Church, Washington, D.C., some years ago. Dr. Greene, the pastor, received into the church on the same morning the Hon. Charles Evans Hughes

a Chinese, and a washerwoman. As he saw the unusual group standing before him, he paused and said, "*My friends, I will have you to notice that at the Cross of Christ the ground is level.*"

—*Moody Monthly*

* * *

All Are Needed

At the Prince of Wales College for African youth at Achimota, Gold Coast, Africa, Alexander Fraser, a Briton, was principal, and Kwegyir Aggrey, an African, was vice-principal. "God knew what he was doing when he made me black," said Dr. Aggrey one day to the writer, flashing into his happy laugh. "He didn't want me to be white or gray, but just black" (which Dr. Aggrey certainly was). "If you are playing the piano you can't play a good tune with the white notes alone; you must have the black ones too. And God wants to play his tunes with his black notes and his white notes together."

—*Black Treasure*

* * *

"Somos Hermanos"

High up in the wild mountain region of Peru, a missionary and a native Indian pastor came unexpectedly upon a group of crude Indian huts. No one was at home, for it was the season when the Indians were away gathering coffee. The missionary looked in one of these huts and was surprised to see a Bible and a song book stuck in one of the rafters. Just then some of the Indians returned, and they were none too pleased to see strangers prowling around their premises. But the Indian pastor knew that the presence of the Bible meant that these Indians had come in touch with a Protestant mission. "They are brothers," he said to the missionary. "That means they know the Gospel." So he called out to the approaching Indians, "We are brothers, your brothers!" Instantly, the attitude of the Indians changed. They knew what that phrase meant. The strangers were invited in, and about fifty Indians gathered around while they sang songs together and prayed and had the pastor tell some Bible stories.

This little incident illustrates admirably what Christianity is trying to accomplish — making brothers of all men. If you go into the wilds of Peru, remember the phrase, "Somos hermanos" — we are brothers. In many places it will work like a charm.

—*Pittsburgh Christian Advocate*

* * *

Fundamentally Settled

In days like these, when chaos appears to be king, and civilization itself sometimes seems verging on collapse, it is something mightily to be desired to have an anchor for the soul — something permanent, abiding, sure, and steadfast, to be tied to.

A man with such an anchor, now a United States Navy officer, recently wrote a letter to his pastor: "Your letter brought back much that has been connected with our church. For almost thirteen years I have been a member; sometimes in better standing than at others. Many times my attendance has not been as faithful as it might have been. But over those years, despite the fluctuating fervor which I applied to it, I can see that the church has been a real rock, a real reference point for me.

"It's just as in navigation — at the beginning of every voyage, you establish your bearing and distance from some fixed mark, and that is your point of departure. We have something in our faith that can fundamentally settle a man, that beneath his surface tides runs like a deep, strong current, never varying in its direction, always surging ahead."

The young lieutenant is absolutely right, of course. *There is nothing in all the world, save the eternal gospel of Christ, that can "fundamentally settle a man."*

—*Home Evangel*

* * *

What a Difference the Gospel Made!

Dr. George Green, home on leave from the mission field, told this experience:

"When I first went out to my mission field in Africa, the boat carried me up a wide, beautiful river flowing through the jungle, and as the sun set and the night came on, I listened with much misgiving to the roll of the war drums. They continued far into the night. The captain of the boat was uneasy and tried to dissuade me from going ashore the next morning, and I admit I was trembling with fear. But I found that "the Lord standeth within the shadows keeping watch above His own." After years of delightful labor I left the jungle on the same boat. As it came down the river, thousands of these same natives gathered on the shores near their villages to say farewell. As the boat came into sight, they broke into song, but not a war song. They were singing the hymn that is a favorite to most of them, 'All Hail the Power of Jesus' Name.' "

—C. Roy Angell, in *the Teacher*

* * *

Who Was Impressed?

In the churchyard of an English cathedral is an inscription carved on a gravestone of a woman who lived in the eighteenth century. After giving the date of her birth and death, there are these words, "She was a cousin of the Duke of Bedford." Think of putting that on a tombstone! Do you suppose God was impressed? Can you imagine that on the arrival of that woman at the pearly gates of Heaven, an angel went before her crying out, "Make way for the cousin of the Duke of Bedford"? We smile and yet we ought to think on the many things on which people pride themselves which make no difference in God's judgment of a life. With God it is not titles or money, or fame, or race, nor even correct opinions about Him which count. A "Who's Who in America" made by God would be very different from the one man makes.

—*New Century Leader*

* * *

The Prince and the Outcasts

When the Prince of Wales visited India there were a number of high caste people who were waiting to shake hands with him, and there was a big barrier separating them from the masses of the people. The Prince arrived, shook hands with those that were presented to him, and then, looking over their heads to the crowds beyond, said, "Take those barriers down." They were taken down, and anyone who liked had free access, and a welcome from the son of the Emperor of India. The next time the Prince came that way, ten thousand outcasts were gathered under the banner inscribed "The Prince of the Outcasts." We have a greater Prince, who said, "Take the barriers away." God's love and favor are for every one who believes in the Lord Jesus.

—*Christian Herald*

* * *

"The Lord Looketh on the Heart"

A weary teacher fell asleep and had a dream. A message had arrived that the Master was coming, and to her was appointed the task of getting all the little children ready for him. So she arranged them on benches in tiers, putting the little white children first, nearest to where the Master would stand, then the little yellow, red, and brown children, and far back the black children. When all were arranged, she looked, and it did not seem quite right to her. Why should the black children be so far away? They ought perhaps to be on the front benches. She started to re-arrange them, but just as all was in confusion, footsteps were heard; it was the Master's tread. He was coming before the children were ready. To think that the task entrusted to her had not been accomplished in time! The footsteps drew near, and she was obliged to look up. Lo, as her eyes rested on the children all shades of color and difference had vanished: the little children in the Master's presence were all alike.

Man makes the mistake of looking upon the outward appearance, forgetting that God looketh on the heart.

— *Christian Herald*

Sold for a Roll of Tobacco

Many years ago a company of slaves were sold by auction in a Nigerian market place, and a poor little boy was placed on the auction block. He had such a miserable appearance that the slave buyers laughed at the suggestion to bid for him, and he was bought for a roll of tobacco. He walked to the coast with a gang of slaves and was put in the hold of a ship bound for America. But the ship was captured by the British, who took the slaves to Freetown and set them at liberty. The little boy was put in the charge of missionaries. Many years later in St. Paul's Cathedral, London, in the presence of church dignitaries and statesmen and nobles there was consecrated the first bishop of Nigeria. It was the little boy who was sold for a roll of tobacco, Bishop Samuel Crowther, who did a wonderful work for God in Nigeria, where his name is still revered as a true hero of the Lord Jesus.

—J. S. Hall, in *the Sudan Witness*

* * *

"It's No Use!"

John Richard Green, fired with the social gospel, whose emphasis is reformation, rather than regeneration, left Oxford's halls, and went down into London's squalid, sin-sodden slums. There he laboured earnestly and unstintingly for a decade. Despairingly, he said, "It's no use. These men will go on drinking and gambling until doomsday!" Defeatedly, he went back to Oxford to write his history of England. Down into these selfsame squalid, sin-sodden slums went William and Catherine Booth. With hearts aglow with the love of God for sinful souls, and with only one Gospel of the grace of God, they lived and preached Christ. "The power of God unto salvation unto every one that believeth!" They won! The story of their labour of love became engraved on the hearts of twice-born men and women, gloriously delivered from sin's ruin and wreckage, "New creation in Christ Jesus."

—W. B. K.

The Gospel's Power

When the Scotsman, Geddie, went to the New Hebrides, the islanders were ignorant, cruel cannibals devoted to war. Later they set this beautiful inscription over Geddie's grave on Aneityum: "When he came to the island in 1848, there was not a single Christian; when he left in 1872, there was not a single heathen."

—Herald of His Coming

* * *

The Same Gospel for the Same Needs

Some months after our arrival in China, an old experienced missionary came to my husband with the following advice: "Do not attempt to speak of Jesus the first time on preaching to a heathen audience. The Chinese have a prejudice against the name of Jesus. Confine your efforts to demolishing the false gods, and if you have a second opportunity you may bring in Jesus." Later, when telling me of the advice that had been given him, my husband exclaimed with hot emphasis, "NEVER, never, NEVER: The Gospel which saved the down-and-outs in the slums of Toronto is the same Gospel that must save Chinese sinners." Years later more than one missionary came to my husband asking, "What is the secret of your power to get men out of such depths of sin?" The reply was, "I simply believe and teach God's Word." Some have replied, "But you cannot preach to a proud Confucian scholar the same as to the common crowd." Then Dr. Goforth would answer: "There is no royal road to God. Rich or poor, Chinese or Canadians, educated or ignorant, all are sinners and must needs come to the same Saviour by the same road."

—Mrs. Goforth Tells How a New Book Was Written

* * *

"Have Seen Gospel!"

A traveler in China asked a native if he had ever read the Gospel. "No," was the answer, "but I have seen it. I have seen a man who was the terror of

his neighborhood with his curses and his violent temper. He was an opium smoker, a criminal, and as dangerous as a wild beast. But the doctrine of Jesus made him gentle and good, and he has left off opium. No, I have not read the Gospel, but I have seen it, and it is good."

—Alliance Weekly

* * *

"Nothing But the Gospel!"

Dr. Baldwin, who was pastor of a church for forty-one years, says, "With another, I testify that at thirty, after examining as best I could the philosophies and religions of the world, I said, 'Nothing is better than the Gospel of Christ.' At forty, when burdens began to press heavily, and years seemed to hasten, I said, 'Nothing is as good as the Gospel.' At fifty, when there were empty chairs in the home, and the mound builders had done me service, I said, 'There is nothing to be compared with the Gospel.' At sixty, when my second sight saw through the delusions and vanities of earthly things, I said, 'There is nothing but the Gospel.' At seventy, amid many limitations and deprivations, I sing:

" 'Should all the forms that men devise
Attack my faith with treacherous art,
I'd call them vanities and lies,
And bind the Gospel to my heart.' "

—Gospel Herald

* * *

A Discouraging "Gospel."

Never can I forget walking along, one night, with a poor consumptive, as we went to hear a lecture on "Consumption — Its Cause and Cure," by a famous expert. The man's heart must have leaped for joy as he told me of the hope he had of leaving his hut and drugs. We listened to the lecture — a fine one; and the lecturer concluded by stating that if we got pure milk, cleanliness, no smoke or dust, and so on, in a hundred years' time we might stamp out the dread disease. The poor consumptive's head drooped when he heard "in a hundred years' time." What was that to him? He wanted an immediate cure. I walked home with him. He was in despair, and shortly afterward he died. Experts are telling us what culture, education, and so on, will do in time to come; but broken men and women want a cure now. We have it! It is the salvation of our Lord and Saviour Jesus Christ. "Now is the day of salvation."

—*London Christian Herald*

* * *

The Unfailing Remedy

A prime minister of England once said: "If I am asked what is the remedy for the deeper sorrows of the human heart, what a man should chiefly look to in progress through life as the power that is to sustain him under trials and enable him manfully to confront his afflictions, I must point to something which in a well-known hymn is called, 'The old, old story,' told in an old, old Book, and taught with an old, old teaching, which is the greatest and best gift ever given to mankind."

—*Sunday School Times*

* * *

Only Broken Natures Know Victory

I remember a flash of righteous indignation that swept over Dr. Scofield's face once as he said, "People say that the bird with the broken pinion never soars as high again.' As if we did not all have a broken wing! For most of us both wings are broken and both legs, and our necks!" So let us just give up this notion that it is the "broken pinion" that is going to keep us from soaring as high as some victorious life Christians can soar. One thing is certain: the bird without a broken pinion is never going to know victory. One qualification you must have for the victorious life is the broken pinion, the broken nature, uttermost weakness. God makes no offer of victory to strong people, people who have not failed, and failed utterly. But for sinners He has a Gospel.

—From *The Victorious Life*, by Charles G. Trumbull

"It Kicks Me"

A missionary in India tells of a Brahman priest who listened to the preaching of the Gospel. He was given a Telugu Testament on condition that he would read it. He did so — then, meeting the missionary, he said in Telugu: "I wish you to take the Book back. As I read it, it kicks me, and makes me feel very unhappy."

—*King's Business*

* * *

An Eye Single

The Apostle Paul was perhaps one of the greatest travelers of his day. He visited many lands, and saw many new scenes in different countries. When he returned he wrote a good deal; his Epistles were widely read by the early churches. And yet, in all the writings of the apostle, there is not one line that is descriptive of the scenery of the countries through which he passed; not a line telling of the wonders of the architecture of his day; not a line describing the customs of the people. Is not this singular? There is a reason for it. The apostle was "blind." As he traveled about he was blind to all else but one thing. On the way to Damascus, when he met the Lord Jesus, He was blinded by the vision of His great glory, and from that time he could see nothing but Him and tell of nothing but His Gospel.

—Rev. R. A. Jaffray, in
The Sunday School Times

* * *

"Our Father"

It is related of the late Mr. Spurgeon that on one occasion he found a boy on the streets, ragged and hungry. Taking him along with him home, the good pastor fed and clothed him, and then, kneeling down, prayed for the friendless boy as only he could pray. Several times in the prayer he referred to the Almighty as "Our Father." When the prayer was finished the boy said, "Did you say 'Our Father'?" "Yes, my boy, your's and mine." "Yes," was the reply, "then we are brothers." "Yes," gravely replied the pastor, and then he talked to him of the Lord Jesus Christ, and finally, on taking leave of him, gave him a letter to a certain boot dealer for a pair of boots. A few days after, Mr. Spurgeon was passing the boot shop, when the dealer saw him and called to him. "I had a strange thing the other day," he said. "A boy came into the shop and asked for a pair of boots, saying that his brother had sent him, and when I asked him who his brother was he said you were." "That is right," said Mr. Spurgeon, "and he is your brother, too, and if you like we will share the cost of the boots."

—*Gospel Herald*

* * *

Both Tramps and Kings Need Him

Not long ago, Prebendary Wilson Carlile died in London at ninety-years of age. Dr. Carlile founded the Church Army, an organization inside the Church of England, working in the slums and with the poor. While at lunch with him several years ago, Dr. Carlile told us one unforgettable thing. Many years before, when King Edward was in his last illness, Dr. Carlile was invited to call on him at Buckingham Palace. Just before that, the king had decorated him for his work with the poor and the outcast. When he entered the bedchamber, and as he approached the king, His Majesty called out faintly, "Well, Carlile, how are your tramps?" Before he had time to reply, the king went on, "Never forget, Carlile, that tramps and kings need the same Saviour!'" Prebendary Carlile did not forget, and he spent his years seeking men in places high and low, telling them of the Christ who died to save them.

—*Moody Monthly*

GRACE

The Open Door

One warm summer afternoon, a bird flew through the open door into a chapel where divine service was being conducted. Full of fear it flew backward and forward near the ceiling and against the windows, vainly seeking a way out into the sunshine. In one of the pews sat a lady who observed the bird, thinking how foolish it was not to fly out through the open door into liberty. At last the bird's strength being gone, it rested a moment on one of the rafters. Then, seeing the open door, it flew out into the sunshine, venting its joy in a song. The lady who had been watching the little bird thought to herself: "Am I not acting as foolishly as I thought the bird was? How long have I been struggling under the burden of my sin in the vain endeavor to get free, and all the while the door of God's grace has been wide open." Then and there the decision was formed to enter in.

—*Expositor*

"It Is Certainly Coming!"

An unbelieving man went to investigate George Müller's orphanage work. The woman who opened the door said, "Have you brought the bread?" He replied, "What bread?" She replied, "The bread for the children. It is five minutes of mealtime." He found many children waiting for breakfast; Mr. Müller was calm. In a few minutes, the woman came rushing back, saying, "The bread has come." There was a cartload. Later, the man learned they needed about 5,000 pounds ($25,000) that day by noon. Mr. Müller confessed, "I don't know where a penny of it is coming from, but it is certainly coming" A letter from India was the entire mail. Opened in the visitor's presence, it contained a draft for the amount needed.

—*Sunday School Times*

* * *

In the Nick of Time

I am never tired of pointing out that the Greek phrase translated, "In the time of need," is a colloquialism, of which the "nick of time" is the exact equivalent: "That we may have grace to help in the 'nick of time.'" Grace just when and where I need it. You are attacked by temptation, and, at the moment of assault, you look to Him, and the grace is there to help in "the nick of time." No postponement of your petition until the evening hour of prayer; but there, man, there in the city street, with the flaming temptation in front of you, turn to Christ with a cry for help, and the grace will be there in "the nick of time."

—G. Campbell Morgan

* * *

The Grace of God — and a Burglar

Valentine Burke, notorious burglar, sat in a cell in a St. Louis jail, awaiting trial. Seeing the headlines of a newspaper, "Jailer at Philippi Caught," being read by another prisoner, he asked to read it, then fumed with rage as he realized that it was the subject of a sermon Moody had just preached in that city. He had noticed, however, the oft-repeated words, "Believe on the Lord Jesus Christ, and thou shalt be saved." He got down on his knees and asked forgiveness, and from that night he was a changed man. Going to New York, he sought to earn an honest living, but failed. Returning to St. Louis, an officer seized him and brought him to headquarters. There he was informed that New York police had shadowed him and reported that he had proved himself straight and honest. He was given a position as a deputy sheriff. Later, Moody visited him in his new position, and Burke showed him some treasured jewels. "Look," he said. "They trust me to guard them. See what the grace of God has done for a burglar."

Moody Bible Institute
—From *Miracles and Melodies*

* * *

Two Miracles

A big, wealthy city church had three missions. On the first Sunday of the New Year, all the members of the mission churches came to the city church for Communion. In those mission churches were some outstanding cases of conversion — thieves, burglars, and so forth — but all knelt side by side at the Communion rail. On one such occasion, the pastor saw an erstwhile burglar kneel beside a judge of the Supreme Court of England — the judge who had sent him to jail, where he had served seven years. After his release he was converted and became a Christian worker. Neither seemed to see the other. After the service, the judge, walking home with the pastor, said, "Did you notice who was kneeling beside me at the Lord's Table this morning?" "Yes," replied the pastor, "but I did not know that you noticed it." Presently the judge exclaimed, "What a miracle of grace!" "Yes, a marvelous miracle of grace," replied the pastor. "But to whom do you refer?" queried the judge. "To So-and-so," said the pastor, mentioning the name of the burglar. "I was not referring to him," said the judge; "I was thinking of myself." "You were thinking of yourself?" "Yes, it did not cost that burglar much to get converted when he came out of jail. He had nothing but a history of crime behind him, and when he saw Jesus as his Saviour, he knew there was salvation and hope and joy for him. But look at me! I was taught from earliest infancy to live as a gentleman; that my word was to be my bond; that I was to say my prayers, go to church, take Communion, and so on. I went through Oxford, took my degrees, was called to the bar, and eventually became a judge. Man, nothing but the grace of God could have caused me to admit that I was a sinner on a level with that burglar! It was harder for me to get converted than for that burglar!"—From a tract, *God's Remedy for Sin*, by F. C. H. Dreyer, of the China Inland Mission.

* * *

One Standard

"I am an old man now," said he. "I am speaking to most of you for the last time, and I tell you from the long experience of my life and from the bottom of my heart, that the only safety lies in Jesus. Go to Jesus Christ with all your problems. That's 'safety first.' "The world needs one standard," he continued, "just as we need one standard yardstick, one standard pound, one standard silver dollar in Washington. Without those simple, often-forgotten standards, what strife, what cheating, what murder wouldn't there be in our land? We need one standard — the saving grace of Jesus — to bring to the world peace. Don't meddle with the Bible. You might just as well go to Washington and cut a piece off that standard yardstick. You'd be no worse than the minister who meddles with the Bible." The speaker was Rev. Russell H. Conwell.

—The S. S. Banner

* * *

Washing the Wool

A clergyman walking near a brook, observed a woman washing wool in a stream. This was done by putting it in a sieve, and then dipping the sieve in the water repeatedly, until the wool became white and clean.

He asked the woman if she knew him.

"Oh, yes, sir," she said; "I shall have reason to bless God to eternity for having heard you preach some years ago. Your sermon was the means of doing me much good."

"I rejoice to hear it. Pray, what was the subject?"

"Ah, sir, I can't recollect that, my memory is so bad."

"How then can the sermon have done you so much good, if you don't remember even what it was about?"

"Sir, my mind is like this sieve: the sieve does not hold the water, but as the water runs through, it cleanses the wool; so my memory does not retain the words I hear, but as they pass through my heart, by God's grace they cleanse it. Now I no longer love sin, and every day I entreat by Saviour to wash me in His own Blood, and to cleanse me from all pollution."

—Christian Digest

"My Grace Is Sufficient for Thee"

The other evening I was riding home after a heavy day's work; I felt very wearied, and sore depressed, when swiftly, and suddenly as a lightning flash, that text came to me: 'My grace is sufficient for thee.' I reached home and looked it up in the original, and at last it came to me in this way, 'My grace is sufficient for thee,' and I said, 'I should think it is, Lord,' and burst out laughing.

"I never fully understood what the holy laughter of Abraham was until then. It seemed to make unbelief so absurd. It was as though some little fish, being very thirsty, was troubled about drinking the river dry, and Father Thames said, 'Drink away, little fish, my stream is sufficient for thee.' Or, it seemed like a little mouse in the granaries of Egypt, after the seven years of plenty, fearing it might die of famine; Joseph might say, 'Cheer up, little mouse, my granaries are sufficient for thee.' Again, I imagined a man away up yonder, in a lofty mountain, saying to himself, 'I breathe so many cubic feet of air every day, I fear I shall exhaust the oxygen in the atmosphere,' but the earth might say, "Breathe away, O man, and fill thy lungs ever, my atmosphere is sufficient for thee.' O brethren, be great believers! Little faith will bring your souls to Heaven, but great faith will bring Heaven to your souls."

—C. H. Spurgeon

* * *

Grace To Save From Ease

Several years ago the Rev. Samuel Chadwick told of a testimony meeting at the close of a revival in his church. One person after another rose to tell of his transformation from a life devoted to lawbreaking, liquor, and all manner of evil. The congregation was profoundly impressed by their witness to the power of the Spirit. At the climax of the meeting a little lady got to her feet and gave the most startling testimony of all! She said: "Jesus saved *me* from a life of ease, luxury, and selfishness, and it took as much grace to save me from my easy chair as it did to save our brother from the gutter."

—*Gospel Herald*

* * *

All of Grace

During his last hours John Knox woke from a slumber sighing, and told his friends that he had just been tempted to believe that he had "merited Heaven and eternal blessedness, by the faithful discharge of my ministry. But blessed be God who has enabled me to beat down and quench the fiery dart, by suggesting to me such passages of Scripture as these: 'What hast thou that thou didst not receive?' 'By the grace of God I am what I am. . . Not I, but the grace of God which was with me.' "

—*Christian World Pulpit*

* * *

Even Though He Had Done Nothing

An old gentleman who came to our house for milk and butter once asked my mother the way of salvation. She quoted John 3:16, but it seemed that that was not enough. He had never had much of this world's goods or opportunities, and the realization that he had never done anything for God troubled him. Then Mother said, "Roe, it's 'by grace through faith' that you are saved, not by works." A new light filled the old man's eyes. "Do you believe that?" he asked. "I certainly do," Mother replied. "Then there is hope for *me*, even though I've never done nothing." She again reminded him of God's mercies and that Christ died for him. A few days later the old fellow took desperately ill. A friendly Christian asked him, "Is it well?" With a smile the feeble voice replied, "By grace through faith I'm ready. Don't you know that Jesus died for me? I only wish I could have lived a little longer so I could do something for Him, but it's all right." Let us beware, Christians, that we don't frustrate the grace of God, for He says, "Whosoever will" may be saved.

—*Sunday School Times*

He Giveth More Grace

He giveth more grace when the burdens grow greater.
He sendeth more strength when the labor's increase.
To added affliction He addeth His mercy,
To multiplied trials, His multiplied peace.

When we have exhausted our store of endurance,
When our strength has failed ere the day is half done,
When we reach the end of our hoarded resources,
Our Father's full giving has only begun.

His love has no limits, His grace has no measure,
His power no boundary known unto men.
For out of His infinite riches in Jesus,
He giveth, and giveth, and giveth, again.

—J. E. Myhill

* * *

His Need His Recommendation

One day Dr. Barnardo was approached by a dirty, little, ragged lad who asked him for admission to the London Orphanage. "But, my boy," said the Doctor, "I do not know you. Who are you? What have you to recommend you?" The lad was quick to seize his opportunity, and held up before Dr. Barnardo his ragged coat, and with a confident little voice he said: "If you please, sir, I thought these here would be all I needed to recommend me." Dr. Barnardo caught him up in his arms, and you may be sure he was welcomed to the orphanage.

—*Wonderful Word*

* * *

"The Unfailing Remedy!"

Bishop Kavanaugh was one day walking through the streets of a city when he met one of its prominent physicians who offered him a seat in his car.

The physician was an infidel. After a while the conversation turned upon religion.

"I am surprised," said the infidel doctor, "that such an intelligent man as you are should believe such an old fable as that."

The bishop made no immediate reply, but some time afterward, said.

"Doctor, suppose that years ago someone had recommended to you a prescription for pulmonary consumption, and given you directions concerning it, and you had procured the medicine and taken it as directed and you had been cured of that terrible disease. Suppose that you had used that prescription in your practice ever since, and had never known it to fail when taken according to directions, what would you say to the man who could not believe in, and would not try your prescription?"

"I should say he was a fool," replied the physician.

"Twenty-five years ago," said the bishop, "I tried the power of God's grace. It made a different man of me. All these years I have preached salvation to others, and whenever it has been accepted I have never known it to fail. I have seen it make the proud man humble; the drunken man temperate, the profane man pure of speech, and the dishonest man true. The rich and the poor, the learned and the unlearned, the old and the young, have alike been healed of their diseases."

"You have caught me fairly, bishop; I have been a fool," said the physician. And that was not the end of it: the infidel doctor became the superintendent of a prosperous Sunday School.

—*Christian Index*

* * *

Man's Work Compared to God's Grace

Longfellow could take a worthless sheet of paper, write a poem on it, and make it worth $6,000 — *that's genius.*

Rockefeller could sign his name to a piece of paper and make it worth a million dollars — *that's capital.*

Uncle Sam can take gold, stamp an eagle on it, and make it worth $20.00 *that's money.*

A mechanic can take material that is worth only $5.00 and make it worth $50.00 — *that's skill.*

An artist can take a fifty-cent piece of canvas, paint a picture on it, and make it worth $1,000 — *that's art.*

God can take a worthless, sinful life, wash it in the blood of Christ, put His Spirit in it, and make it a blessing to humanity — *that's salvation.*

—*Christian Digest*

* * *

"Sneaking Into Heaven!"

I was once asked to visit an old Scotchman who was dying. He was anxious about his soul, for he was unprepared to meet God. After a few visits the truth dawned upon him, and through repentance and faith he experienced the joy of forgiveness, and the assurance of eternal life. Just before he died he said to me, with obvious regrets: "I feel such a *sneak* because I've served Satan all my life and only now at the *end* of my life have I yielded my heart to God." His conscience told him it was a mean, despicable way to serve his Master and Redeemer. It is a comforting thought that God is so ready to receive and pardon us, though we have spurned Him all our days. Salvation is *all of grace*, whether we are saved in youth or in old age.

—Arthur Hedley in *Gospel Herald*

* * *

Grace To Pray

When Joseph Parker, the great London preacher of the last century, was debating one day on the town green with enemies of Christianity, an infidel shouted to him, "What did Christ do for Stephen when he was stoned?" Parker answered — and he said the answer was given him like an inspiration from Heaven — "He gave him grace to pray for those who stoned him." It was the belief of St. Augustine and of Luther that the prayer which was offered by Stephen for those who stoned him, and which Paul must have heard when he held the clothes of those who did the stoning, was used of God for the conversion of the apostle.

—*Watchman-Examiner*

GROWTH

A New Faith and a New Face

"I had five hundred men in my church last Sunday morning," said Dr. J. H. Jowett, "five hundred working-men. One of them has been so frequently in the police court that in our local jail there is one cell that bears his name, and is always waiting for him. He was laid hold of by what we call the Adult School Movement, the Lord Jesus took possession of him, and I think I never heard a more beautiful testimony than one of his friends gave me concerning him. He said, 'You know that man's face is changing every week. He had the face of a beast; it is lighting up, lighting up, like an old cathedral.'"

—*British Weekly*

* * *

The Pull From Above

Haven't you often wondered how the giant redwoods of California draw water to their foliage, often more than 300 feet in the air? "It is not done through pressure from the roots," writes Robert Collier. "It is done by pull from above. All through nature the same law will be found — then the means which the need itself provides." "To grow taller, reach higher!" Have you ever realized that only God can make a man what he ought to be? If you were asked who was the most perfect man who ever lived, you would probably answer, "Jesus Christ." And He was perfect man only because His human exterior was His divine nature. And only as you by faith accept Christ, and He takes up His residence in your soul, will you rise to the heights of character and life that God wills for you. How many men today are living stunted, dwarfed, twisted, inferior lives because they neglect to reach higher? When Gladstone was asked to name the sixty greatest men in history, out of those he named, fifty-six were believers in Jesus Christ as their Saviour and followed Him as their Lord.

—*Visitor*

Safe To Count

Gipsy Smith said: "I was sitting at a table with some preachers, and one, a Scotsman, said, 'How did you get on at your meeting?' I said, Oh, so many passed through the inquiry room. He said, 'Is it safe to count?' I said, 'Well, they counted at Pentecost and put it down at three thousand.' He changed the subject. Later on the Scotsman said, 'Are you married, Mr. Smith?' I said, 'Yes.' 'Any family?' 'Yes.' 'How many?' I replied, 'Is it safe to count?' " When the laughter had subsided the Gipsy added: "You count your children, and the Lord counts His. You made enough fuss when your baby was born. The Lord says there is joy in Heaven over one. The Church doesn't make half enough fuss when one is converted!"

—*Christian Herald*

* * *

Short-Lived Progress

A gourd wound itself round a lofty palm, and in a few weeks climbed to its very top. "How old may'st thou be?" asked the newcomer. "About one hundred years." "About one hundred years, and no taller! Only look, I have grown as tall as you in fewer days than you count years." "I know that well," replied the palm. "Every summer of my life a gourd has climbed up around me as proud as thou art, and as short-lived as thou wilt be."

—*Sunday Circle*

* * *

Onward!

A group of people was climbing the Alps. Two men tried to go higher than the rest and were lost forever. Their friends said: "When last seen, they were going toward the heights. "Oh, if that could be said of every adventure in our lives! Success means to strive constantly, to insist on seeing the invisible, and in spite of clouds and barriers, to keep on toward the heights.

—*Gospel Herald*

263

As the Twig

We, the youth who shock you so,
Ask, "How much did you help us grow?"
You gaze at us with astonishment.
Where were you when the twig was
bent?
Why did you wait? Why did you wait?
If you wanted saplings tall and straight,
You gave us bread. Did that atone
For the days and nights we were left
alone?
You laughed our heroes from their
height
And left them worthless in our sight.
They lost their standards in the dust;
Their weapons dulled with bitter rust.
And when we asked for God, you turned
Our answers back with doubt that
burned.
We watched you tempt the hand of fate.
The world plunged into war and hate
In mockery of brother-love,
Nothing on earth, nothing above!
You blame us for skirting danger's
brink —
We want to feel, for we dare not think.
Who asks good fruit from a well-grown
tree
Must take the time for husbandry.

—Gertrude Ryder Bennett

* * *

How God Grows His Children

I asked the Lord that I might grow
In faith and love and every grace;
Might more of His salvation know,
And seek more earnestly His face.

'Twas He who taught me thus to pray,
And He, I know, has answered prayer;
But it has been in such a way
As almost drove me to despair.

I hoped, that in some favored hour,
At once He'd answer my request;
And by His love's constraining power
Subdue my sins, and give me rest.

Instead of this, He made me feel
The hidden evils of my heart;
And let the angry powers of Hell
Assault my soul in every part.

Yea! more; with His own hand He
seemed
Intent to aggravate my woe;
Crossed all the fair designs I schemed,
Blasted my gourds, and laid me low.

"Lord! Why is this?" I trembling cried;
"Wilt Thou pursue Thy worm to
death?"
" 'Tis in this way," the Lord replied,
"I answer prayer for grace and faith."

"These inward trials I employ
From self and pride to see thee free;
And break thy schemes of earthly joy
That thou mayest seek thy ALL IN
ME."

—John Newton

* * *

A Paradox of Growth

Dr. Bonar once said that he could tell
when a Christian was growing. In proportion to his growth in grace he would
elevate his Master, talk less of what he
himself was doing, and become smaller
and smaller in his own esteem, until, like
the morning star, he faded away before
the rising sun.

—D. L. Moody

* * *

Interpretative Power of Enlarged Experience

When Robert Moffat, in mission
tours in southern Africa moved upward
among the tribes that had no contact
with civilization, he rode in an ox-wagon
and took with him a steam kettle, both
of which were absolute novelties to
them. He told them that in his own country they laid down tracks of steel and
on them drew many ox-wagons with a
great steam kettle at the head of them.
That was his way of describing a train
of cars and a locomotive, by objects
which they had seen. When he set up
his tent and from his lantern threw on
the canvas an image of a train of cars
in motion, they said, "Oh, see the ox-
wagons and the steam kettle!" When he
came to England and brought with him
the son of a chief, and they stepped
into a train at Southampton, the young
lad said, "This is the train of wagons

with the steam kettle." There are natural limits of revelation. God has to use in the description of heaven a nomenclature that is drawn from the experience of earth. To use terms only applicable to heavenly things would be to make Himself unintelligible to man. *There are limits to revelation, found, not in the power of God to declare, but in the power of man to understand. As therefore experience grows in spiritual things, so will spiritual apprehension grow.*

—Arthur T. Pierson, in
The Divine Art of Preaching

* * *

Going Forward

It is impossible to overestimate the importance of growth in grace. To healthy life, growth is absolutely necessary. Indeed, it may be questioned whether there is real, true life at all where there is no growth. It is true in other spheres than the spiritual, whether it be in plant life or animal life, or any other kind of life you choose to mention, that, unless there be growth and development, there is decay and destruction.

—Rev. Hector Mackinnon

* * *

Growing Like Christ

Each day to grow more humble,
    Yet stronger in Thy might;
More valiant, Lord, to carry
    Thy standard for the right.

Each day to grow more gracious
    More sweet and gentle, too;
Yet braver, more courageous,
    More firm, more pure, more true.

That I may grow more like Thee;
    In me Thy Spirit shine;
Transformed from grace to glory,
    Touched by a power Divine.

—M. E. Kendrew

* * *

Onward!

New occasions teach new duties; Time
    makes ancient good uncouth;
They must upward still, and onward,

who would keep abreast of Truth;
Lo, before us gleam her camp fires!
We ourselves must Pilgrims be,
Launch our Mayflower, and steer boldly through the desperate winter sea,
Nor attempt the Future's portal with
    the Past's blood-rusted key.

—James Russell Lowell

* * *

Kings Acting Like Scullions

Instead of acting like kings, many who claim to be sons of God act as meanly as if they were scullions in the kitchen of Mammon. What separation from the world, what heavenly walking with God ought to be seen in those who are chosen to be a peculiar people, the representatives of God on earth and Courtiers of the New Jerusalem above. As the world waxes worse and worse, it behooves men of God to become better and better.   —C. H. Spurgeon

* * *

Go Forward!

Up, then, and linger not, thou saint of
    God!
Fling from thy shoulders each impeding load;
Be brave and wise, shake off earth's
    soil and sin,
That with the Bridegroom thou mayest
    enter in!
    Oh, watch and pray!
Gird on thy armor, face each weaponed
    foe,
Deal with the sword of Heaven the
    deadly blow;
Forward, still forward, in the fight
    Divine;
Slack not the warfare till the field be
    thine.
    Win thou the crown!

—Horatius Bonar, in
The Alliance Weekly

* * *

Stunted

I visited... a proud and happy couple to whose home a little child had recently come. The mother — scarcely more than a girl — brought the baby across to me and, her face literally shining, exclaimed with naive and beautiful enthusiasm, "Isn't he perfect?" He certainly seemed to be, and, in her delightful eyes, he certainly was. But suppose that, in two years' time, the baby is not exactly as he is today! Will she still think him perfect? And, if not, why not? The fact is that even perfection is never perfection in itself. There is always room, within the framework of absolute perfection, for infinite processes of development. As in the case of the baby, stagnation is the tragic evidence of some basic imperfection.

A bud may be a perfect bud; but if, instead of ripening into a shapely and fragrant blossom, it remains a bud, its apparent perfection is simply the camouflage of a hideous deformity.

— *Sunday School Times.*

* * *

No Alternative

The Christian life is like riding a bicycle: if you do not go on you go off.

—W. H. Griffith Thomas

GUIDANCE

What Is a Call?

Mary Lyon, the founder of Mt. Holyoke College, and for twelve years its principal, was wont to say, *"To know the need should prompt the deed."*

William Carey said *his call was an open Bible before an open map of the world,* and he went to India.

Robert Morrison said, "Jesus, I give myself to Thy service. *My desire is to engage where laborers are most wanted,"* and he went to China.

James Gilmour, of Mongolia, decided the question of his field of labor by logic and common sense. *"Is the kingdom a harvest field? Then I thought it reasonable to seek work where the need was greatest and the workers fewest,"* and he went to Asia.

Bishop Alfred R. Tucker, of Uganda, left a secluded artist's studio for the work of Christ. He had been painting the picture of a poor woman thinly clad and pressing a babe to her bosom, wandering homeless on a stormy night in the dark, deserted street. As the picture grew, the artist suddenly threw down his brush, exclaiming, *"Instead of merely painting the lost, I will go out and save them,"* and he went to Africa.

— *Moody Monthly.*

* * *

My Daily Prayer

If I can do some good today,
If I can serve along life's way,
If I can something helpful say,
    Lord, show me how.

If I can right a human wrong,
If I can help to make one strong,
If I can cheer with smile or song,
    Lord, show me how.

If I can aid one in distress,
If I can make a burden less,
If I can spread more happiness,
    Lord, show me how.

If I can do a kindly deed,
If I can help someone in need,
If I can sow a fruitful seed,
    Lord, show me how.

If I can feed a hungry heart,
If I can give a better start,
If I can fill a nobler part,
    Lord, show me how.
        —Grenville Kleiser

* * *

A Guide Who Knows The Way

In Pennsylvaina there is a statue one hundred and twenty feet high, erected to William Penn the founder. When the birds are taking their flight to the sunny South, a great many dead birds are found at the base of this statue. The reason of this is that birds flying in the darkness are apt to strike against the statue and so kill themselves. Examination of the dead birds has shown the birds that meet this sad fate are the young ones who have never taken the journey before. Older birds who have taken the journey before, know about the obstacles and know to avoid them.

How this teaches us the necessity of having a Guide who knows all about the way we are taking and who is able to bring us safely to our journey's end.

— *Gospel Herald*

* * *

"God Moves In Mysterious Way!"

William Cowper, like many of us, was subject to moments of deep melancholy. One night in such a mood he called a cabby and directed him to drive to the banks of the Thames River. The city of London was blanketed with an impenetrable fog, which was, however, no thicker than the despair in the poet's own soul.

For more than an hour the cab driver groped his way along the streets and yet did not find the river. His passenger grew more and more impatient until at last he leaped from the cab, determined to find his watery grave unassisted.

Groping thru the fog, he was astonished when he found himself at his own doorstep. Going to his room he penned the words of that beautiful hymn:

"God moves in a mysterious way His wonders to perform."

— *Gospel Herald*

* * *

The Way-Shower

It is said of Miss Reside, the first woman missionary to Kiowa Indians of Oklahoma, that after she had been with the Indians long enough for them to know what it meant to be a Christian they gave her a new name. They called her *"Aim-day-co."* Chief Bigtree, in explaining this name, said, "When we Kiowas see anyone on the wrong road we call out, *'Aim-day-co'* ("Turn this way"). Our sister came to us from a far land, and found us all on the wrong road and in great danger. She stood in a new road and called to us and said, "Turn this way,' and showed us the Jesus road. God bless Aim-day-co."

—*Sunday School Times*

Better Than Directions

It was a dark, stormy night, and a little child, lost in the streets of the city, was crying in distress. A policeman, gathering from the child's statement enough to locate the home, gave directions after this manner: "Just go down this street half a mile, turn and cross the big iron bridge, then turn to your right and follow the river down a little way, and you'll see then where you are." The poor child only half comprehending, chilled by the wind, and bewildered by the storm, was turning about blindly, when another voice spoke, and said in a kindly tone, "Just come with me." The little hand was clasped in a stronger one, and the corner of a warm cloak was thrown over the shoulders of the shivering child. The way home was made easy. The first one had told the way; this one condescends to be the way.

—*The Expositor*

* * *

Divine Guidance

If it were not for my belief in an overruling Providence, it would be difficult for me, in the midst of such complications, to keep my reason on its seat. But I am confident that the Almighty has His plans and will work them out; and, whether we see it or not, they will be the wisest and best for us. I have always taken counsel of Him, and referred to Him my plans, and have never adopted a course of proceeding without being assured, as far as I could be, of His approbation. I should be the most presumptuous blockhead upon this footstool if I for one day thought that I could discharge the duties which have come upon me since I came into this place, without the aid and enlightenment of One who is wiser and stronger than all others.   —Abraham Lincoln

* * *

The True Way

Dan Crawford once wrote of a native guide who was leading him along a new trail one day. Being somewhat dubious of the direction, he asked his

267

proud guide just where they were going. "The way?" smiled the native.
"You want to know the way? I am the
way!" pointing proudly to his breast,
where the hidden knowledge was locked
up. Says Crawford, "I took my text
from that, sat down with him in the
forest on a fallen tree, and told him of
the Blessed One who could truly say, 'I
am the Way.' " — *Lighted Pathway*.

* * *

"Usin' and Thummin' "

The story is told of a young curate
in the Church of England who was
greatly helped in his understanding of
the Scriptures by frequent conversations with an uneducated cobbler, who
was, nevertheless, well acquainted with
the Word of God. On one occasion
when a friend of his, a young theologian, was visiting him, he mentioned
this remarkable knowledge of the Bible
which the cobbler possessed. The young
theologue, in a spirit of pride, expressed
a desire to meet him, saying he felt
sure he could ask some questions which
he would be quite unable to answer.
Upon being introduced to the man in
his little shop, the question was put,
"Can you tell me what Urim and the
Thummim were?" The cobbler replied,
"I don't know exactly; I understand that
the words apply to something that was
on the breastplate of the high priest.
I know the words mean 'Lights and Perfection,' and that through the Urim and
Thummim the high priest was able to
discern the mind of the Lord. But I
find that I can get the mind of the Lord
by just changing two letters. I take this
blessed Book, and by 'usin' and thummin',' I get the mind of the Lord that
way." — Dr. H. A. Ironside, in the
Moody Church News.

* * *

Only the Sick Ones Would Follow

A friend who was traveling in the
East heard that there was a shepherd
who still kept up the custom of calling
his sheep by name. He went to the man
and said:

"Let me put on your clothes and take
your crook, and I will call them and see
if they will come to me."

And so he did, and he called one
sheep "Mina, Mina," but the whole
flock ran away from him. Then he said
to the shepherd:

"Will none of them follow me when
I call them?"

The shepherd replied: "Yes, sir, some
of them will; the sick sheep will follow
anybody."

I'm not going to make the application; I leave that to you.

—*Moody Monthly*

* * *

Herbert Hoover On Guidance:

There is no other book so various as
the Bible, nor so full of concentrated
wisdom. Whether it be of law, business,
morals or that vision which leads the
imagination in the creation of constructive enterprises . . . he who seeks for
guidance . . . may look inside its covers
and find illumination.

— Herbert Hoover.

* * *

On Time

A gentleman tells of an interesting
visit to the observatory of Harvard
University, just after a new astronomical instrument had been purchased.
According to astronomical calculations
contained in a little book ten years old,
which calculations were based upon observations thousands of years old, a
star was due in a certain position in
the heavens at 5:20 p.m. When the
hour drew near, the instrument was at
once directed to the determined position, and prone on his back under the
eyepiece lay the enthusiastic professor.
It was agreed that when the star
crossed the spider-web line stretched
across the lens of the instrument, the
professor who was watching should
pronounce the word "Here." It was also agreed that the assistant who
watched the second hand of the clock
should let a hammer fall upon a marble
table the instant the clock said it was
5:20. The professor was watching the

star and could not see the clock, while the man with the hammer could not see the star, for he was watching the clock. There was an impressive silence. In the observatory the clock was quietly ticking, but God's earth was moving through space and revolving upon its axis as He bade it do ages ago. Suddenly two sounds broke the stillness. One was the professor saying, "Here," the other the sound of the hammer on the table, and the two sounds were simultaneous — at 5:20 p. m. If God guides the stars and calls them all by their names, does He not guide them and care for each individual who obeys Him?

— *Bible Expositor and Illuminator*

* * *

Markers When They Are Needed

Driving along a Texas road at night, I became uneasy thinking I might have missed a turn two or three miles back. The road was good, but I remembered a fork that I had passed without reading the signs. Mile after mile I drove on. I slowed down with indecision, thinking that I should probably turn around and drive back to that intersection probably ten miles behind me. Then suddenly, in the distance, my headlights picked up a white marker. I increased speed and soon saw the shield that marks the U. S. highways. The figure 82 was clearly visible, and that was the road I wanted, so I continued my way with confidence. In the night of our travel, God frequently gives us reassuring signs. The moment of doubt may arise, we may find ourselves in confusion, then, in His love and grace, He draws us back to the cross. We see the mark of His love, and go on fully reassured in perfect confidence.

— *Eternity*

* * *

Is This the Right Road Home?

Is this the right road home, O Lord?
  The clouds are dark and still,
The stony path is hard to tread,
  Each step brings some fresh ill.
I thought the way would brighter
  grow,

And that the sun with warmth would
  glow,
And joyous songs from free hearts flow.
  In *this* the *Right* Road Home?

Yes, child, this very path I trod,
  The clouds were dark for me,
The stony path was sharp and hard.
  Not sight, but faith, could see
That at the end the sun shines bright,
Forever where there is no night,
And glad hearts rest from earth's fierce
  fight,
  It IS the Right Road Home!
    —Rosalind Goforth, in
      Sunday School Times

* * *

He Leads

He leads us on by paths we did not
  know;
Upwards He leads us though our steps
  be slow,
Though oft we faint and falter on the
  way,
Though storms and darkness oft obscure the day;
  Yet when the clouds are gone
  We know He leads us on.
    —N. L. Zinzendorf

* * *

God's Restraints and Constraints

Many a time in history has supernatural restraint and constraint changed the course of God's servants. Livingstone essayed to go into China, but God suffered him not, and sent him to Africa to be its missionary general, statesman, explorer. Before him, Carey planned to go to Polynesia in the South Seas, but God guided him to India to lay foundations for giving a vernacular Bible to one-sixth of the people of the world. Judson did go to India, but was driven to Burma, where he built up an apostolic church for all time. Barnabas Shaw was thrust out from Boerland, and trusted to God's guidance of his cattle and cart, not knowing whither he went, until the twenty-eighth day brought to him the chief of Namaqualand, his "man of Macedonia," who literally said, "Come over and help us." How many secrets of such leading are

269

yet to be brought to light, thousands of God's servants having been forbidden by Him to follow out their plans because He has had some unexpected door of service to set before them!

—*Illustrator*

* * *

The True God

A man started out through a forest so thickly covered with trees that one day he could not see the sun or sky. After traveling for a long time he knew it was getting night time, so started for what he thought was home. He was so certain that his direction was right that he did not look at his compass. But when he did look at it, he was surprised to find that he was going west when he thought he was going east. He was so sure he was right that he started to throw his compass away. Then he thought, "You have never told me an untruth, and I'll trust you now." He followed the compass and came out right.

We, too, have a compass that will never tell us an untruth. It is God's Word — the Bible. If we always follow it we will be safe. Even though we think we are right, if it tells us something different then let us follow what it says for that is the only safe thing.

—*Gospel Herald*

* * *

The Road to Safety

A news correspondent, forced to jump from a crippled plane over New Guinea, landed safely. He sought a way out of the jungle. Up the mountains, down the rivers, through the thick jungle growth he traveled, only to return discouraged to his starting point. Day by day, week by week, he took one way after another — but there was no road. At last he suddenly came upon a break in the tall grass where apparently some animal had passed. Following the break he found himself on a narrow road! What joy! Later he was found by missionaries and taken to a hospital and the safety of civilization. Think what that road meant to that correspondent! Just

that does the Word of God mean to man as he wanders through the wilderness of a sinful life. Seeking his own ways by himself, he constantly returns to his starting point — still lost, without hope, unable to find the way to eternal life. How good it is to know that there was One who said, "I am the way, the truth, and the life: no man cometh unto the Father, but by me."

—D. J. Evans,
in *Open Windows*

* * *

Needed for the Voyage

A minister was once asked unexpectedly to conduct a service in a country home. He called for a Bible, but none could be found. At last, however, they found one in an old sea chest in the attic. Strange to say, on the outside of the chest were the words, "Not wanted on the voyage." Be sure you make your voyage through life with God's Word as your guide always.

—*Sunday School Times*

* * *

Sealed Orders, But the Captain Aboard

One of our poets, in speaking of our birth, beautifully says, "Every soul leaves port under sealed orders. We cannot know whither we are going, or what we are to do, until the time comes for breaking the seal." But I can tell you something more beautiful than this. Every regenerated soul sets out on its voyage with an invisible Captain on board, who knows the nature of our sealed orders from the outset, and who will shape our entire voyage accordingly if we will only let Him.

—Dr. A. J. Gordon

* * *

Still Under God's Sky

A woman who had to leave her home was traveling to a different part of the country. She cried when she remembered what she was leaving behind her, and her little boy, trying to comfort her, said: "Why, Mother, God's sky is over us yet! It's going right along with us. We shall be all right now!" Let us lift up our eyes to God, who will guide us.

—*Sunday Circle*

Why Forbidden?

Barnabas Shaw reached Cape Town in 1815 with his plans matured to plant there the Gospel of the Son of God. But Dutch rule in Africa was hostile to missionary effort and he was forbidden to preach the Gospel on his chosen field, so in bitter disappointment was compelled to turn his steps elsewhere. He bought a yoke of oxen and a cart, and, putting his goods into it, he and his wife seated themselves therein and headed the lowing kine toward the interior of the country. On the twenty-seventh day of their journey, when they encamped, they discovered a company of Hottentots halting near them. On entering into communication with them they learned that this band of heathen headed by their chief were journeying to Cape Town in search of a missionary to teach them "the Great Word" as they expressed it. Meeting them just in the nick of time proved such a juncture of Providence as had rarely occurred in the history of missions.

—From *Holy Spirit in Missions* by Gordon

* * *

Why Blunder Along

Dr. George Washington Carver was a man of prayer, and in the simplicity of his faith made answered prayer his natural habitat. I asked him if he had ever found prayer for guidance, in connection with his discoveries, to avail. "Of course," he said, "that goes without saying. You see, there is no need for anyone to be without direction, or to wander amid the perplexities and complexities of this life. Are we not plainly told, 'In all thy ways acknowledge him, and he shall direct thy paths'? Why go blundering along on our poor, blind way when God has told us He will

help us? God can always be depended upon. Here is a radio. It is little use standing there unless I turn the dial and tune in on the station I want. Then I will have what I seek. It is all so simple; just opening up the avenues of approach to God through prayer."

—From *Saint, Seer, and Scientist* by J. H. Hunter

* * *

Changing Pastures

I saw a painting of a large boat laden with cattle that were being ferried across an angry, swollen river in time of storm. The artist had so cleverly pictured the dark, threatening clouds and the play of the treacherous, jagged lightning that I immediately concluded that the freight of the poor dumb cattle was marked for destruction. But the title of the painting was simply "Changing Pastures." *Many times we imagine that God's plans mean disaster and affliction, but he is simply "changing pastures," for our good and the welfare of our brethren.*

—*Sunday School Times*

* * *

Shackleton's Testimony

We remember with a thrill the words of Shackelton, the explorer, as he recalled a march with two of his men in Georgia: "When I look back," he said, "I have no doubt that Providence guided us, not only across the snowfields, but across the stormwhite sea. I know that during that long and racking march of thirty-six hours over the unnamed mountains and glaciers of South Georgia it seemed to me often that we were four, not three. I said nothing to my companions on the point, but afterward Worsley said to me, 'Boss, I had a curious feeling on that march that there was another person with us.' "

—*Children's Newspaper*

HABIT

Eagle and Weasel

It is said that a man one day strolling along in the country happened to see a magnificent golden eagle flying up-

ward toward the sky. He watched it with delight and admiration as it strongly mounted upward; but presently he saw that something was wrong with it.

It seemed unable to go any higher. Soon it began to fall, and presently it lay at his feet a lifeless mass.

What could be the matter? No human hand had harmed it. No sportsman's shot had reached it. He went and examined the bird, and what did he find? It had carried up with it a little weasel in its talons, and as it had drawn its talons near to its body for flight the little creature had wormed itself partly out of them and had drunk the lifeblood from the eagle's breast.

How like this it is with sin! It may appear a very small thing one is at first tempted to do; just one glass of wine, but presently a habit has fastened itself upon you and you have it to drag around with you the rest of your life.

—*The Y. C. Companion*

* * *

The Scolding Habit

Scolding is mostly a habit. It is often the result of nervousness and an irritable condition of both mind and body. A person is tired or annoyed at some trivial cause, and forthwith begins finding fault with everything and everybody within reach. Scolding is a habit very easily formed. It is astonishing how soon one becomes addicted to it, and confirmed in it. It is an unreasoning and unreasonable habit. Persons who once get into the way of scolding always find something to scold about. It is an extremely disagreeable habit. It is contagious; once introduced into a family, it is pretty certain in a short time to affect all.

—*Herald of Light and Zion's Watchman*

* * *

She Threw it Away

An old woman was converted in Korea. The visiting missionary and the Bible woman taught her as much as they could and then passed on. The missionary came back many months later.

The old lady told her the following story:

"After you left, I sat in my hut in the evening, puffing away at my dear old pipe and thinking of the wonderful gospel story and of the love of the Saviour to me. As I thought of Him, I felt that I could not sit here with Him (you said He promised to be with me) selfishly enjoying my pipe alone.

"So I held the pipe out to Him and asked Him to share it.

"After some evenings, it came to me that the pipe was very old and dirty and He is so very pure and holy. It was not fit to offer Him. So again I smoked alone. This went on for some time. Then the thought came: 'If it is too old and dirty to offer to Him, then surely it is not fit either for me His follower.' So she threw away the pipe with the explanation, 'If it is not fit for Him, it is not fit for me either.' I don't smoke now."

—*World Dominion*

* * *

A Dangerous Habit

The fault-finding habit is a bad one. It is easily acquired and not readily broken. We live in an imperfect world. Everything is flawed and defective. Institutions all blunder and fall short of the ideal. Persons are all erring creatures and their faults give us offense. But one should not pay too much attention to the faults of others or to the defects of the world in which he lives. He may become a chronic fault-finder, and in that case he will become a grumbler. If he is not careful, he will degenerate into a growler. And if he growls long enough, he will degenerate into a snarler, and in the end he will become a cynic. When a man has become a cynic, he has reached the bottom. There is nothing lower than cynicism. A cynic is of no account either to himself or to anyone else. He is a nuisance and a stumbling block. He did not intend at the start to become a cynic. He began by finding fault, and the habit grew on him until his mind became twisted and his heart sour.

—Dr. Chas. E. Jefferson

* * *

While the Blaze is Young

Not long ago a young man was caught while trying to flee from a post office that he had robbed of several hundred dollars. When his pastor visited him in prison he asked: "Roy, when did you begin to steal?"

The answer was, "I guess I began when I was in the first grade. One day I took some pennies from my brother's bank to buy some candy. He didn't miss them, so I never put them back as I'd intended to. Then I began to take pencils from the fellows' desks and change from the girls' pockets in the coat room. None of the things I took seemed important at the time, but the habit kept growing on me, and here I am."

—*Gospel Herald*

* * *

I Am Habit

It is mighty hard to shake me;
In my brawny arms I take thee;
I can either make or break thee;
    I am Habit!

Through each day I slowly mold thee;
Soon my tight'ning chains enfold thee;
Then it is with ease I hold thee;
    Thus is Habit!

I can be both good and vile;
I can e'en be worth your while,
Or the cause of your bitter cry
    I am Habit!

Oft I've proved myself a pleasure;
Proved myself a priceless treasure,
Or a menace past all measure;
    Thus is Habit!

Harmless though I sometimes seem, yet
My strange force is like a magnet;
Like a great and greedy dragnet;
    I am Habit!

Though you sometimes fear or doubt me
No one yet has lived without me;
I am present all about thee;
    Thus is Habit!

Choose me well when you are starting
Seldom is an easy parting;
I'm a devil or a darling!
    I am Habit!

—*Robert E. Sly, in*
Junior Class Paper

"Attention!"

A practical joker, so the account goes, one day saw a man, who had spent years of service in the English army, going home from the store. He was an aged man who had been for some years out of the uniform of the army.

When the joker suddenly called out, "Attention!" the former soldier stopped, and as his arms snapped to his sides the bundles he was carrying fell to the ground. His military training had been so thorough that it had become a second nature.

Sometimes when we speak of a person's habits we mean his bad habits. But good habits are just as possible to establish as bad habits, and are just as much of a help as bad habits are a hindrance.

—*Gospel Herald*

* * *

Habits

How habits cling to us! The word habit comes from a Latin word which indicates that habits have us, instead of our having them. Instead of saying to a person, "He has a bad habit," we might well say, "A bad habit has him." How necessary then it is to form right habits!

—*Hurlbut*

* * *

H-A-B-I-T

The only way to get rid of a bad habit is to stop it at once. If you try tapering off, this is the result. You drop the "H" and you still have —

A BIT

You think you are getting over it by dropping a little bit, so you go on and drop "A" but you still are —

BIT

That is to say, you are not getting on at all. You are deceiving yourself. You are just where you were. You are still bit by the evil thing. But you go on and drop the "B" and you still have —

IT

And "it" is the sting of habit. "It" has been the trouble all along. You are where you started. Drop "I" and you have —

T

Which stands for temptation. And temptation is a longer word to get rid of than habit. The best way is found in Romans 6:13 — "Neither yield ye your members as instruments of unrighteousness unto sin: but yield yourself unto God."   —*Selected*

* * *

Hard to Change

The well-known sports columnist, Grantland Rice, in his "Sportlight," gave two splendid illustrations of the value of learning things early in life. Mr. Rice spoke to Gene Sarazen, professional golfer of many years' successful competition. He asked Sarazen why he continued to use his old grip on the golf club, when he had learned, as he confessed, of a better one. Said Gene: "It's hard to break old habits. I won the United States Open with this grip when I was twenty-one. I thought then that it was perfect. I found out later that it was not — when it was too late." Rice also interviewed Ty Cobb, the greatest of them all, and asked why, throughout his brilliant baseball career, he held his hands so far apart when batting. "It all started," Cob answered, "when I was a kid of twelve. I was a stringy youngster, and all the bats were too big and heavy for me. I had to hold them that way to swing them. Once you build up habits as a kid, they are hard to change." It is important, you see, to build right habits when you are young. No child is too young to learn about Christ. The earlier, the better — which is a reminder for parents, ministers, Sunday school teachers, and all who work with children, to be faithful to God in respect to children.

     —*Essex*

* * *

A Chained Eagle

A hunter in the Alleghanies one day shot a large bald eagle. The bird measured seven feet two inches across the wings. When the sportsman went to examine his prize, he was astonished to find one of the eagle's claws held firmly in a powerful steep trap to which was attached a steel chain five feet long. Trap and chain had many marks of vicious blows from the eagle's bill, showing how he had vainly endeavored to free himself from them. While they had not been heavy enough to prevent his flying, the hunter believed that they had so impeded and wearied him as to be the cause of bringing the great bird within the reach of his rifle.

Many a fine man with brain and imagination and heart capable of high-soaring flight has been brought within reach of the enemy's gun by some trap of vicious appetite or passion that has held him down from his place among the stars.

How wise the admonition in Hebrews: "Let us lay aside every weight, and the sin which doth so easily beset us."

     —*Fellowship News*

* * *

Easy When We're Young

An old teacher was once taking a walk through a forest with a pupil by his side. The old man suddenly stopped and pointed to four plants close at hand. The first was just beginning to peep above the ground, the second had rooted itself pretty well into the earth, the third was a small shrub, while the fourth was a fullsized tree. The tutor said to his young companion:

"Pull up the first."

The boy easily pulled it up with his fingers.

"Now pull up the second."

The youth obeyed, but found the task not so easy.

"And now the third."

The boy had to put forth all his strength, and was obliged to use both arms to uproot it.

"And now," said the master, "try your hand upon the fourth."

But, lo, the trunk of the tall tree, grasped in the arms of the youth, hardly shook its leaves.

"This, my son, is just what happens with our bad habits. When they are young, we can cast them out more readily with the help of God; but when they are old, it is hard to uproot them, though we pray and struggle ever so sincerely."   —*Heidelberg Herald*

HEAVEN

"A Nice Little Sum Laid Up"

Little Mary was sitting with her Uncle George one afternoon. Uncle George had told her to keep quiet, as he had some accounts to look over, so Mary busied herself with a picture book. For an hour all was still, then Mary heard her uncle say: "There, I have quite a nice little sum laid up against a time of need." "What are you talking about, Uncle George?" asked Mary. "About my treasures, little girl, that I have laid up." "Up in Heaven?" asked Mary. "Oh, no, Mary; my treasures are all on earth — some in banks and some in other places," answered Uncle George. "But haven't you got some in Heaven, too?" asked Mary. "Well, I don't believe I have," said Uncle George thoughtfully. "But run away and play with your hoop now, for I am going out." Uncle George went out and was gone a long time, but all the while he was thinking that, after all, perhaps he was not so well off if he had no treasures laid up in Heaven, to be ready for him when he left this world and his money behind him. He was so impressed with the thought that he wisely decided to lay up treasures in Heaven.

—From *Sparkling Waters*

* * *

Only From Jerusalem to Jericho

"Fine sermon, wasn't it?" asked one of Farmer Peter's friends, referring to a scholarly discourse with which the congregation had been favored that morning by a city preacher. "Maybe," returned Farmer Peter. "Why," persisted the first speaker, "that man knows more about the Bible, and has made a deeper study of Biblical history and geography than almost any other minister in the country." "Has he now?" inquired Farmer Peter mildly. "Well, then, I reckon that the trouble must have been with me. You see, I'd calc'lated I should hear somethin' about the way to Heaven, and I only learned the way from Jerusalem to Jericho."

—*Gospel Herald*

Shut Out

A minister told how one Sunday night when he was quarantined in his house because his child had diphtheria, he watched his church next door; his church that he could not now enter. He saw the lights shining through the windows. He watched the people going in. Then the service started, and he listened to the music. At last he couldn't stand it any longer. Silently, like a thief, he stole out at his back door, and crept up close to a window and listened. Within all was bright; outside he stood in the chill darkness. "I realized for the first time in my life," he said, "what it meant to be *shut out*, what a *terrible* thing it meant to be *shut* out. And some day I should stand at the gate of Heaven. What a terrible thing if *that* door should be shut against me!" God does not want that! Nor do you! But we must not neglect the only means of opening that gate, even the acceptance of him who said, "I am the *way*, the *truth*, and the *life*: no man cometh unto the Father, but by me."

—*Sunday School Times*

* * *

Shut Out Forever!

Many years ago, a man came out from the Jaffa gate, Jerusalem, and stood upon a hillock, shouting with all his might, as if forewarning of danger, and gesticulating wildly, as if to call our attention to what he was announcing. "What is the man saying?" we asked our guide.

"He is shouting, 'Yellah! Yellah!'"

"What does that mean?"

"Come along! Come along!"

We now found we were about to be shut out, and this messenger had come out to warn us that the gate was about to be closed. We made haste, as we did not at all relish the thought of being kept all night outside the walls. We were just in, no more. We entered, and the gate closed behind us. "*The door was shut*" (Matt. 25:10).

The lesson we learned was "Make haste!" — a lesson which some of us never forgot. So near being *shut out* of the earthly Jerusalem! What if it were to be not almost but altogether shut out of the Heavenly City! No time to lose. Too much lost already!

—Andrew Bonar

* * *

"Come Over Here, Father!"

Dr. R. A. Torrey told a touching story about a man in Chicago who had a sweet little daughter. He loved her dearly, but God took the little child away from him. The house was so lonely and he was so angry against God, that he walked up and down in his room far into the night cursing God for having robbed him of his child. At last, thoroughly worn out, and in great bitterness, he threw himself on his bed. He dreamed he stood beside a river. Across the river, in the distance, he heard the singing of such voices as he had never listened to before. Then he saw beautiful little girls coming toward him, nearer and nearer, until at last at the head of the company, he saw his own little girl. She stood on the brink of the river and called across, "Come over here, father!" That overcame his bitterness. He accepted Jesus and prepared to go over yonder where his sweet child had gone.   W. B. K.

* * *

Looking Through the Paling

Some years ago in Dayton, Ohio, a small girl learned to love the Saviour and became an earnest Christian. She loved her father very dearly, but her father was not a Christian, and was not concerned much about the church nor its work.

Each evening as the father would come home from his work, the little daughter would meet him at the gate. The gate was high, and the palings were close together. In order that the child might see through the gate to tell when her father was coming, the father tore off one of the palings from the gate. Each night when the father came home

from work his little Christian daughter was waiting for him, eagerly looking through the paling for his coming.

Finally, the little girl became sick. As she grew worse, the father was heartbroken and did not know what to do. He loved his child more than he did his own life. Just before she died, his little daughter, looking up at her father, said,

"When I get to Heaven I will ask God to pull a paling from off Heaven's gate so I can look through to see you come."

Her last words were, "Papa, I will be looking for you." This greatly touched the father's heart, and he became an earnest Christian.

—*Gospel Herald*

* * *

Are All the Children In?

Are all the children in? The night is falling,
And storm clouds gather in the threatening west;
The lowing cattle seek a friendly shelter;
The bird flies to her nest;
The thunder crashes; wilder grows the tempest,
And darkness settles o'er the fearful din;
Come, shut the door, and gather round the hearthstone —
Are all the children in?

Are all the children in? The night is falling,
When gilded sin doth walk about the street,
Oh, at last it biteth like a serpent!
Poisoned are stolen sweets.
O mothers! guard the feet of inexperience,
Too prone to wander in the paths of sin!
Oh, shut the door of love against temptation!
Are all the children in?

Are all the children in? The night is falling,
The night of death is hastening on apace;
The Lord is calling: "Enter thou thy chamber,
And tarry there a space."

And when He comes, the King in all
His glory,
Who died the shameful death our hearts
to win,
Oh, may the gates of heaven shut about
us,
With all the children in.
—Elizabeth Rosser

* * *

The "Home" We've Not Seen
A refugee from Hitler's Europe tells
of his boyhood when so many tales were
told about America that he felt that all
the family knew this country well. So
settled was this knowledge and love of
the land he had not yet seen that his
mother said to him when he was leaving for America, "You are going home,
I am staying in a foreign land." The
Christian who realizes the tyranny of
life in this world is glad to escape to
the land that is fairer than day. And
when our loved ones go before, we are
forced to say, with tears that are for
ourselves, "You are going Home, and I
am staying in a foreign land."
—*Good News Digest*

* * *

What the Chinese Girl Saw
"Next door to us lived a widow with
her three daughters. The youngest, a
girl of about seventeen, was taken ill
with rapid consumption. As the end
drew near her mother and sisters were
by her bedside weeping. At last all
seemed over. Several moments passed
as the broken-hearted mother gave way
unrestrainedly to her grief. Then suddenly the dying girl opened her eyes
and said distinctly, with joy and peace
written on her face, 'I've come back to
tell you I've seen. I've seen. . . .Oh, it's
wonderful, wonderful!' Then she was
gone. Later, when telling us, the
mother said, 'I could no longer weep,
but only praise.' It is not uncommon
for our Chinese Christians when describing the dying scene of a Christian
friend or relative which they have witnessed, to say they seemed to catch
glimpses of something wonderful just
before passing away."
—Rosalind Goforth, in
Sunday School Times

The Inevitable Alternative
A skeptic once derided a Christian
man by asking him: "Say, George, what
would you say if when you die you found
there wasn't such a place as heaven
after all?"
With a smile the believer replied: "I
should say — well, I've had a fine time
getting there anyway!"
Then the Christian sent a boomerang
back to the skeptic — a question not
quite so easy to answer.
"I say, Fred," he asked, "what would
you say if, when you die, *you found
there was such a place as hell after all?*"
—*Free Methodist*

* * *

The Swan and the Crane
There is an old legend of a swan and
a crane. A beautiful swan alighted by
the banks of the water in which a crane
was wading about seeking snails. For a
few moments the crane viewed the
swan in stupid wonder and then inquired:
"Where did you come from?"
"I came from heaven!" replied the
swan.
"And where is heaven?" asked the
crane.
"Heaven!" said the swan. "Heaven!
have you never heard of heaven?" And
the beautiful bird went on to describe
the grandeur of the Eternal city. She
told of the streets of gold and the gates
and walls of precious stones; of the river
of life, pure as crystal, upon whose
banks is the tree whose leaves shall be
for the healing of all nations. In eloquent terms the swan sought to describe
the hosts who live in the other world,
but without arousing the slightest interest on the part of the crane.
Finally, the crane asked, "Are there
any snails there?"
"Snails," repeated the swan, "no, of
course there are not."
"Then," said the crane, as it continued its search along the slimy banks
of the pools, "you can have your heaven.
I want snails!"
*How many a young person to whom
God has granted the advantages of a
Christian home, has turned his back up-*

on it and searched for snails! How many a man will sacrifice his wife, his family, his all, for the snails of sin! How many a girl has deliberately turned from the love of parents and home to learn too late that heaven has been forfeited by snails!

—D. L. Moody

* * *

"Toward the Sunset!"

"I am trav'ling toward the sunset,
All is calm and all is well;
And the golden tints tow'ring heav'nward,
Are but Nature's crowning spell.
There is quiet midst the shadows,
For the day's turmoil is spent.
Past the noon with all its travail!
Past the hours of stress and strife!
Fleeting ecstasy and triumph,
Mingled in a plodding life.
There is rapture in the sunset
And the pathway, smooth and straight;
I am longing for the sunrise,
Of that glad resplendent day,
Then the climax and the glory
With the earthlife far away."

—Frank Wilford

* * *

"I Own Everything!"

Dr. George W. Truett was entertained on one occasion in the home of a wealthy oil man in Texas. After the dinner the man took him up to the roof of his house and indicated huge fields of oil derricks, and said, "Dr. Truett, that's all mine. I came to this country twenty-five years ago penniless, and now I own everything as far as you can see in that direction." Then he turned to the opposite direction and indicated waving fields of grain and said again, "It's all mine. I own everything as far as you can see in that direction." Then he turned to the east, and pointed to huge herds of cattle and said again, "It's all mine, everything as far as you can see in that direction is mine." One final time he turned toward the west and pointed to a great virgin forest, and said again, "It's all mine. Twenty-five years ago I was penniless, but I worked hard and saved, and today I own every-

thing as far as you can see in this direction, that direction, that direction and this direction." He paused for the expected praise, but to his astonishment it didn't come. Dr. Truett laid a hand lovingly on his shoulder, pointed upward and said, "My friend, how much do you own in that direction?" The man dropped his head in shame and said, "I never thought of that."

—*Western Recorder*

* * *

Why He Didn't Mind the Journey

A small boy sat quietly in a seat of the day coach on a train running between two of the Western cities in the United States. It was a hot, dusty day, very uncomfortable for traveling, and that particular ride was perhaps the most uninteresting day's journey in the whole land. But the little fellow sat patiently watching the fields and the fences hurrying by, until a motherly old lady, leaning forward, asked sympathetically, "Aren't you tired of the long ride, dear, and the dust and the heat?" The lad looked up brightly, and replied, with a smile, "Yes, ma'am, a little. But I don't mind it much, because my father is going to meet me when I get to the end of it." What a beautiful thought it is that when life seems wearisome and monotonous, as it sometimes does, we can look forward hopefully and trustingly, and like the lonely little lad, not "mind it much" because our Father, too, will be waiting to meet us at our journey's end! Father will meet us at the end of the journey — thank God!

—*Bible Expositor and Illuminator*

* * *

Good Night and Goodby

One of God's children, as he was entering life, turned to his Christian wife and daughter, and said "Good night, my dear wife. We'll meet in the morning! Good night, daughter, the separation is but for a short while!" "Then, he said to his unsaved son, "Goodby, son!" "Why," asked the son, "did you say 'Good-by' to me, and 'Good Night' to mother and sister?" "Well, son," said the dying father lovingly and tenderly, "you, through the years, have rejected Christ. The saved and the unsaved have different destinies. The lost are eternally separated from God, and their loved ones 'who die in the Lord." God's Spirit brought deep conviction of sin to the heart of the young son. Weepingly, he said, "Dad, I here and now receive Christ as my personal Saviour, and we will not be separated in the Yonderland!"

—W. B. K.

* * *

Something Else Needed

He was in a hurry when he came into the compound. You could tell his message was important. "My mother is afraid that she is dying, and she would like a Christian to come to see her." "Is your mother a Christian?" we asked. His reply, though just a sentence, revealed the emptiness of religion: "We are Buddhists, but Mother wants something else now." Two Chinese Christian women hurried to the man's house to visit the dying woman. Quietly they told of the love of Christ, and just as quietly she took Him as her personal Saviour. Morning broke on the second day. She could not live. Her son knelt beside her to tell her he would go again to get the doctor. But she raised her hand to stop him and said, "No, Son, I do not wish to get well now, for I would rather go to my new home, where I can be with Jesus." She is with Him now.

—From *The Lifted Light*
China Inland Mission

* * *

The Homeland

"THINK —
Of stepping on shore and finding it Heaven;
Of taking hold of a hand and finding it God's hand;
Of breathing a new air and finding it celestial air;
Of feeling invigorated and finding it immortality;
Of passing from storm and tempest to an unbroken calm;
Of looking up — and finding it HOME!"   —Myrtle Erickson

"They Have Arrived!"

There are Christians of a certain tribe in Africa who never say of their dead "who die in the Lord" that "they have departed!" Speaking, as it were, from the vantage point of the Gloryworld, they trimumphantly and joyously say, "THEY HAVE ARRIVED!" What joy, even in sorrow, is our's when we say of our loved ones, who enter life eternal trusting Jesus, "ABSENT FROM THE BODY — AT HOME WITH THE LORD!"

—W. B. K.

* * *

"Heaven At Last!"

"On the jasper threshold standing,
Like a pilgrim safely landing,
See the strange, bright scenes expanding,
Ah, 'tis heaven at last!

"What a city, what a glory,
Far beyond the fairest story,
Of the ages, old and hoary,
Ah, 'tis heaven at last!

"Christ Himself the living splendor,
Christ, the Sunshine, mild and tender,
Praises to the Lamb we render,
Ah, 'tis heaven at last!"

—*Selected*

* * *

Why She Rejoiced

Though we may have little of this world's goods we have much for which to praise God. A woman was dying in the poorhouse. The doctor bent over her and heard her whisper, "Praise the Lord." "Why, auntie," he said, "how can you praise God when you are dying in a poorhouse?" "Oh, doctor," she replied, "it's wonderful to go from the poorhouse to a mansion in the skies!"

—*The Christian*

* * *

Where He Was Miserable

I heard once of a betting man on his way to some horse races who, by mistake, went on board the wrong steamer. He found himself among a lot of Christians bound for a conference. In the salon, on deck, everywhere, hymns were being sung, and conversations going on of which the things of Christ were the topic. The man felt completely out of place, and his discomfiture ended in his offering the captain a good round sum of money to be put down at the nearest landing place. People talk easily enough about going to Heaven when they die, but they forget that unless they have been made fit for the place, and have received a nature that can enjoy the things of God, they would be as miserable in Heaven as that betting man was among the Christians on the steamer.

—Good News

* * *

Soon to be in Heaven

When Billy Bray was taken with his last illneess, he asked: "Well, doctor, how is it?" "You are going to die." "Glory, glory be to God! I shall soon be in Heaven." He then added in a low tone, and in his own peculiar way, "When I get up there shall I give them your compliments, doctor, and tell them you will be coming, too?"

—The Witness

* * *

The Lights of Home!

A fierce storm was sweeping the great lakes. A steam tug towing a barge began to founder. The captain and his mates took to a small boat. All night long they tossed to and fro, every instant in jeopardy of their lives. In the morning they were rescued by a passing ship. The captain afterward testified that all the long night as they were beaten and tossed by the tempest there was one thing which nerved their arms and kept their hearts from sinking in despair. It was this — shining through the darkness and the storm they saw the lights of home.

—James H. McConkey

* * *

"The Door Is Open"

Dr. T. C. Horton entered an elevator one day and called for the floor at which he wished to stop. Always ready to seize an opportunity to tell what God had done for a world of lost sinners, he turned to the elevator boy, and asked, "Are you bound for Heaven or hell?" "I don't know," the startled young man replied. When the desired floor was reached, the elevator stopped, and the door was opened. But Dr. Horton made no move to go. The elevator boy waited a moment, and then said to him, "Why don't you go? The door is open." "So is the door of Heaven," answered Dr. Horton, walking out, and leaving the young man to make the very obvious application.

—Sunday School Times

* * *

Only a Step

Entering a crowded street car, with his Bible under his arm, a young minister soon became the brunt of sneering remarks and wisecracks from the group of fellows. These remarks continued, and when the minister left the car, one youth said, "Say, mister, how far is it to heaven?" The Christian replied, "It is only a step; will you take it now?"

—Power

* * *

Only Chips

You may spiritualize the foundations and gates, but I do not. An amethyst is an amethyst. I have seen the crown jewels of England, and I admire precious stones. When I go to the office of a merchant in precious stones, he will say to me, "Dr. Buhler, would you like to look at the stones?" Then he spreads out a great, dark purple velvet cushion. Locking the door, he goes to his enormous safe and takes out his diamonds and rubies and emeralds and amethysts, and throws them down, and there before my eyes, is oh, such beauty, such glory! I feast my eyes upon them. Then I remember the Devil would tempt me to covet them, and I say to him, "These are only chips of the great foundations of the City of God."

—Dawn

* * *

Have You the Passport?

Pilgrims need passports. For many years they have been required of travelers entering most countries, and it never has been possible to go from earth to Heaven without one. A passport is "a document issued by the government of a country to one of its citizens or subjects, certifying to his nationality." During his many years of service in Belgium, Ralph Norton kept his American citizenship by renewing his passport at regular intervals. It is a striking fact that this document, so important to Mr. Norton on earth, expired on the day of his operation. But it was fast losing its value in his eyes, for he was no longer "mindful of that country from whence he came out," and his face was turned eagerly toward "a better country, that is, an heavenly." Long before he ever needed an American passport he had, by faith, and "without money and without price," obtained his passport to that Better Country, which never needed to be renewed; and for many years he had been able to say, "My 'citizenship is in heaven.'" He had "boldness to enter into the holiest by the blood of Jesus, by a new and living way, which he hath consecrated for us, through the veil, that is to say, his flesh" (Heb. 10:19, 20). A few weeks after his operation, Mr. Norton, bearing his passport signed by the Sovereign of his own Homeland, triumphantly crossed the Frontier.

—Sunday School Times

* * *

"No Glass Between"

A story is told of a poor boy in London. His parents were dead, and he was the charge of a terrible drunken woman, who forced him to beg, and met him with kicks and cuffs if he brought her too little. His greatest pleasure in life was to see the beautiful things exhibited in shop windows. He knew, though, that these things were not meant for him, for there was always the glass between, and he became reconciled to the thought that he could never have them. The lead soldiers had focused his longing for them — but there was the glass. Alas, he was run over, carried to the hospital, and cared for by Christian charity. He awoke to find himself in a snow-white cot, and he looked into the pleasant face

of a nurse. A few days passed, and then to his astonishment he saw other children playing with toys. Soon he sat up in bed, propped up by pillows, and, wonder of wonders, at his hand was a box of lead soldiers. Slowly he stretched his hand out, touched them, and cried out: "There is no glass between." How will it seem when in the Glory we no longer see "through a glass, darkly"?

—The Expositor

* * *

Whose Fault If We Miss the View?

The two were walking along a suburban road. It could hardly be called a road, it was so deep in mud after a sudden storm. Their feet were clogged, their hats were soaked with the drippings from the trees, and they were still a mile or so from shelter. "Of all the bad roads I ever saw, this is the worst," the man exclaimed. "Oh, look," said the girl. She stood still at the spot where the road turned. Far off, under the rain-washed sky, the towering buildings and gleaming roofs of the city lay as in a picture, soft and clear in the late sunlight. "Isn't it beautiful? And on this muddy road, too! It's like getting a glimpse of the New Jerusalem as one goes plodding along the roads of the world, isn't it? Who cares for the mud after seeing that?" No road is mean or prosaic that has such glimpses. The Christian cannot find a path, no matter how obscure, from which the vision of the city of God cannot be glimpsed every day. If he thinks only of the mud, and never looks toward the view — well, whose fault is it?

—Free Churchman

* * *

Why He Called "Here"

A fierce battle had been fought and the hospital tents were crowded. Surgeons and doctors were hurrying to help and succor. Suddenly from a cot, where lay a youth who had not uttered a sound, came a clear call that rang out in the darkness, "Here." The surgeon ran, thinking he must be in great distress. "What do you want?" the surgeon asked. "Nothing," the young man said, "they are calling the roll in Heaven and I have just answered to my name." There must be a book of life and there must be a book of death. We will be blessed indeed to be able to answer "Here" to our call to the names inscribed in the Lamb's Book of Life.

—*Sunday School Times*

* * *

Samples

A Jewish legend tells us that during the famine in Canaan Joseph ordered his officers to throw wheat and chaff upon the waters of the Nile that the people below might see that there was plenty above. God puts upon the river of life some of the wheat from the heavenly fields in order that we, having a taste of it, may desire more, and seek things that are above.

—From *Heaven on Earth*, by A. C. Dixon

* * *

"Doing God's Business!"

The story is told that when Henry Ward Beecher and a friend were once walking together in a cemetery in Brooklyn, Mr. Beecher said: "Well, I suppose they will be bringing me out here before very long, and leaving me here, but God knows I won't stay here." "Where shall we look for you, Mr. Beecher?" asked his friend. "Somewhere, doing business for God," was the reply.

—George W. Truett

* * *

Not Even the End

A lawyer who knows and loves the Lord tells of a tragic case, in a letter to a friend. "I just got back yesterday from a trip in connection with the sudden death of a client's father. He was a member of a rich and aristocratic family . . . . . I had a delicate and difficult family controversy on my hands for two days, with the silent form of the poor old vacated body in our midst. He was a yachtsman and sportsman, and the pictures of his dogs and boats hung above his casket. His duck guns and Persian rugs were on every hand, and

his trophies; and how futile it all seemed with that greenish white pallor on the still face. When my own father died, it seemed like a beginning; here it seemed like an end."

—*Sunday School Times*

* * *

Worth-while "Foolishness"

When Pepper Martin, the Cardinal's hero of the 1931 World's Series, was asked, "What is your chief ambition?" he answered, "My chief ambition is to go to Heaven!" His flippant questioner guffawed, "You want to play a harp, eh?" "Mister," said Martin, "I don't think that's funny. People don't want to be ignoble, I guess, but they surely are so without thinking. If there is anything foolish in reading the Bible every day and believing its contents; if there's anything funny about wanting to enter Heaven when you leave this life, then I'm afraid that life in this world is not worth living."

—*Now*

* * *

Heaven, The Believer's Homeland!

I had dropped in upon an old friend of my boyhood days. She was one of God's own saints. Rich in experience, she was ripe for the coming glory. She had gone so far in life's pilgrimage that her mind was slightly beclouded, and her memory affected. As I rose to go home she arose also and said, "I want to go home." "But mother," said her daughter, "you are home now." At that she looked a bit dazed. Then looking at me with a tender smile she said with a profound touch of pathos in her voice — "*I want to go home before it gets dark.*"

I opened the door and started homeward. The twilight sky was still aglow with the vanishing glory of the sunset. Beyond it lay the glory of the Father's House. My soul was tingling with the spiritual message my dear friend's words had brought me. What an unspeakable blessing for God's children to reach home before it gets dark! Before the darkness of broken body and failing health; of dimmed senses and clouded faculties; of physical suffering and infirmities; of vanished faces, voices, and fellowships — before all these come, how blessed it is to reach home before it gets dark.

—James H. McConkey

* * *

"A Prepared Place for A Prepared People!"

During the World War a luxurious French villa lay in the path of the oncoming armies. Although deserted, it was shelled and left with great gaping holes in its stone sides. A few swine, which had somehow escaped extermination, rooted their way into the magnificently furnished drawing room. Over the rich, velvet carpet they tracked their muddy feet, overturned the upholstered furniture, tore the expensive draperies and chewed whatever gave any promise of satisfying their hunger. The beauty, the elegance, the cultural characteristics of the place meant nothing to the best nature. They were not partakers of the intellectual or spiritual qualities of the owner.

To the unregenerated millions of earth, the glories of Heaven would be like the French villa was to the swine. They are not partakers of the Divine nature and would have no capacity for enjoying the holy atmosphere of the Glory Land.

—*Gospel Herald*

* * *

"It Comes From Heaven!"

Grand old Hadyn, sick and worn out, was carried for the last time into the music hall, and there he heard his own oratorio of the "Creation." History says that as the orchestra came to the famous passage, "Let there be light!" the whole audience rose and cheered, and Haydn waved his hand toward Heaven, and said: "It comes from there." Overwhelmed with his own music, he was carried out in his chair, and as he came to the door he spread his hand toward the orchestra as in benediction. Haydn was right when he waved his hand toward Heaven, and said: "It comes from there."

—*Sword of the Lord*

* * *

That's What Lets You In

A London waif, cold and hungry, was invited one night, by a city missionary to one of the houses of refuge for little wanderers. He was told to ring the bell, and when they asked him who he was, to say the three words, "In His name." He ventured up the steps and, true to the promise of the worker, received a royal welcome, and with a good supper and a warm bed dreamed that he was in Heaven. A few days after, he was hurt in a London thoroughfare by a passing wagon. The card of the rescue home was found in his pocket, and he was taken to the hospital, and word was sent to the mission. He was tenderly nursed during the few lingering days of his life, and gently taught of that other portal which was also entered "in His name." And often in his last hours he would repeat over and over again, " 'In His name,' that's what lets you in."

—Rev. A. B. Simpson

* * *

The Heavenward Pull!

"I had preached a sermon in an eastern city when a man came to me to say, 'Would you like to shake hands with a redeemed drunkard?' I assured him that I would. He put his hand in mine and said, 'Listen to my story. I once had one of the best positions in this city, but strong drink was my destruction. I was one day helplessly lying in the gutter when some one, taking me by the hand, said, 'If you want to see your boy alive, hurry home! Quickly, I went up to the room where my sin had forced my wife and boy to live, and found that a great truck had passed over the child and he was dying. He took me by the hand and pulled me down by his side and said, 'I will not let you go until you promise to meet me in Heaven,' and, holding my hand, he died. They had to break away his hand clasp from this hand of mine,' said he, holding it up, 'and from that day till this I have felt him pulling me heavenward.' This is true of every one who has a loved one yonder."

—J. Wilbur Chapman

* * *

"Only Glory By and By!"

You are doubtlessly familiar with the story of the retreat of ten thousand Greeks under Zenophon. After great hardships and privations, they finally came to the top of a lofty hill from which, in the distance, they saw the blue waves of the Mediterranean. Its gentle wavelets flashed in the light of the morning sun! From thousands of throats rang the joyous shout, "The Sea! The Sea!" In that time of jubilation, battle-wearied soldiers forgot their months of weary marching and nameless priva-

tions. Yonder were home and their waiting loved ones! Some day, we, too, will come to a "mountain top," from whose vantage point we'll behold the eternal city which hath foundation and whose builder and maker is God. There, the loved ones who have "died in the Lord" are waiting to welcome us into the "everlasting habitations." Then, we'll forget the battles fought, the sorrow and sufferings, the privations and persecutions! Then, we'll know the full meaning of the wondrous words, which say, "For I reckon the sufferings of this present time are not worthy to be compared with the glory which shall be revealed in us." (Rom. 8:18).

"Only glory by and by,
Only glory by and by;
Every heart ache gone forever,
Only glory by and by!"

—W. B. K.

HELL

The "Here" Shapes the "After"

"I'm tired of all this preaching about the hereafter," said one. "I'm living now, and I mean to have a good time. The hereafter isn't here yet." Her companion said: "No, only the first part of it. But I shouldn't wonder if the 'here' had a good deal to do with shaping the 'after.'"

—*Forward*

* * *

What Then?

After the joys of earth,
After its song of mirth,
After its hours of light,
After its dreams so bright —
      What then?

Only an empty name,
Only a weary frame,
Only a conscience smart,
Only an aching heart,
After this empty name,
After this weary frame,
After this conscience smart,
After this aching heart,
      What then?

Only a sad farewell,
To a world loved too well,
Only a silent bed,
With the forgotten dead.
      What then?

Oh, then — the judgment throne,
Then all the woes that dwell
Oh then — the last hope — gone!
In an eternal Hell!

—*Selected*

* * *

Separated!

"I understand you and your wife are going to be separated," said a friend to a well-known judge.

"How dare you insinuate any such thing?" shouted the judge, his face purple with anger. "My wife and I love each other very much."

"Is that so?" queried the friend, "Well, I heard from your doctor that she has only a short time to live, and since I know she is a Christian she will go to be with her Lord. Where are you going when you die?"

The judge stood awhile quietly thinking. His face began to pale as the words took effect.

He cried out, "My God, save me. All these years I have been turning away from Thee. Forgive me, God, and save me."

—*Gospel Herald*

* * *

"Extinguishing" the Bible

An old colored preacher of the South was asked by a Northerner why it was that colored ministers preached so much about hell. "Well, sah," he replied, "I don't knows just why dat am, but I done suppose dat de reason am cause we culled folks haven't got learnin' enough to splanify de tex and extinguish de Bible like you white folks am." We must admit there is more truth than poetry in his statement.

—*Sunday School Times*

* * *

How to Keep Tender

Andrew Bonar and Robert Mac Cheyne were having one of their frequent talks together, talking over the ways of their ministry, when "Mac Cheyne asked me," says Bonar, "what my last sabbath's subject had been. It had been, 'The wicked shall be turned into hell.' On hearing this awful text, he asked, 'Were you able to preach it with tenderness?' "

Shall we repeat Robert MacCheyne's question to one another? When we speak of the destiny of the sinful, or on any one of the awful severities of the Word, are we "able to preach it with tenderness," with a melting heart, with secret tears? They say that Mac Cheyne's severities were terrific, they were so tender! He lived enfolded in the companionship of the Holy Ghost. *He was ever holding converse with Him, and how could he become hard?*

—*Pentecostal Evangel*

* * *

Looking into the Furnace

An old Scotch preacher was passing a glass factory just before going to the church to preach. As a door was ajar,

and it was some time till the service, he stepped inside. One of the large furnaces had just been opened. He gazed into the white, blue, and purple mass of liquid flame until it nearly seared his face. As he turned away unaware of anyone being present, he exclaimed, "Ho mon, what shall hell be like!" A stoker standing in the shadow heard him. Several nights later at the church a man came up to him. "You don't know me, but the other night when you stepped into the furnace room I heard what you said. Every time I have opened that furnace since then the words ring in my mind, 'What shall hell be like!' I have come tonight to find out the way of salvation so that I will not have to find out what hell is like."

—*Christian Beacon*

* * *

A Tragic Death-Bed

A young woman, dying, said to her father, "Father, why did you not tell me there was such a place?" "What place?" "A hell!" He said, "Jenny, there is no such place. God is merciful. There will be no future suffering!" She said, "I know better! My feet are slipping into it at this moment. I am lost. Why did you not tell me there was such a place?"

—*Sunday School Times*

* * *

Time To Resign

On an American troopship, the soldiers crowded around their chaplain asking, "Do you believe in hell?" "I do not." "Well, then, will you please resign, for if there is no hell, we do not need you, and if there is a hell, we do not wish to be led astray."

—*Christian Beacon*

* * *

Not Likely to Catch Up

"You're just out of date," said young Pastor Bate to one of our faithful old preachers who had carried for years, in travail and tears, the Gospel to poor sinful creatures. "You still preach on Hades, and shock cultured ladies, with your barbarous doctrine of blood. You're

285

so far behind, you will never catch up; you're a flat tire, stuck in the mud." For some little while a wee bit of a smile enlightened the old pastor's face. Being made the butt of ridicule's cut did not ruffle his sweetness or grace. Then he turned to young Bate, so suave and said, "Catch up, did you say? Well, I couldn't succeed if I doubled my speed. My friend, I'm not going your way!"
—*Christian Victory*

*   *   *

"Surrender, Or . . ."

Aachen had been surrounded by the American forces. Hitler had sent orders to the Nazi commander to stand and die in the city's defense. But the American commander gave the city an opportunity to surrender before destroying it.

Lt. General Courtney H. Hodges sent an ultimatum to the Nazi commander and to the mayor of this city of 165,000 souls. Then thousands of leaflets were dropped into the city by shellfire, appealing to the troops and citizens of Aachen to surrender and thus prevent needless bloodshed.

"Aachen is encircled," read the leaflets, "American troops surround the city. The German command cannot relieve you.

"People of Aachen! The time has come for honorable surrender. We Americans do not wage war on innocent civilians. But if the leaders insist on further sacrifice, we have no course but to destroy your city.

"There is no time to lose. On our airfields, bombers are waiting for final orders to take off. Our artillery surrounding the city is ready to fire. People of Aachen, act quickly. Tomorrow may be too late. There is only one choice, immediate surrender or complete destruction."

But the Germans did not surrender. Great destruction ensued! How like Christ-rejectors today! They are warned to flee from the coming wrath. They are warned of the doom of Christ-rejectors. Still, they heedlessly hot-foot the road of vice, whose terminus is endless remorse and separation from God! All who go to hell go there as usupers. It

is a prepared place for the devil and his angels. O, how much God has done to save souls from Hell! He gave His Son to die a vicarious death to save men from the eternal burnings!
—W. B. K.

*   *   *

Why Are Men Lost?

A fellow said to me on the train one day, "Oh, you preachers make me sick." "I am not a preacher," I replied; "I wish I were. I don't know enough." He said: "I don't care what you are. You Christians are always talking about a man going to hell because Adam sinned." "No," I said, "you will never go to hell because Adam sinned. You will go to hell because you refuse the remedy provided for Adam's sin. Don't you go to crying about something that has absolutely been taken care of. If you go to hell you will go over the broken body of Jesus Christ who died to keep you out."
—From *The Double Cure*,
by Melvin E. Trotter

*   *   *

A Possibility But Not A Necessity

When a Brooklyn traffic officer handed Miss Margaret Greenberg a ticket, she told him, according to press report, "You can go to hell." When she appeared in court, Magistrate Mark Rudich dismissed the officer's complaint about her language, saying, "It wasn't a command or a wish, but a simonpure statement of a fact, for going to hell *is* a possibility." Multitudes today have forgotten this possibility, or like to deny it. A humorous magazine, poking fun at "advanced theology," remarked, "Nowadays most of the churches and preachers are so advanced that it takes considerable ingenuity to get into hell." It is dubious charity for sinners that obscures or ignores the plain warnings of Jesus.
—*Evangelical-Messenger*

*   *   *

Last Chance

Quite some years ago, Bishop Phillips Brooks became quite ill and would see no visitors. When Robert Ingersoll, the agnostic, heard that his friend was sick, he called at his home to see him and was admitted at once. "I appreciate this very much," said Mr. Ingersoll, "but why do you see me when you deny yourself to all your friends?" "It's this way," answered the bishop. "I feel confident of seeing my other friends in the next world, but this may be my last chance to see you."

—Emery G. Young, in
Coronet

HOLY SPIRIT

There for the Taking

I left the prayer meeting and crept out into the lane, away from town. As I walked I said, "O my God, if there is a man who needs the power of the Holy Ghost to rest upon him it is I; but I do not know how to receive Him. I am too tired, too worn, too nervously down to agonize." A voice said to me, "As you took forgiveness from the hand of the dying Christ, take the Holy Ghost from the hand of the living Christ." I turned to Christ and said, "Lord, I breathe in this whiff of warm night air, so I breathe into every part of me Thy blessed Spirit." I felt no hand laid upon my head, there was no lambent flame, there was no rushing sound from Heaven; but by faith, without emotion, without excitement, I took, and took for the first time, and I have kept on taking ever since.

—F. B. Meyer, in *The Overcomer*

* * *

"Waves of Liquid Love!"

Charles G. Finney says of his own experience, "As I turned and was to take a seat by the fire, I received the mighty Baptism of the Holy Spirit. The Holy Ghost descended upon me in a manner that seemed to go through me, body and soul. I could feel the impressions like a wave of electricity going through and through me. Indeed, it seemed to come in waves and waves of liquid love; for I could not express it in any other way. I wept aloud with joy and love; and I do not know, but I should say I literally bellowed the unutterable gushings of my heart."

In his writings, Charles G. Finney says, "He who neglects to obey the command to be filled with the Spirit, is as guilty of breaking the command of God, as he who steals, or curses, or commits adultery. His guilt is as great as the authority of God is great, who commands us to be filled. His guilt is equivalent to all the good he might do if he were filled with the Spirit."

—*Elim Evangel*

* * *

What Held Up the Revival

Harry Moorehouse, while still a young man, was conducting evangelistic services in a certain city in this country, but there was no revival. God had given precious revivals both in America and in Great Britain, but in this city it was as though he were beating against a stone wall. Day and night he was on his knees searching his heart and crying out, "O God, why is there no revival?" One day he was walking along the street, and the Holy Spirit showed him a large placard on which appeared these words: "Harry Moorehouse, the most famous of all British preachers!" At once he said to himself, "That is why there is no revival!" He went at once to the campaign committee, and said, "Brethren, now I know why there is no revival. See how you have advertised me as the greatest of this and the greatest of that! No wonder the Holy Spirit cannot work! He is grieved and quenched because you haven't magnified the Lord Jesus Christ. 'He' is the wonderful One. I'm just a poor, simple, humble servant, preaching the glorious Gospel, and saying, 'Behold the Lamb of God that taketh away the sins of the world.' "

—*Alliance Weekly*

Our Best—Nothing, Without Him

Mr. Spurgeon once preached what in his judgment was one of his poorest sermons. He stammered and floundered, and when he got through he felt that it had been a complete failure. He was greatly humiliated, and when he got home he fell on his knees and said, "Lord, God, Thou canst do something with nothing. Bless that poor sermon." And all through the week he uttered that prayer. He woke up in the night and prayed about it. He determined that the next Sunday he would redeem himself by preaching a great sermon. Sure enough, the next Sunday the sermon went off beautifully. At the close the people crowded about him and covered him with praise. Spurgeon went home pleased with himself, and that night he slept like a baby. But he said to himself, "I'll watch the results of those two sermons." What were they? From the one that had seemed a failure he was able to trace forty-one conversions. And from that magnificent sermon he was unable to discover that a single soul was saved. Spurgeon's explanation was that the Spirit of God used the one and did not use the other. We can do nothing without the Spirit who helpeth our infirmities.

—Christian Digest

* * *

Strong Enough To Bear the Load

In England, some of our bridges have a red diamond-shaped symbol at either end. It is a warning to those who would cross that the bridge is limited as to the weight it can take. If, therefore, a lorry driver comes with a ten-ton wagon to a bridge which cannot take more than five tons, he must make a detour and find another bridge that is strong enough to bear the load. Some Christians have that diamond-shaped symbol against them, too. God has had to put a warning: "This believer, very energetic, cannot stand the strain of injustice." Hence, when God would use us He cannot, and He must needs find another. Is this the reason you have not fulfilled the purpose God has for you? Is this the reason you are put aside? And do you

feel it to be an impossibility for you to be patient, to suffer unjustly, to forgive in the spirit of Christ? Are you crying out, like Mary, "How shall this be?" Then, hear the answer of that angelic voice: *"The Holy Ghost."*

—King's Business

* * *

How Enemy Was Overcome!

A remarkable visitation of the Spirit, a demonstration of answer to prayer, is recorded by the Rev. Reuben Emerson of Wakefield, Mass. An organized band of infidels was broken up solely through concerted prayer by a few faithful praying Christians. No other means was used. The infidel club held regular meetings to promote their line of thought and attracted many young men of the city. The situation was alarming. It was felt that argument or force would be futile, so they resolved to pray down victory. They were joined by many praying people who learned of their gatherings to pray solely for these spreaders of poison. They claimed the promises and prayed on. One day the infidel leader was brought under powerful conviction. He sought out a Christian and was saved. Then one after another of the band from week to week came under the same conviction. Nearly every member was converted. The whole community acknowledged that it was the work of the divine Spirit. Not a word of controversy or rebuke had been said to these men. Like those at Pentecost, they had asked, "What shall we do?"

—Sunday School Times

* * *

Christ Within

Imagine one without genius and devoid of the artist's training, setting down before Raphael's famous picture of the Transfiguration and attempting to reproduce it. How crude and mechanical and lifeless his work would be! But if such a thing were possible that the spirit of Raphael should enter into the man and obtain mastery of his mind and eye and hand, it would be entirely possible that he should paint this masterpiece; for it would simply be Raphael reproducing Raphael. And this in a mystery is what is true of the disciple filled with the Holy Spirit. Christ by the Spirit dwells within him as a Divine life, and Christ is able to image forth Christ from the interior life of the outward example."

—A. J. Gordon

* * *

For Christians Only

Dr. Torrey used to tell about three persons, a mother, a Sunday School teacher, a Sunday school superintendent, each of whom came to him unknown to the others, and in bitter grief confessed neglecting an impulse to speak to the mother's daughter, who suddenly died. "The Holy Spirit was trying to get the use of three people to save one soul," Dr. Torrey said, "and could not."

—*Gospel Herald*

* * *

In Case of Storm

In a shipping disaster at Samoa, the way in which the British man-of-war *Calliope* escaped, is suggestive. Her machinery was very powerful, and just as she was about to strike the reef, she raised her anchors, and, in the face of the terrible storm, streamed out of the harbor and into the open sea, where she safely outrode the storm. And so in the Christian life, there are times when safety is only to be found in like decisiveness and boldness. Strengthened with all might by His Spirit in the inner man, the soul must bravely go forth to meet its spiritual foes, and boldly attack them.

—C. M. Hawkins, in
Bible Truths Illustrated

* * *

When Moody Preached to the Atheists

In East London during the visit of Moody and Sankey, a hall in the dense working population of that city had been reserved one evening for an address to atheists, skeptics, and freethinkers. Bradlaugh, champion of atheism, hearing of this meeting ordered all clubs he had formed to take possession of the hall. They obeyed and five thousand men marched in from all directions. The atheists laughed when Moody asked the men to choose their favorite hymns for atheists do not sing hymns. Mr. Moody spoke from "Their rock is not as our Rock, even our enemies themselves being judges." He poured in a broadside of telling incidents from his own experience of the deathbeds of Christians and atheists and let the men be the judges as to who had the best foundation to rest their faith upon. He attacked them in their most vulnerable points, their hearts of unbelief. The sermon ended, Mr. Moody announced a hymn, and gave opportunity for all to leave who did not want to stay for the inquiry meeting. Moody was astonished when not one man vacated his seat. After a few words Mr. Moody asked all who would receive Christ to say, "I will." One person, the leading club man, shouted, "I won't!" Moody said: "Men, you have your champion here in the middle of the hall who said, 'I won't.' I ask every man here who believes that man is right to rise and say, 'I won't!' " None arose. "Thank God," said Moody. "Now who'll say, 'I will'?" The Holy Spirit seemed to have broken loose upon that great crowd, and five hundred men sprang to their feet, saying, "I will!" "I will!" till the whole atmosphere was changed, and the battle was won.

—*Alliance Weekly*

* * *

Something Needed Inside

I heard of a poor half-witted fellow whose companion, working beside him, dropped dead. He was found trying to hold up the dead man, trying to make him stand and sit upright. Finding his effort without avail, he was saying to himself, "He needs something inside him." I suspect that is the reason we live at a poor dying rate. We need a living Spirit within to control and uphold us.

—*Sunday School Times*

"Wonderful Harmonies!"

Mendelssohn once visited a cathedral containing one of the most priceless organs in Europe. He listened to the organist, then asked permission to play. "I don't know you," was the reply, "and we don't allow any chance stranger to play upon this organ." At last the great musician persuaded the organist to let him play. As Mendelssohn played, the great cathedral was filled with such music as the organist had never heard. With tears in his eyes he laid his hand upon Mendelssohn's shoulder. "Who are you?" he asked. "Mendelssohn," came the reply. The old organist was dumbfounded. "To think that an old fool like me nearly forbade Mendelssohn to play upon my organ!"

If we only knew what wonderful harmonies the Holy Spirit can draw out of our lives, we should not be content until He has complete possession and is working in us and through us to do His will.

—Senior Teacher, S. B. C.

* * *

Our Aim in Life

The Kurku, a hill tribe in India of some 98,000 people, have as their supreme desire and objective in life to be filled with demons. When filled, they believe, their lives will be immune to attack or harm from the evil forces. Oh yes, they believe in God, a good spirit, who created the world and created them. But he does them no harm, so they worship the evil spirits.

But what would happen if 98,000 of God's people in this land had as their supreme aim in life to be filled with the Holy Spirit? The Church of Christ would awaken, and before very long a veritable stream of missionaries would be going forth that such poor souls as the demon worshippers of India might hear of our Saviour.

—Student Foreign Missions Fellowship

* * *

Filled With the Spirit

On December 26, 1899, at the funeral of D. L. Moody, Dr. Scofield said, "Moody was baptized with the Spirit and knew that he was. It was to him as definite an experience as was his conversion." Moody himself said, 'The blessing came upon me suddenly, like a flash of lightning. For months I had been hungering and thirsting for power in service. I had come to that point that I think I would have died if I had not got it. I remember I was walking the streets of New York. I had no more heart in the business I was about than if I had not belonged to this world at all. Right there, on the street, the fire of God seemed to come upon me so wonderfully that I asked God to stay His hand. I was filled with a sense of God's goodness, and I felt as though I could take the whole world to my heart. This happened years after I was converted.' "

—Elim Evangel

* * *

When the Spirit Leads

The story of missions in more modern times tells of missionaries whose plans have been changed by the Holy Spirit. Judson wanted to go to India, but his course was changed and he went to Burma instead. When David Livingstone was twelve years of age, he read an appeal for missionaries to go to China and he decided to go. His next decision was to be a medical missionary. With this in view he began to complete his medical studies. About the time he was ready to go, the Opium War broke out and Englishmen could not go to China. Robert Moffat was in England at that time telling of the South African mission. Livingstone was interested in Moffat's story and said: "What is the use of waiting for the end of this abominable Opium War? I will go at once to Africa." Thus the Holy Spirit led Livingstone to Africa and the dreadful slave trade was laid bare to the world.

—From God's World Plan,
　　by Mrs. A. L. Aulick

* * *

Everything But Power

A few years ago, I saw a cartoon which all too accurately illustrated the predicament of the Church. A family was leaving on vacation. The car was loaded with baggage and fishing poles, but when the driver stepped on the starter nothing happened. Seeing that the car would not start, the wife spoke up, "I had the footman remove that thing from under the hood so we could carry more baggage — do you suppose that could have anything to do with it?" Yes, lady, that certainly would have something to do with it. But it is very strange that the Church has not discovered that we cannot get anywhere without the power of the Spirit. We have a nice looking car, well streamlined, and with plenty of baggage — but no motor. We are all dressed up to go, but we are not going anywhere . . . . We are faced today with incalculable Satanic power and temptation. Only as we are clothed in the power of Almighty God can we hope to have the victory.

—*Moody Monthly*

* * *

The Greatest Need

"South America needs missionaries full of the Holy Ghost and power. None other need apply. Argentina has plenty of missionaries of the employee type, but few preaching in the power of the Spirit, night after night, to open confession of Christ and abandonment of all sin. My heart bleeds for this need. Are there no young evangelists, their work already owned of God, who will come, pay the price really to dominate the Spanish language, and then pour the oil of God upon these South American multitudes?"

—Norman Lewis, Buenos Aires

* * *

Not Always the Same Method

The Spirit is like the wind. There is mystery, there is power, and we cannot chart the course of the Spirit. He is sovereign to do as He pleases, just as the wind blows where it lists. He did not use the same method or manner with Savonarola and Knox and Luther and Wesley and Moody. Just as there are hurricanes and zephyrs, so the Spirit storms and soothes. He speaks in mighty tornado or gentlest whisper.

The Spirit did not work in the Reformation as He did in the Great Awakening. With Whitefield He blew in one fashion, with Moody in another. The great Awakening was not like the Welsh Revival.

—From *The Wind and the Spirit*, by Vance Havner

* * *

"One Who Falls Down Beside Us"

Miss Estella Myers, a missionary working among the Karre people of French Equatorial Africa, had tried hard to explain to native helpers the meaning of the "Comforter." In order to find something fitting, she had explained the ministry of the Holy Spirit as He encourages, exhorts, admonishes, protects, comforts, and guides the Christian. Finally they exclaimed, "Oh, if anyone would do all that for us, we would say, 'He's the one who falls down beside us.' " When porters, carrying heavy loads on their heads, go long journeys, they may become sick and straggle to the end of the line of carriers. Finally, they may collapse and be killed and eaten by wild animals during the night. If someone passing sees them prostrate there, and stoops to pick them up and help them to safety, they speak of such a person as "the one who falls down beside us." It is this expression which the missionary translator took as the translation of "Comforter" for this is the One who sustains, protects, and keeps the children of God on their journey toward their heavenly Home.

—*Christian Herald*

* * *

"I Only Prayed!"

Newman Hall stood early one morning on the summit of Snowden, in Wales, with a hundred and twenty others who had been attracted hither by the prospect of an unusually grand sunrise. They were not disappointed. As they stood watching the sun tinge the mountain peaks with glory, and sparkle in the lakes, Dr. Hall was invited to preach. He was so overpowered with emotion that he could not preach, but felt moved to pour out his soul in prayer. As he supplicated, the tears rolled down the faces of the people. A superhuman stillness possessed them. Quietly, with solemn awe, they descended the mountain and scattered.

Afterward, visiting this region, the doctor was informed that forty people were converted that morning and had joined the church in that neighborhood. *"But,"* said he, *"I did not say a word to them; I only prayed."*

"Yes, and more wonderful still, they did not know a word you said, for none of them could speak English, only Welsh."

—*Earnest Worker*

* * *

At the Bottom of the Sifter

You see, when Jesus began with His disciples, every one of them was a flesh worker, running on animal heat — *even as you and I.* Two of them, backed by their mother, asked for right and left seats. Were they able to drink Christ's cup; receive His baptism? "Sure! We're able! *Dunametha!* (We're dynamite!)" And Peter was indignant at *their weakness!* So the King set the searchlight on Peter's heart. The Lord let Peter know that *he* was up for collapse: "Satan is going to put *you* in the wheat sifter." "And when thou art converted — when you've hit the bottom and I have lifted you again — strengthen the brethren." Ah, we have sat with Peter in his tossing little boat weeping with him, not for *his* betrayal of our Lord, but for our *own.* And we have cried out, "Alas, dear Saviour, in our flesh there dwelleth no good thing."

—From *FILLED! With the Spirit,* by Richard Ellsworth Day

* * *

Holy Ghost Power

It costs much to obtain the power of the Spirit. It costs self-surrender and humiliation and the yielding up of the most precious things to God. It costs the perseverance of long waiting and the faith of strong trust. But when we are really in that power we shall find this difference, that whereas before it was hard for us to do the easiest things,

now it is easy for us to do the hardest things. James Hervey, the friend of the Wesleys at Oxford, describes the change which took place in him through his anointing by the Spirit: that while his preaching was once like the firing of an arrow, all the speed and force thereof depending on the strength of his arm in bending the bow, now it was like firing a rifle-ball, *the whole force depending upon the powder back of the ball, and needing only a finger-touch to let it off.*

—A. J. Gordon

* * *

Killing the Guide

Sir Samuel Baker relates the following incident: "Many years ago, when the Egyptian troops first conquered Nubia, a regiment was destroyed by thirst in crossing the Nubian desert. The men, being upon a limited allowance of water, suffered from extreme thirst; and, deceived by the appearance of a mirage that exactly resembled a beautiful lake, they insisted on being taken to its banks by the Arab guide. It was in vain that the guide assured them that the lake was unreal, and he refused to lose the precious time by wandering from his course. Words led to blows, and he was killed by the soldiers, whose lives depended upon his guidance. The whole regiment turned from the track and rushed toward the welcome waters. Thirsty and faint, over the burning sands they hurried; heavier and heavier their footsteps became; hotter and hotter their breath as deeper they pushed into the desert, farther and farther from the lost track, where the pilot lay in his blood; and still the mocking spirits of the desert, the afreets of the mirage, led them on, and the lake glistening in the sunshine, tempted them to bathe in its cool waters, close to their eyes, but never at their lips. At length the delusion vanished — the fatal lake had turned to burning sand! Raging thirst and horrible despair! the pathless desert and the murdered guide! Lost! lost! all lost! Not a man ever left the desert, but they were subsequently discovered, parched and withered corpses, by the Arabs sent upon the search."

So sin lures unwary souls from the path of righteousness. The Holy Spirit warns and entreats them. Him they grieve and drive away, and when too late they mourn their folly.

—*Gospel Herald*

* * *

"No Ecstacy, No Fiery Baptism,—But!"

"The Holy Spirit enters the heart, in His fulness, that can boast of nothing but an aching void. Maybe, no ecstacy, no rushing mighty wind, no fiery baptism, but nevertheless, 'the Lord whom ye seek shall suddenly come to His temple.' It is not striving after faith, but resting in the faithful One!"

— Hudson Taylor

* * *

The Holy Spirit's Work

In St. Peter's, Cologne, there are two pictures of the crucifixion of Peter, that stand side by side, and the existence of these two pictures is explained in this way. In the beginning of the 19th century, when Napoleon came and ransacked the city, he robbed St. Peter's of one of those two pictures — the original — and took it away. While the first picture was taken away from the city, the artist, in the absence of the original, painted another picture. In time the original was restored, and the two were placed side by side. Experts now say that there is so little difference between the two pictures you cannot tell which is the original. In the absence of the original, the artist painted another picture of Peter.

Now, that is the glorious work of the Spirit. The Original is absent. *Jesus is in heaven. But the Holy Spirit is here, and He is the master Artist and in the absence of the Original, He is painting the likeness of Jesus upon the unworthy canvas of your life and mine.* May we be worthy copies of the Original! Conformed to His likeness! — Herbert Lockyer, in *The Heritage of Saints.*

How God Led Judson

Adoniram Judson clearly was appointed by the Holy Ghost to the ministry among the heathen. He reached Calcutta in the summer of 1812 full of ardor for preaching the Gospel, only to receive peremptory orders from the British Government to leave the country at once and return to America. With sad hearts the little missionary company retreated to the Isle of France, wondering why what had seemed a wide and effectual door opened to them should now be violently shut. But with unconquerable determination they returned again to India, reaching Madras in the following June. Once more their purpose was thwarted, and once more they were ordered from the country; and being compelled to quit the land, with heavy hearts they fled to Rangoon, to a place which Judson had declared that he regarded with the utmost aversion as a missionary field. There he was permitted to stay, only to find bonds and imprisonments awaiting him. "How mysterious the ways of God!" he must have exclaimed many times. But all is clear now. Judson was forbidden by the Spirit to enter India because God would have him in Burma. There, among its wild tribes, was "a people prepared for the Lord." Park Street Church in Boston, whose call the Spirit constrained Judson to decline, is still a large body, numbering perhaps a thousand members; but the Church in Burma which that same Spirit led Judson to found numbers today thirty thousand communicants.

—A. J. Gordon, in
The Holy Spirit in Missions

* * *

No Competition

A group of clergymen were discussing whether or not they ought to invite Dwight L. Moody to their city. The success of the famed evangelist was brought to the attention of the men.

One unimpressed minister commented, "Does Mr. Moody have a monopoly on the Holy Ghost?"

Another man quietly replied, "No, but the *Holy Ghost* seems to have a monopoly on Mr. Moody."
—*The Chaplain*

* * *

The Spirit-Filled Look

It is related that one day Charles Finney looked at a scoffer, and the scoffer got saved; such was the power of the Spirit in a sanctified life. It is said that Evan Roberts used to look around an assembly, and souls came under conviction; such was the flow of the Spirit's power through a clean channel. The fullness of the Holy Spirit is a reality, and his working partnership is a fact. I walked into a garage one day and found the proprietor swearing at a mechanic. There were two other strangers like myself in the garage at the time, and yet the swearer turned instead to me and apologized. "Don't apologize to me," I said, "you are answerable to God alone for taking his name in vain." That man came under conviction of sin.
—From *Can God — ?* by Edwin Orr

HOME

Mother's Work

Nobody knows of the work it makes,
    To keep the home together:
Nobody knows of the steps it takes
    Nobody knows — but Mother.

Nobody listens to childish woes,
    Which kisses only heal:
Nobody pained by naughty blows,
    Nobody — only Mother.

Nobody knows of sleepless care
    Bestowed on baby brother:
Nobody knows of the tender prayer,
    Nobody — only Mother.

Nobody knows of the lessons taught
    Of loving one another:
Nobody knows of patience sought,
    Nobody — only Mother.

Nobody knows of anxious fears
    Lest darlings may not weather
The storm of life in after years,
    Nobody knows — but Mother.

Nobody kneels at the throne above
To thank the heavenly Father
For the sweetest gift—a Mother's love.
    Nobody can — but Mother.
            — *Selected*

* * *

Tell the Children

Little rows of houses
    On a little street,
Lawns and trees and flowers,
    Fences white and neat.

Little rows of houses
    Full of girls and boys,
Full of shouts and laughter,
    Full of love and noise.

Houses full of children
    Going off to school.
Learning of the nation
    They will one day rule.

Houses full of children . . .
    Have they heard of Christ,
Of a tender Saviour,
    A dear Life sacrificed?

Little rows of houses
    On a little street,
Time is passing over,
    Time with flying feet.

Houses full of children,
    Precious and blood-bought.
Have you told them, neighbor?
    What have they been taught?
            —Martha Snell Nicholson,
                in *Gospel Herald*

* * *

"Is He Talking About You?"

A woman and her little daughter were in a service in which the preacher spoke about how obedience toward God is revealed in the manner in which one attends to the small duties of everyday life. He described how many parents neglect their spiritual duties in the home, how they retire night after night without praying for God's watchful care, and how in the morning they fail to thank Him for rest, protection, and the blessing of the new day. The little girl listened attentively, then turning to her mother, she whispered, *"Mama, is the minister talking about you?"* The simple question pierced the mother's heart. She said nothing, but that night she knelt before her bed, confessed her sin, and asked God's help in carrying out her duties as a Christian mother.

—*King's Business*

* * *

The Girl to Look For

An old gentleman said reflectively: "Once I was young, but now I am old, and I've never seen a girl unfaithful to her mother that ever came to be worth a one-eyed button to her husband. It . . . is written large and awful in the face of a misfit home. If one of you boys ever come across a girl with a face full of roses, who says as you come to the door, 'I can't go for thirty minutes, for the dishes are not washed,' you wait for that girl; sit right down on the doorstep and wait for her. Because some other fellow may come along and marry her, and right there you have lost an angel. Wait for that girl; stick to her like a burr to a mule's tail."

—*Christian World*

* * *

When They Let the Word Speak

One of the fine lawyers in our church told me this story: "A little woman came in my office the other day and said she wanted me to secure a divorce for her. I didn't know her, but I thought I had seen her at our church, so I said to her, 'Huntin' trouble, eh?' She bristled up, and started fighting back with all sorts of self-pitying statements. I let her talk to her heart's satisfaction; and then I said to her, 'If you are determined to break up your home over the silly things you've been telling me, go ahead; but I'm not in that sort of business.' She

got up to leave, but I knew she wasn't leaving. I reached over and took my Bible and started reading some of the New Testament passages about the way a Christian man and woman should regard their marital vows. She stopped me. And she asked me if I would see them together. I pointed to the telephone, and she called her husband. It developed that he had an office in the same building. In five minutes he was in my office. She asked me to read the same passages again. Within less time than it takes me to tell you, they were in one another's arms. He asked me how much he owed me. I told him I would collect weekly, and that the payment would consist of their presence at Sunday school and church and at Training Union. You remember the little couple that joined by letter last Sunday night? They were those people."

—Louie D. Newton, in the *Teacher*

* * *

Home Difficulties

In his biography Pierre Loti tells how, as a small boy, reading stories of sainthood led him to aspire to become a saint. He resolved to imitate Simeon Stylites, who lived on top of a pillar and thereby won a great reputation for sanctity. Accordingly, he mounted a high stool in the kitchen and announced his plan to remain there for forty years. His mother and the cook, however, would have none of his sanctity, and at the end of an hour he was wistfully recording in his diary, "Thus I discovered that it is exceedingly difficult to be a saint while living with your own family." — *Today.*

* * *

Home Fit Place for Jesus

We read of a wealthy man who purchased at high cost a famous painting of Jesus. He sought, with difficulty, an appropriate place for it on the walls of his home. At last he called in an architect who, after carefully examining the house and the picture, said: "Man, you cannot fit this picture into your home! You must make a home to

fit it!" Just as surely we must so order our home life that it would be appropriate to invite Jesus to abide therein.
— *Evangelical Messenger.*

* * *

An Unusual Home

More than two generations back there lived in London a Wesleyan minister, Rev. George B. Macdonald, and his wife. Not being modern, they welcomed to this world six children. Four of the five daughters lived in such a way as to leave well-remembered names.

Alice Macdonald stood one evening beside Rudyard Lake and there pledged her love and life to Lockwood Kipling, a youth headed for India. When a son was born, the parents thought back to the night and scene of their engagement, and they named him, Rudyard Kipling.

Georgianna Macdonald married an artist who later won fame for his skill, Sir Edward Burne-Jones.

Agnes Macdonald likewise married a youthful painter. His name was Edward Poynter, in due time president of the Royal Academy.

Louisa Macdonald turned from the circle of artists and writers around her to marry a quiet Christian engineer. His name was Baldwin, and their son, Stanley Baldwin, has not only been premier of Great Britain, but has for many years been a lay preacher of the Methodist Church.

Thank God for the abiding influences of a really Christian home!
— *Moody Monthly*

* * *

Where His Home Was

A poor widow, taken ill with an incurable disease, was received into an infirmary. Kind friends took her little boy to live with them, and he was treated in every way as if he were their own child. One day, however, he was asked by an acquaintance where his home was. "I live at so-and-so," he replied, "but my home is where Mother is."
— *Sunday School Times*

Shining at Home

Hudson Taylor has said, "A small circle of usefulness is not to be despised. A light that does not shine beautifully around the family table at home, is not fit to rush to a long way off to do a great service elsewhere."
— *Gospel Herald*

* * *

A Roofless House

A Scottish laborer who was a Christian man went to work for a farmer who was not a believer. The latter was a liberal paymaster, but the former stayed with him only a few days. He was asked by a neighbor why he had left. "There was no roof on the house." The Scotsman's meaning may be found in the saying of an old writer, who affirms that a dwelling in which prayer is not lifted up to God daily is like a house without a roof, in which there can neither be peace, comfort, nor safety.
— *King's Business*

* * *

The Home Rules the Nation

For one, I care little for the government which presides at Washington, in comparison with the government which rules the millions of American homes. No administration can seriously harm us if our home life is pure, frugal, and godly. No statesmanship or legislation can save us, if once our homes become the abode of ignorance or the nestling place of profligacy.

The home rules the nation. If the home is demoralized, it will ruin it. The real seed corn whence our Republic sprang was the Christian households represented in the *Mayflower*, or the family altar of the Hollander and the Hugenot.

All our best characters, best legislation, best institutions, and best church life were cradled in those early homes. They were the taproot of the Republic, and of the American churches.
— *Theodore L. Cuyler*

Home

I turned an ancient poet's book,
And found upon the page:
"Stone walls do not a prison make,
Nor iron bars a cage."

Yes, that is true, and something more:
You'll find where'er you roam
That marble floors and gilded walls
Can never make a home.

But every house where love abides
And Friendship is a guest
Is surely home, and home, sweet home,
For there the heart can rest.

—Henry Van Dyke

* * *

What He Missed Most

At the breakfast table, each of the family, even the tiniest one, who was but four years old, repeated a verse from the Bible. Then, joining hands as they stood around the table, they repeated together the Lord's Prayer, closing with a few words of prayer by the father. A guest was much impressed by the scene. A few months later, he was in a university town where the oldest son of the family was attending college. The man talked of his pleasant visit with his family, and then asked, "Would you mind telling me what you miss most, now that you are away from home?" Just for a minute the boy hesitated. It is not easy for a boy to speak his deepest thoughts. But, after a little, he looked up directly into the eyes of his questioner, and answered: "I miss most the handclasp at the breakfast table. If I could feel the close grasp of my father's hand, and repeat with them all the Lord's Prayer, it would begin the day right, and nothing would matter then." He halted a moment, then went on, his tones a bit husky. "The remembrance of those breakfast scenes at home stand between me and more than one temptation. It's what keeps me going straight."

—*King's Business*

* * *

Crime Breeders: Non-Christian Homes

Judge Healy of Detroit, addressing a Young People's Rally, said: "Eighty per cent of the youngsters arraigned in my court came from homes in which there has been no religious training." This is being substantiated time and again by youth leaders and pastors all over the land! There is a terrible ignorance of the basic principles of Biblical morality among our Christian youth. No wonder divorce is abounding since family worship dropped 90%. Be not deceived, there is a vital relationship between the two.

—Norman V. Williams, in,
Family Altar League of America

* * *

"I Am Different"

A young woman lived under very discordant conditions at home. She was dissatisfied, and her discontent was manifest in her face, her manner and the tone of her voice. Trifles irritated her, and had it been possible she would gladly have traveled to the end of the earth to get away from her disagreeable environment. Some time after, a friend met her and saw in her smiling face that a change had taken place. "How are things at home?" he inquired. "Just the same," was the reply, "but *I am different*."

—*Christian Endeavor World*

* * *

Longing for Home

An old Scotchman, who had been a soldier in one of the European wars, was sick and dying in one of our American hospitals. His one desire was to see Scotland and his old home, and once again walk the heather of the Highlands, and hear the bagpipes of the Scotch regiments. The night that the old Scotch soldier died, a young man, somewhat reckless but kind-hearted, got a company of musicians to come and play under the old soldier's window, and among the instruments there was a bagpipe. The instant that the musicians began, the dying old man in delirium said: "What's that, what's that? Why, it's the regiments coming home. That's the tune, yes, that's the tune. Thank God, I have got home once more!" "Bonny Scotland and Bonny

297

Doon," were the last words he uttered as he passed up to the highlands of the better country.

—T. DeWitt Talmage

* * *

Gamblers Recruiting Stations

During the twenty years I was in the game I found that about all the men and women who had filled my houses and bet themselves into ruin were the product of the homes where card playing was encouraged. It is across the friendly poker table or in the bridge game that Satan puts his fiery brand on the young men and women of America. It is in so-called Christian homes that the gambling fever begins. The underworld is not trying to drag innocents down. It does not have to. The homes are turning out more recruits than they can possibly handle. They cannot be chased with an ax. They have secured their worldly wisdom at the dances, card parties, and other social diversions which feature modern social life. There is nothing in the underworld that can furnish them any surprises, and they are more likely to start a redder one of their own.

—An ex-gambler's testimony, quoted in *Moody Monthly*

* * *

A Blessing or a Hindrance?

Marion was a selfish girl. Her own clothes, her own good times, and her own ambitions filled her life until she met the Lord Jesus. Even after she was saved, no one in her family noticed much change in her for some time. She did want to witness for Christ, but most of her thought was still for herself, so her family thought that Marion's religion was only one of her idiosyncrasies. But only two years later Marion surrendered her life unreservedly to the Lord. Soon after, she said: "I am ashamed of my past. I wanted to be a blessing to my family, yet I can see I've been almost as selfish since I was saved as I was before. I think it's my fault that they're not interested in the things of the Lord. Pray that I may really let my light shine for Christ at

home and be willing to do more than my share for His sake." Just a few weeks after this her younger sister said to her one night, when they were preparing for bed, "I want to be a Christian like you are." Marion had really begun to live for Christ, and was she happy!

—Vivian D. Gunderson, in *The Sunday School Times*

* * *

Is He a Member of Your Family?

A college girl wrote home to her parents, who seemed to have expressed some fear as to her religious life at college, "Do not worry; God has been a member of our family too long for me to lose Him now."

—*Moody Monthly*

* * *

The Testing Place

For 120 years Noah preached the Gospel; tell me, how many conversions did he get? Seven. Who were Noah's converts? They were his wife and family. The place where the reality of a man's religion is tested the most is in his own home.

—Rev. Alan Redpath, Pastor, Moody Church

* * *

Great Grace for the Little Things

A minister called at the home of one of the young people of his church. He had never met the girl's people. A very tired and worried looking woman answered the door, and the minister said: "Mary is one of our young folk, and I felt I should call on her people; she's such a bright Christian." "Is she?" was the reply. "Well, sir, Mary is our eldest daughter; we are only too pleased to have her attend church a lot, but I have been sick for a long time, and as soon as Mary gets home from work, she's off again; we see very little of her." "I'm sorry," said the minister, "she seemed to have such grace." "Maybe so," said the mother, "but she doesn't show it here; she must keep it all for outsiders." As the minister was turning away so disappointed, the mother said, "Perhaps, sir, you can show Mary that *it takes great grace for the little things, too.*"

—As told by the minister

* * *

What Makes A Home?

"It isn't the chairs and the books and things,
Or the pictures that hang on the walls;
And it isn't the bird, although gaily he sings,
It's the laughter that rings in the halls;
It's the smile on the face of the mother at night,
And the joy in the little one's eyes,
And our love for each other with all its delight
That makes up the home that we prize."

—*Selected*

* * *

In Our Homes

"Mark Twain" was the pen name of Samuel Clements. As a young man he fell in love with a beautiful Christian girl named Livy and married her. Being devoted to her Lord, she wanted a family altar and prayer at meals after she and Sam were married. This was done for a time and then one day Sam said, "Livy, you can go on with this by yourself if you want to but leave me out. I don't believe in your God and you're only making a hypocrite out of me."

Fame and affluence came. There were court appearances in Europe. Sam and Livy were riding high and Livy got farther and farther away from her early devotion to her Lord. The eventual fall came. In an hour of bitter need Sam Clements said, "Livy, if your Christian faith can help you now, turn to it." Livy replied, "I can't, Sam; I haven't any; it was destroyed a long time ago."

—Dr. Paul S. James, in
Christian Digest

* * *

The Dangers of Home

Statistics show that of the persons killed by falls, more than half died in their own homes. A home should be the safest place in the world, but it would seem to be an especially dangerous place. This is because at home we are off our guard, we are not watching for stumblingblocks. Is not all this true also of spiritual disasters? Our homes are the most frequent witnesses of bad temper, of selfishness, of cruelty, of neglect, of jealousy, of poor faith, of slander, of falsehoods. How many and how terrible are the hazards of our homes!

—*Christian Herald*

* * *

Nobody Would Know

"My father came into our house soon after I was married and looked around," says Dr. Campbell Morgan. "We showed him every room, and then in his rough way he said to me: 'Yes, it is very nice; but nobody will know, walking through here, whether you belong to God or to the Devil.' I went through and looked at the rooms again, and I thought: He is quite right. So we made up our minds straightway that there should be no room in our house, henceforth, that had not some message, by picture or wall text, to tell that we served the King."

—*King's Business*

* * *

The Pastor's Searching Question

Bishop Charles L. Slattery tells the following story he heard in a little church in France: A new pastor had come to the village, and called at a certain cottage. When the husband came home from his work the wife said, "The new pastor called today." "What did he say?" asked the man. "Oh," she answered, "he asked, 'Does Christ live here?' and I didn't know what to say." The man's face flushed. "Why didn't you tell him that we were respectable people?" he said. "Well," she answered, "I might have said only that; only that isn't what he asked me." "Then why," continued the husband, "didn't you tell him that we say our prayers and read our Bible?" The wife replied, "But he didn't ask me that." The man grew more vexed. "Why," he continued, "didn't you say that you were always at church?" "He didn't ask that, either. He asked only, 'Does Christ live here?'"

This man and woman pondered for

many days what the grave pastor meant by his question. Little by little their lives were changed; little by little they grew to expect Christ, not dead but gloriously alive. And some way, they knew not how, through great love and through a willingness to be surprised by the mystery of His radiance, they knew Him. He did indeed live there!

—*Christian Digest*

* * *

The Christian Home

In the family of Andrew Murray, of South Africa, eleven children grew to adult life. Five of the sons became ministers and four of the daughters became ministers' wives. The next generation had a still more striking record in that ten grandsons became ministers and thirteen became missionaries. The secret of this unusual contribution to the Christian ministry was the Christian home.

—John R. Mott

* * *

Home

It takes a heap of livin' in a house to
  make it home,
A heap of sun and shadow, and ye
  sometimes have t' roam
Afore ye really 'preciate the things ye
  lef' behind.
An' hunger for them somehow with
  them allus on yer mind.
It don't make any difference how rich
  ye get t' be,
How much yer chairs and tables cost,
  how great your luxury;
It ain't home t' ye, though it be the
  palace of a King,
Until somehow your soul is sort of
  wrapped round everything.

Home ain't a place that gold can buy,
  or get up in a minute,
Afore it's home there's got to be some
  babies born, and then
Right there ye've go to bring them up
  t' women good and men,
And gradjerly, as times goes on, ye find
  ye wouldn't part
With anything they ever used — they've
  grown right in your heart.

The old high chair, the playthings, too,
  the little shoes they wore,
Ye hoard: and if ye could ye'd keep the
  thum-marks on the door.

Ye've got to weep to make it home, ye've
  got to sit and sigh,
And watch beside a loved one's bed,
  and know that death is nigh,
An' close the eyes of her that smiled,
  and leave her sweet voice dumb.
For these are scenes that grip the heart,
  an' when your tears have dried,
Ye find the home is dearer than it was,
  an' sanctified.
An' tuggin at ye always are the pleasant
  memories
Of her that was, and is no more — ye
  can't escape from these.

Ye've got to sing and dance for years,
  ye've got to romp and play,
An' learn t' love the things ye have,
  by usin' them each day.
Even the roses round the door must
  bloom year by year,
Afore they come a part of ye, suggestin'
  some one dear
Who used to love 'em long ago and
  trained 'em jes' to run
The way they do, so's they would get the
  early mornin' sun.
Ye've got t' love each brick an 'stone,
  from cellar up t' dome,
It takes a heap of livin' in a house t'
  make it home.   —Edgar A. Guest

* * *

What Is Seen in Your House?

A lady had just parted with some friends who had been guests for a few days. She had been happy in having them see her new home and fine furnishings. Sitting down for a moment she noticed her Bible which had not been opened during the friend's visit. Opening the Bible, as it were at random, her eyes fell on the words of Isaiah 39:4, "What have they seen in thine house?" Hezekiah had had visitors. He, too, had been proud of his house, but somehow he had not represented God to his visitors, and God penalized him. Do our guests see a family altar in our homes? Do we wait for a "blessing" at our meals?   —*Garden of Prayer*

Radio and Nerves

Dr. Walter Alvarez, of the Mayo Clinic, declares that radio is not doing the nerves of the American people any good; on the contrary, he says, radio is an enemy of our nervous system. He says that many homes keep the radio going practically all the waking hours with all its cacophony of swing music, "soap operas," murder mysteries, and such like. As a consequence, repose and relaxation are becoming scarcer among radio devotees, and this takes its heavy toll of our nerves.

The "soap operas," which so many millions of housewives and mothers listen to all day long, abound in illicit love, jangling and discordant matrimonial triangles, jealousies, hatreds, and murders aplenty. No one can listen to these fifteen-minute high-tension episodes week in and week out without definite impairment of one's emotional balance. They are merely the old yellow-back novels and ten-cent thrillers etherized.

—Selected

* * *

Daniel Webster's Tribute to His Home

"I did not happen to be born in a log cabin; but my elder brothers and sisters were born in a log cabin and raised in the snowdrifts of New Hampshire, at a period so clearly that when the smoke first rose from its rude chimney and curled over the frozen hills, there was no similar evidence of a white man's habitation between it and the settlements on the rivers of Canada.

"Its remains still exist; I make an annual visit there. I carry my children to it to teach them the hardships endured by the generations which have gone before them. I love to dwell on the tender recollections, the kindred ties, the early affections and the touching narratives and incidents which mingle with all I know of this primitive family abode.

"I weep to think that none of those who inhabited it are now among the living; and if ever I am ashamed of it, or if ever I fail in affectionate veneration for him who reared it and defended it against savage violence and destruc-

tion, cherished all the domestic virtues beneath its roof and, through the fire and blood of a seven years' Revolutionary War, shrunk from no danger, no toil, no sacrifice, to serve his country and to raise his children to a condition better than his own — may my name and the name of my posterity be blotted forever from the memory of mankind!"

—Herald of Holiness

* * *

No Home Here

The following story contains more truth than fiction, and may suggest a cause for the lack of devotional life today. A real estate salesman tried to sell a house to a newly-married couple. Said the wife: "*Why buy a home?* I was born in a hospital, reared in a boarding school, educated in a college, courted in an automobile, and married in a church; get my meals in a cafeteria; live in an apartment; spend my mornings playing golf, my afternoons playing bridge; in the evenings we dance or go to the movies; when I'm sick I go to a hospital, and when I die I shall be buried from an undertaker's. All we need is a garage with bedroom."

—King's Business

* * *

"That House Shall Be Preserved!"

Bishop Coxe tells of visiting an old feudal castle in England, so old that one of its towers dated back to the days of King John. When the Bishop went down to breakfast, he found the young owner of the castle, his family and servants, assembled for morning prayer conducted by the head of the family. As the Bishop lifted his eyes, he noticed high overhead a massive beam that spanned the grand, old hall and bore in old English the following inscription:
That house shall be preserved and never shall decay,
Where the Almighty God is worshipped day by day.
A. D. 1558
Thus for hundreds of years the people of that old castle had turned their faces toward God at the beginning of each day.

—W. B. K.

For This Life Only

"Another evidence of spiritual stupor in this tragic hour is the time employed in most Christian homes to the affairs of THIS life, to preparing meals, washing dishes and keeping the home and dress in strict conformity to worldly standards. Unmindful of the Lord's rebuke to Martha, the daughters of Zion employ most of their time and strength and money in serving the superficial, carnal needs of the Christian Home, while the spiritual needs of their own families and needy humankind are left in utter neglect. Is it any wonder that the work of the Lord is in fearful apostasy and declension because of the need of zealous daughters and stalwart sons of God to be about their Father's business?"

—Sarah Faulkes Moore, in
Family Altar League of America

* * *

God Doesn't Live at Our House

Five-year-old Margaret and her brother were frequent visitors in the home of a neighbor. One of the never-ending wonders over which little Margaret pondered as she visited in Hortense's home was the prayertime. Hortense's daddy read out of the big black book and afterward talked to God as if He were very near and dear to them all. Sometimes the family would join in singing a song of praise. One morning when Margaret had been present at the prayertime, Hortense's mother suggested, "Margaret, don't you pray at your house?" Margaret shook her head sadly and said, "No, you see, God doesn't live at our house like He does at yours." Margaret's home was by no means a so-called underprivileged one. It was an average, middle-class American home. But if the little girl wanted to meet God, the Heavenly Father, she had to go next door. He just wasn't included in her family circle.

Sunday School Digest

* * *

Her Unexpected Neighbor

Margaret Applegarth tells of a young girl leaving Northfield with a desire to do a beautiful piece of service. Upon reaching home she asked her pastor for the name of a lonely person to whom she could bring cheer and happiness. The next day the minister handed her a folded slip of paper and when she opened it, she found written there the name of her own father.

—*Sunday School Times*

* * *

Christian Home, A Seed Plot

In Robert Burns' "Cotters' Saturday Night" we see the ideal picture of Christian home worship at its best. It was from such Scottish homes with their family altars that there went forth the great pioneer missionaries. Robert Moffat, David Livingstone, Alexander Mac Kay — all to Africa; Ion Keith-Falconer to Arabia; John G. Paton to the New Hebrides; James Chalmers to New Guinea; and many others to the uttermost parts of the earth. Christian homes ought to be nurseries for the ministry and the mission fields.

—Chaplain W. Wyeth Willard

* * *

The Responsive Chord!

In the early spring of 1863, the Confederate and Union armies were confronting each other at Spotsylvania. Two bands, one night, began to play sweet music.

A large crowd of the soldiers of both armies gathered to listen to the music, the friendly pickets not interfering, and soon the bands began to answer each other. First the band on the northern bank would play "Star Spangled Banner," "Hail Columbia," or some other National air, and at its conclusion the "boys in blue" would cheer most lustily, and then the band on the southern bank would respond with "Dixie" or "Bonnie Blue Flag," or some other Southern melody, and the "boys in gray" would attest their approbation with an old "Confederate yell." But presently one of the bands struck up sweet plaintive notes, which wafted across the beautiful Rappahannock and were caught up at once by the other band and swelled into a grand anthem which touched every heart "Home, Sweet Home."

At the conclusion of this piece there went up a simultaneous shout from both sides of the river — cheer followed cheer, and those hills, which had so recently resounded with hostile guns, echoed and re-echoed the glad acclaim.

A chord had been struck which caused the hearts of enemies to beat in unison!

—J. William Jones

* * *

The Sanctity of Home

A Christian home should be Heaven begun on earth. It will be if it is the abode of warm and loving hearts. Serene but inspiring is the household which thinks, works, rejoices, and sorrows together; whose personalities are all melted down by Divine grace, uniting them in love. "A lamp," said Robert McCheyne, the great Scottish preacher, "is a very small thing, and it burns calmly, and without noise, and it giveth light unto all that are in the house."

So there are great but quiet influences which, like the flame of a sacred lamp, fill many a home with light and fragrance. A soft, deep carpet not only diffuses a look of ample comfort, it deadens many a creaking sound; so is the peace of a Christian home. A strong curtain wards off the summer heat and the wintry wind; so a sweet family fellowship is a shield protecting all the members. A soft pillow may make some forget their misery, and a tired mind soon forgets its cares in the delights of a comfortable Christian home. Its influence is like the fresh evening breeze at the close of a burning day. There would be fewer aching hearts if there were more Christian homes. When you turn your face homeward, think of Jesus and of Heaven. Our Lord raised three persons from the dead. One was an only son; another, an only daughter; the third, an only brother. Whenever He entered a home He sanctified it with peace and radiant life. Make sure that Jesus is in the sacred presence of your home.

—*Watchman-Examiner*

HONESTY

Be True

Thou must be true thyself
  If thou the truth wouldst teach;
The soul must overflow if thou
  Another's soul wouldst reach;
It needs the overflow of heart
  To give the lips full speech.

Think truly, and thy thoughts
  Shall the world's famine feed;
Speak truly, and each word of thine
  Shall be a fruitful seed;
Live truly, and thy life shall be
  A great and noble creed.

—H. Bonar

* * *

Real Christians

In her book, "Floods on Dry Ground," Eva Stuart Watt describes missionary work in the Belgian Congo, and says: "Even among the enemies of the Gospel

there was growing a secret admiration for those whose lives were out and out for God. The term, 'Bakrustu ya kweli,' was often heard on heathen lips. It means 'real Christians.' Far and wide they were known as men of truth, and men whose prayers got answered. One day the paramount chief had a big court case in which a Christian was charged with hiding a Mabudu prisoner. At the tribunal, the chief said to the accused, 'Tell me, did you hide that man?' 'No, Chief, I didn't.' Then turning to his soldiers, he said, 'You liars, the lot of you! This man is a *Bakrustu ya kweli!* He couldn't tell a lie!' "

—*Sunday School Times*

* * *

How to Give a Good Testimony

A boy, twelve years old, was the important witness in a law suit. One of the lawyers, after cross-questioning him severely, said, "Your father has been telling you how to testify, hasn't he?" "Yes," said the boy. "Now," said the lawyer, "just tell us how your father told you to testify." "Well!" said the boy modestly, "Father told me the lawyers would try to tangle me in my testimony; but if I would just be careful and tell the truth, I could tell the same thing every time."

—*Vermont Chronicle*

* * *

Laying or Lying?

Two men got into an animated argument over which is right, gramatically, to say, "The hen is setting," or "the hen is sitting." Each contended that he was right, and both showed a ready disposition to prove he was right with fistic blows. Finally reason obtained. They agreed to go to Farmer Brown, and put the question to him. Hearing the matter, Farmer Brown guffawed heartily. Then, he said rather contemptuously, "Men, when I see a hen in such a position on a nest, I don't ask whether she is sitting, or setting. I only ask, 'Is she LAYING, or is she LYING?' "

—W. B. K.

* * *

What Impressed Her Creditor

A lady of my acquaintance told me the following experience. She said: "I signed a note for a friend for a small sum of money, but as I had very little, and am a widow with my own living to make, it was a large amount to me. This so-called friend 'skipped' without paying, so I had to pay. Just about this time I was saved, and, in the joy of knowing Jesus Christ, wanted everything in my life to be right for Him. It happened that the money was owing to a Jewish lawyer. I went to see him and told him my circumstances, promising the money would be paid each week as I earned it. I also told him I had just accepted Christ as my Saviour, and for Him, I desired my life to shine. When the last installment of that money was paid that Jew handed back part of the whole sum, saying: "I have had much dealing with people who said they

were followers of Christ. Until now, I have never been much impressed."

—*Sunday School Times*

* * *

A Convincing Conversion

There was in a certain village a very mean man who sold wood to his neighbors, and who always took advantage of them by cutting his logs a few inches under the required four feet. One day the report was circulated that the wood chopper had been converted. Nobody believed the report, for they all declared that he was beyond being reached. One man, however, slipped quietly out of the grocery store where the conversion was being discussed and soon came running back in excitement and shouted: "It's so! He has been!" They all asked, "How do you know?" "Why, I have been over and measured the wood that he cut yesterday. It is a good four feet long!" That testimony convinced the crowd.

—*Moody Monthly*

* * *

An Indian Girl's Short Sermon

A group of travelers gathered around a little Indian girl on the station platform, examining her wares. "You pay two prices for what you buy here," said a man with his hat on one side, who had the air of knowing it all. "But the tourist is robbed everywhere. You might as well make up your mind to be cheated." "This is not cheat," the Indian girl protested, "I make these baskets myself, and they take many days." "Oh, of course, they all declare they are selling cheap," said the man. "And why shouldn't they cheat if they can? I'd do the same in their places." He winked unpleasantly at a man in the crowd. The next remark of the Indian girl was unexpected. " 'For what shall it profit a man, if he shall gain the whole world, and lose his own soul?' " she said in slow English. "That is what they taught us at the mission school, and I will not lie that I may sell my baskets, even though I go hungry." It was a silent company that climbed aboard the Pullman at the conductor's signal. "It was not long for a sermon," said the man with his hat on one side, "but it's the kind of one you can't forget in a hurry."

—*Orphan's Friend*

* * *

Covetousness

Dr. Francis E. Clark told of a friend of his who, when a boy, was in grave danger through covetousness. He wanted fifty cents to go to the circus. Now he had never been to the circus, and try as he would, he was able to earn but thirty-five cents. Several days before the circus he went, as usual, to school in a neighboring town. The fare was fifteen cents. His parents gave him money each day for his ticket. On this particular day the conductor passed him by. His ticket still in his possession, he thought what a simple thing it would be to use it next day, and keep the fifteen cents provided at home for the circus fund. The temptation was awful. "All day the elephant stared at him out of the pages of his Latin grammar, and the giraffes craned their long necks over the tough problems in algebra." All day and all that night (for he could not sleep much) he fought his battle. How he coveted the railroad company's fifteen cents. *But next day he tore up the old ticket and paid his fare.* "*Now as he looks back over a long and honored life, he tells his friends that that was the day of his greatest battle and his greatest victory.*"

—*Sunday School Times*

* * *

A Noble Son

It was a remark overheard in a street car, but it reminded us that there are honorable men in the world. A young man said: "I am very particular about paying my fare. I took a ticket home once when I was a small boy and showed it to my father, saying that the conductor had not taken it, and that I was that much ahead. My father looked at me and said that I had sold my honor for a nickel. That put a new face on it. I always think of what he said when I am tempted to repeat the offense." If all fathers were training their

sons in this way there would be fewer dishonorable transactions in high places.

—*Herald and Presbyter*

* * *

You Can't Fool God

"You can fool the hapless public,
   You can be a subtle fraud,
You can hide your little meanness,
   But you can't fool God!

You can advertise your virtues,
   You can self-achievement laud,
You can load yourself with riches,
   But you can't fool God!

You can criticize the Bible,
   You can be a selfish clod,
You can lie, swear, drink, and gamble
   But you can't fool God!

You can magnify your talent,
   You can hear the world applaud,
You can boast yourself somebody,
   But you can't fool God!"

—Granville Kleiser

* * *

"You Are Not Honest"

A young woman who was one of the leading Christians in a certain church, some years ago went to college. She was president of the young women's society and the teacher of a large Bible class. She came back in her sophomore year, but she avoided the church. The pastor went to her and sought the reason, and she said: "I have lost my faith completely; the teacher of scientific textbooks has shattered my former belief. I believe in the scientific interpretation of the universe." He said to her, "You are not honest!" She flushed to the roots of her hair. "Honesty is the capital stock of scientific thinking; you are not honest!" "What do you mean?" she demanded. "When you go into the laboratory, you conform to conditions, and if you meet the conditions, you get the results." "True." "When did you read your Bible last?" he asked. "Two years ago." "When did you pray last?" "Two years ago." "You are not honest; you are not scientific. *You do not comply with the conditions that nourish faith.* Go home

305

and read your Bible and take up your prayer." And she did, and came back into the ranks.

—Orrin Philip Gifford, in
The Shadow of the Rock

* * *

Could Not Be "Bought"

A recent biography of Stonewall Jackson opened with a fish story. It seems that Tom Jackson was a poor boy, left an orphan early in his life and he made odd sums here and there by selling fish. On one occasion he caught a beautiful bass, and a gentleman of the community, riding by on horseback and seeing the fish, offered him a dollar for it. "No," replied Jackson, "Mr. —— has agreed to take all my fish at fifty cents apiece and he has taken a great number of small ones, and I think that he should have this larger one." The gentleman, still eager for the prize, offered Jackson a dollar and a half, but in resolute courage and thorough-going decision which marked his life to its close, Jackson immediately refused the offer.

—Samuel McPheeters, in
My Tomorrow's Self

* * *

Heinz of "57 Varieties" a Square-Shooter

That Henry J. Heinz, of "57 varieties" fame, was a square-shooter is evidenced by the experience of a new employee. Heinz came upon the man one day at the weigher's platform, checking a farmer's load of apples.

"We are getting you good weight today, Mr. Heinz," said the young man.

"Fine!" said Heinz. "What are you doing for me?"

"Why, you know — a quick eye, a quick hand, and you can always slip over a few pounds extra."

Heinz nodded, but a little later asked the employee to go with him to the office. There he said, "This is the cashier's office. You will get your pay check and leave this place at once."

"But, Mr. Heinz," exclaimed the astonished fellow, "I was saving you money!"

"You were robbing a man who was selling to me," said Heinz. "And you were robbing me of something more

precious." Laying his hand on the other's shoulder, he said, "There is only one way to weigh or to do anything else. Be as square to the other fellow as to yourself."

—*Power*

* * *

The Prospect of Facing the List

William Webb, a butcher of West Worthing, Canada, put up this notice in his window: "This business has been compelled to close owing to bad debts. A list of the names and amounts owing will shortly be shown." Money rolled in; the shop is open again, and business flourishing.   —*Regina Leader-Post*

* * *

Even His Scales Were Converted

While in a town in eastern Poland I went one day in company with one of our missionaries to buy a goose, for goose is the cheapest meat in Poland. The shop was surprisingly clean; the chickens and geese were fat and good-looking. When I asked the shopkeeper about his salvation, his eyes lit up and his face beamed with joy as he answered: "Yes, I am a believer," and, pointing to the missionary, added, "Through your missionary I learned to know Jesus Christ." "How do you know that you are saved?" I asked. "Because my life has been changed completely," he replied. "Now when I sell geese I give correct weight and do not put my finger on the scales. Everything is right now. Even my scales are changed." Other Jews persecuted him, he said, because he no longer attended synagogue or conformed to Jewish traditions. —*European Jew*

* * *

Master Never Out!

A storekeeper went away for the day and left his clerk in charge. A customer came in and asked a favor of the clerk, which meant he would have to do something dishonest. "You can do it, if you want to," argued the customer, "because your master is out." The clerk looked the man straight in the face, and said: "You are mistaken. My Master is Jesus Christ, and He is never out."

—*Sunday School Times*

An Insurance Disagreement

In the *Western Producer* (Saskatoon) recently, there was published a story told by an ex-Reeve of a Mennonite municipality. We reproduce in the words of the man who tells it: "A Mennonite came to see me and asked me to go and inspect his crop which, he said, had been damaged by hail. I asked him if the insurance company had not settled with him, and he replied that it had, but he was not satisfied, and would like to get the opinion of some unprejudiced individual. I told him I did not think it would do any good, but I went out to his farm. After looking over the damage I informed my friend that I estimated that he had been damaged to the extent of about thirty-five or forty per cent. My estimate, he told me, had been very much the same as his own. I asked how much the insurance company had allowed him, and he told me they had assessed the damage at sixty per cent. 'I wanted to make sure,' he said, 'before I sent the money back, that I was overpaid on the damage.' I told him that he need not send it back, but he told me he did not see how any honest man could do anything else. He sent the money back."

—*Evangelical Christian*

*   *   *

Open In All Your Ways

"If you tell the truth," wrote Chinese Gordon to his sister, "you have infinite power supporting you; but if not, you have infinite power against you. The children of kings should be above deceit, for they have a mighty and a jealous Protector. We go to other gods — Baal, etc. — when we lie; we rely on other than God. We may for a time seem to humbug men, but not God. It is indeed worldly silliness to be deceitful. . . . Oh, be open in all your ways. It is a girdle around your loins, strengthening you in all your wayfarings."

—*Christian Beacon*

*   *   *

A Little Girl's Question

A little girl and her brother were carrying a basket of cakes to their grandmother. Curious to see what was in the basket, they very carefully raised the cover and looked in. When their greedy eyes saw the tempting cakes, their mouths fairly watered to taste them. After counting them over several times, they almost made up their minds they might eat just one of them. Nobody would know it, and it would taste so good! While they were gazing at the cakes, and just ready to take one, the little girl looked up in her brother's face, and asked the question, "Can't God count?" This settled the matter; the lid was shut down, and all the cakes were carried to the grandmother.

—*Moody Monthly*

*   *   *

Speak the Truth

Many persons, we fear, are careless about their expressions, and are open to criticism. Exaggeration is a fatal error, and when the guilty party has light, it is sin. "Hundreds at the altar," "scores saved," "a regular torrent of salvation," "never saw anything like it," and similar statements are often wide of the mark.

Again, there is the habit of so coloring a statement that while the truth is spoken, there is a covered lie. The eyes of the world are upon us, and the ears of critics are open to hear; and above all, God is to be taken into account.

Suppressed truth or half-truth, that is meant to mislead, is the meanest kind of lying. "Thou desirest truth in the inward parts."

—*God's Revivalist*

*   *   *

An Acknowledgement That Paid Dividends:

In a Pennsylvania community was a Quaker horse dealer. Said a farmer, on seeing one of this man's horses, "Want to sell?" "Well, I bought this horse for my own use," said the dealer, "but there's no reason why I shouldn't sell him if we can agree on a price." "How much do you want for him?" "I paid $150 for him, and think I'm entitled to a profit of $50. If you want him for $200, he's yours." So the deal was made. The horse was delivered and proved to be very satisfactory to the new owner. A few weeks later, however, he received a check for $50 from the dealer and a note which said: "I told you I paid $150 for the horse. On consulting my records I find I was mistaken. I paid only $100 for him. I told you my profit was $50, therefore I am sending you $50 to make the deal right." The dealer expected no reward for doing what he saw was right according to his light, but the farmer was so pleased that he told the story over and over again and more than $5,000 worth of new business came to him from the advertising.

　　　　　　　　　　　　　—Crown

* * *

The Negro Boy's Surprise

At a slave market in one of the Southern states, a smart, active colored boy was put up for sale. A kind master who pitied his condition, wishing him not to have a cruel owner, went up to him, and said, "If I buy you, will you be honest?" The boy, with a baffled expression, replied, "I will be honest whether you buy me or not."

　　　　　　　—Sunday School Times

* * *

Honesty In Storekeeping

Here is the great innovation in storekeeping which John Wanamaker introduced: You could buy anything in the store and take it home. After you got it home if you did not like it, or the folks did not, or for any other reason you did not want it, you could take it back and your money would be returned without any question, argument, or hemming and hawing! Honesty had at last gotten into store trading. Who could be "stuck" or overcharged when each article had marked upon it in invisible ink, as it were, "If you don't think I'm your money's worth, take me back." Of course, Mr. Wanamaker was imposed upon terribly. Women bought dresses, wore them to parties, and took them back the next day. Others furnished their houses and table for a function, then back with the glassware and china. But crowds filled the store and it grew and grew, and when Mr.

Wanamaker died, his estate was said to be some $40,000,000 or more. Honesty is the best.

　　　　　　　　　—Storekeeper

* * *

Not To Be Trusted

In one of his speeches, Theodore Roosevelt told this little anecdote about the old days when he lived out West on a ranch in the cow country: "There were no fences," he said, "and every calf was branded with the same brand that its mother had, so that the increase of the calves could be totaled. There used to be a ranch law known as the Maverick Law, according to which any calf overlooked in the branding would be branded with the brand of the ranch on which he was found. I was once riding across the country with one of my cowpunchers, when we found a stray calf on another man's ranch. The cow-puncher wanted to brand it with the Roosevelt brand, but I told him I would not stand for it. The cow-puncher said: 'Hold on, old man, I know my business, I always put on the boss' brand,' 'All right,' I said, 'if you do, go back to the camp and get your time.' 'What are you doing that for?' he asked. 'Well,' I answered, 'If you will steal *for* me, you will steal *from* me.'"

　　　　　　　　—King's Business

* * *

Commandments They Understood

Thomas Carthew, a missionary in East Africa, was known to the natives as "Simba," the Lion. Unconventional in his preaching, he was amazingly powerful in his presentation of the truth. Repeating the Commandments one day in the mission church, everything went calmly on until they reached number eight. "Thou shalt not steal," thundered Carthew. "Thou shalt not steal," repeated the colored congregation. There was a pause. "Thou shalt not steal — cocoanuts," announced Cathew. This was an unexpected innovation, and dead silence reigned. "Say it!" demanded the preacher. In hesitating tones came the response. "Thou shalt not steal cocoanuts." "Now say this: 'Thou shalt not steal bananas!' 'Thou shalt not steal

steal bananas!" "Thou shalt not steal — fowls,'" and so on through the whole list of petty pilferings, until the unhappy congregation, which so often had glibly repeated the Commandment, felt most uncomfortable.

—Trail Blazers and Road Makers,
by the Rev. H. S. Hopkins

* * *

If He Had Kept the Dime

A young man employed by our Sunday school board told the following searching story. He was invited at the last minute to preach at a church in Nashville. On sudden impulse he used as his text, "Thou shalt not steal." The next morning he stepped on the bus and handed the driver a dollar bill. The driver handed him back his change. He stood in the rear of the bus and counted the change. There was a dime too much. His first thought was, "The bus company will never miss this dime." Then quickly came the realization that he could not keep money that did not belong to him. He made his way to the front and said to the driver, "You gave me too much change." Imagine his surprise when the driver replied, "Yes a dime too much. I gave it to you purposefully. You see, I heard your sermon yesterday, and I watched in my mirror as you counted your change. Had you kept the dime I would never again have had any confidence in preaching." What a tragedy if he had done the wrong thing! Remember our influence — our shadow-selves — may fall where we can never be.

—Sunday School Builder

* * *

His Own Faulty Standard

A grocer opened his house for cottage meetings and invited an old woman saying, "Mary, you need to get saved." She came, and after different people had spoken, he said, "Here's Mary; I want her to get saved, and then she won't be giving me any more shortweight butter. You know, Mary, I found you cheating me for some weeks; every pound of butter is two ounces short." "Oh, sir," said Mary, "I can tell you how that comes. I lost my pound weight and for five weeks I have used a pound of soap I bought from you as a weight." The grocer said no more.

—Christian Herald

* * *

Sincerity Test

An old Scotch woman said to her pastor, "That was a grand sermon you preached last Lord's Day at the kirk!"

Seeking to test her sincerity he asked, "And what was the text?"

"Ah, meenister!" she replied. "I dinna ken the text or the words. But I came home and took the false bottom out o' my peck measure." *—Power*

* * *

Expensive Butter

In a certain bank there was a trust department in which four young men and one older man were employed. It was decided by the directors that they would promote the older employee and also promote one of the younger men to have charge of the trust department after the older gentleman was removed to his new position. After considering the merits of each of the men, a certain one of the four younger men was selected for the new position and to receive a substantial increase in salary. It was decided to notify him of the promotion that afternoon at four o'clock. At the noon hour the young man went to a cafeteria for lunch. One of the directors was behind him in the line with several other customers in between them. The director saw the young man select his food including a small piece of butter. The butter, he flipped on his plate, and threw some food on top of it to hide it from the cashier. In this way he lied to the cashier about what was on his plate. That afternoon the directors met to notify the young man that they had intended giving him the promotion, but that because of what had been seen in the cafeteria, they must discharge him. They felt that they could not have as the head of their trust department one who would lie and steal. "Honesty is the best policy" both in natural things and in spiritual things. *—Evangelical Christian*

A Famous Coach's Honesty

Probably no man ever had a longer or more distinguished career in the world of sports than the veteran coach A. A. Stagg. For forty-two years he was the idol of students and graduates of the University of Chicago. Yet he is more admired for his rugged character and uncompromising honesty, no matter what the cost.

A successful businessman told how his whole life was changed by a little incident on the baseball diamond. Stagg's champion baseball team was defending its college title. The batter had singled, and one of Stagg's men was racing home with the winning run. Stagg came rushing up to meet him. "Get back to third base," he shouted, "you cut it by a yard." "But the umpire didn't see it," the runner protested. "That doesn't make any difference," roared Stagg. "Get back!" *It cost a game, but a character battle was won.* "When I saw that," said the businessman, "I determined always to play square."

—*United Presbyterian*

Have You Kept Your Promise?

Remember? A number of veterans of Iowa's 113th Cavalry — an outfit that fought superbly in the European war — received Easter cards that really opened their eyes. The front of the card included a sketch of a German battlefield labeled "Easter, 1945." On top, in large letters, was: "REMEMBER?" Then to the right of the sketch was this: "You said then: 'Dear God, if You will bring me safely home, I promise I will live for You, and do what You want me to do' . . . REMEMBER?" On the inside of the card was a family fireside sketch and the following: "Well! *God DID what you asked! He brought you safely home. Now! Have you done what you promised? How about Easter* 1950?" The card was signed by the Rev. Ben L. Rose, pastor of the Central Presbyterian Church, Bristol, Va. He was the chaplain of the 113th.

—*Des Moines Register*

HUMILITY

A Wife's Humility

A drunkard husband, spending the evening with his jovial companions at a tavern, boasted that if he should take a group of his friends home with him at midnight and ask his Christian wife to get up and cook supper for them, she would do it without complaint. The crowd considered it a vain boast and dared him to try it by a considerable wager. So the drunken crowd went home with him and he made the unreasonable demands of his wife. She obeyed, dressed, came down, and prepared a very nice supper just as quickly as possible and served it as cheerfully as if she had been expecting them. After supper one of the men, a little more sober than the others, asked her how she could be so kind when they had been so unreasonable, and, too, they knew she did not approve of their conduct. Her reply was: "Sir, when my

husband and I were married, we were both sinners. It has pleased God to call me out of that dangerous condition. My husband continues in it. I tremble for his future state. Were he to die as he is, he must be miserable forever; I think it my duty to render his present existence as comfortable as possible." This wise and faithful reply affected the whole company. The husband thanked her for the warning and became a serious Christian and a good husband.

—*Sunday School Times*

* * *

That God May Have All the Glory

"I am by birth," said a converted Hindu, when addressing a number of his countrymen, "of an insignificant and contemptible caste, so low, that if a Brahman should chance to touch me, he must go and bathe in the Ganges for the purpose of purification; and yet God has been pleased to call me not only to a knowledge of the Gospel but to the high privilege of teaching it to others. My friends, do you know the reason for God's conduct? It is this: if God had selected a learned Brahman and made him the preacher, bystanders might have said it was the amazing learning of the Brahman and his great weight of character that made him a fruitful soul-winner. But now, when anyone is convinced by my instrumentality, no one thinks of ascribing praise to me; and God, as is His due, has all the glory."

—Tom Olson, in
The Sunday School Times

* * *

One Thing He Needed

At the dinner table of one of the well-known millionaires who had done much for the public good, discussion turned upon the value of prayer. The millionaire said he did not believe in it. He had everything he wished for, so there was no need for him to pray for any favors. The principal of a Scottish university, who was present, said, "There is one thing that you might pray for." "What is that?" "You might pray for humility." Whatever our possessions, we shall be all the happier if we pray for the humble spirit which can thank God for His mercies.

—*Moody Monthly*

* * *

Why She Didn't Want Praise

A young woman recently converted, and whose holy life was noted in the church, sang a solo at one of the services that brought much blessing. The minister commented on it, at length. On leaving the church at the close, she was overheard saying to the minister, "If you please, sir, I don't want you to praise me." "Oh," said the minister in surprised tone, "why not?" "Because," said the singer, "it's Christ I want to glorify. Since I found Him as my Saviour, I want everything about me to point to Him, and when I sing I want people to see Him."

—*Sunday School Times*

Washing Feet of Poorest

In the twelfth century a custom was originated in Bavaria which was carried on every year for hundreds of years. A prince of the royal family knelt before the multitudes on Holy Thursday and washed the feet of the twelve poorest men who could be found. He bathed their feet in a silver bowl and wiped them on a towel of the very finest linen. He spoke kindly to them during the ceremony and gave to each a gift of money.

It is conceivable that a prince might go through this ceremony once a year without being very humble in heart, but if we are to follow the example of our Master, we must be humble in heart as well as in deed every day of the year.

—Olive Bishop Branch, in
Gospel Herald

* * *

No Need To Mention the Name!

One day, crossing a New York City street, a woman became confused, and stepped directly in front of an approaching streetcar. People on both curbs were sick with horror at her sure fate, when a powerful man rushed forward and not only rescued her from the streetcar, but carried her to safety on the sidewalk. It was a miracle of bravery and quick thinking. A policeman said to the hero, "I'll have to report this incident, sir, and I ought to mention your name for valor." "There will be no necessity for mentioning my name." "But I must put down something, sir," the policeman insisted. "Then," smiled the hero, "just put down that a black man did it," and with that he disappeared in the crowd. A ripple of admiration went softly through the crowd. "A black man did it." What modesty! What quiet dignity! What an honor to the whole race of black men! And the man was Dr. Robert R. Morton, President of Tuskeegee Institute!

—*Bible Teacher*,
Southern Baptist Convention

* * *

The Sweetest Music

Have you ever thought of it, that only the smaller birds sing? You never heard a note from the eagle in all your life, nor from the turkey, nor from the ostrich. But you have heard from the canary, the wren, and the lark. The sweetest music comes from those Christians who are small in their own estimation and before the Lord.

—*Watchman-Examiner*

* * *

Big Men

George Washington shocked General Lafayette one morning by merely being, what the father of our country described as, a gentleman. It seems George Washington and Lafayette were talking together when a slave passed. The old colored man paused, tipped his hat and said, "Good mo'nin', Gen'l Washin'ton."

Immediately George Washington removed his hat, bowed and wished the man a pleasant day.

After a moment of shocked silence General Lafayette exclaimed, "Why did you bow to a slave?"

The great man smiled and replied, "I would not allow him to be a better gentleman than I."

—Billie Avis Hoy, in
Gospel Herald

* * *

First, Report to the Lord!

Mr. Moody, when holding meetings at St. Louis at one time, was approached after the service by one of his ushers who told him there was a group of the most influential men and women of the city who wished to be introduced to him. This was very flattering attention, surely. Mr. Moody had just delivered one of his most powerful and effective sermons, and was busy here and there with the inquirers, while this company of distinguished people waited to meet the great evangelist. When Mr. Moody had finished all that the Lord had given him to do, he quietly, and unobserved, slipped out of the rear door and went to his room. Later, in explaining his apparent discourtesy, he said that he feared to tarry for the words of adulation and flattery; he must get back to his room and report first to his Lord

who had sent him forth. Oh, that we were all more obedient and faithful!

—*Gospel Herald*

* * *

Phillips Brooks' Concern

At the time that Phillips Brooks was made a bishop a friend was staying at the house. They were chatting together, when Phillips Brooks said, "R—, if you see any difference in me, you'll tell me, won't you?" It was the vigilance of a great soul who knew the peril of success and prosperity.

—*Sunday School Teacher*

* * *

What God:

An old Godly writer named Flavel, has given us wise words on this matter. He said:

"When God intends to fill a soul He first makes it empty; when He intends to enrich a soul He first makes it poor; when He intends to exalt a soul, He first makes it sensible of its own miseries, wants and nothingness.

—*Watchman-Examiner*

* * *

Can You Qualify?

Charles Fox, writes of " 'God's five-ranked army of decreasing human weakness.' Concerning this army, many of us can qualify if we are

Foolish enough to depend on Him for wisdom;

Weak enough to be empowered with His strength;

Base enough to have no honor but God's honor;

Despised enough to be kept in the dust at His feet;

Nothing enough for God to be everything."

—*Sunday School Times*

* * *

The "Shoemaker's" Reply

Such a remarkable linguist as William Carey could not long remain unobserved by the British Government, who desired to use his gift of languages for its own purposes. Honors were heaped upon him, but the simplehearted, unassuming man accepted only such positions of influence as would open the way for the work so dear to his heart. In the zenith of his fame, his humility was one of his striking characteristics. At a State dinner, some English officer asked with a sneer, "Was not your great Dr. Carey a shoemaker?" Carey overheard the remark, and answered with quiet dignity, "No, sir, only a cobbler." British authority had denied to Carey a landing place on his arrival in India. When this devoted, humble man died, the Government dropped all its flags at half mast in honor of one who had done more for India than all her generals.

—Illustrator

* * *

His All

In a lecture at Mansfield, Dr. Dinsdale T. Young said that the subject of one of his sermon-lectures was Samuel Bradburn, a poor boy, who once worked at a cobbler's bench, and who became a minister and President of the Wesleyan Methodist Conference. At one Conference several ministers spoke of the sacrifices they had made, one saying that he had "given up his all" to take up the work of a Christian minister. Mr. Bradburn then rose, and, to the great amusement of the Conference, said, "Brethren, when I came into the ministry I gave up half a dozen of the best awls that a man ever had."

—Christian Herald

* * *

Keeping Yourself Out of Sight

A little country boy was out fishing with only a switch for a pole and a bent pin for a hook, but he was catching many fish. A city fellow who had spent much time fishing without any success, though he had the best of fishing outfit, came across the boy with his long string of fish, and he asked the boy the reason of his success. The boy said, "The secret of it all is that I keep myself out of sight." We must keep ourselves out of sight if we desire to be a blessing to others.

John the Baptist kept himself out of sight. He said of the Lord, "He must increase, but I must decrease." He

went before the Lord and paved the way for Him and then he stepped aside and let the Lord receive the glory. What a wonderful picture!

—Junior Challenge

* * *

The Test

"I believe the first test of a truly great man is his humility," said John Ruskin. Sir Isaac Newton, when an old man, said, "I am as a child on the seashore picking up a pebble here and a shell there, but the great ocean of truth lies before me!"

—W. B. K.

* * *

The Unexpected Visitor

When Queen Victoria resided at Balmoral Castle she sometimes enjoyed a walk in the district incognito. On one occasion she slipped out by a side gate, accompanied only by her faithful servant John Brown, who followed behind.

Along the road she came on a flock of sheep being driven by a boy, who shouted, "Keep out of the way, stupid old woman!" The Queen smiled, but said nothing, and when her servant came along he informed the lad that she was the Queen. "Ugh, well," said the boy, "she should dress like a queen."

There were those who did not recognize the Son of God because He came in humble form.

—Gospel Herald

* * *

The Nobility of Humility

When Sammy Morris, a Kru boy from Africa, came to America to be trained for Christian service, he did not ask for an easy place. His biographer records this incident of him when he presented himself for matriculation at Taylor University: He revealed a spirit all too rare among Christians. When President Thaddeus C. Reade asked him what room he wanted, Sammy replied, "If there is a room nobody wants, give that to me." Of this incident Dr. Reade later wrote: "I turned away, for my eyes were full of tears. I was asking myself whether I was willing to take what nobody else wanted. In my experience as a teacher, I have had occasion to assign rooms to more than a thousand students. Most of them were noble, Christian young ladies and gentlemen; but Sammy Morris was the only one of them who ever said, 'If there is a room that nobody wants, give that to me.' "

—Alliance Weekly

* * *

The Danger of High Heads

Corn was spread on the ground, and a net stretched at a certain height over the grain to catch some wild turkeys. The fowls went with their heads down, picking the corn. But when they tried to return, instead of keeping their heads down as when they came in, they lifted up their heads and were caught in the net. If you get into Satan's trap, you cannot get out with head erect, for God gives grace only to the humble.

—Sunday School Times

* * *

"Be Clothed With Humility"

Humility will save you from self-consciousness. It will take away from you the shadow of yourself and the constant sense of your own importance. It will save you from self-assertion and from thrusting your own personality upon the thoughts and attention of others. It will save you from the desire for display, from being prominent, from occupying the center of the stage, from being the object of observation and attention, and having the eyes of the world turned upon you.

—Dr. A. B. Simpson

* * *

A Secret of Charles Dicken's Greatness

It is said of Charles Dickens that people who met him for the first time often would never have suspected that he was the most distinguished literary man of his time. He never spoke of himself. He always took a most modest interest in the affairs of others, and they learned with surprise that the man who had just been talking with them so simply and showing such an interest in their affairs was the literary star of his time.

—Dr. A. B. Simpson

* * *

Full Heads Bow Lowest

A farmer and his young son went into the wheat fields at harvest time. As they looked across the waving fields of golden grain, the boy exclaimed, "Look, Father, at those wheat heads that hold themselves up so proudly. They must be the ones that are filled with grain, and I would suppose that those with their heads bowed down are of no account."

"How foolish you are, my son!" the farmer said, and taking some of the heads into his hands, he showed the boy that the heads that stood up so proudly had only a few, poor, shriveled grains or were completely empty, while those that bowed their heads humbly were filled with large, full, golden kernels of wheat.

—Oliver Bishop Branch, in Gospel Herald

* * *

Why God Used Moody

One reason why God continuously, through so many years, used D. L. Moody was because *he was a humble man.*

I think Moody was the humblest man I ever knew in all my life. He loved to quote the words of another: "Faith gets the most, love works the most, but humility keeps the most." He himself had the humility that keeps everything it gets. As I have already said, he was the most humble man when we bear in mind that which was lavished upon him. Oh, how he loved to put himself in the background and put other men in the foreground. How often he would stand on a platform with some of us little fellows seated behind him and as he spoke he would say: "There are better men coming after me." As he said it, he would point back over his shoulder with his thumb to the "little fellows."

Mr. Moody loved to keep himself in the background. At his conventions,

he would push the other men to the front and, if he could, have them do all the preaching.
—Dr. R. A. Torrey

* * *

Why Not Qualify?

One of the last messages of G. Fred Bergen, Director of the Orphan Homes founded by George Müller, was: "Tell my younger brethren that they may be too big for God to use them, but they cannot be too small."
—*Moody Monthly*

* * *

Meeting Conditions

A government official in India, who was engaged in irrigation work, came to the proprietor of a field and told him he was going to make it fruitful. To which the proprietor answered, "You need not attempt to do anything with my field; it is barren and will produce nothing." The official replied, "I can make your field richly fruitful *if it only lies low enough.*"

If you and I are willing to go down, down, down, Christ will fill us with what will bring forth fruit.
—Gordon Watt, in
The Cross in Faith and Conduct

* * *

Sweet Humility

A hundred years ago, Oberlin, the German philanthropist, was journeying through a snowstorm, near Strasbourg, and lost his way. He was rescued from death by a wagoner who came by after he had sunk in the drifts. The man refused any reward. "Tell me your name, at least," said Oberlin. "Tell me," was the reply, "the name of the Good Samaritan." "His name is not recorded," said Oberlin, wondering. "Then let me withhold mine," said the wagoner.
—*Gospel Herald*

* * *

"He That Is Down!"

He that is down need fear no fall.
He that is low no pride;
He that is humble ever shall
Have God to be his guide.
—John Bunyan

Be Lovely and Not Know It

The supreme height of spiritual loveliness is to be lovely and not to know it. Virtue is so apt to become self-conscious, and so to lose its glow.
—John Henry Jowett

* * *

Washington's Humility

A rider on horseback, many years ago, came across a squad of soldiers who were trying to move a heavy piece of timber. A corporal stood by, giving lordly orders to "heave." But the piece of timber was a trifle too heavy for the squad.

"Why don't you help them?" asked the quiet man on the horse, addressing the important corporal.

"Me? Why, I'm a corporal, sir!" Dismounting, the stranger carefully took his place with the soldiers.

"Now, all together, boys — heave!" he said. And the big piece of timber slid into place. The stranger mounted his horse and addressed the corporal.

"The next time you have a piece of timber for your men to handle, corporal, send for the commander-in-chief."

The horseman was George Washington.
—*Watchman-Examiner*

* * *

"He Did Menial Work, Too."

Hsu Chu, a lad of eighteen from a wealthy Chinese family, came to a China Inland Mission hospital to train as a nurse. Elegantly and becomingly clothed, he was a model of Chinese nobility. A few days after he had begun training, the superintendent was called to deal with him. He had been asked to clean some shoes, and indignantly refused, saying he was a gentleman and a scholar and wouldn't do such menial work. The wise superintendent took the boots and cleaned them herself, while Hsu Chu looked sullenly on. Then leading the lad to the office, she asked him to read for her John's Gospel, chapter 13. When he came to verse 14, his face flushed, and his eyes filled with tears as he laid the Book down, and said, "May Jesus forgive me. He did menial work, too." And from that day, no one scrubbed floors, cleaned shoes, or any other humble task more joyfully than Hsu Chu, who followed in the footsteps of his divine Master.

—*Christian Herald*

* * *

To See His Face

When Thorwaldsen, the famed Danish sculptor, had finished moulding the plastic clay for this statue, he went home, leaving the clay to dry and harden. But, during the night, a dense mist rolled in from the sea. When the sculptor returned to his studio the following morning, he thought that his embryonic masterpiece had been ruined. The majestic head of "Kristus," which had been gazing heavenward, now faced downward. The hands of the clay figure, which had been held aloft as though to bless, were now stretched forward in an inviting way. Gazing upon the altered statue, Thorwaldsen suddenly realized that this was the way the figure ought to be. "If you want to see the face of the 'Kristus,' " the sculptor exclaimed, "you must go down on your knees!"

Yes, and if we would see the face of the One whom this statue represents, we, too, must get down on our knees. And all the time He invites us to do so.

—*The Pilgrim*

* * *

Men God Uses

Someone asked about Saint Francis of Assisi how he could accomplish so much. "This may be why," he said; "the Lord looked down from heaven and said, 'Where can I find the weakest, littlest, meanest man on earth?" Then He saw me, and said, 'I've found him; he won't be proud of it; he'll see that I am using him because of his insignificance.' "

—Donald J. MacKay,
in *Unfeigned Faith*

Silent Under Insult

Never allow yourself to answer again, when you are blamed. Never defend yourself. Let them reprehend you, in private or in public, as much as they please. Let the righteous smite you; is shall be a kindness; and let him reprove you, it shall be an excellent oil, which shall not break your head.

"It is a mark of the deepest and truest humility," says a great saint, "to see ourselves condemned without cause, and to be silent under it. To be silent under insult and wrong is a very noble imitation of our Lord. O my Lord, when I remember in how many ways Thou didst suffer, who in no way deserved it, I know not where my senses are when I am in such a haste to defend and excuse myself.

"Is it possible I should desire anyone to speak any good of me, or to think it, when so many ill things were thought and spoken of Thee! What about being blamed by all men, if only we stand at last blameless before Thee!"

—Alexander Whyte

* * *

Small Enough for God to Use

On one occasion someone said to the late Hudson Taylor, the English physician whom God used to establish the China Inland Mission: "You must sometimes be tempted, Mr. Taylor, to be proud because of the wonderful way God has used you. I doubt if any man living has had greater honor." To this gracious word Mr. Taylor made reply, "On the contrary, I often think that God must have been looking for someone small enough and weak enough for Him to use, and that He found me." In days of stress long ago the prophet Zechariah declared an undying truth: "Not by might, nor by power, but by my Spirit, saith the Lord of Hosts" (4:6).

—Dr. Victor Raymond Edman,
President, Wheaton College, in
Bulletin of Wheaton College.

INFLUENCE
(See also: Christian Example)

Touching Others

"The slightest breeze that ever blew
Some slender grass has wavered,
The smallest life I ever knew
Some other life has flavored.

"We cannot live our lives alone
For other lives we touch
Are either strengthend by our own,
Or weakened just as much."

—*Selected*

* * *

Transformed Into His Likeness

Jonathan Goforth was God's radiant servant always. Of all the messages that reached his wife after he had entered the Gloryland, none touched her as the following: A poor Roman Catholic servant in the home where the Goforths had often visited, on hearing of his passing, said to her master, "When Dr. Goforth has been here I have often watched his face and have wondered if God looked like him!" That dear girl saw in his face, sightless though he was, what she hoped for in her Heavenly Father!

—*"Goforth in China,"*
by Rosalind Goforth

* * *

They Knew Him

A missionary, taking up his work in a strange land, began at once to tell his listeners of Jesus. He told of the selfless love, infinite compassion and tenderness, and the healing power of Christ. He was pleased to see the interest his words awakened. He noted the nods and smiles of his audience, as he told of the Man who went about doing good. Finally he asked how many had ever heard of this Man, and the response was eager and complete. It seemed they all *knew* Him. Upon further inquiry, he found out they were thinking of a Christian doctor who had lived among them at one time and had ministered to them in sickness and health. "Yes," they said, "we knew him well — that man." Oh, so to live that even the unlearned and untaught may recognize the Christlikeness in our lives! This is what He wants, and this is what we should strive for.

—*Sunday School Times*

* * *

A Christian First

When Millet, whose "Angelus" captivated the whole art-loving world, was about to depart from his home for Paris where he became the pupil of Delaroche, his pious grandmother said to him, "I would rather see you dead than unfaithful to God's commands." And when he was just coming into his glory as one of the greatest painters of his day, this same godly woman, whose influence made itself felt in every picture he put on the canvas, said to him, "Remember, my son, you were a Christian before you became a painter."

—W. E. Biederwolf

* * *

Mother's Example Wins!

A fine college student, a senior, said to me after I preached a series of evangelistic sermons,

"I have heard all your sermons on the deity of Christ, the inspiration of the Scriptures, the efficacy of the atoning blood and can answer the logic of everyone of them; but a few weeks ago as I stood with our mourning family by the grave of my invalid mother, and as loving friends lowered her crippled little body into the ground, I said, 'I cannot answer the argument and logic of that wonderful life.' " He said "I want that which made my mother what she *was*." And in a few minutes he found that Saviour, not by the power of logic, but by the power of a quiet, godly life.

—L. R. Scarborough, in
A Search for Souls

Mother's Influence

I took a piece of plastic clay
And idly fashioned it one day,
And as my fingers pressed it still,
It moved and yielded at my will.
I came again when days were past,
The form I gave it still it bore,
But I could change that form no more.
I took a piece of living clay,
And gently formed it day by day,
And molded with my power and art,
A young child's soft and yielding heart,
I came again when days were gone,
It was a man I looked upon,
He still that early impress bore
And I could change it nevermore.

—*Selected*

* * *

"An Unceasing Influence!"

My mother, when she had a large
family of children gathered around her,
made a covenant with three neighbors
— three mothers. They would meet
once a week to pray for the salvation
of their children until all were converted. This was not known until after
my mother's death, the covenant then
being revealed by one of the survivors.
We used to say, "Mother, where are you
going?" and she would say, "I am just
going out a little while, over to the
neighbors'." They kept on in that covenant until all their families were
brought into the Kingdom of God, myself the last; and I trace that line of results back to an evening many years before, when my grandmother commended our family to Christ, the influence
going on until this hour, and it will
never cease. — T. DeWitt Talmage

* * *

"Not In Vain Have I Been I"

If this bit of earth may be
Stronger for the strength I bring,
Sweeter for the songs I sing,
Happier for the path I tread,
Lighter for the light I shed,
Richer for the gifts I give,
Purer for the life I live,
Nobler for the death I die,
Not in vain have I been I.

—*Selected*

A Minister's Influence

A century and a half ago there died
a humble minister in a small village in
Leicestershire, England. He had never attended college and had no degrees.
He was merely a faithful village minister. In his congregation was a young
cobbler to whom he gave special attention, teaching him the Word of God.
This young man was later to be renowned as William Carey, one of the
greatest missionaries of modern times.
This same minister had a son, a boy
whom he taught faithfully, and constantly encouraged. The boy's character and powers were profoundly affected by his father's life. That son was
Robert Hall, the mightiest public orator
of his day, whose sermons influenced
the decisions of statesmen and whose
character was as saintly as his preaching was phenomenal. It seemed that the
village pastor accomplished little. There
were no spectacular revivals, but his
faithful witness and godly life had
much to do with giving India its Carey
and England its Robert Hall.

— *Sunday School Times*

* * *

When the Bishop Needed a Young Man

"I will bless thee ... and thou shalt
be a blessing" (Gen. 12:2). A young
man, sorely baffled, called on Phillips
Brooks. The youth had thought about
his problem a hundred times, and knew
just how he would phrase it when he
met the bishop. After a glorious hour
of fellowship, he left with a radiance
in his soul. When he reached home, he
suddenly remembered, for the first time
that he had completely forgotten to ask
the bishop about his troublesome question. "I did not care," he said. "What
I really needed was not the solution of
a special problem, but the contagion of
a triumphant spirit."

—*Stars in the Sky*

* * *

Because You Passed My Way

My load's a little lighter now,
Because you passed my way —
The sun's a little brighter
And the clouds have passed away.

I've found my Saviour nearer,
And each day He grows still dearer,
And I'm on my way to Glory,
Because you passed my way.

I was lost and no one seemed to care
Until you passed my way,
You saw me, and led me to Christ
Oh, what a happy day,
Now I'm living all for Jesus,
And with Him I'll be some day,
For I found a new beginning,
Because you passed my way.

And when in realms of glory,
I see His precious face,
And hear the angel voices
Within that Heavenly place,
I'll remember that sinner,
Who once had gone astray,
Might not be there in Glory,
Had you not passed my way.
                —Eleanor Taylor Rhodes, in
                Gospel Herald

* * *

"Dead Yet Speaketh!"

Dr. William Wallace, Southern Baptist missionary to China, loved the Chinese people and gave his life for them. He could have left Wuchow when the Communists came, as so many others did, but he refused to leave his hospital and the patients. The Communists imprisoned him, tortured him, and later put him to death. When Dr. M. T. Rankin, executive secretary of the Southern Baptist Foreign Mission Board, later visited some of the mission fields, a Chinese gentleman told him that the Communists had not made much headway in Wuchow and attributed this to the memory of Dr. Wallace. He said that other missionaries had had to leave them, but Dr. Wallace was still there.
                —*Various sources*

* * *

A Picture

From Scotland comes this beautiful and touching incident: One of the rough and hardy fishermen of the Northeast coast was long famous — or infamous — for his drinking propensities. When money was in his pocket it was never long before drink had its way with him. A visitor to the little village noticed in this man's cottage a very beautiful picture, Holman Hunt's "Light of the World," and spoke of it.

"Aye, that's a guid picture," said the fisherman and he told this incident about it.

"I was far down with drink," he said, "when one night I went into a saloon and there hung this picture.

"The sight of it sobered me and I said to the innkeeper, 'Sell me that picture; this is no place for the Saviour.' So I gave him all the money I had and brought the picture home. Then as I looked at it again, the words of my old mother came back to me. I dropped to my knees and cried, 'O Lord Jesus, will You pick me up again and lift me out of all of my sin?' "

The prayer was abundantly answered. Today in that little Scottish town the fisherman is the leader in every good cause.

When the visitor asked him if it had not been a struggle, a look of exultation flashed over the rugged face as he replied, "When such a Saviour comes into the heart He takes the love o' drink out of it." — *Youth's Companion.*

* * *

General Lee's Eloquence

Just at evening, before one of the great battles of the Civil War, Gen. Robert E. Lee, perhaps personally more beloved of his armies than any other military leader, rode out to visit the encampment of some of his most hard-pressed companies. The tired men formed and stood at attention as General Lee, on his famous white horse, rode slowly before the ranks. There was utter silence, as every man saluted. The General rode back along the line. He spoke not a word. With the dignity that never left him, he took off his hat, bowed slightly, and slowly rode away. Suddenly a Georgia sergeant, unable to contain himself any longer, literally burst out of the ranks, "Now then," he shouted, "now then, after what the General said, will you fight, or won't you?"
                —*Christian Advocate*

Sharon's Rose

A Persian fable says: One day
A wanderer found a lump of clay
So redolent of sweet perfume
Its fragrance scented all the room.
"What art thou?" was his quick demand,
"Art thou some gum from Samarcand,
Or spikenard in rude disguise,
Or other costly merchandise?"
"Nay, I am but a lump of clay."
"From whence this wondrous sweetness, say?"
"Friend, if the secret I disclose,
I have been dwelling with a rose!"
Meet parable! For will not those
Who love to dwell with Sharon's Rose
Distill sweet scents o'er all around,
Though poor and mean themselves be found?
Good Lord, abide with us, that we
May catch these fragrances from Thee.
—*Young People's Guide*

* * *

What They Thought of Wesley

A story has come down to us from the days of Wesley concerning his work among the miners of Cornwall. Whole villages were transformed from a gambling, swearing, and Sabbath-breaking people to men and women of sobriety and godliness. In every home was to be found a picture of John Wesley, the man whom they all loved. One day a stranger visiting one of these humble homes seeing John Wesley's picture on the wall said, "Whose picture is that?" The old miner reverently lifted his hat and said, "There was a man sent from God, whose name was John."
— *Serving and Waiting.*

* * *

One Man's Influence

David Brainerd was a man of great spiritual power. The work which he accomplished by prayer was simply marvelous. Dr. A. J. Gordon, in giving a sketch of Brainerd's experience, says, "In the depths of those forests, alone, unable to speak the language of the Indians, he spent whole days literally in prayer. What was he praying for? He knew that he could not reach those savages; he did not understand their language. If he wanted to speak at all, he must find somebody who could vaguely interpret his thought; therefore he knew that anything he should do must be absolutely dependent upon the power of God. So he spent whole days in prayer, simply that the power of the Holy Ghost might come upon him so unmistakably that these people should not be able to stand before him. What was his answer? Once he preached and the interpreter was so intoxicated that he could hardly stand up. That was the best he could do. Yet scores were converted through that sermon. We can account for it only by the tremendous power of God behind him.

"William Carey read his life, and he was so moved by it that he went to India. Henry Martyn read his life, and by its impulse he went to India. Payson read it as a young man of twenty years, and he said he had never been so impressed by anything in his life. Murray McCheyne read it, and was powerfully impressed by it.

"The hidden life, a life whose days are spent in communion with God in trying to reach the Source of power, is the life that moves the world. There may be no one to speak a eulogy over them when they are dead; the great world may take no account of them; but by-and-by, the great moving current of these lives will begin to tell, as in the case of this young man."
—*Herald of Faith*

* * *

Is It Wrong to Play With Dolls?

Is it ever wrong for a little girl to play with dolls? Of course not, you answer; but missionaries have found that it is wrong sometimes. The missionaries tell the heathen that it is wrong to worship idols. The heathen see the little daughters of the missionaries playing with dolls, and they think that the dolls are idols, such as they worship in their houses. Ought not the little girls give up playing with dolls until the people know the difference between a doll and an idol? For the sake of those whom their father is trying to teach about the true God, they must give up their own pleasure.

—*Sunday School Chronicle*

* * *

His Best Sermon

In the summer of 1916, there remained in a certain mission station in China a young English missionary whose four brothers were in the British Army, then in combat. Near the mission station two German businessmen had recently moved into a Chinese house. They had come there because of the unfriendly atmosphere in the settlement in which they had been living. One morning one of the German men went for a hike into the hills, and failed to return. His friend could not speak Chinese, and was at a loss to know what to do. The news finally reached the English missionary. This young man knew that all the surrounding hills were infested with mines against the expected approach of the army of a rival war lord. Nevertheless he went in search of the lost man, and did not give up until he recovered the body. That night several of the Chinese Christians were discussing the event. "Brethren," said one of them, "our missionary is a good preacher, we are all agreed; but he never has preached, and never will preach a sermon like the one he has preached today. Though we should forget every word he has ever said, we can never forget *this thing he has done.* He has made the Gospel live before us."

Rations, 100 *Days*

* * *

My Influence

A careful woman I ought to be;
A little fellow follows me.
I dare not go astray.
For fear he'll go the selfsame way.
Not once can I escape his eyes:
Whate'er he sees me do, he tries.
Like me he says he's going to be —
That little chap who follows me.
He thinks that I am good and fine;
Believes in every word of mine.
The base in me he must not see,
The little chap who follows me.

I must remember as I go,
Through summer sun and winter snow;
I'm building for the years to be
That little chap who follows me.

—*Selected*

* * *

What A Pretty Soul!

"Often we say to one another, 'What a pretty frock!' or, 'What an adorable coat!' or, 'What an exquisite gown!' But we seldom say, 'What a pretty soul! What a charming heart!' " Yet the inner life is the thing of highest value. Said an old and wise writer, "Keep thy heart with all diligence; for out of it are the issues of life."

—Margaret G. Sangster

* * *

On and On!

"I shot an arrow into the air,
It fell to earth, I knew not where;
For so swiftly it flew, the sight
Could not follow in its flight.

"I breathed a song into the air,
It fell to earth, I knew not where;
For who has sight so swift and strong
That it can follow the flight of a song?

"Long, long afterward in an oak
I found the arrow still unbroke,
And the song, from beginning to end
I found again in the heart of a friend."

—Longfellow

* * *

What He Could Not Pack

A young minister was leaving a North County town, and was bidding an old lady good-by. "Well, sir," she said, "you'll be busy packing up your belongings, I expect?" "Yes," he replied. "I have only a few things to get into boxes now."

"There's one thing you won't be able to pack up, sir," said the old lady; "you'll have to leave that behind." "I don't know — whatever is that?" questioned the minister. "You can't pack up your influence, sir," she answered quietly.

—*Christian Herald*

Influence

I spoke a word
And no one heard;
I wrote a word,
And no one cared
Or seemed to heed.
But after half a score of years
It blossomed in a fragrant deed.
Preachers and teachers all are we,
Sowers of seed unconsciously,
Our hearers are beyond our ken,
Yet all we give may come again
With usury of joy and pain;
We never know
To what one little word may grow.
See to it, then, that all your seeds
Be such as bring forth noble deeds.
—John Oxenham

* * *

Influence of an Attraction

U. J. J. Leverrier, the astronomer, noticing irregularities in the orbit of Uranus, surmised that these must be due to the influence of an attraction, though hitherto unknown. *The result of his search for this attractive force was the discovery of a new planet, Neptune.*

A Russian graduate told Robert P. Wilder that his discovery of Jesus Christ *was due to observing closely the saintly life of Baron Paul Nicolay*, who founded and led the Student Christian Movement of Russia.

A student in Columbia University said to a Jewish fellow student: "Do you see the light in the face of yonder student?" "Yes," said the Jewess. "Is it not sad that such light must fade?" The Christian replied: "That kind of light will never fade. Would you like to meet her?" "No," said the Jewess, "*I do not want to be converted.*" The girl with the radiant countenance was not aware of being discussed.

—*Christ in the Student World*

* * *

"You Have Something!"

Frances Ridley Havergal was a devoted Christian as well as an accomplished singer. She was a guest at an occasion where many distinguished people, including the king himself, were present. A famous Italian prima donna had been engaged to furnish entertainment for the brilliant audience, and after a number of wonderful renditions, Miss Havergal was asked if she would sing. She paused a moment in uncertainty, then stepped to the piano and made a most exquisite rendering of a difficult aria from one of Handel's oratorios. Then even before the applause ceased, she began to sing to her own accompaniment, the words of one of her most deeply spiritual poems, for which her pen had become so noted:

"O Saviour, precious Saviour,
Whom yet unseen we love,
O Name of might and favor,
All other names above."

Among the first to congratulate her was the renowned Italian artist who said to her, "You have something I do not have, and I want it."

—*Gospel Herald*

* * *

Appearance of Evil

A well-known Christian worker was riding in a dining car one day, and ordered some grape juice. It was brought to him in a glass of a certain type. Instantly he noticed that on the same table opposite him a man had a bottle of claret wine, and a glass exactly like his, filled with a liquid that looked very much like his. "I wondered," he said "how one of my acquaintances would feel if he saw me sitting at a table with a bottle of wine, and a glass in what appeared to be the same drink. How quickly the story of my wine-drinking would have scattered over the country! I got rid of the grape juice as soon as I could." Yes, he was careful, but not needlessly careful, for such incidents give rise to what can easily become a stumbling block. We never do have any liberty to lead people astray.

—Philip E. Howard, Sr.

* * *

One Touch

May every soul that touches mine,
Be it the slightest contact —
Get therefrom some good;
Some little grace; one kindly thought;
One aspiration yet unfelt;

One bit of courage
For the darkening sky;
One gleam of faith
To brave the thickening ills of life;
One glimpse of brighter skies
Beyond the gathering mists.

—George Eliot

* * *

Held, or Holding On?

I was going through Chicago once, when a prominent man called upon me, sat down at the table by my side, and said, "Mr. Moody, I want you to help me"; and the tears rolled down his cheeks. I said, "What! is it possible that you have lost your hope?" "No," he said. "Are you not still superintendent of that large Sabbath-school?" "Yes." "Is there any known sin that has come into your life and separated you from God?" "No." "Then," I said, "what do you want?" "Well," he said, "the fact is, my wife has something that I haven't got. She has something that keeps her in perfect peace, and I have to hold on all the time to keep my religion." That was the difference between those two sisters. Both loved Christ, but Martha was one of these fretful, anxious, worried women.

—From *Moody's Latest Sermons*

* * *

A Proof of the Word

"David, a man after God's own heart!" said an infidel; "a pretty specimen; a liar, an adulterer, a murderer." "You are a proof of the truth of God's Word," quietly answered the one to whom the words were addressed, "for the Bible says that Nathan said to David, 'By this deed thou hast given great occasion to the enemies of the Lord to blaspheme.'"

—*Christian Reader's Digest*

* * *

The Chimes

A traveler had heard so much of the wonderful chimes of St. Nicholas in Amsterdam, that one day he went up into the tower of the church to hear them. There he found a man hard at work before an immense keyboard, thumping and pounding the keys with his hands encased in wooden gloves.

The traveler was almost deafened by the rattle of the blows on the keys and the harsh discordant clangor of the bells above his head, and hurried away wondering why people talked so much of the beautiful chimes of St. Nicholas. The next day at the same hour he was in a distant part of the city sightseeing, when suddenly the air was filled with the mellow music of marvelously clear and full-toned bells.

"We hear the chimes of St. Nicholas," said the guide in answer to his question, and the man wondered no longer why travelers spoke enthusiastically of their melody. But he thought of the man in the tower, and wondered if he ever knew how beautiful his hard work became in the distance.

If in gloomy moments the thought ever comes to you that your life is shut up to a narrow round of hard work which has in it no beauty or sweetness for you or anyone else, let the story of the chimes teach you better.

—*Fellowship News*

* * *

What Sort of Christian Are You?

Henry Ward Beecher was once asked to explain his position on the use of intoxicating liquors by Christians. He replied: "It is just like this. Suppose there is a precipice out by a schoolhouse, where many children are assembled. Suppose that halfway down the precipice there is a spring that I especially enjoy, and, strong man that I am, I can go down safely, by a narrow path, dangerous to many, but not to me. Suppose that the children are determined to go down there after me, and will not believe that the path is dangerous since they see me tread it with impunity. Some of them that try it fall and break their necks and others are maimed for life. Now, what sort of man — much more, what sort of Christian — should I be if, under these circumstances, I persist in going down that dangerous path? Nay, verily, if I have one particle of magnanimity of soul, if I have been at all of Christ, I shall put a good strong fence across that path, and never tread it any more. This is my position on the total abstinence question.

—*Bible Expositor and Illuminator*

* * *

"A Man Named John Wesley Came to These Parts"

A young nobleman found himself in a little village in Cornwall, England, where he sought in vain for a place where something stronger than water could be procured. Impatiently he inquired of an old peasant who was on his way home after a day of toil, "How is it that I cannot get a glass of liquor in this wretched village of yours?"

The old man, recognizing the questioner as a man of rank, pulled off his cap and bowed humbly, but nevertheless there was a proud flash in his eyes as he answered quietly:

"My lord, something over a hundred years ago, a man named John Wesley came to these parts," and with that the old peasant walked on.

—*Gospel Herald*

* * *

Revealing Fragrance

The first Protestant missionary to Japan, during his service in the Land of the Rising Sun, was brought into touch with members of the royal house of that country. During one of his furloughs in England, he was visited in his apartment by some members of the Emperor's family who were touring Europe. They chatted for perhaps an hour and then left. Later in the day another group from Japan called. "Oh," one of them exclaimed, "you have been entertaining royalty here today." "What makes you think so?" the missionary queried. "Why, there is a perfume manufactured in our country for the exclusive use of the royal family. No one else is allowed to use it, and its fragrant odor is in evidence in this apartment, so that we can tell you have had members of the royal house to visit you here." Do we, who are members of the royal family of Heaven, leave behind fragrance which bespeaks the sweet savor of Christ the King of Glory?

—*Bible Expositor and Illustrator*

* * *

Too Hot To Handle

Bishop Evin Berggrav, primate of the Norwegian Lutheran Church, who was under Nazi guard, is reported to have gotten peculiar treatment from his captors. It is said that his 11-man guard was changed constantly to prevent their coming under his strong spiritual influence,

—*The Pathfinder*

INTERCESSION

Evidence of Prayer

I went to a dear old uncle of mine, Isaiah, before I left the Gipsy tent. I wanted him to be converted, but it would not be good breeding for a mere boy to talk to one of his elders. My uncle noticed a hole in the knee of my corduroys, and said, "My dear, it goes right through," I said, "Yes," and showed him the other knee. He said, "Why, it's worse than the other." I said, "Yes, Uncle, do you know how these holes were worn?" "No, my son, how?" I said, "Praying for you!" "Then," he said, "if that's so, it's time I began to pray for myself!" And he did.

—*Gipsy Smith, in*
The Beauty of Jesus

* * *

A Cure for Irritation

The noble character of General O. O. Howard, whose death occurred some years ago, is well known; and he was often referred to as the "Christian Soldier." Concerning General Howard, Dr. F. E. Clark relates this incident: "When first appointed in command of a regiment located at Governor's Island, he used to walk up and down Broadway, New York, where he was jostled in the crowds. This jostling pained and irritated him, as his arm had been amputated at the shoulder. In his fear that this irritation would sour his disposition he used to pray, as anyone ran into him and hurt him, 'God bless him!' This habit became such second nature with him that he was constantly praying for those about him."

—*Ernest Worker*

* * *

"Try It On Me."

An influential lawyer once rose in a meeting of Mr. Earle, the evangelist, and said: "I have often heard of the power of prayer, but I don't believe a word of it: if you want to test it, take me." The evangelist invited him to come to the front. He replied, "I will do nothing of the kind; but, if you have 'power in prayer,' try it on me." In closing the meeting, Mr. Earle invited all present to pray for the lawyer at an hour he named, and asked the lawyer to note the fact. On the third day that man was crying to God for mercy; and, selling his law books, he became a minister of Christ. —*Alliance Weekly*

* * *

Are We Fulfilling Our Priesthood?

Into the great church of the late Dr. Andrew Bonar, in Glasgow, Mrs. M'Intyre, his daughter, led the Welsh evangelist Fred Clarke. No service was in progress. Mrs. M'Intyre pointed out a pew in the rear where as a wee lass her father had seated her one week day as he went into the empty church. After a long wait she stood up to look for her father. He was seated in a pew, his head bent forward. Soon he moved to another, then another, and another. Sometimes she would see him carefully examine the name plates to find the pews he desired. She did not understand it at the time, but as she grew in stature and the pew-holders grew in grace she learned the significance. The shepherd was praying for the sheep in the very spot where each worshiped.

—*Sunday School Times*

Her Service

Dr. J. H. Jowett used to tell of a little servant girl who applied for membership in his church. He asked her what she was doing for her Lord. She explained that she had very little time off and could seldom attend services or meetings; but, she said, she always took the daily paper up to her bedroom with her at night. Dr. Jowett asked what good that did. "Well," she explained, "I always turn to the Births and Marriages and Deaths. I read over each of these births and pray that these little babies may be early led to the Saviour and made a great blessing to their parents; I read of each wedding and pray that these brides and bridegrooms may be very happy and may always be true to each other; and, reading each of the death notices, I pray, one by one, for all the bereaved that they may turn in their sorrow to the only source of lasting comfort."

—*Sunday School Times*

* * *

Released by Prayer

Dr. Torrey in illustrating the definiteness of prayer, tells the following: "Up in a little town in Maine, things were pretty dead some years ago. The churches were not accomplishing anything. There were a few godly men in the churches, and they said, "Here we are, only uneducated laymen, but something must be done in this town. Let us form a praying band. We will all center our prayers on one man; who shall it be?" They picked out one of the hardest men in town, a hopeless drunkard, and all centered their prayers on him. In a week he was converted. They centered their prayers on the next hardest man in town, and soon he was converted. Then they took up another and another, until within a year, two or three hundred were brought to Christ, and the fire spread out into the surrounding country. Definite prayer for those in the prison house of sin is the need of the day.

—*Sunday School Times*

Why He Believed in Her God

A young, delicate, sweetfaced woman, a Salvation Army officer, was appointed to the charge of an Indian village, where the dominance of a certain caste made any sort of missionary effort almost hopelessly difficult. On the face of it no good had been accomplished. But the pale-faced captain set herself to pray. Every morning before the people were astir she crept through the slumbering village to the jungle beyond, with no other companion than her Bible, and on the same spot morning after morning she prostrated herself on her face before God — the God of India, she said in her petitions — to intercede for the souls which sat in darkness around her. And her prayers were answered, though not as she had asked or expected. She died and never saw the fulfillment. One day, a long time afterward, a tall, powerful, handsome Hindu, with luminous eyes and regal bearing, called at the little mud hut which served as the officers' quarters and told to that faithful captain's successor the story, unknown as it was supposed, of the dead woman's prayers. He had followed her to the jungle, and peering through the heavy undergrowth, had seen her throw herself upon her face and cry to the God of India — his country — and shed overflowing tears for the people of his village — her people, she called them. "Then," he said, "I believed that the God of that woman was a real God, and I made up my mind to worship Him." This was the beginning of a great wave of soul-saving in the village.

—Bible Expositor and Illuminator

* * *

Power of Prayer

A woman came to a missionary at Bengalore, asking him to interfere and prevent a certain native Christian from praying for her any more. When asked how she knew that the Christian was praying for her she replied: "I used to perform my worship to the idols quite comfortably, but for some time past I have not been able to do so. Besides, he told me at one time that he was praying for my family, and now my son and two daughters have become Christians. If he goes on praying, he may make me become a Christian, too. He is always bringing things to pass with his prayers. Somebody must make him stop."

—Missionary Herald

* * *

Because He Is the Son

J. Wilbur Chapman once related this story of one of his friends who was a boyhood companion of Robert Lincoln, the son of Abraham Lincoln. He entered the Civil War and went to the front. When Robert Lincoln found that his friend was a private soldier, he said to an acquaintance, "Write, and tell him to write to me, and I will intercede with Father, and get him something better." The young soldier said: "I never took advantage of the offer, but you do not know what a comfort it was to me. Often after a weary march I would throw myself on the ground and say, 'If it becomes beyond human endurance, I can write to Bob Lincoln and get relief; and I would rather have his intercession than that of the cabinet, because he is a son.' " Every true Christian knows that he has the best Friend possible at the court of Heaven in the Son of God, who "ever liveth to make intercession" for us.

—King's Business

* * *

"You'll Get In."

One day a soldier entered the office of President Lincoln and sat down among about fifty others waiting to see the President. While he was waiting, a little boy named Tad came around, and noticed the man dressed as a soldier, and of course that took his fancy, and he talked to the man. The man showed him his empty sleeve: he had lost an arm in the war. That interested the boy. Just to pass the time away, the soldier told the little boy some interesting war stories, and then the little fellow asked the man what he wanted. He said he wanted to see the President. Tad said, "The President is my father. Do you want to see my father?" The soldier said, "Yes." Tad said, "I will get you in," and ran off. Then a secretary came out and notified all those waiting that the President had only two or three minutes to see visitors, and that they might as well go, for he could not see any more that day except the man then with him. All the people got up to leave, except the soldier. The secretary told him that it was useless to wait. But he said, "The President's son was here, and he has gone in to see his father, to ask if I may come in." The secretary said, "You mean little Tad?" "Yes." "Is he in with his father now?" "Yes," "Well, you will get in to see the President all right. If the President's son is there to plead for you, you wait; you'll get in." Beloved, if the Son has gone in to the Father for you, you will get in. There is no doubt. Trust Him.

—From Edward Drew's
published lessons

* * *

A Great Intercessor

More than half a century ago, George Mueller, that prince of intercessors with God, began to pray for a group of five personal friends. After five years one of them came to Christ. In ten years, two more of them found peace in the same Saviour. He prayed on for twenty-five years, and the fourth man was saved. For the fifth he prayed until the time of his death, and this friend, too, came to Christ a few months afterward.

For this latter friend, Mr. Mueller

had prayed almost fifty-two years! When we behold such perseverance in prayer, we feel that we have scarcely touched the fringe of real importunity in our intercessions for others.

—*Earnest Worker*

* * *

Teach Me, Lord, to Intercede!

Lord, I see the countless millions
  In the land far o'er the sea,
Dying with no hope of Jesus,
  Lost through all eternity;
And I feel so weak and helpless
  As I view this desperate need,
Humbly, Lord, I do beseech Thee,
  Teach me, now, to intercede.

Lord, I see my friends and neighbors
  In a death march toward the grave;
Not one thought of Christ, who bought them,
  Nor the priceless gift He gave;
Then I feel my own undoneness
  Viewing thus this crying need,
And I cry with heartfelt anguish,
  "Teach me, Lord, to intercede."

Lord, I have no wealth to bring Thee,
  And my talents are so few;
But I long for all to know Thee,
  Love Thee as we ought to do.
So while men with brains and talents
  Warn the wicked of their need,
I, within my secret closet,
  Close to God, would intercede.

—Anna Van Buren Prat, in
Way of Holiness

JESUS

Keep on the Road

A young man just starting out upon his work in the ministry was one day talking to an aged minister in London who had spent a lifetime in the service. The young man said:

"You have had a great deal of experience; you know many things that I ought to learn. Can't you give me some advice to carry with me in my new duties?"

"Yes, I can," was the response. "I will give you a piece of advice. You know that in every town in England, no matter how small, in every village or hamlet, though it be hidden in the folds of the mountain or wrapped round by the far-off sea, in every clump of farmhouses, you can find a road which, if you follow it, will take you to London.

"Just so every text which you choose to preach from in the Bible will have a road that leads to Jesus. Be sure you find that road, and follow it; be careful not to miss it once. This is my advice to you." The old minister's advice should be followed by every one, who in any capacity, presumes to be a teacher of Divine Truth.   —*Gospel Herald*

* * *

Have You Ever Heard Such?

Said Spurgeon: "I have heard of ministers who can preach a sermon without mentioning the Name of Jesus from beginning to end.

"If you ever hear a sermon of that kind mind that you never hear another from that man. If a baker once made a loaf of bread without any flour in it, I would take good care that he should never do so again; and I say the same of a man who can preach a Christless gospel. Let those go and hear him who do not value their souls; but dear friends, your soul and mine are too precious to be placed at the mercy of such a preacher."

—*Christian Index*

* * *

Jesus

Lonely? No, not lonely
　With Jesus standing by;
His presence always cheers me,
　I know that He is nigh.

Friendless? No, not friendless
　Since Jesus is my friend;
I change, but He remaineth
　True, faithful to the end.

Sadden'd? No, not sadden'd
　By scenes of deepest woe;
I should be if I knew not
　That Jesus loves me so.

Tired? No, not tired;
　While leaning on His breast
My soul has full enjoyment
　Of His eternal rest.
　　　　—Charlotte S. C. Panton

* * *

What They Said About Him:

Renan, the Frenchman, said, "In Jesus is condensed all that is good and ex-

alted in nature." Thomas Paine, the infidel said, "The morality that He preached has not been exceeded by any." Rousseau stated, "If the life and death of Socrates were those of a martyr, the life and death of Jesus Christ were those of a God." The Jew, Disraeli, acknowledged the fact that, "Jesus has conquered Europe and has changed its name to Christendom." Thomas Jefferson, said, "Jesus Christ has given to us the most sublime and benevolent code of morals ever offered to man." The great theologian and Biblical critic, David Strauss, said, "Jesus remains the highest model of religion within the reach of our thoughts. No perfect piety is possible without His presence in the heart."

— *Gospel Herald*

* * *

"Express Image!"

A Chinese Bible woman was preaching Christ to the scholar of a market town, in the market place. He heard her courteously, and after a little said: "Madam, you speak well, but why do you dwell on Jesus Christ? Let Him alone, and tell us about God." Whereat she replied, "What sir, should we know about God if it were not for Jesus Christ?"

—*Sunday School Times*

* * *

Christ Reflects Deity

In the Rospigliosi Palace in Rome is Guido Reni's famous fresco, "The Aurora," a work unequalled in that period for nobility of line and poetry and color. It is painted on a lofty ceiling. As you stand on the pavement and look up at it, your neck stiffens, your head grows dizzy, and the figures become hazy and indistinct. And so the owner of the palace has placed a broad mirror near the floor. In it the picture is reflected and you can sit down before it and study the wonderful work in comfort. *Jesus Christ does precisely that for us when we try to get some notion of God. He is the mirror of Deity. He is the express image of God's person. He interprets God to our dull hearts. In*

Him God becomes visible and intelligible to us. We cannot by any amount of searching find out God. The more we try the more we are bewildered. Then Jesus Christ appears. He is God stooping down to our level and He enables our feeble thoughts to get some real hold on God Himself.

—Frank M. Fairchild, in *Can We Believe?*

* * *

Example — or Saviour?

Socrates taught for forty years, Plato for fifty, Aristotle for forty, and Jesus for only three; yet those three years infinitely transcend in influence the combined one hundred and thirty years of teaching of Socrates, Plato, and Aristotle, three of the greatest men of all antiquity. Jesus painted no pictures; yet the paintings of Raphael, Michelangelo, and Leonardo da Vinci received their inspiration from Him. Jesus wrote no poetry; but Dante, Milton, and scores of the world's greatest poets were inspired by Him. Jesus composed no music; still Haydn, Handel, Beethoven, Bach, and Mendelssohn reached their highest perfection of melody in the hymns, symphonies, and oratorios written in His praise. Thus every sphere of human greatness has been incomparably enriched by the humble carpenter of Nazareth. But His unique contribution to the race of men is the salvation of the soul. Philosophy could not accomplish that — nor art — nor literature — nor music. Only Jesus Christ can break the power of sin; only He can speak "power into the strengthless soul, and life into the dead." The world admires Christ afar off. Some adopt Him as their example and try to pattern their lives after His. A few open the door of their hearts and invite Him in to be their Saviour.
Though Christ a thousand times in Bethlehem be born,
If He's not born in thee, thy soul is still forlorn.　　　*—Bible In New York*

* * *

The Unique Christ

His birth was contrary to the laws of life.

His death was contrary to the laws of death.

He had no cornfields or fisheries but He could spread a table for five thousand and have bread and fish to spare. He walked on no beautiful carpets or velvet rugs, but He walked on the waters of the Sea of Galilee and they supported Him.

Three years He preached His Gospel. He wrote no book, built no church house, had no monetary backing. But after nineteen hundred years, He is the one central character of human history, the Pivot around which the events of the ages revolve, and the only Regenerator of the human race.

Was it merely the Son of Joseph and Mary, who crossed the world's horizon nineteen hundred years ago? Was it merely human blood that was spilled at Calvary's hill for the redemption of sinners? What thinking man can keep from exclaiming: "My Lord and My God!"

—*Watchman-Examiner*

* * *

One Solitary Life!

I am far within the mark when I say that all the armies that ever marched, and all the navies that ever were built, and all the parliaments that ever sat, and all the kings that ever reigned, put together, have not affected the life of man upon this earth as powerfully as has that one solitary life — the life of Christ.

—Phillips Brooks

* * *

Dr. Kelly's Insignia

Dr. Howard A. Kelly was in the habit of wearing a button with a question mark on it. He has bought them and given them out by the hundreds. He uses it as a springboard for a conversation on Christ. A stranger asks, "What does that question mark mean, Dr. Kelly?" He replies, "What is the greatest thing in the world?" Knowing that they are speaking to a physician, some reply, "Health is the greatest thing." Others in answer to the inquiry say, "Money." "No," this great scientist replies, "the biggest question in the world is: *What think ye of Christ?*" Then he proceeds to say a few words for his Christ, the Great Physician. Busy with carrying the burdens of his patients in the hospital, busy with his cares as a physician, but never too busy to speak a word for his Lord.

—*Christian Herald*

* * *

What Think Ye of Christ?

"Pharisees, with what would ye reproach Jesus?"

"He eateth with publicans and sinners."

"And you, Caiaphas, what have you to say of Him?"

"He is a blasphemer, because He said, "Hereafter ye shall see the Son of Man sitting on the right hand of power and coming in the clouds of heaven.' "

"Pilate, what is your opinion?"

"I find no fault in this Man."

"And you, Judas, who have sold your Master for silver — have you some fearful charge to hurl against Him?"

"I have sinned, in that I have betrayed innocent Blood."

"And you, centurion and soldiers, who led Him to the Cross, what have you to say against Him?"

"Truly this was the Son of God."

"And you, demons?"

"He is the Son of God."

"John the Baptist, what think you of Christ?"

"Behold the Lamb of God."

"And you, John the Apostle?"

"He is the bright and morning Star."

"Peter, what say you of your Master?"

"Thou art the Christ, the Son of the living God."

"And you, Thomas?"

"My Lord and my God."

"Paul, you have persecuted Him; what testify you against Him?"

"I count all things but loss for the excellency of the knowledge of Christ Jesus my Lord."

"Angels of Heaven, what think ye of Jesus?"

"Unto you is born a Saviour, which is Christ the Lord."

"And, Thou, Father in Heaven, who knowest all things?"

"This is My beloved Son, in whom I am well pleased."

Dear reader, what think you of Christ?

—*Elim Evangel*

* * *

Face To Face

Two infidels once sat in a railroad train discussing Christ's wonderful life. One of them said, "I think an interesting romance could be written about Him." The other replied, "And you are just the man to write it. Set forth the correct view of His life and character. Tear down the prevailing sentiment as to His divineness and paint Him as He was — a man among men." The suggestion was acted upon and the romance was written. The man who made the suggestion was Colonel Ingersoll; the author was General Lew Wallace; and the book was *Ben Hur*. In the process of constructing it he found himself facing the unaccountable Man. The more he studied His life and character the more profoundly he was convinced that He was more than a man among men; until at length, like the centurion under the cross, he was constrained to cry, "*Verily, this was the Son of God!*"

—D. J. Burrell

* * *

Every Knee Shall Bow

A number of prominent literary men were assembled in a clubroom in London one day a number of years ago. The conversation veered to a discussion of some of the illustrious figures of the past, and one of the company suddenly asked: "Gentlemen, what would we do if Milton were to enter this room?"

"Ah," replied one of the circle, "we would give him such an ovation as might compensate for the tardy recognition accorded him by the men of his own day."

"And if Shakespeare entered?" asked another.

"We would arise and crown him master of song," was the answer.

"And if Jesus Christ were to enter?" asked another.

"I think," said Charles Lamb amid an intense silence, "we would all fall on our faces."

—*King's Business*

* * *

A Rabbi Who Was Conquered

Some years ago two Christian missionaries entered a town in Poland. No Jew would listen to them. At last they sent a challenge to the rabbi for a public debate on whether Jesus was the Christ. For three days the synagogue was crowded, and at last the missionaries were cast out, spit upon, and beaten, and barely escaped with their lives. The rabbi was applauded as a splendid monument of truth. Next Sabbath he did not conduct the worship. Another Sabbath passed with a deputy preacher. Then a notice was issued that Rabbi Goldringer wished to see all the members of the synagogue on the third Sabbath. Amid breathless silence, the rabbi, very pale, arose and said: "Brethren, you are all aware of the recent controversy. You were good enough to acclaim me as victor in that debate. As I have to stand before the Judge of all the earth, I must tell you, let the consequences be what they may, that *I* was conquered; and I am here to say, among all those who know me best, that Jesus of Nazareth is the Messiah of whom Moses and the Law spake."

—*Dawn*

* * *

Proof Enough

A great many people are inclined to discount the history of Jonah and the whale, as told in the Bible. They tell us that they just can't "swallow" it.

One day a man traveling on a train became engaged in a conversation about the Bible with the passenger seated next to him. "If you can prove to me that Jonah was swallowed by a whale, I'll believe all the rest of the Bible," he said.

"What do you think of Christ?" asked his companion.

"That's beside the point," he answered.

"But do you think that Christ was wise?"

"Yes," he said. "I think Christ was the wisest Man that ever lived."

"Well, then, if He was the wisest Man that ever lived, and I could show you that He believed that Jonah was swallowed by the whale, would you believe it yourself?"

"I certainly would," the man answered immediately. So his newly-made acquaintance opened a New Testament, turned to Matthew 12:40 and told the man to read it. He read aloud: "As Jonah was three days and three nights in the whale's belly, so shall the Son of Man be three days and three nights in the heart of the earth."

"It was Christ who said that, He believed the account of Jonah and the whale."

"Thanks, mister," was the reply. "I never saw that before. That's proof enough for me."

If doubters would examine the evidence of the Scriptures, their doubts would fall away into faith.

—*Essex*

* * *

Three Reasons Why China Needs Christ

C. K. Lee, a native Christian leader of China, was in this country a few years ago. One Sunday he spoke in a modernistic church in California. At the conclusion of the message, a young college student propounded this question, "Why should we export Christianity to China when you have Confucianism in your country?" "There are three reasons," was the rejoinder. "First of all, Confucius was a teacher and Christ is a Saviour. China needs a Saviour more than she needs a teacher. In the second place, Confucius is dead and Christ is alive. China needs a living Saviour. In the third place, Confucius is some day going to stand before Christ to be judged by Him. China needs to *know* Christ as Saviour before she meets Him as Judge."

—*Triumphs of Faith*

* * *

Why the Same Text?

The following story came direct to us from the Rev. Mr. Cunningham of South China: One day a well-dressed, intelligent-looking man came to the Street

Chapel. He sat and listened well for some time, then left. This was repeated three consecutive days. Then he rose and addressed the missionary, saying: "I have heard you speak three times and you always have the same text. Why don't you change it?" Mr. Cunningham, somewhat surprised, asked, "What text?" "Jesus Christ," was the reply. After a moment's silence the missionary replied: "Sir, before answering your question, may I ask you: "What had you for dinner today?" "Rice," replied the man. "What food had you yesterday?" Again came — "Rice." "And what do you expect to eat in the future," the missionary asked. "Rice, of course. Rice gives me strength. I could not do without it. Sir, it is — " he hesitated as if for a strong word — "Sir, it is my very life!" The missionary raised his hand, "That is just what I wanted from you. What you have said of rice, Jesus Christ is to our souls. He is the *rice of life*."

—Rosalind Goforth, in
The Christian Digest

* * *

The Carpenter

"The sun beat down on the village,
  And in at the open door;
But the Carpenter's hands were busy,
  For the Carpenter's folk were poor.
The sweat was bright on His forehead,
  As He cut and planed each length;
For, to feed and to clothe His dear ones,
  The Carpenter gave His strength.

"The Carpenter stood in the city,
  And the helpless about Him lay;
The lame man shouted for fleetness;
  The blind man sobbed for the day.
And healing flowed from His fingers;
  At His touch the weak grew brave;
For, to heal and to help the helpless,
  His virtue the Carpenter gave.

"On a lonely hill, Golgotha,
  Men set the cruel Tree;
And crucified the Carpenter
  That day for you and me.
They nailed those hands so holy.
  Those feet they drove the spike —
For, to save the souls of all mankind,
  The Carpenter gave His life."

—*Selected*

Who Is the Man?

A few years ago the principal of the English Mission College at Cairo, Egypt, received a letter from a Japanese Buddhist of the city whose children were attending his school. "Who is John three sixteen? My children are always talking about him?"

The principal sent a note back saying that "John three sixteen" was not a person but a verse out of a book.

He promptly received another letter from the man. "Can you supply me with a copy of the book?"

A copy was sent and although the man was then leaving Cairo, the principal soon received word that the father and all members of the family had become Christians.

—*Wesleyan Methodist*

* * *

We Need More Than an Example

Dr. Joseph Parker on one occasion, referred to the Unitarian conception of Jesus Christ as a great example only, and then went on to say: "We have been to hear Paderewski play. It was wonderful, superb, magnificent. Then we went home and looked at the piano. We would have sold it to the first man who would have been fool enough to buy it. This is the effect of your great examples upon us. I want not only a great example, but a great Saviour, one who can deliver me from my weakness and my sins." To follow a good example in the future will not blot out the black record of the past; we need the blood of Christ's atoning sacrifice to accomplish that. To hear a Paderewski play will not make us like a Paderewski. Could a Paderewski incarnate himself within one, he could play like himself. So the Christian life is not Christ and I, but Christ in me. We need the Christ within to live the Christ without.

—*Moody Monthly*

* * *

Ingersol on Christ

"In using my speeches do not use any assault I may have made on Christ, which I foolishly made in my early life. With Renan, I believe Christ was the one perfect man. 'Do unto others' is the perfection of religion and morality. It is the *summum bonum*. It was loftier than the teachings of Socrates, Plato, Mohammed, Moses or Confucius. It superseded the commandments that Moses claimed to have gotten from God, for with Christ's 'do unto others' there could be no murder, lying, covetousness or war. It superseded Greek patriotism, Roman fortitude, or Anglo-Saxon bravery, for with 'do unto others' bravery and patriotism would not be needed."

—M. D. Landon, in
Homilectic Review

* * *

All Things to All Men

Christ was a home missionary, in the house of Lazarus.

Christ was a foreign missionary, when the Greeks came to him.

Christ was a city missionary, when he taught in Samaria.

Christ was a Sunday school missionary, when he opened up the Scriptures and set men to studying the Word of God.

Christ was a children's missionary, when he took them in his arms and blessed them.

Christ was a missionary to the poor, when he opened the eyes of the blind beggar.

Christ was a missionary to the rich, when he opened the spiritual eyes of Zacchaeus.

Even on the cross, Christ was a missionary to the robber, and his last command was the missionary commission.

—Amos R. Wells

* * *

We Are No Different Today

One evening, at a small literary gathering at which Thomas Carlyle was present, a famous self-righteous lady was bewailing the wickedness of the Jews in not receiving our Saviour, and ended her diatribe by expressing regret that He had not appeared in our day. "How delighted," said she, "we should all be to throw our doors open to Him and listen to His divine precepts. Don't

you think so, Mr. Carlyle?" Thus appealed to, he replied: "No, madam, I don't. I think that, had He come very fashionably dressed, with plenty of money, and preaching doctrines palatable to society, I might have had the honor of receiving from you a card of invitation, on the back of which would be written, 'To meet our Saviour'; but if He had come uttering His sublime precepts, and denouncing the pharisees, and associating with the publicans and lower classes, as He did, you would have treated Him much as the Jews did, and have cried out, 'Away with Him!'"

—Tom M. Olson, in
Sunday School Times

* * *

Christ's Last Will and Testament:

He left His purse to Judas; His body to Joseph of Arimathea; His mother to John; His clothes to the soldiers; His peace to His disciples; His supper to His followers; Himself as an example and as a servant; His Gospel to the world; His presence always with God's children!

—*Selected*

* * *

The Ship That Couldn't Sink

At the time of the sinking of the *Titanic*, one of our great American preachers was in Belfast, Ireland. The *Titanic* had been built in Belfast, and there was a great local pride over the mighty ship. She had been heralded far and wide as "the unsinkable ship." Sixteen members of the church in Belfast, all skilled mechanics, went down with her. The mayor said that Belfast had never been in such grief as that which came over this terrible tragedy. When the news finally was verified that the gallant ship was certainly lost, so deep was the grief that it is said strong men met upon the streets, grasped each other's hands, burst into tears, and parted without a word. The visiting American preached the Sunday after the tragedy in the church to which the sixteen members who had been lost belonged. Not only was the building packed with people, but on the platform were lords, bishops, and ministers of all denominations. In the audience many newly-made widows were sitting, and orphans were sobbing on every side. The great preacher took as his subject, "The Unsinkable Ship." But he did not apply that term to the *Titanic*, which on her first voyage had gone out into the Atlantic and crashed into an iceberg, carrying her precious cargo of human lives down to watery death. No, the preacher's message was about that other "unsinkable ship" — the frail boat on the Sea of Galilee, unsinkable because the Master of land and sea was asleep on a pillow in the after part of the vessel. Thank God He still lives and rides the billows and controls the storms, and when the children of men take their only true Pilot back on board, we will ride out the present storms and He will bring the vessel through to the fair harbor of our hopes.

—*American Fundamentalist*

* * *

Our Lord's Mother — But

A Romanist soldier was lying wounded in France, when a chaplain went near him, and the wounded man said, "I don't want you — you don't believe in 'Our Mother.' " Said the chaplain, "We respect Mary as the mother of our Lord, but you look as if you need the doctor." "Yes," said the man. The chaplain answered, "Will you have the doctor, or the doctor's mother?" *We need Jesus Christ, the great Physician,* more than His mother.

—*Christian Herald*

* * *

Tributes to Christ

Christ is the great central fact of the world's history. All lines of history converge upon Him. All the great purposes of God culminate in Him.

—Charles Spurgeon

* * *

The life of Christ, the holiest among the mighty and the mightiest among the holy, has lifted with its pierced hands empires off their hinges and turned the stream of centuries out of its channel, and still governs the ages.

—Jean Paul Richter

The image of Christ shall never be effaced. It shall be painted in the hearts of men.

* * *

I find the name of Jesus Christ written on the top of every page of human history.

—George Bancroft

* * *

If Christ be not divine, every impulse of the Christian world falls to a lower octave, and light and love and hope decline.

—Henry Ward Beecher

* * *

The True Messiah

A Jewish soldier had heard much about the character and teachings of Jesus. He went to his rabbi and said, "Rabbi, the Christians say that the Christ has already come, when we claim that He is yet to come." "Right," asserted the rabbi. "Well," asked the young soldier, "when our Christ comes, what will He have on Jesus Christ?" "That," said the rabbi, "we do not know!" What else could he say?

—*Moody Monthly*

* * *

When Christ Is in the Right Place

A father, reading his Sunday paper and wishing not to be disturbed by his little girl, cut up a map of the world, gave it to her, and told her to put it together. After awhile she returned with it and every piece was in its place. The father was very much surprised and said: "Why, how did you do it, darling? You don't know anything about geography." The little one replied, "There was a picture of Jesus on the other side, and I knew when I had Jesus in the right place, the whole world would be all right."

—*Eight Bells, Haven of Rest*

* * *

Mender of Broken Hearts

Max I. Reich tells of passing a repairing shop in the window of which was a sign reading: "We mend everything except broken hearts." Brother Reich stepped back and entered the store, and when a beautiful young Jewess came forward to serve him he said: "I saw your sign, and want to ask what you do with people who have broken hearts." "Oh!" she said: "We send them to the hospital." "You are a Jewess, are you not?" Did you ever read Isaiah 57:15? 'For thus saith the high and lofty One that inhabiteth eternity, whose name is Holy; I dwell in the high and holy place, with him also that is of a contrite and humble spirit, to revive the spirit of the humble, and to revive the heart of the contrite ones.' And," continued Mr. Reich, "there was also He who read Isaiah 61:1, in his home-town synagogue at Nazareth. The verse contains the words 'He hath sent me to bind up the brokenhearted.' And," said Mr. Reich, "the Messiah added, 'This day is this scripture fulfilled in your ears.' " (Luke 4:21).

—Rev. Max I. Reich

* * *

If Virtue Walked the Earth

Once, it is said, a Scottish preacher of the modern school closed a sermon with these words, "Virtue is so attractive that, if she were to become incarnate, and walk the world in human form, men would fall down and worship her." The pulpit of that church was occupied the same evening by a different type of preacher, a humble evangelical man, who loved the gospel of a crucified Redeemer. He preached Christ crucified, and at the close of his discourse reminded the congregation of the statement made in the morning by the senior preacher, and then added, "I am sorry to say that Virtue did once walk the world in human form, in the person of the Lord Jesus Christ, and men, instead of falling down and worshipping Him, crucified and nailed Him to a tree."

—*Heart and Life* Magazine

* * *

Daniel Webster's Saviour

This story is told of Daniel Webster when he was in the prime of his manhood. He was dining with a company of literary men in Boston. During the dinner the conversation turned upon the subject of Christianity. Mr. Webster frankly stated his belief in the divinity of Christ and his dependence upon the atonement of the Saviour. One said to him, "Mr. Webster, can you comprehend how Christ could be both God and man?" Mr. Webster promptly replied, "No, sir, I cannot comprehend it. If I could comprehend him, he would be no greater than myself. I feel that I need a superhuman Saviour."

—*Christian Witness*

* * *

The Only Name That Mattered

Mrs. Booth used to tell a beautiful story of a man whose saintly life left its permanent and gracious impress upon her own. He seemed to grow in grace and charm and in all nobleness with every day he lived. At last he could speak of nothing but the glories of his Saviour, and his face was radiant with awe and affection whenever he mentioned that holy name. It chanced that, as he was dying, a document was discovered that imperatively required his signature. He held the pen for one brief moment, wrote, and fell back upon the pillows, dead. And on the paper he had written, not his own name, but the name that is above every name. Within sight of the things within the veil, *that* seemed to be the only name that mattered.

—From *Mushrooms on the Moor*, by Dr. F. W. Boreham.

* * *

The Jockey's Discovery

A retired jockey, whom a mission worker was eager to win to Christ, appeared at a mission service on Palm Sunday. The lesson that evening was that of Jesus entering Jerusalem. After the service the jockey commented on the story. "What a jockey He would have made! I know what He was riding. It was a Syrian colt. I had a drove of those beasts to break once. Jesus sat on one that nobody had ever ridden before. And all those youngsters were running in front and waving palms. Yet Jesus was holding him as meek as anything." The jockey paused a moment, and then

335

said, "I say, if He could do that with a bit of horseflesh, I reckon He could do something with me." —*The Dawn*

* * *

The Incomparable Christ
II Corinthians 8:9

In infancy He startled a king; in boyhood He puzzled the doctors, in manhood He walked upon the billows and hushed the sea to sleep. He healed the multitudes without medicine and made no charge for His services. He never wrote a book, yet not all the libraries of the country could hold the books that could be written about Him. He never wrote a song, yet He has furnished the theme of more songs than all song writers combined. He never founded a college, yet all the schools together cannot boast of as many students as He has. Great men have come and gone, yet He lives on. Death could not destroy Him, the grave could not hold Him.

—Forman Linicome

* * *

"Jesus Lived His Inside Out!"

Said a lad to his dad, "Daddy, Jesus was the only One who dared to live His inside out!" Indeed, He was! "the crystal Christ!" He was the only utterly selfless Personage who ever lived. His WHOLE life was dedicated, without the least alloy of self, to the relief and service of all who stood in need of them. Possessing an infinite capacity for love, He was able to treat every other being's suffering and sorrow as if they were His own. All human woe mattered to Him! —**W. B. K.**

More Than an Example

A big lump of something — a stone supposedly — lay for centuries in a shallow limpid brook in North Carolina. People passing that way saw only an *ugly lump*, and passed on. A poor man passing one day saw a *heavy lump* — a good thing to hold his door ajar — and he took it home. A geologist who stopped at the poor man's door one day saw a *lump* of *gold* — the biggest lump of gold ever found east of the Rockies. Many people looked upon Jesus. Some saw only a Galilean peasant, and turned away. Some saw a prophet, and stopped to listen. Some saw the Messiah, and worshipped. Some saw the Lamb of God, and looked to him to save them from their sins. There are people today who see in Jesus simply a perfect man, and they get nothing more from him than the example of his perfect life. Others looking upon him see the Lamb of God — the divinely chosen sacrifice and Saviour; and realizing that their greatest need is to be saved from their sins they go to him for cleansing. When you look at Jesus what do you see?

—*Expositor*

* * *

"The Three Short Years!"

"The three short years of the public ministry of Jesus have done more to soften and regenerate mankind than all the moralizing of all the moralists, and all the philosophising of all the philosophers since the world began!"

—Leckey

JEW

A Name To Fear

One day when Dr. H. A. Ironside set out for a walk, it began to rain. His umbrella was in need of some repair work, and he noticed an old Jewish handy man with some umbrella parts under his arm and learned that he could fix the umbrella.

Ironside watched as the old man

worked. His face was furrowed and he was obviously poor. When asked the charge, the man replied, "Thirty-five cents."

Ironside gave him the thirty-five cents and then said, "I can imagine you have to do many jobs like this to earn a living. Here is an extra half dollar which I would like to give you in the

name of the Lord Jesus Christ."
The old man was stunned. He replied,
"In the name of Jesus Christ they
burned my house in Russia! In the
name of Jesus Christ they robbed me of
all I had! In the name of Jesus Christ
they drove me and my family out into
the snow! I have been in America four
years, and now for the first time someone speaks to me in the name of Jesus
Christ, and gives me more money than
I ask!"

—*Christian Life*

* * *

God's Chosen People

Forgotten; No; that cannot be:
All other names may pass away,
But thine, MY ISRAEL, shall remain
In everlasting memory.

Forgotten! No; that cannot be:
Inscribed upon My palms thou art,
The name I gave in days of old
Is graven still upon My heart.

Forgotten! No; that cannot be:
Beloved of thy God art thou
His crown forever on thy head,
His Name forever on thy brow.

Forgotten! No; that cannot be:
Sun, moon, and stars may cease to shine,
But thou shalt be remembered still,
For thou art His and He is thine.

—*Horatius Bonar*

* * *

A Jew Who Did Not "Escape."

When traveling in a train in Palestine, Rabbi Slostowski was given a Testament by a Christian Jew. He says,
"That very evening I went to my room
in Jerusalem and began to read the New
Testament. Before I started to read, I
prayed: 'Open thou mine eyes, that I
may behold wondrous things out of thy
law.' I read until three o'clock in the
morning, then kneeled down to pray. I
besought the Lord that he would show
me the truth: which is right and which
is wrong — the Talmud or the New Testament? And for the first time in my
life I prayed *in the name of Jesus!* Following this prayer there came into my

heart such peace and joy as I had never
before experienced. I knew beyond any
shadow of doubt that the Lord Jesus
was the long-foretold Messiah of the
Jews, and the Saviour of the world, and
I accepted him as my own personal
Saviour. After this I went to bed, but
I could not sleep. I still had the new
consciousness of joy and peace and assurance. Then I heard a real voice saying to me: 'Do not escape from me any
more. I will use you to glorify my
Name and to be my witness.' I wish
to point out that it was not imagination,
but a real fact. Immediately I answered: 'Lord, here am I.' From that
time my life has not belonged to myself
but to him. At first I was a secret believer like Nicodemus. Then came the
decision to confess Christ openly—come
what would! Persecutions rapidly followed, but these did not deter me in the
least."

—George T. B. Davis, in
Sunday School Times

* * *

Well-Scattered Treasure

God said time and again that He
would scatter Israel among all the nations of the earth, and I have taken
pains to ascertain whether there are
Israelites to be found in the most remote
parts of the earth. I asked Dr. Peck
whether there were Israelites among
the Eskimos in the Arctic Circle and
he told me there were quite a number
of them. I asked Dr. Crawford, who
worked in Central Africa, and he said
he had found them there. I asked Dr.
Hudson Taylor whether there were any
in China, and he said there were many
of them. I have yet to find the country
where there are no Israelites. You will
remember Christ's own parable about
the hid treasure, how a certain man
found a treasure in a field and then he
did a very remarkable thing, he went
and hid it in the field again, and then
bought the field to get the treasure out
of it. That treasure is Israel.

—Canon F. E. Howitt

* * *

His Rabbi's Message

While riding one day in a New York
subway train, I sat beside a young Jew,

and breathed a prayer for guidance as to how to begin a conversation with him. I handed him a tract, and after he read it I asked him how he felt toward Christ. He tried to dodge the question, but after a few minutes he said this, "I must get off at the next station, but I will tell you what our rabbi told us last Saturday — that he was beginning to think that Jesus Christ, after all, may be our Messiah, and that we have been wrong all these centuries." The Jew smiled as he said it, and then added: "You look surprised; so did every Jew in the synagogue." He then left the train, and I prayed that he as well as the rabbi would soon find the Saviour.

—*Sunday School Times*

* * *

"Rabbi" Duncan's Longing

When "Rabbi" Duncan, the great Presbyterian professor of Hebrew, was dying in Edinburgh, someone told him there was a man in the infirmary whose language no one could speak. "I will learn it, I will learn it," said the dying scholar, "that I may tell him about the Saviour." Have we ever felt a passion like that — a passionate longing to tell every sinner we meet about the Saviour?

—From *The Glorious Company of the Apostles*, by J. D. Jones

* * *

Can Jews Be Converted?

Some years ago a minister of the Church of England in London had attended an early morning prayer meeting in the interest of Jewish missions. Coming out on the street he met a brother clergyman who had just come out of a special service at St. Paul's Cathedral on the anniversary of the conversion of St. Paul. After an exchange of greetings, the minister who had been at St. Paul's asked the other where he had been that morning. He told him of the Jewish mission's prayer meeting, upon which the other showed some surprise that his friend should happen to believe in the possibility of Jews being converted. The other asked him where he had been, and he told him

of the special anniversary service at St. Paul's. "Who was St. Paul?" he asked him. After a moment's hesitation he said, "I suppose you would call him a Hebrew Christian, a converted Jew." "What music did they have?" "Why, Mendelssohn's St. Paul, of course." "Who was Mendelssohn?" "Why, a German." "No, he was a converted Jew," was the reply. "Who was the preacher?" "Dr. Jacobs, Bishop of St. Albin's." This man did not believe in the power of God to convert Jews into the Christian faith, and yet he had been in the church dedicated to the memory of a converted Jew; attended a service in honor of this Jew's conversion; listened to music composed by a converted Jew, and was greeted on that early morning by the Rev. Aaron Bernstein, a converted Jew.

—*Earnest Worker*

* * *

"The Conversion Epidemic Among Jews

At least 204,500 Jews were converted during the past century.

A leading Jewish journalist in a recent article, "The Conversion Epidemic among the Jews," confesses that these converts are not just ordinary persons but men of prominence; not the poor and ignorant who embrace Christ but very often the intelligent and wealthy class. Says he: "It must be acknowledged that in the last century so many hundreds of thousands leave us, I maintain that the number of those who have been baptized, since the death of Moses Mendelssohn to the present day, is not less than 350,000 Jews."

—Rev. Jacob Garternaus

* * *

Interesting Facts:

Ancient Jerusalem lies buried from thirty to one hundred feet below the level of the present city. Jerusalem has been besieged forty-six times. It has been completely razed to the ground seventeen times!

—*Selected*

* * *

Why the Jews Wouldn't Sign

In a costly residential section of the city of Richmond some new owners complained that the singing of a small Christian church near by disturbed them. A petition to be presented to the city council was circulated. It was brought also to a Jewish resident, who said, "Gentlemen, I cannot sign it. If I believed as do these Christians, that my Messiah had come, I would shout it from the housetops and on every street of Richmond, and nobody could stop me."

—*Moody Monthly*

* * *

How to Destroy the Jews

In the diminutive *Christian Witness*, being published in England, we find this interesting note on how to destroy the Jews. The editor requests that Anti-Semitists take notice. He quotes from Jeremiah 31:35-37, in which the Lord declares that if the ordinances of the sun, moon, and stars were to cease, then the seed of Israel should also cease to be a nation. The editor goes on to point out the order in which those who despise Israel should proceed. First of all, they must blot out the sun, cast away the moon, and entirely destroy the stellar universes overhead. Then, and not until then, can they proceed to exterminate the Jewish people.

—*King's Business*

* * *

A Great Galaxy of Jewish Converts

There is a galaxy of great stars of Jewish converts who have won world-wide fame as historians, musicians, philanthropists, statesmen, diplomatists, theologians and missionaries. Let me mention a few in order to persuade even the most skeptical person:

Benjamin Disraeli (Lord Beaconsfield), Prime Minister of England, statesman.

Alfred Eidershein, theologian and writer.

Rev. Christian David Ginsberg, author of the greatest Biblical work of the age, "Massoreth-ha Massorah."

Rev. Ridley Herschell and son, Lord Herschell; Lord Chancellor of England, astronomer.

Rabbi J. Lichenstein, who confessed Christ before his congregation, which he served for forty years, thus stirring all Hungary.

Felix Mendelssohn, distinguished composer.

Joseph Rabinowitz, of Kischineff, whose remarkable conversion stirred all the Jews of Russia. Scholar, philanthropist.

Bishop Shereshewsky, who translated the Bible and prayer-book into Wenli dialect, thereby reaching 250,000,000 heathen souls. Described by Prof. Max Muller as one of the six most learned orientalists of the world. Founder of St. John's College, Shanghai, China.

Sir Arthur Sullivan, author, composer of operas, and church music. Composer of the tune of the popular hymn, "Onward Christian Soldiers."

Joseph Wolff, missionary who traveled the world over with the Gospel message. Son of a rabbi: called "Missionary Shakespeare."

Neander, the "Father of modern church history, a child in spirit, a man in intellect, a giant in learning and a saint in piety, as Philip Schaff characterizes him in his "History of the Christian Church."

L. S. Jacoby, the founder of the Methodist churches on the Continent.

Julius Kobner, a man greatly gifted, who was used of God in the conversion of large numbers in Germany, Holland, Denmark and who, together with Oncken, founded the Baptist churches in these countries.

Isaac De Costa, the poet laureate of the Netherlands, who according to the Encyclopedia Britannica, ranks first among the poets of Holland.

—Rev. Jacob Garternaus

* * *

God of Jew Remind Us Yet!

God of the ancient Hebrew race,
Lord of the Abrahamic Line,
Illumine us that we may trace
Through Holy Writ Thy vast design.
God of the Jew! Remind us yet,
Lest we forget — lest we forget!

These are Thy Chosen People, Lord —
In them all nations shall be blessed
When Israel, redeemed, restored,

Within the Promised Land finds rest.
Thou Hope of Zion, rouse us yet,
Lest we forget — lest we forget!

To them adoption doth pertain,
The covenants, the glory, too;
The promises for aye remain;
The law was given — to the Jew.
God of the fathers, guard us yet,
Lest we forget — lest we forget!

The Holy Ghost moved men of old,
And they, with far prophetic view,
God's great redemptive plan foretold;
The Book was written — by the Jew.
Spirit of Truth, Oh teach us yet,
Lest we forget — lest we forget!

God's love, eternal as His Name,
On them abides, unchanging, true —
Of David's seed Messiah came,
For Jesus Christ was born — a Jew!
Thou Son of God, forgive us yet,
That we forget — that we forget.

—Selected

* * *

A Significant Difference

A prominent Jewish rabbi wrote thus:
"It is not merely that legends have
been woven around his name. Every
great religious genius has been enhaloed
with loving legend. The significant fact
is that time has not faded the vividness
of his image. Poetry still sings his
praise. He is still the living comrade
of countless lives. No Moslem ever
sings, 'Mohammed, lover of my soul,'
nor does any Jew say of Moses the
teacher, 'I need thee every hour.' " What
an admission! And think of that day
when all Israel shall be saved, and the
Redeemer shall turn away ungodliness
from Jacob. Then indeed every Israelite will sing, "My Jesus, I love Thee, I
know Thou art mine."

—Chosen People

* * *

Disraeli's Answer

When some members of the British
House of Commons taunted Benjamin
Disraeli with being a Jew, he replied,
"It is true that I am a Jew, but I would
like the honorable members to know
that when their ancestors were living

in the woods with their bodies painted,
little better than savages, my ancestors
were writing the Book of Psalms and
building Solomon's Temple." That was
a noble and truthful reply. In these
days of anti-Semitic propaganda, it is
well for us to remember that in those
days of paganism and ignorance, the
Jewish people kept alive a knowledge
of God, righteous, holy.

—Christian Herald

* * *

Our Debt to the Jew

The Christian in a special way owes
an incalculable debt to the Jew. The
Hebrew Scriptures are the English Bible, and it is, therefore, not surprising
that popular feeling against the Jew in
this country waned as Puritan love of
the Bible waxed strong. . . . When we
say "Amen" at the close of our devotions, we are speaking Hebrew. When
we look for the "glory of God in the
face of Jesus Christ," we are gazing at
the features of a Jew. When we meet
at the Lord's table to eat the bread and
drink the wine, we are keeping a feast
which was first ordained and observed
by Jews. When we bid our loved ones
a tender, last farewell, we do so rejoicing in the hope of a reunion in the
golden streets of that city which is called
the New Jerusalem. In view of all this,
recognizing the immense debt of Christianity to Judaism, and remembering
that Jesus was born a Jew, it is almost
inconceivable that Christians could favor anti-Semitism.

—British Weekly

* * *

Allenby's Answered Prayer

Allenby Bridge was built to honor Allenby whom God used to miraculously
make conquest of Jerusalem without
the firing of a single gun. It spans
the Jordan River. Allenby told how as
a little boy when he knelt to say his
evening prayers he was taught to lisp
after his mother the closing part of
the prayer, "And, O Lord, we would
not forget Thine ancient people, Israel;
hasten the day when Israel shall again
be Thy people and shall be restored to

Thy favor and to their land." At a reception in London, Allenby said, "I never knew then that God would give me the privilege of helping to answer my own childhood prayers."   —*Chosen People*

* * *

"Lord, Send Messiah!"

Recently in one of the orthodox synagogues of Brooklyn during certain days of repentance and prayer, Jews were seen lying on their faces before God, crying to Him for protection upon their persecuted brethren, especially in Russia. One elderly Jew lifted up his hands toward heaven and in an agony of soul, cried out: "Oh, that Thou wouldest rend the heavens and come down . . . . Lord," he said. "Send Messiah, and should Jesus of the Gentiles be the one, grant us a sign that we may be sure that it is really so, and forgive our guilt toward Him."

—*Herald of His Coming*

* * *

Through Closed Doors

A Jewish woman gave this remarkable testimony in a church in Toronto: She had been living in Constantinople; and one day her husband came home and told her that he had met Jesus of Nazareth, and that He was the Messiah for whom Jewry was waiting. He said he was now His disciple, and he called Him his Saviour and his Lord. She was very angry and set herself to make his life as unhappy as possible. He bore it patiently and said to her, "If only you knew my Lord Jesus, everything would be different." After several months she became convinced that some change had taken place in him, and was convicted in her own soul. She said, "I went up to my room and locked the door, and got down on my knees, and said, 'O God, if Jesus of Nazareth be really my Messiah, let Him introduce Himself to me.' I cannot tell you how, but He came through the shut door as He did on the day of His resurrection, and said, 'I am Jesus whom thou persecutest.' I bowed in His presence and said, 'My Lord and my God'!" How marvelous! The Lord Jesus still proves Himself alive by passing through the closed doors of man's

blindness whenever He hears the earnest prayer of a willing, seeking heart within.

—*Victory Magazine*

* * *

The Healing Jew

This bit from *The Nation* caught my eye. Just think of it, in medicine alone how much we owe to the men of a single race! And sofar as I know not one of these men is an American:

A Nazi with heart disease must not use digitalis, discovered by a Jew, Ludwig Traube. If he has a toothache, a Nazi will not use cocaine, or he will be using the work of a Jew, Solomon Stricker. Nor will he be treated for typhus by the discoveries of the Jews, Widall and Weill. If he has diabetes, he must not use insulin, the discovery of a Jew, Mikowsky. If he has a headache, he must shun pyramidon and antipyrin, discovered by Jews, Spiro and Eilege. Nazis with convulsions must avoid chloral hydrate, the discovery of a Jew, Oskar Liebreich.

—*Justus Timberline*

* * *

Their Wish Terribly Fulfilled

A German woman entered the maternity ward of a hospital in Germany. She saw a picture of Christ in the room, and she asked the nurse to take it down. "I have no authority to take it down," said the nurse. "Then see your superiors, and have it removed as soon as possible," said the woman. The superiors in the hospital said, likewise, that they had no authority to take it down. "My husband is an army officer, and when he comes in a few days, I will get him to see to it that it is taken down." The few days passed and the husband arrived. The German woman told her husband to have the picture taken down. He started to interview one of the authorities, and said, "*My wife and I do not want our boy (both were hoping the new arrival would be a boy), ever to look upon the picture of that Jew!*" And even while he was still speaking, word arrived that a baby boy had just been born to the parents — but, *he was born blind*, hopelessly blind. No, he never *would* look on the picture of that Jew!

—*Chosen People*

341

JOY

The Shining Face

More than seventy years ago, when the great missionary Adoniram Judson, was home on furlough, he passed through Stonington, Conn. In those days the Stonington Line was the principal route between New England and New York, and the boys of the town often played about the wharves in the evening in the hope to catching a glimpse of some famous man.

One evening, one of the boys noticed a man whose appearance excited his curiosity and wonder. Never before had he seen such a light on any human face. Presently it dawned on him that the man was the famous missionary whose picture he had once seen. He ran up the street to the Baptist minister's, to ask if it could really be he. The minister hurried back with him. Yes, the boy was right. But the minister, absorbed in conversation with the missionary, forgot all about the boy who had brought him the news. The boy, silent, eager, unable to tear himself away, stood by and watched that wonderful face.

Many years afterward, that boy, Henry Clay Trumbull, became a famous minister himself, and wrote a book of memories in which was a chapter entitled, "What a boy saw in the face of Adoniram Judson." Doctor Trumbull, too, has passed away, but the light in the missionary's face still shines down the years. Friends to whom Doctor Trumbull told the story told it to others, and the printed pages — who can tell to how many lives they have carried their message.

—*Gospel Herald*

* * *

Three Cheers

A well-known worker among sailors, the late Thomas Boue, once told his hearers of three good cheers, each of which was enjoined by the Lord Jesus Christ. The first is the cheer of forgiveness, as our Saviour said, "Be of good cheer; thy sins be forgiven thee." The second is the cheer of companionship, as Jesus said, "Be of good cheer; it is I; be not afraid." And the third is the cheer of victory, "Be of good cheer; I have overcome the world." These three cheers cover the whole of life, for it is a striking fact that they deal with our past, present, and future. The sin of the past is blotted out for the Christian, the continual fellowship of Christ is offered for the present, and the future will reveal Christ as the conqueror over the world.

—*Toronto Globe*

* * *

Why So Cheerful?

On a train to Liverpool a Christian worker found himself in a crowded compartment seated near two soldiers, one a private, the other a sergeant in his middle thirties. The private was a young lad, ruddy and open of countenance. The Christian worker's heart went out to the boy, and he engaged both of the soldiers in conversation. To his surprise he discovered that they had been through the ordeal of Dunkirk. The younger man appeared particularly happy and cheerful; appeared to look on life as though it were to him a rosy morn. The civilian said to him, "You went through that terrible experience of Dunkirk, yet you seem so happy and cheerful." "Oh, sir," the boy said, "but Dunkirk did a lot for me." "A lot for you? What did it do?" "It brought me to Christ. While I was right in the midst of that conflict, I trusted Him as I had been taught. I was saved, and have been rejoicing in Him ever since."

—*Home Evangel*

* * *

No Money — No Learning — But Joy

A prayer meeting was being held at a mission chapel. A poor coolie came and kneeled. He could not understand even the simple Gospel message. While others were rejoicing, he kept on saying, "Jesus!" which was all the prayer he knew. Soon he rose, and with a happy face, he said: "I am only a poor coolie; I have no money and no learning, but in my heart I have an unable-to-speak-it-out joy."

—*Christian Herald*

* * *

"Not a Single Smile."

A lady told me that as she passed by a church in a London suburb one Sunday, a workingman said to his companion, "Look at 'em, Bill! I've seen a hundred or two people go in there and not a single *smile* among 'em!"

—From *"The Unknown God,"* by One Who Loves Him.

* * *

The Usual Expression

When a certain president of the London Baptist Association began his year of office he was sent to have his photograph taken. The photographer said to him, "Excuse me, sir, but who are you?" He said, "I am a minister." "Oh," said the photographer, "then it will be a solemn expression, please." He asked why. "Well," said the photographer, "it's usual, isn't it?" And that is what the world thinks of some of us. They do not think we are marching to Glory. We do not look like it.

—A. Lindsay Clegg,
at a Keswick Convention

* * *

The Difference

Testified a Scotsman who had found the Lord Jesus Christ as his Saviour, that he was so joyful that he could scarcely find words to express himself. He stood up in a testimony meeting and declared, "I'm happier noo, when I'm *no* happy, than I wis afore when I wis happy."

—*Sunday School Times*

* * *

Crossing Non-existent Bridges

Let us be of good cheer, remembering that the misfortunes hardest to bear are those which never come. — Lowell.

God Is Here

"Strong are walls around me,
   That hold me all the day;
But they who thus have bound me
   Cannot keep God away:
My very dungeon walls are dear
Because the God I love is here.

"They know, who thus oppress me,
   'Tis hard to be alone;
But know not One can bless me
   Who comes through bars and stone.
He makes my dungeon's darkness bright
And fills my bosom with delight."

—Madam Guyon

* * *

Is Your Flag Flying?

Principal Rainy, of whom a child once remarked that she believed he went to Heaven every night because he was so happy every day, once used a fine metaphor about a Christian's joy. "Joy," he said, "is the flag which is flown from the castle of the heart when the King is in residence there."

—*British Weekly*

* * *

Shut In, But —

"A little bird am I
   Shut from the fields of air;
And in my cage I sit and sing
   To Him who placed me there;
Well pleased a prisoner to be,
Because, my God, it pleaseth Thee.

"Oh, it is grand to soar
   These bolts and bars above
To Him whose purpose I adore,
   Whose providence I love!
And in Thy mighty will to find
The joy, the freedom of the mind."

—Madam Guyon

* * *

Dangling by Rope 'Neath Airship

Three men were accidentally carried aloft by the great airship Akron, as they clung to a ground-rope that should have been cast off. The thousands that witnessed the plight of these men were horrified as they watched them holding on in awful desperation while they were being carried higher and higher. The strength of one man failed and he went hurtling down to instant death. Men prayed and cursed by turns. Women shrieked and fainted. Another fell. And when at last the third was safely drawn up to the dirigible, there was unrestrained and universal rejoicing over his rescue. But only rarely indeed does a man's imminent danger of a fall to spiritual death occasion violent grief, or another's rescue to salvation in Christ bring tears and exclamations of rejoicing to an onlooking multitude.

—*Gospel Herald*

* * *

The Result of A Smile:

One Sunday evening, David Livingstone sat in the Aberdeen Music Hall listening to a service rendered by a deputation from the London Missionary Society. When the service was over, Livingstone looked wistfully after the team as they filed out the door. The look on his face so attracted the attention of a congregational minister who was standing nearby, that he stepped quietly to the boy's side and with a smile asked, "My boy, would you like to be a missionary?" Livingstone later said that it was *that smile*, questioning and tender, which led him to make his final decision to serve his Saviour as a foreign missionary.

—*Sunday*

* * *

Does Your Food Agree With You?

At a mission hall in London, a wealthy lady, who was unfortunately deaf, made good use of her riches by providing for the poor some excellent Gospel services. On one occasion a celebrated preacher said to her, "And what part do you take in this noble work?" "Oh," she answered quietly, "I smile them in, and I smile them out again." Soon after this the preacher saw the good results of her sympathy as a crowd of working men entered the hall and looked delighted to get a smile from her. The Bread of Life cannot be recommended to people by those who look as if that food disagreed with them.

—*Sunday School Times*

"Be Supernaturally Joyous!"

George Mueller would not preach until his heart was happy in the grace of God; Jan Ruysbroeck would not write while his feelings were low, but would retire to a quiet place and wait on God till he felt the spirit of inspiration. It is well known that the elevated spirits of a group of Moravians convinced John Wesley of the reality of their religion, and helped to bring him a short time later to a state of true conversion.

The Christian owes it to the world to be supernaturally joyful.

—Dr. A. W. Tozer,
in *Alliance Weekly*

* * *

Her Sacrifice of Praise

It is not to the honor of our gracious Master that we should sit under juniper trees, hang our harps upon willows, and walk about the world in the shadow of death and despair. "I won't be unhappy," said a fine old saint; "it is all I have to give to God and I will praise Him and glorify Him by a happy face and a radiant life."

—A. B. Simpson, in
Alliance Weekly

* * *

The Benefit of Laughter

An eminent surgeon says: "Encourage your child to be merry and to laugh aloud; a good, hearty laugh expands the chest and makes the blood bound merrily along. A good laugh will sound right through the house. It will not only do your child good, but will be a benefit to all who hear, and be an important means of driving the blues away from a dwelling. Merriment is very catching, and spreads in a remarkable manner, few being able to resist the contagion. A hearty laugh is delightful harmony; indeed it is the best of music."

—*Gospel Herald*

* * *

"My Sun!"

One windy day, I visited a girl, kept at home by a lame hip. Her room was on the north side of a bleak house.

"Poor girl," I thought, "what a cheerless life is yours."

"You never have any sun," I said: "not a ray comes in at these windows Sunshine is everything. I love it!"

"Oh," she answered, with the sweetest of smiles, "my sun pours in at every window and through every crack."

I looked surprised.

"The Sun of Righteousness," she said softly. "Jesus — He shines in here, and makes everything bright to me."

—*Gospel Herald*

* * *

Midnight to Noonday

A girl in a mission school in India sang all day as she went about her tasks. When asked why she was so happy, she said: "I have been redeemed from idolatry, and you can never know what that means. I am at liberty. It is like slipping suddenly from midnight darkness into brightest noontide of glory."

—*Sunday Companion*

* * *

Where Is Happiness

Not in Unbelief — Voltaire was an infidel of the most pronounced type. He wrote:

"I wish I had never been born."

Not in Money — Jay Gould, the American millionaire, had plenty of that. When dying, he said:

"I suppose I am the most miserable devil on earth."

Not in Position and Fame — Lord Beaconsfield enjoyed more than his share of both, he wrote:

"Youth is a mistake, manhood a struggle, old age a secret."

Certainly Not in Infidelity —

Thomas Payne cried out during his last moments: "O Lord, help me! God, help me! Jesus Christ, help me!" Voltaire said: "I am lost! I am lost! Oh, that I had never been born!" Colonel Charteris said: "I would gladly give 30,000 pounds to have it proved to my satisfaction that there is no such place as hell."

Not in Pleasure —

Lord Byron, who revelled in pleasure all his days, wrote on his last birthday:

"My days are in the yellow leaf,
The flowers and fruits of life are gone,
The worm, the canker, and the grief
Are mine alone."

Not in Power —

The name of Napoleon, the Great, truly stands prominent for power. Musing, a lonely prisoner on St. Helena, he summarized thus: "Alexander, Caesar, Charlemagne, and myself founded empires. But on what did we found them? On Force! Jesus Christ alone founded His on Love, and today there are millions who would die for Him."

Where then is happiness to be found? Jesus said, "I will see you again, and your heart shall rejoice, and your joy no man taketh from you" (John 16:22).

The answer is simple:

"In Christ Alone"

Taste for yourself, and you will say:
None other Name for me,
There's love and light, and lasting joy,
Lord Jesus, found in Thee."

—*King's Business*

* * *

Sincere Congratulation

The Rev. John Newton one day called to visit a Christian family that had suffered the loss of all they possessed by fire. He found the pious mistress and said: "I give you joy, Madam." Surprised, and ready to be offended, she exclaimed: "What! joy that all my property is consumed?" "Oh, no," he answered, "but joy that you have so much property that fire cannot touch."

—D. L. Moody

* * *

Cheer Up in Reverse

A human being with a heart that is melodious and thankful and humble is invulnerable. You cannot do anything to him. The sources of his joy are very real. While in Florida I went to see an old Negro woman 101 years old. She was bedridden. All her folks, she said, had already died — her husband about fifty years before, and the children one by one. She said they would get along to about fifty or sixty and then they seemed to drop off. There she was, bereft of husband and children, and absolutely helpless. Someone asked me to go to see her and cheer her up. Bless my soul! I had not been there ten minutes until I had her praying for me and cheering me. She said, "I am going to talk to my Pappy in Heaven about you." It was so sweet — so good.

—Dr. C. I. Scofield

* * *

"It Isn't Raining Rain to Me!"

"It isn't raining rain to me,
    It's raining daffodils!
In ev'ry dimpling drop I see
    Wild flowers on the hills!

"A cloud of gray engulfs the day
    And overwhelms the town;
It isn't raining rain to me,
    It's raining roses down!

"It isn't raining rain to me,
    But fields of clover blooms,
Where any buccaneering bee
    May find a bed and roam!

"A health, then, to the happy,
    A fig to him who frets!
It isn't raining rain to me,
    It's raining violets!"

—Robert Loveman

* * *

Smiling In the Storm

An Atlantic liner was caught in a storm. For two days the wind raged. Passengers were frightened. At last an anxious passenger climbed by great effort to where he could see the pilot. Coming back down among the passengers, he spread the glad tidings of peace. Said he, "We are all right. The ship will make port; for I have seen the pilot, and he is *smiling*. With the great Pilot directing our life we can smile on through every storm and smiling, be at peace.

—*Youth's Comrade*

"Count It All Joy."

The missionary reached the little Chinese town shortly after bandits had done their worst. A native Christian showed the ruins of his home; thatched roof, rafters, rude furniture, all turned to ashes. Then, as though it were the last straw, he said, "They even burned my Bible and hymnbook!" And from the ruins, he picked a single page of his Chinese hymnbook, the only thing that had escaped the flames! The missionary took it and read, "Joy to the world, the Lord is come!" It seemed a mockery — this note of joy in the midst of desolation. But if you could have gone to the little chapel and seen the light on the faces of those Christians, who had lost nearly everything, and heard them speak of the home Jesus has prepared for those who love Him, you would know there is joy to the world, because the Lord has come!

—*Sunday School Times*

* * *

The Ridgewarbler

In his "Hunting for the Nightingale in England" John Burroughs tells of listening one black night to the song of the ridgewarbler in the hedge. It was a singular medley of notes, hurried chirps, trills, calls, and warbles. When it stopped singing, a stone flung into the bush set it going again, its song being now so persistently animated as to fill the gloom and darkness with joy. The more he is persecuted the more joyfully he sings. Samuel Rutherford's most gladsome letters are those from his prison. The saints have sung their sweetest when the thorns have pierced their hearts the deepest.

—*Sunday School Times*

* * *

Overflowing Joy

In her book "Floods on Dry Ground," Miss Stuart Watt tells of a revival at an African village named Imbai, which was characterized by intense joy. People would come from far distances with the request, "We want the overflowing joy." Among others, three Walese, semi-pygmies, were sent there by a missionary.

At first, for they were heathen, they were unmoved by the meetings, but later they were awakened by the Holy Spirit, and when asked what they really wanted God to do for them, replied, "The Christians have an overflowing joy. We want God to give that joy to us." When the way of salvation had been made clear to them, they prayed thus, "O God, we don't want our sins any more. Take them away and give us the joy the other people have got in Jesus." When telling their friends about it afterward, they used to add, "And God gave it to us that day."

—*Sunday School Times*

* * *

Religion and Insanity

Because an insane person incoherently dwells on religious questions, unthinking persons jump to the conclusion that often religion is responsible for mental unbalance. Someone wrote Dr. A. B. Richardson, superintendent of an insane asylum in Ohio, for information, perhaps to get confirmation of the notion. Dr. Richardson's answer is worth quoting: "You have asked me an easy question. I have tested that matter thoroughly. There are only two patients in the hospital whose insanity has any relation to religion, and I think from their predisposition to insanity that they would probably have become insane on some other subject if they had not on religion. Now if you had asked me how many people in Ohio are *kept by religion from insanity*, you would have given me a question hard to answer, for they are a multitude. The good cheer, bright hopes, rich consolations, good tempers, regular habits, and glad songs of religion are such an antidote for the causes of insanity, that thousands of people are preserved from insanity by them. But for the beneficial influence of religion, Ohio would have to double the capacity of her hospitals in order to accommodate her insane patients."

—*Moody Monthly*

* * *

Where to Turn Our Eyes

Not long ago there lived an old bedridden saint, and a Christian lady who visited her found her always very cheerful. This visitor had a lady friend of wealth who constantly looked on the dark side of things, and was always cast down although she was a professed Christian. She thought it would do this lady good to see the bedridden saint, so she took her down to the house. She lived in the garret, five stories up, and when they had got to the first story, the lady drew up her dress and said, "How dark and filthy it is!" "It's better higher up," said her friend. They got to the next story, and it was no better; the lady complained again, but her friend replied "It's better higher up." At the third floor it seemed still worse, and the lady kept complaining, but her friend kept saying, "It's better higher up." At last they got to the fifth story, and when they went into the sickroom there was a nice carpet on the floor, there were flowering plants in the window and little birds singing. And there they found this bedridden saint — one of those saints whom God is polishing for his own temple — just beaming with joy. The lady said to her, "It must be very hard for you to lie here." She smiled and said, "It's better higher up." Yes! And if things go against us, my friends, let us remember that "it's better higher up."

—*The King's Business*

* * *

What Won Them

From a mission field comes this testimony: There were many of us small boys in our village in the Belgian Congo. When the missionaries came, we listened to them, marveled at their gentleness, the things they had in their houses, the way they treated the sick, but we did not think of adopting their ways. One day a teacher whom we admired very much went down the river to meet his wife. We waited eagerly to see the new "Mama." But when the canoe returned to our beach some time later, the teacher was alone. His wife had been taken ill on the steamer from Leopoldville and had died before her husband reached her. So our teacher came back to us alone, his heart filled with sadness. But he did not go into

347

his house to weep and wail for weeks as did my people. He carried on his work, preaching to us at every opportunity, saying, "I have joy, because I have Christ." We no longer could be indifferent to the teachings of a man who in his deep personal sorrow showed that he had joy because he had Christ. We wanted to know his Christ. Later, six of my chums and I became inquirers and were baptized. And we learned that in trial and sorrow He was our joy, even Jesus.

—*Secret Place*

* * *

What Restored Dr. Scofield's Joy

In Texas, many years ago, I had visiting me a dear brother in the Lord from Chicago. One morning I was strangely downcast. It was a spiritual depression. I had no indigestion, nothing was the matter with my liver, and there was no way for accounting for that cloud between me and my Father's face. I could have wept. I believe I did. I could not pray. Along about noon it passed away, and there was the shining of His blessed face down in my heart again, and I sang for joy. I said to Johnson, "My dear fellow, I was very depressed." "Yes, I observed it." "I think you went and prayed for me," I said. "No; I ought to have done so; I had a call to; but I did not. But I think your Great High Priest did." I think he prayed something like this: "Father, restore the joy of his salvation; give him the joy of the Lord. I have washed him in my blood and given him my Spirit. Give him joy." It flooded my soul.

—Dr. C. I. Scofield

* * *

Cheerfulness and Health

"Never eat when mad or sad, only when glad," has a scientific basis and significance. Mental conditions depress or stimulate the functions of the various organs of the body. Every cell is influenced favorably or unfavorably by the condition of the mind. "A merry heart doeth good like a medicine," but "by sorrow of the heart the spirit is broken." "Better is a dry morsel, and quietness therewith, than a house full of sacrifices with strife." A change of the mental attitude will cure many a dyspeptic after a corrected diet and other measures have failed.

Of the early disciples of Christ, the record says that they "did eat their meat with gladness and singleness of heart, praising God" (Acts 2:46, 47).

The meal hours should be the most enjoyable time of the day for the family. Nothing of an unpleasant nature should be permitted to be brought up on these occasions. Children should not be arrayed before the father, who has probably been taken away from them during the day, and reminded of their misdeeds during his absence. There is a time to correct children, but the meal hour is not that time. Cheerful topics of an educational and uplifting nature should be dwelt upon. The proverb contains a scientific truth, "Better is a dinner of herbs where love is, than a stalled ox and hatred therewith."

—*Gospel Herald*

* * *

"But, Doctor, I'm That Clown!"

Sometime ago, a poor, nervous wreck called on a famous London doctor. Said the doctor: "You need to laugh. Go down and hear Grimaldi, the famous clown. All London is holding its sides laughing at him." But the visitor straightened himself and said, "Doctor, I am Grimaldi." No, we cannot laugh it off, but there is One Whose cooling, healing touch has still its ancient power:

"Jesus, the Name that calms our fears
And bids our sorrows cease;
'Tis music to the sinner's ear;
'Tis life and health and peace."

—*Gospel Herald*

* * *

Preserved Or Pickled?

Aunt Sophia made this comment concerning Psalm 40:11 — "Let Thy lovingkindness and Thy truth continually preserve me." She said, "Dat is just like the deah Lord. He puts His trusting children right in de big sause pan of His lub, and He sweetens dem with de sweetness of His grace, so dey nebber

get sour. And when you see one who
is cross and fretful and gloomy, bress
you, honey; dey's not preserved, dey's
only pickled."

—*Gospel Herald*

* * *

Spoonsful Of Sunshine!

As a little girl was eating — tiny
little tot she was — she saw coming
through the window a ray of sunlight,
which was focused right on her spoon.
As the little thing put the spoon into
her mouth, she exclaimed with a cheery
laugh: "Look, I have swallowed a spoon-
ful of sunshine." We ought to swallow spoonfuls every day. Everywhere
we go we should scatter sunshine rather
than shadows.

—George W. Truett

* * *

Get a Transfer

If you are on the Gloomy Line,
  Get a transfer.
If you're inclined to fret and pine,
  Get a transfer.
Get off the track of Doubt and Gloom,
Get on a Sunshine Train, there's room,
  Get a transfer.

If you are on the Worry Train,
  Get a transfer.

You must not stay there and complain:
  Get a transfer.
The Cheerful Cars are passing through,
And there is lots of room for you,
  Get a transfer.

If you are on the Grouchy Track,
  Get a transfer.
Just take a Happy Special back,
  Get a transfer.
Jump on the train and pull the rope,
That lands you at the Station Hope,
  Get a transfer.

— *Canadian Baptist.*

* * *

On Laughter

Anatomically considered, laughing is
the sensation of feeling good all over
and showing it principally in one spot.
If a man cannot laugh there is some
mistake made in putting him together,
and if he will not laugh he wants as
much keeping away from as a bear trap
when it is set. Genuine laughing is the
vent of the soul, the nostrils of the heart,
and it is just as necessary for health and
happiness as spring water is for a
trout.

— Josh Billings, in *United Evangelical.*

JUDGMENT

A Starling Which Talked

A lawyer had a caged starling in his
office. The starling had learned to answer when he was called. One morning
a boy named Charlie entered the office.
The lawyer went out for a few minutes,
and when he returned the cage was
empty.

"Where is the bird," he asked the
boy. The boy answered that he didn't
know. "Sonny, that bird was in the
cage when I went out. Where has it
gone?"

Charlie repeated that he did not know
anything about the bird; that probably
the door of the cage was open and the

bird had flown away. At that the lawyer called out, "Starling, where are
you?"

"Here I am," answered the starling,
and the voice came from the boy's pocket.

Imagine Charlie's situation. He had
stolen the bird and hidden it in what he
thought was a safe place. To hide his
guilt he had lied twice; then the voice
came from his pocket to betray him.
There was no way he could deny that
testimony. Not a word could he say.
The bird was a living witness of his
guilt, of his theft and of his lie.

That is what will happen when a
world of guilty sinners who have tried

to hide from God are hauled before the last high judgment bar. Every mouth will be stopped and all will be found guilty before God.

—Missionary Norman Lewis, in, *The Sword of the Lord.*

* * *

What Did You DO?

Possibly, our greatest accountability before God, in the day of judgment, will be for the sins of OMISSION, the things which we should have done, and didn't; the little acts of service we could have rendered; the little acts of kindness we could have shown, and didn't. In Christ's judgment of the nations, it was not so much what they had done, but what they had not done: "For I was an hungered and ye gave me no meat: I was thirsty, and ye gave me no drink!" They took no strangers in; they visited no prisoners. They had lived in calloused indifference to the human need and suffering all about them. They had eaten their morsel alone!

—W. B. K.

* * *

"A Rendezvous with Christ!"

I have a rendezvous with Christ,
And that time not far away,
When all I am and do and say
Shall counted be, and weighed by Him —
I have a rendezvous with Christ
Ere days are run and eyes grow dim.
It seemed 'twere better far
To follow the career I'd chose
Than let some mighty Power
Turn my course at His high will —
And all for self my own days fill:
But I have a rendezvous with Christ!
All other aims in that must pale —
For fatal is it if I fail —
And I to my pledged word am true,
I shall not fail that rendezvous!

—Betty Thornton, in
Sunday School Times

* * *

Just as in the Word

"The morning after reaching Palestine, when setting out for Ramleh, across the plain of Sharon, we saw a shepherd leading forth a flock of white

sheep and black goats, all mingled as they followed him. Presently he turned aside into a little green valley, and stood facing the flock. When a sheep came up he tapped it with his long staff on the right side of the head, and it quickly moved off to his right; a goat he tapped on the other side, and it went to his left. Thus the Saviour's image presented itself exactly before our eyes."

—Prof. J. A. Broadus

* * *

Retaliation

Seth Joshua, one of the leaders of the great Welsh revival of a generation ago once arrived in a town where he was scheduled to preach and found placards everywhere announcing "the Great Seth Joshua." They told all about him but were in reality advertising a stage imitation of the minister at a local theatre that night. Grotesque drawings promised much fun at the expense of this servant of the Lord. That night the theatre was packed and the crowd cheered as the actor came on the stage in perfect imitation of preacher Joshua.

The actor raised his arms as he circled the stage burlesquing the Bible and the evangelist.

The third time around the actor fell with a thud and a hushed audience soon discovered that he was dead.

God will not hold his wrath forever.

—*Sunday*

* * *

Judgment Day Sooner Than He Thought

A Scottish lawyer was a wicked man. Once he hired a horse and, either through accident or ill-usage, killed the animal. Naturally the owner insisted on being paid its value, together with some compensation for the loss of its use. The man of law acknowledged his liability, and said he was perfectly willing to pay, but at the moment he was a little straightened for ready cash. Would the hirer of the animal accept a promissory note? "Certainly," he said. Whereupon the lawyer further said that he must be allowed a long date. "You can fix your own time," said the creditor. Whereupon the wicked man drew the note, making it payable at the Day of Judgment. Eventually the creditor took the matter to court, and there, in defense, the lawyer asked the judge to look at the note. He did so, and then replied: "The promissory note is perfectly good, sir, and as this is day of judgment, I decree that you pay tomorrow." The Negro proverb quaintly expresses a great truth: "The Devil helps the thief every day, but one day God helps the policeman."

—*Methodist Recorder*

* * *

Preaching Judgment

I determined that I would cry aloud against the sins of the people and bring to bear the very fires of hell as a final consequence of their rebellion. For almost two hours I literally flailed the evil doers who sat before me. I called God to witness that the judgment was not far off for them. Concluding, I gave a few moments to the mercy of God but I did that in a stern manner. I was determined that the people should for once stand face to face with the fact of sin and hell. That night the meeting broke and I think I have never experienced such a divine demonstration.

—Charles Finney

* * *

No Fear of Judgment

I do not expect to be judged at the last day. I have no fear of the great white throne. My case has been settled in the Court of Mercy, in which God is judge and Jesus Christ is the advocate. "There is, therefore, no condemnation to them who are in Christ Jesus." "Who shall bring anything to the charge of God's elect?" If you desire to take an appeal from this Court of Mercy to the Supreme Court of Justice you may do so. *I prefer to come to God, the Judge of all, today when I may be represented by such an advocate as Jesus Christ.*

—A. C. Dixon

* * *

What Made Booth Salvationist

Many Christians say with their lips that they believe in the day of accountability, but are as silent as the sphinx when it comes to warning others to flee from the wrath to come. The thing that made William Booth a "fiery" Salvationist was the indicting, taunting statement of an infidel lecturer, who said, "If I believed what you Christians say you believe with reference to the coming judgment and day of reckoning, with the resultant eternal lostness of the impenitent Christ-rejectors, then I would crawl on my bare knees on crushed glass all over London, England, night and day telling men and women to flee from the wrath to come!"

—W. B. K.

* * *

Then What?

Charles G. Finney, a young lawyer, was sitting in a village law office in the state of New York. Finney had just come into the old squire's office. It was very early in the day, and he was all alone when the Lord began to deal with him.

"Finney, what are you going to do when you finish your course?"

"Put out a shingle and practice law."

"Then what?" "Get rich."

"Then what?" "Retire."

"Then what?" "Die."

"Then what?" And the words came tremblingly, "The judgment."

He ran for the woods a half mile away. All day he prayed, and vowed that he would never leave until he had made his peace with God. He saw himself at the judgment bar of God. For four years he had studied law, and now the vanity of a selfish life, lived for the enjoyment of the things of this world, was made clear to him.

Finney came out of the woods that evening, after a long struggle, with the high purpose of living henceforth to the glory of God and of enjoying Him forever. From that moment blessings untold filled his life, and God used him in a mighty way, not as a lawyer but as a preacher, to bring thousands to conversion over a useful period of fifty years.

—*The Church Herald*

KINDNESS

His Practical Interest

In Shanghai, China, it is a common sight to see four or five coolies pulling a heavily laden cart. They get on well enough on the level, but when they come to go up over the bridges they often find it difficult to tug the cart up. As I crossed a bridge I saw a well-dressed Chinese gentleman that I knew go to the assistance of a cart that was stuck, and, laying hold of a rope, give just the extra help that was needed to get the cart to the top of the bridge. I must have caused a good deal of surprise to the passer-by, and not least to the coolies. My friend overtook me a few minutes later, and said, "I am very much interested in the laboring classes." "Yes," said I, "I saw you taking a very practical interest just now." He answered: "That is my work; whenever I see them unable to pull their loads, I help them to the top, and then I have a chance for a few moments to preach the Gospel to them. I tell them, 'It is because I am a Christian that I helped you, because I love Jesus.' And if I see a wheelbarrow upset in the street (a very common sight), I help the man replace his load, then preach the Gospel to him."

—*China's Millions*

* * *

Wordsworth Wields Ax

Wordsworth, the English poet, relates an incident in his early life. Wandering through a wood, he came upon a tottering old man, trying with his mattock to unearth the root of a tree. The task was obviously far beyond his feeble strength, and his patience was at breaking point. The young Wordsworth seized the tool and at one blow severed the tangled root. The old man's gratitude was like an avalanche —

The tears into his eyes were brought,
   And thanks and praises seemed to run
So fast out of his heart, I thought
   He never would be done.

I've heard of hearts unkind, kind deeds
   With coldness still returning;
Alas, the gratitude of man
   Hath *oftener* left me mourning.
      —*Sunday School Times*

* * *

Helping by the Way

My life shall touch a dozen lives
   Before this day is done —
Leave countless marks for good or ill
   Ere sets this evening's sun.
So this the wish I always wish,
   The prayer I ever pray:
Let my life help the other lives
   It touches by the way.
      —*Christian Action*

* * *

Kindness Lives

The late Dr. David McIntyre of Glasgow, who was one of the kindest and humblest men I've ever met, tells a beautiful story showing how a little act of kindness had a transforming influence upon the life of another. Dr. McIntyre was asked to go and conduct the funeral service of a friend of his youth who had lived and labored for half a century in a village on the edge of a bleak Scottish moor. It was his first and only charge. He was greatly loved and missed. Dr. McIntyre tells how he saw one elderly man at the graveside weeping bitterly, and afterwards he tried to comfort him. When calmed down, he told the cause of his tears. Over fifty years previously he was a herd boy, and when driving his herd down a lane a number of cattle rushed past him. All was confusion, and he was full of fear. His experience was insufficient to cope with the situation. Just at that moment the minister, who was straight from college, appeared on the scene and took things in hand. With a quiet patience and a little strategy he gathered the herd together for the lad and went on his way, probably quickly forgetting the incident as he thought on his message for the coming Sabbath. But the lad never forgot — to him it was as though Christ had come to his aid that day. That little kindly act had bound him to Christ, to the church, to his minister for fifty years, and his tears were tears of gratitude for the man of God who had meant so much to his soul.

Kindness is twice blessed; it blesses him who gives and him who takes.

—Sunday School Times

* * *

"Act As Though We Knew It!"

If we knew but half the troubles
  That our neighbor has to bear;
If we knew what caused those furrows
  On his brow, and kept them there —
We should surely try to cheer him
  In some kindly, helpful way,
And there'd be a lot more sunshine
  In the lives of both, today.

If we knew whose feet were standing
  Close beside the narrow stream;
If we knew whose eyes would close soon
  In the sleep that has no dream;
Then perhaps we'd be more tender,
  Lighter judge, more kindly speak —
Oh, why not act as though we knew it —
  For life's cords so quickly break!

—Chester Shuler

* * *

A Sweet Contagion

"Everybody smiled at me. They were all nice people we met out walking," delightedly retorted the tot who had just returned from the park.

"Bless the child, it was her own sweet little smile, ready for everybody, that made them all smile back," laughed the maid who had been along.

If you give good will, you will receive good will in return. Most people will respond to your good opinion of them by thinking well of you. And not the least pleasant thought will come with the knowledge that your smile is helping others, quite as much as their smiles help you.

—The Comrade

* * *

How He Paid for His Supper

In the early days of the settlement of America, an Indian came to the inn at Litchfield, asking for food and a night's shelter, but confessing he had no money to pay. The landlady was driving him away when a man near by directed her to supply the Indian's needs, himself promising to pay. The Indian was very grateful, and said that one day he would repay him. Years later the kindly settler was taken prisoner by a hostile tribe of Indians who carried him far away and enslaved him. One day an Indian came who gave him a musket and ordered him to follow him. Day by day he led him onward, never disclosing the object of their journey nor where it was to end. Then one afternoon they suddenly came upon a beautiful expanse of cultivated fields, with many houses among them. "Do you know this place?" asked the Indian. "Why, of course. Yes. it is Litchfield," said the man. "Yes," said the Indian; "and I was the starving Indian on whom at this very place you took pity. And now that I have paid for my supper I pray you go home."

—Methodist Recorder

* * *

Errands We Can Run

"Mother," said a little boy, "I wish Jesus lived on earth now." "Why, my darling?" "Because I should like so much to do something for Him." "But what could such a little bit of a fellow as you are do for Him?" The child said, "Why, I could run all His errands for Him." "So you could, my child, and so you shall. Here is a glass of jelly and some oranges for poor, old Margaret; I will let you take them, and do an errand for the Saviour, for when upon earth, He said, 'Inasmuch as ye have done it unto one of the least of these my brethren, ye have done it unto me.' Whenever you do a kind act for anybody because you love Jesus, it is just the same as if the Saviour were now living on the earth and you were doing it for Him."

—Homiletic Review

* * *

A Grand Bank

"If I had my wish," said an Old Lady, "I'd like to establish a bank of a very special nature."

"What kind?" asked her companion.

"It would be a Bank of Kindness" was the reply.

"A Bank of Kindness!"

"Yes, that's right, and whenever I heard of a lonely, depressed person I would write a check stating: Please Pay to Bearer one automobile ride or Please Give to Bearer one bouquet of her favorite flowers."

"That's a splendid idea, but couldn't we establish a service on that plane?"

"How?"

"Well, even though we are no longer able to get around much we could make a list of all the people we know who need cheerful attention and we could telephone our active church members to call on these people."

"Now that's really practical. Much better than my Bank of Kindness."

"We would be the Clearing House instead," chuckled the second Old Lady.

"Kindness is the golden chain by which society is bound together."

—Goethe

* * *

Who Are the Meek?

A missionary in Jamaica was examining his school upon a certain verse. He asked a black boy this question: "Who are the meek?"

The boy answered, "Those who give soft answers to rough questions."

—*Western Recorder*

* * *

To Save a Neighbor Embarrassment

Years ago I was stopping in a Roman Catholic village, sixty miles south of our largest hospital in Labrador. On the morning when I was leaving, my hostess apologized for the absence of her husband, who she said had been obliged to leave home early on business. It was not until I arrived at my next stopping place that I discovered the nature of his business. This next village on my winter's round was a Methodist one, and I knew that my host there had fallen on bad times. It was with considerable surprise, therefore, that at my first meal in the cottage I found real sugar for my tea and butter for the loaf. Then the secret came out. My Roman Catholic friend had walked fifteen miles on snowshoes through the dawn of that freezing day, carrying sugar and three cans of milk from his own meager supply, in order that his Methodist friend might not be embarrassed at having nothing to offer "the doctor on his rounds," and that I might have palatable food at the end of my day's work.

—Sir Wilfred T. Grenfell

* * *

How They Knew His Lordship

Some strangers to Lord Schaftesbury were to meet him at a railway station. Asked they, "How shall we know his Lordship?" The answer is challenging: "When you see a tall man getting off the train and HELPING SOMEBODY, that will be Lord Schaftesbury!" Sure enough, a "tall man" alighted from a coach, carrying in one hand his suitcase, and in the other hand the three bundles of a little, old working lady! "They helped every one his neighbour" (Isa. 41:6a).

—W. B. K.

* * *

After a Beautiful Prayer

A beautiful prayer it was, and I thought, "What a good kind of man you must be." But about an hour later, I happened to be coming along the farm, and I heard a hallooing and scolding and finding fault with everybody and everything. I didn't say nothin' for a minute or two. And then I says, "You must be very much disappointed, sir." "How so, Daniel? Disappointed?" "I thought you were expecting to receive a very valuable present this morning, sir, and I see it hasn't come." "Present, Daniel?" — and he scratched his head, as much as to say, "Whatever can the man be talking about?" "You know, sir, this morning you prayed for a Christ-like spirit, and the mind that was in Jesus, and the love of God shed abroad in your heart." "Oh, that's what you mean, is it!" and he spoke as if that weren't anything at all. "Now, sir, wouldn't you be rather surprised if your prayer were to be answered?" "He didn't like it very much," said Daniel, "but I delivered my testimony, and learned a lesson for myself, too."

—From *Times of Refreshing*,
Vol. VIII, by Charles Cullis, M. D.

* * *

The Uneducated Poor Man

This is the testimony of a village carpenter's neighbor: "He cannot talk very well in a prayer meeting, and he hasn't a lot of education. He isn't worth much money, and it's little he can give to the church or to any charity. But a new family never moves into the village that he does not find them to give them a neighborly welcome, and offer any little service he can render. He is always ready to watch with a sick neighbor, and help him in his affairs. He finds a pleasant word for every child he meets. He really seems to have a genius for helping folks in all sorts of common ways, and it does me good every day just to meet him on the street."

—*Sunday School Times*

* * *

Too Late

In this world of hurry, and work, and
  sudden end,
If a thought comes quick of doing kindness to a friend,
Do it that very minute; don't put it off,
  don't wait;
What's the use of doing a kindness if
  you do it a day too late?

—*Selected*

* * *

"I'm Only A General!"

Waiting to board a plane, on which he had a reservation, Brigadier General Theodore Roosevelt, Jr., overheard the piteous plea of a private at the ticket window: "I'm going overseas in three days. I want to see my Ma before I go. I can go home and back only if I travel by plane!" It was explained to him that every seat on the plane was taken. Just then, Brigadier General Roosevelt stepped forward and said, "I'll surrender my seat to him!" "But," protested a fellow officer to the General, "this is a matter of rank!"

"That's right," quickly replied General Roosevelt, "he's a son, I'M ONLY A GENERAL!" God conferred the highest honor upon us when he called us SONS!

—W. B. K.

* * *

Magnanimity of the Blood-Boltered Umsiligazi

Umsiligazi, a great south African chief, placed his left hand on Robert Moffat's shoulder and his right hand on his breast and said, "Machobane, I call you such because you have been my father. You have made my heart white as milk (happy). You fed me when I was hungry, you clothed me when I was naked; you carried me in your bosom." Moffat replied that he had never been conscious of serving the chief in any such way, but Umsiligazi pointed to his two ambassadors and said: "These are great men: Umbate is my right hand. What they heard I heard, what they saw I saw, and what they said, it was Umsiligazi who said it. You fed them and clothed them, and when they were to be slain, you were their shield. You did it unto Umsiligazi, the son of Machobane." *What a commentary on our Lord's words in Matthew* 25:35-39!

—From *Biography of Robert Moffat*,
by Edwin A. Smith

* * *

He Belonged to Some One

A businessman crossed the ferry to New York every day. One day he spoke kindly to a little bootblack who was shining his shoes. After that he noticed that the boy never saw him without wistfully approaching him. The boy would pick up his bundles and brush off his clothing, without expecting any reward. The man was so deeply impressed that one day he asked the boy what inspired him. "Why, sir," he replied, "the first time you met me you called me, 'My boy;' 'till then I had thought I was nobody's boy. I'll do anything for you." So Christ made us know that we are not orphans in a storm, but children of a Father who knows and loves us.

—*Presbyterian*

Deadly Weapon

An old Christian man moved into a community where lived a notoriously disagreeable and contentious neighbor. When informed of the character of his neighbor the old man answered, "If he disturbs me, I will kill him."

His statement reached the ears of the villainous neighbor who in various ways tormented the new settler. But every offense was met with kindness until at last the contentious neighbor was overwhelmed. "I was told that he would kill me, but I did not know he would do it this way."

—William P. King

* * *

He Knows What It Is To Suffer

A fine young Christian recently wrote: "Here I am in the United States again. I thank God for being alive and home once more. When I see you, I will tell you of life in a prison camp. It won't be a pleasant story to hear. I want to forget the twenty-third and twenty-fourth years of my life. . . . However, I don't want you to think that all Japs are cruel. I shall never forget the guard who sneaked me a hard roll one day. Another time he gave me some bread crusts. Another guard was kind — he brought me a handful of potato peelings. They were as kind as they dared to be. I think that hard roll saved my life; I ate a few crumbs at a time, making it last for three days. One thing I have learned: I am going to be very sympathetic with those who are poor, hungry, cold, and in need. When I am able to work again, I plan to put aside some cash each week for such people." The Lord Jesus knows what it is to suffer at the hands of His enemies, and yet He was and is eager to help and ready to forgive them.

—Earl Gardner, in the
Secret Place

* * *

The Blessing Bucher Brought

A soldier, worn out in his country's service, took to playing the violin, for earning his living. He was found in the streets of Vienna, playing his violin. After a while his hand became feeble and tremulous, and he could make no more music. One day, while he sat there weeping, a man came along and said, "My friend, you are too old and too feeble; give me your violin," and began to play most exquisite music, and the coin poured in and in, until the hat was full.

"Now," said the man who was playing the violin, "put that coin in your pocket." The coin was put in the old man's pockets. Then he held his hat again, and the violinist played more sweetly than ever, and played until some of the people wept and some of them shouted. And again the hat was filled with coins.

Then the violinist dropped the instrument and passed off, and the whisper went around, "Who is it? Who is it?" and some one just entering the crowd said, "Why, that is Bucher, the great violinist, known all through the realm; yes, that is the great violinist." The fact was, the artist had taken that man's place, and assumed his poverty, and borne his burden, and played his music, and earned his livelihood. He made a sacrifice for the poor old man.

—*Christian Graphic*

* * *

Comfortable Christians

To others we may give comfort or pain. Some of our natural characteristics are like thorns, and only the grace of God can remove these and polish the rough places so that we become helpful instead of irritating. . . . Dr. Walter Wilson gives this illuminationg note on the Greek word for "comfort." He writes: "In Colossians 4 Paul speaks of Tychicus, Onesimus, Marcus. . . . In referring to them . . . he says, 'which have been a comfort to me.' This word 'comfort' is the word *'paragoria'* in the Greek. From this we obtain our word 'paragoric,' a remedy that stops pain. These men stopped the pain in Paul's heart. Some folks 'give us a pain.' But these friends had the opposite effect."

—*Sunday School Times*

If You Were Busy

If you were busy being kind,
Before you knew it you would find
You'd soon forget to think 'twas true
That some one was unkind to you.

If you were busy being glad,
And cheering people who are sad,
Although your heart might ache a bit,
You'd soon forget to notice it.

If you were busy being good,
And doing just the best you could,
You'd not have time to blame some man
Who's doing just the best he can.

—*Selected*

* * *

A Lesson from a Bird

The naturalist, W. H. Hudson, tells in one of his books about a thrush and a blackbird that always came together, visiting the place where food was put for birds. The blackbird would pick up the crumbs and put them in the thrush's mouth. Then it was noticed that some trap had cut off the thrush's beak close to its head, so that it could not pick up food, and the blackbird was coming to the rescue. Can men afford to let a bird be kinder than they are? Do we not often see men take advantage of another's necessities, instead of going to their relief? How greedily men pick up bankruptcy sales at the smallest possible price, instead of a fair price! How quickly, when a worker is losing his grip on his job, do other workers seek his place, rather than seek to encourage him to do better work! If we know anyone that cannot pick up the crumbs of life, let us pick them up for him.

—*Christian Herald*

* * *

Bread Upon the Waters

There were once two boys working their way through Leland Stanford University. Their funds got low and the idea came to one of them to engage Paderewski for a piano recital, and devote the profits to their board and tuition. The pianist's manager asked for a guarantee of $2,000. The boys proceeded to stage the concert, but the proceeds totaled only $1,600. The boys sought the great artist and told him of their efforts. They gave him the entire $1,600 and a promissory note for $400, explaining that they would earn the amount at the earliest possible moment. "No, boys, that won't do." Then, tearing the note, he returned the money to the boys, and said, "Now take out of the $1,600 all of your expenses, and keep for each of you 10 per cent of the balance for your work, and let me have the rest." The years rolled by. The war came, and Paderewski was striving with might and main to feed the thousands of his beloved Poland. There was only one man in the world who could help Paderewski. Thousands of tons of food began to come into Poland for distribution by the Premier. After the starving people were fed, Paderewski journeyed to Paris to thank Herbert Hoover for the relief sent him. "That's all right, Mr. Paderewski," was Mr. Hoover's reply. "Besides you don't remember how you helped me once when I was a student at college, and I was in a hole."

—*Gospel Herald*

* * *

"If Little Word"

"If any little word of ours
Can make one life the brighter;
If any little song of ours
Can make one heart the lighter;
God help us speak that little word,
And take our bit of singing
And drop it in some lonely vale
To set the echoes ringing."

—*Selected*

* * *

"Never Too Soon"

You cannot do a kindness too soon, because you never know how soon it will be TOO LATE.

—*Emerson*

* * *

A Stranger's Opinion of Lincoln

A rather amusing story is told concerning a traveling book peddler who afterward became a successful publisher. In the autumn of 1830, this peddler called at the door of a log cabin on a farm in Eastern Illinois, and asked for the courtesy of a night's lodging. There was no inn near. The good wife was hospitable but perplexed, "For," said she, "we can feed your beast, but we can't lodge you unless you are willing to sleep with the hired man."

"Let's have a look at him first," said the peddler. The woman pointed to the side of the house, where a lank, six-foot man, in ragged, but clean clothes, was was stretched on the grass, reading a book.

"He'll do," said the stranger. "A man who reads a book as hard as that fellow seems to, has got much else to think of besides my watch or small change."

The hired man was Abraham Lincoln and in later years when he was president the two men met in Washington and laughed over their first meeting.

—*Gospel Herald*

* * *

The Point is Obvious

A chaplain on the battlefield came to a man who was wounded, lying on the ground. "Would you like me to read you something from this Book — the Bible?" he asked the soldier. "I'm so thirsty," replied the man; "I would rather have a drink of water." Quickly as he could the chaplain brought the water. Then the soldier asked, "Could you put something under my head?" The chaplain took off his light overcoat, rolled it, and put it gently under the soldier's head for a pillow. "Now," said the soldier, "if I had something over me! I am very cold." There was only one thing the chaplain could do. He took off his own coat, and spread it over the soldier. The wounded man looked up into his face, and said gratefully, "Thank you." Then he added feebly, "If there is anything in that Book in your hand that makes a man do for another what you have done for me, please read it to me."

—*Moody Monthly*

* * *

Angels' Work

A poor, tired woman with her children entered a parlor car, but the look of relief which had crept into her face

quickly vanished when the porter ordered them out. Frightened, they hurried into the next car. A little boy sitting by his aunt saw them, and said, "Auntie, I want to give them my fruit and sandwiches, they look so hungry." The aunt at first objected, but the little fellow persisted, and found they had not had any breakfast. "God bless you," said the mother, and as the boy started back, the eldest child said, "Mother, is that boy an angel?" "Oh, no!" said the mother, "but he's doing an angel's work."

—*Kindness*

* * *

Bears in the Book

An old couple quarreled so frequently that the whole village knew it. Suddenly they ceased their bickering.

One neighbor approached them to ask what had happened.

"Two bears did it," said the wife.

"Two bears? We thought two bears caused all the trouble."

"Ah," said the husband, "but these are two near bears, which we found in the Bible. 'Bear ye one another's burdens' and 'Forbearing one another in love.'"

—*Sunday*

* * *

"Be Ye Kind"

A personal kindness to St. Paul called forth the immortal letter to the Philippians. A personal kindness to Dr. George R. Stuart, when he was a boy, related itself to his great career as an evangelist. A personal kindness to a boy is back of all the Carnegie Libraries. It has been said of Bishop Lambuth that he had a genius for personal kindnesses.

—*Gospel Herald*

* * *

Small Kindnesses Saved Her Reason

A widow who lives not far from me said to me recently: "I have to go to work every day, and it is late when I get home at night. Sometimes I'm so weary I wish I could just lie down and die. My next-door neighbor is a Christian lady of very quiet and retiring disposition. She isn't well, so can't do very much outside of her own home, but the small kindnesses she showed me this past very cold winter helped to save my reason. She went in and fixed my fire several times to have it nice and warm when I got home, and each time left something tempting for my supper. She took my dog in, when I was forced to remain overnight in the city. She's the kind that feeds the birds and such things — small things? Yes, but how needful!"

—Sunday School Times

* * *

Tact

Wesley and a preacher of his were once invited to lunch with a gentleman after service. The itinerant was a man of very plain manners, quite unconscious of the restraints belonging to good society.

While talking with their host's daughter who was remarkable for her beauty, and had been profoundly impressed by Mr. Wesley's preaching, this good man noticed that she wore a number of rings. During a pause in the meal, he took hold of the young lady's hand, and raising it, called Wesley's attention to the sparkling gems. "What do you think of this, sir," said he, "for a Methodist's hand?" The girl turned crimson.

With a quiet, benevolent smile, Wesley simply said, "The hand is a beautiful hand!" The girl was deeply touched by Wesley's kindness.

—W. B. K.

* * *

Why He Did Not Get the Appointment

President McKinley was considering the appointment of a minister to a foreign country. There were two candidates, their qualifications almost equal. Which one did he appoint? The President told the story of an incident which decided his choice. Years before, when he was a Representative, he boarded a streetcar one night and took the last vacant seat. Shortly afterward an old washerwoman entered, carrying a heavy basket. She walked the length of the car and stood in the aisle, no one offering her a seat. One of the men the President was to consider later, was sitting in a seat opposite where she was standing. He shifted the paper so as

not to see her. Mr. McKinley walked down the aisle, picked up her basket of washing, and gave her his seat. The candidate never knew that this little act of selfishness had deprived him of perhaps the crowning honor of a lifetime.

—Lighted Pathway

* * *

"Not Like Christians"

Two Moslems came in the other day, one with a fractured knee cap. The sufferer was asked if some of his co-religionists would help him by giving something toward the operation expenses. He answered, "Sir, we are not like Christians. When we get into trouble there is no one to help us."

—Sunday School Times

* * *

An Empty Life

In March, 1940 a girl went to the Eddie Martin Airport near Santa Ana, California, and engaged a pilot to take her for a flight to the beach district. She insisted upon using an open plane and riding in the rear cockpit. When nearing Newport Beach, the pilot said, he felt the plane lurch and glanced back to see the girl leap over the side to her death. In the girl's automobile was found a note, which read: *"Forgive me. I just couldn't bear it any longer. It takes courage to die, but it is cowardly to live an empty, ill life."* Behind these words there must have been the agony of a disillusioned life. We may call the poor girl foolish, but that is empty censure now. What was needed was someone's kind and friendly help while she lived. She would never have found life "empty" had some Christian filled her heart with the love of Christ.   *—Watchman-Examiner*

* * *

Your Tones

It is not so much what you say,
   As the manner in which you say it;
It is not so much the language you use
   As the tones you use to convey it.
For words come from the mind,
   And grow by study and art;
But tones leap forth from the inner self
   And reveal the state of the heart.

—The Christian Witness

Different Hands

The Rev. Ira Gillett, missionary in Portugese East Africa, tells the story of a group of natives who had made a long journey and walked past a government hospital to come to the mission hospital for treatment. When asked why they had walked the extra distance to reach the mission hospital when the same medicines were available at the government institution, they replied, "The medicines may be the same, but the hands are different!"

—*Upper Room*

* * *

After He Was Cheated

One day in my boyhood my father paid a neighbor for a ton of coal. We were all away from home when he delivered it. After inspecting the coal bin, I said: "Father, Mr. S. put only a half ton of coal in our bin." Father told me to say no more about the matter. Some weeks later Mr. S. lost his house and all his belongings in a fire. Father sheltered him and his family under our roof; I resented very much having to sleep in the barn loft while the dishonest neighbor rested on my bed. In the morning I heard him talking to Father in the shed below. "You have been kind to me, and a while back I cheated you out of a half a ton of coal," he sobbed out. "I want you to forgive me." He and my father knelt and prayed, and the man gave himself to Christ that morning in the barn.

—True experience of the Rev. G. Baumgartel, Edinburgh, Texas.

* * *

Prayer Meeting for Hoboes

I found five men sitting around a fire under the elevated tracks evidently having breakfast. After passing them I felt I should go back to speak to them. Approaching them I said, "I see you are making your own breakfast. Have you had enough to eat?" "We've got bread and coffee." "Here is fifty cents. Send a fellow over to the store for more food." They looked at me searchingly and asked, "Are you from Moody's?" "My office is there," I replied. "Do you

know what we were talking about just before you came? We were saying that when we were in Sunday school we were told we had to be born again. But we didn't accept it; that's why we are in this terrible condition today. Say, brother, will you pray that we will be converted?" So there around that open fire under the tracks, we wept and prayed with those five men. As we went our way we wondered how many men about us were hungry for the word of salvation. Are we forgetting our Gospel mission?

—Ernest M. Wadsworth, in the *Moody Monthly*

* * *

Meeting Ingratitude

Stephen Merrit gave a free dinner at his mission for homeless men. After sharing with them, he took up his hat to go, and found that someone in a prankish spirit had partially filled his hat with bacon rinds and other table scraps. He was furious for a moment, and in a towering rage he stepped on a chair and delivered a speech. He stormed at the tramps and berated them for their ingratitude. Then suddenly there flashed into his mind the words of the Scripture, "Love suffereth long, and is kind . . . is not easily provoked . . . beareth all things." He lived too near to God to be led astray for long. The Holy Spirit rebuked him within, and the bit of temper passed, and contrition filled his heart. He then and there apologized in all humility, telling the men that he knew he had grieved his Lord. He then invited them all back to another dinner the following night when nearly forty men accepted Christ."

—*Moody Monthly*

* * *

Stretching His Soul

I was just a kid. One spring day Father called me to go with him to Old Man Trussel's blacksmith shop. He had left a rake and a hoe to be repaired. There they were, fixed like new. Father handed over a silver dollar for the repairing, but Mr. Trussel refused to take it. "No," he said, "there's no charge for that little job." But Father insisted that he take the pay, still extending to him the dollar. If I live a thousand years, I'll never forget that great man's reply, "Ed, can't you let a man do something now and then — just to stretch his soul?" That short but big sermon from the lips of that humble, lovable blacksmith has caused us to find, again and again, the great joy and quiet happiness which comes from a little "stretching of the soul."

—R. Lee Sharpe, in the
Alabama Baptist

* * *

Envy, Its Cure

Mr. Moody once told a story which illustrated the only sure plan of getting rid of jealousy.

"There were two businessmen — merchants — and there was great rivalry between them, a great deal of bitter feeling. One of them became a Christian. He went to his minister and said:

" 'I am still jealous of that man, and I do not know how to overcome it.'

" 'Well,' he said, 'if a man comes into your store to buy goods, and you cannot supply him, just send him over to your neighbor.'

"He said he wouldn't like to do that.

" 'Well,' the minister said, 'you do it, and you will kill jealousy.'

"He said he would, and when a customer came into his store for goods which he did not have he would tell him to go across the street to his neighbor's. By-and-by the other began to send his customers over to this man's store, and the breach was healed.

—*The Friend*

* * *

He Dropped the Matter

Two brothers were having some difficulty over a property line. John was very bitter and wrote Alex as follows: "You have cheated and robbed me of that which rightfully belongs to me. You know that the row of poplars is the property line. You have no right to build a fence on my side and claim the ground for yourself. I shall sue you and make you pay every dime it is worth."

Alex was a true Christian. His reply was typical of his character: "Father's will said the property was to be equally divided. By survey I have placed the fence where the division comes. However, both of us are in good standing in this community and I do not want our neighbors to think that we are not Christians. Neither of us can use the ground under the poplar trees, for nothing will grow there. If you will meet me with the surveyors I will allow you to place the fence where you want it, and we will make a permanent record in the surveyor's office that you have 126 feet and I have 118 feet. I have no objection if you want more than your half." John was humbled and ashamed by the generosity and gracious words of his brother. He knew that if the fence were placed where he wanted it all the neighborhood would know and the records would show that he had more than his half. He dropped the matter.

—Walter L. Wilson, M.D.

* * *

The Janitor's Guest

Years ago a Missouri country congregation listened to a sermon by a young preacher who had walked twenty miles to deliver it. Tired, hungry, this youth faltered, floundered, and failed. The people were disgusted; they did not know he had walked the weary miles. When the service was over nobody offered him food or shelter, but as he started down the long road with a breaking heart, the colored janitor asked him to share his humble meal in a nearby shanty. Years passed. The young exhorter became Bishop Marvin of world-wide reputation, and after a full generation he once more stood in that spot to dedicate a great country church. The whole community was assembled; it was a tremendous event in their lives. When the service was ended, many crowded about offering lavish hospitality, but the Bishop waved them all aside, and called the old colored janitor saying, "When I was here years ago I was none too good for you, and I am none too good for you today."

—*Christian Life and Faith*

Where Heaven Is

A certain minister preached one day on Heaven. The next morning he was met by one of his wealthy members, who said:

"Pastor, you preached a good sermon about Heaven. You told me all about Heaven, but you did not tell me where Heaven is."

"Ah," said the pastor, "I'm glad of the opportunity this morning. I have just come from the hill yonder. In that cottage there is a member of your church who is extremely poor; she is sick in bed with fever. If you will go and take her a good supply of provisions and say, 'My sister, I have bought these nice provisions in the Name of our Lord and Saviour:' if you ask for a Bible and read Psalm 23, and then get down on your knees and pray, if you don't see Heaven, before you get all through, I'll pay the bill."

The next morning he said:

"Pastor, I saw Heaven, and I spent fifteen minutes in Heaven, as certainly as you are listening."

—*Gospel Herald*

* * *

On Praying Ground

A Christian man in a place of large responsibility was talking with a friend about a serious disagreement that had arisen between the institution of which he was the head and another man who had been connected with it, but whose relationship to the work had now been severed. This man had written sharp letters, and his letters had been answered in Christian quietness and courtesy. The friend commented on the unusual tone of the letters that had gone in response to the angry accusations. "But," said the friend who had written the letters that were marked by the fruit of the Spirit, "I must keep on praying ground." He realized that, if he replied to the heated, unchristian letters in kind, he would be off praying ground, and not able to pray the matter through with any assurance that God was hearing, leading, and answering.

—*Sunday School Times*

* * *

Living Like You Pray

A little four-year-old daughter, suffering from a severe scolding from her mother was heard to sob pitifully to herself, "I wish Mother loved me as much as she does God. She talks so kind to Him." And immediately one's thoughts flash back to a great man who said, "I owe a great debt to the life of my mother in my early childhood days. She always lived like she prayed."

—*Sunday School Times*

LIGHT

A Blind Man's Testimony

On Glasgow Green, a few years ago, at the conclusion of a gospel address given by a Christian, a man in the crowd asked permission to say a few words. Liberty having been granted, he spoke somewhat as follows: "Friends, I don't believe what this man has been talking about. I don't believe in hell; I don't believe in a judgment; I don't believe in a God, for I never saw one of them."

Then another man asked to be allowed to speak. Permission being obtained, he proceeded as follows: "Friends, you say there is a river running not far from this place, the River Clyde. There is no such thing; it is untrue. You tell me that there are trees and grass growing around me where I now stand. There are no such things, That also is not true. You tell me that there are a great many people standing here. Again I say that is not true; there is no person standing here save myself. I suppose you wonder what I am talking about, but I was born blind; I never saw one of you; and while I talk it only shows that I am blind, or I would not say such things. And you," he said, turning to the infidel, "the more you talk the more you expose your ignorance, because you are spiritually blind, and cannot see."

—Prophetic News

* * *

They Saw the Light

One black stormy night in the combat zone of the southwest Pacific our pilots were out to intercept an enemy warship fleet. Six of my closest friends were in the flight, and at dusk had completed their mission, and all were safe, except it was dark, hazy, and raining, and they were 200 miles at sea, away from their home base, with no beam or homing device to "ride in." Their compasses were not accurate, and they did not know their exact position either. We, on the ground, were listening to them over the radio. As the time approached for them to arrive, we turned on some searchlights, pointing straight up, hoping the pilots could see them. Time came for them to be here, and not an engine could be heard and not a wing light could be seen. Over the radio we could hear: Dick to Jim, "Do you know where we are?" "Pull up, Pete; you're getting too low." "Can you see the field lights anywhere?" "We should be there. Let's start flying in a big circle." "How much gas have you got?" After a few minutes of silence, and with the tension getting greater and greater by the minute, there came over the radio in a clear, relieved, and happy voice: "I see the light! We're saved! I see the light!" We all breathed a sigh of relief. . . . Our prayers had been answered. They had seen the light and followed it home safely. The moral of this true story is self-evident. If you or your friends are still groping blindly in a life of darkness, you are lost and had better begin seeking the light and follow it to salvation.

—Good News

* * *

We Need Light from Heaven

At the Century of Progress exposition in Chicago, light from the star Arcturus was used dramatically to open the gates of the exposition. Every evening during the exposition, the lights on the grounds were turned on by electric impulses from a neighboring state. The crowds standing hushed and breathless each twilight sensed something ageless and eternal as they waited for the lights of the exposition grounds to be set ablaze by a beam of light that had left Arcturus many years before. Today, in the twilight of what seems to be the eve of another Dark Age in the life of mankind, the peoples of the earth are waiting again for a light from Heaven. We can be absolutely confident that if we are receptive to the light that emanates from Jesus Christ, reflected in our own hearts from history, from the Bible, the church, and the Holy Spirit, we need not walk in darkness.

—Quiet Hour

* * *

The Cave and the Sun

There is an allegory written for the little ones, but serviceable to the grown folks: Once upon a time a Cave lived under the ground, as caves have the habit of doing. It had spent its lifetime in darkness. It heard a voice calling to it, "Come up into the light; come and see the sunshine." The Cave retorted, "I don't know what you mean; there isn't anything but darkness." Finally the Cave ventured forth and was surprised to see light everywhere. Looking up to the Sun the Cave said, "Come with me and see the darkness." The Sun asked, "What is darkness?" The Cave replied, "Come and see." One day the Sun accepted the invitation. As it entered the cave it said, "Now show me your darkness!" But there was no darkness.

—Sunday School Times

* * *

Radium Christians

A microscopic speck of radium can, if placed behind a screen of fluorescent metal, be seen to be sending out a stream of sparks forever. These sparks give light and heat, yet (a marvel) it loses no whit of its energy. Like the burning bush, it is a miracle. It emits light and heat at no apparent loss to itself. It is unconsumed, though it is forever pouring out chemical and electrical energies. When placed in the coldness of liquid air, nay, further, when placed in the intense frigidity of liquid hydrogen, all it does is pour out light, and heat. Such ought to be the Christian life — living because Christ lives, a manifestation forever of the life and light of Christ.

—*Sunday School Chronicle*

* * *

Have You a Little Shadow?

Near my home there is a street light. As I was passing by one night, I noticed that as I moved away from the light, my shadow began to lengthen. It increased in length as I moved on and on. Then I went back and stood directly under it, and there was no shadow at all.

When we get away from the Light of the world, we begin to think more highly of ourselves than we ought to think. It is when we are closest to the Light that we get the truest measure of ourselves.

—*The Challenge*

* * *

Where Lights Are Needed

In a South coast town a business girl was having a hard time among her friends because she was a Christian. She was tempted to give up, but a preacher whom she consulted asked, "Where do we put lights?" She was puzzled by the question, so he continued, "We put the lights in a dark place." In a moment she saw his meaning, and realized that God had put her there in those difficult surroundings that she might shine there for her Lord. She determined to be more courageous, and a few weeks later came to the preacher with a group of other girls, all radiant with joy. "Oh," she said, "the thirteenth person from our business house has decided for Christ tonight."

—*Christian Union Herald*

* * *

Reflections

I asked the roses as they grew,
Richer and lovelier in their hue,
What made their tints so rich and bright,
They answered: "Looking toward the light."

Ah, secret dear, said heart of mine,
God meant my life to be like thine,
Radiant with Heavenly beauty bright,
Simply by looking toward the light.
                    —Alfie W. Hallmann, in
                    Christian Youth Herald

* * *

Walking in the Light

A woman in Palestine sat under an olive tree sewing handmade lace on a handkerchief. A woman paused to inquire the price of her work, and to have a conversation. "Do you live here?" "No, I live over the hill. Last night as I walked home a panther followed me, but because I carried a lantern and walked in the circle of light I was safe." "You mean the panther would not attack you while you were in the light?" "That is right, madam." What a lesson is this for Christians!

—*The Conqueror*

* * *

Reflected Glory

An old Negro slave was once addressed by her mistress: "Sybil," she said, "when I heard you singing on the housetop, I thought you fanatical; but when I saw your shining face, I saw how different you were to me." "Ah, Missis," the old woman answered, "the light you saw in my face was not mine, but was 'flected from the cross; and there is heaps more for every poor sinner who will come near enough to catch de rays."

—*Dawn*

* * *

Beauty

Look at a poor little colorless drop of water, hanging weakly on a blade of grass. It is not beautiful at all; why should you stop to look at it? Stay till the sun has risen, and now look. It is sparkling like a diamond; and if you look at it from another side, it will be glowing like a ruby, and presently gleaming like an emerald. The poor little drop has become one of the brightest and loveliest things you ever saw. But is it its own brightness and beauty? No; if it slipped down to the ground out of the sunshine, it would be only a poor little dirty drop of water. So, if the

Sun of Righteousness, the glorious and lovely Saviour, shines upon you, a little ray of His own brightness and beauty will be seen upon you.

—F. R. Havergal

* * *

The Light

A tender child of summers three,
Seeking her little bed at night,
Paused on the dark stair timidly,
"Oh, Mother, take my hand," said she,
"And then the dark will all be light."

We older children grope our way,
From dark behind to dark before;
And only when our hands we lay,
Dear Lord, in Thine, the night is day,
And there is darkness nevermore.

Reach downward to the sunless days
Wherein our guides are blind as we,
And faith is small and hope delays;
Take Thou the hands of prayer we raise,
And let us feel the light of Thee.

—John Greenleaf Whittier

* * *

Gratitude for Deliverance

An Indian chief who had been converted was exceedingly fervent in his prayers and praises during worship and extremely generous in his kindness and gifts to the missionary and his work. The missionary at length asked him why he was so jubilant in his devotions, and so lavish in his gifts. The convert made this pathetic reply: "Ah! you have never been in the darkness!"

—*Sunday School Times*

* * *

A Shining Light

"Have you ever heard the Gospel?" a missionary asked a Chinaman.

"No," was the reply, "but I have seen it. I know a man who was the terror of the whole district. He was at times as fierce as a wild animal, and was also an opium smoker. When he accepted the Jesus' religion, he became quite changed. Now he is meek, and is no longer wicked, and has given up opium smoking. I can see by that, that the Gospel and the service for Jesus are good."

Someone has said: "Lamps do not talk, but they illuminate. Lighthouses make no noise, but they give light."

Thus must the walk of a Christian be a living sermon. Actions speak louder than words.

"Let your light so shine before men, that they may see your good works, and glorify your Father which is in Heaven" (*Matt.* 5:16).

—*Christ for the World Messenger*

* * *

Letting the Light Shine Through

A small child was taken to a cathedral. She sat watching the sunshine through the windows. She asked her mother, "What are these people on the windows?" "They are saints," was the answer. Then the child said, "Now I know what saints are. They are people who let the light shine through."

—*Toronto Globe*

* * *

Shining Faces!

"I once heard Rendel Harris say of the Bible critics: they might tear the volume into shreds, but they could never rub off the light of God from the faces of His people" (Frank Crossley). And it was sehraphic Murray McCheyne who said, "Oh, for the holy shining of the face! and, oh, for the holy *ignorance* of the shining!"

—*Prairie Overcomer*

* * *

"You Are the Lower Lights"

Over half a century ago, it was a stormy night on Lake Erie and a boat was making its way into the Cleveland harbor. The sky was pitch dark.

The captain said, "Pilot, are you sure this is Cleveland? There is only one light." "Quite sure, cap'n." "Where are the lower lights?" "Gone out, sir." "Can you run in?" "We've got to, Cap'n, or die."

The brave old pilot did his best, but, alas, he missed the channel. The boat was wrecked with the loss of many lives. The lower lights had gone out.

From this description of Moody's, P. P. Bliss wrote:

"Brightly beams our Father's mercy
From His Lighthouse evermore;
But to us He gives the keeping
Of the lights along the shore."
　　　　　　　　—*Gospel Herald*

* * *

Light and Comfort in a Japanese Prison

Bishop Heaslett had told a moving story of his prison experiences in Japan. He poignantly describes how one night shortly after his arrest he felt himself completely deserted. He says: "The uncleanness of body, the soiledness of mind, the hopeless isolation; the complete identification of myself with thieves, gamblers, suspects, men who trafficked in women; the ruthlessness of the machine in which I had been caught and in which I was as helpless as a small fly in a large spider's web; above all, what I thought of as being the failure of my friends and their abandoment of me; the accumulated shame and weight of all this brought me that night to bitter tears and the verge of a breakdown." When he had reached what seemed the limit of endurance it was a message from God's Word that brought relief: "*He was numbered with the transgressors.*" He says, "A flood of light and illumination came upon me at that moment. For the first time and through my own experience I knew what our Lord had suffered from His arrest until His crucifixion, as far as the human mind can fathom His experiences."
　　　　　—*Mightier Than the Sword*

* * *

Christian Witness

At a meeting I heard a missionary home on furlough tell of a simple act of his by which he unconsciously saved another's life. He was on board ship and when in his berth, one dark night, he heard that cry — so awful to listen to at sea — "Man overboard." He arose at once from his bunk and took the swinging lamp from its bracket, and held it at the window in his cabin. He could see nothing; but, the next morning, he was told that the flash of his lamp through the port showed to those on deck the missing man clinging to a rope.

He could hardly have held on another minute. The light of the lamp shone just in time to save the man's life.

Have your lamp of truth always burning; and be ready to show the flash of its light, whenever you hear the call for help. On some dark night, you may help to save a poor soul who has fallen into the waves of temptation or despair.
　　　　　　　　—J. W. W. Moeran

* * *

Another Diamond!

The Waldenses adopted various methods by which to disseminate their faith, despite perils and persecutions. Some of them assumed the guise of gem merchants, in order to gain access to people's homes. After the Waldensian had shown his wares and had perhaps made some sales, he would say, "If you promise not to betray me to the clergy and the civil authorities, I will show you another diamond — one that is far more precious and lustrous than the others I have shown you. Its radiant light is able to banish the darkness of your hearts and illumine the path that leads to the heart of God." Then, taking a bundle from the folds of his garment and unwrapping it, he would produce a Bible and seek to lead his auditors into a saving acquaintance with its mighty truths. Thus many entered into the ineffable experience for which every human heart longs, as naturally as the parched fields and drooping flowers crave the advent of the delectable showers.
　　　　　—Rev. Eugene M. Harrison
　　　　　　in *Moody Monthly.*

* * *

Starlight and Sun

A man in Burma found a copy of the Psalms which had been carelessly discarded by a traveler stopping at his house. He started to read it, became more and more interested, and before he had finished resolved to cast his idols away. For twenty years he worshiped the eternal God that David worshiped, God as revealed to him in the Psalms. The Fifty-first Psalm he came to appropriate to himself as his daily prayer.

Then he received from a missionary the first copy of the New Testament he had ever seen. This brought yet greater joy to his heart. He said: "For twenty years I walked by starlight; now I see the sun!" If we were all as faithful to the light we have as was this humble Burman, "our lives would be all sunshine in the sweetness of our Lord."

—*Moody Monthly*

* * *

Light on a Life Raft

Jack Crow of the United States Navy has a remarkable testimony. "My ship was torpedoed. Four other men and myself were on a small life raft for over thirty-two hours. I had my white Testament. I had hardly read from it, but sure did read it on the raft, knowing I was unsaved and would be a lost sinner if death should overtake me. Three of the men made fun of me, but the other man said, 'Buddy, read out loud so I can hear.' Nightfall came, and one by one the three men who scoffed slipped from the life raft, out into a dark eternity, lost. We two prayed that if God would spare our lives, we would live for the Lord Jesus Christ. After what seemed an eternity, a light came out of the darkness, a great distance off. The light came closer. It rested upon us. I did not think of it as a searchlight from a United States destroyer, but as the Light of Jesus Christ shining upon a sinner. Then and there Jesus Christ came into my heart.

—*Baptist Standard*

* * *

Two Suns

A man scoffingly asked, "What advantage has a religious man over anyone like myself? Does not the sun shine on me as on him, this fine day?" "Yes," replied his companion, "but the religious man has two suns shining on him at once — one on his body, the other on his soul."

—C. H. Spurgeon

* * *

Gathering Storm!

A brilliant young attorney had just been admitted to the bar. He was sud-

denly taken ill. The day was gloriously bright and sunshiny. Father called to inquire about his health, and just as he entered the sick man's room, the young attorney said: "How dark it is, the sky is so black. There must be a terrific storm coming." And with those words he passed out into the darkness — alone.

You, who are still outside, *come in! Come in out of the storm!*

—*Christian Index*

* * *

For Dark Places

His lamp am I,
To shine where He shall say:
And lamps are not for sunny rooms,
Nor for the light of day.
But for dark places of the earth,
Where shame and crime and wrong
   have birth.

And so, sometimes a flame we find,
Clear shining through the night,
So bright we do not see the lamp
But only see the light.
So may I shine — His life the flame —
That men may glorify His name.

—Annie Johnson Flint

* * *

Are You Keeping the Light Burning?

Rudyard Kipling and his wife purchased a farmhouse on a mountain slope in an unsettled part of Vermont. One day we are told that they tramped down the mountain back of their house across the valley and up on the next mountain. They came to a tiny house where a woman lived by herself. "Be you the windows across the valley?" she asked. Then she told them how much comfort the lights were to her. Suddenly she looked afraid. "Be you going to stay and keep your lights burning or maybe be you not?" After that day the Kiplings always kept burning the lights in the back of their home. They even took down the curtains and shades so that more light would shine out. As for your opportunity in your community, "Be you going to keep the lights burning?"

—*Secret Place*

When the Last Lamp Goes Out

A man whose youth and early manhood had been spent in evil ways, and who was converted to God, was one night giving his testimony. He had met an old drinking pal during the week who chaffed him for turning pious. "I'll tell you what," I said to him, "you know what I am (he was a lamplighter); when I go round turning out the lights, I look back, and all the road over which I've been walking is all darkness, and that's what my past is like. I look on in front, and there's a long row of twinkling lights to guide me, and that's what the future is since I found Jesus." "Yes," says my friend, "but by-and-by you get to the last lamp and turn it out, and where are you then?" "Then," says I, "why, when the last lamp goes out it's dawn, and there ain't no need for lamps when the morning comes."

—*Sunday School Times*

* * *

Cleaning House!

A little Zulu girl, who had given her heart to Christ, prayed thus:
"O Thou Great Chief, light a candle in my heart that I may see the rubbish, and sweep it out." And along with this little African girl's prayer should go the prayer of William Cowper, the poet:

The dearest idol I have known,
    Whate'er that idol be,
Help me to tear it from Thy throne,
    And worship only Thee.

—*Homiletical Review*

* * *

The Bird and the Mole

Dr. McCook imagines a conversation between a bird and a mole which has just pushed up its head out of the ground: —
"What are you making such a noise about?" he asked the bird as it was swinging and singing on the branch of a tree.
"O, the sunshine, the trees, the grasses, the shining stream yonder, and the white clouds on the mountain side. The world is full of beauty." "Nonsense!" said Mr. Mole; "I have lived in this world longer than you have, and I have gone deeper into it. I have traversed it and tunneled it, and I know what I am talking about, and I tell you there is nothing in it but fishing worms."

Let a man live for himself for all that is "under the sun," Ec. 1:1, 2; let him burrow in the earth and strive to get satisfaction for his soul out of it and he will say with a plash of tears and sobs of secret longing, "My soul hath no pleasure in it," "I hate my life." But let him rise above the sun and bask in the splendor of God's light and presence and he will sing for very joy of heart.

—*Moorehead*

* * *

Do You Look for the Light?

A missionary related her experience in securing a servant for her home. One day a well-dressed Chinese lady came and stated her desire to serve. The missionary demurred, for she wanted someone to make beds, scrub floors, and wash clothes. The lady said that she understood. Somewhat mystified, the missionary hired her. She proved a splendid servant, attended all the meetings, and taught other women to read. On one occasion the missionary, after knocking, entered her room. The servant seemed embarrassed, and acted as if she were hiding some small object. Some days later the same thing happened. Before long she revealed her secret. "Oh, Madam," she exclaimed. "It's coming! The light on my face! I used to see the Christians on their way to the chapel. I noticed how bright their faces were. I wanted that light for myself and thought if I came to work for you I could get some of it. My husband tells me the light is coming, and I was looking in this little mirror to see." Not only did the light show on her face, but the Light shone in her heart. She became a bright and active Christian.

—*China's Millions*

* * *

The Light on the Wall

A young girl had slipped away early to bed one night, weary from the strain of the evening's gayety. She had not yet closed her eyes, when suddenly a light shone upon the opposite wall, revealing a beautiful copy of Plockhorst's "Good Shepherd." The picture stood out sharply and clearly from the darkness of the room. The girl raised herself and looked out through the parted curtains to see whence the light came. It was just a kitchen lamp in the little cottage of a day laborer across the garden. Night after night the light shone, revealing the face of the Savior of men on the wall of that dainty up-stairs room in the luxurious home. But the owner of the lamp never knew it. So do many lives, following the humble, daily routine in the spirit of their Master, often send a revelation of the Savior to those who have great wealth or high position, and of whose lives they know nothing. Many a humble worker has unconsciously given a great man an inspiration to better living.

—Gospel Herald

* * *

A Lighthouse Lesson

A friend told us that he was visiting a lighthouse lately, and he said to the keeper, "Are you not afraid to live here? It is a dreadful place to be in constantly."

"No," replied the man, "I am not afraid; we never think of ourselves here."

"Never think of yourselves! How is that?"

The reply was a good one: "We know that we are perfectly safe, and only think of having our lamps brightly burning, and keeping the reflectors clear, so that those in danger may be saved."

This is what Christians ought to do. They are safe in a house built on a Rock which cannot be moved by the wildest storm; and in a spirit of holy unselfishness they should let their light gleam across the dark waters of sin, that they who are imperiled may be guided into the harbors of eternal safety.

—The Quiver

Light From Above Needed

I recollect a story of Mr. Hume, who so constantly affirmed that the light of reason is abundantly sufficient. Being at a good minister's house one evening, he had been discussing the question, and declaring his firm belief in the sufficiency of the light of nature. On leaving, the minister offered to hold him a candle to light him down the steps. He said, "No; the light of nature will be enough; the moon will do." It so happened that the moon was covered with a cloud, and he fell down the steps. "Ah!" said the minister, "you had better have had a little light from above, after all, Mr. Hume." . . . Better have two lights than only one. The light of creation is a bright light. God may be seen in the stars; His name is written in gilt letters on the brow of night; you may discover His glory in the ocean waves, yea, in the trees of the field, but it is better to read it in two books than in one. You will find it here more clearly revealed; for He has written this Book Himself, and He has given you the key to understand it, if you have the Holy Spirit.

——C. H. Spurgeon

* * *

Another Light in a Dark Street

The Christian Herald (London) tells of a poor woman who had been saved and went home with a joy she had never known before. Some time afterward she testified to her thankfulness to God and said she must leave the street where so much evil surrounded her. The minister looked at her for a moment and said: "What would you think of the Town Council if they took all the lights out of the mean and dirty streets, and set them up only in the well-to-do neighborhoods?" The woman saw the point. Shortly afterward the minister met her and said, "Well, Mrs. Smith, how are things going now?" With a smile she answered, "Oh, very nicely; and there is another light in the street now."

—Sunday School Times

God Knows

I said to a man
Who stood at the gate of the year:
"Give me a light
That I may tread safely into the unknown,"
And he replied,
"Go out into the darkness
And put your hand into the hand of God.
That shall be to you better than a light
And safer than a known way."

—Minnie L. Haskins

* * *

God and the True Scientist

In conversation with Professor S. F. B. Morse, the inventor of the telegraph, the Rev. George W. Hervey asked this question:

"Professor Morse, when you were making your experiments yonder in your rooms in the university, did you ever come to a stand, not knowing what to do next?"

"Oh, yes, more than once."

"And at such times what did you do next?"

"I may answer you in confidence, sir," said the professor, "but it is a matter of which the public knows nothing. I prayed for more light."

"And the light generally came?"

"Yes. And may I tell you that when flattering honors come to me from America and Europe on account of the invention which bears my name, I never felt I deserved them? I had made a valuable application of electricity, not because I was superior to other men, but solely because God, who meant it for mankind, must reveal it to some one, and was pleased to reveal it to me."

In view of these facts, it is not surprising that the inventor's first message was, "What hath God wrought!"

—*Moody Monthly*

* * *

What Is Brightness?

The Rev. Alex Dodds of the Sudan Interior Mission tells the following interesting experience: We had just finished our morning devotional Bible study with the men of the school for the blind. We had been reading "Prophecies and Allusions to Christ as Fulfilled in the New Testament" in the Hausa language. As usual, keen interest was shown, and intelligent questions were asked. Then came a question which at first rather puzzled me. "What is brightness?" How would one answer a blind man? One blind man suggested that it was perhaps like lightning. He had not been born blind. I asked the inquirer if this meant anything to him. He shook his head in instinctive negation. Then I suggested that perhaps it was like that great warm light which made the light of the moon cold by comparison. He knew that the moon "gave off" a feeling of something, but not anything like the heat of the sun, especially as experienced in the Sudan. This seemed to help the man a little. Then came the illuminating description. How we reached this explanation in our exchange of ideas I cannot be quite sure, but it came from the Lord, I know. Brightness is that light which shines in the heart when we put our trust in Jesus as our Saviour. This answered the man's question. From this he was able to visualize brightness, and his face shone as he saw! It was fitting that the blind *millam* (teacher), who instructs these blind men in Braille, closed with this phrase in his prayer, "We do thank Thee, our loving Father, for illuminating our darkened hearts."

—*Moody Monthly*

* * *

A Contrast

A miser, whose ruling passion was strong even in death, exclaimed: "Put out that candle, Marie."

"But, Uncle, suppose you want something."

"Put it out," he gasped, "one does not need light to die!"

Indeed we do. Alas! for those who have it not — for those who have to repeat the dying words of a noted infidel: "I'm taking a leap in *the dark*."

Now for the contrast. A lad lay dying. Said his mother tenderly: "Is Jesus with you in the dark valley?"

"Dark valley!" he whispered, "it's not dark, it's getting brighter and brighter,

Mother. Oh," he murmured, "it's so bright now, that I have to shut my eyes!"

And so he passed away to be with Jesus, who said, "He that followeth me shall not walk in darkness, but shall have the light of life."

—S.J.B.C. in *Assembly Annals*

* * *

Always a Lamplighter

Evangeline Booth relates an experience that she had at the close of an exhaustive day of speaking in London. A messenger asked her to see a man. As she hesitated he pressed her by saying that the man had come from a distance of two hundred miles. Miss Booth replied, "By all means; bring him to me." "But he can't come to you; he is ninety-four years old," the messenger answered. Miss Booth hastened to the old gentleman and he took her hand in both of his and said: "I was the lamplighter for your father when he held his first meeting under cover. I put up the wires and lighted the lamps. Your father placed his hand upon my head and said to me 'My lad, always be a lamplighter for Jesus Christ.' I want you to know that I have always carried the light for my Lord and Saviour." How many of us will be able to say at the close of our little day that we, too, have had this singleness of purpose in bringing the light of Christ to the world in which we live? There are so many good causes that demand our time, strength, and money that often we are bewildered, but always we are needed to carry the light of Christ to a dark and sin-sick world.

—*Secret Place*

* * *

The True Light

Christ, whose glory fills the skies
　Christ, the true, the only Light,
Sun of righteousness, arise,
　Triumph o'er the shades of night;
Dayspring from on high, be near,
Daystar, in my heart appear.

Dark and cheerless is the morn,
　Unaccompanied by Thee;
Joyless is the day's return
　Till Thy mercy's beams I see;
Till Thy inward life impart,
Glad my eyes, and warm my heart.

Visit then this soul of mine;
　Pierce the gloom of sin and grief;
Fill me, Radiance Divine,
　Scatter all my unbelief;
More and more Thyself display,
Shining to the perfect day.

—Charles Wesley

* * *

He Makes It Plain

Do not forget the importance of walking according to the light you have, while seeking for more. If you feel you are called to the work, do not fear as to the way, and the time. He will make all plain. The eye of faith looks to Jesus and walks, in spite of wind and waves, on the water.

—Hudson Taylor

LORD'S DAY

What His "Hallelujah" Cost

Reginald Willis tells of a young man who shouted "Hallelujah" in a revival meeting. The minister looked at him and asked, "Has that 'hallelujah' cost you anything?" "Yes, it has," replied the young man. "I ran a garage and had been offered a contract for Sunday business which would have brought me $2,500 per year. I felt that I could not take any business which would cause me to violate the sanctity of the Lord's Day, so I turned down the offer. I lost the money, but I kept my 'Hallelujah.'"

—*Free Methodist*

* * *

His Last Sunday

Recently the writer's father slipped suddenly away into the better world. It happened on a Monday as he was working with his flowers. On Sunday morning he was not feeling well, but insisted on going to his Sunday school and church. To a daughter he remarked: "One of these Sundays is going to be my last in this world, and I want to be in church that Sunday." By a strange coincidence the writer of this column had just mimeographed his communion letter to his parishioners, and without knowing of his father's remark, had included this quotation: "*It is a poor preparation for one's first Sunday in eternity to have misspent one's last Sunday on earth.*"

—*Moody Monthly*

* * *

His Recommendation

The newspapers some years ago related the following incident to Stephen Girard, the Philadelphia Philanthropist. One Saturday he ordered all his clerks to come on the morrow to his wharf to help unload a newly arrived ship. One young man replied quietly: "Mr. Girard, I can't work on the Sabbath." "You know the rules." "Yes, I know, I have a mother to support, but I can't work on Sabbaths." "Well, step up to the desk, and the cashier will settle with you." For three weeks the young man could find no work; but one day a banker came to Girard to ask if he could recommend a man for cashier in a new bank. This discharged young man was at once named as a suitable person. "But," said the banker, "you discharged him." "Yes, because he would not work on Sabbaths. A man who would lose his place for Conscience' sake would make a trustworthy cashier." And he was appointed.

—*Little Evangelist*

* * *

Was It a Costly Sacrifice?

I know a young fellow in Oklahoma who was intent on going to college, but his folks did not have the money, and he had no work. Finally he got a job in a restaurant for the summer, which promised sufficient earnings to enable him to enter college the next fall. On receiving his first Saturday night's pay envelope, he was ordered to report the next morning at seven o'clock. He had not thought of having to work Sundays, but was told that restaurants must stay open every day, and he must either report for duty next morning or quit. He quit. He had been reared to spend Sunday God's way. College plans were dashed. Then he saw an announcement of a coming examination in his Congressional district for a Rhodes Scholarship. He decided to study at home in preparation for that contest. He won the appointment, and the following fall, instead of going to his state college, he entered Oxford, in England, with a $1,500 appropriation to finance him, through his Rhodes Scholarship.

—*Sunday School Times*

* * *

Sabbath Traditions

During the afternoon, I asked Dr. Klausner (professor in the Hebrew University in Jerusalem) if he would sign my autograph album, to which he replied, "No, I am sorry; but it is the Sabbath." I did not know until I made inquiry that night that the Talmud asserts that writing two words in succession is work, and if a man even signs his name on the Sabbath he has broken the Law. . . . As those of us gathered in his study discussed one subject after another, Dr. Klausner would climb a little stepladder and bring down some heavy tome from his shelves, open it, point to some relevant passage, then return the book and soon take down another. The Talmud says nothing about bringing down books from shelves as work — to write two words would be labor, but to develop a perspiration by reaching up for volumes and vigorously discussing them is not work! This is a perfect illustration of what our Lord meant when he talked about his contemporaries "holding the tradition of the elders" (Mark 7:3).

—From *With my Bible Around the Mediterranean,*
by Dr. Wilbur M. Smith

It Is Man Who Forgets

When Israel forgot her Sabbath, the Lord brought upon the nation the invading force of Babylon, and the covenant people found their solace by the rivers of Babylon but under the iron heel of Nebuchadnezzar. When France forgot her Sabbath, and established a substitute for God's day of worship, the Lord brought upon her nobility the swift judgment of an enraged populace, and the nation went under the iron heel of Napoleon. When England forgot her Sabbath, the armies of Hitler went on the march, and the birth of the land was exchanged for "blood, sweat, and tears." Today the Federal Bureau of Investigation is calling upon the churches of America to use the Sabbath for the saving of youth. "As a law enforcement officer, I am certain that unless children are given the opportunity of participating in the activities which have God as their fundamental objective, we cannot hope to materially reduce crime in our country," declares J. Edgar Hoover.

—Walter C. McCrory,
in the *United Presbyterian*

* * *

Well Spent!

"A Sabbath day well spent
Brings a week of content,
And strength for the toil of the morrow,
But a Sabbath profaned,
Whatever may be gained,
Is a sure forerunner of sorrow."

—*Selected*

* * *

Was It Sabbath Breaking?

Some excellent Sabbath-keepers once accused a Christian railway superintendent of breaking the Fourth Commandment by habitually sending out and sometimes riding on an extra engine on Sunday afternoon. It turned out that the superintendent found the village of M— without any Sunday school, public worship, or Christian leader, and on Sunday afternoon had a Sunday school manned by leaders carried back and forth on that engine after the day's work in their own Sunday schools was over. Oftentimes the superintendent acted as engine driver rather than appoint an employee to this extra Sunday labor. Others may justly do what we could not justly do.

—*Sunday School Times*

* * *

He Couldn't Afford It

A Christian man, an elder in the church, built up in his community a fine business. Among his employees was a young lad of eighteen, only saved a few months. One day a large order came from a rich, but godless, man for goods to be shipped in a hurry. The businessman said to his youthful employee, "I'm awfully sorry, Rob, but this means we will have to work next Sunday." "Mr. A," said the lad, "I heard you tell in church that you never let the Lord down to please your customers." "But what am I going to do?" asked the man. "I can't afford to offend this wealthy customer." And that boy, saved only a few months, said to the mature Christian: "Well, sir, I'm sorry I can't work next Sunday. *I can't afford to offend the Lord.*"

—*Sunday School Times*

* * *

Which Will You Observe?

There is a story told in Benjamin Franklin's autobiography of a clergyman who was ordered to read the proclamation issued by Charles I, bidding the people to return to sports on Sundays. To his congregation's horror and amazement, he did read the royal edict in church, which many clergy had refused to do. But he followed it with the words, "Remember the sabbath day, to keep it holy," and added: "Brethren, I have laid before you the commandment of your king and the Commandment of your God. I leave it to you to judge which of the two ought rather to be observed."

—*Christian Herald*

* * *

A Jew's Challenge to Christians

"I love your English Sunday, your Christian Sabbath, and should be very

373

sorry to see it pass away. If a Jew may be pardoned for making this suggestion to Christians, let me say this: If you sacrifice the Sunday that you have been brought up to respect, you will lose something you will be sorry for the whole of your lives." This was the comment made in the Council Chamber at Middlesborough by Mr. Jules Reubens, a local member, who is a cinema proprietor. Mr. Reubens was speaking against a resolution for Sunday opening of picture houses.

Christian Herald (London)

* * *

A Contrast in Bridge Building

The old town bridge of Tzompantepec had given its humble service since the days of Cortes. No longer could it be depended upon to carry the townspeople with their daily burdens. The authorities announced that all men should gather the following Sunday to build a new bridge. The small group of Protestants had been taught to honor the Lord's Day. Together they discussed the serious problem of their new standards, so different from those of their neighbors. Though few in number, they presented themselves before the village president, offering to build half of the new bridge if only they might be granted the special favor of doing the work on a weekday. Surely the Lord hears the earnest prayers of His children! The request was granted. The Sunday building was a fiesta. Old and young brought their skins of pulque. As the day wore on, bridge building was mixed with carousing. This dilapidated half of the bridge is now compared with the Protestant half — well constructed by a few Christian workers whose consciences would not permit them to build bridges on Sunday!

—Mexico, reprinted in
Record of Christian Work

* * *

Man's Physical Need of a Rest Day

There is a Sabbath law operative in man. Two generations ago, Dr. Haegler of Switzerland, in making tests of the amount of oxygen in the system, dis-covered that more oxygen was lost in a day's toil than was recovered by a night's rest; but the Sabbath made good the cumulative losses of the week of toil. Experience proves that men cannot endure manual toil seven days a week continuously. The Henry Ford Motor Company went back to a six-day work week, not so much because of a shortage of aluminum, but of consideration of health conditions of workers. A company spokesman said that seven days of toil had ill effects on the workers.

—Moody Monthly

* * *

He Knows Both Men and Donkeys

The London costermongers told Lord Shaftesbury that their donkeys which rested one day in seven could travel thirty miles a day with their loads, while those donkeys that worked seven days a week could only travel fifteen miles a day. So you lose seventy-five miles of travel each week by working your donkey every day, and have a sick, seedy-looking donkey in the bargain; while you gain 3,900 miles of travel in a year, and have a sleek, nice-looking donkey, by running him according to the Ten Commandments. What has a donkey to do with the Ten Commandments? Why, don't you remember what it says in Deuteronomy 5:14? . . . He who made both man and the donkey knew what was good for them and so put both man and donkey into the Commandments. Infidelity doesn't know enough to run a donkey without killing it; and as for man, in Paris, where there is no Sabbath, there are more suicides in proportion to the population than in any other city in Christendom.

—Illustrator

* * *

A Serious Problem

"I am a druggist. From the time our little town was founded up until a short time ago, it was a quiet, clean place with its three churches full and everything you could ask for in a town. Sunday was a day of rest and quiet. About five or six years ago, ice-cream parlors began to open Sundays, some grocery stores remained open Sunday mornings. Then came the beer gardens and the picture show, all open on Sunday.

"The demand has been increasing that I also open on Sundays and keep liquor. We have always stood ready to answer any emergency call in times of illness on Sunday. This I believe to be right, but to open my store on Sunday for commercial purposes I feel is wrong. Very little medicine is sold by the majority of drug stores on Sunday. If they were held strictly to the selling of medicine, few drug stores would be open on this day.

"I was brought up by a dear mother to remember the Lord's Day and to keep it holy, to do all my work in six days, and to rest on the seventh and serve my Master. I have tried to do this and have done much work with young people. This decision now faces me, but I feel that if I were to do these two things I would be selling my soul and the price would be too great, and that I had better get out and find something else to do. It seems to me if I did those two things, I would lose the respect of all these young people, as well as doing it in the face of the teachings of my Master, and that would be more than I could bear."

—*Moody Monthly*

* * *

Far More Satisfying

A pastor called two or three times and asked a certain young married man of his church to teach a class of fifteen-year-old boys in the Sunday school, only to be refused. At last the wife of the man urged her husband to tell the minister frankly why he would not teach. It appeared that he played golf on Sunday afternoons, and he felt he could not do that and teach the class, too. Finally he was convinced that here was a real challenge, and that he should renounce the Sunday golf and teach the class. He did so, and after about five months he walked down the aisle of the church with the sixth and last unsaved boy in a class of thirteen, thus bringing the entire class to Christ. After the service the pastor said to the teacher: "Has it been

worth while giving up your game of golf on Sundays, or would you like to spend your Sundays as you formerly did?" There were tears of joy in his eyes and a jubilancy in the tremble of his voice as the man replied: "This is the greatest time of my life. I had rather spend my time telling others about Christ who has done so much for me. I'm sorry that I did not begin teaching years ago instead of wasting my time doing worldly things." If someone some Sunday morning now suggested golf, it was easy to say, "Not today, thank you, I have something more satisfying to occupy my Sundays."

—From *The Christian Use of the Lord's Day,* by J. E. Harris

* * *

Occupation Unchanged

An infidel was introduced by a gentleman to a minister with a remark, "He never attends public worship." "Ah!" said the minister, "I hope you are mistaken." "By no means," said the stranger; "I always spend Sunday in settling my accounts." "Then, alas," was the calm but solmen reply, "you will find, sir, that the day of judgment will be spent in the same manner."

—*Spurgeon's Sermon Notes*

* * *

"The Hens Did It"

Sra. Juana Venegas is a real "character," and has frequently appeared in the pages of this "letter to the Homeland." The other day she placed 500 pesos in the hands of the church officials to be used for the building fund. She said: "The hens did it! I can't get this tithing business through my head, but there were my hens laying eggs on the Lord's Day! Somehow it didn't seem right to use the eggs laid on His day for ordinary purposes, and so for several months I have been setting those particular eggs apart and have sold them separately, and — well, here's the money!"

—*Soldiers and Gospel Mission*

No Sunday Dinner?

There is an uncomfortable bit of truth in the weary comment of an overworked pastor who sighed when he said, "The membership of the average church is the greatest missionary field on earth."

The police records of every city in America will show that the problem of juvenile delinquency is by no means restricted to the slum areas. Children from some of the best homes in every city are falling into the hands of the police and junvenile authorities, for no other reason than that parents are not accepting their responsibilities for their own children.

We venture a positive assertion, in the confidence that hundreds of thousands of American parents need desperately to awaken to its truthfulness: No Sunday dinner, no Saturday night bridge club, no lodge meeting, no Sunday picnic, no out-of-town pleasure trip, no amusement is as important in the life of a parent as the responsibility for providing religious and moral training for his child.

In our opinion there is a serious need for some extremely straight preaching, as well as for some courageous pastoral work at this very point. Thousands of church mothers need to be told in plain terms that no Sunday dinner is as important as their presence in the church school *with their children.* It may even be necessary for someone to say to some parents, *"You have no right to a child you are unwilling to train."*

—*Christian Advocate*

* * *

No Place for Week-Day Tasks

A man . . . was trying to get his Negro servant to do some unnecessary work on Sunday. He reminded the servant that Jesus had said it was lawful to pull an ox or an ass out of a pit on the Sabbath. "Yes, Massa," was the ready reply, "but not if it fell in on Saturday."

—Dr. J. R. Miller

* * *

Our Presidents and the Lord's Day

George Washington in the Revolutionary War, Lincoln in the Civil War and Wilson in the first World War all gave orders relieving troops as far as possible from fatigue duty on Sunday, and giving them opportunity to attend public worship. Hayes and Garfield habitually walked to church that their servants might rest and worship on the Lord's Day. Grant, when at Paris, refused to attend horse races on the Lord's Day. McKinley, when at the opening of the State Centennial of Tennessee, refused a trip up Lookout Mountain, saying, "No, I do not go sightseeing on Sunday." Theodore Roosevelt and Coolidge spoke in appreciation of the Lord's Day; the latter said, "I profoundly believe in the Lord's Day." Hoover, when invited to join a fishing party on the Lord's Day, replied, "The Hoover's never fish on Sunday." President Truman, fishing on the Columbia River, refused to cast a line on Sunday.

—*Christian Digest*

* * *

Courage Rewarded

It was during the stressful days of World War II. The wheels of industry were going night and day, not even stopping on the Lord's Day. To carry the munitions of war to ports of debarkation, great demands were made upon the railroads. Workmen were in great demand. Ministers were asked to work for a railroad whose shops were located in the town where I was pastor of a church. A domineering, godless foreman seemed delighted to make the work as embarrassing and unpleasant as he possibly could. He insisted on my working on Sundays, questioning my patriotism for my observing the Lord's Day as a day of rest and worship. I did not hesitate to tell him where I stood and why! He threatened to demote me, and even have me discharged. Unknowing to both of us, a high official overheard the conversation. This official came to me and highly commended me for my courage and conviction, assuring me protection in my position. May God give to each one of us great courage to stand for that which is right, as we safeguard our Christian heritage which has made us great as a nation, and which is so alarmingly slipping from the consciences of many!

—William A. Tecklenburg,
President, Illinois Regional, I.F.C.A.

* * *

Why Observe Sunday

Question: Why do we observe Sunday as the Sabbath?

Answer: First, of all, we do not. The Sabbath was the seventh day of the week, but Sunday is the first day. These are two entirely different days. The Christian Church observes Sunday, and not the Sabbath, for a number of very good reasons. The first day of the week was the day of our Lord's resurrection and the day when He first showed Himself to His disciples as alive from the dead. It is called by John "the Lord's Day" (Rev. 1:10) and came to be generally so known during the first centuries of Church history. Indeed it never should be referred to by any other name. Not only is the first day of the week the day of our Lord's resurrection, but it was also the day of the descent of the Holy Spirit. Therefore the day is doubly precious to the Christian. It was the day on which Christians gathered for worship in the earliest days of the Church, a practice which has continued down to the present time.

—*Moody Monthly*

A Farm Problem Solved

One Saturday a man who was to help some farmers harvest grain, stopped in, saying he would be at a certain farm on Sunday morning to combine their oats and they would lose their turn if they did not take it then. The farmer and his helpers knew Christ as their Saviour and Lord and did not take care of crops on Sunday. This man was rough and worldly and did not understand their feeling about the Lord's Day. The farmer discussed the unpleasant situation with his helpers and they felt sure God would be displeased and could keep them from having to have the combining done on Sunday. The weather looked very pleasant that evening — only a small, innocent-looking cloud in the South, and the sun was shining. Soon the hired man came to the chicken house door, saying it was sprinkling. God had sent that cloud their way. Soon rain was pouring down. It lasted only a few minutes, but it made the Sunday combining impossible, for the grain was soaked. Sunday dawned beautiful and sunny, and the grain dried out and on Monday it was ready for combining. The thing that made them sure God solved their problem: it rained only on their farm — on either side it was dry!

—*Power*

LORD'S SUPPER

He Sat Down With Judas

An official of the church was visiting a church with whose members he was not well acquainted. He was asked to be one to distribute the bread and wine, and he noted that certain persons sat aside from those who expected to receive these emblems of our Lord's body and blood. He took his part in the service, and observant of the people, saw with surprise that among the noncommunicants sat a deacon he knew sufficiently well to feel sure he was a good man. After the service this official asked the deacon why he had not been

one at the Lord's table. The reply was that he regarded one of the members of that church as untrue and indeed felt this had been proved in certain money transactions he had with that member. The friend quietly said, "Do you consider yourself better than the Saviour? He sat down at His own table with Judas, who, He knew, was a thief." That deacon thought over this and also examined himself lest he be the one at fault in the money transactions. He discovered that he himself was partly to blame, and he made up his differences with that church member; he did not continue away from his Lord's table.

—*Young People's Bible Teacher,*
S. B. C.

* * *

"It's For Saved Sinners!"

A godly old-country pastor was in the midst of his communion service. Suddenly his quick eye detected a woman passing the cup untasted. She sat among the people quietly weeping. At once his kindly heart sensed the situation. For who of us has not at such a time been so conscious of our own unworthiness and sinfulness as to shrink from partaking of that blessed sacrament? But the loving dominie knew the gospel of Christ too well to let one of His little ones suffer thus. He hastened down the aisle. He took the cup from the hands of the serving elder. Stepping up to the weeping woman he pressed it into her hand with the loving, tender exhortation — "Take it, woman; take it. It's for sinners; it's for sinners!"

—James McConkey

* * *

The Little Red Shoes

A couple had lived happily in their married life. Sorrow came, however: their little girl was suddenly taken from them. Their hearts were whelmed with grief. As time passed, husband and wife became estranged from each other. Their former love seemed to congeal into bitter hatred. They lived apart. Coming together, finally, to settle upon the terms of divorcement, they sat in the home where they had spent many happy days. As they sat in sullen silence, their eyes chanced to fall upon a pair of little red shoes which had belonged to their little girl. This reminder of their little girl softened their hearts in tenderness. Ere long, both were weeping for brokenness of heart. God convicted them of their sinfulness and selfishness. Then and there, they renewed their marital vows, and promised God to live for Him, and meet their darling child in Glory! What brought this change? The little reminder, the

little red shoes. As we remember Him, all bitterness vanishes, and the song of our hearts become:

"More love, O Christ, to Thee,
More love to Thee!"

Well did the Lord Jesus know the tendency of our hearts to forget Him. For this reason, and that we might keep green in memory His vicarious death, and promise to return for His own, He has left with His children the Lord's Memorial Supper: "This do in remembrance of Me" (I Cor. 11:24b).

—W. B. K.

* * *

Where Her Pride Was

The following experience was told by a member of the family referred to in this incident. A split in their church had taken place, leaving behind it much bitterness. One Sunday morning a member of the family arose from the breakfast table and said she was going to church. "What?" exclaimed the others, "Are you going back there, after the way our family has been treated! Where's your pride?" The one addressed, quietly answered: "This is Communion Sunday. I am going to sit at the Lord's table and remember His death for me. As for my pride, I haven't any when I survey the wondrous cross, and any bitterness I had has all vanished when I remember He is coming, and perhaps very soon."

—*Sunday School Times*

* * *

Why He Wanted the Cap Lining

A little waif of the streets was admitted to a children's home. He was offered a new outfit, and took a boy's pride in getting a new suit, new stockings, new boots. But when they offered him a new cap he wanted to cling to the old, ragged one he held in his hand. When obliged to part with it, it was noticed by the kindly Sister that he tore out its lining and stuffed it in his pocket. "Why did you do that?" asked the Sister. "Because," he said, with tears in his eyes, "the lining of my old cap was part of my mother's dress. It is all

I've got left of her, and somehow it seems to bring her back." The lining of that torn cap was not merely a circle of faded material, it was a holy symbol. So the bread and wine are sacramental; they are forever holy symbols helping us to realize the presence of Jesus.
—From *His Life and Ours*
　by the Rev. Leslie D. Weatherhead

* * *

"May I Come?"

About twenty of us were preparing to observe the Lord's Supper. "May I come?" asked Yataro Yamaguchi, a Japanese. "Certainly," I replied, "we do not shut anyone out, though ONLY those who know and love the Lord participate at His Table." Hymns were sung. Prayers were made. Scriptures were read. Then Yataro rose to his feet, exclaiming, "I like to pray!"

I felt sorry I had not explained that strangers were not expected to take part and I greatly feared a disturbance which would be in the nature of an anticlimax to what had been thus far a very precious remembrance of the Lord.

But I need not have feared. He prayed much as follows: "O God, I all broke up. One whole year I fight you. I fight hard against Your Holy Spirit. O God, I cannot fight any more. I see Your people eat the bread, drink the wine, tell how Jesus die for sinner like me. O God, I give up. I take Him now for my Saviour. Forgive all my sins. Save me now for Jesus' sake. Amen."

Needless to say, it did not spoil our meeting. As he concluded there was not a dry eye in the little assembly.

Fervently we thanked God for manifesting His grace to this one of another race and a pagan religion.
—Dr. Harry A. Ironside

* * *

Lest We Forget

See this picture. This is my mother. Do you believe me? But my mother is not made of paper. No, she is a real person. Yet when I hold this picture up and say, "This is my mother," it is true, and you all understand what I mean. Now the Lord Jesus said, "This is my body," and the disciples knew just what He meant. He was sitting there at the table when He said it. But they knew that every time they took some of the bread at the Lord's Supper they were to remember that He gave His precious body to die for their sins. And every time they drank of the cup, they were to remember that He shed His precious blood to wash away their sins. In Luke 22:19 we read that the Lord Jesus said, "This do in remembrance of me." He knew how easy it would be for us to forget Him and to forget how much He suffered for us. So He started this little service of remembrance for us to keep. . . . .Every time I take part in the Lord's Supper I say this little poem to the Lord:

In this broken bread we own Thee,
　Bruised for us and put to shame;
And this cup, O Lord, we thank Thee,
　Speaks our pardon through Thy name.

Say this little poem softly to Him when the bread and the cup are passed, and it will give Him joy.
—Vivian D. Gunderson

LOST

The Fate of the "Human Fly"

Some years ago there came to Los Angeles, the great metropolis of Southern California, a so-called "human fly." It was announced that on a given day he would climb up the face of one of the large department store buildings, and

long before the appointed time thousands of eager spectators were gathered to see him perform the seemingly impossible feat.

Slowly and carefully he mounted aloft, now clinging to a window ledge, anon to a jutting brick, again to a cornice.

Up and up he went, against apparently insurmountable difficulties. At last he was nearing the top. He was seen to feel to right and left and above his head for something firm enough to support his weight, to carry him further. And soon he seemed to spy what looked like a grey bit of stone or discolored brick protruding from the smooth wall. He reached for it, but it was just beyond him. He ventured all on a spring-like movement, grasped the protuberance and before the horrified eyes of the spectators, fell to the ground and was broken to pieces. In his dead hand was found a spider's web! What he evidently mistook for solid stone or brick turned out to be nothing but dried froth!

Alas, how many are thinking to climb to heaven on their own, only to find at last that they have ventured all on a spider's web, and so are lost forever. Christ, and Christ alone, can save.

—Dr. Harry A. Ironside

* * *

Not Grief Alone, But Action Needed!

Mary Virginia Lee, a Sunday school worker, arrived one Sunday morning in a beautiful and prosperous southern town. As no one met her at the station, she took a taxi, and driving past the square, noticed automobiles double parked all around the court house. This seemed so strange at such an early hour on the Lord's Day, that she asked the driver what it all meant. He replied, "The men of the town have gathered here to go out in search of a little boy who has been lost since Friday noon. Organized parties have been searching continually night and day ever since. Many have not even slept, but have been constantly seeking the lost child." When they arrived at the home where the worker was to be entertained, she found that her hostess, who was the little lad's Sunday-school teacher, had spent the night with the grief-stricken mother, and her husband had just returned from a fruitless all-night search. The sympathy of the entire town was

aroused. Although many were praying the anxiety grew more tense with every passing hour, and hope was giving way to dread. Throughout the morning services there was a spirit of expectancy but still no news. About noon as the people were returning home from church, some one shouted, "The boy is found!" Immediately loved ones, friends and neighbors hastened to join the happy parents. There was great rejoicing everywhere because the lost boy had been found.

— *Western Recorder*

* * *

A Fatal Point

On the banks of Niagara, where the rapids begin to swell and swirl most desperately preparatory to their final plunge, is a signboard which bears the following sign: "P a s t Redemption Point." Even while one feels the firm soil beneath his feet, a shiver of horror passes through one's soul as he looks off upon the turbulent waters, and realizes the full significance of the sign, "*Past Redemption Point.*" None can go back if past that point.

Sunday School Times

* * *

An Infidel's Final "Assurance"

Sir Francis Newport, the head of an English infidel club, said to those gathered around his dying bed, "You need not tell me there is no God for I know there is one, and that I am in His angry presence! You need not tell me there is no hell, for I already feel my soul slipping into its fires! Wretches, cease your idle talk about there being hope for me! I know I am lost forever."

— *Sunday School Times*

* * *

The Explorer's Last Words

He was found in a lonely hut, dead, with a dishpan which he had used for a desk, across his knees, and in his skeleton hand the following letter, in the writing of which he was evidently engaged when death overtook him.

"The sun is shining, Mother, but I feel so cold. I can still walk a little, but that's about all. There is no blood in me, because I have not eaten for so long. I haven't seen another human being for forty days now. There are some magazines here, but *the stories are so silly.* I have some cards, but *I don't care for solitaire. The only thing I worry about is if God will forgive my sins.*"

Thus ended the career of a young explorer at Long Rapids, Hay River, Alberta, Can. He was about to leap into the dark as far as his eternity was concerned. — *Prairie Pastor.*

* * *

"There Is A Time!"

"There is a time, we know not when,
A place we know not where,
That marks the destiny of men
To glory or despair.

"There is a line by us unseen,
That crosses every path:
The hidden boundary between
God's patience and His wrath.

"To pass that limit is to die,
To die as if by stealth;
It does not quench the beaming eye,
Or pale the glow of health.

"But on that forehead God hath set
Indelibly a mark,
Unseen by man, for man as yet
Is blind and in the dark.

"And yet the doomed man's path below
Like Eden may have bloomed;
He did not, does not, will not know
Or feel that he is doomed.

"He thinks or feels that all is well
And every fear is calmed;
He lives, he dies, he wakes in hell,
Not only doomed — but damned.

"The conscience may be still at ease,
The spirit light and gay;
That which is pleasing still may please,
And care be thrust away.

"Oh! where is this mysterious line
That may be crossed by men,
Beyond which God Himself hath sworn
That he who goes is lost?

"How far may we go on in sin?
How long will God forbear?
Where does hope end? and where begin
The confines of despair?

"The answer from the skies is sent:
'Ye who from God depart,
While it is called today, repent
And harden not your heart.'"
— *Selected*

* * *

Wild Sheep!

"I was a guest at a big sheep ranch. The rancher and I were riding along a ridge, flanking a deep canyon, when three sheep appeared from among the boulders. They stood for a moment with heads up, eyes frightened, one front foot up, poised to run, then crashed through the canyon and were gone.

"I voiced my surprise that wild sheep were still to be found on this ranch.

" 'Not so,' replied the rancher, 'those are the sheep that my herder failed to count in three evenings ago.' Three thousand gentle sheep grazed in the valley below us. Three nights without a shepherd had made this difference!

"In Jesus' parable, it is suggested that the shepherd felt deeply the loss of his sheep or feared what the wolves might do to it. But his distress was also caused by fear of what would happen within the sheep itself.
—*United Evangelical*

* * *

A Matter of Tense

When Hudson Taylor was on his way to China, he was accosted one day by the Ship's captain.

"Taylor, do you think the heathen will be lost if you don't go to China?"

"I think the heathen *are* lost. That's why I go to China."
—*Sunday School Promoter*

Derelicts

"There's a ship floats past with a sway-
ing lurch,
No sails, no crew, no spar;
And she drifts from the paths of her
sister ships
To the place where the dead ships are.
The song of her crew is hushed for aye,
Her name no man can say;
She is ruled by the tide and whatever
wind blows —
And no man knows where the derelict
goes!

"There's a man slinks past with a
lurching gait;
No joy, no hope, no star;
And he drifts from the paths of his
brother men,
To wherever the other wrecks are.
The song of his youth is hushed for aye,
His name but he can say;
He is ruled by the tide and whatever
wind blows,
And no one knows where the derelict
goes!"

— *Harper's Monthly*

* * *

Not Connected

A United Press report out of San Antonio, Tex., tells of a hospital in that
city where it was discovered that the
firefighting system, upon which reliance
had been placed for thirty-five years for
the safety of all its patients in case of
fire, had never been connected with the
city's water main. The pipe that led
from the firefighting system extended
four feet under ground — and there
stopped! An appropriation was immediately made, of course, to hook the
hospital's system to the city water pipes.
In just such a way there are those who,
relying on character, or church membership, or benevolent contributions, or
other works of the flesh have been even
more insecure than were the patients of
the hospital in San Antonio, for it has
been their souls that have been endangered rather than their bodies. Apart

from attachment, by faith, to the source
of the stream of living water, that is,
Christ Himself, there is no safety. It is
in Him that there is life, and in Him
alone.

— *Pilgrim*

* * *

He Was a Loser at Last

A successful farmer, whose flocks and
herds increased, was wont to say to
those who spoke to him about eternal
things, "I must make my fortune first,
then I shall attend to these matters."

One day he took suddenly ill while at
market, and was hurriedly driven home
to be laid on the bed from which he
never rose. To one who sat by his side
during the last hours of life, one who
had often spoken to him on eternal
things, he said in tones of bitter remorse, "I am a loser at last. I have
gained the world, but have lost my soul."

— *Gospel Herald*

* * *

Wrong Orders

Some years ago a passenger train
was rushing into New York as another
train was emerging. There was a head-
on collision. Fifty lives were lost. An
engineer was pinned under his engine,
frightfully injured, and tears were
running down his cheeks. In his dying
agonies he held a piece of yellow paper
crushed in his hand, and said: "Take
this. This will show you that someone
gave me the wrong orders."

Unregenerate men and women will
stand before the Great White Throne
and point to their Modernist preachers,
saying, "Someone gave me the wrong
orders!"

— *Watchman-Examiner*

* * *

Why People Are Not Saved

A mother attended a service in a large
and crowded auditorium accompanied
by her little daughter Mary. In some
manner Mary became separated from
her mother. The mother sent a notice

to the platform which was read: "If there is a little girl named Mary Moore, in the audience, who is lost, will she please raise her hand so that her mother can find her." No little girl lifted her hand, so Mary's mother had the police searching the city for her child. Not finding her, the mother came back and stood at the door of the auditorium as the people filed out. Among the last of them came Mary. Her mother seized her in her arms crying, "Where were you, Mary?" "On the front seat," replied the little one. "Didn't you hear the notice read, 'If there is a little girl named Mary Moore in the audience who is lost, will she please raise her hand so that her mother can find her?'" "Yes," said Mary, "I heard it read." "Why didn't you raise your hand then?" asked her mother. "Why, mother, it couldn't have meant me," said Mary, "for I wasn't lost. I knew where I was." Jesus came to call sinners to repentance because they are saying, "I'm not a sinner, I'm not lost."

—*Wonderful Word*

* * *

Not Far — But Lost!

A young Filipino, travelling in Chicago, registered at the Hotel Sherman. Taking a walk, he became lost. He was ignorant of the name, location, and appearance of the hotel, and so was unable to find it again. Consequently, he selected another room in the Hotel Astor. Unwilling to acknowledge to the authorities that he was lost, he tried for five days to find the place where he had deposited his baggage. Unsuccessful, he finally appealed to the authorities. The police soon found his original registration place, and informed him that for five days he had been living NEXT DOOR to the place where he had left his baggage. Although so near, he lost five days' peace of mind, five days' time, and five days' use of his baggage all because he would not tell an officer that he was LOST. No one should entertain any fears about telling the Lord that they are lost, confessing, "I have gone astray like a lost sheep."

—*Tom Olson*

"If It Were I"

Robert Murray McCheyne, one of the most spiritual Scottish preachers of the last century, was a well-brought-up and carefully trained youth, whose outward life was without blame; in every way respectable, conscientious and well-informed; he knew his Bible, said his prayers, went to church, and was well-satisfied with his own righteousness, forgetting that Scripture has declared, "All our righteousnesses are as filthy rags" in God's sight. While he was away at school a message came telling him of the sudden death of a very godly elder brother. He went home to the funeral, and upon reaching the house of mourning asked to be permitted to go alone into the room where lay the body of his dearly loved brother. As he stood there gazing upon the still, silent form he asked himself the question, "If it were I, where would my soul be?" The answer to his own question honestly given was, "Lost forever." There and then he broke down, gave up all pretension to a righteousness of his own, and found in Christ risen and glorified that righteousness which he celebrates in his little hymn, "Jehovah Tsidkenu."

—*From The Mission of the Holy Spirit*, by H. A. Ironside.

* * *

Is It Nothing to You?

World deaths are 40,000,000 yearly, 109,589 daily, 4,566 hourly, 76 per minute. Two-thirds have never heard the Gospel! "Is it nothing to you?"

—*Selected*

* * *

Misdirected

A terrible blizzard was raging over the eastern part of the States, making more and more difficult the progress of a train that was slowly facing its way along.

Among the passengers was a woman with a child, who was much concerned lest she should not get off at the right station. A gentleman, seeing her anxiety, said:

"Do not worry. I know the road well, and I will tell you when you come to your station."

In due course the train stopped at the station before the one at which the woman wanted to get off.

"The next station will be yours, ma'am," said the gentleman.

Then they went on, and in a few minutes the train stopped again.

"Now is your time, ma'am; get out quickly he said.

The woman took up her child, and thanking the man, left the train. At the next stop, the brakeman called out the name of the station where the woman had wished to get off.

"You have already stopped at this station," called the man to the brakeman. "No, sir," he replied, "something was wrong with the engine, and we stopped for a few moments to repair it!"

"Alas!" cried the passenger, "I put that woman off in the storm when the train stopped between stations!" Afterwards, they found her with her child in her arms. Both were frozen to death! It was the terrible and tragic consequence of wrong direction being given! Still more terrible are the results of misdirecting souls!

—Billy Sunday

* * *

The Very One Christ Came to Save

The brother of Whitefield, the great evangelist, was deeply despondent at times, and felt his utter worthlessness and helplessness. On one such occasion Lady Huntingdon spoke to him about his salvation, and tried to induce him to come to Christ. To all her pleas he answered, "Oh, it is of no use! I am lost! *I am lost!*" "Thank God for that," said she. "Why?" asked the man in astonishment. "Because," said Lady Huntingdon, "Christ came to save the lost, and if you are lost, He is just the one who can save you."

—*Christian Herald*

* * *

A Simple Prayer

One night, after an evening of excitement among worldly people, my eye fell on this sentence: "Every soul not already won to Jesus is already lost."

It was like an arrow of conviction to my soul. An overwhelming sense of my lost and hopeless condition fell upon me, and my soul was hanging over the abyss. I had absolutely no plea but for mercy. Daily I had said my prayers since childhood, but that night, like Saul of Tarsus, I really prayed. The blessed Saviour placed upon my lips, "God be merciful to me a sinner!" In my agony I uttered it with my face upon the floor. And God heard it. He always hears that prayer. That night He lifted me out of the miry clay and planted me upon a rock. He put a new song in my mouth, which I have been singing ever since, even salvation unto my God.

—Dr. James Gray

* * *

Sequel to Salvation Spurned

From her own dying bed an aged woman said to me, very solemnly, "Pastor, I am afraid that my husband sold himself to the devil forty years ago," And then she told me one of the saddest stories I have ever heard. She said that at that time he was very much moved about his own soul. His pastor and many others came to see him and begged him to give himself to Christ and accept Him as his Saviour. She herself pleaded and prayed with him. But he was a member of the state legislature, and he said to her one night, "Wife, I have a scheme to carry through the legislature. It would not do for me to carry that scheme through if I were a Christian man. I am going to see it through, and then I will repent and accept Christ as Saviour." He carried the scheme through but, as she said to me, *from that day he had never apparently had any desire to be a child of God.*

—Arthur T. Pierson

* * *

Perished in Sight of Home!

In the other years, the Government gave plots of ground to settlers who would go and settle upon the land, cultivating it and building a home thereon. A pioneering couple, just married, were among some early settlers in the far north-west. How happy they were! One afternoon, the husband went to a nearby "trading post" for provisions. During the hours of the afternoon, a terrible snowstorm blanketed the whole countryside. Darkness settled down. During the hours of that long night, the wife waved a lantern in the door of their humble cottage, hoping that by its light her lover would find his way safely home. With the coming of the day, searchers set out. Just a short distance from the cottage, they stumbled over the snow-covered, lifeless body of the young husband! He had perished within sight of home. Alas, many, "not far from the kingdom," perish eternally, being without God and without hope!

—W. B. K.

* * *

A Missionary Cry

A hundred thousand souls a day,
Are passing one by one away,
In Christless guilt and gloom.
Without one ray of hope or light,
With future dark as endless night,
They're passing to their doom.

—*Selected*

* * *

The Derelict

The derelict ship is a haunted ship
That sails where the moon rides low;
Her course is determined by the gales
Which buffet her to and fro.

Just like the old ship, adrift at sea,
Sans pilot, sans cargo, and goal,
We sometimes trust to the Winds of
　　Chance
The precious sails of the soul!

—*War Cry*

* * *

Saving the Clothes

Someone has illustrated the value of a soul with a modern parable in this striking manner. A householder took a trip into a far country and left with his servant a child and the child's clothes. After awhile he returned and the servant said to him: "Sir, here are all the child's clothes. They are in ex-

cellent condition — clean, and mended, and pressed. But as for the child, I know not where it is." So in the last day some one will say "Lord, here is my body. I have neglected nothing that belongs to it. It is strong, and well, and beautiful. But as for my soul I have lost it!"

—*The Presbyterian*

* * *

Who Has Found Whom?

In the timber mountains of the Northwest a five-year-old was lost. Night came. The citizens and rangers were searching the caves and mountainsides for him. Snow began to fall. All night the snow laid its blankets, but no Bobby could be found. The next morning the sun came out, and the storm ceased. A weary father decided to come in for a cup of coffee, and when he was within half a mile of home he kicked against what seemed to be a log in the path, but when the snow was jarred a small boy stretched, yawned, sat up from under his snow blankets, and exclaimed, "Oh, Daddy! I've found you at last" Now who found whom? Mortals have an inherited phrase — "So-and so found the Lord." But the Lord has never been lost! Men talk about the search for God. He has asked us to search the Scriptures and to seek His will, but when it comes to salvation it is God who reaches out for us.

—*Conqueror*

* * *

Counterfeit Religion

In South America there is a tree, so travelers say, the leaf of which starving men will chew, because it gives them the most enjoyable sensations of having been fed. Through its influence, all desire for food departs, and a starving person is thus saved from the painful gnawing of hunger. Pain is taken away, but death is not defeated. The leaf contains a drug, but no nourishment. It satisfies a man's craving, but it does not satisfy his need, for in one respect it is a counterfeit of food; it deceives the dying man by assuring him that he has had food, whereas he is dying for lack of it.

This is exactly the danger which attends a form of godliness. It meets and satisfies the inner craving of our religious natures, and yet it is a spiritual drug, plunging us into death when we think we have found life. It satisfies our craving, but it does not provide for our need. It fills, but it does not feed.

—Lionel B. Fletcher, in
Life Quest and Conquest

* * *

Should Not Be Postponed

In 1871 I preached a series of sermons on the life of Christ in old Farwell hall, Chicago, for five nights. I took Him from the cradle and followed Him up to the judgment hall, and on that occasion I consider I made as great a blunder as ever I made in my life. It was upon that memorable night in October, and the court-house bell was sounding an alarm of fire, but I paid no attention to it. You know we were accustomed to hear the fire-bell often, and it didn't disturb us much when it sounded. I finished the sermon upon "What Shall I Do with Jesus?" and said to the audience:

"Now I want you to take the question with you and think it over, and next Sunday I want you to come back and tell me what you are going to do with Him."

What a mistake! It seems now as if Satan was in my mind when I said this. Since then I never have dared give an audience a week to think of their salvation. If they were lost, they might rise up in judgment against me. "Now is the accepted time."

I remember Mr. Sankey singing, and how his voice rang when he came to that pleading verse:

"To-day the Savior calls,
For refuge fly!
The storm of Justice falls,
And death is nigh!"

After the meeting we went home. I remember going down LaSalle street with a young man, and saw the glare of flames. I said to the young man: "This means ruin to Chicago."

About one o'clock Farwell hall was burned; soon the church in which I had preached went down, and everything was scattered. I never saw that audience again.

—D. L. Moody

* * *

Too Late!

Late, late, so late! and dark the night and chill!
Late, late, so late! but we can enter still.
Too late, too late! ye cannot enter now.

No light had we; for that we do repent,
And learning this, the bridegroom will relent.
Too late, too late! ye cannot enter now.

No light! so late! and dark and chill the night!
O, let us in, that we may find the light!
Too late, too late! ye cannot enter now.

Have we not heard the bridegroom is so sweet?
O, let us in, though late, to kiss his feet!
Oh, no, too late! ye cannot enter now.

—Tennyson

* * *

Mixed Audiences

A number of years ago I was invited by a very godly minister to address his congregation on a certain Lord's Day. I said to him, "Doctor, when I come to speak to your people, what kind of audience will I address? Will they be mainly your own members, all Christian people, or many strangers and possibly unconverted people?" I can still see the tears that came into his eyes as he said, seriously and solemnly, "Well, my brother. I think that most of them will be our own people; but I am afraid that very few of our own members are Christians. Therefore, I hope you will come to us with a clear, definite Gospel message, and I shall be praying that God may use it for the awakening and the salvation of many of our people." What a solemn thing to have to make a confession like that! And yet is it not true in many places today? We take too much for granted when we suppose that membership in a Christian church means that one is really a child of God. There must be a second birth; there must be personal faith in the Lord Jesus Christ.

—From *Addresses on First Corinthians* by Dr. H. A. Ironside

* * *

How Christian Dies

An evangelist, seriously sick, sent for the Roman Catholic priest to visit him immediately. A friendship had grown up between the Methodist evangelist and the priest. The priest, thinking he wanted the last rites of the Catholic church, hurried to his bedside. To his surprise, he was greeted by him with, "I'm glad you came. I only wanted you to see how a Christian goes Home to his reward!" With a smile on his calm features, the evangelist passed out of life. Said the priest, "I would give anything I had to die like that. I often fear to close my eyes, not knowing where I shall open them."

—C. E. Gremmels, in *Sunday School Times*

* * *

Civilized But Lost!

A few years ago I was in Japan walking along a broad road which lay outside of the city of Yokohama. As I passed on my way I noticed a Japanese gentleman coming toward me, who, evidently, was of a high and modern order. He was dressed in foreign clothes — a cut-away coat, pressed trousers, highly polished shoes, immaculate linen, a well tied cravat, and a derby hat. His face was bright and very intelligent looking, giving one the idea that he had studied abroad, possibly at Oxford or Columbia University. It was my impression that he was educated beyond all heathenism, and possibly, that he was somewhat Christianized. As he came toward me, he glanced to the left and noticed a wide-open shrine standing beside the road, at the back of which was a large and repulsive looking idol. To my surprise the gentleman stopped, turned to the front of the shrine, took off his derby hat, bowed his head in worship of the idol, mumbled a few prayers, took out a piece of silver from his pocket, threw it with practiced accuracy into a basket which stood before the idol, raised his hand and took hold of a pendant rope, pulled the rope and rang the bell which advised the god that he had prayed and made his offering. Thereupon he turned and went his way.

—Henry W. Frost, in *Revelation*

* * *

Monkey Business

In North Africa the natives have a very easy way to capture monkeys. A gourd, with a hole just sufficiently large so that a monkey can thrust his hand into it, is filled with nuts and fastened firmly to a branch of a tree at sunset. During the night a monkey will discover the scent of food, and its source, and will put his hand into the gourd and grasp a handful of nuts. But the hole is too small for the monkey to withdraw his clenched fist, and he has not sense enough to let go of his bounty so that he may escape. Thus he pulls and pulls without success, and when morning comes he is quickly and easily taken.

Multitudes of human beings — in no way related to the monkey, by the way — have little more sense than he. "For what shall it profit a man, if he shall gain the whole world, and lose his own soul?" the Saviour asked (Mk. 8:36).

—*The Pilgrim*

* * *

Sermon from an Infidel

Peter Stryker never forgot the remark of a learned, legal friend who at the time was an infidel.

"Did I believe as you do," declared the infidel, "that the masses of our race are perishng in sin, I could have no rest. I would fly to tell them of salvation. I would labor day and night. I would speak it with all the pathos I could summon. I would warn and expostulate and entreat my fellow men to turn unto Christ and receive salvation at His hands.

"I am astonished at the manner in which the majority of you ministers tell your message. Why do you not act as if you believed your own words? You have not the earnestness in preaching that we lawyers have in pleading. If we were as tame as you are, we would never carry a single suit."

"I bless God," testified Peter Stryker, "that that remark was made to me. It put fire into my bones which I hope will burn as long as I live. God preached a stirring sermon to me that day by the mouth of my friend, the infidel lawyer."

—*Moody Monthly*

* * *

Wine and the Window

Not long ago, a beautiful and cultured girl, a graduate of one of our great universities, flung herself out of a ten-story window in her home city. She had begun to go with the "fast set," who considered that it is smart and up-to-date to come home at three o'clock in the morning from cocktail parties. That night she took just a little too much and lost her grip on herself. One of the "great" American ladies, lecturing the girls at one of America's foremost women's colleges, told them that the intelligent young woman of today should know what her limit is — just how much liquor she can hold and still keep her poise; and to be careful not to go beyond that limit! Shades of the Bacchanalians! Think of that! Evidently the young woman, mentioned above, had failed to observe "her limit." She had spent a night of sin in that hotel, and when the gray morning came and she realized what she had done, and that she must face her proud family . . . the ten-story window drew her like a magnet. The police officer down there, holding back the crowd while he guarded her mangled form on the pavement, turned to an acquaintance and grimly said: "When you don"t have God, there ain't nothin' to do but *jump!*" If the poor girl could have realized that morning that it was not a window, but a wide open "Door" she could have resorted to — even then! how different it would have been!

—Wade C. Smith, in *Sunday School Times*

388

All Were Lost Alike!

It was a dark, winter's night. The rain was falling fast, and there was nothing more inviting than the warm glow of the fire before which we were sitting.

There was a knock at the front door. The farmer went to answer it, as the rest of the household had gone to their beds.

Coming back to me he said he had heard that all his sheep were missing from the field where they had been placed by him. He must go to find them.

So, having prepared with waterproofs and lanterns, we went forth into the darkness.

In one of the hedges of the field, where the sheep had been left, the farmer discovered what he called "a bolting hole." A strong sheep had worked its way through at that point, and would be followed by all the others.

It was either in the third or fourth field that we came up with the straying animals. And then we found them scattered over the pasture. No two of them seemed to be together. Each had chosen its own course, regardless of the path another had taken. All were lost alike. Then, each had followed its own heart. "All we like sheep have gone astray; we have turned every one to his own way!" ALL sinners are lost alike. But each sinner has gone the way of his own choosing!

—*Watchman-Examiner*

* * *

Case of Nancy Sykes

In Oliver Twist by Charles Dickens, we read the conversation between Rose Maylie, a beautiful, consistent, cultured woman, and Nancy Sykes, of the underworld, wife of Bill, a vile character.

Rose wants Nancy to quit her life of sin and become a Christian.

"No," says Nancy, "it cannot be. If years ago someone like you had touched my life, all might have been different. Now it is too late. Yet, Miss, if there were more like you, there would be fewer like me."

—*Our Youth*

LOVE OF GOD

"He Whom Thou Lovest!"

Dr. P. P. Bliss, the evangelistic singer and composer, said that he wrote the sacred song, "Oh! How I Love Jesus," when he was a young man. Growing older, however, he realized more deeply how insignificant is our love toward God compared to his love for us. Hence, in his later years, he wrote that appealing hymn, which children so love to sing, — and which is good for grownups, too:

I am so glad that our Father in heaven
Tells of His love in the Book He has
   given;
Wonderful things in the Bible I see,
This is the dearest, that Jesus loves me.
     —Sunday School Times

* * *

"God, Loves You, But He Hates Your Business!"

When in Chicago, we passed a saloon. The keeper was outside rolling a hogshead of beer along the street. We passed on but the man with whom I was walking turned, went back and said, "My friend, God loves you. Did you know that"? The saloon-keeper said, "God loves me? Do you know who I am? I am the saloon-keeper. Does God love saloon-keepers? "Yes," said my friend, "God loves saloon-keepers. He hates their business, but He loves them!"
     —Louis T. Talbot

* * *

Love Made the Difference

Someone has illustrated love as the fulfilling of the law in this way: A woman was married to a man whom she did not love. He made her get up every morning at five o'clock, cook his breakfast, and serve it at six o'clock sharp. He made her wait on him, and was exacting in his demands on her time. Her life was made miserable trying to satisfy the requests of her husband. Finally he died. After a few years she married again. This time she married a man whom she really loved. One day while clearing out some old papers, she came across the strict set of rules her former husband had written out for her to obey. Carefully she read them over. "Get up at five. Serve breakfast at six sharp." On and on she read. Then she stopped and thought, and realized that she was fulfilling every single one of his demands, but she had not realized it because this time she was doing it for love's sake. So it is not difficult to serve the Lord Jesus when we really love Him.
     —Sunday School Superintendent

* * *

Some One Who Loved God!

Asked a little bookblack of a lawyer, as he shined his shoes, "Mr. Bartlett, do you love God"? The lawyer was a self-respecting man but not a Christian, and was much taken aback, and said, "Why do you ask me that, Bat"? "Well, me mother'n me got to get out, fer the place we live in'll be torn down. Me grandmother's lame. I dunno whut to do. Yistiddy I heerd two men talkin', an' one said God would help anybody that loved Him, if they'd tell Him they wuz in a hole. I thought I'd lay fer somebody that knowed Him well enough to ask Him." All the embarrassed lawyer could tell the bootblack was to keep trying, and he'd be sure to find somebody who could help him. Then he gave the boy a dollar and hurried away; but after a day of self-examination and reproach, he appeared in a prayer meeting for the first time in years. He frankly told the story without sparing himself. The minister there told the story later at a ministers' meeting, only to find another minister there who knew of a young man awakened to a new life by a question from the same bootblack. Then a third declared that a man who knew how to answer the boy had brought him to his own study. It could not be allowed to end there. The boy was helped to a good lodging for his "family," given patronage, given opportunity for an education, in which he showed so much promise that a lawyer took him in for training. He became a successful member of the bar, and a real helper of other boys, and withal a real Christian man, for he had at last found someone who loved God.

—*Youth's Companion*

* * *

Why They Could Not Sleep

Two missionaries went to a village in Korea in which the Gospel had never been preached. It was noised abroad that they had come, and practically the whole population gathered. The interest of the people was so great that the meeting continued until a late hour. Finally, the missionaries closed the meeting and were shown into an adjoining room for the night. But the people did not go away, and the murmuring of their voices kept the missionaries from sleeping.

Along about two o'clock, one of them went back and said to the people, "Why don't you go home and go to sleep? It is very late and we are tired." The head man of the village answered in substance: "How can we sleep? You have told us that the Supreme Power is not an evil spirit trying to injure us, but a loving God who gave His only begotten Son for our salvation, and that if we turn away from our sins and trust Him, we may have the deliverance from fear, guidance in our perplexities, comfort in our sorrows. How can we sleep after a message like this?"

How could they indeed? And the missionaries, forgetting their weariness, sat down by those poor people and communed with them until the morning dawned.

—*Gospel Herald*

* * *

The Gospel Mirrors

A banker in New York had a great desire to get the Gospel to the soldiers at Sandy Hook, but was not permitted to carry the message to them in person. But his longing desire to help these men was not to be easily thwarted, so he called on a firm which manufactured advertising novelties and had them make several thousand small mirrors about three inches in diameter. On the celluloid back of each of these mirrors he had printed the words of John 3:16. Beneath the words of this inscription was written, "If you want to see who it is that God loves and for whom He gave His Son, look on the other side." These mirrors were distributed among the soldiers with the permission of the officers, and thus each man looking into the mirror would see the object of God's love and the one whom the Saviour came to save.

—From *The Doctor's Best Love Story* by Walter L. Wilson, M.D.

* * *

Herein is Love

A gentleman who was a professed Christian was taken seriously ill. He became troubled about the little love he felt in his heart for God, and spoke of his experience to a friend. This is how the friend answered him: "When I go home from here, I expect to take my baby on my knee, look into her sweet eyes, listen to her charming prattle, and, tired as I am, her presence will rest me; for I love that child with unutterable tenderness. But she loves me little. If my heart were breaking it would not disturb her sleep. If my body were racked with pain, it would not interrupt her play. If I were dead, she would forget me in a few days. Besides this, she has never brought me a penny, but was a constant expense to me. I am not rich, but there is not money enough in the world to buy my baby. How is it? Does she love me, or do I love her? Do I withhold my love until I know she loves me? Am I waiting for her to do something worthy of my love before extending it"?

This practical illustration of the love of God for His children caused the tears to roll down the sick man's face. "Oh, I see," he exclaimed, "it is not my love to God, but God's love for me, that I should be thinking of. And I do love Him now as I never loved Him before." "Herein is love, not that we loved God, but that He loved us" (I John 4:10).

—*Gospel Herald*

All Pervasive!

On the walls of an insane asylum were scrawled the following words by some unknown inmate of the institution:

"Could we with ink the ocean fill,
And were the skies of parchment made,
And every blade of grass a quill,
And every man a scribe by trade;
To write the love of God to man,
Would drain the ocean dry,
Nor could the scroll contain the whole,
Though stretched from sky to sky!"

This anonymous verse is the last verse to the song, "The Love of God!" It so touched the heart of the author of the preceding verses of the song that it became a part of the song.

—Phil. Marquart, M. D.

* * *

Gratitude

One day, we are told, a little girl, the daughter of a printer, who worked where they were printing Luther's translation of the Bible, picked up a small scrap of paper from the floor, upon which were printed these words: "God so loved the world that He gave . . ." the rest of the sentence was torn off, but over and over again the child read, "God so loved the world that He gave . . ." She, and her mother before her, had been taught to fear God as a great Being just waiting to punish them: but now the child said to her mother, who had asked, "What did He give?" "I don't know what He gave, but if He loved us well enough to give us anything, He is not angry with us and we need not be afraid of Him; we can just love and thank Him for whatever He gave us."

—*Gospel Herald*

* * *

Why He Did It

Kazainak was a robber chieftain, living in the mountains of Greenland. One day he came to a hut where a missionary was translating the Gospel of John. He wanted to know what he was doing; and when the missionary told him how the marks he was making were words, and how a book could speak, he wished to hear what it said. The missionary read the story of Christ's suffering; when the chief immediately asked, "What has this man done? Has He robbed anybody? Has He murdered anybody?"

"No," was the reply. "He has robbed no one, murdered no one. He has done nothing wrong."

"Then why does He suffer? Why does He die?"

"Listen," said the missionary. "This Man has done no wrong; but Kazainak has murdered his brother, Kazainak has murdered his child. This Man suffered that Kazainak might not suffer; died, that Kazainak might not die."

"Tell me that again," said the astonished chieftain; and as the missionary again told the story of the love of the Lord Jesus for him, a sinner, he gave his heart to God, having his sins washed away in the Blood of Jesus shed for him, and for every sinner.

—*Gospel Herald*

* * *

The Only Motive Which Will Sustain Us

Hudson Taylor was examining some young people who had volunteered for the mission field. He wanted to ascertain their qualifications for the arduous life toward which they were looking. "And why do you wish to go as a foreign missionary?" he asked one. "I want to go because Christ has commanded us to go into all the world and preach the Gospel to every creature," was the reply. Another said, "I want to go because millions are perishing without Christ, not having even heard of the One Name whereby the lost may be saved." Others gave various answers. Then Hudson Taylor said, "All of these motives, howsoever good, will fail you in times of testings, trials, tribulations, and possibly death. There is but ONE MOTIVE which will sustain you in trial and testing, namely, 'For the LOVE OF CHRIST constraineth us.' (II Cor. 5:14a)."

—W. B. K.

* * *

The Need of Alignment

I walked into an auto repair shop and saw a mechanic looking intently at a car that was lopsided. When I asked him what was the matter with it, he said, "It's all out of alignment. That is, it won't track. The front wheels will go up the middle of the road, and the rear wheels will be way out on one side." Laughingly, I remarked, "What difference does that make, except that it would look a little funny?" My observation almost made the mechanic mad. He answered, "It will make all the difference in the world in the power, because everything in it will be pulling against everything else. There will be a tug of war inside and the power will be cut in half!" When Jesus said, "Thou shalt love the Lord thy God with ALL thy heart, and . . . thou shalt love thy neighbor as thyself," He was insisting that we get our lives in alignment.

—*The Teacher*, S. B. C.

* * *

How They Knew God's Love

We tried to visit the lepers at least once a month, when they gathered out on the grass, and we went over what they had learned and sought to make clear the way of salvation by the use of Gospel posters. Sometimes we asked them questions, to see if they really understood what they were learning. I remember once asking the question, "Just how do you know that the Lord Jesus loves you?" They answered, "Because of you." This truly touched our hearts, and we praised God for the privilege of being His instruments to carry the glad tidings to such as these poor lepers.

—*China's Millions*

* * *

Whom God Loves Best

When the small daughter of the distinguished sculptress, Sally James Farnum, was asked which child was her mother's favorite, the little girl, according to Francis Newton in *This Week*, promptly replied: "She loves Jimmy best because he's the oldest; and she loves Johnny best because he's the youngest; and she loves me best because I'm the only girl!" It would be difficult to find anything which could more lucid-

ly explain God's all-enveloping love for His children. No matter to what heights you have risen or to what depths you have fallen, God loves you best because of some characteristic personal quality which, while it may not be apparent to your fellow men, is known and cherished by your Heavenly Father.

—*Your Faith*

* * *

Supreme Command

During the war between the states, General Lee one day sent word to Stonewall Jackson that the next time he rode in the direction of headquarters the Commander in Chief would be glad to see him on a matter of no great importance. General Jackson received the message and immediately prepared to leave the next morning. Rising very early, he rode the eight miles to Lee's headquarters against a storm of wind and snow, and arrived just as Lee was finishing breakfast. Much surprised, Lee inquired why Jackson had come through such a storm.

General Jackson replied: "But you said that you wished to see me. General Lee's slightest wish is a supreme command to me."

Jesus said: "If a man love me, he will keep my words." And again, "He that hath my commandments and keepeth them, he it is that loveth me."

—W. Everett Henry

* * *

His Preference

The son of Bishop Berkeley once asked his father what was the difference between the cherubim and seraphim. His father replied that the word "cherubim" came from a Hebrew word signifying "knowledge," and that "seraphim" came from a Hebrew word meaning "burning" from which it was inferred that the cherubim were spirits famed for their knowledge, while the seraphim were famed for their burning love. The boy said, "I hope when I die I shall be a seraph, for I would rather love God than know all things."

—From *Pure Religion*,
by Rev. W. L. Mackenzie

The Most Beautiful Thing

The colored sunsets and the starry heavens, the beautiful mountains and the shining seas, the fragrant woods and the painted bowers, are not half as beautiful as a soul that is serving Jesus out of love, in the wear and tear of common, unpoetic life.

—Faber

* * *

Too Busy to Love

A father and his young daughter were great friends and much in each other's company. Then the father noted a change in his daughter. If he went for a walk, she excused herself from going. He grieved about it, but could not understand. When his birthday came, she presented him with a pair of exquisitely worked slippers, saying, "I have made them for you." Then he understood what had been the matter for the past three months, and he said, "My darling, I like these slippers very much, but next time buy the slippers and let me have you all the days. I would rather have my child than anything she can make for me."

Some of us are so busy for the Lord that He cannot get much of us. To us He would say, "I know your works, your labor, your patience, but I miss the first love."

—G. Campbell Morgan

* * *

"To Hear You Say It"

One of Scotland's great preachers, Dr. Alexander Whyte, once told the touching story of an old Scottish woman who lay dying. Her husband, with sorrowful heart, sat holding her hand, and, breaking through a lifetime of reserve, said tenderly, "Janet, if ever a woman was loved, I love you." A smile lit up the face of the dying woman as she replied, "I aye kenned it, John; but oh, to hear you say it!" Christ knew Peter's heart when He addressed the words, "Lovest thou me?" to him . . . He knew that Peter loved him, and was only waiting fearfully, knowing he was unworthy of forgiveness, again to come

near his Lord and show himself a true disciple.

—*Sunday School Times*

* * *

"He Will Get Over It"

Remember when you first fell in love? Observers said, "He will get over it!" That is exactly what occurred with God's children in the Church of Ephesus in the first century: "They got over it!" That is, they "ceased loving Christ first!" God save us from "getting over it!"

—W. B. K.

* * *

He Still Loves Us

There is a strange power in the consciousness of being loved. . . It is said that one of the most distinguished statesmen of the times of the American Revolution was once a hopeless drunkard. He had been engaged to a beautiful girl, but his dissipation had compelled her to break the engagement and sever herself from his influence, which was dragging her down. She had not ceased to love him, or to pray for him. One day she was passing along a suburban road. She saw him lying intoxicated by the sidewalk, his face exposed to the broiling, blistering sun, and swollen with drink and exposure. Her tender heart was moved, and, as she passed by, she took her handkerchief and gently spread it over his stupid, sleeping face. An hour or two later he awoke and saw the handkerchief and her name upon the corner of it. He sprang to his feet, and a glad thrill of hope and courage came to his heart. "She loves me still," he said, "all is not yet lost. For her sake I will redeem my life." And he did. . . . Oh, how much more power there is in the love of Christ to save lost men from despair, if they can only believe that He loves them!

—A. B. Simpson,
in the *Alliance Weekly*

* * *

We Require Loving!

A little girl was making but poor progress toward recovery, though the ailment had been checked and there seemed to be no reason why she should not rapidly improve. But it didn't happen, and the doctor in charge was keenly interested to know why. She was a very sensitive child, easily scared, responding quickly to kindness. Perhaps she was afraid of Nurse or Sister or her unfamiliar surroundings. The doctor decided it was the lack of understanding which was retarding recovery, and so wrote a directive upon the temperature chart: "This child requires loving every four hours." God is even better than that: He says, "I have loved thee with an everlasting love."

—Winship Storey,
in the *Methodist Recorder*

* * *

Letting the Lord Love Her

An old Scotch woman who was alone for the greater part of the day was asked, "What do you do during the day?" "Well," she said, "I get my hymn book, and I have a little hymn of praise to the Lord." Then she added, "I get my Bible and let the Lord speak to me. When I am tired of reading, and I cannot sing any more, I just sit still and let the Lord love me."

—*Moody Monthly*

* * *

A Father's Love and Sacrifice

Many years ago a boy came back to the city from which he had run away some time before. He came riding in a box car, drunk and penniless. The next morning, while his brain was still dull, he stopped a couple of men on the street and asked for money for a meal. One of the men looked closely at him, and then said to the other, "I must ask you to excuse me. I recognize here the son of an old friend, and I must go with him." But what he could not bring himself to

say in the shock of the recognition was that it was his own son who stood there. The father took the boy with him. He arranged his business so he could be away from it, and gave up his life to his son. He never left him day or night, and never by word or sign rebuked him for the past, but put all the strength of his soul into the battle until after six months, one night in a city mission, the boy found Christ and was saved. What a picture the story gives of the divine Father, seeking and striving with wandering children, with no recriminations for the past, only an eager longing that the sinner come back into right relationship with his Maker.

—*Youth's Companion*

* * *

God's Great Love

One time a father wanted to teach his son the lesson of God's great goodness. He took him to the top of a high hill and pointed northward over Scotland, southward over England, eastward over the ocean, westward over hill and valley, and then sweeping his arm around the whole circling horizon, he said, "Johnny, my boy, God's love is as big as all that." "Why, father," the boy replied with sparkling eyes, "then we must be right in the middle of it."

—*Earnest Worker*

* * *

Not Changed by the Wind

C. H. Spurgeon was talking to a farmer who had on his barn a weather vane on the arrow of which was inscribed, "God is love." He said to the farmer: "What do you mean by that? Do you think God's love is changeable — that it veers about as the arrow turns in the wind?" The farmer answered, "Oh, no! I mean that whichever way the wind blows, God is still love."

—*Christian Digest*

LOVE FOR OTHERS

Love Abideth!

You may sit all alone in the great Dresden gallery, in an isolated room dedicated wholly to one great painting,

the Sistine Madonna. You may gaze for hours upon its wondrous picture of tender, majestic motherhood. Yet when Raphael's masterpiece has faded into oblivion the cup of cold water you yesterday gave in the love of your Lord will live forever. You may stand in a single famous chamber in the Vatican gallery where there are four of the world's greatest masterpieces of sculpture. Men call it the most priceless centre of art in the world. Yet when Laocoon, with all its writhing agony, and the Apollo Belvidere, the most faultless carving of the human form in existence, have crumbled into dust, and even the names of their creators have been forgotten, then that humble deed of love you did today, unseen by any eye save that of God, shall abide forever. Yea, when all the waves of human fame, human applause and human flattery have died away upon the sands of time, the tiny wave of love you started in some kind word, some loving ministry, will be rolling and breaking upon the shores of eternity. Every song that floats from your lips in the spirit of love; every word of comfort to the sorrowing; every loving warning and admonition to the wayward; every prayer that goes up out of the love of your heart for a friend in need; every word of cheer and solace to the despondent one; every bit of suffering from criticism and misrepresentation borne in the spirit of love; every mite of silver and gold given for the love of the Master and His suffering ones — every such deed of love, however insignificant it may seem to you, will meet you at the throne of reward, and go with you in your shining train of influence and love all through the countless milleniums of eternity. And does there come a time when your voice of love is silent, your hand of love motionless, your human heart of love no longer throbs, and men say, "He is dead?" Then shall come a voice from heaven saying, "Blessed are the dead that die in the Lord . . . *for their works do follow them.*" Would you build not for time but for a deathless eternity? Then build in love, upon the foundation of Christ.   —James McConkey

* * *

"Love Working Miracles for Mentally Ill!"

The *Chicago Daily News* recently ran the following interesting incident under the heading, "Love Working Miracles for Mentally Ill in Kansas": "A bit of a miracle in the Kansas flatlands is attracting observers from mental institutions throughout the country. They want to learn the secret of the Topeka State Hospital in returning eight of every ten new patients in the last year to useful lives on the outside. The secret is *not* in electro-shock, surgery, group therapy, drugs, or any of the conventional treatments of mental disorders. These play a part, but the *real secret* is contained in a single word: *love!*" Dr. Karl Menninger of the famed brother-team of psychiatrists explains it: "The doctor doesn't cure by any specific treatment. You cure by *atmosphere*, by *attitude*, by *sympathetic understanding* on the part of *every one* in the hospital." Continuing, he said, "By our words and *deeds* at the hospital, we must gently persuade them that society is worth coming back to. There is none of the professional-staff jealousy that *poisons* so many institutions. Everyone is on the team. The hospital attendant's opinion is as readily considered as a nurse's or social worker's."

    —W.K.B.

* * *

Unity Without Being Joined Together

A quarrelsome husband and wife sat before the open fireplace. They lived, or EXISTED, at counter purposes with each other. Sleeping peaceably on either side of the hearth were two cats. Said the husband, "Why can't we thus live in peace with each other?" Replied the wife, "Just tie the tails of those cats together, and fling them over a clothesline, and see what happens!" Two can't walk together except they be agreed. Christians walking separately, can walk peaceably with Christ in their hearts, and with love and good will for everybody. Spirit-filled Christians can agree to disagree without strife and ill-will, their prayer being, "Grace be with ALL THEM that love our Lord Jesus Christ in sincerity" (Eph. 6:24).

    W.B.K.

Said Fritz Kreisler:

I was born with music in my system. I knew musical scores before I knew my A B C's. It was a gift of Providence. Music is too sacred to be sold. I never look upon the money I earn as my own. It is only a fund entrusted to my care for proper disbursement. I reduce my needs to the minimum. I feel morally guilty in ordering a costly meal, as it deprives some one else of a slice of bread — some child, perhaps, of a bottle of milk. My beloved wife feels exactly about these things as I do. In all these years of my so-called success we have not built a home for ourselves. Between it and us stand all the homeless in the world.

— *Prairie Overcomer*

* * *

After She Was Shoved Out

One day I went to see a fellow worker in God's service — a dear Christian, but very impulsive. As we talked together in her hall, I said something she did not like; and she took me by the shoulders and pushed me over the doorstep, shutting the door in my face! I walked home feeling very indignant, but as I waited on the Lord for light, he turned me to John 13:35: "By this shall all men know that ye are my disciples, if ye have love one to another"; and He said, "Will you go to her house tomorrow, and show her love *for my sake?*" I agreed to do so, and handing over my natural indignation to death (His death), I went. The result was unity and peace, instead of division. Then I saw that Satan had tried to separate us, and bring a spirit of bitterness, so as to hinder our uniting in prayer. Praise God, the victory was a very real one, through the working power of our union with Christ in his death. — *Overcomer.*

* * *

"O God, for a Bigger Boat"

The many tragedies at sea, caused by the recent war, and the heroic effort put forth to save the lives in each instance, calls to mind the disaster of *Princess Alice*, which collided with another boat in a dense fog on the river Thames half a century ago. The boat was crowded with excursionists and the loss of human lives was great, about 600 perishing in the dark waters. Dr. Herbert Lockyer tells of an interesting little side light of the tragedy concerning two ferrymen, which is worth repeating.

It appears that these two ferrymen were mooring their boats for the night close at hand, when the crash happened. One heard the crash and the cries, and said, "I am tired and I am going home; no one will see me in the fog." At the coroner's inquest, both had to appear. The first was asked:

"Did you hear the cries?"

"Yes, sir."

"What did you do?"

"Nothing, sir."

"Are you an Englishman? Aren't you ashamed?"

"Sir, the shame will never leave me till I die."

Of the other the coroner asked:

"What did you do?"

"I jumped into my boat and pulled for the wreck with all my might; I crammed my boat with women and children, and when it was too dangerous to take even one other, I rowed away with the cry, 'O God, for a bigger boat!' "

— Dr. Herbert Lockyer

* * *

The Difference

An old Scotch lady who is a sincere Christian told me the following: "I have two daughters who take turns coming in to clean my wee house. Jean comes, and leaves everything shining, but she makes me feel I'm an awful burden to her. But when Mary comes no matter how dull the day, or how low in spirit I'm feeling, she makes everything so cheery, and makes me feel she loves to be with me. They are both Christian

women, ye ken, but aye there's a great difference. Mary has what this puir-world sadly needs, the Christian with the loving heart."
— *Sunday School Times.*

* * *

A Surprising Wish

A man once parked his car on a street. Up came a boy and looked it over. His eyes were wide with admiration of the beautiful car.

"Where did you get this car?" he asked.

"My brother gave it to me," replied the man.

"My, I wish..." The man knew the boy was wishing that he had a new car like that.

But the lad went on and finished the sentence surprisingly: "I wish I could be a brother like your brother was. I have a crippled brother who cannot get out. I would buy him a car like this."
—*The Teacher*

* * *

The Kiss Did It

A Christian woman laboring among the moral lepers of London found a poor streetgirl desperately ill in a cold, bare room. With her own hands she ministered to her, changing her bed linen, procuring medicines and nourishing food, building a fire, and making the poor place as bright and cheery as possible. Then she said, "May I pray with you?" "No," said the girl. "You don't care for me; you are just doing this to get to Heaven." Many days passed, with the Christian woman unwearily kind, the sinful girl hard and bitter. At last the Christian said, "My dear, you are nearly well now, so I shall not come again, but as it is my last visit, I want you to let me kiss you," and the pure lips that had known only prayer and holy words met the lips defiled by oaths and by unholy caresses, and then the hard heart broke. That was Christ's way. Love had conquered where service without love would have been only "sounding brass, or a tinkling cymbal."
— *Christian Digest.*

"What Are You Doing for Others?"

Charles N. Crittenton had made about a half million dollars in business, when God came into his home and took out of it a beautiful daughter only four years of age, the idol of that man's heart. A few days after her burial, he was riding in the elevated train toward his home, and as he thought of little Florence, blinding tears came to his eyes, and this question came to his heart as a voice from heaven: Your daughter is in heaven with the Lord. What are you doing for other men's daughters? He said, "I am doing nothing, but I will." The next year he put $10,000 into the rescue of fallen girls in New York City. The year after, $11,000; and a few years later he gave up his business altogether, capitalized it, and devoted his whole time and strength to going up and down the world telling lost men and women about Jesus Christ and His power to save.
—*Moody Monthly*

* * *

"These Hands"

A young man and a young woman had plighted their troth, and were looking forward to a near wedding day, when the young man was suddenly called to service. From the field of warfare letters regularly came and went, and love shone brightly in all of them. Then letters from the young man abruptly ceased. A few weeks passed and then there came a letter in a strange handwriting. In it the young woman read:

"There has been another battle. I have lost both my arms. I asked my comrade to write this for me, and to tell you that I release you from our troth, for now I will not be able to work and support you."

That letter was never answered. By the next train the young woman journeyed southward. She left the train and went direct to the hospital. Inquiring the location of the young man's cot she quietly approached and suddenly flung herself down by the side of his cot with the passionate words, "I will never give you up. These hands of mine will work for you. We will live our life of love together."

— S. E. DuBois, in *Gospel Herald*

* * *

Offering All They Possess

There is much that is inspiring, as it is pathetic, in the advertisement of a laborer and his wife in a small Michigan town seeking news of a vanished daughter. This humble couple offer to give "all they possess" for news leading to the recovery of the lost child. As an earnest of good faith, they append an inventory of their entire possessions. It is not a long list: a cottage home and furniture worth $1,400 and paid for out of a lifetime's earnings; $200 in the bank, the father's silver watch and the mother's wedding ring. For the restoration to their arms of the loved daughter, they will gladly surrender all. Homeless and penniless they will cheerfully start life all over again. For love, this laborer and his wife find no material price too great to pay, no sacrifice worth counting. They are like the wise man in the parable, glad to sell all that he had in order to buy the pearl of great price.

—*Expositor*

* * *

Somebody to Divide With

A little orphan newsboy was selling his papers on the streets. A man stopped to buy a paper from him. While the man was searching his pocket for a coin he questioned the newsboy as to where he lived. The answer was that he lived in a little cabin way down in the dark district of the city, on the river bank. The next question was, "Who lives with you?" The answer was, "Only Jim. Jim is crippled and can't do no work. He's my pal." The man ventured the remark, "You'd be better off without Jim, wouldn't you?" The answer came with some scorn. "No, Sir, I couldn't

spare Jim. I wouldn't have nobody to go home to. An' say, Mister, I wouldn't want to live and work with nobody to divide with, would you?" That was a short sermon, but it went home.

— *Sentinel*

* * *

Nobility

That day is best wherein we give
A thought to others' sorrows;
Forgetting self, we learn to live,
And blessings born of kindly deeds
Make golden our tomorrows.
Howe'er it seems to me
'Tis only noble to be good;
Kind hearts are more than coronets,
And simple faith than Norman blood.
— Sir Alfred Tennyson.

* * *

Looking Out for the One Following

On the bridge of a British battleship one may see a notice which reads: "Remember the Next Astern." It is intended to be a constant reminder to the captain, as he issues his orders, not to do anything which would be likely to throw the next vessel into difficulties. We Christians would do well to make this our motto. There may be another, perhaps, following just in our wake, and a false move on our part may mean shipwreck for that one. "Remember the Next Astern."

— *Sunday School Times*

* * *

Keeping Soul Out of Dust!

There is a quiet, little man, a vendor of fruits and vegetables, who passes my door every day. One day I picked up a small notebook near the spot where his wagon had stood. On the first page I was much surprised to find these words: "For His Body's sake, which is the Church." Throughout the book were Scriptural quotations and many notations like these: "The following were absent from Bible School last Sunday, be sure to visit them." "Ask about the sick baby." "Leave fruit for the blind lady." "Speak a word of cheer to the old crippled man." "Invite the new family to church services."

The next day I handed the book to the humble fruit peddler, with the query: "I wonder if you dropped this yesterday?" "Yes, indeed," was the answer. "It is my book of reminders, as I call it. I thank you." I told him I had glanced at the contents and expressed my surprise at their unusual character. "Well," he answered, pointing to the first page text, "this is my motive, my reason, for doing things, 'For His Body's sake, which is the Church'." Then with an illuminating smile he added, "You see, it keeps my soul out of the dust."

— *Alliance Weekly.*

* * *

No Farewell to Love
(I Corinthians 13:13)

As an aged Christian lay dying in Edinburgh, a friend called to say farewell. "I have just had three other visitors," said the dying man, "and with two of them I parted; but the third I shall keep with me forever." "Who are they?" "The first was Faith, and I said, 'Goodby, Faith! I thank God for your company ever since I first trusted Christ; but now I am going where faith is lost in sight.' Then came Hope. 'Farewell, Hope!' I cried. 'You have helped me in many an hour of battle and distress, but now I shall not need you, for I am going where hope passes into fruition.' Last of all came Love. 'Love,' said I, 'you have indeed been my friend; you have linked me with God and with my fellow men; you have comforted and gladdened all my pilgrimage. But I cannot leave you behind; you must come with me through the gates, into the city of God, for *love is perfected in heaven*.'" — *Sunday School Chronicle.*

* * *

A Chinese Boy's Unselfishness

An English lady missionary tells the following story of some little Chinese pupils in her mission school: "A class

of small children were reciting the lesson. The youngest of them had, by hard study, kept his place at the head of the class so long that he seemed to claim it by right of possession. One day he missed a word, which was spelled correctly by the boy standing next to him, who made no move toward the first place, saying, 'No, me not go; me not make Ah Fun's heart solly.' That little act meant self-denial, yet it was done so kindly that from several lips came the quick remark, 'He do all the same as Jesus' Golden Rule.'"

— *Brethren Evangelist.*

* * *

Love in Action

Dr. C. H. Parkhurst has a chapter in his book, *Love as a Lubricant*, in which he relates this little story: One day there was a workman aboard a trolley car, and he noticed that every time the door was pushed open it squeaked. Rising from his seat, he took a little can from his pocket, and dropped oil on the offending spot. He sat down again, quietly remarking, "I always carry an oil can in my pocket, for there are so many squeaky things that a drop of oil will correct." Love is the oil which alone can make everyday life in home and business and society harmonious.

— *S. S. World.*

* * *

Her Hand

A devoted Christian wife used to pray for her husband with her hand gently resting on his head when she thought him asleep. After her death it seemed to him that he could still feel that hand upon him, constraining him to be a Christian. It was more than he could resist, and he let that hand guide him to the Saviour. The hand that helps is the hand that has the touch and tenderness of love, and the earnestness and power of prayer.

— *Sunday School Times*

Love Covers

I received a fine letter from a friend in Switzerland. It is difficult for him to write in English, and he naturally was aware of some unique usages of the language. However, he made it all seem very beautiful as he ended with the sentence, "The mistakes you will cover with the coat of love." How necessary it is that we have that great love in our hearts toward our friends! We all make so many mistakes in life! Our real friends always seem to understand because they cover our mistakes with their love.

—L. L. Huffman in *Telescope-Messenger*

* * *

What Are Christians "For"?

A Christian woman who was engaged in work for the poor and degraded was once spoken to by one who was well acquainted with both the worker and those whom she sought to reach.

"It does seem wonderful to me that you can do such work," her friend said. "You sit beside these people, and talk with them in a way that I do not think you would if you knew about them, just what they are, and from what places they come."

Her answer was, "Well, I suppose they are dreadful people. But, if the Lord Jesus were now on earth, are they not the very people He would strive to teach? Would He feel Himself too good to go among them? And am I better than my Master?"

A poor, illiterate person, who stood listening to this conversation, said with great earnestness and simplicity, "*Why, I always thought that was what Christians were for.*" The objector was silenced, and what wonder? Is not that what Christians are for?

—*Christian Herald*

* * *

Giving His Last Biscuit

Sir Ernest Shackleton was asked to tell of his most terrible moment in the Arctic. And he said his worst was one night in an emergency hut. He and his fellows were lying there; he rather apart from the rest. They had given out the ration of the last biscuits. There was nothing more to divide. Every man thought the other was asleep. He sensed a stealthy movement and saw one of the men turning to see how the others were faring. He made up his mind that all were asleep and then stretched over the next man and took his biscuit bag and removed the biscuit. Shackleton lived through an eternity of suspense. He would have trusted his life in the hands of that man. Was he turning out a thief under terribly tragic circumstances? Stealing a man's last biscuit! Then Shackleton sensed another movement. He saw the man open his own box, take the biscuit out of his own bag and put it in his comrade's, and return the man's biscuit and stealthily put the bag back at the man's side. Shackleton said, "I dare not tell you that man's name. I felt that act was a secret between himself and God."

—*Life of Faith*

* * *

Perfect Love

Slow to suspect — quick to trust,
Slow to condemn — quick to justify,
Slow to offend — quick to defend,
Slow to expose — quick to shield,
Slow to reprimand — quick to forbear,
Slow to belittle — quick to appreciate,
Slow to demand — quick to give,
Slow to provoke — quick to conciliate,
Slow to hinder — quick to help,
Slow to resent — quick to forgive.

—*Herald of Holiness*

* * *

A Great Artist's Unselfishness

A beautiful story is told of the artist Turner. Turner's colors were bright and intense enough to almost extinguish the quieter tone. Once when his great picture of Cologne, exhibited in 1826, happened to be hung between two portraits by Sir Thomas Lawrence, himself noticed the injurious effect Turner's bright skies had on his portraits, and felt troubled and mortified. Complaining of the position of his pictures was useless, as once settled, that could not be changed. But one thing could be done, and Turner did it. At that time artists were allowed to retouch their pictures on the walls of the Academy, and Turner "retouched" his to such purpose that Lawrence had no more fear from too close neighborhood. When, on the morning of the exhibition, a friend of Turner's who had before this seen the painting led a party of friends up proudly to see the splendid picture, he started back in amazement. The glorious skies were dull brown — the picture was ruined. Spying Turner, he ran up to him and asked him what had happened to his picture. "Hush!" whispered Turner, "it is nothing. It will all wash off — it's nothing but lampblack. I couldn't bear to see poor Lawrence so unhappy."

—*Moody Monthly*

* * *

At Your Door

One of the best illustrations of this brotherly love is that of Frank Higgins, who was a lumberjack "sky pilot." When he became ill, he was taken to the city hospital, and the fine fellows he had led to Christ sent one of their number along with him to be of any service possible. He was dying from cancer caused by the rubbing of shoulder-straps while carrying heavy loads of Bibles and books from one lumber camp to another. They were to operate on him in the hospital when a big lumberjack said to him, "Frank, you know we love you, and want to help you. Now while the doctors are operating I will be at your door, and if they need a quart of blood or a piece of my bone or skin they can call on me. Now don't forget, I will be at your door."

—*Teacher*, S.B.C.

Why She Kept the Cheaper Job

An example of Christian deference for others was given in an address in Los Angeles by Dr. Will H. Houghton. A number of young women students who were obliged to find part-time employment in order to continue their training at the Moody Bible Institute had placed their names among those of other applicants for positions in a large business house in Chicago. One day the head of the firm communicated with the Institute, saying there was an opening for one young woman at nine dollars a week. The Institute employment manager called the student whose name was first on the list, and advised her to make the change in positions at once, for it would make an increase of three dollars a week in her salary. "But," the girl replied, "is not Miss Brown's name on the list of applicants for this work?" "Yes, it is next to yours. But you have first consideration." "If I make the change can Miss Brown do the work here that I will be leaving?" "No, she is not able to do this kind of work." "Then," continued the student, "if you don't mind, I'll stay here at six dollars and let Miss Brown have the nine-dollar-a-week job."

—*King's Business*

* * *

Carrying Brother

The crossing was muddy, the street was
 wide
And water was running on either side;
The wind whistled past with a bitter
 moan
As I wended my weary way alone.
In crossing the street I chanced to pass
A boy in the arms of a wee, toddling
 lass —
"Isn't he heavy, my sweet little mother?"
"Oh, no," she replied, "he's my baby
 brother."
Thy load may be heavy, thy road may
 be long,
The winds of adversity bitter and strong
But the way will seem brighter if ye
 love one another,
The burden will be light if ye carry a
 brother.

—*Selected*

He Thought of Me

Daniel Webster, going home one day from the law courts, stopped on the way to see his daughter, Mrs. Appleton, who was dying. As he entered the room she looked up and said, "Father, why are you out on this cold day without your coat?" The great lawyer left the room with a sob, exclaiming, "Dying, yet she thinks of me!" That is just what Jesus did. He thought of others all His life.   —*The Dawn*

* * *

"Love Beareth (Covers) All Things!"

During Alexander the Great's brief reign as world conqueror, he decided to have his portrait painted. Accordingly, the finest artist in the realm was called upon to produce the painting, and when he arrived at Alexander's court, the great general requested that the portrait be a full-face pose instead of a profile. This filled the artist with great consternation, for one side of Alexander's face was hideously disfigured by a long scar, the result of a battle wound.

The artist studied his subject for some time, and then a happy solution occurred to him. He seated Alexander at a table, and placing the general's elbow upon it, asked him to cup his chin in his hand. The artist then proceeded to adjust Alexander's fingers so that they covered the unsightly scar. This done, he went to work with paint and brushes.

—*Gospel Herald*

* * *

"Give Me Back My Tears"

One of the mightiest soul winners I ever knew was Colonel Clark of Chicago. He would work at his business six days every week. And every night in the week the year round five or six hundred men would gather together in that mission hall. It was a motly crowd: drunkards, thieves, pickpockets, gamblers and everything that was hopeless. I used to go and hear Colonel Clark talk, and he seemed to me one of the dullest talkers I have ever heard in my life. He would ramble along and yet these five or six hundred men would lean over and listen spellbound while Colonel Clark talked in his prosy way. Some of the greatest preachers in Chicago used to go down to help Colonel Clark, but the men would not listen to them as they did to Colonel Clark. When he was speaking they would lean over and listen and be converted by the score. I could not understand it. I studied it and wondered what the secret of it was. Why did these men listen with such interest, and why were they so greatly moved by such prosy talking? I found the secret. It was because they knew that Colonel Clark loved them, and nothing conquers like love. The tears were very near the surface with Colonel Clark. Once in the early days of the mission, when he had been weeping a great deal over these men, he got ashamed of his tears. He steeled his heart and tried to stop his crying, and succeeded, but lost his power. He saw that his power was gone and he went to God and prayed. "Oh, God, give me back my tears," and God gave him back his tears, and gave him wonderful power, marvelous power over these men.

If we would see the seed that we sow bring an abundant harvest, we must water it with our tears. "He that goeth forth and weepeth, bearing precious seed, shall doubtless come again with rejoicing, bringing in his sheaves with him."   —R. A. Torrey

MIRACLES

The Living Miracle

Highbrows doubt the miraculous in Christianity, but there are many living miracles. "The whole work of the South London Mission in Bermondsey is based upon the power of Jesus Christ to work miracles," says the Rev. Ensor Walters. An agnostic speaker, addressing a gathering of workingmen, laughed at the miraculous element in the Scriptures.

"Has anyone here ever come across a miracle?" he sneered. At last a burly workingman rose and said, "Mates, you knew me when I was a drunkard, and a blackguard. You know the change wrought in me. Am I a miracle?" A great shout of "Yes" nonplussed the speaker, who replied, "Well, my friend, I suppose you mean you turned over a new leaf?" "No," came the swift reply. "Christ turned it over for me."

—*United Methodist Magazine*

* * *

Miracle

Trees, which in winter looked like posts
Against a vacant sky,
Are now arrayed in loveliness.
They mutely testify
To resurrection glory. God
Whispered, "Time now to wake,"
And sleeping nature heard His voice
And felt His power to make
A world of emerald beauty from
The drab of bush and tree.
Each passing year spring seems more
like
A miracle to me!

—Olive Weaver Ridenour

* * *

Better Than Knowing How

"Tell me how He got the song from the seraph and robed it in feathers and got the canary. Tell me, then, what I wish you could tell me, how Jesus came to my gypsy tent. Oh, it is such a mystery to me! I wish somebody would fathom the deep and scale the heights and explain it to me. When there was no Bible, when I could not spell my name, when I was only a little wandering gypsy boy, with my brother and three sisters and my father, without God and without hope in the world — tell me how Jesus came to that old gypsy tent and opened my eyes and made me know He was my Saviour and my Lord. Tell me how, for I do not know. But I know He did it."

—Gipsy Rodney Smith,
in the *Brooklyn Eagle*

George Mueller's Regeneration

At the age of sixteen George Mueller of Bristol, Eng., was imprisoned for theft; and later at the university he lived a drinking, profligate life, acting dishonestly even toward his friends. At twenty years of age he came under the influence of the Bible, and the miracle of regeneration was wrought. He who had been a thief was now so utterly a new creature that in the course of the years he gave away, of the money sent to him for his personal use, no less a sum than $135,000, and when he died his personal possessions were valued at less than $1,000.

—*Christian Digest*

* * *

The Divine Touch

I stood one evening watching the pure white flowers on a vine encircling the veranda. I had been told that the buds that hung with closed petals all day, every evening near sunset unfolded and sent out a peculiar fragrance.

The miracle was more than I had anticipated. A feeling of silent awe possessed me as I saw bud after bud, as if under the touch of an invisible hand, slowly fold back its leaves until the vine was filled with perfect blossoms, most beautiful and sweet. I said, "*If the finger of God laid upon these His flowers can do this in a way beyond the power of human study to explain, cannot the same divine touch, in ways we know not of, do as much for human hearts?*"

—John Hall

* * *

The Right Side

The selfsame net, and the selfsame lake,
And it seemed there was nothing left
    to take;
But the Master said, "Let down your
    net!"
What happened the world can never
    forget —
Ah, the story thrills us even yet!
So many the fish, yet the net did not
    break,

Thus spake the Master — "The right
   side try;"
And the men who had watched the night
   go by
With never a fish for their patient quest,
With never an hour for needed rest,
Gave heed at once to their Lord's behest,
And the miracle saw — the great supply!

When blessings seem scarce, and grow-
   ing less,
And *our* trying results in fruitlessness,
A right side still is surely at hand,
If the heart, attent for the Lord's com-
   mand,
But follow the course that He has
   planned,
Ah, then shall we see how His hand
   can bless.
                  —Wm. M. Runyan

* * *

Point of View

"How can you believe that?" exclaimed a university student coming
upon a classmate reading the Bible.
"Don't you have difficulty with such a
miracle as the dividing of the Red Sea?"

"Yes, I have difficulty with the Red
Sea," was the reply, "but my difficulty
is not how it was divided, but how it
was made. For certainly He who made
it could divide it."
                  —*Christian Digest*

* * *

"Our God Still Able!"

An officer in the first World war gives
this account of God's willingness and
ability to save men from shot and shell
when they will pray. A German machine gun crew had their gun trained
on an angle of our trenches where troops
frequently passed back and forth, and
the casualties were many. As a last resort volunteers were called to storm the
gun in the open. Fifteen men volunteered. They themselves could see at a
glance that most if not all of them must
die. Even if they succeeded in silencing
the gun they would scarcely escape the
hail of lead that would follow them
back to their lines. The young officer
appointed to lead them, a chum of the

one reporting the incident, before going
over, addressed the volunteers as follows: "Men, I am a Christian. Before
every undertaking I pray. Those of you
who are willing, kneel with me and pray
about this one." Then he uncovered his
head and kneeling prayed, asking God
to spare their lives, but if any must go
that their souls might be saved. When
he arose from his knees he noted that
every man of them had knelt with uncovered head. Then they went over the
top and raced for the machine gun nest
amid a hail of lead and steel. They
overcame the gun crew, tore up the gun
and took it with them as they ran back
to their trenches — not a man missing
or seriously wounded. To the men looking on it was a miracle indeed. None
among them will ever say that the day
of miracles is past. God has not withdrawn His "exceeding great and precious promises."
                  —*Gospel Herald*

* * *

A Motor Car Miracle

Formerly our church was built upon a
high bluff. The street in front was wide,
and an experienced driver had no difficulty in turning there. I had not been
driving long enough to have confidence
in myself, and usually sought a safer
turning point. Once I was in a hurry
and tried to make the turn near the embankment. I don't know what happened,
but I found the car going backward at
full speed and the brake would not
work. There was a slight rise before
the drop, but it did not stop the car. All
earthly hope was gone. In my extrem-
ity I called upon the Lord, and the car
stopped instantly with the rear wheels
hanging over the high embankment.
When I reached home I opened my Bible
to find a Psalm of thanksgiving, and my
eyes fell upon these words: "He inclined
unto me, and heard my cry. He brought
me up also out of an horrible pit, out
of the miry clay, and set my feet upon
a rock." The Word made me even surer
that this was a miracle.
                  —*Sunday School Times*

A Prayer Miracle

Newman Hall stood early one morning on the summit of Snowdon with a hundred and twenty others who had been attracted hither by the promise of an unusually grand sunrise. They were not disappointed. As they stood watching the sun tinge the mountain peaks with glory, Dr. Hall was invited to preach. He was so overcome with emotion that he could not preach, but felt led to pour out his soul in prayer. As he supplicated the tears rolled down the faces of the people. A superhuman stillness possessed them. Quietly, with solemn awe, they descended the mountain, and scattered. Afterward visiting this region the doctor was informed that forty people had been converted that morning. "But," said he, "I did not say a word. I only prayed!" "Yes, and more wonderful still, they did not hear a word you said, for none of them can speak a word of English, only Welsh!"

—O. R. Palmer, in
Sunday School Times

* * *

A Miracle in England Harvests

In the opinion of Mr. R. S. Hudson, Minister of Agriculture, the prayer, "Give us this day our daily bread," has been answered by a miracle. That miracle, he explained in a recent speech, is Britain's harvest this year. Mr. Hudson declared that when war broke out, Britain's countryside was dying. Before the war, we were producing less than two tons of food out of every five we were eating. Our pre-war average wheat yield was 33 bushels per acre; but this year the ordinary good farmer was getting 40 bushels; a large number were getting over 50; and some of the champion farmers have reported yields of 80 or even more.

The Minister paid tribute to the work and technical skill which had gone to the production of such mighty yields; "but," he added, "I, at any rate, believe that we've Someone else to thank as well, and from the depths of our hearts. Some Power has wrought a miracle in the English harvest fields this summer, for in this, our year of greatest need, the land has given us bread in greater abundance than we have ever known before. So the prayer, 'Give us this day our daily bread,' has in these times a very direct meaning for us all."

—Dr. T. Wilkinson Riddle, in
Christian Herald (London)

* * *

Transformed!

Far away in the distant hills, North of India, a remote tribe who had never heard of Him were living in the deepest darkness of sin. Lawless head-hunters, in their mountain fastnesses they slew without mercy, their fiendish lust for killing not satisfied till they had decorated their huts with the heads of their fallen enemies. But into those utter depths of heathen darkness there came the Light — *the Light of the Gospel of Christ*, and everything was changed. Missionaries braved the terrors of the mountain fastnesses and the fierce enmity of the head-hunters. Taking their lives in their hands, they turned the Searchlight of God's Holy Word and God's truth upon the blackness of sin. Hearts were broken, sin confessed and put away — men who had loved to slay and kill came to the foot of the Cross for pardon and redemption from their sins. No longer "Head-hunters" there are today, thousands of men and women in these distant Lushai Hills, who, once walking in darkness, have seen the Great Light, they are following Him, and according to His promise they have the Light of Life.

—*Gospel Graphic*

* * *

Salvation's Swift Miracle

A very godless man, noted for his profanity, was one day carrying freight up a gangplank to a big steamer. A man following him accidentally jostled him, and the blasphemer fell into the water, between the wharf and the boat. His last utterance was a horrible oath, a curse upon his comrade. He immediately disappeared. After some time he was rescued from beneath the boat, apparently drowned. Strenuous efforts put forth to resuscitate him were finally successful. With his first breath he cried out, "Praise God, I'm saved!" "Yes, you were pretty nearly gone," someone replied. "Oh," he said, "I don't mean saved from drowning. I mean saved inside. The Lord has taken my sins away." Then he told them when he found himself beneath the boat, he thought the end had come. In these few

seconds he saw himself kneeling again at his mother's side, and heard her prayers for him. His sin, as a high mountain, rose before him, and he cried to God to save him. In that moment he realized forgiveness, and the cleansing of the blood. It was for this that he praised God with his first breath.

—*Alliance Weekly*

MISSIONS AND MISSIONARIES

Every Christian Missionary

When Admiral Foote was in Siam he invited the royal dignitaries to dinner on his vessel. As soon as the guests were seated at the table, he, as was his invariable custom, asked a blessing upon the food. The king in surprise said he thought only missionaries asked a blessing. "True," replied the admiral quietly, *"but every Christian is a missionary."*

—*Earnest Worker*

* * *

Hiding the Book

A colporteur in North India told the Christmas story, and then read it from the Scriptures. One asked, "How long has it been since God's Son was born into the world?" "About two thousand years," the missionary made reply. "Then," asked the villager, "who has been hiding this Book all this time?" Aye, that is it — hiding the Book. For, after all, is not our keeping the Book from those who need it the same as hiding it? What guilt!

—*Christian Digest*

* * *

"It Ought to Be Reversed!"

Our country (the U.S.A.) has only seven per cent of the world's population, yet ninety-three per cent of our theological and Bible school students remain in this country. It ought to be reversed!"

—Rev. T. A. Hege, in
World Conquest

A Prophecy Fulfilled

"Unless we send 10,000 missionaries to the Orient in my generation, we will send a million bayonets during the next!"

—John R. Mott

* * *

One Family's Record

So far as we know, the Scudder family made a missionary record not made by any other family in history. Read this brief statement: "John Scudder and his wife were missionaries to Ceylon and India. Of their ten children who grew to adult life, one died while preparing for the Christian ministry, and nine became foreign missionaries, five being medical missionaries. In 1919, the year marking the centennial of Scudder influence in India, three great grandchildren sailed for that land. Thirty-one descendants have worked in India, while seven others are missionaries elsewhere."

—*Wesleyan Methodist*

* * *

Our Neighbors

"Thou shalt love thy neighbour as thyself" (*Matt.* 19:19).

A gentleman once said to Dr. Skinner, who was asking aid for foreign missions, "I don't believe in foreign missions. I won't give anything except to home missions. I want what I give to benefit my neighbors."

"Well," said the doctor, "whom do you regard as your neighbors?"

"Why, those around me."

"Do you mean those whose land joins yours?"

"Yes."

"Well," said Dr. Skinner, "how much land do you own?"

"About five hundred acres," was the reply.

"How far down do you own it?" inquired the doctor.

"Why, I never thought of it before, but I suppose I own half way through?"

"Exactly," said the doctor; "I suppose you do, and I want this money for the Chinese — the men whose land joins yours at the bottom." Every Christian should say in a higher sense than the heathen poet, "I am a man, and nothing human is foreign to me." To a believer in Christ all men are neighbors.

—*Gospel Herald*

* * *

Not a Question of Liking It

When someone asked a missionary if he *liked* his work in Africa, he replied: "Do I like this work? No; my wife and I do not like dirt. We have reasonably refined sensibilities. We do not like crawling into vile huts through goat refuse. We do not like association with ignorant, filthy, brutish people. But is a man to do nothing for Christ he does not like? God pity him, if not. Liking or disliking has nothing to do with it. We have orders to 'Go,' and we go. Love constrains us."

—*From a local church bulletin*

* * *

A New Viewpoint on Missions

A captain writes: "We may not have wanted to come to India, but it has meant that many thousands of men who would have cherished throughout their lives an entirely wrong conception of missionary work have been able to see that Christian work at first hand. Nothing seems too much for these indefatigable people. Our men have found on Sunday a "little sanctuary' where they may find God, and finding Him can feel again with their loved ones, quiet in mind, strong in spirit. I am writing

from a khaki-colored viewpoint. We have met true and living Christianity here. To see these things is a great revelation that none of us will ever forget."

—*Young People*

* * *

Missionaries Abroad . . .

"Since becoming President, I have come to know that the finest type of Americans we have abroad today are the missionaries of the Cross. I am humiliated that I am not finding out until this late day the worth of foreign missions and the nobility of the missionaries. Their testimony in China, for instance, during the war there, is beyond praise. Their courage is thrilling and their fortitude heroic."

—Franklin D. Roosevelt

* * *

Why They Worshiped Idols

On one of my trips, we camped on the shores of a lake-like river. On a well-wooded hill, I noticed that every third tree had been cut down. "Why do you make idols?" I asked one of the Indians. I shall never forget his reply:

"Missionary, the Indian's mind is dark, and he cannot grasp the unseen. He hears the Great Spirit's voice in the thunder and the storms; he sees evidence of His existence all around, but neither he nor his fathers have ever seen the Great Spirit, and so he does not know what He looks like. Man is the highest creature he knows of, so he makes his idol like a man." Suddenly there flashed across my mind the request of Philip, "Shew us the Father, and it sufficeth us," and the wonderful answer. . . . I opened my Bible and unfolded to them this message. For two weeks I needed no other theme; and as a result they applied these truths to their hearts, burned their idols, and on that spot now stands a little church, while the Indians are transformed by the glorious Gospel of Jesus Christ.

—From *Experiences Among the Indians*, by Egerton R. Young

"How Long Since Jesus Died?"

An aged Mohammedan woman in Bengal asked: "How long is it since Jesus died for sinful people? Look at me; I am old; I have prayed, given alms, gone to the holy shrines, become as dust from fasting, and all this is useless. *Where have you been all this time?*"

The same cry was echoed from the icy shores of the farthest Northwest Territory. An old Eskimo said to the Bishop of Selkirk, "You have been many moons in this land. Did you know this good news then? Since you were a boy? and your father knew? *Then why did you not come sooner?*"

Again, in the snowy heights of the Andes, a Peruvian asked, "How is it that during all the years of my life I have never before heard that Jesus spoke those precious words?"

It was repeated in the white streets of Casablanca, North Africa. Said a Moor to a Bible seller, "Why have you not run everywhere with this Book? Why do so many of my people not know of the Jesus Whom it proclaims? *Why have you hoarded it to yourselves?* Shame on you!"

A missionary in Egypt was telling a woman the story of the love of Jesus, and at the close the woman said, "It is a wonderful story. Do the women in your country believe it?" "Yes!" said the missionary. After a moment's reflection came the reply, "I don't think they can believe it, or they would not have been so long in coming to tell us."

—*Prairie Overcomer*

* * *

Examining A Missionary Applicant

At three o'clock one wintry morning, a missionary candidate climbed the steps to the examiner's home. He was shown into the study where he waited until eight o'clock for an interview.

Upon arriving, the old clergyman proceeded to ask questions.

"Can you spell?"

"Yes, sir," was the reply.

"All right — spell baker."

"Baker — b-a-k-e-r."

"Fine. Now do you know anything about figures?" the examiner inquired.

"Yes, sir — something."

"How much is twice two?"

"Four," replied the lad.

"That's splendid," returned the old man. "I believe you have passed. I'll see the board tomorrow."

At the board meeting the man submitted his account of the interview. "He has all the qualifications of a missionary," he began.

"First, I tested him on self-denial. I told him to be at my house at three o'clock in the morning. He left a warm bed and came out in the cold without a word of complaint.

"Second, I tried him out on promptness. He appeared on time.

"Third, I examined him on patience. I made him wait five hours to see me, after telling him to come at three.

"Fourth, I tested him on temper. He failed to show any sign of it; he didn't even question my delay.

"Fifth, I tried his humility. I asked him questions that a five-year-old child could answer, and he showed no indignation. So you see, I believe this lad meets the requirements. He will make the missionary we need."

— *Selected*

* * *

"My Album . . . Savage Breasts!"

Robert Moffat, father-in-law of David Livingston, being asked to write in a lady's album, penned the following lines:

"My album is in savage breasts
Where passion reigns, and darkness rests
Without one ray of light:
To write the name of Jesus there,
To point to worlds both bright and fair,
And see the pagan bow in prayer,
Is all my soul's delight."

— *Western Recorder*

* * *

Holding the Ropes

The incident is told of a young couple, when bidding farewell to their home country church as they were about to leave for an African field, known as "The White Man's Grave," the husband said, "My wife and I have a strange dread in going. We feel much as if we were going down into a pit. We are willing to take the risk and go if you, our home circle, will promise to hold the ropes." One and all promised. Less than two years passed when the wife and the little one God had given them succumbed to the dreaded fever. Soon the husband realized his days, too, were numbered. Not waiting to send word home of his coming, he started back at once and arrived at the hour of the Wednesday prayer meeting. He slipped in unnoticed, taking a back seat. At the close of the meeting he went forward. An awe came over the people, for death was written on his face. He said, "I am your missionary. My wife and child are buried in Africa and I have come home to die. This evening I listened anxiously, as you prayed for some mention of your missionary to see if you were keeping your promise, but in vain! You prayed for everything connected with yourselves and your home church, but forgot your missionary. I see now why I am a failure as a missionary. It is because *you have failed to hold the ropes.*"

— *Missionary Tidings*

* * *

Read and Weep!

"Approximately nine per cent of the world's population is English speaking; 91 per cent, non-English speaking. Yet, 90 per cent of the world's Christians are to be found among the 9 per cent who are English speaking and only 10 per cent among the far greater number who are non-English speaking. Fully 94 per cent of the ordained preachers minister to the nine per cent, and only 6 per cent to the 91 per cent. Some 96 per cent of the finances are used to minister to the 9 per cent, and only 4 per cent to reach the 91 per cent. IS THIS FAIR? IS THIS THE WORLD VISION OF CHRISTIANITY?"

—Dr. M. A. Dorroch,

Home Director of the Sudan Interior Mission in *Moody Monthly.*

The Argument of the Dying Thief

A minister was conversing with a man who professed conversion. "Have you united with a church?" he asked him. "No; the dying thief never united with the church and he went to heaven," was the answer. "Have you ever sat at the Lord's table of the sacrament?" "No; the dying thief never did and he was accepted." "Have you given to missions?" "No; the dying thief did not, and he was not judged for it." "Well, my friend, the difference between you two seems to be that he was a dying thief and you are a living thief."

—*Sunday School Times*

* * *

Waiting!

Bishop Taylor tells of a village in Africa where he called for a day with his little missionary boat, but was not able to remain or leave a missionary with them. They were bitterly disappointed and long entreated him to alter his purpose and leave a teacher among them. But it was beyond his power, and he sorrowfully left them. As he sailed up the river he saw them standing on the bank beckoning to him with eager entreaty. Two days later he returned, sailing down the stream. As they passed the village, the natives were still upon the banks watching for him. As they saw that he did not intend to land, they became wild in their gesticulation and cries, waving their arms, leaping high in the air, shouting and trying in every way to attract his attention. He felt the appeal in every fiber of his being, but he could do nothing. He had no one to leave, and as he sailed down the river his heart was broken with the sight.

—*The Missionary Worker*

* * *

Her Mistaken Call

A certain young lady in New Mexico had voluteered for foreign mission work. Her pastor was much pleased with her fervent testimonies from time to time. One day he said to the young lady: "I am thinking of some special mission work among the Mexican people in the east part of town. It occurred to me that you would be the logical one to help." The young lady flashed this reply: "But I simply cannot stand Mexicans. You will have to get someone else." Her pastor looked at her thoughtfully, then answered: "If you cannot stand Mexicans, you certainly will not be able to work with Chinese or Negroes or any other race across the seas. You had better pray about this matter and find out whether or not you haven't been mistaken in your call to foreign mission fields."

—Harold Dye in
the Teacher

* * *

A Missionary's Equipment

A life yielded in God controlled by His Spirit.
A restful trust in God for the supply of all needs.
A sympathetic spirit and a willingness to take a lowly place.
Tact in dwelling with men and adaptability toward circumstances.
Zeal in service and steadfastness in discouragement.
Love for communion with God and for the study of His Word.
Some experience and blessing in the Lord's work at home.
A healthy body and a vigorous mind.

—J. Hudson Taylor

* * *

The Unfinished Task

Though our task is not to bring all the world to Christ, our task is unquestionably to bring Christ to all the world.

—Dr. A. J. Gordon

* * *

100,000 Souls A Day!

"One hundred thousand souls a day
Are passing one by one away
In Christless guilt and gloom:
Without one ray of hope or light,
With future dark as endless night,
They are passing to their doom."

—*Selected*

His Last Request

A minister who had recently been called to a prosperous church was met by a prominent woman of the church who said to him, "Doctor, I do not believe in foreign missions." The minister was grieved, but said nothing. A few weeks later, when the congregation was gathered about the Communion table, he took occasion to read the Master's final words to the disciples. "The last words of our friends," said the pastor, "are always precious. It affects us to know what chiefly weighs on their hearts as they are about to leave us. Any message or commission they give us then, we would rather do anything than to fail to heed or execute. It has always impressed me that the thing which weighed most on our Saviour's heart as He was taking His departure, was the world of sinners for which He had died, and the very last request He made of His friends was that they should 'go . . . into all the world, and preach the gospel to every creature.'" Shortly after the close of the service, the same lady approached the pastor, and with tears in her eyes she said, "Doctor, I *do* believe in foreign missions."

—*Illustrator*

* * *

If the Church Fails

Lloyd George, asked by Paul Hutchinson for his estimate of Christian missions, said, "My friend, if the Church fails in its ministry to the world, then the rest of us might as well close up shop."

—*King's Business*

* * *

Do Missions Pay?

A seaman, on returning to Scotland after a cruise in the Pacific, was asked, "Do you think the missionaries have done any good in the South Sea Islands?" "I will tell you a fact which speaks for itself," said the sailor. "Last year I was wrecked on one of those islands, where I knew that eight years before a ship was wrecked and the crew murdered; and you may judge how I felt at the prospect before me — if not dashed to pieces on the rocks, to survive for only a more cruel death. When day broke we saw a number of canoes pulling for our ship and were prepared for the worst. Think of our joy and wonder when we saw the natives in English dress, and heard some of them speak in the English language. On that very island the next Sunday we heard the Gospel preached. *I do not know what you think of missions, but I know what I think."*

—*The King's Business*

* * *

Does It Really Matter?

At an international gathering of young people in New York City, we are told, a young American asked a cultured girl from Burma what was the religious belief of the majority of the Burmese. The young woman informed him that it was Buddhism. The American said quite casually, "Oh, well, that doesn't matter; all religions are the same anyway." The Burmese girl, looking directly at the young man, said, "If you had lived in my country you would not say that! I have seen what centuries of superstition, fear, and indifference to social problems have done for my people. We need the truth and uplift of Christianity. When I became a Christian it cost me something. If your religion had cost you more, you might be more aware of its superiority. My country needs Christ."

—*Gospel Herald*

* * *

The Heathen World

Paint a starless sky; hang your picture with night; drape the mountains with long, far-reaching vistas of darkness; hang the curtains deep along every shore and landscape; darken all the past; let the future be draped in deeper and yet deeper night; fill the awful gloom with hungry, sad-faced men and sorrow-driven women and children.

It is the heathen world — the people seen in vision by the prophet — who sit in the region and shadow of death, to whom no light has come; sitting there still through the long, long night, waiting and watching for the morning.

—Bishop Foster

* * *

The Last Hour

The sunset burns across the sky;
　Upon the air its warning cry
The curfew tolls, from tower to tower,
　O children, 'tis the last, last hour!

The work that centuries might have done
　Must crowd the hour of setting sun;
And through all lands the saving name
　We must, in fervent haste, proclaim.

The fields are white to harvest. Weep
　O tardy workers, as ye reap,
For wasted hours that might have won
　Rich harvests ere the set of sun.

We hear His footsteps on the way!
　O work, while it is called today,
Constrained by love, endued with power,
　O children, in this last, last hour!

—Clara Thwaites

* * *

Is Their Religion Enough?

People who should know better tell me that the heathen are better off as they are, that their own religions satisfy them and meet their need. Is that true? If so, then most certainly we should let them alone. But are they happy as they are?

I am thinking now of that Mohammedan in Algeria who slashed his head again and again with a large knife, until the blood flowed freely, then took newspapers and plastered them on top of his head; finally taking out a match and striking it, he set fire to the papers, hair, and blood. Can you imagine the agony? Why the self-inflicted torture? Because of his religion. He was laying up merit in Heaven. Mohammedanism taught him to afflict himself, and he was doing it with a vengeance. Would you exchange places with him? Would you accept his Mohammedanism and give him your Christianity? Which religion would you prefer? Do you think Mohammedanism brought him peace and comfort and happiness; or the very opposite? I leave you to answer.

I am thinking of the Aborigines of Australia, when a baby is born. The witch doctor must find a victim somewhere, so he seizes on the newborn infant, and in spite of the mother's protests and agonizing appeals, he fills its little mouth with sand until it chokes to death. Why does he do it? Because his pagan religion tells him he must. The spirits have to be satisfied. Does such a religion make that mother happy? Does she enjoy seeing her little baby murdered before her eyes? I think not. Yet you tell her that her religion is good enough for her. Would you exchange places? Would you be willing to be that mother? Again, I leave you to answer.

I am thinking of the Africans who always kill their twin babies, believing them to be demon-possessed. If God should give you twins, would you be willing to have them murdered? You would have to if you lived in Africa, for your religion would compel you to destroy them.

I am thinking of the Hindu widows of India, because of their religion, have to lie down beside their husbands when they have died and allow themselves to be bound and burned alive. Thousands of them have gone into eternity screaming in agony, as they slowly burned to death. Would you exchange your religion for theirs? Do you think it brings them any pleasure, any enjoyment? Yet you tell me to let them alone, that they are better off as they are. What a callous philosophy!

I am thinking, too, of the pagans in Africa, who, when a chief dies, throw his widows — thirty, sixty, or a hundred of them — into the grave with him and bury them alive. Is that a pleasant prospect? Would you be satisfied with such a religion?

Until you, my friend, are willing to accept these religions with their consequences, their abominable practices, for yourself, you ought to be ashamed to say that heathen are better off as they are. Their religions are religions of fear. They know nothing of peace and love. They have no hope. Christianity alone offers them life, abundant life, and that which satisfies the heart.

—Dr. J. Oswald Smith, in
　Sunday School Times

* * *

The Quecha Indians' Groping for God

The Quecha-speaking Indians of Peru worship the sun. This account is taken from the Student Foreign Mission Fellowship News, and, as it says, it "demonstrates pathetically that the human heart cries out for a knowledge of the true God. Each morning the natives gather together in an open place to wait for the rising sun to strike upon a shield of beaten gold which they have raised facing the east. When the first rays of the early sun strike the shield, sending a thousand glancing rays of golden light toward the worshipers, they bow down and cry, "O Sun, we worship thee as God — and if thou be not God — we worship Him who made thee."

—*Independent Board Bulletin*

* * *

"We Would See Jesus!"

"Sahib, we would see Jesus. My village is over yonder three miles away. We have given up idolatry, and we wish to embrace the Jesus religion. Come with me; the entire village is waiting for your coming." Before I could reply another man stepped forward, and then a third, and lo! a fourth, and from the lips of each fell the Macedonian cry. Listen to the last man: "Sahib, this is the fourth year that I have come to you and every time you have sent me away sorrowing. Oh, Sahib, give me a message of hope this time." With a breaking heart I had to say, "Your village is eight miles away, and I dare not even encourage you till I have a teacher for you. Be patient another year."

—*Selected*

* * *

How They Made Sure

The following story was told by a missionary: I remember before going out to India, sitting down with my roommate, now in China, and saying to him:

"What are we going to tell them out there on the field? Are we merely going to tell them *about* Christ? If so, it would be cheaper to send out Bibles and tracts. Can we tell them that we know Jesus Christ saves and satisfies, that He keeps us more than conquerors day by day?" I said: "I am not satisfied. I do not feel that I have a real message such as I need for men out there, nor the experience, nor the power. If we have not, is not the one great thing we need before we leave this country — *to know Him?*" From that day to the end of our student days we rose every morning at five o'clock, spent an unhurried hour with the Word of God, and from six to seven an unhurried hour for prayer. These two hours each day changed our lives and outlook upon our missionary work.

—*Alliance Weekly*

* * *

Where Christ's Heart Is:

When the noble Bruce, hero of Bannockburn, died his heart was extracted and encased in a silver casket by the Black Douglas and carried with the army. Douglas died fighting the Moors. Before he fell he threw the heart of Bruce into the thickest of the fray and urged his soldiers to follow that heart and conquer. Christ's heart is in the densest of heathenism and Christians must have their hearts there if they would feel His heart throb.

—George V. McDaniel, in *Proof*

* * *

Mr. Roosevelt and Missions

Theodore Roosevelt never spoke truer words than those in which he paid tribute to the heroism of the missionaries of the Cross. He said once to a friend: "As high an estimate as I have of the ministry, I consider that the climax of that calling is to go out in missionary service, as your son is doing. It takes mighty good stuff to be a missionary of the right type, the best stuff there is in the world. It takes a good deal of courage to break the shell and go 12,000 miles away to risk an unfriendly climate, to master a foreign language, to adopt strange customs, to turn aside from earthly fame and emolument, and, most of all, to say good-by to home and the faces of the loved ones, virtually forever."

—*Watchman-Examiner*

* * *

Is It True . . .?

One day Mr. Wilfred Grenfell, medical missionary to Labrador, was guest at a dinner in London together with a number of socially prominent British men and women.

During the course of the dinner, the lady seated next to him turned and said, "Is it true, Dr. Grenfell, that you are a missionary?"

Dr. Grenfell looked at her for a moment before replying, "Is it true, madam, that you are not?"

—*Sunday School Promoter*

* * *

"How Long Must We Wait?"

"Long have we sought eternal life,
Years have we waited in sin and strife;
In darkness groped, sad misery's mate.
How long, how long must we wait?

"The aged faint and long for the friend,
Dark shadows gathering bring the end;
Fades now the light, 'tis growing late,
How long, how long must we wait?"

—*Selected*

* * *

First Hand Contact

One of the unforeseen benefits of sending the young people of America to various and far-flung battle fronts all over the world has been that there with their own eyes they have had a sight of foreign missions in action. Writes a soldier from New Guinea, "I had a few mental reservations as to the value of foreign missions, but now I have had all my doubts erased." An officer stationed in the South Pacific confessed, "These people who were head hunters not long ago are so changed it might be beneficial for them to come over and evangelize our civilized Western world a bit."

—*King's Business*

413

Wanted: Men

Ann Judson, pioneer to Burma, once wrote of the kind of missionaries they needed. She said:

"In encouraging young men to come out as missionaries, do use the greatest caution. One wrong-headed, conscientiously obstinate man would ruin us. Humble, quiet, persevering men, men of sound, sterling talents, or decent accomplishments, and some natural aptitude to acquire a language; men of an amiable, yielding temper, willing to take the lowest place; to be the least of all; and the servants of all; men who enjoy much closer religion — who live near God, and who are willing to suffer all things for Christ's sake without being proud of it — these are the men we need."

—*Missionary Digest*

* * *

Home Help

Phillips Brooks was once asked, "What is the first thing you would do if you had accepted a call to become the rector of a small, discouraged congregation that is not even meeting its current expenses?"

"The first thing I would do," he replied, "would be to preach a sermon on, and ask the congregation to make an offering for foreign missions."

Phillips Brooks was never called to that kind of a congregation, but many gatherings today are proving in their own experience that the best way to keep out of debt, develop a healthy spiritual condition, to be a real service to the local community, is to adopt a real missionary policy and make offering for carrying the Gospel of Christ into all the world.

—*Glad Tidings*

* * *

His Compensation

A missionary was asked what compensation he had found in his work for all the sacrifices he had made. He took from his pocket a letter, worn with much handling, and read this sentence from an Oriental student: "But for you,

I would not have known Jesus Christ, our Saviour. Every morning I kneel down before God, and I think of you and pray." "That," said the missionary, "is my compensation."

—Darby Fulton, in *Earnest Worker*

* * *

A Poor Heathen

A certain rich man did not approve of foreign missions. One Sunday at church, when the offering was being received, the usher approached the millionaire and held out the plate. The millionaire shook his head, "I never give to missions," he whispered.

"Then take something out of the plate, Sir," said the usher softly. "The money is for the heathen."

—*The Outlook*

* * *

Don't Let Me Go Back Empty

Robert Moffat, the great missionary to Africa, once told this story:

"A woman came to me after having walked fifteen miles, and said that she wished for a New Testament. I said to her:

"My good woman, there is not a copy to be had."

" 'What! Must I return empty-handed?'

" 'I fear you must.'

" 'Oh,' she said, 'I borrowed a copy once, but the owner came and took it away, and now I sit with my family, sorrowful, because we have no Book to talk to us. Now we are far from anyone else. We are living at a cattle outpost, with no one to teach us but the Book. Oh, go try to find a Book! Oh, my brother, do go and try to find a Book for me! Surely there is one to be found. Do not let me go back empty.'

"I felt deeply for her, for she spoke so earnestly, and I said: 'Wait a little, and I will see what I can do.'

"I seached here and there and at last found a copy and brought it to the good woman. Oh, if you could have seen how her eyes brightened, how she clasped my hands and kissed them over and over again. Away she went with the Book, rejoicing, with a heart overflowing with gratitude."

—*Missionary News*

* * *

John G. Paton's Well

John G. Paton was the hero missionary of the New Hebrides islands in the South Seas. The people were savages, wore little clothing, and lived in a terrible state of sin. Mr. Paton had a time at first in getting the people to believe that he had a message from God.

Finally the water supply ran out on the island because of lack of rain. The natives had never seen a well. Paton proceeded to dig one, and the digging of this well was really the beginning of the conversion of the people. On beginning the well, Paton told the chief that he believed God would give them rain from the hole in the ground. The only fresh water the natives had was that caught when it rained.

When Paton made this statement great excitement prevailed. The chief and others declared that if Paton could bring rain from the hole in the ground, his must be the true God.

Finally the missionary, by digging to some depth, found a spring of living water. The effect upon the people was wonderful. The old chief asked the privilege of preaching a sermon at the Sunday services upon the well. This he did, emphasizing his earnest appeal by excitedly swinging his tomahawk. In the midst of his sermon he cried, "People of Aniwa, the world has turned upside down since the Word of Jehovah is come to this land. Who ever expected to see rain come up through the earth? From this day I must worship Him who has opened up for us this well, and who fills it with rain from below."

During the week following this remarkable sermon great heaps of idols were burned in front of Paton's house. The Christian teaching grew apace, and before many years there was not a heathen left on the island.

—*Missionary Ammunition*

A Short-Visioned Prophecy

The British East India Company said at the beginning of the nineteenth century: "The sending of Christian missionaries into our Eastern possessions is the maddest, most expensive, most unwarranted project that was ever proposed by a lunatic enthusiast." The English Lieutenant-Governor of Bengal said at the close of the nineteenth century: "In my judgment Christian missionaries have done more lasting good to the people of India than all other agencies combined."

—*Church of Christ Advocate*

* * *

What Missionaries Have Done:

1. Every book in the New Testament was written by a foreign missionary.

2. Every letter in the New Testament that was written to an individual was written to a convert of a foreign missionary.

3. Every Epistle in the New Testament that was written to a church was written to a foreign missionary church.

4. The disciples were called Christians first in a foreign missionary community.

5. Of the twelve apostles chosen by Jesus, every apostle except one became a missionary.

6. The only one among the twelve apostles who did not become a missionary became a traitor.

7. The problems which arose in the early church were largely questions of missionary procedure.

8. According to the apostles, missionary service is the highest expression of Christian life.

— *Gospel Herald*

* * *

Burma's "Coming God."

Today in the hills of Burma among the Palaung tribes are scores of little homes in which a corner is set apart as a shrine for the "coming God." The Rev. A. H. Henderson, M. D., describes how these places are swept clean, and no one is allowed to go into them. At night a light is placed in each little shrine. Whenever one of the Palaungs, who live in these hills, is asked why this is done, the answer is always the same, "It is for the coming God." Who this God is or where he may be found they know not, but they live in the hope that some day he will appear. As on that long-ago day in Athens it was Paul's privilege to declare unto the people the one true God, so it is the privilege of the Christian missionary today to carry to these dwellers in the hills of Burma the message of Christ.

— *Expositor*

* * *

Not a Weeping Time

The train from the south slowed down in Waverly Station, Edinburgh, and a little African girl was handed down onto the platform from the open door — then another followed and another and still another. A woman whose white face was more like yellow parchment followed, and gathered the four little African girls around her. The children's eyes were wide open with wonder while the newsboys' eyes were wide open with astonishment. They would have been amazed beyond measure if they had known that this was "Mary Slessor of Calabar," the "Great-White-Ma-Who-L i v e d-Alone," "T h e

White Queen of Okoyong," who had mastered cannibals, conquered wild drunken chiefs brandishing loaded muskets, had faced hunger and thirst under the flaming heat of Africa, had walked unscathed by night through forests haunted by ferocious leopards to triumph over regiments of frenzied savages drawn up for battle, had rescued from death hundreds of baby twins thrown out to be eaten by ants or wild animals and had now brought home to Scotland from Africa, on a much-needed and well-earned furlough, four of these her rescued children. Seventeen years after this her Heavenly Father called her Home to Himself. A fellow missionary conducted her funeral service right in the heart of the district where she had worked for forty-one years. It was a wonderful assembly. All government offices were temporarily closed. Large numbers of people were there, from the highest to the humblest of both races. And there was a great stillness. Suddenly a hysterical native girl began to wail. Old Mammy Fuller, who had loved Mary so much, was standing beside the preacher. She turned to the girl, and said, "Hush, lassie! *Praise God from whom all blessings flow.*" All the people had cause to praise God that day because He had sent Mary Slessor to them and had spared her to serve Him there so many years.

—From *Book of Missionary Heroes,* by Basil Mathews

MOTHERS

Our Good Intentions

I once heard a lady speak at a women's meeting. She said when she was ten years of age, one morning her mother, whom she loved dearly, waked her and asked her to arise and get her father's breakfast, as the mother was quite sick. She said: "I meant to get up; I loved to do things for my mother, but it was only five o'clock, and I was so sleepy that I went back to sleep. Mother did it herself, sick as she was, but she understood why I didn't get up, when

afterward, feeling badly about it, I tried to tell her. She died shortly afterward, but that memory stays ever with me. I don't want to fail anyone who needs me. God grant that I shall not. My cry to Him is that I may never fail to sacrifice, that I may watch with Him."

—Mrs. J. Shields

* * *

Little Mother of Mine

"Sometimes in the hush of the evening hour,

When the shadows creep from the west,
I think of the twilight songs you sang
And the boy you lulled to rest;
The wee little boy with tousled head
That long, long ago was thine,
I wonder if sometimes you long for that
boy,
Oh, little mother of mine.

"And now he has come to man's estate,
Grown stalwart in body and strong,
And you'd hardly know that he was the
lad
Whom you lulled with your slumber
song.
The years have altered the form and life
But his heart is unchanged by time,
And still he is only the boy as of old,
Oh, little mother of mine."

—*Selected*

* * *

Bouquets!

John Quincy Adams said: "All that
I am my mother made me."

Abraham Lincoln said: "All that I
am or hope to be, I owe to my angel
mother."

Dwight L. Moody declared: "All that
I have ever accomplished in life, I owe
to my mother."

Napoleon was a sage when he said:
"Let France have good mothers, and
she will have good sons."

Andrew Carnegie frequently acknowledged the tender interest and influence
of his mother.

Benjamin West declared: "A kiss
from my mother made me a painter."

Henry Ward Beecher once said: "The
memory of my sainted mother is the
brightest recollection of my early
years."

President McKinley provided in his
will that, first of all, his mother should
be made comfortable for life.

Garfield's first act, after being inaugurated President of the United
States, was to stoop and kiss his aged
mother, who sat near him.

Julia Ward Howe, when ninety-one
years of age, said: "We talk of forty

horse-power. If we had forty mother-
power it would be the most wonderful
force in the world."

— *Selected*

* * *

**Dr. C. I. Scofield's Mother's Dying
Prayer**

She and her husband were believing
Christians and worshiped in the Protestant Episcopal church. From the dying mother's lips came a prayer, heard
by the husband and other members of
the family, that the new arrival might
become a preacher of the gospel. Her
dying request was kept a secret, and
only after Cyrus had become a true believer in the Lord Jesus Christ and had
received a definite call to devote his life
to the Christian ministry was he told
of this touching prayer which was so
graciously answered. He remembered
from his earliest childhood that his
father read the Bible to him and to the
family. Thus in his young life was
sown the precious seed of the Word of
God.

— *Moody Monthly*

* * *

She Felt Alone

A little girl was in an orphans' home
and it was observed that she never
cried. One day one of the matrons
asked her, "Why do you not cry? I have
never seen you cry." The little girl replied, "I have no one to cry to since
Mamma died."

It was a glorious thing for every
Christian that Christ said, "Lo, I am
with you alway," meaning every day,
under all circumstances. The Christian
can cry to Him, call upon Him, trust
in Him, and share with Him whatever
joys come into life. — *Baptist Standard.*

* * *

"The Hand that Rocks"
"They say that man is mighty,
  He governs land and sea;
He wields a mighty scepter
  On lower powers than he.

417

"But mightier power and stronger
Man from his throne has hurled,
For the hand that rocks the cradle
Is the hand that rules the world."
— *Selected*

* * *

What It Costs

A woman was calling on a friend whose children were brought in. The caller said, evidently with no thought of the meaning of her words, "Oh, I'd give my life to have two such children," to which the mother with subdued earnestness replied, "That's exactly what it costs."

—S. D. Gordon

* * *

A Mother's Prayers

For many years the mother of Tom Carter prayed that God would save her boy and make a preacher out of him. Her boy was a wicked sinner. He landed in prison, but the mother still prayed for him, believing that God would answer her prayers. One day she received a telegram from the prison, saying that her son was dead.

The mother was stunned for a few minutes. Then she went to her room. There she prayed with her open Bible before her. She said to the Lord, "O God, I have believed the promises Thou didst give me in Thy Word. I have believed that I would live to see Tom saved and preaching the gospel. Now, a telegram says he is dead. Lord, which is true, this telegram or Thy Word?"

She rose from her knees and wired the prison: "There must be some mistake. My boy is not dead." And there was a mistake. Tom Carter was alive! Not long afterward he was saved. When he was released from prison, he became a mighty soul-winner and preacher.

—*Dawn*

* * *

"My Mother Believed in Me!"

"When I was a little mischievous lad,
The neighbors would all agree
That I must be going straight to the bad,
But mother believed in me!

And just because she believed in me,
I couldn't be mean, you see;
For it helps a boy to do right when he
Can say, 'My mother believes in me.'

"To me, as a man, how often there came
Temptations from which I'd flee!
The reason, you know, was always the same —
That mother believed in me.

And so, because she believed in me,
I wouldn't do wrong, you see;
For to disappoint her — ah, that would be
Too bad, when mother believed in me!

"It is not the least of blessings I've had
While passing thro' life, that she,
Though once I was such a mischievous lad,
Could always, believe in me.

My dear old mother has gone from me
To dwell by the Crystal Sea;
If ever I go to her side, 'twill be
Because my mother believed in me!"

—*Selected*

* * *

Give the Smiles to Mother

If you have a smile for Mother,
Give it now.
If you have a kindly word,
Speak it now,
She'll not need it when the angels
Greet her at the golden gate;
Give the smiles while she is living,
If you wait 'twill be too late.

If you have a flower for Mother,
Pluck it now.
Place it gently on her bosom,
Print a kiss upon her brow.
What cares she when life is over,
For the flowers that bloom below.
She will have her share up yonder,
Scattered at her feet galore.

—*Akron Baptist Journal*

* * *

Thomas Edison's Tribute

Thomas Edison paid a beautiful tribute to his mother when he said: "I did not have my mother long, but she cast over me an influence that has lasted all my life. The good effects of her early training I can never lose. If it had not been for her appreciation and her faith in me at a critical time in my experience, I should never have become an inventor. I was always a careless boy, and with a mother of different mental calibre, I should have turned out badly. But her firmness, her goodness, were potent powers to keep me in the right path. My mother was the making of me. The memory of her will always be a blessing."

—Watchman-Examiner

* * *

"She Does Not Love Us Less, but MORE!"

"To think of mother is to recall her unselfish devotion, her limitless, unfaltering love through good and evil report, never wavering, but growing stronger and stronger with the years; and to remember that she asks nothing in return for herself; she asks of us and for us that we be good men and women. If we fail, she does not love us less, but more. Wonderful, constant, miraculous mother's love!"

—John Burke, Former Governor of North Dakota

* * *

Her Son's "Good Night."

I was once spending the night in a beautiful home in a large city, when at about nine o'clock, my host, a gentleman of about fifty-five years of age, arose, saying, "Excuse me, please, for just a few minutes. I am going to say good night to my mother." His mother lived three blocks distant, and for thirty years her son had never failed to go and bid her good night, if he was in the city. "No matter what the weather may be, no matter who his guests are, my husband never fails to run over to his mother's and bid her good night," said the gentleman's wife when he had gone. "Neither he nor she could sleep if this duty had been neglected. When his business compels him to be away from the city, he writes to her every day, if

only a single line. Her mental powers are beginning to fail, and she forgets many things, so that her mind is blank on some points; but when nine o'clock comes she always knows the hour, and says, 'It is time for Henry to come and bid me good night.' "

—Christian Union Herald

* * *

Mothers Make Preachers

When young Matthew Simpson tremblingly broke the news to his widowed mother that he felt called to preach, which would necessitate his leaving the home, she exclaimed with tears of joy: "Oh, my son, I have prayed for this hour every day since you were born. At that time, we dedicated you to the Christian ministry."

Campbell Morgan says: "My dedication to the preaching of the Word was maternal. Mother never told it to the baby or the boy, but waited. When but eight years old I preached to my little sister and to her dolls arrayed in orderly form before me. My sermons were Bible stories which I had first heard from my mother."

—The Voice

* * *

"I'll Be Waiting if He Ever Comes Out!"

Who can understand or fathom the love of God? Who can understand a mother's love? A preacher recently wrote, "I hold in my hand a picture of a little shack outside of the walls of the State Penitentiary at Fort Madison. It is a shack occupied by the mother of a son in the penitentiary for life. She has gone as close to him as she can possibly get and pitched her tent there, saying, "I'll be waiting if he ever comes out.' "

—Florida Baptist Witness

* * *

"It's Mother's Hand!"

There is a beautiful story told of a soldier in World War I who was wounded on the battlefields of France, taken to a hospital, and finally brought back to

419

America. He was in a critical condition when he reached an American hospital — his eyes blinded, his mind beclouded, and his body mangled. And then his old mother traveled many miles to his bedside, laid her hand on his brow. Instantly he said: "It's my mother's hand! I'd know it anywhere!" The mother had not spoken, but he knew the touch of her hand! So it is that Christians who truly know their Lord also learn to recognize and long for "the touch of His hand."

—*Sunday School Times*

* * *

"O, Please, Sir, Read it Again!"

One of our chaplains told this wonderful story: "The Bible brings back the memory and the vision of home. A boy, eighteen years old, was badly wounded. Out of his loneliness came the faces of his loved ones. He was longing to hear their voices, and to see their faces when he died. I read the twenty-third psalm. This day he had had six injections of morphia. While I was reading, I did not watch his face, but, when I had finished, I saw that all pain had gone, that all that expression of suffering had faded away! He said, 'O, please, sir, read it again! While you were reading it, mother was sitting in the other corner of the room, and she smiled at me! Please read it again' ".

—W. B. K.

* * *

Love Never Fails

A mother kept a candle burning in the window every night for ten years. One night, very late, a poor, wretched woman came in from the street. The aged mother said to her, "Sit down by the fire." The stranger asked, "Why do you keep the light in the window?" The old mother replied, "That light is for my wayward daughter. She left home ten years ago. I am praying for her return. I have kept a light in the window for ten years! Others often blame me for worrying about her, but, you see, I love her. I am her mother. Often, in the night, I open the door, and look out into the darkness and cry, 'Lizzie, Liz-

zie!' " The woman from the street began to weep. The aged mother looked closely at her and said, "Why, how cold and sick you seem! You must have trouble enough of your own!" Then suddenly the mother exclaimed, "Can it be? Yes! You are Lizzie! My own lost child! Thank God that you are home again!" How thankful we can be that Mother loves us.

—*The Wesleyan Methodist*

* * *

"Mother o' Mine!"

If I were hanged on the highest hill,
Mother o' mine, O mother o' mine,
I know whose love would follow me still,
Mother o' mine, O mother o' mine.

If I were drowned in the deepest sea,
Mother o' mine, O mother o' mine,
I know whose tears would come down to me,
Mother o' mine, O mother o' mine.

If I were damned of body and soul,
Mother o' mine, O mother o' mine,
I know whose prayers would make me whole,
Mother o' mine, O mother o' mine.

—Rudyard Kipling

* * *

Nothing but Housework?

A busy mother was one day regretting that she could do so little Christian work. "I shall have only a life of housework to show at last," she said rather sadly to a friend one day. "Why, Mother," exclaimed her little daughter, who overheard the words, "all we children will stand up and tell all you've done for us — everything! I shouldn't s'pose they'd want anything better than good mothers up in Heaven!"

And the friend answered: "The child is right. Earth will send to Heaven no better saints than the true Christian mothers who have done their best."

—*Christian Digest*

* * *

Fractions and Mothers

A teacher in one of our public schools put this question to little James in the arithmetic class, "James, suppose your mother made a peach pie, and there were ten of you at the table — your mother and father and eight children — how much of the pie would you get?" "A ninth, ma'am," was the prompt answer. "No, no, James. Now pay attention," said the teacher. "There are ten of you. Ten, remember. Don't you know your fractions?" "Yes, ma'am," was the swift reply of little James, "I know my fractions, but I know my mother, too. She'd say that she didn't want any pie."

—Presbyterian National

* * *

"The Names Have Remained!"

Once years ago J. Sterling Morton, founder of Arbor Day and one of Nebraska's two famous sons in Statuary Hall, drove out to the cemetery to visit his wife's grave. With him he took his three motherless sons. He asked the boys to read the inscription on the newly erected tombstone which consisted of her name, that she was the wife of J. Sterling Morton and the mother of the three sons whose names were chiseled in full. Then the father told the boys that if any of them ever disgraced his mother, he had arranged with a stone-cutter to chisel off his name. Often the sons, who rose to places of eminence, recalled with admiration the warning of their father, but they attributed the real preventive against disgracing their mother to her Christian training and example. The names have remained, but love rather than fear kept them there.

—Moody Monthly

* * *

Only Praise and Gratitude

After one of the terrible battles of the Civil War, a dying Confederate soldier asked to see the chaplain. When the chaplain arrived, he supposed the young man would wish him to beseech God for his recovery; but it was very different. First the soldier asked him to cut off a lock of his hair for his mother, and then he asked him to kneel down and thank God. "What for?" asked the surprised chaplain. "For giving me such a mother. Thank God that I am a Christian. And thank God for giving me grace to die with. And thank God for the Home He has promised me over there." And so the chaplain knelt down by the dying man, and in his prayer he had not a single petition to offer, but only praise and gratitude.

—Christian Herald

* * *

A Mother's Light

A very beautiful story is related of a boat out at sea carrying in it a father and his little daughter. As they were steering for the shore they were overtaken by a violent storm which threatened to destroy them. The coast was dangerous. The mother lighted a lamp and started up the worn stairway to the attic window.

"It won't do any good, mother," the son called after her.

But the mother went up, put the light in the window, knelt beside it and prayed. Out in the storm the daughter saw a glimmer of gold on the water's edge.

"Steer for that," the father said.

Slowly but steadily they came toward the light, and at last were anchored in the little sheltered harbor by the cottage.

"Thank God," cried the mother, as she heard their glad voices and came down the stairway, with a lamp in her hand. "How did you get here?" she said.

"We steered by mother's light," answered the daughter, "although we did not know what it was out there."

"Ah!" thought the boy, wayward boy, "it is time I was steering by mother's light."

And ere he slept he surrendered himself to God and asked Him to guide him over life's rough sea. Months went by, and disease smote him.

"He can't live long," was the verdict of the doctor, and one stormy night he lay dying.

"Do not be afraid for me," he said, as they wept; "I shall make the harbor, for I am steering by mother's light."

—Florida Baptist Witness

Mother to Son

Do you know that your soul is of my
    soul such part
That you seem to be fiber and core of
    my heart?
None other can pain me as you, dear,
    can do;
None other can please me, or praise me,
    as you.

Remember, the world is quick with its
    blame,
If shadows or stain ever darken your
    name.
"Like mother, like son," is a saying so
    true —
The world will judge largely of mother
    by you.

Be yours then, the task — if task it
    shall be —
To force the proud world to do homage
    to me,
Be sure it will say, when its verdict
    you've won:
"She reaped as she sowed: lo, this is her
    son."
               —*Selected*

* * *

"I Will Die — Let My Baby Live!"

I knew him as a brilliant young member of a noted family. He was studying in one of the great universities. His physical development was well-nigh perfect. Tall, broad-shouldered, brawny, graceful in bearing, and quick in movement, he was soon well-known as an athlete. On the field he was invincible in contest, being lion-like in his contact with opponents. But when the games were over, in the hours of study and social intercourse, he was found to be unusually sympathetic, considerate, and kind. In the company of young women he was always the true gentleman, a model of refinement and courtesy. And even in private he never referred to them except in the purest terms. The word Mother was most sacred to him; and whenever that word was used in his presence, he became silent: sometimes he even shed tears.

I inquired of him one day why he was so rough and lion-like in athletics and so gentle at other times, especially toward girls and women. Said he, "I never like to refer to this, but my father told me that when I was being born, mother's case was most serious. Said the doctor, 'I cannot save them both. Decide quickly which one it shall be.' My father stood speechless I was told, not knowing what to say. Mother, who had overheard what the doctor said, said 'I will die: let my child live.' Thus, mother gave her life for me!"
               —Calvin S. Stanley

* * *

God Does Not Lie

God punishes sin. A mother and her little girl of five were visiting. The little girl misbehaved, and her mother said, "Sarah, you must not do that." The child soon forgot and did it again. The mother said, "Sarah, if you do that again I will punish you." Soon the child did it again. When it was time to go home the mother went for her hat, and Sarah was sad for the punishment to come. A young lady noticed it and said, "Never mind, I will ask your mother not to whip you." The reply was, "That will do no good; my mother never tells lies." As God is true He cannot clear the guilty. Punishment is sure.
          —*Christian Union Herald*

* * *

"The Sorest Sense of Loss"

Once I suddenly opened the door of my mother's room, and saw her on her knees beside her chair, and heard her speak my name in prayer. I quickly and quietly withdrew, with a feeling of awe and reverence in my heart. Soon I went away from home to school, then to college, then into life's sterner duties. But I never forgot that one glimpse of my mother at prayer, nor the one word — my name — which I heard her utter. Well did I know what I had seen that day was but a glimpse of what was going on every day in that sacred closet of prayer and the consciousness strengthened me a thousand times in duty, in danger, and in struggle. And when death came, at length, and sealed those lips, the sorest sense of loss that I felt was the knowledge that no more would my mother be praying for me.

—Dr. J. R. Miller

* * *

Spurgeon's Tribute

"I cannot tell how much I owe to the solemn words and prayers of my good mother. It was the custom on Sunday evenings, while we were children, for her to stay at home with us. We sat around the table and read verse by verse, while she explained the Scripture to us. After that was done, then came the time of pleading with God. Some of the words of our mother's prayers we shall never forget, even when our heads are gray. I remember her once praying thus: 'Now, Lord, if my children go on in sin, it will not be from ignorance that they perish, and my soul must bear a swift witness against them at the day of judgment if they lay not hold of Jesus Christ.' "

—*Good Ship Grace*

* * *

Her Day

She cooked the breakfast first of all,
  Washed the cups and plates,
Dressed the children and made sure
  Stockings all were mates.
Combed their heads and made their beds,
  Sent them out to play.
Gathered up their motley toys,
  Put some books away.
Dusted chairs and mopped the stairs,
  Ironed an hour or two,
Baked a jar of cookies and a pie,
  Then made a stew.

The telephone rang constantly,
  The doorbell did the same,
A youngster fell and stubbed his toe,
  And then the laundry came.
She picked up blocks and mended socks,
  And then she blackened up the stove.
(Gypsy folks were fortunate with
  carefree ways to rove!)
And when her husband came at six
  He said: "I envy you!
It must be nice to sit at home
  Without a thing to do!"

—*Selected*

"Mother Is At Prayer!"

Billy Sunday tells of a minister who was making calls. He came to a certain home and asked for the mother but the child opening the door answered, "You cannot see mother for she prays from nine to ten." He waited forty minutes to see that mother, and when she came out of her prayer closet the light of glory was on her face, and he knew why that home was so bright; he knew why her two sons were in the ministry and her daughter a missionary. "All hell cannot tear a boy or girl away from a praying mother," comments Mr. Sunday.

Susanna Wesley, with seventeen children, spent one hour each day shut up with God alone in her room, praying for them — and her two sons, under God, brought revival to England while France weltered in the blood of a ghastly revolution.

—*Baptist Standard*

* * *

Why John McNeil Preached

It is said that when John McNeil, who became himself a great Scotch preacher, had heard a minister preach and had determined to be a Christian, he went to his home and found his mother sleeping. Entering her room he aroused her and told her that he had become a Christian and that he hoped to preach. Putting her arm about his neck she said to him, "Johnny, my lad, I prayed for this before you were born."

—J. Wilbur Chapman

* * *

The Bravest Battle

"The bravest battle that ever was fought,
  Shall I tell you where and when?
On the maps of the world you will find
  it not,
  It is fought by the mothers of men.

"Nay, not with cannon or battle-shot,
  With a sword or noble pen;
Nay, not with eloquent words of thought
  From the mouths of wonderful men!

"But deep in the walled-up woman's
　　heart,
Of a woman that would not yield,
But bravely, silently bore her part,
Lo, there is that battle-field!

"No marshaling troops, no bivouac song,
　No banner to gleam and wave;
But oh, these battles, they last so long,
　From babyhood to the grave.

"Yet, faithful still as a bridge of stars,
　She fights in her walled-up town,
Fights on and on in the endless wars,
　Then, silent, unseen, goes down!

"Oh, ye with banners and battle-shot,
　And soldiers to shout and praise!
I tell you the kingliest battles fought,
　Were fought in those silent ways.

"O spotless mothers in a world of shame,
　With splendid and silent scorn,
Go back to God as pure as you came,
　The kingliest warrior born!"
　　　　　　　—Joaquin Miller

* * *

Making the Children Want "More!"

A mother with three children was
about to leave home for a few days.
Gathering them about her she talked to
them about her absence and their behavior and prayers until she should return. She then poured out her heart
with them in prayer. All heads were
raised and every face was full of sunshine. After a moment's pause a little
two-year-old boy bowed his head down
by his mother's cheek, and said, "More."
When a parent's love and example can
evoke from children a call for more
prayer, the home happiness is assured.
　　　　　　　—*Faithful Witness*

* * *

A Mother's Faith and Godly Resolve

"By faith" Noah became the head of
a wholly believing family in those awful days. What encouragement in that
for believing men and women today!
Mrs. Catherine Booth stood boldly before God and said, "I will not be the
mother of a wicked child!" And she

was not; the Salvation Army stands as a
monument to her faith and to that of
her husband.
　　　　　　　—*Illustrator*

* * *

Through One Mother's Prayers

An old woman with a halo of silvered
hair — the hot tears flowing down her
furrowed cheeks — her worn hands busy
over a washboard in a room of poverty
— praying — for her son John — John
who ran away from home in his teens to
become a sailor — John of whom it was
now reported that he had become a very
wicked man — *praying, praying always*,
that her son might be of service to God.
The mother believed in two things, the
power of prayer and the reformation of
her son. God answered the prayer by
working a miracle in the heart of *John
Newton*. John Newton, the drunken
sailor became John Newton, the sailor-
preacher. Among the thousands of men
and women he brought to Christ was
Thomas Scott, cultured, selfish, and self-
satisfied. Because of the washtub
prayers another miracle was worked,
and Thomas Scott used both his pen
and voice to lead thousands of unbelieving hearts to Christ, among them
a dyspeptic, melancholic young man,
William Cowper by name. He, too, was
washed in the cleansing blood and in a
moment of inspiration wrote "There Is
a Fountain Filled With Blood." And
this song has brought countless thousands to the Man who died on Calvary.
All this resulted because a mother *took
God at His word* and prayed that her
son's heart might become as white as
the soapsuds in the washtub.
　　　　—From *Springs in the Valley*,
　　　　　　by Mrs. Charles E. Cowman

* * *

Prayer Stops Shell Exploding!

When war broke out my husband enlisted. I was left with five children, the
youngest being a baby of eleven months.
Two years later my husband was killed.
My eldest boy was then eighteen, and
he had to join up. Day and night I

prayed for my son's safety. When he came back on his first furlough he had not been home long when he said: "Mother, you've been praying for me." I said: "I have, my son, day and night." He then told me that there had been six of them in a trench when the hissing of a shell was heard. Suddenly the shell dropped in the trench itself, burying its nose in the mud, unexploded. After tense silence, one of the lads said: "Our mothers have been praying for us."

—*Christian Herald, London*

"Always Keep Me Kind and Sweet"

Father in heaven, make me wise,
　So that my gaze may never meet
A question in my children's eyes;
　God keep me always kind and sweet.

And patient, too, before their need;
　Let each vexation know its place,
Let gentleness be all my creed,
　Let laughter live upon my face!

A mother's day is very long,
　There are so many things to do!
But never let me lose my song
　Before the hardest day is through.
　　　　　—Margaret E. Sangster

NATURE

Only God Can Make A Tree

"I think that I shall never see
A poem lovely as a tree;
A tree whose hungry mouth is pressed
Against the earth's sweet flowing breast;
A tree that looks at God all day,
And lifts her leafy arms to pray:
A tree that may in summer wear
A nest of robins in her hair;
Upon whose bosom snow has lain,
Who intimately lives with rain.
Poems are made by fools like me,
But only God can make a tree."
　—Kilmer, the Soldier-Poet, in
　　Christian Monitor

* * *

"If I Could Understand"

"Flower in the crannied wall
I pluck you out of the crannies
I hold you here, root and all, in my hand
Little flower — but if I could understand
What you are, root and all, and all in all,
I should know what God is and man is."
　—Tennyson

* * *

"The Heavens Declare!"

"How do you know whether there be a God?" was once asked of a Bedouin; and he replied, "How do I know whether

a camel or a man passed by my tent last night? By their footrints in the sand." "The heavens declare the glory of God" (Ps. 19:1).

—*Christian Digest*

* * *

"The Winter Scene!"

The lark has flown, the wren is gone,
The robin and the thrush;
The daisy sleeps, the violet hides,
The wind sighs with a hush.

The time has come for frost and ice
To dress the evergreen
With crystal beads and ermine brush,
And deck the winter scene.
　—*Selected*

* * *

Man's Needs and Environment

The atmosphere we breathe is composed of a combination of nitrogen and oxygen suited perfectly to our lungs. The distance of the earth from the sun and moon is scientifically correct for the maintenance of life, health, and happiness. The perpetuity of the rain and snow makes the earth fertile. The tides of the sea keep the shore clean and fresh. Vitamins necessary for bodily existence are provided in abundance.

425

Laws and forces of nature stand ready
to be harnessed for man's use. Nor does
nature exist merely on a subsistence
basis. God has filled the earth with
beauty and charm. There are majestic
mountains and verdant valleys. There
are tall trees and lush carpets of grass.
The moonlight, the stillness of the desert, the melodious thrill of songbirds all
witness that God has made the earth for
our pleasure. Food for man grows plen-
tifully, and beneath the soil are abundant minerals and oils for tools and
fuel. Surely this minute agreement between man's needs and his environmental provision gives evidence of a mir-
acle-working God.

—*King's Business*

* * *

At Eventide

The winter twilight softly steals
Across the glistening snow;
While the evening star adds its splendor
To the mellow after-glow.

The crescent moon brings mystic dreams
Of all that life holds dear,
And nature bows in sweet repose
As the silent night draws near.

Though countless sunsets paint the sky
They ne'er will loose their power,
To draw me nearer to my God
In that peaceful twilight hour.

—H. Margaret Kurtz

* * *

Out in the Fields with God

The little cares that fretted me
I lost them yesterday
Among the fields, above the sea,
Among the winds at play;
Among the lowing of the herds,
The rustling of the trees;
Among the singing of the birds,
The humming of the bees.

The foolish fears of what may happen,
I cast them all away
Among the clover-scented grass,
Among the new-mown hay;
Among the rustling of the corn,

Where drowsy poppies nod,
Where ill thoughts die and good is
born —
Out in the fields with God.
—Elizabeth Barrett Browning

* * *

Summer is Here
Listen!
Summer is here;
Tune in your ear
To the song of the lark;
To the sounds in the dark;
To the symphony played
In the deep forest glade;
Come, join the gay breeze
In its dance through the trees;
To the sweet scented clover,
Come, bumblebees, over
To sup at the dawn
Where the shy spotted fawn
Drinks deep of the stream,
As the sun sheds its beam;
God's love for the world
In each fern that's unfurled,
The message is clear
Summer is here;
Listen!
—Myra Johannesen

* * *

"He Hath Made Everything Beautiful!"
(Eccl. 3:11)
"When God invented beauty
He made such lovely things!
My happy heart is soaring
With every bird that wings.

"His master brush spreads colors
On palettes of the skies
And over ripening grain fields
The haze of autumn lies.

"He gave us for our pleasure
Each lovely flower that blows,
Then added for good measure
The perfume of the rose.

"He knows the singing rapture
That comes with each new Spring—
Oh, when God gave us beauty
He made a wondrous thing!"

—Martha Snell Nicholson,
in *Heaven's Garden*

God Served No Apprenticeships

Scientists tell us that there are nearly a hundred elements in the make-up of our world. These elements have affinities and aversions, and are the playgrounds of opposing forces, yet with all their pulling and pushing there is a nicety of balance that is amazing to thinkers. There may be other elements somewhere in the universe, but another one here might upset the balance of those we have, and certainly if any one of a dozen elements that could be named were taken away, the earth would be a desert. God has just the right number, in the right proportion, and they behave in exactly the right way so that all the pulls balance all the pushes. . . . Most of what man knows, he learned from some other person's experiments or mistakes, and after a fourth of his life spent in school, man fumbles with the mysteries of life and matter — sometimes with an air of profundity. God served no apprenticeships.

—B. H. Shadduck, Ph.D.

* * *

How Poor!

Who walks beside a rosebud
  And does not sense its bloom,
Its lovely form and color,
  Its delicate perfume;
Who walks beneath the heavens
  And does not see the sky,
The sunrise and the sunset,
  The tints that glow and die.

Who treads a rural pathway
  And never hears a bird,
Nor notes the trembling grasses
  A passing breeze has stirred;
Who dwells among his fellows,
  And sees them pass his door,
Nor even hears their heartbeats—
  Is pitifully poor.

—*Kind Words*

* * *

Anthem To God for Autumn

Fields of countless corn shocks,
  All in perfect line,
Like a guard of soldiers,
  Tall and straight and fine.

Pumpkins piled beside them,
  Orange colored shapes,
Frost-killed vines a trailing,
  Like torn and tattered drapes.
A pheasant comes a flying—
  A streak of gorgeous hue—
Blending with the sunset
  Of multi-colors, too.
In the distant wood lot
  A squirrel climbs the trees,
While leaves of gold and crimson
  Are trembling in the breeze.
Oh, when it comes to Autumn
  Is there not special reason
For praising God for beauties
  Of this 'specially lovely Season?

—Roy J. Wilkins, in
Smiles and Sunshine

* * *

Consider the Bee

Here is a little bee that organizes a city, that builds ten thousand cells for honey, twelve thousand cells for larvae, a holy of holies for the mother queen; a little bee that observes the increasing heat, and, when the wax may melt and the honey be lost, organizes the swarm into squads, puts sentinels at the entrances, glues the feet down, and then, with flying wings, creates a system of ventilation to cool the honey that makes an electric fan seem tawdry — a little honey bee that will include twenty square miles in the field over whose flowers it has oversight.

But if a tiny brain in a bee performs such wonders, who are you, that you should question the guidance of God? Lift up your eyes, and behold the hand that supports these stars, without pillars, the God who guides the planets without collision.

—*Selected*

* * *

Rainbow in the Sky

"My heart leaps up when I behold
  A rainbow in the sky;
So was it when my life began;
So is it now I am a man;
So be it when I shall grow old,
  Or let me die!

The child is father of the man;
And I could wish my days to be
Bound each to each by natural piety."
—Wordsworth

* * *

"Into the Woods!"
Into the woods my Master went,
Clean forspent, forspent.
Into the woods my Master came
Forspent with love and shame.
But the olives they were not blind to Him,
The little grey leaves were kind to Him
The thorn-tree had a mind to Him
When into the woods He came.

Out of the woods my Master went,
And He was well-content.
Out of the woods my Master came,
Content with death and shame.
When Death and Shame would woo Him last
From under the trees they drew Him last
'Twas on a tree they slew Him — last,
When out of the woods He came.
—Sidney Lanier

* * *

The Footprints of God

In childhood, how our heart thrilled in reading the story of Robinson Crusoe! He was stranded on an island which he thought to be without human inhabitant, except himself. One day he discovered in the sands footprints of a human being. Following those footprints, he discovered a man, Friday!

Through God's wondrous creation, He has left His footprints. Man, however, in his blindness and unbelief, refuses the evidence of the existence of an infinite Creator. Running riot, his mind comes to glaring foolish conclusions in reference to God's orderly creation. Intellectually, he cannot say that there is no great First Cause, or Master Mind, or Creator of the universe. Man's heart, being deceitful and desperately wicked, says, "There is no God!"
—Phil Marquart, M. D.,
Teacher of Psychology
at Wheaton College

A Winter's Night
"The fleecy snow comes whirling down,
To dress the earth with spotless gown;
The star-shaped flakes, so dazzling white
Present to us a lovely sight.

"The trees that once were brown and bare
Now spread their robes, so soft and fair,
And raise their arms with graceful pose,
Adorned with sparkling winter clothes.

"The home-lights twinkling in the night,
The soft flakes touch with splendors bright;
They send forth colors rich and gay,
Like precious jewels on display.

"The moon and stars, with silvery light,
Add beauty to the glorious night;
And man admires this wondrous scene—
The handiwork of God supreme!

"Dark spots and shadows fade from view,
Smoothed by a gentle hand and true,
Our Heavenly Father, from above,
Thus sends a lesson of His love."
—Martha Grenfell, in
Gospel Herald

* * *

Scenery Cannot Save

Chief Justice Chase was once riding on the train through Virginia. As they stopped at an insignificant town, they told him that Patrick Henry was born there. He stepped out on the platform, and said, "Oh, what a magnificent scene! What glorious mountains! I do not wonder that a place like this gave birth to Patrick Henry." A farmer, overhearing him, said, "Well, stranger; those mountains have been here ever since I can remember, and the scenery hasn't changed much, but I haven't seen any more Patrick Henrys around here that I can remember."
—*Otterbein Teacher.*

* * *

"Show Me Your God"
"Show me your God!" the doubter cries.
I point him out the smiling skies;
I show him all the woodland greens;
I show him peaceful sylvan scenes;

I show him Winter snows and frost;
I show him waters tempest-tossed;
I show him hills rock-ribbed and strong;
I bid him hear the thrush's song;
I show him flowers in the close—
The lily, violet, and rose;
I show him rivers, babbling streams;
I show him youthful hopes and dreams;
I show him stars, the moon, the sun;
I show him deeds of kindness done;
I show him joy, I show him care,
And still he holds his doubting air,
And faithless goes his way, for he
Is blind of soul, and cannot see!
—John Kendrick Bangs

* * *

God's Glory

The heavens declare God's glory,
The wonders of the sky
Repeat each day the message
That He is ever nigh.

The earth takes up the chorus,
The mountains, hills and plains
Stand forth in testimony
That He forever reigns.

The rivers, lakes and valleys
Bear witness of His power;
He speaks through every forest tree
And smiles through every flower.
—Florence Jansson, in
Sunday School Times

* * *

God's Harmony

Everything that God has made was
created "in tune," — the voice of man,
the whisper of the wind, the laughter of
little brooks and the throb of the great
ocean. Nature is harmony, the maintenance of right relations between every
living thing. If we listen with hearing
ears and observe with seeing eyes, we
shall discover that everything in Nature
is full of melody and is alive with divine
rhythms, from the harmonious growth of
the budding leaves to the swing of the
great planets about their lord, the sun.

Not only is the expression of music
universal in Nature but also in man.
Longfellow has fittingly put it that

"Music is the universal language of
mankind." Music has always been the
inspiration and the message-bearer for
all peoples, from the time when Pan
blew the first note upon his reed-pipe
to the cathedral organ of today.
—*Selected*

* * *

"God Made It So!"

Not long ago a group of scientists
were experimenting in Chicago. A female moth of a rare species was placed
in a room. Four miles away a male
moth of the same species was released.
In spite of the din and smoke of the city;
in spite of the distance; and in spite of
the fact that the female was in a closed
room, in a few hours the male moth
was found beating its wings against
the window of the room in which the
female was confined! Explain such
"miracles"? *God made it so!*

Tagged salmon released from Columbia
River points spend four years in the
Pacific, then consistently return to the
spots from which they departed.

Isn't God wonderful? His wisdom
and power are revealed a million ways
in the innumerable miracles of creation
which were planned and executed by
infinite intelligence and might.
—*Christian Victory*

* * *

His Love and Grace

We look with wonder in our eyes
At hills and skies —
In rose of dawn, in sunset-flame,
God writes His Name;
He fills the starlit nights,
The Father of all lights;
The stormy billows shout that He
Is mightier than any sea;
And something in each flower face
Tells to the heart His love and grace.
—*Watchman-Examiner*

* * *

The Artist

When nature with a mission brave
Was by the Lord endowed,
She painted on the sea a wave,
And on the sky a cloud.

And on the land she drew a hill,
And on the hill a tree;
And in the vale she placed a rill
That traveled to the sea.

And then, progressing without doubt
She took a little brush
And in the stream she placed a trout;
And on the tree a thrush.
And on the wave she painted foam,
And roses in the wild;
And in the shelter of a home
A woman and a child.

And did this all perfection bring?
Ah no! Experience shows —
She caused the little thrush to sing;
Gave perfume to the rose.
And best of all, the artist wise
And in her happiest style,
Put love into the woman's eyes
And made the baby smile.
　　　　　　　　　—Grit Story Section

* * *

"Come Little Leaves!"

"Come little leaves," said the wind one
day,
"Come over the meadows with me and
play;
Put on your dresses of red and gold,

Summer is gone, and the days grow
cold."

Soon as the leaves heard the wind's loud
call,
Down they came fluttering, one and all;
Over the brown fields they danced and
flew,
Singing the soft little songs they know.

"Cricket, good-by, we've been friends so
long;
Little brook, sing us your farewell song;
Say you are sorry to see us go —
Ah, you will miss us, right well we
know.

"Dear little lambs in your fleecy fold,
Mother will keep you from harm and
cold;
Fondly we've watched you in vale and
glade;
Say, will you dream of our loving
shade?"

Dancing and whirling the little leaves
went;
Winter had called them, and they were
content.
Soon fast asleep in their earthly beds,
The snow laid a coverlet over their
heads.
　　　　　　　　　—George Cooper

NEGLECT

"Last Chance" — MacArthur

Recently MacArthur said, "We have
had our last chance. If we do not devise
some greater and more equitable system
Armageddon will be at our door. The
problem basically is *theological*, and involves a spiritual recrudescence and improvement of human character which will
synchronize with our almost matchless
advance in science, art, literature, and
all material and cultural developments
of the past 2,000 years. It must be of
the spirit if we are to save the flesh."
　　　　　　　　　—Selected

Good Men Criminally Silent

"All that is necessary for the triumph
of evil is that good men do NOTHING!
　　　　　　　　　—Edmund Burke

* * *

The Silent Voice

In our younger days we used to know
a young lady who had one of the most
glorious singing voices we have ever
heard — a rich contralto with an amazing range, and such volume that it was
necessary for her to hold her throat
when practicing in a small room. She
was a protegee of the great Caruso

and had before her assured success as a concert star. But then one day, singing for a group of her friends, not one of whom had any appreciation of fine music, her voice broke during a difficult score. Her companions, among them a young man to whom she was devoted, laughed at her and teased her unmercifully. An extremely sensitive soul, she put her music away quietly and vowed to herself that she would never sing again.

Strangely, within a few months this girl married that young man who derided her, and for thirty-five years her singing voice has been silent, unless she may sing for herself alone upon occasion.

How many Christians are like that young lady! Possessed of talents which could be used to make Christ known their voices are mute.

—*The Pilgrim*

* * *

What Might Have Been

It isn't the thing you do, dear
It's the thing you leave undone —
That gives you a bit of a heartache
At the setting of the sun,
The tender word forgotten;
The letter you did not write;
The flowers you did not send, dear,
Are your haunting ghosts at night.

The stone you might have lifted
Out of a brother's way;
The bit of heartsome counsel
You were hurried too much to say;
The loving touch of the hand, dear,
And the gentle, winning tone
That you had no time or thought for,
With troubles enough of your own.

Those little acts of kindness,
So easily out of mind,
Those chances to be angels
Which we poor mortals find,
They come in night silence,
Each sad, reproachable wraith,
When hope is faint and flagging
And a chill has fallen on faith.

For life is all too short, dear,
And sorrow is all too great

To suffer our slow compassion
That tarries until too late;
And it isn't the thing you do, dear,
It's the thing you leave undone
That gives you a bit of a heartache,
At the setting of the sun.

—Homer A. Rodeheaver

* * *

No Appetite

One of the incidents of the great Chinese famine was a visit I made to the refugee camp outside the walls of Chinkiang. Mrs. Paxton was taking simple medicines to the sufferers; and, as we made the rounds of the miserable straw mat shelters, within which the starving people hungered on the cold ground, she turned to me with a startled expression and said, "Do you know what most of them are saying? They complain of lack of appetite! Even when they get a bowl of rice from our relief station, they have no appetite." These famine victims were not hungry — because they were starving. They had passed the stage of desire for food. That picture portrays many a soul's state. It has lost interest in or longing for spiritual satisfactions because it is starving.

—*Christian Herald*

* * *

Does Your Bible Make You Sneeze?

Recently I got a peculiar application of the serious text found in Numbers 32:23, "Be sure your sin will find you out," when in a home of a nominal professor. It is nice, when one enters a home, to find several Bibles in that home, scattered here and there.

I picked up the nice, fine Bible which had been received as a present years before and in a little while I began to sneeze. Upon examination I found that the opening of the Bible caused some dust to arise and tickle my nasal passages. I could tell that the Bible had not been dusted for a long time and that it was used only as an ornament. It was a sign of neglect when the dust arose from the Book on the beautiful parlor stand. It might be a good thing

to ask ourselves: "If we opened our Bibles, would the dust make us sneeze?"
—Ural T. Hollenback, in
P. H. Advocate

* * *

"Coming"?

There was an old turnpike man on a quiet country road, whose habit was to shut his gate at night and take a nap. One dark, wet midnight a stranger knocked at his door crying, "Gate! Gate!" "Coming," said the voice of the old man. Then the man knocked again, and once more the voice replied, "Coming." This went on for some time, till at length the stranger grew quite angry, and, jumping off his horse, opened the door and demanded to know why the old man cried "Coming!" for twenty minutes, but never came. "Who's there?" asked the old man in a sleepy voice, rubbing his eyes. "What d'ye want, sir?" Then, awakening, "Bless yer, sir, and yer pardon; I was asleep. I get so used to hearing 'em knock that I answer, 'Coming,' in my sleep, and take no more notice about it." So it is with too many hearers of the Gospel, who hear by habit, and answer God by habit, and at length die with their souls asleep.
—*Sunday School Chronicle*

* * *

"I Shall Not Pass This Way Again!"

I expect to pass through this world but once. Any good, therefore, that I can do, or any kindness that I can show to any fellow-being, let me do it now; let me not defer it or neglect it, for I shall not pass this way again.
—*Selected*

* * *

Opportunity

In one of the old Greek cities there stood long ago a statue. Every trace of it is vanished now. But there is still in existence an epigram which gives us an excellent description of it, and as we read the words we can surely discover what those wise old Greeks meant it should teach to every passer-by. The epigram is in the form of a conversation between a traveler and the statue:

"What is thy name, O statue?"
"I'm called Opportunity."
"Who made thee?"
"Lysippus."
"Why art thou on thy toes?"
"To show how quickly I pass by."
"But why is thy hair so long on thy forehead?"
"That men may seize me when they meet me."
"Why, then, is thy head so bald behind?"
"To show that when I have once passed, I cannot be caught."
—*Christian Press*

* * *

"All I Meant To Do!"

Said yesterday to to-morrow:
"When I was young like you,
I, too, was fond of boasting
Of all I meant to do.
But while I fell a-dreaming
Along the pleasant way,
Before I scarcely knew it,
I found I was to-day!

"And as to-day, so quickly
My little course was run,
I had not time to finish
One-half the things begun.
Would I could try it over,
But I can ne'er go back;
A yesterday forever,
I now must be, alack!

"And so, my good to-morrow,
If you would make a name
That history shall cherish
Upon its roll of fame,
Be all prepared and ready
Your noblest part to play
In those new fleeting hours
When you shall be to-day."
—*The Pacific*

* * *

"I Have Missed It!"

A doctor called to see a patient who was critically ill. When he got to the bedside, the young man said, "Doctor, I don't want you to deceive me; I want to know the truth. Is this illness very serious?" After the doctor had made an examination, he said, "I am sorry to tell you, young man, but you cannot live out the night!" The young man looked up and said, "Well, then, I have missed it at last!" "Missed what?" asked the doctor. "I have missed eternal life. I have been refusing to follow Jesus; although I always intended, some day, to do so. I thought I had plenty of time, and kept putting off the time when I would confess Him." The doctor who was himself a Christian man, said, "It is not too late. Call now upon God for mercy." "No," said the young man, "I have always had a great contempt for any man who would repent when he is dying. He is a miserable coward. I have waited too long, and I have missed it at last." The doctor spent most of the day with the young man, trying to lead him to the Lord; but the young man steadfastly refused, and passed out of this life, whispering these words with his dying lips, "I have missed it!"

—*Gospel Herald*

* * *

Reason for Alarm

Thomas Guthrie used to say: "If you find yourself loving any pleasure better than your prayers, any book better than the Bible, any house better than the house of God, any table better than the Lord's table, any persons better than Christ, or any indulgence better than the hope of Heaven — take alarm."

—*Alliance Weekly*

NEW YEAR

A Happy New Year

A Happy New Year to all today!
Though winds are blowing and skies are gray,
And snow and icicles fill the air;
While mercury stands — I'll not say where —
And each one's thinking "Oh dear! oh dear!
A pretty way to begin the year!"
But it lies with you, I'll whisper it here.

To make me a sad or a merry year;
For all the sunshine that's in the sky
Will not bring smiles if you choose to cry;
Nor all the rain that the clouds can hold
Will tarnish a soul that's bright as gold.
And so, whatever your score may be,
Just please remember, and don't blame me!

—*St. Nicholas*

* * *

What to Forget

"If you would increase your happiness and prolong your life, forget your neighbor's faults. Forget all the slander and unkind remarks you hear each day.

Forget the temptations. Forget all fault-finding, and give a little thought to the cause which provoked it. Forget the peculiarities of your friends and only remember the good points which make you fond of them. Forget all the personal quarrels or histories you may have heard by accident, and which, if repeated, would seem a thousand times worse than they really are. Blot out as far as possible all the disagreeables of life; they will come, but will only grow larger when you remember them and the constant thought of the acts of meanness, or worse still, malice, will only tend to make you more familiar with them. Be more forgiving to others, even as our Heavenly Father is forgiving you daily. Obliterate everything that was disagreeable from yesterday; start out today with a clean sheet, writing upon it for memory's sake only those things which are lovely and lovable and glorify God. Remember that some day we must give an account of our words and deeds and thoughts in the day of judgment. Therefore, let us try to make life beautiful for ourselves and others."

—*Cleremont Herald*

My Guide

The open door of another year
  I've entered by grace divine;
No ills I fear and no foes I dread,
  For a wonderful Guide is mine.
Through joy or chastening though He
  lead,
In tears though my race be run,
Whate'er my lot, this my prayer shall
  be,
  "Not mine, but Thy will be done."

I walk by faith in my heav'nly Guide,
  With fearless, unfaltering tread,
Assured that He, who appoints my days,
  Will daily provide my bread.
He'll send more grace should afflictions
  come,
  And a staff for the pathway steep,
While o'er me ever by night and day
  My Father His watch will keep.

With perfect trust in His love and care,
  I'll walk to my journey's end;
And day by day He will strength renew,
  And peace to my heart will send.
O blessed Guide, walking all unseen,
  Yet close to my side alway,
Do Thou, who guidest my steps aright,
  Lead on to eternal day!
            —Gertrude R. Dugan

*   *   *

A New Year's Resolution

I will, like Paul, *forget* those things which are behind and press forward; like David, *lift* up mine eyes unto the hills from whence cometh my help; like Abraham, *trust* implicitly in my God; like Enoch, *walk* in daily fellowship with my heavenly Father; like Jehoshaphat, *prepare* my heart to seek God; like Moses, *choose* rather to suffer than to enjoy the pleasures of sin for a season; like Daniel, *commune* with my God at all times; like Job, be *patient* under all circumstances; like Caleb and Joshua, *refuse* to be discouraged because of superior numbers; like Joseph, *turn* my back to all seductive advances; like Gideon, *advance* even though my friends be few; like Aaron and Hur, *uphold* the hands of my spiritual leaders; like Isaiah, *consecrate* myself to do God's work; like Andrew, *strive* to lead my brother into a closer walk with Christ; like John, *lean* upon the bosom of the Master and imbibe of His Spirit; like Stephen, *manifest* a forgiving spirit toward all who seek my hurt; like Timothy, *study* the Word of God; like the heavenly host, *proclaim* the message of peace on earth and good will toward all men; and like my Lord Himself, *overcome* all earthly allurements by refusing to succumb to their enticements.

Realizing that I cannot hope to achieve these objectives by my own strength, I will rely upon Christ, for "I can do all things through Christ which strengtheneth me."
            —George Burger

*   *   *

For the New Year

"Ere thou sleepest, gently lay,
Every troubled thought away;
Put off worry and distress
As thou puttest off thy dress.
Drop thy burden and thy care
In the quiet arms of prayer.

"Lord, Thou knowest how I live;
All I've done amiss forgive;
All of good I've tried to do,
Strengthen, bless and carry through.
All I love in safety keep,
While in Thee I fall asleep.

"Ere thou risest from thy bed,
Speak to God whose wings were spread
O'er thee through the helpless night;
Lo, he wakes thee now with light;
Lift thy burden and thy care
In the mighty arms of prayer.

"Lord, the newness of the day,
Calls me to an untried way,
Let me gladly take the road,
Give me strength to bear my load.
Thou my guide and helper be.
I will travel through with Thee."
            —*Selected*

*   *   *

The Art of Forgetting

A London journalist recently told a good story concerning Mr. Lloyd George. Years ago, he said, he and Mr. Lloyd George were enjoying a round of golf together. They had occasion to cross some fields in which cattle were grazing. In his anxiety to catch every word that fell from his illustrious companion's lips, the journalist failed to secure one of the gates through which they passed. Mr. Lloyd George noticed it, paused, went back, and carefully fastened the gate.

Resuming their walk, Mr. Lloyd George asked the pressman if he knew a good old doctor who had recently passed away. "When he lay dying," Mr. Lloyd George continued, "he called his sons and daughters to his bedside and urged them, as they made their way through life, to close every gate through which they passed." Mr. Lloyd George told his companion that he owed more to that sage morsel of philosophy than to any other sentence that he ever heard. Just as there were cattle grazing in the field from which Mr. Lloyd George and his friend had passed — cattle that had no right to stray into the new field that they had now entered — so there are factors in each phase of life that must not be permitted to wander into the next.

—*Watchman-Examiner*

* * *

Farewell Old Year!
I do not know, I cannot see,
What God's kind hand prepares for me,
Nor can my glance pierce through the
    haze
Which covers all my future ways;
But yet I know that o'er it all
Rules He who notes the sparrow's fall.

Farewell, Old Year, with goodness
    crowned,
A divine hand hath set my bound,
Welcome the New Year, which shall
    bring
Fresh blessings from my God and King.
The Old we leave without a tear,
The New we hail without a fear.
    —*Selected*

* * *

The Forward Look!
Lord, make me deaf, and dumb and
    blind
To all, "those things which are behind.'
Dead to the voice that memory brings,
Accusing me of many things.
Dumb to the things my tongue could
    speak,
Reminding me when I was weak.
Blind to the things I still might see,
When they come back to trouble me.
Let me press on to Thy high calling,
In Christ, who keepeth me from falling.
Forgetting all that lies behind —
Lord, make me deaf and dumb and
    blind.
Like Paul, I then shall win the race,
I would have lost but for Thy grace!
Forgetting all that I have done —
'Twas Thee, dear Lord, not I that won!
    —George T. Kenyon, in
    Gospel Herald

* * *

Just One Request
"Dear Master for this coming year
    Just one request I bring:
I do not pray for happiness,
    Or any earthly thing —
I do not ask to understand
    The way Thou leadest me,
But this I ask: Teach me to do
    The thing that pleaseth Thee.

I want to know Thy guiding voice,
    To walk with Thee each day.
Dear Master make me swift to hear
    And ready to obey.
And thus the year I now begin
    A happy year will be —
If I am seeking just to do
    The thing that pleaseth Thee."
    —*Selected*

* * *

"Put Hand in God's Hand"
"I said to the man
At the gate of the New Year,
'Give me a light that I
May tread safely into the unknown,'
And he replied, 'Go out into the darkness
And put your hand into the hand of God.
That shall be to you better than a light
And safer than a known way.'"
    —*Selected*

* * *

"A New Year's Promise"
Another year I enter,
    Its history unknown;
Oh, how my feet would tremble

To tread its paths alone!
But I have heard a whisper,
I know I shall be blest:
"My presence shall go with thee
And I will give thee rest."

What will the New Year bring me?
I may not, must not know;
Will it be love and rapture,
Or loneliness and woe?
Hush! Hush! I hear HIS whisper,
I surely shall be blest;
"My presence shall be with thee
And I will give thee rest."

—*Selected*

* * *

Jonathan Edwards Resolved:

Jonathan Edwards, who was a great and useful man, made five resolutions for himself in his youth, and lived by them faithfully. They are worth studying. Any one who will adopt and follow them will greatly increase his usefulness. The resolutions are as follows:

"1. Resolved: To live with all my might while I do live.

"2. Resolved: Never to lose one moment of time, but to improve it in the most profitable way I possibly can.

"3. Resolved: Never to do anything which I should despise or think meanly of in another.

"4. Resolved: Never to do anything out of revenge.

"5. Resolved: Never to do anything which I should be afraid to do if it were the last hour of my life."

—*Ohio Sunday School Worker*

* * *

A Prosperous New Year!

The New Year lies before me,
A spotless, shining thing,
Bright as the promises of God,
Fresh as the breath of spring.

A year to fill with lovely thoughts,
And kindly, helpful deeds,
Losing all consciousness of self,
In prayer for others' needs.
—*Sybil Leonard Armes*

Recipe for a Happy New Year

Take twelve fine full grown months, see that these are thoroughly free from all old memories of bitterness, rancor, hate and jealousy; cleanse them completely from every clinging spite; pick off all specks of pettiness and littleness; in short, see that these months are freed from all the past — have them as fresh and clean as when they came from the great storehouse of TIME.

Cut these months into thirty or thirty-one equal parts. This batch will keep for just one Year. Do not attempt to make up the whole batch at one time; (so many persons spoil the entire lot in this way) but prepare one day at a time as follows:

Into each day put twelve parts of faith, eleven of patience, ten of courage, nine of work (some people omit this ingredient and so spoil the flavor of the rest) eight of hope, seven of fidelity, six of liberality, five of kindness, four of rest (leaving out this is like leaving the oil out of the salad — don't do it), three of prayer, two of good will and one well-selected resolution. Put in a dash of fun, a sprinkling of play, and a heaping cupful of good humor.

Pour into the whole, love ad libitum and mix with a vim. Cook thoroughly in a fervent heat; garnish with sweet smiles and a few sprigs of joy; then serve with quietness, unselfishness and cheerfulness, and a Happy New Year is a certainty.

—Manuel Barone

* * *

Thought for the Day

"I learn as the years roll onward,
And leave the past behind,
That much I had counted sorrow
But proves that my Lord was kind.
That many a flower I longed for
Had a hidden thorn of pain,
And many a rugged by-path
Led to fields of golden grain."

—O. T. Deever

God in the Tomorrows

The Oriental shepherd was always ahead of his sheep. He was in front. Any attempt upon them had to take him into account. Now God is down in front. He is in the tomorrows. It is tomorrow that fills men with dread. But God is there already, and all tomorrows of our life have to pass before Him before they can get to us.

—F. B. Meyer

OBEDIENCE

"Give to Him that Asketh"

At Banza Mateke, a mission station of the Livingstone Inland Mission, Rev. Henry Richards had a very unusual experience. Never again did he question the truthfulness of Bible statements.

In his efforts to preach the Gospel to the natives about him, he decided to start with the Gospel of Luke. Each day he would translate 10 or 12 verses, and then expound them to his congregation, asking God to bless his efforts.

When he came to the 6th chapter of Luke and the 30th verse a great difficulty appeared. He was confronted with the words, "Give to every man that asketh of thee." He decided it would never do to read this to the people, for notorious beggars that they were, they would ask for everything he possessed.

He turned back to the 1st chapter and started over, to have more time to think what to do. The more he thought about the verse the more he was convinced it meant just what it said. So when he came to it again he read it to the people, and told them what he thought it meant.

At once the natives began asking for his things. Without hesitation he gave what they asked. Soon most of the things he had were in the hands of natives.

Then they talked among themselves, and decided this must be God's man, for never had they seen a man do things like this, and never refuse a request. Then they started to return the things until all had been restored.

It was this *obedience to God's Word* that started the revival among them which soon banished heathenism.

—Ben L. Byer, in
Gospel Herald

Having Our Own Way

"A friend of mine was going down the street and came upon two lads, one of them crying as if his heart would break. My friend said to the other one, 'What is the matter?' 'Nothing, except he just wants to have his own way,' came the answer. My friend walked down the street saying to himself, 'That is just the matter with me and has been for forty years. I have been trying to have my own way and blubbering because I could not have it.'"

—A. C. Dixon, in
Moody Monthly

* * *

How to Understand

In the days of the South, a Negro slave and preacher had an infidel master. The master said to the slave one day, "You are a preacher, Sam?"

"Well, I tells about Jesus some, Massa."

"Well, if you are a preacher, you ought to understand the Bible. Now tell me, what does this mean?" And he opened the Bible and read, "Whom He did foreknow, He also did predestinate" — words that have puzzled wiser heads than the poor slave.

"Well," said the slave, "Massa, where is it?"

"It's in Romans," said the master.

"Oh, my dear Massa; I will explain dis 'ole business to you! It is very simple. You begin with Matthew, and do all the dear Lord tells you to do there, and then you go on to Mark, and Luke, and John; and when you get to that place it is easy enough — but you can't begin there."

—*Preacher's Homiletical Commentary*

The Finger of God

Mr. H. C. Mason tells of the man who in prayer meeting prayed earnestly that God would with His finger touch a certain man. Suddenly he stopped his prayer. A brother asked him, "Why did you change your prayer?" He replied, "Because God said to me, 'You are My finger.' So now I must go and touch the man for God."

—Gospel Herald

* * *

The Greater Innovation

Dr. W. D. Robertson was once approached by a lady who objected to any kind of ritual in church service. She said, "I hear that you are introducing some dreadful innovations in your church service." "Indeed," he replied, "what innovations have we introduced?" "Oh," she said, "I hear that you read the Commandments in your service." "Is that all you heard!" Dr. Robertson replied. "We have introduced a far greater innovation than that. We try to keep the Commandments."

—Earnest Worker

* * *

Those Arbitrary Signposts

An elderly minister was once driving along a country road with a young man who liked to argue on matters of religion. The wise old minister listened to him without much comment as the youth expounded his views, merely saying, bluntly, "So you object to the Ten Commandments!" "N-o," stammered the young man; "not their purpose and object, but — well, here's how it is: a fellow hates to have a 'shall' and a 'shan't' flung in his face every minute. They sound so contrary." The minister slowed down the speed of the car as they passed a road sign: then, speeding up again, he suppressed an involuntary smile as they veered off suddenly to the left. A few minutes later the young man caught at his arm. "You've taken the wrong turn," he pointed out; "that signpost we passed said over that way is Holden." "Oh, did it?" returned the other carelessly. "Well, maybe it is a better road, but I hate to be told to

go this way and that by an arbitrary old signpost." The young man laughed, "I get the point!" And they were soon facing the other way and *following directions that experience had proved to be best.*

—Moody Monthly

* * *

Obedience

Mr. Cecil one day went into a room where his little girl was, bright-eyed and happy as could be. Somebody had just given her a box of beautiful beads. The little girl ran to her papa immediately to show this little gift.

"They are very beautiful, my child," he said, "but now my dear, throw them into the fire."

The little girl looked for a moment. It was a great trial. "Now I shall not compel you to do it; I leave it to you: but you never knew Papa to ask you to do a thing that was not kind to you — I cannot tell you why: but if you can trust me, do so."

It cost a great effort, but the little child began in her own way to think — "father has always been kind to me, I suppose it is right," and she took the box and with a great effort threw it into the fire. The father said no more for some time. The next day, however, he gave her something far more beautiful which she had long desired. "Now," said he, "my child, I did this to teach you to trust in that greater Father in Heaven. Many a time in your life He will require you to give up and avoid what you cannot see the reasons for avoiding, but if you trust that Father as you have trusted me, you will always find it best."

—Gospel Herald

* * *

The Authority For Missionary Work

Dr. Robert Wilder who was the founder of the Student Volunteer Movement, a great missionary movement for the recruiting of missionaries in our colleges and universities, some years ago was in India. He walked into the hotel dining room and the only vacant seat was at a table where there was an army major, a naval officer, together with some other subordinate officers, and their wives.

In the course of the conversation the army major spoke up and said: "Well, I don't see why that these missionaries don't stay at home and mind their own business."

Dr. Wilder said: "Major, I want to ask you a question. Suppose that you received, while you are sitting here at this table, orders from your superior officer to proceed to such-and-such a place with the men under your command and to engage such-and-such an enemy in combat. What would you do? Will you sit here at this table? Would you wait? Why are you in India anyhow?"

The Major's eyes flashed fire as he said: "I will have you to know sir, that as a soldier I am subject to the command of my government. And if my government ordered me to take the men under my command to go to a certain place and to engage the enemy, I would do it though it would cost my life and the life of every man under my command."

Dr. Wilder said: "Major, I am a Christian. Jesus Christ is my King. I serve as a citizen of the kingdom of God. My King arose from the dead, and He gave me a Divine commission. That commission was: 'Go therefore and teach all nations.' And Major, that is why I and the missionaries in India are here. minding the business of our King, and serving under the authority of His government."

—Dr. Luther C. Peak, in,
The Evangelist

* * *

"Standing On The Inside!"

A mother repeatedly told her little boy to sit down. The boy continued to stand, disobeying his mother. Finally, the mother went to him, and plopped him down in a chair. Fuming, the boy said, "I may be sitting down on the OUTSIDE, but I am standing on the INSIDE!" How displeasing to God is mere outward obedience, mere outward conformity to His commandments!

—W. B. K.

He Answered the Call

A little Scotch boy was lying one day in the heather beside a mountain stream. He was looking up at the fleecy clouds and soon fell asleep. As he slept he dreamed and this was his dream. He saw above him a glorious light and from it came a wonderful golden chariot drawn by horses of fire. Down the sky it came faster than the lightning and stopped suddenly at his feet, and although he saw no one he heard a voice that was as sweet as the music of the mountain brook and it said to him, "Come up hither, I have work for thee to do."

The lad rose up to follow the golden chariot, but when he stood upon his feet he awoke, and then he knew it was a dream. But God sometimes speaks in dreams, and the boy never forgot that call from the golden chariot, "Come up hither, I have work for thee to do," and in his waking hours he answered the call and found the work.

This is how he answered the call: One day he went to his room and locking the door he kneeled down beside his bed and said to God: "O Lord, Thou knowest that silver and gold to give to the missionary cause I have none; what I have I give unto Thee. I offer myself; wilt Thou accept the gift?" God did accept the gift, and Alexander Duff, the Scotch lad who had heard the voice calling from the golden chariot, found his work, and became one of the greatest preachers of the missionary Gospel the world ever heard, and one of the first and finest missionaries to the great land of India.

—*Wonderful Word*

* * *

"Too Late Now, Father"

During a series of Gospel meetings held in the schoolhouse of a small village a little girl became very concerned about the salvation of her soul.

She and her father lived next door to the school. He was an unbeliever, and hated everything to do with Christ, and strictly forbade his little daughter to attend any more of the meetings.

The poor child was very distressed, and did not know what to do. She obeyed her father until the next meeting was more than half way through, and then, slipping out without his knowledge, she got through a hole in the backyard fence and ran into the meeting.

It was some time before her father missed her, but when he discovered she had gone, he hurriedly went to the meeting, where he found his little girl on her knees with others, for whom the people of God were praying. So enraged was he that he pushed his way forward and lifted her up to take her from the place. As he raised her in his arms she looked up with a smile and said: "It is too late now, Father, I have given my heart to the Saviour."

This was too much for the hardened man. He, too, sank on his knees, while God's children united in prayer, and very soon he found the Saviour whom he had tried so hard to shut out of his own heart and that of his little child.

    —Gospel Stories for the Young

* * *

When Orders Conflict

A young man about to enter the regular army was conversing with an old soldier. The latter had been giving him some strong advice on the subject of obeying orders. "But suppose, General," said the young man, "orders sometimes conflict. What am I to do in a case like that?" "Well, in the first place," replied the old soldier, "they never will. At least, if they emanate from persons who have the right to order. If you find yourself at some time seemingly subject to such conditions, you may depend upon it that there has been a mistake somewhere. In that case, however, the safe way is to find out who the superior is and obey him."

There are a good many times in ordinary life when at first glance orders seem to conflict. In times like this the safe plan is to take the old soldier's advice and obey the superior. You remember that at one time Peter and John were ordered by the magistrate to quit preaching. I have no doubt that under ordinary circumstances these men would have given heed to the voice of the of-

ficers of the law. But in this case there was the order not to speak, from the magistrates, and the order from God to hold not their peace. They settled the matter by obeying the superior Commander.

    —The Lookout

* * *

Using Both Verses —

"Whatsoever" is one of the most precious words in the Bible. In using it God gives us, in many passages, a sweeping assurance. But the word also has challenging obligations. Dr. Glover of the China Inland Mission called attention to a wonderful promise of our Lord to his disciples as he told them that they had not chosen him, but he had chosen them, "that ye should go and bring forth fruit, and that your fruit should remain: that *whatsoever* ye shall ask of the Father in my name, he may give it you." But, Dr. Glover reminded his hearers, there is another "whatsoever" only two verses earlier, and these two "whatsoevers" must be taken together. "Ye are my friends," the Lord said, "if ye do *whatsoever* I command you." We have no right to ask God whatsoever we will unless we are doing whatsoever he commands. When we fulfill the first, he will fulfill the second.

    — Sunday School Times

* * *

Sousa's Unexpected Pupil

You probably have heard played many times "The Stars and Stripes Forever," a spirited march by John Philip Sousa. Sitting in his hotel room one summer evening, Mr. Sousa heard a hand organ man in the street below playing this, his favorite march, in a slow, dragging manner. He dashed to the street. "Here, here," he called to the sleepy, lazy grinder, "that is no way to play that march!" He seized the handle of the organ and turned it vigorously. The music rushed out, spirited and snappy. The hand organ man bowed low and smiled. The next night Mr. Sousa heard the organ again. This time the tempo was right. Looking out the window, he saw a great crowd gathering about the player. Over the organ on a large card was the grinder's name, and under it, "Pupil of John Philip Sousa." The organ grinder was quick to put into practice what he had learned, and he was proud to have learned from such a great teacher. Saul was quick to ask, "Lord, what wilt thou have me to do?" And you — are you ashamed to let it be known that you are a pupil of the Lord Jesus; and do you put into practice the things you learn of Him?

—*Sunday School Times*

* * *

A Telegram Received but Not Sent

Paul Rader had many a talk with a banker in New York, and he would reply that he was too busy for religion. But he overworked and was sent to a sanatorium for a complete rest. One day God spoke to Paul Rader. The message was quite clear, "Go and speak to S—." Rader caught a train, and went with all speed to the sumptuous sanatorium. As he drew near he saw the banker standing in the doorway. "Oh, Rader," he said, "I'm so glad to see you." "I received your telegram," said Rader. "No," said he, "that is impossible. I wrote a telegram begging you to come, but I tore it up. I did not send it." "That may be so," said Mr. Rader, "but your message came by way of Heaven." He found his friend was under deep conviction of sin; and he pointed him to Christ as a perfect Saviour. That man accepted Christ as *his* Saviour, and his heart was filled with joy. "Rader," he said, did you ever see the sky so blue or the grass so green?" "Ah," said Rader, "we sometimes sing:

"Heaven above is softer blue,
   Earth around is sweeter green;
Something lives in every hue
   Christless eyes have never seen."
Suddenly the banker leaned against Mr. Rader and fell into his arms — dead.

—*Pentecostal Evangel*

* * *

Instant Obedience

Two friends were out walking in the mountains. Following hard at the heels of his master was a faithful dog. The dog's ears and eyes were listening and watching for words of command from his master. In conversation, the master began gesticulating. He raised his arm in the direction of a precipice. The faithful dog, thinking that his master was giving a word of command to him, instantly leapt to his death over the precipice! O, that we were as quick to obey our Master's behests!

—W. B. K.

* * *

When They Hear His Voice

During the First World War several Turkish soldiers attempted to drive away a flock of sheep while their shepherd was sleeping. This occurred on a hillside near Jersalem on a warm day. The shepherd was suddenly aroused and saw his sheep being driven off by the Turkish soldiers. This particular shepherd was sympathetic to the British, and, besides, he did not want to lose his sheep. Singlehanded he could not hope to recapture his sheep by force. Suddenly he had an idea. Standing on his side of the ravine, he put his hand to his mouth and gave his own peculiar call to gather his sheep. The sheep heard it, listened for a moment, then hearing the call again they turned and rushed down one side of the ravine and up the other. It was quite impossible for the Turkish soldiers to stop them, and they could not rush down the ravine in headlong fashion. Soon the shepherd escaped with his sheep to a place of safety before the soldiers had decided what to do. Jesus said, "My sheep hear my voice." They may be temporarily deceived by fake leaders, but they will come rushing back to Him.

—Keith L. Brooks, in
Sunday School Times

* * *

Where He Leads Me

A native of the Congo prayed thus: "Dear Lord, you be the needle and I will be the thread. You go first, and I will follow wherever you may lead!"

—*Christian World Facts*

More Important Than A Profit!

The agent of a powerful and wealthy business house saw an opportunity by which he felt sure he could make an enormous profit for the firm, but in order to do so he would be compelled to disobey the explicit directions which had been given him. He disobeyed his orders and carried through a very successful deal, by which his employers won large profits. If he had obeyed his orders he would have lost. Contrary to his expectations, instead of being commended for his shrewdness he was promptly discharged from their employment. God does not demand of us success, but obedience; it is for us to keep his commandments, and he will take care of the results.

—*Sunday School Times*

* * *

Hearing Ears

Before the beginning of an athletic event, awaited by thousands of fans, a little dog strayed from its master onto the field. From the grandstand on one side of the field, one whistled. Presently, many were whistling to the dog from all sides of the field. In the middle of the field, the little dog, filled with confusion and fright, crouched to the ground. Then, a boy at the end of the field put two fingers into his mouth and whistled shrilly and loudly. The little dog, recognizing his master's call amidst the others, leaped to his feet. With ears erect, the dog ran swiftly to its master.

About God's children following their heavenly Master, Jesus said, "My sheep hear My voice and they follow Me." Let us be swift to discern and obey His voice.   —Howard H. Hamlin, M.D.

* * *

"No Flowers, But A Crown"

I said, "Let me walk in the field."
He said, "No; walk in the town."
I said, "There are no flowers there."
He said, "No flowers, but a crown."

I said, "But the skies are black,
There is nothing but noise and din."
And He wept as He sent me back.
"There is more," He said; "there is sin."

I said, "But the air is thick
And fogs are veiling the sun."
He answered, "Yet souls are sick,
And souls in the dark undone."

I said, "I shall miss the light,
And friends will miss me, they say."
He answered, "Choose tonight
If I am to miss you, or they."

I pleaded for time to be given.
He said, "Is it hard to decide?
It will not seem hard in Heaven
To have followed the steps of your Guide."

I cast one look at the fields,
Then set my face to the town;
He said: "My child, do you yield?
Will you leave the flowers for the crown?"

Then into His hand went mine;
And into my heart came He;
And I walk in a light Divine,
The path I had feared to see.

—George McDonald

* * *

The Acid Test of Obedience

Dr. R. A. Torrey said: "One evening I was told that a minister's son was to be present in my congregation, and though he professed to be a Christian, he did not work much at it. I watched for him, and selected the man in the audience who I thought was he, and selected the right man. At the close of the service I hurried to the door by which he would leave, and shook hands with different ones as they passed out. When he came I took his hand and said: 'Good evening! I am glad to see you; are you a friend of Jesus?' 'Yes,' he answered, heartily. 'I consider myself a friend of Jesus.' 'Jesus said,' I replied, " 'Ye are My friends, if ye do whatsoever I command you.' " His eyes fell. 'If those are the conditions, I guess I am not.' I put the same question to you: Are you a friend of Jesus? Are you doing whatsoever He commands you? Are you winning souls as He commands?"

—*Earnest Worker*

442

"Be Ye Doers of the Word"

There is a story of a missionary in Korea who had a visit from a native convert who lived a hundred miles away, and who walked four days to reach the mission station. The pilgrim recited proudly, without a single mistake, the whole of the Sermon on the Mount. The missionary was delighted, but he felt that he ought to warn the man that memorizing was not enough — that it was necessary to practice the words as well as to memorize them.

The Korean's face lit up with happy smiles. "That is the way I learned it," he said. "I tried to memorize it, but it wouldn't stick. So I hit upon this plan — I would memorize a verse and then find a heathen neighbor of mine and practice it on him. Then I found it would stick."

—*Earnest Worker*

* * *

A Deep Lesson

A lady who had been a Christian worker told Dr. Torrey that she could no longer believe in God, because when her husband was ill she had prayed for his recovery, and God had failed her. Dr. Torrey pointed her to I John 3:22, and asked if she were obeying the conditions land down.

"I am afraid I was not," she admitted.

"Then God has not failed you, but you have failed God," said Dr. Torrey.

So completely did the cloud over her life roll away that when the evangelist said, "Let us pray," she was ready to kneel with him and take the whole matter to the Lord.

The great lesson of life is to be subdued before God.

—Rev. John Macbeath

* * *

Implicit Obedience.

Years ago, says Mr. Ridgway, a young machinist applied to us for a job. We were full, but our next-door neighbor, Mr. Worth, was having trouble to get a young man who would do just what he told him to do. I said to Norman, "You go to see Mr. Worth and tell him

I sent you, and you do whatever he tells you to do; don't put up an argument, but jump in the Brandywine if he tells you to. He took my advice, and later Mr. Worth said to me, "Bill, I have got a fellow at last who will do what I tell him to do." Folks said he was advanced because he stood in Mr. Worth's good graces. As I write he has been advanced and has become the best rolling mills manager in the United States and is employed in a consulting capacity by a large steel mill. He has a large estate on the Hudson.

—William H. Ridgway, in
The Sunday School Times

* * *

No Partial Obedience

When Adoniram Judson graduated from college and seminary he received a call from a fashionable church in Boston to become its assistant pastor. Everyone congratulated him. His mother and sister rejoiced that he could live at home with them and do his life work, but Judson shook his head. "My work is not here," he said. "God is calling me beyond the seas. To stay here, even to serve God in His ministry, I feel would be only partial obedience, and I could not be happy in that." Although it cost him a great struggle he left mother and sister to follow the heavenly call. The fashionable church in Boston still stands, rich and strong, but Judson's churches in Burma have fifty thousand converts, and the influence of his consecrated life is felt around the world.

—*Forward*

* * *

Obedience for Our Own Safety

An aviation cadet, on a practice flight, temporarily stricken blind, in panic radioed that message to his control officer. This officer radioed back, "Follow my instructions implicitly." After keeping the blinded cadet circling the field until the whole field was cleared and an ambulance had arrived, the control officer radioed: "Now lose altitude." "Now bank sharply." "You're coming onto the field now." The cadet brought his plane to a perfect landing, was saved, and later his sight returned. All the Lord is asking of us is implicit obedience.

—Tom M. Olson, in
Sunday School Times

* * *

"What You Want Me To Be"

Probably most people think of being some great thing in some high place. But maybe God desires rather that we be a lowly servant in some quiet place. That requires grace too.

A king went into his garden and found to his amazement wilted and dying trees and shrubs and flowers on every hand. Asking the oak the cause of its withering away he was told that it was dying because it could not be tall like the pine. Turning to the pine he found it drooping because it was unable to bear grapes like the vine. And the vine was dying because it could not blossom like the rose. To his surprise he found the hearts ease blooming as fresh as ever. Upon inquiry as to why it was not dying as were the other things around it he received this reply: "I took it for granted that when you planted me you wanted heartsease. If you had desired an oak or a vine or a rose you would have planted such. So I thought since you had put me here I should do the best I can to be what you want. I can be nothing but what I am, but I am trying to be that to the best of my ability." The story goes that that the king was greatly pleased.

—*Presbyterian Advocate*

* * *

"Pleased to Mind"

"I wish I could mind God as my little dog minds me," said a little boy, looking thoughtfully at his shaggy friend; "he always looks so pleased to mind, and I don't." What a painful truth did this child speak! Shall the poor little dog thus readily obey his master, and we rebel against God, who is our Father, our Creator, our Saviour, our Preserver, and the bountiful Giver of everything we love?

—*Sunday School Times*

The Down Road

Jonah not only paid the fare of the ship in which he tried to run away from God, but he also paid the full price of his disobedience. Notice that in his whole career he was going "down." He went "down to Joppa." From the sweet, free highlands, where he walked and talked with God, to the miasma of the lowlands, he went down. He went "down into the ship," and then down into the sea, and then down into the whale, and then, in the whale, down to the very bottom of the great deep! Disobedience to God means always that we go down. "Down" is the key word to every life that flees from God and duty.

—*The Faith*

* * *

A Lad's Obedience

I don't know how many of you have ever read the life of the Duke of Wellington, but I remember reading, on one occasion, in the life of that remarkable man, that the farmers were complaining of the huntsmen galloping over their fields, and they resolved to keep them out. They locked the gates, then posted men and boys at the gates. Up came a member of the Duke of Wellington's hunting party. There stood the little farmer boy. The gentleman said, "Open that gate." "I must not," replied the boy. By that time, up came the Duke himself. The gentleman said, "Your grace, that boy refuses to open the gate." The Duke looked down, and said, "My boy, open it." "I must not." The Duke said, "Do you know who I am?" The little fellow said nervously, "I believe you are Mr. Duke of Wellington." "Won't you open the gate for me?" "My master told me to open it to nobody." The Duke was so pleased with the boy's implicit obedience that he handed him a sovereign, which is equivalent to a five-dollar bill. As the Duke rode away, the little fellow was overjoyed with his present, and sat on the top of the gate waving his cap. He had done what Napoleon and his army could not do; he had kept the Duke of Wellington out of the fields.

—Dr. Dales Ingles, in
Sunday School Times

Zigzagging Tuckered Him Out!

A farmer drove in to town, and was blamed, at the store where he stopped, for tiring his dog all out by permitting him to follow him. The farmer said: "He is not tired out following me, but by his zigzagging. Not an open gate, or a hole in the fence that he didn't run in and explore. It was his zigzagging that tuckered him out." Judah, instead of following God, took an unsteady course, going into open gates of idolatry and gaps of idol worship. That was their undoing.

—Sunday School Times

* * *

Implicit Obedience

One of the finest tributes ever paid to a devoted animal is told in a story by Archibald Rutledge. By chance he came upon a Negro turpentine worker, whose faithful dog had died a few moments earlier in a great forest fire, because he would not desert his master's dinner pail which he had been told to watch. With tears on his face the old Negro said, "I always had to be careful what I tole him to do 'cause I knew he'd do it." Of how many of us, I wonder, could the Lord say such a thing? Love of God makes us obedient unto Him. What He asks, we give. Where he sends us, we go. While He leads, we follow. Love is not cautious; it is ever brave and generous.

—Upper Room

* * *

Ears That Hear Not

A Karen convert, who came to America, was asked to speak in a meeting on the duty of sending the Gospel to the heathen. He hesitated, and asked, "Do they not know that Christ has told them to do it?"

"Yes," was the answer, "but if you will speak to them, the people will be more interested."

"Nay, nay," he replied, "if they do not mind Jesus Christ, they will not mind me."

—Ram's Horn

His Not to Reason Why

It was part of the duty of a sailor on board a British ship of war to test the electrical system by which the commander signaled his orders from the bridge of the engine room. He had written instructions to carry out these tests every time the ship went into or out of the harbor. One day the ship in question was ordered to sea immediately after entering a certain port. Having tested the bells so recently, the young man decided that a further test was not necessary. But "something went wrong" and a collision was narrowly averted. "Did you test the bells?" asked the officer. "No, sir," replied the delinquent, "I thought" — and he got no further. "You are not here to think, sir: that is my business — and for some days the man had leisure to think in. The commanding officer was right, of course. And God has made it His business to do all the thinking necessary.

—Good News

* * *

How to Make $75

Spurgeon once came to Bristol. He was to preach in the three largest Baptist chapels in the city and hoped to collect three hundred pounds needed immediately for his orphanage. He got the money. Retiring to bed on the last night of his visit, Spurgeon heard a voice which to him was the voice of the Lord saying, "Give that three hundred pounds to George Muller." "But, Lord," answered Spurgeon, "I need it for my dear children in London." Again came the word, "Give that three hundred to George Muller." It was only when he had said, "Yes, Lord, I will," that sleep came to him.

The following morning he made his way to Muller's orphanage, and found George Muller on his knees before an open Bible, praying. The famous preacher placed his hand on his shoulder, and said, "George, God has told me to give you this three hundred pounds." "Oh," said Muller, "dear Spurgeon, I have been asking the Lord for that very sum." And those two prayerful men rejoiced together. Spurgeon returned to

London. On his desk a letter awaited him; he opened it; it contained three hundred guineas. "There!" cried he with joy. "The Lord has returned my three hundred pounds, with three hundred shillings interest."

—*Power*

* * *

Sick Sheep

An Englishman who was traveling in Palestine got to Nazareth in the evening when the shepherds were bringing their flocks to water them at the well. When the sheep had their water the shepherds made a call and their sheep followed them. The Englishman asked the shepherds if the sheep always followed their own shepherds when they called them. "Yes," said the shepherd, "except in one condition." "What is that?" "The sheep that do not follow the voice of the shepherd are the sick sheep. If a sheep is healthy it will always follow the shepherd, but if there is something wrong with the sheep, it will follow anybody."

—Dr. W. H. Griffith Thomas

* * *

Going by the Book

A carpenter, when a companion questioned the correctness of some work he was doing upon a building, pulled out a notebook and looked at it. "I am obeying instructions," he said. "I'm not the contractor, and I'm going by the book." But a little later, when he was ridiculing his friend for the latter's refusal to undertake certain work on the Sabbath, he was surprised to receive his own reply: "I am going by the Book. Someone else is responsible for the final outcome; all I have to do is to obey instructions. If that is the safest way to do when you are building a house, it is the safest way to do when you are building a life."

—*King's Business*

Obedience and Illness

Years ago, out in the country, we knew a girl in her teens who had measles in winter-time. She was put to bed, but was not very sick. Her parents had to drive to town on business. They gave her strict orders to stay in bed and keep warm, but left her with some misgivings, for she was a willful child and had never learned to obey. As soon as they were gone she thought of something she wanted from the unheated upstairs, and in spite of what her parents had commanded, she got out of bed and went up in only her night clothes. Several days later we conducted her funeral, for she had contracted pneumonia and died. We recalled the words of a famous children's specialist: "When it comes to serious illness, the child who has been taught to obey stands four times the chance of recovery that the spoiled and undisciplined child does."

—*Sunday School Times*

* * *

Without a Hat

M. J. Preston, speaking of Thomas J. ("Stonewall") Jackson, and the alacrity with which, if once convinced that a thing was right to do, he did it, mentioned an incident personally witnessed, when Jackson received a challenge to his spirit of self-abnegation in these words: "Imagine now that the providence of God seemed to direct you to drop every scheme of life and of personal advancement, and go on a mission to the heart of Africa for the rest of your days: could you go without demur?" His eyes flashed, as he instantly replied, "I could go without my hat!"

—*Golden Rule*

OLD AGE

Life Begins at Seventy

Between the ages of 70 and 83 Commodore Vanderbilt added about 100 million to his fortune.

Kant at 74 wrote his "Anthropology, Metaphysics of Ethics and Strife of the Faculties."

Tintoretto at 74 painted the vast

Paradise canvas 74 feet by 30.

Verdi at 74 produced his masterpiece "Othello;" at 80, "Falstaff" and at 85 the famous "Ave Maria," "Stabat Mater," and "Te Deum."

Lamarck at 78 completed his great zoological work, "The Natural History of the Invertebrates."

Oliver Wendell Holmes at 79 wrote "Over the Teacups."

Cato at 80 began the study of Greek.

Goethe at 80 completed "Faust."

Tennyson at 83 wrote "Crossing the Bar."

Titian at 98 painted his historic picture of the "Battle of Lepanto."

          —The War Cry

* * *

Life

Let me but live my life from year to year
With forward face and unreluctant soul,
Not hastening to, nor turning from, the goal;
Not mourning for the things that disappear
In the dim past, nor holding back in fear
From what the future veils; but with a whole
And happy heart that pays its toll
To Youth and Age, and travels on with cheer:
So let the way wind up the hill or down,
Through rough or smooth, the journey will be joy.
Still seeking what I sought when but a boy
New friendship, high adventure, and a crown,
I shall grow old, but never lose life's zest.
Because the road's last turn will be the best.

          —Henry Van Dyke

* * *

Saved When Sixty!

"Dr. Metts was once preaching at Inverness. The congregation was already gathered, and he was about to enter the pulpit, when word was brought to him that an aged Highlander, who had been converted at sixty and was now eighty, lay dying. The doctor had often wished to hear the story of this man"'s conversion from his own lips, and now was his last opportunity. The man lived close at hand, but here were over one thousand people waiting to hear the Word of God. There were still two or three minutes to spare, and Dr. Metts determined to visit the aged pilgrim. Going in to the Highlander's house, he said, as he pulled out his watch, 'I have just four minutes; do you think you could tell me in that time how you were converted?' 'Oh,' was the cheerful response, 'I can tell you in two. I became anxious about my soul when I was sixty years of age, and the Lord Jesus Christ came along, and said to me, "Sandy, I'll exchange you." "Exchange, Sandy! and what did you give him?' he asked. And Sandy replied, 'I gave him all the years of my sin, and my sinful heart, and he gave me in turn his righteousness.' "

          —Moody Monthly

* * *

What the Centenarians Wanted

For many years the eminent Dr. Sergei Voronoff of Paris devoted himself to studies of the thyroid gland and various other glands, with a view of defeating death. He hinted that when his researches were completed, men could go to the threshold of the great beyond, then retrace their steps and begin all over. This was hailed with joyful interest by many, for it seemed he was doing something colossal for the good of mankind. Yet somehow the thing had an impious aspect, and with a view of testing its esoterics, the London *Sunday Express* took a poll. It sought not out the sages, but the folks directly concerned with it, the centenarians; they, it was reasoned, would know whether it was as great a boon as it seemed. Almost unanimously they replied that they would have none of it. "I want to go home," said one; and another, "It is dusk, and I am glad of it." To this the rest agreed. Dr. Voronoff, having invented a way to play the same record without rewinding, finds that some at least of the guests have walked out on him.   *—New York World*

An Old Man's Memory

Sir George Burns dotted the Atlantic with the first steamships, and, at the age of ninety-four, was knighted by Queen Victoria. "Men say," he wrote about that time, "that mine has been a most prosperous career. It is true, and I am thankful for it. But, looking back upon life as I do now, this reflection gives me no satisfaction: there is nothing in that fact on which I can rest. But when I read, as I have been reading lately, the letters written by myself seventy years ago, and when I find that, even then, I had definitely decided to serve Christ, that knowledge indeed rejoices my heart in my old age."

—F. W. Boreham's
The Crystal Pointers

* * *

Ready for Death

One dare not postpone his preparations for death until the moment of dying, because it may be too late. There is a story told of an old man who lay dying on a dark and stormy night. The relative watching by his side was much distressed, because on such a night she could send for neither doctor nor minister, and she offered to read to him a chapter from the Bible. But the old man was in such sore pain that he could not listen. *"Nae, lassie,"* he said, *"the storm's up noo, but I thatched my hoose in the calm weather!"*

by W. E. Biederwolf
—From *Awake, O America!*

* * *

Approaching Old Age

Helen Keller was once asked this question: "How do you hope to approach old age?" Characteristic of this, one of the world's most famous women, the following classic answer was given:

"You are the first person who has asked me point-blank how I intend to approach old age. I cannot help smiling — I who have these many years declared that there is no age in the spirit! Age seems to me only another physical handicap, and it excites no dread in me.

"Once I had a dear friend of eighty, who impressed upon me the fact that he enjoyed life more than he had done at twenty-five. 'Never count how many years you have, as the French say,' he would insist, 'but how many interests you have. Do not stale your days by taking for granted the people about you, or the things which make up your environment, and you will ever abide in a realm of fadeless beauty.'

"Then and there I resolved, vestal-like to cherish an inextinguishable flame of youth. I have tried to avoid ruts — doing things just because my ancestors did them before me — leaning on the crutches of vicarious opinion — losing my childhood sense of wonderment. I am glad I still have a vivid curiosity about the world I live in.

"Age, I suppose, like blindness, is an individual experience. Everybody discovers its roseate mountain peaks, or its gloomy depths, according to his or her temperament. It is as natural for me, certainly, to believe that the richest harvest of happiness comes with age as that true sight and hearing are within, not without. Confidently I climb the broad stairway that love and faith have built to heights where I shall 'attain to a boundless reach of sky.' "

—*Gospel Herald*

* * *

How Old Are You?

Age is a quality of mind:
If you have left your dream behind,
    If hope is cold,
If you no longer look ahead,
If your ambition fires are dead —
    Then you are old.

But if from life you take the best,
And if in life you keep the jest,
    If love you hold;
No matter how the years go by,
No matter how the birthdays fly,
    You are not old.

—*Selected*

* * *

Best Years!

When I was seventeen, I used to cut timber with my eighty-year-old grandfather, Nathan Hylton. His hair was as thick and white as clean sheep wool. Six feet tall and weighing two hundred pounds, his shoulders were broader than the length of his axe handle. His arms rippled with muscles knottier and harder than the oak we cut. After Grandpa'd get warmed up, he'd work stripped to the waist; many a winter day I've seen sweat run from his face into his beard and freeze into icicles. "Grandpa, when were your best years?" I once asked him as I stopped to get my wind on the other end of the crosscut saw. "Son, they've all been good years," Grandpa said. "But 'spect I was a better man," he went on, taking a firmer grip on the saw handle, "between fifteen and seventy-five."

—Jesse Stuart, in
Reader's Digest

* * *

The Inner Man Shining Through

A friend and I were speaking of a very fine Christian woman whose testimony for Christ is well known. She is a woman of lovely countenance. I remarked to my friend that this lady's face seemed to grow lovelier in her old age. "Oh," said my friend, "that's her 'inner man' shining through."

—*Personal Experience*

* * *

When to Begin the Picture

A young lady who had become worldly and irreligious, bringing much sorrow to her parents, came to her true self at last by the beauty of character displayed by an old lady to whom she was introduced at an evening party. The old lady's upright, graceful carriage and beautiful expression won the admiration of all. As she crossed the room, the young lady said to a friend, "Oh, what a beautiful old lady. What a picture! How I hope I shall be like that when I reach her age." "Yes, my dear," said her friend. "You may be like her if you wish, but if you would paint such a picture as that by and by you must begin mixing the colors now."

—*The (London) Christian Herald*

"It's Hard to Grow Old Alone!"

I once heard a pathetic story about the Danks family — the people who were responsible for giving the old song *Silver Threads among the Gold* to the world. In 1874 Mr. and Mrs. Danks, with their little brood of children, were a most happy and devoted couple. Both were in their early thirties. Mr. Danks was a song writer of growing reputation. They had beautiful dreams of going down the pathway of life and growing old together. It was in this environment that the inspiration for the song came to him. It became his masterpiece. He dedicated it to his wife.

But the bitter irony of the matter is the fact that marital discord came into the Danks' household. Separation followed. Mr. Danks died in 1903. He was found dead kneeling beside his bed. On an old copy of the famous song he had written these words: "It's hard to grow old alone."

—*Gospel Herald*

* * *

Grow Lovely Growing Old!

"Let me grow lovely growing old,
  So many fine things do;
Silks and ivory and gold,
  And laces need not be new.
There is healing in old trees,
  Old streets a glamour hold,
Why not I as well as they
  Grow lovely, growing old?"

—*Selected*

* * *

Secret of Strength

An exchange says: "It is noted that George Muller, though a man always of delicate constitution physically, began evangelistic tours at the age of seventy, involving a period of seventeen years, and of travel aggregating eight times around the world, and he continued to carry much of the responsibilities of the orphanages besides, until beyond the age of ninety. As a young man his frequent and serious illness and general debility had apparently disqualified him from all military duty and many prophesied early death, or hopeless succumbing to disease; yet at the age of ninety-two he is quoted as saying, 'I have been able, every day and all the day, to work, and with that ease as seventy years ago.' He ascribed his marvelous preservation to three causes: (1) The exercising himself to have always a conscience void of offense, both toward God and toward men. (2) To the love he felt for the Scriptures, and the constant recuperative power they exercised upon his whole being (*Prov.* 4:20); and, (3) To the happiness he felt in God and His work, which relieved him of all anxiety and needless wear and tear in his labors.

—*Watchman-Examiner*

* * *

"Eternal Springtime!"

"I have passed through the springtime of life,
I have endured the heat of its summer,
I have culled the fruits of its autumn,
I am now passing through the rigors of its winter.

At no distant day I see the dawn of an Eternal Springtime.
It comes to meet me. I run to embrace it. All, hail!
Eternal Springtime! Hallelujah!"
—Adam Clarke

* * *

The Right Side Is the Bright Side

A minister fell in company with another traveler. They talked together for some time. Finally the stranger remarked to the minister, "Sir, I think you must be on the wrong side of fifty." "On the wrong side of fifty! No, sir, I am on the right side of fifty." "Surely," the traveler said, "you must be turned fifty." "Yes, sir, but on the right side; for every year I live I am nearer my crown of glory." R. F. Horton relates that Fanny Crosby in her illness remarked, "How can anyone call it a dark valley? It is all light and love!" Then stretching her arms out to Christ, she whispered, "I could run to meet Him!"
—*Sunday School Times*

PARENTAL RESPONSIBILITY

The Monkeys Disagree

"Three monkeys sat in a cocoanut tree,
Discussing things that are said to be;
Said one to the other, 'Now listen you two,
There's a certain rumor that can't be true:
That man descended from our noble race,
The very idea is a disgrace!

" 'No monkey ever deserted his wife,
Starved her babies, and ruined her life;
And you've never known a mother monk,
To leave her babies with others to bunk,
Or pass them on from one to the other,
Till they scarcely knew who is their mother.

" 'And another thing you'll never see,
A monk build a fence around a cocoanut tree,
And let the cocoanuts go to waste,
Forbidding all other monks to taste;

Why, if I put a fence around a tree,
Starvation will force you to steal from me!

" 'Here's another thing a monk won't do:
Go out at night and get in a stew,
Or use a gun, club or knife,
To take some other monkey's life!
Yes, man descended, the ornery cuss,
But, brother, he didn"t descend from us!' "

—*Selected.*

* * *

"I Did Like Mother and It Killed Me!"

What imitators are little children! A small girl watched, with absorbing interest, everything which was happening at mother's card party. She observed how mother was dressed; how she dealth the cards; how the women drank cocktails, and how freely they smoked cigarettes! Next day, the little girl gathered her playmates together to "play party." She dressed herself in some of her mother's clothes. Slipping into her mother's room, she got mother's package of cigarettes. Returning to her little playmates, she put a cigarette in her mouth, struck a match, and, in lighting the cigarette, she accidentally ignited the over-size dress she was wearing. Instantly, she became a "human torch!" A few hours later, her little charred body lay still in death! As she died, she gasped, "I did like mother, and it killed me!"

—W. B. K.

* * *

A Father's Neglect

A father took his little child out into the field one Lord's day, and, it being a hot day, he lay down under a beautiful shady tree. The little child ran about gathering wild flowers and little blades of grass, and coming to its father and saying:

"Pretty! Pretty!"

At last the father fell asleep, and while he was sleeping the little child wandered away. When he awoke, his first thought was:

"Where is my child?"

He looked all around, but he could not see him. He shouted at the top of his voice, but all he heard was the echo. Running to a little hill, he looked around and shouted again. No response! Then going to a precipice at some distance, he looked down, and there, upon the rocks and briars, he saw the mangled form of his loved child. He rushed to the spot, took up the lifeless corpse, and hugged it to his bosom, and accused himself of being the murderer of his child. While he was sleeping his child had wandered over the precipice.

I thought as I read that, what a picture of the church of God! How many fathers and mothers, how many Christian men and women, are sleeping now while their children wander over the terrible precipice right into the bottomless pit!

—D. L. Moody

"Tell Dad? Skip It!"

A young man, who had made a sordid mess of his life, listened hungrily to a minister of the Gospel. As the minister spoke glowingly of the gracious Savior, the Mender of broken things, hope began to revive in the soul of the young man. "Possibly I have not gone too far. There may be help for me!" he soliloquized. His interest was sufficiently revived to seek out the minister for a heart-to-heart talk. The minister listened to the youth as he related the story of years of sinful dissipation and wreckless living. When the story was concluded, the minister said to the young man, "Go now, my boy, and tell your Dad all that you have told me!" An almost savage expression lurked about his twitching, insolent, and defiant lips as the young man said, "Tell Dad what I have told you? Why, I would die and go to hell before I would tell Dad one word of what I have told you. Just skip it!"

Confidence between Dad and Lad had been destroyed. We do not know where the blame lay. We do know, however, that when a father becomes so busy that he has little, or no, time to be a companion to his son, heart-breaking sorrow will probably be the portion of both!

—W. B. K.

* * *

Soul Suicide!

In a testimony meeting, a lawyer stood and spoke thus: "I am sixty-two years old. I want to tell you how I became a Christian: When twenty-four, I married a beautiful Christian girl. I was anything but a Christian. I did not believe in anything or anybody. I tried to break my wife's habit of going to church, but could not. In time, God gave us a baby girl. When the child was young, her mother always took her to Sunday school and church. But when she got to be a young woman, I would take her to night clubs, dances. Thus I weaned her away from her mother! A Sunday morning, Mother knocked on her door, pleading, 'Doris, please wake up. Let's go to church.' 'But, Mother, Father didn't bring me in until three o'clock. Let me off this time. Next time I will go with you.' Years passed. The daughter succumbed to pneumonia! 'Your daughter is dying,' said the doctor, 'will you tell her so?' 'Father, I cannot die! I must not die!' Pleading, she said, 'Father, tell me something. Mamma says if I want to go to Heaven, I must take Christ as my Saviour. You told me all I had to do was to be a good girl. Father, which way shall I take? Your's or Mamma's?' Throwing my arms around her, I said, 'Darling, if you have a moment to spare, for God's sake, for Christ's sake, for your own soul's sake, for Father's sake, TAKE MAMMA'S WAY!"

—*Gospel Herald*

* * *

"As Is the Mother, So Is Daughter!"

I have read the words of the prophet Ezekiel: "As is the mother, so is her daughter." . . . However, I realize as never before that bringing children into this life is a challenge that takes all the manhood and womanhood there is in us. To bring an immortal being into existence, neglect it, mistreat it, and permit a soul to drift in this life, go where it will, do what it may, and then stand by and watch it suffer the pangs of careless sowing — this is almost more than sympathetic parents can endure.

—*Christian Digest*

* * *

Parental Consecration

An evangelist was preaching to the Indians. He had made a strong appeal that assistance be given to other Indians, and a collection was to be taken. Through an interpreter he asked them to make the very best gift they had. When the baskets had been passed down the aisle there came to the front a big Indian, his wife walking by his side and a little bit of a boy between them. Securing the attention of the evangelist, the Indian said, "You told us to give the very best we had to God. Our best is not money, but it is this little child." And without the suggestion of a smile he said, "We could not put him into the basket, so we brought him to you. You may take him away if you please, and we will never see him again. Only re-

member he is God's child."

—J. Wilbur Chapman

* * *

Why He Liked Christiana Best

A little boy asked his mother which of the characters in "The Pilgrim's Progress" she liked best. She replied, "Christian, of course; he is the hero of the whole story." Her son said, "I don't, Mother; I like Christiana best, for when Christian went on his pilgrimage he started alone, but when Christiana went she took the children with her."

—*Sunday School Times*

* * *

Early Training

"The place to begin training your child is in the high chair; the electric chair is too late."

—The Hon. Burton Turkus, Assistant Dist. Atty. N. Y.

* * *

Why the Mother Was Converted

"Mother, are you a Christian?" a little girl asked her mother. "No, Fannie, I am not," replied the mother as she turned and walked away. As the little girl ran off to play, she said, "Well, if Mamma isn't a Christian, I don't want to be one!" The child's indicting words went straight to the mother's heart, and she gave herself, in faith, to Christ.

—W. B. K.

* * *

Memory - Making Days

I must move softly, I must keep
　A watch upon my words and ways,
My children are so small, but these
　Are the dear memory-making days —

The days when their young minds will take
　A clear-cut picture of my face;
Some little word I say will make
　An imprint time will not erase.

My hands, swift-moving through the hours;
　My feet that tread their daily round;
My thoughts (God help me) in their hearts
　Through after years will still be found.

I must walk softly, I must keep
A watch on all I do or say.
Perhaps, thus guarded, I shall make
Some lovely memory today.
—Grace Noll Crowell

* * *

"My Brother's Keeper!"

Dr. George W. Truett was pressing the claims of Christ upon a bright young man who was not a Christian. The boy's father, one of the most distinguished physicians of the city, was also out of Christ. The boy well-nigh worshipped his father. After they had talked for a while he turned to the minister and said, "The best man in this city is not a Christian; why should I be?" The pastor said, "Who is that?" The young fellow answered proudly — "My father is the best man who walks the streets of this city, yet he is not a Christian. Why should I be one?" The next day was Sunday. At the earliest possible hour the faithful pastor was in the physician's office with a great burden upon his heart. "Do you know sir that you are keeping some one else out of the kingdom of God?" "What do you mean," said the doctor. "I mean that your boy told me you were the best man in this city, and that as you did not seem to need Christ in order to be saved he did not see why he should." "Did my boy say that?" said the physician earnestly. "He certainly did" was the reply.

"Pastor what is the first service in your church at which I could make a public confession of Christ?" was the instant question of the father. "This morning at ten-thirty," said the pastor. "I have an important operation at that hour and cannot come. What is the next opportunity available?" "This evening at eight o'clock was the reply." "I will be there." At eight o'clock he was on hand. When the hour came for the decision this splendid man arose, deliberately walked down the aisle, and openly accepted Christ as his personal Savior. As he looked around there stood his boy in the midst of the congregation, with upraised hand, signifying his own decision to accept the same Christ. In a few moments he stood by his father in the same place of open confession and salvation. What a joy to that father who had been leading his own loved boy astray through a false door now to turn him to the true and only Door by which men can enter into the Father's House!

—*Christian Index*

* * *

The Boy Who was Not "With" Her

In an afternoon service in a New England city, a woman rose in the crowded church and passed out of the building. The verse, "For how shall I go up to my father, and the lad be not with me?" had just been quoted, and it went like an arrow into her soul, for she had one boy. He was at high school, and she realized that she had never invited him to be a Christian. She went to his school, waited for him to come out, and said to him, "My son, I've just listened to a text of Scripture that has stirred me through and through. It was this: 'How shall I go up to my father, and the lad be not with me?' I am a Christian, and I have never asked you to be one. I could not wait until you reached home." And he did come, for what boy would not come under such circumstances?

—J. Wilbur Chapman

* * *

What Shall It Profit?

A farmer had an only son whose conversion was the subject of daily thought and prayer. The time of the camp meeting came before it was possible to finish the seeding. When the opening day came the farmer hitched up the wagon and invited the family to go to the meeting. "But, Dad," said the boy, "you aren't going to leave the field by the lane unseeded? It will never be in as good form again this season." "The field will have to take its chances," replied the father. "The meeting has first place." The son was soundly converted. Less than a year later he lay dying, and as the father bent over him the boy's arms went around his neck, and, with shining face, he drew him close. "Oh,

Dad," he whispered, "I'm so glad you let the field wait."

—From *Life's Great Adventure — Prayer,* by Solomon Cleaver

* * *

Quaint Idea?

A mother when asked how she was bringing up her children, replied: "Exceptionally well. On Monday they go to the Scouts; Tuesday, music; Wednesday, dancing school; Thursday, elocution; Friday, singing; Saturday, the movies; and when convenient I take them to Sunday school on Sundays." "May I ask," said the visitor, "what you are doing for their souls?" "For their souls," she said laughing. "What a quaint idea!"

No need of the child is more important than his spiritual needs. To lead him to know and love Christ as his Lord and Saviour and to train him in the Christian way of life is the first duty of the home.

—*Gospel Herald*

* * *

"Have You Spent Sleepless Nights Praying for Them?"

It happened in the country in the home of a deacon. Three children had been born to the family, two of them boys who had come to the years of accountability. A preacher who was holding a meeting in the country church, was stopping in this home. One afternoon, when the fires of evangelism had been burning, the mother in this home said to the preacher, "Why are not my boys saved? The children of other homes are being converted by the score. My boys are interested, but I see no tears; I see no evidences of conviction. Tell me why." The preacher said, "Can you stand a little plain talk?" The mother said, "I can," and the preacher said, "Your boys are dry-eyed and unconcerned because their mother is. Did you ever take either of them aside and talk with him about his salvation?" The mother answered, "Never." "Have you spent sleepless nights weeping over their lost condition?" The mother, sobbing, said, "Never." Then the preacher said,

"The boys are unsaved because their mother has no burden for them!" That night was a momentous night in that home. Next morning, at the breakfast table, with sad and tearful face, the mother refused to eat, saying, "All night long I walked the floor and prayed for my boys. My boys are on my heart and I cannot live unless they are saved!" Both boys that very day were born-again into God's family. Said the boys, "Mother, we heard you when you prayed for us last night, and we are saved now in answer to your prayers!"

—L. R. Scarborough

* * *

Importance of Christian Witness in the Home

Dealing one night with an unsaved young man, Billy Sunday asked, "Is your father a Christian?"

"Don't know; he has been a steward in the church for several years."

"Is your mother a Christian?"

"Don't know; she has been the superintendent of the Sunday school of the same church for some time."

"Have you a sister?"

"Yes, sir."

"Is she a Christian?"

"Don't know; she has charge of the primary department in the Sunday school."

"Do your father and mother ever ask the blessing at the table?"

"No, sir."

"Did your father, mother or sister ever ask you to be a Christian?"

"Mr. Sunday, as long as I can remember, my father, mother or sister never said a word to me about my soul. Do you believe they think I am lost?"

How many of our loved ones, or neighbors or friends could justly bring the charge against us, "They don't act as though they believe we are lost"?

—Mrs. A. C. Peck

* * *

The Price

A daughter of wealthy and worldly parents was fond of the world's pleasures and plunged into them with all the eagerness of youth. One day she was persuaded to attend a Gospel service. The message affected her, and it appeared as though she wanted to be saved. Her parents surrounded her with gay companions and urged her to forget "religion," as they termed it, and return to the world of fashion. When they promised and purchased the "richest dress to be had in the shops," she threw off the concern for her soul and lived only for the world again. In a few weeks she was stricken down with a fatal illness. When she was informed that her case was hopeless, she had a maid bring in that beautiful dress and hang it on a post of her bed. Then she had her weeping parents brought in. Raising her hand, she pointed to the dress and said, "Father, Mother, there is *the price of my soul.*" A few hours later, she passed into eternity.

— Tom M. Olson

* * *

How Will Your Children Remember You?

I vividly recall attending a Rotary meeting in Illinois a few years ago with my friend Gypsy Smith. I was sitting next to him at the speaker's table when suddenly just before he arose to speak, he asked me to mark carefully his closing words. When the moment arrived he lifted high his well-worn Bible. "How many of you men can recall a saintly mother and a godly father who loved this Book, read it, lived it, and seeped it into you?" Practically the entire group, with moist eyes, raised their hands. Then, quietly Gypsy swung home deftly this shaft, "With all your influence today, how many of you are so living that your children will remember you for your faithfulness to this same Book?" It was a tense moment. I felt the impact more than Gypsy did, for I knew a few there whose children are today's problem.

— *The Gideon*

* * *

A Babson Observation

Mr. Roger Babson, world-famous statistician and commentator, has declared: 'I have not been able to find a single useful institution which has not been founded by either an intensely religious man, or by a son of a praying father or a praying mother. I have made this statement before the Chamber of Commerce of all the largest cities in the country, and have asked them to bring forward a case that is an exception to this rule. Thus far, I have not heard of a single one."

— *Selected*

* * *

Go With Children to Church

Someone has asked whether children should be forced to go to church. If by that the implication is pure force, we would say no. The Gospel of compulsion has a definite weakness to it. Force usually begets force, its application engenders resistance. Just because a child is the weaker member in the family it must not be intimidated.

The better way is to persuade a child to go; if done in time it rarely fails. The best way is to say, "John, we are all going to church." The precept of example is contagious.

— *The Evangelical Messenger*

* * *

A Plea To Parents

Dr. W. Leon Tucker told this amazing incident: Dr. Percival, a busy surgeon, was a Christian. He had one daughter, Kitty, whom he loved devotedly. One day she came to her father and told him she was going as a missionary to China. He said, "Kitty, I forbid you ever to to out of my sight." At last she gave up plans for going, and married. She had two darling children. I lived next door to Doctor Percival. One day he told me that he had to give up his surgeon's license because of the condition of his eyes. Later he had to have an operation on his eyes. When the bandages were taken from them, his doctor said, "In two weeks you will be totally blind."

Dr. Percival sent for Kitty and the babies to come. He carefully felt their faces and seemed to get a mental picture of them in his finger-tips. He took me out into the light and "looked at his pastor." It was a sad day in our block, and everyone was weeping.

Months later I went out to lunch with Dr. Percival. I had to help feed him. As he walked home I could see that he wanted to say something. "Say it, Doctor," I said. "Dr. Tucker," he said, "do you think that God is retributive?" I told him I did not believe it. He said, "Tucker, I told Kitty that she could never go out of my sight, but God has taken her from my sight. Wherever you go, plead with parents to keep out of the way when God calls their children into His service."

God has a plan and purpose for each life. Do not stand in the way when He calls!

—Wesleyan Methodist

* * *

The Parental Frown

Chief Justice William H. Waste, of the California Supreme Court, does not hesitate to say that there is a rising tide of lawlessness among the youth of today and that the criminal indifference of parents is largely responsible.

He agrees with President Coolidge that "what the youth of the country needs is not more public control through governmental action, but more home control through parental action."

"Through indifference or because of a generous but ill-considered belief in the dangerous doctrine of 'the new freedom,' parents have given over the reins of authority," says the Judge, "And now they watch with consternation the resulting runaway.

"You cannot give youth the reins and say 'Drive!' without inviting a smash. Youth — I am speaking now of immaturity — lacks judgment. It is dominated to a large extent by the physical urge. Without a guiding hand it will run amuck and smash itself. True religion and good citizenship are inseparable. Supplementing the work of the church is the Sunday school. I am sorry that the Sunday school and the church must often do, unaided, what the home should co-operate in doing."

—The Wesleyan Methodist

Mother's Opportunity

"Mother," said a little child, "how old must I be before I can be a Christian?"

And the wise mother answered, "how old will you have to be darling before you can love me?"

"Why, mother I always loved you. I do now, and I always shall," and she kissed her mother; "but you have not told me yet how old I shall have to be!"

The mother made answer with another question, "How old must you be before you can trust yourself wholly to me and to my care?"

"I always did," she answered and kissed her mother again, "but tell me what I want to know," and she climbed into her mother's lap and put her arms about her neck.

The mother again asked: "How old will you have to be before you can do what I want you to do?"

Then the child answered half guessing what her mother meant, "I can now without growing any older."

Then the mother said, "You can be a Christian now, my darling, without being older. All you have to do is to love and trust and try to please the One who says, 'Let the little ones come unto Me.' "

—Gospel Herald

* * *

A Great Responsibility

When J. Wilbur Chapman nodded courteously and tipped his hat to a neighbor and his wife, Chapman's little boy did the same thing with heart-touching gravity. The neighbor reined up the horse, roared with laughter, and said, "Have the little fellow do it again!" Chapman's eyes filled with tears. "Oh, my friend, it's serious with me. He's watching everything I do."

—The Cross and Crown

* * *

The Hog and the Boy

A few years ago people were gathered about a prize hog that was being exhibited at the Dallas Fair. This creature had just been presented with a blue ribbon, his hoofs had been manicured, and his hair looked as if he had just returned from the beauty parlor. The man who bred and raised that creature was surely a success in that particular. But the one who had this hog in charge was a small boy, possibly twelve years of age. He was sallow-faced, hatched-heeled, hollow-chested, and seemed bent on burning up all the cigarettes in the world as soon as possible. The most arresting part of the whole story was this. The owner of the prize hog was the father of the pathetic boy. What was wrong with this father? Not that it was wrong for him to do well in treatment of animals, but he became so interested in them that he was blind to the best for his boy. He fell into the deadly sin of majoring on minor things.

—*The Covenanter Witness*

* * *

A Whole Family in Heaven

Testified Rev. H. W. Frost, former director of China Inland Mission: "Mrs. Frost and I were married in 1883. God gave us seven children. All but one were married, and there were nineteen grandchildren. But the most remarkable thing of all is that each one of the twenty-eight persons mentioned is a professing Christian, including all the grandchildren. May I add that the supreme joy of our earthly lives is found in the assurance that our whole family will be gathered, in time to come, in

Heavenly places and at the feet of Jesus."   —*Alliance Weekly*

* * *

Godly Influence

Eleven children of Andrew Murray, the saint of South Africa, grew to adult life. Five of the six sons became ministers of the Gospel, and four of the daughters became ministers' wives. The next generation had a still more striking record in that ten grandsons became ministers, and thirteen became missionaries.   —*Alliance Weekly*

* * *

What's Your Answer?

Asked a teen-ager of an editor, "Why is it there are some things that are considered all right for adults to do but if teen-agers do the same things they are considered juvenile delinquents? My parents both smoke and sometimes take a drink. If Dad gets mad, he swears. My uncle has been pinched twice for speeding and the family thought it was funny! These are just a few of the things I've been wondering about. If I were to do any of them, I hate to think what my parents would do to me. I am a fifteen-year-old girl. When I asked Mom and Dad this question, they just said, 'It's different when you're grown up.' I can't see that it is." Neither do I!

—**W. B. K.**

PATIENCE

Let The Blessings Ripen

In the charming little booklet, "Expectation Corner," Adam Slowman was led into the Lord's treasure houses, and among other wonders there revealed to him was the "Delayed Blessings Office," where God kept certain things prayed for until the time came to send them. It takes a long time for some petitioners to learn that delays are not denials. Ah, there are secrets of love and wisdom

in the "Delayed Blessings Department" which are little dreamed of. Men would pluck their mercies green when the Lord would have them ripe. "Therefore will the Lord wait, that he may be gracious unto you."

God's plans like lilies pure and white,
  unfold;
We must not tear the close-shut leaves
  apart;
Time will reveal the calyxes of gold.
  —*Sunday School Times*

"Wait on the Lord!"

"Not so in haste, my heart;
Have faith in God and wait;
Although He linger long,
He never comes too late.

"He never comes too late;
He knoweth what is best;
Vex not thyself in vain;
Until He cometh, rest.

"Until He cometh, rest;
Nor grudge the hours that roll;
The feet that wait for God
Are soonest at the goal."
—*Selected*

* * *

From Bulb to Flower

Henry Ward Beecher said: "If my child asks me for a tuberose, though I plant the bulb immediately, and comply with his request at the earliest possible moment, months necessarily elapse before he gets the flower. So our prayers are not answered at once, not because God would tantalize us, but because the things for which we ask are often so large and require such a development, that there is of necessity a space between the asking and the getting."
—*Christian Herald*

* * *

"Where Else Could I Go?"

"My little boy gave me a great awakening," said an intelligent and spiritually-minded mother. "Jimmy is getting to an age when he often wants to try his own way instead of mine. Then he generally meets with a difficulty that hurts his feelings, and he comes at once to me to have things smoothed out. The other day I caught him up pretty sharply and asked him why he came to me, when he got hurt disobeying me. With big eyes filling with tears he looked his astonishment. 'Why, where else will I go?' he asked. That question cut in deep. I assured Jimmy that no matter what he had done he was always to come to me when he needed help. Then when he had gone to his play, I asked the Lord to open my eyes. I was so

458

often careless of His commandments, and when I got into difficulty I couldn't see why the Lord would let His child get hurt. And to whom did I complain? Why, to the Lord Himself. Wasn't that just like Jimmy? But where else could I go? I never before felt so humble, nor so grateful for my Heavenly Father's patience."
—*New Century Sunday School Teachers' Monthly.*

* * *

Willing To Wait

A rare spirit of acquiescence in the divine will was recently displayed by a poor woman in Atlanta, Ga. She was supported entirely by charity. She had scarcely any education, but had learned a lesson many have failed to learn. Having endured great bodily affliction for many years, her disease reached its last stage, and she lay at the point of death for four or five weeks. Every day, and almost every hour, was thought to be her last, but to the astonishment of all she continued to breathe. Her sufferings were very severe, and, knowing her to be ready for the great change, her friends were almost hoping for the moment of release. One of them said to her, "Well, M—, are you ready to go?" "Yes," she said, "ready to go, but willing to wait!"
—*Moody Monthly*

* * *

Patience . . .

You need never to take a step in the dark. If you do, you are sure to make a mistake. Wait, wait, wait till you have light. Remind the Lord Jesus that as He is counsellor to the Church of God, He will be in your particular case Counsellor and Guide, and will direct you. And if you patiently wait, expectantly wait, you will find that the waiting is not in vain, and that the Lord will prove Himself a Counsellor, both wise and good.
—*George Muller*

* * *

Dr. Goforth's Six-Year Wait

Shortly after arrival in China, Jonathan Goforth received the assurance that Changte would be his field. "For six years, however, our faith was sorely tested. Of all places, Changte seemed most determined to keep out the missionary. And there were other difficulties in the way. . . . So for six years the door to Changte remained fast closed. But during all those years Mr. Goforth never once lost sight of God's promise to him, nor failed to believe it. Again and again, when Mr. Goforth and his colleague visited the city, they were mobbed and threatened, the people showing the utmost hostility. But the day came at last, when the long-prayed-for permission from the presbytery to open Changte was granted. The very next morning found Mr. Goforth enroute for Changte, to secure property for a mission site. Often has he told how, all the way over that day to Changte, he prayed the Lord to open the hearts of the people, and make them willing to give him the property most suitable for the work, Within three days of his reaching Changte he had thirty-five offers of property, and was able to secure the very piece of land he had earlier chosen as most ideal for the mission."   —From *How I Know God Answers Prayer,* by Rosalind Goforth

* * *

Wait

Keep still. When trouble is brewing, keep still. When slander is getting on his legs, keep still. When your feelings are hurt, keep still, till you recover from your excitement, at any rate. Things look differently through an unagitated eye. In a commotion, once, I wrote a letter and sent it, and wished I had not. In my later years, I had another commotion, and wrote a long letter! But life had rubbed a little sense into me, and I kept the letter in my pocket against the day when I could look it over without agitation and without tears. I was glad I did. Less and less it seemed necessary to send it. I was not sure it would do any hurt, but in my doubtfulness, I learned reticence, and eventually it was destroyed. Time works wonders. Wait till you speak calmly, and then you will not need to speak, maybe. Silence is the most massive thing conceivable. Often-times, it is strength in very granduer! WAIT!

—Dr. Burton

* * *

Lincoln's Forbearance

A member of Lincoln's cabinet who frequently disagreed with him about his policies was Secretary Stanton, a man of very pronounced views. One day President Lincoln sent a message of state to Secretary Stanton by a page. On reading the message Secretary Stanton, using violent language as he tore up the message, said, "President Lincoln is a fool!" Returning to the President the page told him what Secretary Stanton had said concerning his message and the President himself. Instead of becoming angry, the President, after a moment's thought, said with a grin, *"Well, perhaps Secretary Stanton is right!"* *Because of his greatness of soul and soft answer, Lincoln completely unarmed the man who so frequently opposed him.*

—Gospel Herald

PATRIOTISM — CITIZENSHIP

"Breathes There A Man?"

"Breathes there a man with soul so dead,
Who never to himself hath said:
'This is my own, my native land!'
Whose heart hath ne'er within him burned,
As home his footsteps he hath turned,
From wandering on a foreign strand?

If such there breathe, go, mark him well;
For him no minstrel raptures swell;
High though his titles, proud his name,
Boundless his wealth as wish can claim;
Despite those titles, power, and pelf,
The wretch, concentered all in self,
Living, shall forfeit fair renown,

And, doubly dying, shall go down
To the vile dust from whence he sprung,
Unwept, unhonored, and unsung!"
　　　　　　—Sir Walter Scott

* * *

Christians, Obey the Law!

A student of a Bible institute was travelling on a highway at a terrific rate of speed. Overtaken by a traffic cop, the student was ordered to curb his car. Timely and golden were the words spoken by the officer to the student. On the student's vehicle were printed the words, "Jesus Saves!" Said the officer, "Your wilful violation of the law; your endangering innocent lives, as well as your own, by the illegal and dangerous speed at which you were travelling, is greatly at variance with the words printed on your car, and brings no honor to the One of whom your motto speaks!"
　　　　　　　　　　—W. B. K.

* * *

The Nation's Strength

I know three things must always be
To keep a nation strong and free.
One is a hearthstone bright and dear,
With busy, happy loved ones near.
One is a ready heart and hand
To love, and serve, and keep the land.
One is a worn and beaten way
To where the people go to pray.
So long as these are kept alive,
Nation and people will survive.
God keep them always, everywhere:
The hearth, the flag, the place of prayer.
　　　　　　　　　—Selected

* * *

"Put Only Americans On Guard To-Night!"

We Americans want leadership that can be trusted, such as we had from General Washington — leadership that is both truthful and trustworthy. When the little and ragged American army was in places of great danger, General Washington gave instructions: "Put only Americans on guard tonight!" That counsel is as sound today as it was then; and the issues at stake are

infinitely larger than even those of 1776.
　　　　—Dr. Victor Raymond Edman,
　　　　President, Wheaton College, in,
　　　　Bulletin of Wheaton College.

* * *

"If They Slip Too Far, the Light Will Go Out of America!"

"The 'New Order,' 'New Freedom,' 'New Day,' 'New Outlook,' 'New Epoch,' 'New Economy,' 'New Deal,' 'New Religion,' 'New Liberalism,' 'New War,' 'New Policy.' We have overworked this word 'NEW' in trying to get out of misery from our 37 years of hot and cold wars, with intervals of hot and cold peace. The practical thing, if we want to make the world over, is to try out the word 'OLD' for awhile. Some OLD THINGS made this country. Some OLD THINGS are slipping. If they slip too far, THE LIGHT WILL GO OUT OF AMERICA! OLD virtues, religious faith, whole truth, integrity, honor in public office, economy in government, individual liberty, willingness to sacrifice. We have a CANCEROUS GROWTH of intellectual dishonesty in public life mostly beyond law. Our great danger is suicide by complaisance with evil!"
　　　　　　—Herbert Hoover, in
　　　　　　　　Headlines

* * *

Lincoln's Bible

Abraham Lincoln's well-thumbed Bible in the Lincoln Museum in Washington, among other things, would abundantly prove that he was a Christian. Listen to him, as on his way to be inaugurated, he utters these impressive words:

"I go to assume a task more difficult than that which has devolved upon any other man since the days of Washington. He never would have succeeded but for the aid of Divine Providence, upon which he at all times relied. I feel that I cannot succeed without the same divine blessing which sustained him, and on the same Almighty Being I place my reliance for support. And I hope you, my friends, will all pray that I may receive the divine assistance without which I cannot succeed, but with which success is certain."

—*Moody Monthly*

* * *

Why Washington Succeeded

You may read in your United States history how George Washington found rest and relief in prayer during the trying times he and his soldiers passed through at Valley Forge. With all the cares and anxieties of that time upon him, he used to have recourse to prayer. One day a farmer approaching the camp heard an earnest voice. On coming nearer, he saw George Washington on his knees, his cheeks wet with tears, praying to God. The farmer returned home and said to his wife: "George Washington will succeed! George Washington will succeed! The Americans will secure their independence!"

"What makes you think so, Isaac?" asked his wife.

The farmer replied: "I heard him pray, Hannah, out in the woods today, and the Lord will surely hear his prayer. He will, Hannah; thee may rest assured He will."

—*Sunday School Times*

* * *

Old Glory

Here's to the Red of it;
There's not a thread of it,
No, nor a shred of it
In all the spread of it
    From foot to head,
But heroes bled for it,
Faced steel and lead for it,
Precious blood was shed for it,
    Bathing it Red.

Here's to the White of it,
Thrilled by the sight of it
Who knows the right of it,
But feels the might of it
    Through day and night;
Womanhood's care for it
Made manhood dare for it;
Purity's pray'r for it
    Kept it so White.

Here's to the Blue of it;
Heavenly view of it,
Star-spangled hue of it,
Honesty's due of it,
    Constant and true.
Here's to the whole of it,
Stars, stripes, and pole of it;
Here's to the soul of it;
    Red, White, and Blue.

—*Selected*

* * *

A Dangerous Omission

The closing part of Lincoln's famous Gettysburg address, reading, "We here highly resolve that these dead shall not have died in vain; that this nation, under God, shall have a new birth of freedom, and that government of the people, by the people, and for the people, shall not perish from the earth," is a wonderful ideal, but are we not in danger of omitting those two vital words, "under God"? "Government of the people, by the people, and for the people" may be little more than a form of tyranny, but government of the people for the people *under God*, is a form of government that honors God, that submits to His righteous rule, and that is exalted thereby.

—*Christian Herald*

* * *

From a Child's Lips

A teacher of children had told them that daddies sometimes allow them to take the wheel of the car, but they always place their hands over their little ones to be sure there will be no mistake. Sometime afterward, a little fellow, eight years old, was asked if he would like to lead in prayer. This is what he said: "Dear Lord, will you please put your hands over the hands of our President, so he will know how to turn the wheel for our country."

—*Sunday School Times*

* * *

"Your Flag — My Flag!"

"Your flag and my flag,
And how it flies today,
In your land and my land,
And half a world away!

Rose-red and blood-red,
Its stripes forever gleam,
Snow-white and soul-white —
The good fore-father's dream.
Sky-blue and true-blue,
With stars that gleam aright —
The glorious guide of the day,
A shelter through the night!

Your flag and my flag
To every star and stripe,
The drum beats, as hearts beat,
And fifers shrilly pipe.
Your flag and my flag,
A blessing in the sky,
Your hope and my hope,
It never hid a lie.
Home-land and far-land,
And half the world around,
Old Glory hears our glad salute,
And ripples to the sound.

Your flag and my flag,
And, oh, how much it holds —
Your land and my land,
Secure within its fold!
Your heart and my heart
Beat quicker at the sight,
Sun-kissed and wind-tossed, —
The red, and blue, and white.
The one flag, the great flag,
The flag for me and you
Glorified all else beside —
The red, the white, the blue!"

—Wilbur D. Nesbit

* * *

Different Motive

Roger Babson, the statistician, was lunching with the President of Argentina. "Mr. Babson," the President said, "I have been wondering why it is that South America with all its natural advantages, its mines of iron, copper, coal, silver and gold; its rivers and great waterfalls which rival Niagara, is so far behind North America.'"

Babson replied, "Well, Mr. President, what do you think is the reason?"

He was silent for a while before he answered. "I have come to this conclusion. South America was settled by the Spanish, who came to South America in search of gold; but North America was

settled by the Pilgrim Fathers, who went there in search of God."
—*Christian Digest*

* * *

Washington at Valley Forge

The sun went down o'er Valley Forge
In the cheerless wintry air;
Day after day the sun went down,
And no man seemed to care;
For day and night alike were fraught
With suffering and disease —
Yet one man rose, when the camp was still,
And went out under the trees.

His heart was heavy, his burden great;
He thought of his hungry men;
He thought of the torn, distracted land
That longed for peace again.
And then he knelt and prayed — but not
To the gods of wood or stone:
He prayed to the God of truth and right,
There under the trees alone.

The stars seemed nearer than before:
A friendlier light they shed;
Great branches like protecting arms
Were stretched above his head;
Something the spirit of earth and air
Whispered in gentle tone —
As the father of his country knelt
There under the trees alone.

When morning came, and, as his wont,
He passed from place to place,
They wondered at the look serene
They saw upon his face.
"What keeps the General's courage up
In doleful days like these?"
They asked, because they did not know
What happened under the trees.
—Samuel Valentine Cole, in
Congregationalist

* * *

The Greatness of America

De Tocqueville of France, over a hundred years ago, visited America. Upon his return home he wrote: "I sought for the greatness of America in her harbors and rivers and fertile fields, and her mines and commerce. It was not there. Not until I went into the churches and heard her pulpits flame with righteousness did I understand the greatness of her power. America is great because she is good; and if America ever ceases to be good, America will cease to be great."

—*Selected*

* * *

MacArthur Is Right!

General Douglas MacArthur, recognizing a spiritual awakening as imperative, says, as quoted by *Moody Monthly*: "History fails to record a single precedent in which nations subject to moral decay have not passed into political and economic decline. There has been either a spiritual awakening to overcome the moral lapse, or a progressive deterioration leading to ultimate national disaster."

—*Prairie Overcomer*

* * *

"Give Me Your Huddled Masses!"

The following words are carved in stone at the base of the Statue of Liberty:
Give Me Your Tired, Your Poor,
Your Huddled Masses Yearning to Breathe Free,
The Wretched Refuse of Your Teeming Shore.
Send These, the Homeless, Tempest-tossed to Me.
I Lift My Lamp Beside the Golden Door.

—Written by a Jewish refugee from Europe.

* * *

"Mothers, Lord, Who Bend the Knee!"

Because we love our country, Lord,
And do revere Thy precious Word;
Because all nations are distressed
And men and women sore perplexed —
Bring back, O God, we pray to Thee,
The mothers, Lord, who bend the knee.

The mothers, Lord, whose lives do shine
With noble deeds, with thoughts sublime;

Who teach their sons to fear Thy Name,
And never stoop to things of shame —
O God on high, we ask of Thee:
Send mothers, Lord, who bend the knee.
—*Walter J. Kuhn*, in
Gospel Herald

* * *

"Only Way Out Is Up!"

On a gray morning during World War One, the Prime Minister of Britain, David Lloyd George, stood grim-visaged before his compeers, members of the British Cabinet. The seriousness of the situation was evident upon the faces of all. Said David Lloyd George, "Gentlemen, we are fighting with our backs to the wall. The only way out is up; our only hope is God; let us pray!" When nations thus turn to God in their trouble, deliverance is not distant.

—*W. B. K.*

* * *

Lincoln's Concern

One day when the Civil War was raging its worst, a minister said to Lincoln, "I surely hope the Lord is on our side." To which Lincoln replied, "I am not at all concerned about that, for I know that the Lord is always on the side of the right; but it is my constant anxiety and prayer that I and this nation should be on the Lord's side."

—*Baptist Standard*

* * *

"Lord, Teach America to Pray!"

And as her flag unfurls on high
Its starry splendor to the sky,
May we, in grateful thanks to Thee
Who gave to us this land so free,
Preserve her freedom in Thy way.
Lord, teach America to pray!

May our good land be true and just,
Her motto e'er "In God We Trust."
May she be guided by Thy Word,
Thy wisdom in her halls be heard.
May all who love her plead today,
Lord, teach America to pray!

—*Selected*

PEACE AND PEACEMAKERS

How He Got Through

A certain mountain in West Africa was held by a tribe of cannibals as their stronghold. Troops had tried to cross the mountain, but had failed. One day a missionary went alone into the enemy's country, calmly climbed the mountain, and reached the other side. Later, he met the captain of the troops. "Do you mean to tell me you have got through untouched?" he said. "How did you do it?" Said the missionary, "You went as men of war; I went as a man of peace."

—*Sunday Companion*

* * *

WANTED: Peace-Takers, Not Peace-Makers:

Now what God seeks is
Peace TAKERS — not peace makers.
Peace has been made, and God is "preaching peace by Jesus Christ" (*Acts* 10:36). And the question is, Will men give up trying to *make* peace, and come as broken-hearted penitents and *accept* the peace made; or, will they continue in unbelief and perish forever? Reader, which will *you* do?

—*Messenger of Peace*

* * *

His Last Word

A young man working on the Limehouse Docks once heard a clergyman named Henderson preach from the text: "Being justified by faith, we have peace with God through our Lord Jesus Christ." Being impressed, he had a conversation afterward in the vestry. Next day he sailed on the steamship *London*, which became a total wreck. Months passed, and a sailor came to the clergyman and said, "Are you Mr. Henderson?" "Yes, I am." "Then," he replied, "I come to you with a message from the dead. I talked and prayed with a young man on board the *London* who had heard you preach from the text, 'Being justified by faith, we have peace with God through our Lord Jesus Christ.' He was in earnest, but he did not seem

to get into the light until a few minutes before the wreck. He and I were told to launch one of the boats and to help man her. While doing so, he said to me, 'Mate, if you get to shore, be sure to tell Mr. Henderson that it's all right; being justified by faith, I have peace with God.' By some accident he failed to reach the boat when the rowers had to pull for their lives from the settling ship. The last thing I saw of that lad he was up in the rigging, waving his hat, and shouting across the waters, 'Being justified by faith, we have peace with God through our Lord Jesus Christ.'" Friend, you may be nearer your wreck than you know.

—*The Dawn*

* * *

Premises Occupied:

A much-beloved man, a leader in a little community of Christian students, lived such a life of serenity and peace that all his student-companions wondered. At length they determined to approach him and ask to be told the secret of his calm. They said: "We are harassed by many temptations, which appeal to us so often and so strongly that they give us no rest. You seem to live untroubled by these things, and we want to know your secret. Don't the temptations that harass our souls come knocking at the door of your heart?" He replied: "My children, I do know something of the things of which you speak. The temptations that trouble you do come, making their appeal to me. But, when they knock at the door of my heart, I answer, 'The place is occupied.'"

—*Methodist Recorder*

* * *

The Old Scotch Elder's Comfort

An old Scotch elder lay dying. One of his friends drew near to the dying saint and asked him, "Weel, Jamie, how lang since is it that ye made yer peace wi' God?" The aged saint said, "Weel, Robin, to tell the truth, I never made my peace wi' God." "But, Jamie, ye ken what I mean — how lang since ye sought and found God?" Again he said, "Oh, Robin, Robin, I never sought and found Him." Then the friend said, "Oh, his mind is gane, and he will never recognize us again." But the old saint opened his lips and said, "Listen! Not I — not I — I never sought Him.

" 'Jesus sought me when a stranger,
Wandering from the fold of God;
He, to rescue me from danger,
Interposed His precious blood.' "
—*Moody Monthly*

* * *

Blowing One's Top!
Keep your temper! Nobody else wants it! When under fire, how easy it is to give offending ones a piece of our minds, which results in our losing our own peace of mind.
—W. B. K.

* * *

The Peace of God
How many thousands of lips have lingered lovingly over those sweet, strong words: "The peace of God, which passeth all understanding, shall guard your hearts and your thoughts in Christ Jesus" (Phil. 4:7, R. V.).

It is God's peace. It acts as an armed guard drawn up around heart and thoughts to keep unrest out. It is too subtle for intellectual analysis, but it steals into and steadies the heart. You cannot understand it, but you can feel it. You cannot get hold of it with your head, but you can with your heart. You do not get it. It gets you. *You need not understand in order to experience. Blessed are they that have not understood and yet have yielded and experienced.*
—S. D. Gordon

* * *

Need Peace of Mind?
Here's How to Get It!
Clark H., 42, is a prominent judge. He said:

"It seems to me that people have more mental disorders today. Or is it just that I have my attention focussed on such things?" he inquired.

"What would you advise as the best way to eliminate psychiatric problems?"

Here's Dr. Crane's answer:

"There would be much less strain on men and women if they teamed up with God as a daily partner. Indeed, in that event, psychiatry would almost pass out of existence.

People who try to live independently and ignore God, are soon overwhelmed with innumerable fears and worries.

They become the typical hypochondriacs, always fretting about gall bladder or ulcer or appendix or impending cancer or insanity.

If more people learned to team up with God, the human race would soon be able to throw off the 50 per cent of its ailments that medical educators admit are psychological."
—Dr. George W. Crane, in,
Chicago Daily News

* * *

"Kept in Perfect Peace"
"Thou wilt keep him in perfect peace
Whose mind is stayed on thee."
I read the dear old promise o'er,
And ask, "Is this for me?"
When troubles throng without surcease,
Can God keep me in perfect peace?

"In perfect peace," when seas run high,
When loud the cutting blast?
When laid upon a bed of pain?
When tears are falling fast?
If Satan all his pow'r release,
Can God still keep in perfect peace?

Yet I recall that far-off night,
Upon a storm-swept sea,
When urgent cries for succor came
From men in jeopardy —
How, instantly, the waves were still
In swift obedience to His will.

O mighty Master of the sea,
Thou art my Master, too!
And Thou, all things, unto Thyself
Art able to subdue —
Thou biddest inner tumult cease;
Thou keepest me "in perfect peace."

—T. O. Chisholm, in
Sunday School Times

How To Prevent A Quarrel

For years two monks lived together in concord and amity. The monotony of their manner of life finally moved one of them to say, "Let us get out of the groove of our humdrum round of daily tasks and do something different — let us do as the world does." Having lived the sequestered life so long, the monk inquired, "What does the world without do?" "Well, for one thing, the world quarrels." Having lived together so long in the bondage of a holy love, he had forgotten how to quarrel, so he queried, "How does the world quarrel?" So the other monk replied, "See that stone. Place it between us and say, 'The stone is mine.' " Willing to accommodate his friend, he said, "The stone is mine." Pausing for reflection and feeling the compulsion of their years of friendship, the monk who suggested the quarrel concluded, "Well, brother, *if the stone is thine, keep it.*" And thus ended the quarrel.

—John R. Riebe

* * *

"Thy Still Dews of Quietness!"

"Drop Thy still dews of quietness,
 Till all our strivings cease;
Take from our souls the strain and
 stress;
 And let our ordered lives confess
The beauty of Thy peace."

—John G. Whittier

* * *

Peace on Earth

Peace on earth, with a world at war?
O what were the angels singing for
That far-away night when the Star
 shown down
With a glorious light on Bethlehem's
 town?

Peace on earth! They were singing of
 Him
Who was born that night to redeem
 from sin;
Who still has the power to cleanse and
 to heal
The contrite heart who is willing to
 kneel.

Peace on earth, amid sorrow and loss?
Yes, peace indeed, at the foot of the
 cross!
Peace in a world that is troubled and
 torn,
Peace in each heart where the Saviour
 is born.

Peace on earth, while the nations rage?
And history is making its darkest page?
Yes, peace on earth, for its steadfast
 light
Is burning in thousands of hearts to-
 night!

—A. H. M.

* * *

Why He Had No Peace

An evangelist preaching in one of our cities became interested in a man in the community of whom he had heard. This man was present at his first two services, and then he disappeared. For three nights he was absent, and then on the sixth he was in his place again. after the service he came up and asked if he could walk home with the evangelist. Then he told his story. Many years before he had wronged one of his best friends. His sin lay like lead on his conscience all those years. In spite of everything he could do he was not able to forget it. The second night he had heard the evangelist say, "God can never give peace to any man who has unrepented sin on his soul." "I heard you say those words," he said, "and I went home afterward. But I could not sleep. I arose in the morning and took a train for the distant city where lived the man I had wronged. I did what I could to make right the evil I had done. That night I had the first night of real peace I have known for years. Yes, I know from awful experience that there is no peace for one who has unrepented sin on his soul."

—*Presbyterian*

* * *

Programme for Peace

Lord make me the instrument of Your
 peace,
Where there is hatred may I bring love,
Where there is malice, pardon,
Where there is discord, harmony,

Where there is error, truth,
Where there is doubt, faith,
Where there is despair, hope,
Where there is darkness, Your light,
Where there is sadness may I bring joy.
Oh Master may I seek not so much,
To be comforted as to comfort,
To be understood as to understand,
To be loved as to love,
For it is in giving that we receive,
It is in losing our lives that we shall
    find them,
It is in forgiving that we shall be
    forgiven,
It is in dying that we shall rise up to
    eternal life.

—Selected

* * *

How to Have Peace

The Chinese have a good proverb, and
it is corroborated by James 4:1. "If
there is righteousness in the heart,
there will be beauty in the character. If
there be beauty in the character, there
will be harmony in the home. If there
be harmony in the home, there will be
order in the nation. When there is order
in the nation, there will be peace in the
world."

—Power

* * *

Open Door to Christ!

Jesus brings music along with the
feast. His coming brings Heavenly music. Next to the Cremona violins, those
made by Jacob Stainer, in the Tyrol, in
the early part of the seventeenth century, are considered the best in the
world, and bring fabulous prices when
one of them is on the market. One of
these instruments was sold in 1791 under strange conditions. A German
Count had heard a gifted musician play
upon a Cremona violin of unusual value,
and spared no pains to secure the instrument for himself. He offered enormous sums; but Alessi, the great violinist, said he would sooner sell his
life. The rumor of the Count's attempt
to get the Cremona went abroad, and
some weeks later an unknown old man
appeared at the castle door with a worn
and shabby violin case under his arm.
The servants refused to admit him.

"Tell your master," he said to them,
"that Heaven's music is waiting at his
door."

The Count received him. The old man
drew from the unworthy case a perfect
instrument, the work of Jacob Stainer's
own hand, and played it so marvelously
that the Count and his people forgot all
about the Cremona. The old man would
only sell his instrument on condition
that he might pass the rest of his life
in the same house with it and play it
once daily. And the Count bought it on
those terms. Touching this incident Dr.
Howard Banks made the comment: "The
melodies of Divine peace can only be
heard in your soul by your opening the
door to Christ, who will come in and
dwell in your heart and daily sweeten
your life with the music of the skies."

—Gospel Herald

* * *

Perfect Peace . . .

I look not back — God knows the fruit-
    less efforts,
The wasted hours, the sinning and re-
    grets;
I leave them all with Him that blots the
    record,
And graciously forgives, and then for-
    gets.

I look not forward — God sees all the
    future,
The road thats short or long, will lead
    me home;
And He will face with me its every trial,
And bear for me the burden that may
    come.

I look not around me — then would
    fears assail me,
So wild the tumult of life's restless sea;
So dark the world, so filled with war
    and evil,
So vain the hope of comfort and of ease.

I look not inward — that would make
    me wretched,
For I have naught on which to stay my
    trust;
Nothing I see but failures and short-
    comings,
And weak endeavors crumbling into
    dust.

But I look up — up into the face of
Jesus!
For there my heart can rest, my fears
are stilled;
And perfect peace, and every hope ful-
for darkness,
And there is joy, and love, and light
filled.

—*Selected*

* * *

Which Were Surprised?

An early American painting shows
the interior of a Quaker meetinghouse.
The simple folk are gathered quietly
waiting for the "presence in the midst."
The door of the meetinghouse has been
pushed open, and there, cautiously entering, are some Indians. Crowding behind them are still more outside. Only
the surprised look of one little girl in
the meeting indicates that anyone is
aware of this intrusion. Indeed, she
would not have considered it intrusion.
The picture is called, "None Shall Make
Them Afraid." This is a picture of an
actual incident in a little Quaker meeting in New York State. The rest of the
story, not shown by the picture, tells
how after meeting was over the Quakers
invited the Indians to go home with
them. The Indians told how they had
crept up to the meetinghouse, cautiously
pushing the door, curious about the
people sitting so quietly, and looking
carefully to see if guns had been stacked
in the corner. Seeing none, they had
said to one another, "These people trust
the Great Spirit." And they did them no
harm.

—*Women's Missionary Magazine*

* * *

A Wise Lad

In his home a pastor was counseling
privately with a man. They heard the
patter of feet. The closed door opened. A
little boy entered the room. The man
turned toward the boy and asked him
a question: "Son, suppose your dad and
mamma would quarrel, what would you
do? Would you, with your mamma fight
against your dad; or would you help
your dad against your mamma?"

After a moment's silence, the following thoughtful answer came from
the son of the pastor: "I would not side
with either. I would stay in between
and try to stop their fighting."

—*Christian Index*

* * *

"Peace Has Been Declared!"

Dr. Dixon tells about a friend of his
who, two years after the Civil War,
went into the mountains of North Carolina to spend a few weeks of his summer vacation. He climbed the mountain
and descended the other side into the
densest valley, and to his surprise
stumbled upon a little cottage, swept
about by a few acres of cultivated land.
On his approach the door was barred
against him. Only after much pleading
was it opened. He found two men living there, who had been its occupants
for nearly three years. They had deserted from the Confederate army, built
themselves a cottage and raised from
the soil enough for the necessities of
life, ever keeping an open eye against
the conscription officers. The war had
now been over for two years; peace had
long since been declared, but they had
not heard it. Your peace has been declared much longer. Have you appropriated it?

—*Dr. W. B. Riley*

* * *

"Peace Where There Is No Peace"

"I know a peace where there is no peace,
    A calm when the wild winds blow;
A secret place, where face to face,
    With the Master I may go.
And I find I'm strong, tho' the days be
        long,
    And sorry the winds may blow,
When I seek the face in that secret place
    Of the Master whom I know.

"Oh, tell me why as the days go by
    And the wild winds blow defeat,
That I do not go to this place I know,
    This place of sure retreat —
This secret place, where face to face,
    The soul and the Master meet."

—*Selected*

God's Peace

We bless Thee for Thy peace, O God,
Deep as th' unfathomed sea,
Which falls like sunshine on the road
Of those who trust in Thee.

That peace which suffers and is strong,
Trusts where it cannot see,
Deems not the trialway too long,
But leaves the end with Thee;

That peace which flows serene and deep,
A river in the soul,
Whose banks a living verdure keep,
God's sunshine o'er the whole.
                            —*Youth's Comrade*

Disappointing the Prosecution

A man bought a farm, and soon after he met his nearest neighbor. "Have you bought this place?" asked the neighbor. "Yes." "Well, you've bought a lawsuit." "How is that?" "Well, sir, I claim your fence line is ten feet on my side, and I am going to take the matter to the court and prove it." The newcomer said, "Oh! don't do that. If the fence is on your side of the line we will just take it up and move it back." "Do you mean it?" "Of course I do," was the answer. "Well," said the man, "that fence stays just where it is."
                            —*Christian Herald*

PERSEVERANCE

When Game Is Hardest

"On the gridiron, on the diamond,
On the link, or on the court,
It's when the game is hardest,
That you get your finest sport!
There's no joy in easy battles,
And no victory in a game,
That is won without a struggle,
And in life, it's just the same!
It is when the going is heavy,
And the pull is all uphill,
And you have to work to conquer,
That you get your finest thrill!"
                            —*Selected*

* * *

There Was One Who Bore All.

A minister, was so harassed by members of his church, and so sharply criticized that he went to his bishop telling him it could no longer be endured, and he would resign. To his surprise the bishop said, "Do your people ever spit in your face?" "No, of course not," he replied. "Do they ever smite you?" "No." "Have they dressed you up, mocked, and befooled you?" "No," he said. "Have they stripped and scourged you, crowned you with thorns — cruci — ?" The minister interposed his reply, "No, God helping me, until they do, I'll hold on."
                            —*Westminster Quarterly*

Perseverance Wins!

Successful men owe more to their *perseverance* than to their natural powers. Gibbon labored twenty years on his *Decline and Fall of the Roman Empire*. George Bancroft spent twenty-six years on his *History* of the United States. When someone asked Lyman Beecher how long it took for the completion of his famous sermon, *The Government of God*, he replied: "About forty years." Everyone admires a determined, persistent man. Marcus Mortan ran sixteen times for the governorship of Massachusetts. At last he was elected by a close majority — a single vote. Such persistence always triumphs in the end.
                            —Nolbert Hunt Quayle, in
                            Alliance Weekly

* * *

Cedar Christians

Jesus, help me to be for Thee,
Just like a big, strong cedar tree;
When all the other trees are bare,
The cedar stands so green and fair,
The wind and storm, the ice and cold
Make it more beauty to unfold,
So I would stand in trial and test,
Just trusting You to do what's best,
Though others fail, Lord, keep Thou me!
May I a cedar Christian be!"
                            —*Selected*

Blessing Brought By Difficulty

Lord Kelvin on one occasion when he was lecturing to his students and an experiment failed to "come off" said, "Gentlemen, *when you are face to face with a difficulty, you are up against a discovery.*" This observation has pertinence quite as much in the spiritual realm as in the scientific field.

—*Moody Monthly*

* * *

Walking With God

Who walks with God must take His way
Across far distances and gray
To goals that others do not see,
Where others do not care to be.
Who walks with God must have no fear
When danger and defeat appear,
Nor stop when every hope seems gone,
For God, our God, moves ever on.

Who walks with God must press ahead
When sun or cloud is overhead,
When all the waiting thousands cheer,
Or when they only stop to sneer;
When all the challenge leaves the hours
And naught is left but jaded powers.
But he will some day reach the dawn,
For God, our God, moves ever on.

—*Western Christian Advocate*

* * *

"Keep On Praying!"

"Though the foe of right oppress,
  Keep on praying;
God is ever near to bless,
  Keep on praying;
Let not fear your heart appall,
Naught of evil can befall,
Stronger is your God than all.
  Keep on praying.

"Pilgrim, have you weary grown?
  Keep on praying;
God is still upon the throne,
  Keep on praying;
He will hear your faithful cry,
He to help is ever nigh,
You shall conquer by and by,
  Keep on praying.

"Christian, has your faith grown weak?
  Keep on praying,
Do the tears roll down your cheek?
  Keep on praying,

Soon you nevermore will sigh,
Tears no more shall dim your eye,
Pray to Him who's ever nigh,
  Keep on praying."

—R. A. Smith, in
Gospel Herald

* * *

"Stedfast, Unmovable"

Tenacity of purpose and tenderness can live in the same heart. Both are good qualities, and when they are controlled by the grace of God one will not drive out the other. Robert Morrison, the first Protestant missionary to China, had both to a remarkable degree. He had to be separated for long periods from his family, but he loved them passionately, and his homecomings were joyous occasions for the household, Marshall Broomhall in his biography of Morrison writes that "with the tenacity of the Borderer he endured, fearing neither the face nor frown of man, undeterred by adversity, bereavement, or contempt. Like the sturdy oak of his native country (England) he weathered many a storm, standing alone, not unmoved, but unmovable when the call of duty demanded."

—*Sunday School Times*

* * *

"Made of Right Stuff!"

"A little brown cork
Fell in the path of a whale
Who lashed it down
With his angry tail.
But in spite of its blows
It quickly arose,
And floated serenely
Before his nose.
Said the cork to the whale:
'You may flap and sputter and frown,
But you never, never, can keep me down;
For I'm made of the stuff
That is buoyant enough
To float instead of to drown!' "

—*Pameii*

* * *

Tongue Reading

There was a man living in a suburb of Kansas City who lost both hands in a premature explosion while blasting stone. His face was much torn. The surgeons did all they could for him — but his eyesight was utterly destroyed. He had been converted only a year or two. The Bible was his delight, and his distress at being no longer able to read it was great. He chanced to hear of a lady in England who read the Braille type with her lips. Some friends ordered for him parts of the Bible in the Moon raised type, and he could hardly wait till their arrival.

But alas! the explosion had destroyed the nerves of his lips — there was no sense of touch there! He wept over the Book and stooped to kiss it farewell, when he happened to touch it with his tongue. His teacher was recalled, and he quickly learned to read the raised characters by running his tongue along them.

"I have read the whole Bible through four times," said he, "and many of the books of the Bible over and over again." That man loved God's Word.

—Power

*   *   *

The Optimistic Frog

Two frogs fell into a deep cream bowl,
One was an optimistic soul;
But the other took the gloomy view,
"We shall drown," he cried, without
    more ado.
So with a last despairing cry,
He flung up his legs and he said
    "Goodbye."
Quoth the other frog with a merry grin,
"I can't get out, but I won't give in.
I'll just swim round till my strength
    is spent,
Then will I die the more content."
Bravely he swam till it would seem
His struggles began to churn the cream.
On the top of the butter at last he
    stopped,
And out of the bowl he gaily hopped.
What of the moral? 'Tis easily found:
If you can't hop out, keep swimming
    round.   *—Selected*

*   *   *

"You'll Do It!"

Somebody said that it couldn't be done,
But he with a chuckle replied
That "maybe" it couldn't but he would
    be one
Who wouldn't say so 'till he'd tried.
So he buckled right in, with a trace of
    a grin
On his face. If he worried, he hid it.
He started to sing as he tackled the
    thing
That couldn't be done, but he DID it.

Somebody scoffed: "Oh, you'll never do
    that,
At least no one has ever done it."
But he took off his coat and he took off
    his hat,
And the first thing we knew he'd begun
    it;
With a lift of his chin, and a bit of a
    grin,
Without any doubt or quibbling;
He started to sing as he tackled the
    thing
That couldn't be done, and he DID it.

There are thousands to tell you it cannot be done;
There are thousands to prophesy
    failure;
There are thousands to point out to you,
    one by one,
The dangers that wait to assail you;
But just buckle in with a bit of a grin,
Then take off your coat and go to it;
Just start in to sing as you tackle the
    thing
That "cannot be done" and you'll DO it.
     —Selected

*   *   *

Conquering Barriers

There is a self-opening gate which is sometimes used in country roads. It stands fast and firm across the road as a traveler approaches it. If he stops before he gets to it, it will not open. But if he will drive right at it, his wagon wheels press the springs below the roadway, and the gate swings back to let him through. He must push right on at the closed gate, or it will continue to be closed. This illustrates the way to pass every barrier on the road of duty. Whether it is a river, a gate, or a mountain, all the child of Jesus has to do is to go for it. If it is a river, it will dry up when you put your feet in its waters. If it is a gate, it will fly open when you are near enough to it, and are still pushing on. If it is a mountain, it will be lifted up and cast into a sea when you come squarely up, without flinching, to where you thought it was. Is there a great barrier across your path of duty just now? Just go for it, in the name of the Lord, and it won't be there.

—Henry Clay Trumbull

* * *

A Jewish Boy's Persistence

A little Jewish boy joined up with the Schoolbag Gospel League, and was so pleased with the Gospel of John that he hastened to headquarters to get one of the other Gospels. Before leaving he gave his heart to the Lord and prayed this prayer, "Oh, Lord, I want to know the truth." A little later, he came to the headquarters with twenty-two cards signed up, and asked for twenty-two Gospels. When he went home with them, his mother asked, "What makes such a bulk in your pocket?" On his telling her, she took the Gospels and destroyed them all, giving the boy a severe beating, and leaving him with cuts on the forehead and cheek. What do you think he did? He went and signed up two more children, then returned to headquarters for twenty-four Gospels. What a missionary was this Jewish boy!

—*Sunday School Times*

* * *

Perseverance

Certain officers approached Napoleon to recommend a young captain for promotion. Napoleon asked them: "Why do you suggest this man?" Their answer was that he through unusual courage and cleverness won a signal victory several days before. "Good," said Napoleon, "but what did he do the next day?" That was the last that was ever heard of the young man.

There are two kinds of people in the world — those who show an occasional burst of brilliancy and those who can be depended upon to do their best every day in the year — in other words the flashers and the plodders. The backbone of a Christian civilization is its dependable people. These are the ones who can

always be counted on no matter what happens, anywhere.

—*Religious Telescope*

* * *

Many Starters — Few Finishers

A missionary sat with the minister of the only church in a small town and watched the passers-by from the seclusion of the parsonage veranda. Said the minister: "That man made a great start a year ago. That young man came out in the meetings last fall. That little girl started when the evangelist was here in the spring." The missionary had seen none of the dozen or so persons of whom the minister spoke in church or Sunday school. At last he said, "You have indeed a great number of starters here, but are none of them planning to finish?" Let us not only start the temples of our Christian lives, but let us finish them.

—*Sunday School Times*

* * *

Don't Quit

When things go wrong as they sometimes will,
When the road you're trudging seems all uphill,
When funds are low and debts are high,
And you want to smile but you have to sigh,
When care is pressing you down a bit,
Rest if you must, but don't you quit.

Life is queer with its twists and turns,
As everyone of us sometimes learns,
And many a failure turns about,
When he might have won had he stuck it out.
Don't give up, though the pace seems slow —
You may succeed with another blow.

Often the goal is nearer than
It seems to a faint and faltering man;
Often the struggler has given up,
When he might have captured the victor's cup.
And he learned too late, when the night slipped down
How close he was to the golden crown.

Success is failure turned inside out —
The silver tint of the clouds of doubt,
And you can never tell how close you
are,
It may be near when it seems afar.
So stick to the fight when you're hardest
hit —
It's when things seem worse that you
mustn't quit.

—*Baptist and Reflector*

* * *

"Be Sure!"

The man who once most wisely said,
"Be sure you're right, then go ahead,"
Might as well have added this, to wit:
"Be sure you're wrong before you quit."

—*Selected*

* * *

"To Yield Is Death"

How Captain Cook and his party of
faithful followers set out upon their
trip in search of the North Pole, is
ever of interest. Dr. Solander, a learned
Swede, and also a man of exceedingly
peppery temper, accompanied them in
the capacity of naturalist. It was the
depth of winter, and a cold south wind,
accompanied by driving snow, surprised
the explorers when some considerable
distance from their encampment. Dr.
Solander therefore called the party
round him, and his face was grave. "I
have had some experience of this in my
own country," he said, "but you have
had none. Now, attend to my advice,
for upon it depends your lives. We must
resolutely set our faces to get back to
the encampment, and with never a stop,
for the danger lies in falling asleep."

"I suppose we shall get horribly tired,
doctor?" asked Lieut. Hodder, the leader
of the party, trying to smile at the unpleasant prospect.

"Of course we shall," answered the
quick-tempered doctor sharply, "but it
will be a chance to see what we are
made of. I warn you, Hodder, that the
men, as their blood grows cold, will ask
to be allowed to rest. Do not permit it
for a moment — urge them — urge them
with blows, with the bayonet, if necessary. Remember, the wish to stop is the
first symptom of the blood refusing to
circulate. To yield to it is death!"

The party moved on; the wind blew,
and the snow fell, and the frost cut
them through and through, yet their
stout hearts held on still. There was no
wish expressed to stop, and if any felt
a longing for rest, none voiced that
longing, but suppressed it and kept it
under by firm, dogged will-power.

—*Christian Graphic*

* * *

Good Timber

'The tree that never had to fight
For sun and sky and air and light,
Never became a forest king,
But lived and died a common thing.
The man who never had to toil,
Who never had to win his share
Of sun and sky and light and air,
Never became a manly man,
But lived and died as he began.
Good timber does not grow on ease.
The stronger wind, the tougher trees,
The farther sky, the greater length
By sun and cold, by rain and snow,
In tree or man good timber grows."

—Douglas Mallock

* * *

Goforth's Closed Doors

Some years ago, a missionary with
Paul's passion, Jonathan Goforth, was
separated from his life's labor in China
when his mission was turned over to the
United Church of Canada. With his missionary wife, at the time weak with illness, with two lady missionaries who
were semi-invalids, with a young man
who did not know the language, this veteran, then nearly seventy years old,
started out for a new field, to preach
Christ where he had not been named.
Five fields in Manchuria they assayed
to enter, and every door was closed. But
his faith was steadfast, and then came
the Macedonian call to northwest Manchuria. Another miracle of modern
missions transpired. Later, nine hundred and eighty-four adults were
baptized in that mission; prior to this
nine hundred and sixty-six. The Lord
of the Macedonian campaign is still
alive.

—*Sunday School Times*

"I Shall Emerge One Day!"

"If I stoop
Into a dark tremendous sea of cloud
It is but for a time. I press God's lamp
Close to my breast; its splendor soon or
    late
Will pierce the gloom; I shall emerge
one day."

              —Browning

* * *

An Indian That Would Not Deny His Lord

The power to control a certain village of Indians in Mexico, is in the hands of the Council of Elders. When Antonio Reyes became a Christian, he was so eager to tell his neighbors of his new-found Saviour that the Council called him to appear before them one dark night. He appeared, and found several Indians armed with guns, sitting by the side of the judge. No time was wasted, for the judge told him that the time had come for him to make a decision: either he must give up his new religion or leave the village. Then the judge ordered the men to shoot Antonio if he did not do one or the other. With a smile Antonio told them that he could not give up Christ. For the first time in his life, he said, he had found One who had filled his heart with joy. Nor could he leave the village until they had come to know Him, too. Months passed filled with persecutions and dangers, yet Antonio stood his ground. Today a little chapel built by the group of believers of that village stands as a monument to the fidelity of an Indian who had come to love Christ more than life.

        —*Sunday School Times*

* * *

"Done For!"

A commanding general in flashing the news of the progress of a battle during World War I, when 4,000 Frenchmen were flung against 30,000 Germans on Plemone Hill, June 1918, reported as follows:

"Bombardment began at midnight;

2:30 A. M. Bombardment worse on our right;

4:15 A. M. After repulsing several attacks, are surrounded on our right;

7:45 A. M. Right has fallen;

10 A. M. Still holding;

11:45 A. M. Enemy masses everywhere. Still holding.

12:05 P. M. Done for!"

His orders were, "Hold the position to death!" He obeyed fully!

        —*Selected*

* * *

"I Can Plod!"

Undoubtedly the world owes a great deal to men of genius, but it is doubtful whether it owes as much to such as to men of dogged perseverance. . . . Perseverance is needed in every phase of the Christian life. Nothing is obtained in the spiritual realm by a hop-skip-and-jump, so to speak.

When William Carey began thinking of going to India as a pioneer missionary, his father pointed out to him that he possessed no academic qualifications that would fit him for such a task. But William Carey answered: "I can plod." . . . Those who accomplish things for the glory of God and the good of humanity are plodders.

        —K. M. McDitchie, in
          Watchman-Examiner

* * *

Press On!

Press on! Though mists obscure
The steep and rugged way,
And clouds of doubt beset,
Soon dawns the brighter day.

Keep on! Though hours seem long
And days deep-fraught with woe,
Let patience have her perfect work
And vanquish every foe.

Hope on! Though all is lost
And storms beat high.
Have faith! Be still and know
That God is nigh.

        —*Selected*

Where Stoutest Timber Grows:

The strongest trees grow not beneath the grass of a greenhouse, or in the protection of sheltered and shaded valleys. The stoutest timber stands on Norwegian rocks, where tempests rage, and long, hard winters reign. And is it not so with the Christian also? Exercise gives health, and strength is the reward of activity. The muscles are seen fully developed in the brawny arm that plies the ringing hammer.

—Gospel Herald

POWER

Wanted: One More Organization

Admittedly, the church is "top-heavy" with man-made organization. How much spiritual and physical energy is needlessly expended, dragging along sundry church organizations! The early church had a MINIMUM of organization and a MAXIMUM of power. The present-day church has a MAXIMUM of organization, and a MINIMUM of power. It seems to me that we need yet ONE additional organization. We could designate this greatly needed organization thus: The S.S.S.S. Society, which, being interpreted, means: The society for the suppression of superfluous societies! What say ye?

—W. B. K.

* * *

God's Standing Challenge

The power of prayer has never been tried to its full capacity in any church. If we want to see mighty wonders of divine power and grace wrought in the place of weakness, failure and disappointment, let the whole church answer God's standing challenge: 'Call unto Me, and I will answer thee, and show thee great and mighty things which thou knowest not."

—J. Hudson Taylor

* * *

Missionary Vision

William Jessup, for fifty years a missionary in Syria, was discouraged because he could not win men to Christ. He decided the difficulty must be in him. He resolved to spend one week by himself with the Word of God. He had not read far when something dawned upon him he had never realized. He had never given God His place in the work of winning others. He had worked in his own strength. He thought of the fall of Jericho. He remembered that God did that so that no man could take credit. After this he took a sheet of paper and wrote down the names of eleven men whom he was seeking to bring to Christ and lifted them to God in prayer, asking God to do the work and use him if he was needed.

One Friday one of the young men came to him under a burden for his sins and was saved. In three weeks all of these men were won. "I will be a different missionary the rest of my life. I realize that it is God who worketh in us to will and to do."

—Gospel Herald

* * *

Night Vigils and Days of Fasting

I have been in that old church in New England where Jonathan Edwards preached his great sermon, "Sinners in the hands of an angry God." He had a little manuscript which he held up so close to his face that they could not see his countenance. He went on and on until the people in the crowded church were tremendously moved. One man sprang to his feet, rushed down the aisles and cried, "Mr. Edwards, have mercy!" Other men caught hold of the backs of the pews lest they should slip into perdition. I have seen the old pillars around which they threw their arms when they thought the day of judgment had dawned upon them. The power of that sermon is still felt in the United States today. But there is a bit of history behind it.

For three days Edwards had not eaten a mouthful of food: for three nights he had not closed his eyes in sleep. Over and over again, he had been saying to God, "Give me New England! Give me New England!" and when he rose from his knees, and made his way into the pulpit they say that he looked as if he had been gazing straight into the face of God. They say that before he opened his lips to speak, conviction fell upon his audience.   —J. Wilbur Chapman

* * *

"Can't Lick God!"

"The day after the great earthquake and fire at San Francisco a newsboy was showing a dazed man the way through the rubble, and as they walked, the lad philosophized — "It took men a long time to put all this stuff up, but God tumbled it over in a minute. Say, mister, 'taint no use for a feller to think he can lick God."

—*The Lord Reigneth*

* * *

A Fireman — Not a Brakeman

We have eased up, put on the brakes, slowed down until we are shorn of power. The story is told in Texas of a bishop who went to the aid of a pastor in a campaign. He put his best into the work. Great crowds came and many were saved. It was a glorious meeting. At the close of it the pastor said: "Bishop, you are a great preacher. The people love you. You are doing a great work, but you must put on the brakes." The bishop looked at him and said, "Brother, you are mistaken. I am not a brakeman; I am a fireman!"

—*Moody Monthly*

* * *

God's Power

Each worker for Christ, in his own particular sphere, meets with many valleys and mountains, crooked places and rough ones, which God alone can deal with. Let him rejoice not only that God's power is equal to the occasion, but also that there are difficulties of such a nature as to make the putting forth of that power a visible and notable thing.

—J. Hudson Taylor

Their Secret of Power

In a letter written to the Roman Emperor Trajan by Pliny the Younger, governor of Bithynia about A. D. 110, Pliny described what he had learned about the Christians and their worship. "They are accustomed to meet," he says, "on a fixed day before daylight to sing a hymn of praise to Christ as God." The troubled governor of Bithynia had tried to explain to the Roman Emperor the reason for the spread of the Christian faith, which was being extended so rapidly that it was leaving the pagan altar deserted. Unwittingly he declared the secret of the power of Christianity and its spread in the world — the Christians worshipped Jesus Christ as God ... Only the Jesus who is the Son of God can redeem us from our sin. . . . Only the Christ who is beyond humanity can be the object of our worship and our eternal hope.

—H. Guy Moore, in
Open Windows

* * *

The Price of Power

Years ago, I was pastor of a church in North London, which is still dear to my heart. Stricken, smitten, and afflicted, I came to the very borderland of eternity; spent a day and a night there expecting to cross over. After I came back to life the first man I went to see was Joseph Parker of the City Temple who to me was always as tender as a mother. I said to him: "I do not understand the experience through which I have passed. I cannot understand the suffering, the sorrow, the breaking of it." He put his two hands on my shoulders and said, "My boy, never mind; your people will get the value; there will come another note into your preaching which you never could have found, if you had not suffered." I went back and said: "If that be so then thank God for all the breaking and all the pain."

A man never finds the throne of power until he has submitted his life wholly to God. That is the great lesson.

—G. Campbell Morgan

Get Rid of the Plugs

God has given the Holy Ghost "to them that obey him." At Keswick many years ago a young student came to me and said he wanted to speak to me about the state of his soul. He told me that the doctrine of the Trinity caused him difficulties, and he begged me to explain it. I answered that this was impossible for me, but that I had the impression that there was something in his life which was upsetting his inward peace and harmony, and that he would never gain strength until he had removed this obstacle. We looked out through the window, away to Skiddaw. I said: "Up there in the hills is the deep lake. We need the water down here in the town. The pipes have been laid, but the water does not flow. The pipes are plugged." Somewhat surprised, the young man left me without saying a word. Some hours later he returned and insisted on seeing me at once. His face shone. "The plug has been removed; the letter is already in the letter box." Many people pray for the fulness of the Spirit, attend conferences, read books about the power of the Spirit, and still do not receive it, because they still cling to some secret sin. Obedience brings joy and blessing.
—From *Simple Talks on the Holy Spirit*, by D. H. Dolman, D. D.

* * *

Strength in Weakness

Lord, by Thy favor Thou hast made my mountain to stand strong. Psalm 30:7.
I could not do without Thee,
I cannot stand alone,
I have no strength or goodness,
No wisdom of my own;
But Thou, beloved Savior,
Art all in all to me!
And perfect strength in weakness
Is theirs who lean on Thee!
—F. R. Havergal

* * *

The Secret of Power

Spurgeon was once asked the reason of his marvelous power in the ministry. Pointing to the floor of the Metropolitan Tabernacle, he said, "In the room beneath, you will find three hundred praying Christians. Every time I preach they gather there, and uphold my hands by continuous prayer and supplications. It is in that room that you find the secret of the blessings."
—*Power*

* * *

The Irresistible Tide

Years ago, during the building of a bridge across a portion of New York's harbor, the engineers were seeking a base for one of the buttresses. They struck upon an old scow full of bricks and stone that had long ago sunk in the mud until practically buried. Divers were sent down to place great chains under the scow so that it could be raised, but every device failed. At last a young engineer assured them it could be done. He brought two barges to the spot, and attached the huge chains, which were around the scow, to beams on the barges. The chains were fastened tightly at low tide. There was nothing else to do but wait, and, as the tide swept up the harbor raising the barges by its mighty power, the buried scow shook, shivered and responded. It was raised by the lift of the Atlantic Ocean! *So it is by the life and lift of the Holy Spirit that our lives are energized, and that which is a hindrance is carried away. Habits and sins that we ourselves would be powerless to uproot, are gripped by the might of the Spirit and taken away, thus enabling our lives to be placed on a sure foundation.*
—*Southwestern Evangel*

* * *

"Power Belongeth Unto God"

The whole secret of why D. L. Moody was such a mightily used man you will find in Psalm 62:11, "God hath spoken once, twice have I heard this, that *power belongeth unto God.*" I am glad it does. I am glad that power did not belong to D. L. Moody; I am glad that it did not belong to Charles G. Finney; I am glad that it did not belong to Martin Luther; I am glad that it did not belong to any other Christian man whom God has greatly used in this world's history.

Power belongs to God. If D. L. Moody had any power, and he had great power, he got it from God.

—R. A. Torrey

* * *

Power Beneath Us

A visitor was once walking along a high part of the shore of the Dead Sea when he lost his balance and fell into the water. He could not swim and, in desperation lest he should sink and be drowned, he began to fling his arms about. At last he was exhausted and felt he could do no more. Then he found something he had not known: the water bore him up. The water of the Dead Sea is so heavy with salt and other minerals that when he lay still in it he found he floated on the surface. He could not drown so long as he resigned himself to the power of the deep. So it is with us. There is a power beneath us and around us waiting to bear us up. We should cease from all our flounderings and fruitless efforts and let the power of God undergird us.

—R. W. H. Shepherd

* * *

Wesley and His Enemies

John Wesley was one day preaching in a rough section of London where ribald pleasures held sway. He was addressing a vast multitude of people when two ruffians appeared at the edge of the crowd. They said one to another: "Who is this preacher? We'll show him. What right has he to come here, spoiling our fun?" They picked up a stone in each hand and belligerently elbowed their way through the crowd until they came within hailing distance of the preacher. They had their hands raised, prepared to hurl the stones at the speaker, when, as Wesley was talking about the power of Christ to change the lives of sinful men, a beauty spread over his face and transformed him with its effulgence. They stood transfigured, their arms poised in air. One turned to the other with a note of awe in his voice and said, "He ain't a man, Bill; he ain't a man." The stones fell from their hands

to the ground, and as Wesley spoke, their hearts were softened. Finally, when the sermon had been completed, the great preacher made his way through the crowd, which parted respectfully for him to pass. One of the ruffians timidly reached out his hand to touch the hem of the preacher's garment, and as he did so, the attention of Wesley was drawn to him and his companion. He put out his hands, placed them on the heads of the two ruffians, and said, "God bless you, my boys," and passed on. And as he did so, one ruffian turned to the other and said with even more awe in his voice, "He *is* a man, Bill; he *is* a man. *He's a man like God.*"

—From — *You Can Win*
by Norman V. Peale

* * *

Unused Power

Some time ago I visited one of our great hydro-electric plants. The guide took me out on the mile-long dam. It seemed good to get away from the whir of the high dynamos. As we stood there, I noticed a lot of water going over the dam, and I said to the guide: "What per cent of the power from this river do you actually transform into electricity, and how much goes over the dam and is lost?"

He shook his head and said: "We don't use even one-hundredth part of it!"

I was stunned. Then I asked myself: "How much of the power of God do I transform into usefulness and how much is unused and lost?"

—M. Trevor Baskerville—

* * *

The Seat of Power

Paganini, the great violinist, came out before his audience one day and made the discovery just before they ended their applause, that there was something wrong with his violin. He looked at it a second and then saw that it was not his famous and valuable violin.

He felt paralyzed for a moment, then turned to his audience, and told them there had been a mistake and he did not have his own violin. He stepped back behind the curtain thinking that it was still where he had left it, but discovered that some one had stolen his and left that inferior one in its place. He remained back of the curtain a moment, then came out before his audience and said:

"Ladies and Gentlemen: I will show you that the music is not in the instrument, but in the soul." And he played as he had never played before; and out of that inferior instrument, the music poured forth until the audience was enraptured with enthusiasm, and the applause almost lifted the ceiling of the building, because the man had revealed to them that music was not in the instrument, but in his soul.

—*Sunday School Times*

* * *

When God Used a "Stammering Tongue.

One day during his great mission in London, Mr. Moody was holding a meeting in a theater packed with a most select audience. Noblemen and noblewomen were there in large numbers, and a prominent member of the royal family was in the royal box. Mr. Moody arose to read the Scripture lesson. He attempted to read Luke 4:27: "And many lepers were in Israel in the time of Eliseus the prophet." When he came to the name of Eliseus he stammered and stuttered over it. He went back to the beginning of the verse and began to read again, but when he reached the word "Eliseus" he could not get over it. He went back the third time, but again the word was too much for him. He closed the Bible with deep emotion and looked up and said, "Oh, God, use this stammering tongue to preach Christ crucified to these people." The power of God came upon him, and one who heard him then and had heard him often at other times said to me that he had never heard Mr. Moody pour out his soul in such a torrent of eloquence as he did then, and the whole audience was melted by the power of God.

—*Sunday School Times*

* * *

Plenty But No Power

There is an interesting story which has come down from medieval times:

The great scholar, Thomas Aquinas, came to the City of Rome to pay his respects to the one who was then pope. In the course of his visit, the pope proudly showed him all the wonders of the papal palace, and took him to his treasury and showed him chests of silver and gold received from every part of the world. With something of a smile on his face he said, "You see, Thomas, we cannot say with Peter, 'Silver and gold have I none.'" Looking the pope in the eyes, Thomas Aquinas fearlessly replied, "No, and neither can we say, 'In the Name of Jesus Christ of Nazareth, rise up and walk.'" Riches had come, but power had gone! Peter and the apostles had poverty and power.

—From *Lectures on the Book of Acts,* by H. A. Ironside

* * *

It's the Power To Keep That's Needed.

Ludwig Nommensen, a pioneer missionary to the Batak tribesmen, was told that he could stay for two years, during which time he studied the customs and traditions that ruled the people. At the end of that time the chief asked him if there was anything in the Christian religion that differed from the traditions of the Batak. "We, too, have laws that say we must not steal, nor take our neighbor's wife, nor bear false witness," the chief said. The missionary answered quietly, "My Master gives the power to *keep* His laws." The chief was startled. "Can you teach my people that?" he asked. "No, I cannot, but God can give them that power if they ask for it and listen to His Word." The missionary was permitted to stay another six months, during which time he taught just one thing — the power of God. At the end of that time, the chief said, "Stay; your law is better than ours. Ours tells us what we ought to do. Your God says, 'Come, I will walk with you and give you strength to do the good thing.'" There are now about 450,000 Batak Christians, with their own independent church organizations.

—*Commission,* a Baptist World Journal

Jesus and I

"I cannot do it alone,
The waves run fast and high,
And fogs close chill around,
And the light goes out in the sky;
But I know that we two
Shall win in the end —
       Jesus and I

"Coward and wayward and weak,
I change with the changing sky;
Today so eager and brave,
Tomorrow not caring to try;
But He never gives in,
So we two shall win —
       Jesus and I."
         —*Selected*

*   *   *

Stabbed Through and Through

Dr. Malan of Geneva, on a trip to Paris, fell into conversation with a chap who began to reason with him about Christianity. The doctor answered every argument with a quotation from the Scriptures — not venturing a single remark or application. Every quotation his companion evaded or turned aside, only to be met by another passage. At last he turned away. "Don't you see I don't believe your Bible? What is the use of quoting it to me?" he screamed. But the only reply was, "If ye believe not that I am he, ye shall die in your sins." Years afterward, Dr. Malan received a letter in an unfamiliar handwriting. "You took the Sword of the Spirit and stabbed me through and through," it read, "and every time I tried to parry the blade and get you to use your hands and not the Heavenly steel, you simply gave me another stab. You made me feel I was not fighting you, but God." At the close Dr. Malan recognized the name of his Paris-bound companion of ten years before.
       —Charles E. Fuller

*   *   *

The Bible

An old Professor of biology used to hold a little brown seed in his hand. "I know just exactly the composition of this seed. It has in it nitrogen, hydrogen, and carbon. I know the exact proportions. I can make a seed that will look exactly like it. But if I plant my seed it will come to nought; its elements will simply be absorbed in the soil. If I plant the seed God made it will become a plant, because it contains the mysterious principle which we call "the life principle." This Bible looks like other books. We cannot understand altogether its power. Planted in good ground, it shows that it has the life.
       —*C. U. Herald*

*   *   *

The Secret of Moody's Power

In the fall of 1871, when Moody was speaking in Brooklyn, *his congregation dropped to eighteen.* Moody despised failure. And then one night, after the service was over, some unnamed woman quietly said to him, "We have plenty of *preaching* in Brooklyn, but if you will *tell us something about the Bible* it will be blessed to us." That broke his unfruitful methods forever. The next afternoon he gave a simple Bible reading, and the ravishing, sweet fires of God at once came down. He had a heart for nothing now but the glory of the Word.

One November night of that year (he was thirty-four), he walked the streets of New York, sobbing, "O God, why don't You compel me to walk close to Thee always? Deliver me from myself! Take absolute sway! Give me Thy Holy Spirit!" So mightily did the Spirit of God come upon him that he had to rush to the home of a near-by friend, and ask for a room where he could be alone, where there followed hours of which it is unlawful to speak, and he seldom did.
       —Wilbur M. Smith

*   *   *

"It Kicks Me"

A missionary in India tells of a Brahman priest, an intelligent and open-minded man, who listened attentively to the preaching. He was given a Telugu Testament on condition that he would faithfully read it. He read it for a month; then meeting the missionary again, he said, in Telugu: "I wish you to take the Book back. As I read it, it kicks me." The Bible convicts of sin.

—*Glad Tidings*

* * *

Dynamite!

A man was sitting on a pile of planks near the Quirinal in Rome. At his feet lay a large package. A couple of officers, passing, noticed the bundle on the pavement. They stopped and asked what it contained, ever suspicious of infernal machines. "Dynamite!" said the man. The officers jumped. One of them gingerly seized the package, the other the man, and both were taken to the police headquarters. When the package was opened it was found to contain — Bibles! "Where is the dynamite?" inquired the officers. "'The word of God is quick, and powerful, and sharper than any two-edged sword,'" replied the colporteur. He was right. "Dynamic" is the exact Greek word that the sacred writer uses for "powerful." The Bible is dynamite toward sin and all unrighteousness.

—*Homiletic Review*

* * *

O, God, Help!

God's strongest saints realize their weaknesses, and appeal to Him for strength. One Sunday morning, as Charles H. Spurgeon passed through the door back of the pulpit in the Tabernacle, and saw the great crowd of people, he was overheard saying, "O God, help!" Strong as he was, he realized that he was insufficient for so great a task as preaching the Gospel in power, unless God should be his Helper.

—*Dr. A. C. Dixon*

* * *

The Secret of Their Power

When William IV of England died, there was a young girl spending the night at the palace. They awakened her and told her that she was now the Queen of England. As soon as she heard the news she dropped on her knees and asked the Heavenly Father to help and guide her through all the years that were to follow. For sixty-four years this girl, who was Queen Victoria, reigned over the British Empire. England never made greater progress than during her reign. A prince of India asked her what was the secret of England's power, and for her answer she quietly picked up a Book from the table near by. "This is the secret," she said. The Book was God's Word, the Bible.

—*George W. Truett*

* * *

A Big Difference

A Buddhist monk in Ceylon, who was acquainted with both Christianity and Buddhism, was once asked what he thought was the great difference between the two. He replied, "There is much that is good in each of them, and probably in all religions. But what seems to me to be the greatest difference is that *you Christians know what is right and have power to do it,* while we Buddhists know what is right but have not any such power."

—*The Expositor*

* * *

Sin Shuts Off the Power!

An incident is told of a certain college which was without any supply of water one morning. The plumber was called and he examined the plumbing, but could find nothing wrong. Yet, there was no water. Next the water department of the city was called and they sent men to investigate the trouble. After much searching they finally found the cause. A mile away from the college, where the small pipe line which supplied the college was connected with the large line going into the little city, there at the junction, they found a huge toad which had been sucked partly into the small line and which had literally shut off all the water. The men who removed the trouble maker suggested that it had most likely got in there first as a little tadpole, but had fed upon the water until it grew and shut off the water.

So it is with sin. Many a Christian has allowed some little sin to sneak into his life, and allowed it to remain there, until he woke up one day, and like Samson long ago, found that the power was gone.   —*Brethren Missionary Herald*

* * *

Knowledge Without Power

The late Dr. George S. McCune, who for many years was engaged in missionary work in Korea, made this statement: "A Korean said: 'We have had a code of morals. We have known what we ought to do, and what we ought not to do, but we have had no power to do what we knew to be right. But when Jesus Christ came into our lives we had power to do right.'"

—*Moody Monthly*

After the Prayer

A new organ, so the story goes, had been installed in a New York City church. A rare and costly instrument it was. The first Sunday it was used, the electric current that was required to operate the console went off at a point early in the service. A hurried call for help brought a mechanic. Soon a note was sent up, and handed to the organist. The note said, "After the prayer, the power will be on!" That mechanic did not realize what depths and heights of truth were in the suggestiveness of those simple words. A prayerless church is a powerless church; a church that mightily prays will mightily achieve for God and His Kingdom.

— *Christian Digest*

PRAISE

"Let It Be of Praise."

A friend of mine was recently summoned to the bedside of his aged mother. More than eighty years of age, she was stricken with what they feared would prove her fatal illness. When her children were gathered in the room, her pastor came; as he was about to lead them in prayer, he turned to the aged saint and asked her what selection of Scripture he should read. She said, "Make your own selection, but let it be of praise." The weakness of old age was on her, and the pain of sickness, but there was no gloom. It was light at eventide. "Let it be of praise."

—James I. Vance, in
Earnest Worker

* * *

Praise Changes Things! Try It!

Mrs. Chas. E. Cowman tells of a missionary in dark China who was living a defeated life. Everything seemed to be touched with sadness and although he prayed and prayed for months for victory over depression and discouragement, his life remained the same. He determined to leave his work and go to an interior station and pray till victory came. He reached the place and

was entertained in the home of a fellow missionary. On the wall hung a motto with these words, "Try Thanksgiving." The words gripped his heart and he thought within himself, "Have I been praying all this time and not praising?" He stopped and began to praise and was so uplifted that instead of hiding away to pray and agonize for days he immediately returned to his waiting flock to tell them that praise changes things. Wonderful blessing attended this simple testimony and the bands that had bound others were loosened through praise.

—J. A. R. in
The Missionary Worker

* * *

Evening Praise

The Alpine shepherds have a beautiful custom of ending the day by singing to one another an evening farewell. The air is so crystalline that the song will carry long distances. As the dusk begins to fall, they gather their flocks and begin to lead them down the mountain paths, singing, "Hitherto hath the Lord helped us. Let us praise His name!"

And at last with a sweet courtesy, they sing to one another the friendly farewell: "Goodnight! Goodnight!" The words are taken up by the echoes, and from side to side the song goes reverberating sweetly and softly until the music dies away in the distance.

—*Selected*

* * *

"When I Do Anything, They Scowl!"

Dr. Ira S. Wile, who has had wide experience in dealing with difficult children, once told me of a particularly interesting case which made him realize the need of praise as a practical doctor's prescription.

"It was a case of twin boys," he said. "One was particularly bright; the other seemed mentally inferior. The father asked me to find the reason.

"When I had gained the child's confidence he told me the story children almost invariably tell in such cases.

" 'Why don't people like me,' he asked, 'the same as they do my brother? When he does anything they smile. When I do anything they scowl. I can't ever seem to do anything as good as he does.'

"I separated those boys as much as possible," said Dr. Wile. "I had them placed in different classes in school. I told their parents to stop using comparisons as a goad upon the backward one, and to praise him for his own little accomplishments. He soon was standing on his own feet.'"

—Princess Alexandra Kropotkin, in *Liberty.*

* * *

"I Thank Thee, O Father"

A servant girl in great anxiety of soul sought the help of her clergyman. All his explanations of the Gospel and application of it for her case, failed to bring peace. She said she had tried to pray, but dared not speak to God. "If you cannot pray," said the clergyman, "perhaps you can praise." He went on to show that it was God who had graciously begun to stir her soul, giving her concern about salvation and some feeling of sorrow for her sins. He told her that she would greatly add to her sins if she failed to thank him for His grace; but if she praised and blessed God for what he had done, she would soon find that He who had begun the good work would carry it on to the praise and glory of His grace. To commence this exercise, he recommended her to go home singing the 103d Psalm, "O thou, my soul, bless God the Lord." She departed with a light heart, singing as she went, "and," said the minister, in telling the story, "She is singing still, praising and praying and rejoicing with joy unspeakable, and full of glory."

—*Gospel Banner*

* * *

"Lift Up Your Heart!"

We thank thee, Lord, for all thy love,
For countless blessings from above;
From north to south, from east to west,
Thy glories shine, and man is blest.

In every zone, in every clime,
We hear thy praise, its happy chime;
For sun and moon and radiant stars,
And all the glory night unbars.

For every flower that decks the way,
For all the birds with songs so gay,
For smiles upon each human face,
For all thy wondrous love and grace.

Lift up your heart, lift up your voice,
Give thanks to God, rejoice, rejoice!
Into his courts we'll make our way,
And praise him on Thanksgiving Day!

—Georgia Tilliam Snead, in
Gospel Herald

* * *

Praise the Lord

Praise Him when the sun is shining,
  When the winds of trouble blow,
When you see no silver lining
  On the clouds that hang so low.

Praise illumines clouds of sorrow,
  Turns the gray skies into gold
Giving promise of a morrow
  Bright with blessings manifold.

Praise Him when your load is heavy
  And the day no comfort brings,
Then your burden God will carry,
  Bear you as on eagles' wings.

God delights to have us praise Him,
　And believe His holy Word;
And He knoweth them that trust Him,
　For they always praise the Lord.
　　　　　—Ida A. Guirey, in
　　　　　　Sunday School Times

* * *

"Praise Ye the Lord"

An aged lady, dearly loved her Lord.
Often her cup of joy overflowed. A favorite expression of hers was, "Praise the
Lord!" In God's house, when the minister preached, she would say, "Praise
the Lord!" Sometimes the minister was
disturbed when "Aunt" Betty said,
"Praise the Lord!" He would lose his
line of thought for the moment. He offered her a pair of blankets if she would
refrain from saying, "Praise the Lord!"
during his sermon. She greatly needed
the blankets, for she was very poor.
She did her best to earn them on the
minister's terms. For many Sundays,
she kept perfectly quiet during the sermon. Then, one day, a visiting minister
came to preach. He preached on forgiveness of sin, with its attendant
blessings and joys. As he preached,
"Aunt" Betty thought less and less of
the blankets, and more and more of the
joys of salvation. Finally, she could
stand it no longer. She cried out,
"Blankets or no blankets, PRAISE THE
LORD!"
　　　　　—W. B. K.

* * *

We All Need Praise

If parents and bosses administered
praise oftener, the psycho-analysts
would get a rest from the overwhelming
rush of patients suffering from inferi-
ority complexes. For we must bask in
the warmth of approval now and then;
otherwise the health of our self-respect
becomes seriously endangered.

As a rule, husbands are blinder than
wives to this need in the home. A survey of rural life uncovered one general complaint made by women living on
farms. As the wife of one prosperous
Ohio farmer expressed it:

"Maybe when I'm a hundred years
old I'll get used to having everything
I do taken for granted. As it is, life
comes pretty hard when you don't hear
a word of thanks for your efforts.
Sometimes I feel like copying the woman who served her menfolk cattle fodder one day for dinner, after waiting 20
years for a word of praise. 'I've never
heard aught to make me think you'd
know the difference,' she said when they
declared she must be crazy."
　　　—Princess Alexandra Kropotkin, in
　　　　　Liberty.

* * *

"I'm Fed Up!"

One New Year's Day a millionaire of
my acquaintance, whose pride it was
never to offer a tip for any service, faced
an unforgettable tragedy. His chief accountant committed suicide. The books
were found to be in perfect order, the
affairs of the dead man — a modest
bachelor — were prosperous and calm.
The only letter left by the accountant
was a brief note to his millionaire employer. It read: "In 30 years I have
never had one word of encouragement.
I'm fed up."
　　　　　— *Gospel Herald*

PRAYER

"Lord, What A Change!"
Lord, what a change within us one short
　hour
Spent in Thy Presence will prevail to
　make!
What heavy burdens from our bosoms
　take!
What parched grounds refresh as with
　a shower!

We kneel and all around us seems to
　lower,
We rise, and all, the distant and the
　near,
Stands forth in sunny outline, bright
　and clear.
We kneel how weak, we rise how full
　of power!

Why therefore should we do ourselves
  this wrong,
Or others, that we are not always strong,
That we are ever overborne with care,
That we should ever weak or heartless
  be,
Anxious or troubled, when with us is
  prayer,
And joy and strength and courage are
  with Thee.

          —*Trench*

* * *

The Power of Prayer

J. Edgar Hoover, director of the F.B.I.,
says: "The spectacle of a nation praying is more awe-inspiring than the explosion of an atomic bomb. The force
of prayer is greater than any possible
combination of man-made or man-con-
trolled powers, because prayer is man's
greatest means of tapping the infinite
resources of God. Invoking by prayer
the mercy and might of God is our most
efficacious means of guaranteeing peace
and security for the harassed and helpless peoples of the earth."

          —*Selected*

* * *

He Answers

I know not by what methods rare,
But this I know, God answers prayer.
I know not when He sends the word
That tells us fervent prayer is heard.
I know it cometh soon or late;
Therefore we need to pray and wait.
I know not if the blessing sought
Will come in just the guise I thought.
I leave my prayers with Him alone
Whose will is wiser than my own.

    —*Eliza M. Hickok, in the*
          King's Business

* * *

Isaac Newton's Testimony

One of the greatest scientists who
ever lived gave this witness to his faith
in God: "I can take my telescope and
look millions and millions of miles into
space; but I can lay my telescope aside,
go into my room and shut the door, get
down on my knees in earnest prayer,
and I see more of heaven and get closer
to God than I can when assisted by all
the telescopes and material agencies on
earth."

          —*The Pilgrim*

* * *

When Tasks Are Hard

In a certain cotton factory there is a
card on the walls of the workrooms that
reads: "If your threads get tangled send
for the foreman." One day a new worker got her threads tangled, and she tried
to disentangle them, but only made them
worse. Then she sent for the foreman.

He came and looked. Then he said
to her: "You have been doing this yourself?"

"Yes," she said.

"But why did you not send for me according to instructions?"

"I did my best," she said.

"No, you did not," the foreman said.
*"Remember that doing your best is
sending for me."*

          —*Moody Monthly*

* * *

George Mueller's Answered Prayer

A Scotch brother said: "I was an intensely worldly man, yet I never found
satisfaction. When my father passed
away, who was a delightful Christian, I
looked over his papers, and saw he had
given large sums of money to Mr. Mueller's orphanage. I said, 'I am sure my
father would like me to help that work.
I will go down.' I went, and there was
a revival on for boys and girls, so I
listened to the message. God saved me.
They said, 'We are not surprised, for at
this Home, for thirty-eight years, Mr.
Mueller never ceased to pray for you.' "

          —*God's Revivalist*

* * *

Why He Wanted to Study Geography

Gulu, a Punjabi Christian, came to
his American friend, and said, "Sahib,
teach me some geography." Astonished,
the American asked, "Why, Gulu, what
do you want with geography at your
age?" "Sahib," gravely answered Gulu,
"I wish to study geography so that I
may know more about what to pray."
Surely that is the antithesis of the
"Bless me and my wife, my son John

and his wife, us four and no more" type of Christian.

—From *The training World Christians,*
by Loveland

* * *

A Child's Prayer

A touching incident is related of a small lad — one of the Glasgow waifs — who, exhausted by disease during the ten years of his young life, was taken into the infirmary for an operation. In a pitiful, tremulous voice he pleaded with the surgeon and medical students, "Will one of you gents put up a wee prayer for a wee boy, just a wee prayer to Jesus for me in my distress?" As there was no response but, a pitying smile, the child himself asked that Jesus would be near. The following day, the operation having been completed with more than usual ease and success, the little patient's relief was evident. "The good Jesus heard your prayer," said the surgeon, as he took the wasted hand. "I kent He wud," was the reply, to which he added, "I will just pray to Jesus for you, doctor."

—*Christian Herald*

* * *

Not Always Answered Our Way

One day a lady was giving her little nephew a lesson. He was generally a good, attentive child, but on this occasion he could not fix his mind on his work. Suddenly he said, "Auntie, may I kneel down and ask God to help me to find my marble?" His aunt having given her consent, the little boy knelt by his chair, closed his eyes, and prayed silently. Then he rose and went on with his lesson contentedly. Next day, almost afraid of asking the question, lest the child had not found his toy, and so might lose his simple faith, she said, "Well, dear, have you found your marble?" "No, Auntie," was the reply, "but God has made me not want to." God does not always answer our prayers in the way we wish or expect, but if we are sincere, He will take from us the desire for what is contrary to His holy will.

—*Home Messenger*

Where He Learned Most

The *Pilgrim* reports Dr. Harry A. Ironside as a young preacher visiting the aged Alexander Fraser and listening enthralled as one truth after another from God's Word was opened up by Mr. Fraser until he could restrain himself no more and cried out, "Where did you learn these things?" "On my knees on the mud floor of a little sod cottage in the north of Ireland," replied Mr. Fraser. "There, with my Bible open before me, I used to kneel for hours at a time, and ask the Spirit of God to reveal Christ to my soul and to open the Word to my heart. He taught me more on my knees on that mud floor than I could ever have learned in all the colleges and seminaries in the world."

—*Christian Digest*

* * *

God's Strange Answers

He was a Christian, and he prayed. He asked for strength to do greater things, but he was given infirmity that he might do better things.

He asked for riches that he might be happy; he was given poverty that he might be wise.

He asked for power that he might have the praise of men; he was given weakness that he might feel the need of God.

He had received nothing that he asked for; all that he hoped for. His prayer seems unanswered, but he is most blessed.

—*The Standard*

* * *

In Stonewall's Camp

An officer once complained to General Stonewall Jackson that some soldiers were making a noise in their tent. "What are they doing?" asked the General. "They are praying now, but they have been singing," was the reply. "And is that a crime?" the General demanded. "The articles of war orders punishment for an unusual noise," was the reply. "God forbid that praying should be an unusual noise in the camp," replied General Jackson.

—*Wesleyan Methodist*

"If Two of You"

In the early years of his ministry, Dr. George W. Truett took the following verse as his text for a morning's message: "If two of you shall agree on earth as touching any thing that they shall ask, it shall be done for them of My Father which is in heaven" (Mt. 18:19). Having quoted his text, Dr. Truett asked:

"Do you believe it?" Of course he did not expect an answer, but one was forth-coming nevertheless. As he paused for a moment that his question might be understood, a very poor member of the congregation, poor in this world's goods but rich in faith, rose to her feet. "I believe it pastor," she said, "And I want you to claim that promise with me." "It staggered me," said the pastor. "I knew I did not have the faith to claim the promise, but before I had time to answer a big burly blacksmith in the congregation rose to his feet; "I'll claim that promise with you, Auntie" he said, and together the two, the poor washerwoman and the blacksmith, dropped to their knees in the aisle and poured out their hearts in prayer for the salvation of the woman's husband. Now it happened that this man was a river boat captain on the Rio Grande, a swearing, foul-mouthed drunken sot, and he was at that moment sleeping off a drunk at home.

That night, for the first time in many years at least, the old river boat captain was in the church and while the pastor preached the woman prayed, not for the salvation of her husband, rather she was thanking God for it, for she seemed to know it would happen that night. And of course when the invitation was given this old foul-mouthed captain came to give his heart to the Lord and he became one of the most dependable and faithful workers in that church.
— *Baptist Standard*

* * *

Judson on Prayer

Adoniram Judson, perhaps the greatest missionary ever sent out from American shores, was emphatic in his insistence upon prayer. I quote his words: "Be resolute in prayer. Make any sacrifice to maintain it. Consider that time is short and that business and company must not be allowed to rob thee of thy God." That was the man who impressed a mighty empire for God.
— *Heart and Life Bulletin*

* * *

God Still Answers!

I can see in my mind's eye a missionary of our church. It is his first visit to Keswick Convention, and he is greatly troubled about a city wholly given to idolatry, where Hindu immorality is rampant, and idolatry spells all kinds of unseemly things. Mr. Hubert Brooks on the platform in his Bible reading, says, "Before they call, I will answer," and this missionary begins to think of that city. No preaching was allowed in that place. He had been knocking on its gates for entrance. No preaching was allowed there, and offenders were imprisoned. Later Mr. Brooks **read:** "The king's heart is in the hand of the Lord, as the rivers of water: he turneth it whithersoever he will." The missionary thinks of the rajah who will not open his gates; he bows his head silently and says, "Now, Lord, the king's heart, the Maharajah is in thy hand, turn it so that these gates may be opened for the preaching of thy Word." The Bible reading ends. On the top of the program there is a suggestion that we should not read our letters until the meeting was over, and this missionary has his letters in his pocket; as he passes out he opens one and reads: "The Maharajah has opened his gates to the preaching of the Gospel, has given us a site for our mission house, and we are free to bring the people to the Lord Jesus Christ." "Before they call, I will answer; and while they are yet speaking, I will hear."

— William Dalgett, in *Moody Monthly*

* * *

How Big Must It Be?

Mr. Spurgeon said: "I remember hearing it said of a godly man: 'Mr. So-and-so is a gracious man, but he is very strange; for the other day he prayed to God about a key he had lost.' The person who told it to me regarded with astonishment the idea of praying to God about a lost key; and he seemed altogether surprised when I assured him that I prayed in like manner. What! Pray about a key? Yes. Please tell me how big a thing must be before you can pray about it? If a certain size is appointed, we should like to have it marked down in the Bible, that we might learn the mathematics of prayer. Would you have it recorded that, if a thing is so many inches long, we may pray about it; but if it happens to be about a quarter of an inch too short, we must let it alone? If we might not pray about little things, it would be a fearful calamity; for little things cause us great worry, and they are harder to deal with than great things. If we might not pray about minor matters, it would be a terrible loss of comfort."

—*King's Business*

* * *

Asking for a Little Dog

Theodore Monod was once telling a little friend about Christ healing blind Bartimaeus. "And what," said he to the boy, "would you have asked from Jesus if you had been blind?" "Oh," said the child, with glowing face and kindling eyes, "I should have asked him for a nice little dog with a collar and chain, to lead me about." How often do we ask for the blind man's dog instead of the seeing man's eyes.

—*Sunday School Chronicle*

* * *

Prayer Does This — and More!

Dr. Hysloop, speaking before the British Medical Association, once said: "The best medicine which my practice has discovered is prayer. The exercise of prayer in those who habitually practice it must be regarded as the most adequate and normal of all the pacifiers of the mind and calmers of the mind and calmers of the nerves.

"As one whose whole life has been concerned with the sufferings of the mind, I would state that of all the hygenic measures to counteract disturbed sleep, depression of spirits, and all the miserable

sequels of a distressed mind, I would undoubtedly give the first place to the simple habit of prayer.

"It is of the highest importance, merely from a physical point of view, to teach children to hold daily communion with God. Such a habit does more to quiet the spirit and strengthen the soul to overcome mere incidental emotionalism, than any other therapeutic agency known to me."

—*The Torch Bearer*

* * *

Some One Prayed

The weary ones had rest, the sad had joy
    That day, and wondered "how?"
A plowman singing at his work had
    prayed,
    "Lord, help them now."

Away in foreign lands, they wondered
    "how"
Their simple word had power.
At home, the gleaners, two or three had
    met
    To pray an hour.

Yes, we are always wondering "how?"
    Because we do not see
Someone, unknown perhaps, and far
    away
    On bended knee.

—*Selected*

* * *

Asking and Receiving

Sir Walter Raleigh once made a request of the Queen and she petulantly answered, "Raleigh, when will you leave off begging?" Sir Walter replied, "When your Majesty leaves off giving,'" and his request was granted. But the God of all grace never grows weary of our asking and never rebukes us for coming.

—Henry W. Frost

* * *

Help From Above

In a large metropolitan hospital there is a surgeon who insists upon having a moment alone before entering the operating room. Because of his great skill many of the younger doctors wondered if there might be a relation between his success and this unusual habit. When one of the interns put the question to the surgeon, he answered, "Yes, there is a relationship, a very close one. Before each operation I ask the great Surgeon to be with me, to guide my hands in their work. There have been times when I didn't know what to do next, and then came a power to go on — power which I know comes from God. I would not think of performing an operation without asking God's help."

—Earl S. Scott, in
Young People's Weekly

* * *

Are You This Busy?

Luther once said: "I am so busy now that I find if I did not spend two or three hours each day in prayer, I could not get through the day. If I should neglect prayer but a single day, I should lose a great deal of the fire of faith."

—*Link and Visitor*

* * *

Work More ON Your Knees

A preacher, while watching a marble cutter at work, exclaimed: "I wish I could deal such clanging blows on stony hearts!" The workman replied: "Maybe you could if you worked like me, *on your knees.*"

—*The Free Methodist*

* * *

All Traced to Kneeling Figures!

D. L. Moody declared, "Every great movement of God can be traced to a kneeling figure!" Therefore, "Ye that make mention of the Lord, KEEP NOT SILENCE" (Isa. 62:6b).

—W. B. K.

* * *

Obituary of Mrs. Prayer Meeting

"Mrs. Prayer Meeting died recently at the First Neglected Church, on Worldly Ave. Born many years ago in the midst of great revivals, she was a strong, healthy child, fed largely on testimony and Bible study, soon growing into world wide prominence, and was one of the most influential members of the famous Church family.

"For the past several years Sister Prayer Meeting has been failing in health, gradually wasting away until rendered helpless by stiffness of knees, coldness of heart, inactivity and weakness of purpose and will power. At the last she was but a shadow of her former happy self. Her last whispered words were inquiries concerning the strange absence of her loved ones now busy in the marts of trade and places of worldly amusements.

"Experts, including Dr. Works, Dr. Reform and Dr. Joiner, disagreed as to the cause of her fatal illness, administering large doses of organization, socials, contests and drives, but to no avail. A post mortem showed that a deficiency of spiritual food coupled with the lack of faith, heartfelt religion and general support, were contributing causes. Only a few were present at her death, sobbing over memories of her past beauty and power.

"In honor of her going, the church doors will be closed on Wednesday nights, save the third Wednesday night of each month, when the Ladies Pink Lemonade Society serves refreshments to the men's handball team."

—*Free Will Echo*

* * *

Prayer Silences Infidel

Arrangements had been made for a lecture by the agnostic lecturer, Bradlaugh, who was a forceful orator, and it was feared by a small group of believers in the city that his visits would cause great spiritual harm to the youth of the place. They covenanted together that they would take hold of God for the hindering of the meeting. The evening came, however, and Bradlaugh appeared on the platform before a capacity audience. Was the prayer of the earnest group to go unanswered? After the introductory remarks by the chairman, the great infidel stepped to the front and began to speak. "Ladies and gentlemen," he said, and then passed his hand over his forehead. A second and a third time he repeated those words, and then, turning to the chairman, he said, "For some reason, sir, my mind seems clouded, and I am unable to continue. I am sorry to disappoint the audience." He sat down. The Chairman apologized, and the audience dispersed. Bradlaugh never returned to the place.

—*Alliance Weekly*

* * *

She Was Worried

A little Chinese girl lived in a school where missionaries teach. When praying one night she said to the missionary: "Do you think God understands Chinese?"

"Oh, yes," replied the missionary. "Why do you ask?"

"Because," said the little girl, "sometimes when I feel bad I like to pray to God in Chinese, and I wonder if He understands, just the same as English."

"Of course," said the missionary, "God knows every language, and it is not the words we say as much as the feeling down deep in our hearts that makes us want to speak of Him. He says in the Bible: 'Before they call I will answer, and while they are yet speaking I will hear.' So speak in any language and He will hear."

—*World Conquest*

* * *

An Alienist's Evaluation of Prayer

Dr. T. Bulkley, the distinguished mental specialist, addressed the British Medical Association in these words, "As an alienist and one whose whole life has been concerned with sufferings of the mind, I would state that of all the hygienic measures to counteract disturbed sleep, depression of the spirits, and all the miserable sequels of a disturbed mind, I would undoubtedly give first place to the simple habit of prayer."

—*Moody Monthly*

* * *

They Did Not Know What to Say

Two African chiefs once came to Dr. Chalmers, a missionary, and said, "We want Christian teachers; will you send them?" Chalmers had no one to send, and told them so. Two years passed, and these two chiefs came again. Dr. Chalmers himself happened to be at liberty, and he traveled over the intervening country and arrived on Sunday morning. To his surprise, he saw the whole village on their knees in perfect silence. He asked one of the chiefs what they were doing, and received the reply, "Praying." "But you are not saying anything," said Dr. Chalmers. "White man," the chief answered, "we do not know what to say. For two years, every Sunday morning, we have met here; and for four hours we have been on our knees, and we have been praying like that, but we do not know what to say." What a picture of waiting nations!

—*Gospel Herald*

* * *

How They Prayed

George Whitefield, the famous English evangelist, said, "O Lord give me souls, or take my soul!"

Henry Martyn, missionary, kneeling on India's coral strands, cried out, "Here let me burn out for God."

David Brainerd, missionary to the North American Indians 1718-1747: "Lord, to Thee I dedicate myself. O accept of me, and let me be Thine forever. Lord, I desire nothing else, I desire nothing more." The last words in his diary, seven days before he died, "O Come, Lord Jesus, come quickly. Amen."

Thomas a'Kempis, 1379-1471: "Give what Thou wilt, and how much Thou wilt, and when Thou wilt. Set me where Thou wilt and deal with me in all things, just as Thou wilt."

Dwight L. Moody: "Use me then, my Saviour, for whatever purpose and in whatever way Thou mayest require. Here is my poor heart, an empty vessel; fill it with Thy grace."

Martin Luther, a few words from his great agony of prayer on the night preceding his appearance before the Diet of Worms: "Do Thou, my God, do Thou, God, stand by me against all the world's wisdom and reason. O do it! Thou must do it. Stand by me, Thou True, Eternal God!"

John McKenzie, a prayer of a young missionary candidate as he knelt on the banks of the Lossie: "O Lord, send me to the darkest spot on earth!"

"Praying Hyde," a missionary in India: "Father, give me these souls, or I die."

Mrs. Comstock, a missionary in India, a prayer of parting when she sent her children home: "Lord Jesus, I do this for Thee."

John Hunt, a missionary to the Fiji Islands, a prayer upon his dying bed: "Lord, save Fiji, save Fiji; save these people, O Lord; have mercy upon Fiji; save Fiji!"

—Wesleyan Methodist

* * *

The Explanation!

The men who have accomplished most for God have been men of prayer. John Wesley was wont to spend at least two hours each day in prayer. Samuel Rutherford rose at three o'clock each morning to wait upon God. John Fletcher was said to have stained the walls of his chamber by the breath of his prayers. The greatest missionaries have been uniformly men of prayer. Think of David Brainerd dying at the age of twenty-nine, and Henry Martyn at the age of thirty-one, and yet their names stand out as among the brightest stars in the missionary firmament. These young men exerted a profound influence not only upon their own generation, but upon all succeeding generations as well. It was not by their actual labors, which were soon cut off, so much as by their prayer life and their resultant saintly characters.

—Gospel Herald

* * *

"The Face Tells"

Dr. Joseph Parker says, "You can tell whether a man has been keeping up his life of prayer. His witness is in his face. That face grows in vulgarity which does not commune with God day by day. It loses beauty. 'The shew of their countenance doth witness against them.' There is an invisible sculptor that chisels the face into the upper attitude of the soul. 'They took knowledge of them, that they had been with Jesus.' Their garments smelled of cassia, and all the fragrant flowers that grow about the feet of the King."

—Dr. Alexander MacLaren

Living As We Pray

I knelt to pray when day was done,
　And prayed "O Lord bless every one,
Lift from every saddened heart the pain,
　And let the sick be well again."

And then I woke another day,
　And carelessly went upon my way.
The whole day long I did not try
　To wipe a tear from any eye.

I did not try to share the load
　Of any brother on the road.
I did not even go to see
　The sick man just next door to me.

Yet once again when day was done,
　I prayed "O Lord bless everyone."
But as I prayed, unto my ear
　There came a voice that whispered
　　clear,

"Pause, hypocrite, before you pray,
　Whom have you tried to bless today?
God's sweetest blessings always go,
　By hands which serve Him below."

And then I hid my face and cried,
　"Forgive me, God, for I have lied.
Let me but live another day,
　And I will live the way I pray!"

—Selected

* * *

How High?

It was time for evening prayers. Buddy's busy day was over, and, with Daddy, he was ready to pray. The usual words were prayed, and the "for Christ's sake, Amen," added; then: "Daddy, how high did we pray? Did God hear us, Daddy?" Daddy was accustomed to the task of trying to answer difficult questions — that rare privilege that daddies have — and tried his best with this one, assuring Buddy that God heard every word; that he always hears everything we say. Soon Buddy slumbered, but Daddy remained awake for a time, thinking about the question of how "high" prayers go. How high we pray is an important thought, because there are things that weigh down our prayers sometimes. Jesus told of several of them — the man, for instance, who, at the altar, remembered something, and had to hasten off to make it right.

—Gospel Messenger

"While the Brother Is Finishing"

It is said that Moody could not stand long prayers in public. At one of his meetings he called on a brother to pray, and he became lost in a eulogy on the Almighty. As Moody saw no landing in sight, he suddenly said, "While the brother is finishing his prayer let us sing number 75." A medical student happened to be bored with the long prayer, and was just reaching for his hat to leave when Moody's sudden switch from the prayer to the song arrested his attention. He put his hat down, remained in the service, and was converted. The student was the famous missionary afterward, Sir William Grenfell.

—*Gospel Herald*

* * *

"Give Him What He Asks!"

It is related of Alexander the Great, that, on one occasion a courtier asked him for some financial aid. That great leader told him to go to his treasurer and ask for whatever amount he wanted. A little later, the treasurer appeared and told Alexander the man had asked for an enormous sum, and that he hesitated to pay out so much. "Give him what he asks for," replied the great conqueror; "he has treated me like a KING in his asking, and I shall be like a king in my giving!"

Greatly grieved must be our God because of the smallness of our requests of Him!

"Thou art coming to a King,
    LARGE petitions with thee bring;
For His grace and power are such,
    None can ever ask too much!"

—W. B. K.

* * *

"I Must Pray More"

A young man had been called to the foreign field. He had not been in the habit of preaching, but he knew one thing, how to prevail with God; and going one day to a friend, he said, "I don't see how God can use me on the field; I have no special talent." His friend said: "My brother, God wants men on the field who can pray. There are too many preachers now, and too few pray-

ers." He went. In his room in the early dawn a voice was heard weeping and pleading for souls. All through the day, the shut door and the hush that prevailed made you feel like walking softly, for a soul was wrestling with God.

To his home hungry souls would flock, drawn by irresistible power. In the morning hours some would call and say: "I have gone by your home and have longed to come in. Will you tell me how I can be saved?" or from some distant place another would call saying: "I heard you would tell us here how we might find heart-rest."

—J. Hudson Taylor, in
    Christian Action

* * *

"Do It Again"

In Nottingham, England, is the Wesleyan Chapel where William Booth, founder of the Salvation Army, was converted. A memorial tablet marks the spot where this notable friend of the friendless received his baptism of spiritual power. Salvation Army leaders from around the world journey to that chapel as a shrine.

One day an aged colored man in the uniform of the Army was found by the minister of the chapel standing with uplifted eyes before the tablet.

"Can a man say his prayers here?" the old soldier asked. "Of course," was the reply. "Of course, a man can say his prayers here."

And the old Army officer went down on his knees, and lifting his hands before the tablet, prayed, "O God; do it again! Do it again!"

—*The Evangel*

* * *

Laying Hold On God!

Mr. Roger Babson in an after-dinner address made the following statement: "Prayer is the greatest unused power in the world, and faith is the greatest undiscovered resource." Faith is a grasping of Almighty power; the hand of man laid on the arm of God; when the things impossible to us become the possible, O Lord, through Thee.

—*Sunday School Times*

Irretrievable Error

A pious but cranky old lady was greatly annoyed because her neighbors forgot to ask her to go on their picnic.

On the morning of the event they suddenly realized their affront and sent a little boy to ask her to come along.

"It's too late now," she snapped. "I've already prayed for rain."

—*Sunday School Times*

* * *

How Moravians Prayed

When God was visiting the Moravians in the early days, they organized at Herrnhut two praying bands, one of men and the other of women, each with twenty-four members. These bands set apart one man and one woman to pray every hour of the day, so that the men in their place and the women in theirs were praying continuously during the twenty-four hours. This double prayer, unbroken through every day, was maintained for a hundred years. During this period there emerged the Moravian Mission movement in which the missionary church grew three times as large as the home church. The Moravians were used to give new light on essential Bible truths to John and Charles Wesley, thus preparing them for the revival that swept England and reached America.

—*Sunday School Times*

* * *

Prayer Track

In a certain West African village the native Christians had no privacy for prayer in their huts. So each Christian made off to the bush, behind his hut, for seasons of prayer. After a while there was a worn track from the hut to the place of prayer. Then if it ever happened that the track became overgrown from want of use, another Christian villager would admonish his neighbor, "Brother, there is something wrong with your prayer track."

—*Power*

* * *

When Praying Hyde Prayed

Dr. Wilbur Chapman wrote to a friend: I have learned some great lessons concerning prayer. At one of our missions in England the audiences were exceedingly small; but I received a note saying that an American missionary was going to pray God's blessing down on our work. He was known as Praying Hyde. Almost instantly the tide turned. The hall became packed, and at my first invitation fifty men accepted Christ as their Saviour. As we were leaving I said, "Mr. Hyde, I want you to pray for me." He came to my room, turned the key in the door, and dropped on his knees, and waited five minutes without a single syllable coming from his lips. I could hear my own heart thumping, and his beating. I felt hot tears running down my face. I knew I was with God. Then, with upturned face, down which the tears were streaming, he said, "O God." Then for five minutes at least he was still again; and then, when he knew that he was talking with God there came from the depths of his heart such petitions for me as I had never heard before. I rose from my knees to know what real prayer was. We believe that prayer is mighty and we believe it as we never did before.

—*Gospel Herald*

* * *

"The Lord Heareth!"

A lifeguard sits all day on the beach watching for persons needing his help. All about him is the noise of hundreds of pleasure-seekers, talking, laughing, shouting — the waves roaring — noises of other types.

"I don't see how," remarked a man one day, "you can hear a cry for help when someone out in the water needs you."

"No matter how great the noise and confusion," replied the guard, "I have never had an occasion when I could not distinguish the cry of distress above all the other sounds."

The gentleman went away thinking about this — and reflecting that it is a lot like that with God. When a soul cries out for His help, amid the babble and storms of life, He never fails to hear.

—W. B. K.

Getting a Church on Its Feet

The quickest way to get a church on its feet is to get it on its knees.

—W. W. Ayer, in
Christian Digest

Tie a Prayer Knot

When you come to the end of your rope, tie a prayer knot, and hang on.

—From *Prayer Proverbs,*
by W. T. McLean

PREACHERS — PREACHING

A Dull Year and Discouraged!

It had been a dull year in the church where Moffat was converted. The deacons finally said to the old pastor: "We love you, pastor, but don't you think you had better resign? There hasn't been a convert this year." "Yes," he replied, "it has been a dull year, sadly dull to me. Yet, I mind me that one did come, wee Bobby Moffat. But he is so wee a bairn that I suppose it is not right to count him." A few years later Bobby came to the pastor and said, "Pastor, do you think that I could ever learn to preach? I feel within me that I ought to. If I could just lead souls to Christ, that would be happiness to me." The pastor answered, "Well, Bobby, you might. Who knows? At least you can try!" He did try, and years later when Robert Moffat came back from his wonder-work in Africa the King of England rose and uncovered in his presence, and the British Parliament stood as a mark of respect. The humble old preacher, who had but one convert, and who was so discouraged, is dead and forgotten, and yet that was the greatest year's work he ever did, and few have equalled it!

—*Young People's Weekly*

* * *

"Fool!"

Henry Ward Beecher often received anonymous letters, among them being a most unusual one with only the word FOOL written on a large sheet of paper. Mr. Beecher took the letter into the pulpit with him. Said he, "I have received many anonymous letters, but I hold in my hand the uniquest one I ever received. The anonymous writer signed his name FOOL but failed to enclose the letter!"

—W. B. K.

"John Wanamaker's Man, Not God's"

In 1904 there came another crisis. I was invited to return to London to take charge of what appeared to be a derelict cause at Westminster. The crisis was created by the fact that the door of opportunity stood wide open before me in this country. Among other things, John Wanamaker, whom I knew well and for whom I had a profound regard, telegraphed me to come to see him. When I did so, he said, "England is already made. This great country is in the making, and we need you here." He then offered, if I would remain, to build an auditorium for me with a Bible school attached, in Philadelphia. I at once told him that I couldn't do it. When he asked why, I said I should become John Wanamaker's man. The greatness of the man is seen in that he at once agreed and gave me his blessing.

—F. B. Meyer

* * *

God Only to Be Remembered

When I was in Northfield . . . I went out early one morning to conduct a camp meeting away off in the woods. The camp dwellers were two or three hundred men from the Water Street Mission in New York. At the beginning of the service prayer was offered for me, and the supplication opened with these inspired words: "O Lord, we thank thee for our brother. Now blot him out." Then the prayer continued: "*Reveal thy glory to us in such blazing splendor that he shall be forgotten.*" It was absolutely right, and I trust the prayer was answered.

—Dr. J. H. Jowett

* * *

"Too Much Time With The Saints!"

An old saint kept grumbling because a preacher did not come to see her often enough. Finally, he said, "Sister, I am too busy trying to save the unsaved among us to spend too much time with the saints. But I promise you that when we get to heaven, I will drop in some morning and stay a thousand years!"

—*Christian Observer*

* * *

The Preacher's Business

G. Campbell Morgan heard this statement made: "The preacher must catch the spirit of the age;" and gave the following answer: "God forgive him if he does. The preacher's business is to correct the spirit of the age."

—*Watchman-Examiner*

* * *

Statesman or Sinner

Daniel Webster, the famous American politician and orator, once spent a summer in New Hampshire, and every Lord's Day went to a little country church morning and evening. His niece asked him why he went there, when he paid little attention to far abler sermons in Washington. He replied: "In Washington they preach to Daniel Webster, the statesman, but this man has been telling Daniel Webster, the sinner, of Jesus of Nazareth." "All have sinned" (*Rom.* 3:23). Preach Christ.

—*Glad Tidings*

* * *

Two Great Pastors

We think of Phillips Brooks as a great preacher, but those fortunate enough to be in his church knew him also as a great pastor. He said one time, "I wish that I could devote every hour of the day to calling on my people. I know of no happier or more helpful work that a pastor can do, and I call as much as I can. How is it possible for one to preach to his people if he does not know them, their doubts, sorrows and ambitions?"

Dr. J. H. Jowett, like Paul, possessed rare powers of sympathy, for which he paid a high price, literally wearing himself out in his ministry. He once said, "At first I could not conduct a funeral without tears. I could not read the Burial Service without my speech being choked; but now I have had so many funerals, have seen so many people in sorrow, and have seen so much suffering, that I can read the Burial Service without tears. Well, perhaps this is part of the gracious providence of God that the burden should be eased, but I don't want the ease of it be at the cost of losing the compassion with my fellow men. I would rather have the tears, I would prefer the choking speech, I would prefer that my not-too-strong body should be tired out, drained out twice a week, if I might only keep my compassion for my fellow men."

—*Gospel Herald*

* * *

A Tall-Enough Preacher

A steward came to the presiding elder and asked for a preacher. "How big a man do you want?" asked the elder. "I do not care so much about his size," said the steward, "but *I want him to be tall enough to reach heaven when he is on his knees.*"

—*Baptist Bulletin Service*

* * *

Terminal Facilities

The BEST time to terminate a sermon is five minutes before any one wants you to stop!

A Christian lad invited his non-church-going boy friend to go with him to his church. The services were strange to the non-church-goer. He asked many questions about different phases of the service. In beginning his sermon, the pastor took out his watch and placed it, with care, on the pulpit. Asked the non-church-goer, "What does that mean?" "Aw, that don't mean nothing!" It should. Always send the sheep of Christ's pasture away wanting more. They are more likely to come back again, and regularly.

—*W. B. K.*

* * *

F. B. Meyer's Temptation

F. B. Meyer told the following experience to a few personal friends: "It was easy," he said, "to pray for the success of G. Campbell Morgan when he was in America. But when he came back to England and took a church near to mine, it was somewhat different. The old Adam in me was inclined to jealousy, but I got my heel upon his head, and whether I felt right toward my friend, I determined to act right. My church gave a reception for him, and I acknowledged that if it was not necessary for me to preach Sunday evenings I would dearly love to go and hear him myself. Well, that made me feel right toward him. But just see how the dear Lord helped me out of my difficulty. There was Thomas Spurgeon preaching wonderfully on the other side of me. He and Mr. Morgan were so popular, and drew such crowds, that our church caught the overflow, and we had all we could accommodate!"

—*King's Business*

* * *

Road To Irreverence

I met a man; and the music of God had gone out of him. With great honesty he told me how the glory had departed. First, he had disliked a preacher's style of preaching. Then he grew to dislike the preacher himself. Irreverance for the minister and his message expanded in the man's heart. Finally he found himself feeling irreverent toward the church where the man spoke Sunday after Sunday.

You see how it is? It is all a sad pattern. We cannot lose reverence for things spiritual without losing reverence for the Author of spirituality — God.

The road to irreverence usually does not begin with disrespect toward God, but disrespect toward the things of God.

—*Young People's Standard*

* * *

Enters Glory "Hitting" On All Cylinders!

The Rev. James Harris, 77, of Oreana, Illinois, collapsed and died at the end of his sermon in a county home for the aged. With his last breath, he said, "I have just one more point to make and then I'll close!" We believe he made that "last point" in the presence of his wondrous Lord!

—W. B. K.

Devotion vs. Talent

D. M. Panton of England writes of a young preacher without much natural ability or education, and certainly not possessed of a striking personality, who seemed to be God's instrument to melt many hearts and get people saved. An old theological professor was asked what he thought of the young man. His answer was: "There isn't enough talent in his sermons to fill a thimble, but there is devotion enough to float Elijah's chariot to Heaven — and that's what does it."

—*Christian Digest*

* * *

Preachers Who Talk Too Much

A wise and observant editor calls attention to those preachers who think they must make "appropriate" remarks. "Recently," says the editor, "we attended a church service at which the pastor introduced every hymn, every scripture reading, every anthem and every part of the service with 'appropriate' remarks. The consequence was that an hour was used up, and the people too before he reached his sermon. Evidently that pastor thinks that he is paid for his much speaking. We are certain that his people would let him off with less.

—*Clipped*

* * *

Isolation or Separation?

"The parish priest of austerity,
Climbed up the high church steeple,
To be nearer to God, and bring His Word,
Down to the people!
In sermon script he daily wrote,
What he thought was sent from heaven,
And dropped it down on the people's head,
Twice one day in seven.
In his age, God said, 'Come down and die,'
And he cried from his high church steeple:
'Where art Thou, Lord?' And the Lord replied,
'Down here among My people.' "

—*Selected*

Preachers' Kids

Pity the P. K.'s, Preachers' Kids? Nay! Rather thank God for them! Said Albert Edward Wiggam: "Preachers' children are among the most fortunate in the world. One-twelfth of all the persons listed in Who's Who in America are children of ministers!" The following were parsonage products: Louis Agassiz, George Bancroft, Henry Ward Beecher, Henry Clay, Jonathan Edwards, Ralph Waldo Emerson, Oliver Wendell Holmes, James Russell Lowell, Samuel F. B. Morse, Francis Parkman, and Harriet Beecher Stowe. The parsonage has contributed to the birth of our Nation, and to its upbuilding. John Hancock, first signer of the Declaration of Independence, was a minister's son. Nathaniel Greene, a general of the Revolution, was the son of a Quaker preacher. A. C. Muhlenberg, first speaker of the first congress of a new-born nation, was a preacher's son. Woodrow Wilson, too, was a minister's son. Herbert Hoover's mother was a Quaker preacher. Six minister's daughters have been "First Ladies of the land!' Our hats off to the Preachers' Kids!

—W. B. K.

* * *

"Thank God That You Can Do That Way"

Dr. Carl Armerding and his son, Hudson Taylor Armerding, were sitting in a meeting. As one of God's servants preached the wondrous Gospel of the grace of God, tears filled the eyes of Dr. Armerding. Said he to his son, "Son, why does a man act like this?" Said the son, "Dad, thank God that you CAN act that way." God, save us from a "dry-eyed" religion!

—W. B. K.

* * *

"The Preacher's Wife"

There is one person in your church Who knows your preacher's life.
She's wept and smiled and prayed with him,
And that's your preacher's wife!

She knows one prophet's weakest point,
And knows his greatest power.

She's heard him speak in trumpet tone,
In his great triumph hour.

She's heard him groaning in his soul,
When bitter raged the strife,
As hand in his she knelt with him —
For she's a preacher's wife!

The crowd has seen him in his strength,
When gleamed his drawn sword,
As underneath God's banner folds
He faced the devil's horde.

But she knows deep within her heart
That scarce an hour before,
She helped him pray the glory down
Behind a closet door!

You tell your tales of prophets brave,
Who walked across the world,
And changed the course of history,
By burning words they hurled.

And I will tell how back of them
Some women lived their lives,
Who wept with them and smiled with them —
They were the preacher's wives!
　　　　　　　　　—Selected

* * *

Why Billy Sunday Was Approved!

An examining committee, composed of ministers, had met to look into the qualifications of Billy Sunday to be ordained as a Gospel minister. Among other questions "fired" at the world-famous baseball player was a request that he identify a well-known church father, defining some of his writings. Billy was "stumped." After fumbling around for a moment, he, with a twinkle in his eye said, "I never heard of him! He was never on my team!" For awhile, indecision characterized the learned theologians. Finally one of them moved that Billy Sunday be recommended for ordination, adding that Billy Sunday had already won more souls for Christ than the whole shebang of them put together!

—W. B. K.

* * *

God, Not a Policeman

Among the first glimpses we get of our God is that of a Seeker: "Adam, where art thou?" (Gen. 3:9). In commenting upon this question to his Bible class, a teacher said, "You can never be a preacher if you read it as though God were a policeman. Read it as though God were a broken-hearted Father looking for a lost child!"

—W. B. K.

* * *

A "De-Flater!"

An influential Christ-rejector was genuinely saved in a church service. The pastor's heart was over-joyed! The edge of his joy, however, was somewhat dulled when he asked the new convert what it was in his sermon that brought him to God. "Ah," said the convert, "It wasn't your sermon; IT WAS YOUR TEXT!"

—W. B. K.

* * *

Hindrances in the Pulpit

Wesley once said, "There are some men who preach so well when in the pulpit, that it is a shame they should ever come out of it; and when they are out of it, they live so illy that it is a shame they should ever enter it."

—*Sunday School Times*

* * *

A Mistaken Interpretation

A young man presented himself to the presiding elder of the Methodist Church and said he desired to become a preacher. On being questioned by his ecclesiastical superior, he replied that the night before he had seen in the sky, written in large characters of gold, the letters P. C. — Preach Christ. As the presiding elder knew the young man well, as a person very excitable, and otherwise utterly unfitted for the work of the ministry, he said to him, "But, my young brother, you are mistaken. P. C. does not mean, in your case, Preach Christ. It means Plough Corn. It will be your calling, and you will be doing God's will most truly if you continue to help your father on the farm."

—From *A Bishop's Message*,
by Rev. Ethelbert Talbot

He Healed Others

The word "others" occurs in the Bible five hundred twenty-two times. Of Jesus it was said, "He healed others."

Dr. Adam Clarke, the great Biblical scholar of two hundred years ago, lies in Westminster Abbey. On his tomb is a candle burned down to near the socket, and around it these words: "In burning for others, I myself, also, have been consumed."

—*Sunday School Times*

* * *

"Don't Run"

As an old minister, five years in my first pastorate and forty-one in the second, I would pass on an encouraging hint to younger brethren. I left my first pastorate scared away by criticism, afterwards to learn the noise had all been made by one man. One man in a church, community, or organization, may by loud and persistent effort create the impression that matters are all wrong and that everybody is demanding a remedy; which puts me in mind of the old story about the "frog farm."

A farmer advertised a "frog farm" for sale, claiming that he had a pond that was thoroughly stocked with fine bullfrogs.

A prospective buyer appeared and was taken late one warm evening to the pond that he might hear the frogs. The "music'" made so favorable impression on the buyer that the sale was made.

Soon afterward the purchaser proceeded to drain the pond in order to catch and market the frogs. To his surprise, when the water was drained out of the pond, he found that all the noise had been made by one old bullfrog.

—G. B. F. Hallock

* * *

What He Remembered

Dr. Theodore L. Cuyler once visited Scotland and made diligent search for someone who had known Robert Murray M'Cheyne. Finally one old man was brought forward.

"Can you tell me," asked Dr. Cuyler, "some of the texts of M'Cheyne?" And the old man made reply, "I don't remember them." "Can you tell me some sentences that he used?" And the reply was, "I have entirely forgotten them." Then said Dr. Cuyler, "Don't you remember anything about him at all?" "Ah!" said the man, "that is a different question. I do remember something about him. When I was a lad by the wayside playing one day M'Cheyne came along, and laying his hand on my head said, 'Jamie, lad, I am away to see your poor sick sister,' and then, looking into my eyes, he said, 'And, Jamie, I am very concerned about your own soul.' I have forgotten his texts and his sermons, Dr. Cuyler, but I can still feel the tremble of his hand and I can see the tear in his eye."

—*Sunday School Journal*

* * *

"Get On Fire!"

"How can I get crowds to attend my services?" asked a young preacher of John Wesley. Replied Wesley, "Get on fire and people will come out to see you burn!"

—W. B. K.

* * *

Why He Did Not Understand

The story is told concerning a prime minister of England that he was invited to hear a distinguished preacher, who at the time was being widely used of God for the conversion of men. It is said that on that occasion the preacher was at his best and the Gospel was preached in demonstration of the Spirit and in power. On leaving the meeting the prime minister was asked how the meeting impressed him, and his reply was, "To tell you the truth, I gave the man my most careful attention from start to finish, but I was wholly unable to understand what the man was talking about." Here was a man with a great mind, able to deal with complex political problems, but wholly unable to receive the plain and simple teachings of the Cross. This proves the truth of what the apostle says: "The natural man receiveth not the things of the Spirit of God: for they are foolishness unto him: neither can he know them, because they are spiritually discerned."

—*Christian Digest*

How He Preached

Richard Baxter gave his ideal of preaching:
"To preach as though he'd never preach again,
And as a dying man to dying men!"

—W. B. K.

* * *

Not What, But Whom?

James Inglis was a graduate of Edinburgh University, learned and eloquent. He became the most popular preacher in Detroit, Mich. Eager listeners filled his church to overflowing. One day when he was preparing sermons for the following Sunday, it seemed a voice said to him, "James Inglis, whom are you preaching?" Startled, he answered, "I am preaching good theology." "I did not ask what you are preaching, but *whom* you are preaching?" Inglis answered, "I am preaching the Gospel." Again the voice said, "I did not ask you what you are preaching; I asked *whom* you are preaching?" Silent, with bowed head, for a long time sat the preacher. Then rousing himself, he cried: "O my God, I am preaching James Inglis. But henceforth I will preach Christ and Him crucified." Inglis went to a chest of drawers in his study, took his eloquent sermons from the files, and burned them one by one. From that day he turned his back upon popularity, and gave himself wholly, by life and testimony, to the task of lifting Christ before men. And God honored his consecration in giving him ever-widening influence.

—*Moody Monthly*

* * *

The Flowers Came Too Late

L. O. Dawson, in his autobiography, tells of an interesting service in a church that had just buried its pastor. On the following Sunday a memorial was held in his honor. A large congregation overflowed the house. One speaker told of his worth as a preacher, another told of his tender ministrations as a pastor, others spoke of him as a citizen, some thought of him as a neighbor, or father, and so on to the end. When it came his turn to speak, Brother Dawson spoke as follows: "All you have said of my dead brother is true. He was a man out of the ordinary and gave of his remarkable powers to your service without stint or reserve. But if you had, while he was yet alive, filled these pews as you have today, he would not now be dead. Empty pews broke his heart, and he did not know of the love of which you have been speaking. *He died for the lack of the things you have today so beautifully said and done.*"

More preachers die from broken hearts than from swelled heads!

—*The Clarion*

* * *

Sleepy Preaching

"If a man sleeps under my preaching, I do not send a boy to wake him up; but I feel that a boy had better come and wake me up."

—Henry Ward Beecher

* * *

Pray for Your Preacher

Dr. John Watson, better known to many as Ian Maclaren, in the early years of his ministry, determined to preach without manuscript. He took into his pulpit a single sheet of paper containing a few notes. Sometimes his memory failed, and he would say: "Friends, this is not very clear. It was clear in my study on Saturday. Now I will begin again." The people never showed any impatience. After a sermon one Sunday morning, a gaunt Highlander elder went to him and said, "When you are not remembering your sermon just give out a Psalm, and we will be singing while you are taking a rest, for we are all loving you and praying for you."

In after years, Dr. Watson said, "I am in the ministry to-day because of the tenderness and charity of those country folks; those perfect gentlemen and Christians."

—*Gospel Herald*

* * *

Why Camouflage?

A young man, brought up to look upon, and to think of "God as God," had listened to a long diatribe on "The Mys-

terious Urge Behind the World." After the service he asked his chaplain, "When you use such statements, *do you mean God?*" "I suppose I do," said the chaplain. "Then *why don"t you say so?*" said the lad. "The Bible never camouflages the name of God or His place in the world."

—J. W. Lipscomb, in the *Southern Methodist Layman*

* * *

"Chariot of Humanity Stuck!"

"When the chariot of humanity gets stuck, as it has done now, nothing will lift it out except great preaching that goes straight to the mind and heart. It is time the Christian churches should act together and act promptly in the name of God and humanity. If the churches fail, I do not know what is going to happen."

—David Lloyd George

* * *

"I Understood Everything He Said."

A child accompanied her mother to a preaching service of Dr. Harry A. Ironside. The little girl listened with rapt attention to the straight-forward, simple Gospel message. Upon leaving the church, the child said to her mother, "Mother, I thought Dr. Ironside was a great preacher." "Yes, darling, he is, but why do you thus talk?" "Why," said the little girl, "I understood everything he said!" Dr. Ironside considered the saying of the child one of the greatest compliments ever paid him.

—W. B. K.

* * *

"The Preacher's Gravest Peril: Restless Scattering of Energies!"

"I am profoundly convinced that one of the gravest perils which beset our ministry is a restless scattering of energies over an amazing multiplicity of interests, which leaves no margin of time or of strength for receptive and absorbing communion with God. We are tempted to be always 'on the run,' and to measure our fruitfulness by our pace and by the ground we cover in the course of a week!

Gentlemen, we are not always doing the most business when we seem to be the most busy. We may think we are truly busy when we are really only restless. A little studied retirement would greatly enrich our ministry."

    —From *The Preacher*:
    His Life and Work, by Jowett

* * *

Resigned and Re-Signed

Dr. Thomas T. Villiers says, "I once heard John Robertson speak. He told us that a year before he had felt he must leave the ministry. He said, 'I struggled all night in prayer with God about the matter, and about the time the eastern light began to stream in the windows, I said, "O God, here is my commission; I resign." But God, in His infinite mercy, said to me, "My son, you need not resign your commission. I will re-sign your commission." And ever since then I have been preaching under a re-signed commission.' "

    —*Wonderful Word*

* * *

How Robert McCheyne Preached

Let the old sexton tell the story. A visitor to the manse where McCheyne lived and church where he preached asked the old man to tell him something of McCheyne — how he studied and how he preached.

The old sexton took him into the study and said, "Sit down, now put your hands over your face, now let the tears fall — that is the way my master studied." They went into the church and up into the pulpit. "Lean over, way over, and stretch out your hands towards the congregation and now let the tears fall — that is the way my master preached."

    —Rev. J. Kenton Parker

* * *

All Need Christ

I read of a minister traveling in the South who obtained permission to preach in the local jail. A son of his host went with him. On the way back the young man, who was not a Christian, said to the minister:

"I hope some of the convicts were impressed. Such a sermon as that ought to do them good."

"Did it do you good?" the minister asked.

"Oh, you were preaching to the convicts!" the young man answered.

The minister shook his head and said, "I preached Christ, and you need Him as much as they."

    —*The Christian Advocate*

* * *

Heap Big Wind

An Indian had attended services one Sunday morning. The sermon, without real spiritual food, had been very loud in spots. The Indian, a good Christian, was not impressed.

When asked how he had liked the sermon, he said: "High wind; big thunder; no rain!"

    —*Marion County Mail*

* * *

Said Dr. Will Mayo:

"I have seen patients that were dead by all standards. We knew they could not live. But I have seen a minister come to the bedside and do something for him that I could not do, although I have done everything in my professional power. But something touched some immortal spark in him and in defiance of medical knowledge and materialistic common sense, that patient LIVED!"

The Mayo Brothers, Doctors Will and Charles, were founders of the world-famed Mayo Clinics. "We're making more money than two people have a right to," said Dr. Charles to his brother. Then they began to disperse, with a generous hand, much of their earnings in co-operating with the Great Physician, Jesus, in wiping away tears of sorrow and suffering from tear-dimmed eyes!

    —W. B. K.

* * *

"We Would See Jesus"

There was a certain kind and diligent pastor who was dearly loved by his people for his gracious spirit, but whose preaching had little power and appeared to be devoid of a vital message. One

501

Lord's day, when he took his place in the pulpit prior to the morning service, he found a slip of paper there with these words only: "Sir, we would see Jesus."

The kind old preacher was hurt at first, gravely so — but for days the words burned in his heart, and because they did, he began to meditate more and more upon the Person of Christ. This began to reflect in his life and in his preaching, and ere long a change in him was felt among his congregation. At length, on another Sunday morning, he again found a slip of paper on the pulpit. This time the message read: "Then were the disciples glad, when they saw the Lord."

—*The Pilgrim*

* * *

An Incorruptible Inheritance

I shall never forget an hour in our home (where there were ten children) when my father sat there before us, and the college question was up. One of the children said to him, "If you had used the great brains you have in the law business, instead of being a preacher, we would all have had a chance to go to college, and you would have had money enough to send us." I saw my dad look out the window. He turned back with tears running down his cheeks, and said, "Yes, that is the truth. I could have done it, but when you woke up in hell you would have cursed me far worse than you do now. Children, money isn't everything; and I will try to leave you an inheritance that is incorruptible, that does not fade away. When I am gone — a poor Methodist preacher — you will know me one thing, and that is that I knew Jesus." Oh, I am glad he didn't sell out to what his children wanted!

—Paul Rader, in
Moody Church News

* * *

You Can Help Your Pastor Succeed

Dr. J. Wilbur Chapman had an experience in his first pastorate in Philadelphia which ought to encourage other pastors and churches to establish the same kind of pastoral support. It is de-

scribed in this clipping from an unknown source:

"Dr. J. Wilbur Chapman in his first pastorate in Philadelphia was visited by a layman who frankly said to him: 'You are not a strong preacher. In the usual order of things you will fail here, but a little group of laymen have agreed to gather every Sunday morning and pray for you.' Dr. Chapman added: 'I saw that group grow to one thousand men gathered weekly to pray for this preacher.' Of course, he had great success. Almost any pastor would succeed if a group of leaders would thus back him up."

—*The Presbyterian*

* * *

Wanted: Hundred Men

John Wesley said, "Give me a hundred men who fear nothing but sin, and desire nothing but God, and I will shake the world: I care not a straw whether they be clergymen or laymen; and such alone will overthrow the kingdom of Satan and build up the Kingdom of God on earth."

—*The Preacher's Magazine*

* * *

The Sermon that Failed

A Methodist layman visited a great city church in Ohio during a business trip. After the service he congratulated the minister on his service and sermon. "But," said the manufacturer, "if you were my salesman I'd discharge you. You got my attention by your appearance, voice, and manner; your prayer, reading, and logical discourse aroused my interest; you warmed my heart with a desire for what you preached; and then — *and then you stopped, without asking me to do something about it!* In business, the important thing is to get them to sign on the dotted line."

—*Record of Christian Work*

* * *

Why There Were No Converts

A minister once came to Spurgeon and said dolefully, "I have been preaching for so many years and hardly have any been converted." "Why, man," exclaimed the great preacher, "you didn't expect that every time you preached a sermon somebody would be converted, did you?" "No, of course, I didn't expect that." "Well," that's why they weren't converted!" Could that be our trouble today?

—*Christian Digest*

* * *

A Homily on Homiletics

One day I was riding along a country highway when I met a farmer with a load of hay so big that it took up the whole roadway. To get around it we almost upset in the ditch. That event furnished me with a valuable homiletic lesson. I said to myself: If that hay were baled it would not take a quarter as much space, and there would be just as much hay. Many sermons are like that load of hay. They need baling. There will be just as much hay, just as much food for your people. Loose hay has thrown many a churchman into the ditch. For *length* remember that you will have other chances to preach; for *fervor*, preach as if this were your last chance.

—Henry B. Williams, in *Watchman-Examiner*

* * *

"Exposing the Scriptures"

After the usual preliminaries, the Negro minister stood, and, opening his Bible on the pulpit, said, "And now, brudders and sisters, I'ze going to expose the Scriptures!" After all, isn't this the bounded obligation, under God, of every minister of the Gospel of the grace of God? "Preach the Word!"

—W. B. K.

* * *

"Young Man, You Can't Preach!"

A young convert tried to preach in the open air. He could not preach very well, but he did the best he could. Someone interrupted him and said, "Young man, you cannot preach; you ought to be ashamed of yourself."

Said the young man, "So I am, but I am not ashamed of my Lord."

—*Moody*

Dangerous Inclusiveness

A brilliant modernistic preacher, who had pleased his audience with flowery oratory as he discoursed glibly of the importance of breadth of view and the danger of bigoted opinions, was bidding farewell to his congregation as he was about to leave them for a new parish. One of his young men approached him, and said: "Pastor, I am so sorry we are losing you. Before you came I was one who did not care for God, man, or the Devil, but through your delightful sermons, I have learned to love them all!"

—Dr. H. A. Ironside

* * *

"Lord, Nudge Me When I've Said Enough!"

A preacher who was popular with his congregation explained his successes as the result of a silent prayer he offered each time he entered the pulpit. It went like this:

"Lord, fill my mouth with worthwhile stuff, and nudge me when I've said enough!"

—*School Activities*

* * *

There Is A Difference!

Aunt Becky was punctuating the Negro preacher's sermon with "Amen! Amen! Praise de Lawd!" as he lit into every sort of sin from murder to shooting craps. Then the parson moved on against snuff-dipping, and Aunt Becky exclaimed to her neighbor indignantly, "Dar now! *He's done stopped preachin' and gone to medlin'!*"

—*Moody Monthly*

* * *

Vivid Preaching

Whitefield's sermons abounded in striking figures of speech and in vivid illustrations. Lord Chesterfield heard him graphically describe a sinner, under the figure of a blind man, going along the edge of a cliff, guided only by his staff. As the blind man came to the edge, suddenly his staff fell from his hand. As Whitefield described the man seeking to recover it and just ready to step into the chasm, Chesterfield bounded from his seat, exclaiming, "O God; he's gone! Save him!"

—*Sunday School Times*

* * *

His Preaching Convicted

In a pew of a great London church one Sunday evening we found a minister of our acquaintance, who, so he told us, had been having the luxury of two Sundays "off." He had spent them in paying visits to some of the great churches of the metropolis. He had listened to one of the most brilliant and popular men in Nonconformity; he had sat under the spell of a silver-tongued preacher of the Church of England. That afternoon he had also heard a great mission preacher, a man of no learning, or rude eloquence, and, as he expressed it, quite antediluvian in his theological view. That service had left an abiding impression on his mind. "What did you think of him?" we asked. "Well, of course," he replied, "for style, and all that, he is not to be mentioned in the same breath with —— and with ——, but, do you know, that man made me feel like a scamp!"

—*Sunday at Home*

* * *

"Yes, Dear, But Remember, I Have Had To Listen To You Five Times Today!"

It was at the close of a Lord's Day, and Dr. Harry A. Ironside had been busy in the King's business. Five times had he spoken. On the way home — how human it all was — a simple question of Mrs. Ironside was turned aside with irritation. The Holy Spirit quickly convicted this man of God. Contritely, he asked his wife's' forgiveness with, "Forgive me. I am quite tired. Remember, I have preached five times today." And then came the answer: "Yes, dear, I know; but remember, I have had to listen to you five times today!"

—*Moody Monthly*

* * *

A Study in Values

Sir Astley Cooper, on visiting Paris, was asked by the chief surgeon of the

empire how many times he had performed a certain feat of surgery. He replied that he had performed the operation 13 times. "Ah, but Monsieur, I have done it 160 times. How many times did you save life?" continued the curious Frenchman, after he had looked into the blank amazement of Sir Astley's face. "I," said the Englishman, "saved eleven out of the thirteen. How many did you save out of the 160?" "Ah, Monsieur, I lose dem all; *but the operation was very brilliant.*" Of how many popular sermons might the same verdict be given! *Souls are not saved, but the services are very brilliant!*

—C. H. Spurgeon

* * *

A Potential Major General

Matthew Culbertson gave up his commission in the United States Army to become a missionary. At Shanghai he did valiant service during the Taiping riots. A minister said to him, "Culbertson, if you were at home, you might be a major general." The missionary replied: "Doubtless I might; men whom I taught at West Point are major generals to-day." And then he added these words with deep earnestness: "But I would not change places with one of them. I consider there is no post of influence on earth equal to that of a man who is permitted to preach the Gospel." He had chosen "the better part," and had no yearning after secular honors.

—*Old Scrapbook*

* * *

When To Stop Boring

Beneath a glass atop a pulpit which Dr. Walter Wilson approached to bring a message occurred these wise words of wisdom, "If after ten minutes you don't strike oil, QUIT BORING!"

—W. B. K.

* * *

"How To Reach the Masses"

Years ago a convention met in Indianapolis to discuss "How to Reach the Masses." One day during that convention a young man stood on a box on a corner and began to preach. A crowd gathered, mostly workingmen going home to their suppers. They were electrified by the sermon. They forgot that they were tired. They forgot that they were hungry.

The crowd became so dense that it had to move. The preacher announced that he would preach again at the Academy of Music. They followed him down the street, singing as they went, and they filled the main floor of the building, sitting with their dinner buckets, while he preached again with such power that they were moved to tears.

But he had only a few minutes to preach because the convention on "How to Reach the Masses" was gathering in the same auditorium. While the convention was discussing how to reach the masses, D. L. Moody was *doing* it! He was preaching the kingdom of God and every man was pressing violently into it!

—Vance Havner, in *Moody Monthly*

* * *

How to Keep Tender

Andrew Bonar and Robert M'Cheyne were having one of their frequent talks together, talking over the ways of their ministry, when "M'Cheyne asked me," says Bonar, "what my last Sunday's subject had been. It had been, 'The wicked shall be turned into hell.' On hearing this awful text, he asked, 'Were you able to preach it in tenderness?'"

—*The Pentecostal Evangel*

* * *

Papa Praying, Mama Packing

A minister received a call from a large church at almost double his current salary. He replied that he would prayerfully consider the matter and give them his decision in a few days. A short time later the pastor's son was asked by an interested friend if his father had decided to accept the offer.

"I don't know," the child replied. "Papa is still praying, but Mama has our things all packed."

—*Selected*

* * *

Preach the Gospel!

A young minister in a college town was embarrassed by the thought of criticism in his cultured congregation.

He sought counsel from his father, an old and wise minister, saying: "Father, I am hampered in my ministry in the pulpit I am now serving. If I cite anything from geology, there is Prof. A—, teacher of this science, right before me. If I use an illustration of Roman mythology, there is Prof. B— ready to trip me up for my little inaccuracy. If I mention something in English literature that pleases me, I am cowered by the presence of the learned man that teaches that branch. What shall I do?"

The sagacious old man replied: "*Do not be discouraged, preach the gospel. They probably know very little of that.*"

—*The Broadcaster*

* * *

Tactful Preaching

The story is told of a clergyman who had just been called to a wealthy church. He wanted to present to them tactfully the facts of the Gospel without hurting anyone's feelings (quite a feat), so he said, "You should repent, to some extent, or else you might be damned, more or less, and possibly go to hell, in a measure." Our pulpits have been overrun by such vacillators. They fluctuate between the north pole of liberalism and the south pole of conservatism. Their ministry is marked by irresolution and indecision. They tread the King's Highway with faltering and hesitating steps, and yet expect people to follow them.

—*Voice*

* * *

Spurgeon Presented Christ

"How did you like Mr. Spurgeon?" asked one of a friend who had just returned from hearing the famous preacher.

The reply was, "I forgot to investigate Mr. Spurgeon; my attention was drawn so closely to the Saviour of whom he was preaching."

—*Watchman-Examiner*

* * *

Clarity Also Needed

A newspaper report of a sermon on I Corinthians 13:1 misprinted the word "charity" making the text read: "Though I speak with the tongues of men and of angels, and have not clarity, I am become as sounding brass, or a tinkling cymbal." Commenting on this, the editor said: "As it appears in print it was not New Testament truth, but it was truth, nevertheless. The people want the preacher to be luminous rather than voluminous, and the preacher who is without clarity will soon be without a congregation.'"

—Immanuel Missionary

* * *

In God's Presence

An old minister of a small church in a country town had one day in his audience a very distinguished statesman. The service went on about as usual, and the old minister preached with his accustomed earnestness and plainness of speech.

At the close of the service, several members of the congregation gathered about him and said: "Brother, we had a distinguished visitor today, but you did not seem at all embarrassed." Whereupon the old man replied, "I have been *preaching in the presence of the Almighty* God for forty years, and do you think with Him as one of my constant hearers, any man can embarrass me by his presence?"

—Power

* * *

Whom He Wanted To Please.—

At a church reception, given a young man who had just been installed as the pastor, a woman went up to the young man and said, "I do not uderstand how you dared attempt the task of pleasing seven hundred people." Quick as a flash he replied: "I did not come to this city to please seven hundred people. I have come to please only One, and if I please Him all will be well."

—Record of Christian Work

* * *

Whom He Saw

A Christian man urged his unsaved friend to go to hear a preacher whom he liked very much. The friend com-

plied with this request. Afterward the Christian asked, "Well, what did you think of him?" "I did not think anything of him," was the reply. The Christian was disappointed until the friend added: "I was so busy thinking of the Christ whom he preached that I did not have time to think of the preacher. And now his Saviour is my Saviour, too."

—Sunday School Times

* * *

Worn Trousers

Two ministers' wives were in conversation, and while they talked they sewed. Said one of the ladies: "I don't know what we are going to do. In our church there seems to be no life, though my husband spends hours preparing his sermons. But the people do not care to hear him, his salary is far behind, interest on the church mortgage is overdue, and we are discouraged."

The other pastor's wife replied: "It is not like that at our church. The pews are filled every Sunday, and Wednesday nights too. My husband gets great joy in visiting his people and praying with them. We have added three new missionaries to our responsibilities this year. God is blessing abundantly."

Both of these ladies were mending their husbands' trousers — the first was working at the seat; the second, at the knees.

—The Anchor

* * *

Why He Passed One Church

I was holding a revival service in a city in Virginia where the people were beautifully hospitable. I went to the home of a young banker and his wife one night after church for refreshments. On the way we passed another large --- church. I remarked, "Maybe its none of my business, but why do you pass this church which is within two blocks of your home to go to the other?" The baker answered: "I live all week among the hard things of life where men are cruel to each other and where might and wrong are forever on the throne and truth and goodness are on the scaffold.

I need to have my spiritual batteries restored; I need to meet God face to face. In the church across the street the music is jazzed; the atmosphere is one of fun and laughter; the sermon is full of jokes, and there is no reverence. I am hungry for something I cannot find over there."

—C. Roy Angell, in
the Teacher

Three Divisions

In preaching on the text, "Adam, Where Art Thou?" a Negro preacher said, "I make three divisions to dis tex': Fustly, ebery man got to be somewhar. Secondly, some men is whar they ought not to be. Thirdly, dey dat is whar they ought not to be, is gwine to find themselves whar day don' want to be."

—W. B. K.

PRESENCE, GOD'S

As If No Other Child.—

Dr. Frosyth told the story of a friend of his who was taken over a sheep farm in Australia at the time of shearing, and how the guide took one little lamb from a pen and placed it in a huge enclosure with some thousands of sheep, where the noise of the bleating sheep and the shouting of the shearers was deafening. The lamb remained still for a moment, then it cried, and its cry was answered by the mother at the other end of the enclosure along which the lamb walked to its mother who came to meet it. "Do not imagine that you are beyond the reach of God," said the doctor. "He sees you as if there were no other child in the whole world."

—*Sunday School Chronicle*

* * *

"Alone, Yet Not Alone!"

"I climbed into a tree," said Dr. John G. Paton of the New Hebrides when the howling savages swarmed about him to take his life, "and was left there alone in the bush. The hours I spent there live all before me as if it were but yesterday. I heard the frequent discharging of muskets, and the yells of savages. Yet I sat there among the branches, safe in the arms of Jesus! Never, in all my sorrows, did my Lord draw nearer to me, and speak more soothingly in my soul, than when the moonlight flickered among those chestnut leaves, and the night air played on my throbbing brow, as I told all my heart to Jesus."

—*Prairie Overcomer*

With Us!

In the silence of my chamber
I may with my Saviour share
All my worries and my troubles,
As I talk with Him in prayer.
When I kneel before my Master,
I can feel His presence there,
And the load of care and sorrow
Seems much easier to bear.
In the silence of my chamber
I find peace, and lose despair,
For the glory of the Saviour
Come to me by way of prayer:
I can feel sweet peace descending
Like a shower from above,
And my heart grows calm and tender
In the blessing of His love.

—*Selected*

* * *

Prayer Fellowship

F. W. Boreham, the writer, tells the story of an old Scotchman who lay very ill. His minister came to see him. As the minister sat down on a chair near the bedside he noticed on the other side of the bed another chair placed at such an angle as to suggest that another visitor had just left it. "Well, Donald," said the minister, "I see I am not your first visitor." The Scotchman looked up in surprise; so the minister pointed to the chair. "Ah," said the sufferer. "I'll tell you about that chair. Years ago I found it impossible to pray. I often fell asleep on my knees; I was so tired. And if I kept awake, I could not control my thoughts from wandering. One day I was so worried I spoke to my minister about it. He told me not to worry about kneeling down. 'Just sit down,' he told me, 'and put a chair opposite you, and imagine Jesus is in it, and talk to Him as you would to a friend.' The Scotchman added, "I have been doing that ever since. And so, now you know why the chair is standing like that."

A week later the daughter of the old Scot drove up to the minister's house and knocked at the door. She was shown into the study, and when the minister came in she could hardly restrain herself. "Father died in the night," she sobbed, "I had no idea death could be so near. I had just gone to lie down for an hour or two, for he seemed to be sleeping so comfortably. And when I went back he was dead. He had not moved since I saw him before, except that his hand was on the empty chair at the side of the bed. Do you understand?" said the daughter. "Yes," said the minister, "I understand."

—Watchman-Examiner

* * *

Father's Voice

In a sketch of his boyhood, the Rev. John McNeill tells the story of an experience with his father. I remember one Saturday night it was nearly midnight when I started to tramp six or seven miles down through the lonely glens to get home. The road had a bad name. This particular night was very black, and two miles outside our little village the road gets blacker than ever. I was just entering the dark defile when, about a hundred yards ahead, in the densest of the darkness, there suddenly rang out a great, strong, cheery voice, "Is that you, Johnny?" It was my father, the bravest, strongest man I ever knew. Many a time since, when things have been getting black and gloomy about me, I have heard a voice greater than any earthly parent cry, "Fear not: for I am with thee." And lo, God's foot is rising and falling on the road before us as we tread the journey of life.

—Christian Herald

* * *

My Father Is Here

I had a friend who was very happy in the possession of a beautiful wife, and a sweet little daughter of the age of

three. Sudden sorrow struck the home when the young wife was killed in a traffic accident, and it seemed that all of the light had gone out of his life forever. The night after the funeral, the young father was putting his baby daughter to bed, and with awkward fingers was buttoning her sleeping garment when the lights suddenly went out all over the house. He suspected that a fuse had blown out in the basement, and said to the baby, "Papa will be right back; you lie still and wait here." But she, frightened at the thought of being left alone, pleaded to be taken with him, so he picked her up in his arms and started through the darkened hallways and down the stairs. The babe snuggled in his arms for a while in silence; but as they entered the basement she tightened her arms about his neck, and said, "It's awfully dark; but I'm not afraid, because my papa is here!" A sob shook the man's whole body. He buried his face in the baby's hair and wept, as he said, "Yes, dear, it *is* dark, indeed; but I also am not afraid, because *my* Father is here!"

—Bible Expositor and Illuminator

* * *

Certainly I Will Be With Thee

Many years ago, a little boy lay on his small bed, having just retired for the night. Before going to sleep, he moved in the direction of the large bed on which his father lay, and said, "Father, are you there?" and the answer came back, "Yes, my son." I remember that that boy turned over and went to sleep without a thought of harm.

To-night that little boy is an old man of seventy, and every night before going to sleep he looks up into the face of his Heavenly Father and says, "Father, are You there?" and the answer comes back clear and strong, "Yes, My son."

Whom need we fear if God our Father be with us?

—Scattered Seed

* * *

His Glorious Companion

The Rev. A. W. Bailey was about to take a trek of several weeks through a difficult field in Africa. It was on the verge of "hunger time." He says, "I had hardly set foot in the native path when four words from Second Kings, two, verse six were flashed into my mind: 'They two went on.' At the same time I was thrilled by the glorious consciousness that the benign, majestic Christ was walking beside me. For nearly seven weeks the trek continued under the blazing heat of the autumn sun of Northern Rhodesia, often in burning thirst, often in deep weariness, but never a day without the deep consciousness of that glorious Presence. I found myself unconsciously stepping out of the African path to let my unseen Guest take the trail. Then, on the day that my water boy induced me to drink the juice of the deadly matupa tree, in resentment for a longer day's trek than he fancied, I had simply to reach out a hand of faith and touch the hem of the seamless Robe and was whole again. My boys in wonder said: 'Truly, sir, that tree is deadly. We use its sap for fish poison. You would have died, had not God intervened.' The great, lasting lesson of the trek was the blessed reality of His presence, and His all-sufficiency for every contingency."

—*Prairie Overcomer*

* * *

God Is Near, and Hears and Feels

Sometime ago, when it became necessary to break her of the habit of sleeping with me, I laid my little child in her crib, kissed her good-night, and turned out the light. She cried long and bitterly, thinking that I did not hear her cry and that I did not love her, not knowing that I was in reality not far away — only hidden by the darkness — and that my mother-heart was aching for her. I indeed heard her cries and longed to do what she wanted, but for her own good I must hide myself.

And so, *in times of affliction, our God indeed hears our cry, is near* (Ps. 23:4), *and feels for us* (Exod. 3:4), *though for our own good He may hide His face and may seem not to hear.*

—Grace C. W. Groben

Alone — but Not Alone.

Even at a very early age we can learn of the fatherly love and care of God and trust ourselves to Him. A little girl named Gloria had a nurse who foolishly gave the child a fear of being in the dark alone. When her mother learned of the child's fear, she set about curing it by telling her that God was another Father as loving as her own daddy, but much wiser and much more powerful. He would care for her wherever she was, in the dark as well as in the light. One evening Mother sent Gloria on a little errand to a sewing room off the hall. It was getting dark and the room was not lighted. " 'Fraid; dark, Mummy; 'fraid," said Gloria. "No, dear," said Mother, "it is not very dark in there, and you know God is in the dark as well as in the light." Thus encouraged, Gloria slowly took two steps toward the room and then stopped. For a moment there was a battle inside her heart, and then, in victorious faith, she cried out, "Dod, O Dod, I'm a-tomin'!" and she paddled boldly on right into the dark room, alone — yet not alone. Being sure her strong and loving Heavenly Father would be wherever she had to go gave her victory over fear. And the same certainty is ever the secret of mastering our fears, whether we be children, youths, or grown men and women.

—Joseph E. Harris, in
The Sunday School Times

* * *

Human Skill — and God's

I was invited by a well-known surgeon to watch a complex operation he was about to perform. As he went through the laborious preparation for the operation he seemed confident, but a little tense. "All set?" I asked, "Almost," he replied, and stopped and bowed his head for a moment. Then, calm and relaxed, he led the way to the operating room. During the operation his hands never faltered. Afterward I said to him, "I was surprised at your praying before you went in. I thought a surgeon relied solely on his own ability." He answered, "A surgeon is only human; he can't work miracles by himself. I'm certain that science couldn't have advanced as far as it has, were it not for something stronger than mere man. You see," he concluded, "I feel so close to God when I am operating that I don't know where my skill leaves off and His begins."

—Kenneth Roberts, in
Reader's Digest

* * *

Whom Are You Going With?

A fine young athlete was considering foreign missions as a life work. He was asked to open a new field in a far distant land. He hesitated and said, "I just can't bring myself to go out there alone." "Would you go there," he was asked, "with a man like David Livingstone?" "Yes," he replied. "Would you go there with a man like Dan Crawford?" "Yes, I'd be glad to." "Then why not go with Jesus Christ?" Jesus calls us not to a life of loneliness, but to a life of companionship with Him in His work. What He actually says is, "Come and we will do it together." One of the most precious, therefore, of all our Master's names is Immanuel.

—Dr. John E. Simpson,
in the *United Presbyterian*

* * *

Vanguard of God

See the glorious morning sunlight
    Flash o'er fields begemmed with dew;
Where the harvest standeth waiting,
    For the laborers are few.
Christian! doth the Master bid thee
    Leave thy friends and leave thy home?
Shrink thou not; He'll only send thee
    "Whither He Himself would come."

Lo, the nations sit in darkness,
    Where no Gospel light is shed,
Thirsting for the Living Water,
    Dying for the Living Bread.
Are there tender ties that bind thee?
    Dost thou love thy land and home?
Yet stay not; the Master sends thee
    "Whither He Himself would come."

—*Selected*

* * *

Why the Bishop Was Not Robbed

When he was a curate, Bishop King of Lincoln, was sent to see a dying man.

The night was dark and the way lonely, and he trudged on only to find, when he reached the house, there was no one ill. He returned perplexed. Years passed, and when he was a Bishop, he visited a man in prison under the sentence of death, and, to his surprise, the criminal asked if he remembered the incident. "It was I," said the man, "who gave the false message. I wanted to lure you out that I might rob you on the lonely road." "Why didn't you attack me there?" said the bishop. The reply was extraordinary: "I hadn't the pluck. I lay in hiding determined to attack you on your way back, but I saw you were NOT ALONE." "But I was alone," said the bishop. "No, you were not," retorted the man. "There was a mysterious looking stranger walking close behind you, who followed you to your house and then disappeared. My chance was gone, and I experienced a sensation I never had before!" Could it be that the angel of the Lord stood by him, and made the FACT known?

—*Sunday School Times*

* * *

Still Under His Care

An old mariners' chart of the east coast of North America and adjacent waters, drawn by an unknown cartographer in 1525, and now in the British Museum, has some interesting and fearful directions on it. The mapmaker wrote across great areas of then unexplored land and sea the following inscriptions: "Here be giants," "Here be fiery scorpions," "Here be dragons." At some time in its career the chart fell into the hands of the scientist, Sir John Franklin. He scratched out the fearful old marking and wrote across the map, "Here is God."

—*Christian Leader*

* * *

Wesley's Memorial

The heart of many a visitor to Westminster Abbey must have been touched by reading the three sayings of John Wesley that are carved on the memorial which has been raised to him and his brother. One is, "I look on all the world as my parish;" another is, "God buries His workmen, but continues His work." The third is his ejaculation, "The best of all is, God is with us!" He uttered it on his deathbed, and then, once more raising his arm, and lifting his voice in grateful triumph, he repeated, "The best of all is, God is with us."

—T. C. M., in
Choice Gleanings Calendar

* * *

The Nearness of His Father

Years ago a little boy was entering school for the first time. The busy mother packed his lunch and told him to go straight up the road across the bridge to the schoolhouse. The boy saw a little fish in the stream below the bridge. He laid down his lunch and started down to the stream to catch the fish, but saw a beautiful butterfly, ran after it, and tried to catch it. It eluded him, leading him farther and farther down the road. When he finally gave up the chase, he could not find the bridge. He decided to pray. He knew only two prayers. The first one was, "Now I lay me down to sleep;" he saw that would not fit his case. The other — the Lord's prayer — was better. He knelt down and said aloud, "Our Father." Instantly he heard a voice behind him; it was his own father, who had followed him because he knew it was his first day in school and he might need help. In telling his experience years later, the boy now grown to manhood said it was the greatest revelation of his life to realize that his Father was so near.

—*Sunday School Times*

* * *

What We Miss.

"Old Father Morris," says his biographer, "had noticed a falling off in his little village prayer meeting. The first time he collected a tolerable audience, he took occasion to tell them something concerning the conference meeting of the disciples after the Resurrection. 'But Thomas was not with them!' said the old man in a sorrowful voice. 'Thomas had got cold-hearted, and was afraid that they would ask him to make the

first prayer; or perhaps,' he continued, looking at some of the farmers, 'he was afraid the roads were bad; or perhaps he thought a shower was coming on!' He went on significantly summing up the common excuses, and then with great simplicity and emotion, he added, 'But only think what Thomas lost, for in the middle of the meeting the Lord Jesus came and stood among them.' "

—From *Calvary to Olivet*,
by C. Stanford

* * *

Not a Visitor

Near the Royal residence at Osborne in the Isle of Wight were almshouses. While visiting an old lady in one of these a gentleman asked her, "Does the Queen ever visit here?" "Oh, yes," was the answer, "Her Majesty comes to see me." "And does the King of kings visit you here?" asked the visitor. "No, sir," said the old lady. "He doesn't *visit*, he *lives* here."

—*Christian Herald* (London)

* * *

His Father's Hand.

A minister says: "I well remember the time when my child, a laddie of three years, had to undergo an operation to save him from becoming totally blind. I was accorded the privilege of being in the room during the operation. My dear child was laid on the operating table. He was extremely nervous, and his body was quivering very much. He called to me: 'Father! Father! Will you stand beside me? Will you hold my hand?' As I took his hand the quivering ceased, the nervousness abated. 'Father,' he said, 'I am not afraid now,' and then turning to the doctor, he said, 'Doctor, you may go on now. I am not afraid!' " So the handclasp of our Heavenly Father begets confidence and strength. We are not afraid when we feel His love-grip.

—*Christian Herald*

* * *

He Goes Before

A young lady leaving for the mission field was sitting by a dear friend in the home church the Sunday evening previous. Suddenly, as if moved by a strong impulse, the friend took the young missionary's Bible and turned to John 10, and underscored part of the fourth verse: "And when he putteth forth his own sheep, he goeth before them." How many times during the years that followed, in days of darkness and difficulty, that promise was a source of power and comfort. "The Lord . . . sent them . . . whither he himself would come."

—Sunday School Times

* * *

Unseen Visitor

"Food is on the table!" said Mr. Ch'eng, motioning us to the entrance of their kitchen. We had come to their humble abode in China, just after they had accepted the Lord Jesus as their Saviour. They had cast out all their gods and asked us to come and give them more instruction in the way of righteousness.

We were hungry as we sat down before a low table on which were placed two dishes. One contained some squash boiled in water, and the other had the poorest kind of rice, all they could afford. Beside it was a rock of black salt, such as is given to cattle in the United States, but which served as their table salt. He dipped it into the dish of squash to season it. I had expected him to ask me to give thanks for the food, but instead he stood up himself, and looking upward to the soot-begrimed ceiling, closed his eyes as he said very reverently, "Please, Heavenly Father, partake with us!"

We were touched in heart at this act of courtesy toward God. When anyone comes in while a Chinese is having a meal the host invariably courteously asks the visitor to partake: "Ch'ing ch' ih fan!" Mr. Ch'eng's sense of God's presence was just that real! Then he bowed his head and thanked God for the food. How real is God to you?

—J. B. Tweter

* * *

The Postman's Confidence

A postman was telling me what a sense of security he felt in his work of delivering the mail. "Why," he said, "all the resources of the Government are pledged to support me in carrying on my work. If I have only one small post card in my bag, no man dares to molest me in its delivery. All the Federal police powers of the United States would be thrown into action if necessary to secure the safe delivery of that post card." And that led me to think how confidently you and I may set forth with our life, our personality, our equipment, such as it is, to deliver the flaming truth of the Gospel. The Word of our Lord is just as much for us today as it was for the disciples, when he said: "All power is given unto me in heaven and in earth. Go . . . and, lo, I am with you alway, even unto the end."

—Sunday School Times

* * *

"There's the Reason"

Some students of the Moody Bible Institute were in a terrible automobile wreck. Their car was demolished. Miraculously, the students escaped with only minor injuries. Their escape from death was a matter of general discussion by those who saw the wrecked car before it was towed from the highway. "How was it possible that the occupants of this demolished car escaped with only minor injuries?" asked one onlooker. A stranger, pointing his finger in the direction of the rear glass in the wrecked car, said, "There's the reason!" Resting flatly against the glass was a booklet-tract, whose title could be plainly seen, "God's Presence with His People!

(As told to the author of the booklet-tract, W. B. K., by Bill Reichman, a graduate of the Moody Bible Institute.)

* * *

Alone With God

Softly fall the shades of evening,
    Twilight spreads her mantle broad,
O'er my soul there comes a longing,
    To be alone — alone with God.
To some quiet place retreating,
    Forbidden is each earthly care,
Closed the door to all but Jesus
    At this sacred hour of prayer.

Alone with God — a holy stillness
  O'er my spirit gently steals,
In the secret of His Presence
  Here my soul His glory feels.
Far above this world's confusion,
  Winged by faith my spirit soars
To the throne — where my dear Saviour,
  In my soul His glory pours.

Alone with God, O blest Communion,
  Naught on earth could sweeter be,
For my soul is lost in rapture,
  When my Saviour speaks to me.
Here He tells me how He loves me,
  How for me His life He gave,
On the rugged Cross He suffered,
  There my soul from sin to save.

Alone with God — could I but tell it,
  As by faith my Lord I see,
And the joy of life eternally
  In that Home prepared for me.
Alone with God — Ah, yes, I love it
  Naught on earth could sweeter be,
For my soul is lost in rapture,
  When my Saviour speaks to me.
  —*Selected*

* * *

Both Great and Small

An infidel saw a Christian walking, and asked him where he was going. "To church, sir." "What to do there?" "To worship God." "Pray tell, whether your God is a great or a little God?" "He is both, sir." "How can He be both?" "He is so great, sir, that Heaven cannot contain Him; and so little that He can dwell in my heart!" The infidel afterward admitted that that answer had affected him more than volumes he had read by gifted authors.

  —*Tom Olson, in*
  Sunday School Times

* * *

"Companied With Him"

What can strip the seeming glory
  From the idols of the earth?
Not a sense of right and duty,
  But a sight of peerless worth.

'Tis the look that melted Peter,
  'Tis the face that Stephen saw,
'Tis the heart that wept with Mary
  Can alone from idols draw.

Draw, and win, and fill completely,
  Till the cup o'erflows its brim.
What have we to do with idols
  Since we've companied with HIM?
  —J. Stuart Holden

* * *

Meditation

I sat and watched the Evening Star
  And my thoughts were full of God —
I felt His breath on the evening breeze,
  His pulse beat through the sod.

I saw His smile on a pansy's face,
  Heard His voice in the night-bird's call;
I knew He had passed through the waving grass —
  As a hush fell over all.

He drew His mantle of dusk about
  Every bush, and flower and clod —
I sat and watched the Evening Star,
  And my thoughts were full of God.
  —Audred Pitts, in
  Wesleyan Methodist

* * *

The Jewish Peddler's Tribute

In the home of parents hung a picture depicting Christ taking the last farewell from his disciples and giving them the supreme promise: "Lo, I am with you alway." One day a Jewish peddler came. It so happened that I was home alone. The Jew looked around in the room; soon his eyes were fascinated by the picture of Christ. Long he gazed upon it. Then turning to me he asked: "Is this your Messiah? Is this your God?" I told him that it was Christ, our Saviour, and described to him the meaning of the picture. "And what does he say?" he asked. I read the promise printed beneath the picture: "And, lo, I am with you alway, even unto the end of the world." The Jew thought for a while, then turning to me he said: "Boy, what a wonderful Messiah you Christians have. He is always with you." Again he gazed into the picture. Then he slowly took his pack, left the room, and still I heard him whispering: "What a wonderful Messiah; he is with you alway." Some Christians often forget what a perfect Saviour we have in Christ.   —*Sunday School Times*

Always!

When David Livingstone sailed for Africa the first time, a group of his friends accompanied him to the pier to wish him *Bon Voyage.* Some of them, concerned for the safety of the missionary, reminded him of the dangers which would confront him in the dark land to which he was journeying. In fact, one man urged Livingstone to remain in England.

In response, David Livingstone opened His Bible and read aloud the portion of our Lord's last recorded words in Matthew's Gospel, chapter 28: "Lo, I am with you alway." Turning to the one who would have prevented his going, the missionary said: "That, my friend, is the word of a Gentleman. So let us be going."

—*The Pilgrim*

* * *

"Still, Still With Thee!"

Still, still with Thee, when purple morning breaketh,
When the bird waketh, and the shadows flee;
Fairer than morning, lovlier than daylight,
Dawns the sweet consciousness, I am with Thee.

—Harriet Beecher Stowe

PRIDE

Refuse and Die

In the "last memorable days of France's liberation" a soldier wrote home: "We have seen many strange sights. Recently we have raced on day after day, meeting great crowds of Germans along the way jumping and shouting for joy at the thought of being taken prisoner! Now and then an old S. S. man is brought in — stern, truculent, and dour. One of these fanatics was carried in the other day, badly wounded. He required an immediate blood transfusion, and was quickly told so by one of the doctors. 'Will it be British blood?' asked the German. 'Yes; good, British blood,' replied the doctor, who added, solemnly, 'If you refuse it, you will die!' 'Then,' answered the proud Nazi curtly, 'I would rather die.' A short time afterward his body was carried out for burial." No wonder the British Tommies exclaimed of this poor, deluded man, "What a fool!" Every day men and women are being fooled even more than this German — fooled into believing that they would rather die without mercy than accept God's salvation, purchased at infinite cost, by the blood of Christ. Surely such an attitude is the height of folly.

—*Good News Digest*

Too Proud To Accept God's Gift

Apparently too proud to accept neighbors' help, an elderly couple died from starvation, exposure, and pneumonia, according to the Associated Press. Opinion on the causes of the deaths was given by Medical Examiner Thomas F. Corriden at the Cooley Dickinson Hospital, at Northampton, Mass. The couple was taken to the hospital from their home in nearby West Cummington where a neighbor said she had been turned away from the door by the husband when she offered assistance. Neighbors finally gained admission to the home and found the man and wife unconscious. Too proud to accept *the* Gift is the reason numbers of persons are on perishing ground today, in a spiritual sense. The Lord Jesus Christ is God's "unspeakable Gift." Eternal life is the free gift of God in Christ Jesus our Lord (Rom. 6:23). Salvation is a gift of God. . . . To be too proud to accept such gifts from such a Giver will mean to perish in a deeper sense than from starvation.

—Tom M. Olson, in *Now*

* * *

"About Out of Cheese"

A drummer called at the country variety store on his monthly sales visit.

"Where's the boss?" the drummer asked of a gangling boy upon whose upper lip a little "goose down" was putting in its appearance. Squawked the boy, "The boss ain't in. I'M THE WHOLE CHEESE!" Eyeing the boy with deserved disdain, the drummer said, "Boy, when the boss comes in, tell him he is about out of cheese!" Beware of inflating pride.

—W. B. K.

* * *

A King's Son

In the early days of slavery in North America, a plantation visitor in the deep south was watching a group of these poor Negroes while they were loading heavy bales on a wagon. One of the slaves stood out above his fellows — head erect, shoulders back and unbowed under the whip-lashes of the overseer, and walking with a strong gait. The visitor inquired about this man, and his host replied: "He is the son of an African king, and he never forgets it."

The Christian is the son and heir of God almighty. Let us never forget it, and live accordingly.

—The Pilgrim

* * *

No Reason To Be Proud

"Two ladies at Shanghai once got to talking about Hudson Taylor, wondering if he was ever tempted to be proud. One of the ladies went and asked Mrs. Taylor. She did not know. But Mrs. Taylor went and asked Mr. Taylor. He was surprised and inquired, 'Proud about what?' Mrs. Taylor replied, 'Why, about the things you have done.' Then immediately came this beautiful answer, 'I never knew I had done anything.' And Mr. Taylor was right; he never had done anything, for it was God who had wrought in and through him.

—China's Millions

* * *

Remember What Thou Wast

A story is told of an Oriental vizier who carried with him a mysterious chest of which no one knew the contents. One man asked him what the chest contained. He was allowed to look inside, but he saw only the common garb of a working man. The vizier said: "Such was I when our Sovereign deigned to lift me from the dust. If ever my heart is tempted with pride, I correct it by looking at these things, and saying, 'Remember what thou wast.'"

—The Quiver

* * *

Self-Measurement

A little boy came to his mother, saying, "Mamma, I am as tall as Goliath; I am nine feet high." "What makes you say that?" asked the surprised mother. "Well, I made a little ruler of my own and measured myself with it, and I am just nine feet high!" There are many people who follow the little boy's method, measuring themselves by some rule of their own. God tells us of those who, "measuring themselves . . . and comparing themselves among themselves, are not wise" (2 Cor. 10:12).

—Pilot

* * *

When We Can't Do For Ourselves

A secular weekly tells the story of a little fellow who had reached that epoch in a boy's life when he gets his first pants, and the uplift unsettled his spiritual equilibrium. Hitherto he had been a devout little Christian and joined his little sister every morning in asking the Lord's help and blessing for the day. But this morning, when he looked at his new pants, and felt himself a man, he stopped his little sister as she began to pray as usual, "Lord Jesus, take care of Freddie today, and keep him from harm," and, like poor Simon Peter, in his self-sufficiency, he cried out, "No, Jennie; don't say that; Freddie can take care of himself now." Little Jennie was shocked and frightened, but knew not what to do; and so the day began. Before noon they both climbed up into a cherry tree, and while reaching out for the tempting fruit Freddie went head foremost down into an angle between the tree and the fence. With all his desperate struggles and those of his frightened sister, he was utterly unable to extricate himself. At last he said

515

to Jennie, with a look of mingled shame and intelligence, "Jennie, pray: Freddie can't take care of himself after all." Just then a strong man was coming along the road, and the answer to their prayer came quickly as he took down the fence and freed Freddie. The boy went forth with a lesson for life, to walk like Peter, with downward head and humble trust in a strength and care more mighty than his own.

—A. B. Simpson

* * *

Indispensable Christians

"He is impossible to get along with, because he thinks he's impossible to get along without," was said of a Sunday school worker. No wonder the result was a dismal failure for the would-be indispensable. The worst idea a Christian can have is that he is absolutely necessary to the work in which he is engaged, that his absence would stop the whole undertaking.

—*Sunday at Home*

* * *

What Prevents Filling

When you come to the Lord, He will never send you away empty unless you come so stuffed full of yourself that there isn't room for any of His blessing.

—*Youth for Christ Magazine*

"And Pour Contempt on All My Pride"

The life and death of our Lord Jesus Christ are a standing rebuke to every form of pride to which men are liable.

Pride of *birth and rank.* "Is not this the carpenter's son?"

Pride of *wealth.* "The Son of man hath not where to lay his head."

Pride of *respectability.* "Can any good thing come out of Nazareth?"

Pride of *personal appearance.* "He hath no form nor comeliness.

Pride of *reputation.* "A friend of publicans and sinners!"

Pride of *learning.* "How knoweth this man letters, having never learned?"

Pride of *superiority.* "I am among you as he that serveth."

Pride of *success.* "He came unto his own, and his own received him not." "Neither did his brethren believe on him." "He was despised and rejected of men."

Pride of *ability.* "I can of mine own self do nothing."

Pride of *self-will.* "I seek not mine own will, but the will of him that sent me."

Pride of *intellect.* "As my Father hath taught me, I speak these things."

Pride in *death.* "He became obedient unto death, even the death of the cross."

—*Gospel Message*

PROCRASTINATION

"I Have Found A Bigger Fool Than I Am!"

A king sent for his jester one day, and presented him with a stick. He said, "Take this stick and keep it until you find a bigger fool than yourself." Lying on his deathbed, the king again sent for his jester. "I am going away," the king said. "Whither?" asked the jester. "To another country," replied the king. "What provision has your majesty made for this journey and for living in the country whither thou goest?" the jester asked. "None," was the answer. The jester handed the king the stick. "Take it," he said. "I have found a bigger fool than myself, for I only trifle with the things of time while you have trifled with things of eternity."

—*Gospel Herald*

* * *

"Too Late!"

A friend of mine, an evangelist, told me of preaching in a prison chapel one Sunday to twelve hundred men. Sitting at the front and apart from the others were two young men barely twenty years old. After the service my friend asked the warden about those two men and was told they had come from the death row and in two days would die in the electric chair. It came over God's servant like a shock that he had preached the last sermon these two young men would ever hear before they went to meet their God.

—Dr. John R. Rice

* * *

Do It Now

He was going to be all that a mortal should be
    —To-morrow;
No one should be kinder or braver than he
    — To-morrow.
A friend who was troubled and weary he knew,
Who'd be glad of a lift, and who needed it, too;
On him he would call and see what he could do
    — To-morrow.

Each morning he stacked up the letters he'd write
    — To-morrow,
And thought of the folks he would fill with delight
    — To-morrow.
It was too bad, indeed, he was busy to-day,
And hadn't a minute to stop on his way;
More time he would have to give others, he'd say
    — To-morrow.

The greatest of workers this man would have been
    — To-morrow.
The world would have known him had he ever seen
    — To-morrow.
But the fact is, he died, and he faded from view,
And all that he left when living was through
Was a mountain of things he intended to do
    — To-morrow.

—*On the Line*

Not Safe To Wait

A woman came to Dr. Chalmers one day and said: "Dr. Chalmers, I cannot get my child to come to her Saviour. I've talked and talked to her, but it's no use." The doctor thought to himself that she must be lacking in wisdom, and said, "Let me talk with your daughter by myself, and we will see what may be done." One day he met the daughter and engaged her in conversation. "You have been bothered a good deal about the matter of your soul's salvation, haven't you? Suppose I say to your mother that you don't want to be talked to about the matter for a whole year, how will that do?" The Scottish lassie hesitated a little and then replied: "Well, I don't think it would be safe to put off the matter for a whole year. Something might happen! I might die before then." "Yes, that's so," replied the doctor. "Suppose we say six months." The daughter didn't think that even that would be safe. "Well, then, how about three months?" After a brief hesitation the daughter replied, "I don't think it is safe to put it off at all." They knelt together and in a few moments the daughter was radiantly saved.

—From *Memorial Addresses*

* * *

A Forgotten Vow

Several years ago a young mother was desperately ill, so to a Christian neighbor she made this vow: "If God will spare my life one more time, I'll be a different woman. I'll take my children to church, and try to raise them the way God would have me do." She recovered completely and for a season remembered her promise, but as time went on she began to drift back into her old sinful ways. One day, while riding with an old friend, they both took a little nip of gin, and that resulted in a fatal auto wreck. The nearest phone to her home was the Christian lady's to whom she had made her vow. When the message was given, the godly woman simply turned from the phone and said, "She, that being often reproved hardeneth her neck, shall suddenly be destroyed, and that without remedy" (Prov. 29:1).

—*Sunday School Times*

Sometime Was Too Late!

Said a young man to the Rev. Mr. Young: "I intend to become a Christian sometime, but not now. Don't trouble yourself about me. I'll tend to it in good time." A few weeks after, the man was injured in a sawmill, and, as he lay dying, Mr. Young was called to him. He found him in despair, saying: "Leave me alone. At your meeting I was almost persuaded, but I would not yield, and now it is too late. Oh, get my wife, my sisters, and my brothers to seek God, and do it now, but leave me alone, for I am lost." Within an hour he passed away, with these words on his lips, "I am lost, I am lost, just because I would not yield when I was almost persuaded."

—*Sunday School Times*

* * *

Frozen Talons

One winter day, a carcass was floating down the Niagara River upon a cake of ice. An eagle, soaring above the river, spied it and dropped down upon it. He sat there leisurely devouring his easy prey. The swift current began bearing him rapidly downward to the fall. But was he not safe? Could he not leap in a moment into mid-air from his dangerous post? Could he not stretch his great pinions and float off into safety at the very brink of the awful cataract? Had he not done that a thousand times before in his bird experience? So he floated on! But by and by came the thundering roar of the great cataract. The cloud of white mist that marked the fatal brink of the fall was towering almost above him. It was time to leave. So he stretched out his great wings for flight. But he could not rise! Unnoted by him his talons, sunken in the ice, and the flesh of his prey, had frozen hard and fast in the bitter winter day, and his FATE WAS SEALED! He flapped his great wings. He struggled with all the power of muscle and sinew. But all in vain. In a few moments he was swept over into the abyss to his death. HE HAD DELAYED TOO LONG! . . . How will YOU escape if you neglect? Your immortal soul is in instant and unceasing jeopardy of eternal death. God offers His Son Jesus Christ as YOUR escape. What will YOU do with Him?

—James H. McConkey

* * *

Do It Now!

"I expect to pass through this world but once. Any good thing, therefore, that I can do, or any kindness I can show to any fellow human being, let me do it NOW. Let me not defer nor neglect it, for I shall not pass this way again!"

—Stephen Grellet

* * *

Don't Wait A Minute

If you have hard work to do,
    Do it now.
To-day the skies are clear and blue,
To-morrow clouds may come in view,
Yesterday is not for you —
    Do it now.

If you have a song to sing,
    Sing it now.
Let the notes of gladness ring,
Clear as song of birds in spring,
Let each day some music bring —
    Sing it now.

If you have kind words to say,
    Say them now.
To-morrow may not come your way,
To do a kindness while you may,
Loved ones will not always stay —
    Say them now.

If you have a smile to show,
    Show it now.
Make hearts happy, roses grow,
Let the friends around you know,
The love you have before they go —
    Show it now.

—*Gospel Banner*

* * *

The Dread Awakening

A distinguished professor of psychology once told his class of a striking case of somnambulism. It was that of a man who, one night went downstairs to the door of the house in which he dwelt, and yet he was asleep all the time. He opened the door and stepped out into the street, and so strong was the somnambulistic trance that still he slept. He passed along the street and out into the open country, and still he slept. Not till his naked feet touched a little stream that crossed his path did he awaken to the darkness of the night and the strange unfamiliar scene. There are souls like that. They never awaken till they touch the cold waters of death, and feel the night winds of mortality arouse them to the darkness of their night and the strange, unfamiliar scenes of eternity and judgment.

—W. M. Mackay

* * *

Delay May Be Fatal

Three men sat in a Chinese evangelistic service in Canton. They were well known round the world: Sun Yat-sen, the great revolutionary leader; Wu Ting-fang, at one time ambassador in Washington; and Admiral Chen, of the Chinese navy.

When the sermon was over, an appeal was made for decisions, and cards were passed through the audience. Admiral Chen had been touched by the message, and was about to write his name on the card, when one of his companions whispered to him: "Don't be in a hurry to take that step; first think it over."

—*Alliance Weekly*

* * *

The Right Time

A group of men were arguing one day as to the best time to cut an ash-stick. One argued that the best time was in the spring when the sap was rising. A walking-stick cut at such a time would be strong, yet supple. Another declared that no time was as good as summer, for then the wood would be at the very top of its form. The third man declared that both his friends were wrong, for the best time to cut an ash-stick was in autumn, when the sap had matured and perfected the wood. The longer they argued the more each was wedded to his own opinion. At last they decided to call in an old farm-servant whose knowledge of nature was only equalled by his homely wisdom. "When is the best time to cut an ash-stick, John?" they inquired.

"When you see it, gentlemen. It may not be there next time you pass that way." Now is the time to get right with God. Now is the time to call him in, to ask him to become Senior Partner in the business of your life. "Now is the accepted time; behold, now is the day of salvation."

—William J. May, in the *Methodist Recorder*

* * *

Mr. Meant-To

Mr. Meant-To has a comrade,
    And his name is Didn't-Do.
Have you ever chanced to meet them?
    Have they ever called on you?
These two fellows live together
    In the house of never-win,
And I'm told that it is haunted
    By the ghost of might-have-been.

—*Selected*

* * *

"Lie By Till Morning!"

The steamship *Central America*, on a voyage from New York to San Francisco, sprang a leak in mid-ocean. A vessel, seeing her signal of distress, bore down toward her. Perceiving her danger to be imminent, the captain of the rescue ship spoke to the *Central America*, asking, "What is amiss?" "We are in bad repair, and going down. Lie by till morning!" "Let me take your passengers on board NOW," said the would-be rescuer. It was night, and the captain of the *Central America* did not like to transfer his passengers then, lest some might be lost in the confusion, and, thinking that they would keep afloat some hours longer, replied, "Lie by till morning!" Once again the captain of the rescue ship called: "You had better let me take them now." "Lie by till morning," was sounded back through the night. About an hour and a half later, her lights were missed! The *Central America* had gone down, and all on board perished, because it was thought they could be saved at another time. While salvation is offered you, now, do not delay to receive Christ!

—Leslie Greening, in
Gospel Herald

"Tomorrow Is the Devil's Motto!"

Colonel Rahl, the Hessian commander at Trenton, was in the midst of a game of cards when a courier brought a message stating that Washington was crossing the Delaware River. Rahl put the letter in his pocket. He did not read it until the game was finished; then he rallied his men, only to die just before his regiment was taken prisoner. Only a few minutes' delay, but he lost honor, liberty, life!

"Tomorrow!" is the devil's motto. Earth's history is strewn with the wrecks of half-finished plans and unexecuted resolutions. "Tomorrow" is the perpetual refuge of incompetency and sloth.

—Nolbert Hunt Quayle, in,
Alliance Weekly

* * *

"You Can't Scare Us!"

Years ago a corps of civil engineers came to a little town in Pennsylvania and went up into the mountains and examined the dam that controlled the waters of the stream that flowed down the valley. They came back to the valley and said to the people of the town, "The dam is unsafe. The people of the valley are in danger." The people said to them, "You can't scare us." That fall the men came back to the valley and examined the dam again, and said to the people in the valley, "We warn you people again, and you are in danger every hour." They laughed again and said, "Scare us if you can." The men went up again in the spring and warned the people, but again the people said, *"That's a chance. We have been hearing that so many times. Scare us if you can."*

It was not fifteen days later that a boy with his horse on the dead run came down into the valley shouting, "Run for your lives! The dam has gone and the water is coming." The people only laughed at him but he did not wait to hear their laughter; he went on down the valley still shouting his warning. In a very few minutes the dirty water came and in less than 30 minutes after struck the town, Johnstown was in ruins with more than 3,700 of those who had been in the town, in the presence of God. You have been reproved many a time yourself frightened many a time yourself and you sit there and say, *"Scare me if you can; get me by frightening me if you can."*

—*Gospel Herald*

* * *

One Night Too Late

One night at a revival meeting a young lady was urged to repent. She said, "I will seek the Lord to-morrow night." The next evening her mother found that she intended to go to a ball, and she begged her not to do so. She replied, "I will go if I die," and went upstairs to dress. A young man came to take her to the ball. She was called, but did not answer. Her mother went to her room and found her sitting before the glass, putting a ribbon in her hair, but she was a corpse! *She waited one night, and lost her soul!*

—*Gospel Herald*

* * *

"Too Late!"

I saw a door
And meant to go
Within the room
Someday.
I looked around
And marked the ground
Lest I forget the way.
When I returned
All was the same
Excepting
Where before a light had been
No light was seen
And God had closed the door.

—*Selected*

* * *

"Sir, I May Be Dead Tomorrow!"

An earnest Christian doctor one day called to see an old man that he had frequently visited before. The old fellow was suffering from an attack of bronchitis. The doctor made the necessary inquiries, and, after promising to get some medicine ready when called for, he was about to say "good-by" when the patient's wife asked, "When must John take the medicine, sir?" "Let me see;

you are not very ill; suppose you begin to take it a month from to-day." "A month from to-day, sir?" they cried in astonishment. "Yes, why not? Is that too soon?" "Too soon! why, sir, I may be dead then!" said the patient. "That is true; but you must remember you really are not very bad yet. Still, perhaps you had better begin to take it in a week." "But sir," cried John in great perplexity, "begging your pardon, but I might not live a week." "Of course you may not, John, but very likely you will, and the medicine will be in the house; it will keep, and if you find yourself getting worse, you could take some. I shan't charge anything for it. If you should feel worse to-morrow even, you might begin then." "Sir, I may be dead to-morrow!" "When would you propose to begin, John?" "Well, sir, I thought you would tell me to begin to-day." "Begin to-day by all means," said the doctor, kindly. "I only wanted to show you how false your own reasoning is, when you put off taking the medicine which the Great Physician has provided for your sin-sick soul. Just think how long you have neglected the remedy He has provided. For years you have turned away from the Lord Jesus. You have said to yourself, "next week," or "next year," or "when I am on my deathbed, I will seek the Lord;" any time rather than the present. And yet the present is the only time that you are sure of. God's offer is only for to-day. "Now is the accepted time; behold, now is the day of salvation." You may be dead to-morrow!

—*Gospel Herald*

*   *   *

Too Late

One evening when Mr. Alexander and I were in Brighton, England, one of the workers went out from the afternoon meeting to a restaurant for his evening meal. His attention was drawn toward the man who waited upon him, and there came to his heart a strong impression that he should speak to that waiter about his soul, but that seemed to him such an unusual thing to do that he kept putting it off. When the meal was ended and the bill paid, he stepped out of the

resturant, but had such a feeling that he should speak to that waiter, that he decided to wait outside until the waiter came out. In a little while the proprietor came out and asked him why he was waiting. He replied that he was waiting to speak with the man who had waited upon him at the table. The proprietor replied, "You will never speak to that man again. After waiting upon you he went to his room and shot himself." Oh, men and women, there are opportunities open to every one of us to-night that will be gone, and gone forever, before another day dawns. The time is short!

—*Dr. R. A. Torrey*

*   *   *

The False Gospel of Delay

A minister of the Gospel determined on one occasion to preach on the text, "Now is the accepted time; behold, now is the day of salvation." While in his study thinking, he fell asleep and dreamed that he was carried into hell and set down in the midst of a conclave of lost spirits. They were assembled to devise means whereby they might get at the souls of men. One rose and said, "I will go to the earth and tell men that the Bible is all a fable, that it is not divinely appointed of God." No, that will not do. Another said, "Let me go: I will tell men that there is no God, no Saviour, no Heaven, no hell."

"No, that will not do; we cannot make men believe that." Suddenly one arose and with a wise mien suggested, "No, I will journey to the world of men, and tell them that there *is* a God, that there *is* a Saviour, that there *is* a Heaven — yes, and a hell, too; but I'll tell them there is NO HURRY; tomorrow will do." And they sent him.

—*Biblical Treasury*

*   *   *

Settled in Time

A young fellow hearing a Gospel address was greatly moved. He was told that if the Spirit of God was working in his heart and conscience it was exactly the time to make his decision. "The time when you hear God's call, is the time you ought to respond.

The young man answered saying, "Right now I take Christ as my Saviour."

He worked at a sawmill in the mountains, and the next morning at work he was singing in his gladness of heart, as only the newborn can sing.

It was about noontime when by an accident he was caught in some of the machinery and badly hurt.

As kindly hands did all that was possible for him, he said, "Send for the preacher who preached in the churchhouse at the foot of the mountains last night."

In a little while the preacher was by his side. Taking his hand he said, "Charlie, I have come; what would you like to say?" "Wasn't it glorious that I settled it in time!" he replied.

Have you settled it?

—*The Messenger of Peace*

* * *

Waiting — For What?

The clock of life is wound but once,
And no man has the power
To say just when the hands will stop;
At late, or early hour.

Now is the only time we own
To do His precious will,
Do not wait until tomorrow;
For the clock may then be still.

—*Selected*

PROFANITY

"Out of the Mouth of Babes"

A young man had been extremely profane, and thought little of it. After his marriage to a lovely Christian girl, the habit appeared to him in a different light, and he made spasmodic efforts to conquer it. But not until some years had passed did he become victor, when the evil was set before him by a little incident. One Sunday morning as he stood before his mirror shaving he inflicted a slight cut and, true to fixed habit, he blurted out the single word, "God!" He was not a little chagrined when he saw reflected in the mirror the pretty image of his three-year-old daughter. Hastily laying down her doll, she exclaimed as she looked expectantly about the room. "Is God here?" Blushing and ashamed, the father said, "Why do you ask that?" "I thought He must be 'cause I heard you speak to Him!" said the child. Then, noticing the sober look on his face, she added, "Call Him again, Daddy; I know He'll come!" The child's trusting words cut to the heart. He caught her up in his arms and for the first time in his life asked God to forgive him and to make him a real Christian from that time forward.

—Keith L. Brooks

What Does Your Language Show?

Sometime ago, a client came into my office, a Southern gentleman who has approximately six million dollars of funds in our investments. During the course of the conversation he used my Lord's name in a way I didn't like, and I stopped him. "Please, sir, that name you just used is the most precious name I know anything about. I love it more than anything in this world, and I don't like to hear that name used in the fashion you did. I am a Christian." What do you think he said? "So am I. I teach a Sunday school class down South." "Well," I said, "you would not have guessed it in a thousand years," and something inside me said, "Are you going to lose this contract?" Just recently this gentleman and his wife were in my office again. He said, "This is the man who gave me such a tongue lashing when I was here before." She turned to me and said: "I am glad you did, because he deserved it. He has been a different man since."

—Erling C. Olsen, in
Moody Monthly

* * *

A Soldier's Testimony:

While traveling by train between Trenton and New York, a soldier sat down beside me. This soldier, a Negro, had been a physician in New Jersey before entering the service. I asked him if he had many opportunities to witness for Christ in camp, and he replied: "The first night in the tent most of the boys were swearing and telling smutty stories. Finally I said to them: 'Gentlemen, all evening you have been taking the Lord's name in vain and telling your filthy stories, and I have said nothing. Now, I am going to talk with God, and, out of respect to Him, I ask you to please be quiet.' I went to my knees in prayer, and not a sound was made. From that hour on, swearing and dirty stories went out the door, and each time I went to prayer, there was silence and respect." —Corp. M. M. T., in *Moody Monthly*

* * *

What He Asked For

One hot summer day a young farmer came from his cornfield hot and tired. He took the name of the Lord in vain, cursing the cornfield for being such a grassy mess. He finally succeeded in cleaning the field thoroughly, the rain came, the sun shone, but the field of corn refused to grow as it should. When harvest time came the farmer complained that he didn't make enough corn to pay the fertilizer bill. His Christian wife calmly asked, "Didn't you ask God to damn that field of corn?" Then the young fellow repentantly remembered his words. God does hear and answer us, and if many profanity users realized just what they were asking for, I believe they would be a little more careful. —*Sunday School Times*

* * *

A "Savage" Protest Against Profanity

An article in a recent issue of the *Chicago American Legion Magazine*, by J. Norman Lodge, Associated Press war correspondent in the Solomon Islands, asks, "Who are these natives we so lightly refer to as savages?" To stress his point, he quoted a notice posted in an American mess hall for United States soldiers: "American soldiers are requested please to be a little more careful in their choice of language, especially when natives are assisting them in unloading ships, trucks, and in erecting abodes. American missionaries spent many years among us and taught us the use of clean speech. Every day, however, American soldiers use bad words, and the good work your missionaries did in our midst is being undermined by your careless profanity." It was signed by a "talking" chief of the Polynesian tribe on Guadalcanal. —*Now*

* * *

What Would George Say Now?

George Washington's Orderly Book of August 3, 1776, included this comment: "The general is sorry to be informed that the foolish and wicked practice of profane swearing, a vice hitherto little known in the American army, is growing into fashion; he hopes the officers will by example as well as influence endeavor to check it and that both they and the men will reflect that we can have little hope of the blessing of heaven on our arms if we insult it by our impiety and profanity. Added to this, it is a vice so mean and low, without temptation, that every man of sense and character detests and despises it." —Mary Stover

* * *

A Fiery Trial

When a man had been converted at a mission in Lincoln, Eng., his associates in one of the foundaries were determined to make him swear. Failing in their purpose, they heated a bar of iron, let the redness fade out, and then passed it on to him to carry to some one.

The man's hand was badly burned, of course, but he didn't swear. He simply said, "Mates, I wouldn't serve you like that!" Then, according to Gipsy Smith, who related the incident, he began to sing:

I'm not ashamed to own my Lord,
   Or to defend His cause;
Maintain the honor of His word,
   The glory of His cross.

"We all slunk away ashamed," one of the other men afterward told Gipsy Smith.

A song instead of an oath — that was a true Christian witness! —*Sunday School Times*

PROPHECY

Beyond Old Age

Mrs. Eliza Kirk of London, England attained the ripe old age of 101. She celebrated the anniversary by removing all mirrors from her home. The reason given for her strange action was: "I like to think of myself as I was, not as I am." The believer can do something vastly superior to removing mirrors. Without attempting to ignore or forget his present appearance, he can place the telescope of prophecy to his eye of faith and see himself as he is going to be (I John 3:2).

—*Now*

* * *

Believing Is Seeing

There is a good story told to the effect that a Jew, being in the company of a Christian, took up a New Testament and opened it to Luke 1:32,33: "The Lord God shall give unto him the throne of his father David: and he shall reign over the house of Jacob for ever." Turning to his Christian friend the Jew asked, "How do you understand that Scripture?" The Christian answered, "Oh, it's figurative language, descriptive of Christ's spiritual reign over the church." "Then you do not take it literally?" asked the Jew. "Certainly not," replied the Christian. The Jew made this further remark, "Then why should you expect me to take literally what precedes, where the Scriptures say that this Son of David shall be born of a virgin? Do you believe that literally?" "Surely," answered the Christian. The Jew continued, "Why do you accept verse 31 as literal, but explain verses 32 and 33 as figurative?" "Because," answered the Christian, "verse 31 has become a fact — Jesus was so born. It was indisputable evidence." "Ah," said the Jew, "I see! You believe the Scriptures when you see them fulfilled. I believe them because they are the Word of God." Who was right in principle?

—*King's Business*

Refusing To Read Will Not Change It

The *Courier* publishes an interesting comment from a Palestine missionary to the effect that the Arabs dislike to buy the Bible because they say it promises to give their land to the Jews, and they say that the promise to Abraham still holds good. They are right concerning the promise, but their refusal to buy and read the Bible will not prevent the fulfillment of its prophecies.

—*Prophecy*

* * *

Something Tremendous Portending

Would to God I could take every unbeliever and scoffer to Israel to see prophecy in fulfillment! People are pouring in by thousands, roads are being built, Cadillacs are all over the place, great new apartment houses are going up in the cities, irrigation lines span the country, and everyone is feverish with activity. I had an old Jewish rabbi as my guide when I "did" Jerusalem. After it was all over, and his voice and my feet were worn out; and he had expatiated at length on all the past glories of the country, I asked him, "But what does all this mean?" His answer was as sincere as it was revealing: "Very few of the people coming into the country are orthodox Jews in the strict sense. Most of us have limited faith in our Scriptures. We are being brought back by blind impulse — just as the birds are drawn to the South for the winter. We feel that something tremendous is portending, something which vitally concerns us, and yet is far larger than the little country of Israel. Something is going to burst which is bigger than an atom bomb." Yes, praise God, the skies are going to burst, and our Lord will appear!

—M. L. Ketcham, in the
Bible Friend

* * *

Which Was the Dotard?

It is a remarkable fact that Sir Isaac Newton, writing on the prophecies of Daniel, said that if they were true, it would be necessary that a new mode of traveling should be invented, for knowledge would be so increased that man would be able to travel at the rate of fifty miles an hour. Voltaire, true to the spirit of skepticism, said: "Now look at the mighty mind of Newton, who discovered gravitation; when he began to study the Book called the Bible, it seems in order to credit its fabulous nonsense, he believed that the knowledge of mankind will be so increased that we shall be able to travel fifty miles an hour! The poor dotard!" Today even a skeptic would have to say, "Newton was a wise philosopher; Voltaire a poor old dotard."

—From *Scriptural Anecdotes*, by Sayles

* * *

A Rabbi Corners a "Christian"

A Jewish rabbi was in conversation with a prominent church dignitary, and the matter of the relationship of the Christian message to the Jewish hope of a Messiah was taken up. "As I understand it," said the rabbi, "you Christians believe that Jesus was the Messiah." The clergyman assured him that this was correct.

"When, then, will this man Jesus fulfill the rest of the prophecies about himself? When will he reign upon the earth? When will he appear in glory?" The reply was that this had been fulfilled by the coming of the Holy Spirit into the hearts of the people. The prophecies, explained the clergyman, must be understood figuratively, or spiritually. But the rabbi persisted.

"But you believe that in the birth and ministry of Jesus the prophecies of the Old Testament about those matters were literally fulfilled?"

"Yes," was the reply.

"Then," said the rabbi, "since you take to yourself the right of making one set of the prophecies literal, and another set figurative, I take the right to declare that both are figurative. I have as much reason to say that the prophecies of the birth of Messiah are to be taken figuratively as you have to say the prohecies of His reign are only figurative."

—*Young People's Full Gospel Quarterly*

* * *

Modern Fulfillment of an Ancient Prophecy

A colonel in the Turkish army once asked Dr. Cyrus Hamlin in Constantinople for a proof that the Bible is the Word of God. In view of the fact that the colonel was a well-traveled man, Dr. Hamlin said to him, "Have you ever been in Babylon?" "Yes," replied the colonel, "and I will tell you a curious incident. The ruins of Babylan abound in game, and I once engaged a sheikh and his group to take me there for a week's shooting. At sundown, the Arabs, to my amazement, began to strike their tents, getting ready to leave. I went to the sheikh and protested, but nothing I could say had any effect. 'It is not safe,' said the sheikh; 'no mortal flesh dare stay here after sunset. Ghosts and ghouls come out of the holes and caverns after dark, and whoever they capture becomes one of themselves. No Arab has ever seen the sun go down on Babylon.'" Dr. Hamlin took out his Bible and read to the officer from Isaiah 13:19,20: "And Babylon, the glory of kingdoms, the beauty of the Chaldees' excellency, shall be as when God overthrew Sodom and Gomorrah . . . neither shall the Arabian pitch tent there." "That is history you are reading," said the colonel. "No," answered Dr.Hamlin; "it is prophecy. These words were written when Babylon was in all her glory." The colonel was silent; and they never met again.

—*Christian Victory*

PROTECTION, GOD'S

Protected

God's Word is sometimes an unexpected protection. A Christian business man recently had surprising evidence of this, and has written about it in a letter to a friend. He had just attended a meeting of the Chicago Camp of Gideons, and was walking along Milwaukee

Avenue when, to quote from his letter: "I was attacked from behind by two youthful bandits, who shoved me into an alley and began to rob me. One of them helped himself to my jade scarf-pin, but, before they located the small amount of money I had with me, the other one ran across my New Testament. 'Oh,' said he to his companion, 'this here guy's a Christian; I guess we hadn't ought to do anything to him.' 'O. K.,' replied the other, and handed me back my pin. Both men then hurried away, leaving me unharmed. How I thank and praise our ever blessed Lord for Psalm 34:7." The Psalmist sang: "The angel of the Lord encampeth round about them that fear him, and delivereth them."

—*Sunday School Times*

* * *

An Angel Hand on the Bridle?

In Central British Columbia, in a very isolated community, a Shantyman missionary was leading an open-air service in front of a general store. Soon the program was interruped by the appearance of a drunken cowboy who spurred his horse in a headlong gallop directly toward the missionary. Not one of the people who stood and watched the scene was aware of the quick inner cry for guidance and help that flashed from the missionary's heart to the throne of God. A split-second decision was reached: "Lord, you are able to protect — if you permit that horse and rider to run me down — Thy will be done." The horse lunged forward until its next step must smash the missionary to the ground. Suddenly it reared on its hind legs, as if encountering an invisible wall of the protection of the Lord. Three times the booze-crazed rider spurred his frothing mount at the missionary, and three times the horse refused to take the final leap that would have spelled serious injury or death to the Shantyman. The service proceeded to a conclusion as if there had been no danger.

—*Sunday School Times*

* * *

Faith and Mercy

A man, crossing a dreary moor, came upon a cottage which he visited. "Are you not afraid to live in this lonely place?" asked the visitor of the occupant. "Oh, no," said he, "for faith closes the door at night, and mercy opens it in the morning!"

—*Gospel Herald*

* * *

The Runaway Buggy

Dr. A. A. Hodge tells this story of the great Dr. Witherspoon, Presbyterian clergyman of the eighteenth century.

One day a man rushed into his presence. "Dr. Witherspoon," he shouted, "help me to thank God for His wonderful providence! My horse ran away, my buggy was dashed to pieces on the rocks, and behold! I am unharmed."

The good doctor smiled benevolently at the inconsistent, imperfect character of the man's religion. "Why," he answered, "I know a providence a thousand times better than that. I have driven down that rocky road to Princeton hundreds of times, and my horse never ran away and my buggy was never dashed to pieces."

Here is a truth few Christians ever grasp. An accident occurs and we have a seemingly miraculous deliverance. Immediately we see God's hand in it and praise Him and tell others of His marvelous act of providence. It never occurs to us to thank Him for the times beyond number when we were spared even the accident.

—Charles E. Bayley, in
The Alliance Weekly

* * *

Where the Bullet Stopped

A lieutenant in the United States Army on some far-off battle front and his buddy were sent out on an important mission. When the enemy discovered them, the lieutenant faced them, saying to himself, "Lord, it's your responsibility now." As he reached for his carbine, a shot from one of them struck him in the breast and blasted him down. Thinking he was dead, his pal grabbed his carbine and blasted away with both guns. He received three bullet wounds, but when he finished not one of the enemy was left. The lieutenant wrote his sister in Pennsylvania: "He was amazed when

I rolled over and tried to get up. The force of that bullet had only stunned me. Dazedly, wondering why, I pulled my Bible out of my pocket and in utter muteness looked at the ugly hole in the cover. It had ripped through Genesis, Exodus, Leviticus, Numbers, and kept going. Where do you think it stopped? In the middle of the Ninety-first Psalm, pointing like a finger at this verse, 'A thousand shall fall at thy side, and ten thousand at thy right hand; but it shall not come nigh thee.' I did not know such a verse was in the Bible. . . In utter humility I said, 'Thank You, precious God.' "

—From leaflet,
"A Lieutenant's Miraculous Escape"

* * *

Unseen Perils

One night a little yacht was cruising among the Western Isles of Scotland when a gale set in from the broad Atlantic and caught the frail craft off a perilous lee shore. There was no shelter at hand, but the old skipper knew of a harbor some distance away, and thought he could make it. And so, through the darkness the little ship plunged on her course amid the wild welter of wind and wave. At length she swung into smooth water, and the passengers turned into their berths and went peacefully to sleep. In the morning the master came on deck and surveyed the scene — a little loch girt about with dark purple mountains. It was a quiet haven; but, looking toward the entrance, he beheld a narrow channel with sharp, jagged rocks jutting here and there, and all awash with boiling surf. He shuddered, and, turning to the old skipper, he exclaimed, "Did we — did we pass there in the darkness?" Our God has brought us hitherto on the voyage of life, and He will never forsake us.

—*Christian World*

* * *

In the Hands of God

When Martin Luther was in the throes of the Reformation and the Pope was trying to bring him back to the Catholic Church, he sent a cardinal to deal with Luther and buy him with gold. The cardinal wrote to the Pope, "The fool does not love gold." The cardinal, when he could not convince Luther, said to him, "What do you think the Pope cares for the opinion of a German boor? The Pope's little finger is stronger than all Germany. Do you expect your princes to take up arms to defend you — you, a wretched worm like you. I tell you No. And where will you be then?" Luther's reply was simple: "Where I am now. In the hands of Almighty God."

—*Christian Digest*

* * *

"For He Careth for You"

Recently it was my pleasure to listen to a Gospel address by an officer of the Royal Navy who had fought in many encounters during the first World War, and came through safely. He read the 91st Psalm every day while aboard ship. With the outbreak of the World War he again was called to the colors. Once more his ship was in conflict with the enemy. While in the line of duty she received a bad hole in her side. That did not deter her nor her crew. In fact, the ship was in several encounters after being struck. This British officer related a most interesting fact. He said the ship's flag had on it these words, "In the care of God." Whenever the ship was in a heavy engagement, the men aboard could look up and see the old flag flying, and take courage. The ship was still "in the care of God."

—From *Walks with Our Lord through John's Gospel,*
by Erling C. Olson

* * *

Many Ways To Fall, But One Way To Stand

Did you ever see Balanced Rock in Colorado? There it stands, pivoted precariously upon its base, held up as if by some invisible hand. As we saw this marvel of nature, we thought of this fact: What an object lesson for God's children! We can fall many ways, but we can stand only in one way. None of God's children is kept from falling but by the encircling and undergirding "everlasting arms!" How heartening to know that our God neither sleeps nor slumbers; that He is ABLE to keep us from falling, and to present us faultless before the presence of His glory, because our lives are foundationed upon the Rock, Christ Jesus!

"On Christ the solid rock I stand,
All other ground is sinking sand!"
—Dr. Joel D. Arnold,
an Hebrew Christian

* * *

Bible Stops Bullet

The Welsh preacher, John Evans, tells of a friend of his who was in the Civil War. This young man received a captain's commission. Though many of the men in the army had little regard for religion, it was fashionable for each soldier to have a Bible.

The captain was ordered with his company to burn a fort. They were exposed to the fearful firing of the enemy. When the conflict was over, he found that a musket-ball had lodged itself in his Bible which was in his pocket. Had it not been for this intervention, he most surely would have been killed. Investigating further, he found that the bullet had lodged in his Bible so as to rest on the verse, "Rejoice, O young man, in thy youth; and let thy heart cheer thee in the days of thy youth, and walk in the ways of thine heart, and in the sight of thine eyes: but know thou, that for all these things God will bring thee into judgment."

This made as deep an impression upon his mind as did the remarkable deliverance itself. He at once turned his heart to God and continued devout to a good old age. He often remarked that the Bible had been the salvation of his body and soul.

Thy Word is power and life;
It bids confusion cease,
And changes envy, hatred, strife,
To love, and joy, and peace.
—*The Burning Bush*

* * *

Whitefield and the Robber

Taking a sizeable sum of money to a widow with a large family, Whitefield asked a friend to accompany him.

The two travelers proceeded on their journey, and before long, encountered

a highwayman, who demanded their money, which they gave. Whitefield now turned the tables on his friend and reminded him how much better it was for the poor widow to have the five guineas than the thief, who had just robbed them. They had not long resumed their travel, before the man returned and demanded Whitefield's coat which was much more respectable than his own. His request was granted, Whitefield accepting the robber's ragged garment till he could procure a better.

Presently they perceived the robber again galloping towards them most furiously; and now fearing that their lives were threatened, they spurred their horses, and, fortunately arrived at some cottages, before the highwayman could stop them. The thief was balked and no doubt, was immensely mortified; for when Whitefield took off the man's tattered coat, he found in one of its pockets a carefully wrapped parcel containing one hundred guineas.
—*Gospel Magazine*

* * *

Not Even A Knock

Testified Olga Kristensen, who spent forty years in China as a Missionary:

"Toward the end of my stay I had nearly eighty refugees at the mission station besides the women living there. One night we heard the bandits approaching. There were shots at the end of the street. We all knew that without intervention, murder and disaster were on the way. I went into my closet and prayed to God for a word to calm myself and the others with me. My tortured soul then found a word I had often read before, but which now had a real meaning for me — 'When thou liest down, thou shalt not be afraid: yea, . . . thy sleep shall be sweet. Be not afraid of sudden fear, neither of the desolation of the wicked, when it cometh.' Could I have a better message? I brought it to all the others and told them to go to rest. When I was going to bed I was tempted to lie down with my clothes on, but after a little struggle I undressed and, lying down, slept soundly. Next morning the dead were lying outside our premises. There had been fighting and murder, but no one had even gone so far as to knock on our door."

—*Free Methodist*

* * *

God's Protection Not Limited

The story is told that during the great Plague in London, several centuries ago, the stricken people were dying by thousands, and all roads leading out were crowded with fugitives. A Negro was helping pack a carriage that stood at a door on Craven Street, Strang. His master was abandoning his town house for his country home. The Negro said to another, "Since my lord leaves London for fear of the plague, his God must live in the country, I suppose." This was not sarcasm, for he had but recently come from Africa, where the gods are supposed to have local shrines and jurisdictions. The nobleman, who overheard the remark, was struck by it. "That ignorant fellow has taught me something that I had well-nigh forgotten," he said to himself. "My God is truly everywhere. He can keep me safe in town as well as in the country. Lord, pardon my mistrust." He remained in London and applied himself to caring for some of the stricken ones, many of whom were utterly alone and helpless, deserted by their relatives and neighbors. The God that Lord Craven trusted preserved him, and the plague did not come nigh his dwelling.

—*Alliance Weekly*

* * *

Why the Italians Did Not Land

Asked by a news correspondent why the Italians were unsuccessful in landing on the Island of Malta, Lt. Gen. Sir Wm. Dobbie replied, "I believe it was God." What would your answer be? Certainly the Italians wanted the island. The savage bombing evidenced that. Both Germany and Italy knew the strategic position this fortress occupied. In fact, the entire course of the war might have been changed if Malta had been taken by the enemy. General Dobbie enlarged upon his comment by telling how he and Lady Dobbie and some others recognized their need of divine intervention and committed the fortress to God.

"Our lives were not important," said he, "but it was important what happened to Malta. It had to stand, and we rested in the confidence that God would enable it to stand."

—*Moody Monthly*

* * *

Why the Engine Stopped

A sergeant-major, converted some time ago in a Salvation Army hut while on duty in the Middle East, had charge of the locomotive which ran between Cairo and Haifa. After his conversion he made it a practice, before starting on each journey, to pray for the safety of the train and of his passengers. On one journey the engine suddenly stopped, for no apparent reason. A civil engineer on the train, as well as the engine staff tried in vain to discover the cause of the breakdown which took place at 3 o'clock on a wet morning. As dawn approached, two workmen came running farther down the line with the news that a rainstorm had made a hole in the permanent way large enough to engulf the whole train had it proceeded. "What luck!" the passengers said. But the driver quietly gave his witness and spoke of the prayer he offered for their safety every time he took his place on the footplate. Strangely enough, as it seemed to the passengers, the engine started without a hitch when the track had been repaired after a fourteen-hour holdup.

—*Alliance Weekly*

* * *

The Charm That Works!

In New York's Chinatown, an American woman walked into a curiosity shop and asked to see some good-luck charms.

The elderly Chinese lady in charge looked at her skeptically and proceeded to lay her wares on the counter.

The customer leaned over the counter and said earnestly, "Would you mind telling me which of these is the best? You see, I have to have one that really works. I have a son in the South Pacific and I want something that will take care of him."

The shopkeeper looked at her for a moment and smiled, "My best good-luck charm I don't have on the counter."

"Well, for goodness sake, let's see it. I want the best thing you have," she countered excitedly. "I'll pay any price." "But it doesn't cost anything. You see, my good luck charm is God. I have three sons and three grandsons in the service myself. But when my boys were born, I dedicated them to God, and every day since they were babies I have asked God to take care of them. He has answered my prayer, and I know He will continue to do so. It's the only charm that works and I recommend it wholeheartedly to you."

—Sunday

* * *

God Controls Fire

A Chinese Christian had been asked to give to a fund to be expended in sacrifice to idols as an insurance of his house against fire. He declined, on the ground that he trusted in the living God, and idols could not save from fire. When the idolatrous ceremony was over, fire broke out in the street where his home was and burned over one hundred and twenty houses. When the flames were coming nearer and nearer to his house they tried to persuade him to remove his furniture, but he refused, and in their presence prayed to God to show that he was indeed the Lord of hosts who could send legions of angels to deliver him, if need be, from so great a calamity. Nearer and nearer came the fire, until only one house stood between his own house and the flames. Suddenly there was a change of wind and his house was saved.

—New Century Leader

* * *

The Night I Prayed

I was awakened one night while my husband was overseas, with an urgent need to pray. My heart was frantic, for something told me he was in grave danger. And through the long hours of the night I was on my knees beseeching God for the safety of my loved one.

The next day the radio blared the news of the "Belgian Bulge" and somehow I was sure my fears had been in this connection. I marked the date and time of the night and resolved to compare notes with my husband when and if I should ever see him again.

He came home a year later and one of the first things I wanted to know was his situation the night when I had prayed. We even took into consideration the changes in time zones and according to his dairy those very hours when I was on my knees, his whole battalion was surrounded by the Germans. Many of his friends were massacred in the much written up "observation" battalion which met such a sad fate but God "Preserved him alive."

—Helen Eisenhart

* * *

"There Shall No Evil Befall Thee"

I was journeying northward after a winter's teaching in the South. As the day went on, our train came upon a wreck. We were held behind it for many hours until the night fell. Then came the order to run around the wreck. As our train ran by the burning wreckage, the passengers from our sleeper flocked to the rear platform to watch the wreck. Under the same impulse I sought the rear of the car. The platform was crowded with spectators. Naturally I stepped across to the front platform of the car adjoining ours. I laid my hands upon the iron rods at the side. Lifting my foot I was about to step out upon the platform. There came a sort of gentle arrest to my spirit which stayed my step for a moment. The next instant I was conscious of a cold breath of air upon my cheek, which should not have been there if the car door were closed. In another instant I realized that someone had left the door wide open, and the platform lifted, and I was about to step out through the darkness from a fast express train to what would have seemingly been certain death. I walked forward, sat down in my berth, pulled my hat over my eyes, and had a quiet, blessed season of thanksgiving with the Lord.

—James McConkey

* * *

Counting on God's Care

When America was young, those brave God-fearing ancestors battled with cold, hunger, wild beasts, and hostile Indians. At the edge of a settlement stood a cabin, the home of an aged Quaker and wife. One evening at family worship, the wife read the Ninety-first Psalm. After prayer and retirement the Quaker asked, "Mother, didst thou leave the latchstring inside tonight?" "Yes, Father, I did," replied the Quakeress. "Well, since thou readest, 'Thou shalt not be afraid for the terror by night; nor for the arrow that flieth by day,' I think we should leave the string outside." The godly Quaker arose, put the latchstring outside and went back to bed, saying, "God will take care of thee and me." Toward midnight the door opened; whispering was heard. 'Twas the chief, consulting with his braves. Soon the door closed and all was quiet. In the morning when the Quaker and his wife looked out, the village lay in ruins. Theirs was the only cabin standing. The Indian chief had gone to their cabin that night with murder in his heart, but was struck by the tiny string dangling on the outside. To him it spelled trust and friendship. But to the aged couple "it was the hand of God."

—Triumphs of Faith

* * *

The Broken Rail

It was past midnight. A strange sense of impending evil came over me. I felt that something strange was going to happen! I told my fireman, "Jim," who is a Christian, and we decided we would kneel down right there on the engine, and pray. Then off we went, having committed our train to Him who sees in the darkness as well as in the light! It was almost morning, when I saw a man running and waving something frantically! I applied the emergency brake, and brought the train to a standstill as quickly as I could. "There's a broken rail just ahead of you," the man shouted. When I saw it, I said to the man: "Thank God for answered prayer, but what made you come out so early?" He said he awoke early, and could not rest until he had started out to examine the railway line! He did not know why, until he discovered the

broken rail! He turned out to be a Christian, so we knelt down on the track, and thanked God for deliverance.

—Dave Fant, Sr., in
Life and Liberty

* * *

The Power of Prayer

I read an incident that occurred during the first settling of the United States when there were plenty of wild Indians and wild animals. The country was thinly settled with white people. There was a young Christian family living in Virginia, consisting of a man, his wife and two small children. One day in the summer after they got their crop done they went to visit their nearest neighbor, eight or ten miles away, the woman and the children on their only horse and the man with his rifle walked beside his family.

In the evening about the time they started for home, there rose a storm and before they reached home dark overtook them. The storm was raging, the lightning was fearfully flashing every few seconds — they could only see their Indian path by the flashing lightning. They got about a mile from their home. All at once the horse stopped and by the flash of lightning they saw a huge panther on a limb of a tree just in front of them, ready to make his spring on the woman and children; (the man started to shoot, but in the morning he had forgotten to take but one load for his rifle and he had used that one.) Just as the animal started to leap, the woman looked up through the fearful clouds, and prayed to the Lord to save them, and at that very moment there came a stroke of lightning, tore the tree up and the wild beast fell dead right in front of them. Such is the power of the Almighty to answer an earnest and faithful prayer.

—Z. T. Caldwell

* * *

God Uses Spider!

When Robert Bruce, the famous emancipator of Scotland, was fleeing from his enemies, he sought refuge in a cave. Although they were hot on his trail, when they reached his hideout a spider had built a web over the mouth of the cave. His pursuers concluded that he could not have entered without first destroying the web. Naturally they presumed that he had fled elsewhere. No wonder Bruce prayed, "O God I thank Thee that in the tiny bowels of a spider You can place for me a shelter, and then send the spider in time to place it for my protection."

—Gospel Herald

* * *

A Child's Confidence

Enroute to China as a missionary, Robert Morrison was taken seriously ill in New York. A kind gentleman took him to his own home, and put him in his own bed. In the same room was a little child, sleeping so quietly in her crib that they decided not to awaken her. Some time afterward the child awakened and turned to her father's bed. She was startled at seeing a stranger there. Gripping the sides of her crib, she stood up and looked at Mr. Morrison steadily for a moment; then rather falteringly she asked, "Man, do you pray to God?" "Oh, yes, my dear," came the quick response, "every day. God is my best Friend." The answer reassured the child. After a moment she sank slowly into her crib, laid her head again upon her pillow, and fell asleep. Morrison said that he never forgot that child's lesson of confidence and faith; and that among the worst hardships and dangers of his missionary work, he was always able to lie down and sleep, a stranger in a strange land, but always under the protection of the Almighty God.

—Youth Companion

* * *

John Wesley's Narrow Escape

When John Wesley was six years old, his father's house was burned with all its contents. All the children were taken to safety except John, and he was forgotten until the roof was almost ready to cave in, then he was heard crying. His father ran to the stairs, but they were so nearly consumed they would not bear his weight; so utterly in despair he fell on his knees and asked God for

help. In the meantime little John had climbed up on a chest. The neighbors, seeing him and with no time to get a ladder, one man was hoisted on the shoulders of another, and he was rescued. A moment later the roof fell in. Then the father cried out: "Come neighbors, let us kneel down; let us give thanks to God. He has given me all my eight children; let the house go, I am rich enough." This incident was so indelibly impressed on John Wesley's mind that under one of his portraits he wrote, "Is not this a brand plucked out of the burning?" God always cares for His own.

—Sunday School Times

* * *

Why the Boxers Fled

Dr. Goodrich . . . was on the lookout on a wall in Peking during the Boxer uprising in China, and saw the enemy approach within a second of achieving its objective, when suddenly the whole attacking force turned and fled in confusion. Some of those who fled were captured, and when asked why they fled, answered: "We saw the walls suddenly swarming with angels in white, and we cried out, 'The gods have come down to fight for the foreigners, and our cause is lost.'"

—Tom M. Olson

* * *

Jehovah's Rain

Dr. John G. Paton of the New Hebrides awoke one night to find the natives firing the church right by his home. Committing himself to God, he went to face the savages. He said, "They yelled in rage and urged each other to strike the first blow, but the Invisible One restrained them. I stood invulnerable beneath His invisible shield. At this dread moment a rushing and a roaring sound came from the south like the noise of muttering thunder. They knew from previous hard experience that it was one of their awful tornadoes of wind and rain. The mighty roaring of the wind, and the cloud pouring in torrents awed them into silence. Some began to withdraw from the scene, all lowered their weapons of war, and several, terror-struck, exclaimed: "That is Jehovah's rain! Truly their Jehovah is fighting for them and helping them. Let us away!"

—From *The Life of John G. Paton*

* * *

Kept by God

Years ago the king of Abyssinia took a man by the name of Campbell, prisoner. He was a citizen of Great Britain. He was carried to the fortress of Magdala, and in the height of the mountains put in a dungeon. No cause was assigned for his confinement. After six months Great Britain found it out. They demanded an immediate release for their citizen. King Theodore refused to release him.

Within ten days, ten thousand soldiers were on shipboard, sailing down the coast. They disembarked and marched seven hundred miles under the blasting rays of a hot sun up the mountains to the dungeon where their subject was held prisoner. They gave battle, tore the gates down, and soon reached the prisoner, lifted him out and placed him on their shoulders and carried him all the way down the mountains and placed him on one of the big ocean vessels which sped him safely home.

Ten thousand soldiers were employed in the release of one man. It took several months to release and return the prisoner. It cost the English government twenty-five million dollars to release that man. The entire government was interested and ready to help him.

The Christian belongs to a better Kingdom than any earthly kingdom. When a man is born again, he becomes a citizen of Heaven. All Heaven is interested in the success of the Christian. God gave His Son to redeem man. He gives His Grace to save and keep him. Angels rejoice when any sinner is saved. All Heaven stands back of the child of God. The Lord will do more for His own than any earthly power can do for any of its subjects. —*Gospel Minister*

* * *

God's Assurance to Ralph Norton

Crossing the Atlantic on the S.S. Philadelphia, in early September, 1917, with the "Black week" just past us, with its fifty-nine sunken boats, Ralph C. Norton was awakened early on Sunday morning by the Holy Spirit, and given a new message from the Word — Psalm 107:30, "So he bringeth them unto their desired haven," which he underscored in his Bible. Another morning, in preparation for the danger that awaited, he opened his Bible and found looking up at him that lovely message of assurance, "No weapon that is formed against thee shall prosper." He knew and accepted it as a faithful word of promise, and as he continued to think on it, the voice of the Spirit came to him very expressly, "Turn over to Job 5:19, 20," and there he read for confirmation, "In famine he shall redeem thee from death: and in war from the power of the sword." He felt and knew that these assurances were not given him for naught, and we talked them over. We had been praying earnestly for safety at sea; all the great work before us in the Belgian Gospel Mission seemed involved. And so it was, that when an agitated and trembling wife burst into the cabin that September morning, and breathlessly cried, "Quick, Ralph, a torpedo has just missed us; we may be attacked again any moment — oh, be quick, don't wait!" he quietly smiled, looking up from his Bible, and tranquilly answered, "Listen, Edith, I was sent down to my cabin just a few moments ago, and bidden again to read Job 5:19, 20 — listen while I read it to you — 'He shall deliver thee in six troubles: yea, in seven there shall be no evil touch thee: In famine he shall redeem thee from death: and in war from the power of the sword.'" And so we faced the perils of the deep, not once, but during seven crossings of the sea during the wartime, and his faithful Word was our guide and our stay, the cloud in daytime, and a pillar of fire by night.

—From *Opened Windows of Heaven*, by Edith Norton.

* * *

God's Watching, the "Father Kind"

I read somewhere of a little boy who was told that the eye of God is always watching us. He thought a minute, and then he said, "I'd like to know what kind of watching it is. Tim Brown watches me in school so he can tell teacher if I whisper and get me bad marks. But Father watches me in a different way. When I am on the beach he keeps watch so I won't get in too deep. I like that kind of watching. Is God watching like that?"

—*Moody Monthly*

* * *

When Christ Holds Us

Two little girls were playing with their dolls and singing, "Safe in the Arms of Jesus." "How do you know you are safe?" asked the older sister. "Because I am holding Jesus with both my hands tight." "That's not safe," said the other. "Suppose Satan came along and cut your hands off?" The child looked troubled, dropped dolly, and thought. Suddenly her face shone with joy. "Oh, I forgot! Jesus is holding me; and Satan cannot cut off his hands, so I am safe."

—*The Expositor*

* * *

Standing On A Cobra!

I neglected that night to take a candle with me into the veranda-shed of my stick-and-mud house which served as a bathroom. Undressing, I removed my right boot. Just as I straightened up, I heard a sound on the outside. Stepping out, I planted my half-bare foot right on the back of a large, spitting cobra! The big brute was over six feet long. It writhed in protest at being thus trodden under foot! I called my boy to bring a candle, and started myself for a shotgun. Approaching the bathhouse cautiously, we saw the cobra with head aloft, eyes blazing, defying the world. The shot gun put an end to his life. Relating the incident several years later to friends in America, they told me that I was constantly in their prayers, and because of their prayers, God wrought a mighty deliverance for me!

—*A. W. Bailey, in Lighted Pathway*

An Experience

A pioneer preacher tells of a personal experience. He says, "In the course of my work in a certain settlement I incurred the ill will of the leader of a gang of horse thieves and bandits, who made his honest boast that he would 'get me.' One afternoon a man was hurt by a falling tree and I was sent for. To reach the lumber camp I had to pass through some rough, cut-over land. It was evening as I entered it, and all at once I was overcome with fear and foreboding, which I could not shake off until I dismounted and laid my trouble before the Lord. I went on unmolested. The next day the head bandit was shot by one of his men, and I was again summoned to a deathbed. The man confessed on the previous night he had lain in wait in the cut-over land, intending to kill me, adding, 'But who were those men who rode with you?' When I said I was alone he screamed, 'You were not! Two men were with you, one on either side, and in all my life I never saw such horses as they rode. Who were they?' The excitement brought on hemorrhage, and he fell into unconsciousness from which he never rallied. But I have never doubted that on the night of my terror God sent me supernatural protection and deliverance."

—*Gospel Herald*

* * *

David Brainerd's Credentials

Tomahawks in hand, the Indians crept toward the strange tent. As they cautiously peered under the flap, their intention to kill was forgotten. There, in the center of the tent was a man on his knees. As he prayed, a rattlesnake crossed his feet and paused in position to strike. But the snake did not strike. It lowered its head again and glided out of the tent. It was a long time later when David Brainerd, the man in the tent, found out why the Indians at the village received him with such honor as they did. He had expected that they would want to kill him. The reason for their change of heart was the report their comrades had brought of the marvelous thing they had seen. The Indians looked upon David Brainerd as a messenger from the Great Spirit, which indeed he was. He had come into the deep forest to preach the Word of God to the savages. Surely it is a good thing that in all good work the protection of God is with the worker.

—*Boys' World*

* * *

When Poison Failed

An Arab woman had been won to Christ from Mohammedanism. Her family coaxed, argued, and threatened to draw her from her new faith, but in vain. Then they concocted a simple, deadly poison, and secretly put it in her food. When she had eaten the meat containing the poison, she realized very quickly what had happened, and knew how deadly it was. She knew she was doomed to death. The poison would first make one very irritable, then very dull; then it would effect the mind still more, and after that the body, till death should come. She was greatly startled and distressed, and did not know what to do. As she sat, without planning to, she began to repeat the Name, the great Name. Not aloud but to herself she repeated with great intensity, "Jesus, Jesus, Jesus." For two or three days she continued and the poison gradually receded from her blood, while the family watched with strange eyes. The poison had never failed before. She told the missionary, "Each time I said that Name, I felt as though there was a wave of life, and in between a wave of death!"   —S. D. Gordon

PROVISION, GOD'S

How We Often Treat the Lord

An incident from the life of that great preacher and hymn writer, Dr. Arnot, is to the point. This preacher was once visiting among his poor sick people in his parish in Edinburgh. Before going up into a certain house he stood back in the street to see whether Betty Gordon, an aged woman, was at home or not. He knew that she was at home because her little flower pots were out upon the window sill and the blind was up. He knew Betty was in, for when she went away she carefully took in the flower pots and pulled down the blinds.

Dr. Arnot knew that she was poor and needy, but he was happy at heart because somebody had given him money that morning to give to the poor, and he had calculated what Betty's rent would amount to for a month, and he had it in his pocket to give to her. He climbed up the winding stone stairs, and, panting, at last reached Betty's door. He knocked. At first he knocked softly, but there was no answer. Then he pulled the bell, and though it rang loudly there was no answer. Then he knocked louder, but there was no answer. At last he said: "Betty forgot to pull the blinds and she has gone out leaving the flower pots there. What a pity!" Then he went down the stairs.

The next morning he went back, because he knew that Betty needed help. He knocked at the door. After a little waiting Betty came and opened it.

"Oh," she said, "is it you, Mr. Arnot? I am so glad to see you! Come in!"

Dr. Arnot went in and sat down. After some conversation he offered prayer, and the sweet face of Betty Gordon, framed with her white hair, looked at him like the face of an angel. But there were tears in her eyes and a little look of care there that he had not seen before.

The kind preacher said: "Betty, why are you crying?"

She was crying in earnest by that time.

"Oh," she said, "Dr. Arnot, I am so afraid of the landlord. He will come, perhaps, today. He came yesterday, and I had no rent, and I dinna open the door. I am afraid of his coming, for he is a hard man."

"Betty, what time did he come yesterday?"

"He came between eleven and twelve o'clock," she said. "I remember, because I looked at the clock, and it was twenty-five minutes to twelve."

"Well," said Dr. Arnot, "it was not the landlord: it was I, and I brought to you, Betty, this money to pay your rent. Take it and be thankful." She looked at him and said: "Oh, was it you? Did you bring that money to pay my rent, and I kept the door shut against you, and I would not let you in? I heard you knocking, and I heard you ringing the door bell, and I said: 'That is the landlord; I wish he would go away.' And it was my ain meenister. It was my ain Lord who had sent ye as His messenger, and I wouldna let ye in." —*Gospel Herald*

* * *

When the Chaplain Prayed

Captain Johnson was serving his men as chaplain on an inland in the South Pacific. He prepared to go on a bombing raid on Jap-occupied islands several hundred miles away. The mission was a complete success. On the homeward course the plane began to lose altitude and the engines seemed to fade out. But God had provided an island, and a safe landing was made. Later they learned that the enemy was just one-half mile in each direction, yet their landing had not been discovered. The staff sergeant came and said, "Chaplain, you have been telling us for months of the need of praying and believing God to answer in time of trouble, and that He does it right away. Now it is your chance to prove what you have been preaching. We're out of gas, base several hundred miles away . . . . and almost surrounded by Japs." Johnson began to pray and lay hold of the promises and believed that God would work a miracle. All afternoon he was on his knees. Night came and the crew slept on the ground. Johnson continued to pray. About 2 a. m. the staff sergeant was strangely aroused and, walking to the water's edge, discovered a metal float, which had drifted up on the beach — a barge on which were fifty barrels of high octane gasoline. In a few hours the crew reached their home base safely. An investigation revealed that the skipper of a U. S. tanker, finding his ship in sub-infested waters, had his gasoline cargo removed so as to minimize the danger of a torpedo hit. Barrels were placed on barges and put adrift 600 miles from where Johnson and the plane crew were forced down. God had navigated one of these barges through wind and current and beached it fifty steps from the stranded men. —*Sunday School Times*

* * *

Even in Mid-Ocean

One Sunday night in April, 1912, an American woman was very weary, yet could not sleep because of an oppression of fear. At last she felt a burden of prayer, and with tremendous earnestness began to pray for her husband then in mid-Atlantic, homeward bound on the *Titanic*. As the hours went by she could get no assurance, and kept on praying in an agony, until about five o'clock in the morning when a great peace possessed her, and she slept. Meanwhile her husband, Colonel Gracie, was among the doomed hundreds who were trying frantically to launch the lifeboats from the great ship whose vitals had been torn out by an iceberg. He had given up all hope of being saved himself, and was doing his best to help the women and children. He wished that he could get a last message through to his wife, and cried from his heart, "Good-by, my darling." Then as the ship plunged to her watery grave, he was sucked down in the giant whirlpool. Instinctively he began to swim under water, ice cold as it was, crying in his heart, "Good-by, my darling, until we meet again." Suddenly he came to the surface and found himself near an overturned life boat. Along with several others he climbed aboard, and was picked up by another lifeboat, about five in the morning, the very time that peace came to his praying wife! Supplication! The prayer that will not take No for an answer; that storms the battlements of Heaven, and brings confusion and defeat to all the powers of hell, even death itself! —*Christian Observer*

* * *

When She Prayed for Thirty Dollars

God answers prayer . . . Let us trust him. A Christian woman was in financial need. She had been talking a good deal to the Lord about it. Her income that month was thirty dollars.

. . . . She began praying for the impossible, asking the Lord for thirty dollars more. The next mail brought her a certain envelope. She writes about it as follows: "I opened the envelope when my husband and I were at breakfast, and my eyes began to feel queer, so that I had to wink fast, and there was a big lump in my throat. The envelope contained a check for $32.84, and instantly there was a little prayer in my heart, 'O dear heavenly Father, I just can't thank You enough.' Why, it just seemed as if the Lord were sitting right by my table." Yes, but why say, "As if the Lord *were?*" For the Lord *was.* And he had been standing right alongside when she had asked for the impossible. Nor is the Lord's bank account all used up yet. He has more checks, and his balance at the bank is large.

—*Sunday School Times*

* * *

Sending Our Prayers

A good man was not only sick, but his absence from work had depleted his pocketbook and he was in dire need of the very necessities of life. He lacked fuel to replenish his winter fires, and he lacked food to invigorate his half-starved body. The church heard of his distress and the deacons came to pray for him. As they were cloistered with the sick man in prayer, suddenly the door opened and as the icy breath of the day, with its blustering snow, swept in the doorway, a youthful voice chimed out, "My father could not come, but he has sent his prayers, and they are out in the wagon!" The prayer meeting was abandoned while the good deacons went out and brought in flour and food in abundance. Then, the youth drove to the coal bin and put in a good supply of coal. —From *General Epistle James,* by Dr. R. E. Neighbour

* * *

God's Ravens

A little boy, having read with his mother the story of how God fed Elijah by the ravens, sat on the wintry night in a fireless room beside a bare table. With a simple, childish trust, he asked his widowed mother if he might set the door open for God's ravens to come in.

"I feel sure they must be on their way," he said. The trustful mother granted the request. The burgomaster of that German town, passing by, was attracted by the sight of the open door, and entered, inquiring the cause. When he learned the reason, he said, "I will be God's ravens!" He relieved their needs then and afterwards.

"Trust in the Lord, and do good; so shalt thou dwell in the land, and verily thou shalt be fed" (Ps. 37:3).

—F. B. Meyer

* * *

Prayer That Brought a Cloudburst

William Hacquist of the Evangelical Alliance Mission tells a story of escape in Boxer days. They had traveled six days and had come to a point where they must choose by land or river for further travel. But, because of drought, there was no water in the Han River at the time. Further, their carriers and escort refused to travel other than on the land route. So a prayer meeting was called in a native inn to ask God's guidance. They felt led to procure two large flat-bottom river boats; they bought food and placed it with their baggage on board. But there was no water. "The place where we stayed was surrounded by high hills. As we prayed and waited, in about mid-afternoon, heavy dark clouds came over the hilltops, and from them came pouring down the heaviest rain I have ever seen. It really looked like a cloudburst. In a very short time the river bed was filled with water, so we could release the boats and nicely float down the river. We later learned why we were led not to travel by land. In a mountain pass, several hundred bandits were waiting to kill us. God sent us the safe way."

—Ernest Gordon, in
The Sunday School Times

* * *

The Stranded Fish

H. Clay Trumbull, in his book, "Personal Prayer," tells of a widow who had a hard struggle providing for her two children. One stormy night, she found she had not one particle of food in the house for the next day's need. She prayed with her children that night omitting to tell them of their need. When morning came, she prayed for their daily bread, assured that her Father could supply it — as He alone knew how. She asked her children to go down to the shore before breakfast, and get some clean sand for their sitting room floor. Before the days of woolen carpets, in the humbler New England homes they were accustomed to strew sand on the floor. When the children had gone, the mother again kneeled and prayed for their daily bread. After this she spread the breakfast table, for which she had no food. Suddenly the children returned without the sand, but bringing gleefully a fine fish, which they had found in a hollow of the beach, as left by the outgoing tide after the storm, and which they together had captured. With a grateful heart she thanked God for His goodness, and prepared the fish for their breakfast. —*Sunday School Times*

* * *

Wood in a Storm

Louisa M. Alcott tells the following story of her kind-hearted and benevolent father and mother:

"One snowy Saturday night, when our wood was very low, a poor child came to beg a little, as the baby was sick and the father was on a spree with all his wages. My mother hesitated a little at first, as we also had a baby. Very cold weather was upon us, and a Sunday to be got through before wood could be had.

"My father said, 'Give half of our stock, and trust Providence: the weather will moderate, or wood will come.'

"Mother laughed, and answered in her cheery way, 'Well, their need is greater than ours, and if our half gives out, we can go to bed and tell stories.'

"So a generous half went to the poor neighbor, and a little later in the evening, while the storm raged, and we were about to cover up our fire to keep it, a knock came, and a farmer who usually supplied us appeared, saying anxiously:

"'I started for Boston with a load of wood, but it drifts so, I want to go home. Wouldn't you like to have me drop the

wood here? It would accommodate me, and you needn't worry paying for it.'

"'Yes,' said Father; and as the man left, Father turned to Mother with a look that much impressed us children with his gift as a seer, 'Didn't I tell you wood would come if the weather did not moderate?'

"My mother's motto was, 'Hope and keep busy,' and one of her sayings was, 'Cast thy bread upon the waters, and after many days it will come back to you buttered.' "　　　　　—*The Christian*

* * *

I Cried — He Answered

One morning I was on my knees praying, asking God to send me $10.00 some way, so that I could buy an automobile license. If I were to preach the next Sunday morning at the penitentiary, I needed means of transportation. And so I prayed and told God that if He wanted me to preach there, it was His problem, and not mine.

While I was talking to the Lord, my wife was cleaning the carpets downstairs. She turned off the vacuum cleaner and shouted upstairs, "Are you praying for $10.00?"

I answered, "Yes."

"Well, quit praying," she said, "Somebody has just shoved it through the letter slot in the door."

—*The Baptist News*

* * *

How Faithful God Is!

Charles Haddon Spurgeon the prince of preachers, telling about his grandfather in one of his sermons, said: "He had a large family and a very small income but he loved his Lord, and he would not have given up his preaching of the Gospel for anything, not even for an imperial crown. He has told me often how the Lord provided for him. He had a little farm to get his living upon it, and he had a cow which used to give milk for his many children, and one day when he came up to the cow it fell back with the staggers and died.

"Grandmother said, 'James, how will God provide for the dear children now? What shall we do for milk?'

"'Mother,' he said, 'God said He would provide, and I believe He could send us fifty cows if He pleased.'

"It so happened that on that day a number of gentlemen were meeting in London, persons whom he did not know, were sitting as a committee for the distribution of money to poor ministers, and they had given it to all who had asked for any; he liked to earn his own money. He did not send in any petition or appeal. Well, after the gentlemen had distributed to all who had asked there was five pounds over, and they were considering what they should do with this balance.

" 'Well,' said one, 'there is a Mr. Spurgeon down at Stambourne, in Essex, a poor minister. He stands in need of five pounds.'

" 'Oh,' said another, 'don't send him five pounds. I will put five to it. I know him. He is a worthy man.'

" 'No,' said another, 'don't send him ten pounds. I will give another five pounds if somebody else will put a fourth five to it.'

"The next morning came a letter to grandfather with ninepence to pay! Grandmother did not like to pay out ninepence for a letter, but there was twenty pounds in it; and as my grandfather opened it he said, 'Now, can't you trust God about an old cow?' "

How faithful God is!

— *Watchman-Examiner*

* * *

Even Before He Called

Some years ago one of our Christian leaders was trying to prepare himself for Christian service, but his funds gave out and it looked as if he would have to leave school. He earnestly asked the Lord to come to his relief if it was His will for him to go on with this preparation. The following day he received a letter containing a 'check large enough to take care of his needs. He was so happy that his prayer had been answered, but Satan whispered to him to look at the date of the letter and he would see that it was not an answer to his prayer as it had been written before he had prayed. This dampened his joy until he remembered that the Lord had said, "Before they call, I will answer." Then he realized that God had

known his need and had prepared the answer even before he had called upon him.

—Sunday School Times

* * *

"The Lord Hath Blessed!"

When our soul is much discouraged
　By the roughness of the way,
And the cross we have to carry
　Seemeth heavier every day;
When some cloud that overshadows
　Hides our Father's face from view,
O 'tis well then to remember
　He has blessed us hitherto.

Looking back the long years over,
　What a varied path! And yet
All the way His hand hath led us,
　Placed each hindrance we have met,
Given to us the pleasant places,
　Cheered us all the journey through,
Passing through the deepest waters,
　He has blessed us hitherto.

Surely then our hearts should trust Him,
　Though the clouds be dark o'erhead;
We've a Friend that draweth closer
　When all other friends have fled.
When our pilgrimage is over,
　And the gates we're sweeping through,
We shall see with clearer vision
　How He's blessed us hitherto.

—Selected

* * *

"God Will Provide!"

Back in the depression days of the early '30s, my husband pastored a small country church. We then had three little children. Many times our weekly income was less than $10. One day, we found ourselves out of bread and with only some rancid bacon grease for shortening. I used it, however, in making hot biscuits and we managed to eat some of them for lunch. Later, as we put the remaining biscuits on the supper table, our five-year-old daughter prayed very earnestly, "Dear Jesus, help us to eat these biscuits or else send us some better ones. Amen!" Later that evening, the doorbell rang. There, at the door, stood a member of our church who had a bakery route. Before we could tell him our story he began unloading his large bakery basket with all kinds of tempting sweet rolls, buns, biscuits, besides dark and white bread. "You know," he said rather apologetically, "I was tired tonight and seven miles out here in the pouring rain seemed so far. I was tempted to wait until tomorrow evening and bring these bakery things on my way to prayer meeting as I usually do." Then he added, "But I was strongly constrained to come tonight! Hope you can use these things!"

—Anne S. Alexander, in *Power*

* * *

God the Giver

A boy was bringing home a loaf of bread. Someone said, "What have you there?" "A loaf." "Where did you get it?" "From the baker." "Where did the baker get it?" "He made it." "Of what did he make it?" "Flour." "Where did

he get the flour?" "From the miller." "Where did he get it?" "From the farmer." "Where did the farmer get it?"

Then the truth dawned upon the boy's mind, and he replied, "From God." "Well, then, from whom did you get that loaf?" "Oh, from God."

—*Moody Monthly*

* * *

The Unexpected Meal

A friend of mine, Miss L. Dennis of the Heart of Africa Mission, spent her Christmas Day as the only European in a Congo village. She was without food at dinner time, and kneeled at her bedside in the tiny one-roomed native hut to pray, "Give me this day my daily bread." As she arose, out flew a little hen with a loud, "Tuck, Tuck, Tuck." She had laid her first egg under the bed.

—*Sunday School Times*

READY

Preparing for Eternity

"Mamma," said a little child, "my Sunday-school teacher tells me that this world is only a place in which God lets us live a while, that we may prepare for a better world. But, Mother, I do not see anybody preparing. I see you preparing to go into the country, and Aunt Eliza is preparing to come here; but I do not see any one preparing to go there. *Why don't they try to get ready?*"

—*Prairie Overcomer*

* * *

"I Am Ready!"

Some time ago we read an account of the death of General Von Hindenburg. The general was not noted for making verbose remarks. Deep waters are quiet. The doctor who was awaiting on him had written a book entitled, *Death in the Lord.* The old general looked up with his dying gaze and said, "Doctor, is death in the room?" "No, General, death is not in the room, but death is walking around in the yard just waiting to come in." "Very well, then I want to talk with the Lord." He reached un-

der his pillow for a small Testament and read, "Let not your heart be troubled; ye believe in God, believe also in me. In my Father's house are many mansions: if it were not so, I would have told you. I go to prepare a place for you. And if I go to prepare a place for you, I will come again, and receive you unto myself; that where I am, there ye may be also" (John 14). He closed the book and put it under his pillow. "Now, Doctor I am ready; open the door and tell death to come in!" He closed his eyes for a time, and opened them for eternity.

—*Gospel Herald*

* * *

Preparation Before the Storm

One winter night in a tiny cottage in a Scottish glen a fine old Scotsman lay dying. The wind howled through the trees and blew the peat smoke into the room. The rain lashed the windows. It was a wild night. Only his daughter and himself were in the house. "Father," said the former, "would ye like me to read the Bible to ye?" "Na, na, lassie," said the old saint, his eyes full of the

light streaming from the other land, "I
theekit (thatched) ma hoose before the
storm began."

—From *In Quest of a Kingdom*,
          by Dr. L. D. Weatherhead

* * *

The Time To Decide

A student came to a Scottish professor, asking him how long he might safely put off decision for Christ. "Until the
day before your death," was the strange
reply. "But I cannot tell when I shall
die," said the youth. "True," replied the
professor "then *decide now.*"

—*Quiver*

* * *

His House in Order

I was spending the night in the home
of a fine old physician. We were in
what he called his "den." Handing me
a book, he said, "Look over that while
I finish a few things here at my desk."
Presently he put down the roller top
of his desk and smilingly turned to me
with this cryptic sentence, "My house
is now in order." After a moment he
continued, "I have a heart ailment;
so every night before I retire I close
up all my affairs. If I do not awaken
in the morning everything is in order.
I am at this minute at peace with God,
my fellow man, and myself."

Years later I met the same sentence
again. A girl had slipped and broken
her neck. The doctors were about to
take her to the operating room. Her
father was on the way from a distant
city. She asked me to give him this message in case she didn't come back from
the operating room, "Tell him my house
is in order."

Just recently I met it once again. A
little hunchback radio operator waited
after the evening service to talk to me.
"I have a feeling I won't come back
this time. I was torpedoed last time.
My ship leaves tonight. I wanted to talk
to somebody about the things of the
other world. But please don't get the
wrong impression. My house is in order."

—C. Roy Angell,
in the Teacher, S. B. C.

The Only Answer

Night after night during the bulge
battle of Europe, Robert Gordon Bolinder of Hackensack, N. J., flew his
P-61 black widow against enemy raiders.
In forty-two combat fights he and his
observer shot down four planes and
were credited with an additional "prob-
able" over the heavily-defended Cologne
plain. Back from the nightmare of the
skies, he packed away his medals — the
American silver star, air medal, nine
oak leaf bronze clusters, five battle stars
in the European theater, and a President squadron citation — and entered
a theological seminary as a divinity
student. Late March brought Bolinder
an invitation to Washington, D. C., to
receive from Lord Halifax the British
Government's coveted Distinguished
Flying Cross. "I was ready to die for
Uncle Sam in combat," Bolinder remarked, "and now I'm ready to burn
out for Christ. I'll be discontent until
I've served Christ as vigorously as I've
served the stars and stripes. Christ is
the answer to the atomic age — and the
only answer. If we had an army for
Christ to carry the Gospel of redemption to the four corners of the globe
with as much zeal as the American Army went out to lick the Germans and
the Japs, the U.N.O. could take a holiday."   —*Christian Life and Times*

* * *

Where Will You Be?

A Christian doctor in London wanted
to arouse his page boy as to the salvation of his soul. One night the doctor
explained to him that "the Lord himself shall descend from heaven with a
shout" (1 Thess. 4:16). He ended the
recital by saying, "When the Lord
comes, you may have my home, John."
The boy looked surprised. "And my
car." John was more surprised. "And
my furniture, and my money." The
boy could only gasp, "Thanks." Alone
in bed he began to think. "If the doctor goes to heaven, what will I do with
his house and car and all the rest?
Where will I be?" He woke up the
doctor and explained his problem, and
before morning he was also ready.

—*Philippine Evangelist*

"Let Us Be Ready"
Will He come in the twilight
When the day is done,
And send, as His herald,
The setting sun?

Will He come at dawning,
When the world awakes,
And all the sweetness
Of the morning takes?

Will it be at noontime
When life runs high
With the sun's bright banner
In the midday sky?

Morning, noon, or evening —
When we do not know;
Let us then be ready
When He comes, to go.
—M. Rawley Lemley, in
Herald of Holiness

"Be Ready"
Will it be as day is dawning
And the world with beauty wakes,
When we feel and breathe the sweetness
Of the morning as it breaks?

Will it be, perhaps, at noontime
As we work and life runs high,
While the sun in brightest banner
Shineth forth in midday sky?

Will it be in fading twilight,
When the day its course has run,
That He'll send to us as herald
Heaven's orb the setting sun?

Be it morning, noon or evening
Neither day nor hour we know;
Only let us all be ready,
When He comes, with Him to go.
—Earnest O. Sellers

REPENTANCE

Repentance Necessary

If there is no repentance, there can be no pardon. Some years ago a murderer was sentenced to death. The murderer's brother, to whom the State was deeply indebted for former services, besought the governor of the State for his brother's pardon. The pardon was granted, and the man visited his brother with the pardon in his pocket. "What would you do," he said to him, "if you received a pardon?"

"The first thing I would do," he answered, "is to track down the judge who sentenced me, and murder him; and the next thing I would do is to track down the chief witness, and murder him."

The brother rose, and left the prison with the pardon in his pocket.
—*Dawn*

* * *

There's A Vast Difference . . .

Between being sorry for sin and being sorry you are "caught."

Between confessing your sins and confessing some other fellow's.

Between seeing your own faults and seeing some other person's.

Between conversion of the head, and conversion of the heart.

Between being led by the Holy Spirit and led by your own imagination.

Between being persecuted for "righteousness' sake," and being persecuted for "foolishness' sake."

Between "contending for the faith" and striving for your own opinion.
—*Christian Digest*

* * *

" 'Tis Not Enough"
" 'Tis not enough to say,
'I'm sorry and repent'
And then go on from day to day,
Just as I always went.

"Repentance is to leave
The sins we loved before,
And show that we in earnest grieve
By doing them no more."
—*Selected*

* * *

A Girl's Simple Definition

A Sunday school teacher told me of a girl in her class of fourteen-year-olds. This girl was saved only a few months, but she had already made progress, and

542

was very eager to learn more about God and His Word. Aware that the girl was unusual, and also that she came from a home where she had little encouragement, the teacher wanted to help her all she could. One Sunday the lesson was on repentance, and she said to the young girl, "Margaret, do you think you could explain to the class what repentance means?" Margaret shyly faced the class, and in a clear voice said: "I think it means this: Before I was saved, I pleased myself, and wasn't a bit sorry for my sins. In fact, I didn't think I was a sinner at all, but when I accepted Christ, I wanted to please Him, above anybody, and was real sorry I ever grieved Him. *I love to please Him now.*"

—*Sunday School Times*

* * *

Doubt or Sin?

Dr. John Sutherland Bonnell tells about receiving a telephone call from on officer who had just arrived at the Pennsylvania Station. The officer had only two days' leave, being on his way to the Pacific, but instead of spending that time with his family he had come all the way to New York for an interview.

Dr. Bonnell put aside his other plans and told him to come over. Across the desk the officer told that he felt he could not go into battle in his present state of mind. He had lost his faith. He was upset by his doubts. He had ceased to pray. Dr. Bonnell interrupted and said, "I am not the slightest bit interested in your doubts. I am not going to waste my time or yours going into them. Tell me about your sins."

A full minute of silence passed without a word. The silence was broken shortly after Dr. Bonnell asked the officer if he had pictures in his wallet of his family. The officer did. The pictures were put on the desk where both could see them and the truth in a burst of tears came out. Repentance was what he needed. Repentance is what this neurotic generation needs!

—*The Presbyterian*

Think It Over:

"True repentance is never too late, but late repentance is seldom true!"

—Matthew Henry

* * *

It Broke Him Down

Dr. Evans, when a student at Moody Bible Institute, began talking to a man at the Pacific Garden Mission, about his soul. The man argued: "I do not believe the Bible. I am an atheist." Evans repeated one verse, "Except ye repent, ye shall all likewise perish." The fellow scoffed, "I told you I didn't believe it." Again Evans quoted, "Except ye repent, ye shall all likewise perish." The man exasperatingly uttered, "You disgusting fellow, what is the use of telling me that?" Again Evans repeated the verse. In anger, the man struck Dr. Evans between the eyes with his fist, sending the Bible one way and Evans the other. God gave him grace. He got up and said, "My friend, God loves you, and 'except ye repent, ye shall all likewise perish.'" The next night that man was in the mission before the meeting began. He confessed: "I could not sleep. All over the wall I read, 'Except ye repent, ye shall all likewise perish.' I saw it on my pillow. When I got up I saw 'Except ye repent,' at the breakfast table, and all through the day it was before me. I have come back to settle it."

—*Gospel Herald*

* * *

"Extraordinary"

A gentleman after attending church one day, said: "Here is gratitude for you; here I and my family have shown this man the greatest kindness, and the return he makes when he gets into the pulpit is to tell us that we are great sinners unless we repent. He preaches that our good works go for nothing before God. This sermon will do very well for a penitentiary; but before a genteel and respectable audience, to tell them that they are sinners is the most extraordinary conduct that I ever met with."

—*Sunday School Times*

Art Thou A Seer?

The penitent can see
  With more than mortal sight;
Earth's wisdom gropes and fails
  Like lame men in the night.
To penitents alone
  Are heavenly things made clear:
The best of lenses is
  A penitential tear.

—Max I. Reich

* * *

What Held Him Back

A. Lindsay Glegg in "Life with a Capital 'L'" tells of once when he was seeking to lead a young man to the Lord. He opened the Bible and went from Scripture to Scripture with him, and yet, somehow, something held the young fellow back. It was getting very late, and Mr. Glegg told him to go to his room, read the same passages again, seek light on them, and return and report the next evening. When the young fellow came there was joy in his face as he exclaimed, "It's all right; at two o'clock this morning I surrendered to Christ." "What kept you back?" He replied: "I am a bookseller, and I sell books — good, bad, and indifferent — and I hand out every day to young people a great deal of literature which, if they read, will drag them down into hell. I had a great battle to fight last night. I have my living to make. But I thought over those Scriptures, and I marked them in red ink in my Bible: and it was two o'clock this morning when God changed my mind; and in a flash I saw the horror of what I was doing. God gave me repentance, and Christ came into my heart, and now the peace of God floods my soul."

—*Sunday School Times*

* * *

The Difference Between Penance and Repentance

A clergyman found some children reading the Douay version of the New Testament, and on noticing a passage in the chapter which was translated "do penance" where the English version rendered the same word by "repent," he asked them if they knew the difference between penance and repentance. A short silence followed, and then a little girl asked, "Is it not this . . . : *Judas did penance, and went and hanged himself; Peter repented, and wept bitterly?*"

—*The Teacher*

* * *

Impossible To Be a Christian

In a small country church, a rich man has for years been the leading elder. The congregation were looking for a new minister, and this elder interviewed each man who preached as a candidate. One of these was a truly born-again man, and his sermon was on "Repentance." Said the elder to him, "I dislike very much hearing our people called sinners." "Are you a Christian, sir?" asked the minister. "Of course I'm a Christian," said the man. "Then you were a sinner, and sought Christ for salvation," said the minister. "Oh, no, I never was a sinner," said the elder. "Well, sir," said the minister, "it's impossible for you to be a Christian then, because it was sinners Christ came to save. *He tells us so Himself.*"

—As told to me by a
      member of the church.

* * *

Which Needs Help?

Self-righteous people know nothing of true repentance. A woman told her minister she would leave the church if a young woman who shared her pew wasn't made to occupy another seat. Said the minister: "Madam, that girl was saved from a terrible life of sin. You say she sits and weeps quietly through the church services, and it annoys you, but it's because her heart is so full of love to her Saviour. Can't you try to understand her?" "No, I can't," said the woman. "People who show emotion over their religion annoy me. I have always lived a good life. I don't make any fuss." "Well, madam," said the minister, "have a talk with the girl; I believe she can help you."

—As told by the minister

* * *

His Unseen Audience

When Mr. C. B. Christopher, recently retired from his post as deputational secretary of the London City Mission, was only fifteen, he conducted his first Gospel services in a village chapel in southern England. In preparation, he rehearsed his addresses in a field. His pulpit was a hayrack; his congregation, a dozen cows! He preached from, "Repent ye therefore and be converted." The cows paid no attention, but he was astonished to find, on the other side of the rack, a man on his knees pleading for pardon and peace. "Tell me more about Jesus," he urged, when he and the preacher met face to face. "I told him the story of redemption," says Mr. Christopher, "and a drunkard, fighter, and demon-possessed man entered into peace and blessing." It was his first soul. What a memorable beginning!

—*London City Mission Magazine*

* * *

Repent and Turn

Acts 26:20

Repent and turn! God calls today;
Oh, do not close thine ear, I pray!

Listen! It is the Voice of love —
Grieve not that tender heart above.

Repent and turn! Now is the hour,
The time of God's redeeming power;
Tomorrow it may be too late.
Just now wide open is the gate.

Repent and turn! Christ shed His Blood
To reconcile thy soul to God!
All has been done; for refuge flee,
Apply the Blood, He'll pass o'er thee.

As when the ancient Israelite,
Upon that dark Egyptian night,
Put on his door the mark of blood,
And so escaped the wrath of God.

My friend, I plead, do thou the same —
Put all thy trust in Jesus' Name!
Not all good works, nor prayers of thine,
Can save apart from Blood Divine.

But that will save! Before Him bow
Repent and turn and trust Him now.
For soon will end the day of grace:
God's wrath is coming on apace.

—*Kingdom Tidings*

REST

No Music in a "Rest!"

"There is no music in a rest, but there is the making of music in it." In our whole life-melody the music is broken off here and there by "rests," and we foolishly think we have come to the end of the tune. God sends a time of forced leisure, sickness, disappointed plans, frustrated efforts, and makes a sudden pause in the choral hymn of our lives; and we lament that our voices must be silent, and our part missing in the music which ever goes up to the ear of the Creator. How does the musician read the "rest"? See him beat the time with unvarying count, and catch up the next note true and steady, as if no breaking place had come in between. Not without design does God write the music of our lives. Be it ours to learn the tune, and not be dismayed at the "rests." They are not to be slurred over, not to be omitted, not to destroy the melody, not to change the keynote. If we sadly say to ourselves, "There is no music in a 'rest,'" let us not forget "there is the making of music in it."

—Mrs. Charles Cowman

* * *

Resting

Resting on the faithfulness of Christ
    our Lord:
Resting on the fulness of His own sure
    Word:
Resting on His wisdom, on His love and
    power:
Resting on His covenant, from hour to
    hour.

Resting and believing, let us onward
    press,
Resting on Himself; the Lord our right-
    eousness!

Resting and rejoicing, let the saved ones sing,
Glory, glory, glory unto Christ our King.

—*Selected*

* * *

Modern Life's Three Words

Someone has said that modern life can be spelled in three words, "Hurry, worry, bury." One thinks of a senator who was asked, as he rushed breathlessly along, "What do you think of the world crisis?" He replied, "Don't bother me; I'm in a hurry to make a radio speech. A crisis like this is no time to think!" The Bible has as much to say about resting as about working. Our Lord would have us come apart and rest awhile, for if we don't, we will come apart!

—Vance Havner

* * *

"Rest in the Lord"

Amidst life's storms and cares and woes,
Amidst the lots and shaft of foes,
Amidst the powers which dare oppose,
    Rest in the Lord.

Be it thy joy, O anxious soul,
Till thou shalt reach the Heavenly goal,
Thy burden on thy Lord to roll,
    Rest in the Lord.

Sickness may try, and losses come;
But thou art on the safe way home:
Thy Father will disperse the gloom,
    Rest in the Lord.

In quiet calm — in Christ's own rest —
Is secret strength for all opprest;
All things are working for the best,
    Rest in the Lord.

Rest in His truth, His power, His grace,
Rest in His knowledge of thy case;
Rest in the sunshine of His face,
    Rest in the Lord.

Rest in His love — it cannot chill;
Rest in His sweet and blessed will;
Rest in Himself; be hushed, be still,
    Rest in the Lord.

—A. C. Thiselton, in
Heart and Life

Recipe for Rest

When at night you sleepless lie,
And the weary hours drag by —
Lift your thoughts to God above,
Bending down to you in love.
Feel His presence by your bed —
His soft touch upon your head.
Let your last thought be a prayer,
As you nestle in His care;
Ask Him all your way to keep,
Then — why then — drop off to sleep.

—*Selected*

* * *

Putting Down Our Whole Weight

To celebrate an old man's seventy-fifth birthday, an aviation enthusiast offered to take him for a plane ride over the little West Virginia town where he spent all his life. The old man accepted the offer. Back on the ground, after circling over the town twenty minutes, his friend asked, "Were you scared, Uncle Dudley?" "No-o-o," was the hesitant answer. "But I never did put my full weight down." We smile at the remark of the old man, but there is no doubt of the fact that there are many Christians who are exactly the same way. They have been offered and have received salvation; they enter Christ, but they never put their full weight down on Him. He's carrying them all the time, but they are tense and unrelaxed in their Christian life and do not know the joy that comes from complete rest in Him. — *Eternity*.

* * *

Too Good To Be True

A little fellow, sent to the country one summer by the *Tribune* Fresh Air Fund, for the first time in his life was shown into a bedroom in the farmhouse where he was to be entertained, and told he was to sleep there. It was like another world to the little fellow, who had always slept in the slums, often in some dark hallway or in the street. As he surveyed the soft bed with its white spread and pillows, he felt sure there must be a mistake. However, for a brief moment or two he ventured to throw himself upon the spread and feel for once in his life he had lain upon a

real bed. But fearing that the rightful owner would come in and find him there, he quietly slipped off and curled himself up on the floor to sleep. In the early morning the farmer's wife came in to see that all was right. She gave a great exclamation as she saw him curled up under the bed. It was only by dint of much physical and mental persuasion that she was able to get him under the sheets and make him believe that it was really for him. Alas, how many of God's children are like that poor little lad, sleeping under the bed when they might be resting on the soft bosom of His love and enjoying the "peace that passeth all understanding." — A. B. Simpson, in
—*Alliance Weekly*

* * *

The Sin of Restlessness

There is a restlessness and fretfulness in these days which stand like two granite walls against Godliness. Contentment is almost necessary to Godliness, and Godliness is absolutely necessary to contentment. A very restless man will never be a very Godly man, and a very Godly man will never be a very restless man.

—D. L. Moody

* * *

Come unto me . . .

Heart that is weary because of the way,
Facing the wind and the sting of the
  Spray,
    Come unto Me, and I will refresh
    you.

Heart that has tasted of travail and
  toil,
Burdened for souls whom the foe would
  despoil,
    Come unto Me, and I will refresh
    you.

Heart that is frozen — a handful of
  snow,
Heart that is faded — a sky without
  glow,
    Come unto Me, and I will refresh
    you.

Heart that is weary, O come unto Me,
Fear not, whatever the trouble may be;
    Come unto Me, and I will refresh
    you.

— Amy Carmichael

* * *

"We Shall Rest!"

"When earth's last picture is painted
And the tubes are twisted and dried,
When the oldest color has faded,
And the youngest critic has died,
We shall rest, and faith, we shall need
  it,
Sit down for an eon or two,
'Till the Master of all good workmen
Shall set us to work anew.
Then those that were good shall be
  happy,
They shall sit in a golden chair,
And splash at a ten-league canvas
With brushes of comet's hair.
They shall find real saints to draw from:
Magdalene, Peter, and Paul.
They shall paint for an age at a siting,
And never get tired at all,
And only the Master shall praise them,
And only the Master shall blame;
And no one shall paint for money,
And no one shall paint for fame,
But each for the joy of the working,
And each in his separate star,
Shall paint the thing as he sees it,
For the God of things as they are."

—Kipling

* * *

The Message on a Wrapping Paper

It was getting near the days of festival, and it was time for him to buy some saffron powder to dye his robes for the great occasion, so the Hindu priest paid a visit to a near-by shop, purchased the powder and took it home. When he undid the package, he found strange words on the wrapping paper — "Come unto me . . . and I will give you rest!" Again and again the words rang through his mind. Was not that what he had been looking for for years? Rest! Had he not tortured himself and made endless journeys for that? Who could give such an invitation? One day he passed on the scrap of paper to another man; to a man who became determined that he would find out where the words came from and who said them. He carried the piece of paper around with him and seized every opportunity of asking folk if they knew anything about such precious words, but with no success. One day Krishna came across a group of Christians preaching in the open air and he stopped to listen. He heard for the first time of One who could save from sin and, joy of all joys, he heard the precious words repeated, "Come unto me . . . and I will give you rest." Krishna is now a devoted servant of the Lord, witnessing to everyone, including the priest who first had the piece of wrapping paper.

—Scripture Gift Mission
News Bulletin

"Burden Bearers"

The camel, at the close of day, kneels down upon the sandy plain, to have his burden lifted off — and rest again.

My soul, thou too, should to thy knees, when day-light draweth to a close, and have thy Lord lift off thy load, and grant repose.

Else how cans't thou tomorrow meet, with all tomorrow's work to do, if thou thy burden all the night, dost carry through?

The camel kneels at break of day, to have his lord replace his load, then rises up anew to take the desert road.

So thou shouldst kneel at morning's dawn, to have Him give thy daily care, assured that He no load too great will make thee bear.

—Selected

RESTITUTION

The Trespassing Hen

A man in New Jersey told me the following circumstances concerning himself and one of his neighbors.

"I once owned a large flock of hens. I generally kept them shut up. But one spring, I decided to let them run in my yard, after I had clipped their wings so that they could not fly. One day, when I came home to dinner, I learned that one of my neighbors had been there, full of wrath, to let me know that my hens had been in the garden, and that he had killed several of them, and thrown them over into my yard.

"I was greatly enraged because he had killed my beautiful hens that I valued so much. I determined at once to be revenged, to sue him, or in some way to get redress. I sat down and ate my dinner as calmly as I could. By the time I had finished my meal, I became more cool, and thought that perhaps it was not best to fight with my neighbor about hens, and thereby make him my bitter enemy. I concluded to try another way, being sure that it would be better.

"After dinner, I went to my neighbor's. He was in his garden. I found him in pursuit of one of my hens with a club, trying to kill it. I accosted him. He turned upon me, his face inflamed with wrath, and broke out in a great fury, 'You have abused me. I will kill all of your hens, if I can get them. I never was so abused. My garden is ruined.'

" 'I am sorry for it,' said I; 'I did not wish to injure you, and now see that I have made a great mistake in letting out my hens. I ask your forgiveness, and am willing to pay you six times the damage.'

"The man seemed confounded. He did not know what to make of it. He looked up at the sky, then down at the earth, then at his neighbor, then at the poor hen he had been pursuing, and said nothing. 'Tell me now,' said I, 'what is the damage, and I will pay you six-fold; and my hens shall trouble you no more. I will leave it entirely to you to say what I shall do. I cannot afford to lose the love and goodwill of my neighbors, and quarrel with them, for hens or anything else.'

" 'I am a great fool!' said my neighbor. 'The damage is not worth talking about; and I have more need to compensate you than you me, and to ask your forgiveness than you mine.' "

—Gospel Herald

Confess — Restore

A bright young girl, at the end of one of my addresses, was waiting, and I said to her: "Come, my girl, I am quite sure that you have got something to see me about." "O," she said, "I have, sir. I remember that three or four years ago, when I was a girl at school, one of my companions asked me to go out and get some candy for her. I got it, but I kept back half the money for myself. That sin has been working in my mind. It seems as if God keeps saying, 'Confess, confess, restore'; but, sir, I have been fighting it for the last month or two. It looks so stupid to do a little thing like that."

She did confess the sin, and the confession was genuine, for it was followed by restitution. The joy-bells of heaven became atingle in her soul again!

—From *The Christ-Life and the Self-Life*, by F. B. Meyer

* * *

"Do You Know that Gold Watch?"

When I was in South Africa a fine, handsome Dutchman, over six feet high, came into my service and God laid His hand on him and convicted him of sin, and the next morning he went to the beautiful home of another Dutchman and said to him: "Do you know that gold watch?" "Why, yes," said the other, "those are my initials; that is my watch. I lost it eight years ago. How did you get it, and how long have you had it?" "I stole it," was the reply. "But you were my friend?" "I stole it, and have worn it." "What made you bring it back now?" "I was converted last night," said the other, "and I have brought it back first thing this morning. If you had been up I would have brought it last night!"

—Gipsy Smith

* * *

A Thief Who Found Christ

A man carrying a big black bag said to Gipsy Smith at Louisville, Kentucky: "I heard you preach on 'stripe washing' and want to get right with God. You see that bag? It is full of money that I stole forty years ago. Every penny I stole is there — a small fortune — and forty years' interest. I am going, though it means traveling many miles, to restore it to its owner." Then he fell on his knees and almost as soon as they touched the floor he shouted, "Glory to God, I have found Him." Though he had not yet handed over the bag, in his heart the thing was done. Later, after restitution had been made, he said, "I am the happiest man in all America."

—From *The Beauty of Jesus*, by Gipsy Smith

* * *

A Religion Worth Having

Dr. F. E. Marsh used to tell that on one occasion he was preaching on the importance of confession of sin and, wherever possible, of restitution for wrong done to others. Afterward a young man came up to him and said: "Pastor, you have put me in a sad fix. I have wronged another and am ashamed to confess it or try to put it right. I am a boatbuilder, and the man I work for is an unbeliever. I have talked to him often about his need of Christ and have urged him to come and hear you preach, but he scoffs and ridicules it all. In my work, copper nails are used because they do not rust in the water, but they are quite expensive, so I had been carrying home quantities of them to use on a boat I am building in my back yard." The pastor's sermon had brought him face to face with the fact that he was just a common thief. "But," he said, "I cannot go to my boss and tell him what I have done, or offer to pay for those I have used. If I do he will think I am just a hypocrite, and yet those copper nails are digging into my conscience, and I know I shall never have peace until I put this matter right."

One night he came again to Dr. Marsh and exclaimed, "Pastor, I've settled for the copper nails, and my conscience is relieved at last." "What happened when you confessed?" asked the pastor. "Oh, he looked queerly at me, and then said, 'George, I always did think you were just a hypocrite, but now I begin to feel there's something in this Christianity after all. Any religion that makes a

549

dishonest workman confess that he has been stealing copper nails, and offer to settle for them, must be worth having."

—*Emergency Post*

* * *

Oddities in the News

Tax collector gets assist from evangelist: Uncle Sam is $1,265 richer because four people got under conviction after hearing Evangelist Billy Graham. Some time ago he got five $100 bills with the request that they be forwarded to the Internal Revenue Collector. In more recent days three others sent $765 tagged as "restitution for shortages" in past income tax reports. "I have been a Christian, but I've backslidden," said a Florida resident, who enclosed $500. "Partly through lack of knowledge and also from wrong advice from an accountant I did not pay certain taxes in full," the letter went on. "But God hasn't let me forget it. So I want to get the money I think I owe into the treasury. . . . I hesitate to send cash to the internal revenue department lest it be a temptation to anyone into whose hands it might fall." . . . None of the letters was signed.

—*Alliance Weekly*

* * *

Gets Religion; Pays 35 Year Old Water Bill

Mrs. A. Lins got around to paying her water bill at last. It was nearly 35 years overdue.

Joseph E. Higgins, city superintendent of water, disclosed that he received a letter from Mrs. Lins, now of Great Falls, Mont. Inclosed was a $2.75 money order and a water bill for that amount covering premises at 4752 N. Hermitage av. from May 1, to Nov. 1, 1917. The property now is occupied by a service station. Her letter read in part: "After 35 years I am paying this past due water bill. I have been converted to the Lord Jesus Christ and have accepted him as my personal Savior and Redeemer, so I wish to right all wrongs as far as possible."

—*Chicago Daily Tribune*

When He Forgot to Shave

Some years ago there came to Chicago a man who sold goods for a New York concern. He had been stealing money from his company until the amount totaled a few thousand dollars. The man had worked out a plan by which he thought to stifle his conscience. He would work hard all day and go out to places of amusement at night, and remain to a late hour.

One day in a Chicago hotel, he was stropping an old-fashioned razor, and, looking for a piece of paper to wipe the blade on, he tore out a page from a Gideon Bible. Starting to wipe the blade, his eye caught these words, "The wages of sin is death." Conviction struck his heart, and smoothing out the page, he read, "The wages of sin is death; but the gift of God is eternal life through Jesus Christ our Lord."

The startled salesman read the Bible for two hours, and then on his knees beside the bed with the Bible open in front of him, he acknowledged himself to be a sinner and in need of a Saviour. He took Christ as his Saviour, and realizing that a new life had been bestowed upon him, he wired the firm in New York that he was returning. He made a confession of the stolen money. He was not prosecuted and not even discharged, but allowed to put back something each month out of his salary.

—*Moody Monthly*

* * *

Stopping in the Middle

Somewhere I read of a little lad, who was kneeling at his grandmother's knee in prayer. "If I should die before I wake," said Donnie — "I pray," — prompted the gentle voice. "Go on, Donnie." "Wait a minute," interposed the small boy, scrambling to his feet and hurrying down stairs. In a few moments he was back again, and, dropping down in his place, took up his petition where he had left it. But when the little white-gowned form was safely tucked in bed, the grandmother questioned with loving rebuke the interruption. "But I did not think what I was saying, Grandmother; that's why I had to stop. You see, I'd set up Ted's menagerie and stood all his wooden soldiers on their heads, just to see how he would tear around in the morning. But, if I should die before I wake, why — I didn't want him to find them that way, so I had to go down and fix them up. There are lots of things that seem funny if you are going to keep on living, but you don't want them that way if you should die before you wake." "That was right dear, it was right," commended the grandmother's voice, with a tender quiver. "I imagine there are a good many prayers that would not be hurt by stopping in the middle of them to undo a wrong."

—Prairie Overcomer

* * *

Sermon Prompts Payments

"I vividly recall having taken goods from your store. However, I shall experience supreme satisfaction in seeing that you are fully reimbursed. I believe that God forgives me, and I now earnestly beg your forgiveness."

This is part of notes being received by 50 startled Louisville store owners from a penitent thief who heard a minister's sermon on repentance. He has scraped until he got $1,200 to cover his conscience debts.

The money represents the value of goods stolen from shops over a period of years. The Rev. Harold Roy Veach has agreed to deliver the payments, ranging from $1 up to $400.   *—Gospel Herald*

* * *

Missing Chocolate!

During the early years of my mother's married life she had a young girl, Ida, helping with the housework and baby sitting. One day Mother left the girl with my four-year-old brother for the afternoon. When Mother returned she noticed that a box of chocolates on the library table had disappeared — only an empty box remained.

She questioned Ida, who said that my brother had eaten them all while she was upstairs cleaning.

Mother accepted this explanation, gave small Bill a little lecture, and dismissed the matter from her mind.

Eighteen years later, and 1500 miles away, we were surprised (there were now three children) to receive in the mail a box of candy from a Mrs. William Brown. Mother puzzled over it until the next day when a letter came, explaining that Mrs. Brown was once Ida, the hired girl of long ago. She went on to say she had lied that day about the candy as she had eaten the chocolates herself. She had recently accepted Christ as Saviour, joined a church, and wanted to make restitution and seek forgiveness, where possible, for wrongs of her old life. Eighteen years had passed but she still remembered the box of chocolates.   *—Power*

* * *

His New Name

My grandfather, who was converted in the mighty revival that swept Northern Ireland in 1859, told me many wonderful stories of that time. One story was of a man noted for cheating at the markets. One day he took a load of goods to the market and sold it to a recently converted man, who witnessed to him of Christ. He scoffed, saying, "Give me my money, and never mind the religion." On the way home great conviction from the Spirit of God came upon him, and he got down from his cart to the ditch on the roadside. As he called on God to have mercy on him, the man to whom he sold the produce came along. He, too, got down and knelt with the man on the roadside. Soon others joined them. The man was saved, and, jumping up, he said: "I've cheated nearly every one of you here today at some time or other, and by God's grace I'll make it right with each of you just as soon as I can. I know they called me the 'cheater' for a nickname, but I've got a new name now, and by His grace I'll adorn it."   *—Personal*

* * *

Finding the Foundlings!

Under the conviction of sin, a wealthy Chicago bachelor sent for a pastor. Said he, "I heard a man preach yesterday, and he told me I must find Christ where I lost Him, and I want to find Him." His tears were flowing like rain.

The pastor said, "That should be easy."

He replied, "It won't be easy for me. I have done things that the people of this city know nothing about. But God knows, and I know. Listen! There is a sweet-faced, beautiful girl lying yonder in a dishonoured grave, and there are two little children, a boy and a girl, who are in a home for foundlings because I hadn't manhood enough to own them and give them my name. And," said he, "you know, doctor, it strikes me, if I am to find Christ I will have to find those children and bring them here and let the people know they are mine."

The minister said, "Yes, it means that."

The rich man replied, "I can do nothing for her now, but I am going to send a message to that distant state for the little ones." He discovered that the little girl had joined her mother, and the little boy was with a farmer. He knew these people were not his parents, and the poor little fellow longed for love.

But it never came to him. They brought him to the big city, and the rich man sat down in a chair, and took the little boy on his knee and said:

"My boy, would you like to see your father?"

The little fellow said, "I don't know, sir."

"Do you think you could love him, even though he did you and your mother a great wrong?"

And the poor little fellow said, "I don't know, sir."

"Well," he said, "look about you. Do you think you could be happy if you lived here with me?"

He said, "I don't know, sir."

Somewhere there the father's heart had a resurrection, and he cried: "Put your arms round my neck, hold me tight, and call me father, though I don't deserve the name!

Turning to the preacher, he said: "I have found Christ in finding my child!"

—Gipsy Smith

RESURRECTION
(See also: Death)

"Do You Plant Corn?"

A missionary lady in Africa was talking to some black men and women. "Jesus died on the Cross for us all," she told them. "Then His body was put in a grave and on the third day He arose from the grave. We, too, shall arise from our graves after our bodies have rested for a time in the ground."

"How can that happen?" asked one old black man. "I do not believe that. What is put in the ground cannot come up."

"Listen to me," said the missionary lady. "Do you plant corn?"

"Yes, I do," he answered.

"Well, what happens when you put the grain of corn in the ground?"

"The grain decays and the corn comes up out of the ground," he replied.

"Very well," said the missionary lady. "The grain decays but the life in the corn doesn't die. It sends up a plant that comes through the soil and grows

several feet above the ground.

"It will be the same with us. When we are dead our bodies will be put into the ground. They will lie there until Jesus comes again. Then He will wake us and we shall arise from our graves. We believe that His Word is true."

"I cannot understand it," said the old black man, "but I believe it now, too, for Jesus has said it."   —*Selected*

* * *

"I Feel It in the Air!"

I know it's Easter time again,
  I feel it in the air.
The breath of spring with woodsy tang,
  And new life everywhere.
And spring glides on with magic touch
  O'er mountain side and glen;
And wakens all the sleeping plants
  For Easter time again.

The brooklets leap from rock to rock,
  As if in joyful play;

The flowers peep from darkened tombs
  To welcome Easter Day.
The birds are swinging on the boughs,
  And trill in ecstasy;
They seem to show the world's great joy
  Of Easter mystery.

Why should we dread the thing called
  death?
It's just an open door,
Where all within is love and peace
  And joy forever more.
"Because I live, you too shall live,"
  We hear the Saviour say.
Let's consecrate our lives anew,
  On this glad Easter Day.

          —Edna Reed

* * *

The Power of Resurrection

I remember that after I had worked in university centers in Portugal I went from there to Norway, and I was a little impressed by the difference among the people. I wondered how one could explain it. Then I remembered that every representation I had seen in Portugal of Jesus Christ was that of an infant in arms, or else someone crucified. We glory in the fact that He was an infant in arms, for everything depends on the incarnation; we glory in the fact that He died on the cross. But the first painting I saw on reaching Norway was that of the empty tomb, the three women and the angel. "He is not here; He is risen." The thought came to me, "May that not explain possibly some of the difference in the types of Christianity in Portugal and in Norway?" *He is risen, and the power is available for you and me,* so that we too can be seated in heavenly places with Jesus Christ, and live a life of victory.

          —R. P. Wilder

* * *

Better Trust in the Living One!

Two little colored boys were slaves to an Arab master. He taught them to believe in Mohammed, whose body, they were informed, was preserved in a coffin in the city of Medina in Arabia. One day these little lads heard a missionary tell about the death, burial, and resurrection of Christ. That night in the darkness of their little hut, they talked the matter over. "What think you?" asked one of them. "Our master tells us that Mohammed is dead, and that his dead body is kept in a coffin; but the white man tells us that Jesus, the Son of God, who came to die for us, rose again and is alive." "I think," replied the other, "that I would rather believe in the Living One." So they did. They were taken to the mission station and taught more about the truth of God as it is revealed in Jesus Christ.

          —*Good News*

* * *

"Please Do Not Give A Moment's Grief to Me!"

My doctor at last has given what has been his real diagnosis of my illness for weeks — an inoperable case of cancer of the pancreas.

Now if he had been a Christian he wouldn't have been so dilatory and shaken, for he would have known, as you and I do, that life or death is equally welcome when we live in the will and presence of the Lord.

If the Lord has chosen me to go to Him soon, I go gladly. On the other hand, I remember that Christ is still the Great Physician. And so in simple faith and trust I say to Him, "Lord, if thou wilt, thou canst make me whole." I await His answer utterly at peace.

Please do not give a moment's grief to me. Think of me only happily, gaily, as I do of you. My interest is as keen as ever in everything over there — Memorial Student center and buildings that are to follow, commencement affairs with all the joy and lightheartedness.

I do not say a cold goodbye, but rather a warm "auf Wiedersehen," till I see you again — by God's power and grace on campus this fall or later in the Blessed Land, where I may be allowed to draw aside a curtain when you enter.

With a heart full of love for every individual of you,

          —Effie Jane Wheeler

(Dr. Effie Jane Wheeler was a member of Wheaton College Faculty for sixteen years. The foregoing, she wrote to Faculty and student body before she entered into the presence of her Lord!)

Resurrection

If the Father deigns to touch with divine power the cold and pulseless heart of the buried acorn and to make it burst from its prison walls, will He leave neglected in the earth the . . . . man made in the image of his Creator? If matter, mute and inanimate, though changed by the forces of nature into a multitude of forms can never die, will the spirit of man suffer annihilation when it has paid a brief visit like a royal guest to this tenement of clay? No, I am as sure that there is another life as I am that I live today!"

—William Jennings Bryan

* * *

Immortality

In the Metropolitan Museum of New York is a monument to Edgar Allen Poe and on it are inscribed these words, "He was great in genius; unhappy in life; wretched in death; but in fame he is immortal."

That is one kind of immortality. But there is a better one; an immortality not for genius, nor of power, nor of earthly greatness of any kind, but an immortality "brought to light," as Paul says, "through the gospel," that comes through devotion to the will of God and service in the name of Christ, that knows nothing of unhappiness in life or wretchedness in death, but *looks out through the stress and the strife of the life that now is, through the doorway of death into the light of heaven, where everlasting woe gives place to a never-ending life of glory and riches and honor before the throne of the living God and our Christ.*

—From *The Man Who Said He Would* by William Edward Biederwolf,

* * *

Daffodils

Daffodils in early spring
Seem to cheer up everything.
Little sermons do they preach,
Valued lessons, too, they teach.

Growing up from murky mire,
Higher thoughts they would inspire.
Though they're planted in the ground
Far above it they are found.

There's a Flower pure and true
Blooming e'er before our view.
From the darkness of the tomb,
Where He lay in deepest gloom,
Jesus rose, His life to pour
Sweetest fragrance evermore.

—*Selected*

* * *

"We Are Seven!"

"Sisters and brothers, little maid,
  How many may you be?"
'How many? Seven in all,' she said,
  And, wondering, looked at me.

"And where are they? I pray you tell?"
  She answered, 'Seven are we;
And two of us at Conway dwell,
  And two are gone to sea.'

" 'Two of us in the churchyard lie,
  My sister and my brother;
And, in the churchyard cottage, I
  Dwell near them with my Mother.'

"How many are you, then" said I
  "If they two are in heaven?"
The little maiden did reply,
  'O master, we are seven!'

"But they are dead; those two are dead;
  Their spirits are in heaven!"
'Twas throwing words away; for still
  The little maid would have her will,
  And say, 'Nay, we are seven!' "

—Wordsworth

* * *

"Vivit! Vivit!"

Luther was once found at a moment of peril and fear, when he had need to grasp unseen strength, sitting in an abstracted mood tracing on the table with his finger the words, *"Vivit! vivit!"* ("He lives! He lives!") It is our hope for ourselves, and for His truth and for mankind. Men come and go; leaders, teachers, thinkers speak and work for a season, and then fall silent and impotent. He abides. They die, but He lives. They are lights kindled, and therefore, sooner or later quenched; but He is the true light from which they draw all their brightness, and He shines for ever more.

—Alexander Maclaren

A Daring Challenge

A certain Hanoverian countess, who lived about a hundred years ago, was a noted unbeliever, and was especially opposed to the doctrine of the resurrection, as indeed every unbeliever might well be, especially if his opposition could alter it.

This lady died when about thirty years of age. Before her death she gave orders that her grave should be covered with a slab of granite; that around it should be placed square blocks of stone, and that the corners should be fastened to each other and to the granite slab by heavy iron clamps.

Upon the covering this inscription was placed:

THIS BURIAL PLACE PURCHASED TO ALL ETERNITY MUST NEVER BE OPENED

All that human power could do to prevent any change in that grave was done. But a little birch tree seed sprouted, and the root found its way between the side stone and the upper slab and grew there. Slowly but steadily it forced its way until the iron clamps were torn asunder, the granite lid was raised, and it is now resting upon the trunk of the birch tree, which is large and flourishing. — *Selected.*

* * *

The Arch of Triumph

The Arc de Triomphe in Paris is a center of radiating life. It is the most magnificent triumphal arch in all the world. From it a dozen of the stateliest and most lovely avenues of the city stretch forth into the far distances. All life floods it; and all life flows out from it. So the world's life has its central Arch of Triumph in Christ's Cross and resurrection. Two mighty bulwarks of stone rise to their tremendous yet graceful height to form the single Arc de Triomphe — two yet one. Neither is complete without the other. "Christ died — and rose again," but the resurrection power gives meaning and power to the cross. — *King's Business.*

* * *

Dr. Hinson's Valedictory

The following is a quotation from the words of Dr. W. B. Hinson, speaking from the pulpit a year after the commencement of the illness from which he ultimately died: "I remember a year ago when a man in this city said, 'You have got to go to your death.' I walked out to where I live, five miles out of this city, and I looked across at that mountain that I love, and I looked at the river in which I rejoice, and I looked at the stately trees that are always God's own poetry to my soul. Then in the evening I looked up into the great sky where God was lighting his lamps, and I said: 'I may not see you many more times, but, Mountain, I shall be alive when you are gone; and, River, I shall be alive when you cease running toward the sea; and, Stars, I shall be alive when you have fallen from your sockets in the great down-pulling of the material universe!'" This is the confidence of one who knew the Saviour. Is it yours?

—*Advent Herald*

* * *

"When the Stars Have Passed!"

The stars shine over the earth,
The stars shine over the sea;
The stars look up to the mighty God,
The stars look down on me.
The stars shall live for a million years,
A million years and a day;
But God and I will live and love
When the stars have passed away.

—Earl G. Hamlett

* * *

"Behold, A Mystery Indeed!"

Behold, a mystery indeed!
The tinted flower that once was seed;
The power of faith, transcending creed;
God! Who appears in direst need.
Once ugly bulb, now lily bloom,
Diffusing fragrance through the room;
A cruel cross, Golgotha's gloom;
A Risen Christ, an empty tomb.

—*Selected*

* * *

Thomas Jefferson's Dead Bible

Congress once issued a special edition of Thomas Jefferson's Bible. It was simply a copy of our Bible with all references to the supernatural eliminated. Jefferson, in making his selections from the Bible, confined himself solely to the moral teachings of Jesus. The closing words of Jefferson's Bible are: "There laid they Jesus, and rolled a great stone to the mouth of the sepulchre and departed." If our Bible ended like that, it would mean the impossibility of other resurrections. But thank God our Bible does not end like that. And the resurrection of Jesus Christ from the dead is our "living hope."

—*Moody Monthly*

* * *

He Will Not Leave Us

In a book by Archibald Rutledge, called, "Children of Swamp and Wood," a nature story, we find this passage referring to our migration —

"And when the time comes for our migration hence to a land unknown, through a misty darkness, He will not desert us. In the rainy night, in that cavernous and monstrous dark, the frailest abide secure. In that flight amid other spheres than ours I believe we shall know what it means to be sustained by Everlasting Arms."

The migration of the birds ends in finding their desired haven. Shall we then doubt the end of our migration when He goes with us all the way? "I will never leave thee nor forsake thee."

—Julia Graydon

* * *

Looking Ahead

It seems but the other day, though full seventy years have passed since then, that I heard two boys talking under my little east window that looked out upon the sea. It was springtime, and good old black Enoch was planting flowers. "I don't like to see seeds bein' planted," said the older boy; "makes me think o' diggin' graves an' buryin' folks." "It don't make me feel that way a bit," said the younger. "I just look ahead and see 'em wake right up into posies."

—*Sunday School Times*

* * *

Who'll See Him First?

Some years ago a minister of my acquaintance said to me: "I have always known and preached the necessity for the new birth, and the Resurrection, but it's only of late years I have come to know of the personal return of the Lord Jesus. It came to me with a great light, while sitting beside an aged member of my congregation — a poor man, yet rich toward God. Just before he died, he sat up in bed and said: 'Pastor, He has been a great Saviour and Lord. I always longed to live to see Him come in person, but now I'm going; but I'll see Him first anyway, for the dead in Christ shall rise first.' "

—*As told to me*

* * *

The Garden Tomb

When the Garden Tomb was discovered in 1885, the godly General Gordon was convinced that this was the place where the body of Jesus had lain. There is a traditional tomb inside the wall of modern Jerusalem, but no certainty attaches to the site. The Garden Tomb, hidden for centuries, was covered with rubbish twenty feet high. When they first cleared the spot, with great caution they gathered all the dust and debris within the tomb and carefully shipped it to the Scientific Association of Great Britain. Every part of it was analyzed, but there was no trace of human remains. If this is the real tomb of Christ, then Jesus was the first to be laid there and he was also the last.

—*Alliance Weekly*

* * *

"Winter Just A Memory!"

Ever see a farm scene
　At joyous Easter time?
With Winter just a memory,
　The whole world seems in rhyme.

The crocus buds a-bulging,
　Just ache to be in bloom,
And morning-glories crowd the fence
　In search of growing-room.

The pigs and piglets softly drowse,
　The cows seem more content,
While calves and lambs all sniff to catch
　The breeze's gentle scent.

"It's Spring," the zephyrs whisper,
The trees repeat it through,
And every blade of grass chimes in . . .
"Happy Easter . . . to You!"
—*Selected*

* * *

The Mistaken Love Letter

I saw a little child's grave without a headstone. A fresh bunch of flowers had been laid there and a little piece of paper held down by a twig. Struck by the unusualness of this, I opened it, and read: "May 30, 1887. Papa has been here." It seemed both sweet and sad. The father's heart had not yet learned to think about the departed as having passed to the Glory overhead. He thought of his child as lonely and shut away, and it might be a comfort to know that "Papa" had been there. It was a little love letter, and gave a beautiful glimpse into a father's heart. It is to be hoped that he may learn to think so much differently about his child — even as I think of those whose cast-off garments of earth are buried near by.
—Frances E. Willard,
in a letter to children

* * *

Where Was the Key?

A little girl died at a hotel where she was stopping with her father. The mother was dead. Just two followed the body to the cemetery, the father and a minister. The man's grief was great. At the grave he took from his pocket a key, unlocked the casket and looked on the face of his child once more, then silently closed the casket, and handed the key to the keeper of the cemetery. On the way back to the city the minister quoted to the broken-hearted man Revelation 1:18, explaining how the Lord Jesus though dead was now alive. "But what is that about the keys?" asked the man. "It means this," said the minister. "You think the key to your little girl's casket is in the hands of the keeper of the cemetery. Let me tell you, the key to your little girl's grave hangs at the girdle of the Son of God, and he will come some morning and use it." Then the light broke through the man's tears, and he saw the glory of the Resurrection. —*Record of Christian Work*

The Lesson of the Lily

Rightly the lily is the flower of Easter. It lies buried in the ooze of pond or stream. There is nothing in the grave of the dead lily that appeals to nostril or eye. But silently the forces of life are working in the dark and the damp to prepare a glorious resurrection. A shaft of green shoots upward toward the sun. This is followed by a cluster of tiny buds. One day the sun smiles with special warmth upon the dank, black ooze, and there leaps into the light a creature of light and beauty: it is the lily, an angel of the earth, whose look is light.
—*Fuel for the Fire*

* * *

An Easter Message

A few years ago a submarine sank off Provincetown. As soon as possible divers descended. They walked about the disabled ship endeavoring to find some signs of life within. At last they heard a gentle tapping. Listening intently they recognized the dots and dashes of the Morse code. These were the words spelled out, "Is there hope?"

"IS THERE HOPE?" This is the constant cry of humanity, and Easter is the answer to that cry.
—*Selected*

* * *

The Difference

A Japanese Baron, through an interpreter, was addressing Bethany Sunday School in Philadelphia. The superintendent, Mr. John Wanamaker, listened in amazement as his distinguished guest was explaining that the teachings of Confucius and Jesus were the same, and there was no need of his changing his faith. The Baron was visiting America to study educational methods, and was deeply interested in the work of Sunday Schools.

After this defense of heathenism before his school, Mr. Wanamaker, distinguished veteran Sunday School leader and great merchant, rose up and spoke what came out of his heart on the spur of the moment. Acknowledging the high moral standards of Confucius, he continued, "There is this vital difference between Confucius and our Lord Jesus Christ. Confucius is dead and buried, and he will remain in his grave till Jesus Christ tells him to arise. But our Christ's grave is empty. He is living. He is here in this room to-day." And taking a little Testament from his pocket, Mr. Wanamaker added with deep emotion, "We have His Words; they are living Words, and we can read them in this Book."

—*Gospel Herald*

* * *

Overwhelming Evidence!

Arnold of Rugby declared: "I have been used for many years to study the histories of other times, and to examine and weigh the evidence of those who have written about them, and I know of no one fact in the history of mankind which is proved by better and fuller evidence of every sort, to the understanding of a fair enquirer, than the great sign which God hath given us that Christ died and rose again from the dead."

—Joseph C. Macaulay, D. D.
in *Moody Monthly*

* * *

In One Triumphant Move

There is a wonderful picture called "The Game of Death," in which a young man is represented as playing chess with the Devil. The Devil, apparently, by the position of the chessmen, has won the game. A noted chess player went to see the picture, and after looking at it, he said, "I can save that fellow!" Then he explained how the chessmen should be moved to win the game. That is what Jesus Christ has done for us. He has, in one move, eternally checkmated the Devil, and snatched the prey from the mighty. By His victory over death Jesus has given us victory over the grave.

—*Sunday School Chronicle*

* * *

From Despair to Joy

It is said that when Harry Lauder received a telegram that his son had been killed on the battlefield he was hurled into a state of despondency that threatened his reason. He raved against a cruel fate that had torn his son from him. Then one day he learned that the boy had become a Christian and was waiting for him on the other side of death. The realization that the life in Christ would blossom anew in the life beyond, because Christ had risen from the dead, lifted him out of black despair. He found a new incentive to live. He exclaimed, "I would that I could picture to you the joy that lies in the assurance of seeing my boy again."

If Easter be not true,
Then faith must mount on broken wing;
Then hope no more immortal spring;
Then hope must lose her mighty urge;
Life prove a phantom, death a dirge —
If Easter be not true.

—Henry H. Barstow, in
Open Windows

* * *

What Broke the Opposition

Our coming to the northern Indians often met with chilly opposition. "We don't want you," they would say. "You white people brought us measles, scarlet fever, smallpox, firewater, and many have died." Trying to address one sullenly indifferent encampment, I breathed prayer for guidance, and after getting my message, I shouted: "Indians, listen to me! I know where all your children are who are not among the living. Many hearts are sad and lonely, but I am so glad that the Great Spirit gives the authority to tell you that you may all meet your children again, and be happy with them forever." At these words a stalwart Indian at the other end of the tent sprang up, threw back his blanket, and rushed toward me, exclaiming: "I had eight children, and they are all dead! My heart is empty, and my wigwam is lonely. They no longer play on the beach, and the canoes are rotting on the sand. I long to see my children again and clasp them in my arms. Tell me, missionary, where they are, and how I can hope to see them. I will do anything you tell me." I turned to the Book, to the Saviour's comforting words, "For of such is the kingdom of heaven." I told them how Jesus had satisfied the claims of justice, and all the children were saved. We may be uncertain about men and women who have become careless, but the children of the white man, red man, and black man are all safe in the paradise of God. Every bit of opposition had vanished, and day after day I opened to them the Scriptures. On that spot, as a result, is a splendid church, with the majority of the people converted.

—From *Experiences Among the Indians,* by Egerton R. Young

* * *

Even Ingersoll Had Hope!

The infidel, Robert Ingersoll, when standing at the grave of his brother, said, "Life is a narrow vale between the cold and barren peaks of two eternities. We strive in vain to look beyond the height. We cry aloud, and the only answer is the echo of our wailing cry. From the voiceless lips of the unreplying dead there comes no word. But in the night of death hope sees a star and listening love can hear the rustle of a wing!"

—W. B. K.

* * *

Christ Sees Us As We Are Going to Be

The story is told of an artist who had in his mind the conception of a great picture. He stretched his vast canvas, and prepared the paint. He painted with great sweeps of his brush as he put in the background. Day after day, he would walk back and forth, putting a daub of gray here, a daub of blue there, and some black there. One day, he came down from the scaffolding to look at what he had done. He kept moving back, back, back. A visitor had come in unnoticed. As the artist moved backward, he bumped right into the stranger. Said the artist, "I didn't know you were here. When did you come in? What do you think of the picture? It is going to be the masterpiece of my life. Isn't it magnificent?" The other said, "I don't see anything there but great daubs of paint!" "Oh," said the artist, "I forgot. You can see only what is there, while I see the picture as it is going to be!"

The blessed Lord Jesus sees us as we are going to be when we awaken with His likeness. Then we shall be like Him, for we shall see Him as He is!

—From *The Epistles of John,* by Dr. Harry A. Ironside

* * *

The Difference

As a missionary finished preaching in a market place in one of the villages of northern India, a Mohammedan stepped up to him and said: "You must admit that we have one thing you have not, and it is better than anything you have."

"And what is it you have?"

"When we go to Mecca," said the Mohammedan, "we at least find a coffin. But when you Christians go to Jerusalem, your Mecca, you find nothing but an empty grave."

Smilingly, the missionary explained, "That is just the difference. Mohammed is dead and in his coffin. And all false systems of religion and philosophy are in their coffins. But Christ is risen, and all power in Heaven and on earth is given to Him. He is alive forevermore!"

—*Sunday School Times*

* * *

"Don't You Believe It!"

It was this blessed hope of unending bliss that rendered D. L. Moody triumphant in life and all-glorious in death. Before his home-going, he said, "Some day you will read in the papers that D. L. Moody is dead. Don't you believe it! At that moment I shall be more alive than I am now; I shall have gone up higher, that is all! I was born of the flesh in 1837; I was born of the Spirit in 1856. That which is born of the flesh may die, but that which is born of the Spirit will live forever!"

—From *Because He Lives,* by W.B.K.

* * *

"Christ in You"

Many years ago we were traveling through a Southern State. It was the month of February and the time of the blossoming glory of the peach tree. By and by our train pulled up by a great peach orchard. In it were a hundred thousand trees. Each individual tree was robed in splendor of pink and white bloom. As the train slowly wheeled past the great orchard the south wind which blew into the car window was heavily laden with the perfume of that vast orchard of blooms. Suppose you had stood on the same spot in the dead of winter. Those peach trees were all in the same place, but how different. There was not a sign of life, or bloom, or beauty. There they were stretching their dead, bare leafless branches toward the winter sky as though in mute appeal for the life, beauty and blossoms to come of which there was yet no sign. Suppose you were to whisper to them, "Peach trees, as you stand here, so dead and dry and blossomless, what is your hope that you will some day be clothed in the splendor and glory of the spring blossomtime?"

If the peach trees could answer you they would call back with one voice, "The peach life that is in us is our hope and glory" — just as Paul tells the Colossians that it is "Christ in you, the hope of glory" (Col. 1:27).

—James McConkey

* * *

The Resurrection Symbolized

There is a story told of a workman helper of the great chemist, Faraday. One day he knocked into a jar of acid a little silver cup. It disappeared, being eaten by the acid. The great chemist came in and put some chemical into the jar, and in a moment every particle of silver was precipitated to the bottom. He sifted it out a shapeless mass, sent it to a silversmith, and the cup was restored, shining brighter than before. *If Faraday could precipitate that silver and recover his cup, I believe God can restore my sleeping and scattered dust.* There are greater miracles of God's than those that He accomplishes through men.

—*Sunday School Times*

* * *

The Blessed Future

The doctor did not think the dying daughter would hear when he said to the mother, "*Poor child; she has seen her best days.*" But she heard him and said, "*No, Doctor, I haven't seen my best days; my best days are still to come when I shall see the King in His glory.*"

—From *The Man Nobody Missed,* by W. E. Biederwolf

* * *

"Trav'ling Toward the Sunset!"

I am trav'ling toward the sunset,
All is calm and all is well;
And the golden tints tow'ring heav'n-
    ward,
Are but Nature's crowning spell.
There is quiet midst the shadows,
For the day's turmoil is spent.
Past the noon with all its travail!
Past the hours of stress and strife!
Fleeting ecstacy and triumph,
Mingled in a plodding life.
There is rapture in the sunset
And the pathway, smooth and straight;
I am longing for the sunrise,
Of that glad resplendent day,
Then the climax and the glory
With the earthlife far away.

—Frank Wilford

* * *

He Lives and Loves Forever

Some time ago a preacher was speaking about the resurrection of Christ, and he said that he had been telling the story of the crucifixion to his four-year-old boy. As he went on with the story, the little fellow looked up with a sad expression on his face, and said, "Did Jesus die, then, Dad?" "Yes," said the father, "He died on the cross." "Oh," said the boy, "He cannot love me now, then." Said the father, in telling this incident, "How I realized the value of the resurrection at that moment, and what a joy it was to be able to say: 'He can love one now, because He rose again from the dead on the third day. He lives, and loves, now and forever.'"

—*Wonderful Word*

* * *

The Believer's Resurrection

A vase closely sealed was found in a mummy pit in Egypt by the English traveler Wilkinson. In it were dis-

covered a few peas, old, wrinkled, and
hard as a stone. The peas were planted
carefully under a glass and at the end
of thirty days they sprang into life,
after having lain sleeping in the dust of
a tomb for almost three thousand years
— a faint illustration of the mortal
body which shall put on immortality.
"Because He lives, we shall live also."

—*Gospel Herald*

* * *

The Power of Praise

When the armies of Napoleon swept
over Europe, one of his generals made a
surprise attack on the little town of
Feldkirch, on the Austrian border. As
Napoleon's formidable army maneuvered
on the heights above Feldkirch, a council of its citizens was hastily summoned
to decide whether to surrender or attempt a defense. In this assembly the
venerable dean of the church arose to
declare: "This is Easter Day. We have
been counting on our own strength, and
that will fail. This is the day of our
Lord's resurrection. Let us ring the
bells and have services as usual, and
leave the matter in God's hands. We
know only our weakness and not the
power of God." The council accepted
his plan, and in a few minutes the
church belfry chimed the joyous bells
announcing the Saviour's resurrection.
The enemy, hearing the sudden peal,
concluded that the Austrian army had
arrived during the night, broke up
camp, and before the Easter bells had
ceased, the danger had been lifted.

—*Lutheran Hour*

* * *

Power in Christ

Within fifty days of the death of Jesus Christ, and the apparent collapse of
His cause, the city of Jerusalem rang
with the clarion cries of men who, with
all boldness, declared that God had
raised Him from the dead, and that
they were His witnesses.

Craven cowards were changed into
courageous confessors, and rude unlet-
tered fishermen from Galilee had become
royal heralds of the King, so that all
who saw them and heard them were
compelled to acknowledge that something had happened which had utterly
transformed their lives.

When questioned by their critics the
Apostles had no hesitancy in making reply. They account for their own boldness by attributing everything to the
Risen Christ.

—Rev. G. H. Lunn

* * *

When You Really Believe It

A little more than a month before
Easter she had returned from the burial
place outside the great city, leaving
there in the silence her fourteen-year-
old boy. Two days later her little girl
gave up the fight, and in less than a
week her baby. Only the three-year-
old escaped. It was diphtheria. When
Easter came she was at church with her
husband and the child. Her face was
pale, but tender and beautiful. She
wore no emblem of her sorrow, and the
lilies and violets on her coat were like
those she had worn every Easter since
I had known her. When the great congregation rose to sing, she sang softly
the words:

The powers of death have done their
  worst,
But Christ their legions hath dispersed.

Her husband stood with his head bowed.
He could not sing. But she touched
his hand as it lay on the back of the
pew, and when they recited the Creed
I heard him saying the words steadily,
"I believe in . . . the resurrection of
the body; and the life everlasting." She
taught her class of girls that day, and
he went to his superintendent's desk, led
his school in worship, and read the
Easter story with only a break now and
then in his fine voice. Amidst the faces
lined with suffering, rebellion, and despair of that Easter congregation, they
had seemed a miracle. A fifteen-year-
old boy, walking home with his father
from the Sunday school said, "Dad, I
guess Mr. and Mrs. L — really believe
it, don't they?" "Believe what?" said
the father. "The whole big thing, all
of it; Easter, you know."

—*Earnest Worker*

"What Has Science to Say?"

Said Dr. Joseph A. Parker: "Some have found fault with me. They say I am old-fashioned and out of date; I am always quoting the Bible; why not turn to science this morning.

"There is a poor widow here who has lost her only son. She wants to know if she will see him again. Science shall give the answer, and I will put the Book away." So he took the Book and put it on the seat behind. "Will this woman see her son again? Where is he? Does death end all? What has science to say?" Here a long pause. "We are waiting for an answer, the woman is anxious." Another long pause. "The woman's heart is breaking. Science must speak. Nothing to say? Surely? Then we must take the Book," and here he reverently replaced it, and with great deliberation opened it and read: "I shall go to him, but he shall not return to me . . . The dead shall arise . . . for this corruptible must put on incorruption, and this mortal must put on immortality. O death, where is thy sting. . . . I saw the dead, small and great, stand before God."

Then, closing the Book, and patting it affectionately, he said, "We will stick to the Book!"

—From *The Lamb Upon His Throne,* by Dr. Joseph Parker

* * *

A Living Saviour

One day an Indian fakir was sitting under a tree when some leaves of a torn book blew his way. They were from a New Testament, and as he read the words on them his heart was strangely warmed, and he set out to look for someone who obeyed the book. He found an Englishman with a black band on his arm, and concluding that this was the distinctive mark of a Christian, the fakir donned one, too. Sometime later he entered into a Christian church for the first time and listened to his first Christian preacher, staying after the service to say that he, too, was a follower of this way, and pointing to the black band as proof. They explained that it was the English sign of the death of a loved one. He mused for a moment, and

then answered: "But I read in the Book that my Loved One has died, so I shall wear it in memory of Him." And so he did, until he heard the story of the Resurrection, and learned that his Loved One was alive forevermore. Then he removed the black band from his arm, and thereafter his shining face was sufficient advertisement of his new allegiance.

—*Methodist Recorder*

* * *

Christ Is Risen — Hallelujah!

Christ is risen! Hallelujah!
  Gladness fills the world today;
From the tomb that could not hold Him,
  See, the stone is rolled away!

Christ hath risen! Hallelujah!
  Blessed morn of life and light!
Lo, the grave is rent asunder,
  Death is conquered through His might.

Christ hath risen! Hallelujah!
  Friends of Jesus, dry your tears;
Through the veil of gloom and darkness,
  Lo, the Son of God appears!

Christ hath risen! Hallelujah!
  He hath risen, as He said;
He is now the King of Glory,
  And our great, exalted Head.

—Fanny J. Crosby

* * *

It's That Simple

Somebody said to Talleyrand, Bishop of Autun during the French Revolution, one of the most astute men who ever lived:

"The Christian religion — what is it? It would be easy to start a religion like that."

"Oh, yes," replied Talleyrand. "One would only have to get crucified and rise again the third day."

—*Power*

* * *

The Resurrection in Nature

Some years ago I kept a marine aquarium. As I stood looking at it one summer day I saw on the surface of the water a tiny creature, half fish, half snake, not an inch long, writhing as in mortal agony. With convulsive efforts it bent its head to tail, now on this side, now on that, springing in circles with a force simply wonderful in a creature so small.

I was stretching out my hands to remove it lest it should sink and die and pollute the clear waters, when, lo, in a moment, in a twinkling of an eye, its skin split from end to end, and there sprang out a delicate fly with slender legs and pale lavender wings. Balancing itself for one instant on its discarded skin, it preened its gossamer wings and then flew out of an open window.

The impression made upon me was deep and overpowering. *I learned that nature was everywhere hinting at the truth of the resurrection.*

—*Moody Monthly*

* * *

"Alas for Him!"

Alas for him who never sees
The stars shine through his cypress trees!
Who, hopelessly, lays his dead away,
Nor looks to see the breaking day
Across the mournful marbles play!
Who hath not learned, in hours of faith,
The truth to flesh and sense unknown,
That Life is ever lord of Death,
And Love can never lose its own!

—John Greenleaf Whittier

* * *

"Come Forth"

Before the tomb Christ stood one day,
And dried the people's tears away
As He spoke forth in mighty voice
That made Judea's hills rejoice,
"Come forth!"

Inside the tomb Christ lay one morn,
Defeated seemed Salvation's Horn,
But God the Father spoke the word,
And this He said, though no man heard,
"Come forth!"

Inside the tomb of sin I lay,
The price of sin I had to pay;
But Christ the Raiser of the dead
Spoke to my poor, bound soul and said,
"Come forth!"

And when the great and final sound
Shall raise our loved ones from the ground,
'Twill be the last time we shall hear
That glorious sound upon our ear,
"Come forth!"

—Louie W. Stokes

* * *

Remembering Only the Cocoon

Arthur Brisbane once pictured a crowd of grieving caterpillars carrying the corpse of a cocoon to its final resting place. The poor, distressed caterpillars, clad in black raiment, were weeping, and all the while the beautiful butterfly fluttered happily above the muck and mire of earth, forever freed from its earthly shell. Needless to say, Brisbane had the average orthodox funeral in mind and sought to convey the idea that when our loved ones pass, it is foolish to remember only the cocoon and concentrate our attention on the remains, while forgetting the bright butterfly.

—Edmund K. Goldsborough, in *Sanctuary Magazine*

* * *

Ten Years or a Thousand

When Rufus Choate, the distinguished American statesman, took ship for England in search of health, a friend said to him, "I feel sure that your health will be restored and that you will be living and at your work ten years from now." "Living ten years from now!" said the great lawyer. "I shall be living a thousand years from now." In a few days Mr. Choate died, but in the sense in which he used the words he did not die.

—*Westminster Teacher*

* * *

Following Dead Gods

A missionary states that on one occasion a number of persons who were hearing him, mostly women, showed great astonishment when he told them that the God he worshipped, and wished them to worship, is a *living God. They* said, *"The foreigner's God is better than ours; ours has no life."*

—*Missionary Herald*

* * *

"Each Covered With Drapery of Snow"

An army chaplain tells of having bivouacked with his brigade upon an open field with nothing over him, or his soldiers, but the cold, cloudy sky. On arising the next morning, all over the field were little mounds like new made graves, each covered with a drapery of snow which had fallen during the night and covered each soldier, as with the winding sheet of death. While he was gazing upon the strange spectacle, here and there a man began to stir, rise, shake himself and stand in momentary amazement at the sight. It was a beautiful symbol of the resurrection.

—*Gospel Herald*

* * *

A Triumphant Funeral

London had never witnessed such a funeral service as was held for Dr. F. B. Meyer in Christ Church Cathedral. There was never a note of defeat, no hint of tragedy, no suggestion of regret, but there were radiant Scripture passages and glorious Easter hymns. At the conclusion of the service, the vast congregation rose as the organist began to play. They stood with bowed heads waiting for the throbbing dirge of the Death March, but instead the organist swung into the triumphal notes of the Halleluiah Chorus. And why should it be otherwise, when a great servant of Christ was standing at attention before his King? That is the faith which is ours today! We worship, not a dead Jesus, but a living Christ, "who hath abolished death, and hath brought life and immortality to light through the gospel."

—*Presbyterian*

* * *

The Only One Who Conquered Death

Dr. Harry Rimmer was traveling in Egypt and, while negotiating with the Secretary of State, a refined and cultured gentleman, he engaged him in conversation concerning religious experience. "We believe that God has given to man three revelations of Himself," said Dr. Rimmer. "We, too, believe that," said the man, who was a Moslem. "We believe that God has revealed Himself in the works of creation. "We, too, believe that." "We believe that God has revealed Himself in a book — the Bible." "We believe that God has revealed Himself in a book — the Koran." "We believe that God has revealed Himself in a man — that man is Jesus Christ." "We believe that God has revealed Himself in a man — that man is the prophet Mohammed." "We believe that Jesus died to save His followers." "We believe that Mohammed died for his people." "We believe," said Dr. Rimmer, "that Jesus is able to substantiate His claims because He rose from the dead." The Moslem hesitated, then his eyes fell, and finally he replied, "We have no information concerning our prophet after his death." Jesus Christ is supreme because He is the only one who ever conquered death and triumphed over the grave. —*Sunday School Times*

* * *

How To Know Easter's Coming:

"Thirty days hath September,"
Every person can remember;
But to know when Easter'll come
Puzzles even scholars some.

When March the twenty-first is past
Just watch the silvery moon,
And when you see it full and round,
Know Easter'll be here soon.

After the moon has reached its full,
Then Easter will be here
The very Sunday after
In each and every year.

And if it hap on Sunday
The moon should reach its height,
The Sunday following this event
Will be the Easter bright.

—*The Friend*

Which Christ?

A very learned man once said to a little girl who believed in the Lord Jesus: "My poor little girl, you don't know whom you believe in. There have been many christs. In which of them do you believe?" "I know which one I believe in," replied the child. "I believe in the Christ who rose from the dead."

—*Sunday School Times*

* * *

Our Living Saviour

Vital Christian experience comes from knowing Jesus as the living Saviour.

Two irreligious young men were discussing the resurrection, telling each other why it was impossible for them to accept the doctrine. Then a deacon of a near-by church walked by, and in a joking way one of the young fellows called to him, "Say, Deacon, tell us why you believe that Jesus rose again." "Well," he answered, "one reason is that I was talking with Him for half an hour this very morning." We may all experience proof of the resurrection of Christ in the acknowledging of His living presence in our lives. No one who knows Jesus personally questions the resurrection.

—*Watchman-Examiner*

* * *

Contrasting Views of Ghandi and Sankey

Some fifteen years before Ghandi's death, he wrote:

"I must tell you in all humility that Hinduism, as I know it, entirely satisfies my soul, fills my whole being, and I find a solace in the Bhagavad and Upainshads that I miss even in the Sermon on the Mount."

Just before his death, Ghandi wrote:

"My days are numbered. I am not likely to live very long — perhaps a year or a little more. For the first time in fifty years I find myself in the slough of despond. All about me is darkness; I am praying for light."

Just before Sankey's homegoing, he wrote:

"I believe in Him who said, 'Verily, verily, I say unto you, He that believeth on me hath everlasting life.'

"I believe in the Son of God with all my soul, might, mind, and strength, and am therefore saved by the word of One who cannot lie. I have only a little longer weary tossing on the billows' foam, only a little longer of earthly darkness, and then the sunshine of the Father's throne. So sure am I of meeting in heaven those of my friends who are following the Lamb, that I send them this final message, that God is love. Good night, good night."

—W. B. K.

* * *

"If Easter Be Not True!"

If Easter be not true,
Then all the lilies low must lie,
The Flanders poppies fade and die;
The spring must lose her fairest bloom,
For Christ were still within the tomb —
If Easter be not true.

If Easter be not true,
Then faith must mount on broken wings,
Then hope no more immortal spring,
Then hope must lose her mighty urge,
Life prove a phantom, death a dirge —
If Easter be not true.

If Easter be not true,
'Twere foolishness the cross to bear,
He died in vain who suffered there;
What matter though we laugh or cry,
Be good or evil, live or die,
If Easter be not true.

If Easter be not true —
But it is true, and Christ is risen!
And mortal spirit from its prison
Of sin and death with Him may rise!
Worthwhile the struggle sure the prize,
Since Easter, aye, is true!

—Henry H. Barstow

* * *

"Yet Shall He Live"

A little girl whose baby brother had just died asked her mother where baby had gone. "To be with Jesus," replied the mother. A few days later, talking to a friend, the mother said, "I am so grieved to have lost my baby." The little girl heard her, and, remembering what her mother had told her, looked up into her face and asked, "Mother, is a thing lost when you know where it is?"

"No, of course not." "Well, then, *how can baby be lost when he has gone to be with Jesus?*" Her mother never forgot this. It was the truth.
—*Junior King's Business*

* * *

"He Tore the Bars Away!"

A stanza from an old hymn says that Jesus Christ "burst the bars" of the grave and "tore its bands away." If a man bursts the bars of state's prison all the police force of the commonwealth is after him to bring him back. If, on the contrary, he has served out his full time, all the power in the state cannot retain him a single hour longer. Jesus Christ must remain in the grave three days "according to scripture," *but after the three days had expired there was not power enough in heaven or in hell to retain Him another moment.*
—A. J. Gordon

* * *

Certainties — Not Speculations

When that great Christian and scientist, Sir Michael Faraday, was dying, some journalists questioned him as to his speculations for a life after death. "Speculations!" said he, "I know nothing about speculations. I'm resting on certainties. 'I know that my redeemer liveth,' and because He lives, I shall live also." —*Gospel Trumpet*

An Anticipated Delight!

One of the anticipated delights of the life beyond is our reunion with those dear ones who have died in the Lord, "whom we have loved long since, and lost awhile."

"And the stately ships go on,
To the haven under the hill;
But O for the touch of a vanished hand,
And the sound of a voice that is still!"
—Alfred Tennyson

* * *

Christ Is Risen

"Oh, we see Him in the springtime,
When each bud and leaf and flower
Bursting from its deathlike sleeping
Speaks of resurrection power!
When all nature wakes in gladness,
Birds sing out their tuneful lays,
And the earth, bedecked with blossoms,
Joins in its Creator's praise."
—*Pentecostal Evangelist*

* * *

Reveille! — Not Taps

A soldier said, "When I die do not sound taps over my grave, but reveille — the morning call, the summons to rise."
—From *Streams in the Desert*,
by Mrs. Charles E. Cowman

REVIVAL

Prayer and Revival

When Finney was conducting a revival in a certain place, a young woman came in from a neighboring town and asked him to go there and preach. "Her utterance was choked with deep feeling." Mr. Finney told her he did not see how he could go, but he looked up the place and found that it was a moral waste, cursed by a minister who had changed to infidelity. The young woman came the next Sunday, and "appeared greatly affected; too much so to converse, for she could not control her feeling." The evangelist consented to go the next Sunday afternoon, and after his arrival at her home he heard her praying in a room above. He remained in that home overnight, and heard her praying and weeping nearly all night. She pleaded with him to come again, and "at the third service the Spirit of God was poured out on the congregation." A spirit of prayer came powerfully upon Mr. Finney, as it had upon this young woman. The spirit of prayer spread, and the revival that followed was so powerful that "nearly all the principal inhabitants of the town were gathered into the church, and the town was morally renovated." This great spiritual movement was started by that young woman's prayers.
—*Gospel Herald*

Birth of the Welsh Revival

The world still feels the influence of the great Welsh Revival which flamed across the tiny country of Wales at the beginning of this century. But few remember just how this mighty spiritual movement began:

A Christian Endeavor meeting was in progress in a small town in Wales when a timid young Welsh girl arose. She was so nervous that she could utter only one short sentence: "O, I do love Jesus!" Then she sat down. The Lord used that earnest testimony to fulfill His own divine purpose. Spiritual fire came down on that young people's meeting, even akin to Pentecost. Quickly it spread through that Church, then through the little town, and on through the whole of Wales. Its influence was soon felt all around the world.

—Thomas DeCourcy Rayner

* * *

Revival

Revive Me (Ps. 138:7)

My love is cold, my faith is small,
My zeal is lacking, doubts appall,
My footsteps falter, oft I stray,
And weakness marks me for its prey.
God of Revival, hear my plea,
Empower, endue, revive e'en me.

Revive Us (Ps. 85:6)

With all Thine own, in Jesus' Name,
We would confess our common shame,
And humbly bow before Thy face,
To seek Thy pardoning, cleansing grace.
God of Revival, God of love,
Refresh, revive us from above.

Revive Thy Work (Hab. 3:2)

Thy workers' hearts are filled with dread;
Thy lost are left, Thy sheep unfed;
Thine enemies Thy work defy,
And things are weak, ready to die.
God of Revival, now we pray,
Visit Thy work in this our day.

They Shall Revive (Hos. 14:7)

Oh, for Thy Spirit's quickening breath!
Reviving from the sleep of death.
Oh, for Thy mighty, ancient power!
Arousing us this very hour.

God of Revival, Thee we praise,
For signs of blessing in our days.

—A. Gardner

* * *

The Right Start

The great revival under Jonathan Edwards, in the eighteenth century, began with his famous call to prayer. The marvelous work of grace among the Indians under Brainerd had its origin in the days and nights that Brainerd spent before God in prayer for an enduement of power from on high for his work. A most remarkable and widespread display of God's reviving power was that which broke out at Rochester, N. Y., under the labors of Charles Finney. It not only spread through New England but to Great Britain as well. Mr. Finney attributed the power of this work to the spirit of prayer that prevailed. The great revival of 1859 in the United States began in prayer and was carried on by prayer more than anything else. "Most revivals," writes Dr. Cuyler, "have humble beginnings, and the fire starts in a few warm hearts. Never despise the day of small things. During my own long ministry nearly every work of grace had a small beginning . . . a humble meeting in a private home . . . a group gathered for Bible study by Mr. Moody in our mission chapel . . . a meeting of young people in my home."

—*Alliance Weekly*

* * *

Prayer for Revival

"Humbly now, O Lord, I pray
Send revival here today.
All my coldness, all my sin,
All my doubtings deep within;
Forgive them, Lord, and cleanse away;
Oh, send revival here today!

"Humbly, Lord, I ask of Thee,
Send this awakening through me;
Emptied out of self and pride,
Thy light no longer will I hide.
And, or dear Lord, use me, I pray,
To bring revival here today!"

Mrs. Charles Bell
—*Moody Monthly*

"Evangelize!"

Give us a watch word for the hour
A thrilling word, a word of power;
A battle cry, a flaming breath,
A word to rouse the Church from rest
That calls to conquer or to death;
To heed her Master's high behest.
The call is given, Ye hosts arise,
Our watchword is Evangelize.

The glad evangel now proclaim
Through all the earth in Jesus' Name
This word is ringing through the skies
Evangelize, Evangelize.
To dying men, a fallen race
Make known the gift of gospel grace
The world that now in darkness lies,
Evangelize, Evangelize.   —*Selected*

* * *

"Do Not Stem Revival's Tide!"

"Has my brother ought against me?
Have I wronged him in the past?
Have I harbored unkind mem'ries?
Have I false aspersions cast?
Have I treated him with coldness?
Passed him by — the other side?
Then, forgive me, oh! my brother,
Do not stem Revival's Tide."

—*Selected*

* * *

Dr. R. A. Torrey's Prescription:

"I can give a prescription that will
bring a revival to any church or community or any city on earth.

"First, let a few Christians (they
need not be many) get thoroughly right
with God themselves. This is the prime
essential. If this is not done, the rest
that I am to say will come to nothing.

"Second, let them bind themselves
together in a prayer group to pray for a
revival until God opens the heavens and
comes down.

"Third, let them put themselves at the
disposal of God for Him to use as He
sees fit in winning others to Christ.
That is all!

"This is sure to bring a revival to any
church or community. I have given this
prescription around the world. It has
been taken by many churches and many
communities, and in no instance has it
ever failed; and it cannot fail!"

—*Gospel Herald*

The Doctor Noticed the Change

During the Welsh Revival of 1904-
1905, a village doctor remarked to a
friend, "Well, the revival is doing me
good anyway." "Do you mean that you
have more patients?" his friend inquired.
"Not at all," the doctor answered; "but
£23 due to me, which I had written off
my books as hopelessly bad debts, have
been paid to me since the revival began."

—From *Stories of Great Revivals*,
by Henry Johnson

* * *

Subtraction Sometimes Important, Also

When I talk about blessing I not only
mean additions, but subtractions, too. A
pastor came to one of his fellow pastors
and said, "We've had a revival in our
church." The other man replied, "That's
good. How many were added to your
church?" "None were added, but ten
were subtracted." That's spiritual prosperity. It may mean subtraction. If
some of our churches had the unconverted deacons subtracted, revival would
come.   —*Moody Monthly*

* * *

Walking Revival!

Newspapermen went down from London to report at first hand the marvelous happenings of the great Welsh Revival at the turn of the century. On
their arrival in Wales one of them
asked a policeman where the Welsh
Revival was. Drawing himself to his
full height he laid his hand over his
heart and proudly proclaimed: "Gentlemen, the Welsh revival is inside this
uniform!" He had caught the holy fire.

—*Power*

* * *

How to Bring Revival

Gipsy Smith was once asked how to
start a revival.

He answered: "Go home, lock yourself in your room, kneel down in the
middle of your floor. Draw a chalk
mark all around yourself and ask God
to start the revival inside that chalk
mark. When He has answered your
prayer, the revival will be on."

—*Missionary Worker*

If

If all the sleeping folk will wake up,
And all the lukewarm folk will fire up,
And all the dishonest folk will confess
    up,
And all the disgruntled folk will sweeten
    up,
And all the discouraged folk will cheer
    up,
And all the depressed folk will look up,
And all the estranged folk will make up,
And all the gossipers will shut up,
And all the dry bones will shake up,
And all the true soldiers will stand up,
And all the church members will pray
    up,
Then you can have a revival.

                            —*Selected*

* * *

Breaking up Things for Christ

I was in revival services in Amarillo, Texas, years ago in a little Baptist church. A contractor got converted. He was building two houses, and had two big crews of men. We were having morning services at ten o'clock. Do you know what he did? He went around to these houses and said to all those carpenters, plumbers, and painters. "Boys, we are having a meeting down at the church." Then he said some good things about the preacher, and said: "I want you to hear him. I will tell you what we will do. Nobody will work on my job here from ten to eleven o'clock. We are all going down to the church on my time." One man said: "I do not care to go to church. I'll stay here and work." "No," the converted man said, "nobody is going to work on my job while the preacher is down in my church trying to have a revival. We are all going down there." So they came in their overalls, and some of them got converted. You know if you really break up a business or break up a roof — if you really go to breaking up things for Jesus — you can have a revival.

                    —*Sword of the Lord*

* * *

The Price of Revivals

A short while before Dr. J. B. Chapman passed away, he was addressing a gathering of preachers, when he said, "We have reached the place where one man plays a handsaw and another gives a 'Life's Story,' gathering a big crowd and we call that a revival. No! that is not a revival; that is a farce. Tears, sweat, and blood are the price of a revival, and some of us are not willing to pay the price."

                    —*Herald of Holiness*

REWARDS

Out of This Life

Out of this life I shall never take
Things of silver and gold I make.

All that I cherish and hoard away
After I leave, on the earth must stay.

Though I have toiled for a painting rare
To hang on my wall, I must leave it
    there.

Though I call it mine and I boast its
    worth
I must give it up when I quit the earth.

All that I gather and all that I keep,
I must leave behind when I fall asleep.

And I wonder often what I shall own
In that other life, when I pass alone.

What shall they find and what shall
    they see
In the soul that answers the call for
    me?

Shall the great Judge learn, when my
    task is through
That the spirit had gathered some
    riches, too?

Or shall at the last it be mine to find
That all I had worked for I'd left
    behind?

                    —*Edgar A. Guest, in,*
                    The United Evangelical

_____

* Used by permission of the copyright owners, Reilly & Lee Co., Chicago

His Well Done

If everything I do each day
　Were written in a book —
If every evening I could see
　How that day's page would look —
I feel that on each passing day
　My record would improve;
My thoughtless deeds I'd rectify,
　All dross I would remove.

"Oh, help me, Lord, to not forget
　My record at Thy throne,
And that my every thought and deed
　Each day to Thee is known.
Dwell Thou within my heart, I pray,
　From dawn to setting sun,
That, when my record is reviewed,
　I may hear Thy 'Well done'!"

　　　　　　　　　　　—Selected

* * *

After

After the crosses — a crown of life;
After weeping — a song;
After the night of sorrow — a bright
　and glorious dawn.

After the heartaches — the comforting;
After the storm — a calm;
After suff'ring and sighing — God's love
　a healing balm.

After the longing — reality;
After wand'ring — the way;
After the pain of parting — the glad
　reunion day.

After the mourning — the oil of joy;
After darkness — the light;
After earth's toil and trials — the
　blessed face of Christ.

　　　　　　　　　　—Eda A. Reid

* * *

A Statue, — or a Shrine?

Several visitors to Paris have commented on the contrast between two prominent statues in that city. Both of them are statues of men whose first name was Louis. The first is of Louis XIV, the absolute monarch. He is remembered today chiefly for his exclamation, "I am the state!" He repre-

sents one of the supreme achievements of greatness through power. His philosophy of life was that the whole nation and the world, in so far as he could compel it, should serve him. A few blocks away is a more unpretentious statue. There is no uniform on this figure carved in stone, no badge of office, no sword, no crown. It is the statue of Louis Pasteur, the servant of humanity and servant of God. His life of unselfish, devoted research conferred immeasurable benefit upon all humanity in all the years to come through overcoming disease and suffering. The statue of the monarch is nothing more than a piece of sculpture; the statue of Pasteur is a shrine, where pilgrims from all over the world bow in grateful homage. It is the uncrowned servant of mankind who wears the real crown of men's love and honor.

　　　　　—Berean Senior Quarterly

* * *

Sent on Ahead

"Poor R — ; I understand that poor R — did not leave much property," said a friend commiseratingly of one who had just died, as he drove home with the minister from the cemetery. "Too bad! He worked hard, and made money, but he was too tenderhearted. I think every beggar in town must have known him." The minister listened politely. "I suppose what you say is right about his having no property, but I imagine, from what I have known of his life, that he must have considerable property to go to."

　　　　　　　　　　　—Forward

* * *

One Suit — But

The contrast between two lives was noted by Dr. Harold E. Luccock. The first was a woman who died in London, famous as "the best dressed woman in Europe." She left almost a thousand frocks, but with each frock she had worn "the same unseeing eyes, the same deaf ears, the same enameled, painted face." The second was a man who died in the same city, with but one suit, blue with a red collar on the coat. He was William Booth, founder of the Salvation Army. He had but one costume, but he lived in a thousand lives.

—*Christian Herald*

* * *

Record On High!

In Malden, near Boston, in a Baptist church, is a marble tablet thus inscribed:

IN MEMORIAM
Rev. Adoniram Judson,
Born August 9, 1788,
Died April 12, 1850,
Malden his birthplace,
The ocean his sepulchre,
Converted Burmans and
The Burman Bible
His monument.
His record is on High.

—*Selected*

* * *

God's Compound Interest

One of the early founders of the Rothschild House, in his younger days borrowed a small amount of money from a friend to help him start in business. Without security to give, he got it on the ground of his need. He went to a distant part of Germany, and many years rolled on. After nearly half a century, when the name of the family and the firm had become world-wide, his old benefactor did not even know it was the same youth he had once befriended. But one day, when he was an old man and his health had broken, his fortune gone and his family dependent upon him, and the darkest shadows gathering about his life, he received a letter from the Rothschild House in Frankfort, summoning him to the bank for an important interview. As he entered the private office of the great banker, he was greeted with a welcome he had little expected. After the old acquaintance had been renewed, the great banker went to his desk and took out a draft for an enormous amount of money, amounting to some hundred thousand dollars, handed it to his old friend, and said, "I have sent for you to pay you the dividends on the stock you entrusted

to my banking nearly fifty years ago." Astounded, the friend refused to take the money, saying that he had no such claim, and could not accept such a gift. "It is not a gift," said the banker, "it is simply the actual profit on the money you gave me, wisely turned over a great many times, until it has actually accumulated this compound interest . . . " As A. B. Simpson said, "There is a day coming when the trust that we have committed to His keeping will be returned to us a millionfold more. We shall find what a good investor of our treasures God is."

— *Gospel Herald*

* * *

Not the Reward, but the Lord

The first Victoria crosses were awarded in Hyde Park, London, in 1857. The following is a description of one of the incidents of their awarding: "A veteran, terribly maimed, came up to receive his medal, and the Queen, flinging down the medal, turned her back upon the troops, and, covering her face with her hands, burst into tears. All the while the maimed man stood still; then the Queen recovered her composure and pinned the medal to his coat. As she did so she spoke some words to him, and the soldier's answer was: 'God bless Your Majesty; we'd bear it all again for Queen and country.'" It was not the medal itself that brought joy to the soldier's heart, but the fact that his service for the Empire was recognized at the hand of his sovereign. Likewise it is not the reward of the Christian that will be his chief delight, but rather the Lord from whom he receives the "crown of life." — *King's Business*.

* * *

His "Well Done"

A young man, having studied violin under a great master, was giving his first recital. Following each number, despite the cheers of the crowd, the boy seemed dissatisfied. Even after the last number, with the shouts louder than ever, the boy stood watching an old man in the balcony.

Finally the old man smiled and nodded approval. Immediately the young man relaxed and beamed his happiness. The plaudits of the crowd meant nothing until he had won the approval of the master. — *Sunday*

* * *

"Cannot Recompense Thee"

There is a marble tablet let into the outside walls of Plymouth's High Street Chapel, bearing luminous words:

Erected by Friends
As a Memorial of their esteem and respect for
JOHN POUNDS
Who, while earning his livelihood
By mending shoes, gratuitously educated
And, in part, clothed and fed
Some hundreds of Poor Children.
He died suddenly
On the first of January, 1839
Aged 72 years
"Thou shalt be blessed: — For they Cannot Recompense thee."
— *Gospel Herald*

* * *

God's Law About Giving

There is a story about a man who put a gold piece in the collection plate at church instead of a penny. When he discovered his mistake he went to the usher and tried to get it back. But the usher objected; he said it would not look well to do that.

"All right," said the giver, "let it go. After all, I've given it to God, and He'll reward me for it."

"Oh, no, He won't," the usher contradicted. "God will reward you for only the penny, for that is all you intended to put in."

Anna had a friend of whom she was very fond. When her friend's birthday came, Anna wanted to make her a substantial gift; but her purse was nearly empty at that time, and she could not spend the money that it would cost to make the gift. So she had to buy something cheaper.

When she gave it to her friend she said, "I had planned to give you something better than this, Grace, but I can't, and I hope you will accept this."

"Of course I will accept it, Anna," Grace told her, "and I shall prize it just as much as the other that you wanted to give me."

These two stories illustrate God's law about giving. It is not the size of the gift, but the size of the giver's heart that is to be considered. According to Jesus' standard, the gold piece that the man put in was worth only a penny.

— *Gospel Herald*

RICHES

The Story of the 8 Rich Men

In 1923, a very important meeting was held at the Edgewater Beach Hotel in Chicago. Attending this meeting were eight of the world's most successful financiers. Those present were:

The president of the largest independent steel company;

The president of the largest utility company;

The president of the largest gas company;

The president of the New York Stock Exchange;

A member of the President's cabinet;

The greatest "bear" in Wall Street;

Head of the world's greatest monopoly; President of the Bank for International Settlements.

Certainly we must admit that here were gathered a group of the world's most successful men. At least, men who had found the secret of "making money." Twenty-five years later let's see where these men are:

The president of the largest independent steel company — Charles Schwab — died a bankrupt and lived on borrowed money for five years before his death.

The president of the greatest utility company — Samuel Insull — died a fugitive from justice and penniless in a foreign land.

The president of the largest gas company — Howard Hopson — is now dead.

The president of the New York Stock Exchange — Richard Whitney — was recently released from Sing Sing Penitentiary.

The member of the President's cabinet — Albert Fall, was pardoned from prison so he could die at home.

The greatest "bear" in Wall Street — Jesse Livermore — died a suicide.

The head of the greatest monopoly — Ivan Kreuger — died a suicide.

The president of the Bank for International Settlements — Leon Fraser — died a suicide.

All of these men learned well the art of making money, but not one of them had learned how to live.

— Louis R. Lurie, in *Journal of Living*

* * *

Few Smiling Millionaires

"Millionaires seldom smile," said Andrew Carnegie. And a few years ago John D. Rockefeller told Dr. Carter Helm Jones at the close of a sermon in Cleveland that great wealth is a burden destroying the real zest of life and banishing peace from the heart.

Truly, there is a better business before us than merely envying the rich.

— *Gospel Herald*

* * *

Lest He Become Obsessed

At a meeting of the Colorado Conference Historical Society, a story was told of a pioneer preacher, who, during the gold rush, had taken a little time off and joined the prospectors in panning for gold. Soon he was giving all his time to the search for gold. Suddenly, realizing his peril, he climbed to a high peak, and opening the handkerchief which contained the gold dust he had washed out so laboriously, he shook it out upon the ground, then held up the cloth that the mountain winds might cleanse it. This story does not mean that there is any disgrace in making money, if it be made honestly. But that Colorado

preacher was becoming obsessed with one desire — to get rich — and he saw it. Let us be sure that the love of money has not gripped us. May we, as Christians, have a keen sense of honor, and practice the principles of stewardship.

— *Upper Room*

* * *

Starving in the Midst of Plenty

We read of a very rich man, worth hundreds of millions of dollars, who was said to have literally starved to death. For many months before he died he was unable to digest any solid food. He gave great banquets, but he could not partake of the delicacies he provided for others. Although he took some pleasure in entertaining foreign princes and important personages, he himself slowly wasted away.

Opulence and luxury are not life, nor can the splendors of this world become an adequate substitute for real living. While we know this, how pitiful is the knowledge that in the realm of spiritual and eternal things there are souls that seem to be withering away.

— *Watchman-Examiner*

* * *

Poverty Amid Riches

A Swedish writer tells of a farmer whose thoughts took living shapes of gold and silver, coins, banks and barns, grains of wheat and corn, cows and pigs. These forms clouded his mind, hiding the beauty of the landscape. When he sat down to read, they settled like bees on the paper, allowing him to read only the market report and the price of cows. Just a fancy? Yes, but based on a subtle psychological fact. If we are to own money and not allow it to own us, we must have a rich soul, else we soon become victims of a strange poverty. The late Robert Horton said the greatest lesson he learned from life was that people who set their minds and hearts on money are equally disappointed whether they get it or whether they don't. It binds alike the poor who crave money and the rich who make it their god.

— *Quiet Hour*

What Good Is It?

It is recorded of one of America's richest men, that before he died he said to a friend: "I don't see what good it does me — all this money that you say is mine. I can't eat it, can't spend it; in fact, I never saw it, and never had it in my hand for a moment. I dress no better than my private secretary, and cannot eat as much as my coachman. I live in a big servants' boarding house, have dyspepsia, cannot drink champagne, and most of my money is in the hands of others, who use it mainly for their own benefit." This is the testimony of one who put his treasure in "a bag with holes."

—*Gospel Herald*

* * *

Service for God Lasts

Roger Babson says —

"One dollar spent for a lunch lasts five hours."

"One dollar spent for a necktie lasts five weeks."

"One dollar spent for an automobile lasts five years."

"One dollar spent in the service of God lasts for eternity"   —*Selected*

* * *

In Death There is Equality

Alexander the Great, we are told, being upon his deathbed, commanded that, when he was carried forth to the grave, his hands should not be wrapped, as was usual, in the cerecloths, but should be left outside the bier, so that all men might see them, and might see that they were *empty;* that there was nothing in them; that he, born to one empire, and the conqueror of another; the possessor while he lived, of two worlds, of the East, and of the West, and of the treasures of both, yet now when he was dead could retain not even the smallest portion of these treasures; that in this matter the poorest beggar and he were at length upon equal terms."

If we live for this world, we shall go out of it empty-handed, but if we live for the next world we shall depart *full-handed,* "rich in faith" and soon to enter upon an eternal inheritance.

—*The United Evangelical*

Gold Gained — Soul Starved

Aga Khan, on the silver jubilee of his leadership of the Ismaili Moslem sect, received from his followers, his weight in silver. On the golden jubilee, in gold; and on the anniversary five years ago, in diamonds. That day in Bombay he weighed 243½ pounds — he received 2½ million dollars. That ceremony was repeated later in East Africa with the same result.

This year on his 75th birthday, he is to receive his weight in platinum. At last reports he weighed in at 240 pounds. At the present price of platinum, he will receive about three million dollars. He is honored by Ismaili Moslems as a direct descendant of Mohammed and a kind of deity on earth.

According to the press, he spends most of his time on the French Riviera, and following the fortunes of his stable of race horses. The total amount of his wealth usually is summed up in the word "fabulous."

—*Gospel Herald*

* * *

Needless Accumulation

Forget not that your first and principal business as a disciple of Christ is to give the gospel to those who have it not. If you cannot go in person, inquire diligently what blood-mortgage there is on your property in the interest of lost souls. I warn you that it will go hard with you when the Lord comes to reckon with you, if He finds your wealth hoarded up in needless accumulations instead of being carefully devoted to giving the gospel to the lost.

—A. J. Gordon

* * *

Riches Where?

D. L. Moody told of a rich man who lay dying. His little daughter was greatly puzzled over what was happening. Her father loved to have her with him, and she had often sat on his bed wondering why her big, strong father was lying helplessly there. One day the heads of his business came to pay their last call. There the rich man lay looking at his little girl when she said, "Father, are you going away?"

"Yes, dear, and I am afraid you won't see me again."

Then the little one said, "Have you got a nice house and lots of friends there?"

The successful man of the world lay silent for a while, and then said: "What a fool I have been! I have built a great business here, but I shall be a pauper there."

—Lionel Fletcher, in
Life of Faith

* * *

The Musings of a Dollar

Money may make three different sorts of speeches.

It may say: "Hold me and I will dry out the foundations of sympathy and benevolence in your soul and leave you barren and destitute. Grasp me tightly and I will change your eyes that they will care to look upon nothing that does not contain my image, and so transform your ears that my soft metallic ring will sound louder to them than the cries of widows and orphans and the wail of perishing multitudes. Keep me, clutch me and I will destroy your sympathy for the race, your respect for the right and your love and reverence for God."

Or it may say: "Spend me for self-indulgence and I will make your soul fat and indifferent to all except your own pleasure I will become your master and you will think that I only am of importance and powerful."

Or it may say: "Give me away for the benefit of others and I will return in streams of spiritual revenue to your soul. I will bless the one that received and the one that gives me. I will supply food for the hungry, raiment for the naked, medicine for the sick and send the Gospel to the benighted. At the same time, I will secure joy and peace for the soul that uses me."

—*Selected*

* * *

"Millionaires Who Laugh Are Rare"

"Comrades was born in poverty, and would not exchange its sacred memories with the richest millionaire's son who ever breathed. What does he know about mother or father? These are mere names to him. Give me the life of the boy whose mother is nurse, seamstress, washerwoman, cook, teacher, angel, and saint, all in one, and whose father is guide, exemplar, and friend. No servants to come between. These are the boys who are born to the best fortune. Some men think that poverty is a dreadful burden, and that wealth leads to happiness. What do they know about it? They know only one side; they imagine the other. I have lived both, and I know there is very little in wealth that can add to human happiness beyond the small comforts of life. Millionaires who laugh are rare. My experience is that wealth is apt to take the smiles away.

—Andrew Carnegie in
Watchman-Examiner

* * *

After His Riches Had Gone

The children of a certain family, during its prosperity, were left in the nursery in charge of servants. When adversity came the servants were discharged and the parents lived with the little ones. One evening, when the father returned home after a day of anxiety and business worry, his little girl climbed up on his knee, and twining her arms around his neck, said: "Papa, don't you get rich again. You did not come into the nursery when you were rich, but now we can come around you, and get on your knee and kiss you. Don't get rich again, Papa."

—*Moody Monthly*

* * *

Money

Dug from the mountain side
  Or washed in the glen,
  Servant am I or master of men.
Earn me, I bless you;
Steal me, I curse you;
  Grasp me and hold me,
A fiend shall possess you.
  Lie for me, die for me,
  Covet me, take me —
Angel or devil,
  I'm just what you make me.

—*Selected*

Affluence Now, Bankruptcy Hereafter

A certain tribe in Africa elects a new king every seven years but it invariably kills its old king. For seven years the member of the tribe enjoying this high honor is provided with every luxury known to savage life. During these years his authority is absolute, even to the power of life and death. For seven years he rules, is honored and surfeited with possessions, but at the end he dies. Every member of the tribe is aware of this, for it is a custom of long standing; but there is never lacking an applicant for the post. For seven years of luxury and power men are willing to sacrifice the remainder of life's expectation. They are only ignorant pagans, yet in the proudest civilization of our day men of intelligence and leadership are now making the same choice between things now and bankruptcy hereafter. Scores and hundreds and thousands are willing to be bankrupts through eternity if they may only win their millions here.

—*Selected*

* * *

The Acid Test

The late Dr. W. B. Riley records how one memorable Sunday, Dr. John A. Broadus, when his ushers were about to take the offering, left his pulpit and walked down to where one usher was beginning his collection, and went along with him and looked at every penny, nickel, dime, quarter, and dollar that went into the basket. You may well imagine that some of the people were angry. Some were confused. Others were shamefaced. Others were filled with amazement. All were evidently surprised. When the collection was over, Dr. Broadus walked back to his pulpit to speak from his morning's text. He said to his congregation: "My people, if you take it to heart that I have seen your offerings this day and know just what sacrifices you have made and what sacrifices you have not made, remember that the Son of God, your Saviour, goes about the aisles with every usher and sees with His sleepless eye every cent put into the collection by His people." Our use of money is often the acid test of our character.

—Dr. William Ward Ayer, in
The Evangel

Money Talks

Let me have a word with you. I am your servant if rightly used. You will become my slave if you persist in misusing me. I am often spoken of as "The root of all evil." This is not fair play. I can be the root of much good if you will use me properly.

Try to put yourself in my place — I don't like to change hands for every little trinket and fancy that come along. I would like to stay with you for a little while. There may be a real mission that I can perform for you some time. On the other hand, I detest being held tightly. It hurts. When there is something urgent, and really useful, let me be on my way. I wasn't intended for you alone. I want to do the greatest possible good.

And, ah, yes, please remember, I like to go to church, too. I am always happy when I can work for the Master of all silver and gold, the One who owns the true riches of all the world.

—M. E. Detterline

* * *

"Think of the Difference"

A young woman was one day visiting an aged man, a friend of her father's, who had been associated with him in early life. The man had been one of those who had run after the world and overtaken it. All it could give he had obtained. Soon he inquired after the state of his friend, whom he knew to be in circumstances of far less external comfort than himself. As he listened to the story of his less-favored friend's patience in suffering, of the cheerfulness with which he could look forward to either life or death, the rich man's conscience applied the unexpressed reproach, and he exclaimed, "Yes, yes, you wonder why I cannot be as happy and quiet, too; but think of the difference. *He is going to his treasure and I — I must leave mine."*

—G. B. F. Hallock

* * *

Abundant Money, But —

An extraordinary story is told by a Swiss lady who was a prisoner for twenty days in a cave of the Alps. She says that she set out for a walk by herself, intending to return to her hotel for lunch. Fascinated by the scenery, she penetrated farther up the gorge, and lost her way. In her wanderings she slipped and fell a long distance, alighting in a cave. At first she congratulated herself on not being dashed to pieces, but in a short time she feared that she was reserved for the worse fate of dying by starvation. There was no way of egress from the cave but from above, and when she attempted to climb, she found the steep sides too slippery to give her any foothold. She shouted for help at intervals all that day and night until she was too hoarse to hear her own voice. She became intensely hungry and thirsty. Some water was trickling out through the rock, some of which she drank, and there was a kind of moss growing on the side of the cave that alleviated the pangs of hunger. She had plenty of money in her purse, but she would gladly have given it all for a mouthful of bread. When found by a peasant, she was almost a skeleton and was quite demented. He carried her to a hospital where she slowly recovered. She will never forget that fearful ordeal. Her situation, with abundant money at her command, yet liable to perish with hunger, is a lesson that we in these times need to learn; that there are times when boundless wealth cannot deliver us.

—*Christian Herald*

* * *

Worthless Money

Tightly clasping a penny in her small hand, a little girl entered a candy store and laying her penny on the counter, she lingered over the different kinds of sweets temptingly displayed, and finally made a choice. Pointing one chubby finger, she said to the clerk, "I'll take that one." "I'm afraid that one is two cents," said the clerk consolingly. Again the child inspected the different candies, and again indicated her selection. "That one is two cents also," the clerk was forced to repeat. Ruefully she turned away and started to leave. "Wait, little girl," called the clerk, "you've forgotten your penny." "I don't want it," was her reply; it won't buy anything." The story reminded us of that prophecy of the day when our gold shall be removed from us, and men will "cast their silver in the streets" (Ezek. 7:17-19). Men will become so exasperated over the uselessness of their money that they will cast it in the streets!

—*Prophecy Monthly*

* * *

The Inspiration to Give

There was a widow of small means, yet of noble liberality. But unexpectedly a legacy was left her, and she was wealthy. But to a cause to which, in her comparative poverty, she had delighted to give five dollars, she now proffered twenty-five cents. When asked why such a strange change, and in her present circumstances, at last she candidly replied: "Ah, when day by day I looked to God for my bread, I had enough and to spare. Now I have to look to my ample income, and I am all the time haunted with the fear of losing it and coming to want. *I had the guinea heart when I had the shilling means; now I have the guinea means and the shilling heart.*"

—*Topical Illustrations*

* * *

Both Jewels and Life — LOST!

Among the discoveries in the ruins of Pompeii was a woman in the act of gathering in her apron rings, bracelets, and other valuable articles of jewelry. Some wealthy persons, aware of the coming destruction, fled, leaving these THINGS behind as worthless in comparison with life. But she, hoping to save both, delayed the time of her flight, and alas! was overwhelmed in the holocaust! Both jewels and life were lost.

—*W. B. K.*

* * *

Consider Nero!

Consider Nero, who had so far exhausted all pleasures he offered prizes for new methods of enjoyment to be devised — he sits on his splendid throne the Emperor of Rome, the conqueror of the world — the porches of his palace a mile long — the ceiling of his banquet halls arranged to shower perfumes upon the travelers — entertainers are gathered from every corner of the world. His crown is worth half a million — his mules shod with silver — a thousand chariots accompany him when he travels — he never wears the same garment twice. But he is peevish, gloomy, miserably unhappy, dissatisfied — because he is unsaved. He dies a suicide.

—*Grace and Truth*

* * *

"He Saved His Life But Lost It"

Two brothers, both well established on their own farms, investigated the possibility of giving their lives for missionary service. One felt he should give up his opportunities for material gain, finish his missionary preparation, and move with his family to the field of South America. They are there today, investing their lives for Jesus Christ. The other brother felt that his material opportunities were too good to sacrifice for Christ, and the hazards of the mission field were too great. He returned to his farm, and a year or two later died accidentally in a fire on the farm. He saved his life and lost it. He clung to his material wealth — but of what profit was it?

—*The Prairie Overcomer*

* * *

Rich, But Can't Eat

Said a rich man regretfully:
"I am not really to be envied. How can my wealth help me? I am 60 years old, and I cannot digest. I would give you all my millions if you could give me your youth and health. I'd gladly sell all to have half my life over again!"

—T. P. O'Connor

* * *

Holding It for Life's Short Day

"The wealthy owner of a large business in Sweden had been a poor boy. His task had been the tending of cattle. One day he wanted to be away and asked his sister to tend the cattle, promising to let her hold for the day a small coin, worth less than two annas, to be returned at night. She consented. The very sight of money was a rarity. She spent a long, hard day caring for his cattle, holding the bright coin, and returned it at night quite content with the day's pay. Later the brother, who had grown very wealthy, was telling the story. He had allowed the love of money to crowd out the Christ passion, to which he was not a stranger. He told the story with great glee, laughing at his sister's simplicity. My friend said quietly, 'That is all you get; you hold your wealth to the end of the day of your life; then you give it up and have as little as before, and the whole of your life is gone!' And the man's startled face showed he quite understood."

—*King's Business*

* * *

Priceless Things

The best things in life money cannot buy. One would not depreciate that value of money. It is a necessary part of our lives, and the ability to make it honestly and to spend it wisely is to be commended. But let us pause and think of those things that money cannot buy. What are they? Prayer, faith, peace, hope, appreciation of the good and the true and the beautiful — those things which we value most. Loyalty, dependability, sincerity and high Christian ideals make character, but where could you buy them?

The world is run on faith — faith in our families, in our work, in our friends — and faith cannot be bought! The sense of the presence of God — our Christian religion — cannot be bought or sold, but it is our most valuable possession, our greatest asset.

"Seek ye first the Kingdom of God, and His righteousness."

These priceless things, which money cannot buy, belong to the Kingdom of God.

—*War Cry*

* * *

A Choice of "Riches"

Some years ago there appeared one day in the same daily paper two accounts, one of an American woman who had just spent $70,000 for Paris dresses; and the other of a woman, a beautiful Christian character, who, being questioned in a legal matter, modestly admitted that she had given many millions of her estate to various righteous causes. "Well," as someone remarked, "it is a matter of taste — Paris gowns or heavenly crowns."

— *Christian Statesman*

* * *

Who Holds the Title?

"Are the lawyers still searching for a clear title to Oakdeen," asked John Kendricks of his friend. "Yes," responded De Costa, "they are still at it." They have traced the title back to Lord Mayor Woodroffe of England, who in 1660 took out a claim. But there is a prior claim, it seems, and I tell my wife that I should not be surprised to see Adam's name appearing on the title deed." "And even then," said Mr. Kendricks, "the title will not be clear; there is a prior claim. "Why, I thought Adam was the first man on this terrestrial ball!" said De Costa in surprise. "If we trace the title deeds of all estates to their origin, we shall find in the most ancient of all land records this entry, 'In the beginning God created the heaven and the earth,' and across every title deed that has been executed is God's signature: 'The earth is the Lord's, and the fulness thereof; the world, and they that dwell therein,'" said Kendricks. "Then, if God's signature is upon all property, where does

man's claim come in," asked De Costa. "We are at best but his tenants, and if we recognize his ownership, we are but squatters," answered Kendricks.

— *Moody Monthly.*

* * *

"De Lawd's Cow"

After many years of preaching the Gospel I sincerely believe that there is hardly any one thing that will soon reveal the character of men and women as the way in which they spend their money. Just tell me what you did with the money that passed through your hands during the past six months and it will not be hard to tell whether you are selfish or unselfish, godly or worldly, generous or grasping. The amount of money you have handled has nothing to do with it. It is the question of your attitude toward it.

Some years ago a couple of stock buyers in the South rode up to the home of an old colored man and noticed a fine milk cow grazing in the yard. One of them said, "Uncle, we would like to buy this cow. Is she yours," The old Negro replied, "No, sah, boss, dat ain't my cow. Hit's de Lawd's cow. I'm jest a-keepin' her fer Him."

That old man had grasped the great principle of stewardship. We really do not own anything. Whatever we seem to possess is just loaned to us for a little while, for "the earth is the Lord's and the fulness thereof."

— *Western Recorder*

ROMANS 8:28

"And we know that all things work together for good to them that love God, to them who are the called according to His purpose" (Romans 8:28).

When He Lost His Home

The story is told of an only survivor of a wreck who was thrown on an uninhabited island. After a while he managed to build himself a hut, in which he placed the little that he had saved from the wreck. He prayed to God for deliverance, and anxiously scanned the horizon each day to hail any passing ship. One day on returning from a hunt

for food he was horrified to find his hut in flames, — all he had had gone up in smoke. The worst had happened it seemed. But that which seemed to have happened for the worst was in reality for the best. The next day a ship arrived. "We saw your smoke signal," the captain said. If our lives are in God's hands "all things work together for good." — *Western Recorder*

Be Patient With God

"God's plans, like lilies pure and white,
   unfold,
We must not tear the close-shut leaves
   apart;
TIME will reveal the calyxes of gold."
                     Selected.

* * *

He Did What He Could

A young man accepted for the African missionary field reported at New York for "passage," but found on further examination that his wife could not stand the climate. He was heartbroken, but he prayerfully returned to his home and determined to make all the money he could to be used in spreading the Kingdom of God over the world. His father, a dentist, had started to make, on the side, an unfermented wine for the communion service. The young man took the business over and developed it until it assumed vast proportions — his name was "Welch," whose family still manufactures "grape-juice." He has given literally hundreds of thousands of dollars to the work of missions. Every job is missionary work when we interpret it by stewardship.
        —*The Presbyterian Advance*

* * *

Miss Saxe's Closed Door

I heard Miss Grace Saxe tell of her call to the foreign field. Her father was not anxious for her to go, but had consented. She had been accepted by a missionary board, her trunks were packed, her ticket bought, and she was ready to sail on a certain morning. The night before, her father was taken very ill, and by morning was not expected to live, and she knew she must give up going that day. She became very rebellious, and could not understand why God permitted the illness, especially when in a few days her father was well again. She was thrown into great darkness, sought her pastor, who had been with her in her experience of her call, and they prayed together for light. So, groping, she went on for days. At the end of a week there came the report of the vessel on which she was to have sailed being wrecked and everyone on board lost. Miss Saxe did not go to the foreign field, but has been a wonderful Bible teacher in this country, and has done missionary work not in her way, but in God's way; even to assisting in a great evangelistic campaign in the Orient. — Mother Ruth, in *The Sunday School Times.*

* * *

"Behind A Frowning Providence"

William Cowper, the great hymn writer, after his attempt at suicide had been frustrated, returned home and wrote:

"God moves in a mysterious way,
   His wonders to perform.
He plants His footsteps on the sea
   And rides upon the storm.

"Deep in unfathomable mines
   Of never-failing skill,
He treasures up His bright designs,
   And works His sovereign will.

"Ye fearful saints, fresh courage take!
   The clouds ye so much dread
Are big with mercy and shall break
   In blessing on your head.

"Judge not the hand by feeble sense,
   But trust Him for His grace,
Behind a frowning Providence,
   He hides a smiling face.

"His purposes will ripen fast,
   Unfolding every hour.
The bud may have a bitter taste,
   But sweet will be the flower.

"Blind unbelief is sure to err,
   And scan His work in vain;
God is His own interpreter,
   And He will make it plain."
              —*Gospel Herald*

* * *

"Glad To Be A Leper!"

Peking missionaries were astounded when an old man said: "I am glad I am a leper! For if I had not been a leper, I never would have come to this hospital and would never have learned to know Jesus. I had rather be a leper with Jesus Christ than be free from leprosy without Him."
        —*Sunday School Times*

Was It the Wrong Port?

Lord Clive, as a young man, in the spirit of adventure set out from his British home for India. The ship upon which he sailed was caught in a terrific storm, and continuous adverse gales drove it far off the course, until it finally limped into a South American harbor. There he had to remain for many months before being able to get passage to India. But during the long wait he acquired the Portuguese language, which qualified him when he did reach India to take an important position with the East India Company, ultimately resulting in his being appointed by the crown as Governor General of India. Do not deplore upsets; they may be God's messengers.

— *King's Business*

* * *

Why God Spoils Our Plans

Sir James Thornhill painted the cupola of that world-famous structure St. Paul's Cathedral in London. He was compelled to work while standing on a swinging scaffold far above the pavement. One day when he had finished a detail on which he had spent days of painstaking effort, he stopped and began to estimate his work. So well had he succeeded that he was lost in wonder and admiration. As he stood there gazing at the structure, he began to move backward slowly in order to get a better view, forgetting where he was. A man who was with him became suddenly aware that one more backward step would mean a fatal fall. Quick as a flash he made with his own brush a sweeping stroke across the picture. The abstracted artist stopped and rushed forward, crying out in anger and dismay; but when his companion explained his strange action the great artist burst into expressions of gratitude.

Some day we shall thank God for every loss sustained in this life, for every shattered idol, for every disrupted plan. — *Gospel Herald*

* * *

God's Harmonies!

A beautiful incident is told by a traveler of his visit to the Cathedral of Pisa. He stood beneath the wonderful dome and gazed with awe upon its graceful proportions. Suddenly, the great dome seemed full of harmony. "The waves of music vibrated to and fro," he said, "loudly beating against the walls, swelling into full accord like the roll of a great organ, and then dying away into soft, long-drawn far-reaching echoes, melting into stillness in the distance. It was only the guide who, lingering behind, had softly murmured a triple chord. But beneath that magic dome, every sound resolves into harmony. No discord can reach the summit of the dome and live; the trampling of feet, the murmur and bustle of the crowd are caught up, softened, harmonized, blended, and echoed back in music." If a dome, the work of man's hands can thus harmonize all discords, can we doubt that under the great dome of Heaven, God can make "all things work together for good to them that love" him? Every affliction, every tear, every grief and sorrow will be blended into harmony within the overarching dome of his grace, and be as the music of Heaven.

— *Christian Life Missionary*

* * *

When We Can't See It

A young lad had his arm broken at a neighbor's home and, lest he would frighten his mother, went to his father's place of business where his eldest brother called a doctor who gave the injured member the necessary attention. Then the two brothers went to tell their mother. A few tears relieved any shock, and then a younger brother about nine years old, always a solemn little fellow, came in with the words, "Well, Mother, 'All things work together for good to them that love God;' this is one of the times when we can't see it, but we know it's true."

—*Sunday School Times*

* * *

"I Learn"

"I learn as the years roll onward,
    And leave the past behind,
That much I have counted sorrow
    But proves that my Lord was kind;

That many a flower I longed for
  Had a hidden thorn of pain;
And many a rocky bypath
  Led to fields of golden grain."
                            —Selected

* * *

Disappointment

"Disappointment — His appointment,"
  Change one letter, then I see
That the thwarting of my purpose
  Is God's better choice for me.
His appointment must be blessing,
  Tho' it may come in disguise,
For the end from the beginning
  Open to His wisdom lies.

"Disappointment — His appointment,"
  "No good thing will He withhold;"
From denials oft we gather
  Treasures of His love untold.
Well He knows each broken purpose
  Leads to fuller, deeper trust,
And the end of all His dealings
  Proves our God is wise and just.

"Disappointment — His appointment,"
  Lord, I take it, then, as such,
Like the clay in hands of potter,
  Yielding wholly to Thy touch.
All my life's plan is Thy molding,
  Not one single choice be mine;
Let me answer, unrepining —
  "Father, not my will, but Thine."
                    —Civic Bulletin

* * *

His Best Year

The confidential secretary of a New
York merchant whose business ran into
thousands of dollars laid before his employer the company's annual financial
report. The merchant had known for
a long time just how it would look. "A
bad year, sir," the young man said in an
effort to speak comfortably, "but business will surely mount before long." In
silence, the merchant scanned the sheet.
Vast losses were tabulated, and the gains
were small. It appeared that, for him,
bankruptcy was imminent. When at
last he spoke, his voice was low and
steady. "It has been a good year, John,
— in spite of everything. I think it is
the best year I have ever had. Every
one of those figures 'in the red' represents hours of agony and prayer. Those

experiences have made me rich in hope,
so rich that I cannot despair over any
other loss. The future looks bright to
me, for God has said that 'no good thing
will he withhold from them that walk
uprightly.' " "May I tell you, sir," the
secretary remarked, "that it was your
steadiness under testing that made me
long to know Christ, as you know Him.
I agree with you, sir; it has been a good
year."   —King's Business

* * *

Looking Back We See

Who can look back on life and see
  Its intricate design;
Its strange and lovely tapestry
  Of changeful hue and line.
And, looking thus, can fail to find,
  In scenes of dull despair
How, still, some threads of brightness
    wind
Among the shadows there?

Who can look back and fail to see,
  When paths had grown most dark,
Most veiled in sombre mystery,
  That still there shone a spark —
A spark that led him on and on,
  Once more into the light.
Who can deny God makes the dawn
  More fair because of night?
                            —Selected

* * *

"It Was Gold!"

The floods washed away home and
mill — all the poor man had in the
world. But as he stood on the scene of
his loss, after the water had subsided,
broken-hearted and discouraged, he saw
something on the bank which the waters
had washed bare. "It looks like gold,"
he said. It was gold. The flood which
had beggared him made him rich. So it
is ofttimes in life. Sorrow strips off
loved possessions, but reveals the treasures of the love of God. We are sure,
at least, that every sorrow that comes
brings to us a gift from God, blessing
which may be ours, if we will accept it.
                            —J. R. Miller

* * *

No Accidents With God

Rowland V. Bingham, founder of the
Sudan Interior Mission, was a man

whose faith in God and His goodness was exercised in practical experience day by day.

Dr. Bingham was very seriously injured in an automobile collision in his sixtieth year — his head was severely cut, and a number of bones were broken. When he came to consciousness on the following day in a hospital, he asked the nurse what he was doing there. "Be very quiet," she replied, "for you have been in a frightful accident."

"Accident? Accident!" Dr. Bingham exclaimed. "There are no accidents in the life of a Christian. This is an incident."

* * *

A Handicap May Be A Blessing

The late President Theodore Roosevelt was very near-sighted. He always carried with him two pairs of glasses of different strength, one for near and the other for distant vision. During his last great political campaign he was shot in the city of Milwaukee by a man called Schrenk. The surgeon who was examining his wound handed him his steel spectacle case with the remark that it was due to its presence in his vest pocket that he owed his life. The case had broken the force of the bullet and had deflected its course from his heart. "Well, now, that's strange," said Mr. Roosevelt as he took the case with the shattered spectacles. "I've always considered the burden and handicap of having to carry those two pairs of glasses, especially these heavy ones that were in this case, as a very sore one, and here at last they have been the means of saving my life." We may not always know in this life the reason for the handicaps with which we may be afflicted. We are certain, however, that they are often blessings in disguise. Milton, blind, was much more of a poet than when he had his full sight. The imprisoned Bunyan was writing for the ages to come. Sometimes lameness comes to a man that he may be slowed up, live much longer and thereby continue his work. Countless are the illustrations which reveal to us that God is in the events of our lives to a greater extent than most of us imagine.

—*Watchman-Examiner*

Had He Lost All?

A young businessman who had been severely tested, and whose heart was again and again tempted to rebellion during the process of trial to which he was submitted, came to a Christian worker. His motherless babes, two and five years old, clung one to either hand. Though still in his early thirties, his hair was snow white from the hours of anguish through which he had passed. An income of twenty thousand dollars a year was gone. His capital was swept away. His home was gone; his car for sale. Stripped of everything but the two loved children, the big, broad-shouldered young father, towering over six feet, in the strength of a capable manhood, looked steadily at the worker, and said, "In looking back upon my sufferings, I find that God makes no mistakes."

—*Sunday School Times*

* * *

Singing If You Can

God never would send you the darkness
  If He felt you could bear the light;
But you would not cling to His guiding
    hand
  If the way were always bright,
And you would not care to walk by faith,
  Could you always walk by sight.

Then nestle your hand in your Father's,
  And sing, if you can, as you go;
Your song may cheer some one behind
    you
  Whose courage is sinking low;
And, well, if your lips do quiver —
  God will love you better so.

—*Selected*

* * *

"Thou Art My Pilot!"

Uncharted is the sea
  On which my bark must sail;
If tempests there shall be,
  Or quiet calms prevail,
I know not; but I know
Whatever wind may blow,
From east, north, south, or west,
'Twill all be for my best;
Fear does not shake my heart.
For thou my Pilot art!

I know that thou wilt all
  Thy promises fulfill,
Whatever may befall,
  'Twill not be for my ill;
I know that thou wilt guide
My bark through wind and tide,
That with my voyage past
I shall reach the port at last:
Fear does not shake my heart,
For thou my Pilot art!

—Wm. Gustave Polack, in
Gospel Herald

* * *

Not All Sweetness

The sound of an egg beater drew me into the kitchen one day, and there I found my mother at work . . . I began to watch what she was doing. I would find out just what she put into that chocolate cake that made it so good. There was chocolate, of course, and I reached for a little crumb that had fallen off the bar . . . It was bitter. I glanced at the other things on the table. There was a cupful of sour milk — surely Mother wasn't going to put that in the cake! . . . I saw her add it, along with some of that awful soda that she had given me once for stomachache. What kind of cake could she possibly make out of such things? . . . My nose turned up, but Mother only smiled and told me to wait and see. We were eating dinner. . . It was true that it looked as good as usual, but I tasted it carefully, a little crumb, then a larger crumb, and finally a whole bite. It couldn't have been better. I forgot all about the sour milk and asked for another piece. Life is not all sweetness — there is much that is bitter, and we cannot believe anything good will come from it. Certainly, all things are not good, but "all things work together for good." This is God's promise to them that love Him. Day by day He is making you what He wants you to be, and He will never put anything into your life by mistake.

—*Gospel Herald*

* * *

Lessons of the Year

For I learn as the years roll onward
  And leave the past behind,
That much I have counted sorrow

But proves that our God is kind;
That many a flower I longed for
  Had a hidden thorn of pain,
And many a rugged bypath
  Led to fields of golden grain.

So the heart from the hardest trial
  Gains the purest joy of all,
And the lips that have tasted sadness
  The sweetest songs that fall.
Then as joy comes after sorrow,
  And love's the reward of pain,
So after earth is Heaven,
  And out of our loss is gain.

—*Selected*

* * *

Absolute Submission

In a home for deaf mutes, a distinguished visitor was watching a class, when he suddenly requested that he might be permitted to ask a question and have the children answer it on the blackboard. And so he had the question translated into their sign language: "Could any of you children tell why it is that God has permitted you to be so strangely and sadly afflicted by the loss of your natural organs of speech and hearing?"

There was a great silence. The principal was much embarrassed. The teachers, feeling that it was a strange and pedhaps improper question to ask, hung their heads.

But one little lad raised his hand, and stepping to the blackboard, wrote: "Even so, Father; for so it seemed good in thy sight."

Tears fell from the eyes of the stranger, and the lesson was never forgotten. This is the foundation of all character and all morals; absolute submission of the will of man to the will of our Father in heaven.

—A. B. Simpson, in
Alliance Weekly

* * *

When We See the Other Side

Dr. Handley Moule, Bishop of Durham, visited West Stanley immediately after a terrible colliery explosion. He addressed the crowd at the pit's mouth, among whom were relatives of the entombed miners. "It is very difficult," he said, "for us to understand why God should let such an awful disaster happen, but we know Him and trust Him, and all will be right. I have at home an old bookmarker given me by my mother. It is worked in silk, and when I examine the wrong side or it, I see nothing but a tangle of threads. It looks like a big mistake. One would think that someone had done it who did not know what she was doing. But when I turn it over and look at the right side, I see there, beautifully embroidered, the letters, 'God is love!' We are looking at all this today," he continued "from the wrong side. Some day we shall see it from another standpoint and we shall understand."

—From *The Meaning of Sorrow*, by Dr. Handley Moule

* * *

Comforting Little Verse
What most you long and hope for
  Might only bring you pain;
You cannot see the future
  God's purpose to explain.
So ever trust thy Master;
  He doeth all things well;
He loveth more than heart can know
  And more than tongue can tell.
—*Selected*

SACRIFICE

How Spurgeon Showed His Love
A few years before the death of Spurgeon, an American lecture bureau tried to engage him to come to America and deliver fifty lectures, speaking in all the large cities of the country. As compensation, the bureau offered to pay all of Mr. Spurgeon's expenses, and all the expenses of his wife and his private secretary to come with him, from the time they left London until they returned, and, in addition, to pay $1,000 per night for each of his fifty lectures. But Mr. Spugeon promptly declined this tempting offer to make $50,000 in fifty days, saying, "I can do better. I will stay in London and try to save fifty souls." No wonder he succeeded so marvelously in winning souls! No wonder that at his death more than 12,000 converts rose up to bless his memory and thank God that Spurgeon ever lived!
—*Good News Broadcaster*

* * *

Nothing Less Than the Best
Before the 1939-45 war a school for the children of "untouchables" in India received a shipment of Christmas presents from English children each year. Each girl received a doll, "whose clothes took off and on!" and each boy a toy. One year the Doctor Sahib from a nearby mission hospital came to distribute the presents and told the children about a village not far away where the children had never heard of Jesus or of Christmas and suggested that they might each like to give one of their old toys to be taken to these other children. They readily agreed, and he came the next Sunday to receive them. The boys and girls filed past him and handed a doll or a toy each. *But* — it was the *new* presents that they gave. When asked why, a girl said, "Think what He gave for us, and what He has done for us. Could we give Him less than our best?" —*Sunday School Times*

* * *

How Livingston Took a Criticism
Misjudged by a fellow missionary, Livingstone gave up his house and garden at Mabotsa, with all the toil and money they had cost him, rather than have any scandal before the heathen, and began in a new place the labor of house and school building, and gathering the people around him. His colleague was so struck with his generosity that he said had he known his intention, he never would have spoken a word against him. Parting with his garden cost him a great pang. "I like a garden," he wrote, "but Paradise will make amends for all our privations here."
—*Dr. Peloubet*

No Ox for Plowing

One day a Korean missionary was with a friend who was traveling through the country. The friend was amused to see in a field a young man pulling a plough and an old man holding the handles.

"They must be very poor," remarked the friend.

"Yes," was the reply. "When the church was being built, they wanted to give something. So they sold their only ox and gave the money. That is why this spring they have to plow like that."

"What a sacrifice!" exclaimed the friend.

"They did not call it a sacrifice," replied the missionary. "They were glad to have an ox they could sell."
—*Union Story Paper*

* * *

She Wanted To Give All

In a Chinese school for blind children there was one girl who seemed too dull and stupid to be taught anything. A lady visitor asked how she might help. The nurse said: "Give that poor little girl a piece of money; she has never possessed a coin of her own." So the child received a five-cent piece, to her great delight. Each day she planned some fresh way of spending it, sometimes keeping it herself, and sometimes giving it to the nurse to take care of for her. Now a meeting was to be held at Foochow for the Bible Society, and this child knew that it supplied the school with Chinese Gospels in embossed type for the blind. She was too ill to go to the meeting, but she asked the nurse to take her five-cent piece and put it in the collection. The nurse said: "Half of it would be enough. It is all you have. Let me change it, and then you can give part and keep part." But the blind child insisted on giving all she had. She said, "No, I have never been able to give God anything before; I want to give it all."
—*Christian Life Sunday School paper*

* * *

Missionary Parents Needed

There was a race of parents that could raise a race of missionaries. Let me give you the instance of an old Moravian woman. A friend called upon her with sadness in his looks. He said to the mother, "Your son is gone." "Is Thomas gone to Heaven through the missionary life? Would to God He would call my son John!" Well, John did become a missionary and he fell. This time the committee were very sad; but before they opened their lips, the old woman anticipated the story and exclaimed, "Thank God! Would that He would call my last son William!" William went, too, and fell; then the noble woman exclaimed, "Would that I had a thousand sons to give to God!" Would that we had a thousand such mothers! Then would our missionary ranks be full.
—*Prairie Overcomer*

* * *

"Go Get Your Scars!"

It is said that when the knights of King Arthur's court, returned from the field of battle, if they did not bear in their bodies some scar of the battle, they were thrust forth by the king, with the command, "Go, get your scar!" How few of us can say with Jesus' faithful warrior, Paul, "I bear in my body the marks of the Lord Jesus" (Gal. 6:17); "Christ Jesus my Lord . . . for whom I have suffered the loss of ALL THINGS" (Phil. 3:8). Remember that when we appear before the judgment seat of Christ, to be judged for the deeds done in the body, Christ is not going to look for medals. He is going to look for SCARS!
—*W. B. K.*

* * *

"And Sailed Through Bloody Seas!"

Do not be indifferent to this thing called *Christianity*. It was created for you by the blood of Christ and preserved for you by the blood of the martyrs.

For almost the first three hundred years Christianity was a forbidden thing. Its adherents were publicly whipped, dragged by their heels through the streets until their brains ran out. Their limbs were torn off, their ears and noses were cut off, and their eyes were dug out with sharp sticks or burned out with hot irons. Sharp knives were run under their finger nails. Melted lead was poured over their bodies. They were drowned, beheaded, crucified, ground between stones, torn by wild beasts, smothered in lime kilns, scraped to death by sharp shells, and killed all day long.

In 1651 in Massachusetts, Rev. Obadiah Holmes, because he held a prayer meeting in his home, was ordered to be whipped by Governor Endicot. So severe was the whipping that for days he could lie only by resting on the tips of his elbows and his knees and yet when the last lash had fallen, he looked at his tormenters and through bloodstained lips cried, "Gentlemen, you have whipped me with roses!"

A redeeming Christ has given you a future filled with hope. Do not look lightly upon this thing called *Christianity*, which cost the Son of God His blood, and millions of His followers their lives.

—Dr. R. W. Ketchum

* * *

At His Mercy

George Atley, a young Englishman with the heart of a hero, was engaged in the Central African Mission. He was attacked by a party of natives. He had with him a Winchester repeating rifle with ten loaded chambers. The party was completely at his mercy. Calmly and quickly he summed up the situation. He concluded that if he killed them it would do the mission more harm than if he allowed them to take his life. So, as a lamb to the slaughter he was led; and when his body was found in the stream, his rifle was also found with its ten chambers still loaded.

—*Heart and Life Bulletin*

* * *

Salvation Army Sacrifices

When the *Empress of Ireland* went down with one hundred and thirty Salvation Army officers on board, one hundred and nine officers were drowned, and not one body that was picked up had on a life belt. The few survivors told how the Salvationists, finding there were not enough life preservers for all, took off their own belts and strapped them even upon strong men, saying, "I can die

better than you can;" and from the deck of that sinking ship flung their battle cry around the world — *Others!*

* * *

How the Apostles Died

All of the apostles were insulted by the enemies of their Master. They were called to seal their doctrines with their blood and nobly did they bear the trial. Schumacher says:

"Matthew suffered martyrdom by being slain with a sword at a distant city of Ethiopia.

Mark expired at Alexandria, after being cruelly dragged through the streets of that city.

Luke was hanged upon an olive tree in the classic land of Greece.

John was put in a caldron of boiling oil, but escaped death in a miraculous manner, and was afterward branded at Patmos.

Peter was crucified at Rome with his head downward.

James, the Greater, was beheaded at Jerusalem,

James, the Less, was thrown from a lofty pinnacle of the temple, and then beaten to death with a fuller's club.

Bartholomew was flayed alive.

Andrew was bound to a cross, whence he preached to his persecutors until he died.

Thomas was run through the body with a lance at Coromandel in the East Indies.

Jude was shot to death with arrows.

Matthias was first stoned and then beheaded.

Barnabas of the Gentiles was stoned to death at Salonica.

Paul, after various tortures and persecutions, was at length beheaded at Rome by the Emperor Nero."

Such was the fate of the apostles, according to traditional statements.

—*Christian Index*

* * *

Already Dead

When James Calvert went out to cannibal Fiji with the message of the Gospel, the captain of the ship in which he traveled sought to dissuade him. "You will risk your life and all those with you if you go among such savages," he said. Calvert's magnificent reply was, "We died before we came here." And yet he would have been the last to talk about a sacrifice; it was not a life of sacrifice, but of real pleasure.

—*King's Business*

* * *

Love's Great Sacrifice

The home of an English family was discovered on fire. They thought everybody was out but the baby. The mother saved her. For years as the child grew up the mother went about the house with her hands covered. The eldest of the servants had never seen her hands uncovered. But the daughter came into her room one day unexpectedly, and the mother sat there with her hands uncovered. They were torn and scarred and disfigured. Instantly the mother tried to cover them as the girl came forward, but she said, "I had better tell you about it. It was when the fire was in the house and you were in your cradle. I fought my way through the flames to get you. I wrapped you in a blanket and dropped you through the window, and somebody caught you. I could not go down the stairway, so I climbed out of the window. My hands were burnt, and I slipped and caught on the trellis work. When I fell, my hands were torn. The doctor did his best, but, my dear, *these hands were torn for you.*" And the girl, who had grown to womanhood, sprang toward her mother, took one hand and then the other, and buried her face in those hands, as she kept saying, "They are beautiful hands, beautiful hands."

—J. Wilbur Chapman

* * *

"The Child Apostle"

When the late Bishop of Madras was visiting Travancore, there was introduced to him a little slave girl by the title of "The Child Apostle." She had won this title by the zeal with which she talked of Christ to others. Her quiet, steady persistence in this had won several converts to Christ. But she had suffered persecution too brutal to re-

late. When she was introduced to the Bishop, her face, neck, and arms were disfigured and scarred by stripes and blows. As he looked at her, the good man's eyes filled, and he said, "My child, how could you bear this?" She looked up at him in surprise and said, "Don't you like to suffer for Christ, sir?"

—*Gospel Herald*

* * *

A Joyous Confirmation

A missionary in Africa writes: "I have dwelt four years alone in Africa, have been thirty times stricken with fever, have been attacked by rhinoceri and lions, have been ambushed by natives, have eaten everything from ants to rhinoceri, but I would gladly go through the same experience again for the joy of teaching these people to know the Saviour who gave His life a ransom for them." — *Gospel Herald.*

* * *

Dog Saves Master's Life!

The dog's name was Joker. One day Joker's master, a missionary, was walking through long grass in Africa. The path was only a foot wide. Curled up on the path was a huge snake! Rearing its head, the snake lunged straight for the missionary's eyes. When the snake was only a little distance from the missionary's face, the faithful dog sprang and got hold of the snake by its neck, not until the snake, however, had buried its fangs in the dog's nose. Joker tried to raise his head, but he could only put out his tongue. Slowly licking his master's hand, the faithful dog turned over DEAD! — W. B. K.

* * *

He Gave All He Had

Madame Chiang Kai-shek tells the story of a hero of the Chinese rice fields during an earthquake. From his hilltop farm he felt the quake and saw the distant ocean swiftly withdrawn from the old shore line, like some prodigious animal crouching back for a leap. He knew that the leap would be a tidal wave. In the valleys below, he saw his neighbors working low fields that would

be flooded. They must be gathered quickly to his hilltop. His rice barns were dry as tinder. So with a torch he set fire to them and rang the fire gong that hung beneath the eaves. His neighbors saw the smoke and rushed to help him. Then from their safe perch on the hill, they saw the waters cover over the fields they had just left. In a flash they knew their salvation and what it cost their benefactor. The monument they erected to his memory is still standing, bearing this motto, "He gave us all he had, and gave it gladly."
—*Young People's Weekly*

* * *

"If You Survive!"

When the Boxer movement, in China, was on, Horace Pitkin was among those whose death had been determined upon by the Boxer crowd. His wife and child were in this country and as they led him out to the place where he was to be beheaded, he said to a friend, "If you survive, tell my son that when he is twenty-five years of age, I want him to come out here and take my place as a missionary of the Lord Jesus."
— Dr. W. B. Riley

* * *

Self-Denial

Too little is known of the self-denial made by men and women, and especially by mothers, for the sake of helping others. Dr. James Franklin, while riding a Pullman, was addressed by a porter who told of how he felt called into the ministry but had ignored it because his brother also had a similar call. They were poor boys and could not see their way clear to prepare for the ministry. The porter said that they decided to work together. He would work and send his money to his brother, who later became Bishop Scott, an outstanding bishop of the Methodist Church. Dr. Franklin met Bishop Scott one day and told him of his having met his brother, a Pullman porter. "Yes," said the bishop, and the tears ran down his cheeks as he continued, "he is my brother, and may God bless him. I owe everything to him." — D. Carl Yoder.

* * *

John Wesley's Sacrifice

John Wesley, a classical scholar and gifted with a virile mind, gave himself fully to God and consecrated all his powers to his service. Possessed of a scholar's love for books, yet he spent the most of his life in the saddle and in the active duties of a most strenuous life. With a passionate love for art, especially for music and architecture, he turned away from their charms to blow the Gospel trumpet with all his might. With a more than ordinary longing for the sweets and comforts of human love, he rose above disappointments which would have crushed ordinary men, forgot his "inly-bleeding heart" (his own expression), and gave himself unreservedly to the work of binding up the broken-hearted. Visiting the beautiful grounds of an English nobleman, he said, "I, too, have a relish for these things; but there is another world." — *Sunday School Times*.

* * *

"I Will Be Your Missionary Still!"

"Recall the twenty-one years of my service; give me back its shipwrecks, give me its standings in the face of death, give me it surrounded by fierce savages with spears and clubs, give it back to me with arrows flying around me, Give it back to me with clubs knocking me down, give all this back to me, and I will be your missionary still."
— Rev. Thomas Chalmers

* * *

Sacrifice and Service

People talk of the sacrifice I have made in spending so much of my life in Africa. Can that be called a sacrifice which is simply paid back as a small part of a great debt owing to our God, which we can never repay? Is that a sacrifice which brings its own best reward in healthful activity, the consciousness of doing good, peace of mind, and a bright hope of a glorious destiny hereafter? Away with the word in such a view, and with such a thought! It was emphatically no sacrifice. Say rather it is a privilege.—Livingstone.

Sufficient

"How much is your salary?" A Mohammedan stood before the mission school teacher who himself had once followed the Crescent instead of the Cross." "Fifty cents a week," came the answer. "Why, you could get ten times that in a government school!" "Yes, but I teach not for money — I teach for God." "Well — but are those all the clothes the missionaries provide? Don't you have a robe also?" The humble teacher looked down at his cotton shirt and trousers. "No, these are sufficient," he replied. The Moslem shook his head. "I never thought there was anything to this Jesus religion," he observed thoughtfully, "but there must be, if a man will give up his robe and his lawful wage for it."

—*Wesleyan Missionary*

SALVATION

"You Wouldn't Let Me!"

Gypsy Smith said that once when a group of gypsies were forced to cross a swollen stream a great number of them were drowned. One young man made a desperate attempt to save his mother who kept clinging to him. Several times he pushed her away, saying, "Let go, Mother, and I can save you." But she would not heed and was lost. At the funeral the son stood by his mother's grave and said over and over, "How hard I tried to save you, Mother, but you wouldn't let me!" How hard God tried to save the Israelites, but they wouldn't let Him, and how often He tries to turn us from our follies, but we refuse to allow Him to do it.

—*Quiet Hour*

* * *

When the Word Dawned

When Dr. Willis R. Hotchkiss went to Central Africa, he had great trouble to find a word that would explain to them the Saviour who died to save them. Over two years had passed, but this magic word "Saviour" he could not translate clearly and adequately. One night he was sitting with some of the natives around their campfire, when Kikuvi, the most intelligent of the natives, began to tell about Mr. Krieger, who had been attacked by a lion and badly torn. Kikuvi had come to his rescue and had driven the lion away. Kikuvi modestly said, "*Bwana nukuthaniwan na Kikuvi* [The master was saved by Kikuvi]." The missionary leaped for joy. At last he had heard the precious word. He immediately changed the verb from the passive to the active form, and said, "*Ukuthania Bwana?* [You saved the master?]" This proving correct, the missionary said: "Why, Kikuvi, this is the word I have been trying to get you to tell me these many days, because I wanted to tell why Jesus, the Son of God, came to this earth." "Oh," Kikuvi interrupted, his black face lighting up as he turned to the missionary: "I see it now. I understand! Jesus came to *kuthania* [save] us from our sins, and to deliver us from the hands of *Muima* [Satan.]" The moment the word "Saviour" had dawned on his darkened vision, all the scattered fragments of truth that had been floating through his mind became one glorious revelation. — From Esther D. Hooey, in *Sunday School Times*.

* * *

Three Things Worth Knowing

D. L. Moody told: "An old man got up in one of our meetings and said, 'I have been forty-two years learning three things.' I pricked up my ears at that. I thought if I could find out in three minutes what a man had taken forty-two years to learn, I should like to do it. The first thing he said he had learned was that he could do nothing toward his own salvation. 'Well,' I said to myself, 'that is worth learning.' The second thing he found out was that God did not require him to do anything. Well, that was worth finding out, too.

And the third thing was that the Lord Jesus Christ had done it all, that salvation was finished, and that all he had to do was to *take* it. Dear friends, let us learn this lesson. Let us give up struggling and striving, and accept salvation at once." — *Moody Monthly*.

* * *

Religion Isn't Salvation

Pandita Ramabai, the noted Christian leader of India, tells how she followed the religions of her country during her childhood days and right up until after she was married and had grown to womanhood, and of how they never satisfied. One day she heard about Christianity, and she said, "That is what I want. Christianity will satisfy the longings of my heart. I will embrace the Christian religion." Accepting Christianity, she sailed for England, where she was baptized and later confirmed. She joined a church in England, and for eight years lived a most exemplary Christian life. One night she happened to be listening to a message on the new birth. Never before had she been told that she must be born again, born from above. She was convicted, and right there and then she accepted Jesus Christ as her personal Saviour, and passed out of death into life. This is her testimony in her own words: "I found the Christian religion," she said, "but did not find the CHRIST of the religion." She had embraced Christianity, but she had not accepted Jesus Christ. — "Salvation versus Religion," in the *Christian Digest*.

* * *

Better Than Gradual Cleansing

The children's father had not yet learned that it was Christ who could make us clean within and Christ who could keep our hearts pure. Little Mary knew it, and so she prayed, "Make me gooder and gooder and gooder till there is no bad left." It is the Lord Jesus who will make us pure within if we let him. — *Illustrator*.

Life Better Than Religion

Christ Jesus came into the world not to establish a religion, but to give life.

In the Gospel of John the word "life" occurs forty-four times, and the word "religion" not once. Dr. Scofield once had occasion to tell a young minister that he did not believe he ever had been born again. In astonishment the young man said, "Why, I got religion ten years ago at such a place." "That is interesting," the older minister answered; "and while you were getting religion, why didn't you get saved?" "Why, isn't getting religion getting saved? Didn't Jesus Christ come to bring religion?" "No. He himself tells us why he came: 'I am come that they might have life.'" The conversation led to the two men kneeling in prayer, and the young minister accepted Christ as his personal Saviour in a real way.

—*Sunday School Times*

* * *

"You Can Lippen Yourself to Him"

In his *Journal*, David Livingstone tells of the home-going of his mother. In her great weakness her mind had been troubled as to her acceptance with God. "Seeing the end was near," he writes, "Sister Agnes said, 'The Saviour has come for you, mother. You can lippen yourself to Him?' She replied, 'Oh, yes.'" "Lippen" is an old English word, stil in use in Scotland. It signifies repose, reliance, rest. This is what the Saviour requires from the sinful seeking soul. Then, let us "lippen" to Him.

—David M. McIntyre, in *Christ the Way*

* * *

When We Cease To Struggle

A drowning boy was struggling in the water. On the shore stood his mother in an agony of fright and grief. By her side stood a strong man seemingly indifferent to the boy's fate. Again and again did the suffering mothed appeal to him to save her boy, but he made no move. By and by the desperate struggles of the boy began to abate. He was losing strength. Presently he arose to the surface weak and helpless. At once the man leaped into the stream and brought the boy in safety to the shore. "Why did you not save my boy sooner?" asked the now grateful mother. "Madam, I could not as long as he struggled. He would have dragged us both to certain death. But when he grew weak and ceased to struggle, then it was easy to save him." It is when we cease from our own works and depend helplessly upon Him that we realize how perfectly able He is to save without any aid from us.

—James H. McConkey

* * *

Necessary — and Enough

In a hospital ward, a lady missionary found an undersized and undeveloped little Irish boy, whose white, wizened face and emanciated form excited her deepest sympathy. His own soul's need was put before him, and he was awakened to some sense of his lost condition, insomuch that he commenced seriously to consider how he might be saved. Brought up a Romanist, he thought and spoke of penance and confessional, of sacraments and church, yet never wholly leaving out Christ Jesus and His atoning work. One morning the lady called again upon him, and found his face aglow with a new-found joy. Inquiring the reason, he replied with assurance born of faith in the revealed Word of God, "O missis, I always knew that Jesus was necessary; but I never knew till yesterday that He was enough!"

—Dr. Harry A. Ironside

* * *

Choosing the Right Priest

The incident occurred in a city restaurant. The men at one of the tables were conversing on the subject of religion, and the argument grew so lively that it was impossible for those at the nearest tables not to hear. The argument was as to whether salvation was by works or grace. A Roman Catholic in the party insisted that no man can know he is saved until he dies, and as a final argument he exclaimed, "Well, all I can say is this, I have placed myself in the hands of my priest, and he is re-

sponsible for my salvation." At this point a gentleman arose from his table, and lifting his hat, said: "Gentlemen, I believe I am well known in the law courts and in this room. I could not help hearing the argument, and I feel bound to say that our Roman Catholic friend is quite logical in what he says. I also have placed myself in the hands of my Priest and He is responsible for my salvation. The mistake our friend has made is that he has chosen the wrong priest. My Priest is the Lord Jesus Christ."

—*Sunday School Times*

* * *

What the Old Clock Needed

A man owned a clock which he prized very highly, but one day it stopped, and he couldn't get it to go again. In order to make it work he tried different things without success. First he tried heavier weights. This, however, did not help, but rather oppressed the machinery. Then he took away the old face and put on a new one, but this made no difference. Still the clock would not go. Then he tried new hands, but this, too, failed to induce the clock to go. The owner's little boy had been an interested spectator of his father's efforts to make the clock go. At last the little boy said, "Daddy, I think the poor clock needs a new inside."

I wonder if any of you have been making good resolutions finding you cannot keep them, trying to do good, but somehow or other you have failed. Stop trying. You must begin with the New Birth. "Ye must be born again." (*John* 3:3,7).

— *Gospel Herald*

* * *

A Problem

A young man distinguished for his mathematical attainments was fond of challenging his fellow students to a trial of skill in solving difficult problems. One day a classmate came into his study, and, laying a folded paper before him, said: "There is a problem I wish you would help me solve," and immediately left the room. The paper was eagerly unfolded, and there, instead of a question in mathematics were traced the lines, "What shall it profit a man, if he shall gain the whole world, and lose his own soul? Or what shall a man give in exchange for his soul?"

With a gesture of impatience, he tore the paper to atoms, and turned again to his books. But in vain he tried to shake off the impressions of the solemn words he had read. The Holy Spirit pressed home convictions of guilt and danger, so that he could find no peace, till he found it in believing in Jesus.

—*Elim Evangel*

* * *

The One Insurance He Had Neglected

A little boy climbed up on his father's knee, and, looking up into his face, asked, "Papa, is your soul insured?" "Why do you ask that question, Sonny?" "Why, Papa, I heard Uncle George say that you had your house insured and that you had insured your barn and your life, but he was afraid you had not thought about insuring your soul and he is afraid you will lose it. Papa, won't you go and get it insured right away?" The father bowed his head and was silent. He owned broad acres of land, and his buildings were all covered with insurance. He had insured his life for the maintenance of his wife and little son; yet not one thought had he given to his own soul. And "what shall it profit a man, if he shall gain the whole world, and lose his own soul?" ,

—*Sunday School Times*

* * *

In the Lamb's Book of Life

In the Chapel of St. George, in Westminster Abbey, is a memorial of World War II. It consists of four bound volumes that contain the names of the 60,000 civilians who were killed in the city of London by enemy action. One volume lies open on the shrine and a light shines down upon the typescript names that appear on that opened page. Each day a page is turned. Thus will the names of those who were rich or poor, titled or of the common people, old or young, healthy or ill, sound of body

or crippled, famous or infamous, stand together to be revealed in the light for all to see as a page of the book is turned each day. It is a book of death. There is another book — the Book of Life. It is in Heaven. In that Book, too, will be found the names of men and women from all classes and conditions on the earth. All will be in the light, and all will be honored of God. For the Book of Life will reveal, in that coming day, the names of those who through faith in God and His Christ will have been regenerated from death to life.

—*Our Hope*

* * *

The Lack

A young artist had wrought long upon an angel statue, and then concealed himself that he might hear what the master Michelangelo would say about it. The master looked upon it awhile, with breathless suspense, and the young artist waited, expecting his verdict. He heard Michelangelo say, "It lacks only one thing." So nearly brokenhearted did the young sculptor become that he could neither eat nor sleep until a friend of his in deep concern for him made his way to Michelangelo's studio and inquired what it was the statue lacked. The great artist said, "Man, it lacks only life; with life it would be as perfect as God Himself could make it." Many cannot see the difference between a man's morality and a Christian's righteousness. Why a moral man should not simply grow better and better until he is good enough to enter the Kingdom of God, they say they cannot see. A man's morality is the mere outward adornment of the flesh; a Christian's righteousness is the fruit of an indwelling Spirit — the Spirit of Christ.

—W. E. Biededwolf, in
"The Man Who Said He Would"

* * *

Struck Down To Be Saved

A telephone linesman gives his friend "Slim" credit for saving his life thus. "Sometimes new poles are green, and watersoaked, and will conduct electricity," he explained. "A short time ago my gang was sent to replace a pole that had been badly burned. The new pole . . . was wet and green, the street was wet, and overhead was a high line carrying 33,000 volts. We were hoisting the new pole. . . . I had thoughtlessly seized the butt end of the new pole as it swung clear of the ground and was guiding it into place when suddenly one of the boys made a run for me and knocked me sprawling. I arose from the sloppy street, wet, muddy, and ready for fight. . . . He pointed aloft to where I saw the new pole had hit the lower high-line wire. I also saw instantly that had he not taken such a quick action in knocking me clear of the pole, I would have been a 'goner.' " Does God not often strike down sinners, as He did Paul on the road to Damascus, that He might get them to listen to His voice and so might become saved from the wrath to come?

—*Gospel Herald*

* * *

A Queen's Faith

John Townsend wrote a letter to Queen Victoria, urging her to read John 3:16; and Romans 10:9-10, so that she might know that the eternal life promised in the Bible is sure both for the present and the future. About two weeks later Mr. Townsend received the following reply:

"Your letter of recent date received, and in reply I would state that I have carefully and prayerfully read the portions of Scripture referred to. I believe in the finished work of Christ for me, and trust by God's grace to meet you in that Home of which He said, 'l go to prepare a place for you.' "

—(Signed) Queen Victoria

* * *

The Indian's Answer

An Indian and a white man were brought under deep conviction of sin by the same sermon. The Indian was immediately led to rejoice in pardoning mercy. The white man was for a long time in distress, almost to despair. But he was at last brought to a sweet sense of his sin forgiven. Some time after, meeting his red brother, he said to him:

"How is it that I should be so long under conviction, when you found peace at once?" "O brother," replied the Indian, "me tell you! There comes along a rich prince. He propose to give you a new coat; you look at your coat and say, 'I don't know; my coat look pretty good, it will do a little longer.' He then offers me a new coat. I look at my old blanket; I say, this good for nothing, and accept beautiful garment. Just so, brother, you try to keep your own righteousness, you won't give it up; but I, poor Indian, had none, so I glad at once to receive the righteousness of God — the Lord Jesus Christ."

—*Scattered Seed*

* * *

His Part — and God's

A colored man rose in a meeting to give his testimony to the saving grace of God. He told how the Lord had won his heart and given deliverance from the guilt and power of sin. He spoke of Christ and His work but said nothing of any efforts of his own. The leader of the meeting was of a legalistic turn of mind, and when the Negro's testimony was ended, he said: "Our brother has only told us of the Lord's part in his salvation. When I was converted there was a whole lot I had to do myself before I could expect the Lord to do anything for me. Brother, didn't you do your part first before God did His?" The other was on his feet in an instant and replied: "Yes, sah, Ah clear done forgot. Ah didn't tell you 'bout my part, did I? Well, Ah did my part for over thirty years, runnin' away from God as fast as evah my sins could carry me. That was my part. An' God took aftah me till He run me down. That was His part."

—Dr. Harry A. Ironside

* * *

To Be Had for the Asking

A few days after the Civil War had been officially ended, a man was riding along a road in West Virginia. Suddenby a soldier, clad in a dirty and tattered Confederate uniform, sprang out of a thicket, seized the horse's bridle, and with twitching face demanded, "Give me bread! Give me bread! I don't want to hurt you, but give me bread — I'm starving." The man on horseback replied, "Then why don't you go to the village and get food?" "I don't dare — they will shoot me," was the soldier's answer. "What for?" inquired the man; "tell me your trouble." Whereupon the Confederate soldier related that he had deserted his company several weeks before. Upon approaching the Union pickets, however, he had been informed that no fugitives from Lee's army were to be taken in. What was he to do? If he returned to his company, he would be shot as a deserter. In desperation he had taken to the woods and lived there on roots and berries until starvation had driven him to the point of madness. The man on horseback listened, and then exclaimed: "Don't you know the war is over? Lincoln has pardoned the whole Confederate army. You can have all the food you want." Taking a newspaper from his pocket, he showed the account of Lee's surrender and the President's proclamation of amnesty. With a shout of joy, the soldier dropped the bridle and ran for the village. That starving deserter did not know that the bread for which he hungered had been available to him for some time and could have been had for the asking. In his ignorance he had been self-deprived. Thus it is with the Bread of Life and many a hungry heart. Oh, if your soul is afflicted with a gnawing emptiness, let me assure you that the Lord Jesus Christ may be had for the asking.

— Dr. Vernon C. Grounds, in
Our Hope

* * *

Only ONE Way!

A woman who was a very busy church worker waited for D. L. Moody after he had told a group of church workers some very plain truths from God's Word. "Mr. Moody," said the angry woman, "do you mean to tell me that I, an educated woman, taught from childhood in good ways, and all my life interested in the church and doing good, must enter Heaven the same way as the worst criminals of our day?" "No, madam,"

said Mr. Moody. "I don't tell you at all: *God does.* He says everyone who would enter Heaven, no matter how good they think they are, or how well educated, or zealous in good works, *must be born again."*

— *Sunday School Times*

* * *

When We Try to Help God

An evangelist could not convince a lady that all the good things she did would not avail in God's sight. Being very wealthy, she gave a supper to some poor people, and also provided clothes for them. An inspiration struck the evangelist, and he said to her: "If one of the guests thanked you very much for the clothes, but said: 'I must make some small return,' and rolled up his old clothes in a parcel and asked you to accept them in return, would you be pleased?" At once she said, "No." Then it dawned on her how useless were all her efforts to make herself better, and she accepted the Lord as her Saviour and King.

—*Christian Herald*

* * *

Second Birth

I never loved the pleasant earth
So much as since my second birth.
The shy forget-me-not's soft blue
Seems bits of Heaven shining through.
The golden buttercup's bright face
Proclaims the glory of His grace.
His precious Blood that washes all
The red of maples in the fall —
My sin forever far away.
As white as hawthorn buds in May —
The saint's new, shining, linen dress —
The robe of His own righteousness.
I touch the pansy's purple face —
His kingly majesty I trace.
Green pastures breathe refreshment, rest,
And sweet communion on His breast;
While bird song from the orchard trees
Suggest celestial harmonies.
I see in river, hill, and glen
New charms since I've been born again!

—Lois Reynolds Carpenter

"Just Ask For Them!"

During the Spanish War, Colonel Roosevelt commanded a regiment of rough-riders in Cuba. He became much attached to his men and was greatly concerned when a number of them fell sick.

Hearing that Miss Clara Barton (the lady who devoted herself to the work of nursing the wounded soldiers) had received a supply of delicacies for the invalids under her care, Colonel Roosevelt requested her to sell a portion of them to him for the sick men of his regiment.

His request was refused. The Colonel was very troubled; he cared for his men, and was willing to pay for the supplies out of his own pocket.

"How can I get these things," he asked. "I must have proper food for my sick men."

"Just ask for them, Colonel."

"Oh," said Roosevelt, his face breaking into a smile, "that's the way, is it? Then I do ask for them." And he got them at once.

Have you asked the Lord Jesus to come into your heart, and save you?

—W. B. K.

* * *

How To Understand Genesis

Pastor Philpott was once asked by a ministerial association to present a paper on the subject, "The Deepest Need of Man." He took care to embody in that address nearly all of the third chapter of Romans, and needless to say his presentation did not meet with the approval of many present. At a farewell supper for a minister, a little later, one took occasion to pick an argument with him about it. He declined to be drawn into a discussion, but his questioner persisted: "Seriously, I have been thinking of what you were saying the other day, and I have been wondering what you would do if one of the students from the college, greatly perplexed, requested you to explain the first three chapters of Genesis. How would you deal with him?" "Well," Dr. Philpott said, "I would ask him if he knew anything about the third chapter

of John's Gospel." "Why, what has that to do with it!" He replied, "Doctor, it has everything to do with it. God does not begin with a sinner at the first three chapters of Genesis. He begins at the third chapter of John — 'Except a man be born again, he cannot see the kingdom of God.' When he has experienced the change of heart that Christ Himself emphasized was absolutely necessary to the understanding of things spiritual, he will have no difficulty whatever with the first three chapters of Genesis."

—*Moody Church News*

* * *

Made — Not Bought

The Rev. Stuart McNairn told in a meeting, that at one town in Argentina, the Roman Catholics had built a magnificent church, but they had not yet been able to open it. Why? Because they could not afford to buy any saints to put in it. But yet a little way down the road in a little mission hall, God was making saints, creating them, not out of plaster, but through the regenerating power of the blood of Christ.

—*Christian Herald*

* * *

Can You Answer This?

A Welsh minister, beginning his sermon, leaned over the pulpit and said with a solemn air. "Friends, I have a question to ask. I cannot answer it. You cannot answer it. If an angel from heaven were here, he could not answer it. If a devil from hell were here, he could not answer it."

Every eye was fixed on the speaker, who proceeded. "The question is this, *"How shall we escape, if we neglect so great salvation?"'*

—*Free Methodist*

* * *

No Hope in Ourselves

I remember shortly after I began to preach I had a large Sunday school. We had the regular Gospel lessons, and I always met my Sunday school teachers and went over the lesson with them.

Whatever else I neglected, I never neglected that. Once I pointed out to them that it was a wonderful lesson for bringing the children to Christ, and I said to them, "Now do it." As I went about next Lord's Day here and there, my heart almost broke. They were asking the children, "Don't you think you ought to be a better boy?" A heathen philosopher could tell a child that. Our message is about a God who "so loved the world that he gave his only begotten Son." Are we telling people, "Don't you think you could be a better boy if you would join the church?"

—Dr. C. I. Scofield

* * *

Stop Trying

I remember a lady in the north of England who became quite angry when I made this statement: "None in this congregation will be saved until they stop trying to save themselves." Down she came from the gallery, and said to me, "You have made me perfectly miserable." "Indeed," I said, "how is that." "Why, I always thought that if I kept on trying, God would save me at some time; and now you tell me to stop trying. What then am I to do?" "Why let the Lord save you."

—D. L. Moody

* * *

More Than a New Coat

"Socialism," declared a street orator, "can put a new coat on a man!" "Jesus Christ," cried a voice in the crowd, "can put a new man in the coat, and that is better still!"

—Onward

* * *

A Prince and a Saviour

A Hindu woman discovered that she was a great sinner and that God is holy and cannot pass by sin. She often said, "I need some very great prince to stand between my soul and God."

After a little while she heard that the Bible contained the account of a Saviour who died for sinners. So she asked a pundit to read the Bible to her. He began at the 1st chapter of Matthew, and as he read the list of names in the geneology of Christ, the woman thought, "What a wonderful Prince this Jesus must be to have such a long line of ancestors." And when the pundit read, "Thou shalt call His Name *Jesus*: for He shall save His people from their sins," the woman exclaimed, "Ah, this is the Prince I want! This is the Prince I want!"

—Gospel Stories for the Young

* * *

"O, Let Him In!"

A picture of the Lord Jesus knocking at the door of a heart was taken one day by a parish visitor to a house where a father and mother lived with their small son. Some impulse made the mother pin the picture up in their little kitchen, and when the small boy came in from school, he was very interested in it. His mother was too busy with the dinner to answer his questions, but presently Father came in from work. "Who is the Man, Daddy, and why is He knocking at the door?" the little fellow asked again and again. The father tried to ignore the question, but it was asked again and again with great persistence, and at last he replied that it was the Lord Jesus Christ knocking at a door. "Then why don't they let Him in?" asked the little boy, wonderingly.

Dinner came just then, and the father managed to change the subect, but again and again during the days which followed the little lad asked the same question: "*Why* don't they let Him in?" The question began ringing in the father's ears, until at last one day he fell on his knees and cried: "Lord Jesus, it's the door of *my* heart at which You are knocking. Please forgive me for keeping You waiting so many years. The door is open — oh, come right in and take possession!"

—Gospel Herald

* * *

The Change Came the Other Way

An Italian woman, whose husband had accepted the Gospel and joined a Protestant church, was asked, "Is it true that your husband has changed his religion?" "No," answered she, "but his religion has changed him. Formerly he had no religion, but now he has accepted one that must be very good, because it has changed him so. You must have noticed that he does not get drunk." — *King's Business*.

* * *

The Blind Man's "Mistake"

There is a story told of a poor blind man who stood on a bridge over a canal in the City Road, London, reading aloud from an *embossed Bible* to any who would listen. A gentleman on his way home stopped on the outskirts of the crowd to see what attracted so many loungers. Just then the poor man, who was reading in the fourth chapter of the Acts, lost his place, and, while trying to find it, kept repeating the last clause he had read. "None other name —none other name — none other name." Some smiled at the blind man's embarrassment, but this gentleman went away very thoughtful. He was at that very moment inquiring the way of life, and in the mood to be influenced by a word spoken in season. The chance word haunted him, and before morning he had surrendered to its power. "I see it all!" he cried. "I have been trying to be saved by my own works, my repentance, my prayers, my reformation. I see my mistake. It is Jesus who alone can save. To him will I look."

—From *The Pastor His Own Evangelist*, by Goodell

* * *

It Goes Deeper Than the Hands

There is a story of a colored man who came to a watchmaker and gave him the hands of a clock, saying: "I want yer to fix up dese hans. Dey jes' doan' keep no mo' kerrec' time for mo' den six monfs." "Where is the clock?" answered the watchmaker. "Out at de house on Injun Creek." "But I must have the clock." "Didn't I tell yer dar's nuffin' de matter wid de clock 'ceptin' de hans? And I done brought 'em to you. You jes' want the clock so you can tinker with it and charge me a big price. Gimme back dem hans." And so saying, he went off to find some reasonable watchmaker. Foolish as he was, his caution is very like that of those who try to regulate their lives without being made right on the inside. And their reason for not putting themselves into the hands of the Lord is very similar to the reason the colored man gave. They are afraid the price will be too great." They say, "We only wish to avoid this or that habit." But the Master Workman says, "I cannot regulate the hands unless I have the heart."

—*The Way of Faith*

* * *

It's a Fact!

A Calcutta paper relates that recently a young Brahman came to the house of a missionary for an interview. In the course of the conversation he said: "Many things which Christianity contains I find in Hinduism; but there is one thing which Christianity has and Hinduism has not."

"What is that?" the missionary asked.

His reply was striking. "A saviour."

—*Power*

* * *

Experience Speaks

An old man, in talking to a young friend of mine, was reminiscing. "Son," he said, "I'd like to tell you about my life. I was christened soon after I was born, and I became a christened sinner. As I grew older, I wandered away from the church and began to engage in the pleasures of the world, and I became a sinful sinner. However, as I began to think about my life, I realized that I should do something about it, and I became a church sinner. Then, one happy day, my life was completely changed when I accepted the Lord Jesus Christ as my own personal Saviour, and I became a saved sinner. You know, son, a saved sinner is the only kind of a sinner that can find real joy in this world, and the only kind of a sinner that the Lord can welcome into Heaven."

— Clifford Bedell

Only Three Minutes!

I went to see a young man who was near his end. Seeing the time was short, I came at once to the all-important subject: "Friend, I see that you are very ill — are you prepared for what is before you?" "Wish I only were," he replied, giving me a look of despair. "If I could but be spared for two or three weeks I believe I might be prepared — but, the doctor tells me, I cannot live but for only a few hours probably." "Three weeks," I said; "why do you want three weeks?" Then he went on to give me his idea of preparation and conversion, and added, "All of which must occupy some weeks." "What!" I exclaimed. "Three weeks in order to be saved? Let me tell you that you may be saved, yes, in three minutes" — and so saying I opened the Word of God and read, "As many as received him, to them he gave power to become the sons of God, even to them that believe on his name." Inviting Jesus into his heart, he was saved instantly! Shortly, he went into eternity thanking and praising the Lord for saving him!

— Dr. A. J. Gordon

* * *

The Rheims Cathedral

The Cathedral of Rheims was known the world over for its sculptured beauty. There was widespread horror when it was destroyed during the war by deliberate bombardment. During the years which have elapsed since the signing of the armistice, great efforts have been carried on for its restoration, and it was reopened and reconsecrated in the middle of July of this year. "Even during the war," says the architect, "the people of Rheims worked indefatigably after each bombardment to save the broken statues, the bits of sculpture, and the slivers of glass from the smashed windows." Now these have again been combined. The famed "smiling angel," which was picked up in 113 pieces, is standing on her old place by the left door, and it is impossible to see where she has been cemented together again. The lead sheets which covered the roof had been melted during the fire which burnt the building. The melted metal poured over the gargoyles, and lodged in many crevices. This was collected and stored, and again has been used for its original purpose. The fragments of glass, carefully preserved, have taken years to piece together. Wherever possible, the original glass has been used; where it no longer exists, the colors have been perfectly matched. The delicate pinnacles and curving Gothic arches rise again in their original grace, though the carved garlands and minute handiwork of thirteenth century workmen has been burned away.

Thus, also, God can take a human life, which has been defaced and almost destroyed by sin, and restore it into a new edifice for the praise of the glory of His grace, if it be only fully yielded to Him. — *Alliance Weekly.*

* * *

Salvation At Hand

A night of terror and danger because of their ignorance was spent by the crew of a vessel off the coast of New Jersey in the winter of 1888. Just before dark a bark was discovered drifting helplessly, and soon struck her bow so that she was made fast on a bar and in momentary danger of going down. A line was shot over the rigging of the wreck by the life-saving crew, but the sailors did not understand that it was a line so connecting them with the shore that they might seize it and escape. All signs failed to make them understand this.

So all night the bark lay with the big waves breaking over it, while the crew, drenched and shivering, shouted for help. In the morning they discovered how unnecessarily they had suffered, and how *all night the line lay right in their reach by which they might have been saved.*

—A. J. Gordon

* * *

Christ Makes the Difference

Heaven above is softer blue,
   Earth around is sweeter green!
Something lives in every hue
   Christless eyes have never seen:

Birds with gladder songs o'erflow,
Flowers with deeper beauties shine,
Since I know, as now I know,
I am His, and He is mine.

           —Wade Robinson

* * *

Carrying or Carried?

Friends, you have all known me as a devout Roman Catholic," said a Belgian who was converted recently. "I used to go to confession and communion, but I had to acknowledge that after all I had no peace. I found that a God whom I could carry" — he meant the wafer given to Catholics at Communion — "was unable to help me. In order to be helped I needed a God who could carry me, and such a God I have found in the person of my blessed Saviour, the Lord Jesus Christ."

        —Sunday School Times

* * *

Only Two Religions

While presenting the Gospel on the street of a California city, we were often interrupted about as follows: "Look here, sir! There are hundreds of religions in this country, and the followers of each sect think theirs the only right one. How can poor plain men like us find out what really is the truth?" We generally replied something like this: "Hundreds of religions, you say? That's strange; I've heard of only two." "Oh, but you surely know there are more than that?" "Not at all, sir. I find, I admit, many shades of difference in the opinions of those comprising the two great schools; but after all there are but two. The one covers all who expect salvation by doing; the other, all who have been saved by something done. So you see the whole question is very simple. Can you save yourself, or must you be saved by another? If you can be your own savior, you do not need my message. If you cannot, you may well listen to it."

        —H. A. Ironside, in
          Gospel Herald

Something More Required

A minister called to see a lady who was uniting with his congregation. After he left, the lady turned to her husband and said, "There must be something wrong." "Why?" asked the man. "That minister made me feel so self-satisfied," she said, "and congratulated me on being what he called a 'good living woman.' I'm sure something more is required of us by God, but I'm so ignorant of the Bible, I don't know what." "From out of my far-away childhood Sunday school memories," said the husband, "there comes to my mind a verse something about 'not of works, lest any should boast.' If I were you I would find out more before you join that man's church." "I will," said the lady, and she did, and found Christ.

        As told by the lady

* * *

He Knew A Good Proposition

I was holding a meeting in St. Louis. At the close of a noon meeting a keen appearing businessman approached me, saying, "You are speaking to the most ungodly man in St. Louis." "Praise God!" I said. "Do you mean to say you are glad that I am bad?" "No," I said, "but I am certainly glad to find a man that acknowledges that he is a sinner." "Mr. Newell, I have been coming to these meetings for four weeks. I did not sleep last night. I have had little sleep for three weeks. I have prayed. I have read the Bible. I have waited here today to have you tell me what I need to do." "Now," I said, "we will turn to the Bible, and I read, 'To him that worketh not, but believeth on him that justifieth the ungodly — '" "That's what I am — 'ungodly' — but please tell me what to do." "This verse tells you," I said, "that *you* are to do nothing save one thing — 'To him that worketh not, but believeth on him.... his faith is counted for righteousness.'" He suddenly leaped to his feet and stretched forth his hand, and said, "Mr. Newell, I accept that proposition!" and off he went without another word. Next noonday I espied his shining face and introduced him to the great audience. This

was his response to my introduction: "I am a businessman, as you know. I know a good proposition. But I found one yesterday that so filled me with joy that I could not sleep a wink all night."
— From *Triumphs of Faith*, by W. R. Newell

* * *

When You Get the "Divers"

A colored preacher reading his Bible got very much concerned about the interpretation of these words. He decided to preach a sermon on "Divers Diseases." Following is an excerpt from the sermon: "If you gets pneumonia, the doctors can cure it. If you gets tuberculosis, they seldom cures you. but when you gets the 'divers' nobody but the good Lord can heal you." We smile at the old Negro's mistakes, but perhaps he preached well after all, for there are many diseases of the soul that only Christ can heal.
— *Teacher* (S.B.C.)

* * *

" 'Tain't Coupled Onto Anything!"

Two travelers, who fancied they were abundantly able to take care of themselves, entered a railway carriage when the train was being made up and found comfortable seats. They had dropped into conversation when a porter looked in and told them to go forward. "What is the matter with this coach?" they asked. "Nothing," he grinned, "only 'tain't coupled onto anything that'll take you anywhere." That is the trouble with many beautiful creeds and theories — they sound well, but they do not take you anywhere. The soul that would journey heavenward must make sure of the coupling. That is it: "Whosoever shall call upon the name of the Lord shall be saved." — *Heart and Life*

* * *

"Thank You Lord!"

A mountain missionary recently dealt with a young woman about her soul. Over and over he repeated God's promises, and repeatedly she declared: "Yes, I believe that!" To give her assurance he inquired, "Then are you saved?" "No,

I don't think I am," she answered faintly.

After many attempts to assure the girl and many seasons of prayer with her, the missionary was at a loss to know what to do next. He invited the girl to his home where another attempt was made by an associate worker. She, too, failed. Before letting the girl go home, the missionary gave her a Bible all her own.

"Thank you," she said gladly.

Quickly the missionary turned to her: "Why don't you say that to the Lord? You thank me for merely giving you a Bible, but you will not thank Him for the precious gift of salvation."

The young woman faltered a moment, then exclaimed: "I see it now."

"Then are you saved?" the missionary asked.

"Yes, I'm saved," she responded joyfully. — *Florida Baptist Witness.*

* * *

What Exposed Their Need

After making an appeal to workers in their factory canteen, an evangelist invited questions. A man stood and said bluntly: "We don't need religion. We have everything we want. We have plenty of money. The firm provides recreation. Food is put before us, and we don't even have to wash the dishes. What need have we of religion?" The evangelist found his reply in a poster prominently displayed which read: "Twelve hundren knives and forks have been stolen, from this canteen during the past month. In the future those who use the canteen must bring their own cutlery." — *Pentecostal Evangel.*

* * *

"Cut It Up By the Roots"

A young minister addressing a rather fashionable audience, attacked their pride and extravagance, as seen in their dresses, ribbons, chains, and jewels. In the evening an old minister preached powerfully on the corruption of human nature, the enmity of the soul against God and the necessity of a change of heart by the regeneration of the Spirit. Late that night as they sat together in private, the young minister said, "Doctor D., why don't you preach against the pride and vanity of people for dressing so extravagantly?" "Ah, son Timothy," replied the venerable man: "while you are trimming off the top branches of the tree, I am endeavoring to cut it up by the roots, and then the whole top will die out." — *Selected.*

* * *

Even An Archdeacon or Bishop

Bishop John Taylor Smith, former Chaplain General of the British Army, ... was preaching in a large cathedral on this text: "Except a man be born again, he cannot see the kingdom of God." In order to drive it home, he said: "My dear people, do not substitute anything for the new birth. You may be a member of a church, ... but church membership is not new birth, and 'except a man be born again, he cannot see the kingdom of God.' ". . . On the left sat the archdeacon in his stall. Pointing directly at him, he said, "You might even be an archdeacon like my friend in his stall and not be born again, and 'except a man be born again, he cannot see the kingdom of God.' You might even be a bishop like myself, and not be born again, and 'except a man be born again, he cannot see the kingdom of God.' ". . . A day or so later he received a letter from the archdeacon, in which he wrote: "My dear Bishop: You have found me out. I have been a clergyman for over thirty years, but I had never known anything of the joy that Christians speak of. I never could understand it. Mine has been hard, legal service. I did not know what was the matter with me, but when you pointed directly to me, and said, 'You might even be an archdeacon and not be born again,' I realized in a moment what the trouble was. I had never known anything of the new birth." He went on to say that he was wretched and miserable, had been unable to sleep all night, and begged for a conference, if the bishop could spare the time to talk with him. "Of course, I could spare the time," said Bishop Smith, "and the next day we went over the Word of God, and, after some hours, we were both on our knees, the archdeacon taking his place before God as a poor, lost sinner, and telling the Lord Jesus he would trust Him as his Saviour. From that time on everything has been different."
— Dr. Harry A. Ironside

* * *

"Christ In Your Name"

"Well, my dear, and what is your name?" The famous Dr. Andrew Bonar, of Scotland, was saying good-by to a medical missionary accompanied by his young sister, and to the latter this question was addressed. "Christine," was her reply. "What a lovely name!" said the aged servant of the Lord. "You, see, my dear, you have Christ in your name, but have you Christ in your heart?" She was silent to that important personal question, but could not forget it. That night after a long talk with her brother, she flung wide open the door of her heart to the Saviour, Christian living and faithful service and has shown by years of consistent living among the Edinburgh students, the reality of her decision.
— *Moody Monthly*

SECOND COMING OF CHRIST

He Is Coming

Great Bible interpreters and great Bible preachers have generally received much comfort from the doctrine of Christ's second coming. Read these words from the pen of Dr. G. Campbell Morgan: "To me the second coming is the perpetual light on the path which makes the present bearable. I never lay my head on my pillow without thinking that, maybe before the morning breaks, the final morning may have dawned! I never begin my work without thinking that, perhaps He may interrupt my work and begin His own. This is now His word to all believing souls, till He come." We are not looking for death, we are looking for Him.

—*Watchman-Examiner*

* * *

What Does "Come Again" Mean?

When I left Australia years ago, I said to my mother, "Mother, if God spares me, I will come back to see you." For years she waited. Had anyone said to her, "Mrs. Talbot, what are you waiting for?" she would have said, "My boy in America is coming back." And suppose this person said to her, "Coming back? What do you mean? Surely you don't expect a personal, visible, actual coming!" "Yes," she would have replied, "that's the way he is coming." Possibly her friend might have said, "Did you ever get letters from him? Do you ever receive gifts? Well, that is what he meant — he is coming in all these things." My mother would have answered, "Why, that isn't what he meant, for he said that *he* would come back!" Some years afterward, I did cross the ocean, walked down the gangplank from the steamer, and said, "Mother, here I am."

—From L. T. Talbot's sermon,
*If Christ Should Not Return
—What Then?*

* * *

Better Than a One-Way Ticket

A Christian woman was once talking to a servant of Christ about the assurance of her safety in the Saviour and said, "I have taken a single ticket to Glory, and do not intend to come back." Whereupon the man of God replied: "You are going to miss a lot. I have taken a return ticket, for I am not only going to meet Christ in Glory, but I am coming back with him in power and great glory to the earth."

—*Sunday School Times*

* * *

"It's There to Stay!"

Dr. W. B. Henson, a Bible-believing minister of the other years, preached a mighty sermon on the second coming of Christ. A group of young ministers heard the message. At the close of the service, they said to Dr. Henson, "We don't see it as you do; we cannot get it out of the New Testament." Replied Dr. Henson, "Of course you can't get it out of the New Testament. It's there to stay!"

—Vance Havner

* * *

"Upon Whom the End of the World Has Come

We are living, we are dwelling
　In a grand and awful time:
In an age on ages telling:
　To be living is sublime.
Hark! The waking up of nations,
　Gog and Magog to the fray:
Hark! What soundeth? Is creation
　Groaning for its latter day?

Will ye play, then, will ye dally,
　With your music and your wine?
Up! It is Jehovah's rally;
　God's own arm hath need of thine.
Hark! The onset! Are ye folding
　Faith-clad arms in lazy lock?
Up! Oh, up, thou drowsy soldier!
　Worlds are charging to the shock.

Worlds are charging, heaven beholding;
　Thou hast but an hour to fight;
Now the blazoned cross unfolding,
　On, right onward, for the right!
On, let all the soul within you,
　For the truth's sake go abroad!
Strike! let every nerve and sinew
　Tell on ages — tell for God!

—Arthur Cleveland Coxe

* * *

Whether You Want It or Not

I remember one night in Stockton, Calif., . . . I was preaching about the coming of Jesus. As I was in prayer I was conscious of a woman getting up and going out, for in those days the skirts would swish whenever a lady walked. It seemed to me that this lady must have gone out in a hurry. When I finished my prayer and went to greet the friends at the door, I found a woman pacing back and forth in the lobby. The moment I came she said to me, "How would you dare to pray like that —

'Come, Lord Jesus?' I don't want Him to come. It would break in on all my plans. How dare you!" I said, "My dear young woman, Jesus is coming whether you want it or not." Oh, if you know Him and love Him, surely your heart says, "Come, Lord Jesus!"
—H. A. Ironside

* * *

The Honor Due Unto His Name

On March 23, 1743, when "The Messiah" was first performed in London, the king was present in the great audience. It is reported that all were so deeply moved by the "Hallelujah Chorus" that with the impressive words, "For the Lord God omnipotent reigneth," the whole audience, including the king, sprang to its feet, and remained standing through the entire chorus. From that time to this it has always been the custom to stand during the chorus whenever it is performed. With spontaneous joy the soul stands to salute Him who "cometh in the name of the Lord." He is "King of kings, and Lord of lords" and to Him we pledge allegiance.
—*Today*

* * *

Our Commander's Signaled Promise

In Sherman's march from Chattanooga to Atlanta and the sea, General Johnston was removed from his command by the Confederates and his army given to the impetuous General Hood. Hood at once marched to the rear of Sherman, threatening his communications and base of supplies at Allatoona, which commanded the pass through the mountains. Sherman sent an order to one of his lieutenants, Corse, to proceed to Allatoona. He himself went as far back as Kenesaw Mountain, and from that eminence on the clear October day could see plainly the smoke of battle and hear the faint reverberation of the cannon. His flag officer at length made out the letters which were being wig-wagged from the garrison at Allatoona, "Corse is here." This was a great relief to Sherman, who then heliographed his famous message, "Hold the fort, I am coming." Among the soldiers in

Sherman's army was a young officer, Major Whittle, who related the incident to P. P. Bliss, the famous evangelist. Taking this incident as his inspiration, Bliss wrote the once well-known hymn, "Hold the fort, for I am coming." The hymn thus inspired has genuine Christian faith in its lines. The Church is to *occupy* until Christ comes.
—*Sunday School Times*

* * *

"A Little While"

"A little while!" and He shall come,
   The hour draws on apace,
The blessed hour, the glorious morn,
   When we shall see His face;
How light our trials then will seem!
   How short our pilgrim way!
Our life on earth, a fitful dream,
   Dispelled by dawning day!

A little while, with patience, Lord,
   I fain would ask, "How long?"
For how can I with such a hope.
   Of glory and of home,
With such a joy awaiting me,
   Not wish the hour were come?
How can I keep the longing back,
   And how suppress the groan?
—*Selected*

* * *

Spiritual Soap and Water

Speaking further of the word "watch," the late Dr. A. J. Gordon used to tell a humorous story that helps to illuminate its meaning in this case. When his children were small it was his custom to spend his summer vacation with them at their old farmstead in New Hampshire. And on one occasion, after being with them for a while, he surprised them by saying that he must return to Boston for an important business engagement. But observing their disappointment at the thought of his absence, he comforted them by adding that he was coming back again, "And," said he, "I will expect you to be at the station watching for me."

The children went to see him off, but hardly had the train moved out of sight before they hastened back to the farm again, and began pleading with their mother to wash their hands and faces and comb their hair, and put on clean aprons, or what not, that they might be ready to return to the station for the afternoon train! Moreover, the importuning was repeated day after day until Dr. Gordon did return. And Mrs. Gordon was wont to say that she never knew her children to be so interested in soap and water in all their lives as they were on that particular occasion!

John's first epistle emphasizes the motive, where it is written, "Beloved, now are we the sons of God, but it doth not yet appear what we shall be: but we know that, when he shall appear, we shall be like him; for we shall see him as he is. And every man that hath this hope in him *purifieth himself,* even as he is pure" (I John 3:1-3).

—*Western Recorder*

* * *

On Guard!

Some day you may visit the interesting and historic French-Canadian city of Quebec. There you will see the Plains of Abraham, where the English forces of General Wolfe won Quebec from the French. When you see the steep ascent that Wolfe's men had to make up the face of the great rocky cliffs, you will be amazed that they succeeded. Mere boys should have been able to hold off a force of soldiers from scaling such cliffs and gaining the heights. Yet Wolfe and his men made the ascent and gained the citadel. Why? Because the overconfident defenders became careless and pleasure-loving; and, one night, when they were off guard, the enemy saw his opportunity, scaled the heights, and took the city. Quebec fell because its defenders failed to keep watch. And for failure to keep watch, thousands are losing the battles of life every day; while, at the last, for failure to keep watch, many will be unready for the return of Jesus Christ.

—*Joseph Harris, in Sunday School Times*

* * *

When the Thrilling News Comes

When those who had upheld the banner of the Cross had almost lost heart, John Knox, who had been banished, accepted the invitation from the truehearted ones and left Geneva for Scotland. When he landed, quick as lightning the news spread — John Knox has come! Edinburgh came rushing into the street. The old, the young, the lordly, and the lowborn were seen to mingle together in joyful expectation. All business, all common pursuits were forsaken. Travelers suddenly mounted and sped into the country with the tidings. John Knox has come! The whole land was moved and stirred with a new inspiration, and the hearts of enemies withered. This was the effect of the presence of a man like ourselves. What will the land feel when the news comes: *"The Son of man* is come! The Son of man is come!"

—*Andrew Bonar, in Sunday School Times*

* * *

The Coming King

Dean Farrar was a privileged personal friend of Queen Victoria, though he seldom referred to the distinction. But on the first anniversary of the accession of Edward VII to the throne of England, during the service in Canterbury Cathedral, he told how the Queen, after hearing one of her chaplains preach at Windsor on the second coming of Christ, spoke to the Dean about it and said, "Oh, how I wish that the Lord would come during my lifetime." "Why does your Majesty feel this very earnest desire?" asked the great preacher. With her queenly countenance lit up with deep emotion she replied, *"Because I should so love to lay my crown at His feet."* —*Light and Life Quarterly*

* * *

When Ye Think Not

McCheyne, the Scotch preacher, once said to some friends, "Do you think Christ will come to-night?"

One after another they said, "I think not."

When all had given this answer, he solemnly repeated this text, "The Son of Man cometh at an hour *when ye think not."* —*Watchman-Examiner*

Is It a Practical Belief?

To recognize the approach of the Day of the Lord is expected of all believers. Just as certainly they are warned that they will not know the day or the hour. The good effect of this expectation is illustrated by the aged colored man who, when asked as to what value his belief in Christ's soon coming had on his life, said, "I'm sitting with my feet untangled."

—Dr. Chafer, in
Sunday School Times

* * *

What They Had Been Praying For

Asked by Dr. George E. Guille what was his attitude on the Lord's Second Coming, Pastor William Anderson, Jr., of Dallas, Tex., answered that he didn't know that he had any attitude on the subject. He wasn't interested. He had been so busy preaching the first coming that he had not had time to think about the Second Coming. "Well," said Mr. Guille, "I only wanted to know whether you loved His appearing." Left alone in his study, "Dr. Bill," as his many friends called him, sat at his desk as if held by an unseen hand, asking himself over and over, "Do I love His appearing?" Then he took up his Bible and read Paul's second letter to Timothy, and other Scriptures, and before he left his desk and his study, was able to say with a swelling heart that he did love Christ's appearing. On getting home, he astonished his wife by telling her he must resign his pastorate, and the reason why. He called his session together, and asked them to join him in asking the Presbytery to dissolve their relation. They were as much amazed as Mrs. Anderson had been. When the pastor explained what had happened to his convictions, that he had become a premillenarian, whereas he had come to their church a postmillenarian, and thought the only fair thing was to resign, one of the elders cried out, "Why, my dear pastor, this is what we have been praying for. Resign nothing! God has answered our prayers!" From that time Dr. Bill Anderson's ministry was transformed, and his pastorate became

so fruitful as to be "spoken of throughout the whole world."
—Dr. W. L. Pettingill, in
Sunday School Times

* * *

He Stayed, and Waited, and Watched

A little boy was told by his father to wait on a corner by a department store, while the father had a tire changed on his car. It turned out that the car required more attention than the man had anticipated, and it took over an hour. The father anxiously hurried back to get his little boy, and found the little fellow right where he had told him to stay. He said to the boy, "Did you think your daddy had forgotten about you?" "Oh, no," was the reply, accompanied by a smile of perfect trust, "I knew you would come just as soon as you could. I wasn't a bit worried. I stayed where you told me, and waited, and watched for you." Dear child of God, worried and confused by present-day world events, you, by the grace of your Lord, can be like that little boy. Have a perfect trust in Him, as you await His coming, watching and waiting in perfect obedience to Him. He has the "times and seasons" in command.
—*Sunday School Times*

* * *

"What If It Were Today!"

A traveler chanced upon a beautiful villa situated on the shores of a beautiful lake in Switzerland far from the beaten track of tourists. The traveler knocked at the garden gate and an aged warden undid its heavy fastenings and bade him enter. The aged man seemed glad to see him and showed him around the wonderful garden.

"How long have you been here?" the traveler asked. "Twenty-four years." "And how often has your master been here meanwhile?" "Four times." "When was he last here?" "Twelve years ago." "He writes often?" "Never once." "From whom do you receive your pay?" "His agent in Mainland." "But he comes here often?" "He has never been here." "Who does come, then?" "I am almost always alone — it is very, very seldom that even a stranger comes." "Yet you have the garden in such perfect order, everything flourishing, as if you were expecting your master's coming to-morrow!" "*As if he were coming to-day, sir, to-day;*" exclaimed the old man.

It is our duty to be ready for our Lord's Coming to-day, though His coming may be far in the future.

—*New Century Leader*

* * *

He Is Near!

I know not in what watch He comes
  Or at what hour He may appear,
Whether at midnight or at morn,
  Or in what season of the year;
  I only know that *He is near.*

The centuries have gone and come,
  Dark centuries of absence drear;
I dare not chide the long delay,
  Nor ask when I His voice shall hear;
  I only know that *He is near.*

I do not think it can be long
  Till in His glory He appear;
And yet I dare not name the day,
  Nor fix the solemn Advent year;
  I only know that *He is near.*

—Horatius Bonar

* * *

To Be Ready

She was a little six-year old, golden haired lassie, with a simple, trusting faith.

One morning, while I was a guest in the home, I found her busily working in her bedroom, carefully putting things to rights for the day, and I remarked to her, "Oh, how nice and neat your room looks, with everything put in order," and her reply came sweetly and simply: "Yes, I am putting it in order, *for Jesus might come today.*"

—*Moody Monthly*

* * *

Confident Before Him

One New Year's night, after close communion with the Lord, I retired and fell asleep. I had one of those rare dreams which leave behind them the impression of the voice of God. In my dream I was gazing into the heavens at night, looking at one of the brightest constellations, when, suddenly there appeared among them a wonderful star as bright as Venus at its brightest. As I gazed upon it, wondering at its strange beauty in that quarter of the heavens, I became conscious that it was rapidly growing larger every moment and swiftly approaching. So fast did it enlarge that it seemed to be literally rushing earthwards. My whole being was stirred with the thought that some stupendous event was happening.

Then there passed over my spirit in my dream a distinct consciousness that the Lord was coming; that this was the Morning Star and He was just behind it. The best part of the dream was that it brought only rest and joy. Startling as was the appearance and certainty of the coming King, there was no fear, but a sweet consciousness that all was right. I was glad He was coming, that in a few moments He would be here. I also had the consciousness that it was all right for those I loved as well as for myself.

Just at that moment I awakened with the quiet sense that God had spoken to my heart with a personal message respecting what His glorious Coming would be to me. Oh, that we may so live each moment that when He shall appear, we may have confidence, and not be ashamed before Him at His Coming.

—A. B. Simpson.

* * *

The Best Authority

A friend of mine who has grown in grace and true Christian experience, amidst hard church opposition, has had, for several years, a fine Bible class of young women. It is in a worldly church, and her teaching, under God, has been richly blessed. One Sunday while she was teaching the lesson on the second coming of Christ, the minister came into the room. In an angry voice he interrupted the teacher and said: "You are well aware we do not believe that doctrine in this church. Who gave you the authority to teach it here?" Holding out her Bible toward the angry minister, and in quiet, yet clear voice, the teacher said, "Here, sir, in God's Word, I find my authority.'"

—*Sunday School Times*

* * *

Prophets That Do not Cry

Two ministers, long friends, met one day after being apart for a time. They discussed their churches; then began to talk on present-day events. Said one, "I don't preach on the Lord's return at all; my congregation doesn't like it. I hear you have many against you for preaching it. I told you years ago there's no use setting people against you." "My friend," said the other man, "by God's grace, I preach His whole Word, and thereby deliver my soul; and if the Lord Jesus comes in my lifetime no one who is left behind will be able to say (as many will, of some ministers) that I did not give out the truth and warn them of what's ahead. How about you?"

—*Sunday School Times*

* * *

They Will Come Back If They Are With Him

In the Fiji Islands, there is a pathetic custom of calling to the dead. The savage climbs a high tree or cliff and, after mentioning his dead friend's name, cries, "Come back! Come back!" We who stand by the graveside of our Christian dead know that one day they WILL come back, when our Lord returns for His own!

—*London Christian Herald*

* * *

What Would He Say?

If He should come to-day
And find my hands so full
  Of future plans, however fair,
  In which my Saviour has no share,
  What would He say?
If He should come to-day
And find my love so cold,
  My faith so very weak and dim
  I had not even looked for Him.
  What would He say?
If He should come to-day
And find that I had not told
  One soul about my Heavenly Friend
  Whose blessings all my way attend,
  What would He say?
If He should come to-day
Would I be glad, quite glad?
  Remembering that He died for all
  And none through me had heard His
  call,
  What would He say?

—*Selected*

SELF CONTROL

"The Old Colonel"

In the other years, there lived in the city of Charleston, South Carolina, a familiar figure, "The Old Colonel!" During his Civil War days, he was famed for his control over others. Those under his command seemed to delight in instantly and cheerfully obeying his commands. At the close of the war, "The Old Colonel" became a "hard" drinker. One day a race riot broke out in that southern city. Soon the situation got beyond the power of the authorities to control it. In the midst of the melee, some one said, "Send for 'The Old Colonel.'" Search was made for him. Finally he was found in a saloon. Putting on his regimentals, he got astride his charger, and swiftly rode away to the scene of the riot. Dashing into the midst of the frenzied mobs, "The Old Colonel" began to give commands. Instantly his orders were obeyed, and the rioters began to disperse! With quiet restored, "the Old Colonel" rode away. Later, he was found "dead drunk" in a saloon. He was an eminent success in controlling others. He was a dismal failure in controlling *himself.*

—W. B. K.

* * *

My Car Under Perfect Control

People say, "Oh, religion — it is all about limitations and restrictions. It means that a man is to be reined in, and

not allowed the legitimate use of his natural possessions and appetittes," Not at all. One of the things we say of a motor car is, "I have it under complete control." What does that mean? That it won't go? You don't suppose that the man who has his car at the side of the road, which absolutely won't run, is inclined to say, "My car is under perfect control." The car that is subject to perfect control will travel easily at its high speed; it will do exactly what is required of it, and do it easily. That is what God does for man under control.
—*Sunday School Chronicle*

* * *

Consecrated Patience

A Quaker had a quarrelsome neighbor whose cow often broke into the Quaker's well-cultivated garden. One morning, having driven the cow from his premises to her owner's house, he said to him, "Friend, I have driven thy cow home once more, and if I find her in my garden again ——"

"Suppose you do," his neighbor angrily exclaimed, "what will you do?"

"Why," said the Quaker, "*I'll drive her home to thee again, friend.*"

The cow never again troubled the Quaker.   —Henry Pickering

* * *

"What About Your Vile Temper?"

A woman came to a servant of Christ and said, "I wish you would go and talk to my husband. He is getting where he never stays home at night. He sets the children such a bad example; and if I talk to him, he slams the door and out he goes!" The minister happened to know something of that home, and said to the woman, "Before we pray for your husband there is something I want to talk to you about. What about your VILE temper? Go to God and say, 'O God, I come to Thee confessing my vile, wicked temper; my bad temper is driving my husband from home; it is alienating my children; my bad temper is bringing dishonour on the name of the Lord. Deliver me from that bad temper, that thus I may be able to present the sweetness and graciousness of

Christ, and so help my husband and children.' " Did she follow this golden advice? Nay! She jumped to her feet and ran out into another fit of temper!"
—From *Addresses on The Second Epistle to the Corinthians,*
by H. A. Ironside

* * *

Inherited Temper

"A bad temper runs in our family." Some people sit down and simply do not try to control their angry outbursts because they confess their fathers had bad tempers before them. Other wiser people make this family trait a warning. "You have the evenest temperament I ever saw!" remarked one girl to another. "I don't see how you manage it." "Manage it?" echoed her friend. "I have to! Maybe you don't know that I come from the Black McGreevys? In a little town we used to live in, the children would run indoors when they saw my father coming down the street. My grandfather struck my grandmother, whom he adored, in a wild fit of temper, so that she was a cripple for life. He never smiled again. With a history like that, what could I expect but a life of insane rages? But I wouldn't be like that. I went to Jesus Christ and I said, 'Dear Lord, I know that I can't control my temper or myself. Take control of my life for me.' And He has."
—*Sunday School Times*

* * *

To Strike Means To Be Beaten

Dr. G. A. Leichliter, of Toronto, Canada, tells this interesting story: "A traveler relates that in Shanghai one day he saw two coolies engaged in a heated argument in the midst of an attentive crowd. The combatants waved their arms, shook their fists and stamped their feet, all the time apparently hurling at each other the bitterest epithets that Mongolian brains could conceive, but never a blow was struck. When the traveler inquired what was the trouble he was told by one of the onlookers that the coolies were 'fighting.' When he expressed surprise at such a fight that could be waged so bitterly and yet without any physical violence the Chinese explained the matter thus: 'You see the man who strikes first is beaten, because thereby he confesses that he has run out of ideas.'"

—*Watchman-Examiner*

* * *

The Lion Tamer's Defeat

Nero, the lion, was the chief attraction of the circus. One of the elephants, passing Nero's cage, chanced to throw the heavy cage's sliding bolt. The door opened! "Back! Nero, back!" Teeth bared, lips curled in a protesting snarl, Nero crouched. "Back! Back to your cage!" The brute crouched lower, his long claws digging nervously in the ground. A few persons hurried from their seats, but most of the crowd sat spell-bound. With his muscles tense, his eyes aglow with anger, his tail lashing from side to side, maddened by his trainer's interference, Nero crouched still lower. Knowing that to hesitate was to lose, the trainer stepped forward, lashing the animal's face with his whip. Nero snarled fiercely, but he paused quivering, irresolute. "Back, Nero!"

The lion's look slowly changed. His eyes blinked under the whip. Then the brute gave up. With a last harsh snarl, he turned and sprang back into his cage. The man had won.

The whole of the story has not been told. One day Nero was without a master; his cage was not rolled out into the arena for his performance. The trainer — the only man whose voice the big lion would obey —— had been taken suddenly ill. Nor did he ever come back. The physicians said his death was due to alcoholic poisoning.

The truth is, the man who was so brave he would face that snarling lion, who was so strong-willed he could make the lion back down before him, was a slave to drink. No one is any stronger than his weakest point.

—*Gospel Herald*

* * *

The Art of Self-Defense

"Do you think it wrong for me to learn the art of self-defense?" asked a young man of his pastor.

"Certainly not," answered the minister. "I learned it in youth myself, and I have found it of great value during my life."

"Indeed, sir! Did you learn the old English system or Sullivan's system?"

"Neither. I learned Solomon's system."

"Solomon's system?"

"Yes; you will find it laid down in the first verse of the 15th chapter of Proverbs, 'A soft answer turneth away wrath.' It is the best system of self-defense of which I know."

—*Western Recorder*

* * *

"I Can Receive No Money That I Have Not Earned": General Robert E. Lee

"The men in the uniform of gray went back to rundown farms, devastated regions, war-scourged cities, impoverished estates. Many of their homes were in ashes; they had to begin all over again. On an April day in 1865, through long lines of weeping men there rode the commander-in-chief of the defeated army, grave of countenance but calm of spirit. All his material possessions were gone; beloved Arlington had passed out of his hands. There came an offer of a home in England, where he might spend the rest of his days in comfort, ease and luxury. He declined it. He refused $25,000 a year, offered him by an insurance company, saying, 'I can receive no money that I have not earned,' and became president of a small and struggling college at a salary of $1,500. He nourished no rancor, showed no bitterness, called upon his former soldiers to support the Union.

"One day a mother put her little child in his arms and asked that he offer a prayer for her first-born. General Lee bowed his head over the child, held him close, handed him back to his mother, saying, 'Teach him to deny himself.'

"When men can meet defeat in such a spirit, victory is present. He who rules his own spirit is greater than he who takes a city."

—Rev. Edgar DeWitt Jones, in
United Daughters of the Confederacy Magazine.

Faith for Little Things

Multitudes of Christians who trust Christ for eternal salvation, who walk through the valley of suffering with Heavenly courage, who face opposition and persecution bravely, belie their Lord before the world by defeat in the small things of life.

Two women live side by side. One has no faith in a Divine Saviour, but she has poise and self-control and shows kindness and thoughtfulness for others. The second woman is a believing Christian, but she is nervous and irritable, easily upset and often selfish in her relations with others. Her neighbors forget her faith and sterling qualities of heart and mind, and judge her Lord by her poor defeated self.

—*Wesleyan Methodist*

* * *

Temper

When I have lost my temper
I have lost my reason too.

I'm never proud of anything
  Which angrily I do.
When I have talked in anger
  And my cheeks were flaming red
I have always uttered something
  Which I wish I had not said,
In anger I have never
  Done a kindly deed or wise,
But many things for which I felt
  I should apologize.
In looking back across my life,
  And all I've lost or made,
I can't recall a single time
  When fury ever paid.
So I struggle to be patient,
  For I've reached a wiser age;
I do not want to do a thing
  Or speak a word in rage.
I have learned by sad experience
  That when my temper flies
I never do a worthy deed,
  A decent deed or wise.

—*Selected*

SELFISHNESS

Pleasurable Co-Operation

The small boy was drawing his still smaller neighbor along the walk in his little wagon. He looked up beaming when a watchful face appeared at the doorway. "I'm trying to make Janie happy, Aunt Mary," he said.

"What a beautiful spirit for the child to have!" exclaimed the admiring aunt. But presently it seemed to her that the boy's effort was not very successful. Wee Jane was evidently afraid to ride and was trying to climb out of the wagon and draw it herself.

"She doesn't like riding, Bobby!" exclaimed the aunt.

"But I want to draw the wagon myself; I want to make her happy doing the things I like to do."

The same spirit lies at the root of much that we like to call kindness to others.

—*London Christian Herald*

Answering the Problem

A lecturer was once asked by a member of his audience, "If a ship was wrecked in midocean, and only a single boat was available, and if there were twenty young, strong, able men on board, and twenty weakly women, would it not pay best, and be best for the world, to save the stronger capable men, and let the rest drown?" And he answered, amid the loud applause of the meeting, "What possible good could twenty such men as that be to the world?"

—*Sunday School Times*

* * *

The Peril of Hoarding

We are told of a man who, knowing the value of water, lived in fear that the supply would become exhausted. He had a farm, and on the farm was a pond of water. Whenever he could do so he would turn every little stream into this pond. When the pond was full he was happy, and when it was getting low he was terribly worried. He would catch in tubs and barrels the rain water that would run from the roofs of his buildings and haul it to the pond. He begrudged the animals the water they would drink. He spent days bringing water and pouring it into the pond. When he was bringing an unusually large quantity one day, he slipped into the pond and drowned.

You say, "How foolish he was!" And all of us say the same thing. But are not many of us doing the same thing?

Here is a person who has set his heart on money. He wants money. He craves money. He would do anything to get money. Yes, but you say, "This is money and not water." True, but there have been times when rich men would have given all the wealth they had for a glass of refreshing water.

—*Lutheran Young People*

* * *

The Danger of Self

The Moorish Palace had a small grotto-like entrance into which we were invited by placards announcing the wonders and beauties, but once inside there were only mirrors, and whichever way you turned you saw only yourself. You looked in one direction and you had grown tall and thin, and in another short and wide. Your face expanded or lengthened in the most astonishing way. In every direction the mirrors lured and deceived you, promising exits where there were none and only bringing the bewildered wanderer face to face with some other distorted reflection of himself — always himself.

There are people who spend their lives in the Moorish Palace. Whichever way they turn they see nothing but self, and soon it grows to be an exaggerated and distorted self. They see it made little by fancied slights and they are resentful. They see it grow into importance by some success and their pride is gratified; and even when they think they are working for God self comes slipping into their foreground.

—*Kate Hamilton, in Queen's Garden*

A Breathing Corpse

"That man may breathe, but never lives,
Who much receives, but nothing gives,
Whom none can love, whom none can thank,
Creation's blot, creation's blank!"

—*Selected*

* * *

Wanting What We Should Not Have

I once heard of a spoiled child who was in a dreadful fit of temper because his nurse would not let him have a valuable vase from the cabinet. Hearing him crying loudly, his mother went into the room and asked, "What do you want, darling?" Said the boy, "I want that!" pointing to the vase. "Yes, darling, you shall have it," said the mother unwisely, but wishing to make him happy. But when she put it before him the child simply lifted up his voice and yelled afresh. "Why, what do you want?" asked the mother again. "I want — I want," said the boy between his sobs, then the words came out with a rush, "I want to have something that I mustn't." So the forbidden tree had a fatal attraction for Eve.

—*Christian Herald*

* * *

Death to Self

In a city he visited during one of his many journeys preaching the Word of God, Dr. A. C. Gaebelein noticed a sign in a small dyeing establishment which read:

*"I Live To Dye, I Dye To Live
The More I Dye The More I Live
The More I Live The More I Dye."*

Read these words aloud, and you will hear a great spiritual truth. The more there is death to self, that much more fully is the Lord Jesus Christ able to live His life in us. "I am crucified with Christ; nevertheless I live; yet not I, but Christ liveth in me" (Gal. 2:20). This kind of living is possible to every believer by full appropriation of all that is his in Christ. "Likewise reckon ye also yourselves to be dead indeed unto sin, but alive unto God through Jesus Christ our Lord" (Rom. 6:11).

—*Moody Monthly*

"Obscuring Christ."

A missionary and his son were to show pictures in a Telugu village. Upon their arrival, they found the only place available for showing the pictures was in front of a Hindu temple. The priest gave his consent for the pictures to be shown there. The missionary noted that the priest, too, was curious to see the pictures. The first picture to be shown was that of Christ, from Hoffmann's "Christ and the Rich Young Ruler." But when the picture was thrown on the screen, it showed only a dim, shadowy face. Upon investigation, the missionary discovered that he had placed his screen directly in front of an idol of Buddha, where a tiny lamp was kept burning. Because the people were anxious to see the pictures, the priest ordered the lamp put out. Then the strong, appealing face of the Christ was clearly visible. So the light of the Christ becomes obscured in our lives if we keep a "lamp burning" to some selfish, worldly desire.

—*Secret Place*

* * *

Lord, Show Thy Hands, Thy Feet!

Lord, when I am weary with toiling,
And burdensome seem thy commands.
If my load should lead to complaining,
Lord, show me thy hands
Thy nail-pierced hands, thy cross-torn hands,
My Saviour, show me thy hands.

Christ, if ever my footsteps should falter,
And I be prepared for retreat,
If desert or thorn cause lamenting,
Lord, show me thy feet.
Thy bleeding feet, Thy nail-scarred feet,
My Jesus show me thy feet.
Oh, God, dare I show thee my hands and my feet?

—*Selected*

* * *

"Hoarding Bounties!"

"Let us gather up the sunbeams,
Lying all around our path;
Get a trust on all the roses,
Give the poor the thorns and chaff.

"And we'll find our sweetest pleasure,
Hoarding bounties of the day;
So the poor will have scant measure,
And ten prices have to pay!

"We'll capture e'en the wind god,
And confine him in a cage;
Thus through our patented process,
We the atmosphere will gauge!

"Then we'll squeeze our little brother,
When his lungs he tries to fill,
Put a meter on his windpipe,
And present our little bill!

"We'll syndicate the starlight,
And monopolize the moon;
Put a royalty on rest days,
A proprietary moon!

"For a right-of-way through ocean spray,
We'll charge just what it's worth,
We'll put our stakes around the lakes,
In fact, we'll own the earth!"

—*Selected*

* * *

The Road to First Place

"Tell me, Higgins, why you're a friend to the likes o' me," said Louis, whom the Sky Pilot had resued from a life of drunkenness and shame. "For Christ's sake, Louis, for his sake." "I would give twenty years of my life if I could have the devotion of the men as Frank Higgins has it," said one of the camp missionaries. "It is yours in the same way Higgins got it," I replied. "Devote yourself to the men, and forget yourself in the devotion." Then I opened an old, old Book, and read again the common-sense Words of One who humbled Himself that we might be exalted, "If any man desire to be first, the same shall be . . . . servant of all."

—Thomas D. Whittles, in
Christian Endeavor World

* * *

When Self Gets in the Way

"Some of us are so full of ourselves," says a writer in the *Canadian Baptist*, "that we cannot see Christ in all His beauty." Some years ago, when I was away on a preaching appointment, my wife and little daughter stayed at the home of a friend. On the bedroom wall, just over the head of the bed in which they slept there was a picture of the Lord Jesus, which was reflected in the large mirror of the dressing table standing in the bay of the bedroom window. When my little daughter woke on her first morning there, she saw the picture reflected in the mirror while she still lay in bed, and exclaimed, "Oh, Mummy, I can see Jesus through the mirror!" Then she quickly kneeled up to take a better look, but in doing so brought her own body between the picture and the mirror, so that instead of seeing the picture of Jesus reflected, she now saw herself. So she lay down again, and again she saw the picture of Jesus. She was up and down several times after that with her eyes fixed on the mirror. Then she said, 'Mummy, when I can't see myself, I can see Jesus; but every time I see myself, I don't see Him.' How true it is when self fills the vision, we do not see Jesus!"

—*Sunday School Times*

* * *

The Self-Centered Wretch.

"Despite those titles, power and pelf,
The wretch concentered all in self;
Living shall forfeit fair renow,
And, doubly dying, shall go down,
To the vile dust from whence he sprung,
Unwept, unhonored, and unsung!"

—*Scott*

* * *

Why the Dead Sea?

We have heard of dead people, dead beasts, dead trees and dead flowers, but is there such a thing as a dead sea? There is and they call it dead because it receives all and gives nothing. This body of water — the most remarkable in the world — is at the southern end of the Jordan Valley in Palestine. It is 47 miles long and ten miles wide, 1292 feet below the sea level and is in one of the hottest regions on earth. It receives 5,000,000 tons of water daily into its bosom from the Jordan river, but gives none out to refresh and nourish the val-

ley below, which has become an arid desert on account of the closefistedness of the sea. Its water is five times as salty as the ocean, is bitter to the taste, oily to the touch and leaves a yellow stain. No fish live in the water, no flowers bloom or fruits grow on its shores, no birds sing in its neighborhood. Its barkless driftwood and shores are incrusted with salt. Its setting is a scene of desolation and gloom, looking as if the curse of God rested on all the region.

It is a striking emblem of the selfish life. Selfishness is the base of all sin.

—*Gospel Herald*

* * *

The Shrine of Self

John S. Hall, veteran missionary of the Sudan Interior Mission, told this amusing account of early days in Africa. The natives were curious of the white man's goods. As yet they had seen only very small mirrors. So they would invite themselves in and breezily go into the missionary's private quarters. On one occasion a big burly native greeted Mr. Hall in the outer room. Then he burst into the bedroom, where Mrs. Hall was seated before her long mirror, and asked her, "How are you?" "I am fine, and how are you?" replied Mrs. Hall. Then this big black fellow, with spear in his hand and a mere goatskin hanging on his side, turned to the mirror and graciously greeted himself, "And how are you, sir?" When he found what he had done he beat a hasty retreat. But what a picture of a man's love of himself! How we bow and bend before the sacred shrine of self. No greetings are quite so gracious.

—*Prairie Overcomer*

* * *

God's Word Is Always Right

We said to a physician friend one day, "Doctor, what is the exact significance of God's touching Jacob upon the sinew of his thigh?" He replied: "The sinew of the thigh is the strongest in the human body. A horse could scarcely tear it apart." Ah, I see, God has to break down at the strongest part of our

self-life before He can have His own
way of blessing with us.

—*Moody Monthly*

* * *

How To Be Miserable

Think about yourself.
Talk about yourself.
Use "I" as often as possible.
Mirror yourself continually in the opinion of others.
Listen greedily to what people say about you.
Be suspicious.
Expect to be appreciated.
Be jealous and envious.
Be sensitive to slights.
Never forgive a criticism.
Trust nobody but yourself.
Insist on consideration and the proper respect.
Demand agreement with your own views on everything.
Sulk if people are not grateful to you for favors shown them.
Never forget a service you may have rendered.
Be on the lookout for a good time for yourself.
Shirk your duties if you can.
Do as little as possible for others.
Love yourself supremely.
Be selfish.
This recipe is guaranteed to be infallible.

—*Gospel Herald*

* * *

Sealed Fountain

In the Roman Forum there used to be a spring called "The Fountain of the Maiden." Until recent years it was impossible to find any trace of it. One day, however, when a lot of rubbish was cleared away from the ruins of the Forum, the old fountain burst forth again. For centuries it had been closed by the refuse that had accumulated. Oh, how many Christian lives are sealed fountains through the hurry and worry of business and pleasure. Where once you were a useful and happy soul-winner, you are today absorbed in your amusements and engagements, and your

life has withered like the streams that sink in the desert and are lost to sight.
—A. B. Simpson

* * *

Why Blind Man Carried Light

How careful we should be that neither by foolish conversation, glaring inconsistencies, religious selfishness, or any other reason, we may cause our brother to stumble or hinder our testimony for Christ. Rather, let us be like the blind man, of whom D. L. Moody used often to tell, who, when asked why he carried a lamp when he could not see to follow its light, naively answered, "I carry it to keep people from stumbling over me."

—A. B. Simpson

* * *

Any Other Selfish Prayers

It is recorded of one man that he prayed the following selfish prayer: "Lord, wilt thou be pleased to preserve me in health today. It is so miserable to be sick; besides I have so much to do. Keep all my family in health, for I need their help. Be pleased also, Lord, to protect my buildings from fire and storm; protect my stock from disease, and especially my horses, for I greatly need their service today. Wilt thou forbid that the bank fail, and I suffer loss thereby, and I pray that thou wilt put it into the heart of neighbor Jones to pay me what he owes me. And wilt thou withhold the rain for a few days until I get my hay all in, and then thou mayst send a shower, as my corn will need it by that time. Now, Lord, do all these things for me, and all else that might be to my interest. Amen."

—*Gospel Trumpet*

* * *

More Than Denying Things

A minister once said: "Campbell Morgan came to this country and preached one sermon that destroyed forty years of my sermons. I had been preaching on the duty of sacrifice, telling how we should deny things to ourselves. In our own family, we often did without this or that, that God might bless us as we gave to His work. What I stressed was denying things to ourselves. Campbell Morgan preached that what we needed to give up was *self* not *things*. My family and I had given up everything under the sun but self. We were proud of what we gave up; we were proud of our humility. It was hard to give up self for crucifixion!"

—*Gospel Herald*

* * *

Is It True Self-Denial?

One morning, as Harry and his parents were sitting at the breakfast table, Harry seemed to be for a while engaged in deep study. Presently he exclaimed, "Father, I have made up my mind not to eat any more salt mackerel."

"Ah, what has brought you to that conclusion?" asked his father, with a look of earnest inquiry.

"Because," continued Harry, "my Sunday School teacher said that we ought to give up something so that we might have money to put in the missionary box."

"Well, but what has induced my boy to choose salt mackerel as the thing he will give up?" asked his father.

"Why," answered Harry, "because mackerel doesn't come very often; and I don't like it very much anyhow."

Have there been some older folk who have tried to practice self-denial in about the same way?

—*P. H. Advocate*

* * *

Broken Christians

A very poor man lived alone in his little hut. One day a wealthy man came to buy his hut. The poor man decided to sell it, and went about the place patching the roof and repairing it carefully, feeling a sense of pride that the rich man should desire his hut. After the money was paid, the new owner began at once to tear down the shack. The poor, bewildered man shouted out to him, "Don't tear down my little home. I have repaired it all so nicely." But the wealthy man replied, "I do not want your shack; I only want the site, this corner lot."

So, beloved, the Lord does not want the self in you patched up. He cannot use you except self is broken down, and you can give Him the site, as it were — an empty life that He can fill with His fulness.

—*Moody Monthly*

* * *

Silent Violin

Liugi Tarisio was found dead one morning with scarce a comfort in his home, but with two hundred and forty-six exquisite violins, which he had been collecting all his life, crammed into an attic. The best were in the bottom drawer of an old rickety bureau. In his devotion to the violin he had robbed the world of all that music all the time he treasured them. Others before him had done the same, so that when the greatest Stradivarius was first played it had had one hundred and forty-seven speechless years. Yet how many of Christ's people are like old Tarisio! In our very love to the church we fail to give the glad tidings to the world; in our zeal for the truth we forget to publish it. When shall we all learn that the good news needs telling, and is all men need to know?

—*Wesleyan Methodist*

* * *

"Spiritual Degeneracy"

Many years ago, quite a number of beehives were carried to the island of Barbados in the West Indies. At first the bees went diligently to work gathering honey for the coming winter. But when those bees found that they were in a land of perpetual summer, they ceased to gather honey. Instead they spent most of their time flying around, stinging the natives. So I sometimes think it is with us. We have what can be called "spiritual degeneracy." God has surrounded us with so many blessings that, instead of working for His glory and for the good of our fellow men, we spend most of our time in living for self. We thrust the sting, when we should be gathering the sweetness of the Gospel life to give out again to starving men.   —*T. DeWitt Talmage*

Finding Life By Losing It

The story is told of Sundar Singh who was traveling with a Tibetan companion on a bitterly cold day. Snow was falling heavily, and both men were almost too frozen to go forward; they felt they would never survive the terrible experience. They reached a steep precipice, and there they saw that a man had slipped over the edge, and was lying, almost dead, on the ledge of rock below. Sundar suggested that they should carry the poor fellow into safety. The Tibetan refused to help, saying it was all they could do to save themselves; and he went on, leaving Sundar behind. With great difficulty the Sadhu managed to get the dying man up the slope and on to his back, and then he struggled on with his heavy burden. Before long he came upon the body of his former companion, the Tibetan. He was dead, frozen to death. On struggled Sundar, and gradually the dying man, receiving warmth from the friction of his own body against that of his rescuer, began to revive, while the Sadhu himself grew warm through his labor. At last they reached a village and were safe. With a full heart, Sundar thought of the words of his Master: "Whosoever will save his life shall lose it: and whosoever will lose his life for My sake shall find it."

—L. E. Maxwell

SERVICE

How Some Want God To Use Them

O, God, use me in an advisory capacity," prayed a Negro who seemed to know nothing of yieldedness to God's will. It is not ours to prescribe to God the day and place in which He, in unerring wisdom, may choose to use us. It is ours to pray as did the Apostle Paul, "Lord, what wilt Thou have me to do?" —W. B. K.

* * *

What Motivates Your Service?

It is said that Wendell Wilkie asked President Franklin D. Roosevelt, when he visited the President in his office in the White House, "Mr. President, why do you keep that frail, sickly man, Harry Hopkins, at your elbow?" Said the President, "Mr. Wilkie, through that door flows daily an incessant stream of men and women who, almost invariably, want something from me. Harry Hopkins wants ONLY TO SERVE ME. That's why he is so near me!" In the light of these splendid words of commendation, let us, who claim to be the servants of Christ, re-examine the motives which enter into our service for Him!"

— Howard H. Hamlin, M. D.

Our Part — and God's

On a slope of the Alps mountains lived a little hunchback, himself an ardent admirer of the beauties about him, but unable to join the climbers. His daily business was to minister to those passing, in the little matters related to their long and arduous endeavor. But one day a famous mountain guide said to him, "How would you like to climb the mountain yourself?" The face of the poor misshapen man beamed, "I should like it very much," he said, "but, of course, I cannot do it." "Let's try it," said the guide; and on the summit the grateful man kneeled down to pour out his soul in gratitude. He did his best; his leader did the rest. — *Christian Standard*

* * *

Her Important Part!

When Milan Cathedral was finished, in the vast throngs of people assembled to witness the dedication was a little girl who was heard to cry out in childish glee, as she pointed to the great building, "I helped to build that!" "What!" exclaimed one of the guards who was standing in brilliant uniform. "Show me what you did." "I carried the dinner pail for my father while he worked up yonder," she replied. Her part, though humble, helped to complete the plans of the architect. In relating this story, Bishop Leonard makes this comment: "Our part in life may seem small, but it should bulk large in our thought when we remember that it is helping to complete the plan of the Divine Architect."

— *Christian Herald*

* * *

Occupied FOR or WITH Jesus?

Martha in the kitchen, serving with her hands;
  Occupied *for* Jesus, with her pots and pans.
Loving Him, yet fevered, burdened to the brim, —
  Careful, troubled Martha, occupied *for* Him.

Mary on the footstool, eyes upon her Lord;
  Occupied *with* Jesus, drinking in His word.
This the one thing needful, all else strangely dim:
  Loving, resting Mary, occupied *with* Him.

So may we, like Mary, choose the better part.
  Resting in His presence — hands and feet and heart;
Drinking in His wisdom, strengthened with His grace;
  Waiting for the summons, eyes upon His face.

When it comes, we're ready, spirit, will, and nerve;
  Mary's heart to worship, Martha's hands to serve;
This the rightful order, as our lamps we trim, —
  Occupied *with* Jesus, then occupied *for* Him!

—Lois Reynolds Carpenter
in *Sunday School Times*

* * *

What She Could

A poor old woman in China, who had been converted, but who seemed unwilling to be baptized, was asked why she hesitated. "Why," she replied, with tears running down her cheeks," "you know that Jesus said to His disciples; 'Go ye unto all the world, and preach the Gospel to every creature.' Now, I am an old woman, nearly seventy years of age, and almost blind. I can tell my husband about Jesus Christ, and I can tell my son and his wife when he has one; I am willing to speak to my neighbors, and perhaps I can go to one or two villages, but I can never go to all the world. Now, do you think He will let me call myself a disciple, if I can do no better?" When she heard that the Lord asked only for the best from each of his followers, and does not require from any one more than he can do, she said gladly: "Oh, then I am ready to be baptized whenever you think best."

—*Gospel Herald*

* * *

Service Evangelism

A missionary in New Guinea returned after several years of service. His friend said to him, "Jones, tell me what you found at your station in New Guinea?"

"Found! I found something that looked more hopeless than if I had been sent into the jungle to a lot of tigers."

"What do you mean?"

"Why those people were so degraded that they seemed utterly devoid of moral sense. They were worse than beasts. If a mother were carrying her little baby, and the baby began to cry, she would throw it into the ditch and let it die. If a man saw his father break his leg, he would leave him upon the roadside to die. They had no compassion whatever. They did not know what it meant."

"Well, what did you do for people like that? Did you preach to them?"

"Preach? No! I lived."

"Lived? How did you live?"

"When I saw a baby crying, I picked it up and comforted it. When I saw a man with a broken leg, I mended it. When I saw people in distress, I took them in and pitied them. I took care of them. I lived that way. And those people began to come to me and say: 'What does this mean? What are you doing this for?' *Then I had my chance*

and I preached the gospel."
"Did you succeed?"
"When I left, I left a church!"
—*Record of Christian Work*

* * *

The Limit in Service

"You are going out to die in a year or two. It is madness!" That is what a tutor in Oxford University, England, said to a brilliant student who was giving himself under the auspices of a missionary society for service in Africa.

It turned out that the young man did die after being on the field only a year, but he had answered his tutor in these wise and weighty words: "I think it is with African missions as with the building of a great bridge. You know how many stones have to be buried in the earth, all unseen, to be a foundation. *If Christ wants me to be one of the unseen stones, lying in an African grave, I am content, certain as I am that the final result will be a Christian Africa.*"
— *S. S. World*

* * *

"Do What You Can!"

"We cannot all be heroes,
And thrill a hemisphere,
With some great daring venture,
Some deed that mocks at fear;
But we can fill a life time
With kindly acts and true;
There's always noble service
For noble hearts to do.

"We cannot all be preachers,
And sway with voice and pen,
As strong winds sway the forest,
The mind and hearts of men;
But we can be evangels
To souls within our reach;
There's always Love's own gospel
For loving hearts to preach.

"We cannot all be martyrs,
And win a deathless name
By some Divine baptism,
Some ministry of flame;
But we can live for truth's sake,
Can do for Christ and dare;
There's always faithful witness
For faithful hearts to bear."
—*Selected*

The Story of Two Brothers

There were two boys in the Taylor family. The older said he must make a name for his family, and so turned his face toward Parliament and fame. The younger decided to give his life to the service of Christ and so turned his face toward China and duty. Hudson Taylor, the missionary, died, beloved and known on every continent. "But when I looked in the Encyclopedia to see what the other son had done, I found these words, 'The brother of Hudson Taylor.'"
—*Gospel Herald*

* * *

"Make Me Like Sam!"

L. L. Legters told the story of Sam, a slave who, as soon as one piece of work was done returned at once to his master's doorstep in order that he might always be ready for his master's bidding, just as we should always be waiting for instructions from our Lord and Master. At some previous meeting of Mr. Legters, a girl who had been impressed with this illustration prayed, "O Lord, make me just like Sam;" and the next morning she awakened with her resolution to be a bondslave of Jesus Christ still flaming in her, the day verse in her Scripture calender was: "Blessed is the man that heareth me, watching daily at my gates, waiting at the posts of my doors."
—*Sunday School Times*

* * *

To What Key Are You Pitched?

A traveling man entered a store where fine glass and chinaware were sold. Addressing the proprietor he said, "I would like to purchase all the glasses that you have in your store which are pitched in the key of "A." The proprietor looked amused, and said, "My friend, I don't buy glasses here because of their musical qualities, so I am not able to select the ones which possess the proper key which you desire!" The traveling man opened his grip and took out a tuning fork; when he struck it against the counter, every glass on the shelves that was pitched to the key 'A" immediately responded to the tuning fork. So, in the Christian heart, the souls of all such as are born of God will respond when the voice of Jesus calls for devoted service for Him.

—*Gospel Herald*

* * *

Faithful Service

Not to be always wanting
    Some other work to do,
But cheerfully to take the task
    Which Christ has set for you,
And to bear the little crosses
    Of humble daily life
With that same dauntless courage
    You meant for nobler strife;
And to share the yoke with Jesus
    Wherever He may lead —
Whether in pleasant pastures
    His tender flocks to feed;
Or whether upon the mountains
    His Blood stains mark your way,
Only to follow Him meekly,
    And to follow all the day,
So, soul, you will be the winner,
    When this day's work is done,
And better fitted for labor
    When tomorrow greets the sun.

—*Silver Cross*

* * *

Greatness Serves

Two boys in a boarding school were assigned similar menial duties, such as clearing tables, mopping floors, and so on. One of the boys was very unhappy at this type of work and would skim through his duties very unsatisfactorily and skip away to play. The other boy, observing this, would very unobtrusively put the finishing touches on his pal's work, and he kept it up for quite some time. Ultimately it was brought to the attention of the faculty and they asked the diligent boy why he was finishing up the negligent boy's work. Was it because he felt indebted to him in some way?" "No," said the worker, "you see, the Bible says that 'whosoever will be great among you, let him be your servant,' and I want to be great, so I thought I would try the Lord's way!"

—*Tom M. Olson*

Neglect of Christ

"My mind was so full of service
    I had drifted from Him apart,
And He longed for the old confiding,
    The union of heart with heart.
I sought and received forgiveness,
    While my eyes with tears were dim,
And now though the work is still
        precious,
    The first place is kept for Him!"

—*Selected*

* * *

Are We Ready?

We must be ready for unexpected calls and new responsibilities. The Samaritan who rode down from Jerusalem to Jericho had nothing to do in the morning but follow that highway, and take care that his beast did not stumble or hurt itself, or get tired out so that it could not finish the journey. . . But, when he came to the place where that unknown pilgrim lay senseless and bleeding beside the road, then, in a moment, the Samaritan's duty changed, and it compelled him to be a rescuer, a nurse, a helper of the wounded.

—*Henry Van Dyke*

* * *

New Discoveries

There is an old Italian proverb, "When God shuts a door, He opens a window." Many of God's saints have come to barriers in life which have eventually meant new and broader fields of service. If we are identified with Christ, distressing circumstances will bring us into new discoveries of the riches of His grace and the treasures of His boundless and eternal love.

—*The War Cry*

* * *

What It Takes to be a Friend

A cowboy explained his idea of Christian living: "Now I'm working for Jim here. If I'd sit around, telling what a good fellow Jim is, and singing songs for him, and getting up in the night to serenade him, I'd be doing just what a lot of Christians do; but I wouldn't suit Jim, and I'd get fired mighty quick. But when I buckle on my chaps and hustle among the hills, and see that Jim's herd is all right and not suffering from lack of water or feed or getting off range and branded by cattle thieves then I'm proving my love and serving Jim as he wants to be served."

—*Courage and Confidence from the Bible*

* * *

Cheap Crosses

During my first year in college a missionary came one night to address the students in the Foreign Missions Fellowship. He testified that as he preached the Gospel upon the streets of Mexico, never a day passed that he was not stoned. He told how that upon the religious feast days and festivals, peddlers would go about the streets selling crucifixes and miniature crosses; and as they passed up and down the city streets their cry would be: "Cheap cross! Cheap cross! Who'll buy a cheap cross?" With a voice of searching conviction he asked, "Is your cross a cheap cross? Is the cross we bear for the sake of our Lord a cheap cross? Paul said, "I bear in my body the marks of the Lord Jesus."

—*Gospel Herald*

* * *

Meaning What We Pray

I prayed: "O Lord, bless all the world,
And help me do my part."
And straightway He commanded me
To bind a broken heart.

I prayed, "Oh, bless each hungry child,
May they be amply fed."
He said, "Go find a starving soul,
And share with him your bread."

"Oh, stir the hearts of men," I prayed,
"And make them good and true."
He answered, "There is but one way —
They must be stirred through you."

Dear friend, unless you really mean
Exactly what you say;
Until you mean to work with God,
It's dangerous to pray.

—*Leola Archer, in*
Sunday School Times

When You Serve for Love's Sake

The mother of one of the girls from a Bible class of mine was sick for two years before she died. Jean was the eldest of six, and several mornings each week she would be up at five o'clock to help her Mother before leaving for her work. Many evenings she set aside for housework that her mother was not able to do. Jean was getting so thin that several of the girls from our class were anxious about her, and one of them said, "You can't keep on working as you have been, Jean; your health will break down." "I don't think it will," answered Jean, "but thank you for being concerned about me. I love helping my mother all I can, *and you know things aren't too hard when you do them for love's sake.*"

—*Sunday School Times*

* * *

All Active!

A minister was once asked by an old-time friend, whom he met in a distant city, "How many members do you have in your church?" "One thousand," the preacher replied. "Really!" the friend exclaimed. "And how many of them are active?" "All of them are active," was the response. "About two hundred of them are active for the Lord; the balance are active for the Devil." In which category do we fall when our pastor catalogs the people of his church? More important, where are we in the Lord's sight? "He that is not with me is against me," said our Lord; "and he that gathereth not with me scattereth abroad" (Matt. 12:30). Line up actively on the Lord's side today.

—*The Pilgrim*

* * *

"You Belong to All These People!"

When little Wilhemina was crowned Queen of Holland, the happy little girl, too young to realize the gravity of the occasion, with thousands of people cheering her, was unable to take it all in and said, "Mamma, do all these people belong to me?" And the mother smiled and said, "No, my dear child, you belong to all these people." We are in the world to serve it with our most unselfish and helpful service.

—Gospel Herald

* * *

A Dog in His Service

A remarkable incident occurred in connection with an encampment of Shantung soldiers located at Shanghai. One day a dog wandered into this camp with some leaves of a book in his mouth. The soldiers caught the dog and read the fragment of the book. It was a portion of the Word of God. They became much interested, and followed the dog to a Christian hospital nearby and asked for more of this kind of literature. This was, of course, gladly given to them. As a result, Dr. Goforth and a Chinese evangelist visited this camp, and two hundred men were enrolled as inquirers. If God can so use the mouth of a dog to deliver His Word, can He not use you and me?

—King's Business

* * *

The Smoke of a Thousand Villages

Robert Moffat, a missionary on furlough in England, was telling about the dark land of Africa. Among those who listened to his accounts of the wonders and needs of that continent was a sturdy young Scot named David Livingstone. He was studying to be a doctor and had decided to give his life to the service of God. But just where and how he could make himself of most use he was not sure. He had planned to go to China as a missionary, but was prevented on account of the opium war.

As he listened to Doctor Moffat's incidents he heard him say, "There is a vast plain to the north, where I have sometimes seen, in the morning sun, the smoke of a thousand villages where no missionary has ever been."

"The smoke of a thousand villages!" Livingstone never forgot those words. Here was something worth while for him to do — something hard and heroic. He longed to go where no missionary had ever been, to give himself in service no one else would attempt.

Filled with the new vision, he went to Doctor Moffat and asked, "Would I do for Africa?"

It was David Livingstone's life decision.

—Message of Light

* * *

Value of Service

A discouraged young doctor in one of our large cities was visited by his father who came from a rural district. "Well, son," he said, "How are you getting along?" "I'm not getting along at all," was the answer. The old man's countenance fell, but he spoke courage and patience and hope. Later in the day he went with his son to the free dispensary. He sat in silence while twenty-five poor unfortunates received help. When the door had closed upon the last one, the old man burst out, "I thought you told me you were doing nothing. Why, if I had helped out twenty-five people in a month, I would thank God that my life counted for something." "There isn't any money in it, though," explained the son. "Money," the old man shouted. "What is money in comparison with being useful to your fellowmen?"

—Gospel Herald

* * *

"Inasmuch"

In serving others, in Jesus' Name, we are, in reality, serving Him. How this truth thrills us in service! In disguise, the Lord Jesus presents Himself in the piteous plea of the hungry, the sick, the homeless ones. This thought is sumed up in the closing verse of a poem:

Then in a moment to my view
The stranger darted from disguise,
The tokens in his hand I knew —
My *Saviour* stood before mine eyes.
He spoke, and my poor name He named:
"Of Me thou hast not been ashamed,
These deeds shall thy memorial be;
Fear not, thou didst them unto Me."

—W. B. K.

S I N

The Eater Eaten

A remarkable story was recently told in the daily press. An oyster fisherman on opening the shell of an oyster, discovered within a fish, three and a half inches long, alive and weakly struggling. The oyster, however, was not to be found, and the fisherman was quite convinced that the fish had entered the open shell, and had been trapped by its closing. Once inside, however, it proceeded to devour the oyster, but being unable to open the shell, would have died in it.

It is not an inapt illustration of certain forms of sin. They enter the life through the door of a careless will. Once thus inside, their eviction is most difficult, and they speedily make themselves master of the premises, eventually destroying the whole life.

—*Moody Monthly*

*   *   *

Watch Sin's Beginnings

In Hampton Court Gardens there are many mammoth oaks well-nigh vanquished by the monstrous coils of ivy which entwine themselves about the trees' trunks like some monstrous serpents entwined about the bodies of their prey. There was a time when the ivy was but a tiny aspirant, asking only a little aid in its upward climb. Had the ivy been denied then, the oaks would have never become the victims of the ivy. Now, there is no untwisting of the coils, and every hour the victor is rendering more vanquished its host.

—W. B. K.

*   *   *

"Hacking at Branches of Sin"

"There are an hundred men hacking at the branches of evil, to one who is striking at the root."

—Thoreau

*   *   *

"Be Sure Your Sin Will Find You Out"

Three men in South Boston posed for a passing photographer. They then refused to pay for the picture, beat the itinerant artist, and tried to smash his camera. Then they ran away, chuckling over their exploit, and ridiculing the plight of their victim. But the photographer had one resource which the three rascals had forgotten — the undeveloped plate in his camera. This he developed and turned over to the police. By means of that telltale bit of paper, the three men were recognized immediately and arrested under a charge of assault and battery, and were soon secure in the grasp of the law. *Sin manufactures its own condemnation. For witness against it, the Judge of all the earth does not need any outside testimony.*

—Albert Thomas Howell

*   *   *

Just Like a Little Sin

A ship once wrecked on the Irish coast. The captain was a careful one. Nor had the weather been of so severe a kind to explain the wide distance the ship had swerved from her course. The ship went down, but so much interest was attached to the disaster that a diver was sent down.

Among other portions of the vessel that were examined was the compass that was swung on deck. and inside the compass box was detected a bit of steel which appeared to be the small point of a pocket knife blade. It appeared that the day before the wreck a sailor had been sent to clean the compass, had used his pocket knife in the process, and had unconsciously broken off the point and left it remaining in the box.

The bit of knife blade exerted its influence on the compass, and to a degree that deflected the needle from its proper bent, and spoiled it as an index of the ship's direction.

That piece of knife blade wrecked the vessel.

Thus one trifling sin, as small as a broken knife point, as it were, is able to rob the conscience of peace and happiness.

—Rev. John McNeil

Little Sins

Years ago there was not a single thistle in the whole of Australia. A Scotchman who very much admired thistles thought it a pity that such a great island should be without that marvelous and glorious symbol of his great nation. He therefore collected a pack of thistle seed, and sent it over to one of his friends in Australia. Well, when it landed, the officers may have said, "Oh, let it in; is it not a little one? It is only to be sown in a garden."

Aye, yes, it was but a little one; but now whole districts of the country are covered with it, and it has become the farmer's pest and plague. It was a little one, but it would have been a blessing if the ship that brought that seed had been wrecked. Take heed of the thistle seed; little sins are like it.

—Spurgeon

* * *

Mostly Hidden

It is computed that only from one-tenth to one-eighth of an iceberg is visible above the water line. A London preacher said, "When you are tempted to judge sin from its superficial appearance, and to judge it leniently, remember that sins are like icebergs — the greater part of them is out of sight!"

—*Moody Monthly*

* * *

Already Inside

I once heard the late Rev. Seth Joshua tell how he met a man who said that he could not swallow what the preachers called "original sin." "My good fellow," said Mr. Joshua, "there's no occasion for you to swallow it — it's inside you already."

—*Christian Herald*

* * *

The Pet Rattler

The Memphis Commercial Appeal carried a news dispatch which told of a Negro man across the river in Arkansas who had a pet rattlesnake. The Negro found the snake as a baby snake. He took it and fed it and made quite a pet of it. The reptile would come when he

whistled. It would eat from his fingers. It would coil around his arm and let him stroke its head with the palm of his hand or with the tips of his fingers.

One day he took it to town to exhibit it among his friends. They marveled at its gentleness — marveled at the way it coiled itself with apparent gentleness around his arm — marveled how it would come when he whistled — marveled that it would eat from his hand. He went back home with his pet. When he got home, suddenly, with only the slightest provocation, the reptile became angry. Quicker than the zig-zag lightning flashes from the bosom of a dark cloud, that pet rattler buried its fangs in the black man's arm. In a few hours the man was dead. In one quick instant, with poisonous fangs, the serpent had written his death in his own blood! Two nights after that, the man who should have been sitting with his family in their humble but happy home was sleeping in the mud of an Arkansas grave. *With such dread cometh such an hour to every man and woman who makes a pet of sin.* So cometh such a horror and death to every man who refuses when God calls. An hour of kindred terror awaits the man or the woman who regards not when God stretches out his hand. A day of dreaded despair like unto that the Negro met when he pulled the pet snake's fangs from his arm and hurled it to the ground, is out yonder somewhere to all who set at naught God's counsel and will none of his reproof. *"Be not deceived; God is not mocked." Turn you at God's reproof. Turn now!* There's danger and death in delay. Let go that sin! Drop it — *now! —*

—Robert G. Lee, in
Whirlwinds of God

* * *

No Harm In It

Some wild ducks found a good feeding place among the reeds growing on the edge of a certain slow running river in South Africa. It was not long before some boys discovered the regular visits of the ducks and planned how to catch them. They began by placing pumpkins in the river above the birds and allowing the river to carry them down to where the ducks were feeding. At first the ducks were nervous and flew away, but soon they decided there was no harm in it, until the pumpkins could almost bump them without disturbing them in any way.

Then came the second part of the boys' plan. Each took a pumpkin, scooped the inside out, made two small holes to see through, and placing them over their heads quietly slipped into the river, showing only the pumpkin above the water. They moved slowly and quietly toward the ducks, caught them by their legs from under the water and killed them.

How many boys and girls are led into sin by saying, "There is no harm in it." The devil likes to deceive boys and girls, just as those boys deceived the ducks. We must always be on the lookout and not let him fool us with questionable things. Jesus will help us to keep out of sin if we ask Him.

—*Gospel Stories*

* * *

Playing With Handles

A little girl, aged four, fell out of a taxi on the way home from a party. She was taken to the hospital, and when she was dying, she said: "I have been a naughty girl. I was playing with the door. I won't do it any more." She must have been a very honest little soul to own up bravely that the shocking business was all her own fault. "I won't do it any more." It was too true. It was her last party. We are all trying the handles of doors in these days, especially the doors marked "liberty" and "happiness." And it sometimes happens that doors fly suddenly open, landing us in the gutter, in disaster and wretchedness.

—*British Weekly*

* * *

Sin's Treacherousness

Some years ago a noted wild beast tamer gave a performance in England. He took lions, tigers, leopards and hyenas through their part of the entertainment astonishing the audience by his complete control over them. As a clos-

ing act, he introduced an enormous boa constrictor, twenty-five feet long. He had bought it when it was only two or three days old and for twenty-five years he had handled it daily, so that it was considered perfectly harmless and completely under his control. The curtain rose upon an Indian woodland scene. The music of an Oriental band steals through the trees, a rustling sound is heard and a huge serpent is seen winding its way through the undergrowth. It stops, its head erect, its bright eyes sparkle, its whole body seems animated. The tamer comes forward and at a signal from him the snake slowly approaches as it has done every day before and begins to coil its heavy folds around him. Higher and higher it rises, until the man and the serpent seem blended into one, and the hideous head is raised above the man. Why we cannot say, but at that very moment the deadly serpent-nature seemed to return. The man gave a scream, the audience burst into applause, but the cheers froze on their lips. The tamer's scream was a deathwail of agony, the cold, shining folds had embraced him for the last time. The audience heard bone after bone crack as they tightened upon him. His plaything had become his master and destroyer. Oh, what a picture of sin! How dreadful is the power of sin.

—E. Gorham Clark, in *Gospel Herald*

* * *

It's Like This...

A woman came to a minister, carrying in her hands a quantity of wet sand. "Do you see what this is, sir?" she said.

"Yes. It is wet sand."

"But do you know what it means?"

"I do not know exactly what you mean by it. What is it?"

"Ah, sir!" she said, "that's me, and the multitude of my sins can't be numbered;" and she gave way to passionate weeping. The minister, calming her, asked her where she had procured the sand.

"At the Beacon."

"Go back, then, and take a spade with you and dig till you raise a good mound, shovel it as high as ever you can, and leave it. Stand back on the shore and see the effect of the waves upon it." The meaning came to the woman. The blood of Christ would wash all her sins away.

—*Christian Digest*

* * *

Something That can Undo

The story is told of a man dying in a London hospital. A Christian visitor asked him, "Is there anything that I can do for you?" The man said, "Not a thing." The question was repeated each day, for several days, and the same answer given. Finally, with the end near at hand, the sick man said in an answer to the same question, "Sir, you ask me if there is anything that you can do for me; there isn't. But tell me — tell me — is there anything that can undo?" What memories of the sins and crimes and failures of the past were in that question! The man was searching for something to take the load off his soul. Thank God there is something that can undo; and the Christian gladly told him of the precious blood of Christ that cleanseth us from all — *all* sin. — *Gospel Herald.*

* * *

Man's Head in Tiger's Mouth!

As a part of a circus act, a man would place his head in a tiger's mouth! He advanced to the tiger and the tiger opened his mouth. While the crowd watched in breathless wonder and horror, the man thrust his head in the open mouth, paused a moment, then slowly withdrew his head from the place of danger and backed from the cage. As he shut the door, the tiger leaped against the bars with terrific force.

Such a foolhardy stunt was sure to attract much attention, and many prophesied that some day that man would pay for his foolishness. Their utterance was fulfilled. In a small town in northern Pennsylvania the man met his doom. While his head was in the tiger's mouth, those powerful jaws closed on him, and before several bullets ended the tiger's life, the man was a corpse.

This takes us in thought to two verses in the Epistle of James: "But every man is tempted, when he is drawn away of his own lust, and enticed. Then when lust hath conceived, it bringeth forth sin; and sin, when it is finished, bringeth forth death." — L. L. Wightman, in *Gospel Herald.*

* * *

The Tenacity of Sin

The following was told in the address of a converted Burman to a group of natives:

"A little banyan seed said to a palm tree: 'I am weary of being tossed about by the wind; let me stay a while among your leaves.' 'Oh, yes,' said the palm tree, 'stay as long as you like,' and by and by forgot the little seed was there. But the seed was not idle. It sent out little fibers and tiny roots, and they crept around the trunk and under the bark and into the heart of the tree itself, and then the tree cried out: 'What is this?' And the Banyan said: 'It is only the little seed you allowed to rest among your leaves.' 'Leave me now,' said the palm tree, 'you have grown too large and strong.' 'I cannot leave you now; we have grown together. I would kill you if I tore myself away.' The palm tree bowed its head and tried to shake the banyan off, but could not, and little by little the palm leaves withered, the trunk shriveled, and only the banyan could be found. *Beware of little sins!*"

—*My Life in Burma*, in
Sunday School Times

* * *

Familiar With Sin?

"Vice is a monster of such frightful mein,
That to be hated needs but to be seen;
But seen too oft, familiar with its face,
We first endure, then pity, then embrace!" — Pope

* * *

Your Secret Sins Will Come to Light

The newspapers of Cincinnati recorded that a poorly dressed woman went to Dr. George Herman asking him to make an X-ray examination of her heart free of cost. She claimed that she was very poor and couldn't pay. The doctor consented to do the work. But when he turned his machine a little below the heart he saw a concealed pocket in which was a purse with five twenty-dollar gold pieces. "Your heart is very bad," he said; "you lied when you said you were poor." In like manner all secret things will come to light before God. — G. A. Swanson.

* * *

Fatal Dalliance!

While in a harvest field, I noticed a spider which seemed intent on minding its own business. A moment later a grasshopper was seen moving along just a few inches from the spider. He crawled slowly in the hot sun, as if on a tour of minute inspection. Gradually he approached the spider until they were but a short distance apart. And then, slowly but with apparent deliberation, the grasshopper reached out with one of his feelers toward Mr. Spider as if to shake hands. Quick as a flash, out went one of the spider's legs, and when he had withdrawn it a web had been attached to the antennae of the grasshopper. Instead of flying away, as he might easily have done, the grasshopper reached out another member, with the same result. Time after time the process was repeated, until the hopper seemed to become aware that he was getting into trouble. By this time he was restless, and his movements were more frequent, but each time he raised an appendage a new web was attached. Finally, in desperation, Mr. Hopper began a real struggle to free himself. But it was too late. At the very moment when he commenced in earnest to attempt his escape, Mr. Spider jumped upon him and rolled him over and over in an ever-increasing coat of web until, within just a few moments, the grasshopper was bound and helpless, and Mr. Spider began his meal. This is just the way many people are entangled with sin — drawn away of their own lust, and enticed (Jas. 1:14).

—Free Methodist

Living on Appearances

Some live on a mere appearance. Drummond writes of the African white ant: "One may never see the insect, possibly, in the flesh, for it lives underground; but its ravages confront one at every turn. You build your house, and for a few months fancy you have pitched upon the one solitary site in the country where there are no white ants. But one day suddenly the doorpost totters, and lintel and rafters come down together with a crash. You look at a section of the wrecked timbers and discover that the whole inside is eaten away. The apparently solid logs of which the rest of the house is built are now mere cylinders of bark, and through the thickest of them you could push your little finger."

Many influences act on Christian character much as these secret pests act upon the beams of houses. *Secret sins silently eat out the pith of the Christian life, and yet everything remains the same to the eye.*

—W. L. Watkins, in
Western Recorder

* * *

"Case Dismissed!"

A southern boy was arraigned in juvenile court for stealing a watermelon. He was guilty. Before passing sentence the judge asked, "Is there anything you wish to say before I pass sentence?" The boy thought for a minute, then said, "Judge, have YOU ever stolen a watermelon?" A painful silence pervaded the court room. Finally, the judge blurted out, "No cross examination allowed! CASE DISMISSED!"

— W. B. K.

* * *

Don't Touch It!

Some years ago in India a little girl whose parents were missionaries came running excitedly to her daddy early one morning. "Oh, Daddy! Come quickly," she said. "I have found the most beautiful string of jewels lying in the grass." The parents had wisely taught this little girl that she must never touch anything that did not belong to her without first asking permission. The father followed the little girl to the dew drenched grass, and she pointed out to him the string of glistening jewels. The "jewels" happened to be a deadly coral snake whose bite would have meant certain death. The only safe thing was not to touch it even though it was beautiful. Sin must never be played with. In its most harmless form it is deadly venomous. The only safe thing is not to touch it.

— *Sunday School Banner*

* * *

"The Bird with the Broken Pinion"

I remember a flash of righteous indignation that swept over Dr. Scofield's face once as he said, "People talk about the bird with the broken wing, — 'The bird with the broken pinion never soars as high again.' As if we did not all have a broken wing! For most of us both wings are broken, and both legs, and our necks!" So let us just give up this notion that it is the "broken pinion" that is going to keep us from soaring as high as some victorious life Christians can soar. One thing is certain: the bird *without* a broken pinion is never going to know victory. One qualification you must have for the victorious life is the broken pinion, the broken nature, uttermost weakness. God makes no offer of victory to strong people, people who have not failed, and

failed utterly. But for *sinners* he has a Gospel.

—From *The Victorious Life*
by Charles Trumbull

* * *

One Thing Pained Him

When the great Chrysostom was arrested by the Roman Emperor, the latter sought to make the Greek Christian recant, but without success. So the emperor discussed with his advisers what could be done to the prisoner. "Shall I put him in a dungeon?" the Emperor asked.

"No," one of his counsellors replied, "for he will be glad to go. He longs for the quietness wherein he can delight in the mercies of his God."

"Then he shall be executed!" said the Emperor.

"No," was the answer, "for he will also be glad to die. He declares that in the event of death he will be in the presence of his Lord."

"What shall we do then?" the ruler asked.

There is only one thing that will give Chrysostom pain," the counsellor said. "To cause Chrysostom to suffer, make him sin. He is afraid of nothing except sin."

—*Baptist Standard*

SINGING

The Singing Marine!

Corporal William Shurts, 21, of F. Company, 5th Marine Regiment, was hit by a sniper's bullet on a Korean hill. He died the next day. His inspirational singing brought cheer and courage to the trenches. His comrades described him as the "man who brought God to the front lines!" His favorite song was "The Old Rugged Cross." How this song enhearted the men in the foxholes! Often, they would join with Corporal Shurts on the chorus. Passing from man to man, William spoke quietly to them of faith in God. "After he talked to us," a comrade wrote, "the dark

night was not so dark, and as you looked up, you thanked God that He had sent a man among you whose belief was so strong that he could PASS IT ALONG!" — W. B. K.

* * *

How Song Saved Sankey's Life:

One Christmas Eve, Ira D. Sankey was travelling by steamboat up the Delaware River. Asked to sing, Mr. Sankey sang the "Shepherd Song." After the song was ended, a man with a rough, weather-beaten face came up to Mr. Sankey and said: "Did you ever serve in the Union Army?" "Yes," answered

Mr. Sankey, "in the spring of 1860." "Can you remember if you were doing picket duty on a bright, moonlight night in 1862?" "Yes," answered Mr. Sankey, very much surprised. "So did I," said the stranger, "but I was serving in the Confederate army. When I saw you standing at your post I said to myself: 'That fellow will never get away from here alive.' I raised my musket and took aim. I was standing in the shadow completely concealed, while the full light of the moon was falling upon you. At that instant, just as a moment ago, you raised your eyes to heaven and began to sing. Music, especially song, has always had a wonderful power over me, and I took my finger off the trigger. 'Let him sing his song to the end,' I said to myself. 'I can shoot him afterwards. He's my victim at all events, and my bullet cannot miss him.' But the song you sang then was the song you sang just now. I heard the words perfectly:

We are Thine, do Thou befriend us,
Be the guardian of our way.

"Those words stirred up many memories in my heart. I began to think of my childhood and my God-fearing mother. She had many, many times sung that song to me. But she died all too soon, otherwise much in my life would no doubt have been different.

"When you had finished your song it was impossible for me to take aim at you again. I thought: 'The Lord who is able to save that man from certain death must surely be great and mighty' and my arm of its own accord dropped limp at my side."

— *Religious Digest*

* * *

No Singing

When the noted agnostic Robert Ingersoll died, the printed funeral notices said, "There will ne no singing." Look not for hymns, anthems, oratorios, carols, and spiritual songs among infidels, agnostics, or skeptics. Without God, without Christ, without redemption, without a divine revelation, and without hope, what have they to sing about?

— *Sunday School Banner*

"The Devil and Good Tunes!"

It was Moody who asked, when criticized for the gaiety of his hymns, "Is the devil to have all the good tunes?"

— W. B. K.

* * *

"I'd Rather Have Jesus!"

Shortly after the Normandy invasion a chaplain's assistant sat at the organ console in one of France's famous cathedrals. The strains of "I'd Rather Have Jesus" drifted through the windowless edifice to reach the ears — and hearts of jeep-riding GI's and the French peasants as they stopped to listen. Another organ — this time at Bauxweiler, France, and the one used by the famous physician and concert organist, Albert Schweitzer — played by the same chaplain's assistant, also responded to the simple strains of "I'd Rather Have Jesus." In a letter to Beverly Shea, the soldier closed with, "I wanted you to know how wonderful I think your song is and to let you know that churches in France and Germany have heard it re-echo through their sacred halls." — *Baptist Standard*

* * *

When He Sang a Drunkard to Sleep

A loud-voiced, drunken man, followed by his wife and small son, swaggered aboard a railroad train that was soon steaming across the lowlands of Scotland. Across the aisle sat a Christian temperance worker who felt led to sing an old hymn with the hope that the drunkard would be quieted and perhaps go to sleep. Soon he was snoring vociferously. After a nap of some hours, he awakened somewhat sobered. As the temperance lecturer left the train, the fellow held out his hand, bade him good-by, and actually thanked him for his singing. Fifteen years passed and the temperance worker was again touring Scotland. After a particularly successful meeting, a well-dressed man and wife came forward and inquired of the speaker if he remembered them. He shook his head. "Why, I'm the man who was drunk that day on the train," confessed the stranger, "and you sang me to sleep. But I never could get away from those hymns, and it wasn't long before they led me to Christ. Our son Joseph, who was also with us that day, is now in school preparing for the ministry." This Joseph was, in years to come, to be the great Dr. Joseph Parker, who was for a long time pastor in one of London's largest churches.

—*American Holiness Journal*

* * *

Singspiration in Africa

Some years ago, a missionary in Central Africa went hunting with his native gun-bearer to secure a fresh supply of meat. It became dark and they lost their direction. Suddenly a strange sound came to their ears, and they saw in the glow of a camp fire an African who had become a Christian. Sitting with his wife, children, and native friends by their camp fire, they were singing "What a Friend We Have in Jesus."

Even to the ends of the earth, where Christianity has penetrated, men, women, and children are singing hymns.

—*Sunday School Times*

* * *

A General's Favorite

General Robert E. Lee was a man of fervent religious spirit, and those who were associated with him in war and in peace recognized the deeply devotional nature of the military man and educator. Two books he constantly used were the Bible and the Book of Common Prayer. His favorite hymn revealed his noble Christian spirit:

How firm a foundation, ye saints of the Lord,
Is laid for your faith in His excellent word!

At the time of his funeral the assembled company sang this hymn.

—*Sunday School Times*

* * *

Her Morning Hymn

A rooming-house keeper called on the city missionary at a certain mission and said to him, "Mrs. J— has a room in my house and she attends this mis-

sion; every morning before she leaves for her work she sings a hymn, something about taking the Cross for a shadow." "Oh," said the missionary, "that's a lovely old hymn entitled, 'Beneath the Cross of Jesus.' I'm glad Mrs. J— sings it; and, tell me, does it help you?" "It sure does," answered the woman. "So much it helps me, that I want to know more about this way of life that makes Mrs. J— so content, and so different from all the other roomers." —*As told by the missionary.*

* * *

Don't Let the Song Go Out of Your Life

A doctor visiting a leper colony heard an aged sufferer singing cheerily; yet he knew that her condition was serious. "Well, Mother," he remarked to her, "you must be feeling pretty well today — you're singing so happily."

She turned a face full of suffering towards him and answered, "O Doctor, my sores hurt so badly I must sing!"

— *Prairie Overcomer*

* * *

Hymns In The Jungle

Here is a report of a soldier's experience in the South Pacific. After a time in Australia, he was sent to New Guinea when operations were begun there. High in the mountains he was wounded in combat. "Imagine," he says, "a dark, stormy, rainy, tropical night and myself, a wounded American soldier, being carried down the mountainside through the thick jungle by a group of natives called Fuzzy-wuzzies, and all the way to hear them singing the Christian hymn,

'Lead, kindly Light, amid the encircling gloom,
Lead Thou me on;

The night is dark, and I am far from home;
Lead Thou me on.'

That was an experience in my Christian life that has meant more to me than anything else." — *King's Business*

Singing In The Dark!

One Christmas, I was in a solitary cell. Suddenly, out of the stillness, from the cell next to mine a beautiful Chinese voice was singing — clear and joyful — "O Come, All Ye Faithful," and then "O, Rest in the Lord," and many other beautiful Christian hymns. A little later I was to be transferred to another prison. I could not sing, but I whistled, "God Be With You Till We Meet Again." Back through the walls came the answer, clear as a flute, "God Be With You Till We Meet Again."

The missionary did not know who the singer was, but we catch the thrill of the Christmas message, coming from our many Chinese friends who are singing in the darkness at this Christmas time. We will not forget them in our prayer. — *The Missionary Link*

* * *

"All Hail The Power of Jesus Name!"

There came the time when George Grenfell, a missionary in Africa, turned into a tributary of the Congo River and met a large group of natives singing powerfully and heartily, in their own language, the moving hymn of *All Hail the Power of Jesus' Name.* And here, only years before, George Grenfell had witnessed scenes of cruelty and hatred. Tears welled into the missionary's eyes as he thought of this. Truly, "All Hail!"

—Will Herman

* * *

In the Dark

In the parish church of a small town on the east of Scotland, the evening service was drawing to a close. The aged pastor had announced the last hymn, when suddenly the lights went out. After a moment of silence the precentor arose from his seat in front and said, "We cannot manage that hymn, sir, but we can all sing 'The Lord's My Shepherd,' in the dark." "Yes, we will take the Twenty-third Psalm," said the pastor. "And let me add, that it is well with every soul that can sing 'The Lord's My Shepherd' in the dark." — *Record of Christian Work.*

The Devil Doesn't Like Praise

"Every day will I bless Thee; and I will praise Thy Name for ever and ever" (Ps. 145:2).

Miss Carmichael, a missionary in South India, tells of a little Hindu girl, only seven years old, who lives in her home and has a great aversion to her share of the household duties, which consists of cleansing the brass water vessels. But one day she came to Miss Carmichael, saying, "Satan doesn't come very close to me if I sing all the time I am rubbing the brasses. He runs away when he hears me sing; so I sing very loud and that drives him away. He doesn't like hymns."

— *Triumphs of Faith*

* * *

They Could Not Bear To Go

Many who sing the old hymn, "Blest be the tie that binds," do not know its history. It was written by the Rev. John Fawcett, who in the eighteenth century was the pastor of a poor little church in Yorkshire. In 1773 he felt obliged to accept a call to a London church. His farewell sermon had been preached, six wagons loaded with furniture and books stood by the door. His congregation — men, women, and children — were in an agony of tears. Looking up, Mrs. Fawcett said: "Oh, John, I cannot bear this! I know not where to go!" "Nor do I," said he, "nor will we go! Unload the wagons, and put everything back." His letter of acceptance was recalled, and he wrote this hymn to commemorate the episode.

—*Sunday Companion*

* * *

Do You Know the Songs?

The story is told of a man who was saved when he was old. He had been a great singer. He had sung many of the world's great songs. He had been applauded and honored by the world. A few days before he died, his daughter saw him weeping as he lay in his bed. She bent over him and asked why the tears were running down his cheeks. "Oh," he said, "I dreamed I was in Heaven, and everywhere I went, people were singing, and they wanted me to sing with them, but I couldn't sing the songs because I didn't know them. I cried so that I wakened crying." As he looked up into her face, he said, "I've sung all my life, but I never learned Heaven's songs."

—*Sunday School Times*

* * *

Their Most Loved Hymn

A native pastor went with his foreign colleague to visit a large leper colony. With their bodies partly protected by sterile robes and their feet thrust into medicated boots, they walked through the cultivated acres, past little homes and gardens, to the great temple. Here permission had been given to hold a service for the Christians. One by one the sufferers came limping in, their swollen faces lifted in happy expectation. Obviously those in the group were believers and so were familiar with the songs of Zion. "What shall we sing? What is your most loved hymn?" inquired the leader, thinking they would call for "I must tell Jesus all of my troubles." To his surprise, the request came at once for something very different:

Singing I go along life's road,
Praising the Lord, praising the Lord;
Singing I go along life's road,
For Jesus has lifted my load!

Thus does the Lord grant His little ones songs in the night also of affliction.

—*Sunday School*

* * *

The Song That Cheers

Haydn, the great musician, was once asked why his church music was so cheerful, and he replied: "When I think upon God, my heart is so full of joy that the notes dance and leap, as it were, from my pen, and, since God has given me a cheerful heart, it will be pardoned me that I serve Him with a cheerful spirit."

—*Gospel Herald*

The Jewish Legend

There is an old Jewish legend which says that, after God had created the world, He called the angels to Him and asked them what they thought of it; and one of them said, "One thing is lacking: the sound of praise to the Creator." So God created music, and it was heard in the whisper of the wind, and in the song of the birds; and to man also was given the gift of song. And all down the ages this gift of song has indeed proved a blessing to multitudes of souls.

—*Maritime Baptist*

* * *

How Scott Was Spared

Wherever India's devoted missionary, Scott, met a heathen, he followed him to his tribe to carry the Gospel. On one such occasion he came across a fierce-looking man and followed him to his tribe — a tribe of wild heathen savages in the interior. He came upon the tribe, dancing about a fire and exciting their fury with a war dance. No chance was he given to speak. Strong muscular arms seized him, and spears were raised, and threatened his life. Scott closed his eyes, raised his violin, and, expecting any moment to meet his Saviour, began playing and singing the words of the hymn, "All Hail the Power of Jesus' Name." He finished the first stanza, went on to the second and the third. No spear reached him. Surprised, he opened his eyes — to find the spears fallen to the ground, and tears in the eyes of these heathen savages. Scott was spared and he spent two years among these people, preaching to them the Gospel of Christ and the mercy of God.

—*The Dawn*

* * *

"Jerusalem, My Happy Home!"

A Scottish mother, who sang, "Jerusalem My Happy Home," so often that her boy learned the words by heart when he was very young, unconsciously made an impression upon his young soul which in after years was the means of bringing him back from sinful wanderings to ask forgiveness for an ill-spent life and to receive pardon. The mother died when her boy was quite young, and he became a wanderer. He came to America, fell in with bad companions, and after years of "feeding on husks," he was carried into a hospital to die. He was a stranger, and would give no account of himself, until one day, when the good nurse was doing something for his comfort in the way of rearranging his pillow, he heard her humming, very low, "Jerusalem, My Happy Home." Instantly his eyes filled with tears, and he said, "Please sing the whole of that hymn to me; it was the only one my mother sang so often when I was a child." All the mother's teachings and prayers came back to him. He sent for a clergyman and asked for prayer. His heart was melted, and at the eleventh hour he found pardon and peace. —*Gospel Herald*

* * *

Blessed Presumption

In one of her letters to a young convert, Frances Havergal comments thus: "Presumption, to speak of Jesus! Is a soldier presumptuous to say what a good general he has? Is it presumption for a liberated slave to tell of his deliveries to his one-time fellow slaves?" She herself would speak for Him anywhere and everywhere, and sing for Him in the most unlikely places. At the first big gathering she went to in Leamington she was asked to sing, and she sang, "Whom having not seen ye love." Everyone was greatly astonished, and there was a profound silence while she was singing, a silence not easily broken when she had finished. Two Christian girls were in her audience, and afterward they told her that they did not know music and singing could be used in the service of the Lord Jetsus Christ. After a talk with Miss Havergal, they made up their minds to put more vigor into their wearisome daily practice, and so fit themselves for this form of service.

—From *Frances Ridley Havengal*, by Esther E. Enock

A Spirit Guided Messenger

Uncle John Vassar, that indefatigable personal worker who was better known during an earlier generation, on one occasion was going from house to house distributing tracts and speaking with the people about Christ. An Irish woman of the city heard of this strange man who was entering houses without an introduction, and was determined she would have none of it. The next day he rang her door bell. When she recognized him she slammed the door in his face. Nothing daunted, he went and sat down on the curb in front of her house and sang this passionate stanza:

"But drops of grief can ne'er repay
The debt of love I owe;
Here, Lord, I give myself away;
'Tis all that I can do."

A short time later this poor woman sought admission to the membership of a local church. As she made her confession before the elders, she could only say between her sobs: " *'Twas those drops of grief. They burned themselves into my heart.*"

—George L. Ruliscon, in *One Altogether Beautiful*

* * *

Singing in the Storm!

Lieutenant E. Williams, representing the Royal Navy, related how he had joined the navy fifty years earlier. Among his many experiences and descriptions was the story of a comrade of his who was on a ship that encountered a hurricane in the Bay of Biscay while headed for Gibraltar. The seas got into the engine room, and volunteers were called out to bale out the water. This young comrade went down. The men came up, tired, and apparently beaten. The ship was rolling in the terrible storm, and all expected to find a watery grave. But this young Christian sailor brought out a little accordion and played and sang:

I've found a Friend; oh, such a Friend!
He loved me ere I knew Him;

He drew me with the cords of love,
And thus He bound me to Him.
And 'round my heart still closely twine
Those ties which naught can sever,
For I am His, and He is mine,
Forever and forever.

New hope came into the hearts of the others as he played and sang. They managed to get back to England, though the ship was listing terribly. Said Lieutenant Williams in his address: "Years afterward I heard some of them tell the story of what wonderful influence came to them in that terrible storm through that young Christian and his singing."

Sunday School Times

* * *

Storms Make Music

I lived in an old house in the country once, where the wind would sometimes whistle around so that I thought I would have to have some music if it must blow like that. So I made a rude Æolian harp of mere sewing silk strung across a board, and placed it under the slightly lifted sash of a north window, and the music was so sweet through all the house when the wild storms came! Is there any north window in your life? Could you not so arrange the three wires of faith, hope, and love that the storms of life would only bring more music into this sad world?

—*King's Business*

* * *

The Value of Singing

A brave little girl was taken to a doctor for a minor, but painful operation. When all was ready, the kindly doctor said, "This will hurt, but you may cry or scream as much as you please." "The little girl looked up at him, smiling, and said, "I would rather sing," which she did with her sweet, childish voice and went through her brief ordeal without sigh, groan or tear.

—*The Presbyterian*

A Gospel Hymn

Dr. H. Clay Trumbull, in his work as a chaplain, once tried to point to Christ a young soldier who was under conviction. But the young man failed to find peace. As he was leaving, Dr. Trumbull gave him a copy of a Soldier's Hymn book. When next they met, the young soldier's face revealed that the change had come. "You tried to make it plain, Chaplain," he said, "yet I didn't get any help. But I opened that little hymn book and read:

Just as I am, and waiting not
To rid my soul of one dark blot,
To Thee whose blood can cleanse each spot,
O Lamb of God, I come!

And then it was all clear to me."

—*Sunday School Times*

* * *

The gods, or God?

Two little Japanese girls of Tokyo were comparing experiences after the earthquake. One had gone with her parents to the Buddhist temple where immense throngs, silent and hopeless, had passed before the idols. "Our parents just looked at the gods and scowled," said the child. The other little girl had attended a service held by a Christian missionary. "Our people looked up to God and sang," she replied. The missionary had read Hebrews 12:26, 27: "Whose voice then shook the earth." Then the people joined with him in singing:

How firm a foundation, ye saints of the Lord,
Is laid for your faith in his excellent Word.

Then with good courage the people turned to the task of rebuilding their homes, and thereby put new hope into all with whom they came in contact.

—*Youth's Companion*

SMALL THINGS

His Touch

I have not much to offer
To Christ, my Lord and King;
No wealth, no might, no wisdom,
No noble gift to bring.
"Five loaves and two small fishes?"
But what alas are they
Among the throngs of hungry
Who crowd life's troubled way?

"Five loaves and two small fishes?"
Not much, dear heart, 'tis true;
But yield them to the Master
And see what He can do!
Placed in His hands of mercy
Thy little will be much.
'Tis not thy gift that matters,
But His almighty touch!

—Avis B. Christiansen

* * *

The Little Tasks

The ceaseless round of little things
Which every dawning brings —
'Tis this, which makes my sum of care
'Tis this, I pray for strength to bear.
Lord, help me through it all to see
How much my duties bring to me.

These never ending tasks I face
Which sometimes seem so commonplace,
The beds I make to make again,
The little windows splashed with rain,
The floors I sweep, the chairs I dust, —
All these I do because I must.

The little garments I repair
And make them fit once more to wear,
The meals I get, the rows and rows
Of dishes every woman knows;
'Tis these, dear Lord, that make me doubt
And fear they'll wear my patience out.

Lord, keep my vision sweet and clear
When irksome days grow dark and drear;
Still let me see their eyes aglow
With love that shall be mine to know;
Help me to sing each morning through,
Because such tasks are mine to do.

For them I sew, for them I bake,
For them these endless pains I take;
Help me to see in all I touch
The little hearts I love so much,
And understand ('tis all I ask)
The meaning of each little task.

—Edgar A. Guest*

* * *

Little Things

Big moments seldom come. Great deeds are rare. Most of the elements that go into the making of a human life are in themselves infinitesimal and of small consequence. The unmediated word, the spontaneous action, the glance and the smile that we think nothing of, are the strands of which a life is woven. Our character is determined by the sum total effect of all these small things upon us. Life is mostly chores, and the one who conducts himself faithfully when he thinks no one is observing is the one whose life will total something worth while. Let us be faithful, then, in small responsibilities. Let us seize the small opportunities. If we take care of the little things in life, the great things will take care of themselves.

—*Gospel Herald*

* * *

Drowned in a Ditch

Sir Ernest H. Shackelton, British naval officer and explorer, after his Arctic explorations, anchored his ship in the River Seine. There, it was lashed by a violent storm. It seemed as if the craft would sink.

Exclaimed the explorer: "Shall I, who have braved the terrors of the broad oceans be drowned in a ditch?" Oftentimes, it is some "mosquito" of discouragement which drowns many of God's children in defeat and despair.

—W. B. K.

---

* Copyrighted. Used by permission of The Reilly & Lee Co., Chicago, Ill.

"No Little Things With God"

I feel permitted to offer up my prayers for everything that concerns me, and I am inclined to imagine that there are no little things with God. His hand is as manifest in the feathers of a butterfly's wing, in the eye of an insect, in the folding and packing of a blossom, in the curious aqueducts by which a leaf is nourished, as in the creation of the world, and in the laws by which the planets move.

I understand literally the injunction, "In every thing make your requests known to God;" and I cannot but notice how amply these prayers have been met.

—Sir Thomas Fowell Buxton

* * *

Great In Little Things

I think that the folks who are faithful in that which is least wear very radiant crowns. They are the people who are great in little tasks. They are scrupulous in the rutty roads of drudgery. They win their triumphs amid small irritations. They are as loyal when they are wearing aprons in the kitchen as if they wore purple and fine linen in the visible presence of the King. They finish the obscurest bit of work as though it were to be displayed before an assembled Heaven by Him who is Lord of light and glory. Great souls are these who are faithful in that which is least!

Our Lord Jesus lived for thirty years amid the little happenings of the little town of Nazareth. Little villages spell out their stories in small events. And He, the young Priest of glory, was in the carpenter's shop. He moved amid humdrum tasks, and petty cares, and village gossip, and trifling trade, and He was faithful in that which is least. He wore His crown on other than state occasions. It was never off His brow.

—J. H. Jowett, in
The Preacher's Magazine

The "One-Note" Musician

"A series of pictures in a popular magazine portrays the story of a one-note musician. . . . He takes his seat in the orchestra with the other musicians, arranges his score, and tunes his instrument. On the arrival of the conductor, the music begins with the leader skillfully bringing in first one group of musicians and then another. After a long time the crucial moment arrives — it is the time when the one note is played. The conductor turns to him and his one note sounds forth. Once more the orchestra plays and the one-note man sits quietly throughout the rest of the concert. . . . *One note only! It may be that our part in life's work may be very small . . . but even that is important.*" It was only a colt, but the Lord had need of him.

—*Secret Place*

* * *

"Tend That for Me"

"Father, where shall I work today?"
  And my love flowed warm and free.
Then He pointed me toward a tiny spot
  And said, "Tend that for Me."
I answered quickly. "Oh, no, not that!
  Why, no one would ever see,
No matter how well my work was done,
  In that little place for me."
And the word He spoke, it was not stern,
  He answered me tenderly:
"Ah, little one, search that heart of thine,
  Art thou working for them or Me?
Nazareth was a little place,
  And so was Galilee."

—*Selected*

* * *

Who We Are — What We Are

The big things of life show who we are. The little things of life show WHAT we are!"

—W. B. K.

* * *

Watch for the Little Things

Watch for the little things
  That brighten any day;
The color of a bird's swift wings,
  The lovely jeweled spray

Of leaves when they are spangled wet
  With dew, and note the grass
Running like music — watch the white
  High-flying clouds that pass.
Watch for the kindly deeds
  That you alone can do;
Help ever with the simple needs
  Of loved ones nearest you,
And when the day with all it brings
  Has swiftly passed away,
'Twill be the little simple things
  That made a lovely day.

—Grace Noll Crowell

* * *

What Almost Defeated Him

Not long ago a stranger met an overland traveler, who had walked on foot from the Golden Gate to New York. He was interested to know what was the greatest difficulty the traveler had encountered in his long journey. He suggested that perhaps the mountains on the trail had been the greatest barrier, but the traveler assured his questioner that it was not that. Then he suggested that perhaps the swollen streams which cut across his road presented the greatest hazard, but it was not that. After a little he said, "What almost defeated me in my journey across the continent was the sand in my shoes." Life is forever tripping over trivial things.

—*Religious Telescope*

* * *

Simple, Little Things

It's the little things we do and say
That mean so much as we go our way,
A kindly deed can lift a load
From weary shoulders on the road,
Or a gentle word, like summer rain,
May soothe some heart and banish pain.
What joy or sadness often springs
From just the simple little things!

—*Selected*

SORROW, SUFFERING, CHASTENING

When Weights Are Blessings

Dr. Lambie, medical missionary, formerly of Abyssinia, has forded many swift and bridgeless streams in Africa. The danger in crossing such a stream lies in being swept off one's feet and carried down the stream to greater depths or hurled to death against the hidden rocks. Dr. Lambie learned from the natives the best way to make such a hazardous crossing. The man about to cross finds a large stone, the heavier the better, lifts it to his shoulder, and carries it across the stream as "ballast." The extra weight of the stone keeps his feet solid on the bed of the stream and he can cross safely without being swept away. Dr. Lambie drew this application: While crossing the dangerous stream of life, enemies constantly seek to overthrow us and rush us down to ruin. We need the ballast of burden-bearing, a load of affliction, to keep us from being swept off our feet.

—*Christian Victory*

"The Right Road Home"

Is this the right road home, O Lord?
  The clouds are dark, and still;
The stony path is sharp and hard,
  Each step brings some fresh hill!

I thought the way would brighter grow,
  And the sun with warmth would glow,
And joyous songs from free hearts flow;
  Is this the right road home?

Yes, child, this very path I trod,
  The clouds were dark for Me;
The stony path was hard to tread,
  Not sight, but faith can see.

But at the end the sun shines bright
  Forever, where there is no night;
And glad hearts rest from earth's fierce
    fight;
  IT IS THE RIGHT ROAD HOME.

—Rosalind Goforth

Wriggling Christians

Our Father, who seeks to perfect His saints in holiness, knows the value of the refiner's fire. An earnest Christian worker had been treated most unkindly, and was crying brokenheartedly when a neighbor came in, and, laying a hand on her shoulder said quietly, "Why, Mrs. —, you're wriggling." Lifting her head the other replied, "I don't think this is a time to be funny." "Oh, I am not that. But don't you know that God has permitted this trouble to touch you, because He sees something in your life that grieves Him, and He has put you in the furnace. When a goldsmith puts gold into the crucible and the fire begins to work on the dross, it begins to wriggle and wriggle, and as the dross is burned out it gets quieter, until at last the surface is so calm that the refiner sees his own face reflected and puts out the fire."

—*Told by a friend.*

* * *

Singing in the Fire

The following incident is related by Mrs. Charles Spurgeon, who was a great sufferer for more than a quarter of a century: "At the close of a dark and gloomy day, I lay resting on my couch as the deeper night drew on; and though all was bright within my cozy room, some of the external darkness seemed to have entered into my soul and obscured its spiritual vision. In sorrow of heart I asked, 'Why does my Lord deal thus with His child? Why does He permit lingering weakness to hinder the sweet service I long to render to His poor servants?' For a while silence reigned in the little room, broken only by the crackling of the oak log burning in the fireplace. Suddenly I heard a sweet, soft sound, a little clear musical note like the tender trill of a robin beneath my window. 'What can it be? Surely no bird is singing out there at this time of the year and night.' My friend exclaimed, 'It comes from the log on the fire!' The fire was letting loose the imprisoned music from the old oak's inmost heart! Perchance he had garnered up this song in the days when all was well with him, when birds twittered merrily on his branches, and the soft sunlight flecked his tender leaves with gold. Ah, thought I, when the fire of affliction draws songs of praise from us then indeed we are purified, and our God is glorified. As I mused, the fire burned and my soul found sweet comfort in the parable so strangely set forth before me. Singing in the fire! Yes, God helping us, if that is the only way to get harmony out of these hard apathetic hearts, let the furnace be heated seven times hotter than before."

—*Sunday School Times*

* * *

"Afterwards"

After the sorrow, after the strife,
After the gruelling cares of life,
After the strain, after the stress,
"The peaceable fruit of righteousness."

After the chastening, after the rod,
After the pruning, the yielding to God,
After the darkness, the grief and distress,
"The peaceable fruit of righteousness."

After the storm, the peace of His power;
After the drought the life-giving shower;
After surrender, the life made selfless;
In "Peaceable fruit of righteousness."

After the roaming, the refuge and Tower;
After the weakness, the sense of new power;
After the waiting, His presence to bless,
In "Peaceable fruit of righteousness."

Fruit of the Spirit, produced by His Hand,
In watching, in waiting, His word of command,
In loving, in serving, in patience and power
Till full is the fruitage and perfect the flower.

—Annie E. Hitt

* * *

Church Built With Stones Thrown

There is a mission in Japan which has a meeting place built by the stones which were thrown at the Christians in years gone by. A mob rushed upon the company and stoned them away. When the time of peace came, the Christians picked up the stones and worked them into their building. God is able to make the wrath of man praise Him.

—*Selected*

* * *

Helped by Being Hurt

Sometimes we are helped by being hurt. A skilled physician about to perform a delicate operation upon the ear said reassuringly, "I may hurt you, but I will not injure you." How often the great Physician speaks to us the same message if we would only listen! Richer life, more abundant health for every child of his, is his only purpose. Why defeat that purpose?

—*Sunday School Times*

* * *

"Betty, Lie Still and Cough!"

Old Betty was converted late in life, and though very poor was active. She visited the sick; out of her poverty she gave to those who were still poorer; collected a little money from others when she could give none of her own, and told many an one of the love of the Saviour. At last she caught a cold and rheumatism, and lay in bed month after month, pain-worn and helpless. A Christian went to see her, and asked if after her active habits she did not find the change very hard to bear, "No, sir, not at all. When I was well I used to hear the Lord say, day by day, 'Betty, go here; Betty, go there;' and I used to do it as well as I could. Now I hear Him say, 'Betty, lie still and cough.' "

—*Gospel Herald*

* * *

Why She Was Changed

A minister tells of one of his members whom he used to visit. She was a little woman of the most ordinary type, but he was never able to touch a single string of sympathy or response in her cold nature. She went away for months. On her return the minister called on her again and found her strangely altered. Her face was radiant with animation. She explained that she had passed

through a terrible trial — everything had gone, and nothing was left her but — God. "Then," she said, "I learned to pray — and I prayed and prayed until *I actually touched him!*" Oh, touch the hem of his garment, and you, too, shall be whole."

—*Australian Sunday School Teacher*

* * *

Where Rehearsed

"And many a rapturous minstrel
  Among the sons of light
Will say of his sweetest music,
  'I learned it in the night.'

"And many a rolling anthem,
  That fills the Father's Home
Sobbed out its first rehearsal
  In the shade of a darkened room."

—*Selected*

* * *

The Spade

"God often digs wells of joy with the spade of sorrow!"

—*Selected*

* * *

The Ministry of Storm

We were going through a great furniture factory, when our guide, the superintendent, pointed out to us a superbly grained and figured sideboard in the natural wood. "I want you to observe the beauty of this oak," he said. "It is the finest selected timber of its kind, and the secret of the intricate and beautiful graining is just this: that the trees from which it was taken grew in a spot where they were exposed to almost constant conflict with storms."

What a suggestive fact! The storm-beaten tree develops the closest and finest and most intricately woven fibers. When it is cut down and the saws lay bare its exquisitely figured grain, the cabinetmaker selects it as the material for his finest work.

So with the human life beset by sorrows, tests and trials. If it stands the storm, how the wind of God strengthens and beautifies it! We need life's stress.

Character cannot be developed into its strongest and most beautiful forms without it.

—B. J., in
Elim Evangel

* * *

If None Were Sick, or Sad

If none were sick, and none were sad,
  What service could we render?
I think if we were always glad
  We scarcely could be tender;
Did our beloved never need
  Our patient ministration,
Earth would grow cold and miss indeed
  Its greatest consolation.
Did sorrow never grieve our heart,
  And every wish were granted,
Patience would die, and hope depart;
  Life would be disenchanted.

—*Selected*

* * *

Looking on the Wrong Side

Dr. G. F. Pentecost was once trying to comfort a woman who had passed through sore trials. Failing in his efforts to cheer her and dispel her doubts, he took up some embroidery upon which she had been working and said, "What a confusion of threads! Why waste time on a thing like that?"

Turning the embroidery over, she said, "Now look at it. You were seeing it from the wrong side."

"That's it, exactly," said Dr. Pentecost. "You are looking at your trials from the wrong side. Turn them over and look at them from the right side — that is, from God's side. The Lord is working out a design of His own for your life, and you must look at things from His point of view, and trust His workmanship."

—Edwin M. Kerlin

* * *

Learning in the Dark

We have read that during World War 1, when it was no longer possible to import those beautiful singing canaries from the Harz Mountains, Germany, a dealer in New York decided to start a system of training canaries to sing. He had bird songs put on records, and these

proved of value. But one day he made a real discovery which meant success. He found that if he covered the cages with thick cloths, completely shutting out the light, the birds learned their song. The song of the Christian originates in the heart, and many a Christian has learned that God sometimes teaches His children to sing in darkness. Verily, "He giveth songs in the night."

—*Moody Monthly*

* * *

Gethsemane

"In golden youth, when seems the earth
A summer land for singing mirth,
When souls are glad, and hearts are
    light
And not a shadow lurks in sight,
We do not know it, but there lies
Somewhere, veiled under evening skies,
A garden each must some time see,
  Gethsemane, Gethsemane,
  Somewhere his own Gethsemane!

"With joyous steps we go our ways,
Love lends a halo to the days,
Light sorrows sail like clouds, afar,
We laugh and say how strong we are,
We hurry on, and, hurrying, go
Close to the border-land of woe
That waits for you and waits for me,
  Gethsemane, Gethsemane,
  Forever waits Gethsemane!

"Down shadowy lanes, across strange
    streams,
Bridged over by our broken dreams,
Behind the misty cape of years,
Close to the great salt font of tears
The garden lies; strive as you may
You cannot miss it in your way,
  All paths that have been, or shall be
  Pass somewhere through Gethsemane!

"All who journey, soon or late
Must pass within the garden's gate,
Must kneel alone in darkness there
And battle with some fierce despair!
God pity those who can not say:
'Not mine, but Thine;' who only pray,
'Let this cup pass,' and cannot see
The purpose of Gethsemane.
  Gethsemane, Gethsemane,
  God help us through our Gethsemane!"

—*Selected*

The Difference

Mozart and a huntsman were once walking together in a forest. A breeze arose. Said the sportsman, "It will startle a hare," but the musician said, "What a diapason from God's mighty organ!" Then when a lark soared singing to the sky, the hunter exclaimed, "What a shot!" But Mozart said, "What would I give if I could catch that trill!" What was the difference? One had his heart attuned to the melodies of God's creation, while the other's ears were deaf to that. Only the pure in heart are attuned to God's messages. Through long years of chastening, Moses had been purified and his spiritual ears opened to God's voice. What a difference between him and Pharaoh! —*Illustrator*

* * *

"I Will Not Leave Thee!"

God is with us in sorrows. There is no pang that rends the heart, I might almost say, not one which disturbs the body, but what Jesus Christ has been with you in it all. Feel you the sorrows of poverty? He "had not where to lay His head." Do you endure the griefs of bereavement? Jesus wept at the tomb of Lazarus. Have you been slandered for righteousness' sake and has it vexed your spirit? He said, "Reproach hath broken Mine heart." Have you been betrayed? Do not forget that He, too, had His familiar friend who sold Him for the price of a slave. On what stormy seas have you been tossed which have not roared about His boat? Never glen of adversity so dark, so deep, apparently so pathless, but what, in stooping down, you may discover the footprints of the crucified One! In the fires and in the rivers, in the cold of night and under the burning sun, He cries, "I am with you; be not dismayed; for I am both thy Companion and thy God!"
—Spurgeon

* * *

Out of Sorrow

Probably the favorite Christmas story, outside of Scripture, is, "The Other Wise Man," by Henry Van Dyke. Said he, "The year had been full of sickness and sorrow for me. Every day brought trouble. Every night was tormented with pain. The heaviest burden was this: That my work, in the world, might be almost ended. It was in one of those lonely nights that this story came to me. I do not know where it came from — out of the air, perhaps. But one thing is CERTAIN: It is not written in any other book, nor is it found in the ancient lore of the East. Yet, I have never felt as if it were my own. It was sent to me, and it seemed as if I know the Giver, though His Name was not spoken!"
—*The Other Wise Man*

* * *

Common to All

Among the parables that Chinese teachers use is the story of a woman who lost an only son. She was grief-stricken out of all reason. She made her sorrow a wailing wall. Finally she went to a wise old philosopher. He said to her, "I will give you back your son if you will bring me some mustard seed. However, the seed must come from a home where there has never been any sorrow." Eagerly she started her search, and went from house to house. In every case she learned that a loved one had been lost. "How selfish I have been in my grief," she said, "sorrow is common to all." —*"How to Face Life,"* by Charles F. Banning.

* * *

Pressed

Pressed out of measure and pressed to all length;
Pressed so intensely it seems beyond strength;
Pressed in the body and pressed in the soul;
Pressed in the mind till the dark surges roll;
Pressure by foes, and pressure by friends;
Pressure on pressure, till life nearly ends.
Pressed into loving the staff and the rod;
Pressed into knowing no helper but God;
Pressed into liberty where nothing clings;
Pressed into faith for impossible things;
Pressed into living a life in the Lord;
Pressed into living a Christ-life outpoured.   —Annie Johnson Flint

"I Broke It's Leg"

A lady was summering in Switzerland. One day she started out for a stroll. Presently, as she climbed the mountain-side, she came to a shepherd's fold. She walked to the door and looked in. There sat the shepherd. Around him lay his flock. Near at hand, on a pile of straw, lay a single sheep. It seemed to be in suffering. Scanning it closely, the lady saw that its leg was broken. At once her sympathy went out to the suffering sheep. She looked up inquiringly to the shepherd. "How did it happen?" she said. To her amazement, the shepherd answered: "Madam, I broke that sheep's leg." A look of pain swept over the visitor's face. Seeing it, the shepherd went on: "Madam, of all the sheep in my flock, this one was the most wayward. It never would obey my voice. It never would follow in the pathway in which I was leading the flock. It wandered to the verge of many a perilous cliff and dizzy abyss. And not only was it disobedient itself, but it was ever leading the other sheep of my flock astray. I had before had experience with sheep of this kind. So I broke its leg. The first day I went to it with food, it tried to bite me. I let it lie alone for a couple of days. Then, I went back to it. And now, it not only took the food, but licked my hand, and showed every sign of submission and even affection. And now let me tell you something. When this sheep is well, as it soon will be, it will be the model sheep of my flock. No sheep will hear my voice so quickly. None will follow so closely at my side.   —James H. McConkey

* * *

"There He Proved Them" (Exod. 15:25).

"I stood once in the test room of a great steel mill. All around me were little partitions and compartments. Steel had been tested to the limit, and marked with figures that showed its breaking point. Some pieces had been twisted until they broke, and the strength of torsion was marked on them. Some had been stretched to the breaking point, and their tensile strength indicated. Some had been compressed to the crushing point, and also marked. The master of the steel mill knew just what these pieces of steel would stand under the strain. He knew just what they would bear if placed in the great ship, building, or bridge. He KNEW because the TESTING ROOM revealed it. It is often so with God's children. God does not want us to be like vases of glass or porcelain. He does not want us to be hothouse plants, but storm-beaten oaks; not sand dunes, driven with every gust of wind, but granite rocks withstanding the fiercest storms. To make us such He MUST bring us into His testing room of suffering. Better the storm waters with Christ than the smooth waters without Him!"

—James McConkey

* * *

Waves That Drive Us Toward God!

A little boy made a boat. He went off in high glee to sail it on the water. But presently it got beyond his reach. In his distress he appealed to a big boy for help, asking him to get it back for him. Saying nothing, the big boy picked up stones, and seemingly threw them at the boat. The little boy thought he would never get his boat back, and that instead of helping him, the big boy was annoying him. But presently he noticed that instead of hitting the boat, each stone went BEYOND it, and made a little wave, which moved the boat a little nearer to the shore. Every throw of the stones was PLANNED, and at last the little boat was brought within reach. How happy the little boy was! Again he was in possession of his treasure!

Sometimes things in our life seem disagreeable and without sense or plan. But let us WAIT awhile, and we shall see that each trial, each striking of a stone upon the quiet water of our life, has brought us NEARER to God!

"Judge not the Lord by feeble sense,
  But trust Him for His grace;
Behind a frowning providence,
  He hides a smiling face!"
—W. B. K.

* * *

The Sweetest Chords

A German baron stretched wires from tower to tower of his castle to make a great Æolian harp. Then he waited and listened to hear the music from it. For a time the air was still, and no sound was heard. The wires hung silent in the air. After a while came a gentle breeze, and the harp sang softly. At length came the stern winter winds, strong and stormlike in their forces. Then the wires gave forth their most majestic music which was heard far and near. There are human lives that, never in the calm of quiet days yield the music that is in them. When the breezes of common care sweep over them they give out soft murmurings of song. But it is only when the storms of adversity blow upon them that they answer in notes of noble victoriousness."

—Dr. J. R. Miller

* * *

When Storm Has Passed

Some years ago, a seventy-five-mile-an-hour hurricane hit the thirty-five-million-dollar Golden Gate Bridge, and bent it twelve and a half feet out of line. Yet the New York engineer said that it was undamaged. "It was built," he explained, "to bend eighteen feet before it will break" Christians are made to stand the storms of life; clouds of adversity do not destroy them, for strong Christian faith outlasts the storm and looks for a sky that will be "cloudless clear after rain."　　—*Secret Place*

* * *

"And It Came to Pass!"

Said an aged Negro, "My favorite words ob de Bible am dese: 'And it came to pass.' And here am de reason: When trouble comes and overflows my soul wid sorrow; when de testings and trials ob life break in their fury ober my head, I turns to God's Word for help and comfort. I don't read very long until I comes across de words, 'And it came to pass.' Dese words teaches me dat de sorrows and troubles didn't come to stay. Dey come to pass.' " Wise indeed was our aged friend! After the sorrows and trials of life will have wrought their soul-refining, character-ennobling purposes, they will pass away: "Weeping may endure for a night, but joy cometh in the morning!"　　—W. B. K.

"This, Too, Shall Pass Away!"

"Art thou in misery, brother? Then I pray
Be comforted. Thy grief shall pass away.
Art thou elated? Ah, be not too gay;
Temper thy joy: this, too, shall pass away.
Art thou in danger? Still let reason sway,
And cling to hope; this, too, shall pass away.
Tempted art thou? In all thine anguish lay
One truth to heart: this, too, shall pass away.
Do rays of loftier glory round thee play?
Kinglike art thou? This, too, shall pass away!
Whate'er thou art, where'er thy footsteps stray,
Heed these wise words: THIS, TOO, SHALL PASS AWAY!"

—Paul Hamilton Hayne

* * *

Frosts Are Needed, Too

A young man was trying to establish himself as a peach grower. He had worked hard and invested his all in a peach orchard which blossomed wonderfully — then came a frost. He did not go to church the next Sunday, nor the next, nor the next. His minister went to see him to find the reason. The young fellow exclaimed: "I'm not coming any more. Do you think I can worship a God who cares for me so little that He will let a frost kill all my peaches?" The old minister looked at him a few moments in silence, then said kindly: "God loves you better than He does your peaches. He knows that while peaches do better without frosts, it is impossible to grow the best men without frosts. His object is to grow men, not peaches."

—*Christian Worker's Magazine*

* * *

Gnarled by the Winds

"They have stood there," the guide said, "for four thousand years. They are the oldest living things. They have been buffeted by the storms of centuries, and their strength comes through withstanding." We were camped in the Sequoia National Park in a clump of the sequoias, gigantic fellows twenty and thirty feet through. They were gnarled old trees, the oldest living things of the world. But they were strong because they had gone through tempests and fires, and had overcome.

So the building of Christian strength comes through being buffeted by winds, flailed by tribulations.

—*Christian Herald*

The Vine Clings in Fiercest Storm

The vine clings to the oak during the fiercest of storms. Although the violence of nature may uproot the oak, twining tendrils still cling to it. If the vine is on the side of the tree opposite the wind, the great oak is its protection; if it is on the exposed side, the tempest only presses it closer to the trunk.

In some of the storms of life, God intervenes and shelters us; while in others He allows us to be exposed, so that we will be pressed more closely to Him.

—B. M. Launderville

SOUL WINNING — PERSONAL WORK

Men Buried Alive!

The passion for souls burned in the breast of Rowland Hill. The people of Wotton called him a madman. This was his defense:

"While I passed along yonder road I saw a gravel pit cave in, and bury three men alive. I hastened to the rescue, and shouted for help until they heard me in the town almost a mile away. No one called me a madman then.

"But when I see destruction about to fall on sinners, and entomb them in the eternal mass of woe, and cry aloud, if perchance they may behold their danger and escape, they say I am beside myself. Perhaps I am, but oh, that all God's children might be thus fired with desire to save their fellows."

—*The Pilgrim*

* * *

At Your Own Door

Sophie had been praying for twelve years to become a foreign missionary. One day, she had so prayed, and the Heavenly Father seemed to say: "Sophie, stop! Where were you born?" "In Germany, Father." "Where are you now?" "In America, Father." "Well, are you not a foreign missionary already?" Then the Father said, "Who lives on the floor above you?" "A family of Swedes." "And who above them?" "Why, some Switzers." "And who in the rear?" "Italians." "And a block away?" "Some Chinese." "And you have never

said a word to these people about My Son? Do you think I will send you thousands of miles to the foreigners and the heathen when you never care enough about them at your own door to speak with them about their souls?"

—*Christian Digest*

* * *

Just One!

Value just one soul. One may be many. Andrew brought Simon — just one. But that one was many, for under God Simon brought three thousand in one day. Joel Stratton, a waiter in a restaurant, brought John Gough to Christ. Just one. And Gough brought many to Christ. Ezra Kimball, a Sunday school teacher, brought Moody to Christ — just one. But that one was many, for Moody rocked two continents for God. But why say more? Just as one digit is valuable in the multiplication table, and one letter in the alphabet, far more valuable is just one soul in God's sight.   —R. G. Lee, in

Watchman-Examiner

* * *

Winning Souls

Someone asked Dr. Lyman Beecher, in his old age, "What is the greatest of all things?" The sturdy veteran replied "It is not theology; it is not controversy; it is saving souls." He had been the king of the American pulpit; but, as he looked back over his noble career, he felt that the greatest good that he had accomplished was in leading guilty and polluted souls to their Saviour.

While David Brainerd, one of the most celebrated of our missionaries, was laboring among the poor, benighted Indians on the banks of the Delaware, he once said, "I care not where I live, or what hardships I go through, so that I can but gain souls to Christ. While I am asleep, I dream of these things; as soon as I awake, the first thing I think of is this great work. All my desire is the conversion of sinners, and all my hope is in God." —*Selected*

* * *

What A Personal Call Did

Dr. A. C. Dixon used to tell the story of a New York pastor who became anxious about a certain banker, a member of his congregation, but to whom he had never spoken directly. One day he went to the banker's office asking for "a ten-minute interview."

"Have you come on business, Pastor?" asked the banker.

"Yes," was the reply, "business for God and eternity. I want to talk to you about your soul."

To the pastor's surprise, the banker replied, "I have been waiting for thirty years for some one to talk to me in this way. Ten minutes, did you say? Come to my house and make it the whole evening." The pastor did so, and the banker was converted. —*Moody Monthly*

* * *

One at a Time

Julia Ward Howe, author of "The Battle Hymn of the Republic," once wrote to an eminent senator of the United States in behalf of a man who was suffering great injustice. He replied: "I am so much taken up with plans for the benefit of the race that I have no time for individuals." She pasted this into her album with this comment: "When last heard from, our Maker had not reached this altitude."

That person who has no interest in individuals, and who never tries to rescue even one lost soul, has a spirit different from that of the Master whose personal words and work make up the bulk of His life record.

"He who waits until he can save many souls will never save one."
—*Michigan Christian Advocate*

* * *

Evangelize!

Give us a watchword for the hour
A thrilling word, a word of power;
A battle-cry, a flaming breath,
That calls to conquest or to death;
A word to rouse the church from rest,
To heed her Master's high behest,
The call is given: Ye hosts arise,
Our watchword is Evangelize!

The glad evangel now proclaim
Through all the earth in Jesus' name;
This word is ringing through the skies,
Evangelize! Evangelize!
To dying men, a fallen race,
Make known the gift of gospel grace;
The world that now in darkness lies,
Evangelize! Evangelize!
—*Henry Crocker*

* * *

"Was That Somebody You?"

Tom Carter, the evangelist, told this in one of his messages: While he was holding meetings in a Pennsylvania town, a young man who had formerly lived next door to the parsonage committed a murder. The whole community was stirred. Mr. Carter and the pastor obtained permission to visit the young man in his cell. After telling him his own story of conversion in a prison, Mr. Carter and the pastor succeeded in leading him to Christ. Then the newly-saved man addressed the pastor and sadly said, "To think I lived next door to you for months and you never told me anything about Jesus until I came here! If you only had, I probably never would have become a murderer."

Are we overlooking any close-by opportunities? —*Evangelical-Messenger*

* * *

Fishers of Men

I watched an old man trout-fishing once, pulling them out one after another busily. "You manage it cleverly, old friend," I said. "I have passed a good many below who do not seem to be doing anything." The old man lifted himself up and stuck his rod into the ground.

"Well, you see, sir, there are three rules for trout-fishing, and it's no use trying if you do not mind them. First, keep yourself out of sight; second, use the right kind of bait; third, have patience."

"Good for catching men, too," I thought, as I went my way.

—Mark Guy Pearse

* * *

Not Bright, — But His Crown Was

Billy Sunday's choir leader, Mr. Rodeheaver, told the following touching story about a boy who sang in his choir. "Joey was not quite bright. He would never leave the tabernacle at night till he could shake my hand. He would stand right next to me until the last man had gone. in order to say good-by. It was embarrassing at times. One evening a man came forward to speak to me. He said, 'I want to thank you for being so kind to Joey. He isn't quite bright, and has never had anything he enjoyed so much as coming here and singing in the choir. He has worked hard during the day in order to be ready in time to come, too, and it is through him that my wife and my five children have been led to the Lord. His grandfather, seventy-five years old and an infidel all his life, and his grandmother have come tonight, and now the whole family are converted.' "

—Sunday School Banner

* * *

The Finger of God

During a season of revival a friend was praying one evening for a certain unconverted neighbor. After this manner he prayed: "O Lord, touch that man with Thy finger; touch him with Thy finger Lord!" The petition was repeated with great earnestness when something said to him: "Thou art the finger of God! Hast thou ever touched this thy brother? Hast thou ever spoken a single word to him on the question of salvation? Go thou and touch that man, and thy prayer shall be answered." It was a voice from the throne.

—Gospel Herald

Was It Worth a Disarrangement?

Dr. Len G. Broughton says: "I remember a few years ago, when I had not as much experience as I have now, and when my enthusiasm perhaps was not as well balanced as it is now, I had been invited to preach in one of the leading churches in one of the great cities. I went into the pulpit conscious that God was with us in a very peculiar sense, and when I finished my sermon the one thing on my mind was the salvation of souls. I did not know whether they had ever had an invitation given there for the confession of Christ, but I did not stop to ask. I stepped down and extended the invitation to any who would accept Jesus then and there to come to the front. Immediately a strong, able-bodied man got up and, with tears streaming down his face, came to the front and took my hand; then another man came. Fourteen grown people confessed Christ that morning. As we went out of the church, the wife of one of the officers, who was also a Sunday school teacher, spoke to an officer of the church, and said: "I greatly enjoyed the sermon until the last, but I do not think that a man should disarrange the order of the service for the sake of having a few people come to the front." The first one who came forward was a railroad engineer who was killed in a wreck that Sunday night.

—From *The Commonplace in Soul-Winning*, by Dr. L. G. Broughton

* * *

Thud of Christless Feet!

The story is told of William C. Burns, the man who mightily blessed Hudson Taylor and Murray McCheyne, of how when he was only a boy of seventeen he visited the city of Glasgow with his mother for the first time in his life. The mother suddenly lost her boy in the crowd and after many anxious moments discovered him in an alley with his head buried in his hands, sobbing with a broken heart. "What ails you, lad?" asked the Scottish mother. "Oh, Mither, Mither," said the country boy, "the thud of these Christless feet on the way to hell breaks my heart." One can understand how he grew up to be the mighty revivalist of Scotland and China.   —Rev. James A. Stewart, in *Alliance Weekly*

* * *

Unfruitful Mountaintop Experience

Blunt common sense always characterized Mr. Moody. Once a man rose in one of his meetings to give his experience. "I have been for five years on the Mount of Transfiguration," he said. Instantly Mr. Moody interrupted him by the sharp question, "How many souls did you lead to Christ last year?" "Well, I don't know," answered the surprised man. "Have you led any?" then came sternly from the preacher. "I — er don't know that I have," said the man. "Then," snapped Mr. Moody, still more sternly, "we don't want that kind of mountaintop experience. When a man gets so high that he can't reach down and save poor sinners, there is something wrong."   —*Methodist Recorder*

* * *

Wilbur Chapman's Poignant Regret

We have an idea that men do not care to talk about their soul's salvation, and so our lips have been sealed. I have possibly the saddest testimony of anyone. I roomed with a man in college for almost two years; I was a student for the ministry and knew that he was not a Christian, and I never warned him once. At the close of my college course he said to me, "Why have you never asked me to be a Christian?" And when I told him that I thought he did not care, he told me that that was the reason he had chosen the room with me, that there had not been a day or night that he was not willing to talk. And then, try as hard as I would to lead him to Christ, I failed.   —J. Wilbur Chapman

* * *

An Artist Named Tucker

A young artist named Tucker painted the picture of a forlorn woman and child out in a storm. This picture took such a hold on him that he laid by palette and brush, saying, "I must go to the lost, instead of painting them."

He prepared for the ministry and for some time worked in the city's slums. At length he resolved, "I must go to that part of the world where men seem to be most hopelessly lost." That young artist was none other than Bishop Tucker, of Uganda, Africa.   —*Power*

* * *

Differing Values

A convert at the Billy Sunday meetings in Scranton, Pa., remarked, "On my farm I raise blooded stock, and there is not a person for miles around who would not go to great lengths to warn me if one of my prize cows got on the railroad track; yet for twenty-five years never a man spoke a word to me about my spiritual welfare."   —*Moody Monthly*

* * *

Find Your Own FIRST!

A minister reports a conversation which he once heard between an evangelist and a young man as they were walking from the tent in which a meeting had been held. The lad had been in the meetings regularly, but had not accepted the Lord Jesus Christ as his Saviour. The evangelist said, "Your mother wants you to be a Christian, for she is a Christian; and your father would be pleased, because he is a Christian, and an officer in the church." The lad was silent for a while; then he said, thoughtfully, "Possibly you may not believe what I say, but neither my father nor my mother has ever asked me to be a Christian, and I never expect to be until they do." The minister added this significant comment: "It is a burning shame that I should be obliged to waste one minute of my time or one ounce of my strength trying to persuade fathers and mothers to speak to their children about Christ."   —*Sunday School Times*

* * *

All Soul Winners

A man seriously hurt in an automobile accident was propped against a tree. A minister happened upon the accident as he came from his study in the nearby church. A number of bystanders, some of whom were members of his church, cried, "Make way, here's a minister." And the crowd made way for the minister, who took care of the spiritual needs of the injured man. Later that minister asked himself, "Why should not any one of my congregation or any Christian be able to help a soul to God?" —*Sunday School Times*

* * *

"Rescue the Perishing"

One time Fanny Crosby, the blind hymn writer, visited the McAuley Mission in New York. She asked if there was a boy there who had no mother, and "if he would come up and let her lay her hand on his head." A motherless fellow came up, and she put her arms about him and kissed him. She went from that meeting and wrote:

"Rescue the perishing, care for the dying,
Snatch them in pity from sin and the grave,
Weep o'er the erring one, lift up the fallen,
Tell them of Jesus the mighty to save."

Some time later, when Mr. Sankey was about to sing this song in St. Louis, he related the incident. A man sprang to his feet in the audience and said, "I am the boy she kissed that night. *I was never able to get away from the impression made by that touching act, I have become a Christian.*"
—*Christian Victory*

* * *

Tact In Soul Winning

"One day I was called to see a dying prospector in a hospital. A companion said to me as I was going in, 'Now don't say anything to him about dying, talk to him of prospecting and claims.' I stood back to see how one prospector would talk to another who would shortly pass over to the other side. But as they talked about the market, new finds, and recalled past experiences, he never paid any attention to them. I then began to speak to him of the *prospect* of spending an eternity with Christ. I told him of the *claim* that Christ had upon him: 'Ye are bought with a price.' As I read and prayed with him he joined me, and then when I asked him if he would like to sing, he said, 'Sing, "*Jesus Loves Me,*

This I Know.' " His mind went back for sixty years, perhaps, to a little country Sunday School, or his mother's knee, where he learned that hymn."
—Wood B. Williston, Anglican Missionary, in *Moody Monthly*

* * *

"The Non-Going Church"

A Supreme Court Judge, whose wife had recently died, attended a little church where his wife was a member for years. The pastor spoke on, "Not the Non-churchgoer, but the Non-going church." Coming to the front, the judge said,

"You're on the right track, sir, go ahead. You're on the right track. My wife passed away last year. The home has been a very lonesome place for me. The other night, as I was standing on the back porch and looking down into the valley, I saw the light of the little church where my wife was converted and where we were married. I called the chauffeur, told him to get the car and take me down to the prayer meeting. There were nine present. At the conclusion of the service the pastor asked me if I had something to say. I did. I said to them: 'You know me, but you knew my wife better. No one has ever asked me personally to become a Christian. I have decided to wait no longer. I am here to ask you to pray for me." —*Christian Index*

* * *

"A Child Shall Lead Them!"

Gipsy Smith pointed a boy to the Lord Jesus who died on the Cross in his place and in his stead. After a while the lad said: "I think I see it — first you bring yourself to Jesus; then you leave yourself with Jesus, and keep going on."

"Yes, that's it," said Gipsy Smith, and the lad went away rejoicing in his new-found Saviour. The next night the evangelist found him in the inquiry-room again, his eyes shining like stars.

"Why Sonny," Gipsy Smith said: "I thought you received Jesus as your Saviour last night!"

"So I did," was the bright reply.

"Then why are you here again tonight?"

"I came to bring my mother," was the simple answer. The next night the same boy was in the inquiry-room once more.

"What brings you here to-night, Sonny?" inquired Gipsy.

"Oh, I came tonight to bring my Grandfather," was the reply.

So three generations were won because a little boy, who found the Saviour, became a personal worker in his own home. 　　　　　　*—Gospel Herald*

* * *

Did It Really Happen?

"Christ before Pilate" and "The Crucifixion," the two masterpieces of the artist Michael Munkacsy, have of late years been exhibited in the Grand Court of the Wanamaker Store, Philadelphia, during the Easter season. One day, a minister of the Gospel was standing gazing reverently at the suffering Christ on the cross, when a well-dressed woman, apparently intelligent, perhaps a foreigner, turned to him and said, impetuously: "Tell me! Did such a thing really happen?" The preacher gazed at her in astonishment. Evidently her ignorance was genuine and, as they stood there together, he preached Christ and him crucified to one who, although surrounded by Christians, had never heard the glad news before.

—A Personal Experience

* * *

Personal Touch

"I laid my hand upon the shoulder of a noble specimen of young manhood and asked him if he was a Christian. He replied, 'No, sir; I have heard you preach every Sunday for seven years without one exception, but I am not a Christian yet.' He is now one of the most faithful members of the church. What seven years of preaching had failed to do, five minutes of heart-contact accomplished."

—Dr. Cortland Myers

* * *

Empty-Handed!

After a month of Christian life, nearly all of which was passed upon a sick bed, a young man, 30 years of age, lay dying. Suddenly, a look of sadness crossed his countenance, and to the inquiry of a friend, he exclaimed: "No, I am not afraid; Jesus saves me now! But oh, must I go — and EMPTY-HANDED?

"Must I go and empty-handed?
Thus my dear redeemer meet?
Not one day of service give Him,
Lay no trophy at His feet?
　　　　　　—W. B. K.

* * *

A Dying Man Challenges Us

A young married man went into a Christian man's office on an errand of business. As he was leaving the proprietor said to him, "My young friend, are you a Christian?" He replied, "I regret to say I am not." That faithful friend then kindly urged him to seek Christ at once, to delay no longer securing the great salvation. The young man thanked him politely and said he would "think of it." In three weeks his widow called at the same office to bring his dying message. Said she: "He thought much of your kind advice, and resolved to seek Christ. He was suddenly taken sick. After a few days he found sweet peace in believing, became entirely resigned to the Divine will, and died in the assurance of faith. 'Tell my friend N.,' said he, 'that I thank him with my dying breath for his faithfulness to my soul.'"

—Baptist Standard

* * *

Are You A Wooden Christian?

Aunt Sophie, a converted scrub woman, used to say that she was "called to scrub and preach." Wherever she went, she would tell others of Jesus, the Saviour. Someone made fun of her by saying that she was seen talking about Christ to a wooden Indian, standing in front of a cigar store. When Sophie heard this, she replied, "Perhaps I did. My eyesight is not good. But talking about Christ to a wooden Indian is not so bad as being a *wooden Christian and never talking to anybody about the Lord Jesus!*" How many souls have *you* brought to the Lord Jesus? Are *you* always busy telling others about the Saviour? 　　　*—Gospel Herald*

Love that Serves

The shepherd counted his sheep; three were missing. The snow was falling fast and he know that those missing would soon perish unless they were found. He called his dog and held up one finger and said, "Go!" Into the storm she went and finally returned with the lamb. He held up his finger and said again, "Go!" She went back again into the storm in search of the missing sheep. Later on he heard the dog return. He put the sheep in the fold and sent the dog forth for the third time, and when she returned he noticed blood on the snow and on her side. He put the sheep away and went to sleep. The next morning he called the dog and she failed to come. Looking in the shed, he found her cold in death. She had battled with wolves in the night as she searched for the lost sheep that her master had sent her out to find. Jesus Christ has sent us forth in search of the "lost sheep;" shall a dog be more faithful to her master than we are to ours? Are we willing to go out into the world and brave dangers and criticisms to be loyal and true to our Master? Will we be faithful unto death?
　　　　　　　　　—*Biblical Echo*

* * *

Africa Bound, but No Souls Won Here

D. L. Moody once met a young fellow on a train. This young man was bubbling over with the prospect of going to Africa and winning the heathen for Christ. Mr. Moody asked him a very pertinent question, "How many souls have you brought to the Lord here at home?" After a brief pause, he answered truthfully, "I do not know of one soul that I have won." —*Gospel Herald*

* * *

Missed: One Opportunity

"When I was a boy of about fourteen years a minister stayed in our home overnight. In the morning as he started on foot for a neighboring village, I went with him to assist with his baggage. I have never forgotten that walk; it comes back to me with a feeling of sadness. One great desire was surging through my soul, and it was, 'I wish he

would talk to me about Jesus and my soul; but he didn't. How much of sin and sorrow I might have been saved from, had he spoken the word I believe God wanted him to speak."
　　　　　　　—*Sunday School Times*

* * *

The Preacher's Steeple Call

"Yes, I want to come into the church; I have been wanting to come for fiftten years," a woman said to the minister when he urged her to confess Christ at the next Communion. "But I'm waiting for Jim. You know he's a good man, yet he doesn't have much use for the church, or — for preachers. He tells me to go ahead, and not wait for him." As the minister left, he said, "Please remember me to Mr. B —— when he comes home. Tell him I hope to have a good talk with him soon." A few weeks later he met Mrs. B —— once more. "Jim made me promise to tell you something for him," she said much embarrassed. "He says if you want to see him so much you will just have to go where he is." "And where is that?" was the inquiry. "Hadn't you better wait a few days before going to him? You see, today he's working on the steeple of the new church." The minister had been challenged to go where Jim was. So he climbed ladder after ladder until he found a much-surprised man. A few minutes were spent in very satisfactory conversation. The next Sunday Jim became a member of the church his wife had already joined. His friends wondered at the change in his life, but the only explanation he would give was this, "The preacher who'll climb two hundred feet of ladder to call on me can have me every time!"
　　　　　　—From *Taking Men Alive*,
　　　　　　　by Charles Gallaudet Trumbull

* * *

Fishing for Big Ones

For the first and second centuries the sign of Christianity was the fish. I decided that a fishhook would be the proper sign to win people to the Lord Jesus Christ, so I had a little golden fishhook made to be worn on the lapel of my coat, and when people ask me what it means I am able to tell them that I am a fisher of men. On the streets of Chicago a little newsboy, from whom I was buying a paper, said, "Mister, do you belong to a fisher club?" I said, "Yes, I surely do." "My," he said, "fishing is nice, isn't it?" "It surely is." The little fellow said, "Do you ever catch any big ones?" "Oh, yes, I have caught 250-pounders." He exclaimed, "Go on!" "Yes," I said, "I have caught 250-pound fish." He said, "Those sure are big." I said, "Yes." Then I leaned a little closer to the newsboy and said, "Sonny, I would rather catch small fish than big ones." He exclaimed, "No!" I said, "Yes, about your size." And he looked at himself, as if he was thinking, "Well, I'm not so small." Then I told him that I was a fisher of men, that I was fishing for souls, and that if he would believe on the Lord Jesus Christ he would be saved. Almost every day as I wear my fishhook on the lapel of my coat some businessman or someone I meet in the elevator, or some person to whom I pause to speak, asks, "Do you belong to a fisher club?" I say, "Yes, the largest fisher club in the world — catching souls for the Lord Jesus Christ."

—*Christian Digest*

* * *

Win Your Friend

Frances Ridley Havergal once told of an experience she had: "During a summer visit just after I had left school, a class of girls about my own age came to me a few times for an hour's singing. Sometimes I accompanied them afterward down the avenue; and whenever I met any of them, I had smiles and plenty of kindly words for each. A few years afterward I sat at the bedside of one of these girls. She told me how she used to linger in the avenue on those summer evenings, longing that I would speak to her about the Saviour. But I never did. And she went on without the light and gladness which it might have been my privilege to bring to her life. God chose other means. But she said — and the words often ring in my ears when I am tempted to let an opportunity slip: "Ah, Miss Frances, I ought to have been yours!"

—*Gospel Herald*

Driving the Nail

When speaking to audiences of American women, Lady Dobbie sometimes used the figure of a nail being driven into a piece of wood. She would say: "Someone places the nail in position by speaking to an individual about Christ as Saviour for the first time. Perhaps this is a mother, or a friend, or a Sunday school teacher. It may have little apparent effect. Then others, as time passes, strike that nail a blow, and drives it in a bit farther, with a word in season about the Lord. Finally someone, perhaps an evangelist, happens to strike the final blow, and the individual is saved. That last person is likely to think he has done a great work, and indeed he has; but he has really done no more than any of the others, each of whom has played a part in winning the other to Christ."

—From *Dobbie, Defender of Malta,* by S. Maxwell Coder

* * *

John G. Paton's Concern for a Cabman

John G. Paton, the great missionary to the New Hebrides, the last time he visited this country spoke in western Ohio to a company of ministers. At the close of the meeting a cab took him and three other ministers to their places of entertainment. It was snowing and blowing fiercely, but when Dr. Paton stepped from the cab he put his hand on the shoulder of the cabman and asked, "Have you given your life to the Lord Jesus Christ?" What an example of love for souls: this old, white-haired patriarch, who had literally transformed the cannibal islands of the New Hebrides from savagedom to Christianity, standing in a blinding snowstorm in (so-called) Christian America, talking to a cabman about his soul! What a life of compassion!

—*King's Business*

* * *

Led by a Dog

A minister who knew the circumstances tells of a good Christian woman who for years had prayed constantly for her husband's conversion with no visible success. She could not even get him to go to church with her; but she had a pet dog that always accompanied her to the church, and sat quietly under the seat. In time the lady died, and the husband could find no comfort anywhere. For several Sundays he noticed the dog leave the house at a certain hour and return at a certain time. One Sunday he followed the dog, which was delighted to have its master with him. The dog trotted along until he came to the church, then bounded up the steps and waited. After standing a few moments the man said, "I'll go in to please the dog; it won't do any harm." He went the next Sunday and the next, the dog always leading the way to the wife's accustomed seat. One morning, after the service, the man arose, and with tears, gave his heart to God, and told of the faithful dog leading him to Christ.

—*King's Business*

* * *

"He Was My Friend"

At the time of Jerry McAuley's funeral, a shabby-looking aged man appeared, approached two men standing near an entrance to the Tabernacle, and asked, as he took off his tall, battered hat if they would take the little bunch of white flowers and have them placed on Jerry's coffin. "And when you drop 'em with the rest," he added apologetically, and his voice trembled, "Jerry, he was my friend, he'll know they come from old Joe Chappy." The little bunch of white flowers was long preserved by Mrs. McAuley. Jerry had said, "When I die, and it may not be long, I want to die on my knees, praying for lost souls . . . . I would rather some poor soul that I was the means of leading to the Lord would put one little rose on my grave than have the wealth of a millionaire.

—From *New York's Most Useful Citizen*, by Don O. Shelton.

* * *

The Sweetest Sound

A beautiful story is told of Dr. John A. Broadus, the scholar and homiletical professor. In his younger days he was converted to Christ in the town in which he lived. Next day he went to one of his schoolmates, Sandy Jones, a red-haired, awkward chap, and said to him, "I wish you would be a Christian; won't you?" And Sandy said: "Well, I don't know. Perhaps I will." And sure enough, after a while, one night in the little church, Sandy Jones accepted Christ. Straightway he stalked across that little meetinghouse, held out his hand, and said, "I thank you, John; I thank you, John." Dr. Broadus went forth from that little town and became a great scholar, a great exegete and theological president. Every summer when he went home (and he hardly missed a year) this awkward, red-haired old farmer, in his plain clothes, with red sand on his boots, would come up, stick out his great, bony hand, and say, "Howdy, John. I never forget you, John." And they say that when Dr. Broadus lay dying, with his family about him, he said: "I rather think the sound sweetest to my ears in Heaven, next to the welcome of Him whom not having seen, I have tried to love and serve, will be the welcome of Sandy Jones, as he will thrust out his great hand and say, 'Howdy, John! Thank you, John; thank you, John.' "

—*Watchman-Examiner*

* * *

In the Blacksmith's Shop

If all Christians had the spirit of Dr. Norman McLeod there would be no trouble about spreading the Gospel. "He never came to my shop," said a blacksmith, "without talking to me as if he had been a blacksmith all his life; but he never went away without leaving Christ in my heart."

—*King's Business*

* * *

"Almost Persuaded"

The address of Paul before Agrippa (Acts 26:26) is at once the model and the despair of the gospel preacher. Perfect in fact, simplicity, dignity and rhetoric. Some one in Rufus Choate's hearing called this address, "Paul's Defense Before Agrippa." "Defense?" said the great advocate. "Why, sir, defense was not in Paul's thought. *His one purpose was to make a Christian of Agrippa, and he nearly succeeded!"*

—C. I. Scofield

* * *

When the Deacons Got Busy

A certain church had gone for more than a year without a single soul being saved. The pastor told his deacons that he thought he should resign. He asked if any of them had tried to win anyone to Christ. None had. Then the pastor said, "Let us make a covenant that if the Lord cannot use us to bring in some souls for Him in the near future, all of us will resign." All agreed. The following Monday one deacon went to his store with a burdened heart. He invited the first clerk he met into his office. They had a heart-to-heart talk, and after prayer he came out a saved man. Then another and another was called in. By late afternoon eleven people had been led to Christ. The other deacons also had been at work and the following Sunday, thirty men were received into the church as a result of the witnessing of deacons who had never before tried to win anyone to Christ. The whole plan of salvation is personal. God provided a personal Saviour, who died a personal death to save lost persons. Therefore it is only natural that one should be a personal witness.

* * *

William Booth — Rudyard Kipling

The Evangelical Christian comments on a statement in Rudyard Kipling's Memoirs, describing his conversations with Booth at one time while touring the British Empire. Kipling writes: "I saw him walking backward in the dusk over the uneven wharf, his cloak blown upwards, tulip fashion, over his gray head, while he beat a tambourine in the face of the singing, weeping, praying crowd who had come to see him off. I talked much with General Booth during that voyage. I expressed my distaste of his appearance at the wharf. 'Young feller,' he replied, bending great eyebrows at me, 'if I thought I could win one more soul to the Lord by walking on my head and playing the tambourine

with my toes, I'd — I'd learn how!' " And so would the Apostle Paul have "learned how" if he had believed it would win any more to Christ in his day.

—*Evangelical Christian*

* * *

"Mind Your Own Business!"

One of God's soul-winning servants became greatly burdened for the salvation of an unsaved girl. She resented his efforts to cause her to see her lostness and need of the Saviour. She told her mother of her displeasure. Said the mother angrily, "The next time he speaks to you about being saved, tell him to mind his own business!"

"But mother," protested the girl, "He talks like this *is* his business!" It IS the business of every born-again believer to do their dead-level-best to bring the lost, perishing ones to Jesus!

—W. B. K.

* * *

Face to Face Talk

I want no great preachers in the field. If I can find a man who can talk face to face with another man, wherever he meets him, then I know how to get missionary work done in America or China.

—Dr. Nevius, Missionary

* * *

Bulldog Evangelism

In evangelistic work in Kentucky, we were using cards reading, "Get right with God," and a group of newsboys attached them to their caps. One day I saw a strange bulldog come along and make friends with these boys. They mauled him to his entire satisfaction, and finally one lad ran to me asking for a card for the dog. He fastened it to the name plate on the collar, which was in keeping with the large size of the dog. Now we were interested in a certain man, and had him on our prayer lists, but had not been able to reach him. That night he came out to the meeting, and as soon as the invitation was given, rushed to the front, fell on his knees, and called upon God to save him. After a new light came on his face and a new song of joy from his lips, I sat by him and asked how it all happened. Said he: "I was not feeling well today, so remained at home from work. I was trying to get some sleep this afternoon, when I was startled by a fierce and prolonged barking at the rear of our house. I finally decided to go and see what it was all about, and as I opened the rear door, in bounded a fierce, ugly-looking bulldog, entirely strange to our neighborhood. At first I was somewhat frightened by the beast, but soon discovered signs of friendliness coming in dog fashion from both ends of this disturber of my peace, so I sat down in a chair, and he immediately and very lovingly came and put his big head in my lap. There, staring me in the face, attached to his collar, was one of those 'Get right with God' cards. I there and then decided that if God was sufficiently interested in me to send that bulldog after me, I'd better give up; and here I am."

—Sunday School Times

* * *

Forgetting Why We Were Sent

A man of seventy-eight, living entirely alone, was recently converted through the efforts of a busy mother. As he was sitting in the park one day, she, an utter stranger, felt impelled to speak to him about his soul's welfare. She found him hungry for spiritual food. As he afterward said to a friend, he "had known for a long time that Christianity was the right thing, only he needed some one to stir him up." I wonder sometimes if we are not faring so sumptuously on sermons and missionary talks and lectures and literature that we are forgetting the Lazarus at our gates. A man's life ought to consist in leading others to Christ."

—Wesleyan Senior Quarterly

* * *

Save Others

Mr. Moody tells of one day seeing a steel-engraving which pleased him very much. He says: "I thought it was the finest thing I had ever seen, at the time, and I bought it." It was the picture of a woman coming up out of the water and clinging with both hands to the Cross of Refuge. "But afterward," he goes on to say, "I saw another picture which spoiled this one for me entirely — it was so much more lovely. It was a picture of a person coming out of the dark waters with one arm clinging to the Cross, but with the other she was lifting some one else out of the waves."

—Sunday

* * *

Should We Enter Uninvited?

"Why did you go to those strange people?" asked a friend of a return missionary. "Did they ask you to come?" "No, they did not ask me." "Then why did you go?" The missionary said: "When I was a young man in college, in going to my room one night, I saw a bright light in a house as I passed. The wind had blown the curtain too close to the gas jet and it was in flames. But because this family had not invited me to warn them, and not wishing to disturb their peace, I passed on to my room." "You did no such thing," said the other. "You wasted no time in crying to them that their house was on fire." "Certainly," said the missionary; "and *the people of the strange land did not invite me, but I knew their danger without Christ, and I knew the peace and joy that comes with knowing him. I was bound, knowing these things, to tell them.*"

—Moody Monthly

* * *

Why the Others Protested

A new missionary on the foreign field was examining some candidates for baptism. He had examined all except one and found their answers to his questions satisfactory. He looked at the last candidate doubtfully, and suggested that as he was so young, he should wait awhile before coming into the church. Immediately the others protested, "Why, he is the one who led us to the Lord!"

—Lightbearer, publication of Sudan United Mission

"I Like the Way I Do It Better Than the Way You DON'T Do It!"

Charles Alexander was accosted by a carping critic: "I don't like the way you do personal work." Replied Alexander, who was well aware of his imperfections, "Neither do I, but how do YOU do personal work?" Shamefacedly, the critic confessed, "Well, I guess I don't do it!" "Well," said Alexander, "I like the way I DO it better than the way you DON'T do it!"

"He that winneth souls is wise," or, "The wise win souls!"

—W. B. K.

* * *

Not Very Tactful, But —

Dr. Len G. Broughton, for years pastor of the Tabernacle Baptist Church, Atlanta, Georgia, told the following incident: "In my church, there was an half-witted young man. To be sure, he 'had zeal without knowledge.' However, he did have a sincere desire to see souls saved. Once, when I was making an appeal for souls at the close of my sermon, this half-witted young man quietly drew up alongside a well-dressed young man, and asked him, "Do you want to go to heaven?" Bluntly, the one approached barked out, "NO!" "Go to hell, then!" said the half-witted young man as he walked away.

God's Holy Spirit used the sincere effort of that young man to awaken the slumbering soul of that haughty sinner, and, ere long, he chose Christ as his Saviour, and heaven as his eternal home.

—W. B. K.

* * *

A Buttonhole Christian

A clerk who had been converted in the meetings invited his employer to attend. One evening he was there and sat across the aisle from Mr. Arthur Tappan. He appeared affected during the sermon, and Mr. Tappan kept his eye on him. After the dismissal Mr. Tappan stepped quickly across the aisle, introduced himself and invited him to stay to the after-meeting. The gentleman tried to excuse himself and get away, but Mr. Tappan caught hold of the button on his coat and said, "Now, do stay; I know you will enjoy it!" and he was so kind and gentlemanly that the man could not well refuse. He stayed and was led to Christ. Afterward he said, "An ounce of weight upon my coat button saved my soul." More "buttonhole Christians" are needed.

—*Gospel Herald*

* * *

No One Thought of the Ones Near By

A great life insurance company in New York invited all its agents throughout the country to a conference in New York, and while in attendance one of the agents from the West insured the barber, the elevator man, and a waiter in the restaurant, all of whom had been employed for years by the insurance company in its great building. No one had thought to offer policies to these men in the home office building! Exactly so. That is the reason the professional evangelist sweeps in so many; he simply improves the chance that has been there all the time. But why must we wait for him?

—*Sunday School Times*

* * *

Interest In Individual Lost

Somehow we have lost our concern for the individual. We have come to think of masses. It is here that we can trace the curse of Communism and Socialism. These ideologies try to obliterate the importance and influence of the individual. Christianity teaches us his value.

But are not we Christians in danger of becoming engrossed with organization? We convene conferences, form societies, issue manuals, pass resolutions with the object of dealing with people en masse. But while we are here and there, the individual goes. We need a baptism of love for souls, a love to win them one by one for the Master.

In the words of Leon Tucker:
"Lord, lay some soul upon my heart,
    And love that soul through me;
And may I nobly do my part
    To win that soul for Thee."

—*Moody Monthly*

"The Weight of a Lost World"

A consecrated Sunday school teacher came to her pastor. She taught a class of young college boys. Twenty-four of them were unsaved. She sat speechless and sobbing before the pastor. "What is the matter?" asked the pastor. She exclaimed, "My boys, twenty-four of them are standing on my heart like the weight of a lost world. I did not sleep any last night. I cannot eat. I must have them or I cannot live!" Prayer followed prayer immersed in tears. In less than two weeks, every one of those twenty-four boys gave glowing, personal testimonies about the saving power of the Lord Jesus!

—W. B. K.

* * *

"I Ring A Door Bell!"

Said Roger Babson, "It is more essential to ring door bells than church bells!" He was right! Let us now say it poetically:

One day I rang a door bell,
In a casual sort of way,
'Twas not a formal visit,
And there wasn't much to say.
I don't remember what I said —
It matters not I guess —
I found a heart in hunger,
A soul in deep distress.
He said I came from heaven,
And I often wondered why,
He said I came to see him,
When no other help was nigh.
It meant so little to me
To knock at a stranger's door,
But it means heaven to him.
And God's peace forever more.

—E. J. Morgan

* * *

One Man the Congregation!

"The longer I live, the more confidence I have in those sermons preached where one man is the congregation; where one man is the minister; where there is no question as to who is meant when the preacher says, "Thou art the man!"

—Henry Ward Beecher

SOWING AND REAPING

A Result of His Sowing

During the Civil War, a man on horseback suddenly found himself confronted with a soldier on sentry guard. The soldier pointed his gun at the other man's breast and said, "Halt! Who goes there?" "A friend," he replied. "Approach, friend, and give the password." "Lincoln," confidently said the man on horseback. There was a dead silence — for it was the wrong password! At length the soldier said slowly and solemnly, "It is the wrong password. If I did not know who you were, your life would pay the penalty of the mistake. At the risk of my own life, I spare yours. Go back and get the right word." The man on horseback thanked the soldier warmly and rode away, returning with the right password, "Massachusetts." "Pass on, all's well," was the immediate reply from the sentry. "I cannot pass," said the rider, "till I have

given you a message. At the risk of your life, you spared mine. Have you the right password for Heaven? "Yes, sir, I have." "What is it?" " 'Jesus Christ,' sir." "Where did you learn that?" "In your Sunday-school long ago in Pennsylvania, sir." God has said, "So shall my word be that goeth forth out of my mouth: it shall not return unto me void, but it shall prosper in the thing whereto I sent it."

—*King's Business*

* * *

Life An Echo

A little boy once went to his mother and said, "Mother, there is a boy out there in the woods and he is mocking me. Everything I say he says over after me. I said 'Hello' and he said 'Hello.' I said 'Who are you?' and he said 'Who are you?' I said 'What is your name?' and he said 'What is your name?'

I was mad and jumped over the fence and went into the woods to find him, but he wasn't anywhere. I said, 'I'll punch your head,' and he said he would punch mine."

The lad's mother said to him, "That is only the echo, my boy. If you had said 'I love you,' it would have said that after you."

—*Gospel Herald*

* * *

A Good Harvest

Many years ago a young man, traveling in one of the Mid-Western States, asked at a farmhouse for a night's lodging, which was gladly granted. Presently another, with his wife, came and asked also for a place in which to spend the night. He was suffering from tuberculosis, was on his way to Colorado, and had only four dollars to get there. The first man offered to give up his room and bed to them, saying he would gladly sleep in the barn or on the floor, which he did. The next morning, as the sick man was leaving, his host gave him a hundred dollars, telling him to use it and not to worry if he was never able to pay it back. Exactly twenty years later, the first man was again in that neighborhood, and decided to see if his former host still lived there. He found him, and as they renewed their acquaintance, another man came to call, and to their surprise, proved to be the other guest of twenty years ago. He had just heard that his generous host had suffered from financial reverses, so came at once, and said to him, "You gave me a hundred dollars when I was in need. Now I am going to repay it by giving you one hundred dollars for each dollar you gave me."

—*Told by the man who was the first guest at the farmhouse.*

* * *

A Christian, But —

Pardon me, Honourable Judge, you see I am a Christian; I am a new man in Christ. It was not my new man but my old man that did that wrong," said the self-excusing culprit on trial. To this the Judge is reported to have replied: "Since it was the old man that did the wrong, we'll sentence him to thirty days in jail. And inasmuch as the new man had complicity with the old man in the wrong, we'll give him thirty days also. *You* will therefore go to jail for *sixty* days."

—*Gospel Herald*

* * *

The Dog Learned Quickly

An old lady rented a furnished villa for the summer, and with the villa a large dog was included. In the sitting room of the villa there was a very comfortable arm chair. The old lady liked this chair better than any other in the house. She always made for it the first thing. But alas! she nearly always found the chair occupied by the large dog. Being afraid of the dog, she never dared hit it to get out of the chair, but instead she would go to the window and call, "Cats!" The dog would rush to the window and bark, and the old lady would quietly slip into the vacated chair. One day the dog entered the room and found the old lady in possession of the chair. He strolled over to the window and, looking out, appeared very much excited, and set up a tremendous barking. The old lady rose and hastened to the window to see what was the matter, and the dog quietly climbed into the chair, which suggests that the deceits we practice on others will, sooner or later, be repaid against ourselves.

—*Religious Telescope*

* * *

"When the Fruit Is Brought Forth"

Nearly a century ago a young girl on the Hudson fell into an evil life and the county records show the history of her descendants. They were 900 in number. Of these, 200 are on the county records as criminals; 9 of her own children served an aggregate term in state prisons of 50 years; and a considerable proportion of her descendants were idiots, lunatics, prostitutes, drunkards, and paupers. History records a corresponding fact: Jonathan Edwards was a man whom the Word of God had changed from sin to holiness. A record of his descendants is known. Out of 1,400 of these, 8 have been presidents of American universities; 100 have been professors; 100 have been ministers of the Gospel; 600 have been doctors; 30, judges; 25, officers in the Army and Navy; and others, mayors, senators, governors, and ambassadors.

—*Dawn*

* * *

Sowing and Reaping

A young man stood upon the trap door of the gallows and pointing to the noose that soon must encircle his neck said — after an eloquent appeal to those of his companions who were standing around to flee from wine and liquor as they would from a serpent — "No harm in it? No harm in it? There is a noose in every glass. Lost reputation, prison doors, cruelty, brutality, murder and death are in it. I sowed my wild oats, but now I must reap the ripened grain. You can see what it is (still pointing at the noose) ; wine did it. It broke my mother's heart, disgraced my sisters, robbed my father of all he possessed, and leaves him a gray-haired brokendown pauper."

—*Gospel Herald*

* * *

"Nails Gone — Scars Remain!"

During my early childhood I had a fiery temper which often caused me to say or do unkind things.

One day, after an argument had sent one of my playmates home in tears, my father told me that for each thoughtless, mean thing I did he would drive a nail into our gatepost. Each time I did a kindness or a good deed, one nail would be withdrawn.

Months passed. Each time I entered our gate, I was reminded of the reasons for those ever-increasing nails, until, finally, getting them out became a challenge.

At last the wished-for day arrived — only one more nail! As my father withdrew it I danced around proudly exclaiming, "See, Daddy, the nails are all gone."

Father gazed intently at the post as he thoughtfully replied, "Yes, the nails are gone — but the scars remain."

—Hazel Farris, Lexington, Kentucky

Sowing As He Could

A businessman in Boston said to himself, "I cannot take part in prayer meetings. I cannot do other things in Christian service, but I can put two extra dinner plates on my table every Sunday, and induce two young men who are away from home to dine with me." He did that for over thirty years, and thus became acquainted with a great number of young men who came to his church, and many of whom became Christians through his personal influence. When he died he was buried in a cemetery thirty miles away, and a special train was chartered to convey his business friends, and there was a special coach on the train for his Sunday guests who had become Christians through his influence. One hundred and fifty of them packed that car from end to end.

—*The Methodist Recorder*

* * *

A Day of Reckoning Coming

Years ago, in old China, lived a man who was a member of the Emperor's orchestra, although he could not play a note. He had obtained his position as a flute player in the royal band by influence, and for many years, whenever the musicians played, he sat with them and held his flute against his lips, pretending to play the plaintive airs and love songs of his native land. But he never dared to blow even softly into the instrument for fear he would cause a discord and be unmasked. For this performance he received a modest salary and managed to live comfortably. But there came a day when it was the Emperor's whim to have each of his musicians play alone. The flutist was dismayed, and as the day approached he became desperate. For a time he took lessons from a professional, but to no avail; he had no musical ear and no talent for the flute. Then he pretended illness, but was afraid he would be betrayed by the royal physician, who was sent to attend him. On the morning of his solo appearance, he took poison and died, rather than face the music. This, then, is the origin of an old Chinese phrase, "He dared not face the music."

—*North Star Baptist*

SYMPATHY

Saved From Dishonor

"An English naval officer," writes C. G. Trumbull, "Has told a grateful story of the way he was helped and saved from dishonor in his first experience in battle. He was a midshipman, fourteen years old. The volleys of the enemy's musketry so terrified him that he almost fainted. The officer over him saw his state, and came close beside him, keeping his own face toward the enemy, and held the midshipman's hand, saying in a calm, quiet, affectionate way, "Courage, my boy. You will recover in a minute or two. I was just like that when I went into my first battle." The young man said afterward that it was as if an angel had come to him and put new strength into him. The whole burden of his agony was gone, and from that moment he was as brave as the oldest of the men. If the officer had dealt sternly with him, he might have driven him to cowardly failure. His kindly sympathy with him dispelled all fear, put courage into his heart and made him brave for battle.

—Sunday School Times

* * *

"Dear Child, I Understand"

"The road is too rough," I said, "dear Lord,
There are stones that hurt me so."
And He said, "Dear child, I understand:
I walked it long ago."

"But there's a cool green path," I said,
"Let me walk there for a time."
"No, child," He gently answered me,
"The green road does not climb."

"My burden," I said, "is far too great,
How can I bear it so?"
"My child," said He, "I remember its weight:
I carried My cross, you know."

And so I climbed the stony path,
Content at last to know
That where my Master had not gone
I would not need to go.

—Selected

"Two Hearts Tugging At One Load"

"Sympathy is two hearts tugging at one load," said Charles A. Parkhurst. True sympathy is usually born in sorrow. Said Henry Giles, "The capacity of sorrow belongs to our grandeur, and the loftiest of our race are those who have had the profoundest sympathies, because they have had the profoundest sorrows." The world hungers for compassion — sympathy. Often we can do nothing but sympathize — suffer with the distressed — but, oh, how it helps!
— *The Voice*

* * *

Didn't Thou Sympathize in The Right Place: Thy Pocketbook?

A farmer had sustained a great loss. In speaking of the loss with a Quaker neighbor, a man expressed concern and said, "I surely sympathize with our mutual friend and neighbor in his loss!" Seriously and thoughtfully, the Quaker asked, "Dost thou sympathize in the right place: THY POCKETBOOK?"

"Let us not love in WORD, neither in TONGUE; but in DEED and TRUTH" (I John 3:18b). — W. B. K.

* * *

"An Understanding Smile!"

It needs so little sympathy
To cheer a weary way,
Sometimes a little kindliness
Lights up a dreary day;
A very simple, friendly word
May hope and strength impart,
Or just an understanding smile
Revive some fainting heart;
And, like a sudden sunlit ray,
Lighting a darkened room,
A sunny spirit may beguile
The deepest depths of gloom.
— *Selected*

* * *

Nobody Cares for Me

Among a large number of persons waiting in the room to speak with Mr. Lincoln, on a certain day in November, 1864, was a small, pale, delicate-looking boy about thirteen years old. The President saw him standing, looking feeble and faint, and said: "Come here, my boy, and tell me what you want." The boy advanced, placed his hand on the arm of the President's chair, and with bowed head and timid accents said:

"Mr. President, I was a drummer in a regiment for two years, and my colonel got angry with me and turned me off. I was taken sick, and have been a long time in the hospital. This is the first time I have been out, and I came to see if you could not do something for me."

The President looked at him kindly and tenderly, and asked him where he lived. "I have no home," answered the boy. "Where is your father?" "He died in the army," was the reply. "Where is your mother?" continued the President. "My mother is dead, too. I have no mother, no father, no brothers, no sisters, and," bursting into tears, "no friends — nobody cares for me."

Mr. Lincoln's eyes filled with tears, and he said to him, "Can't you sell papers?" "No," said the boy, "I am too weak; and the surgeon of the hospital told me I must leave, and I have no money and no place to go."

The President drew forth a card, and addressing on it certain officials to whom his request was law, gave special directions "to care for this poor boy."
— *Gospel Herald*

* * *

The Indians' Sympathy

The Saddle Mountain Mission Indians sent a letter to an Indian agent whose young son had suffered amputation of a leg, in which they said: "Today we have learned that great sorrow has come to your life because your boy, whom you love very dearly, has had to suffer again. We are only poor Indians, and we cannot help you any, but we all feel that we can tell you that we are sorry for you and for him. When a big storm comes, our horses bunch together, and stand with their heads down, trying to keep each other warm. A great storm of trouble has come to you and to us, lately. Let us put our hearts together, and with heads bowed down try to comfort each other under the shadow of the Mighty Rock, Jesus. We are poor Indians and cannot help you any, but we can promise you that we will be good citizens and not give you any trouble. We put our heart beside yours in your trouble, and pray that both you and your boy may meet us some day in the Home Jesus is preparing for us all." — *Sunday School Times*

* * *

If We Knew . . .

There are gems of wondrous brightness
  oftimes lying at our feet
And we pass them walking thoughtless
  down the busy, crowded street;
IF WE KNEW, our pace would slacken, we would step more oft with care
Lest our careless feet be treading to the
  earth some jewel rare.

If we knew what hearts are aching for
  the comforts we might bring,
If we knew what souls are yearning
  for the sunshine we could fling,
If we knew what feet are weary walking pathways roughly laid,
We would quickly hasten forward
  stretching forth our hands to aid.

If we knew what friends around us feel
  a want they never tell,
That some word which we have spoken,
  pained or wounded where it fell,
We would speak in accents tender to
  each friend we chanced to meet,
We would give to each one freely smiles
  of sympathy so sweet.
— *Selected*

* * *

"He Knows!"

"Oh," said a little Scotch woman one morning when I told her that her husband had been slain in battle, "do you think there is any mistake?" "Mistake? I hope I shall get another message." "I don't mean that," she said, "I know my husband is dead. I know it. I feel it in my heart." I said, "What do you mean?" "I mean, is there a God? That is what I mean. Is there a God who loves us like I thought? A God who hears prayers? A God who cares?" Maybe you think she wasn't a Christian to talk like that. But I assure you she was. If you haven't had some hours dark enough to make you ask a question like that, I have had. I understood that little woman, and I said, "God bless you. I know just how you feel." Don't you remember when He was here, once it got so dark that He turned His face to heaven and said, "My God, my God, why hast thou forsaken Me?" Oh, He knows and cares!

— *Moody Monthly*

* * *

"I Understand!"

Hast thou been hungry, child of Mine?
I, too, have needed bread;
For forty days I tasted naught
Till by the angels fed.
Hast thou been thirsty? On the cross
I suffered thirst for thee;
I've promised to supply thy need,
My child, come unto Me.

Perhaps thy way is weary oft,
Thy feet grow tired and lame;
I wearied when I reached the well,
I suffered just the same:
And when I bore the heavy cross
I fainted 'neath the load;
And so I've promised rest to all
Who walk the weary road.

Doth Satan sometimes buffet thee,
And tempt thy soul to sin?
Do faith and hope and love grow weak?
Are doubts and fears within?
Remember I was tempted thrice
By this same foe of thine;
But he could not resist the Word,
Nor conquer pow'r divine.

When thou art sad and tears fall fast
My heart goes out to thee,
For I wept o'er Jerusalem —
The place so dear to me:
And when I came to Lazarus' tomb
I wept — my heart was sore;
I'll comfort thee when thou dost weep,
Till sorrows all are o'er.

— Susanne C Umlauf

* * *

The Comfort of Compasion

There is a lovely letter written by Mrs. Carlyle to that rugged husband of hers in the course of which she tells him how, during a recent illness, she was greatly comforted by her maid. The girl only came into the room, and rubbed her cheek against her mistress's; but it strangely soothed her. "And sometimes," adds Mrs. Carlyle, "I could tell that her cheek was wet, and her tears meant much to me." Jesus, who wept tears at Bethany, also had compassion on the bereaved widow of Nain.

—From *The Uttermost Star*,
by the Rev. F. W. Boreham

* * *

Sympathy That Counted

Dr. Stuart Nye Hutchison tells us about a boy whom he knew who had lost his right hand. He felt so badly about it that he did not want to see anyone. His father said, "I'm going to bring the minister in to see you." The boy said, "I don't want to see him." But the father brought him in. When the boy looked up he saw that the minister had no right arm; there was an empty sleeve. He came over to the boy and said, "I haven't any hand, either. I lost mine when I was a boy, and I know how it feels." It wasn't hard for the boy to get acquainted with the minister who "knew how it felt." So Christ has suffered for us and knows our temptations.

— *Tarbell's Teachers' Guide*

* * *

Sympathy, Not Wisdom, Needed

A rural pastor relates this experience: "A poor mother on a mountain farm met my pastoral visit by bursting into tears, and saying, 'Oh, somehow I felt just as if you would come today. I have so many troubles and problems that I want you to help me out.' Then she told me things that brought tears to my eyes, but the things were beyond my wisdom to solve. I did not know what to say, and was alarmed at the fool I must appear to her. At length she surprised me by saying, 'You have settled my problem so nicely. You have given me just the help I needed.' *Then I knew it was sympathy, not wisdom,* which she needed, for not a problem had I solved." — *Sunday School Times.*

How He Shared Our Infirmities

He who is the Bread of Life began his ministry hungering. He who is the Water of Life ended his ministry thirsting. Christ hungered as man, and fed the hungry as God. He was weary, and yet he is our rest. He paid tribute, and yet he is the King. He was called a devil, and cast out devils.... He prayed, and yet he hears prayer. He wept, and he dries our tears. He was sold for thirty pieces of silver, and redeems the world. He was led as a lamb to the slaughter, and is the Good Shepherd. He died, and gave his life, and by dying destroys death.

— *Christian Index*

TEMPERANCE — ALCOHOL

Present Inmates Released

Two saloon-keepers came into a train where Gypsy Smith, the evangelist, was sitting waiting for the train to start. The two saloon men monopolized all the conversation. Gypsy Smith was hidden behind his newspaper, but he heard them. By and by one of them said, "Mr. Smith, we know you, and we want to say to you that unless you evangelists and ministers stop your knocking at the liquor business, we liquor men will have to go to the poorhouse." "All right," said Gypsy Smith; "when you go in, all the rest of the inmates can come out."

— *Union Signal*

* * *

Nothing New Under the Sun

What Is Drunkenness?
Darkness.
What Is Moderation?
Twilight.
What Is Total Abstinence?
Midday.

What Is Drunkenness?
Slavery.
What Is Moderation?
A chain.
What Is Total Abstinence?
The power which breaks the chain and sets the captive free.

What Is Drunkenness?
A fire.
What Is Moderation?
That which kindles it.
What Is Total Abstinence?
That which puts it out.

What Is Drunkenness?
Death.
What Is Moderation?
The way to it.
What Is Total Abstinence?
Life.

What Is Drunkenness?
Ruin.
What Is Moderation?
Danger.
What Is Total Abstinence?
Safety.

—Rev. James B. Dunn

* * *

Yes, It Warms One!

A patient was arguing with his doctor on the necessity of his taking a stimulant. "But, doctor, I must have some kind of stimulant; I am cold, and it warms me." "Precisely," came the doctor's answer; "see here, this stick is cold," taking up a stick of wood from the box beside the hearth, and tossing it into the fire. "Now it is warm, but is the stick benefited?" The man watched the wood first send out little puffs of smoke and then burst into a flame, and replied, "Of course not; it's burning." "And so are you when you warm yourself with alcohol; you are literally burning up the delicate tissues of your stomach and brain."

—*Sunday School Times*

* * *

No Need To Say, "I'm Sorry!"

The London Daily Mail has a regular feature called the Human Case Book, conducted by Ann Temple. Here is a problem submitted to her:

"I am sixteen, and have made up my mind not to drink, but people make it very hard for me to refuse. They keep on insisting and pressing, and some get scornful and angry if I say, 'I'm sorry, I'd rather have an orangeade.' What's the best way to refuse? — M." Here is the reply: "No need to say, 'I'm sorry.' You invite them to persuade you if you sound apologetic. All that is necessary is a 'Thank you; I only take soft drinks.' . . . If you can just hit the knack of being proud and glad and grateful for being able to hold on to your standards without being awkward or priggish or intolerant, you are just the nicest specimen of human being."

—Maine Civic League Record

* * *

Seasickness on Shore

When Lincoln visited General Grant's camp in Virginia in 1864, he was met by the General and his staff, and on being asked how he stood the trip said, "I am not feeling so well. I got pretty badly shaken up on the bay coming down, and am not altogether over it yet." "Let me send for a bottle of champagne for you, Mr. President," suggested one of the staff officers. "That is the best remedy I know for seasickness." "No, no, my young friend," was the President's reply, "I have seen many a man seasick on shore from drinking that very article."

—Pentecostal Herald

* * *

Unsavory Association

A passenger on a steamer from Bombay to London asked the captain whether liquor could be procured at Zanzibar, where the vessel was to touch. The captain said: "You could get it. I know Zanzibar well, and here the Mohammedans form the greater part of the ruling community, and the Mohammedan law is against the taking of strong drink. The only way in which you can get drink in Zanzibar is by making a declaration that you are a Christian." Is it any wonder that Christian missions make slow headway in lands where the name of Christian is associated with the trade in liquor and narcotics, and where the vices that corrupt the natives are practiced by visitors from so-called Christian countries?

—Christian Advocate

* * *

What a Great Englishman Thought of Liquor

"The only glory in life is to leave the world better for having been in it. Intoxicating drinks do not help us to do that. When I made up my mind that I would be as perfect a citizen as I could be, the first thing I did was to swear off the use of all alcoholic liquors."

—Sir Richard Grenfell

* * *

Strange "Disease"

Some modern psychologists and psychiatrists say that alcoholism is a disease. If so, it is the only "disease" which our nation advertises to the tune of one hundred and thirty million dollars a year; it is the only "disease" which we propagate and encourage by the manufacture of liquors to the tune of three billion dollars a year; it is the only "disease" which we legalize to the extent of licensing 447,000 retail liquor permits each year; it is the only "disease" that God punishes, for He says no "drunkards . . . . shall inherit the kingdom of God" (I Cor. 6:10).

—Evangelical Christian

* * *

Hank Wilson, Famed Ball Player, Gives Warning

"I was at the top of my career. It happened in 1940. That was the year I won the most valuable player award. I received a salary of $40,000. I started to drink heavily. I argued with my manager (Joe McCarthy) and the rest of the players. Then things began to happen.

"I spent the winter in taprooms. When spring training rolled around I was 20 pounds overweight. I couldn't stop drinking. I couldn't hit. That year most experts figured I'd break Ruth's record. But I ended up hitting only 13 home runs.

"I was suspended before the season was over. I drank more than ever. I got booted from one minor league club to another. I worked at odd jobs. Spent all of my money, most of it in bar rooms. Finally I got sick. While I was recuperating in that hospital, I had a lot of time to think.

"There are kids in and out of baseball who think because they have talent they have the world by the tail. It isn't so. In life you need things like good advice and common sense. Kids, don't be too big to accept advice. Be considerate of others. That's the only way to live."

—*Chicago Daily News*

* * *

Beer Mathematics

Said the glass of beer to the bottle of gin: "I'm not much of a mathematician, but I can and I do ADD to a man's nervous troubles; SUBTRACT cash from his pocketbook; MULTIPLY his aches and pains; DIVIDE his property with the liquor traffic, so that FRACTIONS only remain for him. Moreover, I take INTEREST from his work and DISCOUNT his chances for health and success!"

—*Junior Missionary Magazine*

* * *

Time for a New Doctor

On one occasion Dr. John G. Paton was dining with a wealthy friend in England. He noticed that the footman poured out a little whiskey for his host. The gentleman apologized to the missionary and said, "I am accustomed to take a little whiskey for my cough on my doctor's prescription." Doctor Paton said, "How long have you been doing this?" The host answered, "About eight years." "Does your cough seem to get any better?" asked Dr. Paton. "No," answered the man. "Well," said the missionary, "if I had a doctor who prescribed for me for eight years, and he did not cure me, I would quit taking his prescriptions, and get a new doctor."

—*Christian Herald* (London)

The Table Liquor Spreads

The story is told of a poor woman who went to a saloon in search of her husband. She found him there, and setting a covered dish, which she had brought with her, upon the table, she said, "Thinking that you are too busy to come home to dinner, I have brought you yours," and departed. With a laugh the man invited his friends to dine with him; but on removing the cover from the dish he found only a slip of paper, on which was written, "I hope you will enjoy your meal. It is the same as your family have at home."

—*Gospel Herald*

* * *

A Fool in Action

A prize essay, by a Georgia school girl, had this telling statement: "Take one regular, natural-born fool, add two or three drinks of liquor and mix the two in a high-powered motor car. After the fool is thoroughly soaked, place his foot on the gas and release the brakes. Remove the fool from the wreckage. Place in a black, satin-lined box, and garnish with flowers."

—*United Presbyterian*

* * *

His Sobering Choice

"As I entered the office of a well-known merchant," said an American writer, "a thrilling temperance lecture confronted me — a placard nailed to the desk."

WHICH?
Wife or Whisky
The Babes or the Bottles
HEAVEN OR HELL

"The merchant explained, 'I wrote that myself. Sometime ago I found myself falling into the habit of drinking — an occasional glass with a friend. Soon my stomach got bad, my faculties became dulled, and a constant craving for stimulants dominated me. I saw tears in my wife's eyes and wonder on the faces of my children. One day I sat down and wrote that card. On surveying it carefully, its awful revelation burst on me like a flash. I nailed it there and read it many times that day. I went home sober that night, and have not touched a drop since.' "

—From *The Ideal Christian Home*, by Helen S. Dyer

* * *

What the Law Does

The wife of a drunkard found her husband asleep in the kitchen in a filthy condition. She took a photo of him and then placed it on the sideboard beside a photo taken at their marriage. When sober, he saw the two pictures, and awakened to a consciousness of his condition. The office of Law is not to save men, but to show them their state when compared with the divine standard.

—*Sunday Circle*

* * *

General Eisenhower On Beer

General Eisenhower is to be congratulated on his statement that the American fighting man calls for Coca Cola and not for the traditional "beer, beer, beer that makes you feel so queer." The General, in his appearance before the Senate Armed Services Committee, also cited a poll he took of American troops after World War II landings in Italy as follows: "Instead of beer, they wanted Coca Cola, which was easy, because we could import the syrup and make it ourselves."

—*Watchman-Examiner*

* * *

Thin and Blind Rats

A worker who was fond of beer told his wife and child one morning of a dream he had had. He had seen four rats. The first was large, fat, and sleek; two very very thin; and the last was blind. Neither he nor his wife could find any explanation for the dream, but were uneasy, for they had heard that rats brought bad luck.

The little boy, however, had an idea. "The big fat one, Father, was the tavern keeper on the corner who gets all your money. The two thin rats represented

mother and me. But you yourself were the blind one."

—From a French newspaper, Montreal, Canada.

* * *

"Alcohol Cures No Disease!"

There is no single disease in the world, of which alcohol is a cure. Since alcohol cures no disease, it is not a medicine. It has no place in medical practice. It creates only an illusion of vigor which does not exist.

—Dr. Howard Kelly

* * *

Brewers and Soldiers

The *Brewer's Digest* boasted: "One of the finest things that could have happened to the brewing industry was the insistence by high-ranking Army officers to make beer available at Army camps. . . . Here is a chance for brewers to cultivate a taste for beer in millions of young men who will eventually constitute the largest beer-consuming section of our population." How truly this has been fulfilled!

—*Watchman-Examiner*

* * *

"Respectable" Drink!

Three boys brutally bludgeoned a nurse to death to get money to buy "beer and gasoline." They got $1.50. The boy who first knocked her down laughed loudly. The boys denied the use of drugs but said they had drunk a case of beer. The papers said they came from "respectable homes." So — they came from "respectable homes!" They had enjoyed a "respectable" drink, advertised as the beverage of moderation and respectability. They purchased their drink in a "respectable" store, made so by our laws. They read about the drink in "respectable" papers and magazines. So everything about alcohol is respectable; that is, everything but its results.

—*Adult Uniform Lessons*

Dad's Good Liquor!

A fatal accident, involving the lives of four young people, took place upon one of the nation's highways. The evidence that the liquor was the culprit was found in the broken whisky bottles among the debris and mangled bodies of the four youthful victims. The father of one of the girls in frenzied anguish over the untimely death of his beautiful daughter threatened to kill the one who had provided the four young people with liquor, but upon going to the cupboard where he kept his supply of choice beverages, he found a note in his daughter's hand-writing, "Dad, we're taking along some of your good liquor — I know you won't mind."

—*Christian Union Herald*

* * *

Dr. Crane Gives Psychological and Medical Lowdown on Alcohol

Wrote Elaine P., 19, a college sophomore, and a teacher of a Sunday School Class to Dr. George W. Crane, editor of Worry Clinic, Chicago Daily News: "Give me some of the facts about beverage alcohol." Dr. Crane answered thus:

Chronic use of alcohol may cause neuralgia and even paralysis from the resulting neuritis.

It may produce delirium tremens and permanent mental derangement, plus kidney and liver damage, especially if consumed in large amounts.

But the worst danger of alcohol is psychological and can result from only one drink. I refer to the depressing or anesthetic effect upon the nervous system.

From the time you swallow the first drink, it begins to dull your sensitivity.

Like ether, it is an anesthetic. You may not be rendered unconscious by your first few whiffs of ether, but you begin growing groggy.

In the same manner, the first sip of alcohol starts the depressant effect. You don't have to be dead drunk or unconscious for it to do grave injury to your behaviour.

—*Chicago Daily News*

Babe Ruth Refused

Babe Ruth was offered a good sum if he would allow himself to be photographed with a bottle of beer in his hand. The brewer wanted the picture for advertising purposes. It is said that Babe Ruth replied, "No, I have autographed too many baseballs of boys of America to think of helping advertise the sale of beer. Many of these boys regard me as a hero, and I'll not do anything to lessen their esteem of me."

Great! That's a manly utterance! This kind of person in public life seems as rare as the Dodo. May his tribe increase!

—*Selected*

* * *

Brakes Off in America

Duty recently called me hundreds of miles away from home. Having registered at the city's leading hotel, I naturally sauntered toward the once glorious and unusually long lounge. But at the great door I came to a dead stop with a gasp. Over the doorway was a large sign — never there in the old days: "Ladies Cocktail Lounge." A loaded bar ran the vast length of the place, and twelve white-gowned bartenders did the honors! I submit an even dozen bartenders can do plenty of tending to plenty of ladies (with apologies to the word "lady."). In answer to a question about "profits and loss," the bar manager made ready reply: "We count it a very poor day when we do less than $3,000." That is a yearly rate of better than $1,000,000. And this is a "ladies only" bar. It also marks the fact that America is traveling with all brakes off to national suicide. Alexander the Great drank himself to death at thirty-three. Woman with her much more delicate nervous system can beat Alexander's record by years and millions have already entered the contest.

—*Christian Advocate*

* * *

Impossible to Drink Moderately

General Frederick D. Grant, son of President U. S. Grant, said:

"I tried to drink with extreme moderation, because I knew that alcohol is the worst poison a man can take into his system; *but I found out it was an impossibility to drink moderately.* . . . The fact that I indulged at all compelled me to drink on every occasion, or be absurd. For that reason, because moderate drinking is a practical impossibility, I became an absolute teetotaler — a crank, if you please. I will not allow it even in my house. *When a man can say, 'I never drink,' he never has to drink, is never urged to drink, never offends by not drinking;* at least that is my experience. . . . . The hard drinker was once a moderate drinker, and the chances are all against a moderate drinker remaining such, and *I — well, I, for one, don't propose to take such chances.* . . . . If I could, by offering my body a sacrifice, free this country from the demon drink, I'd thank the Almighty for the privilege of doing it."

—*Virginia Call*

* * *

The Greater Danger

An elderly person asked her aged father: "Father, why did you never drink? Was it because you didn't like it?" "No," he replied, "it was because I did like it."

—*Sunday School Times*

* * *

Iceland's Real Freedom

Iceland, about half the size of Missouri, has no jail, no penitentiary; there is no court, and only one policeman. Not a drop of alcoholic liquor is made on the island, and its people are total abstainers, since they will not permit any liquor to be imported. There is not an illiterate person on the island, not a child ten years old unable to read, the system of public schools being practically perfect.

—*Sunday School Times*

* * *

A Piteous Plea

A Pennsylvania farmer, forty-six years old, placed his head on a stick of dynamite, and thus died horribly, a tragic victim of strong drink. He left a note which read: "Dear Jimmy and

Faye, Always remember that Daddy loved you dearly, regardless of what anybody tells you. I just went screwy from drinking and now I am so nervous I can hardly write. Please never drink or play cards, Jimmy. I do hope Faye and you will turn out to be wonderful and good. I hope the Lord takes good care of you and I hope you will both forgive me. I am awfully sorry now, but now it is TOO LATE! Goodby, Daddy."
—W. B. K.

* * *

A Tragic Thing

A swerving car — a driver drunk
A heavy crash — a pile of junk!
A wrecking car — a doctor by
A frightened child — a wife's sad cry!
An orphan child — a widow 'lone;
A new-made grave where pine trees moan!
A tragic thing — may we repent —
A tragic thing — drink's monument.

—G. C. Whitely, in *Western Recorder*

* * *

Example by Proxy

In a home where the father drank at dinner, the pastor was often invited by the mother to dine, in order, as she once explained to him, that her young sons might see that some men were total abstainers, and that they might follow their mother's entreaties and the minister's example.

—*Illustrator*

* * *

Drinking Elders

An elder who was along in years told me this story. When he was a young man, another young man who was a member of the church was summoned before the church session for selling liquor in a saloon near by. He met with the session and listened respectfully to the charge. He admitted that it was true that he did sell liquor, and then added: "But I did not know that it was any more harm to sell it than it is to buy it, and I think I have sold some to every man in this room except the preacher."

—*Christian Observer*

A Fear That Is Not Cowardly

We are sometimes taunted with being afraid of a little alcoholic drink. No one had more courage than the Duke of Wellington, a man who brought more luster on the flag of England than any other man who has ever lived, and yet he was afraid of drink. On one occasion, when he was marching his victorious army across the Peninsula, he halted the whole army. Why? Simply because news had been brought to him that an immense store of Spanish wine lay directly in his line of march. He halted the whole victorious British Army until he had sent on his sappers to blow every single barrel to pieces. He was not a coward; he was not afraid; he saw the danger; he knew the foul, fascinating power of this drug upon both mind and body, and he took measures against his soldiers' being exposed to temptation.

—*Sunday School Times*

* * *

"Drink Not A Disease":

I challenge the concept that alcoholism is a 'disease.'

A victim of epilepsy has a disease, If he has a seizure in public he is absolutely innocent of preconceived intent in the matter.

The situation is utterly beyond his control, and the sympathy he is entitled to is justifiably based upon that fact.

This does not apply to an alcoholic. He doesn't HAVE to get drunk, he merely chooses to get drunk. Everybody knows of people who decided to stop drinking and stopped.

Who ever heard of an epileptic who stopped having seizures because he decided he wasn't going to have any more?

The great amount of attention in scientific quarters, given to the problem of alcoholism, has to my knowledge been seized upon by alcoholics to extend the notion that they have a "disease."

This of necessity places them in a position of lowered moral responsibility.

Why do I mention moral responsibility?

A person under the influence of alcohol is a menace to the welfare of his fellowmen. His acts of commission and omission interfere with the liberties and happiness of others.

When he and the public get sold on the idea that all this results from a "disease" in the sense that polio or cirrhosis of the liver is a disease, and, like the latter, must be coped with as an absolutely inevitable quirk of fate, the net effect is that the alcoholic is condoned in his infantile conduct.

Thus the issue of alcoholism is accepted on the same basis as unwanted pregnancy.

The idea of a "disease" provides the alcoholic with an acceptable excuse to avoid reality

A man in traction and encased in plaster in a hospital for fractures sustained in an accident may be unable to meet his responsibilities because he undoubtedly has a disease.

But I dispute that a man who leaves his pay check in a saloon and reels home to his sad and stricken family does so because he has a disease.

What he has is not a disease but a form of immature, infantile, escapist behavior.

Every alcoholic should be sharply aware that his conduct is productive of disgust, revulsion and outrage on the part of others. The sooner he realizes that fact the better off he and everyone concerned is.

To "Butter Up" an alcoholic with sympathy and assure him that he is blameless because he has a "disease" is precisely the same thing as a bribe to a squalling, spoiled infant.

An alcoholic refuses to face facts and life.

—William Brady, M. D.
Chicago Daily News

* * *

20 D's of Strong Drink

Demands its toll,
Defects the body mechanism,
Decreases chances of success,
Diminishes income,
Deadens noble instincts,
Drowns responsibility,
Desires nothing good,
Delights in evil,
Despises good company.
Deceives its patrons,
Diseases the body,

Drives away self-respect,
Darkens the outlook,
Destroys its user,
Draws misery and woe,
Defies good judgment,
Destroys the body,
Defeats God's plans,
Damns the soul,
"Whosoever is deceived thereby is not wise" (Proverbs 20:1).
—William S. Sharpe

* * *

Alcohol a Slower of Reaction Time.

"It has been shown that the 'reaction time,' or the response by muscular action to a stimulus such as a flash of light, takes an appreciable time, being about one-fifth of a second in a normal person.

"The effect of a small quantity of alcohol, such as a glass of beer, or an ordinary drink of whisky, causes an appreciable lengthening of the 'reaction time,' varying with the individual.

"Then, again, moderate amounts of alcohol affect the judgment and the rapid decision so necessary in a sudden emergency; also they may cause a tendency for a driver to take risks, as in the unsafe attempt to pass a car ahead. The subconscious outlook is also definitely impaired.

—Sir William Wilcox

* * *

He Was Certain of One Thing

Said a member of a church some years ago: "I was talking to a colored man whom I was examining for insurance. I asked him, 'Do you drink alcoholic liquors?' He answered, 'No, I can't say I does; and I can't say I doesn't. But I never done drink to success.'" Did anyone ever "sin to success"?

—*Bible Expositor*

* * *

Alcohol, A Remover

Some one has said that alcohol will remove stains from summer clothes.

This may be true, but stains from summer clothes are not the only things alcohol will remove.

Alcohol will remove the stain all right, but it will remove the summer clothes as well, and also the spring clothes, and the autumn clothes, and the winter clothes.

Alcohol will not only do this for the man who drinks it, but it will do it for all those for whom he is responsible.

Alcohol will remove good food from the dinner table, and shoes from the baby's feet.

It will remove happiness from the home, and then remove the possibility of its ever returning.

It will remove smiles from the face, and laughter from the lips of innocent children.

It will remove school books from the arms and hopes from the hearts of your boys and girls, and then the shoes from their feet, and the warm clothing from their bodies.

Yes, alcohol is a great remover! As a remover of things, alcohol has no equal competitor.

—*Gospel Herald*

* * *

Youth-Destroying Liquor

George W. Crane, Ph. D., M. D., of Chicago, noted writer on psychology and social relations, and the author of daily syndicated newspaper columns nationally disseminated, wrote: "I receive over a thousand letters per day from Americans. These letters clearly show that liquor is destroying the morals of American youth! It is breaking up marriages and contributing to our tragic divorce rate. It is subversive in its influence on functional intelligence, thereby serving as a definite contributing factor to the spread of venereal diseases."

—*Sunday School Times*

* * *

When the Heart Is Opened

A traveler in Scotland once found in a fisherman's hut a striking picture of the Saviour. "How did you obtain possession of this picture?" he asked the owner. He replied: "I was way down with the drink, when one night I went into a 'pub,' and there hung His picture. I was sober, and I said to the bartender, 'Sell me that picture; this is

669

no place for the Saviour.' I gave him all the money I had and took it home. I dropped on my knees and cried, 'O Lord Jesus, pick me up again out of my sin.' " The prayer was answered, and today that fisherman is the grandest man in that little Scottish village. He was asked if he had no struggle to give up liquor. A look of exultation came over his face as he answered, "When the heart is opened to the Saviour, He takes the love of drink out of it."

—*Sunday School Times*

* * *

"Taddie, Lad, Promise Me!"

"Taddie, lad, promise me that you will never drink. Didn't you see how that poor woman was suffering?"

Tad nodded.

"I want you to promise me that you will never drink. I won't ask you to sign a pledge, but give me your word of honor."

Tad put his small hand in his father's and said: "Papa-day, I won't ever drink anything but cold water."

"From this time forth and forevermore," added Mr. Lincoln.

"Forever!" Tad added.

"Now, instead of the written pledge, let us say the 'Mizpah.' Repeat this after me, Taddie: *'The Lord watch between me and thee, while we are absent from one another.'* "

—*The Junior*

* * *

A Brewer Gets Eyes Open!

Frederick Charrington was the son of a wealthy brewer. Upon finishing school, he entered the world-famed brewery of Charrington, Head and Co., London. He was converted by reading the third chapter of John's Gospel.

One day when his conscience was talking to him about being in a brewery business, a woman with a little girl went to a public house and begged her husband to give her some money, for the children were crying for bread. His only reply was to rush out and knock her and the child down. Looking up at the door, the owner saw his name, "Charrington" emblazoned in gold, and wondered how he could say anything to that

man when he thus was responsible for their misery. He said, "I cannot bear it. I will give it up." He did, renouncing a million and a quarter dollars and giving the balance of his life to fighting drink and preaching the Gospel.

—*Gospel Herald*

* * *

The First First Lady who Refused:

The first "First Lady" to go counter to the social custom of serving champagne and other wines at formal White House functions was the wife of President Rutherford B. Hayes, who, in fact, refused to serve any kind of alcoholic beverages.

"I have young sons," she said, "who have never tasted liquor. They shall not receive, from my hand, or with the sanction that its use in my family would give, their taste of what might prove their ruin. What I wish for my own sons, I must do for the sons of other mothers." — *Gospel Herald*

* * *

He Knew His Bible

A boy was on a steamboat making a journey. One day as he sat alone on the deck, looking down into the deep water, two ungodly men (gentlemen I cannot call them) agreed that one of them should persuade him to drink. So the wicked man drew near the boy and in a very pleasant voice and manner invited him to go and drink a glass of wine with him.

"I thank you, sir," said the little fellow, "but I never drink intoxicating liquors."

"Never mind, my lad, it will not hurt you. Come and have a drink with me."

"Wine is a mocker, strong drink is raging, and whosoever is deceived thereby is not wise" was the boy's ready reply.

"You need not be deceived by it. I would not have you drink too much. A little would do you no harm, but would liven you up."

"At last it biteth like a serpent, and stingeth like an adder," said the boy. "And I certainly think it wiser not to play with adders."

"My fine fellow," said the crafty man, "it will give me great pleasure if you will only come and drink just one glass of the best wine with me."

"My Bible says, 'If sinners entice thee, consent thou not,' " was the reply.

That was a stunning blow to the tempter, and he went back to his companion, defeated.

"How did you succeed?" he asked.

"Oh, not at all. The fact is," replied the man, "the youngster is so full of the Bible that I cannot do anything with him."

—*Gospel Herald*

* * *

Lincoln's Wish

On the last day of his life, Abraham Lincoln said, 'With the help of the people, we have cleaned up a colossal job. Slavery is abolished. After reconstruction, the next great question will be the abolition of the liquor traffic. My head and heart and my hand and my purse will go into that work. Less than a quarter of a century ago I predicted that the time would come when there would be neither a slave nor a drunkard in the land. I have lived to see, thank God, one of these prophecies fulfilled. I hope to see the other realized."

—*Youth's World*

* * *

"It Must Be Stopped!"

One night, blue-eyed, three-year-old Joyce Jean Shouse was wandering about a tavern in downtown Louisville, Kentucky, while her mother in an inside room was drinking herself into a stupor with several men. She knew nothing of it when the child, about eleven p. m., left the tavern accompanied by a man who offered her some bubble gum, as reported by witnesses. A week later her ravaged body was found, apparently the victim of a sex fiend, as reported in Association Press dispatches. Local papers stated that the mother had been charged three time previously with being drunk while having the child with her in some drinking place at night. After the tragedy the city alcoholic beverage control administrator, A. J. Bartholomew, stated that he "would wage a personal campaign to keep children out of saloons." How about trying to keep the saloons out of the community?

—*Civic Bulletin*

* * *

God Did Help Him!

A keen-eyed, medium-sized young sea captain stood in the lobby of a large hotel in Hong Kong, conversing with a portly Englishman. "So you have come to trade in the Orient?" the portly one asked. "Well, step into the bar and tell me about your plans." "I am sorry, but I never enter bars, and I don't take alcoholic beverages," the young captain replied. The Englishman's eyebrows rose, and his florid face broke into an unbelieving smile. "Entering the Oriental trade without Scotch and sodas?" "Yes, sir." "Do you expect to be able to do business in the Orient without taking your friends into the saloon and enjoying a friendly drink?" the torrid-faced one laughed. "If you do, God help you!" The keen-eyed young sea captain smiled, and replied, "God WILL help me." And apparently God did. Before his death that young sea captain, Captain Robert Dollar, sat on the tenth floor of the Robert Dollar Building in California street, on San Francisco Bay, where there was always one or more of his great ocean liners and cargo boats, loading or unloading cargoes from industries of almost every nation in the world!

—From *God Will Help Me*, by Walter G. Swanson

* * *

Alcoholism

Dr. Andrew C. Ivy, formerly vice-president of Illinois University, has reported the following facts about the evil of alcoholism:

1. There is an annual loss to industry of more than a billion and a half dollars.

2. There is an annual loss of $585,000,000 to heavy drinkers themselves for days when they are unfit to work.

3. There are 50,000 new confirmed alcoholics every year.

4. There were 5,000,000 arrests for drunkenness in 1951.

5. There were 2,000 deaths due to excessive drinking in 1951. What a tragedy, that 20,000 souls for whom Christ died were ushered into eternity, many unprepared. —*Moody Monthly*

* * *

An English Officer's Opinion

"As an officer I support temperance because I know that officers and men who avoid drink are physically and mentally efficient, their nerves are stronger, they march better, there is less sickness and crime among them, and their power of resistance is strengthened."
—General Sir Reginald Hart

* * *

A Salvationist Speaks Up

"I am against alcohol:

Because I have known unborn babes to be cursed through booze; little children to starve because of booze; young people to be stunted for life through booze; gifted women to become imbeciles through booze; leaders in industry to become beggars in the street because of booze; wedding rings to be sold for booze; fortunes to be squandered for booze; girls to become prostitutes through booze; boys to become criminals through booze; women to be hanged because of booze; men to go to the electric chair because of booze!"
—Catherine Booth

* * *

Lincoln Said

'This legalized liquor traffic, as carried on in the saloons and grogshops, is the tragedy of civilization. Good citizenship demands and requires that what is right should not only be made known, but be made prevalent; that what is evil should not only be detected but de-stroyed. The saloon has proved itself to be the greatest foe, the most blighting curse of our modern civilization, and this is the reason why I am a practical Prohibitionist. We must not be satisfied until the public sentiment of this nation and the individual conscience shall be instructed to look upon the saloon-keeper and the liquor-seller, with all the license earth can give him, as simply and only a privileged malefactor — a criminal."
—*Herald of His Coming*

* * *

Drink Blamed by Expert for Traffic's Toll:

Alcohol is involved to some degree in 40 to 60 per cent of America's annual motor toll of 40,000 dead and 1.5 million injured, according to Lt. Frank M. Andrews, Chief of the Evanston, Illinois, Traffic Police. He made the estimate in an address before Northwestern University Traffic Safety Clinic. Andrews is a member of the National Safety council committee for tests on intoxication and is, perhaps, a leading authority on this subject in this country.

"Police reports show that drinking is involved in 28 per cent of motor traffic casualties," said Andrews, "but any practical person knows that a policeman isn't going to report drinking unless someone he doesn't know looks like he is drunk.

"Of hit and run drivers, 95 per cent of those apprehended promptly have been drinking. Presumably those not arrested soon after the crash also have been drinking."

"There is no doubt that alcoholic beverages are America's No. 1 traffic accident problem."
—Hal Foust, in
Chicago Daily Tribune

TEMPTATION — TESTING

The Man Who was Tempted

A man in a responsible position, entrusted with large sums of money, was one day tempted to put some of the cash to his own account. He knew that it would be a long time before his theft could be discovered. He resisted the temptation, but felt that he must tell somebody the anguish of mind through which he had passed. He went, therefore, to the man who had occupied the position before him, and told him all about the temptation, and how he had almost fallen.

To his surprise, the man did not reprove him, but put his hand on his shoulder in a fatherly sort of way. "I know exactly how you felt," he said quietly. "I went through it all myself when I occupied your position."

How good it is to know that we have One who was "in all points tempted like as we are, yet without sin."

—*Christian Herald*

* * *

The Power of His Name

A native in South Africa had been seduced by a man who had a canteen for selling liquor, and the drink had got hold of him, so that whenever he had a little money he spent it on what he called the "firewater." A missionary lady meeting him one day told him of the Lord Jesus and His power to save him and deliver him from the power of sin. She was away for some time and on coming back the man's wife asked her what she had done to her husband, for she must have bewitched him. He had acted in a way the previous day which he had never done before. She said, "Let us go and ask him." On finding the man the missionary asked him what had taken place the day before and he told her that he had received a little money and was on his way to the canteen to get some "firewater" when he stopped and turned back. On being asked how that happened, he replied it was only a name. The lady asked him what name it was. He said, "May I tell it?" for he thought that the name was a secret talisman not to be uttered to others. "Oh, yes," said the lady, "tell it." "Well, it was Jesus," he said. "I was on my way to the canteen when I stopped and said, 'Jesus, Jesus,' and the spell was broken, for 'whosoever shall call upon the name of the Lord shall be saved.'"

—*Word and Work*

No Matter What Kind of Lions

Within a week after my conversion, I passed by a window of a picture store in St. Louis, and saw hanging there an engraving of a painting of Daniel in the den of lions. The prophet, with his hands behind him, and the lions circling about him, is looking up and answering the king's question. The one thing I was in mortal fear of, in those days, was that I might go back to my sins. I was a drunken lawyer in St. Louis when I was converted, with no power over an appetite for strong drink, and I was so afraid of a barroom or a hotel or a club that when I saw I was coming to one I would cross the street. I was in torment day and night. No one had told me anything about the keeping power of Jesus Christ. I stood before that picture, and a great hope and faith came into my heart, and I said, "Why, these lions are all about *me* — my old habits and sins — but the God that shut the lions' mouths for Daniel can shut them for me." I learned that my God was able. He had saved me, and He was able to deliver me from the lions. Oh, what a rest it was!

—Dr. C. I. Scofield

* * *

The Plimsoll Mark

It was due to the efforts of Samuel Plimsoll (1824-98), British reformer, that the Merchant Shipping Act of 1876 was passed, requiring all ships to bear a mark known as the Plimsoll mark and indicating the maximum load line. By this act the Board of Trade of England was empowered to detain any vessel deemed unsafe, and the amount of cargo was restricted, thus making the long and perilous ocean voyage of those days much safer. Because of his work, Plimsoll became known as the sailor's friend. The Plimsoll mark, with its gradations and figures, may be seen on the bow of ships near the water line as they lie at anchor in a harbor. In God's sight, each of us has a similar mark, though we may not be able to see it. The burdens and responsibilities He gives us may seem unbearable, but He knows our limit, His everlasting arms are underneath, and by His grace we can bear them without sinking. "God is faithful, who will not suffer you to be tempted above that ye are able; but will with the temptation also make a way to escape, that ye may be able to bear it" (1 Cor. 10:13*b*).

—*Sunday School Times*

* * *

Making Provision for the Flesh

One day Bob was given definite instruction by his mother not to go in swimming in the nearby pond. Shortly afterward, Bob was to pass the pond enroute to the ball park. He took along with him his bathing suit, just in case he was tempted! This was making provision for the flesh! How different it was with the aged Negro who said, "When I pass a watermelon patch, I can't keep my mouth from 'watering,' but I CAN RUN!"

—W. B. K.

* * *

Satan Cannot Stand Calvary

There once lived in Dundee, Scotland, a man who had fallen and broken his back as a lad of fifteen. For forty years he lay in his bed and moved only with the most terrible pain. Probably in all those forty years there was not a day when he did not suffer acutely. But day after day God's grace was found sufficient, and many people came to him for cheer and courage in Christian living. One day a visitor asked him, "Doesn't Satan ever tempt you to doubt God?" "Oh, yes," he answered, "he does try to tempt me. I lie here and see my old schoolmates driving along in their carriages, and Satan whispers, 'If God is so good, why does He keep you here all these years?' Then, seeing an old friend walking by in perfect health, Satan fairly screams, 'If God loved you, why did He permit your back to be broken?'" "What do you do when Satan tempts you?" someone asked. "Ah, I take him to Calvary, show him Christ, and point to those deep wounds, and say, 'Doesn't He love me?' And the fact is that Satan got such a scare there 1,900 years ago that he cannot stand to be reminded of Calvary; he flees from me every time." That bedridden saint

had little trouble with doubt; he was too full of the grace of God which is in Christ Jesus our Lord.

—*Sunday School Times*

* * *

How to Look at Temptations

"If only I could see my temptations as I see other people's," said a girl the other day, "they wouldn't be a bit hard to fight. Other people's temptations look so ugly and mean and foolish. But my own temptations come with a rosy light about them, so that I don't see how hateful they are until afterward." There are two ways to see temptations in their true colors. One is to pray about them, to bring them into the clear light of God's presence. The other is to say "How would this look if someone else yielded to it?"

—*Forward*

* * *

A Struggle with Temptation

At school Joe was good in arithmetic but poor in spelling. Mabel was a fine speller and sat opposite him. On examination day Joe forgot many words, and the tempter said, "Look on Mabel's paper; she has them right!"

So Joe copied several, and the teacher saw him. She intended to talk to him after school, for she always thought Joe was honest. Just then the boy who was collecting the papers came to Joe's desk, and she saw him tear his up, and say, "I haven't any!" She knew he had decided to take a zero rather than hand in a dishonest paper. When the school closed, she called Joe and said,

"I saw your struggle, and am proud of a boy who conquered temptation."

—*The Water Lily*

* * *

Who Can Stand Alone?

A minister traveling on a Continental train was the sole occupant of a compartment save for a young man reading a newspaper. The youth was also a Christian, but so weak was his faith, and so many were his temptations, that he told the minister he did not think he would be able to stand life a week longer. The minister took from his pocket a Bible and a penknife, and said, "See, I will make this penknife stand up on the cover of this Bible, in spite of the rocking of the train." The young man, thinking that this was some conjuring trick, watched the proceeding with interest, saying, "I am afraid that it will not be very easy to do that, sir." "But," said the minister, "I am doing it." "Oh, but you are holding it," retorted his fellow passenger. "Why, of course. Did you ever hear of a penknife standing up on its end without being held up?" "I see," was the young man's comment. "I see: *you mean to teach me that I cannot stand unless Christ holds me.* Thank you for reminding me of that."

—*Christian Herald,*
(London)

Over the Falls!

Stewart Anderson, in preaching on temptation, reminds us that Bobby Leach, the Englishman, startled the world by going over Niagara Falls in a barrel without suffering serious harm. Some years later he was walking down the street, slipped on an orange peeling, and was taken to the hospital with a badly fractured leg. Dr. Anderson adds: "Some great temptations, which roar around us like Niagara, may leave us unharmed. But a little, insignificant incident may cause our downfall simply because we are not looking for it."

—From *Battle with Temptation,*
by K. Morgan Edwards

THANKSGIVING

Thank You God
For purple mountains towering high;
For brilliant stars that stud night's sky;
For rosy dawn's whispers of light;
For gorgeous sunsets calling night,
For crimson roses, beauty, rare;
For song bird's music in the air;
For friends and neighbors far and near;
For Christian homes and loved ones dear;
For bended knees at childhood's shrine;
For faith, and hope, and love divine;
For bursting barns filled by thy hand;
For churches lifting spires grand;
For all blessings you understand . . . .
Thank You, God.
—Anna Hughes Varn

* * *

One by One
Perhaps you have heard of the man who wished to dispose of his home. He went to see a friend who was in the real estate business and, describing his house and grounds to the man, asked him to write an advertisement which he could put in the newspapers. His friend did as he was requested and then read what he had written to the home-owner. "Read that again," said the man who wanted to sell his house. His friend obliged, to hear this astonishing remark:

"The house is not for sale. All my life I've wanted a place just like the one you have described. But I never knew I had it until I heard what you have written about it."

There is a grand old song: "Count your blessings, name them one by one." If some of us would do that very thing we should be happier Christians.

—*The Pilgrim*

* * *

I Give Thee Humble Thanks
For all the gifts that Thou dost send,
For every kind and loyal friend,
For prompt supply of all my need,
For all that's good in word or deed,
For gift of health along life's way.
For strength to work from day to day.
I give Thee humble thanks.

For ready hands to help and cheer,
For listening ears Thy voice to hear,
For yielded tongue Thy love to talk,
For willing feet Thy paths to walk,
For open eyes Thy Word to read,
For loving heart Thy will to heed,
I give Thee humble thanks.

For Christ who came from Heaven
above,
For the Cross and His redeeming love,
For His mighty power to seek and save,
For His glorious triumph o'er the grave,
For the lovely mansions in the sky,
For His blessed coming by-and-by,
  I give Thee humble thanks.
                    —Clifford Lewis

* * *

The Only One in Thirty-Five Years.

A soldier in the American Third Army was sent to a rest camp after a period of active service. When he returned to his outfit, he wrote a letter to General George Patton and thanked him for the splendid care he had received. General Patton wrote back that for thirty-five years he had sought to give all the comfort and convenience he could to his men, and added that this was the first letter of thanks he had received in all his years in the Army. There are few points at which human nature is more lacking than in lack of gratitude. Parents must constantly say to children who have received some gift, "Now what do you say?" As we grow older we become hardened to the good things of life and do not think of thanking God who is the giver of "every good gift and every perfect gift." The best rule is the one given by Paul, "In every thing give thanks," and especially "Thanks be unto God for his unspeakable gift."

                    —*Essex*

* * *

"Begins and Ends by Thanking God!"

The Rev. Leslie F. Church related the following story at the annual meeting of the British and Foreign Bible Society:

A friend of his was staying in Yorkshire one very wet Sunday with two other friends. On the way to church he was told they would be the only people there probably, and that the service would be taken by a lay preacher who would have walked fifteen miles over the hills in the pouring rain to get there. "Is he a great preacher?" the friend asked. "No, but he can pray. He

always begins, continues, and ends with thanking God." Sure enough, they were the whole congregation, and the old man came into the pulpit, drenched through with the rain, but punctual. He began his prayer thus: "Almighty God, we thank Thee that it is not always as bad as this."

                    —E. Edmunds

* * *

"In Everything Give Thanks!"

" 'Mid sunshine, cloud or stormy days,
When hope abounds or care dismays,
When trials press and toils increase
Let not thy faith in God decrease —
  'In every thing give thanks.'

"All things we know shall work for good,
Nor would we change them if we could;
'Tis well if only He command;
His promises will ever stand —
  'In every thing give thanks.'

"He satisfies the longing heart,
He thwarts the tempter's cruel dart,
With goodness fills the hungry soul,
And helps us sing when billows roll.
  'In every thing give thanks.' "
                    —*Selected*

* * *

Autumn

We plow the fields and scatter
  The good seed on the land,
But it is fed and watered
  By God's almighty hand;
He sends the snow in winter,
  The warmth to swell the grain,
The breezes and the sunshine,
  And soft, refreshing rain.

He only is the Maker
  Of all things near and far;
He paints the wayside flower,
  He lights the evening star;
The winds and waves obey Him;
  By Him the birds are fed;
Much more to us, His children,
  He gives our daily bread.

We thank Thee, then, O Father,
  For all things bright and good,
The seedtime and the harvest,
  Our life, our health, our food;
Accept the gifts we offer,

For all Thy love imparts,
And, what Thou most desirest,
Our humble, thankful hearts.

—Matthias Claudius, in
The New Illustrator

* * *

Shamed by His Ox

A farmer who had listened to an exposition of the text from Isaiah 1:3, "The ox knoweth his owner, and the ass his master's crib: but Israel doth not know, my people doth not consider," was giving food to his stock, when one of his oxen, evidently grateful for his care, fell to licking his bare arm. Instantly, the Holy Spirit flashed in conviction on the farmer's mind. He burst into tears, and exclaimed: "Yes, it is all true. How wonderful is God's Word! This poor dumb brute is really more grateful to me than I am to God. and yet I am in debt to Him for everything. What a sinner I am!" The lesson had found its way to his heart, and wrought there effectually to lead him to Christ.

—*Sunday School Times*

* * *

Thanks for Comfortable Bed

Thank God for the comfort of a bed,
A pillow soft beneath my head,
The blankets warm, the eiderdown
To cover me when I lie down;
Four walls secure, a roof above,
All prove to me that God is love.

Thank God for the cozy sitting room,
All tidied, clean swept with a broom,
For the one who labors day by day,
For the place of rest, and place of play,
The blazing fire and easy chair:
All tokens of my Father's care.

Thank God 'tis not by these alone
I prove His love; I freely own
A greater proof — at Calvary,
The gift of His own Son for me:
So take from me all earthly bliss,
I still can prove this love of His.

—H. Cockrell, in
Sunday School Times

* * *

Like Mule and Ox

A prominent society man asked a bishop whether it was according to the rules of etiquette to say grace at a banquet table. The clergyman replied: "I do not know much about etiquette, but I remember seeing on the wall of a farmer's home a picture showing mules and oxen at a crib. These were devouring the fodder and scattering some beneath their feet, and over the picture was this inscription:

Who without prayer sits down to eat,
And without thanks then leaves the table,
Tramples the gift of God with feet,
And is like mule and ox in stable.

— *Sunday School Circle*

* * *

The Christian's "Taste Berry"

It is said that in Africa there is a fruit called the "taste berry," because it changes a person's taste so that everything eaten tastes sweet and pleasant. Sour fruit, even if eaten several hours after the "taste berry," becomes sweet and delicious. Gratitude is the "taste berry" of Christianity, and when our hearts are filled with gratitude, nothing that God sends us seems unpleasant to us. Sorrowing heart, sweeten your grief with gratitude. Burdened soul, lighten your burden by singing God's praises. Disappointed one, dispel your loneliness by making others grateful.

Sick one, grow strong in soul, thanking God that He loves you enough to chasten you. Keep the "taste berry" of gratitude in your hearts, and it will do for you what the "taste berry" of Africa does for the African.

—*Expositor*

* * *

A Better Method

"Do you count sheep when you have a hard time getting to sleep at night?" asked Mrs. Bee.

"Why, no, I don't believe I ever do," replied the neighbor, Mrs. Dee.

"Well, I suppose you are one of those lucky persons who never lie awake nights," sighed Mrs. Bee.

"On the contrary," Mrs. Dee replied, "I spend quite a few hours, in the course of a week, in bed but not asleep."

"What do you do to bring slumber?"

"I count my blessings," smiled Mrs. Dee. "If I begin to worry about a younger child, I remember how the older ones improved with years and I pray earnestly for the one on my mind. I can count answers to prayer by the dozen. If I am thinking of money and it troubles me so I cannot sleep, I go back in my book of memories and find time after time when the Lord gave us relief from financial problems. I can truly count my blessings, up to a point where I don't need to try and number them but just relax and *know* that God is still able to deliver me from *anything*, present or future. Eventually, peace and calm replace restless anxiety and I sink into sweet, restful sleep."

"I must try that," nodded Mrs. Bee. "I guess I've tried every method but the right one. Thank you for the reminder."

—James A. Sanaker, in
Gospel Herald

* * *

Sermon by an Insane Man

A visitor in an insane asylum, was accosted by one of the inmates. This patient had full possession of his faculties, but was subject to fits of insanity that made it unsafe for him to be at liberty. The visitor, who had come to preach to those who could comprehend, was startled to have this man come to him with a direct question, "Sir, have you ever thanked God for your reason?" The preacher had never done so, but he vowed that he would be unthankful no longer.

And there are thousands of things besides your reason for which you might well bow your head right now and give a heartfelt prayer of thanksgiving to the Father.

—*Gospel Herald*

* * *

God Hears What We Say

The head of a household at the morning meal had asked the blessing as usual, thanking God for a bountiful provision. Immediately afterward he began to grumble about the hard times, the

poor quality of food he was forced to eat, and the way it was cooked.

His little daughter interrupted him. "Father," she began, "do you suppose God heard what you said a little while ago?"

"Certainly," he replied confidently.

"And did He hear what you said about the bacon and the coffee?"

"Of course" — not quite so confidently.

"Then, Father, which did God believe?"

Even when we as children of God do remember to thank Him for the blessings He pours into our lives, are we not often like this man? Do not our words and our deeds often contrast sharply with the thanks we utter?

—*The Pilot*

* * *

He Came Back to Give Thanks

A minister in England saw a young lad come into his church one weekday and kneel at the altar to pray. The boy remained so long upon his knees that the clergyman was desirous to know more about him. When the lad arose from his devotions the minister asked, "Do you often come here to pray?" "I have been here four times in the last five days," he replied. "Have you some loved one who is fighting at Dunkirk?" asked the minister. "Yes, sir," said the boy, "I have been praying for my daddy. He came home today, and so I came back to thank God for sparing his life," was the simple reply. Like the one leper who was cleansed, he returned to give thanks to God.

—*Alliance Weekly*

* * *

A Thrilling Service

The Methodist Recorder of London tells of a group of survivors of a ship sunk by enemy action, who, on reaching port after being some days adrift on the mighty ocean, cold, hungry, and ill-clad, asked not for food or clothing, but for a minister to hold a thanksgiving service for their safe landing. *The Recorder* states: "The responsible officials at once telephoned to the mayor of the town, who for forty years has been a Methodist local preacher. He at once got in touch with one of the circuit ministers, and also the organist of the circuit chapel, who gladly responded. Within two hours the survivors had a hot meal and were reclothed. At seven P. M., a service was held in a room at the municipal building. How the hearts of these two dozen or more survivors were stirred as they sang *Jesus, Lover of My Soul, Eternal Father, Strong to Save,* and *Abide With Me.* Those present affirm that the memory of that service, including the address, will live with them through all time."

—*Alliance Weekly*

* * *

Strength Supplied in Desperate Need

Sgt. Vernon W. Entrekin relates how he recited the 145th Psalm while dangling by his left foot from a parachute after bailing out of a C-47 transport plane during a swirling snowstorm. Entrekin was one of six aboard the plane when the pilot lost control above Dwight, Nebr. It was his first parachute leap. He had been reading the 145th Psalm just before starting out on the flight. He found himself saying: "The Lord upholdeth all that fall, and raiseth up all those that be bowed down. . . . The Lord is nigh unto all them that call upon him, to all that call upon him in truth." He asked for strength to climb back into the parachute harness which he had failed to fasten securely. Gasping for breath in the icy air, and summoning the last ounce of his energy, Entrekin doubled his body, and caught hold of the harness above his foot. Slowly he was able to climb back to a sitting position while dropping swiftly through the air. Finally he landed with a jolt and unbuckled his parachute harness. He said simply, "Thank you, Lord."

—*Now*

* * *

Suppose the Sun Shouldn't Rise?

There is an imaginative story of that morning when the sun did not rise. Six o'clock came and no sign of dawn. At seven o'clock there was still no ray of light. At noon it was as black as midnight and no bird sang. There was only the hoot of the owl and the swoop of the bat. Then came the black hours of the black afternoon. No one slept that night. Some wept, some wrung their hands in anguish. Every church was thronged to its doors with people upon their knees. Thus they remained the whole night through; then millions of eager, tear-wet faces were turned toward the east. When the sky began to grow red and the sun rose once more there was a shout of great joy. Now millions of lips said, "Bless the Lord, O my soul." Why were these people so thankful? Just because the sun rose after one day of darkness. The very constancy of God's blessings sometimes seems to kill our gratitude. Whereas the wonderful thing about the mercies of God is that they are fresh every morning and new every evening.

—*Henry Alford Porter*

* * *

Just Like a Dog

A little lad of six was invited out to lunch in a neighbor's home. As soon as all were seated at the table the food was served. The little boy was puzzled, and, with a child's frankness, asked, "Don't you say a prayer before you eat?" The host was uncomfortable, and mumbled, "No, we don't take time for that." The lad thought silently for a while, and said, "You're just like my dog! You start right in."

—*Boone Baptist Booster*

* * *

Time for Thanksgiving

When the New England colonies were first planted, the settlers endured many privations and difficulties. Being piously disposed, they laid their distresses before God in frequent days of fasting and prayer. Constant meditation upon distress kept their minds gloomy and discontented, and made them disposed even to return to their fatherland, with all its persecutions. At length, when it was again proposed to appoint a day of fasting and prayer, a plain, commonsense old colonist rose in the meeting and remarked that he thought they had brooded long enough over their difficulties, and that it seemed high time they should consider some of their mercies; that the colony was growing strong, the fields increasing in harvests, the rivers full of fish, the woods full of game, the air sweet, the climate salubrious, their wives healthful, and their children dutiful; above all, that they possessed what they came for, full civil and religious liberty. On the whole, he would amend the resolution for a fast, and propose in its stead *a day of thanksgiving.* His advice was taken.

—Tom M. Olson, in
Now

* * *

The Sin of Ingratitude

One day a man was invited to eat dinner with an old Indian, a highly respected man in the community, and they went to the hotel together. As soon as they sat down to the table he began to eat, but the Indian paused, bowed his head and gave thanks to God for the food. Presently the Indian said to him in his usual drawl:

"Do you know what a man reminds me of who sits down to the table and eats the food that God gives him without thanking God for it?"

"No," said my friend quite abruptly: he didn't care to talk about such matters, and continued to eat.

"Well," said the Indian, "the man who sits down to the table and eats the food that God gives him without thanking God for it, reminds me a good deal of the hog under a chestnut tree eating chestnuts, and doesn't so much as look up to see where the chestnuts come from."

—Noran H. Camp

* * *

The Essential Difference

A Christian general and a judge in India were on a military expedition. When they came to a Mohammendan area they were met by several ladies of a Christian mission. The Indian judge was impressed with these cultured women missionaries, and said, "I cannot understand why these ladies give up their time and risk infection working in this filthy part of town." "It is

rather amazing," replied the general, unless you realize their motive." "Ah, that's just my difficulty." "Their motive is gratitude." "Gratitude! What have our poor people ever done for them that these ladies should feel gratitude? I wish you would explain it for me." "To explain would involve the essential differences between our religions." "I'll listen to you," said the judge. The general gave him a story of a friend in greatest difficulties over money matters and his debt was paid by a kind stranger. Then he explained "Though our debts have been paid and we are free, we owe the deepest gratitude to Jesus Christ our Saviour, who paid them for us, and that explains these missionary ladies. They have only one motive: to prove their gatitude to Him who paid their debts."

—*Power*

* * *

Thankful for Little Things

One morning there was a little puddle by the roadside. Some small brown birds gathered around it and took turns hopping in for a great time of splashing. Then they flew up in the bushes near by and sang gaily, as though pouring out their thanks for the nice bath they had found on a hot, dusty day.

Birds and animals seem to enjoy and appreciate every little blessing that comes their way — a cool drink, a bit of food, a little shade on a hot day, some shelter from a storm.

Don't they rather shame us humans who take so much for granted in our lives? Suppose we try looking about us today to find the little things we should be thankful for.

—M. E. Burkett, in
Gospel Herald

* * *

"These Chaps Wanted to Say, THANK YOU!"

The *Theresa Boyle,* a trawler from Scotland, had been sunk by a Nazi bomber in the North Sea. The crew of ten were able to get away in their lifeboat which was only a small boat. For hours they rowed about hoping someone would see them.

This happened in February. It was terribly cold and they had not much food with them. Forty hours went past and no one had sighted their boat. As the weary hours dragged on, one after another of the men became exhausted and could not help with the rowing.

Ten more hours went past which seemed to them much longer, and hope was beginning to fail when, in the distance, an airplane was seen. Oh, how their hearts beat! Was it a friend or a foe? Soon they recognized it to be a friendly plane. Would they be seen?

The keen eye of the pilot on patrol did not miss them, although their boat was being buffeted by the heavy seas. By this time eight of the men were lying on the floorboard, too weak to row, but just able to wave anxiously at the pilot.

The plane flew low. The men realized they had been seen, and off it went in search of help. It found two mine sweepers, some fifteen miles away, and asked them by lamp signals to follow it. By firing colored lights the pilot guided the mine sweeper to the open boat. It circled round until the men, the entire crew of the sunken trawler, were taken on board — SAVED!

Then it flew off. After going two miles a signal lamp from one rescue ship recalled the plane. "Anything wrong?" signaled the pilot. "No," the reply flickered. "These chaps we picked up just wanted to say *Thank You!*" With this message off flew the plane to carry on its duty of patrol.

Has this story found its answer with you? Have you ever thanked the Lord Jesus for what He has done?

—*Gospel Herald*

* * *

Thinking and Thanking

Sir Moses Montefiore, the Hebrew philanthropist, had as the motto of his family, "Think and Thank." In the old Anglo-Saxon language thankfulness means "thinkfulness." Thinking of all God's goodnesses draws forth gratitude.

—*King's Business*

A Thanksgiving Offering

The parents of a young man who was killed in the World War gave their church a check for two hundred dollars as a memorial to their loved one. When the presentation was made, another war mother whispered to her husband, "Let us give the same for our boy." The father said, "Why, what are you talking about? Our boy didn't lose his life." The mother said, "That's just the point. Let us give it because he didn't."

—*Otterbein Teacher*

* * *

Why He Was Thankful

How often have you ever thanked God for sight? A group of visitors at a summer resort had watched the sunset from the gallery of the hotel. A fat, unromantic-looking man had lingered until the last glow faded, and had seemed thrilled through and through by the beauty of it all. One guest, more observant than the rest, wondered about this, and so at supper she said to this man, who sat next to her, "You certainly did enjoy that sunset, Mr. B. Are you an artist?" "No, madam, I'm a plumber," he responded with a slow grin. "But I was blind for five years."

—*Earnest Worker*

* * *

The Transformation of a Thankful Heart

The story is told of one of the wagon train parties on the Oregon Trail. Water and grass had been scarce for several days. Some of the wagons were broken down, with consequent delays amid the stifling heat. A general feeling of fretfulness had succeeded the early optimism and cheer. So it was decided that, at the next night's stop, a meeting would be held to air their troubles. When the emigrants had gathered around the campfire, one of them arose and said, "Before we do anything else, I think we should first thank God that we have come this far with no loss of life, with no serious trouble with the Indians, and that we have enough strength left to finish our journey." This was done, and then there was silence. No one had any complaints to make. Looked at in such a light, it seemed they really were fortunate. This is the transformation the thankful heart can often make. It enables us to see the real dimensions of many worth-while things that might be passed over.

—*Country Gentleman*

* * *

Thanks for Familiar Things

"I offer thanks for just familiar things;
    The ruddy glory of the sunset sky,
    The shine of firelight as the dusk
        draws nigh,
The cheer song my little kettle sings.

"The woodland music of my giant pine,
    The last sweet tokens that my garden
        yields,
    The mellow tints upon the autumn
        fields,
The far off misty mountain's purple line;

"The sense of rest that home so surely
        brings,
    The books that wait my pleasure, true
        and fine
    Old friendships that I joy to feel are
        mine.
I offer thanks for just familiar things!"

—*Selected*

* * *

Thanking God for All Things

A mother said to me upon the recovery of her child from a serious illness. "Wasn't God good to give us back our child?" I was about to agree with her, when a thought came to me as never before, and to her surprise I said: "Yes; but would not God have been just as good, or just as kind, if your child had not come back to you?" Her answer was doubtful and without enthusiasm. It is easy to give thanks and to speak of God's goodness when we are having our wishes granted and everything is going our way. But, when we realize that we are to thank God for *all* things, we are brought face to face with the serious fact that pleasure, gladness, gratification, are *not* essential features or factors in thanksgiving.

—*Sunday School Times*

Glad, But Not Grateful

Stanford Cobb, missionary to Persia, helped me in another way. Said he, "Do you ever feel thankful when God blesses you?" "Always." "Did you ever tell Him so?" "Well, I don't know that I have." "Well, try it, my young friend, try it. Tell Him so. Tell Him aloud; tell Him so that you are sure you will hear it yourself." That was a new revelation. I found I had only been glad, not grateful. I have been telling Him with grateful feelings ever since, to my soul's help and comfort.

—*Alliance Weekly*

* * *

Thankful Henry

Matthew Henry, the famous scholar, was once accosted by thieves and robbed of his purse. He wrote these words in his diary:

"Let me be thankful first, because I was never robbed before; second, because, although they took my purse, they did not take my life; third, because, although they took my all, it was not much; and fourth, because it was I who was robbed, not I who robbed."

—*Church of Ireland Gazette*

* * *

God's Unspeakable Gift

A bedridden Eskimo said to a missionary, "When you begin to read to me about Jesus, I am as a block of ice; when you finish and go away, I am melted into water."

"The story of Jesus," said an African, "is my hymn, my prayer, my Bible. I weep over it when I can't sing about it, and I sing over it when I can't weep about it. This is true, that I thank God for it from the sole of my foot to the top of my head."

If the Eskimo in Alaska and the Hottentot in Africa are so thankful for the unspeakable Gift, should not all enlightened Americans, and others, give Him the praise due to His matchless name?

—*Arthur F. Ingler*

Thankfulness for a Thorn

George Matheson, the well-known blind preacher of Scotland, now with the Lord, says: "My God, I have never thanked Thee for my 'thorn!' I have thanked Thee a thousand times for my roses, but never once for my 'thorn;' I have been looking forward to a world where I shall get compensation for my cross as itself a present glory. Teach me the glory of my cross; teach me the value of my 'thorn.' Show me that I have climbed to Thee by the path of pain. Show me that my tears have made my rainbow."

—*Moody Monthly*

TIME

The Little Clock

"I just can't go on ticking sixty seconds every minute, sixty minutes every hour, twelve hours every day!"

The clock-maker asked, "Canst thou not tick one tick at a time?"

"Oh, yes," replied the little clock.

"Then that is all that is required of thee," said the clock-maker.

" 'As thy day thy strength shalt be'
This should be enough for thee;
He who knows thy frame will spare
Burdens more than thou canst bear."

—*Gospel Herald*

* * *

The Time Is Short

Oh, my dear friends, you who are letting miserable misunderstandings run on from year to year; you who are keeping wretched quarrels alive because you cannot quite make up your mind that now is the day to sacrifice your pride and kill them; you who are passing men sullenly upon the street, not speaking to them out of some silly spite, and yet knowing that it would fill you with shame and remorse if you heard that one of those men was dead tomorrow; you who are letting your neighbor starve till you hear that he is dying of starvation; or letting your friend's heart ache for a word of appreciation or sympathy, which you mean to give him some day; if you could know and see and feel, all of a sudden, that "the time is short," how it would break the spell! How you would go instantly and do the thing which you might never have another chance to do.

—Phillips Brooks

"I've Shut the Door on Yesterday!"

I've shut the door on yesterday —
    Its sorrows and mistakes;
I've locked within its gloomy walls
    Past failures and heartaches.
And now I throw the key away
    To seek another room,
And furnish it with hope and smiles
    And every springtime bloom . . .
I've shut the door on yesterday
    And thrown the key away —
Tomorrow holds no fears for me,
    Since I have found today.

—Vivien Yeiser Laramore

* * *

He Hadn't Time

Hadn't time to greet the day,
Hadn't time to laugh or play;
Hadn't time to wait a while,
Hadn't time to give a smile;
Hadn't time to glean the news,
Hadn't time to dream or muse;
Hadn't time to train his mind,
Hadn't time to just be kind;
Hadn't time to take a rest,
Hadn't time to act his best;
Hadn't time to pen a note,
Hadn't time to cast a vote;
Hadn't time to sing a song,
Hadn't time to right a wrong;
Hadn't time to send a gift,
Hadn't time to lend or give,
Hadn't time to really live;
Hadn't time to heed a cry,
Hadn't time to say good-bye;
Hadn't time to read this verse,
Hadn't time — he's in a hearse.

—*Grenville Kleiser*

Later Than They Think

The story is told of a man who rushed into a suburban railroad station one morning and, almost breathlessly, asked the ticket agent: "When does the 8:01 train leave?"

"At 8:01," was the answer.

"Well," the man replied, "it's 7:59 by my watch, 7:57 by the town clock, and 8:04 by the station clock. Which am I to go by?"

"You can go by any clock you wish," said the agent, "but you can't go by the 8:01 train, for it has already left."

God's time is moving forward hour by hour, minute by minute. There are multitudes who seem to think that they can live by any schedule they choose and that, in their own time, they can turn to God. But His time is the right time. Now it may be later than they think. Soon it may be too late. "Behold, now is the accepted time; behold, now is the day of salvation" (2 Cor. 6:2).

—*The Pilgrim*

* * *

Living Day At Time

The late Bishop John H. Vincent had the custom of repeating to himself each morning the following simple but far-reaching solution, which may serve as a model for us:

"I will this day try to live a simple, sincere, and serene life; repelling promptly every thought of discontent, impurity, and self-seeking; cultivating cheerfulness, magnanimity, charity, and the habit of holy silence; exercising economy in expenditure, carefulness in conversation, diligence in appointed service, fidelity to every trust, and a childlike faith in God."

—*Christian Observer*

* * *

"Time's Chariot Has Ratchets"

We have only once to live; therefore let us live to some purpose. The day that dawned this morning will never dawn again. The opportunities which it brought with it will never come again; and if we fail to fill it with the service it requires of us there will be no possibility of returning into it to repair the mischief. The wheels of Time's chariot have ratchets on them, and they move only forward.

—William M. Taylor, D. D.

* * *

Time Wasted in "Fussing"

A dear old lady from the country went for the first time on a railway journey of about fifty miles through an interesting, beautiful region. She had looked forward to this trip with great pleasure. She was to see so much, but it took her so long to get her baskets and parcels right, to get her skirt adjusted, her seat comfortably arranged, the shades and shutters right, the anxious questions about all the things she had left behind answered, that she was just settling down to enjoy the trip when they called out the name of her station and she had to get up and hustle out! "Oh, my!" she said, "if I had only known that we would be there so soon I wouldn't have wasted my time in fussing." Dear friend, the wheel of time is flying; the last station is at hand; these things are so trifling. Get your mind on the main business of life; live as you will wish to have lived when you hear the call of the last station, and don't waste any more time "fussing."

—*Earnest Worker*

* * *

Tomorrow

God is in every tomorrow,
  Therefore I live for today,
Certain of finding at sunrise
  Guidance and strength for the way;
Power for each moment of weakness,
  Hope for each moment of pain,
Comfort for every sorrow
  Sunshine and joy after rain.

God is in every tomorrow,
  Planning for you and me;
E'en in the dark will I follow—
  Trust where my eyes cannot see:
Stilled by His promise of blessing,
  Soothed by the touch of His hand,
Confident in His protection,
  Knowing my life-path is planned.

God is in every tomorrow,
  Life with its changes may come;

He is behind and before me;
　While in the distance shines Home!
Home — where no thought of tomorrow
　Ever can shadow my brow;
Home — in the presence of Jesus
　Through all eternity — now.

　　　　　　　　　　　—Selected

* * *

Reductio ad Absurdum

A friend says to me, "I have not time
or room in my life for Christianity. If
it were not so full! You don't know
how hard I work from morning till
night. When have I time, where have I
room for Christianity in such a life as
mine?" It is as if the engine had said
it had no room for the steam. It is as if
the tree said it had no room for the
sap. It is as if the ocean said it had no
room for the tide. It is as if the man
had said he had no room for his soul. It
is as if the life had said it had no time
to live. It is not something added to
life; it is *life.* A man is not living
without it. And for a man to say, "I am
so full in life that I have no room for
life," *you see immediately to what ab-
surdity it reduces itself.*

　　　—From *Flowers of Thought,*
　　　　by Phillips Brooks

* * *

Too Busy

Too busy to read the Bible
　Too busy to wait and pray!
Too busy to speak out kindly
　To some one by the way!

Too busy to care and struggle,
　To think of the life to come!
Too busy building mansions,
　To plan for the Heavenly Home.

Too busy to help a brother
　Who faces the winter blast!
Too busy to share his burden
　When self in the balance is cast.

Too busy for all that is holy
　On earth beneath the sky
Too busy to serve the Master
　But — not too busy to die.

　　　　　　　　　　　—Selected

No Time for God

No time for God?
What fools we are, to clutter up
Our lives with common things
And leave without heart's gate
The Lord of life and Life itself —
Our God!

No time for God?
As soon to say no time
To eat or sleep or love or die.
Take time for God,
Or you shall dwarf your soul,
And when the angel death
Comes knocking at your door,
A poor misshapen thing you'll be
To step into eternity!

No time for God?
That day when sickness comes
Or trouble finds you out
And you cry out for God;
Will He have time for you?
No time for God?
Some day you'll lay aside
This mortal self and make your way
To worlds unknown,
And when you meet Him face to face
Will He — should He,
Have time for you?

　　　　　　　　　—Norman L. Trott

* * *

Time Is Fleeting

In Kensington Gardens, one of London's pleasant open spaces, there stands
elevated a clock which has four dials,
each showing respectively north, south,
east and west, and underneath each dial
is carved in large letters,

"Time Flies"

A very plain and truthful message
this is, and no one living will deny this
plain fact. Many thousands have passed
this clock and have no doubt been glad
to avail themselves of the knowledge of
the hour; but are not the timely words
as to the fleeting of time a plain and
solemn warning to all? Each day brings
us most certainly nearer to the close
of our career here; and the well-known
words are very fitting "brief life is here
our portion."

　　　　　　　　　—Gospel Herald

To-Day

So here hath been dawning
　Another new day:
Think, wilt thou let it
　Slip useless away?

Out of eternity
　This new day is born;
Into eternity
　At night will return.

Behold it aforetime
　No eye ever did:
So soon it forever
　From all eyes is hid.

Here hath been dawning
　Another new day:
Think, wilt thou let it
　Slip useless away?
　　　　　—Thomas Carlyle

* * *

If I Had but One Year

"If I had but one year to live;
One year to love; one year to bless;
One year to better things to stress;
One year to sing; one year to smile;
To brighten earth a little while;
One year to sing my Master's praise;

One year to fill with work my days;
One year to strive for a reward.

"When I should stand before my Lord,
I think that I should spend each day
In just the self-same, plodding way
That I do now. For from afar
The call may come to cross the bar,
At any time, and I must be
Prepared to meet eternity.

"So, if I have a year to live,
Or just one day in which to give
A pleasant smile, a helping hand,
A mind that tries to understand
A fellow-creature when in need,
'Tis one with me — I take no heed,
But try to live each day He sends,
To serve my gracious Master's ends."
　　　　　—Selected

* * *

Just For Today

"Just for to-day, my Saviour —
　To-morrow is not mine,
Just for to-day I ask Thee
　For light and health Divine.
To-morrow's care I must not bear,
　The future is all Thine."
　　　　　—Selected

TITHING

O, The Shame of It:

If the Protestant people of America alone were tithing their incomes we could easily evangelize the entire world and put a copy of the Bible into the hands of every heathen on earth inside of ten years. According to government statistics, we are spending annually in this country six hundred dollars for luxuries for every dollar we spend for missions. We spend in America more for tobacco in a single year than both the United States and Canada have spent for missions since white man discovered America.

　　—From *The Sin We're Afraid*
　　to Mention, by Oscar Lowery

A Faithful Stewart

A manly appearing lad in the village of Barwick, Ga., stood at the teller's window of the bank and said, "I want to put some money in your bank!" The banker who had noticed the boy as a faithful member in the Methodist Sunday school, said, "All right, John. How much do you want to put in?" "Four dollars," the boy replied. "You want the deposit made out to your name?" he asked. "No, sir, make it out to John W. Yates and Company." The banker looked rather quizzical, and asked, "Who is the company John?" "God," the boy replied very reverently. "I got my first month's pay this morning, and I'm starting my tithe account. This is God's money. I'm just handling it for Him.'
　　　　　—*Free Methodist*

A Church of Tithers!

Do you know a church composed entirely of tithers? An account of it would be worth while if you do. Dr. Hugh McKean of Chiengmai, Siam, tells of one in that country. There are 400 members, and every member tithes. They receive 40 stangs (less than twenty cents) and their rice each week. Of this, each gives weekly one-tenth. Because of this they have more for Christian work than any other church in Siam. They pay their own pastor, and have sent two missionary families to spread the Gospel in a community cut off from the outside world. They are entirely responsible for this work and are very earnest about it. They are intensely interested in all forms of Christian work, especially work for unfortunates of every kind, and their gifts for this kind of work are large. They not only have accepted Christ but, having found him good, are making him known to others. And every member is a leper.

—*Moody Monthly*

*   *   *

Handing Out "Tips"

While we were bowling over the roads Henry said to his friend in a casual way, "How would you like to be a porter?" Timothy, busy with driving shook his head decidedly. "Why not?" persisted his friend. "Mostly tips. When I deal with a man I want him to pay me my due, eye to eye; not slip anything into my hand behind my back." "I wonder if that is the way the Lord feels about it?" quietly remarked Henry. "Just what do you mean?" asked Timothy. "Only this: when we give to the Lord without any fixed rule, just when we please, and just as much as we please, I wonder whether He doesn't feel a bit like a heavenly porter. And perhaps we come to feel like the passengers and fall into the habit of giving him whatever spare bit of change we may have handy. I wonder if it wouldn't be better for the Lord and for us if we just looked Him in the eye and gave Him according to some fixed rule."

—*King's Business*

Tithing Her Time

Some months ago a friend of mine told me that her doctor had said she had a very serious trouble, and she added, "My nerves are bad, too. I'm just at the breaking point." Recently, I saw her again. The strained look had left her face, and in its place, there was a look of quiet peace. She said she felt better than she had for years, and was all caught up with her work. When I asked her how it came about, she said: "When I first became a Christian I tithed my income; now I tithe my time, also. I see to it that He has a tenth of my day, for quiet waiting on Him. Truly He has undertaken for my every need, and I praise Him."

—Mrs. J. Shields

*   *   *

Whom Do You Fear Most?

Now it came to pass on a day at noon that I was the guest of a certain rich man. The lunch was enjoyed at a popular restaurant; the waiters were very efficient, and the food was good. Now, when the end of the meal was at hand, the waiter brought unto the host a check. The host examined it, frowned a bit, but made no comment. But as we arose to depart, I observed that he had laid some coins under the edge of his plate. Howbeit, I know not of what denomination the coins were, but the waiter who stood near by, smiled happily, which, being interpreted, means that the tip was satisfactory. Now with such customs we are familiar, and this parable entereth not into the merits or demerits of tipping. But as I meditated on the coins that became tips throughout the nation, I began to think of tips and tithes. For the proverbial tip should be at least a tenth, lest the waiter or waitress turn against you. And as I continued to think on those things, it came unto me that few people who go to church treat their God as well as they honor their waiter, for they give unto their waiter a tenth, but unto God give whatsoever they think will get them by. Verily, doth man fear the waiter more than he fears God? And doth he love God less than he doth the waiter? Truly, truly a man and his money are past understanding!

—Author unknown
Log of the Good Ship Grace

* * *

Before the Heart Hardens

A godly woman unexpectedly received a legacy of $5,000. True to her practice maintained in poverty, she at once put $500 into her tithe box and it was used in the Lord's work. She never mentioned the disposal of the tenth, but after her death there was found entered in her diary the day she received the legacy: "Quick, quick, before my heart gets hard."

—*Choice Gleanings Calendar*

* * *

Which Will You Have?

In the fourth century, Augustine, in a harvest sermon, said: "Our forefathers abounded in plenty because they gave God the tithe and to Caesar tribute. But now, because our devotion has receded, the imposition of taxes has advanced. We are unwilling to share with God, giving Him the tenth, and now, behold . . a taxgatherer takes from us that which God receives not."

—*Sunday School Times*

* * *

Farmers Bring in Tithes

A group of Abernathy, Texas, farmers brought in their tithes. What they brought filled two washtubs with $14,-132.65 in cash and checks — money from the harvest on land they dedicated to God last spring. Each farmer dedicated one-tenth of his acreage.

The First Baptist Church has 500 members. Most of the adult men are farmers on the rolling plains around Abernathy, a town of 1,692, in west Texas, north of Lubbock.

Last spring their pastor, C. A. Kennedy, 35, asked them to dedicate one-tenth of their land to God and see what the returns would be.

They did, each dedicating anywhere from 1 to 68 acres. Kennedy said the farmers who dedicated their land had "phenomenal results."

"There is Albert Hart, with five acres dedicated," the pastor said. "He called me to his farm late in the summer to show that all his acreage was bountiful, but on the dedicated land the cotton stood twelve inches higher than the rest and yielded one and three-quarters bales an acre, compared with an average yield of one bale an acre on his other land.

"He asked me why.

"Why? In Malachi 3:10, it says: 'Bring ye all the tithes into the storehouse, that there may be meat in Mine house, and prove Me now herewith, saith the Lord of Hosts, if I will not open you the windows of Heaven, and pour you out a blessing, that there shall not be room enough to receive it.'

"That is why."

—*Now*

* * *

God's Great Faithfulness

I was preaching one night when at the close of a service a well-dressed man approached me and said, "Dr. Smith, I owe you everything I have in life." I looked at him in amazement. Then he told me this story.

"I was down and out," he began. "I had lost my job. My wife and two daughters had left me. I was dressed in rags. One day I happened to stroll into The Peoples Church during one of your Missionary Conventions. You were speaking, and you were making some of the most astounding statements I had ever heard in my life. You are saying, 'You cannot beat God giving. Give and it shall be given unto you. Square with God and God will square with you.' I sat sat up and listened.

"Just to test your sincerity," he continued, "I filled in one of your cards, promising to give God a certain percentage of all He might give me. That, of course, was easy because I had nothing. To my amazement, within a few hours, I got a job. When I received my first pay, I sent in the amount I had promised. Before long I got a raise. Then I contributed more. Soon I had a new suit of clothes. In due time I got a better job. Presently my wife and daughters came back to me. I continued giving. Before long, all my debts were paid." "Now," he exclaimed, "I own my own home here in Minneapolis and I have money in the bank. All that I owe to you. I found that you were right. I discovered that God was as good as His Word." —Oswell Smith

* * *

"Yes, I Tithe"

Yes, I tithe, and I would like to tell you how it all came about. I had to begin work as a small boy to help support my mother. My first wages amounted to $1.50 per week. The first week after I went to work, I took the $1.50 home to my mother and she held the money in her lap and explained to me that she would be happy if I would give a tenth of it to the Lord.

I did, and from that week until this day I have tithed every dollar God has entrusted to me. And I want to say, if I had not tithed the first dollar I made I would not have tithed the first million dollars I made. Tell your readers to train the children to tithe, and they will grow up to be faithful stewards of the Lord.

—John D. Rockefeller, Sr.

* * *

How Much Shall We Keep?

A servant of God had a little girl whom he was eager should be brought up to serve Him. He wanted to teach her that we should give one-tenth of our possessions to God. One day he called her into his study, where he had arranged ten piles of money. And he said: "You see, I have ten piles of money here. One, two, three, four, five. six, seven, eight, nine — they belong to me; but this tenth one belongs to God." The little girl said: *"Oh, Father, are you going to keep all the nine for yourself?"*

—*King's Business*

* * *

Cakes and Pies versus Paying Tithes

There was a church in our town
   Which thought 'twas wondrous wise.
It tried to pay expenses
   By selling cakes and pies;
But after years of trying
   That plan to raise the cash,
The folks got tired of buying
And the whole thing went to smash.

There was a church in our town,
   And it WAS wondrous wise;
It always paid expenses
   By simply paying tithes.
For when 'twas found the tithe did pay,
   It seemed so very plain:
Forthwith 'twould have no other way,
   Not even once again.

—Rev. Frank Cell, in
   Storehouse Tithing

* * *

Charity Begins . . .

An old Chinese farmer caught in the path of war lost house, tools, equipment, and became a refugee. A missionary loaned him $20 with which he bought a horse and cart and began hauling goods for hire.

The countryside was still dangerous, and he made good wages for his work. Soon he had made an unbelievable sum of $80. He went to the missionary and repaid the $20.

"Now," he said, "I have always given a tithe of my earnings to the Lord. Our church is broken up and scattered. What shall I do with my $8?"

"Eight?" asked the missionary. "Your tithe is only $6. The $20 was a debt."

But the old farmer could not figure that out. All he knew was that at first he had nothing and then he had $80. But the missionary refused to give him advice. "You know of many needs," he said, "If you pray, God will give guidance about it."

Then, one day the old man came in beaming. "I have decided," he said. "Our Lord was a Jew. I have heard that there are many Jewish people who have been driven out of their own country. Will you take this eight dollars and send it somewhere where there are Jews who need help, and let it be used for them? —*The Presbyterian*

* * *

Opened Windows

One of the statements most commonly made is that tithing was intended for the Jew only and does not apply to the Christian living under grace. If this were true, then our Lord would not have said of tithing: "These ought ye to have done" (Matt. 23:23; Luke 11:42).

Our heavenly Father does not promise wealth to every one who tithes, but He does promise to "open the windows of heaven and pour you out a blessing that there shall not be room enough to receive it." Take Him at His word today.

Dr. S. D. Gordon wrote he could never forget his mother's paraphrase of Malachi 3:10. The verse begins: "Bring ye the whole tithe in" and ends, "I will pour" the blessing out till you'll be embarrassed for space. Her paraphrase was this: "Give all He asks: take all He promises."

Tithing pays rich dividends in the home, at school, in business, in the pulpit, on the mission field; in fact, in every walk of life.   *—Tither*

TONGUE

A Harsh Word

One day a harsh word, harshly said,
Upon an evil journey sped,
And like a sharp and cruel dart
It pierced a fond and loving heart.

It turned a friend into a foe
And everywhere brought pain and woe.
A kind word followed it one day,
Sped swiftly on its blessed way.

It healed the wound and soothed the pain,
And friends of old were friends again.
It made the hate and anger cease,
And everywhere brought joy and peace.

And yet the harsh word left a trace
The kind word could not efface,
And though the heart its love regained
It left a scar that long remained.

Friends can forgive but not forget,
Nor lose the sense of keen regret.
Oh, if we would but learn to know
How swift and sure our words can go.

How we would weigh with utmost care
Each thought before it reached the air—
And only speak the words that move
Like white-winged messengers of love.
      —Selected

* * *

Silencing a Gossiper

Jane Parsons was a good woman who was anxious to be at peace with all, and particularly wished to be on good terms with those who lived near her. "But Agnes Saundry was such a 'newsbag' that her calls on Jane were neither few nor far between. Nor did she appear to know the way out when she got in." Jane found Agnes' conversations both unprofitable and disagreeable, for she made free use of other people's names. This made Jane unhappy, so much so that she dreaded the woman's coming. She resolved to lay the matter before her pastor, who at once prescribed a remedy. This was it: Keep your family Bible on the table, and when she has been in the house long enough, ask her to read a chapter or a Psalm and pray with you. Jane followed this excellent advice. So the next time the troublesome woman called, she said to her: "Agnes, you are a good scholar. I wish you would read a chapter or Psalm, and pray with me; it might do both of us good." Agnes excused herself on the ground that she was very busy. She would glady do so another time when she could stay. We scarcely need say that Jane had no further worries with Agnes' gossiping in her house.

      —Christian Life

* * *

The Echo

I shouted aloud and louder
  While out on the plain one day;
The sound grew faint and fainter
  Until it had died away.
My words had gone forever,
  They left no trace or track,
But the hills near by caught up the cry
And sent an echo back.

I spoke a word in anger
To one who was my friend,
Like a knife it cut him deeply,
A wound that was hard to mend.
That word, so thoughtlessly uttered,
I would we could both forget,
But its echo lives and memory gives
The recollection yet.

How many hearts are broken,
How many friends are lost
By some unkind word spoken
Before we count the cost!
But a word or deed of kindness
Will repay a hundredfold,
For it echoes again in the hearts of men
And carries a joy untold.

—C. A. Lufburrow, in
The Classmate

* * *

Reckless Words and Slanderous Darts

"Touch not Mine anointed, and do My prophets no harm." Psalms 105:15. "I would rather play with forked lightning or take in my hands living wires," says Dr. A. B. Simpson, "than speak a reckless word against any servant of Christ, or idly repeat the slanderous darts which thousands of Christians are hurling on others to the hurt of their own souls and bodies.

—*Selected*

* * *

Words Like Arrows

How like an arrow is a word
At random often speeding
To find a target never meant
And set some heart a-bleeding.
Oh, pray that Heaven may seal the lips
Ere unkind words are spoken;
For Heaven itself cannot recall,
When once that seal is broken.

—*The Evangelist and Bible Teacher*

* * *

The Telltale Tongue

Justin Martyr once said, "By examining the tongue of a patient, physicians find out the disease of the body, and philosophies of the mind." The directions that come with a well-known brand of fountain pen say, "When this pen runs too freely it is a sign that it is nearly empty." Is there an application here for us, when our tongues get to running too freely? —*Sunday School Times*

* * *

The Tongue

A biblical writer said, "The tongue can no man tame." A Greek philosopher asked his servant to provide the best dish possible. The servant prepared a dish of tongue, saying: "It is the best of all dishes, because with it we may bless and communicate happiness, dispel sorrow, remove despair, cheer the fainthearted, inspire the discouraged, and say a hundred other things to uplift mankind." Later the philosopher asked his servant to provide the worst dish of which he could think. A dish of tongue appeared on the table. The servand said, "It is the worst, because with it we may curse and break human hearts; destroy reputations; promote discord and strife; set families, communities, and nations at war with each other." He was a wise servant. Solomon said, "Whoso keepeth his tongue, keepeth his soul from trouble."

—J. Whitcomb Brougher

* * *

What A Word Did

'Twas only a word, a careless word,
But it smote the heart of one who heard
 Like a fierce, relentless blow;
The day seemed overcast with gloom,
The sweetest songs seemed out of tune;
 The fires of hope burned low.

'Twas only a word, a loving word,
But a weary, sorrowing heart was stirred,
 And life took brighter hue;
And Faith, triumphant, pruned her wing,

Discouraged souls began to sing,
 And hope revived anew.

Only a word, and yet what power
It holds to better or to mar
 The lives of those who hear.
What power for good — for evil too!
Oh, may our words be good and true,
 And spoken in God's fear.

—Anna L. Dreyer, in
The P. H. Advocate

What Does Your Speech Reveal?

Oh, that my tongue might so possess
The accent of His tenderness
That every word I breathe should bless!

For those who mourn, a word of cheer;
A word of hope for those who fear;
And love to all men, far or near.

Oh, that it might be said of me,
"Surely thy speech betrayeth thee
As friend of Christ of Galilee!"
      —Thomas Robinson, in
        Moody Monthly

* * *

Sent Back for More Work

John Wesley tells us that at Epworth on one occasion a wagon load of Methodists were brought before the magistrates. "What have they done?" asked the magistrate. That was a point the prosecution had not considered. Then said one: "Please, sir, they converted my wife. Before she went amongst them she had such a tongue! But now she is as quiet as a lamb." "Take them back," said the magistrate, "and let them convert all the scolds in the parish!"
      —Mark Guy Pearse

* * *

The Tongue

"The boneless tongue, so small and weak,
Can crush and kill," declares the Greek.
"The tongue destroys a greater horde,"
The Turk asserts, "Than does the
    sword."
The Persian proverb wisely saith,
"A lengthy tongue — an early death!
Or, sometimes takes this form instead,
"Don't let your tongue cut off your
    head."
The tongue can speak a word whose
    speed,
Say the Chinese, "outstrips the steeds."
The Arab sages said in part,
"The tongue's great storehouse is the
    heart."
From Hebrew was the maxim sprung,
"Thy feet should slip, ne'er let the
    tongue."
The sacred writer crowns the whole,
"Who keeps his tongue doth keep his
    soul."
      —Selected

"Ladies Raid Society!"

At the close of a talkative Ladies Aid session at which the ladies had over-indulged in gossiping comments about various members of the community, a young woman who attended for the first time proceeded to call the group the "Ladies Raid Society."
      —*Sunday School Times*

* * *

Only!

Only a seed — but it chanced to fall
In a little cleft of a city wall,
And taking root grew bravely up,
Till a tiny blossom crowned its top!

Only a thought — but the work it
    wrought
Could never by tongue or pen be taught,
For it ran through a life, like a thread
    of gold,
And the life bore fruit a hundred-fold!

Only a word — but 'twas spoken in love,
With a whispered prayer to the Lord
    above,
And the angels in heaven rejoiced once
    more,
For a newborn soul "entered in by the
    door!"
      —*The Christian*

* * *

Cancelling Unkind Words

Some of the older boys and girls doubtless have studied cancellation in school. But there is another kind of cancellation that can be used by the youth of all ages. For example, two boys were speaking of another boy.

"He is slow in games," said one.

"Yes," replied the other, "but he always plays fair."

"He is so stupid at school!" said the first boy.

"But he always studies hard," answered the second.

Thus you see every unkind word spoken by the first boy was cancelled by a kind word from the second. Suppose the next time you hear an unkind word you try to cancel it by putting a kind one in its place.
      —*Gospel Herald*

People Will Talk
You may go through the world, but 'twill
   be very slow
If you listen to all that is said as you
   go;
You'll be worried and fretted and kept
   in a stew,
For meddlesome tongues must have
   something to do —
    For people will talk.

If quiet and modest, you'll have it presumed
That your humble position is only assumed;
You're a wolf in sheep's clothing, or else
   you're a fool;
But don't get excited, keep perfectly
   cool —
    For people will talk.

And then if you show the least boldness
   of heart,
Or slight inclination to take your own
   part,
They will call you an upstart, conceited
   and vain;
But keep straight ahead — don't stop
   to explain —
    For people will talk.
          —*Selected*

* * *

Enquire Diligently!
Dr. McLean tells how he was rebuked and humbled on a certain occasion when he repeated a grave matter he had heard to a friend. His friend opened his Bible to Deuteronomy 13:14 and read: "If thou shalt hear say . . . then shalt thou enquire, and make search, and ask diligently; and behold, if it be truth, and the thing certain that such abomination is wrought among you . . . ."
Then his friend turned quietly to him and asked:
"Have you, dear brother, 'enquired?'"
"Have you 'made search?'"
"Did you 'ask diligently?'"
"Did you try and find out if the story is true?"
"And the thing 'certain?'"
"Is it certain that 'such abomination is wrought among you?'"
Dr. McLean says he could only acknowledge regretfully that he had not

fulfilled one of the six conditions and was repeating the tale from hearsay without making the slightest attempt to act thereon in a Scriptural way.
    —*Watchman-Examiner*

* * *

The Blessed Man!
Said George Eliot, "Blessed is the man who, having nothing to say, abstains from giving wordy evidence of the fact!"   —W. B. K.

* * *

Speak Evil of No Man
A godly minister was approached by one of his church members who wanted to repeat to him some of the wrong-doings of others. The pastor said, "Does anybody else know this but you?" "No sir." "Have you told it to anyone else?" "No." "Then," said the good man, "go home and hide it away at the feet of Jesus, and never speak of it again unless God leads you to speak to the man himself. If the Lord wants to bring scandal upon His Church, let Him do it; but don't you be the instrument to cause it."   —*Christian Herald* (London).

* * *

Words
Forgive me, Lord, for careless words
   When hungry souls are near:
Words that are not of faith and love,
   Heavy with care and fear;
Forgive me for the words withheld,
   For words that might have won
A soul from darkened paths and sin
   To follow Thy dear Son:
Words are such mighty things, dear
   Lord,
   May I so yielded be
That Christ, who spake as never man,
   May ever speak through me.
    —*Spiritual Life*

* * *

Death Or Life In Words
"A careless word may kindle strife,
A cruel word may wreck a life;
A bitter word may hate instill,
A brutal word may smite and kill;
A gracious word may smooth the way
A joyous word may light the day;
A timely word may lessen stress,
A loving word may heal and bless."
    —*Selected*

TRACTS — PRINTED WORD

Be Careful What You Read

One day a gentleman in India went into his library and took down a book from the shelves. As he did so, he felt a slight pain in his finger like the prick of a pin. He thought that a pin had been stuck by some careless person, in the cover of the book. But soon his finger began to swell, then his arm, and then his whole body, and in a few days he died. It was not a pin among the books, but a small and deadly serpent. There are many serpents in the books nowadays; they nestle in the foliage of some of the most fascinating literature; they coil around the flowers whose perfume intoxicates the senses. When the records of ruined souls are made up, oh, what multitudes will be inscribed, "Poisoned by serpents among the books!"

—*Christian Herald* (London)

* * *

Power of the Word

Some time ago a gentleman as he passed along the street was offered a tract. He somewhat curtly refused, saying he did not want to be bothered with any of their evangelistic nonsense; but as the worker pressed him to take it, he did so, though he assured him he would burn it as soon as he got home; and he kept his word, throwing it into the fire and watching it burn. As the thin paper curled up with the heat, his eye caught the sentence: "The Word of the Lord liveth forever," and do what he could he could not rid himself of the words. They buzzed in his ear, they stood out boldly on the white pages of the ledger. Wherever he was, that passage of Scripture haunted him and made him miserable, until unable to bear it any longer, he went to the mission hall, and there finding peace, pardon and salvation, he learned to rejoice that the Word of the Lord did live forever.

—*Christian Index*

* * *

"Pen Mightier Than Sword!"

Dr. Panton tells of "a young Frenchman who had been wounded at the siege of Saint Quentin and was languishing on a pallet in the hospital when a tract that lay on the coverlet caught his eye. He read it and was converted by it. The monument of that man may be seen before the Church of the Consistory in Paris, standing with a Bible in his hand — Admiral Coligny, the leader of the Reformation in France. But the tract had not yet finished its work. It was read by Coligny's nurse who penitently placed it in the hands of the Lady Abbess and she, too, was converted by it. She fled from France to the Palatinate, where she met a young Hollander and became his wife. The influence which she had upon that man reacted upon the whole continent of Europe, for he was William of Orange, who became the champion of liberty and Protestantism in the Netherlands."

—Dr. George W. Truett

* * *

God — Eternity

A young lady who had in her heart a love for souls, gave a tract to a young man in a stage coach in England, and followed the gift with prayer. The young man was on the way to his wedding. He took the little tract and folded it, and then tore it all to pieces, and opening the window threw it out, but a gust of wind blew one piece of the tract back and it lodged on his knee. He wet the end of his finger, took up that torn bit of tract, and read there just one word, "God." He turned it over, and on the other side he could make out the word "eternity." When he reached the home of the young lady he was to marry she met him at the door, and he looked into her face and said, "God! Eternity!" She thought he had lost his reason, but it was the Spirit of God answering the prayer of the young woman who had given the tract. When the circumstances were revealed, before the wedding took place, the bride and groom agreed, together on their knees, to give themselves to Christ.

—From *John Three Sixteen*, by Dr. Wm. A. Rice

1,700 Saved By Reading Tract

Dr. Jacob Chamberlain, of Arcot, India, counted 1,700 people who had been saved by a little tract which he had written, and doubtless, if every Christian who is now living were to testify as to the means of his conversion, we should be astonished at the number who were reached by tracts.

— D. M. Panton, B.A.

* * *

The Futility of Clamor

Wendell Phillips was one of the most polished and graceful orators our country ever produced. He spoke as quietly as if he were talking in his own parlor, and almost entirely without gestures. He had great power over all kinds of audiences. One illustration of his power and tact occurred in Boston. The majority of the audience were hostile. They yelled and sang and completely drowned his voice. Phillips made no attempt to address this noisy crowd, but bent over and seemed to be speaking in a low tone to the reporters who were seated near the platform. The curiosity of the audience was excited: they ceased to clamor and tried to hear what he was saying to the reporters. Phillips looked at the audience and said quietly: "Go on, gentlemen, go on. I do not need your ears. Through these pencils I speak to thirty millions." Not a voice was raised again.

—*Speakers' Library*

* * *

Marvels Wrought by Printed Page!

It was reading Bishop Taylor's *Holy Living and Dying*, that turned John Wesley into a course of life to be shaped by Kempis' *Christian Pattern,* and Law's *Christian Perfection*. It was reading John Fletcher's immortal *Checks to Antinomianism* that changed the popular young church priest into the evangelist — the missionary bishop Dr. Coke, who spread in two continents the doctrine of free grace for every soul of man. — D. M. Panton, B. A.

The Deeper Truth

One morning a Chicago high school teacher, when transferring from one streetcar to another, was handed a tract. Without looking at it she hurried to board her second car. As she passed the conductor, she absent-mindedly handed him the tract instead of her transfer. He glanced at the title and remarked dryly, "Oh *did he?*" She retrieved the tract, surrendered her transfer and hurried to a seat. Then she looked at the leaflet. Its title read, *"Jesus Paid It All." — Moody Monthly*

* * *

Dr. Russell H. Conwell Won Indirectly Through Tract!

"Many decades ago a lady gave some leaflets to two actors. One of the actors, led by this tract to attend church and so becoming converted, was Dr. George Lorimer, pastor of Tremont Temple in Boston. Through his influence, Russell H. Conwell was led into the ministry. Thus the Baptist Temple in Philadelphia, together with the work of the Tremont Temple, and the personal influence of these two notable pulpit speakers, is traceable to one little leaflet in the hands of a woman."

— *Gospel Herald*

* * *

An Unusual Birthday Celebration

John Scudder, a promising young physician in New York, while visiting one of his patients one day picked up a tract on the table and read it. The result was that he and his wife went to India as missionaries. Their nine children all became missionaries in that land. By this time the Scudders have given almost six hundred years of continuous missionary service for India.

— *Earnest Worker*

* * *

J. Hudson Taylor Saved by Reading Tract

J. Hudson Taylor, founder of the great China Inland Mission, was converted through reading a little tract in his father's library when he was fifteen years old. Carelessly, he picked it up to while away the time, but, eighty miles away, his mother was praying for his salvation. Before he laid it down, he was rejoicing in the knowledge of sins forgiven! When we think of the stupendous work of the mission he founded, we marvel that God should have used such a little thing to bring it all about! — *King's Business.*

* * *

"Tracks"

"Well, Ben, how did you like that Tract
I gave to you one day?"
The country parson asked his man
Who kept the weeds away.

"Ah, Massa, it was jes' for me,
It sure did me some good;
I couldn't tell why call 'em 'Tracks'
But *now* I'm sure I could.

"For when I read that little book
It track me everywhere;
It track me down the cellar-steps,
It track me up the stair.

"It track me right out to de barn —
'Nen to de house it comes;
It track me all aroun' de farm —
At las' — it track me 'home.'

"It track me till I 'fessed my sins —
Took dat I stole right back;
It done has tracked me to de Lawd —
God bless yo' fer dat Track!

"I jes' abouten wore it out —
But did yo' want it back?
Its trackin' Mandy! An' I knows
Jes' why you call it 'Track.' "
— Effie O. Foss, in
The Brethren Evangelist

* * *

Tract Power in Africa

Here is an incident that shows how God delights in using the despised things of the world to work out His mighty purposes.

Young Ralph Barton is a poor speaker and knows it. So he seldom tries to speak in public. But he has found a way to witness for his Lord.

Some years ago he wrote some Gospel tracts, had them printed and began to

send them everywhere. One fell into the hands of a poor, simple bushman in West Africa, who had learned to read and write a little. The African understood enough to grasp the fact that he was a sinner in God's sight and that Christ died for him.

He wrote at once to Barton: "I have accepted Jesus as my personal Saviour, caused by reading your soul-striking tract. And presently I am a new-born child. I was totally converted. And now I am going about the towns telling the people what one tract has done in me."

—C. D. Carter

* * *

"Printed Page Never Flinches!"

In scattering divine literature we liberate thistledown, laden with precious seed, which, blown by the winds of the Spirit, floats over the world. The printed page never flinches, never shows cowardice; it is never tempted to compromise; it never tires, never grows disheartened; it travels cheaply, and requires no hired hall; it works while we sleep; it never loses its temper; and it works long after we are dead. The printed page is a visitor which gets *inside* the home, and *stays there*; it always catches a man in the right mood, for it speaks to him only when he is reading it; it always sticks to what it has said, and never answers back; and it is bait left permanently in the pool.

—D. M. Panton, B. A.

* * *

Souls Saved By Tracts

A tract entitled *The Bruised Reed* led to the conversion of Richard Baxter. He wrote *The Saints' Rest* which was blessed to the conversion of Philip Doddridge. Doddridge wrote *The Rise and Progress of Religion in the Soul.* William Wilberforce from reading this book found Christ and wrote his *Practical View.* This book was instrumental in the conversion of Leigh Richmond who wrote "*The Dairyman's Daughter* which has been translated into more than 50 languages, and has been blessed to the conversion of thousands. It is related of Dr. Goodel, that when he was passing through Nicomedia, he left with a stranger a copy of *The Dairyman's Daughter,* printed in the Armenian-Turkish language. Seventeen years afterwards he visited Nicomedia, and found a church of more than 40 members, and a Protestant community of more than 200 persons. That tract with God's blessing did the work.

—Dr. George W. Truett

* * *

The Malay Merchant

A ship commanded by a New England sea captain visiting India was boarded by a Malay merchant, a man of property, who asked him if he had any tracts he could part with. The captain, surprised by the request from a heathen, as he considered him, asked, "What do you want of English tracts? You cannot read them." "True, but I have a use for them nevertheless," said the Malay through his interpreter, "whenever one of your countrymen, or an Englishman, calls on me to trade, I put a tract in his way and watch him. If he reads it soberly and with interest I infer that he will not cheat me; if he throws it outside with contempt, or with an oath of profanity, I have no more to do with him — I cannot trust him."

—*Christian Alliance*

* * *

Just Another House

Down a street in Caracas went a missionary, giving out tracts or dropping them in windows. He noticed a house set back from the street, shut-up looking, forbidding. Why bother? It was just another house. What difference could one make? But he dragged his tired feet to the entrance and dropped his tracts in a small open window. Before he could reach the street again the door was jerked open and a voice hissed, "Sst! Senor, show us your books." In a moment the missionary was inside, preaching the Gospel to the whole family. The girl had received a tract three years before and had cherished the story of Jesus. Now she wanted the big Book with all the stories. She was eager to buy it. And couldn't their house be used for village meetings? When the missionary left, he looked back at the house he might have passed. Just another house? Not at all, but a place which, by God's grace, would be the beginning of another church.

—*Sunday School Times*

* * *

A Great Scholar's Confession

Dr. Valpy, the author of a great many classbooks, wrote these simple lines as his confession of faith:

In peace let me resign my breath,
    And thy salvation see;
My sins deserve eternal death,
    But Jesus died for me.

He gave those lines to old Dr. Marsh, the rector of Beckenham, who put them over the mantel in his study. The Earl of Roden came in and read them, and asked, "Will you give me a copy of those lines?" "I shall be pleased to do so," said Dr. Marsh, and he copied them. Lord Roden took them home and put them over his own mantelpiece. General Taylor, a Waterloo hero, came into the room and read them. While staying with Earl Roden he read them again and again, until he could reply to Roden's remark: "Indeed I do know them by heart; my heart has grasped their meaning." He was brought to Christ by the humble rhyme. He gave the lines to an officer in the army, who was going out to the Crimean War. He came home to die, and when Dr. Marsh went to see him, he said, "Do you know this verse which General Taylor gave me? It brought me to my Saviour, and I die in peace." To Dr. Marsh's surprise he repeated the lines:

In peace let me resign my breath,
    And thy salvation see;
My sins deserve eternal death,
    But Jesus died for me.

—*Sunday School Times*

* * *

"A Torn Leaf"

A clergyman in England asked a dying Christian woman where she found the Saviour; and she gave him a piece of paper torn from an American journal containing part of one of C. H. Spurgeon's sermons. The scrap had been wrapped around a package that came to her from Australia. The words of Spurgeon were read by her and were the means of leading her to Christ.

Commenting on this incident, a writer says, "Think of it; a sermon preached in England, printed in America, in some way coming to Australia, a part of it used as wrapping paper there, coming back to England, was the means of converting this woman."

What an encouragement there is in such an incident for those who preach the Gospel by means of printer's ink! Tracts and religious papers have been wonderfully used of God in the salvation of souls.

—Church of Christ Advocate

* * *

It Hadn't Occurred to Him

The boy was standing before the judge of a juvenile court charged with a crime that had shocked the entire community and had brought grief and misery to his parents. "Where did you get the idea of committing such a deed?" asked the judge. "I read it," replied the lad simply. The judge hesitated a moment, then turned and addressed the boy's father, "Did you ever take the pains to examine the literature your boy was reading?" "Why-er, no — that is, it never occurred to me," responded the man, cut to the quick by the question. Who was to blame? Do you — teacher, mother, father — realize the tremendous influence on character building that is represented by the literature that is falling into the hands of your boys and girls?

—Kings Business

* * *

"Printed Page Deathless!"

Proving that the printed page is deathless, that while we may destroy the tract, the press is able to produce millions more; that the ripple started by a given tract can widen down the centuries until it beats upon the great white throne, Dr. Panton tells of Leigh Richmond who was once traveling in a

coach. "The passengers got out to walk and he began to give a tract to every wayfarer he met. One of his fellow travelers smiled derisively as he saw a tract treated contemptuously by the recipient, torn in two, and thrown down the road. A puff of wind carried it over a hedge into a hayfield, where a number of haymakers were seated, and soon they were listening to the tract read by one of their number who found it. He was observed carefully joining together the two parts which had been torn asunder, but were held together by a thread. The reader was led to reflection and prayer and subsequently became an earnest Christian and a tract distributor himself; and of the rest, within twelve months three became earnest and active Christian workers."

—Clyde Dennis

* * *

A Royal Example

Britain's beloved Queen Mother, Mary, gives us a beautiful example in the practice of tract distributing.

Seth Sykes, the well-known evangelist, tells me that he went into a certain religious book depot, not long ago, to purchase some copies of the widely blessed little tract, *Safety, Certainty, and Enjoyment,* and was informed that fifty extra copies of the tract were being given free to him, because Queen Mary had purchased a supply of these tracts there a little while before, and had paid for an extra fifty, to be given to the next purchaser. The Queen Mother told the salesman that it was her practice to carry several copies with her, for distribution in going from place to place. A beautiful and inspiring exemple indeed! — and one which enhancingly agrees with the Christian character of the gracious woman whom Britain was proud to call queen for a quarter of a century.

—Evangelical Christian

* * *

Heathen Temples Emptied by Tract

Sir Bartle Frere, travelling in India, was amazed to find a small town in which the idol shrines and temples were empty, and the townsfolk professed the

Christian faith. Some years earlier, one of the townsfolk had been given an old garment by an English resident, in a pocket of which, forgotten, lay a Gospel portion with eight or nine tracts in the native language. The life is not in the sower, but in the seed. Even if an infidel scattered the Scriptures, he would only be exploding his own battlements.

—D. M. Panton, B. A.

* * *

The Printed Word

"When a man puts in circulation a good, religious book," said Dr. Stockbridge, "he sets in motion an influence the extent and duration of which he cannot estimate. It is a teacher that requires no outfit, no money for traveling expenses, no salary, is not affected by the climate, is never sick, and consequently has no druggist's or doctor's bills to pay, and experiences no diminution of physical or mental activity because of age. Always ready for work; no blue Mondays; always as bright as the morning stars.

"Books can go and stay where it is not practical for missionaries to live. Our merchant ships carry books and leave them on the islands of the sea, as well as on the shores of continents, years in advance of the arrival of missionaries.

—*The Armory*

* * *

His Appointment

It was nearly nine o'clock in the morning. The train, due at 8:50 a. m., had stopped at the wayside station, taken up the passengers, and steamed away. The stationmaster was settling down again. A gentleman with face red-hot, and temper apparently heated to the same point, came hurrying up. "I would rather have given twenty-five dollars than to have been late this morning. I do not know what is to be done." "There's a comfortable waiting room inside, if you would like to sit down, sir," the stationmaster ventured to say. A table stood in the room with a supply of tracts. Well-chosen and attractive they were. The gentleman chose one and seated himself to read it. A month after this the stationmaster was on the platform. As the train stopped a gentleman leaped out, saying, "Do you remember me?" "I do, sir, you are the gentleman that missed the train and was so troubled about it." "I need not have been. I missed the train that morning, but I found the Saviour. I had been so busy about business that I did not allow myself time to think about God. That tract led me to Jesus Christ. I never knew what happiness was before."

—*Good News*

* * *

Passed on By an Infidel

An infidel received by mail the tract, "Prepare to meet thy God." Angry, he was about to burn it, when it occurred to him that it would be a good joke to send it to a friend, a companion in unbelief. This man was convicted and converted by reading, and in turn sent it to another friend, who was also led to Christ.

—*Biblical Treasury*

* * *

The Answer to a Child's Prayer

A mother in New England was helping pack a box to be sent to India. Her son, aged four, insisted on putting in an offering all his own, a little leaflet entitled "Come to Jesus." His name was written on it with the little prayer, "May the one who gets this soon learn to love Jesus." When the child's leaflet reached that far-off land it was finally given to a Hindu priest who was teaching the missionaries the language. He took it without looking at it, but on his way back to his mountain home he thought of the leaflet, took it out, and read the writing on the outside. The child's prayer so touched him that he was then eager to read further. He soon gave up his idols and became a devoted missionary to his own people. Fifteen years after that, American missionaries visited his mountain village, and there found the converted Hindu priest with a congregation of fifteen hundred people who had learned to love Jesus as their Saviour, through the influence and teaching of that leaflet.

—*Helping Hand*

An Awakening Testimony

I remember hearing the Rev. W. V. Barratt give an account of an experience of his early days in Germany. A boy of ten or twelve he was with his brother distributing tracts from door to door, when at one home his tract was refused and the door discourteously closed. The two boys, obeying the precept of the Lord Jesus, kicked the dust off their feet on the doorstep. Some thirty years afterward he was visiting that part of Germany, when he was called to the bedside of a gentleman who had asked to see him. He was reminded of the incident of thirty years before, and only then learned that the gentleman, inquiring as to the meaning of the boys' singular act, had been convicted of the sin of refusing God's messenger — and had in consequence been led to seek and find salvation.

—Sunday School Times

* * *

Four Prisoners That Needed Release

When Elizabeth came to the throne she set free several prisoners. Presently some courtiers approached her with a petition. "Madam," they said, "we have four prisoners who deserve not to be kept locked up, and we humbly pray for their release." "Who are they?" demanded the Queen. "Their names are Matthew, Mark, Luke and John, your Majesty. They are kept shut up in the Greek language, whereas they should be abroad among the people." The Queen commanded they should be released that they might do service in the English tongue.

—Wonderful Word

* * *

"Last Night, Dancing With Rage, Now Dancing With Joy!"

A young man went home to tell his father of his conversion. The old man worked himself into a fury at his son's presumption in saying he was saved, and turned him out of the house, The son dropped a copy of *Safety, Certainty, and Enjoyment* in the passage. Next morning he returned to see his father. He writes thus: "Last night I left him dancing with rage; and this morning I found him dancing with joy." He was saved through the booklet. The recorder of this adds a sequel. "While traveling in a corridor car with low partitions, I was speaking to the passengers when a head bobbed up, and a young woman said, 'I was saved three weeks ago through reading *Do You Hope or Know That You Have Eternal Life?*' She was the daughter of the man who was so angry at his son's presumption."

—Wm. Luff, in
Gospel Herald

* * *

What A Tract Costing One Cent Did

A son of one of the chiefs of Burdwain was converted by a single tract. He could not read, but he went to Rangoon, a distance of 250 miles. There a missionary's wife taught him to read, and in forty-eight hours he could read the tract through. He took a basket full of tracts, and with much difficulty preached the gospel in his own home, and was the means of converting hundreds to God. He was a man of influence; the people flocked to hear him. In one year 1,500 natives were baptized in Arrecan as members of the church. All this through one little tract! That tract cost one cent. Whose cent was it? God only knows. Perhaps it was the mite of some little girl — perhaps the well-earned offering of some young boy. But what a blessing it was!

—The Evangelical

* * *

Power in the Word

A colporteur in Tanta is reported by the *Bible in the World* as offering the Bible to some Moslems who were sitting in a shop. One of them asked, "Are you a preacher?" "No," was the reply, "I am a colporteur." Then another man said, "Beware! This man is worse than the preacher who speaks to you and goes away. This man leaves you with a book which is able to convert the Moslem!"

—Gospel Herald

* * *

Did You Know:

. . . *that* among the most precious items of cargo on the *Mayflower* on her first trip to America were Pastor John Robinson's tracts?

... *that* the first gospel tracts published in North America were in a "foreign" language devised by John Eliot for the American Indians?

—*Power*

* * *

He Ate It

One Sunday morning he saw a group of men standing at a street corner, and he gave to each of them one of his booklets. One of them, the jester of the party, said, "What's good for the soul must be good for the body," and he screwed up his tract and popped it into his mouth.

Of course, all his friends laughed, but they insisted that he should not only chew it but swallow it that he might get the good that was in it. Not wanting to spoil the joke, he did it.

The tract upset that man most terribly; not his digestion — he was strong and sound in that region — but his soul and conscience. He felt that he had done a silly thing, and a discourteous thing, but worst of all he felt that he had despised God's Gospel and made a jest of it. He was worried about it. The evening came, and he thought he would atone for it by going to the Gospel service. And that night he was saved.

—*High School Christian*

TRUST

The Poor Immigrant

Some men remind me of a poor immigrant who was discovered walking on the tracks of a railroad in New Jersey. On his back he carried a huge bulk and as he trudged on, tired and halt, he resembled Bunyan's pilgrim with his burden. In passing a station an agent ordered him off the track, reminding him he was liable to arrest for trespassing. The man demurred and produced a railroad ticket good for passage from Jersey City to Scranton. The agent looked at him in amazement, and asked why he was walking when he might ride.

The stranger replied that he thought the ticket gave him only the privilege of walking over the road. His right was explained to him, and the tired man with delight boarded the first train for his destination.

Surely the angels must look with wonderment at the thousands who trudge along, anxious and careworn, bearing life's burdens without Divine help and future hope.

Ah, how many of God's children, through distrust and disbelief, fail to "possess their possessions!"

—*Gospel Herald*

"Mother, Is the Moon God's Light?"

A mother and her little four-year-old daughter were preparing to retire for the night. The child was afraid of the dark, and the mother, alone with the child, felt fearful also. When the light was out, the child caught a glimpse of the moon outside the window. "Mother," she asked, "is the moon God's light?" "Yes," said the mother, "God's lights are always shining." The next question was, "Will God blow out His lights and go to sleep?" "No, my child, God never goes to sleep." Then, out of the simplicity of a child's faith, the little one said that which gave reassurance to the fearful mother, "Well, as long as God is awake, I am not afraid."

—*Sunday School Times*

* * *

Trust Him

Trust Him when dark doubts assail thee,
Trust Him when thy strength is small;
Trust Him when to trust Him simply
Seems the hardest thing of all.

Trust Him; He is ever faithful,
Trust Him, for His will is best;
Trust Him, for the heart of Jesus
Is the only place of rest.

Trust Him, then, through cloud and
  sunshine;
All thy cares upon Him cast —
Till the storms of life are over
And the trusting days are past.
                    —*Gospel Herald*

* * *

Trust and Be Not Afraid

"Man," said one Christian Scotsman
to another, "I got a wonderful text in
my reading lesson to-day." "Oh," said
his friend, "let me hear it." "Well," responded the other enthusiastically, "the
text is Psalm 56:3, and it says, 'What
time I am afraid, I will trust in Thee.' "
"Very good," agreed his friend, smiling,
"but I got a better text in my reading
lesson, for in Isaiah 12:2, I read, 'I will
trust, and not be afraid.' "
                    —*Moody Monthly*

* * *

An Indian Girl's Prayer

A teacher among the Sioux Indians
relates the following touching incident:
An Indian baby was dying. She lay
in her father's arms, while near by
stood another little girl a few years older, who was a Christian.

"Father," said the little girl, "little
sister is going to Heaven tonight. Let
me pray." As she said this, she kneeled
at her father's knee, and this little
prayer fell from her childish lips:

"Father God, little sister is coming
to see You tonight. Please open the
door softly and let her in. Amen."
                    —*Gospel Herald*

* * *

Are We Ready to "Jump?

My little boy wished to climb an old
apple tree, so I stood below watching
him as he ascended. The limbs were rotten and began to break under his weight.
He stepped to others and they gave way.
Seeing his plight I held my arms toward
him, though he was far up and called,
"Jump, Buddy, and I'll catch you." He
looked for a moment, then as more limbs
began breaking he said, "Shall I let go
of everything, Daddy, and trust you?"
He jumped and was safe in his father's
arms. That went directly to my heart

as a message of God to me. "Father,
shall I let go of everything, and trust
you?" I let go. I trusted him and wonderfully has he supplied our needs.
                —*Sunday School Times*

* * *

What Am I Now to Believe?

A lady once wrote to a servant of
Christ, "Will you put it down in black
and white what I am to believe?

"I have been told of many different
texts; and they are so many that I am
bewildered.

"Please tell me one text, and I will
try to believe it."

The answer came, "It is not any one
text, nor any number of texts that saves,
any more than the man who fled to the
city of refuge was saved by reading the
directions on the finger posts. It is by
trusting a *Person* — the Lord Jesus
Christ — that we are saved."
                    —*Gospel Herald*

* * *

God Knows the Way

"God knows the way of the righteous,
  Even though it be dark and drear;
He knows when we're tired and weary,
  Our burdens too heavy to bear;
We ask, as the shadows lengthen,
  'Lord, lift Thou this burden of care!'
And often His voice replieth:
  'My child, I placed it for you there!
With grace that is all-sufficient,
  That you might grow stronger in Me,
So trust, weary child, your Father,
  He knoweth and careth for thee!' "
                    —*Selected*

* * *

Leave Tomorrow with God

Would it not be better to leave tomorrow with God? That is what is troubling man; tomorrow's burdens, tomorrow's duties. Martin Luther, in his
autobiography says:

"I have one preacher that I love better than any other on earth; it is my
little tame robin, who preaches to me
daily. I put crumbs upon my window
sill, especially at night. He hops onto
the window sill when he wants his supply, and takes as much as he desires to

satisfy his need. From thence he always hops to a little tree close by and lifts up his voice to God and sings his carols of praise and gratitude, tucks his little head under his wing and goes fast to sleep, and leaves tomorrow to look after itself. He is the best preacher that I have on earth."

—*Gospel Herald*

* * *

Where He Would Be

The late Dr. John B. McFerrin, who in his day was a tower of strength among the Methodists of the South, was lying on his deathbed calmly awaiting the summons to come up higher. His son, who had charge of a circuit twenty miles away, was by his bedside, and when Saturday came was reluctant to leave his dying father, as his Sabbath duties appeared to require. Whereupon the venerable minister said: "My son, I feel a little stronger, and you had better return and fill your appointment tomorrow. If, while you are away, John, I should happen to slip off, *you know where to find me.*" The saint about to depart remembered the words of his Lord, "That where I am there ye may be also."

—*Christian Advocate*

* * *

A Transfer of Trust

A frantic mother called her pastor one day. She had a bad case of "nerves." He thought he heard a child's voice over the phone, so he asked, "Is your child upset and worried as you are?" "Why, of course not," she replied. "But why not?" he asked. "I suppose she puts her trust in me and lets me do the worrying," she answered. "Then make a transference, try to think of yourself as a child of God, and just as your child puts her trust in you, you put your trust in God."

—*Christian Digest*

* * *

When He Feared a Break

A simple man who carried on his business in Manchester, about whose integrity certain rumors were abroad,

was asked, "Do you never fear you will break?" "Ay," said the man emphatically, "I shall break when the Fiftieth Psalm breaks in the fifteenth verse, 'Call upon me in the day of trouble: I will deliver thee.' "

—*Christian Herald*

* * *

Trust versus Doubt

"If we doubt, we don't trust;
If we trust, we don't doubt!"

—*Selected*

* * *

Don't Try to Be Strong; Just Be Still

Hudson Taylor was so feeble in the closing months of life, that he wrote a dear friend, "I am so weak I cannot work; I cannot read my Bible; I cannot even pray. I can only lie still in God's arms like a little child, and trust." This wondrous man of God with all his spiritual power came to a place of physical suffering and weakness where he could only lie still and trust. And that is all God asks of you, His dear child, when you grow faint in the fierce fires of affliction. Do not try to *be strong.* Just *be still.*

—James H. McConkey

* * *

In the Bird's Nest

As if left in grateful appreciation for lives spared, a Sunday school card, carried by a bird to its nest which city workmen saved, is now in possession of Charles Stewart, Secretary of Public Works Department. The limb on which the nest rested was brought down. Cutting had been delayed early in June, for in the little home nestled young robins. Gangs trimming shade trees hadn't the heart to cut this one limb, so they marked it to return at the end of the season. The fledglings had flown when they came back. In the nest was a small card which probably a child had dropped on the way home from Sunday school. Now it was at the bottom of the deserted nest. "We trust in the Lord our God" were the words printed above a pastoral scene.

—*Challenge*

A Bedtime Prayer

Dear Father, now the sky is dim
 With night's blue curtains drawn,
And it is time for peaceful sleep
 Until tomorrow's dawn.

Now quietness is everywhere.
 I hear the lullaby
Of crickets and of sleepy winds.
 The stars blink in the sky.

Now darkness like a downy quilt
 Covers me cozily,
And I am in thy loving care
 And thou art close to me.
—Paul D. March, in
Moody Monthly

* * *

A Heart of Love

Dr. Grenfell tells of an old fisherman, rich in trust, who was "given to hospitality." He was seventy-three years of age, and had fed many hungry folk during the "hard" winters; and when times grew unusually hard, this old man of faith brought forth twelve dirty, well-worn five dollar bills, as a last resort. This money, his entire savings, he gave to the missionary to buy food for needy neighbors. But Dr. Grenfell remonstrated: "You are getting old, and you should not cut the last plank away yet." Then the hardy fisherman of many perils answered: "He'll take care, doctor; guess I can trust Him. It wouldn't do not to have used that sixty dollars, and have sent folks away hungry, would it, doctor? It would look as if I didn't have much trust in Him."
—*Southern Churchman*

* * *

God's Unchanging Word

For feelings come and feelings go,
 And feelings are deceiving;
My warrant is the Word of God,
 Naught else is worth believing.

Though all my heart should feel condemned
 For want of some sweet token,
There is One greater than my heart
 Whose word cannot be broken.

I'll trust in God's unchanging Word
 Till soul and body sever;
For, though all things shall pass away,
 His Word shall stand forever.
—Martin Luther

* * *

Tell Him All

When thou wakest in the morning;
 Ere thou tread the untried way
Of the lot that lies before thee
 Through the coming busy day;
Whether sunbeams promise brightness,
 Whether dim forebodings fall,
Be thy dawning glad or gloomy,
 Go to Jesus — tell Him all!

In the calm of sweet communion
 Let thy daily work be done;
In the peace of soul-outpouring
 Care be banished, patience won;
And if earth, with its enchantments
 Seeks thy spirit to enthrall,
Ere thou listen, ere thou answer —
 Turn to Jesus — tell Him all!

Then as hour by hour glides by thee,
 Thou wilt blessed guidance know,
Thine own burdens being lightened,
 Thou canst bear another's woe;
Thou canst help the weak ones onward,
 Thou canst raise up those who fall;
But remember, while thou servest,
 Still tell Jesus — tell Him all!
—*Selected*

* * *

Eventual Security

"See, Father," said a small boy, who was walking with his father by the river, "they are knocking the props away from the under the bridge. What are they doing that for? Won't the bridge fall?" "They are knocking them away," said the father, "that the timbers may rest more firmly upon the stone piers which are now finished." *God often takes away our earthly props that we may rest more firmly upon Him.*
—*Christian Herald* (London)

* * *

"Called! Held! Kept!"

Frances Havergal, the song writer, lived and moved in the Word of God. His Word was her constant companion.

On the last day of her life, she asked a friend to read to her the 42nd chapter of Isaiah. When the friend read the sixth verse, "I the Lord have called thee in righteousness, and will hold thine hand, and will keep thee," Miss Havergal stopped her. She whispered, "Called — held — kept. I can go home on that!" And she did go home on that. She found His promises unfailing.

—Pentecostal Evangel

* * *

"These Men I Know!"

A great battle was impending. The commander was inspecting his troops. Turning from a mass of undisciplined, inexperienced men before him, he said to one of his generals: "These men I know nothing about." Then, as his eye ran over a body of men who had been with him for a short time and knew something of march, bivouac, and battlefield, he said: "These men *I think* I can trust." Finally he turned to a division of troops who had been with him in all of his campaigns. They were the veterans of his army. They had been baptized in blood and fire in many a fierce and deadly struggle. As they stood before him with set lips and stern countenances, ready, and waiting for the onset of the coming battle, the great commander turned from them with a heart pulsing with pride and confidence, and said quietly to his officers: "These men *I know* I can trust."

How shall we become men and women whom God can trust? How shall we shun the calamity of a continuous spiritual babehood, stunted in growth and blighted in fruitage?

—James H. McConkey

* * *

We Can Trust the King

A skillful surgeon recently undertook the responsibility of performing a serious operation on the eyes of an Eastern monarch which proved highly successful. After the king's recovery the problem of presenting his account puzzled the doctor, for he was dubious as to what figure would correctly estimate the value of the result achieved; as in Eastern countries it is a serious wrong to charge the king more or less than the actual value. Taking a blank billhead the doctor wrote across it: "The king can do no wrong," and respectfully submitted it to the monarch. His answer was a letter enclosing a sum far beyond his highest hopes. When we know not what to pray for, let us leave it to our Heavenly King who doeth all things well.

—Christian Herald

* * *

"If We Can't Hold Out!"

The preacher had delivered himself of one of those eloquent sermons during which he cited all the learned authorities to document his erudite lecture. There were many pretty passages and flights of eloquence — not too much old-fashioned religion. At the end he had quoted Kipling's great poem entitled "If." In this poem he had reached the climax of his lecture. "If you can keep your head when all about you are losing theirs — if you can dare to place all you have in one toss and come back smiling if you lose . . ." Some young war veteran at the back of the auditorium wailed out in a broken, sobbing voice: "But, Brother, suppose we can't hold out? What will help us IF we are not made of the stuff that endures?" The modern erudite preacher had no answer. A little, old, wrinkled lady looked at the young man, and smiled: "I'll tell you, mister. That's where Jesus comes in. Jesus can take all those IF'S and put forward-looking faces on them."

—The Way of The Cross

* * *

Let God Rule

Oliver Cromwell's secretary was dispatched to the continent on some important business. He stayed one night at a seaport town, and tossed on his bed, unable to sleep.

According to an old custom, a servant slept in his room, and on this occasion slept soundly enough. The secretary at length awakened the man who asked how it was that his master could not rest.

"I am so afraid something will go wrong with the embassage," was the reply.

"Master," said the valet, "may I ask a question or two?"

"To be sure."

"Did God rule the world before we were born?"

"Most assuredly He did."

"And will He rule it after we are dead?"

"Certainly He will."

"Then, master, why not let Him rule the present, too?"

The secretary's faith was stirred, peace was the result, and in a few minutes both he and his servant were in sound sleep.   —*Gleanings*

* * *

Revised Version

Five-year-old Mary had been drilled thoroughly on the 23rd Psalm for the Children's day program.

Frightened by the spectators, she began haltingly, "The Lord is my . . ."

"Yes, go on honey," the pastor urged.

Again she started, "The Lord is . . ." The rest was forgotten.

"Come on, darling, you can finish it."

With a deep breath and a big sigh Mary rattled, "The Lord is my shepherd, I should worry."   —*Sunday*

* * *

Everything O. K.

I rather like the small boy's version of the hymn, "Trust and Obey," when he said that at Sunday school they had been singing "Trust and O. K." Good! Everything must be O.K. if the life has been committed to His precious keeping. There is no other way.
—*Expositor*

* * *

That's for Sure

Trust in yourself, and you are doomed to disappointment;

Trust in your friends, and they will die and leave you;

Trust in money, and you may have it taken from you;

Trust in reputation, and some slanderous tongue may blast it;

But — Trust in God, and you are never to be confounded in time or eternity.
—*Power*

More Than Man Can Manage

Sir Robert Peel was found one day praying over a bundle of letters. His friend apologized for disturbing him in his private devotions. "No," said Peel, "these are my public devotions. I was just giving the affairs of state into the hands of God, for I cannot manage them myself."

—*Sunday School Teacher*

* * *

"O, Mommy, Give Jesus A Chance To Work!"

Mother gazed in consternation at the seemingly expanding bump on Bobby's head. Bobby, six-years-old, had just come home from school. "How did you get such a bump? Who hit you?" enquired the anxious mother. "Were you fighting the other children?" Then said the mother, "Come here, let me put cold compresses on it right away!!" Backing toward his bedroom door, little Bobby pleaded, "Jus' a minute, please. I want to talk to Jesus!" His private session over, he went cheerfully to play. But a few moments later, his mother called him for the application of the aforementioned cold compresses. Whereupon, Bobby questioned, "Aw, Mommy, why don't you give Jesus a chance?"

—W. B. K.

* * *

"Though He Slay Me!"

The London City Mission Magazine gives the following touching account of the suffering of one of the thousands of women injured in air raids:

She was buried under the ruins of her little home for six-and-a-half hours, gravely injured, and her little baby daughter was killed. After about five weeks in the hospital she realized she was blinded for life. Her nurse shed tears of sympathy, and the patient comforted her, saying, "No eyes! Oh, but yes I have, nurse. I've got a spiritual vision no bomb can destroy. I've seen Jesus at Calvary, and how precious He is to me now!"

—*Sunday School Times*

Not Half Enough

Mrs. Goforth, well-known missionary to China, relates: "A dear daughter of ours felt hurt that we should have a salary insufficient for our needs, but we assured her that to trust God for what was lacking was not begging. The day came when this daughter and myself took possession of our new home. As we entered the dining room we found a large mail from China on the table. One letter was from the lady in Australia whose gifts in the past seemed always to have met some felt need. Her letter enclosed fifty pounds, with the expressed desire that thirty pounds was to be used for our work in China and twenty pounds was to be used for some personal need. I handed the letter to my daughter, saying: "Shall we not believe that God will undertake for us in time of need? It seems as if our Heavenly Father were beside us saying, 'My child, take this hundred dollars as an earnest of what I shall do for you in the future.'" Tears stood in the eyes of my daughter as she gave back the letter, saying, "Mother, we don't trust God half enough."

—Free Methodist

* * *

"Until I Learned to Trust"

"Until I learned to trust,
I never learned to pray;
And I did not fully learn to trust,
Till sorrow came my way.

"Who deepest drinks of sorrow,
Drinks deepest, too, of grace;
He sends the storm so He, Himself,
Can be our hiding place!"

—Selected

* * *

In the Hollow of His Hand

During an earthquake, a few years ago, the inhabitants of a small village were very much alarmed.

One old woman, whom they all knew, was surprisingly calm and joyous.

At length, one of them said to her, "Mother, are you not afraid?"

"No. I rejoice to know that I have a God who can shake the world."

—New Century Leader

* * *

Safely to the Other Side

A great man once said that of all the experiences of his life that he could remember, there was nothing that gave him such unmixed joy as when, on a crowded street of a great city, a little child looked up into his face, and put his tiny hand in his great one, and said, "Take me across the street to the other side." It was an honor to the strong man to take that trusting child across the street to the other side. Are there not streets ahead for you to cross? Is there some difficulty that you must meet, and do you need a strong arm to take you over to the other side? Put your hand in the hand of Christ. Simple confidence in Him will delight His heart.

—L. S., in
Choice Gleanings Calendar

* * *

Why He Could Sleep

A wild storm was raging around a prairie home. The windows were blown in, and no lights could be kept burning. The mother, grandmother, and three children sat in the darkness in a room on the sheltered side of the house, fearing that any moment it might be swept from its foundation. Suddenly eleven-year-old Walter was missed; he had been holding a whispered conversation with his grandmother a few minutes before. Frantic with fear, the mother called at the top of her voice, but got no answer, and started to grope in the darkness to find him. She found him in his room fast asleep! And when she asked him how he could go to sleep when they were all in danger, he simply replied, "Why, Grandma told me God would take care of us, and I thought I might as well go to bed again."

—New York Observer

UNBELIEF

Why the Limited was Wrecked

Some years ago a fearful railroad wreck took a dreadful toll of life and limb in an Eastern state. A train, loaded with young people returning from school, was stalled on a suburban track because of what is known as a "hot-box." The limited was soon due, but a flagman was sent back to warn the engineer in order to avert a rear-end collision. Thinking all was well, the crowd laughed and chatted while the train-hands worked on in fancied security. Suddenly the whistle of the limited was heard and on came the heavy train and crashed into the local, with horrible effect.

The engineer of the limited saved his own life by jumping, and some days afterwards was hailed into court to account for his part in the calamity. And now a curious discrepancy in testimony occurred. He was asked, "Did you not see the flagman warning you to stop?"

He replied, "I saw him, but he waved a yellow flag, and I took it for granted all was well, and so went on, though slowing down."

The flagman was called. "What flag did you wave?"

"A red flag, but he went by me like a shot."

"Are you sure it was red?"

"Absolutely."

Both insisted on the correctness of their testimony, and it was demonstrated that neither was color-blind. Finally the man was asked to produce the flag itself as evidence. After some delay he was able to do so, and then the mystery was explained. *It had been red,* but it had been exposed to the weather so long that all the red was bleached out, and it was *a dirty yellow!*

Oh, the lives eternally wrecked by the yellow gospels of the day — the bloodless theories of unregenerate men that send their hearers to their doom instead of stopping them on their downward road!

—Dr. Harry A. Ironside

Better Than No Light At All!

I cannot forget the confusion into which I saw a conceited young fellow thrown once, when he turned to an aged minister and, as if challenging discussion, said, "I am told you believe in the inspiration of the whole Bible." The good man answered quietly, "Oh, yes, my friend; and what do you believe in?" A little laugh covered the defeat, but he continued, "But you certainly know what the great scholars say about it?" Again the calm answer met him: "Somewhat; but what did they say to you about your soul?" Now the inquirer grew restive. "They say you are leading men along with a farthing taper in your lantern." To this the aged preacher only said, "Do they say men would see any better if we would let them put the taper out?"

—*Moody Monthly*

* * *

When the Word Critizes Us.

We live in a day when man is criticizing God's Word. Modernism is emasculating it, modern cults are perverting it, and the world is neglecting it. Dr. W. H. Griffith Thomas once said that the word "discerner" in the Greek of Hebrews 4:12, R. V., should be translated "critic" — "a critic of the thoughts and intents of the heart," and he added, "It is the only place in the Bible where the word 'critic' is found, and you notice that it is the Word criticizing us, and if we allowed the Word of God to criticize us a little more, we would criticize it a great deal less."

—*Sunday School Times*

* * *

Something to Die By

A young woman was deeply convicted, felt the weight of her sin and knew that it was separating her from God. She sent for her pastor, who was a godless man. When he arrived she told him about her condition and that she needed the mercy of God. This man who had never known the mercy of God, informed the young woman that she was all excited by overtaxing her mind. He told her that she was all right, and all that she needed was to join the church. She took him at his word and he received her into the church, but only a few months later she again sent for this same pastor. He came into her home, and this time not only found her deeply convicted because of her sin, but seriously ill. To him she said, "Sir, I trusted you in the matter of my soul's salvation. I united with your church, but now I find that my sin is between me and God. Your religion seemed very well as long as I was physically strong, but now I want something to die by. What will you offer me?"

—*Moody Monthly*

Mystery Doesn't Bother in the Dining Room

Did you ever raise a radish? You put a small black seed into the black soil, and in a little while you return to the garden and find the full grown radish. The top is green, the body white and almost transparent, and the skin a delicate red or pink. What mysterious power reaches out and gathers from the ground the particles which give it form and size and flavor? Whose is the invisible brush that transfers to the root, growing in darkness, the hues of the summer sunset? If we were to refuse to eat anything until we could understand the mystery of its creation we would die of starvation — but mystery, it seems, never bothers us in the dining room; it is only in the church that it causes us to hesitate. —*Moody Monthly*

UNSHACKLED

The Way Out

James Bryant came out of a drunken home in which Mother as well as Father were victims of the brewer and he was soon himself a pitiable beer slave. After he was married and had a little son he tried to break away from this habit in his own strength, but failed miserably. A city missionary persuaded him to attend a street meeting. At the close of the meeting Jim told the missionary of his utter helplessness and hopelessness. The missionary replied: "When we were without strength, in due time Christ died for the ungodly;" then added, "As many as received him, to them gave he power to become the sons of God, even to them that believe on his name." On the way home Jim said to himself, "If it is true what this man says, there is a way out." At home he knelt in prayer, repeating the texts the missionary had taught him; but nothing happened. Unable to bear it longer, about three o'clock in the morning he went down on his knees the second time. He repeated the verses and added, "O God, deliver me from this curse. Give me the power to become a child of God." Jim says: "In a moment, He broke the power of canceled sin, He set the prisoner free. It was instantaneous. I rose from my knees, born again by God's Holy Spirit. He took the desire to do evil out of my heart and in its place put the desire to do good. I was a new creature in Christ Jesus."

—*Sunday School Times*

* * *

Transformed Lives!

As Dr. Harry A. Ironside preached in a certain place, he noticed a man in the crowd writing on a card, which he presently handed to the speaker. The man was Arthur Lewis, agnostic lecturer, and he proposed a challenge to the speaker to debate the subject, "Agnosticism versus Christianity," and offered to pay all expenses involved.

Dr. Ironside read the card aloud to his audience and then said: "I accept on these conditions:

"First, that you promise to bring with you to the platform one man who was once an outcast, a slave to sinful habits, but who heard you or some other infidel lecture on agnosticism, was helped by it and cast away his sins and became a new man and is today a respected member of society, all because of your unbelief.

"Second, that you agree to bring with you one woman who was once lost to all purity and goodness, but who can now testify that agnosticism came to her while deep in sin and implanted in her poor heart a hatred of impurity and a love of holiness, causing her to become chaste and upright, all through a disbelief in the Bible.

"Now, sir," he continued, "if you will agree, I promise to be there with one hundred such men and women, once just such lost souls, who heard the gospel of the grace of God, believed it and have found new life and joy in Jesus Christ our Saviour. Will you accept my terms?"

As might be expected, the atheist could only walk away silently.

—*Evangelical Christian*

* * *

"Wake Up, You're Dreaming!"

"Wake up, old man; you're dreaming," yelled a passerby to a converted drunkard who was testifying to the saving power of Christ in a street meeting. The converted drunkard's little daughter, standing nearby, plead thus, "O, please sir, don't wake him up! Before he began dreaming, as you say, he would beat up Mom and me, and didn't provide for us. But now, since he has begun to dream, as you say, he is good to Mom and me, and he brings home his money and provides for us.. O, please sir, let him dream on! Don't wake him up!"

—W. B. K.

* * *

The Incurable Inebriate!

A man named Henry Milans lay in a ward of Bellevue Hospital, N. Y. A group of students stood around his bed, while the instructing professor remarked: "We have discovered in this man all the marked indications of the incurable inebriate. Note the dancing eyes. Note the trembling of the hands and other members of his body. . . . This man can never be cured. He must die as he has lived, a drunkard. Nothing can save him." Not long after, Ensign Hall of the Salvation Army describes

what happened. "Amid the fervent 'Hallelujahs!' of Christians in the hall Milans stumbled forward. . . . The change that took place in him was remarkable. What science was unable to do Christ accomplished in a moment. Nineteen years after his conversion, he testified: 'From that moment to the present I have never been tempted to take a drink of anything with alcohol in it. I should have to learn all over again to love the drink that was for thirty-five years the greatest love of my life.'"

—*The Dawn*

* * *

Made New!

God does not deal in secondhand goods. It is "new" or nothing with Him. So when we bring Him our worthless secondhand lives — our sin-defeated, wrecked, worthless lives — for Him to make whatever improvements He is able to, He has a glad surprise for us. He does not offer to repair or reform; but He offers to create, "to make all things new." It has been well said that "the only way to mend wicked things is to end them."

—*Sunday School Times*

* * *

Born Again!

Clarence Darrow once remarked, "You can make nothing of man but man, selfish, mean, tyrannical, aggressive. That's what man is and a lot more. It is useless to try to change him." *Of the natural man this is true, but "if any man can be in Christ, he is a new creature."*

—*Moody Monthly*

* * *

The New Life

That great California scientist of yours, Luther Burbank, . . . takes a tree that has been going to the bad for some reason or other for years, and at last has become altogether ugly and noxious, and by the shock of a new creation he breaks up all its old habits, turns its energies into fresh channels, and makes of it a lovely and fruitful thing. And if your magician can work that miracle, and break up the habits of the tree and make of it a new thing, beautiful and fruitful, why should it be thought a thing incredible that God can break a man off from his past, and re-create him in the image of righteousness and true holiness?

—*Northfield Calendar*

* * *

Worried About Sins!

A Hindu was worried about his sins. In his despair he came to the priest and asked what he should do to get relief. The priest said, "If you will drive spikes in your shoes and walk five hundred miles, you will get over it." He drove the spikes in his shoes and started on his pilgrimage, suffering intensely at every step.

Once he sat down to rest near where a man was telling how Christ could free men from sin and give them peace. When he heard the good news, he drew off his spike-shoes and threw them as far as he could and cried, "That's what I want, give me Jesus! Give me Jesus!"

—*Sunday School Times*

* * *

"The Human Tiger!"

A French explorer was crossing Africa from the Zambezi, and came into the region of the Barotsi people. He heard stories about the native king Lewanika, whose greatest delight had been to put to death, by newly invented tortures, those who offended him, and who was known as the "human tiger." This French officer came to the station where Pastor Coillard was in charge, and the pastor himself, a Frenchman, entertained him kindly. Then came Sunday. The French officer was absolutely without God, but as a matter of politeness he went to church and sat through the service. When he came out he said, "Monsieur Coillard, who was that remarkable looking man sitting next to me, who listened so carefully?" "That was King Lewanika, the 'human tiger.'" "Was it?" "Yes." "Then if that is what Christ can do, I mean to be His."

—*Hubert Brooke*

Just As I Am

A little girl, anxious about her soul, waited at the close of one of Moody's meetings. One worker advised her to "Read the Bible." Another to "Pray to God." In agony of soul she went home, got on her knees, and cried, "O Lord, I cannot read, I cannot pray; so take me as I am."

—*Gospel Herald*

* * *

"Do You Believe in Your Own Sins?"

A pastor in New York urged an intellectual but dissipated man to become a Christian. The man replied, "I cannot believe in the inspiration of the Bible, in the deity of Christ, or in prayer." "Do you believe in your own sins?" asked the pastor. "Oh, yes," replied the honest soul; "there is no doubt about my being a sinner, and sometimes I am in hell!" "Are you willing to bring your sins to Christ for forgiveness and let Him, whatever you think of Him, take your guilt?" "But," he said, "I can't believe in the inspiration of the Bible, or in the deity of Christ, or in prayer." "Just now," persisted the wise pastor, "I am not asking you to believe these things. You know you are a sinner, and in sin there is a taste of hell. Now, I offer you Jesus Christ as your Saviour from sin. Will you accept Him as such, and leave all questions that puzzle you for future solution?" The man went to his home and that night he accepted the Christ he knew as his Saviour, and came to the meeting the next night to tell the people the joy of forgiveness that was in his soul. After several days of joyful testimony which led others to Christ, the pastor gently asked, "What do you think NOW of the deity of Christ?" "Such a Saviour," he said, with great emotion, "must be divine; if He were not divine He could not have done what He has done for me!"

—*Dr. A. C. Dixon*

* * *

Able to the Uttermost

In a Methodist mission hall there was advertised to sing a men's choir of forty voices. There they were, ranged on the platform, ready to take their part in the service. Their appearance was not that of trained singers. When they sang there was more heartiness than finish about their performance. Their songs were of the Sankey type, and when they came to the refrains there was an abandonment about their singing that was rather alarming. But their faces glowed and their bodies moved to the rhythmic sway of the song. I asked the missionary who they were, and he replied: "Every one of them has been pulled out of the gutter. They were drunkards and profligates but we have won them and saved them. They were a disgrace to the neighborhood, now they are a credit to all and a splendid proof of what Christ can do."

—*Religious Experience*

* * *

"Worth Trying!"

An old, one-eyed panhandler approached a Christian. He had two coppers in a dirty hand. He asked for three more "for a cup of coffee." Said the Christian,

"My brother, you have served the Devil for years, and all he has done for you is to land you here on this street with a lie on your lips, and a thirst in your throat."

I pulled a quarter from my pocket and said, "I am going to give you this, but first I want to tell you about Jesus Christ, who loves you and wants to save you, and make a real man out of you."

He explained the way of salvation. The man said, "If the Lord loves me, as you say, why don't he do something for me?"

"Did you ever ask Him?"

He never had. O, that lost men would ask Him to come into their hearts!

—W. B. K.

* * *

"Then Jesus Came!"

Testified a converted Chinaman, "I was fallen into a deep pit of sin. I was sinking in the mire. I called for help. Along came Confucius. I implored him to reach down and help me. He, however, proceeded calmly to instruct me on right living. He passed on. He could

not save me. Sinking deeper, I cried, 'Help me! Help me now!' Looking up, I saw Buddha. He began to preach to me, saying, 'My son; be quiet, be patient; retire to the inward calm and center of your heart. There you will find Nirvana, eternal rest.! He, too, passed on. I was ready to sink in despair. Looking up again, however. I saw One who said, 'My child, I have come to save you! Will you let me?' Crying out, I said, 'Lord, help me! Lord, save me!' Getting down into the pit, He put His arms about me and lifted me up! He told me that His Name was JESUS! I fell at His feet and said, 'Lord, I will follow Thee!' "

—W. B. K.

* * *

How Christ Saves

A man who had been converted from a sinful life gave this experience of his acceptance with Jesus: "I just crept to the feet of Jesus, and greatly to my astonishment He did not scold me — He knew I had been scolded enough; and He did not pity me; and He did not give me any advice, either. He knew that I had plenty of that. He just put His arms around my neck and loved me. I was a new man."

—*The Presbyterian Record*

* * *

When a Poor Drunkard Went In

I was speaking in a Methodist church in Washington, D. C., and at the close of the service a very fine-looking gentleman came up to me. When he was within ten feet of me, I smelled the liquor on his breath. He said, "Dr. Wilson, can you take me to God and ask Him to do something to me that will make me what I ought to be?" I had never had a man ask me that in my life, and I had been preaching forty-seven years. We knelt together by the front bench, and I prayed: "Lord Jesus, here is a man that liquor has down — sin has him down. You are the Saviour from sin. I am bringing this man to You for You to be his creator, for You to change him and make him what he ought to be. Will you do it?" Then I spoke to the man, and I said, "You ask

Him yourself." "Oh, Jesus, if You can change me, do change me tonight," he prayed. "I want You to do it, and I am coming to You for it." I whispered into his ear, "The blood of Jesus Christ his Son cleanseth us from all sin." The dear fellow bowed his head again and said: "Thank You, Lord Jesus. You came to save me, and I am going to let YOU do it right now." When he arose, the tears were running down his cheeks. His precious wife came hurrying up the aisle. She threw her arms around him and said, "Oh, my prayers are answered!" He said, "Yes, they are, dear; Jesus Christ changed me tonight."

—Dr. Walter L. Wilson, in
"Waves of Truth"

* * *

John Newton's Re-birth

John Newton who ran away to sea, and then to Africa, was sold at last to a negress. He sank so low that he lived only on crumbs from her table and on wild yams dug at night. His clothing was reduced to a single shirt which he washed in the ocean. When he finally escaped, he went to the natives, accepting their base life. It does not seem possible for a civilized man to have sunk so low, but the power of God laid hold on him through a missionary. He became a sea captain; later became a minister. He wrote many hymns sung the world around: "Safely through Another Week," "Come, My Soul," "Glorious Things of Thee Are Spoken," "How Sweet the Name of Jesus Sounds," "One There Is Above All Others."

In the church of London of which he was the pastor, there is still an epitaph which John Newton wrote for himself. It reads: "Sacred to the memory of John Newton, once a libertine and blasphemer and slave of slaves in Africa, but renewed, purified, pardoned, and appointed to preach that Gospel which he had laboured to destroy!"   —*Quiet Hour Stories*

* * *

Getting The "Slums" Out Of Man

It is one thing to get a man out of the "slums." It is an altogether different thing to get the "slum" out of a man. This occurs when a man, through

faith in the Saviour becomes a "new creature in Christ." A missionary from Africa was asked, "Have you gotten those terrible cannibals to a place yet where they do not eat each other?" "No, but we have succeeded in getting them to use knives and forks!"
.   —W. B. K.

* * *

Waiting for Darkness, She Found the Light

One Sunday evening, in his own church, Dr. Hall was delivering a written sermon on temptation, and suddenly felt that his address was unlike his usual style, and too argumentative for many of the people. He paused, looked away from his manuscript, and, appealing with a loud voice to the more distant of his audience, said: "Perhaps among those pressing in at the door there may be someone so miserable as to think of throwing himself over yonder bridge, saying, 'It's too late to tell me not to enter into temptation. I have done it; I am in it. There's no hope for me!' Stop! Stop! There is hope. Christ died for thee. He will forgive. He will save even thee!" A few weeks afterward one of the members of his church told him that he had called to see a woman who had made up her mind to throw herself over Blackfriars Bridge, one Sunday evening, but she thought it was too light and a policeman might stop her; so in order to wait for the darkness she went into the church and stood in the crowd inside the door. Standing there it seemed to her that Dr. Hall had called to her directly to stop, and come to Christ, and she went back to her home to pray, and became a true and happy Christian.

—*Bible Expositor and Illuminator*

* * *

Able to Save to the Uttermost

The Rev. Joseph Hocking writes: "I was the speaker at a Sunday afternoon meeting at Whitefield's Tabernacle. I took for my text the Bible story of the man possessed with a demon. I said that some in my audience that afternoon might be in the condition of that man, drink-ridden, lust-sodden, demon-possessed, and I declared that Christ could

713

even now, as in those far-off days, completely and forever drive out the unclean spirit from such a man. Then something occurred which quite electrified both the large audience and myself. A man in the body of the hall arose and said aloud, 'Sir, I am that man! I am drink-ridden, lust-sodden, demon-possessed! Can your Christ save me?' I answered, 'Yes, *He Can.*' And when the meeting was over the man came humbly and penitently to Christ there and then. He was veritably born again, and became one of the best Christian workers in that mission."

—*Free Churchman*

* * *

"From Mire and Slime of Sin"

The beloved American poet Longfellow could take an ordinary sheet of paper, write some lines on it and make it worth several thousand dollars and we call that genius. A mechanic takes material worth six dollars and makes an article worth sixty and we term that skill. The artist selects a piece of canvas, paints a scene on it and increases its value a thousand times and we say this is art. Jesus Christ reaches down into the mire of sin and picks up the remains of a blasted life and "by the washing of regeneration, and the renewing of the Holy Ghost" He produces "a new creature: old things pass away and behold all things become new" and we call this Salvation.

— *Holiness Missionary Colporteur*

* * *

When God Took Hold of a Convert

Anthony Zeoli, though a Roman Catholic, faithful in attendance at Mass, was also a dope fiend and all-round crook who would pick the pockets of his kneeling fellow worshipers. He says, "I used to pray morning and night. I would not pull off a job with any other criminal except I first prayed about it. I would tell my pals to pray before we burglared a house. When they said they knew no prayer I told them the prayer to pray." Zeoli's career as gangster and gunman in the Philadelphia underworld brought him finally to prison. There a New Testament fell into his hands, which two colored youths, also converts, expounded

to him. As a result, he fell on his knees, crying, "God, be merciful to me a sinner!" It was a fresh illustration of divine mercy, for in a moment the old life and its appetites passed away forever, and Convict 9924 was a new creature in Christ Jesus. The next day he went into the prison yard to preach the Gospel, and the first person he met was the prison chaplain. "I asked him why he didn't tell the prisoners about Jesus and how to get rid of sin. I started immediately to witness to all the convicts, 1,600 of them, and most of all to my companion in crime." The latter was obstinate and refused. Both he and Zeoli left prison at the same time, one to die of an overdose of dope, and the other to become a flaming evangelist. —*Sunday School Times*

* * *

"Only One Line of A Sunday School Verse!"

F. Mitchell, at Keswick, told of an old woman he had met. She said, "I was a terrible drunkard. I used to go out at six o'clock in the morning, as people were going to work, and sing for a few coppers; then I waited for the earliest hour when the public house opened.

"One morning I was making my way back to my filthy, unkempt, and barely furnished home. The thirst for drink was so terrible that I was becoming desperate, and I had two or three hours to wait for the opening of the public house. Arriving home I knelt down on the dirty floor, and the only thing I knew was one line of a hymn — 'Jesus loves me, this I know' — I did not know the rest, and I prayed, 'If that is so, Jesus, do something for me.' Instantly I was set gloriously free."

Mr. Mitchell added: "Some of you Sunday school teachers may take heart from that. You may teach a child a verse of Scripture or a simple hymn containing a divine truth, and he may go out into the world and forget it for years, but the seed is buried there. When I saw this woman, for ten or fifteen years she had been living in a drunkard's home and walking in the midst of old defilement without being touched." —*Keswick Week*

VICTORY

How Will You Enter?

There are two ways of entering port. A ship may come in, waterlogged and crazy, just kept afloat by continual working at the pumps; or it may enter with every sail set, her pennon floating at the masthead. The latter is what Peter, the apostle, desired for himself and those whom he addressed. An abundant entrance is really a choral entrance. The idea may be illustrated from the entrance of a Roman conqueror to his city, whence he had been sent out to war. Amid the crowds of spectators, the procession climbed slowly to the capital, while sweet incense was poured on the air, and music raised her sweetest and most inspiring strains. Will your entrance into Heaven be like that?

—F. B. Meyer

* * *

Invictus — The Captain

Over against W. E. Henley's braggart lines which he entitled "Invictus" ("Unconquered"), are to be set Dorothea's Day's verses, "My Captain," which might be entitled "More than Conqueror":

Invictus

Out of the night that covers me,
Black as the pit from pole to pole,
I thank whatever gods may be
For my unconquerable soul.

In the fell clutch of circumstance
I have not winced or cried aloud,
Under the bludgeoning of chance
My head is bloody, but unbowed.

Beyond this place of wrath and tears
Looms but the horror of the shade;
And yet the menace of the years
Finds, and shall find me, unafraid.

It matters not how strait the gate,
How charged with punishment the scroll,
I am the master of my fate;
I am the captain of my soul.

My Captain

Out of the light that dazzles me,
Bright as the sun from pole to pole,
I thank the God I know to be
For Christ — the Conqueror of my soul.

Since His the sway of circumstance
I would not wince, nor cry aloud.
Under that rule which men call chance,
My head, with joy, is humbly bowed.

Beyond this place of sin and tears,
That life with Him! and His the aid
That, spite the menace of the years,
Keeps, and will keep, me unafraid.

I have no fear though strait the gate;
He cleared from punishment the scroll.
Christ is the Master of my fate;
Christ is the Captain of my soul!

—Selected

* * *

Little — Much

Little of the Word with little prayer is death to the spiritual life. Much of the Word with little prayer gives a sickly life. Much prayer with little of the Word gives emotional life. But a full measure of both the Word and prayer each day gives a healthy and powerful life.   —Andrew Murray

* * *

Crisis and Process

To one who asked him the secret of his service, George Muller said: "There was a day when I died, *utterly died;*" and, as he spoke, he bent lower and lower until he almost touched the floor — "died to George Muller, his opinions, preferences, tastes, and will — died to the world, its approval or censure — died to the approval or blame even of my brethren and friends — and since then I have studied only to show myself approved unto God."

—British Weekly

* * *

"I Fret at Nothing!"

John Wesley's message of salvation by grace through faith turned England

upside down in the eighteenth century. His message of "Christian perfection" has led multitudes of Christians to hunger after holiness of life and to enter into victory. Some find flaws in his theology when he explains holiness, but all testify that he lived a miracle life, free of care when he had a thousand reasons for care, and often with no sense af weariness after herculean labors for Christ. "I feel and grieve," he writes, "but by the grace of God, I fret at nothing."
—Robert C. McQuilkin, D.D., in *Sunday School Times*

* * *

Hudson Taylor's "Exchanged Life"

Hudson Taylor at thirty-seven, already a mighty man of faith and a great missionary warrior, was longing for a victory he did not have. He was often restless and irritated, defeated in his prayer life, a struggling Christian, wondering if there was not something better for him. He read a letter from a fellow missionary of the China Inland Mission, one little known, who told his director out of a full heart how he had come into joy and peace and victory. Hudson Taylor "saw it in a flash," he writes and his "exchanged life" began: the miracle of Christ working out through him. Hudson Taylor was a great missionary and a great Christian to begin with. But that was not the secret of what he found. Quite otherwise. He wrote the guardian of his children in England to teach them in their young years not only God's plan of salvation by grace, through faith, to make them Christians; but God's plan of present salvation by grace, through faith, to enable them to live a victorious life.
—Robert C. McQuilkin, D.D., in *Sunday School Times*

* * *

"Let God"

A young man, who was struggling to let the Lord have His way in his life, knelt to pray. He had been advised to "Let God do the work for him." But as he was kneeling, he cried, "I want to let God have His way, but I can't.

The day before he had cut out of paste-board the letters "LET GOD" and tacked them on the wall. He rose from his knees and with a feeling of defeat and despair, he left the room and slammed the door with a bang, saying, "I can't 'LET GOD.'"

On his return to his room, he was startled to note that the slam of the door had loosened the letter D on the word GOD causing it to fall to the floor, and changing the motto to "LET GO."

"I will, I will, Lord Jesus," he cried and threw himself on his knees at the side of his bed. "I will '*Let go*,' and '*Let God*,' " and he did.
—*Gospel for the Youth*

* * *

Turning Storm Cloud Into Chariot

An eagle sits on a crag and watches the sky as it is filling with blackness, and the forked lightnings are playing up and down. He is sitting perfectly still . . . until he begins to feel the burst of the breeze and knows the hurricane has struck him. Then he swings his breast to the storm, and uses the storm to go up to the sky. Away he goes, borne upward upon it. That is what God wants of every one of His children — to be more than conqueror, turning the storm cloud into a chariot.
—*Sunday School Times*

* * *

Christ for Victory

"We are a supernatural people, born again by a supernatural birth; we wage a supernatural fight and are taught by a supernatural teacher, led by a supernatural captain to assured victory."
—J. Hudson Taylor

* * *

A Branch of the Tree of Knowledge

In a large pottery factory, the foreman, John Foster, was a Christian, and a great temptation came to him while engaged in his work. The president of the concern, who always prepared his formulas in a little private office, was called downstairs, and carelessly laid his formula book lying open on his desk.

716

Foster had to go into the room for some colors, where he saw lying open before him the priceless formula book. It contained secrets of immense value and he could quickly copy some of them. There were plenty of men who would gladly avail themselves of going into business with him if he could produce a chinaware equal to that made at this celebrated pottery. He could be rich. Many thoughts of what he might accomplish passed through his mind, but soon the struggle ended, for he had looked upward. He closed the little book, and holding it aloft, said to himself: "Hallelujah! Victory through Christ!" He then sought the president and handed him the book. He continued a humble decorator with the concern for many years, but there was real joy in his soul in the knowledge that he was right with God.

—Keith L. Brooks

* * *

Not Alone

"I cannot do it alone;
   The waves run fast and high,
And the fogs close all around,
   The light goes out in the sky;
But I know that we two
   Shall win in the end,
      Jesus and I.

I could not guide it myself,
   My boat on life's wild sea;
There's one who sits by my side,
   Who pulls and steers with me.
And I know that we two
   Shall safe enter port,
      Jesus and I."

—*Selected*

* * *

Suggestions for Victorious Living:

Forget each kindness that you do as soon as you have done it.

Forget the praise that falls to you the moment you have won it.

Forget the slander that you hear before you can repeat nt.

Forget each slight, each spite, each sneer, wherever you may meet it.

Remember every kindness done to you whate'er its measure.

Remember praise by others won and pass it on with pleasure.

Remember every promise made and keep it to the letter;

Remember those who lend you aid and be a grateful debtor.

Remember all the happiness that comes your way in living:

Forget each worry and distress, be hopeful and forgiving;

Remember good, remember truth, remember heaven's above you,

And you will find through age and youth that many hearts will love you.

—*Selected*

* * *

"If—"

If you can trust when everyone about you
   Is doubting Him, proclaiming Him untrue;
If you can hope in Christ, tho' all forsake you
   And say 'tis not the thing for you to do;

If you can wait on God, nor wish to hurry,
   Or, being greatly used, keep humble still;
Or if you're tested, still refuse to worry,
   And so remain within His sovereign will;

If you can say, 'tis well, when sorrow greets you,
   And death has taken those you hold most dear;
If you can smile when adverse trials meet you,
   And be content e'en tho' your lot be drear;

If you can be reviled and never murmur,
   Or being tempted, not give way to sin;
If you fight for right and stand the firmer,
   Or lose the battle when you ought to win —

If you can really long for His appearing,
   And therefore set your heart on things above;

Victory in Christ

If you can speak for Christ in spite of
    sneering,
  Or to the most unlovely one show love;

If you can hear the call of God to labour,
  And answer, "Yes" in yieldedness and
    trust,
And go to tell the story of the Saviour
  To souls in darkness o'er the desert
    dust;

If you can pray when Satan's darts are
    strongest,
  And take the road of faith instead of
    sight;
Or walk with God, e'en tho' His way be
    longest,
  And swerve not to the left nor to the
    right;

If you desire Himself alone to fill you,
  For Him alone you care to live and
    be;
Then 'tis not you, but CHRIST Who
  dwelleth in you,
  And that, O child of God, is victory!
        —*Selected*

* * *

Victory

An Indian, in explaining the conflict
of the two natures in man, said, "It
seems to me as though two dogs are
fighting within me: one is a black dog,
and he is very savage and very bad;
the other is a white dog, and he is very
gentle and very good, but the black dog
fights with him all the time." "And
which dog wins?" some one asked.
Laconically, the Indian replied, "Which
ever one I say 'sic him' to!" And it was
well put, for if the will is on the side
of the evil, the flesh will triumph; but
if the will is subdued by grace and subject to the Holy Spirit, the new nature
will control.   —H. A. Ironside

* * *

This Is the Victory!

To feel the tempter's mighty power —
  Without appeal,
To know the pull that money has —
  And never kneel,
To be entranced by honor's glare —
  And have no urge,

To hear the voice of passing pomp —
  And not submerge,
To be uplifted, lauded high —
  And sense no pride,
To gain an orator's great fame —
  And never stride,
To be exalted to the skies —
  Yet self disdain,
To be contemned and set aside —
  And not complain,
    THIS IS VICTORY!
      —R. E. Neighbour, D.D.

* * *

The Tide Is Sure to Win!

On the far reef the breakers
  Recoil in shattered foam,
Yet still the sea behind them
  Urges its forces home;
Its chant of triumph surges
  Through all the thunderous din —
The wave may break in failure,
  But the tide is sure to win!

The reef is strong and cruel;
  Upon its jagged wall
One wave — a score — a hundred,
  Broken and beaten fall;
Yet in defeat they conquer,
  The sea comes flooding in —
Wave upon wave is routed,
  But the tide is sure to win.

O mighty sea! thy message
  In clinging spray is cast;
Within God's plan of progress
  It matters not at last
How wide the shores of evil,
  How strong the reefs of sin —
The wave may be defeated,
  But the tide is sure to win!

      —Priscilla Leonard

* * *

The Incentive Makes a Difference

Your success in life depends on your
motive. There is an old fable about a
dog that boasted of his ability as a
runner. One day he chased a rabbit
and failed to catch it. The other dogs
ridiculed him on account of his previous
boasting. His reply was, "You must

remember that the rabbit was running for his life, while I was only running for my dinner." The incentive is all-important.   —*King's Business*

* * *

What Constitutes Success

Some one gives a prize definition of "success" as follows: "He has achieved success who has lived well, laughed often, and loved much; who has gained the trust of pure women and the love of little children; who has filled his niche and accomplished his task; who has left the world better than he found it, whether by an improved poppy, a perfect poem, or a rescued soul; who never lacked appreciation of earth's beauty or failed to express it; who has always looked for the best in others and given the best he had; whose life was an inspiration; whose memory a benediction.

—*Moody Monthly*

* * *

What A Contrast

Byron wrote before he died:
"My days are in the yellow leaf;
The flowers and fruits of love are gone;
The worm, the canker, and the grief
Are mine alone!"

Paul wrote just before he died: "I have fought a good fight, I have finished my course, I have kept the faith: henceforth there is laid up for me a crown of righteousness."

—*Moody Monthly*

* * *

Where To Cast Your Net

"Did you ever notice," said the old lady, smiling into the troubled face before her, "that when the Lord told the discouraged fishermen to cast their nets again, it was right in the same old place where they had caught nothing? If we could only get off to some new place when we get discouraged, trying again would be an easier thing. If we could be somebody else, or go somewhere else, or do something else, it might not be so hard to have fresh faith and courage; but it is the same old net in the same old pond for most of us. The old

temptations are to be overcome, the old faults to be conquered, the old trials and discouragements before which we failed yesterday to be faced again today. We must win success where we are, if we win it at all, and it is the Master himself, who, after all these toilful, disheartening failures, bids us 'try again.' "

—*Sunday School Times*

* * *

A Bout He Did Not Expect

"Overcome" is a wonderful word in the Greek. In a conflict, it means you have knocked the weapon out of the hand of your adversary. Seth Joshua, a Welsh evangelist, once told this story: "When I was pitching the first tent on the East Moors of Cardiff, on a Saturday afternoon, a burly fellow under the influence of drink came to me and said: 'I say, guv'nor, are you putting up a boxing booth?' 'Yes,' I replied. 'When is the first contest?' 'Tomorrow morning at eleven.' . . . 'Who are going to have the first rounds?' 'I am one of the parties.' 'Who is the other?' 'Beelzebub.' 'Terrible name, but I'll back you, guv-nor.' 'Come here at eleven o'clock tomorrow and we'll see what we can do.' The man came and he was my first convert."

—*British Weekly*

* * *

The Conqueror

No matter how the storms may rage
Upon the sea of life,
No matter how the waves may beat,
No matter what the strife,
The Lord is just the same today
As when He walked the sea,
And He can conquer every storm
That life may send to thee.

The waves are raging everywhere
And men are sore distressed,
But all they need is found in Him
Who giveth perfect rest;
So cast your care upon the Lord,
Whose strength will never fail;
He calms the waves for your frail bark,
His power will e'er prevail.

—*Selected*

VISION

"Eye On Living God"

This story is told by the captain of a ship on which George Müller of Bristol was traveling. During his life he received more than £1,000,000 from the Lord, without advertising — every penny came as an answer to prayer.

"We had George Müller of Bristol on board," said the captain. "I had been on the bridge for twenty-four hours and never left it and George Müller came to me and said, 'Captain, I have come to tell you I must be in Quebec on Saturday afternoon.' 'It is impossible,' I said. 'Then very well, if your ship cannot take me, God will find some other way. I have never broken an engagement in fifty-seven years; let us go down into the chart room and pray.'

"I looked at that man of God and thought to myself, 'What lunatic asylum can that man have come from, for I never heard of such a thing as this?'

" 'Mr. Müller,' I said, 'do you know how dense this fog is?'

" 'No,' he replied, 'my eye is not on the density of the fog, but on the living God who controls every circumstance of my life.' He knelt down and he prayed one of the most simple prayers. When he had finished I was going to pray, but he put his hand on my shoulder and told me not to pray. 'As you do not believe He will answer, and as I believe He has, there is no need whatever for you to pray about it.' I looked at him and George Müller said, 'Captain, I have known my Lord for fifty-seven years and there has never been a single day when I have failed to get an audience with the King. Get up, Captain, and open the door and you will find the fog has gone.'

"I got up and the fog indeed was gone, and on that Saturday afternoon George Müller kept his promised engagement."

—Sunday School Times

* * *

Have You Time?

A visitor to an art gallery noticed a woman on her hands and knees scrub-

bing a floor. "How many beautiful things there are here!" she exclaimed in a friendly tone. "I s'pose so, ma'am, if a body has time to look up," was her answer. With less excuse, many of us go through God's wonderful world in the same way. We have no time to look up and admire the glorious things God has showered around us.

—Christian Herald

* * *

Vision Made the Difference

A friend of mine tells the story of a great naturalist and scientist who, one lovely summer day years ago, went out in the Highlands of Scotland with his microscope to study the heather-bell in all its native glory. In order that he might see it in its perfection, he got down on his knees, and, without plucking the flower, adjusted his instrument, and was soon revelling in its colour, its delicacy, its beauty, "lost in wonder, love, and praise." How long he stayed there he does not know, but suddenly there was a shadow on him and his instrument. He waited for a time, thinking it might be a passing cloud. But it stayed there, and presently he looked up over his shoulder, and there was an old Highland shepherd watching him. Without saying a word, he plucked the little heather-bell and handed it, with the microscope, to the shepherd, that he, too, might see what he was beholding. The old shepherd put the instrument up to his eyes, got the heather-bell in place, and looked at it until the tears ran down his face like bubbles on a mountain stream. And then, handing back the little heather-bell tenderly, he said, "Ay, mon, I wish ye had never shown me that. I wish I had never seen it." "Why?" ased the scientist. "Because," he said, "These rude feet have trodden on so many of them."

—Gipsy Smith

* * *

Look at the Master!

When Leonardo da Vinci finished painting, "The Last Supper," he invited a friend to view it. An "Oh," and "Ah," greeted the artist. The friend was so enamored by the cup that he seemed to be oblivious to all else. Leonardo reached for his brush, dipped it into paint, and, with one bold stroke, wiped out the cup! To the astonished friend, the artist exclaimed, "Fool, look at the Master's face!" The friend almost missed the glory of the painting by looking only at the cup. Today, in the presence of the wonderful gift of God, we need some painter of eternal truth to exclaim, "Look beyond the cup — LOOK AT THE MASTER'S FACE!"

—W. B. K.

* * *

The Upward Look

Above the tumult of the city street, like a sentinel unperturbed, the church spire invites the upward look. It seems to say, "Why hurry so? Why keep your eyes forever on the things below? Why the tense look upon your face as you dodge the crowd that seems to move so slowly? Why that impatient waiting off the curb while the red light taunts you with its forty seconds? Why the irritated honk because the car ahead does not 'jump the light' in the split second between the red and green?

"Stop a moment. Remember, the restlessness of man is dissolved in the peace of God. In his haste man forgets that the mills of God, which never fail, grind very slowly. Man's tense impatience reveals a void where calm and confidence would reign if God were there.

"Look up. The sky is blue, and God is there. He waits to see your lifted eye, to hear the silent cry of your harassed soul, that He may pour into your life the reassurance and the peace which come when He is there."

—Selected

* * *

How Not To Miss the Guidance

Some boys were once trying to see which could make the straightest track across a snowy field. One succeeded in making a perfectly straight track. When asked how he did it he said, "I kept my eyes fixed on the goal, while you fellows

kept yours on your feet." *If "mine eyes are ever toward the Lord," I will walk a straight way.*

—Earnest Worker

* * *

The Eye of Faith

A lady was looking at a picture in the studio of J. M. W. Turner, the greatest of English artists in the first half of the nineteenth century. "Mr. Turner," she said, "I cannot see in Nature what you put in your picture." "Don't you wish you could, madam?" was the calm reply. Only to the eye of the artist does the glory of Nature reveal itself; only to the eye of faith are the beauty and glory of the Lord Jesus revealed.

—Choice Gleanings Calendar

* * *

"Now, Lord, Blot Him Out!"

A Negro minister in the Southland, after presenting a visiting white pastor to his congregation, prayed thus for him: "And now, O Lord, blot him out that we may see JESUS ONLY!"

—W. B. K.

* * *

There's Life In A Look!

"I looked at Him, and He looked at me; and we became ONE forever!" Thus spoke Spurgeon in explaining his conversion from sin to the Saviour. Take hope, ye sin-stricken ones: "Look unto Me, and be ye saved, all the ends of the earth: for I am God, and there is none else" (Isa. 45:22).

—W. B. K.

* * *

"Men Are Like Pigs!"

Said Peter Mackenzie, "Some men are like pigs. They can never look up until laid on their backs!" Examine a pig's eyes and you'll find that this is true. Many, like the muckraker of *Pilgrim's Progress*, are victims of the earthward, downward gaze. God, in goodness, sends affliction, puts man upon his back, that he might look up to God.

—W. B. K.

What Do We See

One was asked to talk to a company of business men about the depression. He tacked up a big sheet of white paper. Then he made a black spot on the paper with his lead pencil, and asked a man in the front row what he saw. The man replied promptly, "A black spot." The speaker asked all present to answer what they saw. All replied, "A black spot." That was what he expected. With calm and deliberate emphasis he said: "Yes, there is a little black spot, but none of you saw the big sheet of white paper. That's my speech. Now you can go home."

—*Quarterly Register*

* * *

Whither Gazing?

Too often we sigh and look WITHIN;
Jesus sighed and looked WITHOUT.

We sigh and look DOWN;
Jesus sighed and looked UP,

We sigh and look to EARTH;
Jesus sighed and looked to HEAVEN.

We sigh and look to MAN;
Jesus sighed and looked to GOD.

—*Selected*

* * *

"So This Is Christianity"

The traveler had been napping, and when the train came to a stop he awakened. "Where are we, porter?" was his question. "We have just crossed the state line, and are now in Maine." It happened that in this emergency stop, his Pullman car was right beside an old automobile junk yard. Piled up and scattered everywhere were pieces of rusty iron and broken cars. "So this is Maine!" said the traveler. Yes, this is Maine, but a very small piece of it. Look up beyond the junk heaps and see the rugged hillsides in the background, and on this side well-kept farmhouses and peaceful cattle grazing. "So this is Christianity!" cries the cynic, surveying the junk heap of broken plans and lives. Oh, no, this is not Christianity! These disorders have pre-empted a little ground, but they exist in spite of Christianity, in spite of Christ. Look up and see the mountains of transfiguration and beatitude.

—*Moody Monthly*

* * *

When the Outlook is Dark Try the Uplook

When the outlook is dark, try the uplook;
These words hold a message of cheer,
Be glad while repeating them over,
And smile when the shadows appear.
Above and beyond stands the Master.
He sees what we do for His sake,
He never will fail nor forsake us,
"He knoweth the way that we take."

When the outlook is dark, try the uplook;
The uplook of faith and good cheer,
The love of the Father surrounds us,
He knows when the shadows are near.
Be brave, then and keep the eyes lifted,
And smile on the dreariest day.
His promise will glow in the darkness.
His light will illumine the way.

—Mary B. Wingate

* * *

Made for the Sky Road

A little lad, listening to the mythical story of Pegasus, the winged horse, exclaimed, "Why did he go on the dirt road when he was made for the sky road?" Are not all Christians made for the sky road? They are disobedient to the heavenly vision when they travel on the dirt road.

—*Record of Christian Work*

* * *

"Fix Eyes Upon Jesus!"

"Since my eyes were fixed on Jesus
I've lost sight of all beside,
So enchained my spirit's vision,
Looking at the Crucified.
All for Jesus, all for Jesus,
Looking at the Crucified."

—*Selected*

* * *

Changed by a Vision

Dannaker, the German sculptor, worked for two years on a statue of

Christ. It looked finished and perfect to him.

To test it he called into the studio a little girl, and pointing to the statue, asked "Who is that?"

She replied promptly, "A great man."

He turned away disheartened, knowing that he had failed.

But he took his chisel and began anew. For six more long years he toiled, and inviting another little girl into his workshop, he stood her before the figure and said, "Who is that?"

She looked up at it for a moment and the tears began to gather in her eyes as she folded her hands across her breast and said, "Suffer the little children to come unto me."

It was enough. Dannaker knew that his task was done. Then the sculptor confessed that during the weary days of those six years, the Christ had come and revealed Himself to him. He had only transferred to the marble the vision he had seen.

Sometime later Napoleon Bonaparte requested him to make a statue of Venus for the Louvre. But he refused. "A man," he said, "who had *seen Christ* can never employ his gifts in carving a pagan goddess. My art is henceforth a consecrated thing."

—*The Presbyterian*

* * *

A "Dirty" Heart, Poor Vision

Preaching in Brighton, England, Rev. Henry Howard said that once he was trying to get up a sermon for children. He said to himself, "What has the heart got to do with seeing?" "I went to the telephone," he continued, "and called the principal doctor in our city. I asked him if there was any disease of the heart that affected the eyes. 'Oh,' he said, 'certainly, Mr. Howard, there is. We call it a "dirty heart"!' 'Oh,' I said, 'that will do for me!' I asked him for particulars, and he explained that it was a disease in which ulcers formed on the inner walls of the heart. There was no pain there, but the blood vessels of the eyes were affected, the eyes became bloodshot, and if there was no cure the blood vessels burst, and the

man became blind. *A clean heart — a clear vision!*"

—*Sunday School Chronicle*

* * *

The Vision of God

The secret of failure is that we see men rather than God. Romanism trembled when Martin Luther saw God. The "great awakening" sprang into being when Jonathan Edwards saw God. Scotland fell prostrate when John Knox saw God. The world became the parish of one man when John Wesley saw God. Multitudes were saved when Whitefield saw God. Thousands of orphans were fed when George Müller saw God.

Is it not time that we got a new vision of God — of God in all His glory?

—*Baptist Standard*

* * *

Unrealized Glory

A story is told of the little daughter of an artist who lost her eyesight in her babyhood. For years she was thought to be incurable. Then a successful operation gave her back her sight. The mother of the child had died some years before, and ever since, her father had been her constant companion and dearest friend. While she lay in a darkened room with bandaged eyes the one thought with her was, "Soon I'll see my dear father." When the days of waiting had passed, and the bandage was removed, at last she looked into the noble, joy-filled face she had so longed to see. She trembled for joy, closed her eyes and opened them to convince herself she was not dreaming. Then, as her father took her into his arms, she exclaimed: "And I had so beautiful a father all these years and did not know it!" Oh, that the bandages might be removed from our eyes, that we might recognize our Saviour in all the beauty of his love!

—*Westminster Teacher*

* * *

Lincoln's Chance

When Abraham Lincoln was a boy he husked corn three days to pay for a second-hand copy of "The Life of Washington." After he had read the book he said, "I don't always intend to delve, grub, shuck corn, split rails, and the like."

"What do you want to be now?" asked Mrs. Crawford.

"I'll be president," confidently said the boy.

"You'd make a purty president with all your tricks and jokes, now, wouldn't you?" said the woman.

"I'll study and get ready, and the chance will come," concluded Abe.

The chance came, and Abraham Lincoln was ready for the biggest job of the Nineteenth Century.

—*Gospel Herald*

* * *

Perverted Use

"I thought it was a pretty fair telescope for one that wasn't very big," said Uncle Silas. "I rigged it up in the attic by the high north window, and had it fixed so it would swing around easily. I took a deal of satisfaction in looking through it — the sky seemed so wide and full of wonders; so when Hester was here I thought I'd give her the pleasure, too. She stayed a long time upstairs, and seemed to be enjoying it. When she came down I asked her if she had discovered anything new." "Yes," she said, "why it made everybody's house so near that I seemed to be right beside them, and I found out what John Pritchard's folks are doing in their out-kitchen. I have wondered what they had a light there for night after night, and I just turned the glass on their windows and found out. They are cutting apples to dry — folks as rich as them cutting apples!" And actually that was all the woman had seen! With the whole heavens before her to study, she had spent her time looking into the affairs of her neighbors! And there are lots more like her — with and without telescopes.

—*Moody Monthly*

* * *

Not Content With a Glimpse

An old Scotch shepherd was nearing his end. A very kind-hearted neighbor

came to see him, and was anxious to know the state of his mind. "Donald," said the friend, "Have you a glimpse of His face now?" "Go away, man," said Donald, "I'll have none of your glimpses. I've had a full view of His blessed face these forty years — why should I be content with a glimpse?"

—*Proof*

* * *

A Parable of the Trees

Once upon a time a man built his house on a spot which commanded a view to the distant mountains and a vast expanse of Heaven's blue skies. Then he said to himself, "I must have trees to shelter and adorn my house; trees make any place more lovely." So he planted a number of fine trees, and these grew up and were admired. But the trees were too many, and were planted too closely, and by and by their lofty tops and interlacing branches shut out the distant view. The mountains were no longer visible from the house, and scarcely a glimpse of the sky could be had.

It is often that way with men's lives. They gather about them earthly interests in order to make their lives more beautiful, more comfortable, more influential, until after a while the glorious mountains of Heaven are shut out and Heaven itself grows dim and unreal.

—*The United Evangelical*

* * *

The Difference!

There is a vast difference between a person with a vision and a visionary person. The person with a vision talks little but does much. The person who is visionary talks much but does nothing.

—*Selected*

* * *

He Flew Too Low!

A great eagle was mortally wounded by a rifle shot. His eye still gleaming like a circle of light, he slowly turned his head and gave one more searching and longing look at the sky. He had often swept these starry spaces with his wonderful wings. The beautiful sky was the home of his heart. It was the eagle's domain. A thousand times he had exploited there his splendid strength. In those far-away heights he had played with the lightnings and raced with the winds, and now, so far away from home, the eagle lay dying because for once he forgot and flew too low.

Is not this a warning for the child of God?

—S. C. Bredbenner, in
Gospel Herald

* * *

Downward Gaze

"A young man once found a five-dollar bill on the street," says William Feather, a well-known writer. "From that time on he never lifted his eyes when walking. In the course of years he accumulated 29,516 buttons, 54,172 pins, 12 cents, a bent back, and a miserly disposition.

"He lost the glory of the sunlight, the sheen of the stars, the smiles of his friends, tree blossoms in the spring, the blue skies, and the entire joy of living."

—*Florida Baptist Witness*

* * *

"Look Up!"

To be distressed, look within;
To be defeated, look back;
To be distracted, look around;
To be dismayed, look before;
To be delivered, look to Christ;
To be delighted, look up.

—Selected

* * *

When We Really See

Something happens to the Christian who really *looks*. It is said of Fred Curtis, a missionary to Japan, that before he went to his field he expressed in a meeting his reason for going: "Woe is me if I preach not the Gospel to the heathen." Immediately one of his friends arose with the remark: "I know what is the matter with Curtis. He sleeps under a missionary chart on which there are 856 black squares representing 856 million heathen, and 190 green squares to represent 190 million Mohammedans. Any man sleeping under such a chart

must decide to become a foreign missionary or have a nightmare every night in the week."   —*King's Business*

* * *

Tennyson's Wish:

When Lord Tennyson was on his death bed, friends at his bedside asked, "Is there anything you wish?" With solemnity, he replied, "Yes, a new vision of God!"

Is not this the need of each one of us? We see man high and lifted up, and his triumphs are thrilling the people. We need, urgently, a heart-transforming, character-ennobling vision, which will cause us to see ourselves as God sees us, and which will cause us to cry out with Isaiah, "Woe is ME! for I am undone; because I am a man of unclean lips, and I dwell in the midst of a people of unclean lips: for mine eyes have seen the King, the Lord of hosts" (Isa. 6:5).

—W. B. K.

* * *

Vital Truth Illustration

He was a good farmer; the furrows in the field he was ploughing stretched like railway tracks to the fence a quarter of a mile away.

"How do you make such straight furrows?" I asked.

"You see that slender pole with a white rag tied to the top of it?" he said in reply. "Well, I set that pole at the point where I want my furrow to end. If I keep my eyes on it all the way across, I can make the furrow almost as straight as a crow can fly; if you get a crook in the first one, the rest have to follow it, for the guiding wheel of the plough runs in the old furrow. Get your first one straight, and the rest will be straight too." The crooked "furrows" in my life have come when I took my spiritual gaze from Christ!

—*Sunday School Times*

* * *

Mole or Lark Outlook?

"How stupid life is!" said the mole,
"This earth is a dull dirty hole!
I eat, I dig, and I store;
But I find it all a bore!"

"The lark sang high in the blue:
"How sweet is the morning dew!
How clear the brooks, how fair the
    flowers,
I rejoice in this world of ours."
                              —*Selected*

* * *

The Secret: Looking Unto Jesus

An Eastern prince had difficulty with
a young man of his court, who was living riotously. The young man was
given his choice between reformation
and death, but he complained that life
was too hard and he could not reform.
The prince ordered the young man to
carry a shell full of oil through the city
streets, with two slaves beside him with
drawn swords ready to execute him if
one drop of oil fell. When the young
man came back the prince said to him,
"What did you see?" "Nothing," said
the young man. "Nothing? Why, it is
the great market day. What did you
hear?" Again the answer was "Nothing." "For," said the young man, "I
had my eyes fixed on the shell of oil. I

could not look or listen, fearing my head
might roll in the dust."

It is when we fix our gaze upon the
Lord Jesus Christ that we will be able
to walk through the temptations of this
life with safety.
                         —Dr. D. G. Barnhouse,
                              in *Gospel Herald*

* * *

Not "It," but "Him."

A missionary one day saw a poor
woman lying prostrate on the ground,
he saw her raise herself and put her
feet where her head had been, and prostrate herself once more; and so she went
on. He went up to her and asked her
what she was doing, and she gave in
answer one Indian word which means,
"A vision of *It*." He knew that woman
was going to travel thousands of miles
in this way to see what she thought was
a sacred flame coming from a mountain.
A great longing came over him that not
only that woman, but all India might
have a vision, not of "it," but of *"Him."*
                              —*Christian Herald*

WAR

Man's Inhumanity to Man

"Many and sharp the numerous ills,
    Inwoven with our frame;
More pointed still, we make ourselves
    Regret, remorse and shame;
And man, whose heaven-erected face,
    The smiles of love adorn,
Man's inhumanity to man,
    Makes countless thousands mourn!"
                              —Robert Burns.

* * *

The Real Enemies

An interesting story is told of a
French soldier, painfully wounded, who
was in charge of the cemetery at St.
Quentin Canal, a cemetery of 37,000
German graves. The French soldier was
strapped up with all sorts of surgical devices.

As he was patiently hoeing rows of
lavender by the acres of black crosses,
he was asked if it were not a strange

circumstance that he who had suffered
so much should be caring for the graves
of his enemies. He was silent for a
minute, then said vehemently, "These
are not my enemies. They never were.
They are the innocents of the war. The
real enemies never approached the
front line."
                              —*Religious Telescope*

* * *

Read and Weep

More than 70% of the National income is expended for past wars, and in
preparation for coming wars.
                              —Harry S. Truman

* * *

Staggering Cost of War

President Eisenhower, in a speech
urging world disarmament said:
"The cost of one modern heavy bomb-

er is this: "A modern brick school in more than 30 cities.

"Two electric power plants, each serving a town of 60,000 population.

"Two fine, fully equipped hospitals.

"Some 50 miles of concrete highway.

"We pay for a single fighter plane with a half million bushels of wheat.

"We pay for a single destroyer with new homes that could have housed more than 8,000 people."

— *Chicago Daily News*

* * *

A Cry Goes Up!

"There's a cry goes up to the ears of God,
From the bleeding earth and the broken sod,
From the battle fields and the long, long row
Of graves where the reddened poppy grows,
From suffering bodies on beds of pain,
From eyes which never will see again,
From the scattered children of Lidice,
From troop ships buried beneath the sea.

"There's a widow's wail and the hungry cry,
Of the child that was only born to die,
In a world where famine stalks the land
And pestilence strikes with a sudden hand.
There are broken homes and broken dreams,
And broken hearts, Dear Lord, it seems
That the broken sob of a broken man
Has come to Thee since the earth began!
When wilt Thou come from the opened sky,
To heal the broken and still their cry?"

— *Selected*

* * *

"A Remorseless Enemy!"

"I hate and fear 'science,' because of my conviction that, for a long time to come, if not forever, it will be the remorseless enemy of mankind. I see it destroying all simplicity and gentleness of life, all the beauty of the world; I see it restoring barbarism under a mask of civilization; I see it darkening men's minds and hardening their hearts."

— Henry Reycroft, a poet

* * *

We Lie in Far Off Lands

In far-off fields strange poppies grow
Between the crosses, row on row
  That mark our place; while in the sky
  The birds, no longer singing, fly,
'Mid planes above and guns below.

We are the dead; short days ago
  We lived, felt dawn, saw sunset glow,
Loved and were loved: and now we lie
  In far-off fields.

O, keep our torch of faith aglow!
To banish war; let nations know
  That, if aggression's hands untie
  The scourge of war, yours will reply,
So long as human blood shall flow.

We are the dead; if to and fro
Across our graves fresh armies go,
  We shall not sleep; to us you owe
  An end of war while poppies grow.
In far-off fields.

— Chaplain Gilbert Darlington

* * *

A Cure For War

A war chief of the Arapaho Indians, "Left Hand," was converted late in life. After he had concluded a very touching talk at a convention in Oklahoma City, an old white-haired preacher arose and said, "Years ago I lived in Denver and enlisted in the army to fight the Indians then on the warpath. At the Battle of Big Sandy, Left Hand led the Arapahos. I sought his blood that day, but today I am his brother in Jesus Christ, our Lord." These words created a profound sensation, so that the great audience called the preacher to the platform, and those two old men, once warriors and enemies on the field of battle, embraced each other with joy. A witness said: "It impressed me so much that I believe that I will be telling the story over and over again after I have been in heaven a million years."

— *Watchman-Examiner*

Without Prince of Peace — Jesus!

With worldly wisdom, skilled in guile,
　Earth's diplomats assemble;
Ignoring Christ, they plot the while,
　And cunningly dissemble.

Peace, peace! they cry; we'll war no
　more,
　But join the nations fast;
To keep the peace and outlaw war,
　Secure we'll be at last.

Without the Prince of Peace, O man,
　How shalt thou learn of peace?
While crafty Satan makes the plan,
　Sin's wars shall never cease.

Thou Lord of Life and Love and Peace,
　I yield my all to Thee;
That wars within my heart shall cease,
　Forevermore to be.
　　　　—John H. Blakely, a Missionary
　　　　in *Sunday School Times*

* * *

Only 268 Years of Peace in 4000 Years

Someone has taken the time to review the history of war and learned that in the last 4,000 years, there have been but 268 years entirely free from war. This of course, only takes into consideration "man's inhumanity to man"; for if man's inhumanity to God were to be considered it would have to be said there has not been a single moment from the fall of man to the present minute, that has been entirely free from war.
　　　　—*Gospel Herald*

* * *

Astronomical!

If the cost of World War II could be prorated among the two billion people of the world, the amount for each man, woman, boy and girl would be $1,708. This amount is exclusive of loss of lives and property.
　　　　—W. B. K.

* * *

Churchill Sees Quick Decision in World War III

"A third world war," Churchill said, "would be different in certain vital aspects from any previous war. The main decision would come in the first month or the first week. The quarrel might continue for an indefinite period but after the first month it would be a broken back war in which no great army could be moved over long distances by land.

"It would begin by both sides in Europe suffering from, in the first stage, what they dread most. The torments which would fall in increasing measure upon the whole civil population of the globe would be indescribable.

"And there is this fact to be remembered — that governments dependent upon long distance commuications on land might well find quite soon they had lost their power to defend themselves."
　　　　—*Chicago Daily Tribune*

WILL OF GOD

Three Kinds of Mission Work

The wife of a missionary, retired and ill, writes this letter, in which is seen the triumph of an unconquered spirit: "He has not spoken for twenty months, has a nurse day and night, and is paralyzed on the right side. One looks and wonders; this is the brain God used and enlarged, this is the hand that wrote the translated Bible — and now he is helpless! But God's Word is not bound; its message is still alive; and some day His faithful servant will walk into the sunrise and sing the songs of the redeemed . . . . I enjoyed *foreign mission* work, then *home mission* work after my husband's retirement, and now I am living in *submission work*. Day by day I have a task, and He gives me strength and grace."
　　　　—*Moody Monthly*

* * *

How Peace Was Won

"With eager heart, and will on fire,
I sought to win my great desire.
'Peace shall be mine' I said. But life
Grew bitter in the endless strife.

My soul was weary, and my pride
Was wounded deep. To heaven I cried:
'God give me peace, or I must die.'
The dumb stars glittered no reply.

Broken at last, I bowed my head
Forgetting all myself, and said:
'Whatever comes, His will be done'
And in that moment, peace was won."
—*Selected*

* * *

When She Obeyed
In my congregation once there was a young lady who was afflicted with bad health. The doctors couldn't locate her trouble. Her parents spent a lot of money consulting specialists and seeking to bring her to health. It was to no avail. One Sunday I preached a message to young people on surrendering to Christ for special service. The young lady came forward and weepingly confessed that she had been fighting such a special call, and said: "As you know, my health has been bad. My parents don't know what is wrong. The doctors can't locate the trouble. But I know. I have known all the time. God is afflicting me because I won't do His will." Following that surrender her health adjusted itself, and she is to-day a trained and gifted nurse in a great hospital.
—From *The Glory of God's Second Call*, by Samuel N. Morris

* * *

Acquiescence in the Divine Will
A rare spirit of acquiescence in the divine will was recently displayed by a poor woman in Atlanta, Ga. She had endured great bodily affliction for many years. Her disease reached its last stage, and she lay apparently at the point of death for four or five weeks. Every day, and almost every hour, was thought to be her last, but to the astonishment of all she continued to breathe. Her sufferings were very severe, and, knowing her to be ready for the great change, her friends were almost hoping for the moment of release. One of them said to her, "Well, M——, are

you ready to go?" "Yes," said she, "ready to go, but willing to wait!"
—*Moody Monthly*

* * *

Submissive to Thy Will
Dear Lord, my heart and life I yield,
Submissive to Thy will;
I only ask that I may have
Some humble place to fill.
I do not yearn for world-wide fame.
But, rather, to exalt Thy name.

I know Thou hast some special task
That Thou wouldst have me do;
Speak now, my Lord, 'tis all I ask
And may I then be true
To all that Thou desirest of me:
Allow me, now, Thy will to see.
—Doris Simerson, in
Gospel Herald

* * *

Pleasing the Father
One day when I was preaching, I asked my own son to stand up. I said: "Robert, stand up. Are you my son?" "Yes, sir." "Well," I said, "Son, you are correct. You are my son; but do you always do that which is right? Do you not sometimes do that which is wrong?" "I expect I do sometimes." "Well, when you do wrong, you are not my son, are you?" "Yes, sir!" "What kind of a son are you then?" "A bad one." "And if you get your just deserts, what do you get?" (He is so big now that he can kiss me on the top of my head, but he knew what he used to get). "Then you are my son no matter how you live?" "Yes, sir." "Then you can go and do as you please?" His answer was, "No, sir — I do not do as I please. I want to live the way you want me to live!"
—R. E. Neighbour.

* * *

"Behind a Frowning Providence"
A story is told of a Christian girl in India, who was about to be married. She was attractive, and one of the most capable girls in the institution. Sores appeared on her hands, and it was discovered that she had leprosy. She was removed from the orphanage and sent

to the leper asylum. She was dressed in her beautiful white flowing garments, as she walked with her brother into that awful place. The women who were there were dirty and filthy, and their faces looked sad and hopeless. When she saw them, she threw her head on her brother's shoulder, and wept and sobbed, "My God," she said, "am I going to become as they are?" She was so distressed, that those about her were afraid she might jump into the well. The missionaries sympathized with her, and asked her if she wouldn't like to be a help to those poor women. A ray of hope came to her and she caught the vision. She started a school, and taught the women to sing, read and write. She could play, so the missionaries bought her a folding organ. Gradually a transformation took place. The houses were made clean, neat and tidy; the women washed their clothes and combed their hair; and that horrible place became a place of blessing.

After being there for some time, she said, "When I first came to the asylum I doubted that there was a God." "Now," she said, "I know that God had a work for me to do, and if I had not become a leper, I never would have discovered my work. Every day I live, I thank Him for having sent me here, and that He has given me this work to do."

—*Gospel Herald*

* * *

Power From Depth

On the coast of Labrador I have seen huge icebergs towering three or four hundred feet in the air. I have seen them sailing due south in the teeth of a strong head wind. They had neither sails nor rudder by which they could track. The secret of it lay in the fact that seven-eighths of the bulk of the iceberg is under water. The great Labrador current moves strongly toward the south. It grips the huge bulk of those icebergs and bears them along no matter how the wind may blow on the surface. The Christian man has a sense of deep underlying agreement with the will of God. His activities lie securely in the will and purpose of the Almighty. He has power which comes from depth.

It is the law within which determines the life without.

—From *Yale Talks*,
by Charles Reynolds Brown

* * *

Lady Huntington's Way

Lord Bolingbroke once asked Lady Huntington how she reconciled prayer to God for a particular blessing with absolute resignation to the Divine will. "Very easy," answered her ladyship: "just as if I were to offer a petition to a monarch, of whose kindness and wisdom I have the highest opinion. In such a case my language would be, 'I wish you to bestow on me such a favor; but your majesty knows better than I if it would be agreeable to you, or right, to grant my desire. I therefore content myself with humbly presenting my petition, and leave the result of it entirely to you.' "

—*The Presbyterian*

* * *

The Will of God

There are peculiar storms in the Indian Ocean — typhoons and monsoons. They are peculiar in that they do not move very rapidly. They do not move practically at all from east to west, or north to south; instead, they play around in a circle.

I was told by a sea captain that before the navigators understood the characteristics of these storms, if they tried to come out of them, they foundered. "Now," he said, "when we run into a monsoon, we locate its center, and we go around it. By and by we narrow the circle; when we get into the center, we are in a dead calm."

This is like God's will. Try to get out of it, and you will find it a destructive force. Get into it, and you are in a calm, and you find it is good, and acceptable, and perfect, as it is so graphically described by the apostle Paul in the twelfth chapter of the Epistle to the Romans. Oh, to stand fully persuaded in all the will of God!

—F. W. Troy, in
Alliance Weekly

Taking Loss as a Christian

A Christian woman recently learned that most of the family possessions and furniture she and her husband owned had been completely destroyed in a warehouse fire. Some of the things were priceless family heirlooms, which no money could replace. The shock was a severe one, but she quietly committed the whole matter to the Lord, and trusted him. A friend of hers, living in the same apartment house, noticed the quietness and entire lack of worry in the face and bearing of the one who had just incurred the heavy loss. Coming up to her, she said, "I didn't know any Christian could take anything this way!" Perhaps the woman had drawn her inference as to Christianity from her observation of most "Christians."

—*Adult Class Quarterly*

* * *

"Thy Will Be Done"

Sweet will of God, I cherish only Thee;
None other will could be the best for me;
In Thee, my all, my ev'ry need I see:
   Be Thou my guide.

If I could choose my path, I would not
   dare;
What seemed to be as best might prove
   a snare
To call me from Thy tender love and
   care,
   And from Thy side.

Thou lovest me, and wilt do what is best;
I'll trust in Thee, and on Thy guidance
   rest;
I'll follow where Thou leadest, and be
   blest
   Till sets my sun;

I will not anxious be, let come what
   may;
Take Thou my hand and lead me in
   Thy way,
Whate'er befalls me, teach me, Lord, to
   say,
   "Thy will be done."

—R. E. Neighbour, D. D.

All Part of God's Plan

The sun is shining in its place,
Each little flower with up-turned face
   Is part of God's great plan,
The stalwart trees all stand erect,
The moon and stars their light reflect,
   But what, we ask, of man?
—*Selected*

* * *

You Can Trust God With Your Business

Queen Elizabeth asked a rich English merchant to go on a mission for the crown. The merchant remonstrated, saying that such a long absence would be fatal to his business. "You take care of my business," replied the Queen, "and I will take care of yours." When he returned, he found that through the patronage and care of the Queen, his business had increased in volume and he was richer than when he left. So every businessman can afford to place Christ's interests first, for the promise is clear and unmistakable. Do Christ's will, and He will look after your welfare.

—From A. C. D., in
   Choice Gleanings Calendar

* * *

A Place Even for "Wrecks"!

Dr. Marshall Craig, preaching in a southern university, pleaded for young men and women to place their all on God's altar. They began to come — the president of the student body, football players, beautiful girls, campus leaders — sincerely, honestly giving themselves to Christ. And then Dr. Craig saw a strange thing. Far back toward the rear of the auditorium, he saw a boy start down the aisle toward the front. And that boy was crawling on his hands and knees. Dr. Craig turned to the president of the university, who said, "It's all right, sir. That boy is one of our students, but he is a hopeless cripple, and the only way he can get around is on his hands and knees." Dr. Craig waited until the boy had made his way to the front, then leaned down to greet him. The young man looked up at the great preacher, and said to him, "Sir, you said God had a place for a man. I know God has a place for these athletes with their muscles of steel; I know God has a place for these campus leaders. But tell me, sir, does God have a place for a wreck like me?" And Dr. Craig told him through his tears, "Son, God has just been waiting for a wreck like you." Oh, my friend, whoever you are, whatever you are, God has a place for you — a will for your life.

—Charles Wellborn's
Baptist Hour Message

* * *

Diamonds At Your Feet!

Russell Conwell tells of an ancient Persian named Al Hafed, who owned a very large farm and was a contented and wealthy man. One evening a Buddhist priest who was visiting Al Hafed told him of the splendor of diamonds which are to be found in some parts of the earth, and of the riches which would come to the man who owned but a handful of these diamonds. At once Al Hafed became discontented, for in the face of such visions of wealth he felt very poor indeed. He must own some diamonds! So he sold his farm and set out to find diamonds. His search carried him fruitlessly to the ends of the earth, until finally, discouraged, penniless, and in rags he threw himself into the sea and was drowned.

In the meantime Al Hafed's successor took possession of his farm. One day when he led his camel out into the garden to drink from the clear brook, he noticed a curious flash in the sands of the shallow stream. He reached in and pulled out a stone containing a beautiful diamond. When he stirred the sands of the garden with his fingers he uncovered other and more beautiful diamonds. Al Hafed was plodding his weary way over the lands of the earth when, on the farm that he sold and left behind were literally acres of diamonds!

Are we satisfied to labor for the Master in the field where He has placed us? Or are we, like Al Hafed, looking to other fields?

—J. W. Reed, in
Gospel Herald

My Best

There is an urge within my breast,
To give the Lord my very best,
In thought, in action, word and deed,
This has become my whole life's creed.

I want to fit into His plan
Be of help to my fellow-man.
Plan the things that I should do
Before my work on earth is through.

It may be out in the darkest night,
Somewhere in the thick of a dangerous fight
That He will send me, ere I'm through,
With all the things I'm supposed to do.

This I know, if I do His will
He will abide and keep me still;
I shall not fear where'er I be
If Jesus, my Savior, pilots me.

—*Selected*

* * *

A Lasting Monument

There were two sons in the Taylor family in England. The older one set out to make a name for the family and turned his attention toward Parliament and prestige. But Hudson Taylor, the younger, chose to give his life to Christ, so he turned his face toward China and obscurity. Hudson Taylor is known and honored on every continent as a faithful missionary and as the founder of the China Inland Mission. But when you look in the encyclopedia to see what the other son has done, you find these words, "The brother of Hudson Taylor." Men may have their names inscribed on marble monuments for feats of fame; some day these monuments will fall in fragments. "But he that doeth the will of God abideth forever" (I John 2:17).

—*Sunday School Times*

* * *

Why He Wanted To Go Back

A returned missionary, home on furlough, was asked, "Do you expect to return to India again?" "In the natural, I can only dislike India," he replied. "Its dirt and filth and heat; its fevers and dreadful diseases, the perpetual fight with mosquitoes; its snakes in our bathrooms, its scorpions in our shoes; its poverty, privations, and hardships; its demon-possessed priests; its sin, degradation, and shame; its anxieties and discouragements are things we can never like. And yet, while I do not wish to seem ungrateful to my friends, I must confess I am not happy here. It is not my friends' fault. The voice of God is calling — calling day and night, sleeping and awake, calling me back to India. I can only be happy in the center of God's will for me, and that place I feel sure is over in hot, dusty India, telling the simple old story of God's love to a multitude of dark-skinned people, whose souls I love with my whole being."

—*Triumphs of Faith*

* * *

God's Plan for Us

What would happen today if you or I should say from the heart, "Lord, work thy will with me"? "Dare we do it? Are we afraid? If so, what do we fear? What is God's will? What does He want to make of us? We have heard the story of the man who dreamed that a man of wondrous beauty and noble bearing approached him. With admiration and envy he gazed and said, "Who is this stranger of so majestic mien?" The answer came, "That is the man God meant you to be.

—*Sunday School Times*

* * *

Better than a Nickel

A little girl approached her father and said, "Father, I want a nickel." The father drew out his wallet and offered her a neat five-dollar bill. But the little girl, not knowing what it was, would not take it. "I don't want that," she said; "I want a nickel." Are there times when we deal with our Heavenly Father as this little girl dealt with her earthly father? Do we sometimes ask for some small favor and refuse his offer of a blessing a hundred times more valuable?

—*Secret Place*

Disappointment

"Disappointment — His appointment."
 Change one letter, then I see
That the thwarting of my purpose
 Is God's better choice for me.

His appointment must be blessing
 Though it may come in disguise,
For the end from the beginning
 Open to His vision lies.

"Disappointment — His appointment,"
 Whose? The Lord's who loves me best.
Understands and knows me fully
 Who my faith and love would test.

For, like loving earthly parents,
 He rejoices when He knows
That His child accepts unquestioned
 All that from His wisdom flows.

"Disappointment — His appointment,"
 No good things will He withhold,
From denials oft we gather
 Treasures of His love untold.

All my life's plan in His molding,
 Not one single choice be mine.
Let me answer, unrepining,
 "Father, not my will, but Thine."
   —*Gospel Banner*

* * *

Blessed Blockades!

Sitting on a fallen tree trunk in the woods I observed a large black ant crawl leisurely along. Interested in seeing what the insect would do I dropped a piece of cracker near it. The falling fragment scared the ant and it started away. I blocked its way with my finger. It started in another direction, and again I blocked it, and finally succeeded in guiding it to the crumb which it immediately seized and began to devour avidly. Doubtless that ant thought the blocking of its chosen path a hardship. It may have been rebellious, wondering what that big creature was trying to do; whereas it was simply a move of a higher intelligence to guide it to something more beneficial than the end of its chosen path. So oftentimes God intervenes and intercepts our advance on the way that seemeth right to us in order that he may direct us to the heav-

enly manna for which he knows our
souls are hungry.
—Rev. Harry S. Laird, in
Homelitic Review

* * *

The Great Architect
When Michelangelo was working on
St. Peter's Cathedral, he had much criticism both from the ecclesiastical authorities and the workmen on the building.
To these critics the great architect said,
in substance: "Even if I were able to
make my plans and ideas clear to you —
which I am not — I am not obliged to
do so. I must ask you to do your best
to help me, and when the work is complete, the conception will be better understood." How necessary it is that men
should pause before criticizing the work
of the Great Architect of the universe.
—Archer Wallace, in
Gospel Herald

* * *

God's Will: the Place of Safety
"Is it safe to work among the lepers?"
was asked of Sam Higginbottom, of India, whose missionary service has been
so blessed to the outcasts whom Christ
asked us specially to remember and heal.
"Yes," was the answer, "it is safer to
work among the lepers, if it's my job,
than to work anywhere else." *A place
of safety outside God's will is too risky
a place for any child of God to contemplate.*
—*Moody Monthly*

* * *

"He Dasn't Quit"
A young man had a class of boys in a
mission Sunday School. Little fellows
they were, and their new teacher's kindness and tact won them to him completely. After awhile the young man
became discouraged with his efforts
among them, and he decided to leave.
He went down early the last Sunday,
and overheard a conversation between
two of the boys. One announced that
he wasn't coming any more; Teacher
was going to quit, and he was going to
quit, too. "Why," said the other boy, "he
dasn't quit. Why, I was the first boy in

his class, and one Sunday he told us kids
that God sent him to teach us, an' he
said God was his boss, and he had to do
wot He said. He's God's man, and he
dasn't quit." And the young man didn't
quit.
—*Record of Christian Work*

* * *

He Got What He Wanted
Dr. A. C. Dixon told the story of a
lady who was traveling with her maid
and child. A wasp got into the carriage
and the child kept crying for it. At last
the lady said to the servant, "What is
the child crying for? Let him have it."
A few minutes later the lady was
startled by an awful scream from the
child, and exclaimed in alarm, "What's
the matter?" "He has got it!" was the
servant's calm reply. So, sometimes in
His great wisdom, God lets us have the
sting and misery of it, and learn through
pain and humiliation that God's will and
way are best.
—From *Windows*,
by McAll Barbour

* * *

Workers With God
A young man entered a florist's shop.
Taking an American Beauty rose out of
a jar, he said, 'See what God has made!'
The clerk of the shop went into the rear
and shortly returned with a wild rose,
fresh and pink, plucked from the countryside. Said the clerk, 'See what God
has made!' Then he held up the American Beauty rose and said, 'See what
God and man have made together.' God
made the forest, but God and man make
the farms and gardens. God made the
quarries, but God and man made the
cathedral.
—*Wesleyan Methodist*

* * *

Just to be Tender
Just to be tender, just to be true,
Just to be glad the whole day through,
Just to be merciful, just to be mild,
Just to be trustful as a child:
Just to be gentle and kind and sweet,
Just to be helpful with willing feet,

Just to be cheery when things go wrong,
Just to drive sadness away with song,
Whether the hour is dark or bright,
Just to be loyal to God and right,
Just to believe that God knows best,
Just in His promise ever to rest,
Just to let love be our daily key,
That is God's will for you and me.

—*Selected*

* * *

Through Deep Waters

One who was passing through deep waters of affliction wrote to a friend: "Is it not a glorious thing to know that, no difference how unjust a thing may be, or how absolutely it may seem to be from Satan, by the time it reaches us it is God's will for us, and will work for good to us?" For all things work together for good to us who love God. And even of the betrayal, Christ said, "The cup which My Father gave me, shall I not drink it?" We live charmed lives if we are living in the center of God's will. All the attacks that Satan can hurl against us, are not only powerless to harm us, but are turned into blessings on the way.

*"In the center of the circle
　Of the Will of God I stand:
There can come no second causes,
　All must come from His dear hand,
All is well! for 'tis my Father
　Who my life hath planned."*

—*Moody Monthly*

* * *

"Lay Me Alongside the Enemy"

It was on a British warship in the Bay of Biscay. The pilot said to the admiral, "It will be an awful night, and there is a lee shore and the wind is rising." The admiral replied: "Sir, you have done your duty in pointing out the danger. Lay me alongside the enemy." When God calls you to duty, let neither prudence nor timidity put in its remonstrance, but let your answer be, "Lay me alongside the hard task, the sacrifice, the danger."

—*Theodore L. Cuyler*

WITNESSING

"I Sho' Loves My Jesus"

A pastor, deeply concerned for the salvation of a Christ-rejecting lawyer, prepared a sermon especially for him, and urged that he attend a designated service. The lawyer accepted the invitation with thanks. He was unmoved, however, by the sermon, and left the service an unsaved man. As he left the church, an illiterate Negro woman, whose heart was filled with the love and compassion of Jesus, approached the learned lawyer, and, with tears streaming down her black face, she said, "I sho' loves my Jesus, and won't you love my Jesus, too?" The dead-in-earnest plea went as a dart directly to the heart of the lawyer, who presently began to rejoice in the Saviour's love and forgiveness! Can we over-estimate the place and power of the personal plea to sinners to surrender to the Saviour?

—*W. B. K.*

No Catch!

During the summertime it is not unusual to observe, all along the Atlantic coastline, men standing on the shore casting with rod and line, hour after hour, without any catch of fish. In fact, not a few have no desire to make a catch, but only to establish a record cast. If memory serves us correctly, a few years ago Ripley's "Believe It or Not" told of a champion bait-and-fly caster who had never caught a fish! There are many Christians, we fear, who must fall into such a category. They possess all the necessary equipment — have been born again, are familiar with the Gospel of Christ, have available all the power of God promised to believers, have the sword of the Spirit — yet they are ineffective witnesses, either because they do not act, or because they depend upon themselves rather than upon the Spirit. —*Our Hope*

Stale or Fresh?

A story is told of an old man who had a wonderful experience twenty-five years ago, so wonderful that he wrote it all down and called it his "Blessed Experience," and when people called on him he would often bring it out and read it through to them. One night, when a friend called in, he said to his wife, "My dear, just run upstairs and bring down my 'Blessed Experience' from the drawer in the bedroom." She went upstairs to get it and on returning she said, "I am sorry, but the mice have been in the drawer, and have eaten up your 'Blessed Experience'!" And a good thing too! If you had a blessing twenty-five years ago, and have not had one since, you had better forget it, and get an up-to-date experience.

—From *Youth with a Capital Why,*
　by A. Lindsay Glegg

* * *

Twofold Testimony

Larry McKenzie, 1951 polio poster boy, whose picture and story have been used by the National Foundation for Infantile Paralysis to help thousands of other stricken children, is also making his testimony as a Christian count in helping others.

In his tour of the country in behalf of the polio drive, the Christian lad frequently told of his love for the Lord Jesus. Now his testimony has been printed in a tract, "Rise Up and Walk," which is being published and distributed by the American Tract Society.

Says Larry in his tract, "I met many famous people on my tour — President of the United States, Harry S. Truman; J. Edgar Hoover, chief of the Federal Bureau of Investigation, and others, but I think often about the time I will meet the Lord Jesus, and until then I really want to serve Him any way I can."

—*Gospel Herald*

* * *

Pershing and MacArthur Testify

We are told that in one of his speeches to the soldiers of the first World War, General Pershing said: "I have known

Jesus Christ now for forty-seven years, and I could not face life without Him. It is no small thing to know that all the past is forgiven, that help is available from God every day." Then continued the stalwart general: "I commend such a Saviour to you."

It is no trifle in this time of tremendous world crisis to have the former Supreme General of the United Nations forces, our own MacArthur, constantly giving concrete evidence of his Christian testimony, "I believe in Jesus Christ."

—*Gospel Herald*

* * *

H. J. Heinz's Testimony

"Looking forward to the time when my earthly career shall end, I desire to set forth at the very beginning of this will, as the most important item in it, a confession of my faith in Jesus Christ as my Saviour.

"I also desire to bear witness to the fact that throughout my life in which there were the usual joys and sorrows, I have been wonderfully sustained by my faith in God through Jesus Christ. This legacy was left me by my sacred mother, who was a woman of strong faith, and to it I attribute any success I may have attained during my life."

—*Power*

* * *

Why He Wanted to Know

On a Southern battlefield a soldier had an artery of his arm shattered severely by the fragment of a shell, and was fast bleeding to death. A passing physician bound up the artery and saved his life. As the physician was leaving, the man cried, "Doctor, what is your name?" "Oh, no matter, said the doctor. "But, Doctor, I want to tell my wife and children who saved me." So when Christ comes to us binding up our spirits and saving our dying souls, there is a longing to tell others what he has done for us.

—*Herald and Presbyter*

* * *

How God Took Care of Gil Dodds

Gil Dodds is the minister's boy who came out of Nebraska to step off the fastest mile ever run on an indoor track. Time 4.10.6. At the end of a race the crowd wondered when he picked up a microphone to acknowledge their applause and said: "I thank the Lord for guiding me through the race, and seeing fit to let me win. I thank Him always for His guiding presence." The rafters of Madison Square Garden must have trembled: these were new words there. "I don't win those races. God wins them. You see, God has given me all I have. I have one great lack. I didn't have the one thing the coaches say a long-distance runner simply *must* have. I couldn't sprint at the end of the mile. But God took care of that. In place of the sprint he gave me stamina." And that is correct. Dodds sprints the whole distance. He sets a killing pace all the way.

—*Christian Herald*

* * *

An African's Witness to Infidels

The Rev. Joseph Tyega, outstanding pastor of the Cameroun, West Africa, came to America for special study at Princeton Seminary. During the Christmas vacation, he underwent an operation in Presbyterian Hospital, New York City. While in bed recuperating, he found himself between a cynical Jew and an equally cynical graduate philosophy student, a foreign diplomat's son. As Mr. Tyega was reading his Bible, the graduate student remarked: "Do you believe that stuff? It's foolish." Whereupon Mr. Tyega replied, "It says right here that philosophers will call it foolish." By the week's end both the graduate student from Europe and the American Jew had accepted Christ as Saviour — through the witness of an African student.

—From *Light from Dark Continent*, by the Rev. Edward Fay Campbell

* * *

The Only Important Scale of Values

Lord Stamp, British authority on economics and finance, was also a Methodist lay preacher. In one of his last speeches which he made before he was killed in a bombing attack, he was talking without noticeable feeling about something connected with the gold standard. Suddenly his tone changed, and he brought his speech to a close with these words: "Before I finish, I should like to say one other thing, and it is this: I have not the smallest interest in what I have been talking about tonight; not the slightest interest in this or any other scale of values excepting only as it may subserve that other scale of values introduced into this planet by Jesus of Nazareth. That is the one and only scale of values which ultimately matters, and which no man now listening to my voice can ever afford to ignore on peril of his soul."

—*Alliance Weekly*

* * *

Why He Couldn't Stop Speaking

Bishop Houghton, speaking at a Pocket Testament League Rally, told the story of a quiet Chinese man who was constantly teased by his friends because he had no tales to tell, nothing to say. Then one day he picked up a little book in the road. It was a copy of the Gospel of St. Luke. He read it through three times, and although he had never met any Christians, he became a Christian, and then, of course, he could not keep the good news to himself. It was not long before his friends almost grew weary of hearing it. They said: "What has happened to you? You used never to speak, and now you cannot stop speaking and telling us all about Jesus." Bishop Houghton commented, " 'We cannot *but* speak of the things that we have seen and heard,' said the early apostles. And today the Christian church is divided into two sets of people, those who say, 'We cannot,' and the others who join with the apostles, and who say, 'We cannot *but* . . .' "

—*Vision and Venture*

* * *

The Monument Moody Wanted

The monument I want after I am dead and gone is a monument with two legs going about the world — a saved sinner telling about the salvation of Jesus Christ.

—D. L. Moody, quoted in *Moody Monthly*

A Cartoonist Speaks for Jesus

Cartoonist Vaughan R. Shoemaker, cartoonist for the Chicago Daily News, creator of "John Q. Public," Pulitzer Prize Winner spoke thus for His Saviour:

"What shall it profit a man if he gain the whole world and lose his own soul?" Any one of us is fortunate if we gain so much as a very small piece of this whole world, much less the whole of it. What if we did? What would it profit us?

I was honest enough with myself back in 1926 to admit I was concerned about my soul. I was simple enough to accept the simple gospel and accepted Jesus Christ as my Saviour.

To this day I have never been sorry. Having had little education or natural ability, for any success I have gained as a cartoonist I must give credit to God. I wouldn't dare start a day without first starting it on my knees, with God, beside my drawing-board. I gain wisdom from Him.

* * *

"Only One Boy"

One of our missionaries to China tells of a boy who "prepared the way" for Jesus in a certain village. The missionary had never visited this village before. "Are there any Christians in your village?" he asked a man. "Only one boy," was the answer. The missionary walked on, and stopping at a house asked for some water. "Have you ever heard of Jesus Christ?" he asked as he took the water. "Oh, yes," was the answer, "there is a boy here who is always talking about Him. He wants me to give up idols, but I dare not do that. But I sometimes think he is right. He is so changed. He used to be selfish and bad-tempered. Now he is unselfish and good-natured, and it is Christ who has made the change." This woman and many others afterward became Christians because of the boy. Like John, he turned many to the Lord God.

—*Earnest Worker*

Talks Christ Only

A religious paper tells of the reporters who rushed to see Pastor Martin Niemoeller, after his release, that they might get some "juicy copy." Instead, they heard a stirring Gospel message and one reporter was heard to say: "Six years in a Nazi prison camp and all he has got to talk about is Jesus Christ."

—*Gospel Herald*

* * *

The Only One He Has

Miss Frances Ridley Havergal, soon after she became a Christian, went to a school at Dusseldorf. Her heart was warm with love for her Saviour, and she was eager to speak for Him. To her dismay, however, she soon discovered that among the hundred girls she was the only Christian. Her first feeling was that she could not confess Christ in that great company of unchristian companions. Her gentle, sensitive heart shrank from a duty so hard. Her second thought, however, was that she could not refrain from confessing Him. "I am the only one He has here," she said. And this thought became a source of strength and inspiration. She felt she was Christ's witness in that school, His *only* witness, and she dare not fail.

—*Sunday School Times*

* * *

Speak Tellingly
"Were half the breath oft vainly spent,
To heaven in supplication sent;
Our cheerful song would oftener be,
'Hear what the Lord has done for me!'"
—William Cowper

* * *

Missionary at Government Expense

During a period of persecution in Korea, a young Christian was falsely accused by police and put in jail as a suspect. When he was placed in solitary confinement, he regretted he was unable to mingle with other prisoners and witness to them. He made it a matter of prayer and was soon banished to one of the neighboring islands. When he was found innocent and released, he said with a beaming countenance: "Just think, I have been longing for a chance to speak of Christ to others, and was mourning because I could not speak in jail. Then God sent me off to an unevangelized island, where there was plenty of work to do, and the government paid for my fare!"

—Tom M. Olson

* * *

A Priest Accepted the Gift

One Sunday morning, a Roman Catholic priest appeared before a congregation of a thousand persons in an Illinois town and said, "My people, I resign my priesthood," though he had been there thirty years. At their earnest request he gave his reasons why he did so: "Last night I spent every hour praising God. All sleep had left me. After reading the New Testament I saw that salvation is in Jesus Christ, and is the gift of God's eternal love. Penance is not in it. Purgatory is not in it. Absolution is not in it. On my knees in my room I accepted the Gift, and I love the Giver, and I walked the room most of the night saying to myself: "I accept the Gift, and I love the Giver'. " And thus for an hour and a half Father Chiniquy expounded to the people the grace of God. At the close of the sermon he asked how many of them would join with him in accepting the Gift and loving the Giver. Every man, woman, and child, except about forty, responded. And that is a Presbyterian church today.

— Dr. A. C. Dixon

* * *

"Must Witness to Our Christian Faith!"

Queen Elizabeth, in a message to the General Assembly of the Church of Scotland, said: "We are very conscious of the need, which was never greater than today, for vigorous witness which it is the privilege of the Church to bear to the abiding principles of our Christian faith. But we are equally conscious that all of us fail in our personal duty unless we all, as individuals, likewise strive to show, by the conduct and example of our daily lives and family relationships, the living reality of our faith and its power to influence, and indeed to shape, the difficult times in which we live."

,   —James R. Adair, in
            Alliance Weekly

* * *

How Others Interpret Our Silence

The following story is told of a case lost in court by the silence of an attorney: "The distinguished Samuel Hoar, father of the late Senator Hoar, once said to a jury that the case was so perfectly plain that he would not insult their intelligence by arguing it. The jury returned in a few minutes with a verdict against him, and when the astonished lawyer asked the foreman how the jury could have returned such a verdict, he received this answer: 'The fact is, Squire, we all agreed that if anything could be said for a case, Squire Hoar could say it, and as you didn't say anything, we concluded to render a verdict against you.' " How often effective testimony for Christ is lost because the one who should give it thinks there is no need of it, while the one who would hear it, because of silence concludes that the matter is not accounted important enough to speak of it!

—*King's Business*

* * *

The General Speaks

I cannot attempt to describe what I owe to the Lord Jesus Christ, nor what He has meant to me throughout my army career (and longer). The knowledge that it is to Him that I owe my eternal salvation has given me a peace which nothing has been able to disturb, while the companionship and help which He has consistently been ready to give me, have been very real and very wonderful.

I would like to bear witness that His help is a most practical and wonderful thing, and I could not contemplate life and its innumerable problems without it. It is a grand thing to be able to take all one's problems to Him, since He promises to give wisdom and direction to those who ask Him. I do most humbly but earnestly commend Him as Saviour and Lord.

—Lt. Gen. Sir Wm. G. S. Dobbie

In Christ and to the World

One of the striking sayings of the late Dr. A. J. Gordon was that the Christian is not to stand in the world and witness to Christ, but to stand in Christ and witness to the world. One such witness, a few evenings ago, had just alighted from his car to open his garage when he was accosted by a stranger who asked him for direction to a certain locality. The information was quickly given, but ere the stranger could get away the Lord's messenger added: "Brother, before you go, we may never meet again, and I should like to ask you, 'Have you a personal interest in the Lord Jesus Christ?' " "No," replied the stranger, "but I would like to have!" Here in the semidarkness of the street of one of our great cities a brief conversation took place, two heads were uncovered, and a soul was introduced to Jesus Christ and definitely accepted Him as his own personal Saviour. Had the brief question not been asked, the individual would have gone on his way, perhaps never to meet the Lord except at judgment.

—*Alliance Weekly*

* * *

The Genuine Ring

In one of Stanley Baldwin's first speeches as a political figure in England ne said, "I remember many years ago standing on the terrace of a beautiful villa near Florence. It was a September evening, and the valley below was transfigured in the long, horizontal rays of the declining sun. And then I heard a bell, such a bell as never was on land or sea, a bell whose every vibration found an echo in my innermost heart. I said to my hostess, 'That is the most beautiful bell I have ever heard.' 'Yes,' she replied, 'it is an English bell.' And so it was. For generations its sound had gone out over English fields, giving the hours of work and prayer to English folks from the tower of an English Abbey. Then came the Reformation, and some wise Italian bought the bell, and sent it to the Valley of the Arno, where after four centuries it stirred the

heart of a wandering Englishman and made him sick for home."

The testimony of a sincere Christian, before his fellowman, will find an echo in the heart of all those who have become followers of the Master.

—Maridel Harding, in
Gospel Herald

* * *

Testimony of Allied Generals

The late Field Marshal Sir Douglas Haig: "The Gospel of Christ is the only hope of the world."

General MacArthur: "I give thanks for God's guidance who has brought to us this success in our great crusade — His the Honor, the Power, and the Glory forever."

General Wavell: "What the men want is a quiet place to read their Bible and turn their thoughts to God."

Field Marshal Montgomery: " I read my Bible every day and I recommend you do the same."

Lt. General Dobbie: "Christ has saved and satisfied me for forty-seven years."
—*The Gideon*

* * *

Worth Sharing

A prominent man in the business world expressed to a friend his keen desire for something real in life. "How about God?" asked his friend. "He is very real to some of us."

"Well," was the reply, "If He is, why don't all of you begin to make Him real to the rest of us? He can't be very real to most Christians, or they wouldn't succeed so well in keeping Him out of all their conversation."

If our religion is worth anything at all, it is worth sharing with others.

—*Prairie Overcomer*

* * *

Salvation Aboard a Transport

There were 7,000 marines and sailors sailing home through the blue Pacific, aboard the U.S.S. *Wakefield*. On a hatch at the stern were seven born-again Christians, including myself, lustily singing good old hymns and Gospel songs. Men swarmed around us until they heard our voices raised in praise to our Saviour; then they scattered, scoffing as they left. But the Lord knew of one boy there who wanted this message. He came to us and asked for a match. We had no match, but each in turn spoke of the Light of the world who had brought each of us out of darkness into His marvelous light. After the testimonies were given, we extended the invitation to this boy, and then we all prayed for him. God melted that boy's heart, and he fell on my shoulder, shedding tears of repentance for his sin. Our little meeting ended that night with not seven but eight fellows singing:

"Thank You, Lord, for saving my soul;
Thank You, Lord, for making me whole;
Thank You, Lord, for giving to me
Thy great salvation, so rich and free."
— Charles Vogel, in *Power*

* * *

The Greatest Bequest

When Patrick Henry's will was read, it was found to conclude with these words: "There is one thing more I wish I could give you. It is the religion of our Lord Jesus Christ. With it, if you had nothing else, you could be happy. Without it, though you had all things else, you could not be happy."
—*Watchman-Examiner*

* * *

Those "Drops of Grief"

Uncle John Vassar, "one of the greatest soul-winners of his century," was going from door to door distributing tracts and speaking with people as opportunity came. An Irish woman heard of this strange man who was entering the houses of the town without introduction, and said, "If he comes to my door he shall not be kindly treated." The next day, with no knowledge of this threat, he rang her bell. When she recognized him she slammed the door in his face. Nothing daunted, he sat upon the doorstep and sang:

"But drops of grief can ne'er repay
The debt of love I owe;
Here, Lord I give myself away;
'Tis all that I can do."

A few weeks later this woman sought admission to a church. As she made her confession before the Elders she could only say between her sobs, " 'Twas those drops of grief. They burned themselves into my heart."
—George L. Rulison

* * *

Christian Doctors Bear Witness!

Said Cecil P. Martin, M.B., Sc.D.:
Science gives us knowledge of our physical bodies and surroundings but no insight into spiritual things. The latter can only come through the Spirit of God giving us an understanding of the revelation of Jesus Christ. Disbelief in Christ arises not from lack of evidence, for evidence is really conclusive, but from our spiritual unwillingness to accept the gospel. Many, therefore, ignore the gospel and try to build a substitute for it out of psychology, sociology, and political ideals; a fruitless task that ends in frustration and disappointment. But to those who take Christ at His Word, He fulfills His promise and manifests Himself in countless ways. They know Him and His power to save, and if this knowledge is not real, then I know not what reality is.

Said Thomas M. Durant, M. D.:
In a day in which men's hearts are full of fear and all about us is unrest and insecurity, the troubled soul finds need of succor which this world's resources cannot provide. The Word of God alone contains the curative prescription for such suffering. Our Lord Jesus Christ says, "Let not your heart be troubled, ye believe in God, believe also in me."

To the one whose "hope is built on nothing less than Jesus' blood and righteousness" there comes the joy of knowing sins forgiven. It is such an one's portion to experience "the peace of God which passeth all understanding" and which keeps men's hearts and minds.

I praise the Lord that, as a physician, He has given me the privilege of testifying to His saving grace and keeping power.

Said John R. Brobeck, Ph. D., M.D.:

So far as I have been able to discover, there is nothing extraordinary about the medical man when his position before God is considered. In God's presence we apparently stand in the same pitiable state as the most worthless, helpless patient in the poorest hospital ward of our various communities. Actually, our condition may be worse than his because as a group we tend to be ignorant of God's Word, and because we seem to have little desire to further our education in this all important direction. It has been my own experience to find, however, that miserable though we be in the sight of Almighty God, He loves us, has revealed His love in the Scriptures, and stands ready to work within us the miracle therein spoken of as the New Birth. I can only express thanksgiving for the love of Jesus Christ my Saviour."

Said Everett D. Sugarbaker, M. D.:

Each time I pray I am overwhelmed at the relationship with God which it is the Christian's privilege to enjoy, a relationship based on greater love than that of earthly father or mother or dearest friend for it was purchased at no less price than the death of His only Son. Pausing at times to contemplate His magnitude and the insignificance of the individual, particularly in this present time, one might find his credulity faltering were it not for the constant reassurances of His abiding love which our Heavenly Father convincingly gives us both in His Word, the Bible, and in our daily experience. My acceptance of Christ as my personal Saviour began this relationship which has become the most precious thing in my life.

Said Paul E. Adolph, M. D.:

"The hearing ear, and the seeing eye, the Lord hath made even both of them." Prov. 20:12.

In my practice of surgery I am always conscious of the limitations of the human senses, both in diagnosis and treatment apart from Divine help afforded in answer to the prayer of faith.

Moreover, the love of Christ shed abroad in my heart constrains me to use every means at my disposal to bring relief to bodily ailments while at the same time I introduce the sick one to our Saviour and Lord, whom to know aright is life eternal.

As I have ministered to both Chinese and Americans, it has brought me great satisfaction to see them find the same joy and peace in Christ which have been my portion in Him.

Said William Chisholm, M.D.:

I believe that Jesus Christ, God manifest in the flesh, died for our sins, that He was buried, and that He rose again the third day according to the Scriptures.

I believe the Bible, the Author of which is the living God, possesses the property of life, and that through the agency of the Scriptures the Holy Spirit imparts the life of God into the human heart, so that men thereby become partakers of the Divine nature. Furthermore, I believe the very best investment one can make of his time is to put at least one hour daily over the words of the Bible. Without these living words in our minds and hearts it is impossible for the Holy Spirit, who works through the words of the Scripture, to bring His lifegiving blessings into our lives.

Said Howard A. Kelly, M. D.:

I believe that all men without exception are by nature sinners, alienated from God, and when thus utterly lost in sin, the Son of God Himself came down to earth, and by shedding His blood upon the cross paid the infinite penalty of the whole world.

I believe he who thus receives Jesus Christ as his Saviour is born again spiritually as definitely as in his first birth, and, so born spiritually, has new privileges, appetites and affections; that he is one body with Christ the Head and will live with Him forever. I believe no man can save himself by good works, or by what is commonly known as a moral life.

I believe Jesus Christ to be the Son of God, without human father, conceived by the Holy Ghost, born of the Virgin Mary.

* * *

Eight Others Got Out Their Bibles

A fine lad entered the Army. He faced a real test the first night he went to bed in the barracks. He had formed the commendable habit of placing his Bible on his bed at home, and kneeling down to read a chapter while having his daily prayer time before retiring. Surrounded by scores of rough men in the one great company room, many of them cursing and jesting loudly, he thought it might be wiser to go to bed and then read his Bible where nobody would notice it. But he told himself, "I am a Christian, and I ought to give these fellows a testimony. I won't strike my colors; I'll do just as I did at home!" So the courageous youngster undressed, got into his sleeping garments, then spread his Bible on his cot. He kneeled down and started to read, and in two minutes the barracks got as quiet as a church. He felt like a goldfish in a glass bowl. . . . After a while the talk began again, and nothing was said about his odd behavior. But the next night when he again opened his Bible and knelt to read, eight other boys dug out their Bibles and did the same. Within a month every man in that outfit would have fought for that boy. They brought their troubles and their questions to him to be settled, and he influenced more men for Christ in that one barracks than

half a dozen chaplains could have moved in a year of Sundays.

—From *Miracles at Morning Cheer,*
by Harry Rimmer

* * *

Witness-Bearing

Dr. G. Campbell Morgan tells of two men, nominal Christians, who worked side by side for five years without finding out, either of them, that the other had ever made a profession of religion. One of them, in telling it to Dr. Morgan, said, "Wasn't it funny?"

"Funny!" said Dr. Morgan, "Why, no. Go find the man and let us get down on our knees before God, *for you have never been born again.*"

—*Earnest Worker*

* * *

No Special Type

In a late publication, Dr. Basil Miller says that Dr. Reuben A. Torrey was won to Christ through the witnessing of a godly mother; Sam Jones, by his own father; George Mueller, by a friend; John R. Mott, by a teacher; George Whitefield, by a book; and Count Zinzendorf, through a certain picture. There is no prescribed type of testimony except that it be Christ-centered and Spirit-directed. Are we in the place where God can use our testimony? Are we making the most of our opportunities of witnessing for Him?

—*King's Business*

WORK

How He Did It

A Chinaman brought a number of his friends to the mission. When asked how he succeeded in getting so many to come, he said, "I got on my knees and talkee, talkee, talkee. Then I got up and walkee, walkee, walkee." Pray and then work. Prayer without works is vain. Praying without working like working without praying, is dead. Let us all talkee and walkee.

—*Gospel Herald*

Tramps Not Wanted

An American was told by an English tourist that he was surprised to find no "gentlemen" in his country. "What are they?" asked the American. The Englishman replied, "People that do not work for their living." "Oh," said the American, "we have some of those here; only we call them tramps." God does not want any tramps, but workers for His glory.

—*Rev. Evan Hopkins*

Is Praying Enough?

When Martin Luther set out on the work which shook the world his friend Myconius expressed sympathy. "But," he said, "I can best help where I am. I will remain and pray while you toil." Myconius prayed day by day, but as he prayed he began to feel uncomfortable. One night he had a dream. He thought the Saviour himself approached and showed him his hands and feet. He saw the fountain in which he had been cleansed from sin. Then looking earnestly into his eyes the Saviour said, "Follow me." The Lord took him to a lofty mountain and pointed eastward. Looking in that direction Myconius saw a plain stretching away to the horizon. It was dotted with white sheep — thousands and thousands of them. One man was trying to shepherd them all. The man was Luther. The Saviour pointed westward. Myconius saw a great field of standing corn. One reaper was trying to harvest it all. The lonely laborer was spent and exhausted, but still he persisted in his task. Myconius recognized in the solitary reaper his old friend Luther. "It is not enough," said Myconius when he awakened, "that I should pray. The sheep must be shepherded; the fields must be reaped. Here am I; send me." And he went out and shared his old friend's labors.

—From *The Fiery Crags*, by Boreham

* * *

A Doctor Who "Worked with God"

In a large metropolitan hospital there is a surgeon who insists upon having a moment alone before entering the operating room. Because of his great skill many of the younger doctors wondered if there might be a relation between his success and this unusual habit. When one of the interns put the question to the surgeon, he answered: "Yes, there is a relationship, a very close one. Before each operation I ask the great Physician to be with me, to guide my hands in their work. There have been times when I didn't know what to do next, and then came a power to go on — power which I know comes from God. I would not think of performing an operation without asking God's help." The surgeon's story spread throughout the country, and one day a father brought his little daughter to the hospital, insisting that the doctor who "worked with God" should operate on his child.

—*Quiet Hour*

* * *

Nazareth Was a Little Place

"Master, where shall I work today?"
  And my love flowed warm and free;
And He pointed out a tiny plot,
  And He said, "Tend *that* for Me."

But I answered quickly, "Oh, no, not there;
  Not any one could see
No matter how well my task was done —
  Not that little place for *me!*"

And His voice, when He spoke, it was not stern,
  But He answered me tenderly:
"Disciple, search that heart of thine;
  Are you working for *them*, or for *Me?*
Nazareth was just a little place,
  And so was Galilee."

—*Selected*

* * *

Second Fiddles

Time and again the persons who occupy first place do little, and the worthwhile things are done by the second-placers. The man who won D. L. Moody to the Lord was a second fiddle, whose name has been forgotten by most people. But what a marvelous work that was! The man who won C. I. Scofield to the Lord was an individual whose name seldom appears in print, but what a mighty work he did! The man who won Spurgeon was an obscure fellow, but his work still bears fruit around the world. There are times when God holds us in second place because there lies the work which he has for us to do.

—*Gospel Herald*

* * *

Her Partnership

An unusual woman was being interviewed by a reporter. Although a widow for years, she had reared six children of her own and twelve adopted children.

In spite of her busy and useful life she was noted for her poise and charm. The reporter asked how she had managed. "You see, I'm in partnership." "What kind of partnership?" She replied, "One day, a long time ago, I said, 'Lord, I'll do the work, and You do the worrying,' and I haven't had a worry since!" Work and trust in God! That's a wonderful partnership. The will to work is priceless. We should beware of our modern schemes to live without honest toil. Everyday duties need never be a burden, however, when we let God carry part of the load. When we let Him do the worrying, we release ourselves from fear and fussiness. When we take Him into partnership, we reinforce our weak efforts by His divine power. No one need feel sorry for himself with the Lord on his side.

—*Sanctuary*

* * *

LeTourneau Says Work!

When should a child start to work? I would say at about the age of three.

I do not believe in the sweat shop or in child labor that deprives a child of his education or the pleasures of carefree hours, and that breaks down his health and stunts his development.

But there is one thing sure: if one does not learn to work as a child he will never do much when he grows up. As for health, I probably sawed as much wood as a boy, and shoveled as much sand in the foundry when I was in my early teens as the next fellow; and I don't know what it means to lose a day through sickness.

Show me a man to-day at the head of affairs who didn't work as a boy. I think that without exception those who get things done to-day are those who learned to work as children.

We need to teach our children the dignity of labor and the pleasure of accomplishment; and that only by determined effort do we create things that are worth while. Not only do sweat and toil keep us out of mischief, but the more we do the bigger kick we get out of doing things.

— R. G. Le Tourneau, in *Now*

No Easy Path to Glory

"It takes a little courage
    And a little self-control,
And some grim determination
    If you want to reach a goal.
It takes a deal of striving,
    And a firm and stern set chin,
No matter what the battle,
    If you're really out to win.

"There's no easy path to glory,
    There's no rosy road to fame,
Life, however we may view it,
    Is no simple parlor game;
But its prizes call for fighting,
    For endurance and for grit,
For a rugged disposition
    And a "don't know-when-to-quit."

—*Selected*

* * *

Already Given

One time a friend was invited to a Scotsman's home for dinner. Tea, of course, was served. When the guest asked that he might have some sugar, the Scotsman said: "Man, the sugar is already in the cup of tea. Stir it up, my friend." We need not so much pray for gifts, as to exercise the gifts God has already given us.

—From *Peloubet's Notes*,
    by Wilbur M. Smith

* * *

The Lord Has a Job for Me

The Lord has a job for me,
But I had so much to do
I said, "You get somebody else
Or wait till I get through."
I don't now how the Lord came out,
But He seemed to get along;
But I had a feeling — sneaking like —
Knowed I'd done God wrong.

One day I needed the Lord,
Needed Him right away,
But He never answered me at all,
But I could hear Him say
Down in my accusing heart,
"Moze, I'se got much to do,
You get somebody else,
Or wait till I get through."

Now, when the Lord He have a job for
me,
I never tries to shirk;
I drops what I has on hand,
And does the Good Lord's work.
And my affairs can run along,
Or wait till I get through;
Nobody else can do the work,
That God marked out for you.
— Paul Laurence Dunbar

* * *

"I'm Scrubbing for Jesus!"
"Sophie, the scrub woman" was questioned one day as she scrubbed the steps of a large New York City building thus: "Sophie, I understand that you are a child of God." "Yes, sir, I'm a child of the King!" "Well, since you are a child of the King, do you believe that God recognizes you as a princess?" "He certainly does," beamed Sophie. "Well, if God is your Father, and you are a princess, and a child of the King, don't you think that it is beneath your level to be found here in New York City scrubbing these dirty steps?" None daunted, Sophie replied, "There's no humiliation whatever. You see, I'm not scrubbing these steps for Mr. Brown, my boss. I'm scrubbing them for Jesus Christ, my Saviour!"
— W. B. K.

* * *

Jesus Christ and We
Christ has no hands but our hands
To do his work today;
He has no feet but our feet
To lead men in His way;
He has no tongue but our tongues
To tell men how He died;
He has no help but our help
To bring them to His side.

We are the only Bible
The careless world will read;
We are the sinner's Gospel,
We are the scoffer's creed;
We are the Lord's last message
Written in deed and word —
What if the line is crooked?
What if the type is blurred?

What if our hands are busy
With other work than His?
What if our feet are walking
Where sin's allurement is?
What if our tongues are speaking
Of things His lips would spurn?
How can we hope to help Him
Unless from Him we learn?
— Annie Johnson Flint

* * *

Refreshed by Working!
I knew a dear man, one of the greatest men for physical exercise I ever saw. He worked hard on the street railroad. I would see him down on his knees, a great big covering over his eyes to shield them from the brilliant light as he welded the steel rails. By Saturday noon he was just worn out, and he would get a bundle of books and off he would go for exercise, over the hills and far away, hunting up poor needy souls, maybe in the county hospital, possibly in the jails, and to poor families. Sometimes he would hear of somebody lying sick and poor and miserable, and he would go to see that one. And you know he had a remarkable way of preaching the Gospel. He would often lay down a five-dollar bill at the side of the bed, if he found out that they had no money to pay the bills. On Sunday he would say, "My! I was worn out yesterday, but I had a wonderful time Saturday afternoon, and I am all rested up!"
— Dr. Harry A. Ironside

* * *

Can't Work Soul to Save
"I cannot work my soul to save
For that my Lord has done;
But I can work like any slave
For love of God's dear Son."
— *Selected*

* * *

Real Love
A little boy declared that he loved his mother "with all his strength." He was asked to explain what he meant by "with all his strength." He said: "Well, I'll tell you. You see, we live on the fourth floor of this tenement; and there's no elevator, and the coal is kept down in the basement. Mother is busy all the time,

and she isn't very strong; so I see to it that the coal hod is never empty. I lug the coal up four flights of stairs all by myself. And it's a pretty big hod. It takes all my strength to get it up here. Now, isn't that loving my mother with all my strength?"

—*Gospel Herald*

* * *

Work!

"Work!
Thank God for the might of it —
The ardor, the urge, the delight of it
Work that springs from the heart's
    desire
Setting the brain and soul on fire
Oh, what is so good as the heat of it?
And what is so glad as the beat of it?
And what is so kind as the stern com-
    mand
Challenging brain and heart and hand?

"Work!
Thank God for the swing of it
For the clamoring, hammering ring of it.
Passion and labor daily hurled
On the mighty anvils of the world.
Oh, what is so fierce as the flame of it?
And what is so huge as the aim of it?
Thundering on through dearth and doubt
Calling the plan of the Maker out.
Work, the Titan; Work, the friend,
Shaping the earth to a glorious end,
Draining the swamps and blasting the
    hills.
Doing whatever the Spirit wills —
Rending a continent apart
To answer the dream of the Master-
    heart.
Thank God for a world where none may
    shirk.
Thank God for the splendor of work."

—*Selected*

* * *

"Stir Me, Lord!"

"Stir me! oh, stir me, Lord, I care not how,
But stir my heart in passion for the world!
Stir me to give, to go — but most to pray;
Stir 'til the blood-red banner be unfurled

What if our hands are busy
lie —
Lands where the Cross was never lifted high.

"Stir me! oh, stir me, Lord! Thy heart was stirred
By love's intensest fire, 'til Thou did'st give
Thine only Son, Thy best beloved One,
E'en to the dreadful Cross, that I might live.
Stir me to give myself so back to Thee,
That Thou canst give Thyself again, through me."

—*Bessie Porter Head*

* * *

Hidden Resources

When Michelangelo was ordered to decorate the walls of the Sistine Chapel, he refused. He had never done any work of that kind, and said he could not do it. But he was told his refusal would not be accepted. When he discovered that there was no alternative without unpleasant consequences, he mixed his colors and went to work. And thus came into being the world's finest painting.

There are few who realize what possibilities are locked up within them until some necessity compels them to attempt something they have always considered impossible.

—*Friendly Chat*

* * *

Earth's Blessing Is Toil

"This is the gospel of labor, ring it, ye bells of the Kirk;
The Lord of love came down from above to live with the men who work.
This is the rose He planted here in the thorn cursed soil;
Heaven is blest with perfect rest, but the blessing of earth is toil."

—*Selected*

* * *

Hunting an Easy Berth

The story is told that a student once wrote to Henry Ward Beecher asking the great preacher "for an easy berth." To this student Mr. Beecher replied:

"Young man, you cannot be an editor; do not try the law; do not think of the ministry; let alone all ships and merchandise; abhor politics; don't practice medicine; be not a farmer, a soldier, or a sailor; don't study; don't think. None of these is easy. Oh, my son, you have come into a hard world. *I know of only one easy place in it and that is in the grave!*"

—L. E. M., in
Christian Union Herald

* * *

How Sir Walter Scott Worked

Sir Walter Scott put in fifteen hours a day at his desk, rising at four o'clock in the morning. He averaged a book every two months, and turned out the "Waverly Novels" at the rate of one a month. Fritz Kreisler, despite his native genius, finds it necessary to devote eight to ten hours a day to practise. One of the Wesleys preached three sermons a day for fifty-four years, traveled 290,000 miles by horseback and carriage, wrote more than eighty different works on many subjects and edited a fifty volume library.

—*Gospel Herald*

* * *

The Busy Man

If you want to get a favor done
  By some obliging friend,
And want a promise safe and sure
  On which you may depend,
Don't go to him who always has
  Much leisure time to plan,
But if you want your favor done,
  Just ask the busy man.

The man of leisure never has
  A moment he can spare;
He's busy "putting off" until
  His friends are in despair;
But he whose every waking hour
  Is crowded full of work,
Forgets the art of wasting time —
  He cannot stop to shirk.

So when you want a favor done,
  And want it right away,
Go to the man who constantly
  Works twenty hours a day.

He'll find a moment, sure, somewhere
  That has not other use,
And fix you while the idle man
  Is framing an excuse.

—*Selected*

* * *

"Just Plain Lazy!"

"Give it to me straight, doc. I can take it! Tell me in plain English what's the matter with me." "Okay, I'll be frank with you. My diagnosis is that you're just plain lazy!" "All right, doc. Now please give me a SCIENTIFIC NAME for it so I can go home and tell my wife!"

—W. B. K.

* * *

Good Timber

The tree that never had to fight
For sun and sky and air and light,
That stood out in the open plain
And always got its share of rain,
Never became a forest king
But lived and died a scrubby thing.

The man who never had to toil
To heaven from the common soil,
Who never had to win his share
Of sun and sky and light and air,
Never became a manly man,
But lived and died as he began.

Good timber does not grow in ease;
The stronger wind, the tougher trees;
The farther sky, the greater length;
The more the storm, the more the
    strength;
By sun and cold, by rain and snows,
In tree or man, good timber grows.

Where thickest stands the forest growth
We find the patriarchs of both;
And they hold converse with the stars
Whose broken branches show the scars
Of many winds and of much strife —
This is the common law of life.

—Douglas Malloch

* * *

Finishing the Task

A friend of mine was building a house in China, and had engaged an old Chinese contractor for the job. The house was nearing completion when my friend received word late one night, requesting him to come at once to the house of the contractor. He found him very ill and in a dying condition, and noticing that the old fellow seemed to be troubled about something, he asked him if all was well between him and his God. The old man replied with a smile that all was well, that his sins were forgiven, and that he was going back to his Heavenly Father. But still feeling that some-thing was troubling him the missionary questioned him further. Finally the old man broke into tears and said: "It's all right with me, Teacher. I am going to the Heavenly Father, but I did not want to go until I had finished the work I started for you. Will you forgive me, Teacher, for not finishing it?" What a great thing if all of us were as much concerned about finishing the work the Master has given us to do!

—*Expositor*

WORLDLINESS

About Master's Business

Edwin Booth was one of America's greatest actors. Dr. Houghton was the rector of "The Little Church Around the Corner," to which Booth and other actors belonged. Said Booth to Dr. Houghton one day, "Doctor, you never use our tickets and come see us play. Don't you like us?" "Mr. Booth, of course I love you all," replied Dr. Houghton, "but if you were taken seriously ill, I hope you would at once send for me. Where would you like the messenger to find me, here in my church about my Master's business, or in a seat in some theater?" "I would like him to find you here, Doctor, — I understand."

—*Sunday School Times*

* * *

Our Life-Giving Atmosphere

We touch the world at so many points, how can we remain unspotted? Scientists tell us of an insect which, though you immerse it in water, yet never touches the water. Enveloped with the element, yet the element never penetrates to the insect itself. The reason of this wonder in nature is that it carries with it into the water its own atmosphere — a bubble of air. Enveloped first in this atmosphere it can bid the other element defiance, and though submerged in it, is untouched by it. Ye are in the world but not of the world. Live in fellowship with Christ. Carry about you the secret atmosphere of communion with thy Lord, and then, though in the midst of abounding sin, thou shalt remain without blemish, unspotted by the world.

—From *Pure Religion*,
by the Rev. W. L. Mackenzie

* * *

Loaded Down With Harmless Things!

Alas, so many Christians are weighted down with so-called "Harmless Things!" D. L. Moody illustrated this truth dramatically in a service: He did not appear on the platform as usual at the beginning of the service, but had Mr. Sankey to say, "Mr. Moody will come onto the platform looking different than you ever saw him at the preaching hour." With their curiosity sufficiently piqued and the time for the sermon at hand, Mr. Moody appeared with a tremendous pack strapped onto his shoulder. He walked slowly across the platform, turned, and walked back. Then he asked the audience, "Do you think I could preach like Jesus wants me to preach with this load on my back? However, it is made up of fine things. There is no whiskey bottle nor a pair of dice in it. It is made up of clothes and many other harmless things. Some of you are trying to serve Christ while you carry a lot of 'weights' on your back. Jesus said you must be different, 'separated' from the world. You must leave some otherwise harmless things beyond."

—C. Roy Angell, in
The Teacher

Bad Company

The crows one spring began to pull up a farmer's young corn. So he loaded his gun and went out to frighten them away. Now the farmer had a parrot, who, when he saw the crows pulling up the corn, flew over and joined them.

Presently, "Bang!" went the farmer's gun, and when he went to see what he had done, he found to his surprise that besides killing three crows he had wounded his parrot.

He took the bird home, and the children asked, "What did it, Daddy? What hurt our pretty Poll?"

"Bad company! Bad company!" answered the parrot, in a solemn voice.

"Yes, that was it," said the farmer. "Poll was with those wicked crows when I fired, and received a shot intended for them. Remember the parrot's fate, children. Beware of bad company!"

—*The Sunday Circle*

* * *

Only One Letter's Difference

"Just one letter of the alphabet makes all the difference between us now," said a recently converted young woman to an unsaved friend, who could not understand the great change that had come over her. "You love the world," she said, "and I love the Word."

—*Word of Life*

* * *

Subject of a Different Kingdom

Dr. Louis Evans tells of a man who entered the hut of a British officer in Africa and found his friend clad in a formal dinner jacket and before him the appointments of a formal dinner. Surprised at this dressing for dinner in the midst of a lot of African savages, the friend expressed fear of the officer's sanity. But he received the explanation that once a week the custom of dressing for dinner was followed because the officer felt that he must not adopt the customs and standards of the natives of Africa. He belonged to the Empire of Britain and he determined to live according to the codes of British conduct no matter how his heathen neighbors lived. So, also, the Christian belongs to

a different empire. He is called unto a life of holiness because God is holy. His behavior patterns are to be taken from Christ, not the world. Ours is the high calling of God in Christ Jesus.

—*United Presbyterian*

* * *

Honoring a Name

The story is told of a soldier in the army of Alexander the Great, who was brought before the great world-conqueror for court martial. When the emperor had listened to the charges and the evidence, he turned to the soldier facing condemnation, and said,

"What is your name?"

"Alexander!" was the reply.

Again the emperor questioned, "What is your name?"

And the second time the soldier answered, "Alexander!"

With a cry of rage, the emperor roared, "I say, what is your name?"

And when the soldier answered for the third time, "Alexander!" the great general angrily replied, "You say your name is Alexander? You are found guilty of your crime as charged, and now you must pay the penalty. *Either change your conduct or change your name, for no man can bear the name of Alexander, my name, and do the things that you have done.*"

—From *Unfeigned Faith*, by Donald J. MacKay

* * *

We Cannot Come!

"Likewise reckon ye also yourselves to be dead indeed unto sin, but alive unto God through Jesus Christ our Lord."

Two fashionable girls, recently converted to God, were asked to a ball, and this is the answer they sent:

"We are sorry to have to refuse your invitation. But the fact is, it is not possible for us to be present with you, for we are dead! We died with Christ a week ago, so we cannot come!"

—*Power*

Lot's Wife

A Denver minister, in a sermon, suggested: When Lot's wife turned back to look at Sodom (*Gen.* 19:26), it was not a glance at the doomed city with a thankful heart that she had escaped. But her eyes lingered upon Sodom, with a question in her heart, "Why did such a catastrophe have to come to such a lovely city?"

The judgment of God fell upon Lot's wife and turned her into a pillar of salt because:

First: Her heart was still in Sodom and she longed to be back there.

Second: Sodom was in her heart and if she had continued up to the mountains (place of God) she would have started another Sodom there.

—*Christian Victory*

* * *

The Bee's Folly

Dr. Edmund gives a good illustration to show the end of the pleasure seeker: "Did you ever read of the bee in the fable, that found a pot of honey ready made, and thought that it would be fine to save all the trouble of flying about the meadows and gathering its sweet stores little by little out of the cups of flowers, and began to sip out of the dish? Then it went in and reveled in the sweets; but when it began to get tired and cloyed, it found — poor bee! — that its wings were all clogged and would not open, nor could it drag its body out of the mass. So it died, buried in pleasure!"

There are many persons, like this bee, that find death in their pleasures.

—George S. Belleau

* * *

Lily Bound

A traveler tells of a peculiar experience that happened to him as he voyaged on the coast of South America. While his ship lay at anchor it became lily bound. The growth of vegetation in that climate is very rapid, and during a few calm days the vessel became the center of a great floating island of beautiful lilies. But the beauty was soon forgotten in the danger. They accumulated so rapidly that the chains became entangled, and yielding to the flow of the tide, the flowery mass caused the vessel to drag her anchor, and to drift in a wrong direction. Eventually the crew had a long and tedious task with hatchets to release their ship from the imprisoning flowers — a picture of the embarrassing effect of eminent success. How often has an accumulation of the gay and golden flowers of opulence and pleasure accounted for the fatal drifting of noble lives!

—Dr. Watkinson

* * *

Unsavory Christians

My sister invited me to a turkey dinner. She had raised the turkeys on her orchard farm. I sat and carved, and the plates were filled. We all took the first mouthful of turkey, then we looked at one another. We could not keep it in our mouths. It tasted like the smell of decayed shrimps. My brother-in-law used the leavings from the shrimp market on the beach, for ground fertilizer, and the turkeys had eaten some of it. We were going to eat turkey, but the turkey had eaten decayed shrimps and the taste had gone all through. There it was, lovely looking turkey, but useless. You may be a Christian and feed on the theaters, but oh, how will your life taste to others? Pity the young person who tries to follow Jesus, and feeds on the stage.

—Paul Rader

* * *

The Bat's Mistake

"No man can serve two masters" (Matt. 6:24). Aesop speaks in one of his fables about a time when the beasts and fowl were engaged in war. The bat tried to belong to both parties. When the birds were victorious, he would wing around telling that he was a bird; when the beasts won a fight, he would walk around them assuring them that he was a beast. But soon his hypocrisy was discovered and he was rejected by both the beasts and the birds. *He had to hide himself, and now only by night can he appear openly. One is our Master, even Christ. Serve Him!*

—*Sunday School Times*

Let Go!

This world holds nothing so dear
   That Christ cannot give us more:
His love, His peace, His joy —
   Far more than heart could implore.
Our lives lose much He has for us
   As we cling to our earthly ties:
In Him are pleasures forevermore,
   Let go — for Christ satisfies!

—*Selected*

* * *

No Place for a Christian

A certain titled British gentleman
was converted. He loved the Lord a
great deal, but he was not well taught
in the Scriptures. He thought that he
could continue in some of his worldly
engagements and still bear a good testimony. On an occasion some weeks
after he gave his heart to the Lord, this
man accepted an invitation to a very
worldly party. Upon his arrival, one
of the guests greeted him with these
words: "I'm so glad to see you and to
know that it isn't true." "I beg your
pardon," he replied, "but I think I don't
quite understand you." "Why," said
the other guest, "rumors were around
that you had been converted a few weeks
ago; I'm so glad you're here and to
know, therefore, that the rumor was un-
founded." "But it is true!" the dumbfounded man ejaculated. Hesitating a
moment, he added. "I see that you think
this party is no place for a Christian
to be. And you are right. You will
never again see me at such an affair,
nor will anyone else." And, bidding his
host and hostess adieu, he departed
from his last world's engagement.

—From *A Doctor In Many Countries,*
   by F. Fothergill

* * *

Saints in Wrong Places

1. A Backsliding Believer — Abram
in Egypt (Gen. 12:10).
2. A Silenced Witness — Lot in Sodom (Gen. 14:12).
3. A Lazy Saint — David on the
house-top (II Sam. 11:2).
4. A Seduced Prophet — The man
of God in the old prophet's house (I
Kings 13:19).

5. A Discouraged Worker — Elijah
under a juniper tree (I Kings 19:4).
6. A Disobedient Servant — Jonah
in the sea monster (Jonah 2).
7. A Miserable Disciple — Peter before the fire (Luke 22:55).

—W. J. Morrison

* * *

Out of Bounds

The old shepherd who offered prayer
in a Welsh revival meeting put it exactly right when he lamented his back-
slidings in these words: "Lord, I got
among the thorns and briars, and was
scratched and torn and bleeding; but,
Lord, it is only fair to say that it was
not on Thy ground; I had wandered out
of Thy pasture."

—Lawson

* * *

What Determines the Weight

Sir Robert Ball, the great astronomer,
said that a man who carries a sack of
corn on earth could as easily carry six
sacks of corn on a globe the size of the
moon. But in a world as vast as the
sun, even to pull out a watch from the
pocket would be to tug at a weight of
five or six pounds. It would be impossible to lift an arm, and if once a man
were to lie down there, he could never
get up again. So, in the spiritual realm,
the weight of our burdens depends upon
the attraction of earth. If the world is
all to us, alas, how true it is that its
burdens crush us!

—*Sunday at Home*

* * *

Who Are the Heathen?

A Chinaman applied for a position as
cook in a western family. The lady of
the house and several other members
of her family were members of a fashionable church, and the Chinaman was
questioned closely.

"Do you drink whisky?"
"No, I Christian man."
"Do you play cards?"
"No, I Christian man."
He was employed and gave great sat-
isfaction. He did his work well, was
honest, upright, and respectful. After

some weeks the lady gave a euchre party and wine was served. John Chinaman was called in to serve refreshments, which he did without much comment. But the next morning he waited on the lady and told her he wanted to quit work.

"Why, what is the matter?" she inquired.

John replied, "I Christian man. I tell you so. I no work for heathen Amelican."

—W. B. K.

* * *

A Peg-Leg Confederate Promises Not to Dance!

It was during the first pastorate of the late Dr. R. E. Neighbour that this humorous incident occurred: The scene of the incident was the First Baptist Church, Americus, Georgia. Preaching on worldly amusements, the preacher closed his message with an invitation to those who danced to come down the aisle, and thus publicly declare "quits'" so far as dancing was concerned. Only ONE responded to Dr. Neighbour's plea: A peg-leg Confederate veteran, who couldn't dance a jig if he wanted to!

—W. B. K.

* * *

Where Contamination Is Inevitable

"I think a Christian can go anywhere," said a young woman who was defending her continued attendance at some very doubtful places of amusement. "Certainly she can," rejoined her friend, "but I am reminded of a little incident that happened when I went with a party of friends to explore a coal mine. One of the young women appeared dressed in a dainty white gown. When her friends remonstrated with her she appealed to the old miner who was to act as guide to the party. 'Can't I wear a white dress down into the mine?' she asked petulantly. 'Yes'm,' returned the old man. 'There's nothin' to keep you from wearin' a white frock down there, but there'll be considerable to keep you from wearin' one back' "

—*King's Business*

No Compromise

A number of years ago in Washington I was returning from visiting friends one cold night in January, when our car stopped suddenly. It showed no disposition to move on, so I asked the conductor what was wrong.

"A car off the track ahead," he said.

As cold as the night was, I got off with him to investigate, and found the car in such a position as to block our progress entirely. I turned to my friend, the conductor, and said: "It seems to me that car is not off the track. If it were, we could go on."

"That's right," he said, "the trouble is it is partly on and partly off."

Those who hinder the work of Christ's kingdom are not only the avowed unbelievers, but those partly on and partly off the track.

—*S. S. Journal*

* * *

Either Give It Up or Get More

A very practical man has confessed: "I have too much religion or too little; I must either give up what I have, or get more. I have too much religion to let me enjoy a worldly life, and too much worldliness to let me enjoy religion." He ended the dilemma triumphantly. He solved the problem by the whole-hearted acceptance of Christ as his living Lord. He put an end to divided loyalty, to doubtful obedience.

—Dr. C. C. Albertson

* * *

How One Man Lost His Chance

A young man, in the very flower of his days, once told the following story, in answer to a question as to why he was not spending his life for God and others.

"I was once," he said, "as you are, a Christian worker, and service for God was a great delight. For many years I gave of my best, and was happy in giving, until one day God called me to launch out in the deep — to forsake all and follow Him fully. But," he continued slowly, "I thought of my wife and two children, of my comfortable home, of my paying business, of all I valued in the homeland, and I looked up to God, and said 'No.' That's three years ago," he said, "and now —"

"Now," I echoed quickly, "what?"

"Oh," he replied with a mirthless laugh, "what's the good of speaking about these things? I don't know why you should have asked me that question; I must go." And he arose and reached out for his hat.

"But," I answered breathlessly, laying my hand upon his arm, "you care still, don't you?"

For a moment he lifted his dark eyes to mine, and never shall I forget his look of remorse. "Care!" he repeated hoarsely; "what's the good of caring now? I'm so involved in business with worldly men that I hardly dare call my soul my own. Both my wife and I have backslidden, and never even go to church; and as for helping others — look, I've lost my chance."

Beware, reader, lest you lose yours.
—*Christian and Missionary Alliance*

* * *

Different Drumbeat!

Thoreau, the naturalist-philosopher, in defending some of his oddities, wrote once, "If I do not keep in step with others, it is because I hear a different drumbeat." The Christian may well say this. If our inner ears have been attuned to the music of the heavens, we hear the drumbeat of the skies, and therefore we must of very necessity seem to the world to be out of step with all that goes on down here which is contrary to the Holy Spirit who dwells within us.

— Dr. Harry A. Ironside

* * *

WORRY

Enjoying Her Worries?

A woman was once being called upon by a victorious Christian, who, after listening to her tale of woe, told her of the way to victory and joy through Christ Jesus. The poor woman listened intently and, when her visitor had finished, looked up with a frightened face and said, "Oh, but I don't want to ever come to the place where I can't worry!" The poor soul seemed to feel a great loss would come to her if she could not worry. She had spent so much of her time in this way, she would be lonely if she stopped and let the Lord carry her and her burdens.

—*Prophetic News*

* * *

Be Not Anxious

Be not anxious about tomorrow. Do today's duty, fight today's temptations, and do not weaken and distract yourself by looking forward to things which you cannot see and could not understand if you saw them. Enough for you that the God for whom you fight is just and merciful, for He rewardeth every man according to his work.

—C. Kingsley

Worry

It is said that J. Arthur Rank has his own special way of handling the problems of worry.

He decided to do his worrying on one single day, Wednesday, and he has what he calls his Wednesday worry club.

When a worry occurs to him on any other day, he writes it down and puts it in a box. And, of course, when he opens the box on Wednesday, he finds that most of the things he was disturbed about have already been settled.

—*The Art of Real Happiness*

* * *

For Tired Nerves

A man, paralyzed by many anxieties, and unable to sleep at night, was so tired in mind and body that he was ready for anything. When he was at the last gasp, he met a Christian friend who told him that if he would only pray about it all, he would find some relief. That night he prayed for the first time for years. He told God everything about himself. And while he was praying he fell asleep. When he woke up hours later he knew he had found his cure. He told his doctor: "I just tell Jesus about my worries. I turn them all over to Him." The doctor replied, "If all my nerve patients would only do that, I should be a poorer man."

—Rev. F. H. Pickering

* * *

"Put Off Worry and Distress"
    (A Bed Time Prayer)
Ere thou sleepest, gently lay
Every troubled thought away;
Put off worry and distress,
As thou puttest off thy dress;
Drop thy burden and thy care
In the quiet arms of prayer.

Lord, Thou knowest how I live,
All I've done amiss forgive;
All of good I've tried to do
Strengthen, bless and carry through;
All I love in safety keep
While in Thee I fall asleep.

—Henry Van Dyke

* * *

Two Things Not to Worry About

There are two things, at least, about which we should never worry. First, the things we can't help. If we can't help them, worrying is certainly most foolish and useless. Secondly, the things we can help. If we can help them, let us set about it, and not weaken our powers by worry. Weed your garden. Pluck up the smallest roots of worry. Watch for their first appearance above the ground and pluck them while they are small. Don't let them get a start. They will crowd out all the beautiful things that ought to grow in our hearts unless we do.

—*Christian Digest*

* * *

"Just As Soon Swear As Worry" — Wesley

There is a little motto that hangs on the wall in my home that again and again has rebuked me: "Why worry when you can pray?" We have often been reminded of the words of the Psalmist, "Fret not thyself because of evildoers, neither be thou envious against the workers of iniquity" (Ps.

37:1). Mr. Wesley used to say that he would just as soon swear as to worry. Worrying is evidence of a serious lack of trust in God and His unfailing promises. Worry saddens, blights, destroys, kills. It depletes one's energies, devitalizes the physical man, and enervates the whole spiritual nature. It greatly reduces the spiritual stature and impoverishes the whole spirit.

— E. E. Wordsworth, in
    Gospel Herald

* * *

Why Worry?

A French soldier in World War I carried with him this little receipt for worry: "Of two things, one is certain. Either you are at the front, or you are behind the lines. If you are at the front, of two things one is certain. Either you are exposed to danger, or you are in a safe place. If you are exposed to danger, of two things one is certain. Either you are wounded, or you are not wounded. If you are wounded, of two things one is certain. Either you recover, or you die. If you recover, there is no need to worry. If you die, you can't worry. SO WHY WORRY?"   —W. B. K.

* * *

Satisfied With Christ

Let me tell you what our Negro washerwoman said one morning when I asked her why she was so happy. "Wall, I'll tell you," she replied, "Ah ain't got no money to lose, so ah never worries about losin' none. Ah ain't got no furniture to lose, for ah gave it to the Lord, and if anythin' happens to it, the Lord did it to His own stuff, not mine. Ah has a fine, healthy body, but if ah gets sick and dies, ah'm goin' to Heaven, and you don't think ah'll worry about that, do you?" She was satisfied with Christ . . . Solomon was worth seven and one-half billion dollars. Do you know what he said? . . . "Vanity of vanities; all is vanity."   —Walter L. Wilson, M.D.

* * *

Feeling Bad When Feeling Good

Said an old lady, "I always feel bad when I feel good, for I know that I'll feel bad after awhile!"

How senseless to thus punish one-self! Worry is a killer! Remember this, "A day of worry is more exhausting than a day of work." Is there a way of escape from the worries and corroding cares of our bothered, burdened world? Yes, there is: "Casting ALL your care upon Him, for He careth for YOU" (I Pet. 5:7).

—W. B. K.

* * *

Worry, Heart's Worst Enemy

"Too many people are living at too fast a pace. Anginal pain may be in-cited by any emotion except PITY. An-ger is the WORST enemy of the heart. It causes more anginal pains and at-tacks than any of the other disturb-ances resulting from emotion!"

— Dr. Newell Clark Gilbert, nationally known specialist in heart diseases.

* * *

The Unworried Christian

Only the life that is truly at leisure from itself can fulfill its ministries rightly. The perfect Christian worker is the unworried Christian, untroubled even about the service he seeks to ren-der. He knows his own inability to change a heart or to convict a sinner. He is sure of his own commission to wit-ness for his Master. And he is so con-fident in the co-working of that Master that he does his part faithfully, and leaves the rest to the Worker that can-not err and does not fail.

How great the glory of an unworried life! It is feeding from the table of the King, and being clothed out of His wardrobe (Matt. 6:25-34). It is genuine, it is reliable, it is practical, it is delight-ful. There are many thus walking by faith, with upward look and rejoicing hearts.

—*Alliance Weekly*

* * *

Worry, A Sin Against God and Our-selves

Worry is not only a sin against God, it is a sin against ourselves. Thou-sands have shortened their lives by it, and millions have made their lives bitter by dropping this gall into their souls every day. Honest work very seldom hurts us; it is the worry that kills. I have a perfect right to ask God for strength equal to the day, but I have no right to ask Him for one extra ounce of strength for tomorrow's burden. When tomorrow comes grace will come with it, and sufficient for the tasks, the trials, or the troubles. God never has built a Christian strong enough to stand the strain of present duties and all the tons of tomorrow's duties and sufferings piled upon the top of them.

—*Moody Monthly*

* * *

Truth About Worry

There is no disputing the fact that, nine times out of ten, worrying about a thing does more damage to those who worry than the actual thing itself.

Modern medical research has proved that worry breaks down resistance to disease. More than that, it actually dis-eases the nervous system — particularly that of the digestive organs and of the heart. Add to this the toll in unhap-piness of sleepless nights and days void of internal sunshine, and you have a glimpse of the work this monster does in destroying the effectiveness of the human body.

It is plain common sense that worry has no rightful place in the lives of most of us.

—Ken Anderson

* * *

Why Worry?

Hannah Whithall Smith tells about a man sliding down a rope into a well. He supposed the rope to be of ample length, but to his dismay he reached the end of it without touching the bottom of the well with his feet. He tried in vain to climb up the rope, and dared not let go for fear of being dashed to pieces. He held on as long as he could, and when utterly exhausted let the rope slip from his grasp. He fell — *just three inches!*

—*Blessed Hope Quarterly*

Lost Them Yesterday

"The little cares that fretted me,
  I lost them yesterday
Among the fields above the sea,
  Among the winds at play.
The foolish fears of what may happen
  I cast them all away
Amid the humming of the bees,
  Amid the clover-scented hay."
  —Elizabeth Barrett Browning

* * *

"Nothing Left to Worry About!"

Let us give up our work, our plans, ourselves, our lives, our loved ones, our influence, our all, right into His hand; and then, when we have given all over to Him, there will be nothing left for us to be troubled about, or to make trouble about.
  —J. Hudson Taylor

* * *

When to Worry

When we see the lilies spinning in
  distress,
  Taking thought to manufacture love-
    liness;
When we see the birds all building barns
  for store,
  T'will then be time for us to worry —
    not before.
  —*Sandy Lake Breeze*

* * *

"Shut Out Yesterdays, and Unborn Tomorrows"

An ocean liner is built so that the captain can, by pressing a button, lower steel doors separating one watertight bulkhead from another. If the hull is pierced in a disaster, this keeps the ship afloat. "In the voyage of life," advised Dr. Osler, world-renowned physician, "learn how to make doors come down and shut out the yesterdays with all their errors and failures. Learn also to lower another door to shut out the unborn tomorrows so that you can live for this day alone. As you move into the next bulkhead, close doors that will shut out both the past and the future."
  —*Chicago Daily News*

* * *

The Bridge You'll Never Cross

It's what you think that makes the
  world
Seem sad or gay to you;
Your mind may color all things gray
  Or make them radiant hue.
Be glad to-day, be true and wise,
  Distinguish gold from dross;
Waste neither time nor thought about
  The bridge you'll never cross.

There's useful work for you to do,
  For hand and brain and heart;
There's urgent human service, too,
  In which to take your part.
Make every opportunity
  A worth-while gain, not loss;
The best is yours, so do not fear
  The bridge you'll never cross.

If life seems drab and difficult,
  Just face it with a will;
You do not have to work alone
  Since God is with you still.
Press on with courage toward the goal;
  With Truth your shield emboss,
Be strong, look up and just ignore
  The bridge you'll never cross.

  —Grenville Kleiser, in
    Christian Leader

* * *

Driving and Worrying Don't Mix

Edward Francis said "I nearly wrecked my car. I was so agitated over the immediate future, that the racing machine reflected my bitter emotions. 'What in the world can *I* do?' I kept asking: 'how will it be possible for *me* to figure a way out of this dark situation?' And just then the other fellow had to do some good driving to avoid my wild car. He was a fine spirited chap, and simply said, 'Excuse me, mister, but you just can't *drive* and *worry*,' then went on. I sat still a moment, and a text popped up: 'Casting all your care upon him; for he careth for you.' And I saw for the first time, that I, a child of God, was mentally living on a hobo basis."

  —From *Filled! With the Spirit*,
    by Richard Ellsworth Day

757

WORSHIP

In Silence

An African native, away from his village, met some missionaries and learned for the first time of the God who loves men. He went back to his tribe carrying the Book which tells of God, but he was unable to read it. When he told the tribe of God, they wanted to do God honor. But how should they worship Him?

They laid the Book on a stump and sat around it in silence, in a meeting that might have reminded us of the old-fashioned silent Quaker meetings. Did such worship touch the heart of God? I am sure it did, far more than much of the cold ritual that many of us are accustomed to go through.

—Wm. Carle, in
Moody Monthly

* * *

The Reason for the Difference

A Nigerian missionary arrived at a Communion service in which four towns were combining, and heard an African addressing the crowded church in a meeting as follows: "I cannot tell you the gladness that is in my heart today. As I walked along the path with the other members from my town I saw that each man held in his hand his Testament and his hymnbook. No man carried a cutlass or a gun. No man walked with fear; every man with faith in you. And yet it is but four years ago that no man from my town would have walked through your town without a cutlass in his hands, and even then he would not have walked alone. Nor would any man from your town have come unharmed through ours. What is the reason for this difference? At that time we worshiped the same gods as you did. Today we worship the same God as you do, but the God we worship today is a God of peace. We have learned that He is our Father, and that we are brothers."

—From *What Is This Christianity?*
by Bishop of Croydon

Keep Out!

I asked an elderly woman once, "If I go to church and the preacher says nothing worth hearing, is it any use for me to go?" "Of course not," she replied curtly. But a young man overhearing our conversation intruded, "I don't see why a man, when he goes to church to worship God, would let a preacher butt in on his worship!"

—*Senior Teacher,
Scripture Press*

* * *

Churches in Prison

Five elders from the Banjo Church in the Amfilo forests were arrested and brought before the local judges at Sayo for trial. Each day the judges said to them, "We do not know why they have arrested you, but pay us a bribe and we will send you home." Each day the elders replied, "Neither do we know why we are arrested, but certainly it is not to pay bribes." With that answer they were marched back to prison. After a week, the local governor called them and said, "If you promise to go back to your village and destroy your church, you will be given your freedom." "How can we destroy the church?" they asked, "It is not our house, but God's." For that they were sentenced to three months' imprisonment in the large disease-ridden, filthy hovel, two hundred feet from the governor's palace.

Where churches were closed, the people gathered under trees and in open fields to continue their worship. When authorities discovered them, they rounded them up and drove them into prisons. So another saying has been started by the believers, "They have closed our churches in the villages, but they are opening new ones for us in the prisons." It is true — for in every courthouse and every prison, there are today groups of witnessing, Bible reading, praying believers.

—Rev. Carl J. Kissling

Neglected Worship

During World War I an Indian maharaja, conversing with an American, asked him, "Do you know why God is punishing the Christians by letting them fight and destroy each other as they are?" Answering his own question, he said, "If I paid as little attention to my religion as most Christians pay to theirs I would expect God to punish me." Then this Hindu prince said that though one per cent of the officials in his employ were British, yet for their sake he kept all his offices closed on Sunday, and had built two Christian churches, that they might have both time and place for worship. But he went on to say that services were held only about once in three months. "What do they do on Sunday?" he was asked. "They are hunting, boating, tennising, racing, and playing cards. If you ask me why God is punishing the Christian nations, I think that there you have the answer."

—*Sunday School Times*

* * *

Dropped by This Generation

Our fathers suffered to gain us freedom of worship. A later generation heedlessly passes by the open door of the church. Little Jane said, "Mother, you know that vase you said had been handed down from generation to generation?" "Yes, dear." "Well, Mother, I'm sorry, but *this generation* has dropped it."

—*Lookout*

* * *

"Ring It Again! Ring It Again!"

A father once told his son that he was going to take him to visit the country church he used to attend as a boy and where he often rang the bell to call the people to the house of God for worship. Great was their disappointment when they found the old church locked and deserted. Looking through a window they could see the long bell rope. The father borrowed a key and opened the door. The little son looked up into his father's face and eagerly exclaimed, "Father, ring it again! Ring it again!" So once again the old church bell rang out. People came from far and near to see what was the matter. He told them what the church had meant to him in his boyhood, and with his help the old church was reopened for worship and service in the community. How we wish that the words of the little lad might resound anew throughout the whole wide world bringing people back to church, "Ring it again! Ring it again!"

—*Moody Monthly*

* * *

Divine Service at Kitchen Sink

In the kitchen of a little apartment in London, the wife of a friend of mine has a little motto over the kitchen sink: "Divine service is conducted here three times daily." I think there is a breath of heaven about that. It is our faithfulness in these small things that enables us to be men that God can trust one day.

—*Rev. Alan Redpath,*
Pastor, Moody Church

* * *

Her Tabernacle

Near Largs, Scotland, there used to live a poor woman with a large family. They lived in a tiny house consisting of a "but and ben." Her husband was a laborer and found it hard to supply the growing needs of his family. To help ease the heavy burden the woman took in washings. Day by day she stood over the tub or the ironing board, with children and chickens about her, earning a little money. But the spiritual life of this woman was so deep and true, in spite of her hard labor, that her influence for good was felt in a remarkable way throughout the whole region. Even the minister would often tether his horse by her door when passing and take a seat by her, as she went on with her work, for the inspiration and help she was to him. One day he said, "My good friend, you always seem so near the Lord. How is it possible when you can never get alone with Him for a quiet prayer?" The woman, with a look of surprise, laid down her iron, seated herself, and said, "Ah, Meenister, that's whar ye mak' the mistake. When I wint tae shut all oot I jist sit me doon in ma chair, an' throw me apron owr ma

heed, an' I'm in ma tabernacle alone wi'
me Lord in a moment."

    —Bible Expositor and Illuminator

* * *

The Secret
I met God in the morning,
When my day was at its best,
And His presence came like sunrise,
Like a glory in my breast.

All day long the Presence lingered;
All day long He stayed with me;
And we sailed in perfect calmness
O'er a very troubled sea.

Other ships were blown and battered,
Other ships were sore distressed,
But the winds that seemed to drive them
Brought to us a peace and rest.

Then I thought of other mornings,
With a keen remorse of mind,
When I too had loosed the moorings
With the Presence left behind.

So I think I know the secret,
Learned from many a troubled way;
You must seek Him in the morning
If you want Him through the day.

    —Ralph Cushman